REFERENCE

Women
in the
Middle Ages

Women in the Middle Ages

in the

Middle Ages

AN ENCYCLOPEDIA

Volume I: A–J

Edited by

KATHARINA M. WILSON

and

NADIA MARGOLIS

GREENWOOD PRESS
Westport, Connecticut • London

Library of Congress Cataloging-in-Publication Data

Women in the Middle Ages : an encyclopedia / edited by Katharina M. Wilson and
Nadia Margolis.
     p. cm.
  Includes bibliographical references and index.
    ISBN 0-313-33016-6 (set : alk. paper)—ISBN 0-313-33017-4 (vol. 1 : alk. paper)—
ISBN 0-313-33018-2 (vol. 2 : alk. paper)
    1. Women—History—Middle Ages, 500–1500—Encyclopedias.   I. Wilson, Katharina M.
II. Margolis, Nadia, 1949–
HQ1143.W643   2004
305.4′09′0203—dc22   2004053042

British Library Cataloguing in Publication Data is available.

Library of Congress Catalog Card Number: 2004053042
ISBN: 0-313-33016-6 (set)
     0-313-33017-4 (vol. I)
     0-313-33018-2 (vol. II)

First published in 2004

Greenwood Press, 88 Post Road West, Westport, CT 06881
An imprint of Greenwood Publishing Group, Inc.
www.greenwood.com

Printed in the United States of America

The paper used in this book complies with the
Permanent Paper Standard issued by the National
Information Standards Organization (Z39.48-1984).

10 9 8 7 6 5 4 3 2 1

This volume is for
Chris

and in memory of
Peter

Contents

Preface

Women in the Middle Ages: An Encyclopedia contains over 300 entries offering both basic and in-depth information on individual women and on broad topics relating to the experience of women in Europe and elsewhere in the world between the second and fifteenth centuries C.E. As such, the *Encyclopedia* is a valuable information resource for students and interested nonspecialist readers as well as for more advanced scholars of medieval culture.

The *Encyclopedia* makes no claim to absolute comprehensiveness; rather, it offers as broad a sampling as possible of medieval women's diverse cultures during the centuries covered. While most other works on medieval women are primarily Anglo- and Eurocentric, with a literary and historical focus, this volume also offers numerous entries with a non-Western focus, covering such areas as China, Japan, India, and the Near and Middle East. Non-Western entries on individuals include Empress Wu, a seventh-century ruler of China; Zoe Karbounopsina, a tenth-century Byzantine empress; Sei Shonagon, a tenth-century Japanese poet; and Mirabai, a fifteenth-century Indian poet. Non-Western entries on broader topics include "Aztec Warrior Women"; "China, Women in"; "Muscovy, Women in"; and "Syrian-Christian Women." In including non-Western subjects, the editors were mindful of the fact that, chronologically speaking, one culture's midpoint is another culture's zenith or nadir. Thus, the seventh century, while a period of economic and cultural expansion in China and the Islamic Middle East, was anything but in the newly emerging Germanic kingdoms of Western Europe. While acknowledging this, this *Encyclopedia*, in deference to its readership and the majority of its material, takes as its chronological parameters for its "Middle Ages" the debatable but useful reference points most familiar to Western-based medievalists, focusing on the era between the decline and fall of Rome (c.400) and the full flowering of the Renaissance in much of Europe (c.1500).

Likewise, and in keeping with the latest research trends, the editors have endeavored to include not only the most recent material on well-known "canonical" persons and topics in literature and history, but also on the more neglected achievements, social classes, occupations, creeds, and even sexual preferences, all in an effort to open new perspectives for understanding and further research on women of the Middle Ages. The entries thus include all manner of medieval women, ranging from affluent patrons to paupers, and from doctors, scholars, and poets to merchants, artisans, and prostitutes. Entries also cover pagan-based legendary and mythical women, Christian and non-Christian saints, visionaries and preachers, cross-dressers and Cathar heretics, empresses and queens, and warriors and slaves. Because of the highly disparate levels of information available on the various topics, the editors' dual goal of accessibility and authority has sometimes been difficult to attain, although in all cases every effort was made to provide the most up-to-date information in the most comprehensible form. If the preponderance of entries still remains with literary, or at least literate, women, it is because these women left the most evidence of their own intelligence, through their own words, whether in sermons, orations, in personal and public letters, poems, plays, or histories.

Furthermore, the editors have also included a sampling of entries examining key ideas and debates that guided medieval historians as these researchers and theorists shaped their notions, and ours, about premodern women. Certain entries, such as the three that explore women in different aspects of the writings of Boccaccio, show how these ideas have evolved in regard to new findings.

The editors sought to enlist contributors exhibiting a variety of scholarly experience and approaches. Most of the contributors are leading experts, even pioneers, in their fields. Although the contributors reflect various schools of thought—for example, some are feminist and others are more conservative—none of them compromises the academic integrity of his or her entry's content. Overall, even in presenting some new viewpoints on women's culture, the editors strove always to make entries informative rather than polemical.

The entries are arranged alphabetically across the two volumes (see the "Abbreviations and Editorial Policy" section for more on the alphabetization of entries). Biographical entries follow the name of the subject with life dates, or, if these are unknown or uncertain, with an indication of generally when the individual lived or was active. Broader topical entries also sometimes include a date designation following the subject heading to allow readers to quickly see the time period under discussion in the entry. For example, the entry on the literary motif of the "Nine Worthy Women" indicates in the title that use of this motif is associated mainly with the fourteenth and fifteenth centuries.

Usually, the entry text is followed immediately by a list of see also references to other related entries in the *Encyclopedia*. The entries conclude with extensive bibliographies broken down by primary and secondary sources when possible. Thus, both specialist and nonspecialist readers will find the bibliographies particularly useful. The *Encyclopedia* also includes cross-references to alternate names or terms in the main A–Z listing, and offers a "Guide to Related Topics" that groups entries into broad subject categories allowing readers to trace main themes and topics, such as "Fairies, Magicians, and Witches" or "Mystics and Visionary Authors," across the two volumes. A detailed subject index also allows access to important names and terms mentioned within entries. The "Abbreviations and Editorial Policy" section lists the abbreviations used in the entries and provides a detailed explanation of how the bibliographies were compiled and can be used. Finally, the *Encyclopedia* is extensively illustrated, with contemporary images accompanying many of the entries.

ACKNOWLEDGMENTS

I should first like to express my gratitude to Elizabeth Petroff, a longtime senior colleague with whom I had the pleasure of teaching in the Comparative Literature Program at the University of Massachusetts, Amherst, back in 1993. Her published work on medieval women visionaries, learned and witty conversation, and personal humanity have all inspired me in bringing this volume, enthusiastically and voluminously begun years earlier by Katharina Wilson, to completion. I also thank Roy Rosenstein and Matilda Bruckner for their help on various aspects of the *trobairitz*. My late husband, Peter K. Marshall, was kind enough to read through and offer advice on Classical and Medieval Latin and Greek titles, citations, and sources. All errors in incorporating such aid are solely my own.

For help in locating contributors beyond those already enlisted by my coeditor, I am indebted to Chris Baswell, Renate Blumenfeld-Kosinski, the late Charles T. Wood, Cynthia J. Brown, Elizabeth A. R. Brown, Elisheva Carlebach; Nancy Coiner, Carolyn Collette, Meg Cormack, Sheila Delany, Eglal Doss-Quinby, Thelma Fenster, Phyllis Granoff, Monica Green, Tom Head, Jo Ann McNamara, Julie Scott Meisami, María-Rosa Menocal, Elizabeth Petroff, Christine Reno, Deborah Sinnreich-Levi; Joe Snow, Jane H. M. Taylor; Ray Thompson, and Bonnie Wheeler, who also provided me with the latest publications from her "The New Middle Ages" series (Palgrave Macmillan).

The research facilities, both online and in situ, at the following institutions have proven unfailingly generous and indispensable: the Four-College Libraries (Amherst, Smith, and Mt. Holyoke Colleges, and the University of Massachusetts at Amherst), Harvard University, Yale University, the University of California at Los Angeles, the University of California at Santa Barbara, the Bibliothèque nationale de France, and the University of Hamburg Library.

Katharina Wilson, her assistants, and students compiled the substantial early basis of the volume. For technical help in the later phases, I thank Sara Upton of the Amherst College Classics Department; Jane Lovett, John Manley, and other staff of the Amherst College Academic Computer Center. Dan Kaden, of Dancer Computers, helped select, set up, and maintain all my machines and peripherals, which he kept from exploding over the years in response to many a frantic phone call.

Among the excellent staff at Greenwood, Gary Kuris, ever since his time at Garland Publishing in the early phases of this project, has always been the determinant, guiding presence. Last but by no means least, my editor at Greenwood, John A. Wagner, has patiently, astutely, and conscientiously helped me through the most crucial phases of this volume's realization.

Nadia Margolis
Leverett, Massachusetts
September 2004

Introduction

Not everyone who writes about women is a feminist, not even if the writer is a woman. Nor are all writers on women misogynistic (hating women), antifeminist (hating feminism), or misogamous (hating marriage). Although traditions interweaving all these tendencies go back to ancient pagan satire, the Christian Church Fathers, the early doctrinal founders of the Church, rendered these traditions into a more systematic misogyny, with Eve and Mary representing Original Sin and Redemption, respectively. Defenders of women find what is perhaps their progenitor in Plato's *Republic* (Book 5), although, like most ancient Greek and some principal Roman sources, the *Republic* would have been unknown before the late fourteenth century because its manuscripts, and the requisite training in Classical Greek, had yet to be recovered. But men have also written about women out of curiosity, or out of a need for thematic symmetry and replenishment after having exhausted the ever-present male configurations within all classes of society, past and present.

Nor were the so-called Middle Ages (a term devised by eighteenth-century historians) necessarily "dark," particularly when we note that Christianity, a source of light to medieval eyes, was maligned as the source of medieval darkness by the anticlerical rationalists of the eighteenth-century Enlightenment. Furthermore, the medieval period extends, according to conventionally held boundaries, for over ten dynamic centuries. Indeed, one of the many fascinating surprises awaiting newcomers to medieval studies is that those characteristics conventionally associated with the so-called Renaissance of the fifteenth and sixteenth centuries were happily flourishing well before then, and not only among men but also among women—albeit privileged and exceptionally talented women. Women participated in many of the great contributions to modern civilization that are considered to have originated in the Middle Ages, for example, romantic love (R. Howard Bloch 1992), parliamentary government, the banking system, universities, and certain literary genres.

Nor did the Middle Ages occur in other parts of the world as they did in Europe. In India, for example, Hindu culture reached its golden age in the early seventh century, when France and parts of Germany, still decades short of the unification achieved by Charlemagne, were being ruled by barbaric Merovingian kings who had only recently established their kingdoms and converted to Christianity. In China, a country with an already longstanding history, the early seventh century saw the beginning of the Tang dynasty, a golden age for Chinese culture overall and an era highly favorable to women's sociopolitical presence, a trend from which Japan also benefited. In the tenth century, the Tang gave way to the Song dynasty, a change that marked a decided downturn in the status of women (see the entry "China, Women in").

In the seventh century, Islamic Arabian culture was on the rise, culminating in the Abbasid golden age from the late eighth to the early tenth centuries. With Baghdad as their new capital, the Arabs overthrew the Christian Vandal and Visigothic kingdoms in North Africa and Spain, forming the Al-Andalus in the latter. Byzantium, the Eastern Roman Empire, remained far more civilized than the Western Roman Empire after 400, preserving imperial culture in its own way, with its own Eastern Orthodox Church (which split from the Roman Catholic Church in 1054). Although its power steadily waned after the Seljuk Turkish victory at Manzikert in 1071, the Byzantine Empire continued proudly until its capital, Constantinople (now Istanbul), fell to the Turks in 1453. But by that time, the West was again on the ascent, particularly in Italy and France. Even within Europe, different lands timed their progress irregularly: medieval practices and traditions, such as serfdom, lasted into the eighteenth and nineteenth century in parts of Eastern Europe, well after other parts of Europe and the Americas had moved into the modern era.

Finally, even at its "darkest" in the fifth to eighth centuries, the Middle Ages did not always bode poorly for women. Meanwhile, in male-designated "renaissances," particularly the major European Renaissance of the fifteenth and sixteenth centuries, women fared less well, as several scholars, such as Joan Kelly in her classic essay "Did Women Have a Renaissance?" (1977 and 1984), have concluded. These scholars point to the fact that women inheriting land under the medieval feudal system or who were guild members in their various trades wielded more public influence than they did later during the Renaissance. Although the Renaissance had a grand aura projected by its literary and visual-arts images of women, those images were created by and for men. Likewise, women in the early Church were allowed to participate more actively in the ecclesiastical hierarchy, as abbesses (heads of monasteries), deaconesses (clergy ranking just below priests), and teachers (see the entries on "Law, Canon" and "Teachers") than they were in later centuries when male clergy assumed greater control.

More modern theories like Kelly's refute the noble-minded pronouncements of Renaissance historians such as Jakob Burckhardt. Seduced by artistic and literary fictions, Burckhardt, in his monumental study, *The Civilization of the Renaissance in Italy* (1860), declared that Renaissance women enjoyed a status equal to that of men, a notion so eruditely enunciated that even Simone de Beauvoir embraced it in her revolutionary book, *The Second Sex* (1949). Although Ruth Kelso's research (1956) disproved Burckhardt, her work has, until recently, received little attention. Newer scholars on the Renaissance and premodern period, like Kelly and Natalie Zemon Davis, along with Classicists specializing in women in Greece and Rome like Mary Lefkowitz, have much to teach us about how we should assess women in the period between their two respective reference points. In sum, these and other historians conclude that we must continue to seek out individual cases to test any global hypotheses about the true situation of women during the Middle Ages.

For example, employing the sacred number three, medieval Christian clerics declared that society consisted of three orders: "those who pray," "those who fight," and "those who work." Women often joined townspeople and Jews in a fourth order, or fourth estate, as it was termed by Shulamith Shahar in *The Fourth Estate: A History of Women in the Middle*

Ages (1983). However, as Shahar and other historians demonstrate, medieval women had their own orders since there were plenty of women who preached and prayed, who worked, and who even fought in military conflicts like the Crusades. Women also added special qualities to these orders and to the ruling class, with queens like Clotilde of the Franks persuading their powerful husbands to convert to Christianity and doing pious and charitable works. Women religious, as if profiting from their marginality and lack of opportunity to train in Latin letters, cultivated direct, nonverbal lines to Christ, made him their spiritual bridegroom, and attained heatedly rapturous states of revelation that their "superior" learned male cohorts could only but record in awe. Some uncommon women whose mastery of literary languages, such as Latin in the West or Classical Arabic within Islamic culture, or of high-level vernacular genres, such as French courtly romance, rivaled their male mentors and thus risked having their authorship disputed. Examples are found in the cases of Heloise, and, to a lesser extent, Marie de France. As religious martyrs, women attained a grisly sort of equality with their male counterparts in gloriously enduring all manner of physical torture. Women who engaged in battle—such as Joan of Arc, who fought the English for Charles VII, or the Aztec women who assisted their men against invaders, or the Lombard princess Sichelgaita (c.1040–1090) who fought alongside her husband against Muslims in Sicily, her fearsome allure recorded by the equally rare (in the twelfth century) female historian, Anna Comnena—frightened their foes by their very "unnaturalness" as armor-clad warriors, even before raising a sword. As workers, women were often capable of executing more meticulous handcrafts with their smaller hands and great patience and stamina, or of providing gentler, more attentive care to the sick and infirm. In *Ale, Beer and Brewsters in England: Women's Work in a Changing World 1300–1600* (1996), Judith M. Bennett illustrated how women (alewives) dominated the brewing industry in England for as long as ale was preferred over beer; when beer took over for several socioeconomic reasons, so did the male brewsters. Many similar cases of medieval women's multidimensional uniqueness have been and continue to be uncovered by historians as they sift through the archives.

Mobility may serve as another measure of women's power and influence. Most recently, Lisa Bitel (2002), who has investigated early medieval European women's lives, including their migratory patterns (400–1100), emphasizes that, since male invaders tended to marry the women of the country they invaded, these nonmigratory women accomplished as much for settlement and assimilation by the stabilizing constancy of their domestic roles despite upheaval as did their more mobile, resettling sisters. In this and other aspects of their existence, women's nonuniqueness was an asset to their societies, though it also erased their presences as individuals.

Equally paradoxically, in contrast to their real-life position, women's individualized personalities, strength, and scope as legendary and mythical entities was overwhelming as these figures alternatingly guided and elevated or demolished men, as exemplified by Beatrice, Medea, Melusine, Natura, the Valkyries, and others. One should not be surprised that such imaginary power in celestial realms translated into women's diminished esteem and influence in the mortal world governed by men. Even when literature and art celebrating supernatural women flourished, we may often view such manifestations as strategies of confinement, both conscious and unconscious. More appalling was the case of witches and certain heretics, in that they could be horribly persecuted for powers they never really had, but were simply thought to possess.

"History favors success," wrote pioneering historian Jo Ann McNamara in the introduction to her volume, *Sainted Women of the Dark Ages* (1992). So, if we wish to speak of women's renaissances, perhaps the most convincing have been those in women's history and literature since the late 1970s. Isolated examples of serious scholarship revising our notions of women's roles in medieval society have existed at least since the suffragette-driven 1890s and early 1900s (Eileen Power's classic 1926 article, "The Position of Women," being one of the best). However, the broader spectrum of the global women's movement in the twentieth century, and especially in the West during the 1970s, attracted more rigorous academic attention to women's history, thereby buttressing work that could otherwise have been dismissed as "hysterical" feminist propaganda. As a result, the 1980s witnessed an immense surge of high-quality historical and literary research and interpretation, translations, and anthologies and sourcebooks—many of which are still valid and useful today.

Peter Dronke's *Medieval Women Writers* (1984) was a major force in developing medieval women's literary studies as a serious discipline. Dronke combined previously unseen primary materials and translations with keenly incisive, yet apolitical, analysis. Also important was the fact that Dronke was, and is, a widely respected male scholar at a world-renowned university who could thus publish with a major university press (Cambridge). Although his view of when the medieval period begins and ends varies by two hundred years at each end from the usual treatments, Dronke's pioneering work stands the test of time. In discussing early women's writing, Dronke emphasizes its lyric depth, thus going beyond the descriptive level and laying the groundwork for the more theoretical approaches of the 1980s and 1990s. Other works over the past two decades have examined the success of medieval women writers coming after those mentioned by Dronke, a glowing example being Earl Jeffrey Richards's translation of Christine de Pizan's *Book of the City of Ladies* (1982, 1998). In rediscovering Christine's 1405 revisionist history of women—a revelation in its own time—Richards rendered the work accessible to the English-speaking world at a propitious time. It was quickly followed by Charity Willard's biography of Christine. Both works were handsomely produced yet affordably priced. A profusion of editions and translations followed, including a second English translation of the *City of Ladies* by Rosalind Brown-Grant (1999), and other translations of Christine in German, Dutch, Italian, Spanish, and Catalan. Thanks to such developments, Christine de Pizan, a poet known mainly to late-medieval French and English specialists up to the 1980s, has become not only part of the undergraduate reading list at many American and European—and even Japanese—universities, but also a literary-critical growth industry beyond feminist concerns. The explosive popularity of authors like Christine also encouraged readers to go back to existing anthologies of lesser-known women writers from earlier or more obscure periods and spaces, such as the women of the early Christian Church translated and anthologized by Patricia Wilson-Kastner's group (1981) and a broader range of women whose works were edited by Marcelle Thiébaux (1987, 1994).

Nonliterate medieval women (i.e., those who were illiterate or who were literate but whose claim to fame lay in other pursuits) have also benefited from the surge, as revealed in studies of guilds, family history, deviant and marginal groups such as prostitutes, women ascetics, doctors, patrons, and lay religious groups such as the Beguines. Volumes such as *Sisters and Workers in the Middle Ages* (1989), edited by Judith Bennett and others, collected and published seminal essays from the 1970s and 1980s. Extremely rich, insightful sourcebook-anthologies, like Carolyne Larrington's *Women and Writing in Medieval Europe* (1995), offered primary materials in translation beyond the usual, enabling the reader to engage as many authentic medieval women's voices as possible. More recently, Carolyn Dinshaw and David Wallace's *Cambridge Companion to Medieval Women's Writing* (2003) provided a series of essays on medieval constructs (e.g., "beneath the pulpit," childhood, marriage, monastic enclosure, widows, and virginity) and authorial personalities and types (e.g., Heloise, Margery Kempe, and the mystics), offering fresh perspectives in readable form.

Multiculturalism, the investigation of cultures beyond the Western nations, represents a still newer field of medieval women's studies; in conjunction with the above-described fields, it extends the boundaries of inquiry still farther. In this domain, much of the innovation lies in linking preexistent but specialized non-Western texts and information with Western analogues, thus opening it to a larger readership. Medieval Islam and Byzantium have so far reaped the most rewards, although interest in China, Japan, and other Asian cultures has increased.

These trends have been at once signaled and nourished by publications like the *Medieval Feminist Forum* (the erstwhile *Medieval Feminist Newsletter*), a cutting-edge research bulletin founded about fifteen years ago and whose editorial base has migrated every few years over a broad geographical range of host institutions within the United States. The *Forum* is now more prosperous than ever, precisely because its brand of feminism has matured with the times, without compromising the journal's intellectual integrity. Its concisely presented, quality scholarship continues to explore and underscore how many current burning issues (such as women and multiculturalism, race, gender, linguistic correctness; the literary "canon"; religion vs. science) also preoccupied medieval minds, and that their discussions may enrich our modern understanding. Many medieval women authors who, even five years ago, lacked so much as an excerpt, whether in their own language or in translation, now have their own Web site devised by research groups or devoted individuals. Although the validity of some of the information on these sites can be uneven at times, the enthusiasm shines forth as another form of the success of medieval women, which, given the relative chronological, cultural, and linguistic distance, often surpasses the popularity of their more modern counterparts.

Abbreviations and Editorial Policy

ABBREVIATIONS AND TERMS
The use of abbreviations is kept to a minimum in these volumes and includes only the few standard usages listed below:

c. = circa

ed. = edition/editor

d. = died

e.g. = for example

et al. = and others

fl. = flourished (used if actual life and death dates are unknown)

n. p. = no named publisher

passim = found various places throughout the cited work

r. = ruled

rev. = revised

trans. = translation/translator

v./vv. = verse/verses

Books of the Holy Bible, when abbreviated, all follow those given in the Revised Standard Version list. Certain well-known series, such as *Monumenta Germaniae Historica* and *Patrologia Graeca*, are italicized and written out in the first citation of an article's bibliography, with the series' operative abbreviation heralded in brackets, and then abbreviated (e.g., MGH, PG) in succeeding references within the same article's bibliography.

ALPHABETIZATION OF ENTRIES
Entries have been arranged alphabetically. Persons are alphabetized by last name unless the first name and "last" name are separated by a particle (e.g., da, de, of, van, von), in which case it is alphabetized by first name; thus, Adelhaid Langmann is found under "Langmann" and Marie de France under "Marie."

NAMES OF PERSONS AND PLACES

Names of more familiar figures and places are given according to their most common English forms. The particles in most foreign names may be translated with the word "of" if the particle links with a town or region that is well known to English speakers (e.g., Eleanor of Aquitaine, Anne of Bohemia, Adela of Blois); otherwise, the authentic particle is retained, as in Katharina von Gebweiler. However, the most commonly accepted scholarly usage is the overriding determinant, and this principle often contradicts the aforementioned usages (and any other consistency rule). Hence, there are entries for Marie de France and Marguerite d'Oingt, but also for Ivetta of Huy and Colette of Corbie. Some versions of names used here, as in the case of Christine de Pizan, reflect the currently accepted version of the name, as opposed to a now-discredited version, in this case, "Pisan." The *trobairitz* (women troubadours) often appear with the names of their places of origin unmodernized, for example, Comtessa de Dia (instead of Die) and Iseut de Capio (instead of Chapieu), although Gormonda of Montpellier is seen just as often as Gormonda de Montpeslier.

Some women are known only by their titles or epithets/first initial, for example, Domna H., Na Prous Boneta, Compiuta Donzella, Frau Ava, and Lady Godiva. In most cases, these women are listed under the name, noun, or initial rather than under the title or adjective, H., Domna rather than Domna H., for example. Cross-references in the main entry listing help ease the reader through such inconsistencies. Whether anglicized or original, common first names often have competing variants, since spelling was not standardized in the Middle Ages (Catherine/Katherine/Katharina; Elizabeth/Elisabeth/Elsbeth; Margaret/Marguerite/Margareta). Again, the form judged by usage over time to be the most common or findable is used in this book, for example, Joan of Arc rather than Jeanne d'Arc, yet Jeanne d'Évreux rather than Joan of Évreux.

TITLES OF WORKS, THEMES, AND CONCEPTS

The titles of works, themes, or concepts are entered under their original or technical language titles and then translated in the entries. However, most are also often cross-referenced from their English or vernacular equivalents, as in the French law, *Jus Primae Noctis*, which entry is cross-referenced from both *Droit du Seigneur* and *Lord's First Night*. Other entries, such as *Belle Dame sans Merci*, are universal in their original language.

SOURCE CITATIONS

As a reference volume, *Women in the Middle Ages* does not use footnotes. However, where specifically necessary, the source-author's name—or, for anonymous works, the work's short title—is given in the entry either as part of the discussion or in parentheses after the pertinent statement in text, for example (Smith) or (*Chanson de Roland*). The reader can then look for the complete citation to the work in the entry's bibliography. If more than one work by the same author is being cited in text, the date of the specific work is given after the author's name—(Jones 1978), for example. The reader can consult the full citation for the author's works in the bibliography as referenced by date. Page numbers are provided in the parenthetic reference only in certain special cases, as in lengthy works without indexes (Jones 1978, 31–32). In cases where a specific edition or translation is being cited, usually for its notes or particular version, the translator's or editor's name is given, prefaced by "ed." or "trans.," but the edition should be sought in the Primary Sources section under the name of the *author* in question. If notes to McNamara's translation of St. Radegund are being cited, then "(ed. McNamara)" will appear at the end of the pertinent in-text statements, but the full citation of the book will be found in the Primary Sources section of the bibliography under Radegund's name, since Radegund is the actual author and McNamara the translator and commentator.

In all practicable cases, all foreign-language works cited in text are given first in their original-language form and then, in parentheses, in English translation. This is also the case with all foreign-language textual citations.

BIBLIOGRAPHIES
The entries' bibliographies are necessarily selective, not comprehensive, and attempt to satisfy the needs of a wide readership. All citations are presented according to a modified version of the *Chicago Manual of Style*. Except in certain cases where unfeasible or unnecessary, all bibliographies are divided into Primary Sources and Secondary Sources.

Primary Sources
Primary sources include printed editions and translations, with each work's most authoritative edition listed first and partial editions and translations coming afterward, crediting the editor/translator. Each is also labeled according to type: "critical edition" meaning the text is in its original language only, as transcribed and reconstructed from medieval manuscripts, with introduction and notes in the modern editor's language; "edition" also means in the original language only unless otherwise described. We have also attempted to signal bilingual editions (original language plus modern-language translation), editions and translations with introductions, commentary and notes (these will almost always contain bibliographies and other aids), and English-only translations (with no original text). Failing the existence of an English translation or bilingual edition, we have cited translations in other modern languages because often these are still more comprehensible, especially given their annotations, than an original, medieval-language edition. We also cite non-English translations when their annotations/commentary are exceptionally good, thus supplementing an English translation.

Certain well-known, older scholarly series containing primary materials—for example, the *Acta Sanctorum* (AASS), the *Corpus Christianorum* (CC), the *Monumenta Germaniae Historica* (MGH), the *Patrologia Latina* (PL), the *Patrologia Graeca* (PG), and the *Patrologia Orientalis* (PO)—are often cited only by title, naming the editor (if identifiable) and, if necessary, the pertinent subseries title, without the publisher and date of the particular volume, since this latter information varies and is unnecessary to effective consultation in reference libraries.

In cases where no printed editions exist, manuscript locations and numbers are provided when possible.

Secondary Sources
The Secondary Source listings in the entries' bibliographies contain only works *about* the topic, including histories and criticism, although many may contain extracts of primary

texts. Not all critical studies listed necessarily agree with the entry author's position on the entry topic, but are mentioned to provide a representative sampling of worthy scholarship and criticism, both old (if still reliable or historically interesting) and new. Certain common reference works such as the *Dictionary of National Biography* (*DNB*) may be cited without author, publisher, or date.

Alphabetical List of Entries

Guide to Related Topics

ABBESSES AND PRIORESSES
Agnes of Assisi, St.
Aldegund, St.
Caesaria, St.
Constance of Castile
Egburg
Gertrude of Nivelles, St.
Gualdrada de' Ravignani
Hazzecha of Krauftal
Heloise
Herrad of Hohenberg/Landsberg
Hild (Hilda), St.
Hildegard of Bingen, St.
Isabel de Villena
Petronilla of Chemillé
Radegund, St.
Theuthild
Umiltà of Faenza, St.

ARTISTS, CRAFTSWOMEN, AND SCRIBES
Artists, Medieval Women
Boccaccio, Women in, *Des Cleres et Nobles Femmes*
Dress, Courtly Women's
Dress, Religious Women's (Western, Christian)
Embroidery
Marcia in the Middle Ages
Scribes and Scriptoria

COMMUNITIES, GROUPS, AND CIRCLES (RELIGIOUS AND LAY)
Beguines
Berthgyth
Bizzoche
Boniface, St., Mission and Circle of
Bugga

Convents
Double Monasteries
Egburg
Eustochium, St.
Ivetta of Huy
Leoba
Mulieres sanctae
Nunneries, Merovingian
Pinzochere
Prous Boneta, Na
Unterlinden, Sisters of

CULTURES (ETHNIC, NATIONAL, AND RELIGIOUS)
Aztec Warrior Women
China, Women in
Desert Mothers
Fatimid Egypt, Women in
Jewish Women in the Middle Ages
Muscovy, Women in
Norse Women
Syrian-Christian Women

DEVIANTS AND MARGINALS
Lesbians in the Middle Ages
Prostitution
Slaves, Female
Transvestism
Witches

DOCTORS, HEALERS, AND CAREGIVERS
Concubines
Elisabeth of Hungary/Thuringia, St.
Fedele, Cassandra
Medea in the Middle Ages
Medicine and Medieval Women

Slaves, Female
Trota and "Trotula"

FAIRIES, MAGICIANS, AND WITCHES
Enchantresses, Fays (*Fées*), and Fairies
Medea in the Middle Ages
Melusine
Morgan le Fay
Valkyries
Witches

FOUNDERS, MISSIONARIES, ASCETICS, REFORMERS, AND RELIGIOUS
Æthelthryth, St.
Agnes of Assisi, St.
Agnes of Bohemia, Blessed
Beguines
Birgitta of Sweden, St.
Bizzoche
Caesaria, St.
Catherine of Bologna, St.
Clare of Assisi, St.
Colette of Corbie, St.
Desert Mothers
Elisabeth of Schönau, St.
Epistolary Authors, Women as
Haider, Ursula
Hild (Hilda), St.
Hugeburc of Heidenheim
Ivetta of Huy
Leoba
Macrina the Elder, St.
Macrina the Younger, St.
Melania the Elder, St.
Melania the Younger, St.
Merici, Angela, St.
Mulieres sanctae
Pinzochere
Porete, Marguerite
Prous Boneta, Na
Rules for Canonesses, Nuns, and Recluses
Syrian-Christian Women
Umiltà of Faenza, St.

HERETICS
Grazida (Grazida Lizier)
Guglielmites
Joan of Arc, St.
Porete, Marguerite
Prous Boneta, Na

HISTORIANS, CHRONICLERS, MEMORIALISTS, AND SAGAS
See also below under Saints' Cults, Lives: Authors and Heroines
Abutsu-ni
Anna of Munzingen
Belle Hélène de Constantinople
Boccaccio, Women in, *De Claris Mulieribus*
Boccaccio, Women in, *Des Cleres et Nobles Femmes*
Cereta, Laura
Christine de Pizan
Comnena, Anna
Egeria
Epistolary Authors, Women as
Hrotsvitha of Gandersheim
Humanists, Italian Women, Issues and Theory
Katharina von Gebweiler/Geberschweier
Laxdœla saga
Leonor López de Córdoba
Paston, Margaret
Perpetua, St.
Place-Names, English, Women in
Sister-Books (*Schwesternbücher*)
Stagel, Elsbeth

LAWS, CUSTOMS, EDICTS, OATHS, PRIVILEGES/PROHIBITIONS, AND RULES
Ancrene Riwle
Celibacy
Dress, Courtly Women's
Dress, Religious Women's (Western Christian)
Footbinding
Hocktide
Jus Primae Noctis
Law, Canon, Women in
Law, Women in, Anglo-Saxon England
Marriage
Penitentials, Women in
Periculoso
Rape
Rules for Canonesses, Nuns, and Recluses
Sachsenspiegel and *Schwabenspiegel*
Teachers, Women as

LITERARY CHARACTERS, GENRES, MYTHS, AND THEMES
Alba Lady
Arthurian Women
Beatrice
Belle Dame sans Merci

Belle Hélène de Constantinople
Brangain
Bride of Christ/*Brautmystik*
Capellanus, Andreas
Chaucer, Geoffrey, Women in the Work of
Criseyde
Danse Macabre des Femmes
Dido in the Middle Ages
Elaine
Enchantresses, Fays (*Fées*), and Fairies
Frauenturnier
Godiva, Lady
Griselda
Guinevere
Humility Topos
Igerne
Isolde
Joan, Pope
Joan of Arc, St.
Judgment of Paris
Kharja
Lady of the Lake
Laudine
Laura
Laxdœla saga
Lunete
Medea in the Middle Ages
Melusine
Minne
Morgan le Fay
Muwashshaḥ
Natura
Nine Worthy Women
Novela Sentimental/Sentimental Romance
Power of Women
Rhetoric, Women and
Tournoiement des Dames
Trobairitz
Trouvères, Women
Valkyries

LOVERS AND BELOVED
Beatrice
Bride of Christ/*Brautmystik*
Christine de Pizan
Concubines
Criseyde
Dido in the Middle Ages
Emma
Francesca da Rimini
Guinevere
Heloise
Isolde
Laura

Margareta von Schwangau
Medea in the Middle Ages
Pinar, Florencia
Rosamond, Fair
Shore, Elizabeth (Jane)
Slaves, Female
Sorel, Agnès
Trobairitz
Trouvères, Women
Yang Guifei

MANUALS OF CONDUCT, MORALS, AND PENANCE
Capellanus, Andreas
Christine de Pizan
Courtesy Books
Dhuoda
Isabel de Villena
Miroir de Mariage (*Mirror of Marriage*)
Penitentials, Women in
Response du Bestiaire
Vertu du Sacrement de Mariage, Livre de la

MARTYRS, SUFFERERS, PRISONERS, AND VICTIMS
Belle Hélène de Constantinople
Cornaro, Caterina
Eleanor of Brittany
Griselda
Ingeborg of Denmark/Isambour of France
Joan of Arc, St.
Malmojades, Les
Perpetua, St.
Porete, Marguerite
Shore, Elizabeth (Jane)
Teresa de Cartagena

MISOGYNISTIC/FEMINIST TOPICS, DEBATES, AND THEORETICAL CONCEPTS
Bride of Christ/*Brautmystik*
Capellanus, Andreas
Christine de Pizan
Frauenfrage
Isabel de Villena
Joan, Pope
Judgment of Paris
Le Fèvre de Ressons, Jean
Le Franc, Martin
Miroir de Mariage (*Mirror of Marriage*)
Power of Women
Response du Bestiaire
Roman de la Rose, Debate of the

Salic Law
Teresa de Cartagena

MOTHERS (ROYAL-DYNASTIC AND THEOLOGICAL)

Aasta of Norway
Childhood and Child-Rearing in the Middle
  Ages
Christine de Pizan
Desert Mothers
Dhuoda
Eleanor of Aquitaine
Igerne
Macrina the Elder, St.
Mary, Blessed Virgin, in the Middle Ages
Teachers, Women as
Yolande of Flanders

MUSICIANS, COMPOSERS, AND MUSICAL GENRES

Chanson de Femme (Women's Song)
Daina
Frauenlied
Hildegard of Bingen, St.
Katherine of Sutton
Music in Medieval Nunneries
Music, Women Composers and Musicians
Theodosia
Trobairitz
Trouvères, Women

MYSTICS AND VISIONARY AUTHORS

Aldegund, St.
Angela of Foligno, Blessed
Ava, Frau
Bake, Alijt
Beatrijs van Nazareth/van Tienen
Bertken, Sister/Berta Jacobs
Birgitta of Sweden, St.
Catherine of Siena, St.
Christina of Markyate
Christina Mirabilis
Clare of Assisi, St.
Clare of Montefalco, St.
Colette of Corbie, St.
Dorothea of Montau, St.
Ebner, Christine
Ebner, Margareta
Elisabeth of Schönau, St.
Elsbeth von Oye
Engelbina von Augsburg
Geertruide van Oosten
Gertrude the Great, of Helfta, St.

Gherardesca of Pisa
Hadewijch
Haider, Ursula
Isabel de Villena
Julian of Norwich
Juliana of Mont-Cornillon
Jutta of Disibodenberg, Blessed
Kempe, Margery
Langmann, Adelhaid
Marguerite d'Oingt
María de Ajofrín
Mechthild of Hackeborn
Mechthild of Magdeburg
Prous Boneta, Na
Rābi'a al-'Adawiyya

RULERS

Popes
Joan, Pope

Empresses
Theodora
Wu, Empress
Zoe Karbounopsina

Queens
Aasta of Norway
Amalasuntha
Anne of Bohemia
Brunhild
Clotilde, St.
Cornaro, Caterina
Dido in the Middle Ages
Eleanor of Aquitaine
Eleanor of Castile
Elizabeth of York
Emma/Ælfgifu
Galla Placidia
Guinevere
Ingeborg of Denmark/Isambour of France
Ingibiorg
Isabeau of Bavaria
Isolde
Jeanne d'Évreux
Margaret of Anjou
Margaret of Scotland, St.
Marie de Brabant
Matilda of Scotland, St.
Radegund, St.
Woodville, Elizabeth
Yolanda of Aragon

Noblewomen
Adela of Blois
Adelaide, Countess of Aumale
Beaufort, Margaret
Chaucer, Alice
Ermengard of Narbonne
Filipa de Lencastre
Jacquetta of Luxembourg
Joan, Fair Maid of Kent
Louise of Savoy
Margaret of Scotland, St.
Margaret of York
Marie de Champagne
Matilda of Tuscany/Canossa
Visconti, Valentina
Yolanda of Aragon
Yolande of Flanders

SAINTS' CULTS, LIVES: AUTHORS AND HEROINES
Baudonivia
Bembo, Illuminata
Bertha of Vilich
Bokenham, Osbern
Chelles, Nun of
Elisabeth of Hungary/Thuringia, St.
Hagiography (Female Saints)
Hrotsvitha of Gandersheim
Marguerite d'Oingt
Maria of Venice (Maria Sturion)
Relics and Medieval Women
Umiltà of Faenza, St.

SCHOLARS, HUMANISTS, THINKERS, AND TEACHERS
Battista da Montefeltro Malatesta
Borja, Tecla
Cereta, Laura
Christine de Pizan
Desert Mothers
Dhuoda
Eleonore of Austria
Epistolary Authors, Women as
Fedele, Cassandra
Gonzaga, Cecilia
Herrad of Hohenberg/Landsberg
Hildegard of Bingen, St.
Hrotsvitha of Gandersheim
Humanists, Italian Women, Issues and Theory
Macrina the Elder, St.
Macrina the Younger, St.
Melania the Elder, St.

Melania the Younger, St.
Nogarola, Angela
Nogarola, Ginevra
Nogarola, Isotta
Novella d'Andrea
Scala, Alessandra
Scrovegni, Maddalena
Teachers, Women as
Varano, Costanza

SPORTSWOMEN
Berners, Juliana

TRADESWOMEN AND WORKERS
Guilds, Women in
Slaves, Female
Spinners and Drapers

VIRGINS
Eustochium, St.
Joan of Arc, St.
Mary, Blessed Virgin, in the Middle Ages
Thecla, St.
Virginity

WARRIORS, PROTECTORS, AND PROTESTERS
Aztec Warrior Women
Frauenturnier
Godiva, Lady
Joan of Arc, St.
Melusine
Teresa de Cartagena
Tournoiement des Dames
Valkyries

WIVES AND WIDOWS
Ava, Frau
Chaucer, Alice
Chaucer, Geoffrey, Women in the Work of
Christine de Pizan
Dorothea of Montau, St.
Dower
Dowry
Emma
Griselda
Guinevere
Ingeborg of Denmark/Isambour of France
Kempe, Margery
Margareta von Schwangau
Marriage
Melania the Elder, St.
Widows

WRITERS (LITERARY), POETS, TRANSLATORS, AND PATRONS
Adela of Blois
Alaisina Yselda
Alamanda
Almuc de Castelnou
Azalais d'Altier
Azalais de Porcairagues
Bietris de Roman
Boccaccio, Women in, *De Claris Mulieribus*
Boccaccio, Women in, *Des Cleres et Nobles Femmes*
Boccaccio, Women in, Works Other than *De Claris Mulieribus*
Carenza, Na
Castelloza, Na
Catalan Women Poets, Anonymous
Christine de Pizan
Clara d'Anduza
Comnena, Anna
Compiuta Donzella
Comtessa de Dia
Cornaro, Caterina
Eleanor of Aquitaine
Elisabeth of Nassau-Saarbrücken
Epistolary Authors, Women as
Ermengard of Narbonne
Eucheria
Eudocia
Filipa de Lencastre
Garsenda of Forcalquier
Gaudairenca
Gormonda de Montpellier
Guilielma des Rosers

H., Domna
Heloise
Hildegard of Bingen, St.
Hrotsvitha of Gandersheim
Iseut de Capio
Izumi Shikibu
Jóreiðr Hermundardóttir í Miðjumdal
Jórunn skáldmær
Katherine of Sutton
Leonor López de Córdoba
Li Qingzhao
Lombarda
Margareta von Schwangau
Maria de Ventadorn
Marie de Champagne
Marie de Compiègne
Marie de France
Mirabai
Murasaki Shikibu
Pinar, Florencia
Proba, Faltonia Betitia
Reyna de Mallorques, La
Rhetoric, Women and
Sei Shonagon
Skáldkonur (Old Norse-Icelandic Women Poets)
Steinunn Refsdóttir
Theodosia
Theosebeia
Tibors
Wallādah
Xue Tao
Ysabella, Domna

Ꜳ

AASTA OF NORWAY (late 10th century–early 11th century). Royal matriarch of Norway, Aasta (Ásta) was the mother of St. Oláf. As with other significant early Scandinavian women of rank, her biography comes down to us from part of the epic chronicles known as the *Heimskringla* (*Circle of the World*), specifically, the sagas of Oláf Tryggvason (*Oláfs saga Tryggvasonar*) and of St. Oláf (*Oláfs saga helga*) commonly attributed to Snorri Sturluson (d. 1241), although their sources and authorship are more complex, as Anne Heinrichs has shown. Daughter of Guthbrand Kúla, Aasta first married Haraldr inn grenske ("Harald of Greenland"), a king in Vestvold, southeastern Norway, and descendant of the great Norse ruler Haraldr hárfargri ("Harald Fair-hair"). According to legend, Aasta's husband, Harald, ventured over to Sweden to negotiate possessions with the wealthy Sigríd, aptly called "the Strong-Minded," a widowed queen. Perhaps because she was annoyed at Harald's proposing marriage simply out of greed for her lands and despite his already respectable married status, Sigríd had him and other chieftains slain in their sleep. Aasta bore Harald's posthumous son, Oláf Haraldsson (c.995), raised him first with her father, Guthbrand, but then married Sigurth Syr ("Sow") Hálfdanarson, king of the lesser domain of Hingkaríki, who became Oláf's stepfather.

Soon thereafter, when Oláf Tryggvason, king of Norway (995–1000), came to convert the kingdom of Hingkaríki, he baptised Aasta, Sigurth, and little Oláf, becoming the boy's godfather. Aasta and Sigurth are described in the chronicles as wise, generous, and noble rulers, from whose union issued Guthorm, Gunhild, Hálfdan, Ingiríth, and Harald. Although current historians tend to downplay Aasta's role, the sagas depict her as a strong, guiding influence on both her second husband and her children, especially Oláf. When the time came for Oláf's first experience aboard a warship at age twelve, it was Aasta who arranged this initiating expedition and ceremonial homecoming as befit her son, now "King Oláf the Stout," whom she pushed and advised toward becoming conquering king and great unifier of Norway. Oláf would fulfill his mother's wishes over the years 1015–1028 as he wrested his kingdom from the Danes and Swedes. His rule would mark a rare interval of relative freedom from outside domination in medieval Norway. He exhibited generosity toward his half siblings, granting land to his half brothers and marrying Gunhild to one of his favorite henchmen, Ketil Kálf of Hringuness. Aasta's other daughter, Ingiríth, also seems to have married well. Oláf became St. Oláf one year after his death in battle in 1030. Having fought alongside him, half brother Harald, Aasta's youngest, also grew up to rule

Norway, from 1047 to 1066. Though appropriately dubbed "Harthràthi" (Hard Ruler), Harald reigned well. He saved Iceland from famine, built churches, founded Oslo, and established coinage, while also being a warrior and one of the last true old-style Viking heroes.

See also Norse Women; *Skáldkonur* (old Norse = Icelandic Women Poets)

BIBLIOGRAPHY

Primary Sources

Haralds saga Sigurdarsonar. In *Heimskringla*, edited by Bjarni Adalbjarnarson, vol. 3: 68–202. Islenzk fornrit, 26–28. Reykjavik, Iceland: Hid íslenzka formritafélag, 1951.

Heimskringla. Edited by Finnur Jónsson. 4 vols. Samfund til uidgevelse af gammel nordisk litteratur, 23. Copenhagen: Møller, 1893–1902. Reprint (as 1 vol.) Copenhagen: Gad, 1911, 1925.

Heimskringla: History of the Kings of Norway. Translated by Lee M. Hollander. Austin: American-Scandinavian Foundation/University of Texas Press, 1964.

Olafs saga saga hins helga: Die "Legendarische Saga" über Olaf den Heiligen. Edited and translated by Anne Heinrichs et al. Heidelberg, Germany: Carl Winter, 1982.

Secondary Sources

Bagge, Sverre. *Society and Politics in Snorri Sturluson's* Heimskringla. Berkeley: University of California Press, 1991. [Good for background and sources, though it never mentions Aasta].

Heinrichs, Anne. Introduction to her edition and translation of *Olafs saga*, listed above.

———. "Oláfs saga helga." In *Medieval Scandinavia: An Encyclopedia*, edited by Phillip Pulsiano et al., 447–48. New York and London: Garland, 1993.

Karras, Ruth Mazo. "Harald hardrádi ("hard-ruler") Sigurdarson." In *Medieval Scandinavia: An Encyclopedia*, edited by Phillip Pulsiano et al., 266–67. New York and London: Garland, 1993.

NADIA MARGOLIS

ABSTINENCE. *See* **Virginity**

ABUTSU-NI (c.1220–1283). A Japanese Buddhist nun known for her spiritual-autobiographical travel poems, Abutsu-ni is particularly remembered for her *Izayoi Nikki* (*The Journal of the Sixteenth-Night Moon*, trans. McCullough; *Diary of the Waning Moon*, trans. Reischauer) during the Kamakura period. Born in Kyoto, as an adolescent, after her parents died and her stepfather had to leave for a distant provincial government post, she served at the court of Princess Ankamon'in (1209–1283) under the name Ankamon'in no Shijo. She married Tamei Fujiwara (1198–1275), by whom she had three children: two sons and a daughter. She met her husband after entering employment (1252) by his family to copy manuscripts of Murasaki Shikibu's *Genji Monogatari*—more familiar to English readers as Lady Murasaki's *Tale of Genji*. Tamei first took her as a minor wife, then as his principal wife after she bore him two children. After being widowed in her late fifties, she became a Buddhist nun under the name Abutsu-ni (the suffix *ni* = "nun"), yet without having to withdraw from the real world. This relative freedom enabled her to engage in the legal dispute over inheritance (both financial and literary, since the Fujiwaras were official custodians of valuable literary manuscripts) arising between Tamei's eldest son by a previous marriage and her eldest son with Tamei, Tamesuke, then age seventeen. To be nearer to the official court and plead on her son's behalf, she moved with only her servants to the eastern capital of Kamakura (south of Tokyo) c.1279, where she remained through four years of legal battles before her death. A judgment handed down in 1289 favored Tamesuke, but more wrangling and reversals ensued into the succeeding century. Her descendents prevailed, however, thus retaining their rights as guardians and disseminators of Japan's literary treasures.

Pilgrimage literature—"Journals of the Path"—was quite popular in thirteenth-century traditional Japanese poetry, as it was simultaneously in Europe. Less escapist than enlightening as it rearranged individual and universal problems and phases over an allegorical (morally symbolic) landscape, pilgrimage writing offered both rationalization and emotional solace in extremely troubled times for both author and reader. Just as Europe was menaced by the Tartar invaders, so too was Japan, which had narrowly escaped the Mongol ravages because of fortuitous bad weather. Another predominant poetic genre, a more subjective, lyric category called *waka*, expresses sentiments surrounding significant phases of human life: temporary or permanent emotional separation caused by love, religious conversion, and death. Abutsu-ni's marriage to Tamei Fujiwara linked her to one of the most distinguished families of Japanese court poets in addition to their status as trusted copyists of other authors' manuscripts; her father-in-law, Fujiwara Teika (1162–1241), was one of the leading *waka* masters. This family belonged to the so-called Reizei school of *waka*, which held their own literary contests at the imperial court. Consequently, Abutsu-ni lacked not for literary models in perfecting her own art, interweaving material from history, literature, and personal experience.

She composed her lesser-known poem, *Utatane* (*Fitful Slumbers*), looking back at an unhappy love affair from her youth and her struggle to overcome its painful aftermath, years later. The fusion of geographical itinerary with subjective evolution characterizing her *Journal* already appears here, along with allusions to her joining the Buddhist convent after her "distaste for the person she had become" because of her love-obsession. She also wrote three prose works: a sort of instructional treatise for her daughter, a memorial tribute to her husband, and an essay on poetics titled *Yoro no tsuru* (*The Crane at Night*), in which she prescribes detailed and accurate descriptions of nature as an essential to good poetry.

Written toward the end of her life, *The Journal of the Sixteenth-Night Moon* was her most ambitious work. Incorporating two main genre traditions (pilgrimage and *waka*) within her poetic journey as the "way of *waka*," or "itinerant poetics," Abutsu-ni began her *Journal of the Sixteenth-Night Moon* on October 16, 1279, and completed it in August of 1280. The text is divided into four parts: prologue, journey, sojourn at Kamakura, and expressions of hope for the success of her son's lawsuit to recover his inheritance, whose outcome she did not live to see. Her movement from Kyoto to Kamakura microcosmically replicates the shift in the center of national power between the two Japanese cities. The first two parts are the most interesting. The narrative opens with an explanation of how, when Abutsu-ni was "blinded by maternal tenderness"—similar to the visions inaugurating European allegorical-journey accounts—the moon appears to her. By the lunar calendar, the moon is at its sixteenth night, when it rises the latest. The poet-narrator compares this delay to her own reluctance to "rise" to her necessary journey. She finally departs, in the wistful season of autumn, bidding a tearful farewell to her previous life and children, each of whom receives his or her own poignantly lyrical poetic exchange with their mother in a series of *wakas*. Traveling at first by oxcart, on arriving at the seven gates of Kyoto, she changes modes of transport by mounting a light horse, or palfrey. She traverses various topographies (like Mt. Miyajiyama, whose summit she had really crossed in 1239, thus prompting memories of her youth here; Mt. Utsu [now, Shizuoka], the melancholy mountain of constant rain), and encounters with figures (a monk-pilgrim who offers to convey a message from her to her beloved Kyoto) and places from Japanese literature (such sites as Fuwa and Kasanui), mythology (such as the first Japanese mythic history, the *Kojiki*, compiled in 711–712, and the *Nihonshoki* [720]), and religion (for example, the Shinto shrine of Atsuta jingu). Nature also plays a role, as when Abutsu-ni's tears of departure relate to autumnal rains and withered leaves—or fiery-colored ones atop an inspirational mountain. The passage from autumn to winter, merged with the image of the moon, is a favorite theme in this work and in other thirteenth-century Japanese poetic journeys. Each stage of this pilgrimage occasions a poetic commemoration, making a total of fifty-five prose and verse *wakas* comprising the *Journal*.

After her death, two volumes of her poetry were published; forty-eight of her poems made their way into imperial anthologies. An allusion to the *Journal* by the celebrated travel poet Basho (1644–1694)—a pioneer in the *haiku* genre, an offshoot of *waka*—reflects the esteem in which her poetry continued to be held by poets centuries later: "The excellent travel accounts of Tsurayuki, Chomei and Abutsu give full expression to the feelings we experience on a journey. Later writers have been unable to progress beyond feeble imitations of their art" (trans. McCullough). Much more recently, Sasaki has demonstrated convincingly the striking parallelisms between Abutsu-ni's life and pilgrimage poetry and that of French protofeminist author Christine de Pizan (1365–1430?), especially in her *Chemin de long estude* (*Path of Long Study*).

See also Christine de Pizan; Egeria; Izumi Shikibu; Murasaki Shikibu; Sei Shonagon

BIBLIOGRAPHY

Primary Sources
Abutsu-ni. [*The Journal of the Sixteenth-Night Moon*]. *Izayoi-nikki*. Critical ed. by Kō Takeda. Tokyo: Meiji-shoin, 1985.
———. *The Izayoi Nikki*. In *Translations from Early Japanese Literature*, by Edwin O. Reischauer and Joseph K. Yamagiwa, pt. 1. Cambridge, Mass.: Harvard University Press, 1951. Reprint 1972. [Also as a separate article: Reischauer, *Harvard Journal of Asiatic Studies* 10 (1947): 255–387]. [With useful commentary].
———. [Excerpts from Section 1, English]. In *Classical Japanese Prose*, edited and translated by Helen Craig McCullough. Stanford, Calif.: Stanford University Press, 1990. [Much supplementary information].
———. [*Fitful Slumbers*]. *Utatane*. In [*Medieval Diaries and Travel Literature*], edited by Hideichi Fukuda, 158–77. Tokyo: Iwanami-shoten, 1993. [Japanese only].
———. *Fitful Slumbers*. Translated by John R. Wallace. In *Monumenta Nipponica* 43 (1988): 391–416.
———. [Prose works, extracts]. *See under* Wallace *below*.
Bashô, Matsuo. [*Backpack Notes*]. *Bashô bunshû*. Critical ed. by S. Sugiura and S. Miyamoto, 53. Tokyo: Iwanami-shôten, 1982.

Secondary Sources
Keene, Donald. *Seeds in the Heart: Japanese Literature from the Earliest Times to the Late Sixteenth Century*. New York: Henry Holt, 1993.
Pigeot, Jacqueline. *Michiyuki-bun: Poétique de l'itinéraire dans la littérature du Japon ancien*. Paris: Maisonneuve & Larose, 1982.

Sasaki, Shigemi. "Voies de savoir et de poésie: poétique du voyage chez deux poétesses de France et du Japon." In *Contexts and Continuities: Proceedings of the Fourth International Colloquium on Christine de Pizan (Glasgow 21–27 July 2000), published in honour of Liliane Dulac*, edited by Angus J. Kennedy et al., 777–93. Glasgow: University of Glasgow Press, 2002. [Compares Christine de Pizan and Abutsu-ni].

Stevenson, Barbara, and Cynthia Ho, eds. *Crossing the Bridge: Comparative Essays on Medieval European and Heian Japanese Woman Writers*. New York and Houndmills, Basingstoke, U.K.: Palgrave, 2000.

Wallace, John R. "Abutsu." In *Medieval Japanese Writers*, edited by Steven D. Carter. Dictionary of Literary Biography, 203. Detroit: Gale, 1999. [Highly informative].

Wren, James A. "Salty Seaweed, Absent Women, and Song: Authorizing the Female as Poet in the *Izayoi nikki*." *Criticism* 39 (1997): 185–204.

SHIGEMI SASAKI

ADELA OF BLOIS (c.1067–1137). The youngest daughter of William the Conqueror (c.1028–1087), Adela, or Adèle, of Blois has long been known as an important literary patron. More recent scholarship focuses on her role as a leading power broker in the volatile politics of the early twelfth century. Conceived shortly after her father's consecration as king of England, Adela was born sometime in 1067 or early 1068. Under the supervision of her mother, Queen Matilda I (Matilda of Flanders, 1031–1083), she was probably raised in Normandy, receiving instruction in Latin and the liberal arts, perhaps alongside her professed sister, Cecilia (d. 1127), at the Abbey of Holy Trinity, in Caen (northern France). In 1081–1082, Adela was betrothed at Breteuil to Stephen-Henry (Étienne, c.1049–1102), eldest son and designated primary heir to Theobald (Thibaud) III, count of Blois, Chartres, Meaux, and Troyes. The couple married at Chartres, probably in 1083 when Adela was fifteen and her husband was in his mid-thirties. (They were certainly married by 1085.) No evidence suggests she received a landed dowry, although the funding Adela provided for Stephen-Henry's participation in the First Crusade is one of several indications that she was endowed with a large wedding gift of cash and other movable goods. Her husband's family, the Thibaudians, granted her a dower including large tracts of forest and at least one castle.

Adela effectively coruled with her husband when he became count of Blois, Chartres, and Meaux in his own right (1089). According to charters and letters, she joined Stephen-Henry on administrative tours and routinely participated in the exercise of all nonmilitary prerogatives of counts, such as controlling property, protecting religious communities, issuing precepts renouncing rights, authorizing grants made by others, and adjudicating disputes at the comital court (court of the count). Among her more notable actions, Adela swore an oath (c.1092), which also bound her husband, to protect Ivo, the illustrious bishop of Chartres (d. 1115); she read out a Latin text to the crowd assembled for the translation of the relics of the sainted Empress Helena (1095); and she founded for the monks of Marmoutier a new priory and settlement in her dower lands (1095–1096). All the while she maintained contact with her birth family and bore five sons and at least one daughter, though she may have had as many as three.

During Stephen-Henry's absence on the First Crusade (1096–1099), Adela ruled with the full lordly authority vested in counts, as she would when he returned to the Holy Land in 1101. After he died in battle at Ramla (now in central Israel) in 1102, she continued to rule proficiently and energetically for eighteen years. As her elder sons came of age, Adela associated them with her in comital lordship, first William (Guillaume), whom she married to Agnès of Sully in 1104 to confirm Thibaudian possession of several strategically located castles, and then Theobald, after his knighting in 1107. At that time she decided that her second son (the future Theobald IV, the Great) would make the better prince and substituted him for the first-born William as their father's primary heir.

A capable and prudent administrator throughout her reign, Adela routinely toured her domains, encouraged the use of written documents, and generated revenue by regulating fairs. Neither two near-fatal illnesses nor lack of knightly training prevented her from intervening decisively in regional power politics as she defended the lands and political autonomy of the Thibaudian counts. She sent knights to fight for the king-designate Louis VI (1101); ordered her men to seize ecclesiastical goods during violent disputes (most notably in 1102–1103 and 1109); defended from attack Hugh, her vassal for the castle of Chaumont-sur-Loire (1109); and allied her sons militarily with her brother, King Henry I of England (r. 1100–1135), in his conflicts with King Louis VI of France (r. 1108–1137), which erupted in 1111, over the status of Normandy. She used her diplomatic acumen, together with her wealth, to settle property disputes at the comital court, to win allies or neutralize enemies in time of war, and to resolve high-level political quarrels (for example, when she orchestrated Henry I's reconciliation to the archbishops Anselm of Canterbury in 1105 and Thurstan of York in 1120).

Adela expressed her piety in wholly conventional terms that embraced both pragmatic and spiritual motives. She used saints' relics to cure fevers, dedicated her youngest son Henry to God, endowed anniversaries for various family members, received Pope Paschal II (1107), and supported new religious movements such as the hermits of Tiron and Cistercian monks. In all, the countess patronized about forty religious communities, two of which were for women. She was also a patron of Latin letters, serving as the subject or dedicatee of diverse compositions by several of the leading literati of her day, most notably Godfroid (Godfrey) of Reims, Hildebert of Lavardin, Baudri of Bourgueil, and Hugh of Fleury. Yet scholars debate the extent to which she actually commissioned any or all of those works or dictated how she was to be portrayed in them. For the most part, these writers praised both her governing skills and feminine virtues, while no extant source criticizes her lordly deeds as inappropriate for a woman.

In April/May 1120, Adela retired to the Abbey of Marcigny, Cluny's sister house in southern Burgundy, where she spent the remaining seventeen years of her life. She intervened in her former counties via sealed letters, preserved her abbey's estates from lay depredators, and became a respected spiritual advisor to her sisters, probably as the nuns' prioress. She died on March 8, 1137, and was buried at Marcigny. Of her children, Odo (Eudes) and Matilda (Mathilde, d. 1120) certainly, and William (d. c.1131–1137) probably, predeceased her. Her son Theobald (Thibaud), after inheriting his father's counties, succeeded his paternal uncle in Troyes, ruling the united Thibaudian domains from c.1125 to 1152; Stephen (Étienne) became King Stephen of England (1135–1154), succeeding his maternal uncle Henry I, and Henry (c.1100–1171) became abbot of Glastonbury (1126) and bishop of Winchester (1129). Her (step)daughter Agnès married Hugh (Hugues) III of Le Puiset (c.1112) and bore Hugh (Hugues) du Puiset, bishop of Durham (1153–1195); the fate of Adela's other (step)daughter, briefly married to Milo II of Bray-sur-Seine, is, like her name, unknown.

See also Dower; Dowry; Relics and Medieval Women

BIBLIOGRAPHY

Primary Sources

Baudri of Bourgueil. *Carmina.* Edited by Karlheinz Hilbert. Heidelberg, Germany: Carl Winter, 1979.

Boutemy, André, ed. "Trois œuvres inédites de Godefroid de Reims." *Revue du Moyen âge latin* 3 (1947): 335–66.

Chartes et documents de l'abbaye cistercienne de Preuilly. Edited by Albert Catel and Maurice Lecomte. Montereau, France: Claverie, 1927.

Guibert of Nogent. *Dei Gesta per Francos.* Edited by Robert B. C. Huygens. *Corpus Christianorum, Continuatio Mediaevalis*, 127A. Turnhout, Belgium: Brepols, 1996.

————. *The Deeds of God through the Franks.* Translated by Robert Levine. Woodbridge, Suffolk, U.K.: Boydell Press, 1997.

Eadmer. *Historia novorum in Anglia.* Edited by Martin Rule. Rolls Series, 81. London: H.M.S.O, 1884.

————. *Eadmer's History of Recent Events in England.* Translated by Geoffrey Bosanquet. London: Cresset Press, 1964.

Gesta Ambaziensium dominorum. In *Chroniques des comtes d'Anjou et des seigneurs d'Amboise*, edited by Louis Halphen and René Poupardin, 74–132. Paris: Picard, 1913.

Hildebert of Lavardin. *Carmina minori.* Edited by A. Brian Scott. Leipzig, Germany: Teubner, 1969.

Ordericus Vitalis. *The Ecclesiastical History of Orderic Vitalis.* Edited and translated by Marjorie Chibnall. 6 vols. Oxford: Clarendon, 1969–1980.

Secondary Sources

Bond, Gerald A. *The Loving Subject: Desire, Eloquence and Power in Romanesque France.* Philadelphia: University of Pennsylvania Press, 1995.

Houts, Elisabeth M. C. van. "Latin Poetry and the Anglo-Norman Court, 1066–1135." *Journal of Medieval History* 15 (1989): 39–62.

LoPrete, Kimberly A. *Adela of Blois, Countess and Lord.* Dublin, Ireland: Four Courts Press, 2004.

————. "The Gender of Lordly Women: The Case of Adela of Blois." In *Studies on Medieval and Early Modern Women: Pawns or Players?* edited by Christine Meek and Catherine Lawless, 90–110. Dublin, Ireland: Four Courts Press, 2003.

————. "Adela of Blois: Familial Alliances and Female Lordship." In *Aristocratic Women in Medieval France*, edited by Theodore Evergates, 9–43, 180–200. Philadelphia: University of Pennsylvania Press, 1999.

KIMBERLY A. LOPRETE

ADELAIDE, COUNTESS OF AUMALE (1029–1090). Also called Adeliza or Adelicia, Adelaide was countess of Aumale (northern French coast) and younger sister of William the Conqueror—William I, king of England (c.1027–1087). Adelaide was the daughter of Duke Robert I of Normandy (r. 1027–1035) and a concubine who may or may not have been Herleve, mother of William, or one Arlette (fl. 1010). Whatever the relationship, Adelaide seems to be the only sibling of William's whose name appears in more than one source.

Norman records show her to have married at least three times. The date of her marriage to her first husband, Enguerrand III, Count of Ponthieu, is unknown. He died in an ambush at St. Aubin near Arques in 1053, leaving her the county of Aumale and a daughter, also named Adelaide, about whom little else is known. The *Domesday Book* records that William gave lands in Essex and Suffolk to his sister as the countess of Aumale. Following Enguerrand's death (1054), Adelaide married Lambert, Count of Lenz. Their daughter Judith (c.1054–after 1086) was later married by William the

Conqueror to Earl Waltheof of Huntingdon in 1070. Shortly after this second marriage, Lambert died in the Battle of Lille, fought between Baldwin of Flanders and Henry III of Germany in 1054. Her inheritance from her two husbands, together with her brother's gift of lands, made Adelaide Countess of Ponthieu, Lenz, and Champagne. She married her last husband, Odo III, the deposed Count of Champagne, sometime before 1070 since in that year, when William gave Odo the earldom of Holderness, the charter identifies him as being married to the Countess of Aumale. After Adelaide's death, Odo conspired against William II in 1094 and was imprisoned in 1096. The date of Odo's death, as well as Adelaide's, is unknown, as is their place of burial.

When their son Stephen was born is also uncertain, since he does not appear in charter until 1090, by which time he became Count of Aumale. In an attempt to depose William III in 1094, Stephen claimed the throne through his descent from Adelaide. Though the coup failed, Stephen appears to have retained his lands and continued in rebellion until Henry I surrendered in 1119.

An otherwise undocumented account of Adelaide appears in the early fourteenth-century *Chronicle* of Thomas Castleford where she is made William's older sister and called Elaine. In this account, she is betrothed by William to Harold, son of Godwin, Earl of Wessex, in exchange for Harold's support of William's claim to the throne. Their wedding solemnized in Normandy, Harold and Elaine/Adelaide then go to England. When King Edward the Confessor subsequently dies and Harold is named to the throne, the new king repudiates his wife, cuts off her hair, and sends her back to her brother. Prompted by this ill treatment of his sister more than by Harold's perjury—according to this legend—William then invades England in 1066.

BIBLIOGRAPHY

Primary Sources
Castleford's Chronicle. Edited by Caroline D. Eckhardt. 2 vols. Early English Text Society, 305–06. Oxford and New York: Oxford University Press, 1996.
Cokayne, George E. *Complete Peerage of England, Scotland.* . . . Vol. 12, edited by Geoffrey H. White. 13 vols. London: St. Catherine Press, 1910–1959.
Magni rotuli Scaccarii Normanniae sub regibus Angliae. Edited by Thomas Stapleton. 2 vols. London: Antiquarian Society, 1840–1844.

Secondary Source
York, Laura. "Adelicia." In *Women in World History: A Biographical Encyclopedia*, edited by Anne Commire et al., 1: 81–82. Detroit: Yorkin/Gale, 2002.

KATHARINA M. WILSON

ADULTERY. *See* **Marriage**

ÆLFGIFU. *See* **Emma/Ælfgifu**

AELIA EUDOCIA. *See* **Eudocia**

ÆTHELTHRYTH, ST. (d. 679). Æthelthryth or Ætheldreda (the modern English form is Audrey) was foundress of the famous monastery at Ely, north of Cambridge, England. She was one of five daughters of Anna, a seventh-century king of East Anglia, and is celebrated as a virgin saint despite having been married twice. Both marriages were politically motivated. The first, probably contracted when Æthelthryth was very young, was to a ruler of the South Gyrwe called Tondberht. It ended on his death soon afterward. The second marriage, contracted in 660, was to the fifteen-year-old King Ecgfrith of Northumbria. He seems initially to have agreed to Æthelthryth remaining a virgin, but later became dissatisfied with the situation, offering estates and money to her advisor, Bishop (and future saint) Wilfrid (634–c.709) if he could persuade her to consummate the marriage. All such attempts failed, and after twelve years, Ecgfrith agreed to allow Æthelthryth to take religious vows. In 672 she entered the monastery of Coldingham, ruled by Ecgfrith's aunt, Abbess Æbbe, and was there consecrated as a nun by Wilfrid. The following year, she returned to East Anglia and founded a double monastery at Ely, near Cambridge, becoming its first abbess. Wilfrid appears to have fallen from favor with Ecgfrith, who expelled him from Northumbria in 678, but he received an estate at Hexham from Æthelthryth herself.

Æthelthryth's life as abbess of Ely was noted for extreme asceticism. She wore wool rather than linen, bathed only before the major religious festivals, seldom ate more than once a day, spent the period from Matins (the first canonical hour of the monastic day) until dawn at prayer in the church unless prevented by illness, and after death was buried at her own wish in a wooden coffin like an ordinary nun. During her later years she had suffered from a large tumor on her neck, but regarded the pain as a welcome penance for the vanity that had led her to wear heavy necklaces in her youth. She died of the plague in 679, seven years after becoming abbess, and was succeeded by her sister Seaxburh.

Sixteen years after Æthelthryth's death, her body was exhumed in the presence of Wilfrid and other witnesses and was found to be completely uncorrupt. Even a wound from the neck tumor, which had been lanced by a physician three days before her death, had miraculously healed to leave only a small scar. Both the original coffin and the clothes in which she had been buried proved to have healing properties, and her body was re-interred in a marble sarcophagus of perfect fit discovered near Cambridge. Her shrine was still intact when Ely was refounded as a monastery by Æthelwold in 970. Many miracles were attributed to her intervention, and her cult, once she became St. Æthelthryth, continued to develop during the late Anglo-Saxon and early Norman period in England. Twelve churches are dedicated to her, all probably postdating another translation of her relics, together with those of her sister Seaxburh, when a new abbey was completed at Ely in 1106. Her shrine was destroyed during the Protestant Reformation in the sixteenth century.

The earliest account of Æthelthryth's life is contained in *Historia Ecclesiastica Gentis Anglorum* (*Ecclesiastical History of the English People*; 4: 19–20) of the Venerable Bede (673–735), and comprises a prose narrative followed by a poem in praise of virginity. This is the source of all later versions, including a vernacular summary in the *Old English Martyrology*. The story was retold by the noted churchman and author Ælfric (955–1020), and is elaborated in the twelfth-century *Liber Eliensis* (*Book of Ely*). The latter must be used with some caution since it contains unreliable information aimed at strengthening the position of the Ely community, as for instance the unsubstantiated statements that the

Isle of Ely was given to Æthelthryth as a marriage gift by her first husband, and that she was consecrated abbess by Wilfrid.

See also Double Monasteries; Penitentials, Women in

BIBLIOGRAPHY

Primary Sources
Aefric. *Ælfric's Lives of Saints*. Edited by Walter W. Skeat. 2 vols. Early English Text Society, o.s. 76, 82. London: N. Trubner, 1881, 1885. Reprinted as one vol., London and New York: Oxford University Press, 1966.
Bede, the Venerable. *Bede's Ecclesiastical History of the English People*. Edited by Bertram Colgrave and R. A. B. Mynors, 390–401. Oxford: Clarendon Press, 1969.
Liber Eliensis. Edited by E. O. Blake. London: Royal Historical Society, 1962.
Old English Martyrology, An. Edited by George Herzfeld, 102–3. Early English Text Society, o.s. 116, London: K. Paul, Trench, Trubner, 1900. Reprinted New York: Kraus, 1973.

Secondary Sources
Butler, Lawrence. "Church Dedications and the Cults of Anglo-Saxon Saints in England." *The Anglo-Saxon Church: Papers on History, Architecture, and Archaeology in Honour of Dr. H. M. Taylor*, edited by L. A. S. Butler and R. K. Morris, 44–50. London: Council for British Archaeology, 1986.
Fell, Christine E. "Saint Æthelthryth: A Historical-Hagiographical Dichotomy Revisited." *Nottingham Medieval Studies* 38 (1994): 18–34.
Griffiths, Gwen. "Reading Ælfric's Saint Æthelthryth as a Woman." *Parergon* 20 (1992): 35–49.
Hollis, Stephanie. "'Some Special Irregularities of Marriage': *Theodore's Penitential* and the Case of St Æthelthryth." In Hollis, *Anglo-Saxon Women and the Church: Sharing a Common Fate*, 46–74. Woodbridge, Suffolk, U.K.: Boydell Press, 1992.
Miller, Edward. *The Abbey and Bishopric of Ely*. Cambridge: Cambridge University Press, 1951.
Ridyard, Susan J. *The Royal Saints of Anglo-Saxon England: A Study of West Saxon and East Anglian Cults*. Cambridge: Cambridge University Press, 1988. [Chapter 6: "The Royal Cults of Ely," 176–210].
Rollason, David. *Saints and Relics in Anglo-Saxon England*. Oxford: Blackwell, 1989.

CAROLE HOUGH

AGNES OF ASSISI, ST. (c.1197–1253). The Franciscan abbess Agnes of Assisi was born in Assisi, in central Italy, to Count Favorino Scifi and one of two younger sisters of Clare of Assisi. In 1211, against violent parental opposition, the fourteen-year-old Agnes left the comfortable Assisi home to join Clare in the Benedictine Convent of Sant' Angelo di Panzo, the latter having taken her vows before her spiritual mentor, the future St. Francis (c.1181–1226) and founder of the Franciscan Order (1209). Sixteen days after Clare fled from her home to the convent, Agnes followed barefoot to observe the Franciscan ideals of perpetual abstinence, constant silence, and "perfect" poverty. This last condition was absolute and noble in a way later approved by Pope Gregory IX in the *privilegium paupertatis*. Agnes, like Clare, was invested with the Franciscan habit, a long, coarse-textured robe with a rope for a belt, by Francis, who accordingly also cut off her hair. Relatives of the two sisters, displeased with their flight and renunciation, attempted more than once to return them home by force, but without success. According to legend, on one such occasion, Agnes managed to thwart the efforts of twelve men to drag her away by miraculously becoming too heavy to carry, until Clare came to her rescue and made peace with their family.

When the nuns of Sant' Angelo asked to join his order and Francis chose Clare to institute the Second Order of nuns in 1212, Agnes assisted in the institution of this new order at the convent of San Damiano, half a mile outside Assisi to the southeast—hence called the Order of the Poor Ladies of San Damiano—before achieving renown as the Poor Clares, the most austere women's order in the Church. In 1219, when the Benedictine nuns at Monticelli, near Florence, asked to join the new Second Order of St. Francis, or Poor Clares, they made Agnes their abbess. Later, Agnes introduced the Rule of the Franciscans into convents across northern Italy at Mantua, Venice, and Padua. She is said to have had a vision of the Christ Child, which is often portrayed in her iconography. Having contributed greatly to the religious communities across northern Italy by furthering the Franciscan Order for women, Agnes died three months after Clare, who had foreseen this.

Today, the Church of Santa Chiara (St. Clare) stands as a testament to the Poor Clares. Begun in 1257, four years after Clare's death, it boasts massive lateral buttresses and a fine rose window, while preserving a simple Gothic interior. It houses the tombs of both Clare and Agnes, surrounded by thirteenth-century frescoes and pictures commemorating the work of the two devout sisters of Assisi. Agnes's feast day is November 16.

See also Clare of Assisi, St.; Convents; Rules for Canonesses, Nuns, and Recluses

BIBLIOGRAPHY

Primary Sources
Agnes of Assisi. "Letter to St. Clare." *The Legend and Writings of St. Clare of Assisi.* Translated by Ignatius Brady, O.F.M. New York: St. Bonaventure, 1953. Reprinted in Petroff (*see below*), 245–46.
"Vita sororis Agnetis, germanae sanctae Clarae." *Analecta Franciscana* 3 (1897): 173–82.

Secondary Sources
Helyot, Pierre. *Histoire des ordres religieux et militaires . . .*, 25–28, 38–42. Paris: Louis, 1792.
Petroff, Elizabeth A., ed. *Medieval Women's Visionary Literature.* New York and Oxford: Oxford University Press, 1986.
Wood, Jeryldene. *Women, Art and Spirituality: The Poor Clares of Early Modern Italy.* Cambridge and New York: Cambridge University Press, 1996.

SANDRO STICCA

AGNES OF BOHEMIA, BLESSED (1203 or 1211–1282). Also known as Agnes of Prague, a member of the Order of Poor Clares and founder of the first Franciscan convent in the Bohemian Lands (what is now western Czechoslovakia), Agnes was born in Prague to Ottokar I, king of Bohemia, and Constance, sister of Andreas II, king of Hungary. She was neither the first nor the only member of the royal Premyslid family to devote herself to pious and intellectual works: her ancestor, Ludmilla (860–921), was the region's first Christian martyr; Wenceslas, duke of Bohemia (d. c.936), had already been canonized, and St. Elisabeth of Hungary was her younger cousin. A century later would come another Premyslid, Anne of Bohemia, popular queen consort to Richard II of England (1367–1400), who fostered the writings of the great English theologian and reformer, John Wycliffe (c.1330–1384), in Bohemia.

Because Agnes was a king's daughter, political demands and necessities determined much of her life. Betrothed at age three to Boheslas, son of Henry, duke of Silesia, she was thus sent off to be raised and educated at the Cistercian abbey of Trebnitz in Silesia (a region encompassing southwestern Poland and northern Czechoslovakia), a convent founded by the Henry's mother, St. Hedwig. When Boheslas died only three years later, however, Agnes had to return to Bohemia. Then promised at age nine to Henry, the son of the expansively powerful Emperor Frederick II (1194–1250), Agnes went to the Austrian court to learn German. It was here that she came to shun the courtly life, turning instead toward an austere one of simplicity and renunciation. As a result, Leopold, duke of Austria, successfully plotted to cancel Agnes's engagement to Henry in favor of his own daughter. Both the fourteenth-century Latin and fifteenth-century German versions of the anonymous *Legend of Blessed Agnes of Bohemia* report how, on her return to the Bohemian court, she devoted herself to God, attended mass, and did penance by wearing a hair shirt beneath her robes. Nevertheless, Wenceslas I, now king of Bohemia, arranged a marriage for her with Frederick II himself, while King Henry III of England (1216–1272) also courted her. Agnes vigorously rejected all such proposals and sought aid from Pope Gregory IX to shield her from a forced marriage. Her case settled without political repercussions, she was now free to dedicate her life completely to God.

Four extant letters from St. Clare to Agnes, written in a clear, affectionate manner between 1234 and 1253, encourage Agnes to pursue her life in continuous relationship with Christ. In Prague, Agnes had a hospice built for the poor, administered by an order known as the Crosiers of the Red Star. Having learned of Franciscan ideals most likely through her association with Francis and Clare of Assisi and the Poor Ladies of San Damiano from the Friars Minor (in Prague since 1225), Agnes obtained permission from Clare and Pope Gregory to establish a Poor Clares convent in Prague. In 1234, she received the veil at Pentecost and was installed as abbess of her convent. After many negotiations, she obtained the cherished Privilege of Poverty for her convent (1247), as Clare had struggled to do for San Damiano. Agnes managed to overthrow the Benedictine Rule in these convents and to replace it with the Rule of St. Francis. This was significant because, until then, the Holy See had regarded the Poor Clares, founded in 1212, as Benedictines, thus compelling them to receive and hold possessions, while the Franciscan credo renounced all property. She played a major role in eliciting the papal bull *Cum omnis vera religio* (*Since all true religion*...; 1253) allowing the sisters to adopt the Franciscan Rule. It was not a complete victory, however, because it did not enforce the vow of poverty unilaterally, but rather left this decision to each individual order. Agnes also allegedly performed numerous miracles in life and after death, ranging from healing the sick and dying to predicting the defeat and death of King Ottokar (r. 1253–1278), her brother's successor, in 1278. She died March 2, 1281 or 1282, and was beatified by Pope Pius IX in 1874.

See also Anne of Bohemia; Clare of Assisi, St.; Elisabeth of Hungary/Thuringia, St.; Rules for Canonesses, Nuns, and Recluses

BIBLIOGRAPHY

Primary Sources
[Anonymous]. *Legenda blahoslavené Anezky a ctyri listy sv. Kláry.* Edited by Jan K. Vyskocil. 2 vols. Prague: Universum, 1932–1934. [Critical ed. of Latin text based on Milan, Biblioteca Ambrosiana ms. H102 with Czech translation].
Clare of Assisi. *Clare of Assisi: Early Documents.* Edited by Regis J. Armstrong. New York and Mahwah, N.J.: Paulist Press, 1988.

———. *Lettere ad Agnese; La Visione dello specchio*. Edited and translated by Giovanni Pozzi and Beatrice Rima. Piccola biblioteca Adelphi, 426. Milan: Adelphi, 1999. [Latin and modern Italian ed. with notes].

Seton, Walter W. *Some New Sources for the Life of Blessed Agnes of Bohemia Including a Fourteenth-Century Latin Version and a Fifteenth-Century German Version*. Aberdeen: Aberdeen University Press, 1915. Reprint Farnborough, Hants., U.K.: Gregg Press, 1966.

Secondary Sources

Butler, Alban. *Lives of the Saints*. Edited and revised by Herbert Thurston, S.J., and Donald Attwater, 1: 462–64. New York: P. J. Kennedy, 1956.

Goorbergh, Edith A. van den, and Theodore H. Zweerman. *Light Shining through a Veil: On Saint Clare's Letters to Saint Agnes of Prague*. Translated by Aline Looman-Graaskamp and Frances Teresa. Fiery Arrow, 2. Louvain, Belgium: Peeters, 2000.

Kybal, Vlastimil. *Svatá Anezka Ceská: historick± obraz ze 13. století*. Pontes pragenses, 8. Brno, Czechoslovakia: L. Marek, 2001.

Polc, Jaroslav. *Agnes von Böhmen 1211–1282. Königstöchter, Abtissin, Heilige*. Munich: Oldenbourg, 1989.

Thomas, Alfred. *Anne's Bohemia: Czech Literature and Society, 1310–1420*. Foreword by David Wallace. Minneapolis: University of Minnesota Press, 1998.

KATHARINA M. WILSON

AILISIA DE BALDO. *See* **Catherine of Bologna, St.**

ALAIS, N'. *See* **Alaisina Yselda**

ALAISINA YSELDA (1190s–c. early 1230s). Alaisina Yselda refers to one or possibly two female troubadours active in the early thirteenth century. Although troubadour expert Pierre Bec argues that "N'Alaisina Yselda," as it appears in original manuscript form, denotes but a single woman ("na" = "lady"), many scholars, after Meg Bogin and then Peter Dronke, have read this as a reference to two sisters, "N'Alais i Na Yselda (or Iselda)," the Provençal for Lady Alice and Lady Isolde—whose names appear together in a single *tenso* (Provençal debate poem) titled, according to its first verse, "Na Carenza al bel cors avinenz" ("Lady Carenza, of fair and lovely form"), and composed of two *coblas unissonans* (stanzas of uniform rhyme scheme throughout) and ending in two *tornadas* (finalizing stanzas addressing the patron or, here, the other speaker). Bruckner's recent edition has sided with Bec in considering her as one woman. The poem centers on a traditional debate-poem question, as Angelica Rieger has demonstrated: the young woman/two young women ask the presumably older and wiser Na Carenza for advice on whether or not they should marry and have children, activities they consider "trop angoissos" ("too anguishing"), or remain virgins. The language of Carenza's response is filled with what appears to be somewhat enigmatic religious allusions as she advises each indeed to take a husband, but one "coronat de scienza" (crowned with wisdom)"—apparently an allusion to Christ—to preserve her chastity and bear fruit from "bon semenza" ("good seed"). This reply thus involves not only traces of Catharism, the entrenched southern-French antimarital heresy, but also the more orthodox Christian concepts, Bride of Christ and celibate marriage, prevalent in Northern medieval cultures.

The woman's/two women's identity remains unknown beyond what the poem tells us. According to Na Carenza, they possessed "neghamenz,/prez et beltatz, iovenz, frescas colors/ . . . cortesia et valors/ sobre tottas las autras conoscenz" ("learning, merit and beauty; youth and fresh complexion . . . courtly manners and worth . . . above all other women I know")—characteristics that would place them in aristocratic ranks. Yet the one attribute she fails to mention that would make them perfect brides for a noble lord or baron is wealth. Such class considerations move Patricia Anderson to view the poem as a satire on the three estates of women according to the opinions voiced by each (Carenza = virgin; Yselda = noble; Alais = peasant). Meg Bogin, whose edition of the poem rearranges the stanzas to emphasize the poem's tripartite, rather than dual, nature, also speculates that the term "serors" (sisters) would suggest their status as nuns. However, were they nuns, their need for advice about marriage would be pointless, since they would already be Brides of Christ. Others, like René Nelli, glean significance from the Cathar elements in Na Carenza's advice. Lacking any poetic sequel or historical information, we do not know Alais and Yselda's decision, but this poem pointedly illustrates the widespread dilemma that many young women faced and the few alternatives open to them. To these women, this brief but incisive poem may well have served as an exemplum.

See also Bride of Christ/*Brautmystik*; Carenza, Na; Celibacy; *Frauenfrage*; Marriage; *Trobairitz*; Virginity

BIBLIOGRAPHY

Primary Sources
Alaisina Iselda. In *Songs of the Women Troubadours*, edited and translated by Matilda Tomaryn Bruckner, Laurie Shepard, and Sarah White, 96–97, 177–79. New York: Garland, 1995. Revised ed. 2000. [Original texts, notes, and English translation].
———. In *Trobairitz: Der Beitrag der Frau in der altokzitanischen höfischen Lyrik. Edition des Gesamtkorpus*, edited by Angelica Rieger, 158–65. Beihefte der Zeitschrift für romanische Philologie, 233. Tübingen, Germany: Max Niemeyer Verlag, 1991. [Original texts, German notes].
Boutière, Jean, and Alexander H. Schutz, eds. *Biographies des Troubadours: Textes provençaux des XIIIe et XIVe siècles*. Revised edition with I. M. Cluzel, 422–24. Les Classiques d'Oc, 1. Paris: Nizet, 1964. [Texts of the original *Vidas*].

Secondary Sources
Anderson, Patricia. "*Na Carenza al bel cors avinen*: A Test Case for Recovering the Fictive Element in the Poetry of the Women Troubadours." *Tenso* 2 (1987): 55–64.
Bec, Pierre. "Avoir des enfants ou rester vierge? Une tenson occitane du XIIe siècle entre femmes." In *Mittelalterstudien: Erich Köhler zum Gedenken*, edited by Henning Krauss and Dietmar Rieger, 21–30. Heidelberg: Carl Winter, 1984.
———. *Burlesque et obscénité chez les troubadours: pour une approche du contre-texte médiéval*, 201–05. Paris: Stock, 1984.
Bogin, Meg. *The Women Troubadours*, 144–45, 178–79. New York and London: W. W. Norton, 1980. Original Paddington Press, 1976.
Dronke, Peter. *Women Writers of the Middle Ages: A Critical Study of Texts from Perpetua (†203) to Marguerite Porete (†1310)*, 101–2. Cambridge: Cambridge University Press, 1984.
Nelli, René, ed. *Écrivains anticonformistes au moyen-âge occitan: 1. La Femme et l'amour*, 256–59. Paris: Phébus, 1977.

JUNE HALL McCASH

ALAMANDA (late 12th century). The woman troubadour (*trobairitz*) Alamanda is named as interlocutor in the first line of a witty *tenso* (debate poem), "S'ie.us qier conseill, bella amia Alamanda" ("If I ask your advice, lovely friend Alamanda"), with Giraut de Bornelh, recognized since the thirteenth century as the "master of the troubadours." Giraut's expertise is thus celebrated in *vidas* (biographies) and *razos* (commentaries) that accompanied the troubadour poems recorded in manuscript anthologies circulating a hundred years after his songs were composed. Only Giraut's name appears in rubrics of the numerous manuscripts that record this *tenso* with its accompanying music, and many critics have considered the *donzella* (maiden) Alamanda a fiction invented by the master poet.

Nevertheless, several factors argue for considering the possibility that Alamanda was not just a fictional *trobairitz*, first and foremost the group of women poets active from approximately 1170 to 1260, whose historical existence can be documented inside and outside the world of troubadour lyric. Within that repertoire, a number of poems exchanged by *trobairitz* develop a similar dramatic situation in which one speaker intervenes on behalf of a lover, to win forgiveness from his beloved *domna* ("lady"). In this *tenso*, Giraut seeks Alamanda's help and asks her to defend him against his lady's accusations (a razo that accompanies the song in some manuscripts names the lady Alamanda as well). The name Alamanda appears repeatedly in a network of intertextual allusions: Bertran de Born composed one of his *sirventes* (political or moral poems) on "the melody of Lady Alamanda" ("el son de N'Alamanda"); in an exchange of *coblas* (stanzas), Bernart Arnaut prefers Lombarda to Giscarda and Alamanda, and Lombarda replies by thanking him for naming her with "two such ladies"; in a dance song dedicated to Beatrice of Provence, granddaughter of Garsenda of Forcalquier (also a *trobairitz*, as attested by one extant song), Guiraut d'Espanha refers to several women troubadours, "Na Tibors de Provenza" and "N'Alamanda." Recent archival research into the history of the Alaman family in southwest France, suggests that the *trobairitz* may have been Alamanda de Castelnou, a noblewoman born c.1160, married to Guilhem de Castelnou, canoness of Saint-Étienne of Toulouse, who died in 1223 according to a tombstone still preserved in the Musée des Augustins in Toulouse. If she were sent as a young girl to the court of the counts of Toulouse (as were many daughters of important vassals at this time), she would have been exposed to considerable poetic activity in a court where Bernart de Ventadorn, Peire d'Alverhna, and other troubadours performed.

However undecided the status of the woman poet remains, the voice of Alamanda recorded in half of the song's eight stanzas and two *tornadas* (envois) plays the game of the debate with vigorous repartee, as she picks up and bats back into Giraut's court the language and themes of his plaints and volleys. Alamanda advises Giraut on how to be submissive to his lady's commands and fends off his anger when the lover transfers onto her the rage he feels against the beloved. With charges of fickleness exchanged on both sides, Alamanda defends the lady, chastises Giraut's prickly way of seeking help, and finally promises to reconcile him with his lady—if he promises to hold onto her love once it is returned to him.

See also Chanson de Femme (Women's Song); *Trobairitz*

BIBLIOGRAPHY

Primary Sources
Alamanda. [Tenso with Giraut de Bornelh]. In *Songs of the Women Troubadours*, edited and translated by Matilda Tomaryn Bruckner, Laurie Shepard, and Sarah White, 42–47, 158–59. New York: Garland, 1995. Revised ed. 2000.

———. In *Trobairitz: Der Beitrag der Frau in der altokzitanischen höfischen Lyrik. Edition des Gesamtkorpus*, edited by Angelica Rieger, 188–94. Beihefte der Zeitschrift für romanische Philologie, 233. Tübingen, Germany: Max Niemeyer Verlag, 1991.

Secondary Sources

Bruckner, Matilda Tomaryn. "Debatable Fictions: The *Tensos* of the Women Troubadours." In *Literary Aspects of Courtly Culture: Selected Papers from the Seventh Triennial Congress of the International Courtly Literature Society*, edited by Donald Maddox and Sara Sturm-Maddox, 19–28. Woodbridge, Suffolk, U.K. and Rochester, N.Y.: D. S. Brewer, 1994.

Chambers, Frank. "Las *trobairitz* soiseubudas." In *The Voice of the Trobairitz: Perspectives on the Women Troubadours*, edited by William D. Paden, 45–60. Philadelphia: University of Pennsylvania Press, 1989.

Paden, William D., Jr. "Some Recent Studies of Women in the Middle Ages, Especially in Southern France." *Tenso: Bulletin of the Société Guilhem IX* 7(1992): 94–124.

Rieger, Angelica. "Alamanda de Castelnou—Une *trobairitz* dans l'entourage des comtes de Toulouse?" *Zeitschrift für romanische Philologie* 107 (1991): 47–57.

Riega, Angelica. "*En conselh no deu hom voler femna:* Les dialogues mixtes dans la lyrique troubadouresque." *Perspectives Médiévales* 16 (1990): 47–57.

MATILDA TOMARYN BRUCKNER

ALBA LADY. A key figure in the poetry of what is now southern France—Provence—a special kind of lady was cultivated by the troubadours for one of their poetic genres called the *alba* (in Provençal), or "dawn-song." Among the female figures invented for troubadour lyric, the *alba* lady emerges as a unique voice defining a new conception of femininity, power, and love in medieval poetry. As a genre, the *alba* (*aube* in Old French, *alva* or *alvorada* in Old Portuguese, *tageliet* in Middle-High German)—all signifying "dawn-song"—expresses the various emotions experienced by illicit or furtive lovers parting at dawn, often wakened by some kind of watchman figure, in time to avoid discovery. The word *alba* (literally, in Provençal, "dawn") appears in the refrain, as the lovers remind themselves to separate, however painful this may be. Like certain other erotic-lyric genres and forms, the *alba* exists in sacred mode as well, recited during the canonical hour of Matins as a prayer for the soul's protection toward the end of night. However, it is the secular, erotic *alba* tradition, particularly that of the twelfth- and thirteenth-century troubadours, that is best known.

Occupying the major singing role—for these poems were usually sung—the lady of the *alba* attains a new level of dramatic significance. Her voice is dignified, expressive, and passionate, rather than the conventional, more subservient, modest tone used by the woman toward the male lover. Because the *alba* was adopted by other European poets (the *trouvères* of Northern France, the German *minnesingers*), this new female voice resonated widely throughout Western Europe. However, no *alba* has as yet been conclusively attributed to a *trobairitz* (woman troubadour), although Bruckner et al., include the anonymous "En un vergier" ("Within a grove") as a possibility. Although the existing body of erotic *albas* is small, a number of masterpieces can be found within it. No poetic forerunners surpass the blend of lyricism, dramatic power, and poignancy of the most accomplished *albas*, which are to be counted among the great love poems of all time. After the three great twelfth- through early-thirteenth-century German poets, Heinrich von Morungen (Lachmann et al. 1977; Hatto), Walther von der Vogelweide (also in Hatto), and Wolfram von Eschenbach (Lachmann et al. 1977; Hatto) composed their *tagelieder*, the form became a cornerstone of German literature. The *alba*'s elegance, musicality, expressiveness, realistic dramatic scenario, and dynamic lady made it an enduring form, outlasting other genres of troubadour love lyric. The genre's flexibility allowed it to find its way into other kinds of narratives both serious and parodic, for example in the thirteenth-century romance *Aucassin et Nicolette* and fourteenth-century Boccaccio's *Il Filostrato*, Chaucer's *Troilus and Criseyde*, *Reeve's Tale*, and *Merchant's Tale*.

The *alba* lady stands out in contrast to the female characters created by the troubadours for other genres because she maintains a courtly stature (and the poet's and audience's respect) while reciprocating her lover's affections. She differs from the lady of the *canso*, the classic troubadour unrequited-love lyric, who, although varied, never speaks. Despite (or perhaps because of) her silence, this *canso* lady, or *domna*, is elevated far above her admirer. Another genre, the *pastorela*, portraying the encounter between knight-errant and voluble shepherdess, is narrated from the viewpoint of the aristocratic knight who attempts to seduce her. Far from the demeanor assumed by the wooer in the *canso* (and in the court), the *pastorela* knight treats the object of his desire as prey, as a creature far beneath him. The mute but perfect *canso* lady and the vocal, unlettered *pastorela* shepherdess, both of whose voices are filtered through divergent modes of controlling male desire, serve as opposite poles from between which the *alba* lady's persona rises to a more independent position; neither virginal nor ravished, she is loving and sensual, while also courtly and dignified. Where the *canso* lady is often repressed, the *alba* lady is outspoken and spontaneously emotional. And where the *pastorela* shepherdess is simple and unsophisticated, even if sometimes full of rustic common sense, the *alba* lady is complex and refined. Her noble bearing remains undiminished as her passion intensifies, mainly because she sees herself as a defender of self-sacrificial, heroic, secret love—rather than mere adultery. Although her song laments a disrupted tryst, it simultaneously celebrates reciprocal love. Mutual love counterbalances the other kinds of love found in the troubadour corpus, such as the unregulated love of the *pastorela* countryside and the unrequited love of the suffering and frustrated *canso* singer. The *alba* lady is a quintessentially courtly lady—a true domna, described in the superlative. In the *alba* titled "Gaita be" ("Good watchman"), for example, Raimbaut de Vaqueiras acclaims her "plus . . . bon e bel" ("the best and most beautiful"); Gaucelm Faidit's or Bertrand d'Alamanon's "Us cavaliers si jazia" ("A knight was lying down"; Appel) praises her as "e so qu'eu plus voilh ai" ("the one of greatest worth"), "la re que plus volia" ("the being most beloved"); while in the *trouvère aube* "Gaite de la tor" ("Watchman of the tower"; Hatto; Rosenberg), one of the most frequently studied Old-French songs, she is "de biauté le monjoie" ("the very summit of beauty"); and "la gensor . . . la mielhs aibia" ("the noblest and best of all creatures") in the *alba* "Ab la gensor que sia" ("To the fairest, noblest lady there is"; Bartsch).

Inevitably, though she sets the standard for courtliness, her active participation in an extramarital love affair, while it does not diminish her ideal-courtly status, moves her to the margin of the real-world court whose mores are defined by Church and state—or even by unworthy troubadour courtiers—rather than by true lovers and poets of *fin'amors* (refined, courtly love). She has risked involvement in an illicit relationship because of her miserable marriage. The *alba* lady's voice thus intersects with and enriches that of the *mal marié/e* (unhappily-married man/woman), enriching this popular theme in both its feudal-legal and poetic-affective dimensions. She has realized that, despite social respectability, her marriage has disempowered her. As the lady of Cadenet's *alba*, "S'anc fui belha ni prezada"

("Once I was fair and prized"), makes plain, marriage has transformed her from "fair and prized" to unappreciated by her husband who, though a wealthy lord, turns out to be lacking in any personal virtues. The institution of marriage itself is often represented in courtly poetry as a business proposition, precluding any claim to courtliness and thus the opposite of *fin'amors*. Yet, the *alba* lady's discourse is unique among the *mal mariées* in that she does not complain so much as explain: she has found a solution, albeit one transgressing against society's cruel (toward individual desires), pragmatic code. The *alba* lady, more articulately than other courtly ladies in love, reveres a code of another kind, invoking the specific principles and employing key terms of *fin'amors*: she disdains ignorance (*desconoissensa*) as well as discourteous (*malamen*) behavior; her churlish husband is "un vilan" in contrast to her lover, who is noble and worthy (*fin'amic, valen*). Her self-portrait is also designed to forestall any hint of ignoble behavior, of *vilania* (boorishness), on her part. She may break her marital vow, and she may bitterly denounce her spouse, but this, within the *fin'amors* ethic, never constitutes *vilania*, the ultimate disgrace. She and her lover exhibit refined manners even under duress; they never part rudely nor does she send him away ahead of time, for such actions would render her unworthy as *fin'amic*. Socioeconomically, this value system carries particular appeal for the dispossessed, since, if honor and value are shifted away from material wealth and property and instead directed towards inner perfection, the disenfranchised have an opportunity for reappraisal, at least in the eyes of sympathizers. *Alba* lovers lay claim to a superior nobility of spirit, actually justifying the consummation of their love on moral grounds.

She is thus simultaneously the domna—a central attraction of the court—and a woman with a secret life to whose rules she has pledged greater fidelity. Her faithful watchman figure (*gayta, guaita*) is her indispensable henchman against the nefarious vigilance of jealous (*gilos*) or prying, gossipy courtiers, not to mention her husband, whose reprisals could be socially, even personally, dangerous in the event of discovery. This drama of good and evil surveillance surfaces for example in the *alba*, "En un vergier sotz fuella d'albespi" ("In an orchard beneath hawthorn leaves"; Appel; Hatto; Bruckner), wherein we find, in addition to the traditional sweet-but-prickly hawthorn signifying the courtly love situation, the lady who is highly "regarded" by many, but as the anonymous poet's double-edged use of *gardar* (to regard, watch) conveys, she is also "guarded" ("per sa beutat la gardon mantas gens" ["for her beauty she is regarded by many"]), imprisoned by the public gaze. The lady of the aforementioned Cadenet's "S'anc fui belha ni prezada," having chosen to recruit a watchman rather than renounce her love despite inherent danger, speaks for all *alba* ladies when she explains: "e murria/s'ieu fin amic non avia/cuy disses mo marrimen" ("I would die/had I not my true love by my side/to whom to tell my sorrow"), duly acknowledging "e guaita plazen/que mi fes son d'alba" ("a pleasing watchman/who warns me of the morrow"). Her watchman, with whom she shares this song, declares his willingness to support and protect true lovers like her. The watchman is not her only sympathizer. W. T. H. Jackson, for example, has argued that the poet's awareness of the complex feelings and events in the *alba* leads him to favor the lovers rather than her husband since, instead of presenting the scene objectively, the *alba* poet offers the woman's point of view. The *alba* poet dramatizes a woman in love, as opposed to the more obviously male-centered experience offered in the *canso*.

Given the *alba* lady's characteristics, it is peculiarly ironic that the first scholars of medieval lyric categorized her status, like her genre, along with the *pastorela*, as "noncourtly"—in contrast to the restrained, stylized, tacit lady of the "courtly" *canso*—according to rigid rules for classification and definition of the genres by origin, theme, and form. Because, like Chaucer's later Wife of Bath (1380s), the *alba* lady expresses emotions so artlessly, early scholars mistook her voice for that of a real woman, a "typical" medieval adulteress, and her genre a reenactment of a real, frequently occurring dawn-parting between lovers. In 1928, Charles Baskerville at first attempted to demonstrate this view on the basis of anthropological studies, and when that proved fruitless, he interpreted the songs themselves as the historical record. However, no documentation exists proving that the *pastorela* and *alba* are indeed taken from real-life customs, although individual encounters between knights and shepherdesses no doubt occurred, and lovers have long lamented parting at dawn. Rather, such scholarly presumption of reality results from the *alba* poets' talent for verisimilitude in character development and dramatization: the very artistry, often labeled by scholars as "folkloric" or "natural," implied by the designation "noncourtly." Tainted by this denigrating terminology, modern critical opinion tends to perceive the *alba* lady's directness and honesty as gullibility, stupidity, or lack of sophistication. Rather than reading her as the poets present her, that is, as a strong, positive role model (in modern feminist terms), even recent critics characterize her as the ultimate victim, abandoned by her lover and despairing of love (Fries; Saville). On the other hand, literary historians have overvalued the mute *canso* lady as *the* troubadour's lady, preferring the safer ground of attempting to decode the mysterious messages hidden beneath her silence—just as with founding troubadour Guillaume d'Aquitaine's famously provocative riddle-poem "Farai un vers de dreyt nien" ("I'll make a poem of absolutely nothing")—hence her prominence in lyric scholarship. Yet as the evidence demonstrates, the *alba* lady, too, is a troubadour's lady, and in her character and voice, the poets provide a far more intriguing, vibrant female figure than in her lyric sisters.

The genre continued to develop after its medieval flowering, especially in Germany and France, where dawn-songs became not only a favored genre of popular poetry but also in high art, such as Scene Two of Wagner's *Tristan und Isolde* (1865). In English, the dawn scene in Shakespeare's *Romeo and Juliet* (c.1596) immediately springs to mind, yet the genre also came into its own as the *aubade*, adopted by poets such as John Donne (1633), whose clever variations on it appear in a number of lyrics. The *alba* reappears abundantly in nineteenth- and twentieth-century English and American poetry. Even modern pop music yields examples. In sum, the *alba* introduced into the Western poetic tradition so fresh and fertile a direction and so vibrant and eloquent a female voice that the form has been continually adapted to a variety of popular and formal media.

See also Boccaccio, Women in, *De Claris Mulieribus*; *Chanson de Femme* (Women's Song); Chaucer, Geoffrey, Women in the Work of; Criseyde; Isolde; Kharja; *Minne*; *Miroir de Mariage* (*Mirror of Marriage*); *Muwashshah*; *Novela Sentimental*/Sentimental Romance; Rhetoric, Women and; *Trobairitz*

BIBLIOGRAPHY

Primary Sources
Appel, Carl, ed. *Provenzalische Chrestomathie*. Leipzig, Germany: Reisland, 1907.
Bartsch, Karl, ed. *Provenzalisches Lesebuch*. Elberfeld, Germany: Friderichs, 1855.
Bec, Pierre, et al., eds. and transs. *Anthologie des Troubadours*. Paris: UGE/"10/18," 1979. [Modern-French translations and original texts].

Bruckner, Matilda Tomaryn, Laurie Shepard, and Sarah White, eds. and transs. *Songs of the Women Troubadours*, xxxix, xli, 189–90. New York and London: Garland, 1995. Revised ed. 2000. [Original texts with English translations]

Cadenet. "S'anc fui belha ni prezada." In *Der Trobador Cadenet*, edited by Carl Appel, 80–81. Halle, Germany: Max Niemeyer, 1920.

Doss-Quinby, Eglal, Joan T. Grimbert et al., eds. and transs. *Songs of the Women Trouvères*. New Haven, Conn.: Yale University Press, 2001.

Goldin, Frederick. *German and Italian Lyrics of the Middle Ages: An Anthology and a History*. New York: Doubleday, 1973.

———. *Lyrics of the Troubadours and Trouvères: An Anthology and a History*. New York: Doubleday, 1973.

Hatto, Arthur T. *Eos: An Enquiry into the Theme of Lovers' Meetings and Partings at Dawn in Poetry*. The Hague: Mouton, 1965.

Lachmann, Karl, et al., eds. *Des Minnesangs Frühling*. Revised by Hugo Moser and Helmut Tervooren. Stuttgart: S. Hirzel, 1977.

Raimbaut de Vaqueiras. "Gaita be." In *The Poems of the Troubadour Raimbaut de Vaqueiras*, edited by Joseph Linskill, 25:261–63. The Hague: Mouton, 1964.

Rosenberg, Samuel N., and Hans Tischler, eds. Chanter m'estuet: *Songs of the Trouvères*, 25–29. London & Boston: Faber & Faber, 1981 [Original texts with notes only].

Walther von der Vogelweide. *Die Gedichte Walthers von der Vogelweide*. Edited by Karl Lachmann and Carl von Kraus, 88–89. Berlin: De Gruyter, 1936.

Secondary Sources

Baskerville, Charles Read. "English Songs on the Night Visit." *PMLA* 36 (1921): 565–615.

Bloch, R. Howard. *Medieval Misogyny and the Invention of Western Romantic Love*. Chicago: University of Chicago Press, 1991.

Bridenthal, Renate, et al., eds. *Becoming Visible: Women in European History*. 2nd ed. Boston: Houghton-Mifflin, 1987.

Fries, Maureen. "The 'Other' Voice: Woman's Song, Its Satire and Its Transcendence in Late Medieval British Literature." In *Vox Feminae: Studies in Medieval Woman's Song*, edited by John F. Plummer, 155–78. Kalamazoo, Mich.: Medieval Institute, 1981.

Gravdal, Kathryn. *Ravishing Maidens: Writing Rape in Medieval French Literature and Law*. New Cultural Studies. Philadelphia: University of Pennsylvania Press, 1991.

Jackson, W. T. H. *The Challenge of the Medieval Text*. Edited by Joan Ferrante and Robert Hanning. New York: Columbia University Press, 1985.

Paden, William D., ed. *The Medieval Pastourelle*. 2 vols. Garland Library of Medieval Literature, 34–35A. New York: Garland, 1987.

Poe, Elizabeth Wilson. "New Light on the Alba: A Genre Redefined." *Viator* 15 (1984): 139–50.

Saville, Jonathan. *The Medieval Erotic Alba: Structure as Meaning*. New York: Columbia University Press, 1972.

Shapiro, Marianne. "The Figure of the Watchman in the Provençal Erotic Alba." *Modern Language Notes* 91 (1976): 607–35.

Sigal, Gale. "Courted in the Country: Women's Precarious Place in the Lyric Landscape." In *Text and Territory: Geographical Imagination in the European Middle Ages*, edited by Sylvia Tomasch and Sealy Gilles, 185–206. The Middle Ages. Philadelphia: University of Pennsylvania, 1998.

———. *Erotic Dawn-songs of the Middle Ages: Voicing the Lyric Lady*. Gainesville: University Press of Florida, 1996.

Spence, Sarah. "'Et Ades Sera L'alba': Revelations as Intertext for the Provençal Alba." *Romance Philology* 35 (1981): 212–17.

GALE SIGAL

ALBIGENSIAN WOMEN. *See* **Grazida (Grazida Lizier)**

ALDEGUND, ST. (c.639–c.684). A late Merovingian saint, Aldegund, abbess of Maubeuge, northeastern France, composed an important autobiography yielding much personal insight into the changing situation of women within the Frankish Church under the influence of St. Amandus (d. c.675), apostle of Flanders. By Aldegund's lifetime, the Merovingian kingdom—begun in the fifth century, first united by the Frankish king Clovis (late sixth century), and named after his legendary ancestor Merovech—extended over most of what are now France, Belgium, and Germany. The equally illustrious King Dagobert (r. 629–639) had just died, leaving the Merovingian domain larger and stronger due to his dynasty's trademark aptitude for inheritance, conquest, governance, and murder. Dagobert also understood the political, as well as spiritual, wisdom in endowing religious communities, and was a generous benefactor to such places as Maubeuge, one of several double monasteries founded between the Somme and the Meuse rivers by members of his circle. Most closely associated with Maubeuge was Nivelles, another double monastery (one inhabited and run by both monks and nuns) established in 640 by Gertrude of Nivelles (628–658), recent widow of Pippin, Dagobert's palace mayor. According to Aldegund's visions, she may have been related to Gertrude and thus also of aristocratic stock.

The daughter of Waldebert, who had possibly served as *domesticus* (subordinate officer) to King Clothar (see Levison, ed.), and Bertilla, Aldegund as a child recounted her holy visions, leading her parents to dedicate her to the Church. However, the precise chronology of her whereabouts and personal contacts is unclear. Aldegund's apparently much older sister, Waldetrude (d. c.688), had been married and bore children, Madelberta and Aldetrude. Both sisters seem to have been "inflamed" with God's love at about the same time. Their mother opposed her daughter Aldegund's desire to consecrate her virginity to Christ rather than to marry conventionally, but was persuaded by Waldetrude to allow her to follow her calling. As for Waldetrude, when Christ's "fire of love" caused her to "sweat with good works," she left her husband, Madelgar, who converted along with her, assuming the monastic name of Vincent of Soignies. More unusual for a female religious of that time was that Waldetrude, who lived as a hermit for a time, was able to establish her own community at Mons (now in Belgium), a fairly difficult feat for a woman unless she had power and connections; Waldetrude did enlist the help of a male relative to aid in building her convent. Another intriguing aspect of Waldetrude's story is that, despite zealous devotion to her new monastic life, she evidently missed the sexual aspect of her previous life (McNamara et al.). As was customary at the time, the sisters' dowry-endowments helped sustain the monasteries to which they attached themselves or founded. If during the sixth century, nunneries were located only within town walls to provide better protection and easier access to religious supervision by priests, the double monasteries of the seventh century enabled nuns, as well as monks, to participate in the monastic colonization of isolated areas. Although one version of her *vita* refutes that she was ever really abbess (*Vita Aldegundis*, ed. Smet, note a), Aldegund became known as both a skillful monastic administrator and spiritual visionary. Her combination of organizational and mystical abilities proved to be very effective for monastic leadership.

Much of our knowledge of Aldegund and Waldetrude comes from the former's autobiography, the *Vita Aldegundis* (*Life of Aldegund*). Comparison of the *Vita Aldegundis* with earlier Merovingian *vitae* like the *Vitae sanctae Radegundis* (*Life of St. Radegund*) shows not only the advanced development of hagiography as a literary form by the mid-seventh century, but also the increased articulation of the female saint's voice. Female saints' lives of the previous century sought to incorporate women's roles in secular society into holy ideals; by contrast, Aldegund's *Vita* further emphasizes feminine mystical experiences in addition to traditional secular womanly duties. Her autobiography's genesis began when, on first becoming a nun, Aldegund dictated her nightly visions to "a certain Subinis," abbot of Nivelles, who added (chs. 20–24) testimony from sisters at Maubeuge and also Waldetrude (Wemple 1987). Aldegund's original account is lost; still available is a summary of that original text written by the anonymous author of the final (second) version, whom modern scholar Jo Ann McNamara suggests might have been a nun under Waldetrude's direction or even Waldetrude's daughter, Aldetrude (see notes to *Sainted Women*). Maubeuge's reputation as a center for teaching children increases the likelihood that this anonymous writer was raised and educated in Aldegund's community. Two printed editions reflect different methodologies in reconstructing these materials: the edition by Corneille Smet is based more directly on the oldest, anonymous (and Subinus's) versions (c.715–718); while that by Wilhelm Levison downplays the *Vita*'s mystical content and adds material from Hucbald of Saint-Amand's ninth-century life of Aldegund (see McNamara et al.; Moreira).

The *Vita Aldegundis* contains the typical hagiographic motifs equating the exalted spiritual life with the mundane necessities of food, water, shelter, clothing, and healing. Thus sanctified and intensified (for example, her fasting, her "precious dress" as "celestial *stola*," her vision promising a "mansion" in Heaven), these analogies form the substance of saintly revelations and miracles. To illustrate how such symbolism was applied, we may take, for example, the episode in which Aldegund kept a fish (a Christian sign since late Antiquity) donated to Maubeuge by a villager in a pond on the nunnery property. Crows (black and evil) attacked the fish. A little lamb (Christ) came out of the field and fought off the crows to save the fish. In another divine configuration, the cloth of Aldegund's habit protected one of her sister nuns from a fire; in yet another, Aldegund healed a gravely ill man by placing the sign of the cross upon him. She also had a vision of St. Amandus ascending to heaven. Her visions were also intensely personalized, to a greater extent than those of other mystics, as Isabel Moreira has demonstrated recently, charting a new direction in nuns' bridal visions (part of the *Brautmystik*—the "Bride of Christ" mystique embraced by her and others), which would provide a model for later mystical women's visions. The popular appeal of Aldegund's visions guaranteed the support of donations to the nunnery. Economic self-sufficiency enabled the monastery to interact— yet remain independent of—the politics of the secular kingdom.

Five days before her death, probably in 684 (van der Essen), her sister Waldetrude experienced a vision of Aldegund carried to her "ethereal seat" by the apostles sent by Christ or a chorus of angels. Aldegund was first buried near Maubeuge beside her parents at their villa called Curtissolra, then later was moved to Maubeuge at the behest of King Theuderic III (although the later *vita* says Sigebert, erroneously, since he predeceased her in 656 [McNamara et al.]) and her niece, the now abbess Aldetrude, a moment that the town would commemorate lavishly thirteen centuries later, in 1984.

See also Bride of Christ/*Brautmystik*; Double Monasteries; Gertrude of Nivelles, St.; Hagiography (Female Saints); Nunneries, Merovingian; Radegund, St.

BIBLIOGRAPHY

Primary Sources

Vita Aldegundis. Edited with commentary by Corneille Smet. In *Acta sanctorum Belgii selecta*, edited by Joseph Ghesquiere, 4: 291–326. 6 vols. Brussels: Mathieu Lemaire, 1783–1794.

———. [Extracts]. In *Sainted Women of the Dark Ages*, edited and translated by Jo Ann McNamara and John E. Halborg et al., 234–63. Durham, N.C.: Duke University Press, 1992. [Highly useful annotated English version].

Hucbald of Saint Amand et al. *Vita Aldegundis.* Edited by Wilhelm Levison. In *Passiones vitaeque sanctores aevi merovingici*, edited by Bruno Krusch, 6: 79–90. *Monumenta Germaniae Historica: Scriptores rerum merovingicarum*, 3–7. 5 vols. Hannover, Germany: Hahn, 1896–1920. Reprint 1977–1979.

Secondary Sources

Bitel, Lisa M. "Women's Monastic Enclosures in Early Ireland: A Study of Female Spirituality and Male Monastic Mentalities." *Journal of Medieval History* 12 (1986): 15–36.

Clarke, H[oward]. B., and Brennan, Mary, eds. *Columbanus and Merovingian Monasticism.* B. A. R. International Series, 113. Oxford: B. A. R., 1981.

McNamara, Jo Ann. "Hagiography and Nunneries in Merovingian Gaul." In *Women of the Medieval World*, edited by Julius Kirshner and Suzanne Wemple, 37–52. Oxford and New York: Basil Blackwell, 1985.

Moreira, Isabel. *Dreams, Visions and Spiritual Authority in Merovingian Gaul.* Ithaca, N.Y.: Cornell University Press, 2000.

Van der Essen, Léon. *Etude critique et littéraire des saints mérovingiens de l'ancienne Belgique.* Louvain, Belgium: Université de Louvain, 1907.

Wemple, Suzanne F. "Female Spirituality and Mysticism in Frankish Monasticism: Radegund, Balthild, and Aldegund." In *Medieval Religious Women, 2: Peace Weavers*, edited by John A. Nichols and Lillian T. Shank, 39–54. Kalamazoo, Mich.: Cistercian Publications, 1987.

———. *Women in Frankish Society: Marriage and the Cloister 500–900.* Philadelphia: University of Pennsylvania Press, 1981.

DUEY WHITE

ALEWIVES/BREWSTERS. *See* **Guilds, Women in**

ALEXIAD. *See* **Comnena, Anna**

ALMUC DE CASTELNOU (c.1140–c.1184 or early 1200s). Almuc was a woman troubadour, or *trobairitz*, to whom only one *cobla* (stanza) is attributed, who may nonetheless have been an important figure in literary circles. Almuc's *cobla* forms half of a *tenso* (debate poem), beginning "Dompna N'Almulcs, si.us plages" ("Lady Almuc, if you please"), written with her friend Iseut de Capio, whose own *cobla* seeks to intercede for Almuc's lamenting lover, identified in the accompanying *razo*, or biographical sketch, as Gigo de Tornon. To Iseut's plea, Almuc replies: "Dompna N'Iseuz, s'ieu saubes/q'el se pentis de l'engan/q'el a fait vas mi tan gran,/ben for a dreichz q'eu n'agues/merce" ("Lady Iseut, if I knew/that he repented of the grave deceit/he has done me,/it would be entirely right for me to show him/mercy"). She withholds her forgiveness, however, stating "mas a mi no.s taing/pos qe del tort no s'afraing/ni's pentis del faillimen" ("but it is not proper for me to be more forgiving/because he does not refrain from the wrong/nor does he repent his fault"). Nonetheless, she is prepared to change her mind, "si vos faitz lui pentir" ("if you make him repent"). If the poem constitutes a modest contribution to the medieval poetic corpus, it does illustrate the power of the lady's will, enhanced for reader by the presence of the purportedly soothing go-between, Iseut, in the love relationship.

Since Almuc de Castelnou has not been conclusively identified, most modern scholars accept two possible women as the *trobairitz* Almuc or Almucs. Jean Boutière and Alexander H. Schutz identified her many years ago as Almodis or Almois, the wife of Guigne de Châteauneuf-de-Raudon (Provençal = Guigo de Castelnou de Randon) in the arrondissement of Mende (Lozère). Nearby stands Chapieu (Castrum de Capione), which could have been the home of her co-protagonist in the poem, Iseut de Capio. This identification, accepted by both Margarita Egan and Matilda Bruckner, appears to be based primarily on evidence provided by the *razo* (commentary) accompanying the poem. If this Almodis is in fact the *trobairitz* Almuc, she must have lived in the early thirteenth century. Her lover, Gigo de Tornon, has been identified as the Gui, lord of Tournon in the Vivarais, who in 1217 supported the bishop of Valence and in 1226 did homage at Avignon to Louis VIII for his lands.

Meg Bogin, on the other hand, deems the razo in question "useless"; proposing an alternative identification of Almuc in accordance with genealogical details on one Almodis de Caseneuve, wife of Giraut I de Simiane, lord of Caseneuve, Apt, and Gordes, who lived in the mid- to late twelfth century. Bogin theorizes, after comparative chronological calculations of biographical data on Almuc, her husband, Giraut, and son, Raimbault, that Almodis must have been born between 1140 and 1147 and that her marriage to Giraut must have taken place between 1152 and 1161 or early 1162. Her son, Raimbaut d'Agoult, as he would come to be known, had accompanied his father on crusade, was himself a troubadour and a patron of poets, as mentioned in twelve poems by his contemporary, the noted troubadour Gaucelm Faidit. Bogin reinforces her case by noting the proximity of Caseneuve, in the Vaucluse, to Les Chapelains, which she identifies with Iseut's home of Capio—instead of Chapieu, signaled in the abovementioned theory. Providing detailed evidence, several scholars (Rieger; Paden; Brunel) have argued that another *trobairitz*, Castelloza, alludes to Almuc in one of the *tornadas* (concluding stanza) of the poem "Ia de chanter" ("I to sing"), in which she refers to her as "Na Miels" ("Lady Best"). The earlier twelfth-century dating would situate Almuc in what Bogin calls "the classical period of troubadour poetry."

Most scholars accept the hypothesis espoused by Egan and Bruckner. Almuc's poem exists in a single manuscript, at the Vatican as Biblioteca Vaticana lat. 3207.

See also Castelloza, Na; Iseut de Capio; *Trobairitz*

BIBLIOGRAPHY

Primary Sources
Almuc de Castelnou. ["Dompna N'Almulcs"]. In *Songs of the Women Troubadours*, edited and translated by Matilda Tomaryn Bruckner, Laurie Shepard, and Sarah White, 48–49, 147, 160–61. New York: Garland, 1995. Revised ed. 2000. [Most authoritative bilingual ed.: original text, English translation, and notes].
———. In *Trobairitz: Der Beitrag der Frau in der altokzitanischen höfischen Lyrik. Edition des Gesamtkorpus*, edited by Angelica Rieger, 168. Beihefte der Zeitschrift für romanische Philologie, 233. Tübingen, Germany: Max Niemeyer Verlag, 1991.

Bogin, Meg. *The Women Troubadours*, 92–93, 165–66. New York and London: W. W. Norton, 1980. Originally Paddington Press, 1976.

Boutière, Jean, and Alexander H. Schutz, eds. *Biographies des Troubadours: Textes provençaux des XIIIᵉ et XIVᵉ siècles*. Revised edition with I. M. Cluzel. Les Classiques d'Oc, 1. Paris: Nizet, 1964.

Chabaneau, Camille. *Les Biographies des troubadours en langue provençale*. Toulouse: E. Privat, 1885.

Egan, Margarita, trans. *The Vidas of the Troubadours*. Garland Library of Medieval Literature, 6B. New York: Garland Publishing, Inc., 1984.

Perkal-Balinsky, Deborah. "The Minor Trobairitz: An Edition with Translation and Commentary." Diss. Ph.D. Northwestern University, 1986. DAI 47 (1987): 2577A.

Schultz-Gora, Oskar. *Die provenzalischen Dichterinnen: Biographieen und Texte*. Leipzig: Gustav Foch, 1888. [See Egan for English translations].

Secondary Sources

Brunel, Clovis. "Almois de Châteauneuf et Iseut de Chapieu." *Annales du Midi* 28 (1915–1916): 262–68.

Jeanroy, Alfred. *La Poésie lyrique des troubadours*. 1: 313, n.2. Toulouse and Paris: Privat, 1934. Reprint Geneva: Slatkine, 1973.

Nelli, René, ed. *Écrivains anti-conformistes du moyen-âge occitan: I. La Femme et l'amour*, 247–49. Paris: Phébus, 1977.

Paden, William D. "Some Recent Studies of Women in the Middle Ages, Especially Southern France." *Tenso: Bulletin of the Société Guillaume IX* 7 (1992): 94–124.

Rieger, Angelica. "*En conselh no deu hom voler femna*: les dialogues mixtes dans la lyrique troubadouresque." *Perspectives médiévales* 16 (1990): 47–57.

JUNE HALL MCCASH

AMALASUNTHA (c.498–535). As the regent of Ostrogothic Italy (526–534) for her son Athalaric, Amalasuntha—also called Amalasuintha, Amalsuentha, or Amalaswintha—was the strong-willed guardian of her father's kingdom who also advocated the dissemination of Classical culture within her realm at a crucial historical juncture between Greco-Roman and medieval European civilizations. Born in Bolsena, Italy, to Barbarian-tribal (Goths, Ostrogoths) nobility, Amalasuntha's lineage destined her to rule. Her father was Theodoric the Great (c.454–526), a scion of the Amal line of Gothic chieftains, who became the Ostrogothic king of Italy. Her mother was Audefleda, sister of Clovis, king of the Franks (r. 482–511), notable for unifying and converting his kingdom to Christianity.

She evidently inherited her passions for power and learning from her father. The death of Attila the Hun in 453 freed the Ostrogoths, his subjects, to benefit from the waning Roman Empire's ascendant eastern half, Byzantium. It was to Byzantium's capital, Constantinople (now Istanbul, Turkey), that Theodoric was sent by his father (461) to serve as a hostage binding a treaty. For ten years, this most sophisticated court provided Theodoric with schooling by Byzantine mentors. By steeping the future ruler in Roman culture, they not only performed their function as imperial tutors but also defused the threat of future barbarism, at least in Theodoric's case. Interestingly enough, Theodoric's sister, Amalafrida, likewise spent a decade in Constantinople as a ward of the state receiving a similarly high level of education. She later became a patron of poets, and her son Theodahad's love of Greek philosophy certainly distinguished him from other Gothic nobles. When Theodoric established his own court, it included Roman scholars with whom the king enjoyed conversing. Though such high-cultural influences did not alter the traditional training of Theodoric's Gothic warriors, it did cause him to provide members of his family with Roman educations and to try to model himself on the ancient Greek philosopher Plato's philosopher-king. Later, when ordered by the Byzantine emperor Zeno (r. 474–491) to liberate the Italian peninsula from the German king Odovacar (r. 476–493)—who had deposed the last Western Roman emperor, Romulus Augustulus (476)—Theodoric first made several years' roughly outlined peace with Odovacar, then, deciding to take Italy over for himself, invited him to a banquet and murdered him, thereby becoming king in 493. Because of the transitional nature of the Roman Empire's Eastern and Western halves, and the rising power of the Barbarian groups as represented in such takeovers, Theodoric is considered the first medieval king (Hollister and Bennett). He ruled Italy as a suzerainty of Constantinople relatively progressively (in Roman style yet allowing Barbarian subjects to preserve their customs) in peace and prosperity for almost forty years. Such was the special atmosphere nurturing Amalasuntha.

Theodoric had an important reason for educating his daughter beyond the norm: since he had no son, Amalasuntha would succeed him. She thus learned to play a role in government in addition to her studies in Classical literature and language. Aside from her Roman Catholic governess named Barbara, the identities of her other tutors remain unknown. Boethius (c.475–c.525) and Cassiodorus (c.480–c.575), two of the kingdom's shining intellects, both served her father, but there is no proof that they contributed to the education of the crown princess. Cassiodorus notes that Amalasuntha was unusual among rulers of his day in needing no interpreters, since she was fully at home in Latin, Greek, and Gothic. St. Gregory, bishop of Tours (538/9–594), by contrast, injects a defamatory episode into this phase of her life: contrary to her mother's wishes that she marry someone of her own royal blood, Amalasuntha took a lover, Traguila, from among her slaves. After pleading with her to no avail, Audefleda dispatched some soldiers who killed Traguila and, after flogging her, sent Amalasuntha back to her mother. Later, the headstrong princess would avenge herself by successfully poisoning her mother's communion chalice. Gregory's story, entirely false, reflects his anti-Arian (the Ostrogoths' form of Christianity, Arianism, deemed heretical by the Church) bias and perhaps a bit of misogyny.

In 515 Amalasuntha wed Eutharic, a distant cousin whose Amal ancestry qualified him for the throne. Eutharic and Amalasuntha soon gave Theodoric a grandson, Athalaric, and also a granddaughter, Matasuntha. After Eutharic's early death in 522, followed by that of Theodoric four years later, the ten-year-old Athalaric became king with his mother serving as regent, the actual ruler. For nine years, Amalasuntha survived plots and thwarted coups, executing rebellious nobles in the process, to preserve the integrity of her father's kingdom. She incurred these perils by striving to maintain a near-impossible balance of good relations among her people, the Ostrogoths, and Byzantium, and then also with the Church. These diplomatic policies filtered down into her prescriptions for dress and mores among her courtiers, who resented the intrusion of Byzantium and the Church into their Gothic way of life (their religion was Arianism). She also attempted to continue her family's new tradition of educating her son as a Roman prince, in both literature and government. Gothic nobles, however, believing such training to be effeminate, wrested Athalaric from her control and immersed him in the manly environment of the Barbarian *comitatus* (a proto-feudal war band ruled by a chieftain), stressing hunting, weaponry, and similar masculine pursuits—including drunkenness and debauchery. This training only shortened his life, so that Athalaric fell ill and died in 534, not yet twenty. Also during that time, she restored the estates of Boethius, the author and minister whom her ailing father had put to death on false charges of treason, to the wronged man's children; she did likewise in other similar cases.

After her son's death, Amalasuntha knew that the Goths would not tolerate a female ruler without at least a male consort. She thus quickly allied herself with her cousin, Theodahad (or Theodat), her aunt Amalafrida's older, philosophy-loving son, in 534, forming a ruling pact with him allowing her the upper hand. Unfortunately, Theodahad lived up to her Gothic adversaries' negative stereotype of learned nonvirility: weak as a warrior (despite his Vandal father) and even as a politician (he was greedy). Shortly after his elevation to the throne, he betrayed her, probably after being bribed by the ambitious Byzantine Empress Theodora (500–548), whose husband, Emperor Justinian (r. 527–565), was hoping peaceably to annex Italy as part of their rebuilding of Constantinople (burned by rioting mobs in 532). The contemporary imperial historian Procopius (500–562) alleges that Theodora sought to eliminate Amalasuntha as a rival for her husband's heart (Amalasuntha had been in diplomatic correspondence with Justinian and also Theodora, separately). However, Procopius was always anti-Theodora and pro-Amalasuntha; just as Gregory of Tours was anti-Amalasuntha and pro-Theodahad in his accounts (plus his Francocentrism completely omits the Byzantine factor). Historians now believe the notoriously resourceful imperial couple may have been playing the co-rulers of Italy against each other.

Amalasuntha was imprisoned on an island in Lake Bolsena, near her birthplace, where, before her supporters might have rescued her, she was strangled, or—by Gregory's account—scalded to death in her bath. Protesting his innocence of her murder, Theodahad blamed the deed on vengeful relatives of three rebellious Goths whom Amalasuntha had executed in 533, or on friends of her mother Audefleda, whom Amalasuntha had supposedly poisoned (Gregory). Justinian, pressed by Theodora as always, decided nonetheless to take advantage of the queen's death in his plans to reconquer the old Roman Empire from the Barbarians. Looking for an excuse to destroy him, the imperial couple ignored Theodahad's plausible story and launched a war to regain Italy both for their empire, under the pretext of avenging Queen Amalasuntha and saving the Church. The treacherous Theodahad was defeated by the famous general Belisarius (c.505–565). Eventually, Byzantium too succumbed to the hyperextension that weakened Rome through such short-lived conquests over a vigorously defiant people like the Vandals, Lombards, and Ostrogoths, for whom Theodoric's premature renaissance unfortunately ended with the death of his daughter, Amalasuntha. Her six surviving letters (preserved by Cassiodorus and Procopius) to Justinian and others demonstrate her diplomatic acumen and impressive epistolary style.

See also Epistolary Authors, Women as; Theodora

BIBLIOGRAPHY

Primary Sources
Amalasuntha. [4 Letters]. In Cassiodorus Senator, *Variae*, edited by Theodor Mommsen, 1: 296, 298–99, 303–04. *Monumenta Germaniae Historica. Auctores Antiquissimorum*, 12. Berlin: Weidmann, 1894. [Original Latin text with commentary].
———. [4 Letters: to Justinian, the Roman Senate, and Theodora]. In *The Writings of Medieval Women: An Anthology*, translated with introductions by Marcelle Thiébaux, 71–84. New York: Garland, 1994. [English translation].
Amalasuntha. [2 letters: to Belisarius, to Justinian]. *See under* Procopius, *below.*
Procopius of Caesarea. [*Gothic Wars*; *Secret History*]. In *Opera omnia*. Critical ed. by Jacob Haury. 4 vols. Munich: K. G. Saur, 2001. [Original Greek text with Latin notes].

———. *History of the Wars; Secret History*. In *Works*, translated by H. B. Dewing, 2: 252–55, 3: 12–43; 6: passim. Loeb Classical Library. 7 vols. Cambridge, Mass.: Harvard University Press; London: Heinemann, 1914–1940. [Bilingual edition, Greek-English].

Gregory of Tours, St. [*Historia Francorum*] *Historiarum libri decem*. Revised critical edition by Bruno Krusch and Wilhelm Levison, Book 3, chapt. 31. *Monumenta Germaniae Historica. Scriptores rerum Merovingicarum*, 1.1, Hannover: Hahn, 1951. [*History of the Franks*, English]: *See above in* Thiébaux trans., 77.

Secondary Sources

[See also notes to editions and translations listed above].

Barnish, S. J. B. *The Variae of Magnus Aurelius Cassiodorus*. Translated Texts for Historians, 12. Liverpool: Liverpool University Press, 1992. [Translated selections with useful commentary].

Burns, Thomas. *A History of the Ostrogoths,* Bloomington: University of Indiana Press, 1984.

Hollister, C. Warren, and Judith M. Bennett. *Medieval Europe: A Short History*. 9th ed. Boston: McGraw-Hill, 2002.

O'Donnell, James J. *Cassiodorus*. Berkeley: University of California Press, 1979.

Riché, Pierre. *Éducation et culture dans l'Occident barbare, VIᵉ–VIIIᵉ siècles*. 4th ed., revised. Paris: Seuil, 1995.

Wolfram, Herwig. *History of the Goths*. Revised and translated by Thomas J. Dunlap. Berkeley: University of California Press, 1988.

KATHARINA M. WILSON

AMAZONS. *See* **Nine Worthy Women; Valkyries**

ANCRENE RIWLE (c.1225). *Ancrene Riwle*, or *Ancrene Wisse* (*Rule for Anchoresses*) was a guide composed in the West Midlands of England for three natural sisters of good family by their spiritual director, a male religious, possibly an Augustinian canon or Dominican friar. *Anchorites* (males) or *anchoresses* (females) are terms for those who withdraw from the world to devote themselves to solitude in prayer and self-mortification like hermits. Anchoresses, however, tend to be more strictly confined to cells than hermits. The vernacular *Ancrene Riwle*, though orthodox in theology and conservative in religious discipline, reflects this movement of popular spirituality and is thus an important document in the social history of England in the later Middle Ages. Although written by a man, it is especially valued in the study of medieval women's cultural roles and personal experience, as adapted from his main sources, Saints Augustine (354–430), Gregory the Great (c.540–604), Bernard of Clairvaux (1090–1153), and Ailred of Rievaulx (1109–1167). It is also a distinguished example of early Middle English prose.

The Dominicans and other preaching orders first came to England in the early 1220s as part of a larger spiritual movement sponsored in part by the Fourth Lateran Council of 1215, which sought to promote a more active moral self-awareness and responsibility among ordinary lay people. Anchoritism grew sharply in the thirteenth century and reached its peak in the fourteenth. Even so, in 1377, only 214 anchorites are recorded for the entire country, considerably less than one percent of those who sought a religious life. Women chose anchoritism more often than men. Although not a member of any religious order, the three sisters for whom this guide was written were nonetheless inspired as young women to enclose themselves in separate but adjacent anchorholds, or cells. The cells were of widely varied sizes, but their dimensions are prescribed in similar "rules" as twelve-feet square. The cell contained three windows: (1) a "squint" in the wall of the church to which the anchorhold was attached and through which the recluse could observe the mass and receive communion; (2) a "parlour" window that opened onto the churchyard or street—shuttered and curtained in black with an embroidered white cross—through which she could speak with her confessor and other visitors; and (3) a service portal through which she communicated to her maidservants, of whom she was allowed two: one to attend to her personal needs and one to run errands. Furniture would have included a bed, table, chair, crucifix, stoup (basin) of holy water, images of the Virgin and other saints, a few edifying books in English and French, tableware, and sewing equipment.

In England, such solitary self-confinement was a venerable institution going back to early Anglo-Saxon times, widespread throughout the country but never very common. The ritual of enclosure itself would have included the administration of the last sacrament—Extreme Unction—followed by a sprinkling of dust and a sealing of the cell from without, as if of a tomb.

Some anchoresses lived to a considerable age, however, and were by no means cut off from their communities, least of all from those on whom they depended for charitable patronage, spiritual guidance, and physical support.

Ancrene Riwle is divided into eight sections, each one treating an aspect of spiritual discipline: devotions, the five senses, the inner feelings, temptations, confession, penance, love of Christ, and more practical considerations. In his preface, however, the author suggests that there are really only two rules: (1) the more important, an inner rule to govern the heart—that is, the emotional life of the anchoress, and (2) an outer rule to govern the exigencies of living an enclosed life. He calls the first "the lady rule," whose purpose is to cultivate love, humility, patience, and other virtues in the recluse; the second is the "handmaiden" rule, whose duty is solely to facilitate the former, flexibly adapting like a good servant to the changing requirements of her mistress. The devotional regimen—the schedule of liturgical hours and prayers—prescribed for the sisters is a fairly ambitious, even severe, one, but the author's tone remains that of affectionate, familiar solicitude for their honor, health, and well-being. His style, too, is brisk and colloquial, with a certain felicity of expression and neatness of phrase. Invoking the analogy of Mary and Martha in the Gospels, he tartly remarks, "Martha has her job: let her be. You should sit with Mary stone-still at God's feet and listen to Him alone." He is full as well of lively circumstantial advice about the life of a recluse. He recommends a modest vegetarian diet but discourages fasting without permission. In fact, he gently frets that the sisters are taking less nourishment than they should. He is even stricter against various ascetic and mortifying practices:

> Let no one put on any kind of belt unless by her confessor's leave, nor wear any iron, or hair, or hedgehog skins, nor beat herself with these or with a leaded scourge, nor draw blood from herself with holly or brambles, without her confessor's leave; let her not sting herself with nettles anywhere, nor beat herself on her front, nor do any cutting, nor take at one time over-harsh disciplines to extinguish temptations. . . . Some women are ready enough to wear breeches of haircloth very well knotted on, the legs very tightly laced down to the feet. But always best is the sweet and fragrant heart: I would rather you bore a harsh remark well than a harsh hairshirt.

The women are reminded to wear warm, well-made shoes and clothes of "skins well-cured; and have as many as you need for your bed and to wear," and to keep themselves clean: "Wash yourself wherever there is need as often as you want, and your things, too—filth was never dear to God, though poverty and plainness are pleasing." The rudeness that the women are enjoined to ignore is embodied primarily in the character of Slurry, the cook's boy, who presumably brought them their vegetable stew. The author has other practical advice about their social interactions. He warns, for instance, against their becoming a magnet for "down-and-outs," especially since the anchoresses themselves are supported by a benefactor: "A recluse must live on charity as moderately as ever she can and not gather in order to give—she is not a housewife, but a church anchoress. . . . Under the semblance of good, sin is often hidden. Let her not want to have a reputation as a generous anchoress, nor, so as to give much, be any greedier to have more." Such restraint also affects her choice of wardrobe ("In God's eyes she is more lovely who is for love of him unadorned outside"), since feminine display is a spiritual snare, a distraction from true goodness. Even wimpling (the headdress required by most convents), when unnecessary, can offend against this strict plainness: "If anything covers your face from a man's eye, be it a wall, be it a cloth in a well-closed window, an anchoress can well do without other wimpling." Anchoresses were permitted small pets, but not livestock, since these involved too much responsibility. Even seemingly innocent favors, like keeping things safe for people, can become disruptive of her serenity of heart. For the same reason, she should avoid the temptation to become overly instructive of children who come to visit, though it is her duty lovingly to guide and teach her own maids.

The anchoress's most important relationship, of course, is with God, which the author dramatizes using the imagery of courtly romance. Christ comes to the recluse as a royal knight who has long loved her as "a poor lady of good family living in a far off country closely besieged by her enemies, her land completely devastated and she utterly destitute inside a castle of earth." He is killed rescuing her, but miraculously rises from the dead. She is urged to accept him, as a noble lady her humble knight-errant. The author is quite explicit in suggesting that her feelings should go beyond gratitude to a frank sublimation of erotic desire: "After the mass-kiss, when the priest consecrates, there forget all the world, there be entirely out of the body, there in gleaming love embrace your beloved, who has alighted into the bower of your breast from heaven, and hold him tight until he has granted you all that ever you ask." The author encourages the deeper cultivation and arousal of such feelings: "Think whether you ought not readily to love the king of joy, who so spreads out his arms towards you and bows down his head as if to offer a kiss. . . . Stretch your love to Jesus Christ and you have won him. Touch him with as much love as you have at some time felt for a person, and he is yours to do with all you wish." As Mary in the Gospels, the anchoress has chosen the "better" part of woman's life on earth (see Luke 10.42). She pursues with concentrated devotion the presence of God, in comparison to which other objects of desire, all other human occupations, are ephemeral distractions. In the worldview and value system of her culture, the anchoress has undertaken the most worthy and demanding of vocations. Even so, the development of bizarre mortifications or other obsessive behaviors was clearly recognized as a danger in the life of a solitary, one from which the author seeks assiduously to protect his friends. The author concludes by wishing the sisters their ultimate goal—that God may give them "nothing less than himself completely"—and by asking a modest favor in return: that they say a Hail Mary for the author whenever they read this work.

The interest of this rule derives in large part, then, from the insight it affords into the social identity and inward consciousness of female recluses. Women who had dramatically separated themselves from the societies in which they lived, who sought to experience the presence of divine being beyond their own world, but who nonetheless still lived in that world, remained significant members of their communities and an inspiration to both men and women who could not hope to imitate the severity of their commitment. *Ancrene Riwle* was copied many times in the thirteenth and fourteenth centuries, and was translated into both French and Latin. It remained an important work of English devotional writing into the early sixteenth century. To a modern reader, the charm of this work lies in its sensible, sincere advice, its modesty and humanity, given the supreme value her culture placed on the anchoress's transcendent goals. In these pages, the enclosed life seems no longer a perversion or distortion of human community or character, but a sympathetic and admirable, possibly even heroic, undertaking on the part of these women.

See also Beguines; Convents; Julian of Norwich; Rules for Canonesses, Nuns, and Recluses

BIBLIOGRAPHY

Primary Sources
Ancrene Wisse: MS. Corpus Christi College Cambridge 402. Edited by J. R. R. Tolkien. Early English Text Society, o.s. 249. London: Oxford University Press, 1962.
Ancrene Wisse: Guide for Anchoresses. Translated by Hugh White. London: Penguin, 1993. [All passages quoted above are from this translation].
Anchoritic Spirituality: Ancrene Wisse and Associated Works. Translated by Anne Savage and Nicholas Watson. Classics of Western Spirituality. New York: Paulist Press 1991.
Ancrene Riwle: Introduction and Part I. Edited and translated by Robert W. Ackerman and Roger Dahood. Binghamton, N.Y.: Medieval and Renaissance Texts and Studies, 1985. [Based on British Library MS Cleopatra C. VI, an earlier ms.].
[Ancren Riwle] The English Text of Ancrene Riwle: The 'Vernon Text,' edited from Oxford, Bodleian Library MS Eng. Poet.a. I. Edited by Arne Zettersten and B. Diensberg. Introduction by H. L. Spencer. Oxford: Oxford University Press, 2000.
Ancrene Wisse: Parts Six and Seven. Edited by Geoffrey Shepherd. 1959. Reprinted Exeter: University of Exeter, 1985. [Also based on Corpus Christi MS.].

Secondary Sources
[See also notes to above editions].
Clay, Rotha M. "Further Studies on Medieval Recluses." *Journal of the British Archæological Association* 16. 3rd ser. (1953): 74–86.
———. *The Hermits and Anchorites of England.* London: Methuen, 1914.
Dobson, E. J. *The Origins of Ancrene Wisse.* Oxford: Clarendon Press, 1976.
Elkins, Sharon K. *Holy Women of Twelfth-Century England.* Chapel Hill: University of North Carolina Press, 1988.
Georgianna, Linda. *The Solitary Self: Individuality in the Ancrene Wisse.* Cambridge, Mass.: Harvard University Press, 1981.
Grayson, Janet. *Structure and Imagery in Ancrene Wisse.* Hanover: University of New Hampshire Press, 1974.
Millett, Bela. "The Origins of *Ancrene Wisse*: New Answers, New Questions." *Medium Ævum* 61 (1992): 206–28.
———, and Jocelyn Wogan-Browne, eds. *Medieval English Prose for Women.* Oxford: Clarendon Press, 1990.
Petroff, Elizabeth Alvilda, ed. *Medieval Women's Visionary Literature.* New York: Oxford University Press, 1986.
Robertson, Elizabeth. "Medieval Medical Views of Women and Female Spirituality in the Ancrene Wisse and Julian of Norwich's Showings." In *Feminist Approaches to the Body in Medieval Literature.*

Edited by Linda Lomperis and Sarah Stanbury, 142–67. Philadelphia: University of Pennsylvania Press, 1993.

Wada, Yoko, ed. *A Companion to* Ancrene Wisse. Cambridge, U.K.: D. S. Brewer, 2003.

Warren, Ann K. *Anchorites and Their Patrons in Medieval England.* Berkeley: University of California Press, 1985.

CRAIG R. DAVIS

ANDREAS CAPELLANUS. *See* **Capellanus, Andreas**

ANGELA MERICI, ST. *See* **Merici, Angela, St.**

ANGELA OF FOLIGNO, BLESSED (c.1248–1309). A Franciscan visionary author known as "Mistress of Theology," Angela (Angelina) was born in the city of Foligno, near Assisi, in the province of Umbria. Like many well-born young women of her time, she was at first attracted to the Third (Tertiary) Order—a local voluntary penitent movement independent of convent rules—for respectability, while, as she herself acknowledged, leading a life of moral disorder and mundane pursuits until her late thirties. However, after Angela lost her husband, children, and mother within the same brutal interval, her Franciscan devotion became more sincere: she experienced a crisis of conscience, causing such overwhelming remorse that she abandoned her dissolute ways. Her conversion, occurring in around 1285, appears to have been fostered by Francis himself, answering her prayers for the grace of a complete break with her past. In the summer of 1291, having sold all of her possessions, forty-three-year-old Angela professed and truly embraced the life of a penitent Tertiary Hermit. After a pilgrimage to Assisi that same year, at around the time of the feast of St. Francis (October 4), a violent mystical seizure overcame her, enabling her to experience the presence of the Holy Trinity. Angela soon thereafter came across a Franciscan friar, "Frater A.," possibly an uncle—Fra Arnaldo (Brother Arnold)—who became her confessor and scribe, since she herself was illiterate.

It was Arnaldo who preserved her spiritual upheavals and visions, translating faithfully her Umbrian dialect into Latin as she dictated the mystical visions comprising her autobiography to which Arnaldo gave the name of *Memoriale*, emphasizing the first part, but which is now known as the *Liber de vere fidelium experientia* (*Book of Experiences of the Truly Faithful*), translated in an English version as the *Divine Consolations*. The *Liber de experientia* represents Angela's personal mystical experience in thirty steps; the last ten condensed by Arnaldo into seven. Begun in 1292 and brought to conclusion in 1298, on its approval by eight theologians of the Minoritic (Franciscan) Order and by Cardinal Giacomo Colonna, the *Liber de experientia* describes her mystical itinerary in terms of thirty steps, beginning with the early moments of her conversion to the summit of her mystical experiences of the divine. She frames her entire interior experience within three spiritual periods or "transformations": (1) transformation in the will of God, (2) transformation with God, (3) transformation within God and God in the soul. The book divides into three treatises: the "Memorial" first tells of her inner life involving nineteen penitential steps, from becoming a Tertiary—committing herself to poverty, recognizing and overcoming her limitations—to finding solace in God's goodness; the second, or "Visions," relates her visions during the next seven steps, in which she perceives herself as wooed by the Holy Spirit during her pilgrimage to Assisi; the third part, also called the *Instructiones* (*Instructions*) on evangelical, or gospel-centered doctrine, consists in a collection of thirty-six letters inspired by further visions and addressed to her followers, plus stories and notes connected with her apostolic activity. Throughout these phases and transformations, Angela's language mirrors her emotions as she narrates them throughout her experience—from deepest sorrow and despair to heights of devotional elation—in a voice as unique as her structuring of this work. Her use of imagery transcends all previous authors' evocations of the physical: for example when she tells of how Christ offers her his wound so that she may drink his blood, or of how her joints became unstrung during the elevation of the host during communion—examples of eucharistic ecstasy. Centuries before critics would coin the term "writing the body," Angela accomplishes just that in her book, as she strives to unite herself literally body and soul with God in both discourse and deed. Elizabeth Petroff characterizes her mystical narrative as "violent, gestural, performative: she does not sing of her love; she acts it out publicly." Scholars such as Rudolph Bell and Caroline Bynum, focusing more closely on how mystics eschewed such bodily requirements as nourishment, provide persuasive insights into the paradoxes of Angela's fasting, obsession with the Eucharist (Body of Christ), and charitable work in feeding the poor.

Angela's affecting yet systematic re-creation of her revelations guaranteed the instant popularity of her work, which was widely copied. Also because, as Peter Dronke avers, she did not "lay claim to any new belief, any idea that challenged the prevailing world-picture of theologians of her time"—"however extravagant her emotional utterances," her *Liber de experientia* received a second approval from Cardinal Colonna, between 1309 and 1310, to include her other writings compiled after her death in Foligno on January 4, 1309. Its oldest manuscript, from Assisi (ms. 342), dated c.1350, enjoyed a wide diffusion in Italy and throughout Europe not only during the Trecento but especially in later centuries, with printed editions appearing in Alcalà in 1502, Venice in c.1510, Paris in 1598, and Cologne in 1601. Her works came to be endorsed by the greatest theologians of the thirteenth through eighteenth centuries, among them Ubertino da Casale (d. c.1330), in his *Arbor Vitae Crucifixae Jesu* (*Jesus, Tree of the Crucified Life*; Venice, 1485), St. Francis de Sales (d. 1622), Bossuet (d. 1704), Fénelon (d. 1715), and St. Alphonsus Liguori (d. 1787). Pope Benedict XIV (r. 1740–1758) ranks her among the greatest mystics of the ages, an equal of St. Teresa of Avila (1515–1582) and St. John of the Cross (1542–1591), while Pope Pius XII (d. 1958) considered her "the greatest Franciscan mystic." Angela was beatified—as indicated by the title of Blessed—by Pope Innocent XII in 1693; her feast day is celebrated by the Franciscan Order and by the city of Foligno on January 4.

See also Catherine of Siena, St.; Clare of Assisi, St.; Hildegard of Bingen, St.; Kempe, Margery; Penitentials, Women in; Porete, Marguerite; Umiltà of Faenza, St.

BIBLIOGRAPHY

Primary Sources
Angela of Foligno. *Le Livre de la Bienheureuse Soeur Angèle de Foligno.* Edited by Paul Doncoeur with M. Faloci-Pulignani. Paris: Bibliothèque d'ascétique et de mystique, 2. Paris: l'Art catholique, 1925. [Latin text with modern French translation].

―――. *Le Livre de l'expérience des vrais fidèles.* Edited by Martin-Jean Ferré and Léon Baudry. Paris: E. Droz, 1927. [Latin text of *Book of Experience* with modern French translation].

―――. [*Memoriale*] *Angela of Foligno's Memorial.* Edited and annotated by Cristina Mazzoni. Translated from Latin by John Cirignano. Library of Medieval Women. Cambridge and Rochester, N.Y.: D. S. Brewer, 2000.

―――. *Angela of Foligno: The Complete Works.* Translated and edited by Paul Lachance. Preface by Romana Guarnieri. Classics of Western Spirituality. Mahwah, N.J.: Paulist Press, 1993. [Supersedes 1909 trans. by Mary G. Steegmann].

―――. [Selections, in French]. *L'Expérience de Dieu avec Angèle de Foligno.* Introduction and selected texts edited and translated by Paul Lachance. L'Expérience de Dieu (series). Saint-Laurent, Québec: Fides, 2001.

Secondary Sources

Bell, Rudolph. *Holy Anorexia.* Chicago: University of Chicago Press, 1985.

Blasucci, A. "La B. Angela da Foligno 'Magistra Theologorum.' " *Miscellanea Franciscana* 48 (1948): 171–190.

Bynum, Caroline Walker. *Holy Feast and Holy Fast: The Religious Significance of Food to Medieval Women.* Berkeley and Los Angeles: University of California Press, 1987.

Dronke, Peter. *Women Writers of the Middle Ages: A Critical Study of Texts from Perpetua (†203) to Marguerite Porete (†1310).* Cambridge: Cambridge University Press, 1984.

Ferré, Martin-Jean. "Les principales dates de la vie d'Angèle de Foligno." *Revue D'histoire franciscaine* 2 (1925): 21–34.

Finke, Laurie. "Mystical Bodies and the Dialogics of Vision." In *Maps of Flesh and Light: New Perspectives on the Religious Experience of Medieval Women,* edited by Ulrike Wiethaus, 28–41. Syracuse, N.Y.: Syracuse University Press, 1992.

Lachance, Paul, O.F.M. "The Mystical Journey of Angela of Foligno." *Vox Benedictina* 4 (1987): 9–39. Reprint, *The Mystical Journey of Angela of Foligno.* Peregrina Papers. Toronto: Peregrina, 1990.

―――. *The Spiritual Journey of the Blessed Angela of Foligno According to the Memorial of the Frater A.* Studia Antoniana, 29. Rome: Pontificium Athenaeum Antonianum, 1984.

Petroff, Elizabeth Alvilda. *Body and Soul: Essays on Medieval Women and Mysticism.* New York and Oxford: Oxford University Press, 1994.

―――, ed. *Medieval Women's Visionary Literature,* 236–38, 254–63. New York and Oxford: Oxford University Press, 1986.

Schmitt, Clement, O.F.M., ed. *Vita e Spiritualità della Beata Angela da Foligno, Atti del Convegno di Studi per il VII Centenario della Conversione della beata Angela da Foligno (1285–1985), Foligno, 11–14 dicembre, 1985.* Perugia, 1987.

SANDRO STICCA

ANNA COMNENA. *See* **Comnena, Anna**

ANNA OF MUNZINGEN (early 14th century). Anna of Munzingen was Prioress of the Dominican nunnery at Freiburg im Breisgau, Germany (founded in 1234), as documented for the years 1316, 1317, and 1327. Known especially as the principal author of the Adelhausen Sister-Book, Anna was descended from a highly respected patrician family at Freiburg, from which various members had served as mayors and city councillors since 1300.

In 1318, Anna composed the *Chronik* (chronicle) section of Adelhausen *Schwesternbuch* (Sister-Book of the Adelhausen Convent), a collection of thirty-seven *vitae* (biographies) or *Nonnenleben* (nun's lives) of her fellow sisters and their mystical experiences. It was originally composed in Latin, but this text has been lost. Only the Middle-High German translation survives, the earliest manuscript of which dates from 1345–1350. Anna identifies herself as the chronicle's author in the first person in the Freiburg manuscript of this work in one memorable passage—the book's colophon (end-text)—professing her ardent piety, her desire to be as perfect a person as possible, and her hope that her book will be read after her death. She reports the sisters' holy lives, their visions, revelations, and other divine blessings in a language at times formulaic but often vividly insightful in expressing the sisters' theological and ministerial concerns. Anna also takes pains to be accurate and to present her material objectively, while carefully reaffirming the sisters' spiritual and practical self-reliance and thus independence from the friars without seeming resentful toward the more privileged latter. This chronicle was soon followed by similarly styled *Nonnenleben* by other nuns for their respective convents' Sister-Books, such as those by Katharina von Gebweiler, Elsbeth Stagel, and Christine Ebner. Since the nuns were not privileged like the friars to participate in sermon activities, this kind of instructive, even hortatory, recounting of mystical experiences proved to be an ideal avenue for the more gifted writers like Anna.

In 1327, Anna also had a register composed of the nunnery's properties. Little else is known of her life.

See also Ebner, Christine; Katharina von Gebweiler/Geberschweier; Sister-Books (*Schwesternbücher*); Stagel, Elsbeth

BIBLIOGRAPHY

Primary Source
Anna of Munzingen. "Die Chronik der Anna von Munzingen." Edited by J. König. *Freiburger Diözesanarchiv* 13 (1880): 129–236.

Secondary Sources
Blank, Walter. "Anna von Munzingen." In *Die deutsche Literatur des Mittelalters, Verfasserlexikon,* edited by Kurt Ruh, et al., 1: 365–66. 2nd ed. Berlin and New York: de Gruyter, 1978.
Garber, Rebecca. *Feminine Figurae: Representations of Gender in Religious Texts by Medieval German Women Writers, 1100–1375.* Medieval History and Culture, 10. New York and London: Routledge, 2003.
Lewis, Gertrud Jaron. *By Women, for Women, about Women: The Sister-Books of Fourteenth-Century Germany.* Studies and Texts, 125. Toronto: Pontifical Institute of Mediaeval Studies, 1996.

ALBRECHT CLASSEN

ANNE DE BEAUJEU. *See* **Louise of Savoy**

ANNE OF BOHEMIA (1366–1394). A radiant figure in internationalizing court culture, Anne (sometimes called Anne of Luxemburg) promoted an exchange between her native Bohemian (now Czech) culture, and that of England, where she reigned as queen consort to Richard II (1367–1400). Born in Prague on May 11, 1366, Anne was the eldest daughter of Charles IV (1316–1378), Holy Roman Emperor, and his fourth wife, Elizabeth of Pomerania (1347–1393). Anne's brothers both claimed the title of Holy Roman

Anne of Bohemia shown with a white deer, one of her Attribute symbols. Stained glass in Boston Parish Church. © Charles Walker/Topfoto/The Image Works.

Emperor: first Wenceslaus IV (1361–1419), king of Bohemia and supporter of the religious reformer Jan Hus (John Huss); after Wenceslaus died of rage in the power struggle, Sigismund I (1368–1437) succeeded him. She was not only of an extremely influential—though not particularly wealthy—family but also highly educated, being conversant in Latin, French, Czech, German, and later, English. Scholars like Alfred Thomas ascribe her intellectual interests and their encouragement to the climate of "profeminine humanism" at her family's court and at Prague's university. This progressivism would apply to women's expanded role in government and not merely in literary discussions at court.

Anne was thirteen years old when her brother King Wenceslaus negotiated her marriage to King Richard II as part of a politically promising alliance between the Holy Roman Empire and England. Anne's circle had refused offers from a minor German prince, Frederick of Meissen, and from King Charles V of France (1337–1380) for his son, the future Charles VI (1368–1422). Anne's mother, Empress Elizabeth, did not send her daughter to Richard until 1381, at age fifteen, perhaps because of civil strife in England and potential dangers posed by French resentment over Bohemian rejection of their marriage-alliance proposal. Indeed, after Anne's arrival in Brussels that fall, French ships loomed ready to kidnap the princess but were recalled, permitting Anne and her entourage to cross the Channel safely to Richard's court. The chronicles agree that the marriage between the two fifteen-year-olds, on January 14, 1382, developed into an exceptionally happy one, thus inspiring various later romantic retellings. However, the marriage did not fulfill any of the political and economical reasons for which it had been arranged: Bohemia did not join in the war against France and the union produced no heir to guarantee the succession of the English Crown.

But the alliance would produce more profound and enduring transformations for Richard's and Anne's respective domains, as demonstrated most convincingly by the recent work of Alfred Thomas. Fourteenth-century Bohemia was enjoying an unprecedented period of cultural dynamism, as evidenced by its flourishing intellectualism, diplomacy, secular literacy with an attendant increase in vernacular literature (works in medieval Czech and related tongues rather than in Latin or Old Church Slavonic), and a new awareness (though not necessarily tolerance) of differences in ethnicity and gender as well as class. England, too, had entered a period of discontent and strife. Despite an initially hostile reception there because of the new queen's foreignness and lack of a dowry, Anne nevertheless gained great popularity through her learned piety and reputation as a peacemaker and intercessor. She was perhaps already attuned to problems of social unrest from her own country's situation: a less felicitous aspect of cultural progress. Her positive influence helped to offset her husband's at times highhanded style during a reign troubled by Wat Tyler's Peasants' Revolt (which had delayed Anne's bridal arrival in 1381), contention between the king and rebellious barons leading to a direct challenge of the king's authority in the events of the "Merciless Parliament" (1388)—a quarrel with the city of London (1392)—and the Black Death.

She was also a generous patron of literature and the arts, beyond merely contributing a cosmopolitan aura to the English court, and inspired works consistent with her benevolent-intercessor image (Strohm). Geoffrey Chaucer (c.1340–1400) became the most famous of her beneficiaries and dedicated his *Legend of Good Women* (F-text, lines 496–97) to her, in a relationship most fully analyzed by David Wallace. The cultivated queen also studied the gospels, and was thought to own copies of the New Testament in Latin, German, and Czech; an illuminated Book of Hours was also done for her (Penketh), now at Oxford, Bodleian Library (MS Lat. Liturg. fol. 3). When she met John Wyclif (c.1328–1384), she became deeply interested in his theological works and fostered his criticism of the Church, pope, and clergy, including his demand that the Church renounce its worldly possessions and that the Bible be translated into the vernacular (which Wyclif accomplished for the English by his milestone translation of the Latin Vulgate Bible). Anne's circle played a key role in transmitting Wyclif's teachings to Prague where they fell on fertile ground: Johann Hus (1369?–1415), a protégé of Anne's brother Wenceslaus, became the head of a new reform movement—the Hussites—that for many years would strongly affect religion and politics throughout Europe. Unlike the analogous Lollard movement in England, the Hussites in Bohemia received more support from women (beguines and nuns), who seized on this movement as an opportunity to acquire more access to religious texts through the vernacular, as John Klassen has shown. Anne's later renown among Protestants (sixteenth century) as "Good" Queen Anne also derived in part from a considerable number of individual pardons granted, supposedly in her name, to the rebels of the Peasants' Revolt of 1381.

At her death from the plague in June 1394, Richard was so overwhelmed with grief that he ordered the destruction of the palace of Sheen, a royal retreat along the Thames where she died. Her bronze effigy (1395) and remains are at Westminster Abbey. A now more isolated and arrogant Richard continued his difficult rule, later marrying Isabelle of Valois to extend his rule to his native land of France while also negotiating with Ireland, only to be deposed (1399), then probably murdered by his rival and cousin, Henry of Bolingbroke (1367–1413), who ruled as Henry IV. It was the latter's son, Henry V (1387–1422), who had Richard interred at Westminster beside Anne.

See also Agnes of Bohemia, Blessed; Joan, Fair Maid of Kent

BIBLIOGRAPHY

Primary Sources
[See also extracts from record quoted in Strohm in Secondary Sources].
Chaucer, Geoffrey. *Legend of Good Women*. In *The Riverside Chaucer*, edited by Larry D. Benson. Boston: Houghton Mifflin, 1987.
Historia Vitae et Regni Ricardi Secundi. Edited by George B. Stow. Philadelphia: University of Pennsylvania Press, 1977.

Secondary Sources
Bell, Susan Groag. "Medieval Women Book Owners: Arbiters of Lay Piety and Ambassadors of Culture." In *Sisters and Workers in the Middle Ages*, edited by Judith Bennett et al., 135–61. Chicago and London: University of Chicago Press, 1989.
Klassen, John M. *The Nobility and the Making of the Hussite Revolution*. East European Monographs, 47. Boulder, Colo. and New York: East European Quarterly/Columbia University Press, 1978.
———. *Warring Maidens, Captive Wives, and the Hussite Queens: Women and Men at War and Peace in Fifteenth-Century Bohemia*. East European Monographs, 527. Boulder, Colo. and New York: East European Quarterly/Columbia University Press, 1999.

Penketh, Sandra. "Women and Books of Hours." In *Women and the Book: Assessing theVisual Evidence*, edited by Jane H. M. Taylor and Lesley Smith, 266–81. London and Toronto: British Library/University of Toronto Press, 1996.

Saul, Nigel. *Richard II*. New Haven, Conn.: Yale University Press, 1997.

Steel, Anthony. *Richard II*. Cambridge: Cambridge University Press, 1941.

Strohm, Paul. *Hochon's Arrow: The Social Imagination of Fourteenth-Century Texts*. Princeton, N.J.: Princeton University Press, 1992.

Thomas, Alfred. *Anne's Bohemia: Czech Literature and Society, 1310–1420*. Foreword by David Wallace. Minneapolis: University of Minnesota Press, 1998.

Wallace, David. *Chaucerian Polity: Absolutist Lineages and Associational Forms in England and Italy*. Figurae. Stanford, Calif.: Stanford University Press, 1997.

KATHARINA M. WILSON

ARTHURIAN WOMEN (5th century–15th century). The place of women in Arthurian literature—the enormous body of poetry and prose related to the legends of King Arthur and his Knights of the Round Table—underwent significant evolution throughout Europe during the Middle Ages. These transformations could vary according to the cultural and linguistic context of each retelling of a given tale or episode. French Arthurian romance, new in the twelfth century, is often credited with having made women characters integral to Arthur's world for the first time. Chrétien de Troyes, called the creator of the Arthurian romance, imagined a fictional court in which women figured importantly in the narrative of the romance and came to play roles central to its meaning, albeit not unproblematically. As other authors re-created Arthurian romance material in several languages (principally English, French, German, Italian, the Scandinavian tongues, Spanish, and Welsh), the women characters, in passing from one literary culture to another, demonstrated great adaptability while retaining certain constant features.

The Arthurian lady generally earns praise for her beauty, followed by such qualities as courtliness, loyalty, and wise action. Often she is an example to the hero, the vehicle for his education into adulthood. Yet a certain ambiguity of presentation can obscure a purely positive reading of her character. It is not always clear, for example, that the lady or her influence is unambivalently welcomed. Sometimes the key women characters of Arthur's world constitute a zone of vulnerability for the kingdom; the tradition of Guinevere's (or Guenevere's) abductions constitutes but one example. The illicit passion of Guinevere and Lancelot and that of Iseult (Isolde) and Tristan afford parallel stories of the human transgression of Christian values that figures in the kingdom's downfall. On the other hand, however, the fairy women who stand outside the Christian pale and who play a prominent role in Arthurian literature act on their own, do not marry, and often take lovers. They can be powerful adversaries of the human world as well as its equally impressive helpers. In the *lai* (short romance) of *Lanval*, Marie de France, a twelfth-century French author, cast Arthur's court as the problem from which Lanval's fairy lover heroically rescues him. The famous Morgan le Fay, initially Arthur's benevolent healer but soon his sworn enemy, flourished in both the human and otherworld spheres; she was only rarely depicted as married and had more lovers than either Guinevere or Iseult, though this was not always looked upon favorably. Finally, a number of female characters described as human nonetheless retained fairy qualities. Laudine, for example, the heroine of Chrétien's romance of *Yvain, or the Knight of the Lion*, is mistress of a magic spring.

Three queens attend the dying King Arthur, and an angel bears the Holy Grail.
Courtesy of North Wind Picture Archives.

While Arthurian women characters often prove to be satisfyingly challenging, they can
sometimes disappoint modern readers. Stories are almost never told from the female
character's point of view, and compared with the male characters of Arthurian legend,
Arthurian women are less fully or clearly drawn. As against Arthur's well-developed
genealogy and bastard birth and Lancelot's nurturance by the Lady of the Lake, events
that share in universal myths of the hero's birth, only the occasional female character
enjoys a genealogy, and it is a sketchy one at best. Female characters seem to lack a heroic
dimension. That is, when male characters falter or err, their heroism appears diminished;
but when female characters stray, there may be a fall from virtue but not, it seems, from
heroism.

Doubling—the "splitting" of a character into two characters, or the copying of traits
from one character to another, sometimes to present the character's opposite face—can
affect a female character's identity. The character of Iseult, wife of King Mark of Cornwall
in the legend of Tristan and Iseult, probably presents the best-known instance: in addition
to the second Iseult, called Iseult of Brittany or Iseult of the White Hands, whom Tristan
marries, there is Gottfried von Strassburg's Queen Isolt, a strong mother figure, not to be
confused with her daughter, Princess Isold, who falls in love with Tristan. Morgan is
sometimes conflated with Morgause, Arthur's half-sister. The name Elaine is shared
among three separate and important characters. Guinevere, too, is doubled by a character
known as the False Guinevere, whose appearance, not generalized in the legend, is limited

to the French Vulgate Cycle of the thirteenth century. Where three Guineveres figure in one of the Welsh *Triads*, a body of teaching in the bardic schools in which each item occurs in a triple grouping, a mythological origin has been posited, because characters that show such "multiple personalities" may well be derived from depictions of deities, who could be portrayed in single or in triple form. Finally, the individuality of Arthurian women characters can blur before the many nameless, endlessly replicated fairy women who flit through medieval Arthurian romance, from Chrétien to Malory, and whom the reader is often hard-pressed to distinguish from one another. From another angle, the Arthurian woman's diminished capacity for direct physical violence can distinguish her from men, since these women are "non-knights," as Richard Kaeuper has argued, pointing to the knights' repeated vows never to commit rape as part of their chivalric code.

The best-known Arthurian women—after Guinevere, Iseult, and Morgan—include the second Iseult, and Brangain, the first Iseult's loyal confidante; Elaine, the Maid of Astolat; Elaine of Corbenic, mother of Galahad; Enid, Erec's patient wife; Laudine, the lady who owned a magic fountain and was loved by Ywain; Lunette, her confidante; the Lady of the Lake, known variously as Nymue, Nyneve, Niviane, or Niniane, or Viviane; and, the Loathly Lady.

See also Alba Lady; Brangain; Elaine; Enchantresses, Fays (*Fées*), and Fairies; Enid; Guinevere; Igerne; Isolde; Lady of the Lake; Laudine; Lunete; Marie de France; Morgan le Fay

BIBLIOGRAPHY
[Since Arthurian literature encompasses such an extensive list of primary sources that has produced abundant critical literature, only those works specifically mentioned in the entry above are cited here, in their most recent and accessible editions and translations; the secondary sources have been similarly selected].

Primary Sources
Béroul. *Le Roman de Tristan*. Edited and translated by Stewart Gregory. Faux titre, 57. Amsterdam, Netherlands and Atlanta, Ga.: Rodopi, 1992. [Bilingual ed., Old French-English].

———. In *Tristan et Iseut: les poèmes français, la saga norroise*. Edited by Daniel Lacroix and Philippe Walter. Lettres gothiques. Paris: Livre de Poche, 1989. [Bilingual, with Modern French trans. and notes].

Chrétien de Troyes. *Yvain, ou le chevalier au lion*. Edited by David F. Hult. Lettres gothiques. Paris: Livre de Poche, 1994. [Bilingual, with Modern-French trans. and notes].

———. *Yvain, the Knight of the Lion*. Translated by Burton Raffel. Afterword by Joseph J. Duggan. New Haven, Conn.: Yale University Press, 1987.

Malory, Sir Thomas. *Morte Darthur*. Edited by John Matthews. London: Cassell, 2000.

Marie de France. *Lanval*. In *Lais de Marie de France*, edited by Laurence Harf-Lancner, 134–67. Lettres gothiques. Paris: Livre de Poche, 1990.

———. *Lanval*. In *Lais of Marie de France*, translated with notes by Glyn S. Burgess and Keith Busby, 73–81, 139–55. London: Penguin Books, 1999. [English trans. and original Old-French text].

Secondary Sources
Fenster, Thelma S., ed. *Arthurian Women: A Casebook*. Arthurian Characters and Themes, 3. New York: Garland, 1996. [Collection of critical essays on wide-ranging aspects, with introduction].

Kaeuper, Richard. *Chivalry and Violence in Medieval Europe*. Oxford: Oxford University Press, 1999.

Krueger, Roberta. "Women, Arthurian." In *The New Arthurian Encyclopedia*, edited by Norris Lacy, 524–26. Garland Reference Library of the Humanities, 931. New York: Garland, 1991.

Wheeler, Bonnie, and Fiona Tolhurst, eds. *On Arthurian Women: Essays in Memory of Maureen Fries*. Dallas, Tex.: Scriptorium Press, 2001.

Wynne-Davies, Marion. *Women and Arthurian Literature: Seizing the Sword.* Houndmills, Basingstoke, U.K.: Macmillan; New York: St. Martin's, 1996.

THELMA S. FENSTER

ARTISTS, MEDIEVAL WOMEN. The data now available to us on the lives of medieval women artists depends on two critical historical considerations. First, until the recent advent of new critical theories of art history, such as feminist art history, for example, the simple fact of the existence and importance of women artists had been largely ignored or distorted by the decidedly masculine voice of earlier art-historical scholarship of the eighteenth through early twentieth centuries. Second, the seeming anonymity of women as artists in the Middle Ages derives in part from medieval artistic, or, more accurately, craftsman traditions, which generally were unconcerned with the specific personalities of individual artists. What we therefore have available to us today consists in valuable yet fragmentary evidence of the existence and particular work of medieval women in the visual arts. This is not to say that the field is meager, but rather that we should be cautious in interpreting whatever scholars have gleaned from the historical record. Such findings merit consideration not as comprehensive history but rather as part of a continuing history, whose many informational gaps are gradually being filled.

Thamar (Timarete) painting her picture of Diana, c.1400–1425. © The British Library/Topham-HIP/The Image Works.

In the Middle Ages, women's lives were often ruled by men. Nevertheless, within the rigid structure of medieval society women carried on creative lives in the visual arts both as artists and patrons. Many of these women's works surviving from this period were commissioned by or dedicated to Church officials or by members of the nobility. For the most part, the art industries allowed to medieval women were what has been termed in modern scholarship the "domestic arts" of weaving, embroidery, and needle work, as well as the important art of book illumination.

As in Western art in general, and particularly in the earlier periods of the Middle Ages, the cloistered world of monasteries and convents was an important center of both learning and artistic development. The first extensive cycle of illuminated miniatures attributed to a woman is most likely that known as the Gerona Apocalypse, produced in Spain, probably in the double monastery of San Salvatore in Tavára. Dated c.975, the manuscript, which art historian Meyer Schapiro has qualified as "one of the great achievements of medieval art," contains the illustration of a late-eighth-century commentary on the Apocalypse by a Spanish priest named Beatus of Liébana, and is currently preserved in the treasure of the cathedral at Gerona. Like many of other surviving copies of Beatus's Apocalypse commentary, this manuscript's illustration style is classified as Mozarabic, in that its most salient characteristics exemplify Christian art of the tenth and eleventh centuries under Moorish (North-African, Islamic) rule. The Gerona Apocalypse manu-script contains the names of various persons responsible for its production. The colophon, or concluding statement, bears the names of two painters: *Ende pintrix et dei aiutrix frater Emeterius et presbiter* ("Ende, painter and servant of God, and Emeterius, brother and priest"). The woman painter's name was thus En or Ende, depending on whether the qualifying noun is read *pintrix* ("painter") or *depintrix* ("depictor")—either of which is possible in Latin. It is significant that she is named, as "painter and servant of God" before her male collaborator, Emeterius, a priest. To sort out which images were painted by Ende, scholars have consulted another existing manuscript of the Apocalypse produced slightly earlier, now in the Archivio Historico Nacional in Madrid, which is known to have been illuminated by Emeterius.

Unfortunately, this Beatus manuscript is badly damaged, making the identification of the style of the illuminations difficult to decipher. It can safely be assumed, however, that Emeterius' style was similar to that of his master, Magius. By comparing the images of a manuscript known to have been done by Magius—in New York's Pierpont Morgan Library, MS 644—to the images of the Gerona Apocalypse, many scholars have con-cluded that it was Ende who was, in fact, the chief illuminator, which would explain why her name appear first in the colophon. Both deserve the praise bestowed on their work by Schapiro, who describes their unique accomplishment in merging tight, frame-oriented, Classical Roman elements with the highly colored, simplistic shapes of primitive art together with a standard of "perfection" and "completeness." "In fusing the primitive and the advanced," Schapiro goes on, "this art is like the text of the Beatus commentary itself—a prophetic vision of world history edited in a small mountain village."

Other early mentions of individual medieval women artists include the fifth-century St. Melania, who was praised for her calligraphic talents. An early medieval *vita* (biog-raphy) of the courageous English missionary to Germany, St. Boniface, tells how the saint requested Eadburg, the eighth-century abbess of Thanet, near Kent, England, to make him a copy of the Epistle of St. Peter in gold letters "so that her words might shine in gold to the glory of the Heavenly Father" (Larrington).

Female monasteries of this period were aristocratic institutions, since they were often founded for the daughters of royal or noble families. The parents of two nuns, Harlinde and Renilde, founded for them the nunnery at Maas-Eyck, in Flanders (Belgium). The two sisters' mid–ninth-century vita praises them for their prodigious labors of writing and painting that would "seem laborious even to robust men." Germaine Greer cites the discovery of an evangeliary (book containing the Four Gospels) by these two women in the sacristy of the parish church at Maas-Eyck and the subsequent exhibition of this manuscript at the Brussels Exhibition of 1880. The earliest major convent scriptorium to have been identified is that of the eight-century scriptorium of Chelles, in northern France, a canonical convent directed by Gisela, sister of Charlemagne. Surviving work from Chelles as cited by Bernhard Bischoff includes a commentary of the Psalms signed by nine women scribes. In this early period, many of these canonical convents, like Ende's San Salvatore and this one at Chelles, were part of double monasteries: religious com-munities of men and women, overseen by women.

At this same time, the main artistic pursuits of women who were not specifically cloistered lay in embroidery and needlework. Typically, ladies of powerful royal and noble families were skilled in these arts. Examples of such women include Ermengard (ninth century), wife of Holy Roman Emperor Lothar I, and noted for her embroidery on the life of St. Peter. Judith of Bavaria (802–843), mother of Charles the Bald, was said to have worked a cloak for Louis the Pious. Charles the Bald's wife, Ermentrude, was also renowned for her needleworking skills. In the late tenth century, the French queen Adelaide, wife of Hugh Capet and mother of Robert the Pious, embroidered a golden chasuble (a bishop's Eucharistic robe), as well as two gold cloaks and two silver cloaks, all as gifts of the royal family for St. Denis. An embroidered stole, currently in the treasury of Durham Cathedral, England, was made for St. Cuthbert in 934 by Queen Aelflaed. In the eleventh century, the biographer of Edward the Confessor notes how Edward's wife, Edith, was skilled in spinning and embroidery. These crafts of weaving and embroidery, although much devalued today as "minor arts," were much esteemed in the Middle Ages. The sumptuous works created by these women paid homage to certain families' wealth and position. The giving and receiving of such items mattered greatly in terms of the shifting political allegiances within and among powerful dynasties.

By the end of the eleventh century, as women were becoming more visible, we see increasing numbers of women artists recorded, as well as some self-portraits. Mostly associated with female monastic foundations, these women artists exhibit an expanding sense of their own skill and importance. Examples of autographed works by specific women include a manuscript of the highly influential encyclopedic work titled the *Etymologiae* (*Etymologies*) by the sixth-century Spanish bishop, Isidore of Seville, completed in 1134, now at the British Library in London (MS Harley 3009), that contains the signatures of eight women: Sibilia, Vierwic, Gerdrut, Walderat, Hadewic, Imgart, Uota, and Cunegunt. An illuminated manuscript of the Sermons of St. Augustine, now in the Grand Ducal library at Wolfenbüttel, Germany, has been well documented as the work of Ermengarde, a nun in the convent of St. Adrian at Lamspringe, Germany, who is mentioned in sources dating from 1178–1214. Guda, who wrote and painted the twelfth-century Homilary of St. Bartholomew, now preserved at Frankfurt-am-Main, Germany (Stadt-und Universitäts-Bibliothek, MS Barth 42), painted and signed her self-portrait, describing herself as a "*peccatrix mulier*" ("sinful woman"), suggesting that she was not cloistered but rather a laywoman or Beguine—belonging to a community of devout laywomen. Another laywoman illuminator, Claricia, signed her self-portrait on a manuscript produced in the late twelfth century at Augsburg, now at the Walters Art Gallery in Baltimore (MS W 26). Shown swinging from the letter "Q," Claricia, with her free-flowing hair and fashionable attire, was clearly not a nun but most probably a well-born young lady, perhaps sent to Augsburg for her education.

As is often the case with ancient works such as these, multiple artists could carry the same name—and even come from the same region or town—thereby sowing confusion. For example, Diemudis, who painted her self-portrait in the initial "S" of a thirteenth-century music manuscript from Wessobrunn in Bavaria, now in Munich (MS Clm. 23036), has sometimes been confused with an early twelfth-century Diemudis of Wessobrunn, who is known from a sixteenth-century text that lists forty-five books by her hand. Yet another Diemudis signed a missal (Munich MS Clm 11004). This sharing of the same name by women of the same monastery points to continuing traditions of manuscript illumination at these female monasteries. For example, the convent of Augsburg has been associated with the names of several female book hands. This tradition extended from the twelfth century, with Claricia's self-portrait, to the later Middle Ages, as embodied in a fourteenth-century

Gospel book from Augsburg containing, among its illuminations, a portrait of an unnamed nun.

Other signed portraits of women artists from this period include one from an astronomical treatise, dated to 1154. In its dedication illumination, the scribe Guta, canoness of Schwarzenthann, Germany, and the illuminator Sintram, canon of Schwarzenthann's brother monastery of Marbach, are shown flanking the image of the Virgin.

Two of the most important monastic women of the twelfth century, Herrad of Hohenberg (or Landsberg) and Hildegard of Bingen (both in what is now Germany), made significant contributions to the visual arts of this period. Herrad, abbess of Hohenberg (in Alsace, France) from 1167 until her death in 1195, directed the creation of one of the greatest of the illuminated medieval encyclopedias, the *Hortus Deliciarum* (*Garden of Delights*), tragically destroyed in 1870, and known to us today only through traced drawings from 1818. An enormous book, originally containing 636 miniatures on 325 folios, it illustrated the entire span of salvation history. Although most scholars no longer believe that Herrad was the illuminator of these images—it was probably painted c.1205, a decade after Herrad's death—her spirit and direction are evident in the manuscript's many images, part of what she called the "mellifluous honeycomb," representing her divine inspiration. The other great female monastic figure of the twelfth century, Hildegard of Bingen (1098–1179), composed music and wrote treatises on topics ranging from theology to science and medicine. One of her best-known works, the *Scivias* (from Latin *scire* = "to know"), a compilation of thirty-five visions, contained an illumination for each vision. The earliest know copy of the *Scivias*, produced at Trier, Germany, and not at Bingen, has been missing from the library at Wiesbaden since World War II. This manuscript was produced prior to Hildegard's death in 1179 and apparently under her direction. Although, as with the *Hortus Deliciarum*, it is unproven and perhaps unlikely that Hildegard painted these images, she obviously inspired their execution, given their resemblance to her visionary writings.

By the thirteenth century, the art of bookmaking began to change. As the demand for books grew among the wealthier populations of growing cities, secular scriptoria (nonmonastic workshops consisting of scribes and illuminators making copies of certain manuscripts) emerged in large, urban areas. These precursors of printing presses (that is, pre-Gutenberg, 1456) were better situated to address the growing demand for books, especially luxurious illustrated books, thus supplanting in importance the more isolated monastic venues of book production.

Contemporary documents addressing the customs and laws of crafts guilds in this period have become an important source of evidence of women's participation as illuminators in these new professional scriptoria. Records such as tax registers and guild lists demonstrate that in large towns and cities throughout western Europe, from the end of the thirteenth century until the second half of the fifteenth century, women had established themselves as independent workers in crafts such as bookmaking and book illumination. The Parisian tax register of 1292 cites a certain Thomasse as an "inn keeper and illuminator." Other artists noted in this particular tax roll include Aaeles, "*la tapicière*" ("tapestry maker"), who is recorded as having done business on the rue de Verneuil. She was taxed 19s for her rug and tapestry craft. Aalis, "*l'ymaginière*" ("image-maker") also appears in a rare citation for what can be interpreted as a female painter and/or sculptor, in the 1292 list. In Bologna, a woman, Donella, is said to have worked as an illuminator around the year 1271. Agnes of Avion (in northern France) is known to have received payment in 1380 for a series of tapestries done for Yolanda of Soissons. A Bruges, Belgium, guild list cites one Berlinette Yweins as an illuminator. Probably one of best-known named professional woman illuminators is Anastaise (Anastasia), extolled by Christine de Pizan (Anastaise was probably Italian-born, like herself) in her revisionist history of women, the *Cité des dames* (*City of Ladies*) (1404/5), for her "skill and cunning in the making of vignettes for illustrated books and landscape scenes for tales... [so that] in Paris none fails to commend her." Unfortunately, although Christine confirms that Anastaise executed ornamental borders for some manuscripts produced in her atelier (workshop; Hindman), and though some scholars believe Anastaise may even have illuminated a copy of the *Cité des dames* given by Christine to Isabeau of Bavaria, queen of France, there are no extant works proven to have been done by this artist.

Many women illuminators owed their ability to work to their male relatives who supported them, as feminist historian Germaine Greer has delineated. For example, Bourgot (late 1300s) worked as an illuminator with her famous father, Jean le Noir, whose patrons included Countess Yolanda of Bar, King John II, the Good (d. 1364) and his son, King Charles V of France (d. 1380). A fourteenth-century list of professional painters in Cologne includes the names of "*Johannes illuminator*" ("John, illuminator") and "*Hilla uxor eius*" ("Hilla, his wife"). Master Honoré, the head of an important thirteenth-century Parisian scriptorium, employed both his daughter, who is not named, and her husband, Richard de Verdun. In Flanders, a great center of book production, women were included as illuminators in the "family business." Margarethe van Eyck, the sister of Jan and Hubert van Eyck, appears to have worked with them in the first half of the fifteenth century, although it is unclear as to the exact nature of her participation. Other female relatives of famous men include Cornelia Cnoop, the wife of Gérard David, who worked as a miniaturist, and Clara, the sister of Robert de Keysere, who has been cited as the illuminator of de Keysere's missal executed for Charles V.

Although within this environment of professional workshops the importance and influence of female monastic scriptoria declined, examples remain of their continuing production. For example, Agnese, abbess of the ancient foundation of Quedlinburg, in Germany, from 1184 to 1205, is reported to have written and illustrated several manuscripts including a Gospel book. Other examples of later monastic production include a gradual, created by the nun Elisabeth, under the first abbess, Agnes, Countess of Freyssing around 1232 for the Cistercian nuns of Seligenthal, now in the British Library (Add. MS 16950), as well as an illuminated manuscript, the *Codex Gisele*, now in the Cathedral library of Osnabruck, which has been attributed to Gisele von Kerssenbroeck, and dated 1300, the year of her death.

Convents continued to produce books not only for themselves but for the larger market of producing commissions for others, mainly other foundations. A nun, Giovanna Petroni, was the director of the scriptorium of Santa Maria in Siena. She and her fellow nuns were known to have accepted commissions for other churches in the period of the late fourteenth century. We know of names of two nuns from the fifteenth-century scriptoria at the monastery of San Giacomo in Ripoli; Angelica Miniberti, who signed a *Collectarium*, and Angela de'Ruccellai, a copyist. An artist's self-portrait appears in an Italian Breviary, the *Breviarium cum Calendario*, from 1453, now in Vienna (Österreichische Nationalbibliothek, fol. 89). The *Breviarium*'s highly competent artist, known for the manuscript's luxuriant, leafy borders, was Maria Ormand or Ormani, who describes herself as "hand-maid of God, daughter of Orman and writer of this book" (Greer).

German nuns also continued to produce books in their scriptoria in the period of the later Middle Ages. Among them are Kunigunda, a nun at the convent of St. Katherine in Nuremberg, who completed a Bible in 1443, Margareta Imhoff, Margaretha Cartheuserin, who together illuminated a winter missal in 1452, as well as Barbara Gwichtmacherin, who is known to have worked with Margaretha Cartheuserin. Sibylla de Bondorff, a Franciscan nun, wrote and illustrated in 1478 a biography of the famous theologian, St. Bonaventure (1217–1274), now in the British Library.

The creative lives of women in the Middle Ages extended to their patronage of the visual arts. Matilda of Canossa and Tuscany, who ruled over a large portion of central Italy from 1069 to her death in 1115, was instrumental in the rebuilding of the Cathedral in Modena at the end of the eleventh century. She is repeatedly mentioned in an illustrated manuscript concerned with the cathedral's reconstruction (*Translatio Corporis Sancti Geminiani*, Archivio Capitolare del Duomo di Modena MS O.II.11), and appears, as well, in the illustrations for the text. The legendary Eleanor of Aquitaine (c.1122–1204), queen of France then England, played a significant role as patron of the arts throughout her life. Her connection with Abbot Suger encompasses both documentary evidence of her donation of liturgical objects to the Abbey of St. Denis and theories as to her more substantial patronage of the rebuilding of the Royal Abbey. Eleanor also gave generously to the double monastery at Fontevrault (or Fontevraud). Records of her specific endowments date from 1152, the year of her marriage to King Henry II of England, and again in 1170 and 1185.

Within the confines of medieval society, women found expression in their patronage of art through their roles as daughters, wives, widows, and consorts of powerful men. One of the most significant forms of art patronage for women in the Middle Ages concerns commissioning and collecting of books. From the early Middle Ages to the fifteenth century, but particularly in the later period, medieval wills and inventories of libraries and households have documented the patronage of women bibliophiles. In the eleventh century, the Countess of Anjou paid in sheep, rye, wheat, and millet for a copy of the sermons of Haimo. Mahaut, Countess of Artois, an important bibliophile, paid a female scribe, Maroie, twenty-five sous in 1312 for a Book of Hours. Margaret of Flanders and her husband, Philip the Bold, Duke of Burgundy, were known to have employed up to sixty artists and artisans for their new library at Germolles. Margaret of Provence (d. c.1280), wife of Louis IX, commissioned Jean de Vignay to translate Vincent de Beauvais's *Speculum Historiale* (*Mirror of History*) from Latin into French. An illumination in a fourteenth-century copy, c.1333, shows both Margaret's and Louis's orders for this work, hers in the French vernacular and Louis's in Latin. Isabeau of Bavaria's patronage included the appointment of one of her court ladies, Katherine de Villiers, to oversee the collection and purchase of books. As Susan Bell has shown, women patronized book manufacture in part because of their central role as teachers of their children. Isabeau of Bavaria's accounts include a Book of Hours and an alphabet psalter (book of Psalms) for her daughters, Jeanne and Michelle, in 1398 and 1403, respectively. Another alphabet book commissioned by the Countess of Leicester in about 1300 is presently in the Bodleian Library at Oxford (MS Douce 231). By the fifteenth century, women patrons such as Margaret of York, wife of Charles the Bold of Burgundy and patron of the prodigious printer and translator William

Caxton, were instrumental in the new process of publishing printed books. It was Margaret who commissioned the first book ever printed in English, Caxton's translation from Latin of the *Recuyell of the Historyes of Troye (Collected Histories of Troy)*, in 1475.

Evidence exists as well for the patronage of medieval women in both architectural foundations and the commissioning of altarpieces and other church decoration. Although women were not allowed openly to negotiate contracts for art production, there is documentary evidence, most prominently in Italy, that noble women in cloistered environments, along with widows and consorts of powerful men, were able through the exercise of public piety to commission works of art directly. For example, Maria de'Bovolini, a wealthy widow, requested a large crucifix from the Paduan painter Guariento for the church of San Francesco in Bassano, Italy, c.1350. Church account books from 1370 and 1371 record payment by the Benedictine nuns of San Pier Maggiore in Florence for a high altar. Fina Buzzacarini, the consort of Francesco il Vecchio da Carrara of Padua, Italy, ordered the construction of a chapel in honor of Santo Lodovico in the Benedictine convent of San Benedetto in Padua. An inscription placed by her sister in 1394 reads in part: "this chapel was built . . . by the illustrious and generous lady, Donna Fina de'Buzzacarini of good memory." Testaments such as this should help to remind us of the many examples, much yet undiscovered, of the direct participation of women in the rich artistic life of medieval Europe.

See also Chaucer, Alice; Chelles, Nun of; Christine de Pizan; Double Monasteries; Eleanor of Aquitaine; Embroidery; Guilds, Women in; Herrad of Hohenberg/Landsberg; Hildegard of Bingen, St.; Marcia in the Middle Ages; Margaret of York; Matilda of Tuscany/Canossa; Melania the Younger, St.; Scribes and Scriptoria

BIBLIOGRAPHY

Primary Sources

King, Margaret L., and Albert Rabil, Jr., eds. *Her Immaculate Hand: Selected Works by and about the Women Humanists of Quattrocento Italy*. Medieval and Renaissance Texts and Studies, 20. Binghamton, N.Y.: State University of New York Press, 1983.

Larrington, Carolyne, ed. *Women and Writing in Medieval Europe: A Sourcebook*. London and New York: Routledge, 1995.

Secondary Sources

Adams, Carol, et al., eds. *From Workshop to Warfare: The Lives of Medieval Women*. London: Cambridge University Press, 1990.

Bell, Susan Groag. "Medieval Women Book Owners: Arbiters of Lay Piety and Ambassadors of Culture." In *Sisters and Workers in the Middle Ages*, edited by Judith M. Bennett et al., 135–61. Chicago: University of Chicago Press, 1976.

Bradley, John W. *A Dictionary of Miniaturists, Illuminators, Calligraphers, and Copyists*, 3 vols. [1887–1889] New York: Burt Franklin, 1958.

Broude, Norma, and Mary D. Garrard., eds. *Feminism and Art History: Questioning the Litany*. New York: Harper & Row, 1982.

Carr, Annemarie Weyl. "Women Artists in the Middle Ages." *Feminist Art Journal* 5 (1976): 5–9, 26.

Casanovas, Jaime Marques, et al. *Apocalypse of Gerona*. Preface by Meyer Schapiro. Olten and Lausanne, Switzerland: Urs Graf Verlag, 1963.

Caviness, Madeline. "Artist: To See, Hear, and Know All at Once." In *Voice of the Living Light: Hildegard of Bingen and Her World*, edited by Barbara Newman, 110–24. Berkeley and Los Angeles: University of California Press, 1998.

————. Hildegard as Designer of the Illustrations to Her Works." In *Hildegard of Bingen: The Context of Her Thought and Art*, edited by Charles Burnett and Peter Dronke, 29–62. London: Warburg Institute, 1998.

De Winter, Patrick. "Christine de Pizan, ses enlumineurs et ses rapports avec le milieu bourguignon." In *Actes du 104ᵉ congrès national des sociétés savantes (1979)*, 335–75. Paris: Bibliothèque Nationale, 1982.

Fox, Matthew. *Illuminations of Hildegard of Bingen*. Santa Fe, N.M.: Bear & Co., 1985.

Gathercole, Patricia May. *The Depiction of Women in Medieval French Manuscript Illumination*. Studies in French Civilization, 17. Lewiston, N.Y.: Edwin Mellen Press, 2000.

Gaze, Delia, et al., eds. *Dictionary of Women Artists*. 2 vols. London and Chicago: Fitzroy Dearborn, 1997.

Greer, Germaine. *The Obstacle Race: The Fortunes of Women Painters and Their Work*. New York: Farrar, Straus & Giroux, 1979.

Hamburger, Jeffrey. *Nuns as Artists Nuns as Artists: The Visual Culture of a Medieval Convent*. Berkeley: University of California Press, 1997.

Havice, Christine. "Approaching Medieval Women through Medieval Art." In *Women in Medieval Western European Culture*, edited by Linda E. Mitchell, 345–86. New York and London: Garland, 1999.

————. "Women and the Production of Art in the Middle Ages: The Significance of Context." In *Double Vision: Perspectives on Gender and the Visual Arts*, edited by Natalie Harris Bluestone. London: Associated University Presses, 1995.

Hindman, Sandra L. *Christine de Pizan's "Epistre Othéa": Painting and Politics in the Court of Charles VI*. Toronto: Pontifical Institute of Mediaeval Studies, 1986.

Hughes, Muriel J. "The Library of Philip the Bold and Margaret of Flanders, First Valois Duke and Duchess of Burgundy." *Journal of Medieval History* 4 (1978): 145–88.

Kibler, William W., ed. *Eleanor of Aquitaine. Patron and Politician*. Austin: University of Texas Press, 1976.

King, Catherine. "Medieval and Renaissance Matrons, Italian Style." *Zeitschrift für Kunstgeschichte* 55 (1992): 372–93.

McCash, June Hall, ed. *The Cultural Patronage of Medieval Women*. Athens: University of Georgia Press, 1996.

————, ed. *Women's Literary and Artistic Patronage in the Middle Ages*. Athens: University of Georgia Press, 1996.

Matter, E. Ann, and John Coakley, eds. *Creative Women in Medieval and Early Modern Italy. A Religious and Artistic Renaissance*. Philadelphia: University of Pennsylvania Press, 1994.

Miner, Dorothy. *Anastaise and Her Sisters*. Baltimore: Walters Art Gallery, 1974.

Munsterberg, Hugo. *A History of Women Artists*. New York: Clarkson N. Potter, 1975.

Newman, Barbara. *Sister of Wisdom. St. Hildegard's Theology of the Feminine*. Berkeley: University of California Press, 1987.

Perkinson, Stephen. "*Engin* and *Artifice*: Describing Creative Agency at the Court of France, ca. 1400." *Gesta* 41:1 (2002): 51–67.

Petersen, Karen, and J. J. Wilson. *Women Artists: Recognition and Reappraisal from the Early Middle Ages to the Twentieth Century*. New York: Harper & Row Publishers, 1976.

Polaczek, Barbara. *Apokalypseillustration des 12. Jahrhunderts und weibliche Frommigkeit: die Handschriften Brussel, Bibliothèque Royale Albert 1er, Ms. 3089 und Oxford, Bodleian Library, Ms. Bodl. 352*. Weimar, Germany: Verlag und Datenbank fur Geisteswissenschaften, 1998.

Schapiro, Meyer. *See under* Casanovas, *above*.

Slatkin, Wendy. *Women Artists in History, from Antiquity to the Present*. 3rd ed. Upper Saddle River, N.J.: Prentice-Hall, 1997.

Smith, Lesley, and Jane H. M. Taylor, eds. *Women and the Book. Assessing the Visual Evidence*. London and Toronto: British Library/University of Toronto Press, 1996.

Stafford, Pauline. *Queens, Concubines, and Dowagers: The King's Wife in the Early Middle Ages*. London: Batsford Academic & Educational, 1983.

Uitz, Erica. *The Legend of Good Women: Medieval Women in Towns and Cities*. Mt. Kisco, N.Y.: Moyer Bell, 1988.

Wheeler, Bonnie, ed. *Representations of the Feminine in the Middle Ages.* Feminea Medievalia, 1. Dallas, Tex.: Academia, 1993.

JEANNE FOX-FRIEDMAN

AUDREY, ST. *See Æthelthryth, St.*

AVA, FRAU (d. 1127). A Benedictine recluse who lived near Melk, Austria, Frau Ava (Mistress Ava) was the first woman poet known by name to have composed in German. Her simple poems all dealt with biblical themes, mainly from the New Testament, the best known of her works being the *Leben Jesu* (*Life of Jesus*), while also reflecting distinctly feminine concerns.

Since we have so few facts about her life, we turn to her own writing for insights about her life and personality. From her work we learn that she had been married, presumably to a lesser lord, and had at least two sons; the elder son and her husband died in the Crusades in the Holy Land. Out of grief, as well as economic necessity, she became a hermit or anchorite near Melk (or Mölk), in lower Austria, on the Danube. Convent rules necessitated her surrendering her surviving son, aged about ten, to the care of the Benedictine monks at the magnificent abbey there, founded 1089. She probably took to writing her poems on the Gospels as a form of consolation. Since she did not know Latin, she had to rely on her son, by then well educated by the Benedictines, to translate or paraphrase the Vulgate (Latin Bible) as material—what she calls the "Sinn" ("Sense")—for her vernacular (Old-High German) poems, which her son then transcribed into a manuscript and later carried about with him on his travels.

Eventually, this late-twelfth-century manuscript turned up in the library of the Chorherrenstift at Vorau, in the province of Styria, central Austria, as part of a larger collection of precious early German literature and history texts known as the Vorauer Handschrift, Codex 276–II.X (labeled "V" in scholarly editions of her works). Sometime in the fourteenth century a Middle-High German copy was made, the so-called Görlitzer Ava-Handschrift, kept in the Oberlausitzischer Gesellschaft der Wissenschaften, MS A.III.I.10, in Görlitz (and thus labeled "G"), on the river Neisse, now in East Germany. Though this Görlitz manuscript is now lost, G. J. A. Will (1765) and Joseph Diemer (1849) managed to preserve its text before it disappeared. Since neither single manuscript contained all of Ava's poems, and even seemed to complement each other, scholars produced complete editions by combining both manuscripts throughout the past two centuries, culminating in the longtime standard edition by Friedrich Maurer (1966), eventually replaced by Kurt Schacks (1986). Moreover, the recent work of Barbara Gutfleisch-Ziche (1997) has contributed greatly to our understanding of the role of the illumination cycle of the *Leben Jesu*, reconstructed and photographed by Piper (1888) from the lost Görlitzer manuscript, in Ava's spiritual message.

Ava's work (1120–1125), a sort of continuous devotional epic, comprises five books: *Johannes der Taufer* (*John the Baptist*, 446 vv.), *Das Leben Jesu* (*Life of Jesus*, 2268 vv.), *Die sieben Gaben des heiligen Geistes* (*Seven Gifts of the Holy Ghost*, 150 vv.), *Der Antichrist* (*The Antichrist*, 118 vv.), and *Das jüngsten Gericht* (*The Last Judgment*, 406 vv.). As is evident from the outset, Ava uses the terms "God," "Son of God," and "Jesus Christ" synonymously. To her, they were all the same person/substance—that is, the Trinity—a doctrinal point questioned less vehemently in the early twelfth century than it had been earlier.

In Ava's evocation of the mission of Christ, two distinct themes, each associated with some sort of unjust privation, not only provide clues to her character but also seem to answer her own inner needs based on personal experience. The first is Ava's deep concern for women, as reflected in her allusions to no less than nine New Testament stories in which women play a major role. In these, she also observes Christ's treatment of them as he moved about in a society that, like her own, had little compassion for women's plight, granting them few rights and no legal protection, just as Ava most probably suffered personally by losing her dower rights (inheritance) after her husband's demise. Her compassion for women's misfortunes thus derives from her prereclusive past. Ava was left destitute when her husband failed to return from the Holy Land because she had no right of inheritance: her husband's fief, invested as a freehold, simply reverted back to her husband's overlord, who was entitled to do with it whatever he wished (returning it to Ava would have required immense generosity). Remarriage without some sort of dowry would have been difficult financially; emotionally, too, it might have been troubling, assuming she and her late husband truly loved and respected each other; also spiritually, given Ava's apparent predisposition to piety, since, by canon law, a second marriage was allowed but lacked the sanctity of the first or of devoting one's widowhood to celibacy. Entering a convent, a second alternative, was also difficult for Ava because of her little son. She could, and she actually did, give the child to the Benedictine monks, but her convent's typically strict and rigid rules would have prevented her from ever seeing him again. These combinations of circumstances convinced Ava to become an ascetic recluse, despite the privations inflicted on her soul and body: frequent fasting, exposure to the cold, and near-constant prayer. She endured this harsh life for several years before returning to spiritual peace by composing her Gospel, in which she dramatically presented the birth, life, and death of Christ with impassioned effectiveness, even though her language remained simple.

The second theme is that of blindness, for among the miracles Jesus performed, Ava concentrates on recounting those dealing with lost and restored vision. Ava's preoccupation with lost sight may be seen as something more than her fixation on biblical figurative language of conversion (such as we find in Acts 9, when Saul the Jew is struck blind before seeing the light of Christianity and becomes Paul) and arising from her reclusive past, spent living in her cell, in almost total darkness, very much like a blind person. Her *claustra* (enclosed space) had only a small opening through which to look out into the world; she had only candlelight by which to read and write. It is also very possible that near the end of her life Ava actually lost her eyesight completely because of such conditions, and was thus condemned to stare into empty darkness. Ava might then have longed for death, and if she remembered the teachings of her last three books—on the Seven Gifts of the Holy Spirit, the Rule of Antichrist, and the Last Judgment—she must have felt assured that her plea for mercy and God's grace would be answered. The urgency of her plea for redemption is vividly demonstrated in her eschatological vision (vision of the hereafter). When, in closing, she finally gives advice to her readers, young or old, on how the good life can and should be lived, Ava believes that all who have lived by the "good rule" would be granted salvation. By the grace of God, she asserts, this salvation will be given to *wir* ("us")—and evidently she counts herself among the saved.

Finally, it must be pointed out that before Ava, no one had attempted a task as demanding as setting down the Gospel story in the vernacular. In an age where few women, or men for that matter, possessed the requisite literacy and learning for such an undertaking, and when one considers that the Church frowned on any lay interpretation or translation of Scripture in the vernacular, Ava's work emerges as bold and courageous as well as a remarkable phase in German religious writing. Nowadays, Ava, a source of Austrian national cultural pride, is honored by the preservation of the convent tower—now called the Avaturm ("Ava-Tower")—in which she supposedly died at Kleinwien near Göttweig, Lower Austria (February 7, 1127), and by an annual literary prize, the "Ava Preis." Most recently, she was the subject of an historical novel for young readers, *Frau Ava*, by Lene Mayer-Skumanz (2002).

See also Childhood and Child-Rearing in the Middle Ages; Convents; Dower

BIBLIOGRAPHY

Primary Sources

Manuscripts Facsimiles
[Vorau MS]. *Die deutschen Gedichte der Vorauer Handschrift, Cod. 267- Teil II) Chorherrenstiftes Vorau.* Edited with introduction by Karl K. Polheim. Graz, Austria: Akademische Druck, 1958.
[Görlitz MS]. "Vom Leben und Leiden Jesu, vom Antichrist und dem jüngsten Gericht." In *Fundgruben für Geschichte deutscher Sprache und Literatur*, edited by August H. Hoffmann, vol. 1: 127–204. Breslau (Wroclaw, Poland): Grass, Barth, 1830. Reprint Hildesheim, Germany: G. Olms, 1969.
[Illustrations to *Leben Jesu* from the *Görlitzer Handschrift* reproduced in Gutfleisch-Ziche, *see under* Secondary Sources].

Texts
Ava, Frau. *Die Dichtungen der Frau Ava.* Critical edition by Kurt Schacks. Wiener Neudrucke, 8. Graz, Austria: Akademische Druck, 1986. [See Schacks's Concordance, to accompany this text, below in Secondary Sources].
———. "Ava: Das jüngste Gericht." In *Frühe deutsche Literatur und lateinische Literatur in Deutschland, 800–1150*, edited by Walter Haug and Benedikt Konrad Vollmann, 728–51. Bibliothek deutscher Klassiker, 62. Frankfurt, Germany: Deutscher Klassiker Verlag, 1991.
———. *Das jüngste Gericht.* In *Frühmittelhochdeutsche Literatur: Mittelhochdeutsch, neihochdeutsch*, edited and translated (Modern German) with commentary by Gisela Vollmann-Profe. Universal-Bibliothek, 9438. Stuttgart, Germany: Reclam, 1996. [Bilingual ed. Medieval German and Modern German].
———. *Die Dichtungen der Frau Ava.* Edited by Friedrich Maurer. Altdeutsche Textbibliothek, 66. Tübingen, Germany: Max Niemeyer, 1966.
———. "Die Gedichte der Ava." Edited by Paul Piper. *Zeitschrift für deutsche Philologie* 19 (1887): 129–96, 275–318.
———. "*Vorauer Handschrift*: VII, a: vom Leben Jesu, b: vom jüngsten Gericht." In *Deutsche Gedichte des 11. und 12. Jahrhunderts*, edited by Joseph Diemer. Vienna: Braumüller, 1849. Reprint Darmstadt, Germany, 1968.
———. [Poems, Illustrations]. In *Die geistliche Dichtung des Mittelalters*, edited by Paul Piper, pt. 1. Deutsche National-Literatur, 3.1. Berlin and Stuttgart, 1888.
———. *Ava's New Testament Narratives. "When Old Law Passed Away."* Translated with introduciton and notes by James A. Rushing, Jr. Medieval Texts in Bilingual Editions. Kalamazoo, Mich.: Medieval Institute, 2003. [New translation based on Maurer's edition with information overview and illustrations from manuscripts V and G].

————. *The Gospel of Jesus According to Mistress Ava.* Translated by Teta E. Moehs. Senda de estudios y ensayos. New York: Senda Nueva de Ediciones, 1986. [English and German. Based on Maurer's edition].

Secondary Sources

Boswell, John. *The Kindness of Strangers: The Abandonment of Children in Western Europe from Antiquity to the Renaissance.* New York: Pantheon, 1988.

Domitrovic, M. "Die Sprache in den Gedichten der Frau Ava." Ph.D. Diss., Universität Graz, 1950.

Goody, Jack. "Inheritance, Property and Women: Some Comparative Considerations." In *Family and Inheritance,* edited by J. Goody, Joan Thirsk, and E. P. Thompson. Cambridge, Mass.: Harvard University Press, 1976.

Greinemann, Sr. Eleoba, O.S.B. "Die Gedichte der Frau Ava. Untersuchungen zur Quellenfrage." Dissertation, Universität Freiburg im Breisgau, Germany, 1968.

Gutfleisch-Ziche, Barbara. *Volksprachliches und bildliches Erzählen biblischer Stoffe: Die illustrierten Handschriften der Altdeutschen Genesis und des Leben Jesu der Frau Ava.* Europäische Hochschulschriften. Series 1: Deutsche Sprache und Literatur. Frankfurt, Germany: Peter Lang, 1997. [Excellent analysis and documentation; illustrated].

Herlihy, David. "Land, Family and Women in Continental Europe, 701–1200." *Traditio* 18 (1962): 89–120.

Hintz, Ernst Ralf. "Frau Ava (?–1127)." *German Writers and Works of the Early Middle Ages: 800–1170.* Dictionary of Literary Biography, 148: 39–44. New York and London: Gale Research, 1995.

Kienast, Richard. "Ava Studien I; II." *Zeitschrift für deutsches Altertum und Literatur* 74 (1937): 1–36; 277–308.

————. "Ava Studien III." *Zeitschrift für deutsches Altertum und Literatur* 77 (1940): 85–104.

Schacks, Kurt. *Lemmatisierte Konkordanz zu den Dictungen der Frau Ava.* Bern, Switzerland and New York: Peter Lang, 1991.

Siemsen, Anna. *Frauenleben im Mittelalter und geistliche Dichtung.* In Siemsen, *Der Weg ins Freie.* Frankfurt: Büchergilde Gutenberg, 1950.

Zöllner, Erich. *Geschichte Österreichs.* 8th ed. Vienna: Verlag für Geschichte und Politik, 1990.

ALBRECHT CLASSEN

AZALAIS D'ALTIER (early 13th century). A woman troubadour (or *trobairitz*), Azalais d'Altier composed a *salut d'amor,* "Tanz salutz e tantas amors" ("So many greetings and so much love"), a love letter in the form of a poem, which appears in one manuscript (V) without rubric. Azalais identifies herself by name in her salutation (v. 6) and appears to address another *trobairitz,* Clara d'Anduza, evoked metaphorically in the request that she be true and clear ("clara," v. 98) to her lover. Intertextual allusions link the *salut* and Clara's one extant song, "En greu esmai et en greu pessamen" ("In grave distress and great trouble"), which may have been composed as a response. As an example of the way one lady addresses another in the context of troubadour lyric, Azalais's poem usefully demonstrates how the troubadour's language of love and praise can be adapted to the language of friendship between women. The poem opens with elaborate praise of the addressee, whom Azalais has never seen but the lover's descriptions of her have been so compelling that Azalais is certain that she would recognize her. The opening gambit thus offers a variation on the theme of *amor de lonh* (love from afar), here linking the two ladies through the male lover.

The poem in rhymed octosyllabic couplets may be associated by its subject with a number of debate songs in the troubadour repertoire in which the lover himself or another lady seeks forgiveness and reconciliation with the beloved. In this case, Azalais intervenes on the side of Clara's unnamed lover, who admits his unspecified fault but begs forgiveness based on his loyalty and submission, as well as on the depth of his suffering since he was cut off from her. Azalais suggests that if his lady does not forgive him, she will be seen by other lovers as inconstant, subject to scorn like Briseida who abandoned Troilus for Diomedes (probably an allusion to Benoît de Sainte-More's *Roman de Troie*, a twelfth-century French adaptation of Dictys and Dares's fifth- or sixth-century Latin accounts of the Trojan War).

In a long *razo* (commentary) on "Anc mais non vi temps ni sazo" ("I never saw the time or season"), Clara's lover is identified as Uc de Saint Circ, poet and author of troubadour *vidas* (biographies) and *razos*. The same narrative commentary refers indirectly to Azalais's intervention: she is mentioned by name in the song's *tornada* (envoi). As is frequently the case when no historical evidence can be found to locate the woman poet's identity outside the world of poetic exchange, there has been some debate about the authenticity of Azalais. The intertextual play of the poems themselves, as well as the *razo*, may nevertheless suggest that these three figures, like many other groups of troubadour poets, patrons, and lovers, form a kind of literary circle in which the participants enjoy playing the games of love in song.

See also Clara d'Anduza; Criseyde; *Trobairitz*

BIBLIOGRAPHY

Primary Sources
Azalais d'Altier. ["Tanz salutz . . . "]. In *Songs of the Women Troubadours*, edited and translated by Matilda Tomaryn Bruckner, Laurie Shepard, and Sarah White, 124–29, 187–88. New York: Garland, 1995. Revised edition, 2000.
———. In *Trobairitz: Der Beitrag der Frau in der altokzitanischen höfischen Lyrik. Edition des Gesamtkorpus*, edited by Angelica Rieger, 681–84. Beihefte der Zeitschrift für romanische Philologie, 233. Tübingen, Germany: Max Niemeyer Verlag, 1991.

Secondary Sources
Poe, Elizabeth Wilson. "A Dispassionate Look at the Trobairitz." *Tenso: Bulletin of the Société Guilhem IX* 7 (1992): 142–64.
———. "Another *salut d'amor*? Another *trobairitz*? In Defense of *Tanz salutz et tantas amors*." *Zeitschrift für romanische Philologie* 106 (1990): 425–42.
Rieger, Angelica. "*En conselh no deu hom voler femna*: Les dialogues mixtes dans la lyrique troubadouresque." *Perspectives Médiévales* 16 (1990): 47–57.
———. "Was Bieris de Romans Lesbian? Women's Relations with Each Other in the World of the Troubadours." In *The Voice of the Trobairitz: Perspectives on the Women Troubadours*, edited by William D. Paden, 73–94. Philadelphia: University of Pennsylvania Press, 1989.

MATILDA TOMARYN BRUCKNER

AZALAIS DE PORCAIRAGUES (late 12th century). Azalais de Porcairagues is one of the *trobairitz* or women troubadours. Not a single authentic document has been discovered that contains the name of this woman troubadour, probably born either in Portirangues (or Portiragnes), near Béziers, or in Porcairagues—in what are now the Hérault and Gard *départments* (sections), respectively, in southeastern France, on the Mediterranean coast. She was a well-educated noblewoman. Azalais's very short and perhaps fictitious *vida* (biography) tells us she wrote many songs about her lover, one Gui Guerrejat ("Guy the Warrior") (c.1140–c.1177?), fifth son of Guilhem VI of Montpellier (near Azalais's homeland) and a cousin of Raimbaut d'Aurenga (or Raimbaut d'Orange; c.1144–1173).

Her ties to Raimbaut's court, an extremely important center in the evolution of Occitan (southern-French) poetry, are confirmed in various poems, her *vida*, and other documents. For Azalais was actually in love with Raimbaut himself, as attested in a popular *canso* (song) included in six songbooks. Raimbaut reciprocated by dedicating a dozen compositions to a lady, whom he calls simply his *joglar* or *belh joglar*, and treats as a friend or confidante.

Her poem, "Ar em el freg temps vengut" ("Now we have come to the wintry season"), interpreted by Aimo Sakari as a previously written *canso* transformed into a lament on the death of Raimbaut (Sakari 1949, 1987; Bruckner et al., xxi). This same poem may have been addressed to the powerful viscountess and troubadour patron, Ermengard (Ermengarda) of Narbonne (1127?–1196?), since verses 49–52 instruct the *joglar* to bring the poem to Narbonne, also on the Mediterranean coast of France. In this instance, Azalais is thus one of the very few female lyricists who address themselves not directly to the lover but to an audience (in this case, Ermengard) other than the beloved. Her reader's expectations of a love song are fulfilled by means of a *Natureingang*, in that she involves nature into her love relationship (such as the allusion to winter's approach). However, in other poems she does address the lover directly, as "amics" ("friend, beloved"). Azalais's poems, in their technique, also show evidence of a poetic relationship with the Countess of Die, or Comtessa de Dia, even though this fellow poet is not named (Bruckner et al.).

As one finds in other *trobairitz*, Azalais appropriates certain troubadour *topoi* (commonplaces, motifs), for example, when singing her lover's praise or appearing preoccupied with self-justification. Underlining the essential paradox of her femininity within a poetic system created by men, she speaks out and proves her complete awareness of her charm and courtly virtues. More significant still in "Ar em el freg temps vengut" is the fact that she takes sides in the widespread debate on the social status to be required of a lover. Despite derision by others—especially other troubadours—she has chosen a lover "who is lord over all" (vv. 25–26), and whose fidelity refutes those who caution ladies against giving their hearts to men of high rank. At the same time, while placing herself at her beloved's mercy—a reversal of the canonical male poet's submission to his lady—she pleads that no unrealistic demands be made of her. Her lover's supposed promise not to require anything untoward of her has sometimes been read as an allusion to the *assag*: a chastity test of whose true existence this poem may be the sole proof. Her aristocratic lover's discretion or indiscretion plays an unusually decisive role because he is not her social inferior. In all, and however much scholars debate her real message, Azalais reveals her skill at "establishing multiple links with fellow troubadours" (Bruckner et al.).

See also Alba Lady; *Chanson de Femme* (Women's Song); Comtessa de Dia; Ermengard of Narbonne; Music, Women Composers and Musicians; *Trobairitz*

BIBLIOGRAPHY

Primary Sources
Azalais de Porcairagues. "Ar em el freg temps vengut". In *Songs of the Women Troubadours*, edited and translated by Matilda Tomaryn Bruckner, Laurie Shepard, and Sarah White, esp. 34–37. New York: Garland, 1995. Revised ed., 2000.

———. In *Trobairitz: Der Beitrag der Frau in der altokzitanischen höfischen Lyrik. Edition des Gesamtkorpus*, edited by Angelica Rieger. Beihefte der Zeitschrift für romanische Philologie, 233. Tübingen: Max Niemeyer Verlag, 1991.

Boutière, Jean, and Alexander H. Schutz, eds. *Biographies des Troubadours: Textes provençaux des XIIIe et XIVe siècles*. Revised ed. with I. M. Cluzel. Les Classiques d'Oc, 1. Paris: Nizet, 1964.

Secondary Sources

[See also extensive notes to above editions, especially Rieger and Bruckner et al.].

Sakari, Aimo. "A propos d'Azalais de Porcairagues." In *Mélanges de philologie romane dédiés à la mémoire de Jean Boutière*, edited by Irénée M. Cluzel and François Pirot, 1: 517–28. Liège, Belgium: Soledi, 1971.

———. "Azalais de Porcairagues, le *joglar* de Raimbaut d'Orange." *Neuphilologische Mitteilungen* 50 (1949): 23–43, 56–87, 174–98.

———. "Azalais de Porcairagues interlocutrice de Raimbaut d'Orange dans la tenson *Amics, en gran cossirer?" Neophilologica Fennica* 45 (1987): 429–40.

———. "Le Thème de l'amour du 'ric ome' au début de la poésie provençale." In *Actes et mémoires du IIIe Congrès International de Langue et Littérature d'Oc (Bordeaux, 3–8 Sept. 1961)*, 2: 88–94. Bordeaux: Université de Bordeaux, Faculté des Lettres, 1965.

———. "Un vers embarrassant d' Azalais de Porcairagues." *Cultura Neolatina* 38 (1978): 215–21.

Shapiro, Marianne. "The Provençal *Trobairitz* and the Limits of Courtly Love." *Signs* 3.2 (1978): 560–71.

HERMAN BRAET

AZTEC WARRIOR WOMEN

AZTEC WARRIOR WOMEN (15th century). The Aztec warrior women of ancient Mexico, specifically the Tlatelolcan, fought not so much with conventional weapons as with signs of their gender, both bodily parts and tools of their domestic roles, as recorded by later historians like Diego Durán (c.1580). Examination of these anomalous women— since normal Aztec women were exclusively domestic and reticent—reveals some essential characteristics of the Aztec (Mesoamerican) view of ideal, normal femininity as well as the negative, abnormal variety exhibited by the Tlatelolcan women. It also invites examination of Aztec societal attitudes toward female aggressiveness, which Cecelia Klein has demonstrated as a "gender paradox."

During a desperate moment in battle (1473), the king of the Tlatelocan people, on seeing his armies hopelessly subdued by the Tenochtitlan (people of the Aztec capital now buried under Mexico City), commanded some women and small boys to remove their clothing and run naked into the fray. The boys threw burning sticks, but it was the women who offered a more fearsome counterattack: they approached the enemy exposing their private parts; some slapping their abdomens and genitals, others squeezing their breasts and splattering milk over their enemies. Another related account describes the women'sheads— Aztec women's headdress and coiffure being one of the culture's enduring hallmarks—as covered in brightly colored feathers, and their lips a lurid red as though they were prostitutes. They were also said to be carrying shields and sharp stone (obsidian) clubs while screaming insults and obscenities at the Tenochtitlan aggressors. This inspired some of the reticent, still-clothed women to come forth and imitate their sisters by flaunting their nether regions; others launched various domestic women's-work implements (e.g., brooms, spindles, weaving-loom parts) at their foes. Yet another account, by Barlow, differs by depicting the women of Tlatelolco during that same episode as dressed and armed as conventional soldiers and who took prisoners (Barlow 1987). This battle, which the

Tlatelolcans lost nonetheless, was one of several involved in the eventual Aztec conquest of the Valley of Mexico, in that country's central region, absorbing subgroups like the Tlatelolcan, prior to being invaded by the Spaniards (early 1500s).

A principal challenge for scholars of ancient Aztec culture is weighing the evidence, at once abundant—thanks to the sixteenth-century Spanish chroniclers' meticulous documentation of Aztec history, dress, and customs, some of whom, like Bernardino de Sahagún, knew the native language (Nahuatl)—but also variously biased, depending on the overt or unconscious political agenda or outlook informing each chronicler's perspective (Klein 1994; Brown). But once research on these sources has sifted out the biases, the above-described episode remains no less dramatic, given the fact that normal Aztec society's gender-role assignments were sharply compartmentalized: women cleaned house, provided and prepared the food, did the spinning and weaving; men, raised as warriors, were forbidden to do any domestic work, including so much as touching women's tools for these tasks, for fear of being thought of as unmanly. Each gender's set of responsibilities, properly fulfilled, constituted the source of male and female honor within their society and love from their spouses. Icons of their respective duties marked each sex from birth. Boys, whose umbilical chords were buried on the battlefield, were signaled by darts and a shield, while girls, whose umbilical chords would be interred next to the hearth, would be signified by a spindle and broom, as seen in illustrated manuscripts and paintings. Aztec women raised warriors but were not themselves called to fight; these women were expected to be meek and mild. They were not even allowed to accompany their husbands into the war zone to act as cooks and servants (though they did prepare food for their men to carry and help them in other ways, but only from home), unlike their Inkan counterparts in Peru. Aztec prostitutes, however, were allowed to follow the warriors (Klein). Aztec society expected men, by unsurprising contrast, to be courageous in battle, with any sign of cowardice specifically condemned as "effeminate," and even "homosexual" in their language, Nahuatl, as recorded by Bernardino de Sahagún in his *Florentine Codex* (10: 24). Similar circumstances are found in Classical Roman literature, for example, in Virgil's *Æneid* and even more so in Virgil's medieval French reworking, the *Roman d'Eneas* (*Romance of Æneas*, c.1160) and later French medieval political literature. Aztec women could become priestesses, but aristocratic women could never become rulers, except nominally, immediately relinquishing rulership rights to male relatives. Yet the woman's presence as crucial link in this lineage of power was essential to ennobling the government (Klein 1994; Gillespie).

Several tales of warrior women occur in pre-Hispanic Aztec legend, almost always as the losing side in battle—doubtless as part of the moral message of the dominant Aztec norm, victorious over lesser peoples degraded by these aberrant, "immoral," "unfeminine" women. This sort of stereotyping is deeply rooted in Aztec mythology, in hideous, evil women-warrior figures like Coyolxauhqui ("Bells-on-the-Cheek"), the murderously rebellious sister of the Aztec war god Huitzilopochtli ("Hummingbird-Left"), who eventually conquered and abandoned her. Coyolxauhqui symbolized the militaristic woman as pretender to the throne, another evil stereotype.

Klein notes, however, that in one incident, occurring earlier than the Tlatelolco war, before the founding of Tenochtitlan, Aztec women courageously helped in successfully defending their camp against the enemy Tepanecs (Klein, 115; Berlin and Barlow, 43). Thus, female aggression, even in Aztec culture, has its positive side, and that this aspect too has its mythohistorical validation, in Chimalma ("Shield"), the female caretaker of the above-mentioned war god Huitzilpochtli. There were also "Shield-Woman" deities probably dating back to pre-Aztec times (Klein 1994; 1993). Though belligerent, these women were defenders of the state, and thus virtuous. Within this paradoxical system, potentially threatening emblems of evil female aggression were translated into acceptable metaphors, as reflected in ritual, literature, and legend. A normal woman's "shield" was her virginity, her weapons were household implements, and sexual intercourse was equated with warfare and conquest. So long as women waged war using their properly female attributes, and in defense of the state and their men, this female militancy was condoned.

See also Frauenturnier; Joan of Arc, St.; Nine Worthy Women; Prostitution; *Tournoiement des Dames*; Valkyries; Virginity

BIBLIOGRAPHY

Primary Sources
Barlow, Robert H. *Tlatelolco, Rival de Tenochtitlan.* Edited by Jesús Monjarás-Ruiz et al. In *Obras de Robert H. Barlow*, 1. Mexico City: Universidad de las Américas, Puebla, 1987.
Berlin, Heinrich, and Robert Barlow. *Anales de Tlatelolco y Códice de Tlatelolco.* Mexico City: Porrúa, 1980.
Durán, Diego. *Historia de las Indias de Nueva España e Islas de la Tierra Firme.* Edited by Angel M. Garibay. 2 vols. Mexico City: Porrúa, 1967.
Sahagún, Bernardino de. *The Florentine Codex: General History of the Things of New Spain.* Translated by Arthur J. O. Anderson and Charles E. Dibble, vols. 6, 10, 8, 12. Monographs of the School of American Research, 14. 13 vols. Santa Fe, N.M.: School of American Research/University of Utah, 1953–1982.

Secondary Sources
Brown, Betty Ann. "Seen but Not Heard: Women in Aztec Ritual—the Sahagún Texts." In *Text and Image in Pre-Columbian Art: Essays in the Interrelationship of the Verbal and Visual Arts*, edited by Janet C. Berlo, 119–54. B. A. R. International Series, 180. Oxford, U.K.: B. A. R., 1983.
Gillespie, Susan. *The Aztec Kings: The Construction of Rulership in Mexican History.* Tucson: University of Arizona Press, 1989.
Joyce, Rosemary A. *Gender and Power in Pre-Hispanic Mesoamerica.* Austin: University of Texas Press, 2000.
Klein, Cecelia F. "Fighting with Femininity: Gender and War in Aztec Mexico." In *Gender Rhetorics: Postures of Dominance and Submission in History*, edited by Richard C. Trexler, 107–146. Medieval & Renaissance Texts & Studies, 113. Binghamton, N.Y.: MRTS, 1994.
———. "The Shield-Women: Resolution of an Aztec Gender Paradox." In *Current Topics in Aztec Studies: A Symposium in Honor of H. B. Nicholson*, edited by Alana Cordy-Collins and Douglas Sharon, 39–64. San Diego, Calif.: San Diego Museum of Man, 1993.
Rodríguez-Shadow, María J. *La mujer azteca.* 4th ed. Colección Historia, 6. Toluca, Mexico: Universidad Autónoma del Estado de México, 2000.

NADIA MARGOLIS

B

BAKE, ALIJT (1415–1455). Alijt (or Aleyt) Bake was a Middle-Dutch author of spiritual treatises that tended toward mystical and spiritual autobiography. She was an Augustinian canoness regular—a semimonastic member of the female clergy bound by a rule, in this case, the fourth-century rule of St. Augustine of Hippo. Born December 13, 1415, in Utrecht or its vicinity, Alijt came, at an early age, under the influence of two women: one, a religious recluse with whom she also lived for some time, and the other, a hospital sister, most likely affiliated with the hospital (then a shelter, or hospital in the modern sense, associated with a monastic order) of Saints Barbara and Lawrence. In 1440, Bake felt called to enter the convent of Galilee in Ghent, northern Belgium. This convent of Augustinian Canonesses Regular was founded in 1430 by the Dutch-born Jan Eggaert, and joined the growing Congregation of Windesheim in 1438. The Windesheim canons and canonesses functioned as the chief religious representatives, complementing the secular role of the Brethren and Sisters of the Common Life, in promoting the *Devotio Moderna* (Modern Devotion), a movement of revival and intensification of the spiritual life through methodical meditation, originating in the Netherlands at the end of the fourteenth century and spreading throughout much of Europe thereafter. Bake was thus nurtured by and participated in a decisive period in the religious history of the Low Countries and Europe as a whole.

Her novitiate at Galilee was highly educational, but also full of tension and conflict. She read extensively, including mystical texts, which may have exacerbated a natural tendency toward quasi-mystical experiences and visions. Some of these informed her of her spiritual superiority to all the other convent sisters. Whom was she to obey, the inner voice speaking to her or the prioress? While readying to leave the convent to join the Poor Clares (a mendicant Franciscan order founded by Clare of Assisi) as a possible remedy, Bake had a vision in which Christ entrusted her with an important mission: to instigate a spiritual reformation within her own religious order. In obedience to that vision, or revelation, Bake took her vows on Christmas Day of 1441. Four years later, in 1445, she was elected prioress of the convent of Galilee to succeed Hille Sonderlants, its first prioress. Her election as prioress indicates a number of things: that she had put behind her the singular behavior characterizing her novitiate, that she was a born leader, and that she was able to convert her fellow canonesses, her "dearest children," away from Sonderlants's asceticism to her own demanding mystical pursuits through her treatises and (according to some scholars) oral addresses, or conferences. Because of the divisive impact of her mysticism on the convent, as manifested in certain of these writings, Bake was relieved of her position as prioress, forced to leave Galilee, and to enter Facons priory, a sister convent of Augustinian Canonesses Regular at Antwerp, Belgium. In her *Brief uit ballingschap* (*Letter from Exile*), of 1455, sent by Bake from Antwerp to the rector of Galilee, a close personal friend, she describes how, contrary to regulations, she was driven from her convent by so-called, unspecified "wise and learned men," presumably visitors sent from Windesheim to verify conditions at Galilee. In the letter Bake also requests the rector to plead her case at the next general chapter meeting of the Congregation of Windesheim. However, not long after Bake wrote this letter, she died, not quite forty years old, on October 18, 1455. That same year the general chapter of the Congregation of Windesheim issued a decree forbidding canonesses to write speculative, visionary or mystical treatises.

Although Alijt Bake demonstrably deserves a place among major late-medieval visionary authors of spiritual treatises and autobiography, she did not begin to attract scholarly interest until the latter half of the twentieth century. Efforts to analyze and appraise her works have been frustrated by their complex history of transmission among different manuscript copyists and printings, resulting in variant texts and confusing multiple titles for the same work. Another impediment lay in the problem of correct attribution, arising both from Bake's habit of reworking earlier writings (whether originally hers or of other authors) and from her censure by Windesheim, thereby causing some of her works to be circulated anonymously. The most recent and thorough investigation into her authorship is that by Wybren Scheepsma (1992–1997). A total of six, possibly seven, works penned by her are currently known to us. A reliable manuscript for most of these is in Brussels, Belgium, at the Bibliothèque Royale, bearing the numbers 643–644. In chronological order, these works are: a collection of four (or three, or five, depending on the source used; Bake herself numbers them at five) *kloosteronderrichtingen*—instructions for cloistered, or "coenobitic," communities; then four longer, separate works: *De vier kruiswegen* (*The Four Ways of the Cross*), her autobiography mentioned earlier (*Mijn beghin ende voortganck*), the above-cited letter, *De brief uit ballingschap*, and *Van de memorie der passien ons Heren* (*On the Recollection of the Passion of Our Lord*). In another case, some doubt surrounds the authenticity of a lengthy treatise entitled *Een Merckelike Leringhe* (*A Notable Lesson*). Her works reflect both general and specific influences. The general influences, especially with regard to Bake's mystical views, can be traced back to German-Netherlandish mystics—sometimes referred to as the Rhineland mystics—of whom Hadjewich of Antwerp (d. 1260), Beatrice (Beatrijs) of Nazareth (d. 1268), Meister Eckhart (d. 1328), Johannes Tauler (d. 1361), Jan van Leeuwen (d. 1378), Jan van Ruusbroec (d. 1381), and Rulman Merswin (d. 1382) appear to have played the most direct role in shaping her mysticism. Furthermore, Ruusbroec, writing in Middle-Dutch, coined much of the mystical terminology used by Bake and others writing in the vernacular. Other influences, not surprisingly, are St. Augustine (354–430) and Bernard of Clairvaux (d. 1153), both of whom Bake cites frequently. A more detailed analysis of her works follows.

She composed her first of her above-cited works, the three (or four, or even five, as explained below) conferences, on the eve of Holy Week in the year 1446, to provide the canonesses with suitable literature for the week between Palm Sunday and Easter Sunday. We may term them "conferences" because they are patterned after sermons by

Jordan of Quedlingburg. Bake herself qualifies them as "crumbs from the table of the wise and honorable teacher Jordanus," while also elaborately commenting on them (Scheepsma). Rudolf van Dijk (1992) suggested that they were first delivered orally. It was their modern editor, Bernard Spaapen (1966–1969), who first gave them their titles as an aid to readers.

The first instruction consists in two parts, divided by Spaapen into two separate works: *De louteringsnacht van de actie* (*The Purifying Night of the Active Life*) and *De weg der victorie* (*The Way of Victory*). The theme of both parts is that the active life can have a profoundly cleansing and purifying effect on the soul; that it can, in fact, lead to a "radical destruction of the self," an important step in Bake's spiritual ascent. The *Weg der victorie*, furthermore, is a summary of the much longer *Een Merckelike Leringhe*, which may or may not have been written by Bake.

The theme of the third (second) instruction, titled *Van zesderhande manieren van heilige onverschilligheid* (*Of Six Ways of Holy Indifference*), is that the donkey on which Christ rode into Jerusalem on Palm Sunday displayed a sixfold holy indifference, or equanimity, from which the good Christian must learn as well as imitate. Spaapen published it as *De weg van de ezel* (*The Way of the Donkey*).

The fourth (third) and final instruction, *De lessen van Palmzondag* (*The Lessons of Palm Sunday*), explores, firstly, the reasons why Christ wept on his entry into Jerusalem and, secondly, the motives for Christ's acceptance of an honor that he had previously rejected. Bake finds the reasons for Christ's acceptance of the honor bestowed on him on Palm Sunday in the belief that "while the virtue of humility is good, resignation is a great deal better." Because of the two themes treated here, Spaapen again divided it in two, as he had with the first instruction, to make the five alluded to by Bake.

Yet, there is a true fourth or fifth instruction left untouched by Spaapen, and recently edited by Scheepsma: *De trechter en de spin* (*The Funnel and the Spider*). In Brussels, in Bibliothèque Royale mss. 643–644, it follows the previously described instructions or conferences. Earlier authorities regarded *De trechter* as an epilogue to the four (three) instructions by Bake, but Scheepsma considers it a separate treatise in its own right. The work is so named because Bake portrays herself as the "funnel" through which God pours out his grace on the sisters of her convent. In this, her role is not merely passive; she also depicts herself as the "spider" weaving a web to "catch" souls for Christ. Should she not succeed, she will die a spiritual death.

Then came her most important and widely circulated work after her death, *De vier kruiswegen* (*The Four Ways of the Cross*), written in 1446 or thereabouts, is indebted, for both organization and content, to the anonymous *Der mynnender sielen boegaert* (*The Loving Soul's Orchard*). In one of its manuscripts (Brussels, Bibliothèque Royale mss. 643–44) it is inserted in the above-mentioned *De weg der victorie* and thus constitutes part of the coenobitical instructions. *De vier kruiswegen* was inspired by a vision, frequently referred to in her autobiography, experienced by Bake on Ascension Day (fortieth day after Easter) in the year 1446. The four ends of the cross stand symbolically for the four ways in which Christ's passion may be contemplated and shared, leading the believer to "Christ's perfection and his likeness." Those proceeding through the four stages are labeled, respectively: (1) beginners, (2) *profecti* ("those who have progressed"), (3) contemplatives, and (4) *animae nudatae* ("denuded souls"), as they move from superficial physical to increasingly profound internalization of Christ's suffering, then probing, through Christ, the privileged hiddenness of God. The fourth, and final, way is one of total surrender, requiring that one denude oneself of all the spiritual gains and treasures acquired by means of the first three ways. It is akin, then, to the so-called "dark night of the soul" beyond which lie illumination and union, to such an extent that "there will hardly be any distinction between the divine Spirit and hers (Bake's) except that one is uncreated and the other created." In some manuscripts, *De vier kruiswegen* is followed by an appendix titled *Van een lichteren weghe* (*Of a less burdensome way*).

Mijn beghin ende voortganck (*My [Spiritual] Beginning and Progress*), written in 1451, constitutes the second part of Bake's autobiography, the first part of which, titled *Het boek der tribulaciën* (*The Book of Tribulations*), is deemed lost. *Mijn beghin ende voortganck* covers only a brief, but difficult and decisive, period in Bake's life, from the time she entered Galilee as postulant, or preliminary stages of candidacy, in the Augustinian order (1440) to around Christmas 1441, when she took her vows. It was during this period that she underwent a mystical transformation process, part of which involved a three- or four-stage imitation of Christ. This process was dominated by two visions: the first on Christmas Day 1440 and the second on Ascension Day 1441. The first vision forms the subject of the *Een merkelike leeringhe* (*A Notable Lesson*); the second would inspire *De vier kruiswegen*. Consequently, *Mijn beghin ende voortganck* also provides the key to interpreting the latter work, as well as her peculiar brand of "night mysticism" (*nachtmystik*) characterizing her ascent to God. As such, it provides a milestone in the history of spiritual autobiography as well as in that of spirituality in general. In composing her autobiography, Bake relied on a spiritual diary she had been keeping for many years. Even so, the autobiography frequently diverges from the strict chronological order of events, because Bake allows herself to be carried away by her own enthusiasm. As Robrecht Lievens observes, the autobiography is written in a lively, moving, often agitated style, revealing a high-strung, spirited, intelligent, and sensitive woman.

De brief uit ballingschap (*The Letter from Exile*), dated 1455, was written from Antwerp to the rector of Galilee where Bake had been prioress. We know that Bake had been exiled to Antwerp, to a sister convent, because of her mystical views. Because of her numerous references in this letter to *De vier kruiswegen*, we can pinpoint this treatise as the crucial work causing her expulsion. The letter, then, is essential to understanding Bake's teachings while also furnishing key biographical information.

Closely related to—indeed a synopsis of—her autobiography, *Mijn beghin ende voortganck*, is a brief work titled *Van die memorie der passien ons Heren* (*Of the Recollection of the Passion of Our Lord*), probably composed around 1455 and possibly not by Bake herself (Scheepsma). As a summary, it restricts itself to the essentials of Bake's spiritual ascent through the imitation of Christ.

Finally, Brussels Bibliothèque Royale mss. 643–44 contains the disputed (in terms of its authorship) long treatise *Een Merckelike Leringhe* (*A Notable Lesson*), also known as *Boecxken vander passien ons heren* (*Little Book [Treatise] on the Passion of Our Lord*), between two of Bake's other works. Some scholars, such as Gaston Peeters, hold that the *Boecxken* is a reworking of an earlier, similarly named work, titled *Bouxkijn vanden inwendeghen navolghen des levens ende der passien ons heren Jhesu Christi* (*Treatise on the Inward Imitation of the Life and Passion of Our Lord Jesus Christ*) and dates from the period immediately following Bake's election as prioress in 1445. However, the oldest text of the *Bouxkijn* is a printed edition from 1514, with no known existing manuscripts.

Furthermore, as we have seen, Bake summarized it in a work certainly by her, *De weg der victorie*. In addition, *Een Merckelike Leringhe* contains a metaphoric cluster also found in *Mijn beghin ende voortganck*: when she exhorts her reader to carry a cross, out of solidarity with Christ, to the end, and having reached Golgotha she must, out of solidarity with Christ once more, remove her garments. These garments, seven in number, are the internal defects that "cleave like leprosy to the soul." For such reasons, Scheepsma believes *Een Merckelike Leringhe* to be an authentic work by Bake. Previous scholars have attributed other tracts to Bake, but these hypotheses have since been discredited.

One would expect Bake's powerful visionary voice to exert influence after her death. Generally, writings by adherents of the *Devotio Moderna* first circulated extensively within the Devotionalist movement before they were widely read beyond its confines. Yet, the small number of manuscript copies of her works suggests the failure of Bake's writings to catch on even within the movement. In search of reasons for this neglect, we recall how her contentiously mystical teachings at the convent of Galilee helped provoke that decree issued in 1455 prohibiting canonesses from composing speculative and mystical treatises. Her unique mysticism thus ironically contributed to her posthumous near-oblivion. Judging from the quantity of fifteenth- and early sixteenth-century manuscripts of Bake's works, *Der vier kruiswegen* was the most widely transmitted of all her writings beyond the convent, while her autobiography (*Mijn beghin ende voortganck* and the missing part) may have been widely read at Galilee, since the only manuscript of the autobiography found so far was transcribed at Galilee in 1705. It was copied from an older manuscript completed at Galilee in 1613 that, presumably, was based on the autograph, or copy made by Bake herself. Until the 1960s, none of Bake's writings would appear in print, except for the *Boecxken vander passien ons heren* printed in 1514 (of dubious authorship), probably because it is her least mystical, and thus least threatening, work. As a mystic and writer, Bake does not perhaps equal the two great women writers and mystics of the thirteenth century who also wrote in Dutch, Beatrijs van Nazareth and Hadewijch, but her qualities as both mystic and writer are such that her works merit greater attention than they have received in the past.

See also Beatrijs van Nazareth/van Tienen; Bertken, Sister/Berta Jacobs; Clare of Assisi, St.; Hadewijch; Rules for Canonesses, Nuns, and Recluses

BIBLIOGRAPHY

Primary Sources

Manuscripts of Alijt's Works
Brussels, Belgium. Bibliothèque Royale mss. 643–44.
Nijmegen, Holland. Albertinum (earlier: Huissen), *Bibliotheca Praedicatorum*, ms. 4.

Early Printed Editions of Alijt's Works
Wouter, Nijhoff, and Maria E. Kronenberg, *Nederlandsche bibliographie van 1500 tot 1540*. The Hague: Martinus Nijhoff, 1923–1971, items 445–47, 2532 and 0207–08.
De brief uit ballingschap. Edited by Bernard Spaapen. *Ons Geestelijk Erf* 41 (1967): 351–67.
De lessen van Palmzondag. Edited by Bernard Spaapen. *Ons Geestelijk Erf* 42 (1968): 225–61.
De louteringsnacht van de actie. Edited by Bernard Spaapen. *Ons Geestelijk Erf* 42 (1968): 374–421.
De trechter en de spin. Edited by Wybren Scheepsma. *Ons Geestlijk Erf* 69 (1995): 222–34.
De vier kruiswegen. Edited by Bernard Spaapen. *Ons Geestelijk Erf* 40 (1966): 5–64.
De weg der victorie Edited by Bernard Spaapen. *Ons Geestelijk Erf* 43 (1969): 270–304.

De weg van de ezel. Edited by Bernard Spaapen. *Ons Geestelijk Erf* 42 (1968): 5–32. [Incomplete ed. See Brussels, Bibliothèque Royale mss. 643–44, vols. 166c–71a and 177a–77c for complete text].

Mijn beghin ende voortganck. Edited by Bernard Spaapen. *Ons Geestelijk Erf* 41 (1967): 209–301, 321–50.

Van die memorie der passien ons Heren. Edited by Wybren Scheepsma. *Ons Geestlijk Erf* 68 (1994): 145–67.

[*Van zesderhande manieren van heilige onverschilliaheid*]. See above, under *De weg van de ezel*.

Secondary Sources

Axters, Stephanus. *Geschiedenis van de vroomheid in de Nederlanden. Vol. III: De Moderne Devotie*, 159–67. Antwerp, Belgium: De Sikkel, 1956.

Bollmann, Anne. " 'Een vrauwe te sijn op mijn selfs handt'. Alijt Bake (1415–1455) als geistliche Reformerin des innerlichen Lebens." *Ons Geestelijk Erf* 76 (2002): 64–98.

Dresen, Grietje. *Onschuld fantasieën. Offerzin ein heilsverlangen in feminisme en mystiek.* Nijmegen: SUN, 1990.

Kohl, Wilhelm, Ernest Persoons, and Anton G. Weiler, eds. *Monasticon Windeshemense, Teil 1: Belgien*, 236–67. Brussels: Archives et Bibliothèques de Belgique/Archief- en Bibliotheekwezen in België, 1976.

Lievens, Robrecht. "Alijt Bake van Utrecht." *Nederlands Archief voor Kerkgeschiedenis* n.s. 42 (1957– 1958): 127–51.

Peeters, Gaston J. *Frans Vervoort O. F. M. en Zijn Afhankelijkheid*, 24–52. Series 4, 99. Ghent: Koninklijke Vlaamse Academie voor Taal- en Letterkunde, 1968.

Scheepsma, Wybren. *Deemoed en devotie. De koorvrouwen van Windesheim en hun geschriften*, 175– 201, 251–64. Amsterdam: Prometheus, 1997.

———. "Mysticism and Modern Devotion—Alijt Bake's (1415–1455) Lessons in the Mystical Way of Living." In *Spirituality Renewed. Studies of Significant Representatives of the Modern Devotion*, edited by Hein Blommestijn, Charles Caspers and Rijcklof Hofman, 157–68. Louvain, Belgium; Paris, France; and Dudley, Mass.: Peeters, 2003.

Van Dijk, Rudolf. "De mystieke weg van Alijt Bake (1415–1455)." *Ons Geestelijk Erf* 66 (1992): 115–33.

Van Mingroot, Eric. "Prieuré de Galilée à Gand." In *Monasticon belge*, edited by Ursmer Berlière and Emile Brouette, vol. 7.4: 761–94. Bruges, Belgium: Abbaye de Maredsous, 1984.

GERRIT H. GERRITS

BALTHILD. *See* Chelles, Nun of

BARNES OR BARNE, JULYANS OR LULYAN. *See* Berners, Juliana

BATTISTA DA MONTEFELTRO MALATESTA (1383–1450).

An Italian humanist and scholar, Battista was the youngest daughter of Antonio da Montefeltro, lord of Urbino, in central Italy. She married Galeazzo Malatesta in 1405. In 1429, her husband succeeded to the lordship of Pesaro. After her husband's assassination two years later by rebellious citizens, Battista returned to Urbino. Her dedication to the study of Classical Antiquity was well established by the time of her marriage, for also in 1405 the renowned humanist Leonardo Bruni (1369–1444) addressed to her his oft-cited letter, "De Studiis et litteris" ("Studies and Letters"), which sets out precepts of education for women.

Latin grammar and letters, Bruni tells her, are the irreplaceable foundations of learning; she should study Latin writers and emulate them, focusing on religion, morals, history and poetry. She need not, on the other hand, concern herself with arithmetic, geometry, or astrology, more so because these disciplines are minor than because they are unsuitable for women. Most emphatically, she should avoid the study of "rhetoric" or oratory, since public speaking was not appropriate for women. Margaret King and Albert Rabil point out that the only gender-specific instructions Bruni gives to women who would be learned are to restrict their studies to the private realm and to concentrate on religion more than their male counterparts.

Battista had occasion to go public, however, when she delivered an oration in Urbino to the Emperor Sigismund in 1433. In it, she implored him to restore Pesaro to her family and to free her son-in-law Pier Gentile Varano, father of Costanza Varano, from prison. The Latin text of her address is powerful and ably constructed, demonstrating a mastery of persuasive strategies. She is shrewdly deferential and self-deprecatory, emphasizing her dependency on the emperor's power and justice: "Relying...both on your imperial benignity and the privilege [accorded me by] my devotion...I shall proceed, even if inelegantly, to what I wish to say."

She heightens the pathos of her sorrow, referring to her son-in-law as her son: "I beg your Majesty that you...release from the dark servitude of prison my innocent son." She subtly emphasizes the emperor's responsibility for her son-in-law, "whom Count Richard humbly entrusted to you on my behalf," as well as what he stands to gain by ruling in her favor: "you will have innumerable people who will praise your fame forever." Last but not least, of course, she deploys a brilliant array of winning compliments: "God has lent divinity to your countenance," she tells him, "a monarch decorated with a wondrous radiance of virtues." Her petition was ultimately unsuccessful, however; her son-in-law was killed in prison. Battista also conducted a correspondence with her father-in-law, some of which has been preserved.

See also Cereta, Laura; Fedele, Cassandra; Humanists, Italian Women, Issues and Theory; Scala, Alessandra; Scrovegni, Maddalena; Varano, Costanza

BIBLIOGRAPHY

Primary Sources
Battista da Montefeltro Malatesta. ["Oration to the Emperor Sigismund." Latin text]. In *Bibliotheca codicum manuscriptorum Monasterii Sancti Michaelis Venetiarum prope Murianum*, edited by G. B. Mittarelli, 701–02. Venice, 1779.
———. "Oration to the Emperor Sigismund." In *Her Immaculate Hand: Selected Works by and about the Women Humanists of Quattrocento Italy*, edited and translated, with an introduction, by Margaret King and Albert Rabil, Jr., 35–38. Medieval & Renaissance Texts & Studies, 20. Binghamton, N.Y.: MRTS, 1983.
Bruni, Leonardo. "De Studiis et litteris." In *Leonardo Bruni.Opere letterarie e politiche*, edited by Paolo Viti. Classici latini. Torino: UTET, 1996.
———. "De Studiis et litteris." In *Vittorino da Feltre and Other Humanist Educators, Essays and Versions: An Introduction to the History of Classical Education*, by William H. Woodward, 119–33. Cambridge, U.K.: Cambridge University Press, 1897. Reprint New York: Columbia University Teachers College, 1963. [English translation only].

Secondary Sources
[See notes to Primary Source editions above].

REGINA PSAKI

BAUDONIVIA (fl. first half of 7th century). The first female author of saints' lives in Europe, Baudonivia was a nun of the convent of the Holy Cross in Poitiers, France. She is known only from her composition of a *Life of St. Radegund* (c.518–587), the queen who founded the convent, written between 609 and 614 to supplement an earlier life of the saint by the Latin poet Venantius Fortunatus (c.530–c.610). From it we learn only that Baudonivia had been a member of the community from an early age, "the smallest of the small ones Radegund nourished familiarly from the cradle as her own child." Written in a simple but forceful Latin, a far cry from the flowery eloquence of Fortunatus, her work is now appreciated as an excellent example of the hagiographer's art— biographies of the saints. It is also remarkable for being the earliest life of a Christian saint known to be by a female author.

Radegund belonged to the high nobility of the Thuringians, a Christianized Germanic people inhabiting the region around the Ruhr Valley, who were conquered in 531 by the Franks, another Christianized Germanic

The nun Baudonivia writing the life of St. Radegund. Folio 43v of eleventh-century manuscript *Life of Saint Radegund*. From Abbey of Sainte Croix, France. © The Art Archive/Bibliotheque Municipale Poitiers/Dagli Orti.

people who dominated the northern part of modern France. The victorious Frankish king Chlotar I won the rights to the young princess, although he did not marry Radegund until around 540. In the early 550s, Radegund left her husband and the royal court in a politically and religiously acceptable manner, that is, to live a life consecrated to virginity and religious works on a country villa. Around 560, Chlotar helped her found the convent of the Holy Cross in the city of Poitiers. She had her friend Agnes installed as abbess, while she herself lived in a private cell attached to the cloister until her death in 587. Although she adopted an ascetic lifestyle, she maintained a certain freedom from the strict obedience enjoined on the rest of the community who followed the Rule of Caesarius of Arles. Outliving her husband by some twenty-six years, she retained her ties to the leading nobles and ecclesiastics of the Frankish realm. She also developed a deep friendship with Venantius Fortunatus, an Italian man of letters who established himself in Poitiers around 567, acted as her agent, and composed his *Life of Radegund* shortly after the saint's death. Beginning in 589, a revolt ripped the community of the Holy Cross apart for several years.

It was at least two decades later, and after the death of Fortunatus, that Baudonivia composed her work to "make known what [he] omitted in his fear of prolixity." An earlier scholarly opinion emphasized the differences between Baudonivia's portrait of Radegund and that offered by Fortunatus. More recent commentators have tended to assign any differences to the changed circumstances of convent of the Holy Cross between the two dates of composition. In any case, it is certain that Baudonivia was particularly attentive to Radegund's political connections, so important to the original status and continuing survival of their convent. In particular, Baudonivia provided a detailed narrative of what was perhaps the most enduring gesture of the queen on behalf of the convent, that is, the acquisition of a relic of the True Cross from the Byzantine emperor. In the process, Baudonivia specifically compared Radegund to Helena, the mother of the Roman emperor Constantine the Great (d. 337). Helena (d. c.330) was traditionally credited with the discovery of the True Cross and thus served as a model of female power that was both saintly and imperial. Radegund had placed the relic in the convent's church where it served, as Baudonivia recognized, as a challenge to the power of Poitiers's bishop. Baudonivia may have written in part to diffuse the continuing effects of the events of 589.

In any case, Baudonivia's work became firmly linked to that of Fortunatus. The two are included together as two books of a continuous work in almost all early manuscripts. In this "dual-author" form the work gained a modest popularity. Thus, Baudonivia was not only the first, but also one of the most widely circulated female hagiographers in medieval Europe.

See also Hagiography (Female Saints); Lesbians in the Middle Ages; Nunneries, Merovingian; Radegund, St.; Rules for Canonesses, Nuns, and Recluses

BIBLIOGRAPHY

Primary Sources

Baudonivia, *Vita s. Radegundis*. Edited by Bruno Krusch. *Monumenta Germaniae Historica. Scriptores rerum merovingicarum*, 2: 358–64, 377–95. Hannover: Hahn, 1888. Intervening pages contain the work of Venatius Fortunatus].

———. [English translation]. In *Sainted Women of the Dark Ages*, edited by Jo Ann McNamara and John Halborg et al., 86–105. Durham, N.C.: Duke University Press, 1992. [Fortunatus's work accompanies this section].

Secondary Sources

Carrasco, Magdalena. "Spirituality in Context: The Romanesque Illustrated Life of St. Radegund of Poitiers." *Art Bulletin* 72 (1990): 414–35.

Coates, Simon. "Regendering Radegund? Fortunatus, Baudonivia, and the Problem of Female Sanctity in Merovingian Gaul." In *Gender and Christian Religion*, edited by R. N. Swanson, 37–50. Studies in Church History, 34. Rochester, N.Y.: Boydell Press, 1998.

Consolino, F. E. "Due agiografi per una regina: Radegonda di Turingia tra Fortunato e Baudonivia," *Studi storici* 29 (1988): 143–59.

Gäbe, Sabine. "Radegundis: sancta, regina, ancilla. Zum Heiligkeitsideal der Radegundisviten von Fortunat und Baudonivia." *Francia* 16 (1989): 1–30.

Leclercq, Jean. "La sainte Radegonde de Venance Fortunat et celle de Baudonivie." In *"Fructus Centesimus": Mélanges offerts à Gérard J. M. Batelink*, edited by A. A. R. Bastiaensen, 207–16. Steenbrughe, Belgium: Kluwer, 1987.

Kitchen, John. *Saints' Lives and the Rhetoric of Gender: Male and Female in Merovingian Hagiography.* New York: Oxford University Press, 1998.

Weston, Lisa. "Elegiac Desire and Female Community in Baudonivia's *Life of Saint Radegund*." *Same Sex Love and Desire among Women in the Middle Ages*, edited by Francesca Canadé Sautman and Pamela Sheingorn, 85–99. New York: Palgrave, 2001.

Whatley, E. Gordon. "An Early Literary Quotation from the *Inventio S. Crucis*: A Note on Baudonivia's *Vita S. Radegundis* (BHL 7049)." *Analecta Bollandiana* 111 (1993): 81–91.

THOMAS HEAD

BEATRICE (13th century). Beatrice is exalted as the redemptive beloved in the *Divina Commedia* (*Divine Comedy*), *Vita Nuova* (*New Life*), and *Convivio* (*Banquet*) of the Florentine poet Dante Alighieri (1265–1321). She is a fundamentally problematic figure. Following the short biography of Dante and commentaries on the *Commedia* by Giovanni Boccaccio (c.1313–1375), literary historians tend to accept that she did exist or was at least inspired by someone who did, a daughter of Folco Portinari. If Dante's poetic Beatrice was in real life Beatrice Portinari, then she was born in 1266, married to Simone de' Bardi in 1287, and died in 1290. Her effect on Dante's life and work was incalculable, out of all proportion to her years or to any literal relationship between her and the poet.

Dante's *Vita Nuova* (1290) presents Beatrice as a predestined force in the poet's life, encountered at the age of nine and exercising an unremitting power over him long past her death. He describes her as the compelling focus of his amorous and poetic life, his love object, the source of his poetic production, and the element that makes sense of his entire being. At the end of the "little book" (*libello*), as he calls the *Vita Nuova*, Dante suspends the project, deferring further speech about Beatrice until he can "more worthily speak of her [...] I hope to say of her what has never been said of any woman." Critics have of course taken this to refer to the *Commedia*.

The *Convivio* (begun 1304–1307), an unfinished vernacular treatise meant to offer authoritative interpretations of Dante's own poems, recounts an enigmatic lapse in loyalty to Beatrice, in favor of a so-called "noble lady." The treatise glosses this figure as Lady Philosophy, and the poet's brief and foolish allegiance to her as a temporary distraction from theology. Both the *Vita Nuova* and the *Convivio* purport to delimit the identity and significance of Beatrice, but their real accomplishment is precisely to set the reader within an interpretative itinerary of the poet's contriving.

The *Divine Comedy* posits Beatrice as the temporal and causal starting-point of the pilgrim's journey to the Otherworld, and its goal (*telos*) as well. In Dante's fiction, Beatrice sends Virgil to rescue the despairing pilgrim and guide him through Hell and Purgatory to her. Once he has reached the Earthly Paradise, at the summit of the mountain of Purgatory, she replaces Virgil and guides the pilgrim through the various dimensions of Paradise to a stage just short of the beatific vision. There she leaves Dante the pilgrim-narrator to St. Bernard's guidance.

Beatrice's centrality in the *Comedy*'s itinerary makes her quite literally the key to arriving at a reading of the poem as a whole. Any adjustment, however minuscule, to the symbolic freight we attach to Beatrice entails a massive reconfiguration of what we understand the

Dante's dream upon the death of Beatrice. In the dream he is led by Love to
behold the beautiful Beatrice on her deathbed and to give her a final kiss, 1872.
© The Art Archive/Tate Gallery London/Eileen Tweedy.

poem to mean. Critics and readers have elaborated an enormous range of interpretative
possibilities for this figure, ranging from the literal and historical (a mortal woman, lost but
greatly loved) to the strictly allegorical (theology, revelation, philosophy, faith, poetry),
to the more fluidly symbolic (a sign of love, the poet's own soul). Aldo Vallone offers a
thorough and succinct overview of how Beatrice has been interpreted since the mid-
fourteenth century, and opts with Singleton to read Beatrice as a figure for divine grace.

We can ultimately say little with certainty about Beatrice. The poet intends us to find
her a cryptic sign and deploys her as a call to interpretation, a challenge to our understanding. Still invested with all the human dimensions of mortality, lived history, and
idolatrous sexual desire, Beatrice is clearly not only a saved but also a salvific (saving)
figure, "the Christ-event in his spiritual biography" (Schnapp). The two fundamentally
contrasting sets of connotations attaching to her have engendered fundamentally opposed
readings of the *Commedia*, and will continue to do so as time opens up new interpretative
possibilities for Beatrice.

See also Boccaccio, Women in, *De Claris Mulieribus*; Dido in the Middle Ages;
Laura

BIBLIOGRAPHY

Primary Source
Dante Alighieri. *Opera/Works*. [There are numerous editions of the original Italian texts and English
translations continue to appear].

Secondary Sources
Harrison, Robert P. *The Body of Beatrice*. Baltimore: Johns Hopkins University Press, 1988.

Pelikan, Jaroslav. *Eternal Feminines: Three Theological Allegories in Dante's Paradiso.* New Brunswick, N.J. and London: Rutgers University Press, 1990.

Picchio Simonelli, Maria, et al., eds. *Beatrice nell'opera di Dante e nella memoria europea, 1290–1990: atti del convegno internazionale, 10–14 dicembre 1990.* Florence: Cadmo, 1994.

Schnapp, Jeffrey. "Dante's Sexual Solecism: Gender and Genre in the Commedia." In *The New Medievalism*, edited by Marina S. Brownlee et al., 201–25. Baltimore: Johns Hopkins University Press, 1991.

Vallone, Aldo. "Beatrice." In *Enciclopedia dantesca* 1: 542–51. Rome: Istituto della Enciclopedia Italiana, 1970.

Wallace, David, ed. *Beatrice Dolce Memoria, 1290–1990: Essays on the Vita Nuova and the Beatrice-Dante Relationship.* Special issue of *Texas Studies in Literature and Language* 32.1 (1990).

REGINA PSAKI

BEATRIJS VAN NAZARETH/VAN TIENEN (1200–1268). Beatrice van Nazareth was a Cistercian nun and author of the Middle-Dutch mystical treatise *Van seven manieren van minnen* (*On the Seven Ways of Loving*). We are rather well informed about the life of Beatrijs van Nazareth thanks to a Latin *Vita* (*Life*) written not very long after her death by the anonymous confessor of her convent, based on her own diary, now lost, and of oral testimonies of older nuns, among whom was her older sister Christine. She was born in 1200, probably as the youngest child of a middle-class family in Tienen in the duchy of Brabant, spanning what are now Belgium and the Netherlands. When in 1207 her mother, Gertrude, died, her father, Bartholomew, put her under the care of a small group of beguines in the neighboring town of Zoutleeuw, where teachers instructed her in the liberal arts. However, when her father observed in the eight- or nine-year-old child certain signs of a religious vocation, he sent her for further education to the Cistercian nuns' convent of Florival in Archennes, near Wavre (now in Belgium), for which he was acting as a general manager.

On April 16, 1215, after long and persistent urging and considerable time before she had reached the minimum age of eighteen, Beatrijs succeeded in being admitted as a novice. Soon after her profession in 1216, she was sent to the Cistercian convent of La Ramée (in Jauchelette, near Jodoigne), to learn the art of copying liturgical manuscripts. There she struck up a lifelong spiritual friendship with the mystic Ida of Nivelles, who predicted her election by God as His Bride. Four years after her return to Florival, before November 1, 1221, she moved to the new convent of Maagdendaal in Oplinter near Tienen, where she was to stay for more than fourteen years. Early in May 1236, she transferred to the newly founded convent of Nazareth, near Lier. There she exercised the office of prioress until her death on August 29, 1268.

As with so many other female mystics in the thirteenth century, Beatrijs's spiritual life was characterized by stern ascesis—self-denial, shunning all physical comfort and pleasure— by the imitation of Christ, a strong devotion to the Eucharist, and by ecstatic phenomena like the gift of tears, irrepressible laughter, and visions. Striking experiences, thoughts, and meditation schemes were written down by her in her *liber vitae*, a kind of diary or workbook, which chiefly must have contained information from the years before her transfer to Nazareth. This document was already lost in the Middle Ages, but the content can still be recovered in some degree, as her hagiographer included it to a large extent, in an adapted form, in his *Vita*. The only text of Beatrijs herself that has survived is the small treatise,

Van seven manieren van minnen (*On the Seven Ways of Loving*), probably written in Nazareth (c.1250), and that constitutes, together with Hadewijch's *Brieven* (*Letters*) and *Visioenen* (*Visions*), the oldest surviving prose in Dutch.

Whereas Beatrijs's liber vitae must have been a private document for personal use, *Seven manieren* offers an objectifying, didactic synthesis of mystical life. From the first sentence—"There are seven ways of loving, coming from and returning to the Most High"—one learns that Beatrijs considers love to be a cycle, which comes from God to the soul, and that returns with the soul to God, an idea she probably borrowed from the French theologian William of Saint-Thierry (d. 1148).

Beatrijs then describes the seven ways in which the soul experiences love as follows. The first manner of loving is the desire to receive the original likeness to God, which was granted to man at Creation: the soul wants to return "in that purity and in that freedom and in that nobility in which it was made by its creator to his image and likeness." In the second manner, love is described as a service to God without any self-interest: one serves Him "disinterestedly and freely, from love alone, without any other motive and apart from any reward of grace or glory." In the third manner, love is experienced as a real infernal pain because the soul desires what it cannot obtain, and with its limited powers, it cannot serve love as much as it wants. The fourth and the fifth manners form a diptych. On the one hand, love is experienced as an immense sweetness that fills the soul with confidence about its election. When this sweetness disappears, however, a violent storm blows up in the soul, an unquenchable passion for the final fruition, with physical consequences: "And thus her veins seem to her to burst open, her blood to boil up, her marrow to be dissolved, her limbs to be weakened, her breast to be on fire, and her throat to be parched, in such a way that her face and all her members perceive an interior fire and experience a tumult of love." In the sixth manner, love has completely taken possession of the soul, so that all its actions are in agreement with God's will: "And then the soul is like the mistress of the house who directs well the whole household, adorns it wisely, prudently, beautifully. With foresight she watches over it, with intelligence she safeguards it, and with discernment she manages it. She brings in and takes out, she acts and omits." The seventh manner finally describes the superhuman desire to rise up from earthly exile and to be united with God in everlasting glory.

Beatrijs's treatise has come down to us, anonymously, in three manuscripts: Brussels, Koninklijke Bibliotheek, 3067–73 (ms. B); The Hague, Koninklijke Bibliotheek, 70 E 5 (ms. H); Vienna, Österreichische Nationalbibliothek, 15258 (ms. W). Only in 1925, the Jesuit Leonce Reypens was able to prove Beatrijs's authorship on the basis of a comparison with the Latin adaptation of it in ch.14, pt. 3 of the *Vita Beatricis: De caritate Dei et .vij. eius gradibus* (*On God's Charity and its 7 Steps*). Since then, Beatrijs's treatise constitutes, alongside Hadewijch's work, a second important testimony in Middle Dutch of the thirteenth-century religious women's movement in the Low Countries.

See also Bake, Alijt; Beguines; Bertken, Sister/Berta Jacobs; Bride of Christ/*Brautmystik*; Hadewijch

BIBLIOGRAPHY

Primary Sources
Beatrijs van Nazareth. *Vita Beatricis. De autobiografie van de Z. Beatrijs van Tienen O. Cist. 1200–1268.* Edited by Leonce Reypens. Studiën en Tekstuitgaven van Ons Geestelijk Erf, 15. Antwerp: Ruusbroec-Genootschap, 1964.

————. *Beatrijs van Nazareth. Van Seuen Manieren van Minne.* Edited by Leonce Reypens and J. van Mierlo. Leuvense Studieën en Tekstuitgaven, 12. Louvain, Belgium: De Vlaamsche Boekenhalle, 1926.

Beatrijs van Nazareth. Van Seuen Manieren van Heileger Minnen. Edited by Herman W. J. Vekeman en J. J. Th. M. Tersteeg. Klassiek Letterkundig Pantheon, 188. Zutphen, Netherlands: Thieme, 1971. [Edition based on Brussels ms.].

————. *Seven manieren van minne.* [Middle-Dutch version] Edited with an introduction by Rob Faesen. Kapellen, Belgium: Pelckmans, 1999.

Translations, Dutch and English

————. *Vita: The Life of Beatrice of Nazareth, 1200-1268.* Translated and annotated by Roger de Ganck. Cistercian Fathers Series, 50. Kalamazoo, Mich.: Cistercian Publications, 1991.

————. *Vita: Hoezeer heeft God mij bemind. Beatrijs van Nazareth (1200–1268). Vertaling van de Latijnse Vita.* Edited by Herman W. J. Vekeman. Mystieke Teksten en Thema's, 7. Kampen: Kok and Averbode/Altiora, 1993.

————. In *Mediaeval Netherlands Religious Literature*, edited by Eric Colledge, 17–29. Bibliotheca Neerlandica, 2. Leiden, London and New York: Sijthoff, 1965.

————. "The Seven Steps of Love by Beatrice of Nazareth." Translated by Mary Josepha Carton. *Cistercian Studies* 19 (1984): 30–42.

————. "Beatrijs van Nazareth." Translated by Theresia de Vroom. In *Women Writing in Dutch*, edited by Kristiaan Aercke, 61–92. Women Writers of the World. New York: Garland, 1994.

————. [Select Excerpts]. In *Beguine Spirituality: Mystical Writings of Mechtild of Magdeburg, Beatrice of Nazareth, and Hadewijch of Brabant.* Edited and introduced by Fiona Bowie. Translated by Oliver Davies. New York: Crossroad, 1990.

Secondary Sources

Axters, Stephanus. *Geschiedenis van de vroomheid in de Nederlanden.* Vol. I: *De vroomheid tot rond het jaar 1300*, 223–38. Antwerp, Belgium: De Sikkel, 1950.

Bradley, Ritamary. "Beatrice of Nazareth (c.1200–1268): A Search for her True Spirituality." In *Vox Mystica: Essays on Medieval Mysticism in Honor of Professor Valerie M. Lagorio*, edited by Anne Clark Bartlett, 57–74. Cambridge, U.K.: Brewer, 1995.

de Ganck, Roger. *Beatrice of Nazareth in her Context.* 2 volumes in 1 [without a specific title]. Vol. 3: *Towards Unification with God.* Cistercian Studies, 121 & 122. Kalamazoo, Mich.: Cistercian Publications, 1992.

Ruh, Kurt. *Geschichte der abendländischen Mystik.* Vol. II: *Frauenmystik und Franziskanische Mystik der Frühzeit.* Munich: Beck, 1993, 137–57.

Vekeman, Herman W. J. "Beatrijs von Nazareth. Die Mystik einer Zisterzienserin." In *Frauenmystik des Mittelalters*, edited by Peter Dinzelbacher and Dieter R. Bauer, 78–98. Ostfildern, Germany: Schwabenverlag, 1985.

Wackers, P. "Het interpolatieprobleem in de 'Seven Manieren van Minnen' van Beatrijs van Nazareth." *Ons Geestelijk Erf* 45 (1971): 215–30.

Willaert, Frank, and Marie-José Govers. "D. Anhang. 1. Beatrijs van Nazareth (van Tienen)." In *Bibliographie zur deutschen Frauenmystik des Mittelalters. Mit einem Anhang zu Beatrijs van Nazareth und Hadewijch*, edited by Gertrud Jaron Lewis, 325–50. Bibliographien zur deutschen Literatur des Mittelalters,10. Berlin: Erich Schmidt Verlag, 1987.

FRANK WILLAERT

BEATRITZ DE DIA (late 12th century). Beatritz (or Beatrix) de Dia was a noblewoman of Die, in the present-day Drôme region of southeastern France, and thus is often confused with the Comtessa de Dia. She also became countess of Valentinois by marrying Guillaume I count of Valentinois (1158–1189), who descended from a minor branch of the family of the counts of Poitou (therein the source of confusion with the Comtessa de Dia). Several Provençalists (specialists in southern-French culture and language) believed her to have been one and the same as the Comtessa de Dia, but this belief is no longer widely held. Although chronologically possible with respect to each poet's lifetime and venue, the fact that Die did not come under Valentinois control until after 1186 offers one basis for refuting this identification.

See also Comtessa de Dia

BIBLIOGRAPHY

Primary Source
Gabrielle Kussler-Ratyé. "Les Chansons de la Comtesse Béatrix de Dia." *Archivum Romanicum* 1 (1917): 161–82.

Secondary Source
Cluzel, Irénée M. "Comtessa de Dia." In *Dictionnaire des Lettres françaises: Le Moyen Age*, edited by Robert Bossuat et al., 216–17. Paris: Fayard, 1964. [Concisely reviews various scholarly opinions on the identity of Beatritz].

HERMAN BRAET

BEATRITZ DE ROMAN. *See* **Bietris de Roman**

BEAUFORT, MARGARET (1443–1509). An important patron and benefactor, author of ordinances, letters, and devotional works, and mother of King Henry VII of England, Lady Margaret, Countess of Richmond and Derby, was born on May 31, 1443, at Bletsoe, Bedfordshire, England. A direct descendent of the powerful John of Gaunt (1340–1399), Margaret benefited politically and financially from several marriages, became a great landowner and administrator, and matriarch of the House of Tudor: in sum one of the most illustrious women in late- fifteenth- and early-sixteenth-century England. Much of our eyewitness knowledge of Margaret comes from the preacher John Fisher (1469–1535), as of about 1494 her confessor and advisor, who would later become bishop of Rochester, vice-chancellor of Cambridge University, and was eventually canonized. His "mourning remembrance," delivered a month after she died, has been a major source for the numerous later biographies of her.

In 1450, the then six-year-old Margaret was married to John de la Pole, of distinguished family but aged only seven; this child marriage was dissolved in 1453. She then (1455) married Edmund Tudor, earl of Richmond, whom she considered her first husband; he died the following year. In January 1457, their child, the future Henry VII, was born. Two other politically strategic marriages followed: on January 3, 1458, she married Sir Henry Stafford (d. 1471), and in June 1472 she married Thomas, Lord Stanley, later Earl of Derby (d. 1504).

In political affairs, she took an active part in the complex situation surrounding the Wars of the Roses (1455–1485), the interdynastic war of royal succession between the houses of Lancaster (whose symbol was the red rose) and York (white rose). She played a key role in Buckingham's rebellion (1483) aimed at replacing the ruthless King Richard III (York) with her son, Henry Tudor, Earl of Richmond. Although this uprising failed, the

Lancastrians then won a decisive victory at Bosworth (1485), in which Richard III was killed and her son, Henry, became king that same year. By arranging in 1483 her son's marriage to Elizabeth of York (1486), Margaret both elevated her own family's status and helped to restore peace between the houses of York and Lancaster. After Henry VII acceded to the throne, Parliament passed an act granting her the right to act "by the name of Margaret, Countess of Richmond," as if she were a *femme sole* (single woman), which allowed her to hold property in her own name and gave her other legal rights.

Lady Margaret's formidable political and economic power as the king's mother also exercised a kinder side, especially in later life. Her extensive acts of piety and charity were much celebrated, perhaps most eloquently in John Fisher's monumental eulogy, affirming:

> All England for her death had cause of weeping: the poor creatures [...] to whom she was always piteous and merciful; the students of both universities to whom she was as a mother; all the learned men of England to whom she was a very [true] patroness [...] all good priests and clerks to whom she was a true defendress; all the noble men and women to whom she was a mirror and example of honor; all the common people of this realm for whom she was in their causes a common mediatrix.

Fisher describes Lady Margaret's daily worship and penitential practices in detail: she took vows, became a "Sister" of many religious houses, and heard several Masses a day. Like many late-medieval nobles, only more so, she endowed chantries (chapels; expenses of church services) at Wimborne Minster and Westminster Abbey. She established two lectureships in divinity, one at Oxford and one at Cambridge (now known as the Lady Margaret Professorships), to promote the study of theology and raise the standards of the clergy. She also established a preachership at Cambridge. Influenced by Fisher, she re-founded Gods House as Christ's College, Cambridge, and subsequently re-founded the hospital of St. John as St. John's College, Cambridge, although funding for St. John's was completed only after her death.

Well educated for a woman of her time, she knew some Latin (regretting not having learned more) and was fluent in French. Fisher tells us, "right studious was she in books which she had in great number both in English and in French." Her will and records of various gifts received supply further evidence of her library and literary interests. Relative to such pursuits was her patronage of printing in its early days. She supported the three greatest early English printers: William Caxton (c.1422–1491), and his successors Richard Pynson (d. 1530) and Wynkyn de Worde (d. 1534?), the last styling himself her printer by 1509. At her request, Caxton translated and printed a thirteenth-century French romance, as *Blanchardin and Eglantine* (1489), which he had sold to her long before. He also printed a collection of prayers, *The Fifteen Oes* (*Fifteen O's* [because each prayer begins with the vocative "O," as in "O blessed Jesus..."]; 1491), at the request of Margaret and her daughter-in-law, Elizabeth of York; this version includes two special prayers for Henry VII. In 1509, at her request, Worde printed *Ship of Fools*, an English prose version of German author Sebastian Brandt's popular verse reworking of a satirical allegory, his 1494 *Das Narrenschiff*, later an influential text for the Protestant Reformation. Also for Margaret, Worde printed an elegant edition of the life of St. Ursula, translated from Latin. Other books printed with her support include two Church service books (the rite according to Hereford and Sarum [Salisbury]), Fisher's sermons on the seven penitential psalms (originally preached in her presence), his funeral sermon on

Henry VII, and the *Scala Perfectionis* (*Ladder of Perfection*) by Cambridge-affiliated contemplative writer Walter Hylton or Hilton (c.1343–1396) in 1494. She was particularly attached to this last work on the active and contemplative lives, and she and Queen Elizabeth gave a copy to a lady-in-waiting, with autographed inscriptions.

Lady Margaret's own writings further attest her many accomplishments in both political and spiritual lives. Ordinances drawn up by her survive, as do several letters and her translations of two devotional works, printed several times in the early sixteenth century. Until 1499, she signed her name as "M Richmond," thereafter as "Margaret R." Her will—of major importance because of her role as patron and benefactor—has also been printed. All these works are in English. Another text, the Latin statutes of Christ's College Cambridge, must have been a collaborative work with John Fisher. The ordinances that she prepared for the reformation of ceremonial mourning dress (1493) show her interest in ceremonial and the organizational ability characterizing the management of her household, her will, and the *Statutes of Christ's College* (1506), which, like her will, reveal the depth of her commitment to the advancement of faith and learning. Both the prudent administrator and the quick-witted lady are present in her more personal letters, as is her ability to turn a phrase. Seven other printed letters are essentially business letters or letters of suit. Of these, the best known are two letters to Henry VII, both dealing with a longstanding suit over a ransom payment owed by the house of Orleans. The second one, written from Calais, France, on her son's birthday, is considered a most polished example of epistolary style from that period, combining business with affection by addressing the king as her "good heart," her "very joy," and her "dear heart," while acknowledging his help and requesting additional support.

Her translations combine her piety, her concern to encourage literacy and foster printing, in bringing continental devotional works, especially French ones, to an English-speaking readership. Fisher's account leads us to believe that for Margaret, translation was an alternative devotional act whenever she wearied of prayer; a good work for "the profit of other." In selecting which books she should translate, she opted for the most spiritually stimulating. Among these is *The Imitation of Christ*, her translation of a French version of the fourth book of *De imitatione Christi*, a most influential Latin spiritual manual (1426) often attributed to German ascetic Thomas à Kempis (c.1380–1471). Her translation accompanied William Atkinson's translation of the other three books, printed in 1503 by Pynson and later by Worde. In translating the section "De Sacramento" ("On the Sacrament [Eucharist]") from the *Imitation*, she rendered a topic particularly close to her heart. Fisher remarks that she received the eucharist (the most important sacrament, signifying the body of Christ) almost twelve times a year. Fisher bore witness at her deathbed to her interpretation of the sacrament, confessing that it contained Christ, the son of God, who died for wretched sinners upon the cross. The text itself is a series of diffuse meditations about the proper receiving of the sacrament; for Margaret, this entailed the receiver's passionate humility and self-mortification. Her *Mirroure of Golde for the Synfull Soule* (first printed c.1506) was an Englishing, again through a French intermediary version, of the Latin *Speculum aureum animae peccatricis* (*Golden Mirror for the Sinful Soul*), attributed to the Netherlands theologian and mystic Denis the Carthusian, or Dionysius Carthusianus (Denis de Leeuwis, 1402–1471), or to Jacobus de Gruytrode (fl. 1470–1475). Like her *Imitation*, the *Mirror* proved popular, judging by the number of subsequent issues and editions. Written for the laity, her *Mirror* fosters an attitude *de contemptu mundi* (of contempt for the world) and is divided into seven chapters after the seven days of the week to facilitate its easy use: "The sinful soul, soiled and defiled by sin, may in every chapter have a new mirror wherein he may behold and consider the face of his soul." Chapter 5, for example, invokes the filth of false riches and vain honors, all finally equalized by death, as she draws on the *danse macabre* (dance of death) theme as well: "And where be the emperors, kings, dukes, princes, marquis, earls, barons, noble burgesses, merchants, laborers, and folk of all estates? They be all in powder and rottenness: and of the most great there is no more but a little memory upon their sepulcher in letters contained. But go see in their sepulchers and tombs, and look if thou canst well know and truly judge which is the master and which is the varlet; which bones be of the poor and which be of the rich."

Despite her ardently professed misgivings about the world, however, Lady Margaret was a survivor, and she lived to see both her son and her grandson crowned kings. She died on June 29, 1509, at Westminster, and was buried in Henry VII's chapel in Westminster Abbey. Her tomb, with its full-length portrait effigy by Florentine sculptor Pietro Torrigiano (1472–1528), is still in place. In an elegy written in 1516, John Skelton exalted her above three legendary queens—Tanaquil (a 7C B.C.E. queen of Rome) and the valiant Old Testament queens Abigail and Esther)—as the preserver of the people and the king.

See also Danse Macabre des Femmes; Elizabeth of York; Margaret of Anjou; Woodville, Elizabeth

BIBLIOGRAPHY

Primary Sources
["STC" + number indicates items found in the *Short Title Catalogue of Books Printed in England, Scotland [. . .]1475–1640*. Compiled by A. J. Pollard et al. Revised by W. A. Jackson et al. 3 vols. London: Bibliographical Society, 1976–1991].
Fisher, John. *The English Works*. Edited by J. E. B. Mayor. Part I. Early English Texts Society, extra series [= EETS, e.s.] 27. London: N. Trubner, 1876.
Margaret, Countess of Richmond and Derby, trans. [Dionysius Carthusianus]. *The Mirroure of Golde for the Synfull Soule*. London, 1506[?]. Other eds. London: John Skot, 1522; London: Wynkyn de Worde, 1526. STC 6894.5. *See also* 6895, 6896, 6897, and 6897.5.
————, and Atkinson, William, transs. *The Earliest English Translation of the "De Imitatione Christi."* Critical edition by John K. Ingram. EETS, e.s. 63. London: Kegan Paul, Trench, Trübner, 1893. [Complete texts of both translations].
————, trans. [*Imitation* and *Mirrour*—Extracts]. *Early Tudor Translators: Margaret Beaufort, Margaret More Roper and Mary Basset*. Selected and introduced by Lee Cullen Khanna. Ashgate: Aldershot, U.K., 2001.
————. [Will] Appendix. In *Collegium Divi Johannis Evangelistae* [St. John's College, Cambridge], edited by Albert C. Seward. Cambridge: Cambridge University Press, 1911.
Rackam, Harris, ed. *Early Statutes of Christ's College, Cambridge*. Cambridge: privately printed, 1927.

Secondary Sources
Ballard, George. *Memoirs of Several Ladies of Great Britain*. Oxford: W. Jackson, 1752. Reprints London: T. Evans, 1775. Edited with introduction by Ruth Perry. Detroit: Wayne State University Press, 1985.
Cooper, Charles Henry. *Memoir of Margaret, Countess of Richmond and Derby*. Edited by J. E. B. Mayor. Cambridge: Cambridge University Press, 1874.
Jones, Michael K. and Malcom G. Underwood. *The King's Mother: Lady Margaret Beaufort, Countess of Richmond and Derby*. Cambridge: Cambridge University Press, 1992.
Lloyd, A. H. *The Early History of Christ's College*. Cambridge: Cambridge University Press, 1934.
Powell, Susan. "Lady Margaret Beaufort and Her Books." *The Library* 6th series 20 (1998): 197–240.

Seward, Desmond. *The Wars of the Roses through the Lives of Five Men and Women in the Fifteenth Century.* London: Constable; New York, Viking, 1995.

Simon, Linda. *Of Virtue Rare: Margaret Beaufort, Matriarch of the House of Tudor.* Boston: Houghton Mifflin Company, 1982.

Underwood, Malcolm G. "Politics and Piety in the Household of Lady Margaret Beaufort." *Journal of Ecclesiastical History* 38 (1987): 39–52.

Warnicke, Retha M. "The Lady Margaret, Countess of Richmond: A Noblewoman of Independent Wealth and Status." *Fifteenth-Century Studies* 9 (1984): 215–48.

ELIZABETH MCCUTCHEON

BEAUTIFUL LADY WITHOUT MERCY. *See Belle Dame sans Merci*

BEGUINES (13th century). Their name deriving from the French *Béguines*, these were pious women in northern Europe (especially Flanders and the Rhinelands) who sought alternative forms of a religious life. At the same time, they became the targets of attacks both by the ecclesiastical authorities, who feared new forms of piety no longer under their complete control, and by misogynistic satirical poets for whom these women became representative of all that was wrong with women in general.

Demographically there seems to have been a surplus of women (at least in the age group before marriage) around 1200 due to men perishing in wars and the crusades and many men entering the priesthood (Simons 1989, 71; Bolton, 147). This group of women had few choices, since the lifestyle of the single working woman was not yet common in medieval Europe. Living in a nonenclosed community of women in an urban environment thus became a new option for those who for various reasons could or would not enter a convent and yet desired a life of poverty, chastity, and devotion. One of the major obstacles preventing women from joining an established order was the increasing reluctance of male monastics to occupy themselves with the *cura monialum*, or the pastoral care of female religious. With the major orders closed to them, women, who also may not have had the requisite dowry for a traditional convent, began to form pious associations.

Though there was no official founder of the beguine movement, an early protector, Jacques de Vitry (James of Vitry), played a crucial role in gaining acceptance for this new pious lifestyle. In 1215–1216, he wrote the *Vita* (*Life*) of Marie d'Oignies (Mary of Oignies), who had died in 1213, and presented her as one of the *mulieres religiosae* (or *mulieres sanctae*), or religious women, whose saintly life could serve as an example against the heresies spreading in the south of France. It is not clear if Mary was a beguine, although in the last years of her life she was surrounded by other pious women. In fact, most of the dozen or so saintly women of the diocese of Liège at the time were Cistercians, and it is very difficult to define a purely beguine-type piety or mysticism (Lauwers, 65–67; Peters).

Indeed, the word "beguine" was not used before the 1230s (McDonnell, 157). Its origin is obscure. Some believe it is derived from a variation on the word Albigensian (the Cathar heretics named from the southern French city of Albi); or from the Flemish *beggen* ("talk too much") or *bag* ("to beg") [Schmitt, 64]); or from the beige color of the beguines' garments; or from Lambert le Bègue (a theory now discounted [Lerner 1983, 158–59]). The thirteenth-century chronicler Matthew Paris was stumped as to the word's etymology. The term for groups of beguines eventually became "beguinage," again, from the French *béguinage*. A beguinage was a retreat, especially well adapted to an urban society where women living in common could "pursue chastity without a vow [. . .] and earn a livelihood by suitable work" (McDonnell, 131). This basic definition of a beguinage underlines the urban character of the beguinage (although many women were of rural origin [Simons 1989, 73]) and the fact that women exercised a profession, most often spinning, weaving, and embroidery or caring for the sick, the dying, and the dead. The women lived in poverty and chastity, but since they were not bound by any vows could abandon the beguinage to marry. The size of a beguinage varied greatly, from two inhabitants to several hundred (Simons 1989, 78–84). One of the largest beguinages was supported by Saint Louis in Paris in the second half of the thirteenth century and is said to have sheltered eight hundred women. This pattern of "towns within towns" (Lerner 1983, 159) became dominant during this time. But other possibilities existed: a beguine could also live at home and work at the beguinage during the day, and there is some evidence of beguines adopting a life of wandering mendicancy. These "women on the loose" (Passenier) were especially vulnerable to clerical and satirical attacks.

In 1216, Jacques de Vitry succeeded in obtaining papal approval for the communities of religious women who would later be called beguines in the diocese of Liège, and in 1233, Pope Gregory IX assured his protection of these women in the bull *Gloriam virginalem* (*To the glory of virginal women*). But in the same year, a synod in Mainz passed legislation against those beguines who would not remain in their houses, wanted to become itinerant beggars, or publicly preach doctrinal errors. It was this danger of the unenclosed woman that led to increased hostility toward beguines; yet their numbers continued to increase, and their piety was admired by many. The council of Vienne (southern France) in 1311–1312 issued restrictive decrees against the beguines that were published in the canon-law statutes known as the *Codex iuris canonici* in 1317 under the elliptical titles *Ad nostrum* (*To our own*) and *Cum de quibusdam mulieribus* (*In the case of certain women*), but these decrees did not lead to the dissolution of most beguinages. Pope John XXII in his *Racio recta* (*Correct Reasoning*) distinguished between good (enclosed) and bad (on the loose) beguines. This distinction allowed for the toleration of beguine houses. Papal legislation remained vague until the fifteenth century, but finally, beguinages became accepted parts of European culture, and until recently, there were a number of active beguinages.

The double role seen by Pope John XXII was reflected in the literature dealing with the beguines. Texts like *La Règle des fins amants* (*Rule for Good Lovers*) show a praiseworthy beguine spirituality that rivals that of the best theologians of Paris (Newman). Another text that distinguishes between good and bad beguines, or those who are obedient and those who are hypocritical and lecherous, is the *Songe du Paradis* (*Dream of Paradise*) (not the one by Raoul de Houdenc). The male-authored hagiography of the beguines is of course positive but also "contains and controls" them by fitting them into orthodox molds (Lauwers). The negative view comes to the fore in the satirical poetry that targeted the beguines (Blumenfeld-Kosinski). One of the earliest attackers of beguine piety was Gautier de Coincy (d. 1236), the Benedictine prior of St. Médard and the author of a large collection of miracles of the Virgin. His wrath was directed against the hypocrisy of the beguines and beghards whose communal life he saw as licentious and even unnatural. Gautier's hostility toward new forms of piety, often depicted as false and overwrought, is typical of a conservative clerical milieu. But the beguines were also attacked by poets associated with the university, such as Jean de Meun and Rutebeuf. In the 1260s and 1270s, they scolded against the hypocrisy and easy life of the beguines. Faux Semblant (False Seeming) in Jean de Meun's *Roman de la Rose* (c.1275) keeps intimate company with Atenance Contrainte (Forced Abstinence) who is depicted as a beguine. Rutebeuf devotes several poems to the beguines (c.1260–1280), indicting their close and thus suspicious relations with the mendicants, their pretense of mystical experiences, and their exaggerated tearful devotions. Their hypocrisy is evident, according to Rutebeuf, in their lack of perpetual vows and the ease with which they can abandon their pious lives. Beguines were also accused of wanting to read the Bible in the vernacular and of preaching in public places, practices either associated with heresy (Lerner 1972) or reserved for the male clerical establishment. The polemical context of these attacks is the hostility of the university clerks toward the mendicants who, they believed, usurped many of their rights with the support of the French king who also favored the beguines. The association of beguines and mendicants thus worked to the women's detriment. But despite much hostility both the mendicants and the beguines continued to flourish and became integral parts of European culture.

Of the striking female poets and thinkers of the time like Beatrice of Nazareth, Hadewijch, Mechthild of Magdeburg, or Margaret Porete—who was burned as a heretic in Paris in 1310—some belonged to an established order or had only tangential connections to the beguines. Margaret was called a beguine at her trial, but we know nothing of her social origins and contacts. The whole question of beguine mysticism needs to be reexamined.

See also Beatrijs van Nazareth/van Tienen; *Frauenfrage*; Hadewijch; Law, Canon, Women in; Mechthild of Magdeburg; *Minne*; *Mulieres sanctae*; Porete, Marguerite; *Roman de la rose*, Debate of the; Virginity

BIBLIOGRAPHY

Primary Sources

Blannebekin, Agnes. *Agnes Blannebekin, Viennese Beguine. Life and Revelations*. Library of Medieval Women. Translated by Ulrike Wiethaus. Cambridge, U.K.: D. S. Brewer, 2002. [Based primarily on the German translation by Peter Dinzelbacher and Renate Vogeler (1994)].

Christ, Karl, ed. *La Règle des fins amants*. In *Philologische Studien aus dem romanisch-germanischen Kulturkreise*, edited by Bernhard Schädel and Werner Mukertt, 173–213. Halle, Germany: Niemeyer, 1927.

Douceline, St. *The Life of St. Douceline, a Beguine of Provence*. Edited and translated by Kathleen Garay and Madeleine Jeay. Cambridge, U.K.: D. S. Brewer, 2001. [Translation of an anonymous southern-French Beguine life with useful introduction and commentary].

Gautier de Coinci. *Les Miracles de Nostre Dame*. 4 vols. Edited by V. Frederic Koenig. Geneva: Droz, 1961–1966.

Guillaume de Lorris and Jean de Meun. *Le Roman de la Rose*. 3 vols. Edited by Félix Lecoy. CFMA Paris: Honoré Champion, 1965–1970.

Jacques de Vitry and Thomas de Cantrimpré. *Two Lives of Marie d'Oignies*. Translated by Margot King. 4th ed. Toronto: Peregrina, 1998.

Rutebeuf. *Oeuvres complètes*. Edited by Michel Zink. 2 vols. Paris: Classiques Garnier, 1989.

Secondary Sources

Blumenfeld-Kosinski, Renate. "Satirical Views of the Beguines in Northern France." In *New Trends in Feminine Spirituality: The Holy Women of Liège and Their Impact*, edited by Juliette Dor, Lesley Johnson, and Jocelyn Wogan-Browne, 237–49. Turnhout, Belgium: Brepols, 1999.

Bolton, Brenda. "Mulieres Sanctae." In *Women in Medieval Society*, edited by Susan Mosher Stuard, 141–58. Philadelphia: University of Pennsylvania Press, 1976.

Galloway, Penelope. "'Discreet and Devout Maidens': Women's Involvement in Beguine Communities in Northern France, 1200–1500." In *Medieval Women in their Communities*, edited by Diane Watt, 92–115. Cardiff: University of Wales Press, 1997.

Grundmann, Herbert. *Religious Movements in the Middle Ages.* Translated by Steven Rowan. Notre Dame, Ind. and London: University of Notre Dame Press, 1995.

Hilka, Alfons. "Altfranzösische Mystik und Beginentum." *Zeitschrift für romanische Philologie* 47 (1927): 121–70.

Lauwers, Michel. "Expérience béguinale et récit hagiographique. A propos de la *Vita Mariae Oigniancesis* de Jacques de Vitry (vers 1215)." *Journal des Savants* 1989: 61–103.

Lerner, Robert. "Beguines and Beghards." In *Dictionary of the Middle Ages*, edited by Joseph Strayer, 2: 157–62. New York: Charles Scribner's Sons, 1983.

———. *The Heresy of the Free Spirit in the Later Middle Ages.* Corrected and revised reprint. Notre Dame, Ind.: University of Notre Dame Press, 1972.

McDonnell, Ernest. *The Beguines and Beghards in Medieval Culture, with Special Emphasis on the Belgian Scene.* New Brunswick, N.J.: Rutgers University Press, 1954.

Neel, Carol. "The Origins of the Beguines." *Signs* 14 (1989): 321–41.

Newman, Barbara. "*La mystique courtoise*: Thirteenth-Century Beguines and the Art of Love." In Newman, *From Virile Woman to WomanChrist: Studies in Medieval Religion and Literature*, 137–67. Philadelphia: University of Pennsylvania Press, 1995.

Passenier, Anke. "'Women on the Loose': Stereotypes of Women in the Story of Medieval Beguines." In *Female Stereotypes in Religious Traditions*, edited by Ria Kloppenborg and Wouter J. Hanegraaff, 61–88. Studies in the History of Religion, 66. Leiden, New York, Cologne: E. J. Brill, 1995.

Peters, Ursula. *Religiöse Erfahrung als literarisches Faktum. Zur Vorgeschichte und Genese frauenmystischer Texte des 13. und 14. Jahrhunderts.* Tübingen, Germany: Max Niemeyer, 1988.

Schmitt, Jean-Claude. *Mort d'une hérésie. L'Eglise face aux béguines et aux béghards du Rhin supérieur du XIVᵉ au XVᵉ siècle.* Paris: Mouton, 1978.

Simons, Walter. "The Beguine Movement in the Southern Low Countries: A Reassessment." *Bulletin de l'Institut Historique Belge de Rome* 59 (1989): 63–105.

———. *Cities of Ladies: Beguine Communities in the Medieval Low Countries, 1200–1565.* Philadelphia: University of Pennsylvania Press, 2001.

Suydam, Mary. "Visionaries in the Public Eye: Beguine Literature as Performance." In *The Texture of Society: Medieval Women in the Southern Low Countries*, edited by Ellen E. Kittell and Mary A. Suydam, ch. 6. The New Middle Ages. New York: Palgrave Macmillan, 2004.

RENATE BLUMENFELD-KOSINSKI

BEIER, DOROTHEA (d. 1464). A German mystic, Dorothea was born in Sagan, Lower Silesia (now in Poland), and married Jakob Beier, a cobbler. After her husband died, Dorothea lived at first in Steinhausen, near an Augustinian Church in Sagan, a town that forbade the use of holy objects to all. Later, shortly before her death, she moved to a convent in Freystadt, also in Lower Silesia. Categorized as a *Leidensmystikerin* ("suffering woman mystic"), a type of female mystic whose experience was characterized by great pain and passion for Christ, she was known to engage in deep contemplation and meditation. She recorded her numerous visions for posterity, particularly at the urging of an Augustinian monk, Simon Arnoldi. After her death, Arnoldi compiled her visions and experiences into a Latin volume titled *Liber spiritualis gracie* (*Book of Spiritual Grace*). It is considered a unique source of religious psychology especially for the study of piety and mysticism in Silesia.

See also Mechthild of Hackeborn

BIBLIOGRAPHY

Primary Source

"*De quodam devotaria.*" In *Scriptores rerum Silesiacarum*, edited by Gustav Adolph Stenzel, vol. 1. 17 vols. in 12. Breslau [Wroclaw], Poland: Josef Max, 1835–1902. Reprint Hildesheim, Germany: Olms, 2003. [Contemporary historical record of Dorothea].

Secondary Sources

Neue deutsche Biographie. Historischer Kommission der Bayerischen Akademie der Wissenschaften. vol. 13. Berlin: Duncker & Humblot, 1982.

Sloger, Juliet, ed. *Women Writers of the Middle Ages.* Robbins Library. Rochester, N.Y.: University of Rochester, n.d. (c.1998). Web site: http://www.lib.rochester.edu/camelot/womenbib.htm.

EDITH BRIGITTE ARCHIBALD

BELLE DAME SANS MERCI (1424–). A female literary typology, originating as a poem by Alain Chartier (c.1390–1430) composed in Paris around 1424, hinges on one commonplace of European love literature: the femme fatale who toys with her lover. His "Beautiful Lady without mercy" has the alluring eyes, mouth, and dress to rival any romance heroine; she shows all the disdain of the *domna* (lady) of troubadour lyric. This lady combines physical beauty and emotional torment in a way that exemplifies the sadomasochistic character of much of the earliest secular writing about love. But she also enjoys a long life as a cult figure. Making appearances in Renaissance erotica and Romantic complaints in the line of Keats, she even reemerges as pop culture's "man-hating woman," celebrated today by Aretha Franklin, Madonna, and others.

What distinguishes Chartier's Beautiful Lady from her many avatars is her uncompromising talk. In this dialogue poem, it turns around the lover's laments about her indifference to focus on her separateness. He is long suffering; immobilized by her fierce look, caught in her nets (vv. 226, 260; Laidlaw 339–40). She is even-tempered, responding with measured words and noncommittal gestures. At stake is her franchise or freedom (v. 286). Chartier's poem plays with the time-worn trope of women's mercilessness by adding a quality of detachment. Respecting the rituals of love service does not oblige this lady to submit to the lover's advances. On the contrary: it frees her to stand apart. The negative character of female indifference mutates into a potential asset—the mark of the Lady's emotional and social independence.

Such a positive assessment of woman's franchise comes under pressure in the ongoing rounds of dialogue. It is trapped in a vicious circle of words between lover and lady. *Male Bouche* (Badmouthing), *Faulx Semblant* (Deceitful Appearance), *Longue Langue* (Exaggerated Talk): all those symbols of language's dangerous force are associated in turn with the Beautiful Lady. She becomes allied with slander—the evil underside of courtly language. By the end of the poem, when the dialogue breaks off and the lover appears to die of anger, franchise has been implicitly stigmatized. The *envoi*, or final dedicatory stanza, warning against slander and admonishing women for their cruelty, underlines this judgment.

Chartier's *Belle Dame* has long been placed in a conservative lineup of late medieval courtly poetry. Like the verse of his earlier contemporary, Eustache Deschamps, it appears nostalgic for the good old days when heartless ladies relented and lovers were, in the end, vindicated. It rehearses the formulas for tortuous passion, darkening them with the melancholy typical of fourteenth-century poets Nicole de Margival's or Oton de Grandson's writing. It was taken as an anthem for that retro fraternity of courtiers, the *Cour Amoureuse* (Court of Love), founded in Charles VI's time to revive the sport of idolizing women.

In Paris, however, Chartier's poem was also implicated in the factionalism that split Charles VII's milieu. During this particularly brutal phase of the Hundred Years War, it was politicized. To which side did it belong? Armagnac or Burgundian, royalist or English partisan? Since Chartier was the king's secretary and diplomat, his poem has commonly been read as a royalist anthem. "*Je suis France et France vueil estre* (I am France and France wish to be)." When the Belle Dame asserts her freestanding status, she sounds nothing so much as the country personified, issuing a rallying cry. This *femme France* (France as a woman) could well represent a poignant early expression of a nation divided and occupied.

It is important to situate the *Belle Dame* in yet another Parisian context: the literary controversies that engaged so many writers during the fifteenth century. The best known case is the debate around Jean de Meun's *Roman de la Rose* (1401–1404). Launched a generation earlier by Jean de Montreuil and Christine de Pizan, it unleashed a series of polemical letters that argued the merits and faults of the allegory. Literary style versus defamatory effects, poetic license versus social accountability: the debate came to a head, and in keeping with the adversarial rhetoric of polemics, was never resolved. What mattered finally was less a consensus than a combat. And that combat made the aesthetic and ethical questions surrounding a poetical work a matter of public concern.

Chartier's poem triggered a similar controversy involving a circuit of writers inside and outside the court in Paris. The first to react was an anonymous group of courtiers who objected to the way "the book called *La Belle Dame sans mercy* spreads rumors in the Court of Love, disrupts the quest of humble servants and snatches from you [women] the happy name of mercy" (Laidlaw, 362). Their charge was relayed by three women: Katherine, Marie, and Jehanne. The poet came back quickly with another poem, *l'Excusacioun aus dames* (*Apology to the Ladies*), which in turn sparked *La Response des dames faicte a maistre Alain* (*The Ladies' Response to Alain*). In the decade following 1424, the controversy escalated with other responses made by provincial poets such as Baudet Hérenc and Achille Caulier. Their *Dame leale en amours* (*Lady Loyal in Love*), *Cruelle femme en amours* (*Woman Cruel in Love*), as well as the works *Erreurs du jugement de la belle dame sans merci* (*Errors in Judgment of the Beautiful Lady without Mercy*) and *Jugement du povre triste amant* (*Judgment of the Poor Sad Lover*) created another onslaught of polemical writing over an allegory. Unlike the debate of the *Rose*, the *Belle Dame* debate happened, for the most part, poetically. It was conducted in French alone. It had none of the learned humanist or scholastic aura that surrounded the *Rose* debate. It was embroiled in national politics. As it evolved, it quit the capital and fanned out across a territory in disarray. Against this menacing backdrop, the *Belle Dame* affair signaled, above all, poetry under fire.

At the heart of this controversy lies the problem of injurious language ("*parole injurieuse*" *Excus.* l. 180). It revolves around what kind of courtly lady Chartier's poem represents. More importantly, it tackles how those representations can do injury. It concentrates attention on the destructive action of language, and on its effects. By introducing this problem, the *Belle Dame* affair picked up the charge of defamation made by Christine de Pizan in the *Rose* debate and extended it still further. Both the courtiers' objection and the women's response created a juridical framework in which Chartier's poem was to be tried for a crime of writing that, while well known throughout premodern Europe, had yet to be applied to a poetical work. Identifying the *Belle Dame* as a case of injurious language confirmed the forensic rhetoric typical of so much courtly writing. Simulating a trial for defamation broke new ground.

The *Excusacioun aus dames* fielded the indictment by claiming autonomy for poetic writing. This defense was mounted deftly, confined as it was to Cupid's Court of Love. Within this mythical setting, Chartier stood corrected on two scores. Not only does his second poem repeat the standard clerical attack against deceptive writing; here the figure of the merciless woman is exposed as simply un-believable. The *Excusacioun* also argues for a distinct ontology for poetry. It brackets its language as well as that of the *Belle Dame* in a separate sphere off limits: "If I dared to say or imagine that any lady was merciless, I would be a false liar and my word injurious" (ll. 177–80). Placed safely within an "if" clause, these works operate in a realm where the truth claim does not pertain in an empirical way. They cannot be judged false. They cannot, by definition, defame women. Buttressed further by the new humanist apologies of poetry, they appear invulnerable to all such legal, political charges.

That defamation and poetic autonomy were the key sticking points for the *Belle Dame* controversy is borne out by the way it continued to evolve. In later poems, the persona of the merciless woman—and not her creator—was tried over and over again. She was held accountable in ways that both clarify and intensify the struggle over poetic writing. The *Cruelle Femme en amour*, presents a courtroom scene where the allegorical persona, Truth, testifies that she has been supplanted in representing the woman by the figure of Fiction. The very criterion alluded to in the *Rose* debate and hanging over the *Belle Dame* affair emerged explicitly. It was named as the final potent defense. The concept of fiction, with all its prestigious philosophical and legal backing, was mobilized against the accusation of verbal injury. But that accusation was itself deepened. In the *Cruelle Femme* and other poems, it became a matter of treason or *lèse-majesté*. Verbal injury was redefined in extremist terms, those of attacking that mysterious sign of royal authority—majesty. Once fiction and treason were introduced simultaneously, pitted one against the other, the stand-off over poetry was polarized. This standoff certainly betrayed the political machinations behind the controversy. Such terms slung back and forth could well be symptomatic of a dynastic conflict that used issues of fiction as a cover. But the standoff raised as well the intractable question of poetry's accountability to the public sphere. In late medieval France as indeed elsewhere, there was no easy adjudication for centuries to come.

Why does this question center and founder on the representations of women? Chartier's *Belle Dame* does not provide a clear answer. Yet the controversy around it does epitomize how the symbolic value of the female figure was contested in premodern culture, and in ways that embedded the literary in civic life. Not only could she embody a novel national figure in the making, Chartier's *Belle Dame* also proved to be a testing ground for the powers and limits of fiction. In this manner, it heralded the early modern *Querelle des femmes* (Quarrel about women) where women's representation was bound up closely with the public sphere.

See also *Alba* Lady; Chaucer, Geoffrey, Women in the Work of; Christine de Pizan; Criseyde; *Miroir de Mariage* (*Mirror of Marriage*); *Roman de la Rose*, Debate of the

BIBLIOGRAPHY

Primary Sources
Chartier, Alain. *The Poetical Works of Alain Chartier*. Edited by J. C. Laidlaw. Cambridge: Cambridge University Press, 1974.

————, Baudet Herenc, and Achille Caulier. *Le Cycle de* La Belle Dame sans Mercy. Critical edition and translation [Modern French] by David F. Hult with Joan E. McRae. Champion Classiques, Moyen Âge. Paris: Honoré Champion, 2003. [Authoritative texts and commentary].

Secondary Sources
Angelo, Gretchen V. "A Most Uncourtly Lady: The Testimony of the Belle Dame sans mercy." *Exemplaria* 15 (2003): 133–57.

Beaune, Colette. *The Birth of an Ideology: Myths and Symbols of Nation in Late-Medieval France*. Translated by Susan Ross Huston. Edited by Fredric L. Cheyette. Berkeley: University of California Press, 1991. Originally *Naissance de la nation France*. Paris: Gallimard, 1985.

Berthelot, Anne. "'*La Belle Dame sans mercy*' ou la dame qui ne voulait pas jouer." In *Actes du colloque du Centre d'etudes médiévales de l'Université de Picardie Jules Verne*. Greifswald: Reineke Verlag, 1994: 13–21.

Blanchard, Joël. "Artefact littéraire et problematisation morale au XVe siécle." *Le Moyen Français* 17 (1985): 7–47.

————. "L'Entrée du poète dans le champ politique au XVe siècle," *Annales E.S.C.* 41, no. 1 (January–February 1986): 43–61.

Brami, Joseph. "Un lyrisme de veuvage: Etude sur le "je" poétique dans "La Belle Dame sans mercy." *Fifteenth-Century Studies* 15 (1989): 53–66.

Brown, Cynthia J. *Poets, Patrons, and Printers: Crisis of Authority in Late Medieval France*. Ithaca, N.Y.: Cornell University Press, 1995.

Cayley, Emma J. "Collaborative Communities: The Manuscript Context of Alain Chartier's *Belle Dame sans mercy*." *Medium Ævum* 71 (2002): 226–40.

Cerquiglini-Toulet, Jacqueline. *La Couleur de la mélancholie: La Fréquentation des livres au XIVe siècle, 1300–1415*. Paris: Hatier, 1993.

La Cour amoureuse, dite de Charles VI: Etude et édition critique des sources manuscrites. 3 vols. Paris: Léopard d'or, 1982–1992.

Galigani, Giuseppe. *L'Effimera conquista dell'ideale 'La Belle Dame sans merci'*. Pisa: ETS, 1984.

Gauvard, Claude. "Christine de Pizan et ses contemporains: L'Engagement politique des écrivains dans le royaume de France aux XIVe et XVe siècles," in *Une femme de lettres au moyen âge: Études autour de Christine de Pizan* edited by Liliane Dulac and Bernard Ribémont, 105–28. Orléans: Paradigme, 1995.

Giannasi, Robert. "Chartier's Deceptive Narrator: *La Belle Dame sans mercy* as Delusion." *Romania* 114 (1996): 362–84.

Hult, David F. "La Courtoisie en décadence: L'Exemple de la *Belle Dame sans merci* d'Alain Chartier." In *Progrès, reaction, décadence dans l'Occident médiéval*, edited by Emmanuèle Baumgartner et Laurence Harf-Lancner, 251–60. Geneva: Droz, 2003.

Johnson, Leonard W. *Poets as Players: Theme and Variation in Late Medieval French Poetry*. Stanford, Calif.: Stanford University Press, 1990.

Kibler, William W. "The Narrator as Key to Alain Chartier's *La Belle Dame sans mercy*." *The French Review* 52, no. 5 (April 1979): 714–23.

Laidlaw, James C. *See under* Chartier, Alain, *in* Primary Sources *above*.

Meyensberg, Regula. *Alain Chartier prosateur et l'art de la parole au XVe siècle*. Berne: Francke, 1992.

Piaget, Arthur. "*La Belle Dame sans mercy* et ses imitations," *Romania* 30 (1901): 28–35; 323–51; 31 (1902): 322–49; 33 (1904): 183–99; 34 (1905): 379–416.

Poirion, Daniel. "Lectures de la *Belle Dame sans mercy*." *Mélanges de langue et littérature médiévales offerts à Pierre LeGentil*. Paris: S.E.D.E.S, 1973: 691–706.

————. *Le Poète et le prince: L'Evolution du lyrisme courtois de Guillaume de Machaut à Charles d'Orléans*. Paris: Presses Universitaires de France, 1965.

Solterer, Helen. "The Freedoms of Fiction for Gender in Pre-Modern France." In *Gender in Debate from the Early Middle Ages to the Renaissance*, edited by Thelma S. Fenster and Clare A. Lees, 135–63. New York: Palgrave/Macmillan, 2003.

———. *The Master and Minerva: Disputing Women in French Medieval Culture* Berkeley: University of California Press, 1995.

Walravens, C. J. H. *Alain Chartier*. Amsterdam: Meulenhoff-Didier, 1971.

HELEN SOLTERER

BELLE HÉLÈNE DE CONSTANTINOPLE (14th through 17th centuries). The legend of the handless maiden—a significant mutilated-female typology—began with *La Belle Hélène de Constantinople* (*Fair Helen of Constantinople*), of a French *chanson de geste* (heroic epic poem) composed around the mid-fourteenth century in northern France. Its roots go back to some of the most intriguing early female folktale typologies: the innocent, persecuted heroine exemplified by Griselda, a character popularized by the mid-fourteenth-century Italian poets, Petrarch and Boccaccio (in his *Decameron*), and in the Middle-English Chaucer's *Clerk's Tale*; the falsely accused, exiled queen, often abandoned on a rudderless vessel, as with Chaucer's Constance in the *Man of Law's Tale*; and—most disturbing and memorable—the beautiful maiden who mutilates herself to escape marriage, usually by cutting off her hand(s), as developed in literate form in Philippe de Rémi's *La Manekine* (*The Girl without Hands*; 1230–1240). All of these tales or, as in *La Manekine*, initiation romances, propose to instruct as well as entertain; they are therefore *exempla*: stories with moral lessons. Complementing the self-mutilation motif, there often arise those of incest, betrayal by a mother-in-law, and monstrous progeny. Belle Hélène's story combines all of these themes and more.

Hélène is the daughter of the legendary King Anthony of Constantinople; her mother, niece of Pope Clement, has died in childbirth. When Hélène is fourteen years old, her father falls obsessively in love with her and offers Clement help in defending Rome against Saracen attacks in return for papal dispensation to marry her. After an angel has reassured him that the marriage will not be consummated, the pope reluctantly agrees. Hélène escapes by boat and finds refuge in a Christian convent in the otherwise still-pagan Flanders. The church bells miraculously begin to toll at her approach, but she soon has to flee the amorous designs of the "Saracen" (pagan) king of Flanders. When she embarks again, the vessel is first attacked by pirates and then shipwrecked, leaving Hélène as the only survivor stranded on the coast of England. Hélène eventually captivates and marries the young English King Henry, against his mother's wishes. Meanwhile, her father is searching all over Europe for his daughter.

Two years after his wedding with Hélène, King Henry departs to protect Rome against renewed Saracen attacks. In her husband's absence, Hélène gives birth to twins. Her conniving, evil mother-in-law falsifies the letter announcing the event—and Henry's reply—in an attempt to have mother and children condemned to burn at the stake. Instead, Hélène's right arm is cut off and given to one of the twins to guard as the three are cast out to sea in a rudderless boat. Stranded on the island of Constance, the children are abducted by a wolf and a lion, respectively, while their exhausted mother is asleep. Unable to find them, Hélène departs with a merchant vessel to France. The boys are found and raised by a hermit until they are sixteen years old when they set out to find their mother. After several adventures they are baptized by the archbishop Martin of Tours and given the names Martin and Brice. In their travels, the twins meet up with Anthony and Henry, who have meanwhile joined forces to search for Hélène. Father and grandfather recognize the twins as kin with the help of Hélène's arm, faithfully carried around by Brice. Meanwhile, Hélène wanders destitute through France and Italy, fleeing her father and her husband whom she believes are trying to kill her. The two men fight numerous battles, culminating in the liberation of Jerusalem from the infidel (Saracens). Both sides finally meet and reconcile thanks first to a prophecy from St. George, received by Hélène's father and husband, promising that they will find Hélène after they have also conquered the city of Castres in Italy, and converted the countries of Flanders and Scotland to Christianity. Indeed, after over thirty years, they find her in Tours. Hélène's severed arm, miraculously preserved all this time, has now been reattached to her body by her son, the future St. Martin. All proceed to the climactic reunion with the pope in Rome. Hélène and Henry spend their last days in that city and are buried there. Brice marries a Saracen princess and succeeds Henry and Anthony on the thrones of England and Constantinople. Martin will become the future St. Martin and assume the archbishopric in Tours, to be succeeded by his nephew, St. Brice. This already convoluted tale is further enriched by two subplots relating the adventures of two Saracen princesses, their marriages to Frankish knights, and their conversion to Christianity, a popular theme in the chansons de geste.

Most of the critical literature concerns itself with questions of origin and affiliation. Various motifs, such as the evil mother-in-law, substitution of letters, and severed limbs as proof of the heroine's demise, show the influence of folklore and occur in over twenty analogues (Roussel 1998). The oldest of them is the *Vitae Duorum Offarum* (*Lives of the Two Offas*), in which Offa is not only the name of an important eighth-century Mercian (Anglo-Saxon) king, but also a word whose etymology (offa = Latin for "premature or aborted fetuses" or "lumps") may play a subtle role, as in so many folk-tale-based texts. These *Vitae* and related works of Anglo-Saxon origin are cited by scholars like Suchier as probable sources for *La Belle Hélène de Constantinople*. The "maiden without hands" and "innocent persecuted heroine" motifs continued to recur in modern French, Italian (e.g., Italo Calvino's "Olive"), German (especially in the Grimm brothers' legends and *märchen* [fairy tales] of 1812–1816), English, and Russian folklore, later spreading to French-Canada and American Indian (Iroquois, Micmac) tribal lore (Bernier; Harvey; Jones).

Historically, Hélène's story is set against the extensive backdrop of Holy War. Saints and miracles aid the Christians, while the infidels are deserted by their gods and are either killed or convert and join the Christian knights. The poem thus pursues the same aim as its protagonists: the spread of Christianity and the glorification of the Crusades.

The oldest extant manuscript of this epic can be found in Arras, Bibliothèque Municipale MS 766 (previously 742), which also contains the earlier religious works, *La Vie de St. Alexis* (*The Life of St. Alexis*) and *Le Trespas de Notre Dame* (*The Life and Death of Our Lady*). The story of Hélène is by far the longest, composed in over 15,000 alexandrines (twelve-syllable verses, the standard heroic verse form in French) divided into *laisses* (stanzas) of uneven lengths. The text purports to be a 1471 copy of a text from 1401 and shows influence of the Picard dialect. There are three manuscripts in verse form containing the poem of *La Belle Hélène de Constantinople*, besides a two-page manuscript describing the battle of Castres. Also in existence are four manuscripts in prose: one by Jean Wauquelin, written in 1448 for Philip the Good, Duke of Burgundy (1396–1467), as he contemplated one more crusade to recapture Jerusalem. This manuscript follows the verse tradition very closely. Three other manuscripts, all quite similar to each other, follow the same plot line, but show more deviations, especially in names. These texts have served as principal models for the later popular romance versions of the tale.

See also Boccaccio, Women in, Works Other than *De Claris Mulieribus*; Chaucer, Geoffrey, Women in the Work of; Griselda; Melusine

BIBLIOGRAPHY

Primary Sources
Calvino, Italo. "Olive." In Calvino, *Italian Folktales*, 255–61. New York: Pantheon, 1983.
Chaucer, Geoffrey. *Clerk's Tale, Man of Law's Tale*. In *The Works of Geoffrey Chaucer*, edited by F. N. Robinson, 101–14, 62–75. New Cambridge ed. Boston: Houghton Mifflin, 1961. [With excellent notes and commentary].
Grimm, Jacob L. C., and Wilhelm Carl. [English Version]. "The Girl without Hands." In *The Complete Grimms Tales*, 160–66. New York: Pantheon, 1972.
La Belle Hélène de Constantinople: Chanson de geste du XIVe siècle. Edited with commentary by Claude Roussel. Textes Littéraires Français, 454. Geneva: Droz, 1995.
Philippe de Rémi. *La Manekine* In *Oeuvres poétiques de Philippe de Rémi, Sire de Beaumanoir*. Edited with commentary by Hermann Suchier, vol. 1. Société des Anciens Textes Français. Paris: Firmin Didot, 1884.
———. Modern French translation with commentary by Christiane Marchello-Nizia. Preface by Donatien Laurent. Moyen âge series. Paris: Stock + Plus, 1980.
Wauquelin, Jean. *La Belle Hélène de Constantinople: Mise en prose*. Edited by Marie-Claude de Crécy. Geneva: Droz, 2001.

Secondary Sources
Bernier, Hélène. *La Fille aux Mains Coupées, conte-type 706*. Archives de folklore, 12. Québec: Presses de l'Université de Laval, 1971.
Black, Nancy, B. "La Belle Hélène de Constantinople and Crusade Propaganda at the Court of Philip the Good." *Fifteenth Century Studies* 26 (2001): 42–51.
Däumling, Heinrich. "Studie über den Typus des 'Maedchens ohne Hände' innerhalb des Konstanze-Zyklus." Inaugural-diss. Univ. Munich. Munich: C. Gerber, 1912.
Harvey, Carol J. "Courtly Discourse and Folklore in *La Manekine*." In *The Court and Cultural Diversity: Selected Papers from the Eighth Triennial Congress of the International Courtly Literature Society, Queen's University of Belfast, 26 July–1 August 1995*, edited by Evelyn Mullally and John Thompson, 395–403. Woodbridge, Suffolk, U.K.: D. S. Brewer, 1997.
Jones, Steven Swann. "The Innocent Persecuted Heroine Genre: An Analysis of Its Structure and Themes." *Western Folklore* 52 (January 1993): 13–41.
Jones-Wagner, Valentina. "La Belle Helene de Constantinople: The Text of the Female Body in a Fourteenth-Century *Chanson de Geste*." Ph.D. diss., City University of New York, 2001.
Krappe, Alexander Haggerty. "La Belle Hélène de Constantinople," *Romania* 63 (1927): 324–53.
Lücke, E. "Das Leben der Constance bei Trivet, Gower, and Chaucer." *Anglia* 14 (1892): 77–112, 149–85.
Roussel, Claude. *Conter de geste au XIVe siècle: inspiration folklorique et écriture épique dans la Belle Hélène de Constantinople*. Geneva: Droz, 1998.
Schick, J. "Die Urquelle der Offa-Konstanze-Saga." *Britannica. Festschrift für Max Foerster zum 60. Geburtstag*, 31–56. Leipzig: B. Tauchnitz, 1929.
Schlauch, Margaret. *Chaucer's Constance and Accused Queens*. New York: New York University Press, 1927. Reprint, New York: Gordion, 1969.

Suard, Francois, "Chanson de geste et roman devant le materiau folklorique: Le Conte de la Fille aux Mains Coupées dans la *Belle Helene de Constantinople, Lion de Bourges* et *La Manekine.*" *Mittelalterbilder aus neuer Perspektive*, edited by Ernst-Peter Ruhe and R. Behrens, 364–77. Munich: Wilhelm Fink Verlag, 1985.

Suchier. *See above under* Philippe de Rémi *in Primary Sources.*

VALENTINA JONES-WAGNER

BEMBO, ILLUMINATA (c.1410–1496). Illuminata Bembo, the daughter of a prominent Venetian noble family, was a nun of the Franciscan order of Poor Clares and author of the *Specchio de Illuminazione* (*Mirror of Illumination*), the primary biographical source for St. Catherine of Bologna (Caterina Vegri/Vigri; 1416–1463), the celebrated visionary from the convent of Corpus Domini at Ferrara and Bologna.

Illuminata entered the monastery of Corpus Domini in Ferrara in 1430. Catherine of Bologna, a novice mistress of the same monastery since 1426, soon gained renown for her pious teaching and visions. When, in 1456, Catherine became the abbess of a new monastery in her native Bologna, some of the nuns of Corpus Domini in Ferrara, including Illuminata, followed her there. By 1472, Illuminata, having succeeded Catherine as abbess of the community, composed the *Specchio de Illuminazione* in Italian at an unknown point after Catherine's death in 1463. This very personal portrait of Catherine differs significantly in tone from her "official" life, written in Latin by Catherine's confessor for use in the canonization procedures, which did not occur until the early eighteenth century. Although the *Specchio* does recount such events as the beginnings of the new community in Bologna, it is less a biography than a meditation on the spiritual life of the saint intended for the continued instruction of the community's members. It tells not only of the Catherine's visions and devotional practices, but also describes how she acted as a spiritual director for the nuns of her community, including reminiscences about conversations between the saint and Illuminata herself, who had lived in an adjoining cell. The manuscript of the work was kept and used at the monastery, where it remains today, but was not printed until more than three centuries later. A shorter version of Catherine's life, edited by Van Ortroy, is also probably the work of Illuminata.

The *Specchio* reflects the memory of a great teacher composed by a student attempting to continue her work. It provides a remarkable portrait of life in a vigorously reformed convent of the fifteenth century.

See also Catherine of Bologna, St.; Clare of Assisi, St.

BIBLIOGRAPHY

Primary Sources

Bembo, Illuminata. *Specchio d'illuminazione sulla vita di s. Caterina da Bologna.* Edited by Silvia Mostaccio. Caterina Vigri, la santa e la città, 3. Florence: SISMEL edizioni del Galluzzo, 2001.

Santa Caterina Vegri: Le Sette Armi spirituale. Edited by Cecilia Foletti. Padua: Antenore, 1985. [Definitive critical, extensively-annotated edition also providing background source texts].

Van Ortroy, Fernand. "Une vie italienne de sainte Catherine de Bologne." *Analecta Bollandiana* 41 (1923): 386–416.

Secondary Sources

McLaughlin, Mary Martin. "Creating and Recreating Communities of Women: The Case of Corpus Domini, Ferrara, 1406–1452." *Signs* 14 (1989). Reprint in *Sisters and Workers in the Middle Ages*, edited by Judith Bennett et al., 261–88. Chicago: University of Chicago Press, 1989.

Spano, S. "Per uno studio su santa Caterina da Bologna." *Studi medioevali* 2 (1971): 713–59.

THOMAS HEAD

BERNERS, JULIANA (c.1388–c.1420s). Also known as Lulyan Barne, Julyans Barnes, or Julyans Bernes, Juliana Berners is purported to be the earliest known woman angler and the author of a volume combining lore on falconry, hunting, and heraldry known as *The Boke of St. Albans*. Printed in 1486 by an anonymous schoolmaster printer, *The Boke of St. Albans* consists mainly of four treatises: on hawking, hunting, coat armor, and blazing of arms—along with related information. The colophon, or closing inscription, ending the treatise on hunting (this is the second treatise and the only one in verse) states: "Explicit Dam Julyans Barnes in her boke of huntyng" ("Here ends Dame Julyans Barnes in her book of hunting"). The famous Alsatian-born printer Wynken de Worde's 1496 reprint contains a similar inscription (altering "Barnes" to "Bernes"), as do two mid- to late-fifteenth-century manuscripts: "Explicit Iulyan Barne" (Magdalene College Cambridge, Pepys Library MS 1047), and "Explicit JB" (British Museum London, MS. Harley 2340). Although all of these versions may draw on a still earlier manuscript, now lost, there is no direct relation between either manuscript containing an inscription and *The Boke of St. Albans*.

Except for the fact of the intriguing inscriptions, all information about Juliana Berners is antiquarian surmise or even pure fabrication. If anyone so named did live in the late fourteenth and early fifteenth centuries, it is not known when or where she was born or died, to what family she belonged, or whether she actually wrote the hunting portion of the *Boke* or perhaps compiled or transcribed some portion of it. We do not even know the preferred spelling of her surname: Barnes, Bernes, and Berneys were all common during this period, and Berners was not settled on until the seventeenth century. At that time, too, the ambiguous gender of "Iulyan/Julyans" was feminized, following one early tradition that "Dam Julyans" of the *Boke* was a woman. It is also possible, however, that the schoolmaster printer mistakenly identified the author with the dame who, within the treatise, gives hunting instructions to her "dere chylde." In sum, the name (Juliana Berners?), the sex (female?), the lineage (daughter of Sir James Berners of Rodding, Essex?), and the occupation (Prioress of Sopwell Abbey?) of the author/compiler of *The Boke of St. Albans* are all speculative and likely to remain so unless some local record or lost manuscript surfaces. Until then, although we might wish to claim for Juliana Berners the distinction of being the first English woman writer to be published in print, such a claim cannot be made with any confidence.

The *Boke of St. Albans* itself, its popularity attested by the existence of at least twenty later editions and versions through the seventeenth century, is a compilation of the gentleman's arts. The hunting portion, containing the cryptic colophon, derives mainly from two sources, an English translation (reputedly the oldest English hunting treatise) of Guillaume Twici's *La Venerie* (*The Craft of Venery* [Hunting]) and *The Master of Game*, a translation done c.1406–1413 by Edward, second Duke of York (1373?–1415) of the first thirty chapters of the French *Le Livre de Chasse* (*The Book of Hunting*, c.1388) by Gaston Phébus (Gaston III, Count of Foix and Béarn; surnamed "Phoebus" for his blonde hair; 1331–1391). The hunting treatise, which recasts these sources by conflating a dialogue between a master and his man with a set of instructions from a dame to her child(ren) or son(s), was in later centuries understood as the work of Sir Tristram (based on Tristan of the Arthurian Round Table, notable in several versions of his legend for his hunting expertise), since he is cited as her authority by the dame herself. Short proverbs, precepts, and poetry round off this treatise, along with lists, such as collective terms (e.g., a "cherme" of goldfinches). The *Boke*'s other treatises, on hawking and heraldry, are similar in style, composition, and concerns, so it is reasonable to assume that one person, perhaps even the unidentified Julyans Barnes, might have had a hand in these as well. However, no evidence whatsoever connects Juliana Berners with the treatise on fishing, inserted between the two heraldry texts in the edition of 1496. In fact, stylistic evidence argues against such a connection.

Nonetheless, the overall lack of sure evidence regarding the life and authorship of Juliana Berners has not deterred various publishers—from the illustrious Wynken de Worde in the fifteenth century, through various British and Scottish nineteenth-century fish and game enthusiasts, to the editors of the American magazine *Sports Illustrated* in the twentieth century—from reproducing her works under her name. Via numerous World Wide Web sites, the fame of Juliana Berners, however undeservedly named as the author of the first English flyfishing manual, continues to spread. There is even an Arizona women's fishing association named in her honor.

BIBLIOGRAPHY

Primary Sources
Barnes, Julians. *Boke of hunting.* Edited by A. Gunnar Tilander. Cynegetica, 11. Karlshamn, Sweden: E. G. Johanssen, 1964.
Berners, Juliana. *The Boke of Saint Albans, containing the treatises on hawking, hunting, and cote armour: printed at Saint Albans by the schoolmaster-printer in 1486, reproduced in facsimile.* Introduction by William Blades. London: Elliot Stock, 1881.
———. *The treatyse of fvsshvnge with an angle: being a facsimile reproduction of the first book on the subject of fishing printed in England by Wynkyn de Worde, at Westminster in 1496.* Introduction by M. G. Watkins. London: Eliot Stock, 1880.
Edward, 2nd Duke of York. *The Master of Game.* Edited by William A. and F. Baillie-Grohman. Foreword by Theodore Roosevelt. New York: Duffield, 1909.
Gaston III Phébus, Count of Foix. *Le Livre de chasse.* Edited by A. Gunnar Tilander. Cynegetica, 18. Karlshamn: E. G. Johanssen, 1971.
Hands, Rachel. *English Hawking and Hunting in* The Boke of St. Albans: *A facsimile edition of sigs. a2–f8 of* The Boke of St. Albans *(1486).* London: Oxford University Press, 1975.
Twici, Guillaume. *La Venerie de Twiti* [French and English versions]. Edited by A. Gunnar Tilander. Cynegetica, 2. Uppsala, Sweden: Almqvist & Wiksell, 1956.

Secondary Sources
Dictionary of National Biography 2: 390–92.
Fery-Hue, Françoise. "Gaston Phébus." In *Dictionnaire des Lettres Françaises: Le Moyen âge,* edited by G. Hasenohr and M. Zink, 482–83. Paris: Livre de Poche, 1992.
Hands, Rachel. "Juliana Berners and *The Boke of St. Albans.*" *Review of English Studies* n.s. 18 (1967): 373–86.
Jacob, E. F. "The Books of St. Albans." *Bulletin of the John Rylands Library, Manchester* 28 (1944): 99–118.
McDonald, John, with Sherman Kuhn, Dwight Webster, and the editors of *Sports Illustrated. The Origins of Angling.* Garden City, N.Y.: Doubleday, 1963.

SYLVIA TOMASCH

BERTHA OF VILICH (early 11th century). A nun of the Benedictine convent of Vilich (or Willich), near Bonn, Germany, Bertha composed, albeit anonymously, the *Vita sanctae Adalheidis* (*Life of St. Adelheid*). Adelheid was the daughter of Count Magingoz of Guelder, who founded Vilich in 983; she served as the first abbess of Vilich and later as abbess of the convent of St. Mary in Cologne until her death sometime between 1008 and 1021. (This abbess should not be confused, as she sometimes is, with her older contemporary the Empress Adelheid [d. 999], who was also celebrated as a saint and whose life was composed by Abbot Odo of Cluny.) Bertha began her work shortly before 1056, dedicating it to Archbishop Anno II of Cologne, a benefactor of her community.

Bertha entered the community of Vilich well after Adelheid's death and obtained much of her information from the abbess's former servant, Egilrad. Bertha's work betrays many of the ideological concerns of the pro-imperial German church, focusing on Adelheid's contact with and influence on the nobility, most particularly the imperial family, and her advocacy of the Benedictine Rule as an instrument of reform. Bertha was likely influenced not only by the traditions of Vilich itself, but by Abbot Wolfhelm of Brauweiler (d. 1091). Wolfhelm was an important monastic reformer in the Rhine Valley, who defended Emperor Henry IV in the Investiture Controversy and opposed Berengar of Tour's theory of the Eucharist. He was regarded locally as a saint, and it is to his biographer, Conrad, that we owe a few bits of biographical information about Bertha, including the observation that she "shone in the knowledge of literature."

See also Hagiography (Female Saints); Rules for Canonesses, Nuns, and Recluses

BIBLIOGRAPHY

Primary Source

[For a full list of editions of Bertha's work, see *Bibliotheca hagiographica latina*, no. 67. Brussels: Société des Bollandistes].

Bertha of Willich. *Vita s. Adalheidis.* In *Monumenta Germaniae historica, Scriptores in folio*, edited by Oswald Holder-Egger, 15: 755–63.

———. *Mater Spiritualis: The Life of Adelheid of Vilich.* Translated by Madelyn B. Dick. Toronto: Peregrina Publishing, 1994.

Secondary Sources

Manitius, Max. *Geschichte der lateinischen Literatur des Mittelalters*, 2: 469–70. First ed. Munich, 1911. Reprint Munich: Beck, 1976.

Schlafke, Jakob. "Leben und Verehrung der heiligen Adelheid von Villich." In *1000 Jahre Stift Villich 978–1978: Beiträge zu Geschichte und Gegenwart von Stift und Ort Villich*, edited by Dietrich Höroldt, 77–97. Bonn: Röhrscheid, 1978.

Worstbrock, Franz Josef. "Bertha von Vilich." *Die deutsche Literatur des Mittelalters Verfasserlexicon.* 2nd revised ed. by Kurt Ruh et al., 1: 800ff. Berlin and New York: Walter de Gruyter, 1978.

THOMAS HEAD

BERTHGYTH (mid- to late century). A third-generation member of Boniface's mission in Germany, Berthgyth (Anglo-Saxon = "Berhtgyth") composed passionate, spiritual letters in Latin. The Anglo-Saxon abbot of Nursling, Wynfrith (c.675–754), known as Boniface after 719 on moving to northern Germany, established a diocese based at Hessen with the commission of Pope Gregory II and some support from Charles Martel, king of the Franks. There he remained until his martyrdom in 754, actively recruiting assistants—many of whom were women—in his mission to convert the Germanic tribes. He founded churches and abbeys, most notably Fulda, introducing the traditions of Anglo-Saxon learning and Roman administrative methods in Germany. Since women played an important part in the religious aspect of Anglo-Saxon culture, Boniface infused this innovation into German monasticism by fostering the building of double monasteries in Germany to promote his educational and missionary aims. His activities and those of his male and female assistants are recorded in a series of letters, published collectively as the Boniface Collection, although they are found in six manuscripts.

One of the women writers represented in the Boniface Collection of greatest interest to modern readers is Berthgyth, who belonged to what might be called the third generation of the Boniface mission: the first generation having consisted of Boniface's English-based female associates, notably Egburg, while the second was comprised of women answering Boniface's invitation to his missionary work in Germany, among whom were Leoba and Berthgyth's mother Cynehild. Berthgyth's generation were women born or who at least received their religious education in Germany.

The few biographical details known about Berthgyth are provided by Otloh's eleventh-century *Life of St. Boniface*. Otloh recounts that the women members of Boniface's mission included Cynehild (maternal aunt of St. Lull, Boniface's successor) and her daughter Berthgyth, both educated in the liberal arts and therefore sent to head monasteries in Thuringia. It is difficult to judge Berthgyth's age or to date her letters; presumably, however, she was a contemporary of Lull, who died in 786. Peter Dronke has suggested that Berthgyth was born in the 740s and wrote her letters in the 770s. Christine Fell, however, believes that Berthgyth's letters should be dated after the death of Lull because they indicate that Berthgyth feels bereft of companionship. She believes that such a feeling would have been unlikely during the lifetime of Lull, Berthgyth's first cousin, given the importance of kinship among the Anglo-Saxons.

Berthgyth owes her writerly identity to two signed letters in the Boniface Collection; a third unsigned letter from a nun to her brother is usually attributed to her. The letters are to her "*fratri unico*" (only brother) Baldhard (d. 796), Abbot of Hersfeld, possibly active in missionary work himself. The letters are composed in good, if simple, Latin, clear in syntax and diction. Some are in *prosimetrum*, or poetically enhanced prose, marked by parallelism, assonance, and rhyme. Their use of rhymed and alliterative octosyllabic couplets recall the *carmen rhythmicum* (rhythmical/rhymed song) in the treatise *De metris* (*On Poetic Meter*) of the famous bishop Aldhelm (c.640–c.709), Boniface's predecessor as premier epistolary author in England, although Berthgyth indicates that she learned to write such poetry from her *magistra* (female teacher), evidence of a tradition of women writing poetry and teaching the art of metric composition.

Berthgyth's letters express her longing for a visit from her brother; they lament the fact that she is alone, without kindred, in a foreign country. The emotion expressed is plaintive and deeply personal, despite the stylized form of the letters. Dronke compares them to female-voiced or -authored vernacular songs, known as *Frauenlieder* [women's songs] or *winileodas* (friend's/lover's songs), and likens their expression of emotion to two Old English elegies, "The Wife's Lament" and "Wulf and Eadwacer." Fell also finds similarities between Berthgyth's letters and Old English poetry, but more in the poetry of exile, especially "The Wanderer," which expresses the exile's need for the help of God in the absence of earthly protectors.

As both literary works and historical documents, Berthgyth's letters reward closer study, as pioneered by Dronke and Fell. While exemplifying how effectively an educated woman could use the techniques of Aldhelm's *De Metris* when given the opportunity, they also afford a glimpse of the private emotions underlying the public life of a woman missionary in Germany.

See also Boniface, St., Mission and Circle of; Bugga; Double Monasteries; Egburg; *Frauenlied*; Leoba

BIBLIOGRAPHY

Primary Sources
Boniface, St. *Die Briefe des heilgen Bonifatius und Lullus.* Edited by Michael Tangl. *Monumenta Germaniae Historica: Epistolae Selectae,* 1. 2nd ed. Berlin: Weidmann, 1955.
————. *Epistolae merovingici et karolini aevi.* Edited by Ernst Ludwig Dümmler, vol. 1: 428–30. Berlin: Weidmann, 1891. Reprint, 1957.
————. *Sancti Bonifacii Epistolae. Codex Vindobonensis 751 des österreichischen Nationalbibliothek.* Edited by Franz Unterkircher. Graz, Austria: Akademische Druck und Verlagsanstalt, 1971. [Facsimile ed. of Vienna ms.].
————. *The English Correspondence of Saint Boniface.* Translated by Edward Kylie. New York: Cooper Square, 1966.
————. *The Letters of St. Boniface.* Translated by Ephraim Emerton. Records of Civilization, 31. New York: Columbia University Press, 1940. Reprint, New York: Octagon, 1973.
Otloh. *Life of St. Boniface.* In *Vitae Sancti Bonifatii,* edited by Wilhelm Levison. *Monumenta Germaniae Historica, Scriptores Rerum Germanicarum,* 57. Hannover and Leipzig, Germany: Hahn, 1905.

Secondary Sources
Dronke, Peter. *Women Writers of the Middle Ages: A Critical Study of Texts from Perpetua (†203) to Marguerite Porete (†1310).* Cambridge: Cambridge University Press, 1984.
Fell, Christine E. "Some Implications of the Boniface Correspondence." In *New Readings on Women in Old English Literature,* edited by Helen Damico and Alexandra Hennessey Olsen, 29–43. Bloomington: Indiana University Press, 1990.
————. "The Religious Life." In *Women in Anglo-Saxon England and the Impact of 1066,* edited by Christine Fell. Oxford: Basil Blackwell; Bloomington: Indiana University Press, 1984.

ALEXANDRA HENNESSEY OLSEN

BERTILLA, ST. *See* **Chelles, Nun of**

BERTKEN, SISTER/BERTA JACOBS (1426/27–1514). Recluse and Middle-Dutch mystical author, Berta Jacobs was born in Utrecht, the Netherlands, in 1426 or 1427 as the illegitimate child of a priest, Jacob of Lichtenberch, who belonged to a powerful Utrecht family. Her father was dean of the chapter of Saint Peter and from 1423 to 1425, vicar general of the diocese. When Bertken was about twenty-four years old, she entered the Utrecht convent of "Jerusalem" as a regular canoness, that is, as a semi-monastic female clergy member bound by a rule. This convent belonged to the congregation of Windesheim, which exerted a profound influence on monastic life in the Netherlands and in Germany during the later Middle Ages. In 1456 or 1457, she had herself immured in a cell, built at her own expense, on the south side of the choir of a church in Utrecht, the Buurkerk. There she lived for fifty-seven years, until her death on June 25, 1514. When, on the next day, she was buried in her cell amid great public interest, a bottle containing a short Latin biography was put in her coffin. As a number of copies and a Dutch translation from that time are still extant today, this biography constitutes our most important source of information about her exterior life.

Her writings were collected and published in two booklets not long after her death. The oldest edition known to us was published in 1516 by the Utrecht printer Jan Berntsz. Other editions were brought out soon after by Jan Seversz in Leyden and Willem Vorsterman in Antwerp. A manuscript from about 1480 attributes one song to her, which was not transmitted by print.

The first book, *Een seer devoet boecxken van die passie ons liefs heren Jhesu Christi tracterende* (*A Very Devout Booklet on the Passion of Our Lord Jesus Christ*), consists mainly in a series of Hours on the Passion. In this small work, one can distinguish three parts. The first part, the introduction, contains three meditations: the first about God's incarnation and his life on earth until the Last Supper, the second about the Last Supper itself with the washing of the feet, the third about Jesus's agony in the Garden of Gethsemane. Each meditation is followed by a prayer in which the soul—referring to Christ's treatment of, respectively, Mary Magdalene, the Canaanite, and the Samaritan woman—dares to ask him for mercy. Part 2, as it appears from the headings in the Leyden and Antwerp editions, consists in the Seven Canonical Hours (the seven prayer services dividing each day, from early morning throughout the night, in most Christian monasteries), during which the events of Christ's Passion are considered (Matins and Lauds—the capture, Prime—Jesus before Pilate and Herod, Terce—the flagellation, Sext—the crucifixion, None—the death on the cross, Vespers—the descent from the cross, and Compline—the entombment). Each of these meditations is followed by a prayer involving a confession and/or a mystical prayer. As in the Leyden and Antwerp editions, the last part of the introduction (1) is called an Hour ("the First Compline") as well, and because it also contains a confession and a mystical prayer in addition to the plea for mercy mentioned above, some scholars have assigned it to the middle part (2), so that in the end, one arrives at eight hours in total. Part 3 consists of a prayer, which concludes Bertken's Passion book.

The second work, *Suster Bertkens boeck dat sy selver gemaect ende bescreven heeft* (*Sister Bertken's Book, Made and Written by Herself*) consists of several rather heterogeneous texts: a short prayer to Jesus; a preparation and a thanksgiving for Holy Communion; a meditation on Jesus's Passion, followed by a prayer; a treatise on Christmas Eve; a mystical dialogue between the loving soul and her beloved Bridegroom Jesus, greatly inspired by the Song of Songs; finally, eight songs, among which the allegorical poem in fourteen distichs "Ic was in mijn hoofkijn om cruyt gegaen" ("I went to my small garden for herbs") has become a classic.

Best known among Bertken's prose writings is her "Tractaet vander Kersnacht" ("Treatise on Christmas Eve"), perhaps inspired by a vision. It shows some influence of Birgitta of Sweden's Christmas vision and has some resemblances with two other Middle-Dutch prose-works: a Christmas vision by the Windesheim male mystic Hendrik Mande (c.1360–1431) and an anonymous vision in a manuscript from the sixteenth century. It is comprised of two individual parts. The first part describes the inner experiences of Mary at the Nativity, and is very carefully structured. It shows how, before Jesus's birth, the Virgin goes through three phases (burning desire, ecstatic jubilation, *unio mystica* [mystical union]), which, after the supreme moment of the Nativity, come back in reverse order, so that from heavenly experience, Mary is gradually brought back to earthly reality. This tripartition bears a striking resemblance to the structure of Hadewijch's visions. The influence of the Middle-Dutch mystical tradition and of contemporary mystical writings is evident in the important role attributed to the Holy Trinity and from the parallelism presented between the Nativity and the birth of Christ within the soul. The second part then describes Joseph's strange experiences outside the room in which the Nativity takes place. Thus, the same event is now described from without, and from a more "earthly" point of view. The marvel Joseph sees—an annex burning without being consumed—refers to Moses and the burning bush, traditionally interpreted in medieval exegesis as a prefiguration of Mary's virgin motherhood. By this miracle, Jesus's foster father is not only convinced of Mary's divine election, but he is also presented as a venerable figure. So, this part of the treatise can be interpreted as a kind of rehabilitation of Joseph, in later medieval literature too often depicted as a ridiculous cuckold.

Although the size of Bertken's output is rather small, she must be considered as one of the most interesting mystical authors of the Low Countries. Her oeuvre, however, still awaits a thorough study of her sources and comparative analysis with the works of other mystics of the later Middle Ages.

See also Bake, Alijt; Beatrijs van Nazareth/van Tienen; Birgitta of Sweden, St.; Bride of Christ/Brautmystik; Hadewijch; Rules for Canonesses, Nuns, and Recluses

BIBLIOGRAPHY

Primary Sources

Bertken, Sister. *Een boecxken gemaket van suster Bertken die LVII iaren besloten heeft gheseten tot Utrecht in dye buerkercke, naar den Leidschen druk van Jan Seversen opnieuw uitgegeven met aanteekeningen en een inleiding door Joh.a Snellen.* Herdrukken van de Maatschappij der Nederlandsche Letterkunde, 3. Utrecht, Netherlands: Oosthoek, 1924.

———. *Een boecxken gemaket ende bescreven van suster Bertken die lvij iaren besloten heeft gheseten tot Utrecht in die buerkercke, naar de eerste uitgave van Jan Berntsz. Utrecht 1516.* Edited with an introduction and notes by C. Catharina van de Graft. Zwolse drukken en herdrukken van de Maatschappij der Nederlandse Letterkunde te Leiden, 9. Zwolle, Netherlands: Tjeenk Willink, 1955.

———. *Een boecxken van dye passie ons liefs heeren.* Leiden, Netherlands: Jan Seversz, c.1515.

———. *Suster Bertken. Twee bij Jan Seversz in Leiden verschenen boekjes ('s-Gravenhage, Koninklijke Bibliotheek, 227 G 46).* Introduction by A. M. J. van Buuren. Utrecht: UTI, 1989. [Facsimile ed. of above with notes].

———. [Translations, English] "Poetry from behind Bars: Some Translations from the Dutch Recluse Sister Bertken (1427–1514)." Translated by H. Vynckier. *Mystics Quarterly* 14 (1988): 143–53.

Secondary Sources

Ampe, Albert. "De geschriften van Sister Bertken." *Ons Geestelijk Erf* 30 (1956): 281–320.

———. "Nog eens de geschriften van Zuster Bertken." *Handelingen Koninklijke Zuidnederlandse Maatschappij voor Taal- en Letterkunde en Geschiedenis* 14 (1960): 9–46.

Meeuwesse, Karel. "Zuster Bertkens passieboekje." In *Dancwerc. Opstellen aangeboden aan prof. dr. D. Th. Enklaar ter gelegenheid van zijn vijfenzestigste verjaardag,* 208–21. Groningen: Wolters, 1959.

De Jong, Martien J. G. "Het kerstvisioen van Zuster Bertken." In De Jong, *Vrede ende vrolicheyt. Kerstfeest in de middeleeuwen,* 214–55. Baarn: de Prom, 1985. [With an edition and translation of the treatise into Modern Dutch].

Heeroma, Klaas. "Het ingekluisde lied." In Heeroma, *Spelend met de spelgenoten. Middelnederlandse leesavonturen.* Fakulteitenreeks, 12, 256–76. The Hague: Bert Bakker/Daamen, 1969.

Van Aelst, J. J. "'Geordineert na dye getijden.' Suster Bertkens passieboekje." *Ons Geestelijk Erf* 69 (1995): 133–56.

Van Buuren, A. M. J. " 'Nu hoert ic sal enen nyen sanc beginnen.' Een lied van Suster Bertken." *De Nieuwe Taalgids* 83 (1990): 212–23.

———. " 'Jhesus, den ic vercoren heb boven al dat ye gewert.' Een lied van Suster Bertken," In *Tegendraads Genot.* Opstellen over de kwaliteit van middeleeuwse teksten, edited by Karel Porteman, Werner Verbeke, Frank Willaert, 149–60. Louvain: Peeters, 1996.

FRANK WILLAERT

BESTIAIRE D'AMOUR (RICHARD DE FOURNIVAL), ANONYMOUS RESPONSE TO. *See Response du Bestiaire*

BIETRIS DE ROMAN (late 13th century). Bietris de Roman was a woman troubadour (*trobairitz*) of Provence; she is also called Bieris, Beatritz, and in manuscripts, "Na Bietris" ("na" = short for *Domna* or *Domina* = Lady). Nothing is known of her life. Like another troubadour, Falquet de Romans, she may have been a native of Romans-sur-Isère, near Montélimar, in what is now la Drôme, in southern France. No other poet alludes to her by name.

The only surviving composition attributed to her, "Na Maria, pretz e fina valors" ("Lady Maria, the virtue and pure worth"), has been frequently discussed. It may be the sole extant example of a medieval love poem written in the vernacular by one woman to another. Confronted with this problematic text, one critic contended that the author's name should be read as N'Alberis, as the feminine counterpart of Alberico da Romano, an Italian troubadour of the thirteenth century (see Zufferey; Rieger). Others have tried to identify the addressee as the Virgin Mary, thus allowing for a mystical interpretation. But "Na Maria, pretz e fina valors" contains a number of amorous *topoi* (commonplaces, motifs) quite consistent in tone and style with the classical courtly lyric in expressing both admiration and longing, besides warning the recipient against false lovers. In fact, the same formula might well have been used by a male troubadour hiding behind the female pseudonym—the choice of which might be construed as reflecting his esteem for all women—while composing a rather conventional piece. Indeed, the text presents no specifically feminine features, or "textual femininity." If a woman did truly write it ("generic femininity"), speculation nevertheless remains open. For the poem does not permit for any certainty about what the reader is witnessing: a typical display of feminine emotion, but without any erotic overtones. Are we to read this as an exceptional homoerotic relationship (Bec), or merely as a poem expressing "entirely normal, even conventional" affection between women of equal social rank and good manners (Rieger 1989)? Perhaps we are to read it as a provocative and/or playful counter-text superficially respecting the literary code to break all the more with the broader cultural model.

See also Lesbians in the Middle Ages; *Trobairitz*

BIBLIOGRAPHY

Primary Sources

Bietris de Roman. "Na Maria, pretz e fina valors." In *Songs of the Women Troubadours*, edited and translated by Matilda Tomaryn Bruckner, Laurie Shepard, and Sarah White, esp. 32–34. New York: Garland, 1995. Revised ed., 2000.

95

————. In *Trobairitz: Der Beitrag der Frau in der altokzitanischen höfischen Lyrik. Edition des Gesamtkorpus*, edited by Angelica Rieger. Beihefte zur Zeitschrift für romanische Philologie, 233. Tübingen: Max Niemeyer Verlag, 1991.

Secondary Sources

Bec, Pierre. *Burlesque et obscénité chez les troubadours: Le contre-texte au moyen âge.* Paris: Stock, 1984.

Nelli, René. *Écrivains anticonformistes au moyen-âge occitan. Anthologie bilingue. 1: La Femme et l'amour.* Paris: Phébus, 1977.

Rieger, Angelica. "Was Bieris de Romans Lesbian? Women's relations with Each Other in the World of the Troubadours." *The Voice of the Trobairitz: Perspectives on the Women Troubadours*, edited by William D. Paden, 73–94. Philadelphia: University of Pennsylvania Press, 1989.

Zufferey, François. "Toward a Delimitation of the Trobairitz Corpus." In *The Voice of the Trobairitz: Perspectives on the Women Troubadours*, edited by William D. Paden, 31–43. *See above entry.*

HERMAN BRAET

BIRGITTA OF SWEDEN, ST. (1303–1373). One of the most extraordinary figures of the Catholic Church, Birgitta authored an influential book of revelations, sermons, and prayers, and was the founder of the Birgittine (Bridgettine) Order. The daughter of Birger Persson, governor and provincial judge of Uppland, central Sweden, and Ingeborg Bengtsdotter, Birgitta (also called Brigida, Brigritta) was born in Finsta Castle near Uppland, the youngest of seven children. After her mother died in 1314, Birgitta's father sent her to live with her maternal aunt and godmother, Karin Bengtsdotter, who was entrusted with the child's education and upbringing. Two years later, in 1316, at barely fourteen years of age and in deference to paternal authority, Birgitta agreed to marry Ulf Gudmarsson, an eighteen-year-old prince who then took his bride to live with him luxuriously in the castle of Ulfasa.

Although we can only theorize about the impact of her mother's untimely death on her spiritual development, we can certainly divide Birgitta's religious life into two distinct periods: the first preceding and the second following the death of her husband in 1344. This transformation derived from Birgitta's attitude toward her virginity and not out of dislike for her husband. In fact, counter to conventional expectations, Ulf seems to have indulged, and then eventually assimilated, his bride's saintly tendencies to an impressive degree. Hence, during her first year or more of matrimony, she convinced her husband to postpone consummation and pray instead. When they finally did engage in intercourse, it was only after promising God in their prayers that it would be without lust and sensual pleasure and that their children, eventually eight in all, born between 1319 and c.1334, would become as devout as their parents. Along with rearing their children and running an extensive household, she also supervised a small charitable hospital near the castle. Of their four girls and four boys (a gender distribution remarkably close to that of Birgitta and her own siblings: three boys and four girls), second daughter Karin, or Katarina, would achieve spiritual renown in her own right as St. Catherine of Sweden. Cecilia, Birgitta's youngest, would become a nun dedicated by her mother, only to flee the convent to marry, with the help of her brother Karl.

The years 1335 through 1339 saw Birgitta living and serving at the royal court, at the behest of the new king Magnus Eriksson, as tutor and lady in waiting to his bride, Blanche of Namur. But the young queen turned out to be frivolous and an unrewarding pupil, and Birgitta finally resigned to join her husband on a pilgrimage to Santiago de Campostella in

1341. The momentous spiritual effect of this long journey, together with early signs of Ulf's fatal illness en route through Arras, soon resulted in the couple's decision to embrace monastic life: Ulf took steps to enter the Cistercian monastery of Alvastra in 1342, only to die in 1344. Birgitta took up residence in a building attached to the monastery. Dyan Elliott notes the difference between each spouse's commitment to chastity: whereas Birgitta viewed her sexual abstinence/activity/abstinence cycle as informing her salvation history in response to personal-devotional versus marital, then religious vows, Ulf "agreed to chastity only after the marriage had produced eight children and his health had failed him on return from Santiago de Campostella." As pilgrims, they also had taken a vow of chastity. Before dying, Ulf placed a ring on his wife's finger as a symbol of his eternal love. Soon after his death, however, she removed the ring since she wished to bury with her husband all traces of carnal love. This erasure, however, does not include her children, for as Jeannette Nieuwland emphasizes, Birgitta managed to incorporate motherhood within her personal scheme of sanctity, following the Virgin Mary's example. Indeed, holy motherhood formed part of her larger accomplishment of living very full secular and spiritual lives, with each complimenting the other, as reflected in her written revelations.

Losing her husband liberated her to fulfill herself as an ascetic visionary. The years between 1344 and 1346 were marked by profound religious introspection and intense meditation on the Passion of Christ and on the Compassion of the Virgin. While praying in her cell at Alvastra in 1345, she experienced her first visions of Christ that would lead her to an intensely mystical illumination throughout the rest of her life. Having given away most of her material possessions, Birgitta also decided to found a new religious order of men and women dedicated to the cult of the Passion of Christ and the Compassion of His mother. As Birgitta herself notes in the eighth book of her *Revelaciones* (*Revelations*), the rule of the new order was dictated to her in a vision by Christ, specifying, for example, that the women's habit would carry the distinguishing emblem of five red flames arranged in a crown-like form on their veil; the men would wear the red flames on their capes. After she had convinced the Swedish bishops of the authenticity of her visions, the bishops helped her to gain the king's support. He granted her the old castle at Vadstena, on the shores of Vattern Lake, as the site of the Birgittine convent. Not content simply to approach the king for the sake of her order, she also had a delegation of bishops convey strong messages to the pope in Avignon urging him to return to Rome and intervene in the Hundred Years War. They may well have taken a copy of the Birgittine Rule to the pope for his approval. But because she had also instigated a crusade that failed against pagans in southern Sweden, she lost the royal support, and even that of her confessor St. Mattias of Linköping, so carefully cultivated by her. With the aid of another consoling, guiding vision of Christ, Birgitta thus decided to visit Rome herself (1349–1350), await the pope's return and to try to secure the approval of her order by the Holy See. While in Rome, she spent her time at daily prayer, in works of mercy, penance, and study, including learning Latin—all intended to honor the Passion of Christ. She also undertook visits to several shrines including Assisi, Benevento, Salerno, and Bari. She continued to pester various popes, saying that Christ commanded them to return to Rome, which Pope Urban V did do in 1367. The pope also sanctioned her new order in 1370, stipulating that it be placed under the Rule of Augustine. Yet to her dismay, Urban, unable to tolerate Italy's political unrest, moved back to Avignon that same year. Birgitta then began preparations for the final pilgrimage of her life, a visit to the Holy Land, which she began in the spring of 1372, reaching Jerusalem on May 13, 1372.

On her return from such a demanding journey, Birgitta died in Rome on June 23, 1373, without having returned to her homeland to witness her convent's inauguration at Vadstena. It would nonetheless go on to become the most important medieval cloister in Sweden. Her relics were first interred at the church of the Poor Clares of Viminal in Rome, and then finally transported mostly to Vadstena in 1374. They were later joined by those of her daughter Catherine and Master Peter. Her few other remnants are at Stockholm, Rome, and, more doubtfully, France, according to Bygden's study.

St. Birgitta's most important writing is the *Revelaciones*, recording the approximately 600 visions and voices experienced by her in periods of mystical ecstasy. Beginning with her time in Alvastra around the time of her husband's death, the cycle of revelations reflect her Italo-Roman sojourn, her various pilgrimages, and those connected with the Passion of Christ and the Life of the Virgin. Written originally in Swedish as the *Uppenbarelser*, they were then translated into Latin mostly by Prior Peter, a Cistercian monk at Alvastra and other confessors, although, according to her *vita*, or life story, she always read over the transcribed text herself at the end of each session. After Birgitta's death, as dictated by another vision of Christ, her friend and confessor Bishop Alfons of Jaén edited her complete works, referring to her as "apostola et prophetissa Dei." The *editio princeps* (first edition) of 1492 grouped the *Revelaciones* into eight books. To the *Revelaciones* proper were added a supplementary collection called *Revelaciones Extravagantes*, the *Regula Sancti Salvatoris* (*Rule of the Holy Savior*)—the rule of her order—and, with her confessor, Master Peter Olovsson, the *Sermo Angelicus de excellentia Beatae Mariae Virginis* (*Angelic Sermon on the Excellence of the Blessed Virgin*) adapted for liturgical use in the daily services in the Birgittine convent. She also composed four prayers (*Quattuor oraciones*). Several versions of her biography have been compiled from contemporary sources as supporting documentation justifying her canonization, decreed by Boniface IX, on October 8, 1391. October 8 is now her feast day.

Birgitta's book of revelations, replete with biblical imagery (Piltz) and echoes of Albertus Magnus and others, so captivated the devout public that the great English mystic Margery Kempe would pattern her work on it competitively, as G. Cleve has analyzed. Further, if negative, testimony to its power can be found in the famous French theologian Jean Gerson's mistrust of these revelations and those of other female mystics, except for Joan of Arc, as Caroline Bynum reminds us.

See also Celibacy; Childhood and Child-Rearing in the Middle Ages; Convents; Dorothea of Montau, St.; Hildegard of Bingen, St.; Joan of Arc, St.; Kempe, Margery; Rules for Canonesses, Nuns, and Recluses; Widows

BIBLIOGRAPHY

Primary Sources
Acta et Processus Canonizacionis beate Birgitte. Edited by Isak Collijn. Samlingar utgivna av Svenska Fornskriftsällskapet, ser. 2, Latinska skrifter 1. Stockholm: Almqvist & Wiksell, 1924–1931. [Her canonization from mss. from Stockholm (Kungliga), Vatican (Ottobonensis) and London (British Library/Harley) manuscripts; includes *Vita* of Birgitta by Master Peter and Prior Peter].
Sancta Birgitta. *Opera minora*: 1. *Regula salvatoris*; 2. *Sermo angelicus*; 3. *Quattuor oraciones*. Edited by Sten Eklund. 3 vols. Samlingar utgivna av Svenska Fornskriftsällskapet, ser. 2, Latinska skrifter, 8: 1–3. Stockholm/Uppsala: Almqvist & Wiksell, 1972–1977.
———. *Revelaciones, Liber I*. Edited by Carl-Gustaf Undhagen. Samlingar utgivna av Svenska Fornskriftsällskapet, ser.2, Latinska skrifter 7: 1. Stockholm: Almqvist & Wiksell, 1977.

———. *Revelationes Sanctae Birgittae, olim a Card. Turrecremata. . . .* Antwerp, Belgium: Petrus Bellerus, 1611. [For ed. of Books 2, 3, and 8].

———. *Revelaciones, Liber IV.* Edited by Hans Aili. Samlingar utgivna av Svenska Fornskriftsällskapet, ser.2, Latinska skrifter, 7: 4. Stockholm: Almqvist & Wiksell, 1992.

———. *Revelaciones, Liber V: Liber Questionum.* Edited by Birger Bergh. Samlingar utgivna av Svenska Fornskriftsällskapet, ser.2, Latinska skrifter 7: 5. Uppsala: Almqvist & Wiksell, 1971.

———. *Revelaciones, Liber VI.* Edited by Birger Bergh. Samlingar utgivna av Svenska Fornskriftsällskapet, ser. 2, Latinska skrifter 7: 6. Stockholm: Almqvist & Wiksell, 1991.

———. *Revelaciones, Liber VII.* Edited by Birger Bergh. Samlingar utgivna av Svenska Fornskriftsällskapet, ser.2, Latinska skrifter 7: 7. Uppsala: Almqvist & Wiksell, 1967.

———. *Revelaciones Extravagantes.* Edited by Lennart Hollman. Samlingar utgivna av Svenska Fornskriftsällskapet, ser. 2, Latinska skrifter 5. Uppsala: Almqvist & Wiksell, 1956.

———. *Birgitta of Sweden: Life and Selected Revelations.* Edited by Marguerite T. Harris. Translated with notes by Albert Kezel. Introduction by Tore Nyberg. New York: Paulist Press, 1990. [Books 5, 7, Four Prayers; *Life* by Prior Peter and Master Peter].

———. *Saint Bride and Her Book: Bridget of Sweden's Revelations.* Translated and edited by Julia B. Holloway. Focus Library of Medieval Women. Newburyport, Mass.: Focus Press, 1992. Reprint Woodbridge, Suffolk, U.K and Rochester, N.Y.: D. S. Brewer, 2000. [Based on a Middle-English version].

Gerson, Jean. *De examinatione doctrinarum.* In *Joannis Gerson . . . Opera omnia,* edited by Ellies Dupin, 1:14–26. 5 vols. Antwerp, 1706.

Secondary Sources

Atkinson, Clarissa. *The Oldest Vocation: Christian Motherhood in the Middle Ages.* Ithaca and London: Cornell University Press, 1991.

Børreson, Kari E. "Birgitta's Godlanguage: Exemplary Intention, Inapplicable Content." In Nyberg, *see below.*

Bygden, A., N. Gejvall, and C.-H. Hjortsö. *Les Reliques de Sainte Brigitte de Suède: Examen médico-anthropologique et historique.* [Offprint from *Bulletin de la Société royale des lettres de Lund* 3 (1953–1954): 93–228]. Lund: Gleerup, 1954.

Bynum, Caroline W. *Holy Feast and Holy Fast: The Religious Significance of Food to Medieval Women.* Berkeley: University of California Press, 1987.

Cleve, G. "Margery Kempe: a Scandinavian Influence in Medieval England?" In *The Medieval Mystical Tradition in England,* edited by Marion Glasscoe, 163–78. Woodbridge, Suffolk, U.K.: D. S. Brewer, 1992.

Elliott, Dyan. *Spiritual Marriage: Sexual Abstinence in Medieval Wedlock.* Princeton, N.J.: Princeton University Press, 1993.

Fraioli, Deborah A. *Joan of Arc: The Early Debate.* Woodbridge, Suffolk, U.K., and Rochester, N.Y.: Boydell Press, 2000.

Nieuwland, Jeannette. "Motherhood and Sanctity in the Life of Saint Birgitta of Sweden: An Insoluble Conflict?" In *Sanctity and Motherhood: Essays on Holy Mothers in the Middle Ages,* edited by Anneke B. Mulder-Bakker. New York and London: Garland, 1995. [Excellent notes and analysis].

Nyberg, Tore, ed. *Birgitta: Hendes vaerk og hendes klostre i Noren.* Odense Studies in History and Social Science,150. Odense, Denmark: Odense Universiteitsforlag, 1991.

Opitz, Claudia. *Frauenalltag im Mittelalter: Biographien des 13. und 14. Jahrhunderts.* Ergebnisse der Frauenforschung, 5. Weinheim, Germany: Beltz, 1987.

Piltz, Anders. "Uppenbarelserna och uppenbarelsen: Birgittas förhållande tell bibeln." In Nyberg, *see above.*

Redpath, Helen M. D. *God's Ambassadress: St. Bridget of Sweden.* Milwaukee, Wisc.: Bruce, 1947.

Voaden, Rosalynn. *God's Words, Women's Voices: The Discernment of Spirits in the Writing of Late-Medieval Women Visionaries.* Woodbridge, Suffolk, U.K. and Rochester, N.Y.: University of York Medieval Press/Boydell Press, 1999.

Warner, Marina. *Alone of All Her Sex: The Myth and the Cult of the Virgin Mary.* London: Weidenfeld & Nicolson; New York: Alfred Knopf, 1976.

SANDRO STICCA

BIZZOCHE (13th–14th centuries). The *bizzoche* (sing.: *bizzocha*) were Italian counterparts to the beguines of France, Germany, and the Lowlands. These laywomen led religious lives of poverty and chastity, either communally in a *bizzocheria* (similar to French *béguinage*) or in their own homes, yet without taking monastic vows and without being enclosed in a monastery. They appear to have burst forth, almost mysteriously, from out of the female penitential movement, the same new energy generating the Mendicant (begging) Orders of Franciscans, such as Saints Francis and Clare, and Dominicans, in the early thirteenth century. Concomitantly, the growth of medieval cities produced a surge in urban eremitism (eremites = recluses), drawing its members primarily from the unmarried virgins or widowed aristocracy and lesser nobility. The *bizzoche*'s free agency away from the cloister and growing popularity disturbed Church officials who feared not being able to control them, all the more so because they preached a direct relationship to God through meditation on Christ's Passion without the Church's mediation.

Spreading throughout many Italian towns as wandering beggars preaching the Gospel, the *bizzoche* were often confused with the *pinzochere*, a contemporary Italian penitential group who did take vows and wear a habit but lived in their own homes. Some prominent *bizzoche* convents and cells were in Montefalco, Foligno, Spoleto, and in Perugia. The Second Council of Lyons (1274) expressed concern for their chastity, given their wandering, uncloistered ways, and the potentially heretical nature of their teachings. The Franciscans and Dominicans tried to bring them under Church control (and protection) by giving them rules by which to govern their communities, so as to absorb them into the Church hierarchy as Third Orders (First and Second Orders being enclosed orders of monks and nuns, respectively), especially after the papal decree of *Periculoso* (1298) and a bull, *Apostolicae sedis* (1309), ordering the perpetual enclosure of all nuns. During the fourteenth century, the Third Orders, which did not impose enclosure except on their "regular" (living by rule) branches, provided an effective outlet for the energy driving the *bizzoche*, who continue to manifest themselves to this day.

See also Ancrene Riwle; Angela of Foligno, Blessed; Beguines; Clare of Assisi, St; Clare of Montefalco, St.; Convents; *Mulieres Sanctae*; *Periculoso*; *Pinzochere*; Rules for Canonesses, Nuns, and Recluses

BIBLIOGRAPHY
Guarnieri, Romana. "Pinzochere." In *Dizionario degli Istituti della Perfezione*, edited by Guerrino Pelliccia and Giancarlo Rocca, 6: 1721–49. Rome: Edizione Paoline, 1980.
Sensi, Mario. "Anchoresses and Penitents in Thirteenth- and Fourteenth-Century Umbria." In *Women and Religion in Medieval and Renaissance Italy*, edited by Daniel Bornstein and Roberto Rusconi, 56–83. Translated by Margery J. Schneider. Chicago: University of Chicago Press, 1996. Original *Mistiche e devote nell'Italia tardomedievale*. Naples: Liguori, 1992.

NADIA MARGOLIS

BLANCHE OF CASTILE (1188–1252). Queen and regent of France, mother of Louis IX, Blanche was the daughter of Alfonso VIII, king of Castile, and Eleanor of England. At the age of twelve, she was married to the French prince Louis, whose brief reign as Louis VIII (1223–1226) ended with his death during the Albigensian Crusade, the longstanding holy war against politically rebellious and heretical lords of southern France. Because the eldest of the royal couple's four sons, Louis IX, was still in his minority when the king died, Blanche was appointed regent. She continued to exert a strong influence in the political and religious life of France even after her son ascended to the throne.

According to the chroniclers of the period, his mother's piety contributed greatly to the education of the future Louis IX, St. Louis (1215–1270). Blanche was renowned for her charitable works and her endowment of religious houses, especially those of the Cistercians. Her reputation as a protector of the poor helped the royal family gain popular support. In some cases, she even appears to have favored the causes of the lower classes over those of the Church. For example, a contemporary anecdote recounts that the queen intervened personally to free a large group of peasants who had been imprisoned for refusing to pay a special tax levied by the cathedral chapter of Paris. Blanche's charity also extended to the Jews, as when Louis IX, influenced by Franciscan advisers, authorized the burning of the Talmud in 1240–1248, she demonstrated tolerance toward the Jewish delegation that came to court to plead against Louis's hostile policy.

Blanche proved to be a shrewd and capable ruler. During the early years of her regency, she managed to quell armed rebellions against her regency fomented both by barons in northern France and the Albigensian lords of Languedoc, in the south. The recently widowed queen maintained a network of alliances with powerful noble houses, but steered away from a second marriage that would ally her too closely with one faction. Her tenacious policies held the threat of English incursions into northern French territory, especially Normandy, in check and pursued neutrality in the conflicts between the papacy and the German emperors erupting on France's eastern borders.

Adenet le Roi, poet, musician, and minstrel recites *Roman de Cleomades* before Mathlide of Brabant and Queen Blanche of Castile. © The Art Archive.

Louis took on more of the duties of government after his marriage to Marguerite of Provence, a match that his mother helped to arrange when he turned twenty-one. Blanche did not willingly cede power to either her son or daughter-in-law, however, with both women disliking each other. In 1248 Louis IX, having vowed to participate in the Crusades, set out on an ill-fated expedition to the Holy Land, leaving the affairs of state once again in the queen mother's care. Blanche initially opposed his decision for reasons that continue to perplex historians, yet she proved instrumental in financing her son's troops. After he was captured in Egypt and held for ransom, she raised money by negotiating with Church officials in Paris to extend their payments of the clerical tax. Blanche was equally resolute in her dealings with the papacy; she vigorously rejected the ambitions of Pope Innocent IV to redirect the crusading forces against the German

Conrad IV (Hohenstaufen), king of Germany, Sicily, and Jerusalem, by threatening French knights with exile if they joined the papal forces.

Toward the end of her life, despite her diminishing overall involvement in government since Louis's marriage, Blanche acted decisively to protect the claim of another son, Alphonse, to succeed as count of Toulouse in 1249, and against riots led by peasants from northern France and Flanders entering Paris, proclaiming themselves a crusade in support of the king. Although she had originally been well disposed toward these *Pastoureaux* ("Shepherds"), as they were called, in 1251, the violence wrought by several of their groups caused her to order suppression of the movement. The news of her death in November 1252 did not reach Louis, still engaged in military campaigns in the Holy Land, until months after the fact. His resultant, almost paralyzing grief, plus the absence of Blanche's firm, competent hand in government, allowed stability to give way to a period of chaos in France.

See also Dower; Jewish Women in the Middle Ages

BIBLIOGRAPHY

Primary Sources
Christine de Pizan. *Livre de la Cité des Dames* (1: 13.2 and 2: 65.1). Edited by E. J. Richards. Introduction and Italian translation by Patrizia Caraffi. 2nd ed. Milan: Luni, 1998.
———. *The Book of the City of Ladies*. Translated by E. J. Richards. Foreword by Natalie Z. Davis. 2nd rev. ed. New York: Persea, 1998. [pp. 34, 207–08].
———. *The Book of the City of Ladies*. Translated with notes by Rosalind Brown-Grant. London and New York: Penguin, 1999. [See pp. 32, 191–92].
Joinville, Jean, Sire de. *Histoire de Saint Louis*. Edited by Natalis de Wailly. Paris: Adrien Le Clerc, 1867.
Paris, Matthew. *Chronica majora*. Edited by Henry R. Luard. 7 vols. London: Longmans, 1872–83. [Esp. vols. 3–5].
———. *Chronicles of Matthew Paris: Observations of Thirteenth-Century Life*. Edited and translated by Richard Vaughan. Gloucester, U.K.: A. Sutton; New York: St. Martin's, 1984. Reprint, 1993.
Psautier de Saint Louis et de Blanche de Castille; 50 planches reproduisant les miniatures, initiales, etc., du manuscrit 1186 de la Bibliothèque de l'Arsenal. Paris: Impr. Berthaud frères, 1909. [Reproduction of the psalter supposedly made for Blanche and owned by Louis, also on Web site: gallery.euroweb.hu/html/zgothic/miniatur/1200-250/03f_1200.html].

Secondary Sources
Bertrand, René. *La France de Blanche de Castille*. Paris: Robert Laffont, 1977.
Decaux, Alain. *Histoire des Françaises*. 2 vols. Paris: Perrin, 1972.
Delorme, Philippe. *Blanche de Castille: épouse de Louis VIII, mère de Saint Louis*. Histoire des reines de France. Paris: Pygmalion, 2002.
Heer, Friedrich. *The Medieval World: Europe, 1100–1350*. Translated by Janet Sondheimer. New York: Praeger; London: Weidenfeld & Nicolson, 1962.
Jordan, William C. "Blanche of Castile." In *Medieval France: An Encyclopedia*, edited by William W. Kibler and Grover A. Zinn. New York and London: Garland, 1995.
———. *Louis IX and the Challenge of the Crusade: A Study in Rulership*. Princeton, N.J.: Princeton University Press, 1979.
Lehmann, Andrée. *Le Rôle de la Femme dans l'histoire de France au Moyen âge*. Paris: Berger-Levrault, 1952.
Nelson, Janet L. "Medieval Queenship." In *Women in Medieval Western European Culture*, edited by Linda E. Mitchell, 179–208. Garland Reference Library of the Humanities, 2007. New York and London: Garland, 1999.
Pernoud, Régine. *La Reine Blanche*. Paris: Albin Michel, 1972.
Sivéry, Gérard. *Blanche de Castille*. Paris: Fayard, 1990.

DIANA L. MURPHY

BOCCACCIO, WOMEN IN, *DE CLARIS MULIERIBUS*

(c.1362–1375). Giovanni Boccaccio (1313–1375), one of the three great Italian poets of his time (along with Dante and Petrarch), produced significant works for the history of, and attitudes toward, women. Chief among these were his two catalogues: the *De claris mulieribus* (*Famous Women*), and, to a lesser extent, the *De casibus virorum illustrium* (*The Fates of Illustrious Men*; 1355–1360), in that the latter mainly includes men's lives, with some women's lives. These works belong to an old tradition of exemplary biography for public edification fostered in ancient literature, ranging from Old Testament books of courageous women Ruth and Esther, to the ancient (eighth century B.C.E.) Greek historian Hesiod, and epic poet Homer in his *Iliad* and *Odyssey*, to their Roman incarnations, like Ovid's first-century B.C.E. *Heroides* (imagined poetic love letters between heroes and heroines) and Virgil's epic for the Roman republic, the *Aeneid* (19 B.C.E.). With the classical-humanistic rediscovery of Greek and Latin literature came the recultivation of enumerative genres like the catalogue

Four scenes from a Middle-French version of Boccaccio's *De Claris Mulieribus*. *Left to right*: Boccaccio writing, presenting his book, a messenger presenting a letter to a woman who is combing her hair, and a queen with four attendants playing musical instruments. Artist unknown, c.1400-1425. © The British Library/Topham-HIP/The Image Works.

or pantheon, and florilegium (anthology), in the Middle Ages and Renaissance, as a way toward recapturing the glory of these past civilizations. Since one of the achievements of Boccaccio's early Renaissance culture was to reconcile the best of pagan antiquity and Christianity for the betterment of secular civic life, his biographies were taken from among nonsaints as well as saints, thereby contributing a secular hagiography to balance and complement the religious saints' lives.

Another phase to be considered in the evolution of catalogues of women leading to Boccaccio's is that of double-edged encomium/invective. That is, the tradition of authors purporting to defame women or defend them, with equal insincerity, as a sort of satirical game. St. Jerome's fourth-century catalogue, the *Adversus Jovinianum* (*Against Jovinian*), was highly influential as a model of both form (catalogue) and satirical style for the Middle Ages. Jerome, the famous Latin translator of the Bible, launched his catalogue with the pretext of rebutting one Jovinian, a heretical monk whose tract revaluing the vices and virtues on an equal plane, and decrying chastity as unnatural, has been lost to modern times, and scholars continue to debate the seriousness of Jerome's intent in his misogynistic argument. The irreverent French scholastic Jean de Meun, in his continuation (c.1275) of the early-thirteenth-century *Roman de la Rose* (*Romance of the Rose*) and Boccaccio show themselves to have inherited this learned, yet tongue-in-cheek polemical style: it is difficult to see where they actually stand but the reader becomes at once enlightened and entertained in trying to determine these authors' positions.

Boccaccio's *De claris mulieribus*, one of the first medieval compilations of famous women's lives, served as a reference book and literary model. Its portrayal of feminine nature and reintroduction of the learned catalogue genre from Classical Antiquity made it a standard reference work for scholars who valued the wealth of information presented in convenient form. Its idea of woman was transmitted all over Western Europe, a textual transmission guaranteeing the catalogue's importance for the tradition known as the *querelle des femmes*, or "quarrel about women," which apparently began with Christine de Pizan (1364/5–1430?), a disgruntled (because of his tone) but admiring (because of his work's potential) reader of Boccaccio, and continued into the intellectual-literary salons of the seventeenth and eighteenth centuries, especially in France. Yet, until recently, this work was seldom studied or even read, especially in comparison to Boccaccio's masterpiece, a compendium of one hundred tales in Italian known as the *Decameron* (c.1351–1353), in which several scholars have examined a connection to the *De mulieribus*; indeed, Christine de Pizan, for example, used both as sources for her *Livre de la Cité des dames* (*Book of the City of Ladies*) of 1404–1405.

De claris mulieribus belongs to Boccaccio's later career, which was devoted to producing scholarly Latin compilations on learned subjects. Completed from between 1361/2 and 1375 in nine separate editorial stages, its most direct inspiration was the catalogue of famous men, *De viris illustribus*, by Petrarch (Francesco Petrarca [1304–1374]), which Boccaccio's preface acknowledges as his model. Boccaccio also acknowledges two other purposes: his desire to give pleasure to his friends and the novelty of the task. While a long tradition exists for such catalogues of men, he knew of nothing comparable for Antiquity's famous heroines, who were, he felt, equally deserving of remembrance. Since Boccaccio's vernacular work is dominated by women, to whom the *Decameron* is dedicated, *De claris mulieribus* may have also represented a unique opportunity for its author to continue exploring the subject of his earlier works (women) within the form and language of his later ones.

In its organization and use of sources, *De claris mulieribus* follows the generic traditions of the scholarly florilegium. Its prologue elucidates a purpose (to celebrate long-neglected heroines), a methodology (to introduce the culture of Antiquity to the literate vernacular public, if only in excerpted stories from ancient texts), and moral vision (to offer examples of proper and improper female conduct). Its 106 heroines, most of whom are pagan, do not systematically illustrate any set of definite themes, but Boccaccio does impart a normative definition of feminine nature through certain patterns in his *exempla*, or moralized tales. He offers a tremendously diverse picture of women in many roles: virgin, wife, widow, whore, philosopher, ruler, scholar, courtesan, even pope. But this diversity masks deep ambiguities in the book's attitude toward its subject, ambiguities that center on woman's connection to virtue, civic life, and cultural history. All three are central to the legacy of *De claris mulieribus* for the history of attitudes toward women.

The most fundamental of these issues is woman's capacity for virtue, which was often debated in medieval letters. It is difficult to specify any one position for Boccaccio on this point, because *De claris mulieribus* never depicts women as simply virtuous or simply vicious. This equivocation is suggested by the word *claris* in its title, which, as the author notes, was used instead of the more usual *illustris* because it connotes infamy as well as fame, notoriousness as well as notoriety. On the negative side, the author's depictions frequently rely on misogynistic constructs inherited from Classical and patristic traditions. The heroic *virago*, whose impressive achievements demonstrate her masculine spirit; the feminine hero, whose chastity, obedience, and silence epitomize female submission; and the evil temptress, whose malevolence and aggressive sexuality challenge the male status quo are all present in the text. Andrea Acciaiuoli, to whom the *De claris* is dedicated, for example, is praised for her accomplishments but regarded as more male than female, as her name's derivation from the Greek word for man (*andros*) demonstrates, or so Boccaccio's false etymology has us believe ("Dedication," para. 5; see note ed. Brown, xix). The first chapter, appropriately enough, speaks of Eve, "Our First Mother," and, in evoking the apple in traditional misogynistic fashion, he is nonetheless more egalitarian than his patristic counterparts, blaming her for fickleness, foolishness, and her ability to appeal to the same instincts within her husband, as causes of their expulsion from Eden. Yet there is something poignant in his last lines, showing her and Adam toiling in Hebron until she "reached old age, tired out by her labors, waiting for death." It must have been fascinating for Boccaccio as secular author to re-create Genesis in inaugurating what are in a sense his "creation myths" of women, replete with various typologies. Among these, the submissive wife, Sulpicia, married to Fulvius, illustrates perfect chastity not only because she is faithful but also because she is quiet, retiring, and self-effacing (ch. 85). His portrayal of Cleopatra (ch. 88), who illustrates woman at her worst, is so overwhelming that Boccaccio feels called on to invent exempla to illustrate it, in the tradition of moral conduct manuals, or even the Bible.

However, Boccaccio does exhibit genuine admiration for deserving women, whom he sometimes not only praises but does so differently from his predecessors. His most striking innovation is to include women painters, writers, artists, sculptors, and scholars. Suetonius and Jerome had made similar additions in their collections of famous men, but no one before *De claris mulieribus* had thought of doing the same thing in a catalogue of women. Perhaps more important, Boccaccio's catalogue also bases its praise on its heroines' deeds rather than their beauty, nature, or good fortune. In the manner of the first-century Greek biographer Plutarch's *Mulierium virtutes* (*Virtues of Women*), which he may have known to some extent, Boccaccio frequently shaped his *encomia* (praise) by certain rhetorical strategies, balancing a woman's good points from nature and fortune against her good points of character. Women were traditionally judged in terms of the former, and rhetoricians held the latter to be more representative of character. Boccaccio, like Plutarch, incorporates both sets of qualities. While the Florentine's reliance on *notatio*, or noting, of such qualities is not consistent, his use of it paved the way for more equitable presentations of women.

The relationship between the *mulier clara* and her community is also complex in its moral depiction. Boccaccio lauds some heroines for their self-isolation from public life (Sulpicia), but not others (Sempronia, Eve, Nicostrata). Sometimes their civic participation is beneficial (Nicaula), sometimes not (Sempronia). Two traditional patterns often appear: the good wife who remains at home and pledges her life to her husband, and the manly, virtuous woman who defends the male status quo. Since the former divorces feminine virtue from civic life and the latter divorces femininity from civic virtue, both contribute to a long philosophical tradition advocating woman's exclusion from public power.

Boccaccio also justifies woman's subjection by references to her depravity. He demonstrates how the ill effects of sexual promiscuity often extend to affairs of state, thus, Clytemnestra murdered her king, Helen began a war, and Athaliah butchered the entire royal family of Israel. There are examples basing woman's insufficiency for public life on greed (Athaliah, Procris, Medusa), dissolution (Clytemnestra, Cleopatra, Agrippina, and Olympia), and disobedience (Iole, Eve, and Sempronia). Cleopatra's biography teaches that nothing is more disastrous for social harmony than the rule of a woman insatiable in all respects. Not only did she murder her brother, seduce Julius Caesar, and corrupt Mark Anthony—all in the name of politics—she also devastated her kingdom by stripping its temples of treasures and bringing ruin in the war against Rome. Her aggressive lust for sexual conquest is explicitly equated to her lust for territorial conquest, and that connection makes her a negative epitome: of woman's unsuitability for power.

Oddly, even women's virtues can bring about the same results. One of the most puzzling aspects of this catalogue is Boccaccio's citing of ingenuity/wit/cleverness (*ingenium*) as grounds for both censure and praise. Ceres's invention of agriculture is credited with both the rise of civilization and the end of the Golden Age. The Roman courtesan Sempronia, the philosopher Leontium, and the apocryphal Pope Joan ruin their associates by their wits, but the cleverness of Minerva, the Sibyls, Sappho, Cornificia, Proba, Thamaris, and Irene are sources of enrichment. Naturally, these ambiguities reflect similar equivocations concerning woman's morality. Both attitudes compromise the collection's relationship to cultural history.

This connection between the heroines and history is best judged by comparing Boccaccio's catalogue of heroines with his catalogue of famous men, *De casibus virorum illustrium*. The two were often thought of as similar works, due to the above-mentioned similarities, yet each belongs to a separate tradition. The *De claris* is very loosely organized. Conceived as an episodic series of sketches arranged in vaguely chronological order, it has almost no literary predecessors in Boccaccio's eyes. His preface and conclusion contain reservations about the book's structure and purpose; such remarks were standard medieval formulae, but Boccaccio's reiterated statements betray an understandable anxiety over the greater risk of errors—in the *De claris*, the result of nine stages of redaction—than in more established genres (see introductions by Brown and Zaccaria to their respective editions). In contrast, the *De casibus* is tightly organized and controlled. Its form (the dream vision) and central topic (fortune and providence) link it with an established form for moral and political pronouncements, especially with two Late-Antique examples, supremely influential in the Middle Ages: Macrobius's commentary (fifth century) on Cicero's *Somnium Scipionis* (*Dream of Scipio*) and Boethius's *De Consolatione Philosophiae* (*The Consolation of Philosophy* [524]). Also significant is the fact that, while Boccaccio plays with the verbal resonances in both his works' titles, as we have seen with the double-edged *claris* in the *De claris mulieribus*, the *De casibus virorum illustrium* indicates a universal viewpoint—*virorum* here means "of mankind" and not simply "of males." In plan and execution, then,

De casibus virorum illustrium is more ordered, more unified, more conventional, and more linked to universal verities than the *De claris mulieribus*.

In conclusion, Boccaccio's catalogue transmits a mixed message, oscillating between virtue and vice, constructive and destructive social influences. Moreover, its failure to present its subject as linked to cultural history perpetuates a subtle but powerful form of exclusion. Despite several interesting and important innovations, the work is more often misogynistic, however subtly and amusingly, than not; yet less misogynistic than other medieval treatments of women. It remains one of the first catalogues of women to posit a feminine fame based on women's deeds. It also influenced many important defenses of womankind, including Christine de Pizan's *Cité* mentioned earlier, and Heinrich Agrippa von Nettesheim's *De nobilitate et praecellentia foeminei sexus* (*The Nobility and Excellence of the Feminine Sex*) c.1509—both radically revisionist in favor of women. More compendia followed Boccaccio's in the next three centuries, often citing him as a source. As his equivocations portend, his ideas would resound through authors on both sides of later *querelles des femmes*. If *De claris mulieribus* did not articulate a new definition of femininity, it helped to popularize a fresher perspective to be developed by his successors. His *De casibus* would be translated soon after its appearance, for example, into Spanish by Pero Lopez de Ayala (1332–1407) *Los acaecimientos & casos de la Fortuna que ovieron muchos principes & grandes senores* and also *Caida de los principes*. An anonymous French cleric would translate the *De claris* into the *Des cleres et nobles femmes* into French (1401; Paris BnF fr. 12420); the French humanist Laurent de Premierfait (d. 1418) would render the *De casibus* into his *Cas de nobles homes et femmes* (note the Frenchman's inclusion of both genders, as opposed to the Spaniard's male-centered titles). Premierfait's work would be rendered into Middle-English verse as the famous *Fall of Princes* by John Lydgate (1370?–1451?). The German Hieronymus Ziegler (1514–1562) would do likewise for his country's vernacular, as Claes de Grave would for the Netherlands (1526), among other examples illustrating the rapid popularity of Boccaccio's catalogues of women.

See also Boccaccio, Women in, *Des Cleres et Nobles Femmes*; Boccaccio, Women in, Works Other than *De Claris Mulieribus*; Bokenham, Osbern; Chaucer, Geoffrey, Women in the Work of; Christine de Pizan; Criseyde; Dido in the Middle Ages; *Frauenturnier*; Griselda; Medea in the Middle Ages; Nine Worthy Women; Proba, Faltonia Betitia; *Roman de la Rose*, Debate of the

BIBLIOGRAPHY

Primary Sources
Boccaccio, Giovanni. *De casibus virorum illustrium*. Edited by Pier Giorgio Ricci and Vittore Branca. In *Tutte le Opere di Giovanni Boccaccio*, edited by Vittorio Zaccaria, vol. 9. I classici Mondadori. Milan, Italy: Arnoldo Mondadori, 1983.
———. [*De casibus virorum illustrium*. Dutch]. *Vanden doorluchtighen mannen ende haren wercken*. Antwerp: Claes de Grave, 1526.
———. [De casibus virorum illustrium. Medieval Spanish]. *The Text and Concordance of Giovanni Boccaccio's* De casibus virorum illustrium, *Translated by Pero Lopez de Ayala HSA MS. B1196*. Edited by Eric Naylor. Spanish series, 102. 6 microfiches. Madison, Wisc.: Hispanic Seminary of Medieval Studies, 1994. [Based on the 1476 Bruges ms. of Ayala's translation].
———. [*De casibus virorum illustrium*. German]. *Fornemste Historien vnd Exempel von widerwertigem Gluck, mercklichem und erschrocklichem Vnfahl, erbarmklichen Verderben vnnd Sterben, grossmachtiger Kayser, Kunig, Fursten, vnnd anderer namhafftiger Herrn* [. . .] *Ioannem Boccatium* [. . .] in Latein beschriben [. . .]. Translated by Hieronymus Ziegler. Augsburg, Germany: Hainrich Stainer, 1545.

————. [*De casibus virorum illustrium*. Middle French]. *Laurent de Premierfait's Des cas des nobles hommes et femmes, Book 1, translated from Boccaccio*. Critical edition by Patricia May Gathercole. University of North Carolina. Studies in the Romance languages and literatures, no. 74. Chapel Hill: University of North Carolina Press, 1968.

————. [*De casibus virorum illustrium*, Middle English trans. Lydgate]. Here begynneth the boke calledde John Bochas, descriuinge the falle of princis, princessis [and] other nobles, tra[n]slatid i[n]to Englissh by John Ludgate[. . .]. London: Richard Pynson, 1494.

————. *Famous Women*. Edited and translated by Virginia Brown. I Tatti Renaissance Library, 1. Cambridge, Mass.: Harvard University Press, 2001. [Modern critical bilingual ed. Latin and English. Latin text based on ed. Zaccaria, *see below*].

————. *De mulieribus claris o Delle donne famose*. Edited by Vittorio Zaccaria. In *Tutte le Opere di Giovanni Boccaccio*, edited by Vittore Branca, vol. 10. *Florence*: Arnoldo Mondadori, 1967–1970.

————. *Boccace, Des cleres et nobles femmes: Ms. Bibl. nat. 12420*. Edited by Jeanne Baroin and Josiane Haffen. 2 vols. Paris: Les Belles Lettres, 1993–1995. [Original Middle-French version from Paris, BnF MS 12420 and facing Modern-French translation].

————. *Forty-six Lives, Translated from Boccaccio's* De claris mulieribus *by Henry Parker, lord Morley*. Edited by Herbert G. Wright. Early English Text Society. Original series, no. 214. 1943 (for 1940). Oxford: H. Milford/Oxford University Press, 1943. [Reproduces much of the Latin original in notes].

Secondary Sources

Angeli, Giovanna. "Encore sure Boccace et Christine de Pizan: remarques sur le *De mulieribus claris* et le *Livre de la Cité des dames* ("*Plourer, parler, filer mist Dieu en femme*" I, 10)." *Le Moyen Français* 50 (2002): 115–25. [Detailed discussion of Boccaccio's technique].

Boccaccio in Europe: Proceedings of the Boccaccio Conference, Louvain, December 1975. Edited by Gilbert Tournoy. Symbolae Facultatis Litterarum et Philosophiae Lovaniensis, Series A, 4. Louvain: Louvain University Press, 1977.

Bozzolo, Carla. *Manuscrits des traductions françaises d'oeuvres de Boccacce, XVe siècle*. Padua, Italy: Antenore, 1973.

Branca, Vittore. *Boccaccio: The Man and His Works*. Translated by Richard Morges and Denise J. McAuliffe. New York: New York University Press, 1976.

Cerbo, Anna. "Il 'De mulieribus claris' di Giovanni Boccaccio." *Arcadia, Accademia Letteraria Italiana, Attie e Memorie* 7 (1974): 51–75.

————. "Didone in Boccaccio." *Annali Istituto Universitario Orientale, Napoli, Sezione Romanza* 21 (1979): 177–219.

Fenster, Thelma S., and Clare A. Lees, eds. *Gender in Debate from the Early Middle Ages to the Renaissance*. New York: Palgrave/Macmillan, 2003.

Godman, Peter. "Chaucer and Boccaccio's Latin Work." In *Chaucer and Boccaccio*, ed. Piero Boitani, 269–95. Medium Ævum Monographs, n.s., 8. Oxford: Society of Mediaeval Languages and Literature, 1977.

Jordan, Constance. "Boccaccio's In-famous Women: Gender and Civic Virtue in *De mulieribus claris*." In *Ambiguous Realities: Women in the Middle Ages and Renaissance*, edited by Carole Levin and Jeanie Watson, 25–47. Detroit: Wayne State University Press, 1987.

Kallendorf, Craig. "Boccaccio's Dido and the Rhetorical Art of Virgil's *Aeneid*." *Studies in Philology* 82 (1985): 401–15.

McLeod, Glenda. *Virtue and Venom: Catalogs of Women from Antiquity to the Renaissance*. Foreword by Charity Cannon Willard. Ann Arbor: University of Michigan Press, 1991.

Phillippy, Patricia. "'Establishing Authority': Boccaccio's *De Claris Mulieribus* and Christine de Pizan's *Livre de la Cité des Dames*." *Romanic Review* 77 (1986): 167–95.

Wright, H. G. *Boccaccio in England: From Chaucer to Tennyson*. London: Athlone, 1957.

Zappacosta, Guglielmo, and Vittorio Zaccaria. "Per il testo del 'De Claris Mulieribus.'" *Studi sul Boccaccio* 7 (1973): 239–270.

GLENDA K. MCLEOD

BOCCACCIO, WOMEN IN, *DES CLERES ET NOBLES FEMMES*. The book titled *Des cleres et nobles femmes* is the anonymous 1401 French translation of Boccaccio's influential Latin catalogue of women, *De mulieribus claris*, sometimes also written *De claris mulieribus* (*Famous Women*, c.1361–1375). Its manuscript tradition, as the most popular verbal and visual dissemination of Boccaccio's work, also merits separate mention as an important phase in the representation of women in Western culture.

Boccaccio's textual gallery comprises portraits of 106 women drawn, apart from three biblical and six medieval heroines, from ancient mythology and literature, and especially from Roman history. As a consummate humanist, Boccaccio culled the histories of these women's civilizing inventions and most noteworthy achievements, whether famous or infamous, from a variety of classical sources. He then infused the most memorable facts of their lives with his own prescriptive comments. Despite the conservative, at times even derisive, views on the "nature" of women expressed in its didactic additions, Boccaccio's *De mulieribus claris* marks an important departure from earlier treatises on women by enlarging considerably the spheres in which women are acknowledged to have intervened, and especially by depicting them as self-determined historical agents.

The favorable reception of these lives among the later medieval literati encouraged Boccaccio to compose two such catalogues—the other being the earlier *De casibus virorum illustrium* (*On the Fates of Illustrious Men*, c.1355–1360)—commemorating not only famous men but also a few women. It also spawned several vernacular translations, critical responses, and reworkings notably by Chaucer and Christine de Pizan. The *Cleres et nobles femmes* is often incorrectly attributed to Laurent de Premierfait, translator of both the *De casibus* (as *Des cas des nobles hommes et femmes*, 1400; rev. 1409) and, with Antonio d'Arezzo, the *Decameron* (1414). Laurent's rendering of both genders replacing Boccaccio's *virorum* ("of men") in the title, *"des nobles hommes et femmes"* (*Of noble men and women*), shows a growing interest in great women's lives via lexical recognition while responding to the *Querelle des femmes* (*Quarrel over women*) sparked during that time, most notably by the Debate of the *Roman de la Rose* (Debate of the *Romance of the Rose*, 1401–1404). The translation of the *De mulieribus claris*, in which we note the choice of *"clara"* ("bright, shining") over the traditional, male-centered *"illustris"* ("illustrious"), must be seen against this background as well.

Despite the uninspired quality of its language, the *Des cleres et nobles femmes* remains both a product of and a monument to the vibrant and socially diverse humanist milieu of early-fifteenth-century Paris. The translation was perhaps commissioned by the wealthy merchant of Lucchese (Italy) origins, Jacques Raponde, who sold several lavish manuscripts to Philip the Bold, duke of Burgundy, including what has come down to us as the earliest surviving copy of the *Cleres femmes* (Paris, Bibliothèque nationale de France MS fr. 12420). The high regard in which fifteenth-century readers held this work is attested by the fact that copies of it were bound into the same volume as those containing female saints' lives (female hagiography serving as a generic-discursive model for Boccaccio, although he excludes saints themselves) or with Christine de Pizan's *Cité des Dames* (*City of Ladies*, in turn modeled on Boccaccio's *De mulieribus claris* and Italian *Decameron*, recast in overtly feminist-revisionist terms).

More than with the original Latin text and its Italian translations, the French volumes, all produced for noble patrons, men and women alike, were profusely illustrated (up to 109 miniatures within a single book). Among the first to center on women alone, these secular cycles propose an innovative iconography of women envisioned in a wide variety of social and marital ranks, occupations, and activities: governing, hunting, fighting, nursing, pleading, painting, reading, writing, and so forth. By contrast, the mostly male pictorial cycles of *Des nobles hommes et femmes* are less creative, focusing on wars, struggles, and other forms of violent behavior. And while the *Des cleres femmes* heroines' range of action bore scant relation to reality in everyday society, these unique images, as much as the text they interpret, bear vivid testimony to late medieval attitudes toward women and continue to suggest an alternative model of historical writing in which women play a leading, rather than a supportive, role.

See also Boccaccio, Women in, *De Claris Mulieribus*; Boccaccio, Women in, Works Other than *De Claris Mulieribus*; Chaucer, Geoffrey, Women in the Work of Christine de Pizan; Dido in the Middle Ages; Joan, Pope; Marcia in the Middle Ages; Medea in the Middle Ages; *Roman de la Rose*, Debate of the; Scribes and Scriptoria

BIBLIOGRAPHY

Primary Sources

Boccaccio, Giovanni. *Boccace, Des cleres et nobles femmes: Ms. Bibl. nat. 12420.* Edited by Jeanne Baroin and Josiane Haffen. 2 vols. Paris: Les Belles Lettres, 1993–1995. [Original Middle-French version from Paris, BnF ms. 12420 and facing Modern-French translation].

———. *De mulieribus claris o Delle donne famose.* Edited by Vittore Branca. In *Tutte le Opere di Giovanni Boccaccio,* edited by Vittorio Zaccaria, vol. 10. Florence: Arnoldo Mondadori, 1967, 1970. [Original Latin text in modern ed.; notes in Italian].

———. *Famous Women.* Edited and translated by Virginia Brown. I Tatti Renaissance Library, 1. Cambridge, Mass.: Harvard University Press, 2001. [Modern ed. with original Latin and facing English translation].

Secondary Sources

Avril, François, ed. *Boccace en France: De l'humanisme à l'érotisme.* Paris: Bibliothèque Nationale, 1975.

Benson, Pamela. *The Invention of the Renaissance Woman: The Challenge of Female Independence in the Literature and Thought of Italy and England.* University Park: Pennsylvania State University Press, 1992.

Bozzolo, Carla. *Les Manuscrits des traductions françaises d'œuvres de Boccace (XVe).* Padua, Italy: Antenore, 1973.

Branca, Vittore. *Boccaccio visualizzato: Narrare per parole e per immagini fra Medioevo e Rinascimento.* 3 vols. Torino: Einaudi, 1999.

Buettner, Brigitte. *Boccaccio's Des Cleres et nobles femmes: Systems of Signification in an Illuminated Manuscript.* Seattle and London: University of Washington Press, 1996.

Bumgardner, George H. "Christine de Pizan and the Atelier of the Master of the Coronation." *Seconda Miscellanea di studi e ricerche sul Quattrocento francese,* edited by Franco Simone, 37–52. Chambéry, France and Torino, Italy: Centre d'Études franco–italien, 1981.

Dulac, Liliane. "Un mythe didactique chez Christine de Pizan: Sémiramis ou la veuve héroïque." *Mélanges de philologie romane offerts à Charles Camproux.* Montpellier, France: CEO, 1978.

Hagedorn, Suzanne C. *Abandoned Women: Rewriting the Classics in Dante, Boccaccio, and Chaucer.* Ann Arbor: University of Michigan Press, 2003.

Jordan, Constance. "Boccaccio's In-Famous Women: Gender and Civic Virtue in the *De Mulieribus claris.*" In *Ambiguous Realities: Women in the Middle Ages and Renaissance,* edited by Carole Levin and Jeanie Watson, 25–47. Detroit: Wayne State University Press, 1987.

McLeod, Glenda. *Virtue and Venom: Catalogs of Women from Antiquity to the Renaissance.* Ann Arbor: University of Michigan Press, 1991.

Perkinson, Stephen. "*Engin* and *Artifice*: Describing Creative Agency at the Court of France, ca. 1400." *Gesta* 41 (2002): 51–67.

Phillippy, Patricia A. "Establishing Authority: Boccaccio's *De Claris mulieribus* and Christine de Pizan's *Le Livre de la Cité des Dames*." *Romanic Review* 77 (1986): 167–93.

BRIGITTE BUETTNER

BOCCACCIO, WOMEN IN, WORKS OTHER THAN *DE CLARIS MULIERIBUS*

(14th century). The *De claris mulieribus* deals specifically with the agency of women in history and, therefore (especially in its influence on Christine de Pizan), commands our interest as an important document in women's literary history. It abounds with feminist issues relating to equality, authority, agency, creativity, and the gendering of power. But the *De mulieribus* is far from Boccaccio's only contribution to medieval literature about women, for he wrote endlessly about women in every possible manifestation of desire, victimization, triumph, evil, and virtue. Therefore, however we define feminism, any reader interested in the history of the depiction of the female in European medieval literature finds infinite variety and conflict in Boccaccio's work. As a medieval incarnation of Ovid (c.43 B.C.E.–17 C.E.)—the great Roman poet of love's tricky psychology—Boccaccio examines men and women in the games of love, exploring the sinful, the playful, the bawdy, the noble, and the divine as comprehensively and as paradoxically as any other medieval author. He writes of female heroism, tragedy, helplessness, and both his narrators and characters alternately adore and despise women. No summary or paraphrase, therefore, can cover the variety of female experience and the diverse views of women he offers. Throughout the vast gamut of his work—romances inspired by Classical Greek and Roman authors, his earthy *Decameron* stories (c.1351–1353), and his later parodic and hortatory (urging) works—Boccaccio, like his English contemporary, Chaucer (c.1343–1400), can provide us with Christian moral drama, then carnival burlesque—and women, accordingly, are in the thick of it all. Feminist scholars will find much to confront but very little on which to agree; it becomes at once imperative to study Boccaccio's women and yet impossible to define or even to characterize his "attitude" toward women, his "feminism," or, for that matter, his "misogyny." This quandary derives to a great extent from the intertwined influences of his Florentine contemporary, Dante (1265–1321) and Classical Roman—though irreverent—Ovid. In confronting and attempting to reconcile each poet's complex depiction of women as both rational and sensual, Boccaccio himself creates dynamic, elusive, and often contradictory portraits of women.

Boccaccio denies us a unified ideology toward not only women but also men and human desire in general. He alternately shows lovers at their most noble, virtuous, treacherous, or lecherous, across various genres in diverse historical and geographical settings. Above all, Boccaccio is a servant of love, and love can ennoble humans or drive them to base animal lust. In so demonstrating, he also invents new genres and invigorates older ones; his language enriched—never stultified—by his vast and varied learning. For example, while studying canon law in Naples, he composed his early *Caccia di Diana* (*Diana's Hunt*) of 1336–1338, the first Italian hunting poem. The *Caccia* allegorically tells the story of female sexuality, describing how a group of young huntresses follow Diana until Venus takes

Two scenes from Boccaccio's *Decameron*. *Left to right*: "The Procession to the Garden," and "The Narrators of the Tale." Courtesy of North Wind Picture Archives.

command and turns their prey into obedient, humble young suitors. In the Christian-allegorical *Ameto*, also called the *Commedia delle ninfe fiorentine* (*Comedy of the Florentine Nymphs*)—the first Italian romance with dominant pastoral elements—of 1341–1342, a shepherd, Ameto, encounters seven women, who turn out to be the seven virtues leading him to heavenly wisdom. From a modern feminist perspective, these allegories may appear rigid, essentializing (assuming a de facto "womanliness" based on latent sexist stereotyping rather than on unbiased reasoning), and thus hampering female expressivity. In truth, they betray the Classical Greco-Roman, Christian, and medieval Italian social influences nurturing Boccaccio as he turns to study human sexuality and both the socialization and the purification of passion—two of his principal themes.

Similar themes surface in the pastoral poem *Il Ninfale fiesolano* (*Nymph Song of Fiesole*) (1346–1349), which describes the trauma of seduction and childbirth suffered by a young devotee of Diana, goddess of the hunt. In his three greatest classical romances—the *Filostrato* (from Greek = "One overcome by love"), the *Filocolo* (from Greek = "Love's Labor"; 1337–1339), and the more martial-epic *Teseida* (*Book of Theseus*; 1340–1342), Boccaccio depicts women buffeted by history, war, male authority, and warrior culture. In the early masterpiece, the *Filostrato*, Boccaccio has given us Cressida, mother of Chaucer's most complex character, a woman torn by desire, family, and history. She is compelled to seek her own way to survive Ovid's remedies, that is, find a new love. The *Filocolo* depicts the quest for healthy married love between Florio and Blancifiore, filtered through stories of *bono* (good) and *malo* (evil) classical love lore. The *Teseida* (source of Chaucer's *Knight's Tale*) opens with Theseus's conquest and domestication of the Amazons. It then continues to explore the Amazon Emily and her irrational effect on two, smitten, imprisoned warriors, while the woman herself confronts her unwanted divine destiny as wife to one of the warriors. Theseus's acts display male desire to control the dangerous independent female principle and to "socialize" it by the institution of marriage, setting the gender paradigm—the role playing—that will inform all subsequent drama within the tale. Feminist analysis of these texts can focus on the roles of marriage in premodern culture and the ordering of both male and female desire by socializing and rationalizing religious forces. How can women negotiate desire in a world of male might and social, moral, and divine imperatives? As Boccaccio traces these conflicts, much female strength and dignity emerge.

The more popular *Decameron* offers a series of stories about marriage, sex, and gamesmanship that invite further inquiry into female subjectivity. In the narrative frame we have female narrators whose ideas of female frailty (in which the women themselves only half believe) would shock some modern feminists as essentialist and full of the women's self-contempt, symptomatic of Boccaccio's overall sexism and lack of enlightenment. Hence the need to situate Boccaccio within his own sociohistorical context—not ours—to avoid such foolishly anachronistic readings and to interpret the female speakers' subversions as part of Boccaccio's love of trickery and deceit, as studied by Guido Almansi and others. Of the one hundred stories themselves, some may seem vulgar, bawdy, or antifeminist, and indeed they are, but we must appreciate the role of folktale genres and fabliaux-style play in assessing the feminist issues at hand. Many characters and narrators advocate antifeminist assumptions, maintaining the fundamental sexual depravity of both men and (even more so) of women. Female desire and wit (whether for doing good or making mischief) display themselves in many ways: a curious Arab teenager learns happily how to "put the devil back into Hell"; a clever princess avoids an unwanted marriage by disguising herself as an abbot and finding her own man; a woman named Zinevra escapes unjust execution and works in male disguise to reunite with her (undeserving) husband; a princess lost at sea takes eight lovers before she gets back on course to her planned spouse, whom she nonetheless manages to convince of her virginity; a scorned princess invents false rape charges to ruin the man she cannot have, but then repents; the women in various fabliaux-like tales betray their wan, impotent husbands for hale and hearty men who never rest from pleasing them abed; some nuns say "bah" to their chaste marriage to Christ and share a virile gardener; a woman uses an innocent friar as a pimp; one women becomes a nun; a nun sleeps with a priest; one woman kills her lover; another is killed by hers. Thus fidelity, adultery, reunion, and murder abound.

Chaucerians find Boccaccio to have been a key source for the *Franklin's Tale* and *Clerk's Tale*, as do Shakespeareans for *All's Well That Ends Well*, among others. Such works resonate with the issues of female strength, ingenuity, and responsibility. Of particular note in the *Decameron* is the wise and brilliant Ghismonda, who fights for sexual freedom with stunning oratory (which, the narrator blissfully informs us, is free of womanly wailing). Her dignified suicide shames her tyrannical father into despair over killing her lowborn but honorable lover. But in a later work on female desire, the *Elegia di Madonna Fiammetta* (*Elegy of Lady Fiammetta*), Boccaccio writes extended satire (for an additional reading see Mariangela Causa-Steindler's introduction to her edition of this work) in the endless monologue of a scorned adulterous aristocrat who dramatizes herself as a tragic victim of male deceit. Fiammetta, contradicting her own story, at one point pretends to have struggled and been overpowered on their first night together.

Which of these female experiences are real, which evoke power, and which hide real disempowerment and propagate myths destructive to women? Such feminist-critical questions tend to confuse more than clarify, since they equate literary history with social history. But literary history is also the history of imagination. In particular, reading male writings that seemingly celebrate female desire, whether in bawdy fabliaux or lofty chivalric romance, may doubly bind the reader. On the one hand, we want to cheer for women who gain mastery of language and desire, who put men in their place, or who heroically transcend male-imposed strictures and institutions. Yet on the other hand, on remembering these tales to be the work of a male author, we wonder if these empowered heroines are simply pawns in a subtle game of reversing the antifeminist coin to reflect not the author's sympathy with female desire but merely his clever virtuosity at romantic fabrication. The author's success at this distortion thus ends up reinforcing misogynistic will rather than softening it. But then again, such potentially reductive arguments obscure the more complex nature of Boccaccio's sexual poetics. Male authorship does not de facto produce misogyny nor does it delimit feminist critical study.

Moving to Boccaccio's narrative, and seemingly personal, level, we observe how potential women readers, and the women in his own pseudo-autobiography, figure into his meta-romantic drama. This level raises issues concerning female sensitivity to male pain, female command of the male heart, mind, and pen, and the role of woman as artistic inspiration. Boccaccio aims the *Filocolo* at young women who "carry in their soft breasts the burning flames of more hidden loves." The *Teseida* is dedicated to Fiammetta (Boccaccio's version of Ovid's Corinna) who charms him even in her "unwarranted disdain" and who figures, as does he, as a character in the poem, presumably Emily. Boccaccio's hope is that the story will warm her cold heart and restore her to him, as he paints himself into the sexual drama and allows us to see his own resultant amorous sorrows.

In contrast to all the dedications and homages to imperious women as worthy and even dominant, Boccaccio also composed one of the most virulent antifeminist tracts in medieval literature, the *Corbaccio* (late 1350s), decried by Ernest Hatch Wilkins, for example, as a "sorry anticlimax" to his masterpiece, the *Decameron*. Wilkins qualifies the *Corbaccio* as "in form a pseudo-Dantesque vision"—that is, seemingly patterned on the work of that epic admirer of Beatrice, Dante—while insidiously taking the opposite side in regard to female nobility. The last of Boccaccio's Italian-language fictions (see Hollander 1988), the *Corbaccio* also takes its cue from Ovid's *Remedia amoris* (*Remedy for Love*; 1 B.C.E.–2 C.E.), which portrays the female body as foul and disgusting: an effective cure for silly male passion. The word *corbaccio* has been translated as either "scourge" or, as Anthony Cassell defends it, "dirty crow," denoting its female target. That the *Corbaccio* comes toward the end of Boccaccio's career leads us to perceive this as his final word on women, perhaps part of his overall guilt at having been a languid, lascivious medieval Ovid, since literary fictive self-indulgence is merely another dimension of carnal abuse. But Robert Hollander argues that the *Corbaccio* is a finely wrought literary joke, not an impulsive venting of spleen. Its brand of medieval "remedial" or "curative" antifeminist literature functions according to the rules of excess typical of its genre. The proposed attacks are therefore partly comic; the sustained condemnation derives from rhetorical, not personal, misogyny; yet the total effect no doubt stands in opposition to Boccaccio's gentle (*gentile*) praise of women.

In confronting his complex body of writing, scholars have wrestled with Boccaccio's ethical poetics and tried to trace the moral drama in which he, as amorous narrator, inscribes himself. Hollander discerns moral conflict and a Christian distrust of desire in all of his work. Janet Smarr, focusing on the shifting role of the various characters named Fiammetta, displays the diversity of female identity and the complexity of Boccaccio's response to his own love of women and to his conception of his own identity as a love poet. Boccaccio's female poetics is at once personal, Christian, and moral. Fiammetta can be Eve, Mary, Laura, or Ovid's Corinna, all displaying virtue and inspiration or serving as a parodic example of the folly of love's enslavement. Fiammetta's multiple manifestations display Boccaccio's comprehensive ambiguous portraiture of women and the problems feminist scholars face in confronting any one of these conflicting shifting depictions, through what Smarr calls a "doubling of viewpoints."

Boccaccio was neither absolutely feminist nor misogynist, despite strong evidence of each tendency in his writings. All attempts to compartmentalize him ideologically and stylistically fail miserably. In his numerous tales of love, he offers a veritable explosion of representations of female desire. But what constitutes "authentic" female desire and who can define it? These questions, so impossible to answer, should thus be bracketed. Judgment, essentialism (mentioned toward the beginning of this article), retroactive criticism, or "presentism" (privileging early texts that seem to anticipate our modern political goals and needs) would constitute misuse of literary history and doom any understanding of Boccaccio as a medieval Ovidian, Dantesque, Christian author.

Ultimately, and specifically with reference to Boccaccio's influence on Chaucer, it is perhaps Boccaccio's disarmingly articulate and capable female characters who leave the most decisive and durable mark on the history of women's representation in literature. This group would include the oratorical Ghismonda of the *Decameron*, the infinitely changing Cressida of the *Teseida*, and the queenly Fiammetta presiding over that most esteemed section of the *Filocolo*, episode 4: the "Thirteen Most Pleasant and Delectable Questions of Love." Throughout his works, Boccaccio attributes the Ovidian traits of trickery, unquenchable desire, and sovereignty to women. Perhaps this last is the highest honor, in the secular sense, that a medieval servant of the servants of love (for such is Boccaccio's poetic persona) can bestow on his creation, the supreme rank of *doctor amoris* (doctor of love). In general, Boccaccio's women are not only dominant but also, to borrow from the Caribbean folk song, "smarter than the man in every way." His portrayal of women as self-determining agents in their romantic lives, while they also struggle against social obstacles is his principal contribution to Western literature, thereby providing some of the most important medieval documentation for the history of gender studies and feminist analysis.

As Wilkins summarizes most comprehensively, the above-analyzed works—especially the *Decameron*—exerted much influence, in multiple genres, over later authors even outside Italy, as evidenced in French, German, and Spanish imitators such as La Fontaine, Sachs, and Lope de Vega. English medieval and later authors range from Gower and Lydgate in the fifteenth century to seventeenth- and eighteenth-century emulators Aphra Behn, Dryden, and Swift; then nineteenth-century British writers George Eliot, Tennyson, and Byron, joined by the American poet Longfellow; and, more recently, the 1970 film (*Decameron*) by the Italian director Pasolini.

See also Beatrice; Boccaccio, Women in, *De Claris Mulieribus*; Boccaccio, Women in, *Des Cleres et Nobles Femmes*; Chaucer, Geoffrey, Women in the Work of; Christine de Pizan; Criseyde; Griselda; Laura; *Miroir de Mariage* (*Mirror of Marriage*); Nine Worthy Women

BIBLIOGRAPHY

Primary Sources
[For works lacking a bilingual edition, the original Italian or Latin reference has been given first, followed, after a semicolon, by the modern English version, if any].
Boccaccio, Giovanni. *Ameto, L'* (*Comedia delle ninfe fiorentine*). Edited by Antonio E. Quaglio. In *Tutte le opere*, vol. 2 (1964); L'Ameto. Translated by Judith Serafini-Sauli. Garland Library of Medieval Literature, 33B. New York: Garland, 1985.
———. *Amorosa Visione*. Translated by Robert Hollander et al. Introduction by Vittore Branca. Hanover, N.H.: University Press of New England, 1986. [Bilingual edition].

———. [*Caccia di Diana*]. *Diana's Hunt/Caccia di Diana: Boccaccio's First Fiction*. Edited and translated by Anthony K. Cassell and Victoria Kirkham. Philadelphia: University of Pennsylvania Press, 1991. [Bilingual edition].

———. *Corbaccio, Il.* Edited by Giorgio Padoan. In *Tutte le opere* (see below), vol. 5 (1994); *The Corbaccio, or, The Labyrinth of Love*. Edited and translated by Anthony K. Cassell. Urbana: University of Illinois Press, 1975. Revised edition, Binghamton, N.Y.: MRTS, 1993.

———. *Decameron*. Edited by Vittore Branca. In *Tutte le opere* (see below), vol. 4 (1976); *The Decameron*. Translated by G. H. McWilliam. Harmondsworth, Middlesex, U.K. and New York: Penguin, 1972.

———. *Elegia di Madonna Fiammetta*. Edited by Carlo Delcorno. In *Tutte le opere* (see below), vol. 5, pt. 2 (1994); *Elegy of Lady Fiammetta*. Translated and edited by Mariangela Causa-Steindler and Thomas Mauch. Chicago: University of Chicago Press, 1990.

———. *De casibus virorum illustrium*. Edited by Pier Giorgio Ricci and Vittorio Zaccaria. In *Tutte le opere* (see below), vol. 9 (1983).

———. [*De mulieribus claris*] *Famous Women*. Edited and translated by Virginia Brown. I Tatti Renaissance Library. Cambridge, Mass. and London: Harvard University Press, 2001. [Bilingual edition].

———. *Filocolo, Il.* Edited by Antonio Quaglio. In *Tutte le opere* (see below), vol. 1 (1964); *Il Filocolo*. Translated by Donald Cheney with Thomas G. Bergin. Garland Library of Medieval Literature, 43B. New York: Garland, 1985.

———. *Il Filostrato*. Italian text edited by Vincenzo Pernicone. Translated with an introduction by Robert P. apRoberts and Anna Bruni Seldis. Garland Library of Medieval Literature, 53A. New York: Garland, 1986. [Bilingual edition].

———. *Ninfale fiesolano*. Edited by Pier Massimo Forni. Milan: Mursia, 1991; *Nymphs of Fiesole*. Translated by Joseph Tusiani. Rutherford, N.J.: Fairleigh Dickinson University Press, 1971.

———. *Teseida delle nozze di Emilia*. Edited by Alberto Limentani. In *Tutte le opere* (see below), vol. 2 (1964); *The Book of Theseus*. Translated by Bernadette Marie McCoy. New York: Medieval Text Association, 1974.

———. *Tutte le opere di Giovanni Boccaccio*. Vittore Branca, general editor. I Classici Mondadori. 12 vols. Milan: Arnoldo Mondadori, 1967–1998. [Projected series of authoritative critical texts of all Boccaccio's works, in original Italian or Latin only; not all volumes have appeared; see above under specific works].

Chaucer, Geoffrey. *Canterbury Tales*. Edited by F. N. Robinson. In *The Riverside Chaucer*, edited by Larry D. Benson. 3rd edition. Boston: Houghton Mifflin, 1987.

Shakespeare, William. *All's Well that Ends Well*. Edited by G. K. Hunter. The Arden Shakespeare. Walton-on-Thames, Surrey, U.K.: Thomas Nelson, 1997.

Secondary Sources

Almansi, Guido. *The Writer as Liar*. London and Boston: Routledge & Kegan Paul, 1975.

Bergin, Thomas G. *Boccaccio*. New York: Viking, 1981.

Bloch, R. Howard. *Medieval Misogyny and the Invention of Western Romantic Love*. Chicago and London: University of Chicago Press, 1991.

Boitani, Piero. *Chaucer and Boccaccio*. Oxford: Society for the Study of Mediaeval Languages and Literature, 1977.

Branca, Vittore. *Boccaccio: The Man and His Works*. Translated by Richard C. Monges and Dennis J. McAuliffe. Edited by Dennis J. McAuliffe. Foreword by Robert C. Clements. New York: New York University Press, 1976.

Calabrese, Michael. "Feminism and the Packaging of Boccaccio's *Elegy of Lady Fiammetta*." *Italica* (1997): 20–42.

———. "Men and Sex in Boccaccio's *Decameron*." *Medievalia et Humanistica* (forthcoming).

Hagedorn, Suzanne C. *Abandoned Women: Rewriting the Classics in Dante, Boccaccio, and Chaucer*. Ann Arbor: University of Michigan Press.

Hanning, Robert. "Before the 'Shipman's Tale': The Language of Place, the Place of Language in *Decameron* 8.1, 8.2." In *Place, Space and Landscape in Medieval Narrative*. Edited by Laura Howes. Tennessee Studies in Literature. (forthcoming).

Heinrichs, Katherine. *The Myths of Love: Classical Lovers in Medieval Literature*. University Park: Pennsylvania State University Press, 1990.

Hollander, Robert. *Boccaccio's Last Fiction, Il Corbaccio*. Philadelphia: University of Pennsylvania Press, 1988.

———. *Boccaccio's Two Venuses*. New York: Columbia University Press, 1977.

Kirkham, Victoria. *The Sign of Reason in Boccaccio's Fiction*. Florence, Italy: Leo Olschki, 1993.

Marcus, Millicent. "Misogyny As Misreading: A Gloss on *Decameron* VII, 7." *Stanford Italian Review* 4 (1984): 23–40.

———. "Seduction by Silence: A Gloss on the Tales of Masetto (*Decameron* III, 1) and Alatiel (*Decameron* II, 7)." *Philological Quarterly* 58 (1979): 1–15.

Nolan, Barbara. *Chaucer and the Tradition of the Roman Antique*. Cambridge Studies in Medieval Literature, 15. Cambridge, U.K., and New York: Cambridge University Press, 1992.

Potter, Joy. "Woman in the Decameron." In *Studies in the Italian Renaissance: Essays in Memory of Arnolfo B. Ferruolo*, edited by Gian Paolo Biasin et al., 87–103. Naples: Società Editrice Napoletana, 1985.

Smarr, Janet Levarie. *Boccaccio and Fiammetta: The Narrator as Lover*. Urbana: University of Illinois Press, 1986.

Suzuki, Michio. "Gender, Power and the Female Reader: Boccaccio's *Decameron* and Marguerite de Navarre's *Heptameron*." *Comparative Literature Studies* 30 (1993): 231–52.

Tournoy, Gilbert. *Boccaccio in Europe: Proceedings of the Boccaccio Conference, Louvain, December 1975*. Symbolae Facultatis Litterarum et Philosophiae Lovaniensis, Series A, 4. Louvain, Belgium: Louvain University Press, 1977.

Vacca, Diane. "Converting Alibech: 'Nunc spiritu copuleris.'" *Journal of Medieval and Renaissance Studies* 25 (1995): 207–27.

Wilkins, Ernest Hatch. *A History of Italian Literature*. Revised edition by Thomas G. Bergin. 2nd printing. Cambridge, Mass. and London: Harvard University Press, 1978.

MICHAEL CALABRESE

THE BOKE OF ST. ALBANS. *See* Berners, Juliana

BOKENHAM, OSBERN (1393–post-1463). Osbern Bokenham composed the first all-female legendary (collection of legends, often saints' lives) in English, popularly known as *Legendys of Hooly Wummen*, in which he mentions several women patrons. He earned a master of theology degree from Cambridge University and then became Augustinian friar resident at Clare Priory in Clare, Suffolk. This was the oldest Augustinian establishment in England (from 1248), with several important women donors from the noble Clare and de Burgh families. One of them, Joan of Acre, daughter of King Edward I, was buried at the priory in 1305 and venerated as a saintly woman by pilgrims and the local populace. Another, Elizabeth de Burgh, founded Clare College at Cambridge University (mid-fourteenth century).

According to statements in the unique manuscript (London, British Library Arundel 327), the untitled legendary was composed between 1443 and 1447. Its present working title, *Legendys of Hooly Wummen*, supplied in 1938 by its Early English Text Society editor, Mary Serjeantson, is a phrase from the text. Sources and influences include Augustine's *De doctrina Christiana* (*On Christian Doctrine* [c.400]), James of Voragine (Jacopo da Varagine)'s *Legenda Aurea* (*Golden Legend*, thirteenth century), Chaucer's life of St. Cecelia (the *Second Nun's Tale*) and *Legend of Good Women* (later fourteenth century),

John Capgrave's life of St. Catherine (early to mid-fifteenth century), various Latin lives, probably the *South English Legendary*, and a wide range of secular and religious poetry, scholarship in various fields, and doctrinal and liturgical materials.

The idea of an all-female legendary had several partial antecedents: lists of female saints concluding Holy Week litanies, early Latin legendaries divided by sex, and the third section of Christine de Pizan's *Livre de la Cité des Dames* (*Book of the City of Ladies*, 1404–1405). Doubtless Bokenham knew all of these. However, he had a particular reason for his authorial choice: service to his landlord, Richard, duke of York (1411–1460) and lord of the Honor of Clare. Richard's strongest genealogical claim to the throne of England came from Edward III's son Lionel of Clarence (1338–1368), and to Richard via female transmission at two points. The incumbent, usurping, and always insecure Lancastrians—represented during most of Bokenham's adult life by the intermittently insane Henry VI—relied on their descent from John of Gaunt, a younger son than Lionel, but head of an all-male line. Lancastrian propaganda, exemplified in the dynastic treatises of the jurist Sir John Fortescue (c.1394–c.1476), depreciated the nature of women and their ability to transmit rule, while Yorkists emphasized female virtues and abilities to support women's right and capacity to transmit rule. Such reproductive politics had figured in political writing for over a century before Bokenham wrote, as an aspect of the Hundred Years War between England and France (1337–1453), a war lasting throughout Chaucer's lifetime and most of Bokenham's, which would end during another dynastic-succession conflict within England, the Wars of the Roses (1455–1485). The claim of Edward III to the throne of France through his mother, the French princess Isabel in the 1330s, had generated discussion of women's ability to transmit rule or indeed to rule. Fifteenth-century French theorists developed the myth of the so-called Salic Law to legitimize their anti-distaff position.

It is thus no accident that Bokenham's women saints—far from being meek, silent sufferers—debate with scholars, advise kings, taunt their persecutors, preach effectively to convert thousands, walk on water, heal the sick, raise the dead, and, as the author says, provide models of exemplary behavior for men and women alike. The patrons named in Bokenham's text were members of the local East Anglian gentry and nobility. Katherine Denston was born Katherine Clopton, daughter, half-sister, and wife to prosperous and influential men in the neighborhood. Katherine Howard was a benefactor and lay sister of Clare Priory; her husband, John Howard, an ardent Yorkist, eventually became duke of Norfolk. Katherine Howard's daughter Elizabeth married John Vere, earl of Oxford; they accompanied Richard of York to France in 1441. Agatha Flegge was the wife of John Flegge, a local official and retainer of Richard in France. Lady Isabel Bourchier was sister to Richard of York. Her husband, Henry viscount Bourchier, was also royally descended; he would become treasurer of England and earl of Essex. The couple made land grants and other gifts to the priory, and Lady Isabel commissioned Bokenham's version of Mary Magdalene's life. I have not located any information about Isabel Hunt.

Aside from the legendary, Bokenham composed the *Mappula Angliae* (literally, "small towel" but here, *A Little Map/Book of England*), a translation of part of Ranulf Higden's *Polychronicon* (*Multiple Chronicle*, c.1364). In the *Mappula*, Bokenham claims to have compiled a long prose legendary (not the *Legendys*), which may be the *Gilte Legende*, an apparently anonymous work of the mid-fifteenth century, extant in eight manuscripts. He was probably responsible for the translation of the Latin poet Claudian's political panegyric for his patron Stilicho, "De consulatu Stilichonis" ("On the Consulate of Stilicho," c.395) made at Clare in 1445, which turns the late classical encomium into propaganda on behalf of Richard of York. He may have composed the verse "Dialogue at the Grave [of Joan of Acre]" (1456), which rehearses Richard's pedigree and progeny. In the legendary, Bokenham claims to have written a Latin verse life of St. Anne, but this has not been found. The *Liber de angelis* (*Book of Angels*) at Cambridge University Library, a pamphlet of magical charms and spells attributed in the manuscript to "Bokenhamus," is certainly not Osbern's work.

See also Christine de Pizan; Hagiography (Female Saints); Salic Law

BIBLIOGRAPHY

Primary Sources
Bokenham, Osbern. [Claudian's panegyric, Translation of]. "Eine Mittelenglische Claudian-Setzung (1445)." Edited by Ewald Flugel. *Anglia. Zeitschrift für englische Philologie* 28 (1905): 255–99, 421–38.
———. "Dialogue at the Grave." In *Clare Priory. Seven Centuries of a Suffolk House*, edited by Katherine W. Barnardiston. Cambridge: W. Heffer & Sons, 1962.
———. *Legendys of Hooly Wummen*. Edited by Mary Serjeantson. Early English Text Society. o. s. 206. London: Henry Milford, 1938.
———. *A Legend of Holy Women*. Translated with commentary by Sheila Delany. Notre Dame, Ind.: University of Notre Dame Press, 1992.
———. "*Mappula Angliae* von Osbern Bokenham." Edited by Carl Horstmann. *Englische Studien* 10 (1887): 1–34.
Capgrave, John. *Life of St. Katherine of Alexandria*. Translated by Karen A. Winstead. Kalamazoo, Mich.: TEAMS/Medieval Institute, 1999.
[Various legends]. *Chaste Passions: Medieval English Virgin Martyr Legends*. Edited and translated by Karen A. Winstead. Ithaca, N.Y.: Cornell University Press, 2000.

Secondary Sources
Delany, Sheila. *Impolitic Bodies. Poetry, Saints and Society in Fifteenth-Century England: The Work of Osbern Bokenham*. New York: Oxford University Press, 1998.
Reames, Sherry. "The Sources of Chaucer's 'Second Nun's Tale.'" *Modern Philology* 76 (1978) 111–35.
Winstead, Karen. *Virgin Martyrs: Legends of Sainthood in Late Medieval England*. Ithaca, N.Y.: Cornell University Press, 1997.

SHEILA DELANY

BONETA, NA PROUS. *See* **Prous Boneta, Na**

BONIFACE, ST., MISSION AND CIRCLE OF (early to mid-8th century). The Anglo-Saxon missionary, St. Boniface (c.675–754), the "Apostle of Germany," attracted a number of learned Anglo-Saxon nuns with whom he corresponded in Latin. Despite certain similarities, Boniface's relationship with his circle, as conveyed in these letters, differed markedly from St. Jerome's (late fourth century) with his Roman devotees like Eustochium. In the course of these exchanges, Boniface's women followers, under his tutelage and by his example, forged a significant phase in the development of female literacy, in addition to contributing to the spread of Christianity in Germany. These women were named (spellings vary even more than given here) Aelffled/Ælflad, Egburg/Ecburga, Eangyth, Bugga/Bucge/Heaburg, and Leoba/Lioba. Berthgyth/Berhtgyth, though she left no extant correspondence with the saint, also figures significantly among them for her three passionate letters to her brother, Balthard, related to Boniface's co-worker, Lul. We also have a letter from Boniface to Berthgyth's mother, Cynehild (see Dronke). Some of these women accompanied Boniface across the Channel to Germany on his papally ordained missions to the northern lands; others seem to have remained in England. Christine Fell notes that the English women's houses provided books necessary to Boniface's religious establishments in Germany, as evidenced in Boniface's letter to Eadburg, abbess of Thanet. Leoba was probably the most accomplished of his co-missionary correspondents, also becoming abbess of Tauberbischofsheim.

Boniface's correspondence numbers some 150 letters (contained in the manuscript at Vienna, Österreichische Nationalbibliothek 751, later edited by Michael Tangl). The only letter in the group from one woman member to another woman is that by Aelffled, abbess of Whitby to Adola of Pfalzel, commending to her an English pilgrim, written in stately and formal prose (see Olsen). Otherwise, the letters from the women to Boniface, though very respectful, are quite emotional, some striving for a more elegant Latin style, which they hoped to improve after Boniface. The motivation for this pursuit derives from the learned and dynamic Anglo-Saxon scholar St. Aldhelm (d. 709), bishop of Sherborne, whose own Latin style was flamboyantly permeated with echoes of most known Latin authors, combined with his native Anglo-Saxon poetic tradition. It was Aldhelm who introduced the rhymed eight-syllable couplet, which became a popular verse form.

As Alexandra Olsen and Peter Dronke each assert, the letters of the Boniface Circle reflect much about these women's mental states in rather gloomy, isolated circumstances. Yet their letters manage to combine love, reverence, and spiritual intensity. Boniface died a martyr to his cause in Frisia, murdered by brigands at Dokkum (now in northern Netherlands).

See also Berthgyth; Bugga; Egburg; Epistolary Authors, Women as; Eustochium, St.; Humility Topos; Leoba

BIBLIOGRAPHY

Primary Sources
Berthgyth. [Letters to Balthard]. Translated extracts in Dronke, 30–33. *See below*, Secondary Sources. [Translated from Latin originals Tangl, *see below, next entry*; useful, since other translations of Boniface exclude Berthgyth].
Boniface et al. *Die Briefe des Heiligen Bonifatius und Lullus.* Edited by Michael Tangl. *Monumenta Germaniae Historica* [MGH]. *Epistolae selectae*, 1. Berlin: Weidmann, 1916. Second ed., 1955.
———. *Briefe des Bonifatius und Willibalds Leben.* Edited by Reinhold Rau. Darmstadt: Wissenschaftliche Buchgesellschaft, 1968.
———. *The English Correspondence of St. Boniface.* Edited by Edward Kylie. New York: Cooper Square, 1966.
———. *The Anglo-Saxon Missionaries in Germany: Being the Lives of SS. Willibrord, Boniface, Sturm, Leoba and Lebuin.* . . . Translated and edited by Charles H. Talbot. Spiritual Masters. London: Sheed & Ward, 1954. Reprint 1981.
Vitae Sancti Bonifatii. Edited by Wilhelm Levison. MGH. *Scriptores Rerum Germanicarum*, 57. Hannover: Hahn, 1907.

—————. *The Letters of St. Boniface.* Translated by Ephraim Emerton. Records of Civilization, 31. New York: Columbia University Press, 1940. Reprint, New York: Octagon, 1973.

Secondary Sources
Dronke, Peter. *Women Writers of the Middle Ages: A Critical Study of Texts from Perpetua (†203) to Marguerite Porete (†1310).* Cambridge: Cambridge University Press, 1984.
Fell, Christine. "Some Implications of the Boniface Correspondence." In *New Readings on Women in Old English Literature,* edited by Helen Damico and Alexandra H. Olsen, 29–43. Bloomington: Indiana University Press, 1990.
—————. *Women in Anglo-Saxon England.* Oxford: Oxford University Press, 1984.
Larrington, Carolyne. *Women and Writing in Medieval Europe: A Sourcebook.* London and New York: Routledge, 1995. [Also contains translations of Boniface's letter to Eadburg and Leoba's to him, among other materials].
Olsen, Alexandra H. http://www.umilta.net/boniface.html. [Informative Web site with contemporary images].
Romain, Willy-Paul. *Saint Boniface et la naissance de l'Europe.* Preface by Georges Duby. Paris: Laffont, 1990.

NADIA MARGOLIS

BOOKS OF SISTERS. *See* **Sister-Books** (*Schwesternbücher*)

BORJA, TECLA (1435–1459). A poet, singer, and scholar praised by poets of Valencia (eastern Spain) and Italy, Tecla Borja (or Borgia) was born in Valencia. She was the niece of Pope Callistus (or Calixtus) III (1378–1458) and sister of Pope Alexander VI (1431–1503). Her only surviving poem is a response to a piece addressed to her by her illustrious male compatriot from Gandia (province of Valencia), Ausias March (c.1397–1459).

See also Catalan Women Poets, Anonymous; Isabel de Villena; Malmojades, Les; Reyna de Mallorques, La; *Trobairitz*

BIBLIOGRAPHY

Primary Source
March, Ausias. "Debat." In *Poesies,* edited by Pere Bohigas, 133. Barcelona: Barcino, 1959.

Secondary Sources
Badia, Lola. "Tecla Borja." In *Double Minorities of Spain: A Bio-Bibliographical Guide to Women Writers of the Catalan, Galician, and Basque Countries,* edited by Kathleen McNerney and Cristina Enríquez de Salamanca, 79. New York: Modern Language Association, 1994.
Massó i Torrents, Jaume. "Poetesses i dames intel.lectuals." In *Homenatge a Antoni Rubió i Lluch,* 1: 411–14. Barcelona, 1936.

KATHLEEN MCNERNEY

BRANGAIN. Brangain (Brangien, Brangaene) is Iseult's confidante in the story of Tristan and Iseult. In a number of versions it is she who accidentally gives the fatal love potion to the young couple, thus leading them into adultery. She takes on a particularly significant role in the Old French poem by Thomas d'Angleterre, composed in the second half of the twelfth century, and in Gottfried von Strassburg's Middle-High German redaction of the very early thirteenth century. In the first, where Brangain is far from a mere compliant servant, there is a certain amount of strife between her and Iseult. In Gottfried's story, she assumes a courtly and wise demeanor, sometimes alert when the heroine is not. Of special note is the episode in which Gottfried's Isolde has ordered the murder of Brangaene, who cleverly talks her way out.

See also Arthurian Women; Isolde

BIBLIOGRAPHY

Primary Sources
Gottfried von Strassburg. *Tristan*. Critical edition by Reinhold Bechstein and Peter Ganz. 2 vols. Deutscher Klassiker des Mittelalters, 4. Wiesbaden, Germany: Brockhaus, 1978. [Middle-High German text].
———. *Tristan, with Surviving Fragments of the* Tristran *of Thomas*. Translated with introduction by Arthur Thomas Hatto. Baltimore: Penguin, 1960. Reprint, 1972.
[Various authors]. *Tristan et Iseut: les poèmes français, la saga norroise*. Edited by Daniel Lacroix and Philippe Walter. Lettres gothiques. Paris: Livre de Poche, 1989. [Bilingual, with Modern-French trans. and notes].
———. *Tristan, with Surviving Fragments of the* Tristran *of Thomas*. Translated with introduction by Arthur Thomas Hatto. Baltimore: Penguin, 1960. Reprint, 1972.
———. *The Romance of Tristan and Iseult*. Translated by Hilaire Belloc. Vintage Classics. New York: Vintage Books, 1994. First published London: George Allen & Unwin, 1903.

Secondary Sources
Fenster, Thelma S., ed. *Arthurian Women: A Casebook*. Arthurian Characters and Themes, 3. New York: Garland, 1996. [Collection of critical essays on wide-ranging aspects, with introduction].
Grimbert, Joan Tasker, ed. *Tristan and Isolde: A Casebook*. Arthurian Characters and Themes, 2. New York and London: Garland Publishing, 1995. Reprint, New York and London: Routledge, 2002. [Important collection of essays by major scholars in the field].

THELMA S. FENSTER

BRAUTMYSTIK. *See* **Bride of Christ/*Brautmystik***

BRIDE OF CHRIST/BRAUTMYSTIK. *Brautmystik* is the concept invoking bridal and erotic imagery to express the union of the soul with God. It is a central idea of mysticism, that is, the deliberately nonrational (and therefore "mysterious") approach to knowing God or any Ultimate Reality. Although it is also referred to as "nuptial" or "bridal mysticism" and manifests itself in various European medieval authors, with it roots even in the Old Testament, the German label, *Brautmystik*, is most often used because it was most fully cultivated by the medieval German mystics, *particularly* women.

Brautmystik depicts the soul as the bride of Christ, or the soul as the bride of God, and the marriage union of God and soul. The concept has its origin in the biblical marriage symbolism of both Old and New Testaments. In the Old Testament, Jehovah God is seen as married to the Nation of Israel: "For your Maker is your husband; the Lord of hosts is his name" (Isaiah 54: 5); before lambasting Israel as a "harlot" for her apostasy, recalls her love for Him "as a bride" (Jeremiah 2: 2); and "And I will betroth you to me forever; I will betroth you to me in righteousness and in justice, in steadfast love, and in mercy. I will betroth you to me in faithfulness; and you shall know the Lord" (Hosea 2: 19–20). In the New Testament, the image of the bridegroom is transferred from Jehovah to Christ, as in these examples "And Jesus said to them, 'Can the wedding guests mourn as long as the bridegroom is with them? The days will come, when the bridegroom is taken away from them" (Matthew 9: 15). The image of the bride is also sometimes transferred to the Church: "I [Paul] feel a divine jealousy for you, for I betrothed you to Christ to present you as a pure bride to her one husband" (2 Corinthians 11: 2); "for the marriage of the Lamb has come, and his Bride has made herself ready" (Revelation 19: 7); "And I saw the holy city, new Jerusalem, coming down out of heaven from God, prepared as a bride adorned for her husband" (Revelation 21: 2).

The early Church thinkers as far back as Origen (c.185–c.254), in his then-controversial belief in the purified soul's mystical union with Christ, and Church Fathers like St. Augustine (354–430) expanded the symbolism from the Incarnate Christ and the Church to the union of believers with the risen Christ. St. Anselm (1033–1109), though more rational in his theology, nonetheless saw the Church as a free, loving, and beloved bride, which should not let herself be involved in earthly or political affairs.

But it was the brilliantly eloquent twelfth-century French Cistercian mystical theologian, preacher, and future saint Bernard of Clairvaux (1090–1153) who imprinted *Brautmystik* as a major devotional construct—through his mystical fervor and poetic, even erotic, language—upon the religious imagination in a way that would end up appealing especially to women. Bernard interpreted the Song of Songs as symbolic of God's love or Christ's love for the Church. Not to be outdone, the major female theologian of this period, the German St. Hildegard of Bingen (1098–1179), devotes five visions in her great prose work, *Scivias* (= "Know the Ways") glorifying the (female) allegory of the Church (Ecclesia), Mary, and Woman in general as one worthy of Christ's love. As Barbara Newman (1987) observes, the Bride of Christ serves as a fitting remedy to what Hildegard perceived as her corrupt times, which she termed *muliebre tempus* ("an effeminate age"), thus using both positive female themes (Ecclesia's purity/Mary's virginity; God's charity and wisdom as feminine) and male misogynist-based pejoratives ("effeminate"—still used today, if more vulgarly) to delineate and promote her ideal. Hildegard's *Brautmystik*, therefore, carried bridal imagery beyond Bernard's rhetorical, sentimental exploitation to symbolize all that was positive about women (also the most virtuous aspects of humankind), to counter all their vulnerability to defilement (as evidenced in Eve), whether as persons or as symbolic of the evolving Church. Despite her achievement, lest one be tempted to read Hildegard as a proto-feminist, she nevertheless agreed with the male tradition holding women to be unsuited for the priesthood: always a (contemplative) bride but never a (active) priest.

For twelfth-century mystics in general, the concept underwent a change from Bride as Nation of Israel, from Bride as the Church (collective), to the Bride as a specific individual, with the example of Mary as the bride par excellence, to the individual soul. Through contemplation and mystical ascent, the Believing Soul becomes intimately united to God in Love and Grace. Inherent in the *Brautmystik* is the concept of the *unio mystica*, or the fusion of souls, in which the soul of the Believer is made one with God, without losing its identity. It is a total union involving the transformation of the substance of the soul by sanctifying grace and the transformation of the faculties by divine light, according to the influential German theologian and preacher, Meister Eckhart (c.1260–1328), and his disciples Johannes

Tauler (d. 1361) and Heinrich Seuse (Henry Suso; c.1295–1366). Fueled by such teachings, whether directly or indirectly, the marriage of the soul was seen to transform itself further, as in the case of German mystics as Margareta Ebner (1291–1351) and Christine Ebner (1277–1356), whereby the union of the soul with God becomes more than a mere spiritual betrothal. Nuns at revolutionary convents like Helfta, some major examples being Gertrude the Great (1256–c.1302) and the beguine, Mechthild of Magdeburg (d. 1282), envisioned a consummate union of love with Christ, in which religious passion became imbued with a sensuous love for God with a fixation on the wounds of Christ. But not all Beguines (laywomen leading religious lives) shared Mechthild's enthusiasm for this image, notably Marguerite Porete (d. 1310), who preferred to address Christ as her "overflowing and abandoned love, courtly for my sake without measure" (Newman 1995, 152). German mystical women felt so intensely married to Christ that they either rejected all offers of marriage, especially in the case of remarriage (for example Adelhaid Langmann and Dorothea Beier), or, if already married, the woman came to view her earthly husband as a *nebenbuhler*, or rival, to her soul's relationship with God and, thus felt a great relief when he died. These mystical women then either entered a cloister or gave themselves wholeheartedly to their mystical experiences and to acts of great selflessness and sacrifice.

It is important to note that, during the twelfth century, an intriguing crossover took place between religious and secular sensibilities and expressive levels. Just as the so-called "courtly love" (*fin'amors*) poets borrowed from the devotional thematic and symbolic repertory to ennoble their love for their ladies without sacrificing the poignancy of their passion—distancing it as far from *concupiscentia* (lust) as possible—so religious writers, such as St. Bernard and later the nuns of Helfta, incorporated courtly lyrical motifs and even eroticism to enhance the impact of their teachings. Male preachers were making Ecclesia more seductive to the masses, and women mystics could unite with Christ more directly than any male mystic. Accordingly, *Brautmystik*, especially as related to *Minne* (the German version of *fin'amors*) appears in both secular and religious literature. Jaroslav Pelikan, in discussing the "Church as *Bella sposa*" (Italian *Brautmystik*) theme as one of the "Eternal Feminines," cites the Florentine poet Dante (1265–1320), in his *Divina Commedia* (*Divine Comedy*), as a dramatic, non-German, secular example of this crossover *Brautmystik* in extolling his mortal beloved, Beatrice. Since he rarely uses the word *sposa* ("bride") otherwise, it is significant that Dante, via the ascending use of the bridal metaphor, equates Beatrice with Mary and the Church, in *Paradiso* (*Paradise*) 25: 111 ("la mia donna [. . .] come sposa tacita et immota" ["my Lady [. . .] just like a bride, silent and motionless); *Purgatorio*, 20: 97–98 ("quell'unica sposa / del Spirito Santo' ["that only bride of the Holy Ghost"]; and *Paradiso* 11: 32–33 ("la sposa di colui ch'ad alte grida,/ dispose lei col sangue benedetto" ["the bride of Him who, with loud cries, wedded her with his sacred blood"], respectively.

Since *Brautmystik* was not the only gendered mystical construct, Caroline Bynum's situating of bridal imagery in relation to other motifs (such as that of the maternal Jesus), at least within Cistercian spirituality, rewards consideration. For example, Bynum notes that maternal names for God did not appear in the same texts with devotion to the Virgin; in the *Showings* or *Revelations* of Julian of Norwich (c.1342–post-1416), an important visionary, Mary is given but a minor role, and we find virtually no bridal imagery; among the nuns of Helfta, those emphasizing an attachment to *Brautmystik* tend not to revere Christ as mother. Not surprisingly, Hildegard, too, had eschewed the theme of Christ as mother, along with other popular images relating to spiritual motherhood, such as Ecclesia's breasts nourishing the faithful (Bynum; Newman 1987). Hildegard preferred to ground her theology in the Trinity as a whole rather than in any one of its persons.

See also Beguines; Beier, Dorothea; Birgitta of Sweden, St.; Catherine of Siena, St.; Ebner, Christine; Ebner, Margareta; Gertrude the Great, of Helfta, St.; Hildegard of Bingen, St.; Julian of Norwich; Langmann, Adelhaid; Mechthild of Magdeburg; *Minne*; Porete, Marguerite; Virginity

BIBLIOGRAPHY

Primary Sources

Bernard of Clairvaux. *Sermones super Cantica Canticorum.* Edited by Jean Leclerq, Henri Rochais and C. H. Talbot. Introduction, translation (French), and notes by Paul Verdeyen and Raffaele Fassetta. Paris: Éditions du Cerf. 1996. [Authoritative bilingual ed., Latin-French].

————. *St. Bernard's Sermons on the Canticle of Canticles.* Translated by Ailbe J. Luddy. 2 vols. Ann Arbor, Mich.: University Microfilms, 1978. Original Dublin: Browne & Nolan, 1920.

Dante Alighieri. *Dante's Purgatorio; Dante's Paradiso.* Edited and translated by John D. Sinclair. 2 vols. Galaxy Books. New York: Oxford University Press, 1971. Original 1939.

Eckhart, Meister, et al. In Wentzlaff-Eggebert, Friedrich-W. *Deutsche Mystik zwischen Mittelalter und Neuzeit.* 3rd ed. Berlin: de Gruyter, 1969. Original 1947.

————. *Meister Eckhart: The Essential Sermons, Commentaries, Treatises and Defense.* Translation and introduction by Edmund Colledge and Bernard McGinn. Classics of Western Spirituality. London: SPCK, 1981.

Hildegard of Bingen. *Scivias.* Edited by Adelgundis Führkötter and Angela Carlevaris. *Corpus Christianorum, Continuatio Medievalis* [=CCCM], 43–43a. Turnhout, Belgium: Brepols, 1978.

————. *Scivias.* Translated by Mother Columba Hart and Jane Bishop. Classics of Western Spirituality. New York: Paulist Press, 1990.

Mechthild of Magdeburg. *Das fliessende Licht der Gottheit.* Edited by Hans Neumann. Munich: Artemis, 1990.

————. *The Flowing Light of the Divinity.* Translated by Christiane Mesch Galvani. New York: Garland, 1991.

Porete, Marguerite. *Le Mirouer des simples ames.* Edited by Romana Guarnieri and Paul Verdeyen. CCCM, 69. Turnhout: Brepols, 1986.

————. *The Mirror of Simple Souls.* Translated with commentary by Ellen Babinsky. New York: Paulist Press, 1993.

Secondary Sources

Aumann, Jordan, O. P. "Dionysian Spirituality and Devotio Moderna." In *Christian Spirituality in the Catholic Tradition,* ch. 7. Online: http://www.op.org/domcentral/study/aumann/cs/cs07.htm. [Informative overview].

Bynum, Caroline W. *Jesus as Mother: Studies in the Spirituality of the High Middle Ages.* Berkeley: University of California Press, 1982.

Garber, Rebecca. *Feminine Figurae: Representations of Gender in Religious Texts by Medieval German Women Writers 1100–1375.* Studies in Medieval History and Culture, 10. New York and London: Routledge, 2003.

Newman, Barbara. "*La mystique courtoise:* Thirteenth-Century Beguines and the Art of Love." In Newman, *From Virile Woman to WomanChrist: Studies in Medieval Religion and Literature,* 137–81. The Middle Ages. Philadelphia: University of Pennsylvania Press, 1995.

————. *Sister of Wisdom: St. Hildegard's Theology of the Feminine,* 196–249. Berkeley: University of California Press, 1987.

Pelikan, Jaroslav. *Eternal Feminines: Three Theological Allegories in Dante's Paradiso*. Mason Gross Lectures. New Brunswick, N.J. and London: Rutgers University Press, 1990.

Volfing, Annette. "Dialogue und Brautmystik bei Mechthild von Magdeburg." In *Dialoge im Mittelalter*, edited by Nikolaus Henkel et al. Tübingen, Germany: Max Niemeyer, 2003.

EDITH BRIGITTE ARCHIBALD

BRIDE-PRICE. *See* **Dowry**

BRIDGET OF SWEDEN, ST. *See* **Birgitta of Sweden, St.**

BRIDGETTINE/BIRGITTINE ORDER. *See* **Birgitta of Sweden, St.**

BRISEIDA. *See* **Criseyde**

BRUNHILD (d. 613). Known also as Brunhilda, Brunichildis, and Brunehaut, Brunhild was queen of the Franks; she was endowed with indomitable will, intelligence, and statesmanship. Brunhild was born in Visigothic Spain, the daughter of Athanagild, king of the Visigoths, and Goiswinth. She married Sigibert I of Metz, a king of the Franks (560/61–575). She was the favorite of historian Gregory of Tours (538/9–594) and an Arian (Arianism being an early, but heretical, form of Christianity), but was converted by the bishops and the king who begged her to accept the Church. Her marriage was a felicitous one; Brunhild and Sigibert had three children, two daughters, Ingund and Clodosind, and a son, Childebert. Sigibert was in contention his own half-brother, Chilperic I (c.537–584) for greater portions of their late father's realm. The conflict intensified after Chilperic had his previous wife, Galswintha, Brunhild's sister, killed to marry the lower-born Fredegund (d. 597), a nonfavorite of Gregory of Tours and thus the most notorious of King Chilperic's wives. When her husband was murdered by agents of Queen Fredegund (575), Brunhild suffered overwhelming anguish and grief. Although her son Childebert, then aged five, was proclaimed Sigibert's successor (as Childebert II), Brunhild was taken by Chilperic from Paris to Rouen, her daughters were held in custody at Meaux, and her treasure was seized.

Merovech, the son of Chilperic by his first wife, Audovera, rescued Brunhild by marrying her in 575, an account of which survives from Gregory of Tours's later eulogy of Brunhild. But Brunhild soon realized that she could more easily exercise power as regent for her son if Merovech were confined to a monastery. Merovech was eventually murdered by his servant at his own request when his father was about to capture him as he escaped from the monastery.

The animosity between Brunhild and Fredegund would last through some three generations, as the following episodes will show. Moreover, Brunhild understood clearly that to maintain her influence at her son's court, she could not yield her position to a younger woman. She therefore broke off the engagement of her son Childebert II to the Bavarian princess Theudolinda, and accepted—some believe she even arranged—the marriage of

Childebert to his former mistress, Faileuba, a self-effacing woman. Queen Faileuba's only deed mentioned by Gregory of Tours—her discovery of a plot to have her husband marry another woman and have his mother ousted from his court—suggests that she was under the protection of Brunhild.

By opening relations with Spain, Byzantium, and the papacy, Brunhild was emerging as a key figure in Austrasian politics (Austrasia then encompassing the northeastern part of the Frankish Merovingian kingdom) during her son's minority. The foreign connections developed by Brunhild with Spain and Byzantium were cemented through the marriage of her daughter, Ingund, to the Visigothic prince Hermengild, and through Brunhild's concern for the fate of Ingund's son, Athanagild, who was placed in Byzantine hands when his mother died in Africa. Brunhild's friendship with Pope Gregory I (the Great, c.540–604) may also be regarded as an extension of the ties she cultivated with influential Frankish and Burgundian Churchmen. Nor did Brunhild neglect to build relations with her in-laws. The Treaty of Andelot, concluded with King Gunthram in 587, procured for Childebert II the kingdom of Burgundy.

Her correspondence sheds light on other aspects of her politics and personality. Addressed to the Byzantine emperor Maurice (c.539–602) and his wife Anastasia, her letters express concern for her grandson Athanagild's fate. Pope Gregory the Great's letters to her also attest her high station, in his addressing her as "the good and Christian woman" of whom he asks various favors: to protect certain priests and bishops, to hold synods to help purge the realm of sinners, to receive the papal legate graciously, and to accept the religious Gregory sent to her. Furthermore, the pope extols Brunhild's role in the foundation of the church, monastery, and poorhouse of Autun (in Burgundy).

The enmity between Brunhild and Fredegund continued even after King Chilperic I died in 584: Fredegund tried to have Brunhild murdered several times, first by a cleric who, after being flogged, was sent back to Fredegund, then by two clerics who began to shiver after being told of Fredegund's plan so that she had to drug them. After their failed attempt, they were thrown into prison in Soissons and, despite their confessions, put to death.

After the death of Childebert II and division of his kingdom, Brunhild suffered insults from Bilichild, her former slave and now wife of her grandson Theudebert II of Austrasia, and then expulsion from Austrasia in 599 by aristocratic adversaries, like Arnulf of Metz and Pepin of Landen, who disapproved of Brunhild's efforts to Romanize the government. Yet these misfortunes only strengthened the dowager queen's resolve to rule. She then sought to prevent the marriage of her other grandson, Theuderic II, ruler of Burgundy to the Visigothic princess, Ermenberta. Her fixation on this issue and her attempts to avenge the humiliation she had suffered in Theudebert's kingdom led to her eventual downfall. With the help of Protadius, her purported lover whom she managed to have nominated mayor of Burgundy in 606, Brunhild almost succeeded in carrying out her plans. But the mayor was assassinated by a faction of the nobility opposed to war with Austrasia. Although Brunhild prevailed and punished the conspirators, and managed temporarily to reunite Burgundy and Austrasia (612), her intrigue over Theuderic II's marriage plans and her banishment of Desiderius, the bishop of Vienne (who dared to criticize her policy of surrounding the young king with concubines) did not enhance her popularity. The chronicler Fredegar (mid-600s) blamed her for the stoning of Desiderius.

Whatever her role in that tragic affair may have been, her subsequent quarrel with the Irish monk Saint Columban (or Columbanus, d. 615) reinforced her reputation as a vengeful and troublesome woman. When he visited the court in 611, Columban refused to bless Theuderic's children on the grounds that they were the offspring of prostitutes (presumably the concubines lamented by Desiderius). Outraged, Brunhild chased the saint from the court and the kingdom.

After the sudden death of Theuderic II in 613, Brunhild found herself without any supporters. Betrayed by the mayor of the palace, Brunhild had no alternative but to try to make peace with Clothar II of Neustria in another attempt to secure the regency for herself during the minority of her great-grandsons. But Clothar, son of Chilperic I and Fredegund, was not inclined to mercy. When the dowager went to visit him, Clothar subjected her to a cruel and humiliating death. Tortured and paraded before the army as a lowly criminal, then tied to the feet of an untamed horse that dragged her along the ground until she was torn from limb to limb, in a final act of contempt, the once-proud queen was thrown into the fire. Both the anonymous *Liber Historiae francorum* (*Book of the History of the Franks*) and Ionas (or Jonas) of Bobbio, in his life of Saint Columban, impute many atrocities to her, thereby diminishing sympathy for her horrible demise.

See also Amalasuntha; Chelles, Nun of

BIBLIOGRAPHY

Primary Sources
Brunhild. [5 Letters]. *Epistulae Austrasicae.* Edited by Wilhelm Gundlach, 26–30, 44, 139–50. *Monumenta Germaniae Historica* (= MGH). *Epistolae merowingici et karolini aevi*, 3. Berlin, 1892. [Latin text only].
Gregory of Tours. *Historia Francorum.* Critical ed. by W. Arndt and Bruno Krusch, 4: 27–28, 51; 5: 1–3, 14, 18, 39; 6: 40, 46; 8: 18–21, 28, 31; 9. 4: 16, 20, 24. MGH. *Scriptores rerum merovingicarum*,1. Hannover, Germany: Hahn, 1884. [Latin text only].
———. *History of the Franks.* Translated with commentary by Ormonde M. Dalton, vol. 2. Oxford: Oxford University Press, 1927.
Fredegar. [*Chronicles*, orig. Latin]. In MGH. *Scriptores rerum merovingicarum*, edited by Bruno Krusch, 2: 1–193. Hannover: Hahn, 1888.
———. *The Fourth Book of the Chronicle of Fredegar with Its Continuations.* Edited and translated by J. M. Wallace-Hadrill. London: Nelson, 1960.
Ionas of Bobbio. *Ionae Vitae sanctarum Columbani, Vedasti, Iohannis.* Edited by Bruno Krusch. MGH. *Scriptores rerum germanicarum in usu scholarum*, 4. Hannover: Hahn, 1905.
Liber Historiae Francorum. Edited and translated by Bernard S. Bachrach. Lawrence, Kans.: Coronado Press, 1973. [Bilingual ed.].

Secondary Sources
Ewig, Eugen. "Die frankischen Teilungen und Teilreiche (511–613)." *Akademie der Wissenschaften und Literatur. Abhandlungen der geistes- und sozialwissenschaftlichen Klasse* 9 (1952): 651–715.
Kurth, Godefroid. "La reine Brunehaut." In Kurth, *Études franques*, 1: 265–356. 2 vols. Paris: Honoré Champion; Brussels: A. Dewit, 1919.
Nelson, Janet L. "Queens as Jezebels: The Careers of Brunhild and Balthild in Merovingian History." In *Medieval Women*, edited by Derek Baker, 31–77. Studies in Church History. Subsidia, 1. Oxford: Basil Blackwell, 1978.

SUZANNE FONAY WEMPLE

BRYNHILD. *See* **Valkyries**

BUDDHISM. *See* **China, Women in (400–1450); Wu, Empress**

BUGGA (fl. early to mid-8th century). Also known as Bucge, or Heaburg, the Anglo-Saxon nun Bugga corresponded with the future St. Boniface (c.675–c.754), the great English missionary leader, called the "Apostle of Germany." She was the daughter of Eadburg (or Eadburga), famous abbess of a convent in Thanet (for which reason the town is now called Minster-in-Thanet), near Kent, who had also exchanged letters with Boniface. Bugga's one known existing letter was written c.720 from England to Boniface in northern Germany.

Because Bugga was a fairly common name in Anglo-Saxon England in the eighth century, it is thanks to determination of her mother's identity that this Bugga has been identified as one of Boniface's correspondents. Little is known of Bugga's life, except that she met Boniface in Rome in 738 or 739, and she outlived him by some years as abbess of a monastery in Kent. Boniface died at the hands of the Frisian brigands in 754. Since Archbishop Bregwin mentions her after her death as *honorabilis abbatissa*—in his letter to St. Lull (d. 786), the Anglo-Saxon bishop of Mainz, Germany—sometime between 759 and 765, we might deduce that she succeeded her mother at Thanet. Other glimpses of these women's lives come from a letter by her mother, Eadburg, to Boniface, lamenting their poverty and lack of friends due to their monastic isolation. More positively, Boniface had written Eadburg in 717 about a mystical experience of a monk under her predecessor, and later (c.732) requested from her a copy of the *Epistles* of St. Peter in gold lettering, which attests the high esteem in which he held Eadburg's scriptorium (Fell; Emerton; Larrington).

As a testimony to both eighth-century Classical Latin learning and (certain) women's literacy, Bugga's letter to Boniface reflects the remarkable level of literacy characterizing Boniface's circle of women correspondents whose studiousness and expressivity sometimes approached that of the monks. Bugga's unique brand of Latin bears traces of the complex, amplified, ornate style usually associated with Adhelm (c.640–c.709), abbot of Malmesbury, then bishop of Sherborne. Aldhelm, dubbed by many "the first English man of letters," was well schooled at his hometown of Wessex in the available Classical Latin canon, though, like his compatriot Bede (673–735), this was acquired more through grammarians' compilations than by reading the major authors firsthand. Aldhelm does seem nevertheless to have possessed direct knowledge of Virgil, Pliny, Cicero, and Juvenal—no small feat for those times (Reynolds and Wilson). Aldhelm also infused his school Latin with Anglo-Saxon touches, as did his Irish and Frankish contemporaries. Because Aldhelm, a future saint, was also a religious reformer and monastic founder, his numerous works found a ready audience and his style was quite influential. Interestingly enough, however, Boniface himself, though he had been a student under Aldhelm, wrote in a less pretentious, cleaner, and more poetic Latin style, which his protégées hoped to emulate.

In terms of content, Bugga's letter also reveals much about the relationship between Boniface and his women followers. She begins by addressing Boniface as "venerable servant of God, endowed with many symbols of spiritual gifts, and most worthy priest of God," while portraying herself as "Bugga, humblest housemaid of God," and pledging her "enduring" and, later, "unfeigned," affection. In general, she is asking Boniface for his protection. More specifically, she alludes to a book she had evidently promised him, the *Sufferings of the Martyrs*, which she promises to send him as soon as she can obtain it. In return, she asks that Boniface "comfort my insignificance by sending me, as you promised in your dear letter, some collection of the sacred writings." She also requests that he say Mass for a deceased member of her family, and closes by announcing her donation, to be borne by the same messenger as the one carrying him this letter, of "fifty *solidi* [gold coins] and an altar cloth," apologizing for its slight worth but assuring him it is the best she can do (cited from trans. Emerton, 40–41).

See also Boniface, St., Mission and Circle of; Scribes and Scriptoria

BIBLIOGRAPHY

Primary Sources
Aldhelm, St. *Aldhelm: the Prose Works*, edited by Michael Lapidge and Michael Herren. New York: Barnes & Noble, 1979.
Boniface, St., and Bugga et al. [Letters: Bugga to Boniface]. In *Patrologia Latina*, edited by J.-P. Migne, 89: 690. [Boniface to Bugga]. 89: 729–31.
———. [Letters]. In *Die Briefe des heilgen Bonifatius und Lullus*, edited by Michael Tangl. *Monumenta Germaniae Historica* [=MGH]. *Epistolae Selectae*, 1: 15–18. 2nd ed. Berlin: Weidmann, 1955. [Latin Text only, more authoritative than *Patrologia*].
———. In *Epistolae merovingici et karolini aevi*, edited by Ernst Ludwig Dümmler, MGH 1: 428–30. Berlin: Weidmann, 1891. Reprint 1957.
———. In *The Letters of St. Boniface*, translated by Ephraim Emerton, 40–41. Records of Civilization, 31. New York: Columbia University Press, 1940. Reprint, New York: Octagon, 1973.
———. *The English Correspondence of Saint Boniface*. Translated by Edward Kylie. New York: Cooper Square, 1966. Original London, 1924.

Secondary Sources
Fell, Christine. "Some Implications of the Boniface Correspondence." In *New Readings on Women in Old English Literature*, edited by Helen Damico and Alexandra H. Olsen, 29–43. Bloomington: Indiana University Press, 1990.
———. *Women in Anglo-Saxon England*. Oxford: Blackwell, 1984.
Larrington, Carolyne. *Women and Writing in Medieval Europe: A Sourcebook*. London and New York: Routledge, 1995.
Olsen, Alexandra H. http://www.umilta.net/boniface.html. [A most informative Web site for women of Bugga's milieu linking to women in other medieval contexts].
Reynolds, L. D., and N. G. Wilson. *Scribes and Scholars: A Guide to the Transmission of Greek & Latin Literature*. 3rd ed. Oxford: Clarendon Press, 1991.

SR. JANE PATRICIA FREELAND

BURGINDA (fl. early to mid-8th century). Burginda was a nun who copied manuscripts and composed a learned letter, and about whom not much else is known. Her correspondence with an unnamed youth places her sometime around 700. Even the name Burginda is uncertain and seems to be more indicative of English, rather than German, lineage. The only evidence of her literary activity is a letter written and signed by her in the manuscript's margin (De Hamel, 31–32), appearing at the end of an early English manuscript containing a commentary by the fifth-century abbot Apponius on the *Canticum canticorum* (*Song of Songs*). Because Burginda's letter, a sort of mini-commentary attached to Apponius's commentary, is itself highly learned—replete with quotations from Virgil and other Classical Latin authors, along with early Christian authors—some scholars doubt the letter to have been written in her hand because of its various spelling errors, rather unseemly in such a literate author. The letter also contains an anonymous literary work in Latin. Nonetheless, Burginda has been credited with it, and she is now cited among the sparse ranks of medieval women scribes.

See also Boniface, St., Mission and Circle of; Scribes and Scriptoria

BIBLIOGRAPHY

Primary Sources
Apponius. *Apponii in Canticum canticorum expositionem*. Edited by Bernard de Vregille and Louis Neyrand. *Corpus Christianorum, Series Latina*, 19. Turnhout, Belgium: Brepols, 1986. [See pp. 391–463].
———. *Commentaire sur le Cantique des cantiques*. Edited and translated with introduction and notes by Bernard de Vregille and Louis Neyrand. Paris: Éditions du Cerf, 1997–1998. [Bilingual ed. Latin-French].

Secondary Sources
De Hamel, Christopher. *Illuminated Manuscripts*. Oxford: Phaidon, 1986.
"Burginda." In *Lexikon des Mittelalters*, edited by Robert Auty et. al., vol. 2. Munich and Zurich: Artemis, 1981.

EDITH BRIGITTE ARCHIBALD

C

CAESARIA, ST. (fl. 502–pre-542). An early Merovingian saint, Caesaria was the mother superior of the St. Jean (St. John) monastery in Arles, southern France, completed in 512. Because she influenced her brother, Caesarius, bishop of Arles (502–542) in writing the monastery's constitution, or rule (*regula*), as it was called—theirs was the first rule composed exclusively for women. She and her (apparently) unrelated, but eponymous, successor, Caesaria II, or the Younger (fl. 542–561), with whom she is often confused, became important female figures in early Western monasticism.

Both siblings, Caesarius and Caesaria I, had committed themselves to the religious life early on. Before leading the St. Jean community, Caesaria had lived in a house established in Marseilles by the Scythian monk, John Cassian (c.360–c.430), himself the author of a rule, known briefly as the *Institutes*. For his part, the learned Caesarius had been nurtured at the flourishing abbey at Lérins (founded c.410)—a small island (now Saint-Honorat) off Cannes, southern France. In formulating his *Regula sanctarum virginum* (*Rule for Holy Virgins*), Caesarius combined the scholarly tradition of Lérins with the community spirit characterizing St. Augustine's rule (part of which was intended for women) and his own knowledge of Cassian. Caesarius's rule advocated feminine participation in monastic governance and his nuns' institutional independence from women belonging to the early Church of Gaul. Three main points followed in Caesaria's community beginning in 512, according to their rule, were: exemption from episcopal control (governance by the Church bishops); economic self-sufficiency; and prohibition of nuns' sewing, weaving, and needlework in favor of more intellectual and contemplative pursuits. Much of the Rule's text pertains to claustration, or strict enclosure of nuns within the cloister walls, allowing few, if any, visitors from the outside. This severe but practical measure, inherited from some earlier monasteries, provided a safe, separate, feminine community during the unsettled, dangerous times of barbarian Europe. The closed house's womb-like ambience also fostered the necessary serenity for the contemplative life and spiritual perfection.

The practices of the St. John's were adopted by other independent, aristocratic foundations north of Arles, most notably by the convent of St. Croix (Holy Cross) in Poitiers, established c.660 by Queen, and later St., Radegund (d. 587). Caesaria II corresponded with Radegund about the daily exercise of the Rule for their respective communities, also providing the queen with a summary/copy of it. The comments in her letters to Radegund reflect Caesaria's support for other contemplative foundations and serve to document the kind of "networking" activities in which these early women founders engaged for the good of their houses. Caesaria, as the more experienced abbess, advises Radegund on various matters: for example, when she urges the ascetic queen to ease for her nuns' sake the bodily austerities she inflicts on herself for Lent, and likewise for their devotions in general; Radegund should not expect her "daughters" to be able to tolerate such an austere regimen as she herself does. In another letter, Caesaria insists on the primacy of reading and learning in convents following Caesarius' Rule: "You must read and listen assiduously from the divine lessons [. . .] to gather from them precious daisies for your ears to make from [these precious lessons] rings and bracelets." Finally, constant prayer must be supported by charitable works.

In the end, it was Caesaria the Elder who was canonized; her feast day is January 12.

See also Radegund, St.; Rules for Canonesses, Nuns, and Recluses

BIBLIOGRAPHY

Primary Sources
Caesaria II (the Younger). [Letter to Radegund]. In *Monumenta Germaniae Historica. Epistolae Ævi Merovingici Collectae*, 2: 450. [Latin text only].
———. [Letter to Radegund]. "Caesaria the Insignificant, . . ." In *Sainted Women of the Dark Ages*, edited and translated by Jo Ann McNamara, John E. Halborg et al., 112–18. Durham, N.C.: Duke University Press, 1992.
Caesarius of Arles. [*Regula sanctarum virginum*]. In *Œuvres monastiques*, introduced, edited and translated (*French*) by Adalbert de Vogüé and Joël Courreau. 2 vols. Paris: Éditions du Cerf, 1988.
———. *Rule for Nuns*. Translated with introduction by Mary McCarthy. Studies in Medieval History, n.s. 16. Washington, D.C.: Catholic University of America Press, 1960.

Secondary Sources
[See also notes to editions and translations above].
Ranft, Patricia. *Women and the Religious Life in Premodern Europe*. New York: St. Martin's, 1996.
Schulenberg, Jane T. "Strict Active Enclosure and Its Effect on the Female Monastic Experience, 500–1100." In *Medieval Religious Women, 1: Distant Echoes*, edited by John A. Nichols and Lillian T. Shank, 51–86. Kalamazoo, Mich.: Cistercian Publications, 1984.

DUEY WHITE

CANTIGAS DE AMIGO. See *Chanson de Femme* (Women's Song)

CANTIGAS DE SANTA MARIA. See **Mary, Blessed Virgin, in the Middle Ages**

CAPELLANUS, ANDREAS (late 12th century). Andreas Capellanus, or André le Chapelain, authored the best-known treatise on love, usually called the *De amore* (*On Love*), an enlightening yet controversial document. Like many medieval authors, he is difficult to identify definitively, since so little real information exists about his life. Because of the way in which Andreas describes himself in the text, and because of certain of the work's references and allusions, critics until recently have assumed that he was a chaplain at the court of Countess Marie de Champagne (1145–1198). Since Marie was the daughter of King Louis VII of France (1120–1180) and Eleanor of Aquitaine (1122–1204), was married to Count Henry the Liberal, and became a celebrated literary patron to whom the renowned Chrétien de Troyes (fl. 1165–1191) dedicated his romance, *Lancelot, le Chevalier de la charrette* (*Lancelot, the Knight of the Cart*), venerating the adulterous love affair between Lancelot and Guinevere, Marie's patronage of Andreas seems a logical surmise. This especially as Marie also figures in Andreas's treatise; and certain charters that form the court of Champagne bear the signature of one "Andreas."

Despite these facts, more recent criticism has cast doubt on this identification. Some believe that Andreas was a member not of Marie's court at Troyes (the capital of Champagne in northeastern France) but of the royal court of Philip II Augustus (1165–1223), at Paris. Others hold that "Andreas" is a pen name, and that his status implied by his name—that of chaplain (a priest, in charge of a chapel, often appointed to high dignitaries of Church and state)—may be only a fictive post at the literary-imaginary court of the King (or God) of Love. Similar speculation revolves around Gualterius (Walter), the young friend to whom Andreas dedicates the work. Disagreements have also arisen concerning the date of the *De amore*'s composition (also called *De arte honeste amandi* [*Art of Honest Loving*]), but it seems most likely that the work was written in the 1180s, at the height of the flowering of northern French courtly literature of love.

Although it is difficult to pin down the *De amore*'s precise authorship and date, it is clear that the work is linked intimately to the medieval courtly tradition, both in Latin (the language in which the treatise was composed) and in the vernacular (whether Old French, Middle-High German, etc.). Such a tradition represents an abstract, personalized emotion like love in highly formalized, even learned terms. Andreas makes explicit reference to texts of many kinds, from the Bible (both Old and New Testaments) and the writings of the Fathers of the Church to numerous classical (and thus pagan) authors, as well as to medieval secular works such as the love debate and the courtly romance. The *De amore* treats the subject of "courtly love" (a now disputed term, but still without a better alternative)—the type of love for its own sake (hence Andreas's term "honest love"), unfettered by the usual feudal marriage contracts—idealized by poets at court. Various love situations are presented as a series of legal cases to be judged by a fictive tribunal of famous real-life women of the time (twelfth century), many prominent in literary circles, including not only Marie de Champagne but also Eleanor of Aquitaine, Isobel of Vermandois (a cousin of Marie, and wife of Philip of Flanders [or Philippe d'Alsace, 1144–1191], Chrétien's other known patron), and Ermengard, viscountess of Narbonne (c.1130–1196?), a patron of the major Provençal troubadours. But the *De amore*'s most basic literary foundation is the *Ars amatoria* (*The Art of Love*) and *Remedia amoris* (*Cures for Love*) of Ovid, the first-century Roman poet whose works on love were among the best-known literary texts of the Latin Middle Ages because their unequaled value as models for deftly yet powerfully expressing the psychology of love. The *De amore* forms a part of a pervasive tradition of imitation and adaptation of Ovid's amatory texts underlying all twelfth- and thirteenth-century courtly love literature.

The *De amore* is composed of a brief preface and three books; the first is by far the longest. In the preface, Andreas explains that his young friend Gualterius, having recently fallen victim to the tender passion, has asked for a treatise on the art of love. Despite his reservations, Andreas agrees to write on this subject, since Gualterius is more likely to proceed cautiously if he is instructed in this art than if he is not. This reservation on Andreas's part, though it seems here to be only a literary commonplace, is in fact an essential element of the work, as the third book makes plain.

The treatise proper begins with Book One. Andreas defines love as a kind of suffering (*passio*) that develops from seeing, and then thinking obsessively about, a person of the opposite sex. (Love is, in Andreas's view, invariably heterosexual.) Gualterius is told that love is fearful by nature and that it completely preoccupies the lover; its Latin name (*amor*) is derived, following the authoritative sixth-century etymologist Isidore of Seville, from *hamus* (hook), because love catches the lover as a fisherman catches a fish. Only people who are neither too old nor too young (men between fourteen and sixty, women from twelve to fifty) are suitable for love, which cannot exist without physical beauty and sexual vigor. Lovers are also usually to be found only among the upper classes, because these alone enjoy the requisite wealth and leisure to pursue love.

The bulk of Book One is composed of dialogues between couples of various levels of the aristocracy, with an occasional commoner thrown in. In each dialogue, Andreas prescribes the approach the man should take in attempting to persuade the woman to accede to his requests. The exchange examines, in legalistic terms, the theory, difficulties, and conditions of love. In no case is it apparent that the woman is persuaded to give her consent. One of the dialogues—that between a nobleman and a noblewoman—contains an allegory that describes the rewards and punishments reserved for three types of women—the judicious, the promiscuous, and the reluctant—in the afterlife. It then goes on to reveal the twelve precepts of appropriate behavior for lovers, who are enjoined, for example, to avoid greed, maintain chastity, and keep their love secret. In another dialogue, a couple from the upper nobility discusses the place of clerics in love. Here the man, a cleric, argues that he need behave with no more moral circumspection than any other Christian, and hence is permitted to love; his partner is skeptical. The relationship of love and sex, money, and prostitutes is also discussed.

Book Two, like the second book of Ovid's *Ars amatoria*, addresses the subject of keeping love alive, a feat accomplished by maintaining courtly behavior and avoiding selfishness, duplicity, impotence—and marriage. Other situations surprising or problematic to modern readers emerge. For example, Andreas excuses infidelity among men but condemns it among women as the *vetus error*, the "primeval sin." And he reveals that, although he is a cleric, he is a hopeless victim of love. This declaration is followed by judgments on various cases of love, many of which are pronounced by the women mentioned previously. The book concludes with a miniature courtly romance culminating in the revelation of thirty-one *regulae amoris* (i.e., "rules for loving" or "regular occurrences in love"). Some of these are jarring (e.g., I: "Marriage is no excuse for not loving"); others are commonplaces (XV: "Every lover grows pale when he sees his partner"). Courtliness, jealousy, and allusions to the medieval medical tradition of lovesickness (the lover's loss of appetite and irregular heartbeat) make up the bulk of the other rules.

The final book begins with another address to Gualterius. Here Andreas explains that he has written about the art of love because of his affection for his friend, but he urges the young man to avoid putting his precepts into practice. With this suggestion, Andreas begins a radical about-face. In Book Three, *De reprobatione amoris* (*The Condemnation of Love*), he contradicts every favorable proposition the first two books enunciated. Love, Andreas declares, is denounced by the Bible, harms friendship, and causes murder: it enslaves the lover, causes endless suffering, leads frequently to murder and adultery, and imperils the soul. Women, furthermore—though they had earlier been presented as beloved, teachers, and judges—are now condemned, in inflammatory terms, as miserly, envious, greedy, gluttonous, fickle, devious, disobedient, rebellious, gossipy, licentious, evil, and unfaithful. At the end of the text, Andreas begs his young friend to follow his advice, renounce the world, and prepare his soul to be ready for the second coming of Christ.

In attempting to analyze Andreas's treatise, we are most struck by its profound discontinuity. Both Andreas's judgments on love and women and also his narrator's own pose are self-contradictory, and yet the work makes no effort to resolve its intrinsic conflict. From the Middle Ages (when copiers, adapters, and translators of the text often modified or suppressed either the pro-love or the anti-love sections, according to each version's specific bias) to the twentieth century (when critics have viewed this work either as a defense or as a condemnation of courtly love), readers have tended to read the *De amore* as a manifestation of one or the other of the extreme positions it contains. Andreas himself notes that his work contains a "*duplex sententia*" (a double meaning). This very duplicity aptly reflects the position of medieval secular love literature: vehemently condemned by ecclesiastical morality and celebrated by courtly poets. Andreas does not attempt to reconcile these two positions, since it would be impossible to do so. He does, however, far more than most writers on either side of the ideological division, allow free expression from both sides.

Another aspect of the *De amore*'s discontinuity is to be found in the complex ways in which it represents the politics of gender. On the one hand, the work seems to have been aimed primarily, or even exclusively, at a masculine readership, as several of its features strongly suggest: its Latin composition (few women in the twelfth century were trained in the language of the Church), its male-inscribed reader (Gualterius), and its reception (it was often read and cited by male members of the clergy). At the same time, the text is obsessed with the feminine. Andreas teaches Gualterius the art of reading so that the young man may be able to decipher thoughts and behavior of members of the female sex, women govern the first book's dialogues and the second book's debates on love, and it is women who pose the fundamental threats to men's happiness and salvation in Book Three.

But in the midst of the traditional opposition of male and female, which, like so much of the text, has its roots in Ovid's *Ars amatoria*, Andreas places a third category: the clergy. Following an important medieval tradition, Andreas's characters attempt to prove that clergymen are, in their ability to love, at least the equals of their lay brethren, and perhaps even superior to them. Nevertheless, their arguments prove unconvincing. In fact, the clerics of the *De amore* are presented with a remarkable number of characteristics that the author has attributed to disgraced members of the female sex. The lechery and gluttony with which Andreas charges women in Book Three, for example, are in fact sins traditionally ascribed to the male monastic community. Moreover, when Andreas argues that a churchman may sin in his *actions* provided that his *sermons* conform to propriety, he is brandishing as a clerical virtue the hypocrisy he labels as women's most dangerous vice. And when Andreas declares, in Book One, that male clerics may engage freely in love while involving nuns in such an activity is strictly forbidden, and when he goes on to reveal the fact that he himself has nearly violated this interdiction, it becomes clear that no classification, principle, or rule about gender or love in his text is stable. Women, the laity, and clerics are all embroiled in the text's play of morality and immorality, desire and fantasy.

The *De amore* has had a complex history of transmission and reception. It survives in a dozen manuscripts dating from the thirteenth to the fifteenth centuries, and which are found in libraries across Europe. Two Renaissance editions date from the fifteenth and early seventeenth centuries. The most recent full redaction, from which subsequent translations derive, dates from 1892. Numerous medieval translations and adaptations survive. In France, the work was twice translated from Latin into French in the thirteenth century, from which Jean de Meun cites in his continuation of the *Roman de la Rose* (*Romance of the Rose*, c.1275). But this vernacular tradition was abruptly halted in 1277, when Etienne Tempier, bishop of Paris, explicitly condemned the *De amore*, along with 219 philosophical propositions judged heretical, and forbade their teaching on pain of excommunication. Elsewhere in Europe, however, the *De amore* remained popular. Many references to it are contained in German ecclesiastical texts. It was also translated into Catalan and Tuscan in the fourteenth century, now accessible in modern printed editions.

While the *De amore* is not considered to be the artistic equal of the works of Chrétien de Troyes or of the *Roman de la Rose*, the questions it raises, its broad frame of reference, and its willingness to confront (if not to resolve) the fundamentally disparate attitudes of ecclesiastical and literary writers toward secular love accord this text an important role in the medieval courtly tradition.

See also Arthurian Women; Christine de Pizan; Eleanor of Aquitaine; Ermengard of Narbonne; Guinevere; Marie de Champagne; *Minne*; *Roman de la Rose*, Debate of the; *Trobairitz*; *Vertu du Sacrement de Mariage, Livre de la*

BIBLIOGRAPHY

Primary Sources
Andreas Capellanus. Trojel, E. *Andreae Capellani Regii Francorum De Amore Libri Tres*. Copenhagen: Gade, 1892. Reprint Munich, 1972.
————. Walsh, P. G., ed. and trans. *Andreas Capellanus on Love*. Duckworth Classical, Medieval and Renaissance Editions. London: Duckworth, 1982. [Bilingual Latin-English ed.].
————. *The Art of Courtly Love*. Translation, introduction, and notes by John Jay Parry. Records of Civilization. New ed. New York: Columbia University Press, 1990. [English version only].

Secondary Sources
Allen, Peter L. *The Art of Love: Amatory Fiction from Ovid to the "Romance of the Rose."* Philadelphia: University of Pennsylvania Press, 1992.
Benton, John. "Clio and Venus: An Historical View of Medieval Love." In *The Meaning of Courtly Love*, edited by Francis X. Newman, 19–42. Albany: State University of New York Press, 1968.
Jaeger, C. Stephen. *Ennobling Love: In Search of a Lost Sensibility*. The Middle Ages. Philadelphia: University of Pennsylvania Press, 1999.
Karnein, Alfred. *De amore in volkssprachlicher Literatur: Untersuchungen zur Andreas-Capellanus-Rezeption im Mittelalter und Renaissance*. Germanisch-romanische Monatsschrift, Beiheft 4. Heidelberg: Carl Winter, 1985.
Moi, Toril. "Desire in Language: Andreas Capellanus and the Controversy of Courtly Love." In Moi, *What Is a Woman? And Other Essays*, ch. 9. Oxford and New York: Oxford University Press, 1999.
Monson, Don A. "Andreas Capellanus and the Problem of Irony." *Speculum* 63 (1988): 539–72.

PETER L. ALLEN

CARENZA, NA (c.1190–c. early 1230s). Na Carenza—"Na" being a Provençal form of the Latin "Domina," meaning "Lady"—is the wise-woman figure and possibly a coauthor, of the *tenso* (Provençal debate poem) titled "Na Carenza al bel cors avinenz" ("Lady Carenza, of fair and lovely form"), after its opening verse. Modern scholars including Matilda Bruckner underscore the difficulty of analyzing this poem because of its scribe's ignorance of Provençal and thus the poem's proper structuring. Following Bruckner's edition, and a traditional debate-poem theme (Rieger), the young and beautiful sisters, N'Alais and Na Iselda—or, if we follow Bec's and Bruckner's reading, they are but one woman named Alaisina Yselda—turn(s) to Na Carenza for advice on whether to marry or remain virgins in the poem's first *cobla* (stanza).

Na Carenza then responds via her own *cobla*, advising the sisters to take a husband "coronat de scienza" ("crowned with wisdom"), for "Retenguta.s pulsel'a cui l'epos" ("she who has him as a spouse remains a virgin"). She also seems to counsel the young woman/ women toward becoming Brides of Christ or to embrace spiritual—that is, celibate— marriage, and also requests rather enigmatically that she/they remember and pray for her when they are "en l'umbra de ghirenza" ("in the protective shadow")—an allusion that Bruckner connects to certain Psalms while also acknowledging René Nelli's attribution of such elements to Catharism, the antimarriage heresy of southern France, from whence this poem originates. We should also note that Meg Bogin, then Peter Dronke, follow a different ordering of the stanzas in their analyses that perceive this exchange as a tri-partite, rather than two-part, conversation among the three women, thus heightening the distinction between possibly satirical (Anderson; Bec 1984) and serious voices.

See also Alaisina Yselda; Bride of Christ/*Brautmystik*; Celibacy; *Frauenfrage*; *Trobairitz*; Virginity

BIBLIOGRAPHY

Primary Sources
Carenza. In *Songs of the Women Troubadours*, edited and translated by Matilda Tomaryn Bruckner, Laurie Shepard, and Sarah White, 96–97, 177–79. New York: Garland, 1995. Revised ed. 2000. [Original texts, notes, and English translation].
———. In *Trobairitz: Der Beitrag der Frau in der altokzitanischen höfischen Lyrik. Edition des Gesamtkorpus*, edited by Angelica Rieger, 158–65. Beihefte der Zeitschrift für romanische Philologie, 233. Tübingen, Germany: Max Niemeyer Verlag, 1991. [Original texts, German notes].
Boutière, Jean, and Alexander H. Schutz, eds. *Biographies des Troubadours: Textes provençaux des XIIIᵉ et XIVᵉ siècles*. Revised ed. with I. M. Cluzel, 422–24. Les Classiques d'Oc, 1. Paris: Nizet, 1964. [Texts of the original *Vidas*].

Secondary Sources
Anderson, Patricia. "*Na Carenza al bel cors avinen*: A Test Case for Recovering the Fictive Element in the Poetry of the Women Troubadours." *Tenso* 2 (1987): 55–64.
Bec, Pierre. "Avoir des enfants ou rester vierge? Une tenson occitane du XIIᵉ siècle entre femmes." In *Mittelalterstudien: Erich Köhler zum Gedenken*, edited by Henning Krauss and Dietmar Rieger, 21–30. Heidelberg: Carl Winter, 1984.
———. *Burlesque et obscénité chez les troubadours: pour une approche du contre-texte médiéval*, 201–5. Paris: Stock, 1984.
Bogin, Meg. *The Women Troubadours*. New York and London: W. W. Norton, 1980. Original Paddington Press, 1976.
Dronke, Peter. *Women Writers of the Middle Ages: A Critical Study of Texts from Perpetua (†203) to Marguerite Porete (†1310)*, 101–2. Cambridge: Cambridge University Press, 1984.
Jeanroy, Alfred. *La Poésie lyrique des troubadours*, 1: 355. Toulouse and Paris: Privat, 1934. Reprint Geneva: Slatkine, 1973.
Nelli, René, ed. *Ecrivains anticonformistes au moyen-âge occitan: 1. La Femme et l'amour*, 256–59. Paris: Phébus, 1977.

JUNE HALL MCCASH

CASTELLOZA, NA (early 13th century). Of this important Provençal (southern-French location and language) woman lyricist (*trobairitz*), three miniature portraits have been preserved. But about Na Castelloza's life ("Na" = shortened *Domna* or *Domina* = Lady) and identity almost nothing has been established, not even the origin of her name, of which there is no other instance. Her name may be either a derivation from a place name or signify simply "the lady worthy of—or possessing—a castle." Her thirteenth-century *vida* (biography), perhaps totally fictitious, claims she was a noblewoman born in the Auvergne region in south-central France, and wife to one Turc de Mairona (probably Provençal for Meyronne, in the present *département* of the Haute-Loire, south-central France). Turc appears to have been a famous warrior, named in an anonymous poem of 1212. Yet, she addressed her love songs to another noble, Armand de Breon, from the nearby Puy de Dôme area, said to have been in love with her. Another *vida*, now lost and almost certainly unreliable, suggests as her lover the otherwise unknown troubadour Pons de Merindol (Vaucluse, south-central France), besides mentioning her presence at the court of Beatrice de Savoy—who married the earl of Provence, Raimon Berenguer, in 1219 or 1220. Recent scholars have revised these last two details, arguing instead that Castelloza was more likely to associate with the court of Dalfin d'Alvernha—or Dauphin of Auvergne—Count of Clermont (c.1155–1235; see Paden, ed. "Poems" 1981; Rieger).

Three songs are ascribed to Castelloza, with a fourth, the anonymous "Per ioi que d'amor m'avegna" ("To delight in any joy that love might bring"), attributed to her by scholars William Paden (ed. "Poems" 1981) and Angelica Rieger based on stylistic and manuscript evidence (it is only in what is called MS. N, in New York, Pierpont Morgan Library 819). This body of surviving work makes her perhaps, after the Comtessa de Dia (Countess of Die), the *trobairitz* with the most extensive preserved work. In one composition, "Ia de chantar non degra aver talan" ("I should never have the wish to sing") she addresses her fellow poetess Almucs de Castelnou (early thirteenth century), deformed in manuscripts as, for example. "Dompna Na Mieils" (see Rieger). Another appears to bear a close relation to a *canso* (song) written by the troubadour Peirol (fl. c.1197), this being the only text containing any trace of formal imitation. The other poems are unique both for their original rhyme schemes and their syllabic formulae.

Like other women troubadours, Castelloza reverses the male poets' cultural model and its asymmetrical dynamics of gender. Castelloza's lady thus becomes the suitor and main speaker; the knight now assumes the more passive role as beloved recipient. Certain troubadour motifs are retained: assuming the role of supplicant, she speaks about dying of love, she promises fidelity as her *amic* (beloved male)'s vassal, and asks to be rewarded for her love-service. Also like her fellow troubadours, she incorporates the mixed terminology from the feudal, legal, and religious lexicons to represent their relationship. Castelloza, in having her male friend play the role normally given to a haughty, unfaithful lady, likewise embraces the traditionally male suitor's suffering so long as it is inflicted by him, her beloved; she considers his cruelty an honor to her. The feeling of affliction is pervasive, because the writer's universe is fundamentally negative, especially in the texts of manuscript N. Yet in MS A (Vatican City, Biblioteca Vaticana, lat. 5232), the element of joy rivals that sorrow in importance. Her poetic expression is replete with contradiction and paradox. As with some troubadours, grief and sorrow become a source of satisfaction.

Na Castelloza's uniqueness becomes apparent when compared to other Provençal poetesses. Whereas throughout the inverted hierarchy they retain part of the former dominant position, she freely admits that her beloved deserves a lady of higher lineage. While thus seeming to appropriate the part of the troubadour love-servant, she may be reversing the stereotype of the amorous female in all popular, that is, pre-courtly genres of European women's song—such as *Frauenlieder, chansons de malmariée, chansons de toile*—showing the woman totally subservient to man. On the other hand, while complaining that the more she sings, the worse she fares in love, this writer focuses her self-awareness in both the artistic and the erotic. When she signals her unconventional stance as a woman who usurps the male prerogative to declare her love—while simultaneously doubting her right to compose at all—she not merely anticipates criticism but seeks social, perhaps also aesthetic, approval for her discourse. Finally, when pretending to "have set a very bad example for other women in love," this "dark lady in song" may thereby have focused on her true audience.

See also Almuc de Castelnou; *Chanson de Femme* (Women's Song); Comtessa de Dia; *Frauenlied; Trobairitz*

BIBLIOGRAPHY

Primary Sources
Boutière, Jean, and Alexander H. Schutz, eds. *Biographies des Troubadours: Textes provençaux des XIIIe et XIVe siècles*. Revised ed. with I. M. Cluzel. Les Classiques d'Oc, 1. Paris: Nizet, 1964.
Castelloza. [Poems]. "The Provençal Trobairitz Castelloza." Edited and translated by Peter Dronke. In *Medieval Women Writers*, edited by Katharina M. Wilson, 131–52. Athens: University of Georgia Press, 1984.
———. "The Poems of the *Trobairitz* Na Castelloza." Edited by William D. Paden. *Romance Philology* 35 (1981): 158–82.
———. In *Songs of the Women Troubadours*, edited and translated by Matilda Tomaryn Bruckner, Laurie Shepard, and Sarah White, esp. 18–29. New York: Garland, 1995. Revised ed., 2000.
———. In *Trobairitz: Der Beitrag der Frau in der altokzitanischen höfischen Lyrik. Edition des Gesamtkorpus*, edited by Angelica Rieger. Beihefte zur Zeitschrift für romanische Philologie, 233. Tübingen: Max Niemeyer Verlag, 1991.

Secondary Sources
[See also notes to above editions].
Bruckner, Matilda T. "Fictions of the Female Voice: The Women Troubadours." *Speculum* 67 (1992): 865–91. Reprint, revised, in *Medieval Women's Song*, edited by Anne L. Klinck and Ann Marie Rasmussen, 127–51. Philadelphia: University of Pennsylvania Press, 2002.
———. "Na Castelloza, *Trobairitz*, and the Troubadour Lyric." *Romance Notes* 25 (1985): 239–53.
Siskin, H. Jay, and Julie A. Storme. "Suffering Love: The Reversed Order in the Poetry of Na Castelloza." In *The Voice of the Trobairitz: Essays on the Women Troubadours*, edited by William D. Paden, 113–27. Philadelphia: University of Pennsylvania Press, 1989.
Van Vleck, Amelia E. "'Tost me trobaretz fenida': Reciprocating Composition in the Songs of Castelloza." In *The Voice of the Trobairitz*, ed. Paden (*see above, under* Siskin), 95–111.

HERMAN BRAET

CATALAN WOMEN POETS, ANONYMOUS (14th and 15th centuries). Two love poems written by women appear in the late fourteenth and late fifteenth centuries, both contained in Miscellaneous Medieval Poetical Manuscripts belonging to the Biblioteca de Catalunya in Barcelona. The first, "Axí cant és en muntanya deserta" ("There when on a desert mountain") appears in MS 8 and is a rhetorical poem presented at one of the annual poetry competitions at Toulouse, a major southern-French cultural foyer earlier frequented by the troubadours. The poet compares a series of extreme natural settings—a desert mountain, the four winds—to her desperate love. The second, found in MS 1744, is "Ab lo cor trist envirollat d'esmay" ("My sad heart is shrouded in chagrin") in which the poet, who has lost her love to death, declares an end to *fin'amor* ("fine love," that is, courtly love for love's sake, outside of contractual marriage) for her. Another anonymous lament appears in the early fifteenth century, containing the following plaintive verses:

> No puc dormir soleta, no/¿Què em faré, llassa,
> si no mi's passa?/Tant mi turmenta l'amor![...]
> Anit vos he somiat/que us tenia en mon braç.
> ¿Què em faré, llassa? (ed. Castellet and Molas, 181)

> (I cannot sleep all alone, no/What shall this unlucky
> one do/if I don't get over it?/Love torments me so!
> [...] /Last night I dreamed of you,/that I had you in
> my arms./What shall I do, poor me?)

See also Borja, Tecla; Isabel de Villena; *Malmojades, Les*; Reyna de Mallorques, La; *Trobairitz*

BIBLIOGRAPHY

Primary Sources
Catalan Woman Poet I. "Axí cant és en muntanya deserta." "Contribución al estudio de los poetas catalanes que concurrieron a las justas de Tolosa." *Boletín de la Sociedad Castellonense de Cultura* 24 (1950): 304–05.
Catalan Woman Poet II. "Ab lo cor trist envirollat d'esmay." "El plant amorós 'Ab lo cor trist...'" (Assaig de restauració d'un text corrupte)." Edited by Jaume Vidal Alcover. In *Estudis de Llengua i Literatura Catalanes IV Miscel.lània Pere Bohigas*, 2: 85–89. Montserrat, Spain: L'Abadia, 1982.
Catalan Woman Poet III. "No puc dormir soleta, no." *Ocho siglos de poesía catalana: Antología bilingüe*. Edited by J. M. Castellet and Joaquim Molas, 181. Madrid: Alianza, 1969. [Catalan texts and Spanish trans.].

Secondary Sources
Badia, Lola. "Anonymous Catalan Medieval Woman Poet I" and "Anonymous Catalan Medieval Woman Poet II." In *Double Minorities of Spain: A Bio-Bibliographical Guide to Women Writers of the Catalan, Galician, and Basque Countries*, edited by Kathleen McNerney and Cristina Enríquez de Salamanca, 46–47. New York: Modern Language Association, 1994.
Massó i Torrents, Jaume. "Poetesses i dames intel.lectuals." In *Homenatge a Antoni Rubió i Lluch*, 1: 408–11. Barcelona, 1936.
Riquer, Martí de, and Lola Badia, eds. *Les poesies de Jordi de Sant Jordi*, 273. Valencia: Tres i Quatre, 1984.

KATHLEEN MCNERNEY

CATALINA OF LANCASTER. *See* **Leonor López de Córdoba**

CATHAR WOMEN. *See* **Grazida (Grazida Lizier)**

St. Catherine of Bologna with Three Donors.
© Courtauld Institute Gallery, Somerset House, London/
www.bridgeman.co.uk.

CATHERINE. *See also under* **Katherine**

CATHERINE OF BOLOGNA, ST. (1413–
1463). Mystic, reformer, teacher, and most famous member of the Corpus Domini monastery,
Catherine was born Caterina Vegri, or Vigri, in
her mother's native city of Bologna, northern Italy. Thereafter she spent most of her life
in Ferrara, family home to her father, probably Giovanni Vegri, thought to be the son
of Bonaventura Vegri, accused of apostasy
(McLaughlin). The most prominent members of
the Vegri line included notaries, lawyers, and
judges favored by the ruling Este family. As a
young girl, according to her first biographer,
Illuminata Bembo, Caterina spent several years
at the ducal court as a companion to the young
Margherita d'Este, apparently developing there
her noteworthy literary, musical, and artistic
skills later highlighting her visionary writing.

From the age of thirteen, Caterina devoted
herself to the religious life, entering in 1426
what was then the community of pious laywomen known as Corpus Domini, founded in
1407 by Bernardina Sedazzari, a woman of strong
and independent character, in the San Salvatore
quarter of Ferrara. Despite original plans and
papal sanctions, Bernardina's community neither formally adopted the monastic rule of St.
Augustine nor were its members, laywomen known as *pinzochere*, strictly enclosed. Like
other lay communities of this kind, women could continue leading ordinary, nonmonastic
lives yet without dependency on male authority. This arrangement afforded security
and respectability to widows and the unmarried, who often brought any dowry or other
personal funds into the group's financial support structure. These women led simple lives of
prayer and domestic activity while also engaging in charitable works such as caring for the
sick, orphaned, and impoverished, especially young girls.

After Bernardina's death in 1425, Corpus Domini experienced a series of changes, making
its early history a remarkable case study in the spiritual quests of early fifteenth-century
Italian religious women. By the time Caterina arrived, a struggle for leadership had been
mounted between the faction led by Lucia Mascheroni, Bernardina's designated heir and
successor, who wished to keep the community in its relatively free, congenial state, and that
of Ailisia de Baldo, another important figure in the community, who advocated adherence to
the stricter Augustinian rule and enclosed way of life. Although a commission of local clerics
did its best to reconcile the two powerful factions, in the end it was Ailisia and her companions who had to depart, moving on to establish a disciplined Augustinian community,
Sant' Agostino, which became a flourishing center of monastic reform in northern Italian

cities. Lucia Mascheroni's leadership of Corpus Domini was soon challenged once more by the intervention of a patrician matron influential in Ferrarese society, Verde Pio da Carpi. Through her benefactions and machinations, Verde managed to capture Corpus Domini, transforming it into a monastery of reformed Clarisse, or Clarists—nuns following the austere rule of St. Clare—ruled by Verde's sister, formerly a Clarist nun in Mantua.

During these troubling changes, Caterina Vegri matured from an impressionable young girl into a thoughtful and spiritual young woman. She ardently supported the strictest version of the rule of St. Clare and its commitment to reformist Franciscan ideals, yet also remained emotionally attached to the maternal Lucia Mascheroni, who guided her first, happy years. Caterina vividly expresses the profoundly wrenching pain of these divided loyalties in Corpus Christi's leadership troubles, and their ensuing conflicts—among which her being accused of apostasy like her putative grandfather (though she was soon absolved)—in her visionary, semi-autobiographical treatise titled *Le Sette Armi spirituali* (*The Seven Spiritual Weapons*, 1438). Writing for her sisters, especially for her novices, she presented her own experience, despite usually alluding to herself in the third person, as a dramatic example of the constant tests, temptations, and weapons inherent in the spiritual battle. Showing little concern for the asceticism typical of other mystics, Caterina focuses on overcoming temptations of mind and spirit more than those of the flesh and the world. The lifelong, inner spiritual battle for which her "weapons" would arm her sisters aimed to subdue the will and the self, to attain conformity with Christ—not in his physical suffering—but in his obedience and humility. In her final, most powerful, vision, that of the Last Judgment, she sees herself among the saved, which her friends interpreted not as presumption but as a sign of divine favor. A young, dedicated novice mistress teaching in the community, Caterina wisely kept these written reflections (rather a book of visions-à-clef, in that she invokes via thinly veiled imagery certain key real-life figures like Verde, then still alive) hidden for a quarter-century, until the moment of her death, whereupon she entrusted the manuscript to the priest in attendance at her deathbed.

Underscoring her reputation for holiness, this "small book" and her years of teaching and reformist activity mark Caterina Vegri's place in late medieval spirituality and monastic history, especially that of Italian religious women. Without ever attaining a rank higher than that of novice mistress at Corpus Domini in Ferrara, for more than twenty years she nevertheless molded the religious life of her community by the teaching that helped to make it a vital center of Clarist reform in northern Italy. As her own spiritual renown grew, her community in Ferrara increased remarkably in numbers, from perhaps twenty to more than a hundred in two decades. Her fame as a "second St. Clare" also led a new Corpus Domini in her native Bologna to choose her as its first abbess in 1456. There, on her death in 1463, her sisters observed the physical signs of her sanctity, particularly the sweet fragrance and incorruption of her body when it was disinterred after a brief burial, which is still claimed today for her remains in Corpus Domini, Bologna. Illuminata Bembo, her close friend, succeeded her as abbess there and wrote two biographies of her. A few years after Caterina's death, this community acquired a printing press and published the first of several editions of *Sette Armi*, making it a fifteenth-century best-seller. Although Illuminata completed the longer version of her biography of Caterina, *Specchio de illuminazione* (*Mirror of Illumination*), in around 1469, it was not printed until 1787, when it was published with *Sette Armi*. With her incorrupt body as the icon of her community and the focus of civic pride, Caterina became a "community saint" in a double sense, inspiring her sisters and fellow citizens throughout the lengthy and arduous campaign finally culminating in her canonization in 1713. Corpus Domini is still an active community today whose records have attracted scholarly interest in recent decades.

See also Beguines; Bembo, Illuminata; Clare of Assisi, St.; Hagiography (Female Saints); Petronilla of Chemillé; *Pinzochere*

BIBLIOGRAPHY

Primary Sources
Bembo, Illuminata. *Specchio de illuminazione* (1469). First published 1787. *See under* Vegri, *below.*
Samaritani, Alberto. "Ailisia de Baldo e le correnti reformatrici femminili di Ferrara nella prima meta del sec. XV." *Atti e memorie della Deputazione provinciale Ferrarese di Storia patria*, ser. 3, 13 (1973): 91–157. [Includes texts of sources on Corpus Domini].
Vegri, Santa Caterina. *Le Sette Armi sprituale.* Edited by Cecilia Foletti. Padua, Italy: Editrice Antenore, 1985. [Critical ed. with texts of additional sources on Caterina, plus excellent introduction].

Secondary Sources
Martinelli, Serena Spanò. "La Biblioteca de 'Corpus Domini' bolognese: l'inconsueto spaccato di una cultura monastica femminile." *La Bibliofilia* 88 (1986).
———. "La Canonizzazione di Caterina Vigri: un problema cittadino nella Bologna dei Seicento." In *Culto dei santi, istituzioni et classi sociali in età preindustriale*, edited by Sofia Boesch-Gajano and Luciana Sebastiani, 719–33. L'Aquila, Italy: L. U. Japadre Editore, 1984.
———. "Per un studio su Caterina da Bologna." *Studi medievali*, ser. 3. 12 (1971): 713–59.
McLaughlin, Mary Martin. "Creating and Recreating Communities of Women: The Case of Corpus Domini, Ferrara, 1406–1452." *Signs* 14 (1989). Reprint in *Sisters and Workers in the Middle Ages*, edited by Judith Bennett et al., 261–88. Chicago: University of Chicago Press, 1989.

MARY MARTIN MCLAUGHLIN

CATHERINE OF SIENA, ST. (c.1347–1380). Caterina da Siena was a Dominican Tertiary who authored 383 extant letters, twenty-six prayers, and a treatise. Catherine was born the twenty-third child of the dyer Jacopo Benincasa, and his wife, Lapa Piagenti, in Siena, Italy. At the age of six, she experienced her first religious vision and began extensive prayer rituals. Soon she vowed her virginity to her Lord. When Catherine reached the age of twelve, however, her mother tried to prepare her for marriage, against which she soon revolted by cutting off her hair. She claimed to have a spiritual cell in her heart into which she could resort for her meditations. In a dream she envisioned St. Dominic, who promised her entrance to his order. Despite much resistance on the part of her parents, she was finally allowed, in 1364 or 1365, to become a Tertiary (religious of the Third Orders: voluntary penitents) of this order, who cared for Siena's sick and impoverished. In her secluded life she experienced many more visions, particularly of Christ, who taught her to read and write and promised to take her as His bride in spirit in 1367. Not long afterward she formed the nucleus of a group of friends and disciples, who became accustomed to calling her "mother." From 1370 onward, at Christ's calling, she began to lead a more active life, gradually developing a lively correspondence with an astoundingly vast range of people, eventually including the pope, the emperor, bishops, dukes, and princes, among other representatives of all social classes. To maintain this vast correspondence, she often dictated her letters to secretaries.

As of 1374, the Master of the Dominican Order, Elias of Toulouse, appointed the Dominican Raymond of Capua (Raimondo delle Vigne da Capua, c.1330–1399) as her confessor. Under Raymond's guidance, Catherine began to widen her ministry to deal with such international affairs as the Crusade against the Turks, Church reform, and later, the Great Schism of the Church (1378–1417), which she had striven so tirelessly to avert. Such extraordinary activities and influence on the part of a woman inevitably aroused suspicion, and she was soon accused of hypocrisy and was slandered by the authorities at Siena. Yet when summoned to Florence to defend herself at the General Chapter of the Dominicans, she managed to attain full exoneration. Raymond would write a life of Catherine after her death, the *Legenda Major* (1385–1395).

Saint Catherine of Siena receiving the Stigmata. Courtesy of North Wind Picture Archives.

At various times throughout her brief life, reports of her association with miraculous events enhanced her saintly reputation. Her involvement in political affairs, however profound and passionate, was always for religious reasons alone and indeed would gradually destroy her health. In 1376 she appeared in Avignon, sent on behalf of the Florentine city-state to negotiate a peace between them and Pope Gregory VI. Although the war continued until 1378, Catherine was influential enough to push Gregory to move the Curia (the papal court and its functionaries) back to Rome in the same year of 1376. While attending church in Pisa in 1375, she was stigmatized (took on the wounds of Christ) as a sign of divine approval of her campaign for the Crusades. In January 1377, she returned to Siena and continued working for her political concerns, since the well-established order of her world seemed to collapse. In 1378, the well-meaning Pope Gregory died and was replaced by Urban VI, with whom Catherine, by then in Rome herself, had less success in promoting her case, while remaining loyal to him nonetheless. With the advent of the Great Schism and the sharp division of the church, Catherine experienced a severe physical breakdown, and died on April 29, 1380. Her body was buried in the Church of the Minerva in Rome; her head was interred at San Domenico in Siena.

Catherine's spirituality is dominated by a pronounced veneration for the Virgin Mary and also the influence of St. Francis of Assisi (1181/82–1226). Like Francis, she voluntarily dedicated herself to caring for the sick, particularly the lepers; she received the stigmata (wounds suffered by Christ on the Cross) and practiced extreme asceticism. However, she did not impose such rigorous practices on her followers.

She composed her book, the *Dialogo* (*Dialogue*), comprised of four treatises synthesizing her teachings, as her testament to the world, allegedly having dictated it in five days while in a state of ecstasy. Although the authenticity of most of her letters cannot be absolutely confirmed, a total of 383 have come down to us, articulating her transcendent spirituality, her keenly individual personality and politics. They are remarkable documents of a strong-willed, devout woman possessing a clear insight into political necessities and ideals in face of a world losing its unity and stability. Through her letters she created a literary forum for both her spiritual and her worldly political concerns. Her theological theory is deeply founded on the concept of love as emphatically symbolized by Christ crucified and His blood, and of God as her lover. Her mystical visions and experiences permeate all her treatises in the *Dialogue*. In clear opposition to the scholastic (more rationalist) theology expounded by Thomas Aquinas (c.1225–1274), she held that God had created man not in general, but only man in whom God wanted to see himself. Catherine was canonized in 1461 (her feast day is now April 29). As a further mark of the Church's esteem for her, she was declared a Doctor of the Church in 1970.

See also Bride of Christ/*Brautmystik*; Clare of Assisi, St.; Virginity

BIBLIOGRAPHY

Primary Sources
Catherine of Siena. *Il Dialogo della divina provvidenza ovvero Libro della divina dottrina*. Edited by Giuliana Cavallini. Rome: Edizioni Cateriniani, 1968. Revised ed., Siena: Cantagalli, 1995.
———. *The Dialogue*. Translated and introduced by Suzanne Noffke. Preface by Giuliana Cavallini. Classics of Western Spirituality. New York: Paulist Press, 1980.
———. *Le lettere di S. Caterina da Siena*. Edited by Niccolo Tommaseo. 4 vols. Florence, 1860. Revised ed. Piero Misciattelli. 6 vols. Siena: Giuntini & Bentivoglio, 1913–1921. Reprint Florence 1939–1940. New ed. by the Centro Nazionale di Studi Cateriani. Presented by Gabriella Anodal. Rome, 1973.
———. *The Letters of St. Catherine of Siena*. Translated with an introduction and notes by Suzanne Noffke. 2 vols. MRTS, 202. Tempe, Ariz.: Arizona Center for Medieval & Renaissance Studies, 2000–2001. [vol. 1, first ed. MRTS, 52. Binghamton, N.Y.: CEMERS, 1988].
———. *The Prayers of Catherine of Siena*. Translated by Suzanne Noffke. New York: Paulist Press, 1983.
Raimondo da Capua (Raymundus de Vineis) [*Legenda Major*]. *Beati Raymundi Capuani . . . Opusculae et litterae*. Edited by Hyacinthe-Marie Cormier. Rome: Typographia polygotta, 1899.
———. *Life of Catherine of Siena*. Translated by Conleth Kearns. Wilmington, Del.: Michael Glazier, 1980.

Secondary Sources
Baldwin, Anne. *Catherine of Siena: A Biography*. Huntington, Ind.: Our Sunday Visitor Publications, 1987.
Beckwith, Sara. *Christ's Body: Identity, Culture and Society in Late Medieval Writings*. London and New York: Routledge, 1993.
Cross, F. L., and E. A. Livingstone. "Catherine, St, of Siena." *Oxford Dictionary of the Christian Church*, 304b–305a. 3rd ed. Oxford and New York: Oxford University Press, 1997.
Gorce, Maxime. "Catherine de Sienne." In *Dictionnaire de Spiritualité*, 2: 327–48. Paris: Beauchesne, 1953.
Luongo, Francis T. "Catherine of Sienna: Rewriting Female Holy Authority." In *Women, the Book, and the Godly*, edited by Lesley Smith, 1: 89–103. Cambridge, U.K.: D. S. Brewer, 1995.
———. "The Politics of Marginality: Catherine of Siena in the War of Eight Saints." Ph.D. diss., University of Notre Dame, 1998.

Noffke, Suzanne. *Catherine of Siena: Vision through a Distant Eye.* Collegeville, Minn.: Liturgical Press/ Michael Glazier, 1996.

ALBRECHT CLASSEN

CELIBACY. Celibacy, the voluntary renunciation of marriage and/or abstinence from sexual intercourse, has often inevitably intertwined itself with the related virtues of chastity and virginity in the evolution of the ideal, carnally and spiritually pure Christian cleric and also monks of other faiths such as Buddhism. In the early period, celibacy was also transmitted to all cultures converted to Christianity (e.g., the Near East and North Africa, especially from the first through the fifth centuries) and also in later cycles of missionary activity around the world. Its observance bore special consequences for women, both as celibates themselves and as spouses and other relatives of men in the clergy pledged to abstain from sex as celibacy laws evolved.

Combat of love and chastity. Fifteenth century. © The Art Archive/ National Gallery London/Eileen Tweedy.

The practice of celibacy was advocated in the first century by the apostle Paul (e.g., 1 Cor. 7) when he asserted that marriage was permissible but celibacy or chastity was better. Paul, realizing that even good Christians could not practice complete sexual abstinence, reserved celibacy for the strongest believers. Paul's view of women as deceivers and transgressors responsible for the Fall shaped his entire perspective on women's role in the burgeoning Church; his relegation of women to passive, silent subordinates to men, whose saving grace was to bear children in marriage (and thus were excluded from celibacy; see 1 Tim. 2: 15), was extremely influential among later theologians. A perhaps less misogynistic side of Paul's emphasis on abstinence, even among laypeople, and celibacy among the clergy, is its function in preventing distraction from prayer, arguably a holdover from the Old Testament and pagan ideal of ritual purity. Later theologians such as Gregory of Nyssa (c.330–c.395) believed that it was easier to avoid marriage altogether than to marry and abstain from sexual contact. In general, these early Church Fathers condoned sex only for producing children, and even in this act all carnal desire must be absent. Chastity, virginity, and abstinence therefore became prerequisites for saintliness because

147

they elevated men and women above common, routinely lustful mortals. Maintaining lifelong virginity for maidens, abstinence for married women, and celibacy for widows—when confronted by temptation to violate these states—qualified women for lower ecclesiastical offices and sainthood.

Despite such moral-philosophical considerations, much of the need for celibacy was first shaped, like the rules of marriage and sexual conduct, by socioeconomic realities. Just as marital morality sought to prevent extramarital sex because it produced illegitimate children—which created additional expense, complicated inheritance and other structures—in the necessarily stricter terms of Church governance, marriage among the priesthood was problematical: marriage produced children, and with that, inheritance rights threatening Church property. Thus, in 529, the great Roman lawgiver, Emperor Justinian, ruled that no man with children or grandchildren could become a bishop, to protect Church property from being taken over by clerics' families. It was also believed that having families would distract bishops from their many duties. To determine rules of celibacy, much wrangling occurred during earlier Church Councils (the earliest being Elvira, c.306) and with papal decrees to promote higher-clergy celibacy, if not clergy-wide celibacy rejected at the Council of Nicaea (325), even as far as Africa. During this formative phase, the Western and Eastern Churches would each come to incorporate different levels of celibacy. In the West, Pope Leo I (the Great; d. 461) allowed married clergy to remain married after ordination provided the couple lived "as brother and sister."

In the Eastern Church in Byzantium, with its capital in Constantinople (the eastern half of the Roman Empire, which would later split from Rome in 1054), the Church Council of Trullo (692) in Canon 13, supplemented Justinian's law by requiring celibacy of all higher clergy, with varying degrees of success in its enforcement. While Eastern bishops had to be celibate, their lower clergy, such as parish priests, were chosen exclusively from married men (see Callam). By contrast, the Western Church moved increasingly toward celibacy among all levels of its clergy.

Early Christianity (first and second centuries) attracted women because it allowed them more participation in the clergy than the Antique Graeco-Roman traditions. As deaconesses and traveling prophets, these women could mediate between the public Church ministry and the private communities (MacDonald; McNamara). From the first century, celibate religious women had their own cult heroines—women as repulsed by male sexual brutishness as they were captivated by spiritual devotion and purity—on whom to model themselves: Cecilia, who before being martyred (c.180), had converted her husband on their wedding night; Potamiaena (d. early third century), whose executioner converted after experiencing vision of her after her death; Felicity, a celibate widow, martyred 162 for publicly preaching and converting her listeners to Christianity; and, perhaps most memorably in that she kept a vivid diary of her ordeal, the Roman matron Perpetua, stripped and martyred in an African amphitheater in 203 for her ascetic Christian beliefs. Celibate women's orders then formed, the first devised by the African Church Father Tertullian (c.160–c.225), a brilliant rhetorician and key exponent of virginity and chaste widowhood in a manner surpassing the orthodox Church's rules. While all Church Fathers prized virginity among women, Tertullian recognized in celibate widows an untapped "second virginity," and thus an important segment of church membership and even the ministry, since, like virgins, celibate (unmarried as well as abstinent) widows could become deaconesses—a lower-clergy role, just below that of priests, but an active one (McNamara).

Because they were so effective, these celibate teaching women (the two conditions for women prohibited by Paul in 1 Tim. 2: 12–15, for example) caused anxiety among the male clergy. Since they were not defined—nor bound, therefore—by marital status, they enjoyed much freedom of movement, becoming leaders of their communities, thus usurping the men. The women's lowly but vital (as it turned out) position in the Church hierarchy also liberated and empowered them, even when being martyred, such as Perpetua in her famous declaration during her martyrdom: they had become men (McNamara, ch. 5). Fears arose that they would embrace heretical sects or found their own. As a result, the higher-ranking bishops and priests began to try to contain them within a more conservative, established (orthodox) Church. By this later containment, the male Church hierarchy excluded women from sacred spaces (Schulenburg in Frassetto).

On the subject of marriage in the early orthodox Church, Justin Martyr (c.100–c.165) advocated continence for married and unmarried Christians alike, since sex existed only for producing children. For St. Clement of Alexandria (c.150–c.215), who may himself have been married, chastity meant marital fidelity rather than abstinence; he viewed the good Christian family—the married parents and children—as a self-contained congregation, marriage as a union of two people wishing to lead a Christian life. These early Fathers give women more equality than in Paul's view of marital roles.

In Gaul (ancient France), married deaconesses, and the wives of priests and bishops, were often ordered to sleep in chambers separate from their husbands'. By the eleventh century, they even occupied different residences. Though bishops were forbidden to marry after ordination, if one were ordained after marriage, he had to vow lifelong sexual abstinence (*conversio*), as did his wife in some cases. Chaperone figures in the form of clerics were often present in the married clerics' residences as a further means of surveillance, both day and night. Radegund, a Merovingian queen and saint (sixth century), although married, was praised by her biographer, Fortunatus, because she expressed disdain for the conjugal bed, always finding some excuse not to join her husband and instead donning a hairshirt and going off to pray (Fortunatus). Also during the sixth century, in Wales, the married couple and future saints Gwynllyw and Gwladys were convinced by their son St. Cadoc to separate and pursue a life of chastity (Schulenburg in Salisbury).

Those who broke the rules by marrying or having concubines were punished in various ways depending on the severity of their offense: they could be barred from higher office and from exercising their office, required to do public penance, or face being deposed.

In distinction to the above-described, monastic men and women (monks and nuns) living in their own communities realized quite naturally that celibacy was a key to their order's identity and a measure of their devotion. Because most of these were ascetic to some degree, celibacy offered another form of self-mortification, along with fasting, uncomfortable clothing, exposure to cold, physical labor, and constant prayer and/or charitable works. This aura of self-denial and extreme piety enhanced the prestige of the monastic way of life above that of other clerics.

The progress of such discipline, to which celibacy was essential within the Western Church, began seriously to waver during the seventh and eighth centuries and then was restored during the Carolingian era (reign of Charlemagne, r. 768–814; crowned emperor 800), only to disintegrate, like much of Charlemagne's empire, after the emperor's death. Vast numbers of married clergy by then made it difficult to enforce the old rules, and upper-level Churchmen were none too restrained either. This disarray provoked several councils and attempts at reform, most notably those of Pope Leo IX (r. 1048–1054) and especially of Gregory VII (r. 1073–1085), who, like the monastic reformers, understood how celibacy could liberate the Church government from lay control. Gregory thus revived the old celibacy rules and their rigorous implementation. Gratian, known as the father of canon law for having provided the first systematic code, the *Decretum* (1142), along with decrees by the First, Second, and Fourth Lateran Councils (1123, 1139, and 1215) gave the Gregorian reforms further impetus into the fourteenth century. Clerics, even subdeacons, were now forbidden to marry after ordination, and celibacy was made a condition for ordination. Gregorian penalties were now more zealously executed: offending clergy were not only deposed but their children were made serfs of the Church.

In Scandinavia at about this same time, celibacy, which conflicted too much with native morality, was not widely upheld among the Icelandic clergy. Thorlákr Thórhallsson (1133–1193) and Gudmundr Arason were both bishops (*byskups*) who were revered as saints, partly by reason of their sexual abstinence. The late thirteenth-century *Thorlak's saga* documents its hero's attempts to regulate Icelandic marriages in accordance with Christian teachings. That Icelandic priests often married, had children, and also kept concubines indicates a weakness in Christian influence in Iceland (Itnyre, in Salisbury, 152–53; Jochens).

The virginity and chastity of single nuns is well documented. As for late-medieval married women who became saints and their approach to celibacy, Dyan Elliott describes the cases of Birgitta of Sweden (1303–1373), Dorothea of Montau in Germany (1347–1394), and Margery Kempe in England (c.1373–c.1440), among others. In all of these women, the conjugal debt (sex in marriage) produced varying degrees of revulsion and an inner need to do penance by ascetic practice (self-mortification and even self-torture). The inward turmoil felt by these women would also sometimes manifest itself through horrific visions conjuring forth the evil of fleshly desire and its fulfillment.

Despite a late-medieval decline in respect for the laws of celibacy, probably occasioned by the ravages of the Hundred Years War (1337–1453) between France and England, and Black Death (begun 1347) devastating much of Europe, with additional theological dismay wrought by the Great Schism of the Church and its resultant popes and anti-popes (1378–1417). But even during this period, the Western Church adhered to its strict, clergy-wide rules for celibacy, despite some theologians' urging a less stringent regime closer to that of the Eastern Church. Because the Western Church had difficulty in enforcing these rules, sexual misconduct simply joined other scandalous actions such asusury (moneylending at interest) and simony (sale and purchase of Church offices) tainting even the upper clergy—corrupt practices that Gregory's reforms had almost eradicated centuries earlier—which would eventually bring about the Protestant Reformation and Catholic Counter-Reformation in the sixteenth century. Celibacy has resurfaced in the twenty-first century as a topic of fervent debate within the modern Church.

See also Convents; Dorothea of Montau, St.; Hagiography (Female Saints); Kempe, Margery; Law, Canon, Women in; Marriage; Mary, Blessed Virgin, in the Middle Ages; Norse Women; Perpetua, St.; Radegund, St.; Rules for Canonesses, Nuns, and Recluses; Syrian-Christian Women; Teachers, Women as; Virginity; Widows

BIBLIOGRAPHY

Primary Sources
[See also texts discussed in Secondary Sources].
Clement of Alexandria, St. *Paedagogus*, 3: 4. Edited by M. Marcovich and J. van Winden. Supplements to Vigiliae Christianae, 61. Leiden, Netherlands and Boston: Brill, 2002.
———. *Stromata.* Sources chrétiennes, 30, 38. Various editors. Paris: Éditions du Cerf, 1951–1954. [See esp. Bks. 3–4].
———. *Stromata, IV.* Critical edition by Annewiese van den Hoek. Translated (French) by Claude Montdésert. Sources Chrétiennes, 463. Paris: Éditions du Cerf, 2001. [Greek original, French trans., and notes].
———. *Stromateis*, Books 1–3. Translated by John Ferguson. The Fathers of the Church, 85. Washington, D.C.: Catholic University of America Press, 1991. [English text and notes].
Fortunatus, Venantius. *De Vita Sanctae Radegundis*, Edited by Bruno Krusch. *Monumenta Germaniae Historica, Scriptores rerum merovingicarum*, 2: 1. 5, 366–67. Berlin: Weidmann, 1885.
———. In *Sainted Women of the Dark Ages*, edited and translated by Jo Ann McNamara and John E. Halborg et al., 73. Durham, N.C.: Duke University Press, 1992.
Justin Martyr, St. *Apologia*, 1: 29. In *Apologie pour les Chrétiens.* Edited and translated (French) by Charles Munier. Paradosis, 39. Fribourg, Switzerland: Éditions universitaires, 1995. [Greek original and French trans. with introduction and notes].
———. In *Works.* Translated by Thomas B. Falls. Fathers of the Church, 6. New York: Christian Heritage, 1948.
Perpetua, Vibia, St. *Passio Sanctarum Perpetuae et Felicitatis, Latine et Graece.* Edited by C. I. M. I. van Beek. Florilegium Patristicum, 43. Bonn, Germany: P. Hanstein, 1938. [Shorter ed.: authoritative Greek and Latin texts].
———. [*Passio*]. "Prisoner, Dreamer, Martyr." In *The Writings of Medieval Women: An Anthology*, edited and translated by Marcelle Thiébaux, 3–22. Garland Library of Medieval Literature, 100B. 2nd ed. New York and London: Garland, 1994. [Entire text in English only, useful commentary].
Tertullian. *Ad uxorem.* In *Opera*, 2. *Corpus Christianorum. Series Latina*, 2. Turnhout, Belgium: Brepols, 1954. [See esp. 2: 8].
Thorláks Saga Byskups. In *Byskopa Sögur*, 1. Edited by Gudni Jonsson. Reykavík, Iceland: Íslendingasagnaútgáfan, 1953.

Secondary Sources
Audet, Jean-Paul. *Mariage et célibat dans le service pastoral de l'Église: histoire et orientations.* 2nd ed. Magog, Québec: Éditions des Sources, 1999.
———.Translated [from 1st ed.] by Rosemary Sheed. London: Sheed & Ward; New York: Macmillan, 1968.
Callam, Daniel. "Celibacy." In *Dictionary of the Middle Ages*, edited by Joseph R. Strayer, 3: 215–18. New York: Scribner's 1983.
Coppens, Joseph, A. M. Charue et al., eds. *Sacerdoce et célibat: études historiques et théologiques.* Bibliotheca Ephemeridum theologicarum Lovaniensium, 28. Gembloux: Duculot; Louvain, Belgium: Peeters, 1971.
———. *Priesthood and Celibacy: Historical and Theological Studies.* Milan and Rome: Ancora, 1972. [English translation of above-cited work].
Elliott, Dyan. *Spiritual Marriage: Sexual Abstinence in Medieval Wedlock.* Princeton, N.J.: Princeton University Press, 1993.
Frassetto, Michael, ed. *Medieval Purity and Piety: Essays on Medieval Clerical Celibacy and Religious Reform.* New York and London: Garland, 1998.
Gray, Janette. *Neither Escaping nor Exploiting Sex: Women's Celibacy.* Homebush, N.S.W., Australia: St. Paul's, 1995.
Itnyre, Cathy J. "A Smorgasbord of Sexual Practices." In Salisbury, 145–56. *See below.*
Jochens, Jenny. "The Church and Sexuality in Medieval Iceland." *Journal of Medieval History* 6 (1980): 377–92.

MacDonald, Margaret Y. *Early Christian Women and Pagan Opinion: The Power of the Hysterical Woman*. Cambridge: Cambridge University Press, 1996.

McNamara, Jo Ann. "A New Song: Celibate Women in the First Three Christian Centuries." *Women & History* 6–7 (1983): entire issue.

Salisbury, Joyce E., ed. *Sex in the Middle Ages: A Book of Essays*. Garland Casebooks, 3. New York and London: Garland, 1991.

Schulenburg, Jane T. "Gender, Celibacy, and the Proscriptions of Sacred Space: Symbol and Practice." In Frassetto, *see above*.

———. "Saints and Sex, ca. 500–1100: Striding Down the Nettled Path of Life." In Salisbury, 203–31. *See above entry.*

Shorter, Aylward. *Celibacy and African Culture*. Nairobi, Kenya: Pauline Publications, 1998.

NADIA MARGOLIS

CERETA, LAURA (1469–1499). Unlike most other humanist letter-writers, the Italian Laura Cereta wrote extensively, in erudite Latin, to members of her family, about personal matters, including memories of childhood. These have survived as precious documents for her time and milieu, so that we know great deal more about her personal life than we do about other women humanists, and indeed about many male humanists.

Born in late August or September of 1469 to Silvestro Cereta, an attorney and magistrate, and his wife, Veronica di Leno, in Brescia (in Lombardy, northern Italy), Laura was the eldest of six children in this upper-middle-class family. She recalls her childhood as an extremely happy one in which she received the affection and attention of her entire family and household. Her earliest education she received from women—nuns—during a two-years convent stay beginning at age seven. Most standard accounts of her life tell us that when she returned home at around age nine, her father became her teacher, which reflects more about standard convention in representing the education of humanist women (one thinks of Christine de Pizan [1364/5–1430?], for example, educated by her father, Thomas) than the actual truth. Indeed she contradicts this convention in her own letter, the most autobiographically informative one (to friend and mentor Nazaria Olimpica), in which she tells of how her father, fearing she would grow coddled and lazy at home, soon took her away from her mother's warm embrace and returned her to her strict and learned woman preceptor for further instruction in Latin (see Robin trans. notes) and Greek, and mathematics, astrology, sacred literature, and philosophy. Two years later, however, at age eleven, her father brought her back home to help care for her younger siblings. At home she pursued her studies on her own, composing learned Latin letters to her mother and sisters whenever free time from domestic duties allowed.

This situation, so typical of the intellectual woman's quandary even today, nurtured her lasting concern for women's education. Her correspondence suggests that she saw herself as writing both within the larger, male-defined, humanist culture, and within a specifically feminine construction of humanist conventions. Like her humanist brothers, she expressed an avid determination to achieve immortal fame through her letters; unlike them, she sought to express and establish herself by connecting as well with other women and with the range of conventionally "feminine" experiences—domestic duties, needlework—that more often operated in humanist women's and men's writings as antitheses to humanist learning. Unlike Cassandra Fedele (1465/6–1558), for example, she does not oppose, but rather juxtaposes, the sewing needle and the pen.

At fifteen, Cereta married a Brescian merchant, Pietro Serina, owner of a shop in Venice, and during his absences from their household she came to include him among her many intimate correspondents. Around the same time, she began to correspond as well with noted attorneys, physicians, priests, and members of literary circles in Brescia and throughout the Veneto region (in northeastern Italy), including the grammarian Giovanni Olivieri and the classical scholar and historian Lodovico Cendrata, a pupil of Guarino da Verona (1370–1460) and also a correspondent of Isotta Nogarola (1418–1466). She also sought out cultivated women like herself; while her attempt to initiate an intellectual friendship with the most famous among them, Cassandra Fedele, apparently failed, Cereta did manage to forge literary friendships with other women like herself. The letters to her husband are very personal, discussing accusations of insufficient affection or expressing concern over his inordinate grief at his brother's death. She wrote as well to her brothers, sisters, father, and mother; while these letters have a certain personal quality to them, however, they also have the quality of set pieces characteristic of letters to other correspondents. The letter to her mother is a classic pastoral; the letters to her brothers deal with their education and urge them to study. Cereta's letters to other correspondents treat standard humanist topics and tropes: the relationship between virtue and classical learning, contemporary political issues (particularly war), friendship, and marriage as a social institution.

Only eighteen months after they were married, Serina died of a fever, perhaps a species of plague. Cereta's subsequent letters are filled with outpourings of grief and loss, to which she continues to allude in later correspondence. She nevertheless continued to write to many people, men and women alike, on a variety of subjects. She is the only humanist woman whose writing activity seems to have been almost entirely unaffected by marriage and domestic duties, although she says at one point that to find time for literary pursuits, given her responsibilities to her parents and siblings as well as to her own household, she often reads and writes at night, sometimes until nearly morning. In spite of this fragmented study schedule, however, she did continue to write and avowedly to pursue fame through literature throughout and after her marriage.

Toward the end of her brief career, she wrote to one of her priestly friends, Brother Tommaso of Milan, whose replies to Cereta's letters are also extant. Their correspondence deals primarily with the difficult relationship between secular learning and Christian truth, and it seems to have had the effect on Cereta of causing her ultimately to abandon her studies, at least on the humanist and literary model, at the ripe age of eighteen. By that time, however, she had also collected and arranged her letters to send them, suitably dedicated, to Cardinal Ascanio Maria Sforza, the duke of Milan's younger son, to attract his literary patronage; the result of this effort is uncertain. Whether because of Sforza's failure to respond, or because of Brother Tommaso's urgings toward the religious life, or because of the death of her father soon after the publication of her letters, or for some other reason about which we cannot even speculate, she then apparently ceased to write. Or else, if Cereta did write more, we no longer possess her work. She lived for another eleven years, dying at the age of thirty in 1499.

There is much about Cereta's letter book—containing eighty-two Latin letters and a dialogue on the death of an ass—that is unique. Although she takes up standard humanist subjects, more than other humanist women, her simultaneous, explicit goals are to pursue the classic male reward of lasting fame through literary achievement, and to discuss the particular problems that women face in pursuing that same objective. Unlike any other woman of her time and place, she writes invectives, all of which deal in one way or another with the issue of the relationship between a woman's virtue and her learning. In one she defends herself fairly straightforwardly against what appear to have been disparaging comments about her accomplishments. In the other three, however, she deliberately contrasts the learned and virtuous women of the past and present with women who are concerned only with personal adornment, with their bodies and their attractiveness to men. She admits that learned women are rare, but also accuses men of failing to acknowledge women's accomplishments, and of expecting so little of women that they can hardly be expected to accomplish much on their own. So long as men persist in requiring their women to function almost exclusively as ornaments, she writes to one Augustinus Aemilius, and since men have greater strength and responsibility in the world, women's failure in true virtue and learning must be laid at their door. She does not take the victim's way out, however; she also attacks women who despise learning and virtue. She calls on all women to persist in the difficult but rewarding pursuit of true virtue contained in classical studies, and invites them to imitate such Classical exemplars as the Egyptian Zenobia, Athena, Sappho, Proba, and Sempronia, as well as her contemporaries Niculosa of Bologna, Isotta Nogarola, and Cassandra Fedele. Although Cereta can be seen as attacking women for the same sorts of defects that her male contemporaries did, she goes beyond conventional detractions to argue that women can choose a better and more virtuous way, and that together they can establish a community of scholars and a tradition of study that is distinctly theirs.

See also Fedele, Cassandra; Humanists, Italian Women, Issues and Theory; Nine Worthy Women; Nogarola, Isotta; Proba, Faltonia Betitia; Scala, Alessandra; Scrovegni, Maddalena

BIBLIOGRAPHY

Primary Sources
Cereta, Laura. *Laurae Ceretae Brixiensis feminae clarissimae epistolae*. Edited by Jacopo Filippo Tomasini. Padua: Sebastiano Sardi, 1640. [Latin text only, with biography by Tomasini].
————. In Vatican City, MS Vat. lat. 3176. cart 3. XVI. [16C ms., the only source containing all Cereta's known extant works].
————. *Laura Cereta, Collected Letters of a Renaissance Feminist*. Edited and translated with introduction and notes by Diana Robin. The Other Voice in Early Modern Europe. Chicago and London: University of Chicago Press, 1997. [English text only, based on above originals, with excellent commentary].

Secondary Sources
Caccia, Ettore. In *Storia di Brescia, II: La dominazione veneta (1426–1575)*, edited by Giovanni Treccani degli Alfieri, 486, 494–96. Brescia, Italy: Morcelliana, 1963.
Palma, M. "Laura Cereta." In *Dizionario biografico degli italiani*, 23: 729–30. Rome, 1979.
Rabil, Albert, Jr. *Laura Cereta: Quattrocento Humanist*. Medieval and Renaissance Texts and Studies. Binghamton, N.Y.: Center for Medieval and Early Renaissance Studies, 1981.
————. "Laura Cereta." In *Italian Women Writers: A Bio-Bibliographical Sourcebook*, edited by Rinaldina Russell, 67–75. Westport, Conn. and London: Greenwood, 1994.
Robin, Diana. "Cassandra Fedele's *Epistolae* (1488–1521): Biography as Ef-facement." In *The Rhetorics of Life-Writing in Early Modern Europe: Forms of Biography from Cassandra Fedele to Louis XIV*, edited by Thomas F. Mayer and D. R. Woolf, 187–203. Ann Arbor: University of Michigan Press, 1995.

———. "Laura Cereta." In *The Feminist Encyclopedia of Italian Literature*, edited by Rinaldina Russell, 46–48. Westport, Conn. and London: Greenwood Press, 1997.

Rossi, Ottavio. *Elogi historici di bresciani illustri*, 196–200, 226–28. Brescia: Bartolomeo Fontana, 1620.

JENNIFER FISK RONDEAU

CHAMPION DES DAMES. See **Le Franc, Martin**

CHANSON DE FEMME (Women's Song). The *chanson de femme*, or, in German, *Frauenlied*, is a modern generic term designating a medieval love lyric whose speaker is female. Historically, the expression has been used to describe two principal groups of lyric: anonymous songs of a popular or popularizing tradition, and songs known to have been written by male court poets. Hence the category generally excludes the female-voiced lyrics of known women writers such as Christine de Pizan and the Countess of Die.

Evidence of the woman's song in medieval Europe precedes the extant texts: Church councils protested against *puellarum cantica* ("girls' songs") as early as the sixth century, and Charlemagne issued a capitulary (ordinance) in 789 forbidding abbesses and nuns to compose *winileodas* (Germanic = "songs for a friend"). Though these lyrics have not survived, two Old English poems of the tenth-century Exeter book may contain remnants of the early *winileoda* tradition: "Wulf and Eadwacer" and "The Wife's Lament"—that appear to be woman's songs of lament and separation, but some scholars continue to question both their context and their speakers' gender (Dronke, 1968, 1984), or as uniquely forceful evidence of a wife's anger toward her estranged husband (Niles). Other early texts include two eleventh-century Latin lyrics from the *Cambridge Songs* manuscript: "Levis exsurgit zephirus" ("Zephyr [the west wind] arises gently") and "Veni, dilectissime" ("Come, most beloved") both of which contain echoes of the Song of Songs, as noted by the *Cambridge Songs*' editor, Karl Strecker, and later, Peter Dronke (1968).

The first surviving female-voiced lyrics in Romance dialect come from eleventh-century Muslim Spain (al-Andalus). Arabic and Hebrew *muwashshaḥât*, strophic poems generally composed of five stanzas expressing the male point of view, often conclude with a *kharja*, a couplet in a Romance vernacular spoken by a woman or a young girl often in a tone quite distinctive from the male-voiced *muwashshaḥ*. These *kharjas* (or, in Spanish, *jarchas*) resemble later peninsular woman's songs in both tone and theme: the female lover is active, frank, and impassioned, and she frequently addresses her song of rapture, desire, or lament to a confidante figure, whether the narrator's mother or girlfriend. Such features also characterize many thirteenth-century *cantigas de amigo* ("songs for a friend"), Galician-Portuguese lyrics composed by male court poets in northwestern Spain and Portugal. Ramón Menéndez Pidal believed that the *jarchas*, the *cantigas de amigo*, and the later Spanish *villancicos* derived from a common Iberian tradition of woman's song. Other scholars extend the shared ancestry to all romance-language-speaking countries—or even all of Europe—perceiving the Arabic tradition to play an essential role in Western medieval literary development, as Leo Spitzer, Peter Dronke (1968), and María Menocal explain from complementary strands of the continuum. From the twelfth century on, the chanson de femme survives in a variety of languages and genres. The oldest German *Frauenlied* is the anonymous "Du bist min, ich bin din" ("You are mine, I am yours"), which concludes a Latin letter written by a nun to her clerkly admirer. Other German *Frauenlieder* of the twelfth and thirteenth centuries survive in the *Carmina Burana* and the Heidelberg Manuscript A, some of which are composed in a strophic form similar to that of the *Nibelungenlied* and traditional ballad-stanzas. Female-voiced German lyrics were also produced by known male poets, including Kürenberc, Meinloh von Sevelingen, Dietmar von Eist, Kaiser Heinrich, and Walther von der Vogelweide (in Lachmann et al.), which Dronke (1968) has compared with Romance, Hispano-Arabic, and English lyrics, finding the strongest affinity to reside between the English and German lyrics, by reason of their ability to convey intense emotion within a concise verse form, particularly the Germans. William E. Jackson (in Plummer) divides the *Frauenlied* into three principal categories: the monologue, the dialogue; and the *Wechsel* (a form in which both a woman and a man speak, but not to each other).

The *Carmina Burana* collection also contains a small number of medieval Latin woman's songs. Anne H. Schotter (in Plummer) separates these lyrics into two groups according to their representation of the female speaker. Only a few offer a serious treatment of the woman's suffering, having been modeled on the figures in the first-century B.C.E. Latin poet Ovid's *Heroides*, a collection of fictitious love letters between famous heroes and heroines of Antiquity, emphasizing women lovers' bereavement. Most of the *Carmina* are indebted to the more cynical, misogynistic tradition of the *Ars Amatoria* (*Art of Loving*), a more widely disseminated work also by Ovid. The spirit of these medieval Ovidian songs parallels that of Goliardic poetry—the irreverent, vibrant poems by wandering, tavern-frequenting anonymous clerics (tenth through thirteenth centuries)—since it invites the audience to laugh at the deceived woman's expense, implying complicity between the shrewd male lover and the poet.

Prominent among the French forms is the *chanson de toile* or *chanson d'histoire*, a lyrico-narrative piece usually composed in assonanced strophes, or *laisses*, with a refrain. The name chanson de toile (song of the cloth) derives in part from the poem's typical narrative configuration: the speaker is often a young girl engaged in spinning, sewing, or embroidery with her mother. From behind the outwardly passive yet distinctly feminine task of spinning, women lovers in the *chanson de toile* are allowed more active roles in love situations than in male-centered lyrics. Evidence gleaned from fictional romances suggests that the songs may also have been preserved, transmitted, and received within these narratives while also enhancing episodes within the plot (Huot; Boulton). As a major example, the thirteenth-century romance, *Le Roman de la rose ou de Guillaume de Dole* by Jean Renart (thirteenth century), as Sylvia Huot emphasizes, serves as "one of the most diverse anthologies of Old French song known today." In this story, a mother sings a supposedly old-fashioned chanson de toile while she and her daughter pursue their embroidery. This song, "Fille et la mere se sieent a l'orfrois" ("Mother and Daughter are Seated at Their Handiwork"), is cited in full and is the earliest known chanson de toile. It is possible, however, that the text reflects an older tradition that precedes its written record. Most of the surviving chansons de toile are anonymous and appear in the important collection of troubadour (southern-French lyric poet) and trouvère (northern-French lyric poet) lyrics known as the *Chansonnier français de Saint-Germain-des-Prés*, which includes "Bele Yolanz en ses chambres seoit" ("Fair Yolande Sat in Her Room") and "En un vergier, lez une fontenele" ("In an Orchard near a Fountain"). Other texts, of questionable authorship, appear as lyric insertions in thirteenth-century narratives such as Jean Renart's, though not as extensively. The French tradition also includes other types of songs: the *chanson d'ami* (song for a friend), the *chanson de mal mariée* (song of an unhappy wife), *chanson pieuse* (pious song), and the *aube* (Provençal *alba*, "dawn song"). As a secondary generic feature, the woman's song frequently manifests itself in the *chanson de croisade* (Crusade song), *pastourelle* (pastoral poem), *virelai, ballette, motet*, and *rotruenge*. Known male poets such as Guiot de Dijon (early thirteenth century) and Guillaume de Machaut (c.1300–1377) are responsible for a small number of female-voiced French lyrics, Machaut particularly in his *Voir Dit* (*True Poem*, c1365), a forerunner to the epistolary novel.

Thirteenth-century Portugal was perhaps the most fertile ground for the medieval woman's song in Europe. The *cantigas de amigo* were composed by male poets such as Martin Codax (fl. c.1230) and his contemporaries, Pero Meogo and Martin Padrozelos. On the whole, these songs exhibit less narrative progression than the French chansons, exploiting instead the lyric expressiveness of repetitive patterns. Occasionally the lover is present and engages in dialogue with the *amiga* (female friend); most often, however, the young girl addresses her complaint to a confidante, who may be a female companion or even an animal. In a celebrated piece by Pero Meogo, the speaker poignantly questions the deer—"hinds on the hillside"—about her fate as abandoned lover. Whereas earlier scholarship dwelled on the seemingly uncomplicated emotions portrayed in these songs, Kathleen Ashley (in Plummer) emphasizes the courtly conventions that render these *cantigas de amigo* the female-voiced counterparts to the cantigas de amor.

Finally, research on the insular tradition of woman's song has only begun. The type exists in a large number of Old Irish lyric and lyrico-narrative works from 800 to 1500, as catalogued by Ruth P. Lehmann (in Plummer). Middle-English forms consist primarily of carols and certain lyrics embedded in narrative works; a noteworthy example of the latter category is Chaucer's *Troilus and Criseyde* (c.1385).

Many unanswered questions remain concerning the origins, influence, and social context of the medieval *chanson de femme*. While some specialists maintain that the extant songs reflect a "popular" or "pre-courtly" tradition that may have engendered the courtly canso, Pierre Bec (1974) describes the surviving texts as "popularizing." Shifting attention away from historical sources, recent feminist scholarship has begun to question the longstanding automatic attribution of "femininity" to any lyric voices associated with unstable positions (Burns et al.). Closer textual analyses of the *chansons de femme* will thus contribute to a greater appreciation of female subjectivity in medieval texts.

See also *Alba* Lady; Boccaccio, Women in, Works Other than *De Claris Mulieribus*; Chaucer, Geoffrey, Women in the Work of; Christine de Pizan; Comtessa de Dia; Criseyde; *Daina*; Embroidery; *Frauenlied*; Kharja; *Minne*; *Miroir de Mariage* (*Mirror of Marriage*); Music: Women Composers and Musicians; *Muwashshaḥ*; *Novela Sentimental/ Sentimental Romance*; *Trobairitz*; *Trouvères*, Women; Wallādah.

BIBLIOGRAPHY

Primary Sources

Bec, Pierre. *La Lyrique française au moyen âge (XIIᵉ–XIIIᵉ siècles)*. 2 vols. Paris: Picard, 1977–1978.

[*Cambridge Songs*]. *Die Cambridger Lieder*. Edited by Karl Strecker. *Monumenta Germaniae Historica: Scriptores rerum germanicarum*, 40. Berlin: Weidmann, 1926; 2nd ed. 1955.

Cantigas d'amigo. In *Crestomatia arcaica*. Edited by José J. Nuñes. 6th ed. Lisbon: Livraría Clássica/ Teixera, 1967.

[*Cantigas*, etc.]. *Bella Domna. Woman as Saint, Lover, Poet and Patron*. London: Hyperion, 1988. CDA 66283. [Compact disk of Galician, Provencal, Old-French songs].

[*Cantigas*, etc.]. In *Wanderers' Voices: Medieval Cantigas and Minnesang*. Performed by The Newberry Consort. Paris and Los Angeles: Harmonia Mundi France, 1993. HMU 907082. [Compact disk with texts and transs.].

Carmina Burana. Edited by Alfons Hilka and Otto Schumann. 3 vols. Heidelberg, Germany: Carl Winter, 1930–1941. [Latin texts].

[*Chansons de femme*]. In *Ave Eva: Chansons de femmes des XIIe et XIIIe siècles/Songs of womanhood from the 12th and 13th centuries*. Performed by Brigitte Lesne. Paris: Opus 111, 1995. OPS 30-134. [Compact disk with texts and transs.].

[*Chansons de femme, chansons de toile*]. In *Chanter m'estuet: Songs of the Trouvères*. Edited by Samuel N. Rosenberg and Hans Tischler, esp. 2–23; and passim. Bloomington: University of Indiana Press, 1981. [Texts, notes, music].

Chansonnier français de Saint-Germain-des-Prés. Edited by Paul Meyer and Gaston Raynaud. Société des Anciens Textes Français. Paris: Edouard Champion, 1925.

Codax, Martin. *O som de Martin Codax: sobre a dimensão musical da lirica galego-portuguesa (seculos XII–XIV)*. Edited by Manuel Pedro Ferreira. Lisbon: Unisys, 1986. [Folio-volume with sound disk; see also in above *cantigas* collections].

Doss-Quinby, Eglal, Joan T. Grimbert, Wendy Pfeffer, and Elizabeth Aubrey, eds. and transs. *Songs of the Women Trouvères*. New Haven, Conn. and London: Yale University Press, 2001. [Introductory essay, texts, music, commentary, and notes].

Dronke, Peter. *Medieval Latin and the Rise of the European Love-Lyric*. 2 vols. Oxford: Oxford University Press, 1968.

———. *Women Writers of the Middle Ages: A Critical Study of Texts from Perpetua (†203) to Marguerite Porete (†1310)*. Cambridge: Cambridge University Press, 1984.

Exeter Book, The. Edited by George P. Krapp and Elliott V. K. Dobbie. New York: Columbia University Press, 1936 [Anglo-Saxon text of "A Wife's Lament," "Wulf and Eadwacer"].

Goldin, Frederick, ed. and trans. *German and Italian Lyrics of the Middle Ages: An Anthology and a History*. New York: Doubleday, 1973.

———. *Lyrics of the Troubadours and Trouvères: An Anthology and a History*. New York: Doubleday, 1973.

Guiot de Dijon. *In Chanter m'estuet, above*.

Lachmann, Karl, and C. von Krause, eds. *Des Minnesangs Frühling*. Revised ed. by Hugo Moser and Helmut Tervooren. Stuttgart, Germany: S. Hirzel, 1977.

Machaut, Guillaume de. *Le Livre dou Voir-Dit/Book of the True Poem*. Edited by Daniel Leech-Wilkinson. Translated by R. Barton Palmer. Garland Library of Medieval Literature, 106. New York: Garland, 1998.

Meogo, Pero. *O cancioneiro de Pero Meogo*. Edited by Xose L. Mendez Ferrin. Vigo, Spain: Galaxia, 1966.

[*Muwashshah, kharja*]. In *Hispano-Arabic Poetry: A Student Anthology*. Edited by James T. Monroe. Berkeley: University of California Press, 1974.

Renart, Jean. *Le Roman de la rose ou de Guillaume de Dole*. Edited and translated by Regina Psaki. Garland Library of Medieval Literature, 92A. New York: Garland, 1995.

Zink, Michel. *Belle: Essai sur les chansons de toile, suivie d'une édition et d'une traduction*. Paris: Honoré Champion, 1977.

Secondary Sources

Bec, Pierre. "Le Type lyrique des *chansons de femme* dans la poésie du moyen âge." In *Études de civilisation medievale (IXe–XIIe siècles): Mélanges offerts à Edmond-René Labande*, 13–23. Poitiers, France: C.E.S.C.M., 1974.

Boulton, Maureen. *The Song in the Story: Lyric Insertion in French Narrative Fiction, 1200–1400*. Philadelphia: University of Pennsylvania Press, 1993.

Buescu, Maria L. Carvalhão. *Literatura Portuguesa Medieval*. Lisbon: Universidade Aberta, 1990.

Burns, E. Jane, Sarah Kay, Roberta L. Krueger, and Helen Solterer. "Feminism and the Discipline of Old French Studies: *Une Bele Disjointure*." In *Medievalism and the Modernist Temper*, edited by

R. Howard Bloch and Stephen G. Nichols, 225–66. Baltimore: Johns Hopkins University Press, 1996.

Grimbert, Joan T. "Songs by Women and Women's Songs: How Useful is the Concept of Register?" In *The Court Reconvenes: Selected Proceedings of the Ninth Triennial Congress of the International Courtly Literature Society*, edited by Barbara K. Altmann and Carleton W. Carroll. Cambridge, U.K.: D. S. Brewer, 2003.

Huot, Sylvia. *From Song to Book: The Poetics of Writing in Old French Lyric and Medieval Narrative Poetry.* Ithaca, N.Y.: Cornell University Press, 1987.

Klinck, Anne L. "The Oldest Folk Poetry? Medieval Woman's Song as 'Popular' Lyric." In *From Arabye to Engelond: Medieval Studies in Honour of Mahmoud Manzaloui on His 75th Birthday*, edited by A. E. Christa Canitz and Gernot Wieland, 22–52. Ottawa: University of Ottawa Press, 1999.

———, and Ann Marie Rasmussen, eds. *Medieval Woman's Song—Cross-Cultural Approaches.* Philadelphia: University of Pennsylvania Press, 2002.

Lorenzo Gradín, Pilar. *La canción de mujer en la lírica medieval.* Monografías da Universidade de Santiago de Compostela, 154. Santiago de Compostela, Spain: Servicio des Publicacións, 1990.

Menéndez Pidal, Ramón. "Cantos romanicos andalusies, continuadores de una lirica latina vulgar." *Boletín de la Real Academia Española* 31 (1951): 187–270.

Menocal, María Rosa. *The Arabic Role in Medieval Literary History.* Philadelphia: University of Pennsylvania Press, 1987.

Mölk, Ulrich. "Chansons de femme, trobairitz et la théorie romantique de la genèse de la poésie lyrique romane." *Lingua e stile* 25 (1990): 135-46.

Niles, John D. "The Problem of the Ending of 'The Wife's Lament'." *Speculum* 78 (2003): 1107–50.

Plummer, John F., ed. *Vox Feminae: Studies in Medieval Woman's Songs.* Studies in Medieval Culture, 15. Kalamazoo, Mich.: Medieval Institute, 1981. [Contains an extensive bibliography as well as articles on individual topics].

Spitzer, Leo. "The Mozarabic Lyric and Theodor Frings' Theories." *Comparative Literature* 4 (1952): 1–22.

Zink, Michel. *Le Moyen Âge et ses chansons.* Paris: Fallois, 1996 [Especially pp. 135–60].

CATHERINE M. JONES

CHANSON DE TOILE. *See Chanson de Femme (Women's Song)*

CHANSON D'HISTOIRE. *See Chanson de Femme (Women's Song)*

CHAUCER, ALICE (1404–1475). Best known as Duchess of Suffolk, in eastern England, Alice Chaucer was also an important landholder and administrator, and a remarkable fifteenth-century political figure, a connoisseur, a patron of literature, and the possessor of a significant book collection. Generally recognized as the granddaughter of the renowned Middle-English poet Geoffrey Chaucer (c.1343–1400) and Philippa Roet (d. c.1387), supposedly attached to the court of Edward III as "a *domicella* ["domestic damsel"] of the chamber to Queen Philippa" (*Chaucer Life Records*; Pearsall), Alice was the daughter and sole heir of Thomas Chaucer (d. 1434) and Maud, or Matilda, Burghersh (d. 1437). Maud's parents were Ismania Hanham, or Hanaps (d. 1420), and Sir John Burghersh (d. 1391), unsuccessful claimant to the baronial house of Kerdeston. In addition to being Sir John's co-heir, Maud had prominent family connections at Richard II's court. She brought to her marriage numerous lands and holdings, especially the manor of Ewelme, which became the principal Chaucer residence. Thomas Chaucer was a respected soldier and statesman, chief butler to Richard II and Henry IV, a loyal and trusted servant to Henry V, speaker of the House of Commons in Parliament and, after the rise of that important noble family, the Lancastrians (House of Lancaster), Thomas became a foreign emissary of the king and the recipient of a lifetime appointment as constable of Wallingford Castle. Known for his interest in literature, Thomas Chaucer entertained local gentry with similar tastes (Ruud; Baugh; Moore).

In 1413 or 1414, Alice was betrothed and probably married to Sir John Phelip, or Philip, from near Dennington, Suffolk, who died in France in 1415, after the Battle of Harfleur (Baugh; Anderson), despite the English victory over this Normandy port. Sometime between 1421 and 1424, Alice became the second wife of the illustrious Thomas Montagu (or Montacute), fourth earl of Salisbury and count of Perche (France). One of the foremost English military leaders during the Hundred Years War, a councilor of the duke of Bedford's in France, a royal councilor in England, and a diplomat, Thomas was also a recognized literary patron. His father, John, third earl of Salisbury, had written verse praised by Christine de Pizan (in her *Advision* [*Vision*] of 1405–1406), who had subsequently sent her son, Jean Castel, to reside in the Salisbury household, seemingly as a companion and aid to Thomas Montagu (Laidlaw).

Thomas's literary and military interests functioned as a potent combination, together with Alice's assets, in the couple's acquisition of prestige and influence. Yet Thomas Montagu was frequently absent from England because of heavy military campaigning in France. However, Alice, now countess of Salisbury, accompanied him to France on at least one occasion in 1424, the wedding of Jean de la Trémouille and Jacqueline d'Amboise. This grand celebration, held at the Paris palace of Philip, duke of Burgundy, was attended by many leading French and English aristocrats, among them John, duke of Bedford, and Anne of Burgundy; William, earl of Suffolk; and Thomas, Lord Scales (as noted by chronicler Jean de Wavrin, c.1445). At the peak of his military career, Montagu died at the siege of Orléans (1428), a victim of Joan of Arc's spurring the French to unexpected victory, leaving but one child by his first marriage, Alice Montagu, about the same age as her stepmother, Alice Chaucer. Alice Montagu would later wed Richard Neville (d. 1460). Their son was Richard Neville (d. 1471), earl of Warwick who would become so powerful as to be nicknamed "the Kingmaker."

In 1430 or shortly thereafter, Alice Chaucer, still in her early twenties, married William de la Pole (1396–1450), earl of Suffolk, a prominent English military leader in France, serving as second in command to the earl of Salisbury and then as commander in chief of the English forces, and who had been captured in 1429 by Joan of Arc's troops. Through his military prowess and political skills, William rose to become marquis, and then duke. In the course of this ascent, he served as major advisor to King Henry VI, thereby becoming one of the most powerful men in the English realm. Another important factor in William's soaring career was his marriage to Alice, for in addition to wealth, dowers and other inheritances from her earlier marriages and later from her parents, Alice brought William de la Pole important family connections. Through her paternal grandmother, Philippa (c.1340–1387)—sister of Katherine Roet Swynford (1350–1404), first mistress, then wife of John of Gaunt (1340–1399)—Alice was a cousin to the powerful Beauforts, and thus related to Henry IV and the subsequent Lancastrian kings. In 1442, Alice bore a son and heir, John de la Pole, second duke of Suffolk (d. 1491/2), temporarily allied by a child marriage with Margaret Beaufort, Suffolk's infant ward. Alice's union with William de la Pole may also have yielded another son, William, and a daughter, Anna.

In 1444, Suffolk, principal English negotiator in the truce between England and France, was instrumental in arranging the marriage between Henry VI and Margaret (c.1430–1482), daughter of King René of Anjou. In November of that year, Alice and her husband arrived in France with an impressive entourage of more than three hundred to escort Margaret to England. Because of unexpected delays, Alice, her husband, and their companions stayed in France for almost five months, ultimately participating in a French wedding ceremony with Suffolk serving as proxy for the English king. After returning to England, Alice Chaucer de la Pole became principal attendant of the queen for many years, even after Suffolk's death in 1450. As part of Margaret's close circle, Alice was acquainted with several prominent noblewomen including Margaret, countess of Shrewsbury; Beatrice, Lady Talbot; Jacquetta of Luxembourg, dowager Duchess of Bedford and later wife of Richard Wydeville (or Woodville); and Jacquetta's daughter Lady Elizabeth Wydeville Grey, future queen of Edward IV. As countess, marchioness, and later duchess of Suffolk, Alice attained prestigious standing at court, wearing the robes and ensign of the Order of the Garter on several occasions between 1432 and 1433.

Substantial documentary evidence suggests that the marriage between Alice and William de la Pole was based on strong mutual attachment. It was purportedly out of affection for his wife that Suffolk had made Alice's Ewelme his primary residence; additionally, many grants to Suffolk also include her (Archer). This bond endured even while political turmoil (including charges of treason against William, because of military losses in France) besieged them, culminating in William's imprisonment, then impeachment before the House of Commons despite his eloquent pleas. Sentenced to exile, while departing from Dover, he was abducted from his boat and beheaded in 1450. When naming her sole executor of his estate, William states in his will that "above al the erthe my singuler trust is moost in her" (*North Country*; Archer), while in a letter written shortly before his assassination, William advises his son to be true to God, his king, and "youre ladye and moder," to obey and listen to "hyr councelles and advises in alle youre werks" (*Paston Letters*; Napier).

Alice's administrative talents, so helpful during her marriage, met with even greater challenges throughout her nearly three decades as a widow (Archer 1992; Anderson), beginning with Suffolk's sudden demise when she was in her mid-forties, with a seven-year-old son. Working rapidly in the ensuing months, she succeeded in maintaining her dower lands (those inherited from previous husbands) and jointure in the de la Pole estates (that portion set aside for her as William's widow), and also recovering the rest of William's lands, naming her officers (personnel helping her govern her domains), and securing the wardship (a kind of custody) of her son John. Like other large landowners of the time, Alice managed her estates with the aid of a council, which she astutely chose, keeping close personal control of administrative functions (Archer). One measure of her success is the extent of her estates, with residences not only at Ewelme but also at Wingfield, in Suffolk, and the Manor of the Rose in London (Stow; Meale). Her overall holdings, it has been claimed, were comparable to those of the duke of York, one of the wealthiest landowners in mid-fifteenth-century England (Metcalfe).

Endowed with intelligence and personal strength, Alice also developed political skill, which helped her withstand the growing opposition and attacks, fanned by Yorkists, against her husband's policies as royal advisor (Virgoe), and subsequently during the turbulent period of Wars of the Roses (a battle for the throne between the Houses of Lancaster [whose badge was the red rose] and York [white rose], 1455–1485). Two months after Suffolk had been impeached by the House of Commons and subsequently murdered, Alice was also indicted at the Guildhall, probably under the influence of the populist rebel Jack Cade before he himself was executed in that same year (1450). The charge of treason against Alice was repeated before Parliament months later. Despite all this, however, Alice was acquitted and remained attached to the court.

As duchess of Suffolk, Alice needed to contend with problems in a political sphere extending beyond her domains. She and Thomas of Scales (c.1399–1460) worked to fill the political gap left at court by her husband's death, particularly since, despite earlier promises, the king granted de la Pole lands to others, at least temporarily. Sometimes blamed for her lack of loyalty to the Lancastrians in the 1450s and 1460s (Napier), Alice's policies have, nonetheless, been praised as sound (Thomson). Significantly, perhaps, Margaret of Anjou was temporarily placed in Alice's custody at Wallingford in 1461. Moreover, Alice and the duke of York negotiated the 1460 marriage between her son, John de la Pole, and York's daughter, Elizabeth Plantagenet, sister of the future Edward IV. Even after John de la Pole came of age, Alice, the dowager duchess, continued to play an active role in estate management and politics, working closely with her son (Archer; Thomson; *Paston Letters*).

Alice Chaucer's great wealth is also reflected in the high quality of her possessions as recorded in various inventories. The tapestries, fine fabrics, jewels, precious metalwork, and books these documents describe are appropriate to a connoisseur and bibliophile, a taste she seems to have shared with her last two husbands (Napier; Goodall; *Descriptive Catalogue*). Like them, she was a patron of literature and noted book owner, as evidenced in a 1446 inventory listing twenty-one books brought from her Wingfield residence to Ewelme. The inventory includes several books related to religious services (e.g., a Mass book, antiphonals, processionals, and a book of collects); a manual for princes, presumably by Vincent of Beauvais (c.1194–1264); a copy of the *Quatre fils Aymon* (*Four Sons of Aymon*), also titled *Renaut de Montauban*, a popular Old French feudal-rebellion epic (late thirteenth century); works by the important English moral-historical poet John Lydgate (c.1360–c.1451), the French diplomat and moral-philosophical translator Guillaume de Tignonville (d. 1414), and, most revealingly, several titles by the Italian-born French feminist moral-political author and lyric poet, Christine de Pizan (1364/5–1430?). In addition to the inventoried volumes, works by these and other authors, including Geoffrey Chaucer, William de la Pole, John Montagu, and the admired French-English lyric prisoner-poet Charles d'Orléans (1394–1465), have been discovered or conjectured as once in her possession (McCracken; Pearsall; Meale; Manly and Rickert; Seymour). In one poem, an intricate word-puzzle encodes her name, "Alyce," corresponding to her authenticated signature (Jambeck).

As her library also indicates, Alice shared the religious sensibilities of her time during her married life and as a widow. She performed many benefactions, most notably to the Church of St. Mary, the Almshouse, and School at Ewelme, and perhaps Eton (Napier; Goodall). Her affinity for certain saints, especially manifest within the Ewelme church, reflects itself in representations of the Virgin Mary, Mary Magdalene, and St. Catherine with her wheel in churches and schools funded by her. St. Catherine, revered for having been spared martyrdom at the torture wheel by angels, seems to have been a particular favorite of Alice, who used the "Catherine wheel"—the insignia of her Roet grandmother's family (Roet, from the French "rouet" = "[spinning] wheel")—as one of her seals.

Alice Chaucer's remains lie in a magnificent three-tiered alabaster tomb in the Church of St. Mary at Ewelme. Probably planned by her before her death, it commemorates her ancestry, formidable worldly status, and her piety.

See also Beaufort, Margaret; Christine de Pizan; Dowry; Hagiography (Female Saints); Jacquetta of Luxembourg; Joan of Arc, St.; Margaret of Anjou; Paston, Margaret; Woodville, Elizabeth

BIBLIOGRAPHY

Primary Sources

Chaucer Life Records. Edited by Martin M. Crow and Clair C. Olson. Oxford: Clarendon Press, 1966.

Christine de Pizan. *Le Livre de l'advision Cristine.* Edited by Christine Reno and Liliane Dulac. Études christiniennes, 4. Paris: Honoré Champion, 2001.

CP=Cokayne, George E. *The Complete Peerage of England, Scotland, Ireland and Great Britain, and the United Kingdom Extant Extinct or Dormant.* New ed., revised by the Hon. Vicary Gibbs et al. 13 vols. London: Saint Catherine Press, 1910–1959.

Descriptive Catalogue of Ancient Deeds in the Public Record Office. Vol. 5. London: H.M. Stationery Office, 1906.

Hoccleve, Thomas. *Selections from Hoccleve.* Edited by M. C. Seymour. Oxford: Clarendon Press, 1981.

[Jean de Wavrin]. Jehan de Waurin. *Recueil des croniques et anchiennes istories de la Grant Bretaigne, a present nommé Engleterre.* Edited by William Hardy. 3 vols. London: Longman, 1864–1891.

Lydgate, John. *Minor Poems of John Lydgate.* Edited by Henry Noble MacCracken. 2 vols. Early English Text Society, e.s. 107; o.s. 192. London: Kegan, Paul, et al., 1911. New ed. London and New York: Oxford University Press, 1934.

North Country Wills, Being Abstracts of Wills Relating to the Counties of York, Nottingham, Northumberland, Cumberland, and Westmorland, at Somerset House and Lambeth Palace. 1383–1558. Edited by J. W. Clay. Surtees Society. Durham: Andrews; London: Bernard Quaritch, 1908.

The Paston Letters, A.D. 1422–1509. Edited by James Gairdner. 6 vols. London: Chatto & Windus, 1904. Reprint Stroud: Alan Sutton, 1986.

Stow, John. *A Survey of London.* 2 vols. Edited by Charles L. Kingsford. Oxford: Clarendon Press, 1908. Reprint 1971.

Secondary Sources

Aldwell, S. W. H. *Wingfield, Its Church, Castle and College.* Originally printed 1925. Reprint Athens, Ga.: Wingfield Family Society, 1994.

Anderson, Marjorie. "Alice Chaucer and her Husbands." *PMLA* 60 (1945): 24–47.

Archer, Rowena E. "'How ladies . . . who live on their manors ought to manage their households and estates': Women as Landholders and Administrators in the Later Middle Ages." In *Woman Is a Worthy Wight. Women in English Society c.1200–1500,* edited by P. J. P. Goldberg, 149–81. Gloucester, U.K.: Alan Sutton, 1992.

Arn, Mary-Jo, ed. *Charles d'Orléans in England (1415–1440).* Cambridge, U.K.: D. S. Brewer, 2000.

Baugh, Albert C. "Kirk's Life Records of Thomas Chaucer." *PMLA* 47 (1932): 461–515.

Begent, P. J. "Ladies of the Garter." *The Coat of Arms* n.s. 7 (1989): 16–22.

DNB = *Dictionary of National Biography.* Edited by Leslie Stephen and Sidney Lee. London: Smith, Elder, 1894–.

Dunn, Diana. "Margaret of Anjou, Queen Consort of Henry VI: A Reassessment of Her Role, 1445–53." In *Crown, Government and People in the Fifteenth Century,* edited by Rowena E. Archer, 107–43. Stroud, U.K.: Alan Sutton; New York: St. Martin's, 1995.

Goodall, John A. *God's House at Ewelme: Life, Devotion and Architecture in a Fifteenth-Century Almshouse.* Aldershot, U.K. and Burlington, Vt.: Ashgate, 2001.

Griffiths, Ralph Alan. *The Reign of Henry VI: The Exercise of Royal Authority, 1422–1461*. Berkeley and Los Angeles: University of California Press, 1981.

Guide to St. Mary's Church, Ewelme, and the Almshouse and the School. Abingdon, U.K., n.d.

Jambeck, Karen K. "The Library of Alice Chaucer, Duchess of Suffolk: A Fifteenth-Century Owner of a *Boke of le Citee de Dames*." *The Profane Arts/Les Arts profanes* 7.2 (autumn 1998): 106–35.

Laidlaw, J. C. "Christine de Pizan, the Earl of Salisbury and Henry IV." *French Studies* 36 (1982): 129–43.

MacCracken, Henry Noble. *See above, in* Primary Sources, *under* Lydgate.

Manly, John M., and Edith Rickert, eds. *Descriptions of the Manuscripts*. Vol. I of The Text of the Canterbury Tales. Chicago: University of Chicago Press, 1940.

McFarlane, K. B. "Henry V, Bishop Beaufort and the Red Hat, 1417–1421." *English Historical Review* 60 (1945): 316–48.

Meale, Carol M. "Reading Women's Culture in Fifteenth-Century England: The Case of Alice Chaucer." In *Mediaevalitas: Reading the Middle Ages*, edited by Piero Boitani and Ana Torti, 81–102. Cambridge: D. S. Brewer, 1996.

Metcalfe, Carol A. "Alice Chaucer, Duchess of Suffolk, c.1404-1475." Diss. B.A., University of Keele, 1970.

Moore, Samuel. "Patrons of Letters in Norfolk and Suffolk." *PMLA* 27 (1912): 188–207; 28 (1913): 79–105.

Napier, Henry Alfred. *Historical Notices on the Parishes of Swyncombe and Ewelme in the County of Oxford*. Oxford: James Wright, 1858.

Pearsall, Derek. *John Lydgate*. London: Routledge & Kegan Paul, 1970.

Richardson, Malcolm. "The Earliest Owners of *Canterbury Tales* MSS and Chaucer's Secondary Audience." *Chaucer Review* 25 (1990): 17–32.

Ruud, Martin B. *Thomas Chaucer*. Minneapolis: University of Minnesota Press, 1926.

Thomson, J. A. F. "John de la Pole, Duke of Suffolk." *Speculum* 54 (1979): 528–42.

Virgoe, Roger. "The Death of William de la Pole, Duke of Suffolk." *Bulletin of the John Rylands Library* 47.2 (March 1965): 489–502.

Watts, John. *Henry VI and the Politics of Kingship*. Cambridge: Cambridge University Press, 1996.

Willard, Charity Cannon. *Christine de Pizan: Her Life and Works*. New York: Persea Books, 1984.

KAREN K. JAMBECK

CHAUCER, GEOFFREY, WOMEN IN THE WORK OF (late 14th century).

Throughout his prolific and varied career, Geoffrey Chaucer (c.1343–1400), the most important author of the English Middle Ages, wrote about women. His two earliest surviving poems (pre-1372), An ABC, also titled *La Priere de Nostre Dame* (*Prayer to Our Lady*) in some manuscripts, and the *Book of the Duchess*—probably an elegy for Blanche, first wife of Chaucer's powerful patron, John of Gaunt (1340–1399)—celebrate the two ideals of femininity: the religious, venerated in the Madonna, and the secular, as embodied in the courtly heroine. The first book of the *House of Fame* (1372–1380) retells the story of Dido and Aeneas, displaying Chaucer's interest in the great heroines of the classical past, the injured or abandoned woman and the ambiguities of literary tradition. The *Parliament of Fowls* (1380–1386) debates the meaning of love between the sexes through the allegorical Garden of Love, with its pains and pleasures, the sultry and disturbing temple of Venus, the avian assembly presided over by Nature with her concern for procreation, the competition of the noble eagles for one reluctant female, and the more relaxed and direct attitudes of the lesser birds toward the subject of mating. Chaucer's longest complete work, *Troilus and Criseyde* (1380–1386), contains his longest and most complex portrait of any character, his Criseyde, the faithless heroine who stirs sympathy as well as censure. Chaucer's narrator expresses concern near the end of the poem lest the ladies in his audience be offended at this story. He protests that he would rather write about such virtuous women as Penelope (faithful wife of the wandering Ulysses in the ancient Greek poet Homer's *Odyssey*) and Alceste (self-sacrificing wife of Admetus in Euripides' classical Greek tragedy of 438 B.C.E., *Alkestis*). Chaucer fulfills this plan in the *Legend of Good Women* (1380–1386), in which, at Alceste's suggestion, the narrator promises to atone before the indignant God of Love by writing stories of good women betrayed by bad men. His last work, the *Canterbury Tales* (1387–1392), consists of a prologue and a collection of thirty stories related on a pilgrimage by various characters including a Prioress, an unnamed Second Nun, and a much-married widow: Alison, the Wife of Bath. There are allusions to—and complaints about—the wives of some of the married

The Wife of Bath. MS, Gg 4.27, University Library, Cambridge. Courtesy of North Wind Picture Archives.

pilgrims: the guildsmen, the Miller, the Merchant, and Harry Bailly, the host. Many of the stories are about love and marriage. In the religious and didactic tales, saintly heroines such as Constance and Cecilia represent Christian ideals of women.

Chaucer uses a number of standard late-antique and medieval genres, both religious and secular: the devotional poem, the saint's life, martyr's *passio* (passion, as in Christ's, during torture), sermon, meditation, dream vision, debate, epic, romance, and *fabliau* (comic, cynical, often lewd tale), and framed narratives (group of carefully arranged tales occasioned by a specific situation or "frame," like Boccaccio's *Decameron* set against the Black Death and this event's thematic potential). Several stock female characters recur within these genres, such as the distant courtly lady of romance and the sly, adulterous wife of the comic fabliau. Chaucer, however, experiments with genre, questioning the views of life and the presentation of character conventionally found in them. Blanche, in the *Book of the Duchess*, unlike the disdainful courtly heroines, is moderate and reasonable, with no desire to impose extravagant ordeals on her male admirers. The *Merchant's Tale* is a romance exposed as a fabliau: we find the marriage of the elderly knight, January, to the "fresh" maiden, May, and her predictable affair with the squire Damien equally squalid, but we also question the cynicism and misogyny of the Merchant himself, as shown in his comments attacking love, marriage and women. The Wife of Bath produces a feminist Arthurian romance in which a knight commits rape, is judged by a court of women, and condemned to death unless he can find the answer to a question: What do women most desire? The Prioress embodies a mistaken notion about genre: she models herself, with her pretty manners and almost seductive appearance, as much on a heroine of romance as on the Madonna, an understandable error when the two are presented so similarly in the poetry of the time.

Different genres are also traditionally associated with different levels of style and different ranks of society. Chaucer's social range is comprehensive. In the religious poems, the romances, and dream visions he writes of goddesses (Fame, Fortune, Nature, Venus), royalty and aristocracy (Mary, queen of Heaven; Dido, queen of Carthage; Constance, an emperor's daughter; Emily, an Amazon princess). His heroines are usually royal or noble—Blanche, the lady eagle, Dorigen, Cecilia—but he also treats women ennobled by marriage, such as patient Griselda, who is hideously mistreated by her husband the marquis to "test" her virtue. These heroines—with the exception of Criseyde, the most interesting—are perfectly chaste, often reluctant to marry, devoted within marriage, devastated by threats to their chastity. Chaucer's fabliau-type tales usually have a bourgeois cast: we meet wives of carpenters, merchants, millers. These are very different in that they are unabashedly sensual and untroubled by adultery, as in the *Shipman's Tale*, willing to exchange sexual favors for money both extramaritally and within marriage. The cast of the *Canterbury Tales* also reflects the increased social mobility of the later fourteenth century. Just as Chaucer himself, the learned layman from a mercantile background moving in court circles and holding high offices, becomes a new man, so also there are new categories of women. The Wife of Bath seems to be a businesswoman, a *femme sole* (self-sufficient single woman), her cloth-making surpassing that of male workers even at Ypres and Ghent (renowned textile centers in the Low Countries), her competitive spirit extending to being first in church at the offering. Social climbing and rivalry are themes informing many of the tales and their frame. The guildsmen on the pilgrimage have ambitious wives. The Prioress strives to be courtly in her behavior.

Chaucer operates within and examines the prevailing contemporary taxonomies of women. The female pilgrims of the *Canterbury Tales* exemplify the two roles assigned to women—nun and wife—in sharp contrast to the more varied professions of the men. Neither the Prioress nor the Wife of Bath fits her role perfectly: the former breaks the rules of her order with her personal adornment, her spoiled pets, and her very presence on the pilgrimage; the latter rebels more overtly with her defense of marriage, remarriage, and female domination. The Wife of Bath is obviously usurping one of the most authoritative masculine roles, that of the preacher. Married women are categorized by the three stages of their lives in relation to men: maidens, wives, and widows.

Chaucer, who was conversant with the philosophical and theological debates of his time on such problems as free will, emphasizes how little freedom is enjoyed in the first two stages of women's lives. His virginal heroines—Emily, Constance, Cecilia—are usually unwilling to marry but are nonetheless handed by one patriarchal figure to another. Marriage is a "cage" in the *Miller's Tale*. In the *Clerk's Tale*, Griselda is required to give up her will entirely to her husband. Some of Chaucer's characters feel keenly that this is compatible with neither love nor justice. In the *Franklin's Tale*, Dorigen and Averagus negotiate a marriage of equality and shared freedom, a bold experiment nearly ending in disaster. Motherhood is represented mainly as a vulnerable condition, reflecting perhaps the suffering of the ideal Madonna as well as the infant mortality rate at that time. The minor character of the wife in the *Summoner's Tale* mentions the recent death of her child almost casually. Constance, set adrift with her baby in a rudderless boat, prays to the Virgin Mary, who has suffered even more on account of her own son. The *Prioress's Tale*, whose narrator and young hero utter hymns to the Virgin, recounts the murder of a widow's only child, underscoring the dual pathos of her plight as twice bereaved: of husband, then of child.

Widowhood in Chaucer's England could, however, be an enviable time of relative freedom and affluence. One of many contradictions in the Wife of Bath's character is her desire for a sixth husband when her own experience has taught her, just as well as the authority of the Church, the "wo that is in mariage." Chaucer's other most interesting widow, Criseyde, values being her own woman, though whether she is free is one of the main problems of the poem. She cannot be easily classified. On the one hand, critics have argued that her relationship with Troilus constitutes a marriage and, on the other, that she is willfully loath to surrender the prized condition of widowhood.

This portrait seems deliberately vague about categories. The narrator mentions that he knows neither her age nor whether she has children. Criseyde, to judge from the volume of critical debate on her, also eludes the starkest binary division of women into "good" and "bad," though both the narrator and the God of love assume that readers will classify her as the latter. The Wife of Bath, as usual, turns the tables by classifying her husbands as three good, two bad. Various polemical attempts are made to quantify. In the *Merchant's Tale*, Pluto and Proserpina supernaturally echo the antagonism of the sexes: he arguing that he knows "ten hondred thousand" tales of female wickedness and quoting Solomon's pessimistic maxim that he found one good man in a thousand but no good women at all. Proserpina rebuts him with a list of good women and in the *Legend*, the God of Love tells the poet that he has in his books numerous good women to write about, twenty thousand indeed more than he knows. Even if the good women of the *Legend* seem more victimized than virtuous, in the *Canterbury Tales* the exemplars of courage, wisdom, and charity are female. Overall, Chaucer foregrounds good women more than good men, with the graver, more didactic *Tales* advocating that men follow women's example and counsel.

Chaucer is deeply concerned with women's relationship to literature as readers and listeners, writers and subjects. He addresses the women in his audience directly in *Troilus*, and we first see Criseyde at home listening to the story of Thebes, an ironic backdrop to her own situation. Female authorship was rare, though the Second Nun mentions her own role as transmitter of the story of St. Cecilia, herself an energetic preacher and polemicist for the faith. There is a pointed example in *Troilus*: while Criseyde agonizes about whether to accept Troilus's love, her niece Antigone sings a song about the joys of this relationship, written by one of the best and happiest women in Troy, as if this were a better testimony than the possibly self-interested love poems by men. Criseyde herself is literate and writes love letters to Troilus. The heroines of the *Legend* also compose letters: even Philomela, raped then silenced by her assailant cutting out her tongue, weaves the story of her assault on a tapestry. That other weaver, the Wife of Bath, may well be illiterate but is steeped in literary and theological tradition. Her climactic fight with her fifth husband breaks out over the book of wicked wives, which he insists on reading, battering her with the verbal weapons of clerical and misogynist literature. Her question, "Who peyntede the leon?" ("Who painted the picture of the lion?")—since the picture of the lion being killed by a man would look quite different if painted from the lion's point of view—raises the issue, much discussed nowadays, of women's relation to a literary tradition established mainly by male authorship. Chaucer is unusual, perhaps unique, among medieval English writers in his consciousness that male authors have a problematic and responsible relationship to their female subjects.

See also Arthurian Women; *Belle Dame Sans Mercy*; Boccaccio, Women in, *De Claris Mulieribus*; Boccaccio, Women in, *Des Cleres et Nobles Femmes*; Boccaccio, Women in, Works Other than *De Claris Mulieribus*; Chaucer, Alice; Childhood and Child-Rearing in the Middle Ages; Christine de Pizan; Criseyde; Dido in the Middle Ages; Embroidery; Griselda; *Miroir de Mariage* (*Mirror of Marriage*); *Natura*; *Roman de la Rose*, Debate of the; *Vertu du Sacrement de Mariage, Livre de la*

BIBLIOGRAPHY

Primary Source
Chaucer, Geoffrey. *The Riverside Chaucer.* Edited by Larry D. Benson. 3rd ed. Boston: Houghton Mifflin, 1988.

Secondary Sources
Biscoglio, Frances M. *The Wives of the Canterbury Tales and the Tradition of the Valiant Woman of Proverbs* 31: 10–31. San Francisco: Mellen Research University Press, 1993.
Cox, Catherine S. *Gender and Language in Chaucer.* Gainesville: University Press of Florida, 1997.
Crane, Susan. *Gender and Romance in Chaucer's Canterbury Tales.* Princeton, N.J.: Princeton University Press, 1994.
Delany, Sheila. *Medieval Literary Politics: Shapes of Ideology.* Manchester and New York: Manchester University Press, 1990.
———. *The Naked Text: Chaucer's Legend of Good Women.* Berkeley and Los Angeles: University of California Press, 1994.
———. *Writing Woman: Women Writers and Women in Literature, Medieval to Modern.* New York: Schocken, 1983.
Dinshaw, Carolyn. *Chaucer's Sexual Poetics.* Madison and London: University of Wisconsin Press, 1989.
Dor, Juliette, ed. *A Wyf Ther Was: Essays in Honour of Paule Mertens-Fonck.* Liège, Belgium: Université de Liège, 1992.
Fradenburg, Louise O. "The Love of Thy Neighbor." In *Constructing Medieval Sexuality*, edited by Karma Lochrie, Peggy McCracken, and James A. Schultz, 135–57. Medieval Cultures. Minneapolis and London: University of Minnesota Press, 1997.
Hallissy, Margaret. *Clean Maids, True Wives, Steadfast Widows: Chaucer's Women and Medieval Codes of Conduct.* Westport, Conn.: Greenwood, 1993.
Hansen, Elaine Tuttle. *Chaucer and the Fictions of Gender.* Berkeley and Los Angeles: University of California Press, 1992.
Mann, Jill. *Feminizing Chaucer.* Woodbridge, U.K. and Rochester, N.Y.: D. S. Brewer, 2002.
———. *Geoffrey Chaucer.* Hemel Hempstead, U.K.: Harvester Wheatsheaf; Atlantic Highlands, N.J.: Humanities Press, 1991.
Martin, Priscilla. *Chaucer's Women: Nuns, Wives and Amazons.* London: Macmillan; Iowa City: University of Iowa Press, 1990.
McDonald, Nicola F. "Chaucer's Legend of Good Women, Ladies at Court and the Female Reader." *Chaucer Review* 35 (2000): 22–42.
Percival, Florence. *Chaucer's Legendary Good Women.* Cambridge Studies in Medieval Literature, 38. Cambridge: Cambridge University Press, 1998.

PRISCILLA MARTIN

CHELLES, NUN OF (c.625–679). The Nun of Chelles was an otherwise unnamed nun who composed, in Latin, the older version of the life of Queen Balthild (c.625–679), whose realm, then called Neustria, comprised the western portion of the Merovingian Frankish kingdom. The nun lived in the monastery founded by Balthild at Chelles, not far from Paris, in the Eastern Merovingian Frankish kingdom then named Austrasia (sixth to eighth centuries). Her so-called *A Vita* (*A Life*) of Balthild is noteworthy since these were usually written by male members of a community. Yet, if we examine this *Vita* carefully, we discover that at the time it was written the Chelles monastery did not have male members. The text does not mention the presence of monks while the queen was alive. It does speak of priests being at the bedside of the dying Balthild, but their function was purely sacramental. Balthild called them and when they came, she asked the sisters to leave. A different version emerges from the *Vita Bertilae* (*Life of Bertilla*), composed somewhat later. Bertilla was installed as abbess by Queen Balthild herself, at the recommendation of Genesius, bishop of Lyon. Under Bertilla, Chelles emerged as an important link between the Frankish lands and the British Isles, as begun in the previous century, and thus played a key role in training Anglo-Saxon nuns and missionaries and in converting the local population.

For her part, the English-born Balthild had led a remarkable life by beginning in servitude, after being taken from her homeland as a slave during a raid, and brought to Neustria to serve as a chambermaid to the palace mayor. Somehow (the hagiographers—writers of saints' lives—are discreet on this aspect), she later became the wife of King Clovis II of Neustria and Burgundy (639–657), after whose death and with the support of her former owner, the mayor, she ruled as regent for her son Clothar III, with whom she reigned jointly and effectively. She also extended her realm by marrying her younger son, Childeric, to the daughter of the deposed queen of Austrasia, whom Balthild later helped restore to power as regent until Childeric could assume the throne. But not all of her maneuvers were successful. After suffering defeat in a complex power struggle involving the astute Ebroin (the new palace mayor) and ecclesiastical officials, Balthild was forced to retire to Chelles.

On entering Chelles, Balthild did not replace Abbess Bertilla, who outlived her patroness by twenty-six years (dying in around 705), and thereafter invited monks to join the community. Thus, the Nun of Chelles's *Vita* also relates the founding of Chelles as a double monastery, with the nuns and monks performing different tasks and with its own rule distilled from those of Benedict, Caesarius, and others.

Naturally, hagiographers such as the Nun of Chelles focus more on Balthild's gaining permission to convert (her conversion's authenticity adds another mysterious facet to her story) and her reign as a saintly queen than as an ambitious political figure. According to the Chelles authoress, she exhibited motherly qualities as a queen not only toward her own offspring but also toward the young men in her court, for whom she acted as "optima nutrix" ("most aristocratic nurturer"), while with the indigent she was "pia nutrix" ("gentle nurturer"). As regent, Balthild was an instrument of God's direction of harmony between warring princes. As a member of the monastery, Balthild knew well that the sisters had to offer prayers to God not only for the king and queen but also for the royal officials. With the magnates now running the kingdom, divine help was needed for a broad constituency if Chelles were to serve as "God's earthly helper."

The authoress may have finished her work after the first monks were admitted to Chelles. The "dilectissimi fratres" ("most beloved brothers") to whom she dedicated the composition, were not, however, the brothers of the monastery. They were probably the monks of Corbie, a northern-French monastery also founded by Balthild (657) and where Balthild's friend, Theudefrid, continued to serve as abbot for some time after her death. Corbie would become one of the most influential Benedictine abbeys during Charlemagne's reign (771–814).

The *Vita* shows that the authoress knew Baudonivia's *Vita S. Radegundis* (*Life of Saint Radegund*) because the same triple theme found in the *Vita S. Radegundis* appears also in her own work: the motherly disposition of Balthild; her function as peacemaker between the hostile kingdoms; and the extension of this mission to Chelles, which by her presence becomes the source of concord between God and the royal court. To reproach her for imitating Baudonivia would be useless, since both women came from similar backgrounds. Balthild, like Radegund, was brought up to serve the family, the aristocracy, and God as a mediator of conflicts—a role better understood by a woman than by a man. The Nun of Chelles imitated Baudonivia in general thematic structure, but for the specifics she found her own context.

See also Baudonivia; Double Monasteries; Hagiography (Female Saints); Radegund, St.

BIBLIOGRAPHY

Primary Sources
Nun of Chelles. *Vita S. Balthildis reginae.* Edited by Bruno Krusch, 477–508. *Monumenta Germaniae Historica*(= MGH), *Scriptores rerum merovingicarum* (= SRM), 2. New ed. Hannover, Germany: Hahn, 1977–1979.
———. "Balthild, Queen of Neustria." In *Sainted Women of the Dark Ages*, edited and translated with commentary by Jo Ann McNamara and John E. Halborg et al., 264–78. Durham, N.C.: Duke University Press, 1992. [Useful introductions, notes, and English text].
Vita Bertilae, abbatissae Calensis. Edited by Wilhelm Levison, 95–109. MGH. SRM, 6. Hannover: Hahn, 1977–1979.
———. "Bertilla, Abbess of Chelles." In *Sainted Women of the Dark Ages*, 279–88. *See above under* "Balthild...."

Secondary Sources
Nelson, Janet T. "Queens as Jezebels: The Careers of Brunhild and Balthild in Merovingian History." In *Medieval Women*, edited by Derek Baker, 31–77. Studies in Church History: Subsidia, 1. Oxford: Basil Blackwell, 1978.
Wemple, Suzanne Fonay. *Women in Frankish Society: Marriage and the Cloister, 500 to 900.* The Middle Ages. Philadelphia: University of Pennsylvania Press, 1981.

SUZANNE FONAY WEMPLE

CHILDHOOD AND CHILD-REARING IN THE MIDDLE AGES. The study of childhood, and medieval childhood in particular, is a relatively recent event in historical and cultural studies. As a convenient signpost, we may take 1960, the date of Philippe Ariès's *L'Enfant et la vie familiale sous l'ancien régime*, to mark the beginning of the systematic study of affective life and of social institutions, and the beginning of a focus on children and the notion of childhood. Although earlier studies on children and childhood in the ancient and medieval world are valuable for their observations (cited in the bibliographies to Ariès and his successors), the basic issues in the debate on the nature of childhood in the Middle Ages were identified in a few influential studies spawned in part by the English translation of Ariès's book. Ariès's perspective, as it applied to the Middle Ages, is based on two main propositions: that the ancient and medieval world lacked a concept of childhood as a distinct stage in human life, and that emotional bonding in these ages differed strikingly from our notions about relationship, for parents in premodern times protected themselves from the pain of grief by not caring about their children. Despite their essential denial of love to medieval children, and even of a conceptual existence to childhood in this period, Ariès's views were positive and idealizing, if sometimes frustrating to a public requiring more of a psycho-history than his social history.

Ariès's theories on childhood inspired passionate scholarly interest, ranging from emulation to refutation, since their inception and over the ensuing decades. Ariès himself would later confess to insufficient grounding in the medieval period, since it was but one small phase of his book, which he would try to emend in the 1973 edition, in the wake of reactions from leading social historians Pierre Riché, J. L. Flandrin, and Emmanuel Le Roy Ladurie. Yet, his later emulators retained the daring of the vintage Ariès more than the revised one. For example, Edward Shorter claimed ancient mothers were indifferent to children younger than two and that lower-class parents used the cradle as a stupefying device. Likewise

Children's education: girls learning to spin, boys to fight. Folio 40v of *Le Livre des Bonnes Moeurs* (*Book of Good Manners*), fifteenth-century manuscript by Jacques le Grant. © The Art Archive/ Musée Condé, Chantilly/Dagli Orti.

with influential nonscholars such as Elisabeth Badinter, a popular essayist asserting that premodern societies were devoid of love for children, that they spurned and even feared them. However, the more qualified of Ariès's successors embraced a variety of evolving trends in social and other types of history and their ever-expanding sources—legal, clerical (foundling homes), and private records, including canon and secular law; depictions of children in literature and the visual arts; encyclopedias and manuals of family life, child-rearing and education; plus, on the more religious side, models from saints' lives, records of pilgrimage shrines, records of miracles (see Ronald Finucane), materials collected for validating canonization, and transcripts from canonization trial proceedings. These newer, more balanced syntheses have greatly enriched our understanding of childhood in the Middle Ages and the significance of medieval commentators on childhood such as Vincent of Beauvais (d. 1264), Aldobrandino of Siena (d. 1287), Francesco da Barberino (1264–1348), and Jean Gerson (1363–1429), with Christine de Pizan (1364/5–1430?) being one of the few women to touch on the topic of childhood and mothering in several of her works, as Bernard Ribémont has shown.

Among Aries's successors, Lloyd De Mause, an important critic of Ariès in the 1970s, opted for a psychoanalytic approach in his *History of Childhood* in that the "history of childhood is a nightmare from which we have only recently begun to awaken. The further back in history one goes, he maintains, the lower the level of child care, and the more likely children are to be killed, abandoned, beaten, terrorized, and sexually abused." Thus his task is to "provide an overview of the history of infanticide, abandonment, nursing, swaddling, beating, and sexual abuse . . . [to demonstrate] how widespread the practice was in each period." Although other contributors to this volume carry these ideas further, their insights also mitigate their dark view of medieval childhood. Yet among these, Mary Martin McLaughlin examines records in saints' lives and memoirs, "the personal, biographical and autobiographical or self-revealing works which grew more abundant during these centuries [eleventh and twelfth] manifesting the rising self-awareness[. . .]in the culture of this age." She finds "clear signs, especially from the twelfth century onwards, of tenderness towards infants and small children, interest in the stages of their development, awareness of their need for love." As exemplars of medieval attitudes toward children in this period, she points to the writings of Anselm of Canterbury and Vincent of Beauvais, both of whom argued for the gentle treatment of children. She touches only briefly on infanticide, seeing it primarily as a response to illegitimacy.

Two later studies, without claiming to be histories of childhood, nonetheless offer distinct important perspectives enabling us to resolve the apparent contradiction between appalling conditions for children and the documented presence of caring adults knowledgeable in child development and childhood needs: those by John Boswell and Clarissa Atkinson. Boswell's reexamination of infanticide, exposure, and abandonment of society's defenseless members shows these to be society's worst offenses against children. He attempts to understand the apparently widespread abandonment of children, while discounting the notions "that there was no concept of 'childhood' in premodern Europe, and that parent–child relations in previous ages were for this and other reasons (such as the high infant mortality rate) inherently and categorically different from those of the modern West." Plausible as these hypotheses may seem, Boswell continues, "such theories do not account well for the available evidence." In fact, Europe seems to have discovered the individual and the child in the twelfth century, the same century in which the greatest number of children were abandoned or exposed. After discussing Greek, Roman, Muslim, and Early Christian examples of abandonment, Boswell turns to the specifically medieval phase of his survey: the institution of oblation—the donation of a child as a permanent gift to a monastery, whether as an orphan, a dispossessed heir (due to illegitimacy or rival heirs), but most often among the lower classes to relieve impoverished parents of the burden of the child's upkeep. Boswell shows oblation to be a uniquely medieval response to many of the same economic and social problems that plagued earlier societies and threatened their children, a response shaped by the new medieval values of Christian morality and spirituality in regard to helping the poor and defenseless to resolve a perennial moral dilemma: "Oblation constituted a compromise between a highly developed moral system and primitive social structures." We may consider oblation a form of abandonment, as did some medieval children, but the Middle Ages in general seemed to consider oblation an alternative to abandonment. Thus we have the contradiction that Boswell observes: "Although the eleventh and twelfth centuries mark a low point in abandonment of children in Europe (outside Scandinavia), they were also witness to the fullest flowering of oblation and it is likely that these developments are more than co-incidentally related."

Atkinson studies such economic-biological versus moral-spiritual quandaries in child-rearing in another light, in her investigation of the idea of Christian motherhood. She tends to accept the idea that family relations are culturally constructed rather than purely biologically driven, without denying this clear biological basis to a society's care for its infants, while probing the lengthy evolution of motherhood as biological, spiritual, and theological fact. Her discussion of the values of motherhood and family in the twelfth century is the most relevant for our purposes. There is no doubt, she says, that "the insecurity and real dangers of medieval childhood created powerful, persistent fantasies of protection and rescue by an omnipotent, loving mother." In discussing the picture of children and parents given in the collection of miracle stories associated with the Virgin Mary at Chartres, she tells us:

> The numerous children and infants in the stories present a poignant and complicated glimpse of medieval childhood [. . .]. Their presence in such numbers, with the assumption that they and their circumstances are touching and pitiful, argues against the "indifference" to children sometimes attributed to medieval adults. On the other hand, the stories do not supply evidence of careful and empathic parenting—far from it: Mary is a much more satisfactory parent than any of the adults.

Two comprehensive studies of medieval childhood represent more current scholarly directions in this field, one by Danièle Alexandre-Bidon and Monique Closson, and the other by Shulamith Shahar. The materials cited in both studies contradict Ariès's theory of indifference toward small children. Shahar is convinced that "a concept of childhood existed in the mid- and late Middle Ages, that scholarly acknowledgement of the exis-tence of several stages of childhood was not merely theoretical, and that parents invested both material and emotional resources in their offspring" (145). Both studies begin with describing medieval marriage and sexual practices. Succeeding chapters discuss preg-nancy, labor, and infancy. Since reconstructing the history of childhood for past ages is obviously difficult, both Shahar and Alexandre-Bidon, and Closson recognize the hazards involved in drawing conclusions from material never expressly intended to provide in-formation about childhood and does so only peripherally. Nevertheless, these two studies and in other recent scholarship have systematically explored such sources as handbooks on marriage, medieval encyclopedias—especially those by Vincent of Beauvais and Bar-tholomaeus Anglicus [Bartholomew the Englishman]—, the writings of the mystic Ray-mond Lull on child-rearing, and Italian family record books. Another primary source for Alexandre-Bidon and Closson is manuscript illumination, mostly devotional (books of hours, breviaries, etc.), profusely and carefully catalogued in their book.

What is unique about Alexandre-Bidon's and Closson's study is that the two authors focus primarily on the details of the material life of children and parents. As they say in conclusion, an alternate title for their book would be *Petit manuel de puériculture médiévale* [*Little Manual of Medieval Child Care*], for this is just what they provide. Alexandre-Bidon and Closson attempt to determine what medieval people actually did in private by looking a penitentiaries, those guides for priests, telling what kind of leading questions confessors should ask to find out what their parishioners were doing in bed, and what penances to prescribe if the couple was sinning—no oral sex, no sodomy, no "animal" positions, and no sex on forbidden days, which accounted for almost half the calendar year. No sex was permitted during pregnancy either. Succeeding chapters discuss pregnancy, labor, handling the newborn (the two baptisms), nursing, hygiene: diapers and swaddling bands, bathing. We are told in detail of how babies were fed, how "pap" was prepared as an infant's first solid food. Evidence is provided on the use of "nursing horns," necessary before bottles were available if the mother died and a wet nurse could not be found. (Nursing horns were hollowed out animal horns used like bottles now, evidently more frequently used than American scholarship has suggested.) The stage of teething was evidently of concern, for practical reasons because babies cried a lot during teething, and for philosophical reasons because medieval people thought that all a baby's first teeth had to come in before he or she could learn to talk. They used teething rings but no pacifiers. Considerable attention is devoted to the matter of cradles and cribs, as well as to various kinds of clothing for babies.

Other chapters are concerned with the baby after the first year. The authors summarize the evidence concerning learning to walk and to talk; both these events seem to have occurred later than in modern infants. To assist in walking, and probably to prevent crawling, babies used various types of walkers, all of which are described and illustrations provided from manuscript illumination. Since babies had to be carried everywhere by working mothers and fathers, the authors present various kinds of equipment for carrying babies on one's back while working in the fields, carrying a baby when riding on a mule or horse, baskets for babies to be attached to the side of a mule for longer journeys, and so on. Attention is given to the role of the father in caring for young children, a surprise, since there is so little mention of fathers and children in medieval literature. The conclusions drawn about punishment of babies are also a surprise; the authors stress that the cardinal rule was "Don't let babies cry." The idea was to nurse them, feed them, or change them if they cry. Only a bad mother beats her infants. For older children, probably over three, punishment seems to have been left up to fathers. Childhood ends when permanent teeth come in.

There is a sizable section on toys for children. Although objects like toys do not last long enough to be discovered by archeologists, there is evidence of their existence in paintings and manuscript illumination, and in account books of royal families showing what toys were commissioned for princes and princesses. For very small babies, there were rattles and various objects on which to suck or bite. Older children were given toys associated with their gender roles and their future responsibilities; thus, girls received little sets of dishes and cooking pots, and dolls of various kinds, and boys were given hobby-horses and swords. Both sexes were given windmills and kites. Class-defined toys are also documented: one princess got a little princess doll on horseback, accompanied by a little page doll; ordinary children contented themselves with rag dolls. There seems to have been very few objects that we would really term toys for children under the age of two, which the authors explain as being due to the fact that children under two were played with by adults and constantly watched until they could walk. Once they could walk, they were pretty much on their own, and then they acquired more toys. We are reminded that once a child was two, there was probably another child on the way or already born, and the mother could no longer devote much time to the toddler.

In addition to this rather linear model of child development, Alexandre-Bidon and Closson at each stage try to deal with differences in treatment of infants according to class and rural-urban environment. The authors are aware that their evidence is predominantly upper class and urban, but they provide a surprising amount of evidence about rural families and poor families. In the section on illness, the authors look at pilgrimage data reflecting the popularity of pilgrimages to certain saints to cure illnesses of children, to assess medieval people's love for their children and the lengths to which they would go, regardless of class, to find help for them. Atkinson and Boswell analyze similar source material in their studies of motherhood and abandonment, respectively.

Medieval people emerge from this study as quite enlightened about infancy. For the first two years of their life, children seem to have been carefully and lovingly cared for; their world was almost entirely a feminine one, and many children had two caretakers, their biological mother and their wet nurse. According to Alexandre-Bidon and Closson, there was much attention to cleanliness; here the system of using swaddling bands is explained so that it is clear that a baby could be removed from swaddling bands to change diapers just as easily as clothes could be removed now. In the absence of safety pins it seems to have been the swaddling bands that held the diapers in place. Swaddling bands immobilized the babies more than now, and that may be connected with the desire to prevent them from crying. Shahar questions the reliability of the conclusions of Alexandre-Bidon and Closson in this area, as in many other respects, by citing evidence that to many observers, medieval babies were hopelessly filthy and that swaddling practices encouraged disease and infection.

Shahar's study, as its title, *Childhood in the Middle Ages*, indicates, was the first truly inclusive work on this subject. Her initial chapters look at developmental models of the stages in childhood and explore the treatment of infancy and early childhood. After two chapters devoted to the issues of abandonment, and to sickness, handicaps, bereavement, and orphanhood, she turns to education in the second stage of childhood and factors in personality formation. Class issues in education govern the contents of the final chapters, covering education in the nobility, in urban areas, and among the peasantry. A short appendix examines the relevance of Freudian thought on incest to our understanding of medieval childhood.

Not to be outdone, Alexandre-Bidon's newer book, with Didier Lett, stresses social theory and history along with the iconographic approach of the former's first book on childhood, to map out a history of symbolic place of the child in both life and death, in Christendom, and then in real-life terms within all social classes and occupations (whether as apprentices, slaves, or spies). Alexandre-Bidon and Lett conclude overall that, despite much misery, hardship, and exploitation (from their labor to their urine in certain kinds of manufacturing), medieval children were also surrounded by a considerable affection.

Nicholas Orme, another very recent voice on medieval childhood, approaches his topic from a more late-medieval-early-Renaissance Anglocentric perspective as he delineates each stage of a child's experience from its conception, then gestation within its mother—including the use of relics or amulets and other charms to ensure its survival through birth—and its baptism and subsequent phases of development up to adolescence, with all attendant ceremonies (e.g., naming, swaddling, weaning) and prevailing beliefs (folkloric and theological), among which: the female fetus assumes a soul at about ninety days, in comparison to about forty-six days for the male. Orme uses a more restricted range of hard evidence, both chronologically and generically, than Alexandre-Bidon, but his use of iconographic material is impressive, as is his discussion of toys (the males' being more interesting) and songs, making even his more general conjectures worthy of attention. He concludes that, at least in late-medieval England, seemingly 42.5 percent of children died before age ten; childhood marriage, infanticide, and cruelly demanding apprenticeships were quite rare.

One notes in almost all of the above studies a lack of attention to the real situation of Jewish children as opposed to medieval Christian anti-Semitic propaganda: that the Jews routinely killed Christian children and used their blood to make matzoh, of Jewish cannibal mothers, and so forth. Some Jews supposedly saw the "truth" of Christianity after seeing a child's bleeding corpse. Such accounts represent a curious conflation of Abraham's Sacrifice from the Old Testament and the Eucharist (the body of Christ in the Host, or communion wafer) in the Gospels, along with Ecclesia's (the Catholic Church's) triumph over blind Synagoga (both female allegorical figures popular in medieval art) as exemplified most memorably in Chaucer's *Prioress's Tale.* Paradoxically enough, Atkinson's avowedly Christian-centered work perhaps offers the most information on medieval Jewish children within their own cultural context, relating scriptural precepts and examples (especially the story of Isaac's miraculous birth to the aged Sarah) to real-life practice wherever possible, and asserting children's status as spiritual and material blessings to the household, especially male children. Compared to Christian teachings, sexual expression for both genders, within marriage, received higher moral approval since it helped to guarantee the survival of the Jewish people. Even less evidence exists for medieval Islamic views on childhood, particularly Muslim females, given their lower station in life compared to that of men, following their theology. Shahar, for instance, notes the lack of obstetrical treatises—in a culture otherwise renowned for its scientific knowledge—because such tasks were left to illiterate midwives and not true doctors, that is, men.

Most recently, Daniel Kline synthesizes and demonstrates the usefulness of a responsible feminist literary-theoretical approach to Western medieval female childhood in reading standard literary works as historical documents; primarily Middle-English writings such as Chaucer's *Prioress's Tale* and *Physician's Tale,* the dream-vision poem *Pearl,* and the so-called N-Town plays. By glossing such literature with modern educational-historical studies and medieval courtesy manuals (see his bibliography), Kline analyzes *Pearl* as a defense of children advocating their revaluation in society as blessedly innocent. The N-Town Nativity Plays reveal much about customs surrounding infant girls, their birth, and education. Chaucer's Prioress epitomizes essential teachings from courtesy manuals; his *Physician's Tale* "problematizes the multiple tensions of growing up female in late medieval England"; poetic romances like *Floris and Blancheflur,* while allowing girls to enjoy educational travel adventures on a par with boys, nonetheless relegates girls to "objects of exchange between men, facilitating patriarchal power as potential mothers and wives." From such works, Kline draws several conclusions about medieval attitudes toward childhood, for example, that female children, because their labor did not earn income and because they required a dowry to marry properly, caused their parents to lose money. Sons brought in money through labor from an early age. But more generally and pervasively, these (mostly male) authors "struggled with conflicting imperatives" in their evocations of female children: girls deserved good care to become healthy, caring wives mothers essential to preserving society and lineage; yet they were also ill-treated physically and coerced into severely restricted lives because of that same society's prejudice against them.

All in all, most scholars would now agree that no society can survive without seeing to the needs of its young, and without awareness of childhood's developmental stages from birth to adulthood. Most also agree that by the twelfth century, at least in Europe, childhood and the family existed as distinct concepts, and that these concepts bore social consequences, including the deep affection many parents felt toward their children. Accordingly, the high infant mortality rate marking the Middle Ages is now attributed to the complex interplay of economics, limited medical skills, food quality and distribution rather than to parental contempt for children. In all, as Barbara Hanawalt (2002) has recently argued, the study of medieval childhood has made much progress, yet much also remains to be done.

See also China, Women in; Courtesy Books; Griselda; Medicine and Medieval Women; Teachers, Women as; Virginity

BIBLIOGRAPHY

Primary Sources

Aldobrandino of Siena. *Le régime du corps*. Edited by Louis Landouzy and Roger Pépin. Preface by Antoine Thomas. Paris: Honoré Champion, 1911.

Bell, Susan Groag, ed. *Women from the Greeks to the French Revolution*. Stanford, Calif.: Stanford University Press, 1973. [Useful anthology excerpting treatises pertinent to childhood and other aspects of women's lives.]

Chaucer, Geoffrey. *The Riverside Chaucer*. Edited by Larry D. Benson. 3rd ed. Boston: Houghton Mifflin, 1987.

Christine de Pizan. *Livre des Trois Vertus*. Edited by Charity Willard and Eric Hicks. Bibliothèque du XVe siècle, 50. Paris: Honoré Champion, 1989. Reprint 1997.

————. *Treasure of the City of Ladies*. Translated by Sarah Lawson. Harmondsworth, U.K.: Penguin, 1985.

Floris and Blancheflu. In *King Horn, Floriz and Blanchflur, The Assumption of Our Lady*, edited by J. Rawson Lumby; re-edited by George A. McKnight, 71–110. E.E.T.S., o.s. 14, 1886. London: Oxford University Press, 1901.

Francesco da Barberino. *Del reggimento e de' costumi delle donne (Reggimento e costume di donne)*. 2nd ed. Edited and revised by Giuseppe Sansone. Roma: Zauli, 1995.

Gerson, Jean. *L'Education des dauphins de France*. Edited by Antoine Thomas. Paris: Droz, 1930.

[N-Town Plays]. Peter Meredith. *The Mary Play from the N-Town Manuscript*. New York: Longman, 1987.

Pearl. In *Poems of the Pearl Manuscript*, edited by Malcolm Andrew and Ronald Waldron. York Medieval Texts, 2nd series. Berkeley: University of California Press, 1978.

Vincent of Beauvais *De eruditione filiorum nobilium*. Edited by Arpad Steiner. Cambridge, Mass.: Mediaeval Academy, 1938. Reprint New York: Kraus, 1970.

Secondary Sources

Alexandre-Bidon, Danièle, and Monique Closson. *L'enfant à l'ombre des cathédrales*. Lyon, France: Presses Universitaires de Lyon/CNRS, 1985.

————, and Didier Lett. *Les Enfants au Moyen Age : V^e–XVe siècles*. Preface by Pierre Riché. Paris: Hachette, 1997.

————. *Children in the Middle Ages: Fifth to Fifteenth Centuries*. Translated by Jody Gladding. Notre Dame, Ind.: University of Notre Dame Press, 1999.

Ariès, Philippe. *L'Enfant et la vie familiale sous l'ancien régime*. Paris: Plon, 1960. Revised ed., 1973.

————. *Centuries of Childhood: A Social History of Family Life*. Translated by Robert Baldick. New York: Knopf, 1962.

Atkinson, Clarissa. *The Oldest Vocation: Christian Motherhood in the Middle Ages.* Ithaca, N.Y.: Cornell University Press, 1991.

Badinter, Elisabeth. *L'Amour en plus. Histoire de l'amour maternel, XVIIe–XXe siècles.* Paris: Flammarion, 1980.

Barron, Caroline M. "The Education and Training of Girls in Fifteenth-Century London." In *Courts, Counties, and the Capital in the Later Middle Ages,* edited by Diana E. S. Dunn, 139–53. New York: St. Martin's, 1996.

Blumenfeld-Kosinski, Renate. *Not of Woman Born: Representations of Caesarian Birth in Medieval and Renaissance Culture.* Ithaca, N.Y.: Cornell University Press, 1990.

Boswell, John. *The Kindness of Strangers: The Abandonment of Children in Western Europe from Late Antiquity to the Renaissance.* New York: Pantheon, 1988.

Bynum, Caroline W. *Jesus as Mother: Studies in the Spirituality of the High Middle Ages.* Berkeley: University of California Press, 1983.

Crawford, Sally. *Childhood in Anglo-Saxon England.* Stroud, U.K. and Dover, N.H.: Sutton, 1999.

De Mause, Lloyd, ed. *The History of Childhood.* New York: Harper, 1974. Reprint Northvale, N.J.: Aronson, 1995.

Derevenski, Joanna Sofaer, ed. *Children and Material Culture.* London and New York: Routledge, 2000.

Elias, Norbert. *The Civilizing Process: Sociogenetic and Psychogenetic Investigations.* Revised ed. London: Blackwell, 2000.

L'Enfant au Moyen-âge. Special number of *Sénéfiance,* 9 (1980). Aix-en-Provence: CUER MA; Paris: Honoré Champion, 1980. [Important collection of studies in various disciplines, in French].

Finucane, Ronald C. *The Rescue of the Innocents: Endangered Children in Medieval Miracles.* New York: St. Martin's Press, 1997.

Flandrin, J.-L. "Enfant et société." *Annales—E. S. C.* 19 (1964): 322–29.

Goodich, Michael. *From Birth to Old Age: The Human Life Cycle in Medieval Thought, 1250–1350.* New York and London: University of Haifa, 1989.

Haas, Louis. *The Renaissance Man and His Children: Childbirth and Early Childhood in Renaissance Florence 1300–1600.* New York: St. Martin's, 1998.

Hanawalt, Barbara. *Growing Up in Medieval London: The Experience of Childhood in History.* New York: Oxford University Press, 1993.

———. "Medievalists and the Study of Childhood." *Speculum* 77 (2002): 440–60.

Kline, Daniel T. "Female *Childhoods.*" In *The Cambridge Companion to Medieval Women's Writing,* edited by Carolyn Dinshaw and David Wallace, 13–20. Cambridge: Cambridge University Press, 2003.

Le Roy Ladurie, Emmanuel. *Montaillou, village Occitan de 1294 à 1324.* Paris: Gallimard, 1975. (esp. ch. 13).

Lett, Didier. *Famille et parenté dans l'Occident médiéval au Ve–XVe siècles.* Paris: Hachette, 2000.

Marcus, Ivan G. *Rituals of Childhood: Jewish Acculturation in Medieval Europe.* New Haven, Conn.: Yale University Press, 1996.

McLaughlin, Mary M. "Survivors and Surrogates: Children and Parents from the Ninth to the Thirteenth Centuries." In De Mause, 101–81.

Orme, Nicholas. *From Childhood to Chivalry: The Education of the English Kings and Aristocracy, 1066–1530.* London: Methuen, 1984.

———. *Medieval Children.* New Haven, Conn.: Yale University Press, 2001.

Ribémont, Bernard. "Christine de Pizan et la figure de la mère." In *Christine de Pizan 2000: Studies in Honour of Angus J. Kennedy,* edited by John Campbell and Nadia Margolis, 149–61. Amsterdam: Rodopi, 2000.

Riché, Pierre. *Education et culture dans l'Occident barbare (VIe–VIIIe siècles).* Paris: Seuil, 1962.

———, and Danièle Alexandre-Bidon. *L'Enfance au Moyen âge.* Paris: Seuil/BnF, 1994.

Schultz, J. A. *The Knowledge of Childhood in the German Middle Ages, 1100–1350.* Philadelphia: University of Pennsylvania Press, 1995.

Shahar, Shulamith. *Yaldut bi-yeme ha-benayim.* Tel-Aviv, Israel: Devir, 1990.

———. *Childhood in the Middle Ages*. Translated by Chaya Galai. London and New York: Routledge, 1990. Reprint 1992.

Shorter, Edward. *The Making of the Modern Family*. New York: Basic Books, 1975. Reprint 1977.

Trexler, Richard C. "The Foundlings of Florence, 1395–1455." *History of Childhood Quarterly* 1 (1973–1974): 259–84.

———. "Infanticide in Florence: New Sources and First Results." *History of Childhood Quarterly* 1 (1973–1974): 98–116.

ELIZABETH A. PETROFF

CHINA, WOMEN IN (400–1450). In the long span of Chinese history, the period from 400 to 1450 would not be labeled "medieval" (see Mou in Mou, ed.). China was a large and populous region during these centuries, its population ranging from a low of perhaps 40 million to well over 100 million. There was considerable change in political organization, with China sometimes divided into more than one state, and some ruling houses non-Chinese. The four major dynastic periods are the Northern and Southern dynasties (420–589), Tang dynasty (618–907), Song dynasty (960–1276), and Mongol Yuan dynasty (1215–1368). During these centuries there were major changes in almost all aspects of Chinese social, economic, and cultural histories, such as the decline of aristocratic domination of the government, the expansion and commercialization of the economy, and the rise of Neo-Confucian philosophy, and these broad historical changes had much to do with changes in women's situations. The Tang is viewed by many scholars as a high point of women's social and political influence, a time when women were prominent as power-holders at the imperial court—for example, the Empress Wu and Yang Guifei—and as poets in the entertainment quarters, such as Xue Tao. By contrast, the Song has generally been seen as a time when women's situations took a turn for the worse, when footbinding spread, elite women stayed out of public life, and widows began to feel greater pressure not to remarry.

Conceptions of Gender. The principles of gender differentiation most pervasive in this period of Chinese history were ones inherited from classical times. The differences between men and women were often summed up by reference to *yin* (dark, passive, female) and *yang* (bright, assertive, male), the pair of complementary forces that account for movement and change in the cosmos. Underlying the theory of yin and yang is the assumption that all things are interrelated and interdependent; no part has a life of its own for each is shaped by and helps to shape other constituent parts in a continuum of interactions of yang and yin. All things contain some yin and some yang, although in most cases one predominates. In divination manuals and treatises on biology, medicine, weather, or other natural phenomena, yin and yang were generally treated as equally essential and important. In Confucian models of social relations, however, it was tacitly accepted that yang is superior to yin, that action and initiation are more valued than endurance and completion. Thus yin-yang cosmology was used to explain gender hierarchy, making male dominance a matter of nature. The *Classic of Filial Piety for Girls*, written in Tang dynasty times, states: "Yin and yang, gentle and tough, are the beginnings of heaven and earth. Male and female, husband and wife, are the beginnings of human social relations. . . . The wife is earth and the husband is heaven; neither can be dispensed with. But the man can perform a hundred actions; the woman concentrates on a single

This Tang Dynasty figurine depicts an elaborately dressed female musician or lady of the court. © The Art Archive/Musée Cernuschi Paris/Dagli Orti.

goal." In the eleventh century, Sima Guang elaborated: "Yang sings out and gives life to things; yin joins in and completes things. Therefore wives take as their virtues gentleness and compliance and do not excel through strength or intellectual discrimination."

Almost as important to conceptions of gender as yin and yang were the distinctions between inner and outer. The classic *Book of Rites* called for punctilious attention to the "separation of male and female." Men and women should spend most of their time out of the company of each other, and when they had to be together, should observe a general avoidance of physical contact. The importance of women staying out of sight of men was underlined in the *Analects for Girls*, a primer written in Tang times, in this way: "Inner and outer each have their place. Males and females gather separately. Women do not peak through the walls, nor step into the outer courtyard. If they go out, they must cover their faces. If they look out, they conceal their forms." In the twelfth century, the leading Confucian philosopher Zhu Xi cited with approval the saying from the *Book of Rites*: "Men do not discuss inside affairs nor do women discuss outside affairs."

As these passages make clear, notions of inner and outer were not simply notions of how things are in nature, but how they should be in a morally correct social order. Still, for most of those who left written record, these ideas were not simply ideas. Women aged from about ten to forty made efforts to avoid being seen by unrelated men. By Song times, it was not uncommon for them to cover their faces with veils if they had to travel about, or shield their faces with a sleeve if caught unawares. Wives in upper-class households who had any interest in the men's activities stayed behind screens and listened to conversations with guests without joining in.

Women's Social Roles. The conceptual framework of yin and yang, inner and outer, did not prevent women from occupying a variety of social roles. Outside the family, women could enter religious orders, both Buddhist and Taoist. Older commoner women, especially widows forced to support themselves, could take on such occupations as midwife, matchmaker, innkeeper, or shopkeeper, or they could earn money through spinning, weaving, or raising silkworms at home. There was also a sizable market for young women to serve as musicians or prostitutes in the entertainment quarters or to enter homes as maids and concubines. Poor families could raise money by selling a daughter to brokers who would arrange her placement. Sometimes the parents expected to get her back after a number of years, at which time they would arrange a marriage for her.

Still, the vast majority of women lived out their lives in the basic familial roles of daughter, wife, daughter-in-law, mother, mother-in-law, widow, and grandmother. Usually in their late teens, they moved from the household into which they were born to another family of comparable class standing to become a wife. Thus, the structure and organization of the family and marriage systems had enormous importance in both how others treated them and how they thought of themselves. In broad comparative terms, the Chinese family in this period was patrilineal (descent from father to son), patriarchal (men owned and ruled all), and patrilocal (home is where the male line is). The descent line from father to son to grandson was taken to be the core of the family: family property, family names, and obligations to ancestors were all transmitted along the patriline. Property was vested in the men in the family; tenancies, houses, furniture, and most other property was conceived as family property; when transmitted to the next generation, only the sons received shares. Legally, senior generations had authority over junior ones, and husbands had authority over wives. Since sons had to stay home to continue the descent line, wives were brought in for them. Marriage thus moved a girl from one family to another, from subordination to her father to subordination to her husband and his parents.

Marriage in this period was legally monogamous. Tang and Song legal codes specified a year of penal servitude for anyone who took a second wife when he already had one. Both men and women could legally remarry if the first marriage ended by death or divorce, but not before. Rights to initiate divorce, however, were not equal. Wives were not free to divorce or abandon their husbands at will, but men could divorce wives on a wide variety of grounds, including talkativeness and barrenness. Husbands could also take concubines, monogamy restricting them to one wife at a time but not to one woman. Wives were generally selected for sons from among a family's peers, often with attention to the value of the connection created, but men who could afford them could choose their own concubines, and normally selected women from the lower classes who had for one reason or another entered the market for women.

However, women could hold property in this system. If they had no brothers, they might inherit the family property and have a husband brought in for them. Moreover, most daughters who were married out were given dowries that they could treat as their private property once they were married. Moreover, as wives and mothers, they often managed the family property of their husbands and sons. But women's power in the family seldom rested primarily on property. The emphasis on filial piety in Chinese culture did not apply only to fathers, but to mothers as well. And the patrilocal marriage system that forced young women to move from one home to another also kept grown sons at home with their mothers. The women with the most influence in family affairs thus were generally the older women who as mothers could expect deference if not devotion from their children and grandchildren.

Changes over Time. Women's opportunities inside and outside the family in this period of Chinese history, as in any other, were shaped by overall developments in the society and economy. The urbanization of the eighth through thirteenth centuries increased the opportunities for women to earn money, whether working in their homes spinning or weaving, or working in shops, inns, or other urban establishments. The spread of footbinding was facilitated by the growth of urban culture, and the interpenetration of the scholarly and urban cultural spheres. With the development of printing and the decline in the cost of books, women's literacy and levels of education increased. By the Song period, one woman in the educated class attained a reputation as a poet equal to her male contemporaries. Changes both in the structure of the ruling class and the commercialization of the economy led to an escalation of dowries, so that by Song times women often came into marriage with substantial property. The laws on family division were modified to take these changes into account and to assure that orphaned daughters received significant shares of family property.

At least as important as these changes in social, political, and economic order were changes in ideas, tied to the evolution of both Buddhist and Confucian ideologies. By the Song dynasty, within Buddhism, the bodhisattva (one who renounces Nirvana, the Buddhist spiritual analogue of Paradise, to save others) Guanyin came more and more to be conceived as a compassionate woman who offered a view of feminine spirituality and a focus for women's devotion. Within Confucianism, patrilineal principles came to be if anything more emphasized than before, as ancestral rituals were revitalized and the organization of descent groups promoted. At the same time, leading thinkers emphasized how crucial it was for widows, even if young and childless, to refuse to remarry out of fidelity to their husbands. Once they had entered a family as a wife, in other words, they were to consider themselves as a permanent member of that patriline.

Changes in Chinese culture and social practices attributable to the continual contact and conflict with non-Chinese peoples and states to the north have yet to be studied adequately. Some scholars argue that women held more power under the northern nomadic peoples (the Xianbei, Turks, Khitans, Jürchens, and Mongols) and that the relative prominence of women in Tang times reflects the hybrid, Sino-foreign culture of the ruling elite of the period. Other scholars argue that these non-Chinese societies, while organized along principles different from the Chinese, were just as patriarchal, and certainly placed their highest value on the very masculine quality of prowess in martial arts. In areas of mixed population there was, without doubt, considerable cultural borrowing both ways (such as greater tolerance of levirate marriages—in which a man marries his brother's widow—among Chinese during the Mongol Yuan dynasty), but in the long term this foreign impact did little to alter the basic structure of the Chinese family and gender systems.

See also Childhood and Child-Rearing in the Middle Ages; Courtesy Books; Dower; Dowry; Footbinding; Li Qingzhao; Marriage; Wu, Empress; Xue Tao; Yang Guifei

BIBLIOGRAPHY

Birge, Bettine. "Chu Hsi and Women's Education." In *Neo-Confucian Education: The Formative Stage*, edited by Wm. Theodore de Bary and John W. Chaffee. Berkeley: University of California Press, 1989.

Birrell, Anne M. "The Dusty Mirror: Courtly Portraits of Woman in Southern Dynasties Love Poetry." In *Expressions of Self in Chinese Literature*, edited by Robert E. Hegel and Richard C. Hessney. New York: Columbia University Press, 1985.

Cahill, Suzanne. "Performers and Female Taoist Adepts: Hsi Wang Mu as Patron Deity of Women in T'ang China." *Journal of the American Oriental Society* 106 (1986): 155–68.

———. "Practice Makes Perfect: Paths to Transcendence for Women in Medieval China" *Taoist Resources*, 2. 2 (1990): 23–42.

Chung, Priscilla. *Palace Women in the Northern Sung, 960–1126.* Monographies du T'oung Pao, 12. Leiden: E. J. Brill, 1981.

Ebrey, Patricia Buckley. *The Inner Quarters: Marriage and the Lives of Chinese Women in the Sung Period.* Berkeley: University of California Press, 1993.

———. "Shifts in Marriage Finance from the Sixth to the Thirteenth Centuries." In *Marriage and Inequality in Chinese Society*, edited by Rubie S. Watson and Patricia Buckley Ebrey. Berkeley: University of California Press, 1991.

———. *Women and the Family in Chinese History.* Critical Asian Scholarship. London and New York: Routledge, 2003.

———. "Women, Marriage, and the Family in Chinese History." In *The Heritage of China*, edited by Paul Ropp. Berkeley: University of California Press, 1990.

Franke, Herbert. "Women Under the Dynasties of Conquest." In *La Donna nella Cina Imperiale e nella Cina Repubblicana*, edited by Lionello Lanciotti. Florence: Leo S. Olschki, 1980.

Holmgren, Jennifer. "Imperial Marriage in the Native Chinese and Non-Han State." In *Marriage and Inequality in Chinese Society*, edited by Rubie S. Watson and Patricia Buckley Ebrey. Berkeley: University of California Press, 1991.

———. "Widow Chastity in the Northern Dynasties: The Lieh-nü Biographies in the *Wei-shu*." *Papers on Far Eastern History* 23 (1981): 165–86.

———. "Women and Political Power in the Traditional T'o-pa Elite: A Preliminary Study of the Biographies of Empresses in the *Wei-shu*." *Monumenta Serica* 35 (1981–1983): 33–74.

Kelleher, Theresa. "Confucianism." In *Women in World Religions*, edited by Arvind Sharma, 135–59. New York: State University of New York Press, 1987.

Levering, Miriam L. "The Dragon Girl and the Abbess of Mo-shan: Gender and Status in the Ch'an Buddhist Tradition." *The Journal of the International Association of Buddhist Studies* 5.1 (1982): 19–35.

Mou, Sherry J., ed. *Presence and Presentation: Women in the Chinese Literati Tradition*. New York: St. Martin's, 1999. [Collection of essays by major scholars on a multidisciplinary array of topics].

Murray, Julia K. "Didactic Art for Women: The *Ladies' Classic of Filial Piety*." In *Flowering in the Shadows: Women in the History of Chinese and Japanese Painting*, edited by Marsha Weidner. Honolulu: University of Hawaii Press, 1990.

Spade, Beatrice. "The Education of Women During the Southern Dynasties." *Journal of Asian History* 13.1 (1980): 15–41.

Widmer, Ellen, and Kang-i Sun Chang, eds. *Writing Women in Late Imperial China*. Stanford, Calif.: Stanford University Press, 1997.

PATRICIA BUCKLEY EBREY

CHRISTINA OF MARKYATE (c.1096–post-1155). Christina was an English recluse renowned for her asceticism, her spiritual counsel, and her prophetic visions. Born to a wealthy Anglo-Saxon family in Huntingdon, a market town north of London, she was named Theodora at baptism, but later came to be called Christina, "the name of her creator," as a sign of her betrothal to Christ. Although Christina appears in several contemporary texts, her story is known primarily through an anonymous life composed by a monk of St. Alban's who was clearly well acquainted with the holy woman. The only extant manuscript of that work is incomplete, ending with events of 1142. Recent research, however, suggests that very little of the text has been lost.

Even as a child Christina was notably pious. Her hagiographer noted that "as she had heard that Christ was good, beautiful, and everywhere present, she used to talk to Him on her bed at night just as if she were speaking to a man she could see." On a family pilgrimage to St. Alban's, a nearby abbey, she was inspired by the example of the monks to take a vow of marriage to Christ. While still in her teens, however, her beauty attracted Ralph Flambard, the bishop of Durham and royal chancellor, who attempted to seduce her. Frustrated by his failure, he prompted a local youth of high standing to propose marriage. Christina resisted the match on the grounds of her prior vow, but under extreme pressure from her family, including physical violence, was eventually betrothed. When she continued to disdain the betrothal (tantamount to marriage in contemporary practice) as invalid, she was kept in custody by her parents for over a year. The bishop of Lincoln enforced her betrothal after a bribe from Christina's father.

Christina was sustained by visions, particularly of the Virgin Mary, but she was also supported and counseled by a number of local religious figures. The array gives a sense of the variety of spiritual advisors to be found in one region of England. The first was Sueno, a canon from Huntingdon, who served as Christina's confidant during her youth. During her confinement, Christina also turned to Eadwin, a hermit living outside town. This man, after consulting the archbishop of Canterbury, arranged Christina's escape from her family that she might live with a female recluse named Alfwen. Later, Christina moved a short distance to live under the tutelage of the famed hermit Roger at Markyate, spending the best part of four years hidden in a cramped hole behind his cell to avoid scandal. Meanwhile, her betrothal was annulled by the archbishop of York who took her under his protection.

After Roger's death, Christina returned to Markyate to reside in his hermitage. She became fast friends with Geoffrey, abbot of nearby St. Alban's, to whom she provided much advice on both spiritual and practical matters, often based on her visions. It was Geoffrey who convinced a reluctant Christina to take formal monastic vows and later founded a new convent for nuns at Markyate, of which Christina became the first prioress. A beautifully illuminated psalter made for Christina in the St. Alban's scriptorium survives. An illumination at the head of Psalm 105 depicts the holy woman interceding with Christ for the abbot and his monks. Her fame spread, and eventually Christina came to the attention of King Henry II (1133–1189) and Pope Adrian (or Hadrian) IV (d. 1159)—the sole English pope—for whom she embroidered a pair of sandals.

The life by the monk of St. Alban's provides insight into the social and psychological struggles of twelfth-century holy woman. Eschewing a concern with miracles, the author instead focused on the torments and comfort that came from vivid visions of the devil, the Virgin Mary, and Christ. A fine example of the growing concern with affective emotions in the literature of that period, the text provides an extraordinary portrait of a woman's spiritual growth. It also chronicles the development of the intense friendship between the recluse and the abbot of St. Alban's, a relationship in which the woman was often ceded the authoritative role. At the heart of the text is Christina's marriage to Christ. The author reflects Christina's own certainty that she had been personally called to such a relationship. As she stated at one of her trials, "If I do all in my power to fulfill the vow I made to Christ, I shall not be disobedient to my parents. What I do, I do on the invitation of Him whose voice is heard in the Gospel." That marital bond and the visions that accompanied it provided Christina's authority. As a "bride of Christ," Christina served—in a manner similar to that of male hermits—as spiritual advisor and arbiter of disputes. She died sometime after 1155 at Markyate Priory, England. Celebrated locally as a saint, she was never canonized.

See also Ancrene Riwle; Bride of Christ/*Brautmystik*; Marriage

BIBLIOGRAPHY

Primary Sources

[Christina's Life]. In *Gesta abbatum monasterii s. Albani*, edited by Henry Riley, 1: 97–105. 3 vols. Rolls Series, 28. London, 1867.

The Life of Christina of Markyate, a Twelfth-Century Recluse. Edited and translated by Charles H. Talbot. Oxford: Oxford University Press, 1959. Reprint 1987.

The St. Alban's Psalter. Edited by Otto Pächt, C. R. Dodwell, and Francis Wormald. Studies of the Warburg Institute, 25. London: Warburg Institute, 1969.

Secondary Sources

Cartlidge, Neil. *Medieval Marriage: Literary Approaches, 1100–1300.* Woodbridge, Suffolk, U.K. and Rochester, N.Y.: D. S. Brewer, 1997.

Fanous, Samuel, and Henrietta Leyser, eds., *Christina of Markyate.* London and New York: Routledge, 2004.

Head, Thomas, "The Marriages of Christina of Markyate." *Viator* 21 (1990): 71–95.

Hostetler, Margaret. "Designing Religious Women: Privacy and Exposure in The Life of Christina of Markyate and *Ancrene Wisse*." *Mediaevalia* 22 (1999): 200–231.

Holdsworth, Christopher. "Christina of Markyate." In *Medieval Women,* edited by Derek Baker, 185–204. Studies in Church History. Subsidia, 1. Oxford: Basil Blackwell, 1978.

Karras, Ruth Mazo. "Friendship and Love in the Lives of Two Twelfth-Century English Saints." *Journal of Medieval History* 14 (1988): 305–20.

Koopmans, Rachel. "The Conclusion of Christiana of Markyate's Vita." *Journal of Ecclesiastical History* (2000): 663–98.

Warren, Ann. *Anchorites and Their Patrons in Medieval England.* Berkeley: University of California Press, 1985.

THOMAS HEAD

CHRISTINA MIRABILIS (1150–1224). Christina Mirabilis ("the Astonishing"/ "Marvelous"), also known as Christina of St. Trond, was a Flemish religious woman known for her prodigious self-abuse and other bodily exploits—even by the standards of other medieval mystics in this time of innovative spiritual energy—as part of her ardent desire to form a mystical union with Christ. By turns associated with various orders—Cistercian, Benedictine, and Premonstratensian—she remained in truth a laywoman and was thus freer to pursue her extreme style of devotion than if she had been a cloistered nun bound by monastic rule. Likewise, although she has been occasionally revered as "St. Christina" or "Blessed Christina" because of her immense popularity, even now, there is no evidence of a formal canonization process.

According to her *vita* (life) by Thomas de Cantimpré, a Dominican theologian from Louvain, she was born to respectable parents in St. Trond (in Flemish = Sint Truiden), Limbourg province—though more modern sources say Brusthem, near Liège—both in eastern Belgium, the youngest of three orphaned sisters. Her two pious elder sisters raised her, so that all three desired to enter the religious life. At about age twenty-two she experienced a severe cataleptic seizure, leaving her in a deathlike state; indeed, those around her thought she had died and held a funeral for her. However, during the funeral Mass, she not only recovered, but her body levitated from out of her coffin to the roof of the church, causing all but her sisters to flee the service.

Later, returning with her sisters, she recounted her vision of traveling to Hell, Purgatory, and Paradise, stating that she had been sent back to help save other souls in Purgatory. Supposedly, she could literally sniff out sinful people by their odor, which meant that most people smelled foul to her. To escape this she would hide in ovens and closets, roll herself up into a ball of wax, climb trees, rocks, and towers, or simply fly upward and away from them to pray, hanging from the branch, precipice, or rafter. Like many ascetics, she dressed in rags, ate little and badly, slept on stones, and begged for sustenance. But in her newfound wish to free the souls of departed loved ones in Purgatory by means of her own bodily suffering, she surpassed all others in self-mortification: she rolled around in fires, stood in ice water for hours, lay inside tombs for long periods, bound herself to a millwheel dragging her underwater, and yet, while experiencing great pain, showed no evidence of bodily injury. During her sufferings she continued to receive revelations, visions, prophecies, and ecstasies. She also had an otherworldly singing voice, strangely emitted from her body, as if to disobey the existing prohibition against women singing in public places that much more gloriously. Naturally, although some construed such deeds as reflecting her holy empathy with the suffering souls in Purgatory, increasing numbers of others considered her insane and, out of both fear and loathing, persecuted Christina as one possessed by demons. This cruel treatment simply provoked her toward more physical marvels, however. Moreover, she lived to age seventy-four.

One of her most memorable bodily feats involved exuding fluids from her breasts, as reported by Thomas de Cantimpré. Having fled persecution out to the desert, she became hungry and thus prayed. God responded by making her "virginal breasts" flow with milk, which sustained her for nine weeks. Later, when she was chained by her sisters and friends in a cellar as a mad person, her breasts emitted healing oil that, after curing the sores of one of her sisters, brought about her release. But as Caroline Bynum leads us to ask, are such descriptions rooted in Christina's reality, or should we read such curing-fluid imagery as part of Thomas's hagiographical (saintly biographical) style, since he mentions it in another of his holy women's lives, that of St. Lutgard (Bynum 1987, 122–23)? Religious women's unique ability to provide food and healing oil amid great privation, plays a major role in the emerging identity of holy women, as distinct from holy men. Taken together with her other acts of bodily self-abuse, Christina may be seen as an extreme example of what Elizabeth Petroff notes as a prevailing "dissatisfaction with traditional body-soul stereotypes" among female mystics who, while contemplating Christ's body on the Cross, used their own bodies to provide "visible evidence of her ecstatic experiences" (notes to Thomas's "Life," Petroff ed.).

She was also capable of politically prophetic visions, as in 1213, when the duke of Brabant was about to do battle. Claiming to have seen the sky filled with swords and blood, she rushed to the monastery of St. Catherine's in St. Trond, warning the nuns to go and pray for their loved ones about to be killed. Later, she became counselor to that monastery.

News of this extraordinary woman reached a local nobleman, Count Ludwig (Louis) of Looz, who "began to love her in his heart," in Thomas's words, and sought her out as spiritual advisor. In this capacity, she would weep for him or meet with him at his palace to scold him in a maternal way for his transgressions against the Church and other sins. She also assisted Ludwig at his death, during which he confessed all his lifetime's sins to her.

Christina's own death at St. Catherine's at St. Trond was appropriately recorded, as she first curses her body as a mortal prison too slow to release her, then verbally caresses it and predicts its purification and ascent into heaven with her soul. Bynum cites this scene to affirm that "Christina's words express much of what a thirteenth-century woman and her hagiographer [Thomas] assumed about female body: source of temptation and torment, body is also a beloved companion [. . .] essential to the person herself and will be perfected and glorified in heaven" (Bynum 1992, 237). The recently expired Christina is then called back fervently by her grief-stricken companion, Beatrice, whom she rebukes for having interrupted her death, and then, after blessing her and all the sisters gathered, died for the third and final time, as Thomas tells us. In writing of such women, Thomas's contemporary and fellow hagiographer, Jacques de Vitry (James of Vitry) warns us that, in reading their lives, one should "admire the fervor, not imitate the works" (cited in Bynum 1987, 85, 336).

Although never officially canonized, Christina is remembered with a feast day, July 24, and has been deemed the patron saint of the mentally ill and also of mental-health caregivers. She has also inspired certain minor poets, songwriters, and, not surprisingly, several Web sites.

See also Beguines; Hagiography (Female Saints); Juliana of Mont-Cornillon; Mechthild of Magdeburg

BIBLIOGRAPHY

Primary Sources

Thomas de Cantimpré. *Vita Beatae Christinae Mirabilis Trudonopoli in Hasbania*. Edited by J. Pinius. In *Acta Sanctorum . . . editio novissima*, July, vol. 5 (Paris, 1868): 637–60. [Latin text; also online http://www.peregrina.com/translations/Christina_L.html].

———. "*Life of Christina of St. Trond, Called Mirabilis* by Thomas de Cantimpré." Translated with introduction and notes by Margot King with David Wiljer. Toronto: Peregrina, 1999; 2000.

———. "*Life of Christina of St. Trond, Called Mirabilis* by Thomas de Cantimpré" [Excerpts of King trans. above]. In *Medieval Women's Visionary Literature*, edited by Elizabeth Alvilda Petroff, 36, 175, 184–89. New York: Oxford University Press, 1986. [Pioneering anthology with insightful, informative commentary].

Secondary Sources

[See notes to King trans., and to Petroff ed., above].

Bynum, Caroline W. *Fragmentation and Redemption: Essays on Gender and the Human Body in Medieval Religion*. New York: Zone Books, 1992.

———. *Holy Feast and Holy Fast: The Religious Significance of Food to Medieval Women*. Berkeley: University of California Press, 1987.

Finke, Laurie A. "Mystical Bodies and the Dialogics of Vision." In *Maps of Flesh and Light: The Religious Experience of Medieval Women Mystics*, edited by Ulrike Wiethaus, 28–44. Syracuse, N.Y.: Syracuse University Press, 1993.

Holsinger, Bruce W. *Music, Body, and Desire in Medieval Culture*. Figurae. Stanford, Calif.: Stanford University Press, 2001.

Wiethaus, Ulrike. "The Death Song of Marie d'Oignies: Mystical Sound and Hagiographical Politics in Medieval Lorraine." In *The Texture of Society: Medieval Women in the Southern Low Countries*, edited by Ellen E. Kittel and Mary A. Suydam, ch. 7. New York: Palgrave Macmillan, 2004.

EDITH BRIGITTE ARCHIBALD

CHRISTINA OF ST. TROND. *See Christina Mirabilis*

CHRISTINE DE PIZAN (1364/5–c.1430). The first professional woman writer in French literature, Christine de Pizan excelled in a great variety of genres, from courtly lyric to political and religious treatises, "publishing" with astounding success and influence, both esthetically and intellectually. Many of the original copies of her works are thus masterpieces of book and manuscript production as well as milestones in literature and moral or political thought.

The abundant autobiographical content inserted into many of her works provides us with an unusually complete story for an early woman author, as Christine relates both

Christine de Pizan presenting her book to Isabel of Bavaria, Queen of Charles VI of France. Courtesy of North Wind Picture Archives.

personal historical facts and her emotional reactions to them, all often recast according to her self-identification with heroes and heroines from her vast reading. Her father, Tommaso di Benvenuto da Pizzano, taught astrology—of the type known as judicial astrology, then a respected science for predicting future events—at the University of Bologna in northern Italy. After moving his family to become an advisor to the Republic of Venice, joining an old colleague, Tommaso Mondino da Forlì, Tommaso da Pizzano married Mondino's daughter, from which union Christine was born. Shortly thereafter, when King Charles V of France invited him to Paris to become royal "physician" (scientist-advisor) and councilor in 1368, Tommaso da Pizzano became "Thomas de Pizan" and the three-year-old Christine was thus brought to Paris with her parents and two brothers. Thomas would remain a major presence throughout his admiring daughter's life, both as an acclaimed scientist and for having educated her beyond the conventional limits of her gender. Her mother, by comparison, barely receives mention and seems to have been simply a traditional, beloved maternal force. In 1379, fifteen-year-old Christine married a young royal notary, Etienne du Castel. However, the happy couple soon suffered misfortune: King Charles's death in 1380 weakened the position of Thomas de Pizan, who died around 1389, leaving many debts. Shortly thereafter, Etienne du Castel succumbed suddenly to an epidemic, leaving Christine a young widow and sole support of her mother, three children, and a niece; her two little-known brothers, Paolo and Aghinolfo, quickly abandoned them to reclaim family properties in Italy. Christine stayed with her charges in

Paris, enduring constant legal battles to fend off creditors and protect what little patrimony remained. Many of her first lyric poems, such as the *Cent ballades* (*One Hundred Ballades*), composed in around 1394, recall her painful solitude and lost happiness.

However, her untimely widowhood also seemed to liberate her literary and scholarly talents as she strove to earn a living. She would pen several hundred lyric poems, adding a new voice to the already highly conventionalized courtly poetic forms of *ballade*, *rondeau*, and *virelai*. At the same time, her intellectual-allegorical autobiography, the *Advision* (*Vision*) of 1405 informs us, she took up the studious routine to which her father had introduced her by reading all available works on history and philosophy. This prepared her for more "serious" genres, as she saw them, which dominated the highly productive phase of 1400–1413: complex prose histories, like her biography praising her father's patron combined with a discourse on ideal monarchy, *Le Livre des fais et bonnes meurs du sage roy Charles V* (*The Book of the Deeds and Good Practices of the Wise King Charles V*), 1404, and moral-political manuals including the *Enseignemens a son filz* (*Moral Teachings to her Son*) and *Proverbes moraux* (*Moral Proverbs*, 1400–1401); through the more ambitious *Livre du Corps de policie* (*Book of the Body Politic*, 1407), the *Livre de Prod'hommie de l'homme* (*Book of Human Integrity*), and its alter-ego, the *Livre de Prudence* (*Book of Prudence*) of 1404–1405; along with the military-scientific *Livre des Fais d'armes et de chevalerie* (*Book of Feats of Arms and Chivalry*, 1410) and anti–civil war treatise *Livre de la Paix* (*Book of Peace*, 1412–1413), countering the emotionalism of her *Lamentacion* on this subject from 1410. All of these works aspired in some way to educate the French nobility to survive, perhaps even end, the Hundred Years War (1337–1453) between France and England and the civil strife with which it divided France. As if it were not brazen enough for a woman to treat such traditionally masculine topics, Christine's most famous prose works overtly revised preexisting models in favor of women, as in the learned fortress defending women's honor called the *Livre de la Cité des dames* (*The Book of the City of Ladies*) of 1404–1405—freely inspired by Boccaccio but more positively didactic than the Italian on the topic of female virtue—and its conduct-manual extension, the *Livre des Trois vertus* (*Book of the Three Virtues*), also known as the *Tresor de la Cité des dames* (*Treasure of the City of Ladies*) written in 1405. Much of her poetry from this stage followed the didactic narrative mode also, as in the *Livre du Chemin de long estude* (*Book of the Path of Long Study*) of 1402–1403—a pilgrimage, inspired by Dante's *Inferno* and Boethius' *Consolation of Philosophy*, culminating in a political debate—and *Livre de la Mutacion de Fortune* (*Book of Fortune's Transformations*), 1403—23,000 lines of literary autobiography prefacing a universal moralized history. The *Mutacion* attracted her commission by Duke Philip of Burgundy to write the biography of his brother, Charles V.

Throughout her authorial evolution, we find her appropriating not only beneficial models but also those male authors she found informative but evil, precisely because of their seductive gift for teaching misogyny as truth. Most notable among this clerkly majority was Jean de Meun, the vastly learned yet cynically ironic thirteenth-century continuator of Guillaume de Lorris' celebrated allegorical tale of love, the *Roman de la Rose*. Angered by certain Parisian humanists' reverence for Meun, while finding support among others, Christine participated in the notorious Debate of the *Roman de la Rose* (1401–1404), the first *querelle des femmes* (disputes over the vices and virtues of women) in French literary history. Even before the epistles addressed to her adversaries, she had written the *Epistre au Dieu d'amours* (*Epistle of the God of Love*) on May Day 1399, then her *Dit de la Rose* (*Tale of the Rose*) in 1402 during the debate. Her militant defense of women, embraced by literate women for centuries thereafter, caused certain nineteenth-century male critics to brand her a "bluestocking." Yet it was Christine's faith in marital happiness, plus her belief in the moral responsibility of learned authors toward their public, that drove her attacks on Meun. Her feminism thus differs markedly from its twentieth-century counterpart, a fact that has not deterred many recent American and British feminist analyses of her from abusive extremes.

Despite her political commitment, she never renounced lyric composition, often cautioning women about the misery awaiting them in the idealized dilemma of courtly love, whether in her debate poems of around 1400—the *Debat de deux amans* (*Debate of Two Lovers*), *Livre des Trois Jugemens* (*Book of the Three Judgments*), and *Dit de Poissy* (*Tale of Poissy*)—or in some of the *Autres balades* (*Other Ballades*) from 1402 to 1407, the pastoral *Dit de la Pastoure* (*Shepherdess's Tale*) of 1403, two *Complaintes amoureuses* (*Lover's Complaints*) and *Cent Ballades d'amant et de dame* (*One Hundred Ballades between Lover and Lady*) of 1407–1410. In two book-length works—the *Epistre Othea a Hector* (*Epistle of Othea to the Trojan Prince Hector*), a collection of Classical mythological tales with allegories and moral explanation written in about 1401, and the *Livre du Duc des vrais amans* (*Book of the Duke of True Lovers*) of 1404–1405, a proto-epistolary novel of an unhappy love affair—Christine mixes prose and poetic forms to great effect. These instructive writings, though often "stitched" or "mortared" together, as she herself analogizes, from well-known male authorities, nonetheless bore Christine's unique style in both voice and content. The consummate professional, Christine presented her works beautifully in high-quality illuminated manuscripts whose material composition, transcription, and illustration she herself conceived, supervised, and in the finest examples copied herself in her elegant hand. These books attracted powerful and generous patrons among the French royal family: John, Duke of Berry, and Philip the Bold, Duke of Burgundy; along with Philip's son, John the Fearless, and John's nemesis, Louis, Duke of Orleans; as well as Charles VI, the dauphin Louis de Guyenne, and Queen Isabeau of Bavaria, to whom Christine would offer the most complete and lavish collection of her works, now British Library Harley MS 4431, completed after 1410. Yet despite Christine's increasing esteem and influence among such lofty notables, their gradual demise, along with the effects of continued violent confrontation between the dukes of Burgundy and Orléans, not forgetting the ravages of the Hundred Years War, threatened her newfound position. As did other writers of the time, Christine expressed concern about the role of the monarchy amid this turmoil. In 1405, she even directly addressed Queen Isabeau in an *Epistre a la Reine* (*Epistle to the Queen*), urging her to resolve the explosive conflict among the French princes. Similarly, she invokes the duke of Berry's help in a *Lamentacion sur les maux de la France* (*Lament on the Ills of France*) in 1410.

The need for personal solace caused by relentless war also compelled her to try her hand at religious works during this phase, beginning with her two *Oraisons* (*Orisons*, or prayers)—one "to Our Lady," the other "on the life and Passion of Our Lord"—and enumerative prayer to the Virgin, *Les Quinze Joyes Nostre Dame* (*Fifteen Joys of Our Lady*), of 1402–1403. In 1409, she merged her admiration for Petrarch with the penitential psalms in the *Sept psaumes allegorisés* (*Seven Allegorized Psalms*). These early devotional efforts set the stage for the more somber and pious tone of her later years, as evidenced in the *Epistre de prison de vie humaine* (*Epistle of the Prison of Human Life*) of 1414–1418, a

Christian consolation addressed to Marie de Berry and all widows of the disastrous battle of Agincourt (1415), and the *Heures de contemplacion* (*Hours of Contemplation*) of around 1420, a meditation on Christ's Passion and Mary's grief, quite similar to an epistle composed by Jean Gerson on the same topic. Christine would lose her own son, Jean de Castel, a royal officer and courtly author, in 1425.

Fortunately, the bright hope for France's victory over English domination during the Hundred Years War arose in the form of a warrior maid, which at least briefly revived Christine's spirits sufficiently to celebrate and affirm the Maid of Orléans's authenticity in the *Ditié de Jehanne d'Arc* (*Story of Joan of Arc*) in July 1429 from her retreat at Poissy. It is her last known work.

See also Abutsu-ni; *Belle Dame sans Merci*; Boccaccio, Women in, *De Claris Mulieribus*; Boccaccio, Women in, *Des Cleres et Nobles Femmes*; Boccaccio, Women in, Works Other than *De Claris Mulieribus*; Griselda; Isabeau of Bavaria; Joan of Arc, St.; *Roman de la Rose*, Debate of the

BIBLIOGRAPHY

Primary Sources
[Primary sources are listed by name of the editor of all critical editions and translations of Christine's works containing important commentary as well as of standard texts].
Altmann, Barbara K., ed. *The Love Debate Poems of Christine de Pizan.* Gainesville: University Press of Florida, 1998.
Blumenfeld-Kosinski, Renate, ed. and trans., and Kevin Brownlee, trans. *The Selected Writings of Christine de Pizan.* New York: W. W. Norton, 1997. [Critical anthology of translated extracts with reprinted essays].
Cerquiglini, Jacqueline, ed. *Cent Ballades d'amant et de dame.* Bibliothèque médievale. Paris: "10/18", 1982.
Fenster, Thelma S., ed. *Le Livre du duc des vrais amans.* Medieval and Renaissance Texts & Studies, 124. Binghamton, N.Y.: MRTS, 1995.
———, and Nadia Margolis, transs. *The Book of the Duke of True Lovers.* New York: Persea, 1991. [With extensive commentary].
———, and Mary C. Erler, eds. and transs. *Poems of Cupid, God of Love.* Leiden, Netherlands and New York: E. J. Brill, 1990. [*Epistle of the God of Love* and *Tale of the Rose* in original Middle French, with English translation and notes].
Forhan, Kate L., trans. *The Book of the Body Politic.* Cambridge: Cambridge University Press, 1994.
Hicks, Eric, ed. *Le Débat sur le Roman de la rose.* Paris: Honoré Champion, 1977.
———, and Thérèse Moreau, transs. *Le Livre de la Cité des Dames.* Paris: Stock, 1986.
———, and Thérèse Moreau, transs. *Le Livre des Faits et Bonnes Mœurs du roi Charles V le Sage.* Paris: Stock, 1997 [Modern-French translation and commentary; excellent feminist preface].
Kennedy, Angus J., ed. *Le Livre du Corps de policie.* Études christiniennes, 1. Paris: Honoré Champion, 1998.
———, and Kenneth Varty, eds. and transs. *Le Ditié de Jehanne d'Arc.* Oxford: Medium Ævum, 1977.
Parussa, Gabriella, ed. *L'Epistre Othea.* Textes Littéraires Français, 517. Geneva: Droz, 1999.
Rains, Ruth Ringland. *Les Sept psaumes allégorisés of Christine de Pisan.* Washington, D.C.: Catholic University of America Press, 1965.
Reno, Christine, and Liliane Dulac, eds. *L'Advision Cristine.* Études christiniennes, 4. Paris: Honoré Champion, 2001.
Richards, Earl Jeffrey, trans. *The Book of the City of Ladies.* New York: Persea, 1982.
———, ed., and Patrizia Caraffi, trans. *Città delle dame.* Milan: Luni, 1997. 2nd rev. ed. 1998 [Original French with Italian trans. and notes].
Roy, Maurice. *Œuvres poétiques de Christine de Pisan.* 3 vols. Paris: Firmin Didot, 1886–1896. Reprint New York: Johnson, 1965.

Solente, Suzanne. *Le Livre des Fais et bonnes meurs du sage roy Charles V*. 2 vols. Paris: Honoré Champion, 1936–1940.

———. *Le Livre de la Mutacion de Fortune*. 4 vols. Société des Anciens Textes Français. Paris: Picard, 1959–1966.

Tarnowski, Andrea, ed. *Le Chemin de long estude*. Lettres gothiques. Paris: Livre de Poche, 2000.

Varty, Kenneth, ed. *Christine de Pisan. Ballades, Rondeaux and Virelais: An Anthology*. Leicester, U.K.: Leicester University Press, 1965. [Original Middle-French only, based on the better manuscript than Roy (*see above*) though only selections, with useful notes and glossary].

Willard, Charity C., with Eric Hicks, eds. *Le Livre des Trois Vertus*. Bibliothèque du XVe siècle, 50. Paris: Honoré Champion, 1989.

———, ed. *The Writings of Christine de Pizan*. New York: Persea, 1994.

———, ed., and Sumner Willard, trans. *The Book of Deeds of Arms and Chivalry. Christine de Pizan*. University Park: Pennsylvania State University Press, 1999.[Other eds. and trans. in bibliographies by Kennedy and Yenal, listed below].

Secondary Sources

Altmann, Barbara K., and Deborah McGrady, eds. *Christine de Pizan: A Casebook*. New York and London: Routledge, 2003.

Brabant, Margaret. *Politics, Gender & Genre: The Political Thought of Christine de Pizan*. Boulder, Colo.: Westview, 1992.

Brown-Grant, Rosalind. *Christine de Pizan and the Moral Defence of Women: Reading Beyond Gender*. Cambridge: Cambridge University Press, 1999.

Campbell, John, and Nadia Margolis, eds. *Christine de Pizan 2000: Studies on Christine de Pizan in Honour of Angus J. Kennedy*. Faux Titre, 196. Amsterdam, Netherlands and Atlanta, Ga.: Rodopi, 2000. [Contains substantial bibliography].

Desmond, Marilynn, ed. *Christine de Pizan and the Categories of Difference*. Medieval Cultures. Minneapolis: University of Minnesota Press, 1998.

Dulac, Liliane, and Bernard Ribémont. *Une femme de lettres au Moyen Age: Études autour de Christine de Pizan*. Medievalia/Études christiniennes. Orléans: Paradigme, 1995.

Forhan, Kate Langdon. *The Political Theory of Christine de Pizan*. Women and Gender in the Early Modern World. Aldershot, U.K. and Burlington, Vt.: Ashgate, 2002.

Harding, Carol E. "'True Lovers': Love and Irony in Murasaki Shikibu and Christine de Pizan." In *Crossing the Bridge: Comparative Essays on Medieval European and Heian Japanese Woman Writers*, edited by Barbara Stevenson and Cynthia Ho, 153–73. New York and Houndmills, Basingstoke, U.K.: Palgrave, 2000.

Hicks, Eric, et al., eds. *Au champ des escriptures: IIIe colloque international sur Christine de Pizan, Lausanne, 18–22 juillet 1998*. Études christiniennes, 6. Paris: Honoré Champion, 2000.

Hindman, Sandra. *Christine de Pizan's "Epistre Othea": Painting and Politics at the Court of Charles VI*. Toronto: Pontifical Institute of Mediaeval Studies, 1986.

Kennedy, Angus J. *Christine de Pizan: A Bibliographical Guide*. 3 vols., continuing. London: Grant & Cutler, 1984; 1994; Woodbridge, U.K.: Tamesis, 2004. [Generally more scholarly, better for non-U.S. sources than Yenal].

———, et al., eds. *Contexts and Continuities: Proceedings of the Fourth International Colloquium on Christine de Pizan (Glasgow 21–27 July 2000), published in honour of Liliane Dulac*. 3 vols. Glasgow: University of Glasgow Press, 2002. [Most recent large collection of essays to date].

Mühlethaler, Jean-Claude, Denis Billotte et al., eds. *"Riens ne m'est seur que la chose incertaine": Études sur l'art d'écrire au Moyen Age offertes à Eric Hicks[. . .]*. Geneva: Slatkine, 2001. [Contains many essays on or relating to Christine].

Ribémont, Bernard. *Sur le chemin de longue etude*. Études christiniennes, 3. Paris: Honoré Champion, 1998.

Richards, E. J., ed. *Christine de Pizan and Medieval French Lyric*. Gainesville: University Press of Florida, 1998.

———, et al., eds. *Reinterpreting Christine de Pizan*. Athens: University of Georgia Press, 1992.

Solente, Suzanne. "Christine de Pisan." *Histoire littéraire de la France* 40 (1969): 335–422.

Stevenson, Barbara, and Cynthia Ho, eds. *Crossing the Bridge: Comparative Essays on Medieval European and Heian Japanese Woman Writers.* New York and Houndmills, Basingstoke, U.K.: Palgrave, 2000.

Willard, Charity Cannon. *Christine de Pizan, Her Life and Works.* New York: Persea, 1984. [A good starting point].

Yenal, Edith. *Christine de Pizan: A Bibliography.* 2nd ed. Metuchen, N.J. and London: Scarecrow, 1989. [Stronger for U.S.-based sources].

Zimmermann, Margarete, and Dina De Rentiis, eds. *The City of Scholars: New Approaches to Christine de Pizan.* Berlin and New York: de Gruyter, 1994.

LILIANE DULAC

CITIES AND URBAN PROBLEMS. *See* Dower; *Frauenfrage*; Guilds, Women in

CLARA D'ANDUZA (early 13th century). Clara d'Anduza, woman troubadour (*trobairitz*), lived in the first third of the thirteenth century and may have been a noblewoman of the house of Anduza, a court that hosted many troubadours in the late twelfth and early thirteenth centuries. She is one of the few women poets who composed *cansos* or love songs, the most prestigious of the lyric genres exploited by the troubadours. Her single extant *canso*, "En greu esmai et en greu pessamen" ("In grave distress and great trouble"), survives only in manuscript C; a rubric identifies Clara as the author. Addressed to her beloved, the poem describes her suffering and attributes her separation from her *amic* to the harm done by *lauzengier* (slanderers). She promises unfailing fidelity (a motif she shares with many *trobairitz*) and complains that grief and anger make it impossible to accomplish with her verses what she desires. Her closing comment reveals the kind of self-reflexivity typical of troubadour lyric. Like many troubadour lovers, she plays skillfully with the language of love, pain, and desire, as she associates heart, body, and self through the ambiguous meaning of Old Provençal *cor/cors*.

Intertextual evidence links this song metrically and thematically with a number of troubadour poems, most particularly with Azalais d'Altier's *salut d'amor*, "Tanz salutz e tantas amors" ("So many greetings and so much love"), and Uc de Saint Circ's "Anc mais non vi temps ni sazo" ("I never saw the time or season"). A lengthy narrative commentary (*razo*) on Uc's song (which may have been composed by Uc himself) identifies him as Clara's secretary and would-be lover. It also introduces another lady (named Azalais d'Altier in the envoi to Uc's poem), who intervenes on the lover's behalf to ask for his lady's forgiveness and restore their love. Azalais's *salut* performs just that function, and Clara's *canso* may be seen as her response. As is typical in troubadour lyric, these poems play across the boundaries of life and art, fiction and feeling. They involve the participants as well as the public in the literary game of love as practiced in the courts of southern France.

See also Azalais d'Altier; *Trobairitz*

BIBLIOGRAPHY

Primary Sources

Boutière, Jean, and Alexander H. Schutz, eds. *Biographies des Troubadours: Textes provençaux des XIIIe et XIVe siècles.* Revised ed. with I. M. Cluzel. Les Classiques d'Oc, 1. Paris: Nizet, 1964.

Clara d'Anduza. ["En greu d'esmay..."]. In *Songs of the Women Troubadours*, edited and translated by Matilda Tomaryn Bruckner, Laurie Shepard, and Sarah White, 30–31; 151–52. New York: Garland, 1995. Revised edition 2000.

———. In *Trobairitz: Der Beitrag der Frau in der altokzitanischen höfischen Lyrik. Edition des Gesamtkorpus*, edited by Angelica Rieger, 574–76. Beihefte zur Zeitschrift für romanische Philologie, 233. Tübingen, Germany: Max Niemeyer Verlag, 1991.

Secondary Sources

Gégou, Fabienne. "*Trobairitz* et amorces romanesques dans les 'Biographies' des troubadours." In *Studia Occitanica in Memoriam Paul Remy*, edited by Hans-Erich Keller, 2: 43–51. Kalamazoo, Mich.: Medieval Institute Publications, 1986.

Poe, Elizabeth Wilson. "A Dispassionate Look at the Trobairitz." *Tenso: Bulletin of the Société Guilhem IX* 7 (1992): 142–64.

———. "Another *salut d'amor*? Another *trobairitz*? In Defense of *Tanz salutz et tantas amors*." *Zeitschrift für romanische Philologie* 106 (1990): 425–42.

———. *Compilatio, Lyric Texts and Prose Commentaries in Troubadour Manuscript H (Vat. Lat. 3207)*. The Edward C. Armstrong Monographs on Medieval Literature, 11. Lexington, Ky.: French Forum, 2000.

MATILDA TOMARYN BRUCKNER

CLARE OF ASSISI, ST. (1193/94–1253). The founder of the Poor Clares, the women's Franciscan order, Clare (or Clara) was born into an aristocratic and moderately affluent family in the northern Italian town of Assisi. During her teens she came under the charismatic spell of a man some ten years her senior, Francis, the son of a merchant family from the same town. Hearing a reading from the Gospel of Matthew (10: 7–9) on the feast of St. Matthias in 1208, Francis of Assisi (1181/2–1226) had undergone a radical religious conversion. At the center of his, and eventually Clare's, spirituality stood the twin ideals of voluntary poverty and of the apostolic life, that is of following Christ in the manner of the original apostles through the renunciation of wordly goods and the preaching of God's kingdom. By 1210, Francis had begun to gather a group of followers, the nucleus of what was to become the Order of Lesser Brothers, more commonly known as the Friars Minor or Franciscans. Clare almost certainly heard Francis preach in Assisi's cathedral during that year. In 1211, rejecting a marriage arranged by her relatives, she secretly left home to join Francis's band; her sister Agnes soon followed her example. Francis provided San Damiano, a church located outside the walls of Assisi, as a convent for the sisters and other women who steadily joined them.

During the next few years, these women worked closely with Francis's Lesser Brothers. Clare herself was instrumental in convincing Francis of the importance of an active as opposed to contemplative career, spreading the message of poverty through preaching and example. Misogynistic values in society and the Christian church, however, prevented the acceptance of women preaching or otherwise engaged in an active ministry. Clare and her Poor Sisters became institutionally separate from Francis and his Lesser Brothers, living a cloistered life in San Damiano and other convents. While poverty would remain central to their spirituality, the outward form of their life resembled that of traditional monasticism far more than that of male mendicants. Officially known as the Second Order of St. Francis, they would come to be commonly called Clarissas or Poor Clares in honor of their first abbess and leader.

While the order grew, it did so under strict supervision by male clerics. Since the Fourth Lateran Council (1215) had prohibited the introduction of new rules for the religious (or monastic) life, Clare and her sisters followed versions of the Rule of St. Benedict prepared for them by Cardinal Hugolino (official protector of the Franciscan orders) and Pope Innocent IV. The existence of six different versions developed between 1219 and 1252, however, suggests considerable tension between the women and their male supervisors. These monastic documents contained little about the practice of poverty so central to the Franciscan ideal. Around 1250, Clare set about remedying that problem by composing an original rule for her order. In the sixth chapter, Clare boldly stated a requirement of near absolute poverty, admonishing her sisters "not to receive or hold onto any possessions or property acquired through an intermediary or even anything that might reasonably be called property." She grounded this commitment in the words of Francis, by quoting a "form of life" that the saint had allegedly granted to the Convent of San Damiano. This rule was given conditional approval in 1252, but did not receive papal authorization until two days before Clare's death. An annotation in the margin of the original says that it was then brought to the saint on her sickbed and that she kissed it repeatedly in joy over its acceptance. Clare also pro-

St. Clare of Assisi, founder of the Poor Clares order, holding a lily and warding off armies of Frederick II with monstrance. © The Art Archive/Museo Tridentino Arte Sacra Trento/Dagli Orti (A).

vided an autobiographical reflection in a *Testament* composed (if Francis's *Testament* is any guide) during her final sickness. Finally, her order cherished a blessing that the saint delivered to her sisters on her deathbed. While the authenticity of the latter two documents has been much debated by scholars, the editors of the critical edition of Clare's work accept both as genuine. The Latinity of both the *Rule* and *Testament*, however, were almost certainly improved by scribes at the papal chancery where they were copied.

The only other writings to survive from Clare's hand are four letters sent to Agnes, a daughter of the King of Bohemia. In 1232, a group of Franciscan friars in Prague on a preaching tour had inspired the princess to enter the religious life. Over the course of the next decades she entered into a correspondence with Clare, seeking advice as to how a woman might follow Francis's vision. Clare's letters, laced with biblical quotations, give some sense of how she struggled with the same issues in her own career. Another letter to Ermentrude of Bruges is certainly not original, but probably a summary of authentic letters from Clare to this Flemish Beguine made in the seventeenth century by the Franciscan scholar Luke Wadding.

Clare was canonized in 1255, two years after her death, by Pope Alexander IV. The text of the inquest into her life (*processus canonizationis*) conducted for that purpose was discovered in the early years of the twentieth century. A life of Clare, apparently by a contemporary and usually, although not certainly, ascribed to Francis's biographer,

Thomas of Celano (c.1190–1260) also survives. Along with her own writings, these documents provide the clearest insight into Clare's life. Her piety was exceptionally pragmatic, focused on the practice of the ideal of poverty. The hagiographic sources made no mention of the visions common among female saints of the thirteenth century. Instead, the witnesses stressed humility and her devotion to the ideal of poverty, as well as the miracles (from cures to the protection of the convent of San Damiano against Muslim troops in the employ of Emperor Frederick II) that were accomplished through her prayers. Clare always sought, by her own admission, to be a faithful follower of Francis. Yet it would be wrong to deny her originality. Tenaciously and against much opposition, she managed to adopt in difficult circumstances the charismatic ideals of Francis into an institutionalized lifestyle for women that was acceptable to a misogynist ecclesiastical hierarchy.

See also Agnes of Assisi, St.; Agnes of Bohemia, Blessed; Beguines; Hagiography (Female Saints); Rules for Canonesses, Nuns, and Recluses

BIBLIOGRAPHY

Primary Sources
Clare of Assisi. *Claire d'Assise. Écrits.* Edited by Marie-France Becker, Jean-François Godet, and Thaddée Matura. Sources Chrétiennes, 325. Paris: Éditions du Cerf, 1985.
———. *Early Documents.* Translated by Regis Armstrong. Revised ed. St. Bonaventure, N.Y.: Franciscan Institute Publications, 1993.
———. *Francis and Clare: The Complete Works.* Translated by Regis Armstrong and Ignatius Brady. New York: Paulist Press, 1982.
Opuscula sancti Francisci, Scripta sanctae Clarae: concordance, index, listes de fréquence, tables comparatives. Edited by Jean-François Godet. Corpus des sources franciscaines, 5. Louvain, Belgium: Université catholique de Louvain, 1976. [Useful concordance and index, etc. to Clare's and Francis's works].
Lazzeri, Zeffirino, ed. "Il processo di Santa Chiara d'Assisi," *Archivum Franciscanum Historicum,* 13 (1920): 403–507. [Records of Clare's canonization process].
Thomas of Celano(?). *Legenda sanctae Clarae virginis tratta dal ms. 338 della Bibl. communali di Assisi.* Edited by Francesco Pennacchi. Assisi: Metastasio, 1910.
Omaechevarria, Ignacio, ed. *Escritos de Santa Clara y Documentos Contemporaneos.* 2nd ed. Biblioteca de Autores Cristianos, 314. Madrid: Editorial Catolica, 1982. [Other contemporary documents].
Vorreux, Damien, ed. *Sainte Claire d'Assise: Biographie, écrits, procès et bulle de canonisation, textes de chroniquers, textes législatifs, tables.* Paris: Éditions franciscaines, 1983.

Secondary Sources
Bartoli, Marco. *Clare of Assisi.* Translated by Sr. Frances Teresa. Quincy, Ill.: Franciscan Press, 1993. Original *Chiara d'Assisi.* Rome: Istituto storico dei Cappuccini, 1989.
Brooke, Rosalind, and Christopher Brooke. "St. Clare." In *Medieval Women,* edited by Derek Baker, 275–87. Studies in Church History. Subsidia, 1. Oxford: Basil Blackwell, 1978.
Menesto, Enrico, ed. *Chiara di Assisi: Atti del XX Convegno internazionale.* Atti dei Convegni della Società di studi francescani, n.s. 3. Spoleto: Centro italiano di Studi sull'alto Medioevo, 1993.
Covi, Davide, and Dino Dozzi, eds. *Chiara, francescanesimo al femminile.* Collana "Studi e ricerche," 1. Rome: Edizioni Dehoniane, 1992.
De Villapadierna, Isidoro, and Pietro Maranesi, eds. *Bibliografia di Santa Chiara di Assisi: 1930–1993.* Rome: Istituto storico dei Cappuccini, 1994.
Grau, Englbert. *Leben und Schriften der heiligen Klara.* Werl, Westphalia, Germany: Dietrich Coelde Verlag, 1997.
Gieben, Servus. *L'iconografia de Chiara d'Assisi / Clare of Assisi: Iconography.* Italia Francescana, 1. Rome, 1993. [Also appended to orig. ed. of Bartoli, *see above*].

Kuster, N. "Thomas von Celano und Klaras Armut in San Damiano. Beitrag zu einer Neuinterpretation der beiden Franziskanusviten und zu Diskussion über den Verfasser der Klaralegende." *Wissenschaft und Weisheit* 59 (1996): 45–80.

Movimento religioso femminile e francescanesimo nel secolo XIII. Assisi: La Società, 1980.

Marini, Alfonso, and Beatrice Mistretta, eds. *Chiara d'Assisi e la memoria di Francesco*. Città di Castello: Petruzzi, 1995.

Peterson, Ingrid. *Clare of Assisi: A Biographical Study*. Quincy, Ill.: Franciscan Press, 1993.

Van den Goorbergh, Edith, and Theodore Zweerman. *Light Shining through a Veil. On Saint Clare's Letter to Saint Agnes of Prague*. Translated by Aline Looman-Graaskamp and Frances Teresa. Louvain: Peeters, 2000.

THOMAS HEAD

CLARE OF MONTEFALCO, ST. (c.1268–1308). A saint, mystic, and abbess, Clare was also known as St. Clare of the Cross (Santa Chiara della Croce). While most sources give the year 1268 as the birthdate of St. Clare of Montefalco, in central Italy, daughter of Giacoma and Damiano, according to Butler's *Lives of the Saints* she was born in 1275, a date that has theological significance because it thus puts her death at age thirty-three, the same age at which Christ was crucified. Her association with Christ is emphasized further in the hagiographic record by the report that symbols of the Passion—including the crucifix, the crown of thorns, the three nails, and the lance—were found in her heart during a postmortem examination. Because of these miraculous signs, Berengarius (*Ital.*: Berengario di Donadio [or] di Sant'Africano; *Fr*: Béranger de Saint-Affrique), the vicar general of Spoleto opened an investigation into Clare's life in 1309. Despite his initial suspicion that such signs of divine favor were a hoax, Berengarius became convinced of her sanctity and initiated the process that would result in her canonization nearly six hundred years later. He composed a *vita* (saint's life) from which much of her biography has been reconstructed.

Clare spent most of her life as a cloistered nun, although there is some dispute concerning whether she belonged to the Franciscan or Augustinian order, since each claims her. The first phase of her religious vocation developed within a secular community of Tertiaries (belonging to the Third Order and thus usually attached to Mendicants or other penitential movements) under the leadership of her sister Giovanna. As Tertiaries, the women and girls of the community were influenced by their contacts with the Franciscans. In 1290, however, Giovanna became the abbess of the convent of Santa Croce, which adopted the Augustinian rule. When Giovanna died, Clare reluctantly accepted the position as her sister's successor. She proved to be a capable administrator who was able to combine her preference for the contemplative life with active service. Like other mystics, Clare was noted for her visionary fervor and ascetic practices. As with other members of penitential orders, she rejected any bodily comforts, engaged in protracted fasts, and performed acts of mortification of the flesh. Clare was also known for her charitable work in support of the poor, ill, and diseased. A number of miraculous cures were believed to have derived from her intervention. In addition, she took on public roles such as that of peacemaker during a political crisis between Montefalco and the neighboring city of Trevi.

A popular cult sprang up in Clare's region of Umbria, in central Italy, immediately after her death. In fact, there is some evidence that St. Clare of the Cross, as she was called, was often invoked in place of St. Clare of Assisi, whose cult had been established at an earlier date. However, there were three unsuccessful attempts to legitimate Clare of Montefalco as a saint before Pope Leo XIII finally approved her official canonization in 1881. Her feast day is celebrated on August 18.

See also Clare of Assisi, St.; Hagiography (Female Saints); Penitentials, Women in; Rules for Canonesses, Nuns, and Recluses

BIBLIOGRAPHY

Primary Sources
Berengarius. *Vita di santa Chiara da Montefalco.* Edited by Michele Faloci-Pulignani. Rome, 1885.
————. *Life of St. Clare of Montefalco.* Translated by Matthew J. O'Connell. Edited by John E. Rotelle. Augustinian Series, 9. Villanova, Pa.: Augustinian Press, 1999.
Butler's Lives of the Saints. Edited by Herbert Thurston, S.J., and Donald Attwater. Vol. 3. New York: P. J. Kenedy and Sons, 1956.
Fonti per la Storia di S. Chiara da Montefalco. Edited by Claudio Leonardi and Enrico Menestò. 2 vols. Perugia: Regione dell'Umbria; Florence: Nuova Italia, 1984. [In Latin and Italian. Sources on Clare's life, including hagiography and canonization process].

Secondary Sources
Bynum, Caroline Walker. *Holy Feast and Holy Fast: The Religious Significance of Food to Medieval Women.* Berkeley: University of California Press, 1987.
Frugoni, Chiara. "Female Mystics, Visions, and Iconography." In *Women and Religion in Medieval and Renaissance Italy*, edited by Daniel Bornstein and Roberto Rusconi, 130–64. Chicago and London: University of Chicago Press, 1996.
Goodich, Michael. "The Contours of Female Piety in Later Medieval Hagiography." *Church History* 50.1 (1981): 20–32.
Holmes, George. *Florence, Rome, and the Origins of the Renaissance.* Oxford: Oxford University Press, 1986.
Menestò, Enrico. "The Apostolic Canonization Proceedings of Clare of Montefalco, 1318–19." In *Women and Religion in Medieval and Renaissance Italy*, edited by Daniel Bornstein and Roberto Rusconi, 104–29. Chicago and London: University of Chicago Press, 1996.

DIANA L. MURPHY

CLEMENCE OF BARKING (fl. late 12th century). The Benedictine nun and Anglo-Norman poet-translator at Barking Abbey is known by only one reference: the signature that appears at the end of her verse life of St. Catherine: "Jo ki sa vie ai translatee,/Par nun sui Clemence numee./De Berkinge sui nunain./Pur s'amur pris cest oevre en mein" (vv. 2689–92; "I who have translated her life am called Clemence by name. I am a nun of [the abbey of] Barking. For the love of her [= Catherine] I took this work in hand"). Clemence may also have been the author, as MacBain argues (1958), of an anonymous Anglo-Norman verse life of Edward the Confessor, composed at Barking between 1163 and 1170 (ed. Södergård 1948).

Founded in the seventh century and dedicated to the Virgin Mary, the royal abbey at Barking (now a suburb of London) became home to a prestigious tradition of female sanctity and learning. Following a mid-twelfth-century property dispute, the abbacy fell vacant from 1166 to 1173, when Henry II appointed Mary, the sister of Thomas Becket (c.1120–1270), as abbess as part of his reparations for the archbishop's murder (Elkins). Guernes de Pont-Sainte-Maxence thanks Mary, in the epilogue to his nearly contemporary life of St. Thomas, for gifts of clothing and a horse. By 1179, Henry had replaced Mary with his own natural daughter, Maud; the latter has been identified as the dedicatee of Adgar's *Gracial* (ed. Kunstmann).

Clemence's life of St. Catherine reflects the sophisticated "feminist" culture of Barking Abbey. She faithfully translates the Latin prose source, the version known as the *Vulgata*, into Anglo-Norman octosyllabics, but does not hesitate to intervene with reflections of her own. These passages reveal her as a talented poet, enthusiastically committed to the celebration of the virgin martyr, St. Catherine, as a patron of women's spiritual and intellectual vocations. Clemence further associates Catherine with the Virgin Mary, queen of heaven, who presides over a *grant compaignie* (great assembly) of saints, in which the choir of consecrated virgins, including those of Barking, will ultimately find due place (vv. 1727–84). Here and elsewhere, Clemence's phraseology echoes that of other Anglo-Norman saints' lives of the period, notably those of Lawrence, George, Edward the Confessor, and Mary the Egyptian. Clemence also echoes the *Tristan* of Thomas of Britain (late twelfth century), whose discourse is parodied by the Roman tyrant in her poem (vv. 2165–57); Thomas again may have influenced the lyricism of Catherine's address to her heavenly spouse (vv. 1357–70; Robertson). Clemence's *St. Catherine* thus offers a remarkable synthesis of clerical and courtly elements, representative of the twelfth-century Anglo-Norman literary community.

See also Hagiography (Female Saints)

BIBLIOGRAPHY

Primary Sources
Adgar. *Le Gracial*. Edited by Pierre Kunstmann. Ottawa: Éditions de l'Université d'Ottawa, 1982.
Clemence of Barking. *The Life of St. Catherine of Alexandria by Clemence of Barking*. Edited by William MacBain. Anglo-Norman Text Society, 18. Oxford: Blackwell, 1964.
———. In *Virgin Lives and Holy Deaths. Two Exemplary Biographies for Anglo-Norman Women. The Life of St. Catherine. The Life of St. Lawrence*. Translated with commentary by Jocelyn Wogan-Browne and Glyn S. Burgess. Everyman Library. London: J. M. Dent; Rutland, Vt.: Charles E. Tuttle, 1996.
Thomas of Britain. *Tristran*. Edited and translated by Stewart Gregory. Garland Library of Medieval Literature, A, 21. New York: Garland, 1991.
La Vie d'Édouard le Confesseur: Poème anglo-normand du XIIe siècle. Critical ed. by Östen Södergård. Uppsala, Sweden: Almqvist & Wiksells, 1948.

Secondary Sources
Batt, Catherine. "Clemence of Barking's Transformations of *Courtoisie* in *La Vie de sainte Catherine d'Alexandrie*." In *Translation in the Middle Ages*. Edited by Roger Ellis. *New Comparisons* 12 (1991): 102–33.
Calin, William. *The French Tradition and the Literature of Medieval England*. Toronto: University of Toronto Press, 1994.
Elkins, Sharon. *Holy Women of Twelfth-Century England*. Chapel Hill, N.C. and London: University of North Carolina Press, 1988.
MacBain, William. "The Literary Apprenticeship of Clemence of Barking." *Journal of the Australasian Universities Language and Literature Association* 9 (1958): 3–22.
———. "Five Old French Renderings of the *Passio Sancte Katerine Virginis*." In *Medieval Translators and Their Craft*, edited by Jeanette Beer, 41–65. Studies in Medieval Culture, 25. Kalamazoo, Mich.: Medieval Institute Publications, 1989.
Robertson, Duncan. *The Medieval Saints' Lives: Spiritual Renewal and Old French Literature*. The Edward C. Armstrong Monographs on Medieval Literature, 8. Lexington, Ky.: French Forum, 1995.

————. "Writing in the Textual Community: Clemence of Barking's Life of St. Catherine." *French Forum* 21 (1996): 5–28.

Wogan-Browne, Jocelyn. "'Clerc u lai, muïne u dame': Women and Anglo-Norman Hagiography in the Twelfth and Thirteenth Centuries." In *Women and Literature in Britain, 1150–1500*, edited by Carol M. Meale, 61–85. Cambridge Studies in Medieval Literature. Cambridge: Cambridge University Press, 1993.

DUNCAN ROBERTSON

CLIFFORD, ROSAMOND. *See* Rosamond, Fair

CLOTILDE, ST. (470–548). The Frankish queen known in Modern French as Clotilde, in Merovingian Latin as Clothild or Crothilda, and in English as Clotilda, is credited with having converted her husband Clovis (c.466–511), king of the Salian Franks, to Christianity (c.496). Clovis, in turn, would be revered for inaugurating the future realm of France as a Christian kingdom. Clotilde was inspired in her pious deeds by St. Genovefa—Genevieve, patron saint of Paris (423–502)—both women becoming religious heroines in attempting to civilize their people amidst the violence and personal losses of the Barbarian invasions and complex royal politics. Clotilde's main biographical source is an anonymous early tenth-century *vita* (life) based on information from Gregory of Tours's *Historia Francorum* (late sixth century) and Hincmar of Reims's life of St. Remigius (later ninth century), Remigius (Rémy) having been the bishop of Reims who baptized Clovis.

Born in Lyons, Clotilde was the younger daughter of King Chilperic of Burgundy, who was murdered by his brother Gundobad, who kept her at his house while exiling her sister. The beautiful Burgundian princess attracted the attention of the king of the Franks, and, after negotiations via a Frankish envoy disguised as a pilgrim who charmed Clotilde at Mass and gave her lavish gifts to convince Gundobad, she and Clovis were married c.492. Clotilde, a Catholic Christian, immediately endeavored, via a wedding-night lecture, to convert Clovis, who, like many barbarians, was either still pagan or more likely Arian: a primitive form of Christianity by then condemned as heretical by the Church. Finally, and thanks to a miraculous victory over the Alemanni, which her husband believed was caused by her, Clotilde succeeded in effecting the conversion of Clovis and 3,000 men, plus his sister Albofled, who would marry Theodoric the Ostrogoth (c.455–526), whose daughter, the future queen in Italy, Amalasuntha (c.494–535), would also convert. This legendary baptism of Clovis occurred in about 496, as Gregory of Tours records, though modern historians suggest that it might have occurred as late as 508. Meanwhile, King Clovis, through law and diplomacy, his policies often bolstered by murder and warfare (although his reputation for brutality has benefited from some revision [Daly]), managed to unify his kingdom as never before. As he doubtless realized when deciding to convert, his kingdom's Catholic Christianity set it apart from and above the other barbarian kingdoms that later renounced their Arianism in favor of Catholicism (Hollister and Bennett). Clotilde and Clovis had three sons and two daughters.

After Clovis's death in 511, and the resultant infighting among her sons for control of the kingdom, Queen Clotilde, eager to escape the horrendous atmosphere at court, often visited the abbey of St. Martin at Tours, eastern France. She founded the abbeys of

Andalys and Chelles. Both her daughters were very devout: her namesake daughter Clotilde, under her mother's influence, established a pattern of Christian princesses acting as missionaries to the courts of the Arian kings they married—a phenomenon historian Jane Schulenburg has labeled "domestic proselytization." The vita mentions the tragic death of the younger Clotilde, attempting in vain to convert her Visigothic husband, but omits Telechild, or Teutechild, who became a nun and founded the monastery of St. Peter at Sens, France (trans. McNamara et al.). After young Clotilde's death, Queen Clotilde retired to St. Martin of Tours, where she continued her acts of religious piety and charity until her death. Her great-granddaughter, Queen Bertha, by welcoming missionaries to Kent, England, c.579, would help to spread Christianity in that region. Clotilde's Feast Day is June 3.

See also Amalasuntha; Hagiography (Female Saints); Salic Law

BIBLIOGRAPHY

Primary Sources

Gregory of Tours, St. [*Historia Francorum*] *Historiarum libri decem*. Revised critical ed. by Bruno Krusch and Wilhelm Levison, book 2. ch. 37. *Monumenta Germaniae Historica. Scriptores rerum Merovingicarum* [= MGH.SRM], 1.1, Hannover, Germany: Hahn, 1951.

Vitae S. Clotildae. Edited by Bruno Krusch. MGH.SRM, 2: 349–51. Hannover: Hahn, 1888.

———. "Clothild, Queen of the Franks." In *Sainted Women of the Dark Ages*, edited and translated by Jo Ann McNamara and John E. Halborg et al., 38–50. Durham, N.C.: Duke University Press, 1992. [Highly useful annotated English version].

Secondary Sources

Daly, William M. "Clovis: How Barbaric, How Pagan?" *Speculum* 69 (1994): 619–64.

Hollister, C. Warren, and Judith M. Bennett. *Medieval Europe: A Short History*. 9th ed. Boston: McGraw-Hill, 2002.

Livingstone, E. A., ed. *The Oxford Dictionary of the Christian Church*. Original editor F. L. Cross. 3rd ed. Oxford: Oxford University Press, 1997.

Schulenburg, Jane T. *Forgetful of Their Sex: Female Sanctity and Society, ca. 500–1100*. Chicago: University of Chicago Press, 1998.

Van de Vyver, A. "La Chronologie du règne de Clovis d'après la légende et d'après l'histoire." *Le Moyen Âge* 53 (1947): 177–96.

NADIA MARGOLIS

COBLASWECHSEL (POETIC EXCHANGE). *See* **Alamanda; Azalais d'Altier; Carenza, Na; Garsenda of Forcalquier; Lombarda; Maria de Ventadorn; Ysabella, Domna**

COLETTE OF CORBIE, ST. (1381–1447). St. Colette, from Corbie, in Picardy (northern France), founded the Colettines, a reformist branch of the Poor Clares (women's Franciscan order, founded c.1215), a unique example of a reform originating first in the female branch of an order and then influencing the male branch (see Ranft).

Though Corbie was associated with its widely revered monastery since the seventh century, known especially for its library, scriptorium, and school of the Carolingian era (ninth century), Colette's own development did not integrate this aura, however. What would move her instead would be more pressing problems: the decline of the once-vital Poor Clares, a mendicant (begging) order for women dedicated to poverty, profound spiritual meditation, and good works; she was also troubled by the effects of the Great Schism of the papacy (1378–1417). She was born to well-off parents. Her father, Robert Boelet, worked as an artisan, and her mother was extremely pious. Because they were in their fifties at her birth on January 13, 1381, they named their long-awaited child Nicolette, in honor of St. Nicholas. They died in close succession when Colette was eighteen, whereupon she lived with her guardian, Dom de Roye, the Benedictine abbot of Corbie. When de Roye urged her to marry, she refused and gave all her belongings to the poor.

She began her religious career as a beguine or Tertiary at Amiens. Briefly defined, beguines were laywomen leading religious lives but not cloistered, nor did they take vows; tertiaries were usually lay penitents belonging to the Third Order of monks and nuns (the First Order being enclosed monks, the Second, enclosed nuns), attached to mendicant orders such as the Franciscans and Dominicans, whose lives were otherwise similar to the Beguines'. She later decided to pursue a more austere, enclosed and spiritually intense life and thus joined the monastery of Poor Clares at Moncel, northwest of Paris. Seeking still greater austerity and purity than what their rule offered (since the Church had seriously altered Clare's rule after her death), Colette became an anchorite in 1402 (significantly on September 17, the Feast of the Stigmata of St. Francis), living as an avowed ascetic recluse, in a walled cell with but a small grill opening for air and light, in the church of Notre Dame of Corbie for three or four years, until she experienced rapturous visions of both Sts. Francis and Clare, in around 1406, instructing her to reform the Three Orders of St. Francis (see *Acta Sanctorum*). These commands she interpreted as founding a new monastery of Poor Clares (one accommodating all Three Orders), taking care to obtain papal approval. To assist her in this endeavor, she enlisted Henri de Baume as confessor and spiritual guide, a learned cleric capable of counseling her on how to convince the pope of the authenticity of her visions. During this era of the papal Schism, France had its own pope at Avignon, while another reigned in Rome. Colette and Henri were successful in presenting their mandate at Avignon to Pope Benedict XIII, who, citing Innocent IV's approval of the original Poor Clares, along with his favorable opinion of Colette's devotion and obedience, granted his approbation in 1406, making her superior general of all future Poor Clare convents.

Colette's first reformed monastery was completed by 1408. Property was granted in 1412 for the construction of another one, near Dole (northeastern France), with the further help of the Franciscan friars. These same friars then joined her reform movement, comprising her First Order (enclosed men), later called "Colettan" houses, while the Second Order (enclosed women) would be called "Colettines" as more houses were built throughout France. Like all monastic founders, Colette devised a rule, and submitted it to the Franciscan minister general, Guillaume de Casal (William of Casal) who approved it most enthusiastically, as did the famous humanist, Pope Pius II (r. 1458–1464) later.

Colette's special talents as a monastic founder lay in her ability to realize her visionary experience—evidently occurring with almost debilitating force, what Johan Huizinga, following the philosopher William James's terminology (in *The Varieties of Religious Experience* [1902]), categorized as the "theopathic state" typical of politically influential late-medieval visionaries—in active, practical ways. Despite her supersensitive nature, she was obviously an attentive, resourceful administrator and astute negotiator and advisor, who not only paved the way for her own reforms despite potential Church-hierarchy and community resentment, but also frequented and counseled the Burgundian court and Yolanda of Aragon (c.1381–1442) in their political designs (Lopez; Forceville). Her Colettines carried her reforms beyond France to the Low Countries, Italy, and Germany, as did the Colettans, though the latter met with more disputes from rival movements within the Franciscan order. She established seventeem convents before her death in Ghent, Flanders (Belgium). Among several notable Italian women nurtured by the Colettines who would go on to become founders in their own right was Catherine of Bologna (1423–1463) founder of Corpus Domini. Her Colettine Sisters remained especially active in France.

Colette of Corbie was canonized in 1807. Her Feast Day is March 6.

See also Birgitta of Sweden, St.; Catherine of Bologna, St.; Clare of Assisi, St.; Convents; Rules for Canonesses, Nuns, and Recluses; Yolanda of Aragon

BIBLIOGRAPHY

Primary Sources
Acta Sanctorum Martii, 1: 540–601, esp. 561–62. [Describes her visions, etc.].
Colette. *Documents sur la Réforme de Sainte Colette en France*. Edited by Ubald d'Alençon. *Archivum Franciscanum Historicum* 2 (1909): 447–56; 600–612; vol. 3 (1910): 82–97. [Original language only].
———. [Documents relevant to her reform]. Translated in *The First Rule of St. Clare and the Constitution of St. Coletta*. London: Thomas Richardson, 1875.
———. *The Testament of St. Colette*. Translated by Mother Mary Francis. Chicago: Franciscan Herald Press, 1987. [Translation of *Exhortation de sainte Colette à ses soeurs*].
Pius II. Bull *Solet annuere*. Translated in *The First Rule of St. Clare*, esp. 107–15. *See above.*
William of Casal. "Lettres inédites de Guillaume de Casal à Sainte Colette de Corbie et notes pour une biographie de cette sainte." *Études franciscaines* 19 (1908): 460–81; 668–91.
———. [First Letter to Colette]. Translated in *The First Rule of St. Clare*, 96–97. [*See above*].

Secondary Sources
Forceville, Philippe de. *Une grande figure politique de la première moitié du XVe siècle: Ste Colette de Corbie et son alliance avec Yolande d'Anjou*. Paris: A. & J. Picard, 1958.
Huizinga, Johan. *The Autumn of the Middle Ages*. Translated by Rodney Payton and Ulrich Mammitzch. Chicago: University of Chicago Press, 1996. Original *Herfsttij der Middeleeuwen*, 1924.
Livingstone, E. A., ed. *The Oxford Dictionary of the Christian Church*. Original editor F. L. Cross. 3rd ed. Oxford: Oxford University Press, 1997.
Lopez, Élisabeth. *Petite vie de Sainte Colette*. Paris: Desclée De Brouwer, 1998.
———. *Culture et sainteté: Colette de Corbie, 1381–1447*. Travaux et recherches/CERCOR. Saint-Étienne, France: Publications de l'Université de Sainte-Étienne, 1994.
Ranft, Patricia. *Women and the Religious Life in Premodern Europe*. New York: St. Martin's, 1996.

NADIA MARGOLIS

COMNENA, ANNA (1083–post-1148). Anna Comnena, or Komnene, was one of the first women historians and a key literary figure of Byzantium, the Eastern Roman Empire as of 330, in which the primary language was Greek instead of Latin and whose religion, by Anna's time, was Greek Orthodox, centered at Constantinople, instead of Roman Catholicism. The eldest daughter of Emperor Alexius (original Greek: Alexios) I Comnenus (1048–1118) and Empress Irene (Eirene), Anna married Nicephorus Bryennius (Nikephoros Bryennios) and conspired with her mother to have him made emperor instead of her brother John II

Comnenus (1088–1143), whom her father had declared as his successor. Unsuccessful in this attempt, and mercifully pardoned, Anna withdrew to a monastery and began to write an account, in Greek, of her father's life and achievements, the *Alexiad* (*Alexias*). Because she had received a broad education in both the classics and scriptural writings, she was able to make good use of her privileged access to the royal archives and life at court in composing her history, which renders it extremely valuable to modern historians of Byzantium.

Completed sometime after 1148, the *Alexiad* covers the period 1069–1118 in fifteen parts or books. As its title suggests, it is centered on her father and resembles an epic in certain ways, such as its adulatory tone, glorifying Alexius and his family. The work draws on an impressive array of models and sources. From among the ancient authors, Anna owes most to diverse major Greek historians Thucydides (460–400 B.C.E.), Polybius (Polybios, c.202–125 B.C.E.) and the later Plutarch (Ploutarchos, c.46–120 C.E.), but she tells us she knew the works of the fifth-century B.C.E. Aristotle and Plato and makes numerous classical allusions. As for later sources, the *Alexiad* draws on the *Chronographia* (Chronography) of the Byzantine philosopher and theologian Michael Psellus (Psellos, c.1019–c.1078) and is a continuation of the history up to 1079 written by her husband, Bryennius. In many instances, Anna also writes from personal knowledge. For all of these reasons, she falls more within the humanist, rather than the Byzantine religious, tradition of historiographers. However, when she praises her father's persecution of the heretics and in other similar moments, she reflects Greek Orthodox animosity toward such groups as the Bogomils, and even toward the Western Church (Roman Catholic) and its Crusades, as potentially detrimental to the Byzantine Empire.

In portraying Alexius as the ideal Byzantine emperor, Anna therefore shows him to be godly, fatherly, and wary of the West. The Byzantines' first encounter with the Crusaders is described: it seems the former were not impressed. The narrative is laced with irony and sarcasm, and the author is vigorously self-assertive. Despite its somewhat defective chronology, the *Alexiad* is one of the best historical works of the Byzantine age and is the main source for our knowledge of this crucial period. As an example of the *Alexiad*'s later literary influence, the great Scottish novelist Sir Walter Scott frequently refers to it in his romance, *Count Robert of Paris* (c.1800).

The *Alexiad* is also important from the linguistic point of view as it exhibits the significant gap developing between demotic (everyday usage) and literary Greek. Anna Comnena does not write in the contemporary language used by many other writers, but attempts a neo-Attic (more archaic, noble) style based on her knowledge of classical writers. This is moderately successful in the area of vocabulary (in spite of the numerous contemporary technical terms, foreign words, and colloquialisms), but less so in the realm of style and syntax. Among its modern incarnations, the *Alexiad* has been translated into Modern Greek, French, German, Swedish, and Russian, as well as English.

BIBLIOGRAPHY

Primary Sources
Anna Comnena. *Alexias*. Critical ed. by Diether R. Reinsch and Athanasios Kambylis. Corpus fontium historiae byzantinae, 40. 2 vols. Berlin and New York: de Gruyter, 2001. [Bilingual ancient Greek-English scholarly edition].
——. *The Alexias of the Princess Anna Comnena*. Translated by Elizabeth A. S. Dawes, London: Routledge & Kegan Paul, 1928, 1967.

—————. *The Alexiad of Anna Comnena*. Translated by Edgar R. A. Sewter. Harmondsworth, Middlesex, U.K.: Penguin, 1969, 1976.

Secondary Sources

Barrett, Tracy. *Anna of Byzantium*. New York: Delacorte Press, 1999. [For younger readers, based on the *Alexiad*].

Buckler, Georgina. *Anna Comnena, A Study*. Oxford: Oxford University Press/Humphrey Milford, 1929, 1968.

Dalven, Rae. *Anna Comnena*. Twayne World Authors. New York: Twayne, 1972.

Gouma-Peterson, Thalia, ed. *Anna Comnene and Her Times*. Garland Reference Library of the Humanities. Garland Casebooks. New York: Garland, 2000. [Collection of essays by important scholars].

DAVID LARMOUR

COMPIUTA DONZELLA (13th century). La Compiuta Donzella di Firenze, meaning "the accomplished damsel of Florence," is the name given to the author of three fine Italian sonnets of the thirteenth century. She is the first woman known to compose Italian verse. Although critics once maintained that Compiuta Donzella was not really a name but a self-assertive pseudonym, and that the poems were written by a male poet, scholars now tend to believe that a poet of this name really existed (see Kleinhenz; Cherchi). The name Compiuta appears frequently in documents of the period. Her poems are found in only one manuscript, but a significant one, the Vatican Library Codex A 3793.

One sonnet is a complaint about being forced by her father to marry against her will. It is known by its first line, "A la stagion che'l mondo foglia e flora" ("In the season when the world's in leaf and flower"), beginning with the conventional invocation to Nature often seen in medieval lyric, but to which, after the first seven joyous verses, she adds a different twist—heralded by "e me" ("but in me")—in lamenting over the last seven verses not unrequited love, but almost its opposite, at least superficially: her father's insistence that she take a husband. As Christopher Kleinhenz reminds us in regard to this poem's context, medieval marriage arrangements often had less to do with love between the betrothed than with the property their union would consolidate. This poem documents what must have been the sentiments of many a thoughtful, talented young woman in similar circumstances, whether because they loved a man other than the parentally chosen one or wished never to marry at all. The second sonnet is often presented in anthologies as an extension of the first. Beginning "Lascia vorria lo mondo, e Dio servire" ("This world I'd wish to leave and God to serve"), it expresses her (so far as we know, unfulfilled) desire to become a nun and thereby become the bride only of Christ, a frequent female mystical motif. Joseph Tusiani assesses her first two sonnets as memorable for their contrasting portrayals of the "ideal world she envisions and the tyranny of a society she abhors." The third poem is part of her reply in a *tenzone* (debate poem) with an anonymous poet addressing her as "Gentil donzella somma ed insegnata" ("Gentle damsel, in sum most learned") and later as "Compiuta Donzella" (see Kleinhenz).

Little is known about Compiuta Donzella besides what she tells us in her very skilled poems. She lived in Florence, Italy, in the thirteenth century, and she is addressed with admiration in a letter (no. 5) by another poet of the thirteenth century, Guittone d'Arezzo (c.1230–1294). He may also have sent her the *canzone* (lyric poem) "Se di voi donna giente" ("If from you, gentle Lady . . ."). A poet known as Master Torregiano, or Torrigiani, sent her two sonnets praising her learnedness and poetic gifts as a "maraviglia" ("marvel"). These are extant, and we know that one of her three sonnets was penned in reply to his correspondence. Two canzoni were dedicated to her by another poet, perhaps Chiaro Davanzati (c.1230–c.1280). Luigi Russo observes that in her poems we see "a life and a character that we do not encounter in any other poems of the period," and that she expresses "a sincerity of expression and a fullness of emotion that seem almost modern." On the other hand, Achille Tartaro dismisses her poetry as "a poor thing, unworthy of the excessive praise of the romantics." In general, however, critical reception has been positive, even among venerable conservative male literary historians including Ernest Hatch Wilkins. Kleinhenz, coming thirty years after Russo, considers her poems unique for their time, even among her women-voiced (male poets assuming female personae) contemporaries: Compagnetto da Prato, Rinaldo d'Aquino (c.1220–1281), Giacomino Pugliese, Cecco d'Angiolieri (c.1260–c.1313), and Rustico Filippi (c.1230–1295). Her poems are among the first in the Tuscan school, and precede the *dolce stil nuovo*, the "sweet new style," made famous by Guido Guinizelli (c.1240–1276), Guido Cavalcanti (c.1255–1300), Dante Alighieri (1265–1321), and others in the later thirteenth century. The manuscript in which her poems appear is a collection of some of the finest poetry of the period, and the fact that we have praises of her by three other poets suggests that she was quite well known and respected in her day. The first two of the sonnets described above continue to be widely anthologized, whether in Italian or in translation.

See also Beatrice; Bride of Christ/*Brautmystik*; Catalan Women Poets, Anonymous; *Chanson de Femme* (Women's Song); Marriage; *Trobairitz*; *Trouvères*, Women

BIBLIOGRAPHY

Primary Sources
[A select sampling. Her poems are found in almost every anthology of medieval Italian poetry].
Compiuta Donzella. [*Sonnets*]. In *I Classici Italiani*, edited by Luigi Russo, 1: 66–68. Florence: Sansoni, 1963. [Italian text and commentary].
———. [2 *Sonnets*]. In *Poeti del Duecento*, edited by Gianfranco Contini, 1: 434–35. Milan and Naples: Ricciardi, 1960.
———. [2 *Sonnets*]. Translated by Christopher Kleinhenz. *See below, under* Secondary Sources. [Reproduces Contini's Italian text also].
———. [*Poems*]. In *The Defiant Muse: Italian Feminist Poems from the Middle Ages to the Present*, edited and translated by Beverly Allen et al., 2–5. New York: Feminist Press, 1986.
———. [2 *Sonnets*]. In *The Age of Dante: An Anthology of Early Italian Poetry*, introduced and translated by Joseph Tusiani, 155–56. New York: Baroque Press, 1974.
Guittone d'Arezzo. [Letter to Donzella]. In *La Prosa del Duecento*, edited by Cesare Segre and Mario Marti, 52. Milan and Naples: Ricciardi, 1959.

Secondary Sources
Azzolina, Liborio. *La Compiuta Donzella di Firenze*. Palermo, Sicily: Reber, 1902.
Cherchi, Paolo. "The Troubled Existence of Three Women Poets." In *The Voice of the Trobairitz: Perspectives on the Women Troubadours*, edited by William D. Paden, 198–209. Philadelphia: University of Pennsylvania Press, 1989.
Chiari, Alberto. "La Compiuta Donzella." In Chiari, *Indagini e letture*, Series 2: 1–7. Florence: F. Le Monnier, 1954.
Kleinhenz, Christopher. "*Pulzelle e maritate*: Coming of Age, Rites of Passage, and the Question of Marriage in Some Early Italian Poets." In *Matrons and Marginal Women in Medieval Society*, edited by Robert R. Edwards and Vickie Ziegler, 89–110. Woodbridge, U.K.: Boydell Press, 1995.

Tartaro, Achille. "Guittone e i rimatori siculo-toscani," In *Storia della letteratura italiana. Le origini e il duecento*. Milan: Garzanti, 1965.

Tusiani, Joseph. *See above, under* Primary Sources.

Wilkins, Ernest Hatch. *A History of Italian Literature*. Revised ed. by Thomas G. Bergin. Cambridge, Mass.: Harvard University Press, 1978. Original 1954.

ELIZABETH A. PETROFF

COMTESSA DE DIA (c.1150–c.1215). The Countess of Die is possibly the earliest and definitely the most famous woman troubadour, or *trobairitz*. As with so many other trobairitz, actual historical evidence remains elusive: we know that she came from Dia or Die (in the present *département* of the Drôme, southeastern France) and was a contemporary of another trobairitz, Azalais de Porcairagues. "Comtessa" might be a mere forename (see Jeanroy), but on the other hand, the poetess is perhaps to be identified with Isoarde, not Beatritz, as many Provençalists claimed (see, e.g., Kussler-Ratyé, ed.), who died in 1212–1214. This daughter of Isoard, Count of Die was entitled to be addressed as "Countess" of Die; she was married to Raimon d'Agout. If one relies on her possibly fictitious *vida*, or biography, she was the wife of one Guilhem (William) of Peitieus. However, five men could have answered to that name in that period, among whom the Count of Valentinois. Also, the place name of Peitieus may refer not to Poitiers but to Mount Peytieux, in southern France.

The Comtessa, if she was indeed Isoarde, according to Walter Pattison's 1952 theory extrapolating from her vida, fell in love with and addressed her poems to Raimbaut d'Aurenga, more likely Raimbaut IV of Orange (d. 1218), a lesser-known poet and namesake grandnephew of the famous troubadour Raimbaut III of Orange (d. 1173). But this association may derive merely from scholars imagining her as the great troubadour's partner in a notable love-debate poem, or *tenso*: "Amics, en gran cosirier/sui per vos e en grieu pena" ("Friend, I'm in great distress/over you, and grievous pain"), whose roles are labeled anonymous *domna* (the Comtessa's possible part) and Raimbaut d'Aurenga. Recent scholars point to similarities in metrics and intertextuality (discernible textual echoes and dialoguing among a group of authors) among the Comtessa, Azalais de Porcairagues, and Raimbaut; yet also that, while Raimbaut figures in her vida, the Comtessa does not appear in his, nor in other pertinent documentation (see Bruckner et al., eds.).

There are four miniatures portraying her. Four of her songs have survived, along with the music for one of them ("A chantar m'er de so q'ieu no volria"). Within these poems, the Comtessa already succeeds in shifting the posited asymmetrical roles in the male lyric. Vacating the post of an adored but silent idol, having the man function in his turn as a passive audience, she assimilates herself within her narrator, the lover-poet, to reveal her own emotions. The need to speak manifests itself despite the speaker's wishes: "A chantar m'er de so q'ieu no volria" ("I must sing that which I would prefer not to"), as one of her *cansos*, or poems ("songs"), begins.

She borrows a few motifs from the traditional courtly repertory as she reflects upon her friend's faithlessness and reproaches him for his pride, although her verse evinces mostly a marked optimism; it celebrates joy and youth while defying all wicked-minded slanderers and spies who meddle in others' love affairs. Some older critics, like Jeanroy, are taken aback by the overt manner in which the Countess sometimes expresses her erotic side—as in stanza two of "Estat ai en greu cossirier" ("I have been sorely troubled"):

Ben volria mon cavalier	I'd like to hold my knight
tener un ser en mos bratz nut,	in my arms one evening, naked,
q'el s'en tengra per ereubut	for he'd be overjoyed
sol q'a lui fezes cosseillier;	were I only serving as his pillow,
car plus m'en sui abellida	and am more pleased with him
no fetz Floris que Blanchaflor;	than Floris with his Blanchefleur.
eu l'autrei mon cor e m'amor,	To him I grant my heart, my love,
mon sen, mos huoills e ma vida.	my mind, my eyes and my life.
(ed. Bruckner et al.; translation slightly modified)	

The same may be said about a few troubadours. Yet the envisioned physical relations are projected into the realm of desire and thus represented as unattainable. One may also mention the startling directness causing the poetess to add, no doubt by way of provocation, that she would like to hold her lover instead of her husband: "sapchatz gran talan n'auria/qe.us tengues en luoc del marit" ("Know that I'd feel a strong desire to have you in my husband's place"; vv. 21–22). But her need to trust him, perhaps in a distinctively trobairitz manner (see Robbins), is equally evident in the ensuing, final lines: "ab so que m'aquessetz plevit/de far tot so qu'eu volria" ("provided you had promised me/to do everything I wished").

Unlike other Provençal women lyricists, for example Na Castelloza, this writer posits herself between male and female poetic strategies. Nowhere does she completely renounce the exalted privilege of a *domna* placed at the summit of love's hierarchy. Aware, no doubt, of her own social rank, she cannot but expect her *amic* (beloved man) to return her passion. In retaining for herself—by way of a double reversal—the praise of the lady offered elsewhere by the male discourse, she does what no man would dare: her friend finds himself being reminded of her many qualities, of her beauty and her lineage. As Matilda Bruckner (1992; 2002) has observed, the comtessa "enjoys experimenting with a variety of self-images from song to song, and even within a single song." Less rigid in persona and demand for fidelity than Castelloza, the comtessa "plays with the sexual balance of power." We also notice that if she sings her own praise, it is not out of vanity, but because it is through these virtues that she might retain her lover. While looking for the best of both systems, the Comtessa rejects the laws of discretion and proclaims she, unlike male poets, does not want her love for a worthy man to be kept a secret, as she avers in "Estat ai en greu cossirier" (vv. 4-5): "e vuoil sia totz temps saubut/cum eu l'ai amat e sobrier" (I want it known for all time/how exceedingly I loved him").

See also Azalais de Porcairagues; Beatritz de Dia; Castelloza, Na; *Trobairitz*

BIBLIOGRAPHY

Primary Sources
Boutière, Jean, and Alexander H. Schutz, eds. *Biographies des Troubadours: Textes provençaux des XIIIe et XIVe siècles*. Revised ed. with I. M. Cluzel. Les Classiques d'Oc, 1. Paris: Nizet, 1964.
Comtessa de Dia. [Poems]. In "Les Chansons de la Comtesse Béatrix de Dia." Edited by Gabrielle Kussler-Ratyé. *Archivum Romanicum* 1 (1917): 161–82.
———. In *Songs of the Women Troubadours*, edited and translated by Matilda Tomaryn Bruckner, Laurie Shepard, and Sarah White, esp. 2–13. New York: Garland, 1995. Revised ed. 2000.

———. In *Trobairitz: Der Beitrag der Frau in der altokzitanischen höfischen Lyrik. Edition des Gesamtkorpus*, edited by Angelica Rieger. Beihefte zur Zeitschrift für romanische Philologie, 233. Tübingen, Germany: Max Niemeyer Verlag, 1991.

Secondary Sources

Bruckner, Matilda T. "Fictions of the Female Voice: The Women Troubadours." *Speculum* 67 (1992): 865–91. Reprint, revised, in *Medieval Women's Song*, edited by Anne L. Klinck and Ann Marie Rasmussen, 127–51. Philadelphia: University of Pennsylvania Press, 2002.

Cluzel, Irénée M. "Comtessa de Dia." In *Dictionnaire des Lettres françaises: Le Moyen Age*, edited by Robert Bossuat et al., 216–17. Paris: Fayard, 1964. Revised by Geneviève Brunel-Lobrichon, in the rev. *Dictionnaire*, edited by Geneviève Hasenohr and Michel Zink, 324–25. Paris: Livre de Poche, 1992.

Dronke, Peter. *Women Writers of the Middle Ages: A Critical Study of Texts from Perpetua († 203) to Marguerite Porete (†1310)*. Cambridge: Cambridge University Press, 1984.

Faucheux, Christian. *Etude sémantique et syntaxique de l'œuvre de la Comtesse de Die, Signum* 1.1–2 (1974): 1: 1–7; 2: 5–16.

Ferrante, Joan. "Notes towards the Study of a Female Rhetoric in the Trobairitz." In *The Voice of the Trobairitz: Essays on the Women Troubadours*, edited by William D. Paden, 63–72. Philadelphia: University of Pennsylvania Press, 1989.

Gravdal, Kathryn. "Metaphor, Metonymy, and the Medieval Women Trobairitz." *Romanic Review* 83 (1992): 411–26.

Huchet, Jean-Charles. "Les Femmes troubadours ou la voix critique." *Littérature* 51 (1983): 59–90.

Jeanroy, Alfred. *La Poésie lyrique des troubadours*, 1: 313–16, Toulouse and Paris: Privat, 1934.

Kasten, Ingrid. "The Conception of Female Roles in the Woman's Song of Reinmar and the Comtessa de Dia. In *Medieval Women's Song*, ed. Klinck and Rasmussen, 152–67, *see under* Bruckner *above*.

Kay, Sarah. "Derivation, Derived Rhyme, and the Trobairitz." In *Voice of the Trobairitz*, ed. Paden, 157–73. *See under* Ferrante *above*.

Pattison, Walter T. *The Life and Works of the Troubadour Raimbaut d'Orange*. Minneapolis: University of Minnesota Press, 1952.

Rieger, Dietmar. "Die französische Dichterin im Mittelalter: Marie de France—die 'trobairitz'—Christine de Pizan." In *Die französische Autorin von Mittelalter bis zur Gegenwart*, edited by Renate Baader and Dietmar Fricke, 29–48. Wiesbaden, Germany: Athenaion, 1979.

Robbins, Kittye Delle. "Woman/Poet: Problem and Promise in Studying the *Trobairitz* and Their Friends." *Encomia* 1 (1977): 12–14.

HERMAN BRAET

CONCUBINES. The practice of men having concubines—concubinage, in which the man has a sexual relationship, usually cohabitational, with a woman outside the bond of marriage—existed during the Middle Ages in various societies around the world. The following discussion focuses primarily on its development in the medieval Christian West, and in its very different manifestation in medieval Islam. Because it was a more stable relationship than that involved in prostitution or fornication, the concubine usually benefited from a special status.

In Western societies, the principal overall distinction between concubinage and marriage, whether accepted in a particular society or not, is that, because it is extramarital, on the man's death, the children from such a union and their concubine mother had inferior legal standing to that of legal children and wives. Concubinage had existed in Ancient Rome as a real institution, a legally and socially acceptable union minus the formalities and class concerns (since the concubine usually came from a lower class than the man) involved in marriage. On the other hand, the Germanic tribes, though they too indulged in some sort of concubinage, did not appear to designate it as a specific social entity. In later Roman times, however, certain restrictions resembling those applied to marriage also came to pertain to concubinage, such as prohibiting consanguinity (a close relative could not be a concubine), and eventually, informal polygamy: a respectable man could not be both married and have a concubine, but could choose one status or the other. In sum, Late Roman concubinage increasingly resembled marriage according to law. The esteemed Roman jurist, Herennius Modestinus (early third century), for example, equated any lifelong partnership with marriage, and thus one in which the couple shared legal rights.

Perhaps surprisingly, in the West, early Christianity exerted little influence at first, although Christian Roman emperors—those beginning with Constantine (r. 306–337) and especially as codified by Justinian, for civil law (*Digesta*, 25.7), in 529, invoking natural law as its basis—further legally aligned concubinage with marriage to the extent that all unions were presumed marriages unless formally specified otherwise. The Church hesitated to condemn concubinage outright since, as a form of stable monogamy—a crucial tenet of Christian doctrine—it was better than promiscuous alternatives and thus should be encouraged. The First Council of Toledo (400) actually permitted Christians to have concubines so long as these men were not married. However, Church Fathers such as St. Augustine of Hippo (354–430) argued vehemently against this right, typically after having enjoyed his concubine up until his own conversion and then dismissing her. Augustine was seconded by Pope Leo I (d. 461), known for advancing the papacy's influence throughout Africa, Spain, and Gaul (now France and Belgium), as well as the Western Roman provinces and, like the bishop of Hippo, was a key figure in formulating Church doctrine. The majority of Church officials adopted this strict interpretation, though not always rigidly, but inasmuch as they could impose it on the lay population during the Early Christian period. The limitations of their influence is demonstrated by the fact that, during the Merovingian and Carolingian periods of the Frankish Empire (fifth through ninth centuries), concubinage was widespread among these rulers, whose children often enjoyed inheritance rights on a par with legitimate children (Stafford).

When Gratian—known as the Father of Canon Law for compiling the first systematic collection of laws for the Church, or canon law, in his *Decretum* (c.1141)—was trying to assemble and reconcile the various canons for this corpus, he had to deal with the contradictory positions they conveyed concerning concubinage. In the end, Gratian's solution to these disparities was monumental in its balance between real-world viability and Christian-doctrinal fidelity: concubinage was a valid marriage contracted privately by mutual verbal consent but without ecclesiastical (Church ceremony) and legal formalities (dowry, etc.). This same ambivalence would inform, though with gradual modification, the Western Church's policy toward concubinage thereafter (Helmholz).

Because it considered concubinage a form of private marriage, and private marriages valid, medieval canon law was often kinder to children of concubinage than were some prevailing civil codes (more regionalized). However, the union had to be proven through some kind of tangible private contract. The children of a provably contracted union could therefore inherit from their mother, and even their father if the latter died without children from legal marriage; those without such proof enjoyed no rights. By decree of Pope Alexander III (1172), concubinage could subsequently be legitimized by formal marriage.

In terms of the real existence of concubinage in Europe, legal treatises and court records reflect scattered incidents of concubinage among both clergy and laity. In England, for example, the great legist Henry de Bracton (d. 1268) alludes to a party's "legitimate concubine" in his *De legibus et consuetudinibus Angliae* (*On the Laws and Customs of England*). In Castile, Spain, in the secular corpus compiled in the thirteenth century under King Alfonso X El Sabio ("The Wise"), titled *Las Siete Partidas* (*Seven Parts*) we find concubinage laws called *barragania*, as well various thirteenth- through fifteenth-century Italian statutes (Poulmarède; Barna).

The medieval Church's lenient attitude toward concubinage continued until the hardening necessitated by the challenge of the Protestant Reformation's attacks on Church corruption and laxness. The resultant Catholic Counter-Reformation, whose principles were embodied in the determinations of the Council of Trent (1545–1563), ruled that those living in concubinage could not take Communion.

Islamic concubinage was much more clearly defined and universally accepted than in the West, as Shaun Marmon has analyzed in her classic study. Although their concubines were always slaves, offspring of concubinage were considered free and legitimate through their father. This characterizes a society that prized children, especially male heirs, as a vital aspect of family continuity. Any inferiority ascribed to concubine offspring seems to derive more from concerns of racial purity (pure Arab blood possibly mixed with foreign slave blood), and was more characteristic of earlier Islam. Such early prejudice disappeared after the Abbasid revolution (750), whose social attitudes increasingly favored the children of slave concubines and free, aristocratic fathers so that these offspring came to dominate the ruling class. Once a concubine bore her master a child, even if it did not live, she attained elevated status as *umm al-walad* ("mother of the child"), and could not be resold or even given away. Concubines giving birth to future rulers could themselves rise to great wealth and influence; the most outstanding example being the sultan's concubine Shajar al-Durr, who even ruled Egypt for a brief time in the mid-thirteenth century and contributed to the emergence of the Mamluk rulers, slave sultans who would rule Egypt for 250 years (1250–1517).

Slaves had the right to marry each other, with the master's consent, in which case the master relinquished his sexual rights over the bride. Thus the married female slave could no longer be a concubine.

The Muslim bible, the Quran (or Koran), superseding the Old and New Testaments in its scope, allowed sexual access to an unlimited number of slaves as well as to a maximum of four wives. The crime of adultery, punishable by death, is imputed only when a man engages in sex with a woman who is neither his wife nor his concubine. Because she was a slave, a concubine was purchased and thus owned by her master/consort, who could cancel the sale if he soon found some aspect of her physically repugnant or that she had been frequently fornicating. As in marriage, and also in Western concubinage, consanguinity between master and concubine was prohibited, nor could a man have two concubines who were sisters. The concubine also could not be a pagan.

Although concubinage sometimes functioned as an alternative to marriage (e.g., for financial reasons) and despite the above-mentioned rights enjoyed by concubines and their children, this institution never replaced marriage in Islamic society. While the concubine's prestige came from her role as child bearer, a wife's prestige and rights were based on her own pedigree and property; her husband had obligations to her, while he had none to his slave concubine.

See also China, Women in; Fatimid Egypt, Women in; Ingibiorg; *Jus Primae Noctis*; Law, Canon, Women in; Law, Women in, Ango-Saxon England; Marriage; Norse Women; Prostitution; *Sachsenspiegel* and *Schwabenspiegel*; Slaves, Female

BIBLIOGRAPHY

Primary Sources

Bracton, Henry de. [*De legibus*]. *Bracton on the Laws and Customs of England.* Translated with commentary by Samuel E. Thorne. 4 vols. Buffalo, N.Y.: W. S. Hein, 1997. [Latin and English].

[Gratian]. *Corpus iuris canonici.* Edited by Emil Richter. Revised by Emil Friedberg. 2 vols. Leipzig, Germany: Tauschnitz, 1879. Reprint Graz, Austria: Akademische Druck, 1955.

[Justinian]. *The Digest of Justinian.* Edited by Paul Krüger and Theodor Mommsen. Translated by Alan Watson. 4 vols. Philadelphia: University of Pennsylvania Press, 1985. [Latin and English ed.].

Las Siete Partidas. Translated by Samuel P. Scott. Edited by Robert I. Burns. The Middle Ages. 5 vols. Philadelphia: University of Pennsylvania Press, 2001. [See esp. vols. 3–4].

Secondary Sources

Barna, Gianluigi. "Un contratto di concubinato in Corsica nel XIIIe secolo." *Rivista di storia del diritto italiano* 22 (1949): 43–56.

Brundage, James A. "Concubinage and Marriage in Medieval Canon Law." *Journal of Medieval History* 1 (1975): 1–17.

———. *Law, Sex and Society in Medieval Europe.* Chicago: University of Chicago Press, 1987.

Helmholz, R. H. "Concubinage, Western." In *Dictionary of the Middle Ages,* edited by Joseph R. Strayer, 3: 529–30. New York: Scribner's, 1983.

Marmon, Shaun E. "Concubinage, Islamic." In *Dictionary of the Middle Ages,* edited by Joseph R. Strayer, 3: 527–29. *See above entry.*

Poulmarède, Jacques. "Concubinage." In *Dictionnaire du Moyen Âge,* edited by Claude Gauvard, Alain de Libera and Michel Zink, 328. Quadrige. Paris: Presses Universitaires de France, 2002.

Salisbury, Joyce E., ed. *Sex in the Middle Ages.* Garland Medieval Casebooks, 3. New York and London: Garland, 1991. [Important essays by major scholars, concubinage mentioned passim].

Sellar, W. H. D. "Marriage, Divorce and Concubinage in Gaelic Scotland." *Transactions of the Gaelic Society of Inverness* 51 (1981): 463–78.

Stafford, Pauline. *Queens, Concubines and Dowagers: The King's Wife in the Early Middle Ages.* Athens: University of Georgia Press, 1983.

Ullmann, Walter. *Law and Politics in the Middle Ages: An Introduction to the Sources of Medieval Political Ideas.* Ithaca, N.Y.: Cornell University Press, 1975.

NADIA MARGOLIS

CONFRATERNITIES/FRATERNITIES. See **Guilds, Women in**

CONSTANCE. *See Belle Hélène de Constantinople;*
Griselda

CONSTANCE OF CASTILE (d. 1478). A Spanish abbess and author of devotional treatises, Constance of Castile (Constanza de Castilla) was born to a noble family and raised in the prison where her father, Prince Juan, spent most of his adult life. Her legitimate royal lineage posed a potential threat to the descendants of the usurper of the

Castilian throne, which may explain why her cousin, Queen Catherine, placed her in the Dominican convent of Santo Domingo el Real in Madrid, perhaps around 1406. By 1416, Constanza had already been elected abbess, and her young age suggests that the queen may have influenced the election. Constanza was proud of her royal birth, and those she dealt with acknowledged it by mentioning her in documents as both princess and prioress.

Constanza's royal blood gave her great influence at court. Her leadership and the crown's patronage made possible the era of her convent's greatest material splendor. Constanza supervised a building program that resulted in the completion of the community's main chapel and the construction of the convent church and refectory. She governed Santo Domingo el Real as prioress for some fifty years, stepping down in 1465, probably because of her advanced age. She died in 1478.

The prayers, devotional treatises, and liturgical offices written by Constanza are brought together in Manuscript 7495 of the Biblioteca Nacional (Madrid). In some cases the rubrics indicate that Constanza is copying out a well-known prayer or translating texts written by an Apostolic Father, as is the case of the letters of St. Ignatius of Antioch. Nonetheless, folio 82v contains a sort of bibliography in which Constanza explicitly identifies herself as the author of many of the works copied in the manuscript, naming specifically the initial *Oración* (*Prayer*), the *Oras de los clavos* (*Hours of the Nails*), the *Quinze gozos* (*Fifteen Joys*), the *Siete angustias* (*Seven Sorrows*), and the *Letanía de la Virgen* (*Litany of Our Lady*) (ed. Wilkins).

Folio 82v also contains passages in which Constanza pauses to reflect on her works and on herself as author. She views her compositions as a means of praising and serving God. Perhaps because of her royal descent, Constanza voices little anxiety over the question of authorial authority. Although she uses the topos of false modesty, emphasizing her ignorance and her status as a sinner, unlike other medieval women writers she does not relate such formulas of humility to her female gender, adopting instead the more generic and thereby not gender-specific status of sinner. At the end of the *Oras*, Constanza renounces any passage that may be contrary to the teachings of the Church, attributing such lapses to her weakness and to the evil influence of Satan. Although frailty and susceptibility to diabolical temptation were negative attributes commonly ascribed to women in the Middle Ages, it is once again significant that Constanza fails to associate her shortcomings with her female gender.

In Constanza's version of the *Quinze gozos*, the Joys are the pretext for a series of petitions asking for the Virgin's intercession. While Constanza includes the more or less traditional seven Joys, eight additional Joys give her version its particular orientation by emphasizing and extolling the Virgin's maternity. Thus, Constanza beseeches the Virgin's intercession by virtue of the joy with which she carried Christ for nine months in the tabernacle of her belly, the joy and sweetness with which she gave birth to the Son of God, the joy of being the mother of God, the joy of the milk of her breasts, and the joy she experienced while diapering, nursing, cradling, and kissing Christ. One must assume that Constanza's insistence on the Virgin's experience of motherhood is a conscious choice on her part, for other long versions of the Joys amplify the traditional seven differently. Constanza thus creates for her female audience a poetic world without adult men in which she celebrates such female bodily functions as nursing and such maternal activities as diapering and cradling.

Constanza's most ambitious work, her *Oración*, is an extended meditation on the life of Christ, divided into forty-four chapters, to be recited before Communion. Although the text's first-person voice is twice identified with that of Constanza, its rubric indicates that the author envisions her work as being read by other persons as well, most likely the other nuns in her convent. Such other users of the text are asked to remember Constanza in their prayers so that she can receive part of the benefits that Christ will give them for reciting it. This means that it is not the composition of the prayer that its author regards as particularly meritorious for her salvation; rather, the writing of the prayer is an effort that will eventually be rewarded through its recitation by other pious readers.

In each chapter, after briefly evoking a significant incident of Christ's life, Constanza observes that He accomplished such and such a deed for her benefit and, in the process, illustrated some particularly desirable virtue. Theologically, the *Oración* concentrates on the Passion and thereby on the suffering humanity of Christ, but also calls attention to the Virgin Mary's *compassio*. Constanza's identity as both princess and prioress is also evident. Ever conscious of her family ties, she prays for the souls of her departed royal relatives. In her capacity as prioress, Constanza asks God to bless the nuns in her charge, and the very composition of the work is directly related to her role as leader and teacher of the community.

Public preaching was reserved for the friars of the First Order of St. Dominic, while the nuns of the Second Order remained cloistered and derived their identity above all from their life of prayer. Thus, the devotional texts that make up Constanza's collected works represent a crucial aspect of the community's daily existence and are central to the prioress's self-image and to that of her companions as Dominican nuns.

See also Convents; María de Ajofrín; Mary, Blessed Virgin, in the Middle Ages; Teresa de Cartagena

BIBLIOGRAPHY

Primary Source
Constanza de Castilla. *Book of Devotions. Libro de devociones y oficios*. Edited by Constance L. Wilkins. Exeter Hispanic Texts, 52. Exeter, U.K.: University of Exeter Press, 1998.

Secondary Sources
Huélamo San José, Ana María. "El devocionario de la dominica Sor Constanza." *Boletín de la Asociación Española de Archiveros, Bibliotecarios, Museólogos y Documentalistas* 42: 2 (1992): 133–47.
Surtz, Ronald E. *Writing Women in Late Medieval and Early Modern Spain: The Mothers of Saint Teresa of Avila*. Philadelphia: University of Pennsylvania Press, 1995.

RONALD E. SURTZ

CONVENT CHRONICLES. *See* **Sister-Books** (*Schwesternbücher*)

CONVENTS. The term *convents*, deriving from Latin *convenio* ("to assemble, meet") and *conventum* ("agreement"), signified an association united by a common purpose. Ecclesiastically, it can mean either the domicile of the association or the community itself, of either gender, though in modern times it is applied more exclusively to women religious.

The two orders in the European Middle Ages whose houses originally were called convents, especially in Italy, were the Mendicant orders, so-called because their members were forbidden to own property and therefore sustained themselves by begging and working in the towns, where they would preach and hear confession. The original Mendicant Friars were the Dominicans and Franciscans. The very first house that St. Dominic (c.1172–1221) created in Prouille, France, in 1207 was a female institution, as was San Damiano, established by St. Francis (1181/2–1226) in Assisi for St. Clare (1193/4–1253) in 1212. In their founders' minds, these convents did not represent new forms of female monasticism. They multiplied rapidly, and their members struggled at length in the thirteenth century before they were accepted—in a

The Cistercian nuns at Valladolid receiving their charter from Queen Maria de Molina. Courtesy of North Wind Picture Archives.

sense, "promoted"—as the Second Order of the Preachers and the Second Order of Friars Minor. (The First and Second Orders consisting of professed men and women, respectively, and the Third Orders were secular penitents and originally, Mendicants.)

The main preoccupation of St. Dominic, born in Caleruega (Castile, Spain), was to convert the Cathars, a powerful heretical sect through much of Mediterranean Europe, around Fanjeaux, in southwestern France, their stronghold with several houses of heretics. Here, Dominic first assembled twelve women who were converted to a life of prayer and satisfaction, and in 1207, he obtained episcopal (i.e., from the Church bishops) permission to establish at Prouille, in the church of Notre-Dame a convent for them, to be directed by a nearby male community. He obtained donations for his project; for example, the church of St. Martin of Limoux was a gift from Viscount Berengar of Narbonne. He could thus build a double monastery, reserving its spiritual direction for himself and giving temporal administration over the female convent to Guillelmine Fanjeaux, its prioress until her death in 1225.

Dominic, in his capacity as a canon, probably gave a *regula* (rule)—a set of spiritual and administrative guidelines—to the female community (1213) at Prouille. Whether this rule conformed to others of the time, particularly the female Cistercian rule (named for the strict Benedictine order founded at Cîteaux, France, in 1098) or resembled the female Premonstratensian rule (from St. Norbert, founder of Prémontré, northern France, in 1120; resembling the Rule of St. Augustine), we do not know, since its details have not come down to us. In 1215, a papal protection of Prouille's goods followed, and in 1216, the clerks depending on Dominic, prior of St. Romain of Toulouse, were established as an Augustinian canonical order, with Prouille mentioned as a dependency of St. Romain. Because it was the first house Dominic founded, even before St. Romain, Prouille's status remained ambiguous because of its separate origins from the bull (papal decree) normally governing all convents in St. Romain: their founding and privileges. Prouille's standing was finally settled in 1218, when a papal bull recognized it as an independent community, belonging to the Preaching Order.

Dominic established a female convent in Madrid in 1218, and in 1219, he reunited in Rome in San Sisto (St. Sixtus) some sixty sisters from Santa Maria de Tempulo, San Bibiano, and some smaller communities. Eight sisters from Prouille supervised the Rome facility and assured that the customs were observed. Six brothers saw to their spiritual needs. Their rule resembled the rule of Prouille slightly modified by Dominic in 1220–1221. In 1223, the general of the order, Jordan of Saxony, established the convent of Sant' Agnes in Bologna, for which he tried to obtain the rule from Prouille, but the latter could not find the text of its rule. Thus he turned to San Sisto, whose rule of thus became the form of life of the Second Order of the Dominicans, resembling the Premonstratensian rule. Humbert of Romans, general of the order from 1254 to 1263, at the chapter general of Valenciennes (France) in 1259, gave the *Constitutions of the Nuns of the Order of Preachers*, resembling the San Sisto rule, to all the female convents. The sisters had to accept it, but the provincials could add *admonitiones* (suggestions and corrections) to it that further regulated the life of the Dominican nuns.

Prouille was divided into two convents, with two separate churches, the female St. Maria and the male St. Martin. The female choir was split off from the church. The female convent had a *hospitium* (lodging) where the sisters' parents could take a meal but could not sleep. All the sisters shared a common dormitory, and there was an infirmary. They shared the cellar (provisions storehouse) with the brothers. The brothers' convent had a secular apothecary, and numerous other dependencies, such as workshops and granges, supervised by the friars.

The whole order, both the masculine and feminine parts, was directed by a master general. Subordinate to him were the provincials, and, at the head of each community were the priors, who supervised the male and the double houses. In the case of a double house (male and female religious), the prior had total spiritual jurisdiction, guarded the cloister of the female convent, visited the female convent annually, directed its chapter, and corrected all the sisters, including the prioress. He appointed the confessors, the chaplains, and the procurators. The latter directed the agricultural exploitation of the double monastery. The females also oversaw vassals of the convent.

The prioress exercised immediate authority over the sisters. She was elected by the sisters, generally for three years, and was confirmed by the provincial or the master-general. If the prioress was not chosen within a month, she was selected by the provincial. The prioress presided over chapter meetings, saw that the rule and discipline were observed, and directed the sisters at work. In some convents, the prior and prioress shared administrative duties, selecting eight sisters to help them. Elsewhere, the prioress was assisted by the subprioress, the mistress of the novices (new members), the cellaress (keeper of the cellar, i.e., provisions), and the supervisor of the rule. Nuns were admitted usually at age eleven and education continued until age fourteen. Certain female convents received members as young as seven and admitted them to the profession at twelve. Some female convents also had *conversae* (lay sisters) who helped with the lower jobs.

Although no other female community on the Prouille model was founded in France until 1283, in Italy and Germany the development of such convents occurred very rapidly. Nevertheless, in 1224, it was decided at the chapter general of Paris that the foundation of female houses was to be suspended. The Lombard provincial wanted to withdraw from Sant' Agnes of Bologna all the brothers but in 1226 Honorius III forbade the chapter to abandon the sisters of Bologna. The question was raised again in 1228 and 1235, and the Dominican brothers stopped serving the sisters. Only Prouille and Madrid were able to obtain from Pope Gregory IX (1236) a plan to have a prior and four brothers at their convent. In 1238, Raymond of Peñafort (c.1180–1275), master-general (and later, saint), acquired from Gregory IX a decree that he would not incorporate any more female houses into the Dominican order. But Innocent IV from 1244 to 1252 gave licenses to nineteen female convents. However, in 1252 and 1253, once again the female convents came under the supervision of the bishops. The situation lasted until 1267 when Clement IV withdrew the 1253 privilege of Innocent IV that was renewed by Alexander IV in 1259, which reconstituted the government of the sisters by the brothers, making it somewhat easier for the priors to accommodate their program to the women's convents. The priors did not have to live in the monastery but could nominate chaplains who did.

As of 1303, there were forty-two female convents in Italy, seventy-four in Germany, thirteen in France, eight in Spain, six in Bohemia, three in Poland, and three in Hungary. The Dominican historian Bernard Gui (c.1261–1331) spoke of two in Scandinavia, but actually there were two in Sweden and one in Denmark. In England, the first Dominican female convent was founded in 1356. Since the Council of Trent (1545–1563) these convents fell under the episcopal jurisdiction.

The Dominicans also had to accept Gregory IV's wish that they supervise the convents of St. Marie-Madeleine, founded by Canon Rodolphe of the Cathedral of Saint-Maurice at Hildesheim, central Germany in 1225. Gregory IX in 1227 regulated the order and imposed on it the rules of Citeaux. But in 1232, he changed his mind and gave the rule of St. Augustine, following San Sisto of Rome. Thus, the Order of the Penitents had to accept the government of the Order of Preachers, except in towns where there was not a house. There they relied on different Augustinian communities.

St. Francis was not as efficient an administrator as St. Dominic but he was joined by one of the most respected women saints, Clara (Clare), who advocated absolute poverty and complete dependence on God. After Clare's ordination at Portiuncula (Santa Maria degli Angeli), their favorite chapel near Assisi in 1212, St. Francis installed her in a Benedictine monastery of San Paolo, then in the small house at Sant'Angelo in Panzo near Assisi, and finally at San Damiano in Assisi, which had as its mark from the start, poverty and claustration (enclosure). In 1215, St. Francis gave Clare and her companions a *formula vitae* (prescription for life), resembling the text he probably composed for the brothers. Unfortunately, we have only two passages from it surviving in Clare's writings. Since it was not detailed, in 1215 St. Francis adopted the Rule of St. Benedict for the sisters, modified by his earlier *formula vitae*. Following Francis's death in 1226, Clare continued to defend their ideals of devout poverty and composed a rule of strict observance that was accepted for her convent, San Damiano, by Clement IV shortly before her death in 1253.

The story of the Second Order of St. Francis—called variously Poor Clares, Poor Ladies, Poor Recluses, Order of San Damianó, the Clarisses (in France), Order of St. Clare—paralleled that of the Dominican sisters; the friars were reluctant to care for them despite the sanctity of the nuns' lives. The Clarisses had to fight for fifty years before it became acceptable for the friars to work for them, "not out of duty but out of love."

Clare's determination to adhere to the principles set down by St. Francis caused such concern that Pope Honorius III appointed Ugolino of Segni (or Hugolino Segni), a personal friend of St. Francis, as cardinal protector of both male and female Franciscans (1218). Ugolino in turn had Honorius issue a bull placing all Poor Clare houses under papal ownership. Ugolino also extended a new rule, basically Benedictine, to the female communities that came to be founded in rapid succession after San Damiano: Monticello near Florence, Monteluce near Perugia, Santa Maria near Siena, and Santa Maria di Gattaiola in the diocese of Lucca. This rule, however, omitted two essential points: deepest penury and spiritual direction by the Friars Minor. Soon also, Ugolino changed his mind about spiritual direction. He appointed Brother Pacifique as visitor and entrusted the Minors with governing the Poor Clares, still without fulfilling the privilege of poverty. Meanwhile, in 1227 Ugolino assumed the papacy as Pope Gregory IX, and in 1228, upon arriving in Assisi for the canonization of St. Francis, he offered property and income to all the Poor Clares, urging them to renounce their vow of poverty. This was rejected by Clare who then obtained from the pope an order, not a bull, allowing the sisters of San Damiano to live in absolute indigence. Nevertheless, Ugolino's rule remained in effect in most female houses of San Damiano until 1248.

Many of the communities were not poor. For example, Spello in 1232 accepted at the urging of the papacy a good part of the abbey of San Silvestro in Subiaso. Or at Milan, the community of Poor Clares was founded in 1223 when the convent was built on the land next to the church of San Apollinare. Subsequently, the church and more land were given to the sisters, and in 1233, they had received the hospital of San Biagio of Monza with all its possessions. In 1246, the hospital of San Giorgio became the nuns' property. Despite their proclaimed poverty, their convent was flourishing: in 1236 there were forty nuns, and in 1251, this number increased to sixty.

Some convents, of course, did follow the principle of poverty. The famous house at Prague was established by Agnes, daughter of the King of Bohemia (1203/1211–1282). She was engaged to Emperor Frederick II but appealed to the pope and then entered the community and became abbess in 1234, believing in strict poverty. At first, Gregory IX was adamant. He refused to confer such a rule on the convent, and in 1235 he gave the Hospital of St. Francis to the sisters. Fortunately, Agnes found a helpful ally in Clare. They sent the pope letter after letter, and finally, in 1238, the pope granted the convent at Prague the same privilege of poverty that he had conferred on San Damiano. Agnes then proceeded to write a rule, but the pope rejected it. Another royal lady, Isabella, the sister of King (later, St.) Louis IX of France (1214–1270), composed a rule for the convent she founded at Longchamps, Paris. Her rule was accepted for other foundations in 1263 by Urban IV, but its influence remained limited, being adopted only at Cordelières-de-Saint-Marcel in Paris, Blois, Toulouse, and Palestrina.

Gregory's successor (ignoring Celestine IV's two-year reign), Pope Innocent IV (r. 1243–1254) conceived of the plan of having the brothers supervise the sisters. He charged the order's general with the direction, visitation, and correction of the sisters in 1245. In addition, he gave a rule to the sisters giving all responsibility for them to the friars. But the lovely dream did not materialize. Innocent IV was attacked from both sides: the brothers thought the charge too onerous; the sisters objected to the limitation of the cardinal protector and the mitigation of the *privilegium paupertatis* (privilege of poverty).

Finally, Urban IV, together with the minister-general of the Franciscans, Bonaventure (theologian and future saint, c.1217–1274) appeased the two sides. Urban wrote a rule according to which the Friars Minor had to protect the Poor Clares. Bonaventure told the sisters that the brothers accepted this out of fraternal love and intervened only in convents willing to sign the "instrumentum nostrae libertatis" ("instrument of our liberty"). The brothers thus had only spiritual direction; they were only assistants to the cardinal protector. Despite the publication of the rule of Urban IV in 1264, the situation remained difficult. The sisters accepted the rule only to avoid falling under the jurisdiction of the bishops and losing all their privileges. Later, however, the bull of Boniface VIII (1298) gave the sisters all immunities enjoyed by the friars. Their government depended on the cardinal protector who had to have the help of the provincials naming the visitors. Further, each house was to have a chaplain to hear confession and administer the sacraments. While it was desirable that he be selected from among the Friars Minor, the cardinal protector could appoint anyone to that office.

As we have seen, the Rule of St. Clare insisted on "lady poverty," and it had some of the brothers to do begging for her. Moreover, they took a vow of total silence, which yielded only in moments of dire necessity. Very strict abstinence also prevailed: no wine, never any cooked food on Wednesdays and Fridays, and fasting on bread and water four days a week at Lent, and three days a week during Advent and at vigils if one wished. The sisters, including the abbess, slept on boards in a dormitory. The clothing and the haircut also followed the gravest discipline.

For Ugolino, the Rule of St. Benedict was also the foundation but he extended it with directions concerning the entrance into the convent and an examination of the qualities of the postulants. But he did not say anything about the novitiate (probationary period for a new member, or novice), age of admission, or the *numerus clausus* (required number of enclosed members). In addition, he included that exit from the convent was possible only if one was called to make a new foundation. No one was to enter the house without papal authorization. Innocent IV supplemented Ugolino's rule with certain provisions: that divine office was to be said by a Franciscan; the name of St. Francis had to be mentioned during the service; the duration of the novitiate must be regulated. Urban IV's rule of twenty-six chapters was extensive and minutely detailed while containing scant doctrinal innovation. To the three vows, he united those of perpetual and absolute enclosure. He urged against old, infirm, and inept postulants, and prescribed the dates of confessions and the sacraments to be administered to the ill. He covers the vow of silence but also recreation, to be spent in pious conversation. He dictated how the abbess should be elected, her confirmation, and her holding a weekly chapter. Travel to Rome was forbidden under penalty of excommunication. A convent could expect the official visitor once a year, who was empowered to depose the abbess if he found her unsatisfactory, and also receive the suggestions of the sisters and direct the chaplains and the converts.

By 1400, there were about 400 convents, of which about 250 were in Italy. The communities in France and Spain were the next most numerous. In Germany there were only about twenty-five convents. England had only three houses as of 1364–1365, and there is no trace of Poor Clares in Scotland or Ireland. Poland, Dalmatia, and Hungary had a significant number of convents, and there were houses in Cyprus, Crete, and Negropont (now Euboea and Chalcis, Greece). The convents varied in size: Cracow and Naples had at least 250 nuns, but they were exceptionally large; most larger houses contained fifty to eighty members, and the smallest only three. It has been estimated that around 1400 there were about 15,000 sisters.

In the fourteenth century, many houses fell short of the ideals Urban IV set for them. Thus in the early fifteenth century, the reforms of St. Colette of Corbie (1381–1447), who was born at the famous Benedictine monastery at Corbie, Picardy (France), became quite popular. She was first a Beguine; she then entered the Poor Clares at Moncel, but found the rule too lax and therefore became a recluse. But her visions of St. Francis complaining about the slackening of his order proved more than she could bear. She requested once again the cancellation of her vows to found a community where she would live like St. Clare with her companions. Indeed, by her death in 1447, Colette restored seventeen monastic houses in France for her branch, which became known as the Colettine Poor Clares.

In Italy, the preaching of St. Bernardino of Siena (1380–1444) and St. John (Giovanni) Capistrano (1386–1456) was so inspirational that several female convents decided on correction and placed themselves under the oversight of the Observantines or Observants (Fratres de Observantia, founded 1368)—Franciscans seeking to "observe" their rule with extreme and relentless rigor—in the fifteenth century. A number of the Benedictine and Augustinian orders also began to adopt the strict discipline of the Poor Clares. In Spain, the Conceptualists, founded in Galina by Beatrice, left the Cistercians after Beatrice's death (1495) and bound themselves to the rule of the Observants. In France at about the same time, the Order of Annunciation was linked with the Observants, although it developed as an exclusively feminine order.

See also Agnes of Bohemia, Blessed; *Ancrene Riwle*; Beguines; Chelles, Nun of; Clare of Assisi, St.; Colette of Corbie, St.; Double Monasteries; Dress, Religious Women's (Western, Christian); Guglielmites; *Periculoso*; Rules for Canonesses, Nuns, and Recluses; Scribes and Scriptoria

BIBLIOGRAPHY

Primary Sources
Benedict, St. *RB 1980: The Rule of St. Benedict in Latin and in English.* Edited and translated by Timothy Fry et al. Collegeville, Minn.: Liturgical Press, 1981. [More recent editions in English only].
Francis, St. [Rule, etc.]. *Écrits.* Edited by Kajetan Esser. Translated [Modern French] with notes by Théophile Desbonnets. Sources Chrétiennes, 285. 2nd ed. Paris: Éditions du Cerf, 2003. [Original Latin text with Modern French trans. and notes; Esser also critically edited Francis's complete works, 1976, etc.].
Gui, Bernard. *See below* in Hinnebusch.
Jordan of Saxony. *Life among the Saints. The Letters of Bl. Jordan of Saxony to Bl. Diana of Andalo.* Translated by Kathleen Pond. London: Bloomsbury, 1958.
———. *The New Life of St. Dominic.* Translated by E. McEniry. Columbus, Ohio: Columban Press, 1926.

Secondary Sources
Coakley, John. "Gender and Authority of Friars: The Significance of Holy Women for Thirteenth-Century Franciscans and Dominicans." *Crusade History* 60 (1991): 445–20.
Discry, Fernand. "La Règle des pénitents de Ste. Marie Madeleine, d'après le ms. de St. Quirin de Huy." *Académie royale de Belgique. Bulletin de la Commission royale d'histoire* 121 (1956): 85–145.
Fontette, Micheline de. *Les Religieuses à l'âge du droit canon. Recherches sur les structures juridiques des branches féminines des ordres.* 89–151. Bibliothèque de la Société d'Histoire Ecclésiastique de France. Paris: J. Vrin, 1967.
Hinnebusch, William A. *The History of the Dominican Order.* 2 vols. Staten Island, N.Y.: Alba House, 1966–1973.
Moorman, John R. H. *A History of the Franciscan Order; from its Origins to the Year 1517.* Oxford: Clarendon, 1968.

———. *Medieval Franciscan Houses.* St. Bonaventure, N.Y.: Franciscan Institute, 1983.

Ranft, Patricia. *Women and the Religious Life in Premodern Europe.* New York: St. Martin's, 1996.

Stoud, Debra L. "The Production and Preservation of Letters by Fourteenth-Century Dominican Nuns." *Medieval Studies* 53 (1991): 309–20.

Venarde, Bruce L. *Women's Monasticism and Medieval Society: Nunneries in France and England, 890–1215.* Ithaca, N.Y., and London: Cornell University Press, 1998.

SUZANNE FONAY WEMPLE

Portrait of Caterina Cornaro, wife of King James II of Cyprus, dressed as St. Catherine of Alexandria, c.1542. © Alinart/Art Resource, NY.

CORNARO, CATERINA (1454–1510). Caterina Cornaro was queen of Cyprus. Born to a prominent Venetian family owning property and important commercial interests on the island of Cyprus, Caterina was educated at the Convent of St. Benedict in Padua. She remained there until 1469, when a marriage was arranged for the celebrated beauty with James II of Cyprus. They were married in 1472. Despite his illegitimate birth into the ruling Lusignan family, James had usurped the throne from his half-sister Charlotte of Lusignan and her husband Louis of Savoy in 1460. On James's marriage to Caterina, the Venetian senate formally adopted the bride and provided her dowry, thus enabling the republic to gain influence in Cyprus while supporting James's tenuous reign. Although the bride was welcomed in Famagusta with great ceremony, on June 5, 1473, James II was killed in a conspiracy. Their son, born after his death, was proclaimed King James III, only to die in 1474, whereupon Caterina reigned for a number of years, fending off, with the aid of the Venetian navy, various threats to depose her. Not surprisingly, her principal rival for the crown of Cyprus was Charlotte of Lusignan, who persisted in fomenting diplomatic intrigues from the moment she was overthrown against James, then Caterina as Venetian puppets, making the widowed queen's status little better than that of a prisoner in her own realm, both protected and completely dominated by Venice. Charlotte's nearly thirty years of plotting finally succeeded to the extent that, in 1489, the Venitian government persuaded Caterina, a queen without an heir, to retire and cede her rights to the doge of Venice.

As her reward for this gesture, she received certain lands in Cyprus, and also the fiefdom and castle of Asolo, near Treviso, where she lived for the next twenty-one years, establishing there the brilliant court, renowned for fostering arts and letters, as described by the humanist Cardinal Pietro Bembo. Her beauty, tragic situation, and love of the arts continued to inspire artists and composers throughout the centuries, notably in Giorgione's contemporary portrait of her (finished by Titian), now in the Uffizi, and in two nineteenth-century operas, by Donizetti, Balfe, and Halévy.

See also Rosamond, Fair; Shore, Elizabeth (Jane)

BIBLIOGRAPHY

Primary Sources
Bembo, Pietro. *Gli Asolani*. Edited by Giorgio Dilemmi. Florence: Accademia della Crusca. 1991.
————. *Gli Asolani*. Translated by Rudolf B. Gottfried. Bloomington: Indiana University Press,
1954. Reprint Freeport, N.Y.: Books for Libraries Press, 1971.

Secondary Sources
Antinoro-Polizzi, Joseph A. *Lady of Asolo: A Pictorial History of the Life and Times of Caterina
Cornaro*. Rochester, N.Y.: Ayers Printing, 1985.
Brion, Marcel. *Caterina Cornaro, reine de Chypre*. Paris: Albin Michel, 1945.
Campolieti, Giuseppe. *Caterina Cornaro, Signora di Asolo*. Milan, Italy: Camunia, 1987.
Crane, T. F. *Italian Social Customs of the Sixteenth Century and Their Influence upon the Literatures of
Europe*. New Haven, Conn.: Yale University Press, 1920.
Hunt, David, et al., eds. *Caterina Cornaro*, London: Trigraph/Bank of Cyprus, 1989.

CHARITY CANNON WILLARD

CORPUS DOMINI. *See* **Catherine of Bologna, St.**

COUNTESS OF DIE. *See* **Comtessa de Dia**

COURTESY BOOKS (12th–15th centuries). Courtesy books or manuals are part of
conduct literature, which, in its most positive light, provides systematic guidelines for
success in the world to men and women, each manual usually aiming at a specific class,
milieu or profession, and gender. Women's manuals, almost always in the vernacular, usually dealt with maintaining a household—whether a castle, manor, or urban dwelling—
along with rules of etiquette appropriate to that class and setting. Because almost all were
authored by men, these manuals for women have come to be seen by modern scholars as
yet another vehicle of patriarchal containment, one eliciting voluntary submission to
architectural and bodily enclosure for both pragmatic and spiritual reasons, in a way
analogous to monastic rules for nuns. Although some sort of conduct manual existed
in cultures around the world—for example, the *Classic of Filial Piety for Girls*, written in
Tang dynasty China, and the Talmud's teachings for Jewish women—this discussion
focuses on European courtesy books, since these were the most numerous and influential.
However, a striking characteristic in all courtesy manuals for women, regardless of nationality, is the similarity of their basic prescriptions.

The principal categories of sources for the European manuals derived from Old and
New Testament literature (especially the so-called Wisdom Books and Gospels), and
distillations of Classical Roman moralists circulating in various medieval compilations.
Such materials include biblical exempla (moral tales), the so-called *dicta* of Cato and
Solomon, letters of the Church Fathers (early founders of orthodox Church doctrine)—
particularly Tertullian (d. c.225), in *Ad uxorem* (*To Wives*), *De cultu feminarum* (*On the
Cult of Women*), *De monogamia* (*On Monogamy*); Ambrose of Milan (d. 397) in, for
example, *De virginibus* (*On Virgins*), *De institutione virginis* (*On the Education of Virgins*);
Jerome (d. 420), for example, in his *Epistula ad Eustochium*, or letter to Eustochium

extolling virginity; and Augustine (d. 430) in *De sancta virginitate* (*On Holy Virginity*) and *De bono viduitatis ad Juliam* (*To Julia on Being a Good Widow*)—and collections of proverbs and customs. Certain medieval religious moral works, rather like monastic rules composed in Latin, such as the learned Anglo-Saxon Aldhelm (d. 709) in *De laudibus virginitatis* (*In Praise of Virginity*) advocated virginity and the "second virginity" (chastity for widows) as the highest virtue for women, who were also counseled to lead rather ascetic lives.

In secular literature, an interesting representation of women's role in chivalric training is Chrétien de Troyes's *Perceval, ou le Conte du Graal* (*Perceval, or The Story of the Holy Grail* [c. 1185]), a courtly romance about the education of young Perceval, an aspiring ideal knight, whose first authority for good conduct is his mother—whom he must learn to cease citing to avoid annoying his male mentors, as he progresses. Quasi-manuals, or "arts," of love also appeared, such as those by the French cleric Andreas Capellanus, or André le Chapelain (*De amore*, late twelfth century), and Juan Ruiz (d. 1250), archpriest of Hita (*El Libro de buen amor* [*The Book of Good Love*]), but these were rather tongue-in-cheek, with the latter being more of a picaresque autobiography with allegorical moral-spiritual interludes, closer to Jean de Meun's irreverent continuation to the *Roman de la Rose* (*Romance of the Rose*, 1265–1275).

More serious and manual-like in tone and design were the medieval French translations (thir-

Woman combing her hair while her husband admires her in bedroom. Folio 6R of 1475 French manuscript book of miniatures. © The Art Archive/Musée Condé Chantilly/Dagli Orti.

teenth century) of the Roman poet Ovid (43 B.C.E.–17 C.E.), especially his *Ars amatoria* (*Art of Loving*) and *Remedia amoris* (*Love's Remedy*)—the anonymous *Clef d'Amors* (*Key of Love*) and Jacques d'Amiens's *L'art d'amors* and *Li remedes d'amors*—for these "trained" men and women to become objects of sexual pleasure while following the chivalric code. Also popular, originating in Muslim Spain was Ibn Hazm's elegant Arabic treatise on love, known in English as the *Ring of the Dove* (early eleventh century). Courtly literature replaced the Church Fathers' *virginitas* with *fin'amors* (refined, "courtly" love) as the ideal woman's virtue.

By contrast, and although they owe much to these patristic (Church Fathers) and courtly traditions, true courtesy manuals, especially those of the later Middle Ages (fourteenth to fifteenth centuries), were destined for men and women in the real world, with practical, everyday concerns; hence their composition in the vernacular (nonmonastic women rarely learned Latin) and their decidedly practical approach and structure. Conduct manuals not only help the reader to succeed in his or her sphere, and furnish husbands with capable domestic partners, but they also help society at large to keep its members—particulary women— in their proper place.

Probably the first true conduct manual, while remaining in the courtly, *fin'amors* tradition, was the troubadour Garin lo Brun's *Ensenhamen* (*Instructions*) of the late twelfth century in Occitan (or Provençal, the language of southern France), the title signaling a mini-genre of which there are eight by different authors (Krueger 1995; Monson). Garin begins typically enough by advising women to be clean and to dress neatly. He diverges from religious rules in having them wear soft, attractive clothing. They should comport themselves gracefully, speak minimally and in well-modulated tones, and adapt to their companions' moods. Garin, a bit self-interested, allows his women to flirt, but only with trustworthy and discreet men—and to be kind and generous with troubadours. Other pertinent *ensenhamen* are those by the famous Lombard (northern-Italian) troubadour Sordel (*Ensenhamen d'onor* [*Instruction in Honor*], early to mid-1200s), which, being more Platonic than erotic, emphasizes a woman's protection of her honor, and by the Catalan troubadour Amanieu de Sescar (*Ensenhamen de la donzela* [*Instructions for a Damsel*], c.1280), ingeniously reproducing typical lovers' conversation for purposes of demonstration. Many of the earlier, more courtly advice books were written in verse to enhance their appeal to courtiers.

In northern France, the authors tended to be clerics rather than courtiers, thus portending a sterner, more austere, neo-patristic outlook than that of their southern counterparts, especially toward women. Étienne de Fougères, chaplain to King Henry II of England and bishop of Rennes, France, in his *Livre des Manières* (*Book of Manners, Ways and Means*, 1174–1178) enumerates all the various estates and classes of society, rather daringly pointing a critical finger at each, as he places women at the bottom of his social ladder, after peasants and merchants, lamenting that they cannot all be as worthy as his patron and dedicatee, the countess of Hereford. Robert of Blois (fl. mid-1200s), in his more menacingly titled *Chastoiement des Dames* (*Ladies' Chastisement*), recommends temperance in dress, diet and drink, and obedience to the husband. Yet Robert is in the world enough to at least counsel women on handling flirtatious advances. Another northern cleric, Durand of Champagne, composed the first mirror for princesses (those for princes already being quite abundant), the *Speculum Dominarum* (*Mirror for Women Rulers*), in which he adapted his profession's patristic values to secular, royal needs. Queen Jeanne de Navarre (Joan of Navarre, 1273–1305), wife of the French king Philippe le Bel (Philip the Fair, 1268–1314) had commissioned this work of Durand, who was her confessor. Not surprisingly, Durand focused on developing the princess's spiritual rather than administrative qualities, exhorting her to be merciful toward her subjects' requests, to cultivate piety, faith, hope, and charity. That Durand penned his advice in Latin betokens his belief, like Jerome's, that women should be educated according to a curriculum that included Latin. Yet even this princess must obey her husband. Since the *Speculum*, being in Latin, hardly ventured beyond the court in its influence, it was soon translated into French, its readers' rank also somewhat universalized, as the *Miroir des Dames* (*Mirror for Ladies*, fourteenth to fifteenth centuries), attaining sufficient popularity to warrant another translation later by Ysambert de Saint-Léger during the early sixteenth century for the Renaissance.

From the late thirteenth century onward, courtesy books extended their audience beyond the ranks of noblewomen to those of the rising middle class. Furthermore, most of these treatises were composed by the envisioned reader's family members, for example, fathers to daughters, of which three survive: those by Louis IX, Geoffroi de La Tour Landry, and an unnamed middle-class Spanish father. The king of France, Louis IX (St. Louis, 1214–1270) intended his *Enseignements à sa fille Isabelle* (*Instructions for His Daughter Isabelle*) as a complement to his larger treatise to his son, the future Philippe III, the *Enseignements à Philippe*, both done c.1267–1268. Louis's advice reflects his deep piety and love of justice, grounded in his biblical patristic and philosophical readings. Geoffroi de La Tour Landry (c.1330–c.1405), author of the *Livre du Chevalier de La Tour Landry pour l'enseignement de ses filles* (*Book of the Knight of La Tour Landry for the Instruction of His Daughters*), was a nobleman of Anjou (western France) who fought in the Hundred Years War. Together with his general reading and life experience, Geoffroi also borrowed from an anonymous Franciscan treatise, the *Miroir des bonnes femmes* (*Mirror of Good Women*, thirteenth century) for its vivid hagiographical episodes used to illustrate his practical counsel urging modesty, propriety, humility, silence (except in wisely advising her husband in private), chastity, and once married, uncompromising fidelity. He strongly warns against sexual temptation, vanity in dress, and general overindulgence, depicting the harsh punishments awaiting disobedient women. Geoffroi does favor education, provided the reading material is moral and Christian. One of the most popular courtesy books ever, the *Livre du Chevalier de La Tour Landry* was translated into Middle-High German (c.1450) and Middle English. The fifteenth-century Spanish *Castigos y do[c]trinas que un sabio dava a sus hijas* (*Chastisements and Doctrines of a Wise Man to His Daughters*) follows a similar vein.

Several treatises purport to be from mothers to daughters, but their authorship by actual women, rather than male authors posing as women, has not been conclusively determined. The Italian *Dodici avvertimenti che deve dara la madre alla figliuola quando la manda a marito* (*Twelve Warnings a Mother Should Give Her Daughter Demanded in Marriage*, c.1300) appears to represent a more feminine point of view in its emphasis on how to avoid a husband's wrath. A German poem, *Die Winsbeckin* (1200s), a female counterpart to *Der Winsbecke* for young men, is cast as a dialogue between a Bavarian noblewoman and her daughter (see Rasmussen). It recommends moderation overall but takes a less stern view of courtly love than its French male contemporaries, arguing that, when properly pursued— by avoiding false, deceitful suitors—love can be a serious, ennobling passion that need not be incompatible with marriage. The anonymous Middle-English *Good Wife Taught Her Daughter* (1300s) is also structured as a dialogue, but this time between a middle-class mother and daughter. Like Geoffroi de La Tour Landry, this work extols modesty, piety, obedience to her husband, and chastity, together with advice on thrifty household management and strict, thorough education of one's children. In light of the prescriptions given here compared to those for noblewomen, middle-class women enjoyed more freedom than aristocratic women: they could go into town on their own and sell their wares—provided they did not attend such unsavory events as wrestling matches or loiter in taverns. Similar concerns characterize the contemporaneous *Good Wyfe Wold a Pylgremage* and *The Thewis of Gud Women* (*The Customs of Good Women*).

A third type of familial conduct manual, by an older husband for his young wife, conveyed upper-middle-class values in the *Mesnagier de Paris* (*Householder of Paris*, 1392–1394) in an intriguing way from the outset. The aged husband/teacher announces that he will transform the nuptial bedroom nightly into a private classroom, his adolescent wife into his "virgin" pupil, in reviewing her daily conduct using the vocabulary of correction and chastisement, to avoid humiliation before outsiders. This exhaustive, three-part compendium combines moral wisdom with details of household management: housekeeping, gardening, cooking, training of servants, horses, and hawking. Though as staunchly moral as Geoffroi de La Tour Landry, the Mesnagier is more sympathetic toward the special needs of his youthful wife/pupil, as when he yields to her natural love of fine apparel, so long as it is dignified. He also advocates that she remarry after he (most likely) predeceases her. Another significant departure from the conservative standard is his welcoming of her advice to him, in private (La Tour Landry also allows this), citing examples of how wives can help husbands avoid foolish actions. Assuring her he would never test her as Walter did Griselda in Boccaccio's tale (mid-1300s), his general underlying strategy in this work is however, as always, containment and molding.

Certain courtesy books addressed women of all classes, thus affording a more complete picture of later medieval women's lives. One of these was actually composed by a woman. The earlier example, a poem by the Florentine, Francesco da Barberino (1264–1348), *Del reggimento e costumi di donna* (*On the Conduct and Manners of Women*, c.1310), lists some fifty rules treating the entire course of a woman's life from girlhood through old age, with special provisions according to each class and occupation, ranging from lay sisters, slaves, bakers, and produce merchants to beggars, shopkeepers, weavers, church attendants, and tavern-keepers. Francesco also discusses prenatal care, beauty, and the need for solace in time of crisis; he counsels on love problems, and even offers conversational tidbits and riddles. Such accommodation of variety is a distinctive feature of this otherwise decidedly masculine, conservative set of teachings. The one conduct manual known to have been by a woman, the prolific Italian-born French author Christine de Pizan's enormously popular *Livre des Trois Vertus* (*Book of the Three Virtues*, 1405–1406), often known by its sixteenth-century title *Tresor de la Cité des Dames* (*Treasure of the City of Ladies*), in a sense answers all her male precursors, yet without being disturbingly revolutionary. Dedicated to Duchess Marguerite of Guyenne, the *Trois Vertus* renders the principal message of Christine's revisionist history of women, the *Cité des Dames* (1404–1405), into practicable form for women of all classes, from the point of view of an exceptionally learned woman equally experienced in life's joys and harsh realities. Her spectrum of society extends from prostitutes to nobles; married, unmarried, and widowed; mostly secular but referring to nuns as well. Because of events in her own life, Christine was able to sympathize with and advise in three significant domains—widowhood, women's rights, and how women both commit and suffer from various forms of fraud, vanity, and envy—far beyond what male-authored manuals accommodate. She recommends that women avoid making enemies and to strive constantly to remain in favor with husbands, family, and friends. In a fourth theme, Christine stresses that women of all ranks and professions must fulfill their duties with dignity and competence to avert detractors, whether in household management and child-rearing or supervision of an estate, business, or country in her husband's absence. Finally, she warns against *fin'amors* in its usual form, the extramarital affair, because the woman always loses out on all levels much more than the man due to society's double standard. Better to seek the safety and pleasure of a stable family life over the passing thrill of *fol amors* ("foolish love"), causing the permanent loss of her reputation and all else she has worked for; *fin'amors* makes for beautiful poetry but practical misery. Although Christine often disappoints modern readers by espousing fundamentally conservative principles, including tolerating an occasionally brutal husband, she does so to protect her female readers in the long run: this is how life is; any disruption to the normal order of things will incur bad repercussions; real progress happens slowly. The successful woman knows how to exploit hypocrisy's mechanisms (e.g., dissimulation, discretion) without succumbing to hypocrisy itself. She does encourage virtuous women to be more educated and active in family and public life, in itself an innovative and constructive ideal for her time. The *Trois Vertus* was soon translated into several European languages, as were several of Christine's other moral-didactic and works, two of which were mirrors for princes, though very different from each other in style and substance: the earlier *Epistre que Othea la desse envoya a Hector de Troye* (*Epistle of the Goddess Othea to the Trojan Prince Hector*, 1400–1401) and the *Livre du Corps de Policie* (*Book of the Body Politic*, 1407); for her son she did the the *Enseignements moraux* (*Moral Instructions*, 1401–1402), plus other didactic works dedicated to rulers as part of Christine's one-woman plan to stem the tide of civil unrest and the Hundred Years War.

Men continued to instruct women nonetheless, as in the anonymous French *Miroir aux dames* (c.1450)—not to be confused with the above-mentioned *Miroir des Dames* translation of Durand's *Speculum* or the Franciscan *Miroir des bonnes femmes*—begins as a manual of good conduct, by a fair-minded male author addressing himself to "all women." But closer reading exposes it as a vituperation against current women's fashion: the high, multicornered headdress and dresses with revealing gauze front bodice panels that give women the appearance, and morally destructive force, of devils. The *Miroir's* quirky petulance, perhaps not without irony, make for amusing reading, as it bears all the marks of a once-dominant critical voice—that of the conservative male cleric—on the wane.

In the early French Renaissance, Anne de France (1460–1522), daughter of King Louis XI, would derive inspiration from both St. Louis's *Enseignements* and Christine's *Trois Vertus* for her manual to her fifteen-year-old daughter, Susanne, in c.1505. So successful was Anne as an example of noble female conduct and preceptor to her daughter that other nobles sent their new wives and daughters to be educated by her (Willard). Although not allowed to succeed her father because of her gender by Salic Law, her immense capabilities as princess were therefore not wasted. In sum, no matter what the era, social sphere, or authorial intention, courtesy books would prescribe and inculcate women with the need for the "chaste body, the silent mouth, and the closed door." Learning self-regulation co-evolved with learning to run a household, just as for men acquiring self-control was a prerequisite to controlling others (Salih).

See also Capellanus, Andreas; Celibacy; Childhood and Child-Rearing in the Middle Ages; China, Women in; Christine de Pizan; Dress, Courtly Women's; Dress, Religious Women's (Western, Christian); Eustochium, St.; Griselda; Law, Women in, Anglo-Saxon England; Paston, Margaret; Power of Women; Rules for Canonesses, Nuns, and Recluses; *Sachsenspiegel* and *Schwabenspiegel*; Salic Law; *Vertu du Sacrement de Mariage, Livre de la*; Virginity.

BIBLIOGRAPHY

Primary Sources
Anne de France. *Les Enseignements d'Anne de France, duchesse de Bourbonnois et d'Auvergne, à sa fille Susanne de Bourbon.* . . . Edited by Alphonse-Martiel Chazaud. Moulins, France: C. Desrosiers, 1878. Reprint Marseille: Laffitte, 1978.
The Babees Book, Aristotle's ABC, Urbanitatis, Stans Puer ad Mensam, The Lytille Childrenes Lytil Boke, The Bokes of Nurture of Hugh Rhodes and John Russell, Wynkyn de Worde's Book of Kervynge, The Booke of Demeanor, The Boke of Curtasye, Seager's Schoole of Vertue, etc. etc. with some French and

Latin Poems on Like Subjects and Some Forewards on Education in Early England. Edited by Frederick J. Furnivall. Early English Text Society [= EETS]. Original series, 32. London: N. Trübner & Co., 1868. Reprint New York: Greenwood Press, 1969.

Barberino, Francescoda. *Reggimento e costumi di donna.* Critical ed. by Giuseppe Sansone. Topazi, 3. 2nd ed. Rome: Zauli, 1995.

Castigos y do[c]trinas que un sabio dava a sus hijas. Edited by Hermann Knust. Revised by Hernán Sanchez Martínes de Pinillos and Nicasio S. Miguel. Tesis "Cum Laude," L: 8. Madrid: Fundación Universitaria Española, 2000. [Ed. based on Madrid Escoriál MS by Knust originally published in Madrid, 1878].

Christine de Pizan. *Le Livre des Trois Vertus.* Critical ed. by Charity Willard and Eric Hicks. Introduction and notes by Charity C. Willard. Bibliothèque du XVe siècle, 50. Paris: Honoré Champion, 1989.

———. *The Treasure of the City of Ladies, or The Book of the Three Virtues.* Translated with an introduction by Sarah Lawson. Harmondsworth, U.K. and New York: Penguin, 1985.

———. *A Medieval Woman's Mirror of Honor: The Treasure of the City of Ladies.* Translated with introduction by Charity C. Willard. Edited with introduction by Madeleine P. Cosman. New York: Bard Hall/Persea, 1989.

Dodici avvertimenti che deve dara la madre alla figliuola quando la manda a marito. Edited by Pietro Gori. Rome [?]: Salani, 1885.

Durand de Champagne. *Speculum dominarum.* Edited by A. Dubrulle. Diss. Ph.D., École des Chartes, 1988. *See also below under* Ysambert de Saint-Léger.

Ermengaud, Matfré. *Le Breviari d'amor.* Edited with introduction by Gabriel Azaïs. 2 vols. Geneva: Slatkine Reprints 1977. Original Béziers, 1862–1881. [Provençal text, French intro].

Étienne de Fougères. *Le Livre des manières.* Edited by R. Anthony Lodge. Textes Littéraires Français, 275. Geneva: Droz, 1979.

Garin lo Brun. [*Ensenhamen*]. *L'Ensengnament alla dame.* Critical ed. and translation (Italian) by Laura R. Bruno. Filologia occitanica. Studi e testi, 1. Rome: Archivio Guido Izzi, 1996. [Original Provençal with Italian translation and commentary].

Geoffroi de La Tour Landry. *Livre du Chevalier de la Tour Landry.* Edited by Anatole de Montaiglon. Bibliothèque Elzevirienne, 52. Paris: P. Jannet, 1854.

———. *The Book of the Knight in the Tower.* Translated by William Caxton, Edited by M. Y. Offord. EETS. Supplementary series, 2. London and New York: Oxford University Press, 1971.

———. *Der Ritter vom Turn.* Translated by Marquardt vom Stein. Edited by Ruth Harvey. Texte des späten Mittelalters und der frühen Neuzeit, 32. Berlin: Erich Schmidt, 1988. [Original Middle-High German text, Modern German and English commentary].

The Good Wife Taught Her Daughter, The Good Wyfe Wold a Pylgremage, The Thewis of Gud Women. Edited by Tauno Mustanoja. Suomalaisen Tiedeakatemian toimituksia, B: 61, 2. Helsinki: Suomalaisen Kirjallisuuden Scuran, 1948.

Louis IX (St. Louis). *Enseignements à Isabelle.* In *The Teachings of Saint Louis.* Critical ed. by David O'Connell. Studies in Romance Languages and Literatures, 116. Chapel Hill, N.C.: University of North Carolina Press, 1972.

Lydgate, John. *Table Manners for Children/Stans puer ad mensam.* Translated with introduction by Nicholas Orme. Foreword by Lotte Hellinga. Salisbury, U.K.: Perdrix Press, 1989. [Facsimile of Caxton's print of Lydgate (In Huntington Library) with Modern English trans.].

Le Mesnagier de Paris. Edited by Georgina E. Brereton and Janet M. Ferrier. Translation (French) and notes by Karin Ueltschi. Lettres gothiques. Paris: Livre de Poche, 1994. [Bilingual Middle French-Modern French with abundant notes].

Le Miroir aux Dames. Edited and introduced by Arthur Piaget. Neuchâtel, Switzerland: Attinger, 1908. [Middle-French text, Modern French notes].

Queene Elizabethes Achademy: A Booke of Precedence, etc., with Essays on Early Italian and German Books of Courtesy. Edited by Frederick J. Furnivall. EETS. e.s., 8. London: N. Trübner, 1869.

Robert de Blois. *Chastoiement des dames.* In *Robert de Blois, son œuvre didactique et narrative. Étude linguistique et littéraire.* Paris: Nizet, 1950.

[Winsbeckin]. *Winsbeckische Gedichte nebst Tirol und Fridebrant.* Edited by Albert Leitzmann. 3rd ed. revised by Ingo Reiffenstein. Altdeutsche Textbibliothek, 9. Tübingen, Germany: Max Niemeyer, 1962.

Ysambert de Saint-Léger. *Le Miroir des dames.* Critical ed. with introduction and notes by Camillo Marazza. Lecce, Italy: Milella, 1978. [Original sixteenth-century French text from Paris BnF MS fr. 1189 with Modern French commentary].

Secondary Sources

Ashley, Kathleen M. "Medieval Courtesy Literature and Dramatic Mirrors of Female Conduct." In *The Ideology of Conduct: Essays on Literature and the History of Sexuality*, edited by Nancy Armstrong and Leonard Tennenhouse, 25–38. New York: Methuen, 1987.

———, and Robert L. A. Clark, eds. *Medieval Conduct.* Medieval Cultures, 29. Minneapolis: University of Minnesota Press, 2001. [Landmark volume with essays by major scholars].

Bornstein, Diane. *The Lady in the Tower: Medieval Courtesy Literature for Women.* Hamden, Conn.: Archon Books, 1983.

———. *Mirrors of Courtesy.* Hamden, Conn.: Archon Books, 1975.

Dronzek, Anna. "Gendered Theories of Education in Fifteenth-Century Conduct Books." In Ashley and Clark, *see above.*

Hentsch, Alice A. *De la littérature didactique du moyen âge s'adressant spécialement aux femmes.* Halle, Germany: Universität Halle-Wittenberg; Cahors, France: Coueslant, 1903. Reprint Geneva: Slatkine, 1975.

Krueger, Roberta L. "Courtesy Books." In *Medieval France: An Encyclopedia*, edited by William W. Kibler and Grover Zinn, 265–67. New York and London: Garland, 1995.

———. "'Nouvelles choses'": Social Instability and the Problem of Fashion in the *Livre du Chevalier de la Tour Landry*, the *Ménagier de Paris*, and Christine de Pizan's *Livre des Trois Vertus*." In Ashley and Clark, *see above.*

Monson, Don A. *Les Ensenhamens occitans: essai de définition et de délimitation du genre.* Bibliothèque française et romane, C: 75. Paris: C. Klincksieck, 1981.

Nicholls, Jonathan. *The Matter of Courtesy: Medieval Courtesy Books and the Gawain Poet.* Woodbridge, U.K.: D. S. Brewer, 1985.

Rasmussen, Ann Marie. "Fathers to Think Back Through: The Middle High German Mother-Daughter and Father-Son Advice Poems Known as *Die Winsbeckin* and *Der Winsbecke*." In Ashley and Clark, *see above.*

Salih, Sarah. "At Home, Out of the House." In *The Cambridge Companion to Medieval Women's Writing*, edited by Carolyn Dinshaw and David Wallace, 124–40. Cambridge, U.K. and New York: Cambridge University Press, 2003.

Sponsler, Claire. *Drama and Resistance: Bodies, Goods, and Theatricality in Late Medieval England.* Medieval Cultures, 10. Minneapolis: University of Minnesota Press, 1997. [See especially ch. 3].

Stiller, Nikki. *Eve's Orphans: Mothers and Daughters in Medieval English Literature.* Westport, Conn.: Greenwood Press, 1980.

Willard, Charity C. "Anne de France, Reader of Christine de Pizan." In *The Reception of Christine de Pizan from the Fifteenth through the Nineteenth Centuries*, edited by Glenda K. McLeod, 59–70. Lewiston, N.Y.: Edwin Mellen Press, 1991.

GLENDA K. MCLEOD

COURTS OF LOVE/COURS D'AMOUR. *See* **Capellanus, Andreas; Marie de Champagne**

CRESSIDA. *See* **Criseyde**

Cressida talking with Pandarus by a window. From a fifteenth-century French manuscript copy of *Filostrato* by Boccaccio, translated into French by Pierre de Beauveau. Douce 331 fol. 15r. © The Art Archive/Bodleian Library Oxford/The Bodleian Library.

CRISEYDE. Criseyde (also Briseida, Cressida, Criseida, or Cresseid) is commonly known today as the unfaithful lover of Troilus because she transferred her affections to Diomede during the Trojan War. Benoît de Sainte-Maure first related this version of her story in the *Roman de Troie* (*Romance of Troy*), a French romance inspired by the story of the Trojan War and written about 1165–1170. Boccaccio and Chaucer adapted their versions of the story from Benoît. Boccaccio used the name Criseida in the Italian *Il Filostrato* (from Greek = "One overcome by love") written about 1336–1338, and Geoffrey Chaucer rewrote a version of Boccaccio's poem in English as *Troilus and Criseyde* in the mid-1380s. Finally, Robert Henryson related her death in *The Testament of Cresseid*, a Scottish poem written about 1470. There are also several other versions of her story, most notably in the Sicilian author Guido delle Colonne's *Historia destructionis Troiae* (*History of the Destruction of Troy*), completed in 1287, as well as a number of French prose versions, all adapted from Benoît's romance, and a French translation of Boccaccio, the *Roman de Troyle* (*Romance of Troilus*), by either Pierre or Louis de Beauvau (c.1383–1385), which Chaucer may also have used.

Briseida's story does not begin with Benoît. She appears in Homer's *Iliad* (eighth century B.C.E.) and other works in Greek and Latin, both in Antiquity and the Middle Ages before the twelfth century. Benoît seems to have known her principally through Dares, the alleged Trojan author who related the fall of Troy in a sixth-century prose chronicle titled the *De excidio Troiae historia* (*History of the Fall of Troy*). In it, Briseida appears as the sole woman in the descriptive catalogue of major Greek figures in the Trojan War. There is no explanation for her appearance as a Greek in this catalogue, and Dares says nothing about her life or family. The Homeric version reports the existence of two women, one the daughter of Brises, the other of Chryses—hence the patronymics Briseida and Criseyde—both of whom are concubines captured as spoils of war. Briseida reappears in Ovid, especially in his fictional series of love letters between mythological lovers entitled the *Heroides* (Letter iii), in a first-century Latin version of the *Iliad* known as the *Ilias latina* (*Latin Iliad*), and in the fourth-century chronicle, *Ephemeridos belli troyani* (*Chronicle of the Trojan War*), ascribed to a Greek author called simply Dictys. Briseida's name appears here and there in other works in which she conforms to the pre-Benoît tradition representing her as an abducted captive and concubine. One other important element preceding Benoît is a reference in Dictys to a Trojan woman Diomede is bringing back to his city, Argos—information that provokes the anger and jealousy of his wife—but Dictys says nothing further about the Trojan woman.

Briseida is already in love with Troilus when Benoît's version of her story begins. Almost immediately she is obliged to leave him and go to the Greek camp as part of an exchange of prisoners. To motivate the exchange, Benoît also makes Calchas her father; it is he who obtains her transfer from Troy to the Greek camp in the exchange of prisoners. Calchas, a Trojan seer, has earlier gone over to the Greeks on Apollo's order. Once among the Greeks, Briseida is courted by Diomede, gradually falling in love with him while setting aside her now hopeless love for Troilus. Still, she takes close to two years to transfer her affections and loyalty from Troilus to Diomede. Unlike later authors, Benoît focuses on her change of heart rather than on Troilus's growing awareness of her infidelity. Her affair with Troilus seems to be open and to bring her no shame. But her love for Diomede is another matter. The *Troie* narrator makes Briseida an example of unfaithful women. But he suggests the possibility of a second opinion on her conduct by reference to a queen (perhaps Eleanor of Aquitaine) who would have rejected his views and read Briseida in the context of the forced exchange of women in the Middle Ages. In the end, Briseida is anxious about her reputation for infidelity, but opts for Diomede because she has no other alternative, least of all any hope of ever being reunited with Troilus.

In *Il Filostrato* Boccaccio focuses on the love story for which the Trojan War serves only as a backdrop. He also invents the beginning of Troiolo's love and courtship of Criseida, which Benoît does not relate. He introduces Pandaro as Criseida's cousin, Troiolo's friend, and go-between or strategist in promoting his affair with Criseida. For her part, Criseida quickly decides to love Troiolo and actively participates in the first and second assignations, of which there are only three before she is sent to the Greek camp. She meets him in her home, comes to greet him after dismissing her entourage, and leads her lover to her bedroom on their first night together. Secrecy is important for them, unlike Benoît's lovers' situation in the *Roman de Troie*. However, once appearances are saved, Criseida participates actively in making the affair very pleasant for both lovers. After Criseida passes to the Greek camp, we hear relatively little about her after her new love for Diomede begins. Her transfer of affection to Diomede is, therefore, as uncomplicated as her first love for Troiolo; indeed, it is swift compared to Benoît's Briseida. The story elicits the narrator's reflections on women, as he compares and contrasts Criseida with his own lady, named Filomena, for whom he is writing the *Filostrato*. Perhaps this is an adaptation of Benoît's juxtaposition of Briseida and a virtuous queen.

In *Troilus and Criseyde*, Geoffrey Chaucer follows by and large Boccaccio's plot-line, including his focus on Troilus rather then Criseyde after her transfer to the Greek camp. She is still manipulated by Pandarus, here her uncle and an older man, and seduced by Troilus, albeit willingly, rather than courted and cooperative, as in Boccaccio. But Chaucer also restores some distinctive features of Benoît's version that Boccaccio had eliminated, notably a greater emphasis on her sense of guilt and responsibility for being unfaithful to Troilus. Chaucer's Criseyde evinces more conventional moral sense than her predecessors, and she is more introspective. Thus, although Pandarus's manipulations and Troilus's seduction are effective, she also admits to the latter a conscious personal decision to acquiesce in the seduction when they consummate their love. Nonetheless, Chaucer's Criseyde is more conscious of the harm discovery and gossip can do to their love than is her Italian counterpart.

None of these authors continues Criseyde's story beyond her affair with Diomede, although it was surely fraught with uncertainties since, in Benoît and the pre-Benoît tradition, Diomede was a married man. In Robert Henryson's *Testament of Cresseid*, Diomede abandons her after a brief affair. Deprived of all support and honor, Cresseid turns to a wanton life. The gods afflict her with leprosy (a venereal disease in the Middle Ages) after she blames them for her fate. Cresseid is then ostracized and dies a death that superficially punishes her for her inconstant life: the victimizer is the victim of fortune. But Henryson is not interested in the misogynist (anti-female) reading of her life. His Cresseid is indeed the victim of fortune. She is so badly disfigured by her disease that Troilus does not recognize her when he catches sight her during a truce. Yet something about her reminds him of his former love, and he generously gives her much gold as alms. Cresseid herself does not recognize her former lover. When she learns afterward who her momentary benefactor was, she dies. When Troilus learns her identity, he has her buried in a beautiful grave. Only Henryson has Troilus visit the Greek camp during a truce, a device Shakespeare will use in *Troilus and Cressida*. One wonders why earlier authors ignored this motif in their versions of the story.

In all these works, Criseyde or Briseida is exemplary in one of two ways. On the one hand, she exemplifies the inconstant woman. In the Piedmont marquis Thomas III of Saluzzo's *Livre du Chevalier errant* (*Book of the Wandering Knight*, 1390s), Brexis, or Briseida, is expelled from the court of love for infidelity, despite Diomede's defense of her conduct. On the other hand, references to her in catalogues of good or bad women are surprisingly rare; she does not often exemplify the unfaithful or inconstant woman. Women writers are especially critical of her conduct. Azalais d'Altier, an early thirteenth-century *trobairitz*, or woman troubadour, recalls Briseida's inconstancy to dissuade another women, perhaps the trobairitz Clara d'Anduza, from changing lovers. At the turn of the fifteenth century, Christine de Pizan condemns her in the *Mutacion de Fortune* (*Mutations of Fortune*, 1403) and the *Epistre Othea* (*Epistle of Othea*, 1399–1400) probably on the evidence of the thirteenth-century adaptation of the *Troie* found in the *Histoire ancienne jusqu'à César* (*Ancient History to the Time of Caesar*). Briseida is not named among the virtuous women in Christine de Pizan's feminist pantheon, the *Cité des dames* (*City of Ladies*, 1404–1405).

In the four major versions of her story treated above, her exemplary inconstancy is an instance of changeable humanity and the effects of fortune or destiny on love and free will. Human potential for change is itself problematic, no matter where it occurs and whom it hurts (see Mann). As time passes, even short spaces of time, human beings change with circumstances. In this context, authors like Benoît and Chaucer make Criseyde or Briseida not merely an example of inconstancy or false love but also a human problem. Her actions, thoughts, and sentiments stir feelings of pity and disapproval for the almost inevitable ways of the fallen or errant humanity in everyone. These are the sources of Chaucer's and Henryson's pity for their heroine's fate.

Criseyde or Briseida is, therefore, an example, a figure whose story could well appear in any medieval catalogue of exempla. As in her story, she is available for transfer into any context her fate may be made to illustrate. For the misogynist, her betrayal of Troilus may exemplify woman's perversity. For the medieval woman author, she may illustrate a woman's betrayal of her sex by a retreat from the moral fortitude and constancy that define the virtuous woman as much as the virtuous man. Benoît de Sainte-Maure does both, using Briseida first to justify his misogyny, then, afterward, to evoke the image of a woman of virtuous strength, a queen whose fortitude outshines Briseida's weakness. Boccaccio moves along similar lines in contrasting his own lady with Criseida. Criseyde's case thus raises the issue of human constancy, thereby obliging the reader or audience introspectively to resolve the issue on one side or the other. While elevating Briseida from the captive concubine of antique tradition to a noblewoman, Benoît invents a story about Briseida's change of heart. Briseida changes, but her change does not occur in a few days. It takes place over time as she fluctuates between two loves, the one for Troilus that becomes impossible, the other for Diomede that is new and appears attractive. Benoît's Briseida and her incarnations are all victims of superhuman powers and human mutability. They are aware of the bad example they set and sincerely regret it. These characteristics of Benoît's Briseida are variously rewritten by subsequent authors in the diverse, yet interfacing contexts of misogyny, human inconstancy, and destiny.

It is instructive to compare Briseida's career with that of her Trojan countryman, Aeneas, the hero of Virgil's Latin epic of the founding of Rome, the *Aeneid* (19 B.C.E.). Aeneas is an exile and a widower when he meets Dido, herself a widow and exile, and both begin a fateful new love. Both Boccaccio and Chaucer make Criseyde a widow. Both she and Aeneas have a new love—Troilus and Dido, respectively. But parental and divine authority forces them to leave their new love in spite of sincere attachment to their lovers. Again both find a new love—Briseida in Diomede, Aeneas in Lavinia. But there is a major difference between Briseida and Aeneas. He is a man, she a woman, and that difference seems to separate their fates. When Aeneas, a traitor to the Trojans in some traditions (including Benoît's *Troie*), leaves Troy, he goes on to found Rome. Briseida too passes from Troy to the enemy. She then disappears from her story after giving herself and her love to Diomede. Except in Henryson: there she is herself betrayed and becomes an exemplary victim of human change and destiny.

See also Arthurian Women; Azalais d'Altier; *Belle Dame Sans Merci*; Boccaccio, Women in, Works Other than *De Claris Mulieribus*; Chaucer, Geoffrey, Women in the Work of; Christine de Pizan; Clara d'Anduza; Dido in the Middle Ages; Medea in the Middle Ages; *Trobairitz*

BIBLIOGRAPHY

Primary Sources
Azalais d'Altier. *See under* Secondary Sources, *under* Poe, *below.*
Benoît de Sainte-Maure. *Le roman de Troie*. Critical ed. by Leopold Constans. 6 vols. Sociéte des Anciens Textes Français. Paris: Firmin-Didot, 1904–1912.
———. *Le Roman de Troie*. Extracts edited and translated by Emmanuèle Baumgartner and Françoise Vielliard. Livre de Poche: Lettres Gothiques. Paris: Librairie Générale Française, 1998.
Boccaccio, Giovanni. *Il Filostrato*. Edited by Vittore Branca. In *Tutte le opere*, general editor, Vittore Branca, vol. 2. Milan, Italy: Arnoldo Mondadori, 1964.
———. *Il Filostrato*. Edited by Vicenzo Pernicone. Translated by Robert P. apRoberts and Anna Bruni Seldis. Garland Library of Medieval Literature, A53. New York and London: Garland, 1986.
Chaucer, Geoffrey. *Troilus and Criseyde*. Edited by Stephen A. Barney. In *The Riverside Chaucer*, general editor, Larry D. Benson. 3rd ed. Boston: Houghton Mifflin, 1987.
Christine de Pizan. [*Cité des Dames*]. *Città delle dame*. Original Middle French edited by E. Jeffrey Richards. Translated (Italian) by Patrizia Caraffi. 2nd ed. revised. Milan, Italy: Luni, 1998.

————. *Epistre Othea*. Critical ed. by Gabriella Parussa. Textes Littéraires Français, 517. Paris: Droz, 1999.

————. *Livre de la Mutacion de Fortune*. Critical ed. by Suzanne Solente. 4 vols. Société des Anciens Textes Français. Paris: Picard, 1959–1966.

Clara d'Anduza. *See under* Secondary Sources, *under* Poe, *below.*

Henryson, Robert. *The Testament of Cresseid*. In *The Poems*, edited by Denton Fox. Oxford, U.K.: Clarendon Press, 1981.

Ovid. *Heroides*. Edited by Henri Borneque. Translated (French) by Marcel Prévost. Paris: Les Belles Lettres, 1991.

Roman de Troyle, Le. Edited by Gabriel Bianciotto. Publications de l'Université de Rouen, 75. 2 vols. Rouen, France: Université de Rouen, 1994.

Thomas III, Marquis of Saluzzo. *Le Livre du Chevalier errant*. Critical ed. by Marvin James Ward. Diss. Ph.D. University of North Carolina, Chapel Hill 1984. Ann Arbor, Mich.: UMI, 1984.

Virgil [P. Vergilius Maro]. *Aeneid*. In *Opera*, edited by R. A. B. Mynors. Revised ed. Oxford Classical Texts. Oxford, U.K.: Clarendon Press, 1972.

————. Translated by C. Day Lewis. Anchor Books. Garden City, N.Y.: Doubleday, 1952.

Secondary Sources

Benson, C. David. "Critic and Poet: What Lydgate and Henryson Did to Chaucer's Troilus and Criseyde." *Modern Language Quarterly* 53 (1992): 23–40. Reprinted in *Writing after Chaucer: Essential Readings in Chaucer and the Fifteenth Century*, edited by Daniel J. Pinti, 227–42. New York: Garland, 1998.

Boitani, Piero, ed. *The European Tragedy of Troilus*. Oxford, U.K.: Clarendon Press, 1989.

Engels, L. J. "Hector" and "Troilus." In *A Dictionary of Medieval Heroes. Characters in Medieval Narrative Traditions and Their Afterlife in Literature, Theatre and the Visual Arts*. Edited by Willem P. Gerritsen and Anthony G. van Melle. Translated by Tanis Guest, 139–45, 283–85. Woodbridge: Boydell Press, 1998.

Hansen, Inez. *Zwischen Epos und höfischem Roman: die Frauengestalten im Trojaroman des Benoît de Sainte-Maure*. Beitrage zur romanischen Philologie des Mittelalters, 8. Munich: Wilhelm Fink Verlag, 1971.

Jung, Marc-René. *La legende de Troie en France au moyen âge*. Romanica Helvetica, 114. Basel, Switzerland and Tübingen, Germany: Francke Verlag, 1996.

Kelly, Douglas. "The Invention of Briseida's Story in Benoît de Sainte-Maure's *Troie*." *Romance Philology* 48 (1995): 221–41.

Mann, Jill. *Geoffrey Chaucer, Feminist Readings*. Atlantic Highlands, N.J.: Humanities Press International, 1991.

Mieszkowski, Gretchen. "The Reception of Criseyde 1155–1500." *Transactions of the Connecticut Academy of Arts and Sciences* 43 (1969–1973): 71–153.

Minnis, Alastair, and Eric J. Johnson. "Chaucer's Criseyde and Feminine Fear." In *Medieval Women: Text and Contexts in Late Medieval Britain: Essays for Felicity Riddy*, edited by Jocelyn Wogan-Browne, Ann Hutchison, Arlyn Diamond et al., 199–216. Turnhout, Belgium: Brepols, 2000.

Nolan, Barbara. *Chaucer and the Tradition of the "Roman Antique."* Cambridge Studies in Medieval Literature, 15. Cambridge: Cambridge University Press, 1992.

Payen, Jean-Charles. *Le motif du repentir dans la littérature française médiévale (des origines à 1239)*, 286–292. Publications romanes et françaises, 98. Geneva: Droz, 1968.

Poe, Elizabeth W. "Another *salut d'amor*? Another *trobairitz*? In Defense of *Tanz salutz et tantas amors*." *Zeitschrift für romanische Philologie* 106 (1990): 314–37.

Wetherbee, Winthrop. *Chaucer and the Poets: An Essay on Troilus and Criseyde*. Ithaca, N.Y. and London: Cornell University Press, 1984.

DOUGLAS KELLY

CROSS DRESSING. *See* **Transvestism**

D

DAINA. The *daina* is Latvian folksong, arguably created mainly by women. Any folk literature is by its very nature anonymous and thus can be assumed to contain a fair proportion of material emanating from women, either as authors or as transmitters, although differences between these two categories in the oral tradition are frequently difficult to establish. In the Latvian *daina*, however, women's influence is dominant to a greater degree than seems to be the case in many other national areas and other forms of folk literature. Since the *daina* bears discernible medieval roots, one is entitled to view it as a product of medieval, and mainly female, authorship, albeit anonymous.

In terms of versification, the *daina* is usually trochaic (having two syllables, accent on the first, per metric foot), occasionally dactylic (having three syllables, accent on first, per metric foot), and contains four lines, with four metric feet in each line. Although it can be more properly regarded as a distich (two-line poem) of eight feet per line, the standard convention has always been to print it as a four-line poem. Because of its laconic style and also for other reasons, the *daina* was considered difficult to render into English, as demonstrated in the wide-ranging efforts at English translation included in Uriah Katzenelenbogen's work. More recently, however, we have the creative renditions of the *dainas* by Eso Benjamins, in which the translator follows a method he calls "agglomeration and selection," in which he infuses *daina* material into longer-metered poems more conducive to graceful English; the result being remarkably faithful to the wording and the spirit of the original short ones. These English versions are eminently readable and should convince the reader unfamiliar with Latvian of the *dainas'* great poetic worth.

As is common in folk literature, the cumulative number of *dainas* is impossible to ascertain. The first, and still classic, collection compiled by Krišjānis Barons (1835–1923) between 1894 and 1915, contains 35,789 "original" songs as well as numerous variants. Later research compiled close to a million *dainas* and their variants, which form part of the Latvian national folklore archives. Because the *daina* has always been the backbone, the flesh and blood, of Latvian culture, the monumentality of Barons's life's work on *dainas* earned him the lofty appellation, frequently encountered even in otherwise unemotional contexts such as literary histories, of Barontēvs (Father Barons). Most of the work done on the *daina* has been published in Latvian, with a small proportion of scholarship in Russian, Czech, and German. In Latvian the most important work is that of Ludis Berzīņš.

Philological evidence indicates that the *daina* goes back to before the eighth century, and through the subsequent centuries it changed relatively little. Although references to folksongs from the Latvian territory do appear in medieval sources, actual quotations are first preserved in documents connected with witches' trials in 1584, and the earliest full printed text of a folksong appears only in 1632. The latter, however, was found in the same form by Barons more than a quarter of a millennium later when he encountered it in the still-vital oral tradition.

The Baltic region (Latvia, Lithuania, Estonia, etc.) was one of the last to be Christianized in Europe, having long resisted the new religion. Tenacious native beliefs and religious practices endured despite the missionary efforts of German conquerors in the twelfth century, and as late as 1649, the date of publication of the Protestant missionary Einhorn's *Historia Lettica, das ist Beschreibung der Lettischen Nation* (*Lettish* [= Latvian] *History, that is, a Description of the Latvian Nation*), there is evidence of undiminished devotion on part of the Latvians to their pagan deities, and preeminently their goddesses. Not surprisingly then, the *daina*, although vigorously repressed, especially in its mythological manifestations, by foreign invaders striving to impose this totally different religion, Christianity, nevertheless preserved numerous vestiges of its most basic beliefs, such as tree animism. Mythological *dainas* are not as numerous as other kinds, but references to pagan deities, above all Laime, the goddess of good fortune, as well as occasionally her counterpart Nelaime (Bad Fortune), appear with great frequency in songs that can in no ordinary sense be classified as mythological. Equally popular is the figure of Jānis, an amalgam between a pre-Christian male deity and St. John the Baptist, but he appears exclusively in songs connected with the traditional Latvian midsummer festival.

It has been estimated (see Bücher) that women composed between 61 and 77 percent of all *dainas*, and observers of traditional Latvian customs in the eighteenth and nineteenth centuries agree that men did not usually indulge themselves in song; for women it formed constant accompaniment to their daily activities. For example, *dainas* like no. 118 attest to the view that it is the man's part to be silent. The internal evidence for female authorship is certainly strong. Since the *daina* typically expresses itself in the first person singular, the gender of the speaker is frequently identifiable as female, Latvian language being highly inflected. In addition to this, the songs contain many references to areas of experience or objects undeniably restricted to women, and mention of a father's authority, although frequent, is far less prominent than a sense of the all-pervasive influence of the mother and the everlasting bond between her and her offspring. The family has always been the traditional center of Latvian social life, and Latvian folksong, although overtly patriarchal in line with standard Indo-European practice, has in the Baltic area always been subtly dominated by the figure of the mother. The loss of political autonomy in the thirteenth century may well have reinforced the importance of the woman as the center (if not the head) of the family, as well as furthered the short, domestically oriented *daina* as the main form of poetry instead of (possibly lost) more heroic poems of preeminently male authorship. Yet another feature of the *daina*—and a most notable one—is its extraordinary predilection for diminutives, morphological formations used to express tenderness, affection, and other emotional nuances. Such vocabulary is by no means the property of women alone, yet as one of the most outstanding means of expression in the *daina*, it is often regarded as a factor that contributes to its notably feminine ethos.

This does not mean that the *daina* suffers from qualities frequently attributed to a feminine outlook: sentimentality, emotionality, and an overall narrowness due to limited experience. The emotion expressed in these songs, while frequently profound, is also very disciplined. They are "feminine in character . . . masculine [in] conception" (Andrups and Kalve), and appeal equally to men and women. Their imagery is powerful and very concise, expressing a deep, truly pagan love of nature and a demanding work ethic, while describing the influence of social forces, mainly familial, on the speaker. Relatively little interest is given to romantic love—indeed, the word "love" is conspicuous by its absence. Nor is uniquely individual experience their focus. This genre celebrates the collective and generic, rather than the particular and extraordinary. Hence, one of their most notable functions in Latvian culture is the inculcation and reinforcement of ethical values, yet without seeming heavily didactic. The *daina*'s exemplary role is thus analogous to that of the Latvian matriarch—the *mater familias*—the moral center and teacher of the family, by example as well as by precept.

See also *Chanson de femme* (Women's Song); *Frauenlied*; Music, Women Composers and Musicians; *Muwashshaḥ*; *Skáldkonur* (Old Norse-Icelandic Women Poets)

BIBLIOGRAPHY

Primary Sources
Barons, Krišjānis. *Latvju dainas*. 8 books in 6 vols. Jelgava, Latvia: H. I. Drawin, 1894–1915. Reprint Riga, Latvia: Liesma, 1985.
Benjamins, Eso. *Dearest Goddess: Translations from Latvian Folk Poetry*. Arlington, Va.: Current Nine, 1985.
Švābe, Arveds, Karlis Straubergs, and Edite Hauzenberga-Šturma. *Latviešu tautas dziesmas*. 12 vols. Copenhagen: Imanta, 1952–1956. [Edition with more modernized spellings, critical essays].
Melngailis, Emilis. *Latviešu muzikas folkloras materiali*, vols. 1–3. Riga: Liesma, 1951. [Offers probably the richest collection of pertinent music (about 4,500 melodies)].

Secondary Sources
Andrups, Jānis, and Vitauts Kalve, *Latvian Literature*. Translated by Ruth Speirs. Stockholm: Goppers, 1954.
Berziņš, Ludis. *Ievads latviešu tautas dzejā: metrika un stilistika*. Vol. 1. Riga, 1940. 2nd ed. Chicago: Baltu Filologu Kopa, 1959.
Biezais, Haralds. *Die Hauptgöttinnen der alten Letten*. Uppsala, Sweden: Almqvist & Wiksells, 1955.
Beldavs, A. V. "Goddesses in a Man's World, Latvian Matricentricity in Culture and Spheres of Influence in Society." *Journal of Baltic Studies* 8 (1977): 105–29.
Bücher, Karl. *Arbeit und Rhythmus*. 4th ed. Leipzig: Reinicke, 1909. 6th ed. 1924.
Katzenelenbogen, Uriah. *The Daina*. Introduction by Clarence A. Manning. Chicago: Lithuanian News, 1935. [Deals with the Lithuanian as well as the Latvian *daina* in selections and critical study].
Rūķe-Draviņa, Velta. "Einige Beobachtungen über die Frauensprache in Lettland." *Orbis* (1952): 53–73.

ZOJA PAVLOVSKIS-PETIT

DANSE MACABRE DES FEMMES (1482–1519). The *Danse macabre des femmes* (*Death's Dance of Women*) represents another type of pantheon, parade, or catalogue of women, in this case by providing a female complement to a distinctive visual arts and literary theme of the fifteenth century, the *Danse macabre* (or *macabré*), which first appeared in the *Danse macabre des hommes*—a display of how death overtakes men from all levels of society, from kings to paupers and fools (see Huizinga). The women's version again features death as the great social leveler of women ranging from queens to merchant women to prostitutes to, finally, the fool. The value of the *Danse macabre des femmes* is more historical-documentary, especially in its manuscripts' and printed editions' striking combination of image and text for morally-instructive purposes, than literary.

This "parade" reveals more than the predictable attitudes toward women; the accompanying illustrations furnish much information on women's dress and deportment along the various social ranks, occupations, and physical conditions. The different manuscripts and printed editions of the *Danse* also reflect the high level of literacy and artistic refinement among a growing number of upper-class women, especially powerful patrons like Anne of Brittany, queen of France (1477–1514) and Margaret of Austria, regent of the Netherlands (1480–1530), who actively sponsored works promoting women's elevated status during the late fifteenth and early sixteenth centuries.

The first *Danse macabre des hommes*, thought to have been authored 1424 by the noted chancellor of Notre Dame of Paris, Jean Gerson (1363–1429), with illustrations on the walls of the Church of the Innocents, was destroyed, with some vestiges, believed to have been copies, remaining at the Chaise-Dieu in Amiens (northern France). The first published edition, therefore, the men's *Danse* was printed by Guyot Marchant in September 1485. In July 1486, the renowned printer published, along with a new edition of the men's, the first printed edition of *Danse macabre des femmes*, of which a (nonillustrated) manuscript, now in Paris, Bibliothèque nationale de France fr. 1186, had already been executed in 1482. It is important to note that this first version of the women's *Danse*, containing thirty examples (the most minimal version of all seven from 1482–1519), differs from the more extensive Guyot Marchant print of 1486. The other printed edition, also by Marchant (1491), joins its predecessor in articulating the full didactic, text-image scheme for the death dance. The single illuminated manuscript, Paris, BnF. fr. 995 (no date but c.1500), containing thirty-two sumptuous (despite, or because of, their topic) miniatures within forty-four folios along with verse text, was patterned on the printed editions. The differences between the prints and the manuscripts often derive from the differences between print culture and manuscript culture, as Sandra Hindman demonstrates.

In a manner reminiscent of Dante's *Divina Commedia* (*Divine Comedy*, 1321), as well as a morality play, *La Mort* (Death) leads the characters along, speaking to them and us as the work unfolds; another speaker figure, *L'Acteur* (Authority), also plays an important role in elucidating the work's message. Many of the women "dancers" express an awareness of the damnation or salvation awaiting them. The aspect of social satire, alternating with grim reality, is more salient in the women's *Danse* than in the men's. The only negative stereotypes in the *Danse macabre des femmes* are those of the Witch and the Whore— yet not without a degree of sympathy—and *Baillive* (the Gossip).

Though not great literature in terms of its verses, this appropriation of yet another previously male-centered genre is creative by simply existing, joining the Roman author Ovid's *Heroides* (first century B.C.E.), the *Tournoiement des Dames/Frauenturnier* (*Tournament of Ladies*, thirteenth to fifteenth centuries), Boccaccio's *De casibus virorum illustrium* (*The Fates of Illustrious Men and Women*) and *De claris mulieribus* (*Famous Women*, c.1362–1375), Chaucer's *Legend of Good Women* (c.1385), Christine de Pizan's *Epistre Othea* (*Epistle of Othea*), *Mutacion de Fortune* (*Mutations of Fortune*), and *Cité des Dames*

(*City of Ladies*, 1404–1405), and Martin le Franc's *Champion des Dames* (*The Ladies' Champion*; 1440–1442), and others in enumerating women of all varieties and virtues. As Ann Harrison, the *Danse*'s modern editor and authority, suggests, because of the nature of its content and the cultural contexts its tradition represents, this *danse macabre* reveals itself to be more a "Woman's Dance of Life."

See also Boccaccio, Women in, *De Claris Mulieribus*; Bokenham, Osbern; Chaucer, Geoffrey, Women in the Work of; Christine de Pizan; *Frauenturnier*; Le Franc, Martin; Nine Worthy Women; *Tournoiement des Dames*

BIBLIOGRAPHY

Primary Sources
La Danse macabre de Guy Marchant. Edited by Pierre Champion. Chefs d'oeuvre du livre français, 2. Paris: Quatre Chemins, 1925.
The Danse Macabre of Women. Edition, translation, introduction by Ann Tukey Harrison with Sandra L. Hindman. Kent, Ohio and London: Kent State University Press, 1994. [Original Middle-French with English translation of BnF. fr. 995 plus commentary on all mss. and prints, with reproductions of the miniatures].

Secondary Sources
[See commentary to above edition].
Alexandre-Bidon, Danièle, and Cécile Treffort, eds. *À Réveiller les morts: la mort au quotidien dans l'Occident médiéval.* Preface by Jean Delumeau. Lyon, France: Presses Universitaires de Lyon, 1993. [Important volume containing articles by major scholars].
Huizinga, Johan. *The Autumn of the Middle Ages.* Translated by Rodney Payton and Ulrich Mammitzch. Chicago: University of Chicago Press, 1996. Original *Herfsttij der Middeleeuwen*, 1924.

NADIA MARGOLIS

DEATH'S DANCE OF WOMEN. *See Danse Macabre des Femmes*

DE CLARIS MULIERIBUS. *See Boccaccio, Women in, De Claris Mulieribus*

DESCHAMPS, EUSTACHE. *See Miroir de Mariage (Mirror of Marriage)*

DES CLERES ET NOBLES FEMMES. *See Boccaccio, Women in, Des Cleres et Nobles Femmes*

DESERT MOTHERS (4th–5th centuries). In early Christian times, it was common to cite the authority of a highly esteemed source as a "father" or "mother," respectively; hence, for example, the Fathers of the Church (Basil, Gregory of Nazianzus, Augustine, Jerome et al.) because their writings constituted the theological "birth" of the Church. Likewise with certain ascetics, the so-called Desert Fathers, and their female counterparts, the Desert Mothers, since many of them were living literally in the desert, for example, in the Egyptian Scetis (the southern Nitrian desert), or in another lonely place metaphorically resembling a desert.

The Early Ascetics. The ascetic movement of early Christianity was promoted by men as well as by women, as documented by a great number of Late Antique sources (see Albrecht 1986; Elm). The vast material includes anecdotal narratives, biographical summaries as well as extended vitae, scholarly treaties on asceticism, rules for monastic life and *apophthegmata*: the sayings or teachings of famous ascetics.

Though there were other types of women ascetics—those who followed ascetic lifestyles within normal households—this discussion attempts to treat the solitary ones. Occasionally, however, drawing sharp distinctions is difficult, and in cases where, even in the desert, it happened that a man and a woman who had dedicated themselves to continence lived together. But as a general rule, the Desert Fathers and Mothers of the fourth and fifth centuries were anchorites and hermits, living as solitarians or in loose communities. In time, monasteries and convents in the strict sense developed in the desert. A particular feature of early Syrian asceticism were wandering ascetics; the ones who chose each to live alone literally atop a pillar, with food brought by disciples or sympathetic onlookers, were called, from the Greek, *stylites* (= "pillar").

Accounts of the most typical Desert Mothers are found in various compilations. One, *Apophthegmata Patrum* (*Sayings of the Fathers*) also known as the *Alphabetical Collection* or *Gerontikon*, in Greek, documents the monastic communities of Egypt. Although not edited before the late fifth or early sixth century (presumably in Palestine), much older material was included. Another similar collection, available only in a Latin translation (sixth century), is the *Vitae Patrum* (*Lives of the Fathers*). The *Historia Monachorum in Aegypto* (*History of the Monks in Egypt*) is a kind of travel itinerary of the late fourth century, transmitted in both Greek and Latin translations. Other related sources include Palladius's *Paradise* (generally known as his *Lausiac History*, since it was dedicated to a certain Lausiacus, fifth century) and Theodoret of Cyrus's *Philotheos historia*, or in Latin, *Historia Religiosa* (*Religious History*, fifth century). The first equivalent collection of Western origin was the *Dialogues* of Gregory the Great in the late sixth century. Such collections of short lives and sayings of famous ascetics were passed on among later generations for the education of monks and nuns.

Although all of the aforementioned collections include more materials on men than on women, at least some of them were conceived on an egalitarian basis. Thus, the author (or later editor/redactor) of the *Lausiac History* stressed that this collection concerned "male and female Fathers." Out of seventy-one chapters, twenty deal with, as is clear from the titles, one or two prominent female ascetics (see Jensen 2003; 2001–2002). Later generations have sometimes singled out this significant, if relatively scarce, material on the "Mothers" from the original collections and assembled it into separate *Materika*, collections dealing with female ascetics only (see *Meterikon*, ed. Tsames). Particularly influential was the Greek *Apophthegmata* collection, containing the sayings connected with three mothers—Sara, Syncletica, and Theodora—alphabetically among the father's names.

In the ascetic milieu of formative Christianity, spiritual maturity and competence counted more than other more or less socially determinative categories. Such prioritization overrode economic class distinctions, in that well-to-do women and men chose to share the living conditions of the lower social strata with regard to food, dress, or personal hygiene. Other determinants—education, age, and gender—were also at least deemphasized. Authority was granted to the "spiritual father" or to the "spiritual mother," irrespective of their previous social position in the real world, which the ascetics had deliberately renounced.

It also became possible for women to transcend their social position as women, in accordance with the whole gender ideology common throughout the ancient Mediterranean, which allowed that, just as Egyptian desert monks, who were by natural age children, could be respected as fathers by gray-haired monks due to a superior spiritual maturity, so could women assume the spiritual rule over men by the same criterion. Also, incorporating vestiges of the real world perspective, within the ascetic scheme it could even serve as a special exercise in humility for a man to be subordinated to the spiritual care of a woman. That the categories of man and woman were not abolished altogether, even among ascetics, is shown eloquently in an episode connected with a female ascetic called Sara: Two anchorites come to see her, but as they are about to leave, they are overcome by the temptation to humiliate her. So they say to Sara, "See to it that your thoughts shall not become proud and you say: 'Look there, the hermits come to me, though I be but a woman.'" While misogyny is discernible here as in some other passages attributed to male ascetics, the sayings of the mothers are obviously free of such tendencies. Sara's answer, however, reflects the self-confidence of a female anchorite, in highly male-centered language: "According to nature I am a woman, but not according to my thoughts" (in *Apophthegmata*, "Sara," no. 4; *PG*, 65: 420/trans. in *Sayings*). Some testimonies have Sara utter as well: "It is I who am a man, you who are women" (Guy, 34).

The ascetic movement's ambivalence toward gender manifests itself in other ways. Since Antique Greek and Roman authors, New Testament Apocrypha (books outside the canonical New Testament), and patristic (by the Church Fathers) texts usually equated being a man with being a more perfect human, there existed a tendency to define female martyrs, ascetics, spiritual mothers, or any good female Christians as "quasi-men" or "manly women." According to the apocryphal Gospel of Thomas (Logion 114), Simon Peter's request that Mary (presumably the Magdalene) leave the followers of Jesus is rejected by the Lord's promise to make her "male" that she, too, might rise to heaven. The egalitarian ethic, therefore, opposes the historically more effective hierarchic conception, which is revealed not only in the construct of "the female man of God" (see Cloke), but also in the tendencies inside the ascetic movement toward misogyny (image of woman as seducer), separation of sexes (against spiritual partnerships and mixed monasteries, rules of seclusion), and general sexual pessimism. According to the theological "construct of the 'sexless' *parthenos*" ("virgin," applied to both sexes), ascetic life can lead to a "radical transcendence of gender" (Jensen 2003) over to the "heavenly way of life," and the *bion angelikon* (life of angels). In other words, transcendence of one's own sexuality in the ascetic life allows for the realization—echoing the old baptismal formula (from Galatians 3: 28): "there is neither male nor female"—that between men and women living in asceticism there should exist absolute equality, while in practice they would come to treat each other freely as "brothers and sisters."

Spiritual Motherhood. In principle, all provisions pertaining to spiritual fatherhood were equally valid for spiritual motherhood, as evidenced by the interchangeable use of the titles *abbas* (father) and *amma* (mother), *geros* (old man), and *graida* (old woman). These titles denote levels of spiritual maturity of either sex and their commensurate ability to guide spiritual lives. In the *Apophthegmata* collection, the spiritual child (Greek: *teknon*) receiving guidance corresponds to the same degree to an *abbas* as to the *amma*—irrespective of age and gender, as in "Abbas Zacharias," and the above-mentioned Sara

(*Amma Sara*). Those seeking advice from them could be other ascetics, or men and women living in the world, and also people just turning from worldly life to an ascetic lifestyle. Experienced ascetics attracted pupils who stayed with them, thus learning not only by words, but by sharing the life of their spiritual father or mother.

As a rule, the sayings ascribed to women correspond in origin and transmission process to that of their male colleagues, which indicates the real existence of situations affording spiritual mother-and-child relationship reflected within a spiritual teacher–pupil rapport among women as with men. The sayings were transmitted orally at first, and then transcribed as written documents through a process like that preserving the words of Jesus. For the sayings of Theodora and Sara, we could appropriately assume much authenticity. More problematical cases include sayings attributed to St. Syncletica, to whom we shall return: from their appearance in the framework of the *Apophthegmata* collection, they seem to have been lifted out of the *Syncletica-Vita* (*Life of Syncletica*).

A characteristic feature of male as well as female sayings is the spiritual experience behind them, their origins in personal ascetic practice—a source of charismatic appeal for the advice-seeker. In most cases, the reported scene ends in a sentence, comparable in linguistic shape to that of the neighboring ancient Oriental proverbs. With these it often shares the figurative language of the parable. Symbolic actions of prophetic meaning can also be found in the *Apophthegmata* tradition. Certain mnemotechnical (mechanics of memory) aids, for transmission and learning by heart, are a further significant feature (see Lilienfeld): The most typical ones—those of pregnant brevity, the simile, the enumeration—occur in traditions connected with both men and women.

An equally important feature is the recurring reference to the Bible, "behind which lies the knowing of large portions of the Holy Scripture by heart" (Lilienfeld). Not only is the specific Christian dimension of the guidance by the Desert Fathers and Mothers apparent here, it also reveals the high level of culture of the monastic milieu, so often disregarded by older research.

Desert Mothers: Real-Life Examples. From the above-mentioned, authoritative *ammas* of the *Apophthegma* collection, Theodora and Sara emerge as obviously historical figures. The reference point for determining Sara's lifetime is the testimony of Abbas Paphnutius (fourth century), who had lived for sixty years by the banks of the Nile as a hermit. Theodora was probably a leader of a female community close to Alexandria. Theodora can be dated accurately to the turn of the fifth century, as shown by her relationship to the Archbishop Theophilus of Alexandria (d. 412). She must have been a highly cultured woman of well-to-do background, who was obviously familiar with the theological controversies of her time. In her sayings, Theodora raises questions of biblical exegesis and dogmatic issues, for example, when she debates the Manichean sect's hatred of the body and also argues about the resurrection of the dead. In another saying ascribed to her, the presence of the paritetic (virgin-monk) formulation is remarkable (*Apophthegmata*, Theodora, no. 1, 5, 10). Later hagiographic tradition portrays her even as the author of books.

Returning to Syncletica, cited as a problematic case for authenticity, this is ironic, since she is the Desert Mother about whom we have the most biographical details. The vita of Syncletica describes her as the abbess of a convent giving spiritual advice to her nuns. However, we can only cautiously rely on the vita as a historical source because it presents her as a female pendant to St. Antony and a follower of St. Thecla (Albrecht 1986). It is probable that Syncletica's *vita*, modeled on the that of St. Antony, was compiled around a well-known name associated with a preexistent tradition of reported sayings. Syncletica's case is, however, useful, even if no Desert Mother named Syncletica actually lived, because it does attest the existence of women like her in that milieu.

From the *Apophthegmata* collection, we learn that Syncletica, Theodora, and Sara are not the only women amid numerous *abbas*, but they were the only named ones. Traditions connected with other female ascetics did not preserve any female names, though they did record their deeds. So we read about such anonymous examples as an anonymous hermit taken for a monk in her lifetime (*Apophtegmata*, "Bessarion," no. 4: PG, 65: 140–41), a penitent prostitute who chose to live as a recluse within a community of other religious women guided by an anonymous *amma*, and a virgin (*Apophtegmata*, "Serapion," no. 1; PG, 65: 413–16), who lived together with an anchorite (*Apophtegmata*, "Kassian," no. 2; PG, 65: 244). In any case, the women of the Egyptian Scetis commemorated in the *Apophthegmata* collection are not the only ones worth mentioning, we have chosen them as a representative segment. In our introduction, we pointed to other select ascetic sources referring to additional female ascetics, who, though not all of them lived literally in the desert, are presented in a manner similar to the accounts of Theodora, Sara, and Syncletica, that is, via recreating short episodes from their lives as well as with sayings. Considering this, the information on "desert mothers" is less ample than that referring to the male ascetics and their numbers might have been smaller than that of male anchorites—still, more information is at hand than handed over by conventional (Church) historiography.

See also Syrian-Christian Women; Teachers, Women as; Thecla, St.

BIBLIOGRAPHY

Primary Sources

Apophthegmata Patrum. In *Patrologia Graeca*, edited by J.-P. Migne [= PG], 65: 71–440. [Greek text only].
———. *The Sayings of the Desert Fathers: The Alphabetical Series*. Translated and introduced by Benedicta Ward. Foreword by M. Anthony. Cistercian Studies, 59. New ed. London: Mowbray. 1981. Original New York and London: Macmillan, 1975, 1980.
———. *Les Sentences des Pères du désert: Collection anonyme*. Translated (French) and Introduced by Lucien Regnault. Sablé-sur-Sarthe, France: Abbaye St.-Pierre de Solesmes, 1981.
Athanasius of Alexandria, [*Life of St. Antony*]. In PG, 26: 837–976. [Greek text only].
———. *Life of Antony*. Translated by Tim Vivian and A. N. Athanassakis et al. Foreword by Benedicta Ward. Cistercian Studies, 202. Kalamazoo, Mich.: Cistercian Publications, 2003.
Pseudo-Athanasius of Alexandria, [*Life of St. Syncletica*]. In PG, 28: 1485–1558. [Greek text only].
———. *Vie de Sainte Synclétique*. Translated by Odile B. Bernard. Foreword by Lucien Regnault. Spiritualité Orientale, 9. Bégrolles-en-Mauge, France: Abbaye de Bellefontaine, 1972.
Gregory the Great. *Dialogues*. Edited and translated (French) by Adalbert de Vogüé and Paul Antin. Sources chrétiennes, 251, 260, 265. 3 vols. Paris: Éditions du Cerf, 1978–1980. [Bilingual Latin-French ed.].
Historia monachorum in Aegypto. Critical ed. by André-Jean Festugière. Subsidia hagiographica, 34. Brussels: Société des Bollandistes, 1961. [Greek text, French notes].
Meterikon. Diegeseis, Apophthegmata kai Bioi ton hagion meteron tes eremu, asketerion kai hosion gynaikon tes Orthodoxu Ekklesias. Edited by Demetrios G. Tsames. Thessaloniki, Greece: Ekdoseis Adelphotetas "Hagia Makrina," 1990.
Palladius [*Historia Lausiaca*]. *The Lausiac History of Palladius*. Edited by Cuthbert Butler. Texts and studies, 6. 2 vol. Cambridge: Cambridge University Press, 1898–1904; Reprint Hildesheim: G. Olms 1967. [Greek text, English commentary].

————. *The Lausiac History.* Translated Robert T. Meyer. Ancient Christian Writers, 34. Westminster, Md.: Newman Press, 1965.

Theodoret of Cyrrhus [*Philotheos historia*]. *Histoire des moines de Syrie.* Critical ed. with notes and introduction by Pierre Canivet and Alice Leroy-Molinghen. Sources Chrétiennes, 234, 257. 2 vols. Paris: Éditions du Cerf. 1977–1979. [Bilingual Greek-French ed.].

————. *A History of the Monks of Syria.* Translated with introduction by Richard M. Price. Cistercian Studies, 88. Kalamazoo, Mich.: Cistercian Publications, 1985.

Thomas, Gospel of. *The Gospel According to Thomas.* Edited and translated by Antoine Guillaumont et al. Leiden, Netherlands: Brill; New York: Harper, 1959. [Bilingual Coptic-English ed.].

Vitae Patrum. In *Patrologia Latina*, edited by J.-P. Migne, 73: 855–1022.

————. *The Desert Fathers.* Translated by Helen Waddell. New Introduction by M. Basil Pennington. New York: Vintage, 1998.

Secondary Sources

Albrecht, Ruth. *Das Leben der heiligen Makrina auf dem Hintergrund der Thekla-Traditionen. Studien zu den Ursprüngen des weiblichen Mönchtums im 4. Jahrhundert in Kleinasien.* Forschungen zur Kirchen- und Dogmengeschichte, 38. Göttingen, Germany: Vandenhoeck & Ruprecht, 1986.

————. "Die Anfänge des weiblichen Mönchtums. Ein Versuch." *Erbe und Auftrag* 76 (2000): 388–400.

————. "Frühes weibliches Mönchtum." In *Aufbruch der Frauen. Herausforderungen und Perspektiven feministischer Theologie*, edited by Birgit Janetzky, Esther Mingram and Eva Pelkner, 50–65. Münster, Germany: Edition liberación, 1989.

Cloke, Gillian. *This Female Man of God: Women and Spiritual Power in the Patristic Age, AD 350–450.* London and New York: Routledge, 1995.

Elm, Susanna. *"Virgins of God": The Making of Asceticism in Late Antiquity.* Oxford Classical Monographs. Oxford: Clarendon Press, 1994.

Frank, Karl Suso. "Asketinnen in den Apophthegmata Patrum." *Erbe und Auftrag* 77 (2001–2003): 211–25.

Guy, Jean-Claude. *Recherches sur la tradition grecque des Apophtegmata Patrum.* Subsidia hagiographica, 36. 2nd ed. Brussels: Société des Bollandistes, 1984. Original 1962.

Hausherr, Irénée. *Spiritual Direction in the Early Christian East.* Translated by Anthony Gythiel. Foreword by Kallistos Ware. Cistercian Studies, 116. Kalamazoo, Mich.: Cistercian Publications 1990. Original *Direction spirituelle en Orient autrefois.* Rome, 1955.

Jensen, Anne. "Frauen in der Asketengeschichte "Das Paradies" von Palladios (Historia Lausiaca)." *Erbe und Auftrag* 77 (2001–2002): 99–116.

————. *God's Self-Confident Daughters: Early Christianity and the Liberation of Women.* Translated by O. C. Dean, Jr. Louisville, Ky.: Westminster John Knox Press, 1996. Original *Gottes selbstbewußte Töchter. Frauenemanzipation im frühen Christentum?* Freiburg, Germany: Herder, 1992. New ed. Theologische Frauenforschung in Europa, 9. Münster: LIT, 2003.

Lilienfeld, Fairy von. *Spiritualität des frühen Wüstenmönchtums: Gesammelte Aufsätze 1962 bis 1971.* Edited by Ruth Albrecht and Franciska Müller. Oikonomia, 18. Erlangen, Germany: Lehrstuhl für Geschichte und Theologie des christlichen Ostens, 1983.

Petersen-Szemerédy, Griet. *Zwischen Weltstadt und Wüste: Römische Asketinnen in der Spätantike. Eine Studie zu Motivation und Gestaltung der Askese christlicher Frauen Roms auf dem Hintergrund ihrer Zeit.* Forschungen zur Kirchen- und Dogmengeschichte, 54. Göttingen: Vandenhoeck & Ruprecht, 1993.

Swan, Laura. *The Forgotten Desert Mothers. Sayings, Lives and stories of Early Christian Women.* New York: Paulist Press, 2001.

Ward, Benedicta. *Apophthegmata Matrum.* Texte und Untersuchungen zur Geschichte der altchristlichen Literatur, 129 [= Studia Patristica, 16]: 63–66. Darmstadt, Germany: Wissenschaftliche Buchgesellschaft, 1985.

Zanetti, Ugo. "Apophtegmes et histoires édifiantes dans le synaxaire arménien." *Analecta Bollandiana* 105 (1987): 167–99.

EVA MARIA SYNEK

DHUODA (fl. c.843). Author of an extraordinary *Liber Manualis*, or handbook, of advice for William, her fifteen-year-old warrior son, the Duchess Dhuoda lived in ninth-century Uzès in the south of France. She reports that she composed the book from November 30, 841, to February 2, 843, while William was far from home serving his overlord. William's father was Bernard of Toulouse, a prominent fighter and feudal magnate, who had ordered his son William to pay feudal homage to young king Charles II the Bald (823–877) after the Battle of Fontenoy-en-Puisaye, on June 25, 841. Bernard hoped the gesture would make amends for his own lack of support in this fray and help the family regain their fiefs in Burgundy. Bernard's reputation as an alleged traitor and adulterer placed his relatives in severe jeopardy during a period marked by violence, when the disintegrating Carolingian empire, founded by Charlemagne in 800, was torn by internecine wars and foreign invasions. In her husband's absence, Dhuoda had her own feudal obligation to maintain the defense of Septimania, the region along the southern-French coast, even as she kept up her program of study and writing.

In perilous times, Dhuoda's book reveals a mother's worry for her son. Yet, she cleverly adorns her work with lyrics, acrostics, numerology, word play, and etymologies to entertain him, as she instructs him in pious and practical matters befitting the conduct of a well-born youth. Dhuoda expects her son to fraternize with great men, offer counsel in the king's hall, sit in courts of judgment, befriend pilgrims, widows, and orphans, pray assiduously at all hours, collect books, and read prodigiously. She counsels William in the pleasures and techniques of reading; she evidently loves to read herself. Her creative compilation draws on a range of literary types. The *Liber Manualis* is a long letter, following epistolary conventions. It also contains lyric poems, probably her own. Elaborate versifying lay within her grasp as she amply demonstrates. She relies on the Bible, especially the Psalms. She uses patristic (by the Church Fathers: early founders of Church doctrines, fourth through 5 centuries) commentaries, popular prayer books, and treatises on the vices and virtues. Among her authorities are "Doctors of the Church" St. Augustine (354–430) and St. Gregory the Great (c.540–604), and the encyclopedist Isidore of Seville (c.560–636). Her book is also a *genealogia* (Book 10), legitimizing the family's importance through brief rosters of recently dead kinfolk. She gives heed to William's relatives ostensibly for the purpose of prayer, though possibly with an eye to improving the family's fortunes.

Dhuoda's book belongs most clearly to the *speculum* or "mirror" genre, a work giving advice to princes and aristocratic youths. Favored in Dhuoda's day, this genre had many exemplars, represented by the works of, for example, the eighth- and ninth-century Carolingian scholars Alcuin, Einhard, and Jonas of Orléans, and encapsulated in the vernacular in Hrothgar's speech to Beowulf. The medieval model was St. Augustine's virtuous prince, in *The City of God* (5.24). Although a female precedent for Dhuoda's work exists in the seventh-century Herchenefreda, who sent a few short admonitory letters to her ecclesiastical son, Dhuoda's fully developed treatise is unique among mirrors of conduct. Not only does she educate her child as woman and mother, she insists on her special maternal role, not available to a male advisor. She wittily plays on the image of her own book as mirror; when her son refers to its pages, he can, through reading and prayer, gaze upon her as he would an image in a mirror.

Pierre Riché's editorial division, which finds general acceptance among scholars, organizes the *Liber Manualis* into five pithy personal introductions, a table of chapters, and eleven books. Dhuoda's *Incipit textus* (the text begins) announces her intent and explains her title, through word play; *Incipit liber* (the book begins) salutes William, lamenting her maternal plight; *Epigrama* (verse inscription) weaves her name and William's in acrostics; *Incipit prologus* (the prologue begins) defines the work as a "mirror"; *Praefatio* (preface) inscribes family facts, including the place and date of Dhuoda's wedding and the birthdates of sons William and Bernard, an unusual strategy for this time; and *Incipiunt capitula* (the chapters begin) is a chapter list that does not always match the actual chapters.

Book 1 addresses the love of God, and unfolds numerological correspondences among biblical and theological events. Book 2 discourses on the Trinity, on the three virtues of faith, hope, and charity, and on prayer. This last topic reflects the currently popular prayer manuals.

Book 3 establishes the patriarchal dynamic of the work as it applies in the world. From the reverence for God emanates feudal and filial veneration. Scriptural examples contrast Isaac's submission with Absalom's disobedience, intended to provoke an analogy in the reader's mind with the contemporary turmoil wrenching apart the imperial family of Louis the Pious and his sons. William owes unconditional love and loyalty to his biological father, Bernard. To his feudal lords, the boy owes thoughtful counsel, an obligation that has its material benefits. If William can make himself indispensable to his lord as a trusted counselor, he can advance his own career and gather dependable vassals of his own. He should press his advantage, respect men in power, and attach himself to the most forceful men of rank.

Book 4 is a treatise on the vices and virtues, another popular genre. The book also comments on the seven gifts of the Holy Spirit and on the eight Beatitudes, both scales of virtuous conduct that appear in varying forms throughout the Bible (most familiarly in Matthew 5:3–11 and Luke 6:20–22). Numerology recurs, with a meditation on their sum of fifteen.

Book 5 assesses human ordeals—wrongdoing, temptation, hardship, persecution, adversity, affliction, sickness—none of which must keep William from reverencing God. Book 6 enumerates fifteen stages to perfection, citing again the seven gifts of the Holy Spirit and the eight Beatitudes. Book 7 introduces the Augustinian idea of the double birth (carnal and spiritual) and the double death (temporal and eternal), stressing the importance of mothers.

Book 8 takes up William's specific prayer obligations: he must pray for clergy and kings, his overlord and his father, the souls of departed family members, and notably his uncle, the late Tedderic, his godfather and material benefactor. Book 9 numerologically treats the four letters of ADAM and the fifteen benedictions.

Book 10 summarizes. Lyrics open and close this section. Opening lyrics play on William's age, while acrostic verses based on his name review his mother's counsels. The ending contains Dhuoda's name acrostically plaited into her epitaph. Within this lyric frame, Dhuoda begs William to pray for the family, naming both herself and nine deceased forebears. Book 11 returns as an afterword, abbreviated from a current treatise, with directives on reciting the Psalms.

Dhuoda's husband and son William met tragic ends. Bernard was slain, accused by Charles the Bald of treachery; William was killed at age twenty-four when he turned against Charles and tried to seize the city of Barcelona. Dhuoda's younger son Bernard lived on, vengefully beleaguering Charles and earning the nickname of Hairy Paws ("the Fox"). One tradition claims that a descendent of Dhuoda's became William the Pious, duke of Aquitaine, founder of Cluny (909/10).

In addition to the human appeal of the *Liber Manualis* as a document arising out of ill-fated family circumstances, Dhuoda's book commands attention: (1) as a compendium of literary genres and traditions valued in the period, (2) as a record of the political and military scene of the post-Carolingian world, (3) as an overview of the religious conduct judged appropriate for the pious layman, (4) as an early educational guide for a juvenile of the warrior class, and (5) for its revelation of the status of at least one educated woman of the ninth century.

See also Childhood and Child-Rearing in the Middle Ages; Christine de Pizan; Courtesy Books; Teachers, Women as

BIBLIOGRAPHY

Primary Sources

Dhuoda. *Liber manualis. Handbook for her Warrior Son.* Edited and translated by Marcelle Thiébaux. Cambridge Medieval Classics, 8. Cambridge: Cambridge University Press, 1998. [Latin text and English translation, with notes].

———. *Manuel pour mon fils.* Edited by Pierre Riché. Translated by Bernard de Vrégille and Claude Mondésert, S. J. Sources chrétiennes, 225bis. Revised ed. Paris: Éditions du Cerf, 1991. Original 1975. [Latin text and French trans., with notes].

———. *Handbook for William: A Carolingian Woman's Counsel for her Son.* Translated with an introduction by Carol Neel. Regents Studies in Medieval Culture. Lincoln and London: University of Nebraska Press, 1995. Reprint Washington, D.C.: Catholic University of America Press, 1999. [English trans. only, with notes].

———. *Liber Manualis. Educare nel Medioevo. Per la Formazione di mio Figlio Manuale.* Edited by Inos Biffi. Translated by Gabriella Zanoletti. Introduction by Simona Gavinelli. Milan: Jaca Book, 1982. [Latin text, Italian notes and trans.].

Secondary Sources

Armstrong, Grace Morgan. "Engendering the Text: Marie de France and Dhuoda." In *Translatio Studii: Essays by His Students in Honor of Karl D. Uitti for his Sixty-Fifth Birthday*, edited by Renate Blumenfeld-Kosinski et al., 27–49. Faux titre, 179. Amsterdam: Rodopi, 2000.

Cherewatuk, Karen. "*Speculum Matris*: Dhuoda's Manual." *Florilegium* 10 (1988–1991): 49–63.

Dronke, Peter. *Women Writers of the Middle Ages: A Critical Study of Texts from Perpetua (†203) to Marguerite Porete (†1310).* Cambridge: Cambridge University Press, 1984.

Jaffee, Clella I. "Dhuoda's Handbook for William and the Mother's Manual Tradition." In *Listening to Their Voices: The Rhetorical Activities of Historical Women*, edited with an introduction by Molly Meijer Wertheimer, 177–98. Columbia: University of South Carolina Press, 1997.

Mayeski, Marie Anne. *Dhuoda. Ninth Century Mother and Theologian.* Scranton, Pa.: University of Scranton Press, 1995.

MARCELLE THIÉBAUX

DIDO IN THE MIDDLE AGES. There were three main strands of tradition from Classical Antiquity that influenced the story of Dido in the Middle Ages. One of these threads, a very potent force in literature, stemmed from the moving depiction by Virgil (70–19 B.C.E.) of the love of Dido and Aeneas in Books 1 and 4 of his epic poem of the founding of Rome, the *Aeneid* (19 B.C.E.). Aeneas, on his way from the ruins of Troy to Italy, was driven by a storm off course to Carthage, where he and his followers were hospitably welcomed by Queen Dido, who had fled from the city of Tyre and had founded Carthage. The hero dallied there with Dido, but was finally warned by Jupiter through Mercury of his higher goal to reach Italy, thus to make possible the eventual founding of

Aeneas relating his story to Dido. Courtesy of North Wind Picture Archives.

Rome. Dido, aware of Aeneas's imminent departure, bitterly denounced his infidelity, placing a curse on him and his descendants. She built a funeral pyre, committing suicide with the sword that had been a gift from Aeneas. She is a truly tragic figure, generous in her love for Aeneas, but frenzied in her abandonment by him and a victim of his loyalty to his greater destiny. In Book 6, when Aeneas encounters Dido's shade in the Mourning Fields of the Underworld, he pities her and tries to explain his leaving her. She angrily turns away from him and rejoins her former husband, Sychaeus, whose love equals hers. A second model for the interpretation of Dido's story, stemming from and countering Virgil's version, is the treatment by Ovid (c.43 B.C.E.–17 C.E.) in his book of epistolary dialogues between famous mythological lovers, the *Heroides* (Dido figures in ch. 7). She sends a letter to Aeneas, in elegiac couplets, urging him to delay sailing from Carthage and not to risk the dangers of the deep. She rues her shame and dishonor, but cannot bring herself to hate him. In carefully wrought rhetorical figures, she bewails her tragic dilemma, arousing the reader's sympathy for her and contempt for Aeneas's cruelty. A third vital strand of the Dido legend was that handed down by historians, who denied that Dido and Aeneas were contemporaries. The oldest extant account of the historical Dido (under the name of Theisso; Elissa in Phoenician) is an excerpt from the Greek historian Timaeus of Tauromenium (mid-third century, B.C.E.). A more detailed version is found in Justin's epitome (third century, C.E.), or abridgement, of the Augustan historian Pompeius Trogus. Here Dido is the intrepid and resourceful queen who escaped from pursuit by her wicked brother Pygmalion, the murderer of her husband Acherbas (also known as Sicharbas or Sychaeus). After she founded Carthage, Iarbas, the powerful neighboring king, demanded her hand in marriage. Her story is developed around a series of clever deceptions, culminating in her stratagem of building a funeral pyre, dedicated to the memory of her former husband, which she mounted and then killed herself with a sword.

The Latin Christian Apologists, particularly Tertullian (c.160–c.240) and Jerome (c.348–420), had studied in pagan schools of rhetoric and were skilled in the use of the *exemplum virtutis* (moral-instructional tale of virtue). In vigorous exhortation of Christian women, they cited Dido, according to the historical account, as an example of chaste widowhood. Playing on the biblical injunction, "it is better to marry than to burn" (I Cor. 7.9), they said of Dido that "she preferred to burn rather than to marry a second time" ("maluit ardere quam nubere"), which we find in Jerome, *Adversus Iovinianum* (*Against Jovinian*), 1.43; to be compared to Jerome's *Epistle* 123, and also in Tertullian's *De Monogamia* (*On Monogamy*, 17). St. Augustine (354–430) in the *Confessions* (1.13.20–22) recalls being compelled by his teachers of grammar to learn the wanderings of Aeneas and to weep over hapless Dido, who killed herself for love. Yet he reveals his adherence to the Christian view of Dido's chastity by remarking "if I should ask these teachers whether Aeneas truly came to Carthage as the poet says, the less learned will answer that they do not know, while the more learned will deny that it is true."

There were champions of Dido who blamed Virgil for defaming her character. An epigram attributed to Ausonius (fourth century), but now believed to have been written by Giorgio Merula (c.1424–1494), depicts Dido as speaking from her portrait: "Oh envious Muse, why did you goad Virgil against me, so that he would invent the loss of my chastity?" ("invida, cur in me stimulasti, Musa, Maronem,/fingeret ut nostrae damna pudicitiae?"; Ausonius, *Epigram*, 118).

The late fourth-century Virgilian commentator, Servius, widely quoted in the Middle Ages, included aspects of the historical Dido in his glosses on the *Aeneid*. In his commentary on *Aeneid* 1.267, Servius refers to Virgil's anachronism, observing that the poet disregarded history in having Aeneas visit Carthage, which was founded sixty years before Rome, just as Troy fell 340 years before the founding of Rome. He concedes, however, that Virgil changed history not through ignorance but for the purpose of poetic art. He also explains that Dido was truly named "Elissa," but after her death was called "Dido," that is "virago" ("manly woman"), in the Punic language because of her brave death on the pyre, built, as explained in the historical version, to escape marriage with Iarbas. Servius expounds the language and basic meaning of Virgil's text, but occasionally he comments on Dido's conduct. When she reveals to her sister Anna, "I recognize the traces of my olden passion" (*Aeneid* 4.23), the Servius remarks: "bene inhonestam rem sub honesta specie confitetur" ("she confesses something dishonorable under an honorable guise"). He glosses *Aeneid* 4.69, "hapless Dido burns with love and wanders through the whole city," with the comment: "furor enim est amor, in quo nihil est stabile" ("for love is madness, in which nothing is stable"). Another important handbook for the Middle Ages was the moralistic and allegorical *Expositio Vergiliana continentia secundum philosophos moralis* (*An Explanation of Virgil's Work According to Moral Philosophers*) by Fulgentius (late fifth century to early sixth century). From the description in *Aeneid* 4, one can gain an idea of the work's extravagant style: Aeneas, the spirit of adolescence, "is inflamed by love, and, driven by storm and cloud, as though in confusion of mind, commits adultery." Dido, the cause of this upheaval, is briefly named when her shade "now void of passion and its former lust" ("quasi amoris atque antiquae libidinis umbra lam uacua"), is confronted by Aeneas in *Aeneid* 6. Strongly influenced by Fulgentius, and quoted with equal enthusiasm by medieval writers, was the twelfth-century commentary on the first six books of the *Aeneid* attributed to Bernardus Silvestris of Tours (twelfth century). Here likewise, Dido bears the responsibility for leading Aeneas astray: "Abandoned, she dies, and burned to ashes, she passes away" ("Dido deserta emoritur et in cineres excocta demigrat").

A high point of Virgilian exegesis as a moral exercise was achieved by Cristoforo Landino (1424–1498) in his *Disputationes Camaldulenses* (*Disputations at the Monastery of Camaldoli*) of 1472. Refining and enlarging on the commentaries of Fulgentius and Bernardus Silvestris and sharing in the Platonism of his Florentine contemporaries, Landino saw in the first six books of the *Aeneid* a path, progressing through a series of temptations and impediments, to the *summum bonum* ("highest good"). The episode of Dido is one such hazard on this journey. She represents not only sensual passion, but also, when she and Aeneas take shelter in the cave, the descent into the lust of political power, from which the hero must emerge to reach his goal of Italy.

Distinct from the commentary tradition is an aspect of Virgilian influence seen in a medieval historical compendium, the *Excidium Troiae* (*Fall of Troy*). This work, the earliest manuscript of which is dated in the ninth century, is a prose reworking of a considerably earlier composition, using Greek as well as Latin sources. It contains an adaptation of the wanderings of Aeneas from the fall of Troy to his arrival in Italy, in chronological rather than in Virgil's artificial order of events, and without a visit to the Underworld. Lacking in the *Excidium Troiae* is any attempt at allegorical or moral interpretation. Instead of a lofty hero seeking perfection while undergoing a series of trials, one finds an Aeneas who, when accused by Dido of wanting to leave her, unscrupulously lies and says that he has no such intention. He steals away from Dido while she is asleep and leaves his sword at the head of her bed. Here she is not the model of chaste widowhood, but rather one eager to gratify herself with love for Aeneas. She also has a place in the thirteenth-century prose work, the *Histoire ancienne jusqu'à César* (*Ancient History to the Time of Caesar*), which encompasses ancient history from Genesis through Roman times. This work interweaves Justin's account of the historical Dido into a series of paraphrases of Virgil's *Aeneid* (see Monfrin). Among medieval chronicles that include Dido, we also find the Spanish *Primera Crónica General* (*First General Chronicle*) in the later thirteenth century, wherein the learned King Alfonso X (The Wise, 1221–1284) gives special emphasis to a marriage between Dido and Aeneas.

As for more poetic or literary works, three *Carmina Burana* dealing with Dido's love for Aeneas illustrate the genre of the medieval lyric (Nos. 98, 99, and 100). Outstanding is No. 100: Dido's lament beginning "O Decus, o Libie regnum, Kartaginis urbem!" ("O glory, O Libyan realm, O city of Carthage!"), surviving from the twelfth century in manuscripts from the later twelfth and early thirteenth centuries. She deplores the grief that Aeneas has caused her and expresses concern for her subjects, the Tyrians, now vulnerable to foreign invaders because of her love affair with such a "foreigner," the Trojan Aeneas. Yet in deciding to die, she remains true to her love for Aeneas. Sychaeus is not mentioned, though Iarbas is. Several details, such as Scylla's "mad rage" and the giant Cyclops's "gore" menacing Aeneas and his men, as well as addresses to her sister Anna and to Palinurus, recall the *Aeneid*, while her rhetorical expressions of feeling suggest Ovid's *Heroides* 7. The intensity of her sentiments and her determination to die for love mark the lyric as a memorable extension of classical precedents.

The twelfth-century Norman romance, *Roman d'Eneas* (*Romance of Aeneas*), provides a refashioning of Virgil's epic, colored by Ovidian sentiment. It presents a queen inflamed by love and tormented by the madness of her passion, unrequited by the poem's courtly hero (Margolis). Dido's portrayal in the *Roman* is marked by four laments, based on speeches in *Aeneid* 4, matching and perhaps going beyond Virgil in erotic feeling (Dronke). The first elaborates her wish to have a child by Eneas; the second pictures her unfulfilled dream of a love shared between them; in the third, she utters a series of anguished questions, asking why the course of their love and her unfaithfulness to her former husband happened as they did; the fourth begins with her plaint to the *dulces exuviae*, the "dear relics": the hero's sword, his clothing, and the bed they shared. Dido rehearses her guilt and fame as a heroine, finally ending with words of forgiveness for Eneas (*Aeneid* 4.651). Even though she pardons him, contrary to Virgil's story, she does rebuff him in their encounter in the Underworld. The medieval romancer, however, because of her infidelity, does not permit her to rejoin Sychaeus in death. The flame that kindles her pyre is metaphorically the flame that has fired her love for Eneas.

The great Italian poet Dante (1265–1321) in his treatment of Dido in the *Divina Commedia* (*Divine Comedy*) and *Convivio* (*Banquet*) intensifies Dido's medieval legacy. His reading of her in the *Divine Comedy* gains significance given Virgil's role as primary guide to Dante the pilgrim-narrator through the Hell and Purgatory, the first two-thirds of this spiritual epic. Even as Virgil placed Dido in the Underworld in the Mourning Fields among sorrowing heroines and not among the suicides, so Dante put Dido, not in Canto 13 of the *Inferno* (*Hell*), but rather in the company of Semiramis, Cleopatra, and Helen in Canto 5, among the lustful: "that other is she who killed herself for love and broke faith with the ashes of Sychaeus" ("L'altra e colei, che s'ancise amorosa/E ruppa fede al cener di Sicheo," *Inferno* 5.61–62; compare to *Aeneid* 4.552: "non servata fides cineri promissa Sychaeo" [she did not keep her avowed faith with the ashes of Sychaeus"]). In the third and final book of the *Divine Comedy*, *Paradiso* (*Paradise*), even though Virgil the guide must recuse himself from this Christian heaven because of his pagan status, Dido is mentioned among those who loved, but ill-advisedly (*Paradiso* 9.97–98). Dante perceives her as having wronged both Sychaeus and Creusa, Aeneas's wife lost during the burning of Troy, thus in the latter case bringing a charge against her not raised by Virgil. Dante's more aridly philosophical, unfinished *Convivio* 4.26.2 interprets Dido's presence allegorically: Aeneas must leave her to resume his mission, to take the path of virtue. In his Latin political treatise, *De Monarchia* (*On Monarchy*) 2.3.14–16, Dante symbolically defines the phases of Aeneas's imperial mission by naming his three wives: Creusa in Asia, Dido in Africa, and Lavinia in Europe.

Dante's later contemporary, Petrarch (1304–1374), showed the way to praise the chaste Dido in preference to Virgil's treatment. In *Il Trionfo della Castità* (*Triumph of Chastity*, vv. 10–12, 154–159), Petrarch twice honors Dido among his examples of chastity for having died out of loyalty to her former husband and not, as commonly believed, because of vain passion. He composed a lengthy Latin allegorization of the love of Dido and Aeneas in his *Epistolae de Rebus Senilibus* (*On Old Age*) 4.5 (in Petrarch, *Opera quae extant omnia*), which expresses the fall of virtuous man because of sins of the flesh. He goes on, however, to discuss the historical aspects of the episode. He explains that Dido was born three centuries after Aeneas's death and cites Augustine's *Confessions* to indicate that Aeneas never came to Carthage. Petrarch introduced the story of the chaste Dido in Books 3.418–29 and 4.2–6 of his epic, *Africa*. Also, as Craig Kallendorf demonstrates, Petrarch, without actually citing *Aeneid* 4, based the tragic love story of Sophonisba and Massinissa in *Africa* Book 5 on Virgil's Dido and Aeneas.

That third great medieval Italian author, Boccaccio (1313?–1375), refers both to the historical and the Virgilian Dido in several diverse works in verse and prose, in Italian and in Latin. In two early poems, the *Amorosa Visione* (*Amorous Vision*) and in *L'Elegia di Madonna Fiammetta* (*Elegy of Madonna Fiammetta*), he depicts the Virgilian heroine, who, suffering the pangs of love and cruel abandonment, evokes the reader's profound compassion. In *Esposizioni sopra la Commedia di Dante* (*Explanations of Dante's* Divine Comedy) on Canto 5 (*Espos. litt.* 6583), Boccaccio treats both versions. In several paragraphs he elaborates the account of Justin with dramatic details, while offering only a brief outline of events in Virgil's story. Out of respect for Virgil, Boccaccio states, he would accept the *Aeneid*'s version, as does Dante, were not the chronology contradictory to the prevailing authority, Eusebius's *Chronicle*. Citing Eusebius' three dates for the founding of Carthage, Boccaccio notes that none of these coincides with the time of Aeneas. He concludes that Dido was chaste. Chapter 42 of Boccaccio's *De Claris Mulieribus* (*Famous Women*) exerted a wide influence on later writers. His account follows Justin closely, except for a reference to the coming of Aeneas, but adds that Dido did not see him and deemed that she should die rather than be unfaithful to her former husband. Boccaccio ends his chapter with a sermon on chastity, reminiscent of Tertullian and Jerome. Dido is also one of the examples appearing in a vision in Boccaccio's *De Casibus Virorum Illustrium* (*On the Fates of Illustrious Men and Women*, 2.10–11). The events of her arrival in Carthage, told in full detail, are familiar from Justin's account. Dido appears in the garments she wore to her death on the pyre. She calmly reflects on having deceived the avarice of her brother, on her good fortune in her flight, on the noble city that she founded, and on the number of her people—then she collapses in anguish and tears. A second chapter sings her praise, emphasizing her manly strength and the womanly grace of her chastity. Especially in his great mythological compendium, the *Genealogia Deorum Gentilium* (*Genealogy of the Gods*), Boccaccio makes clear the antithesis between the Virgilian and the historical Dido. In Book 2.60, he treats the two versions of her story; later (6.53) he warns that not everyone believes the account in the *Aeneid*. However, he defends Virgil in a crucial passage of the *Genealogia*, 14.13. Boccaccio replies to the charge that poets are liars and that Virgil told a false story about Dido. He argues that the fictions of poets are not intended to deceive since they do not claim to relate the literal truth. Since Virgil was learned, Boccaccio goes on, he realized that Dido was virtuous and preferred to die by her own hand than to break her vow of chastity, but under the veil of poetry he told a story that was similar to that of the historical Dido in many ways. Virgil's purpose was fourfold: (1) to tell of the arrival of Aeneas in Africa, in the eighth-century Greek poet Homer's poetic manner, beginning in the middle of the story, (2) to show to what passions human weakness is subject, that firm strength can overcome them, and how Dido was endowed with special qualities to attract Aeneas, (3) to honor the Julian family of Augustus by the praise of Aeneas, and (4) to magnify Rome through its wars against Carthage, as prefigured in Dido's imprecations. Thus, in explaining Dido's function, Boccaccio vindicates Virgil and through him all poets.

In the early fourteenth-century *Ovide Moralisé* (*Moralized Ovid*), a lengthy and influential French adaptation of the *Metamorphoses*, the story of Dido and Aeneas is told in some three hundred verses. They include a lament by Dido, based on *Heroides* 7. Although Ovid's *Metamorphoses* 14.78–81 devoted only a few verses to Aeneas's stay in Carthage, the French poem greatly enlarges the Dido episode, making use of Virgil's *Aeneid*. To this tradition likewise belongs the *Ovidius Moralizatus* in Latin prose, which forms Book 15 of the *Reductorium morale* (*Moral Re-examination*) by the influential French moralist and translator-commentator Pierre Bersuire (d. 1362).

The finest medieval English poet, Geoffrey Chaucer (c.1343–1400), in *The House of Fame* (1379–1380), is influenced by both Virgil and Ovid. He borrows from a number of classical and medieval Latin authors and French love poets to present a strongly partisan case on Dido's behalf. Despite the disclaimer in Book 1 that he would not "speke of love" (vv. 247–48), in a dream vision in Venus's temple of glass, Chaucer summarizes the *Aeneid*, devoting special attention to the story of Dido and Aeneas, viewed in a series of "graven" scenes. Dido was deceived by Aeneas's fair appearance; her fault was in loving a stranger too soon (1.267–70). Eventually, by recalling Mercury's command to seek Italy, the poet excuses Aeneas for leaving Dido (1.427–32). Chaucer tells of Dido's love again in *The Legend of Good Women*. The third life in the *Legend* is inscribed, "Incipit Legenda Didonis martiris Cartaginis Regine" ("Here begins the Legend of Dido, martyred queen of Carthage"). She is depicted as gentle, noble, and "that fayrer was than is the bryghte sonne" (v. 1006), and generous in her lavishing of hospitality and gifts on Aeneas and his men. In the scene in the cave, Aeneas swears to remain true to her, and Dido takes him as her husband, also swearing lifelong devotion (vv. 1238–39). Yet, Aeneas wearies of his love for her and determines to leave. Chaucer borrows from the *Excidium Troiae* the details of his treacherous departure, using much the same wording in having Aeneas leave his sword at the head of Dido's bed. *The Legend of Dido* concludes with her letter to Aeneas as adapted from Ovid's *Heroides* 7.

John Gower (1325?–1408), a contemporary of Chaucer, also follows Ovid's *Heroides* in having the forsaken Dido compose a letter to Aeneas. In the *Confessio Amantis* (*The Lover's Confession*) 4.77.142, Aeneas is portrayed as the lover guilty of the sin of sloth, who by not returning to Carthage causes Dido to take her own life by the sword. A few years later John Lydgate (c.1370–c.1450) presented the chaste Dido in the *Fall of Princes*, a reworking of the late fourteenth-century French translator Laurent de Premierfait's *Des Cas des Nobles Hommes et Femmes* (*On the Fates of Illustrious Men and Women*), itself an expanded version of Boccaccio's *De Casibus Virorum Illustrium*. Lydgate praises Dido as the model of virtue, a guide for all widows, whose dying boast was, "For I have but one husband, as God willed it" (v. 2118). William Caxton (c.1422–1491) printed in 1490 the *Eneydos* (*Aeneid*), a translation of a French prose text, the *Livre des Eneydes* (*Book of the Aeneid*), based ultimately on Virgil's *Aeneid*. He knew of the historical and chaste Dido through Boccaccio and praised her, but did not attempt to reconcile the historical version of her story with that of Virgil.

An ardent defender of Dido was Christine de Pizan (1364–1430?), known as the first professional woman of letters. She deployed the example of Dido in several of her works when pleading the cause of feminism against misogynistic elements of her time and, on a love-lyrical level, in warning women that the illicit nature of the much-extolled (by males poets) "courtly love" inevitably damages women. Her poem, *Epistre au Dieu d'Amours* (*Epistle of the God of Love*, 1399), contains sixteen ten-syllable verses depicting Dido as the victim of Aeneas. Again in *Le Livre de la Mutacion de Fortune* (*The Book of Fortune's Mutations*, 1403), she emphasizes the treachery and unreliability of men and praises the masculine traits of Dido. As the founder of Carthage, Dido merits a place in Christine's revisionist history of women, the *Livre de la Cité des Dames* (*Book of the City of Ladies*, 1405). Part 1, chapter 46 relates Dido's life through the founding of Carthage, with details stemming from Justin and Boccaccio and from the French account in the *Histoire Ancienne*. Lady Reason, one of the allegorical guide figures for Christine the narrator, stresses Dido's prudence as a city-builder and lawgiver. In part 2, chapter 56, Christine, countering the misogyny of the early thirteenth-century Matheolus' *Lamentationes* (*Lamentations on the Evils of Women*) and Jean de Meun's *Roman de la Rose* (*Romance of the Rose*, c.1275), cites Dido as representing "d'amour ferme en femme" ("a woman steadfast in love"). She is more constant in love than Aeneas, whose secretive, treacherous nocturnal departure Christine vividly evokes. Not only is his betrayal a transgression against love, but at the very least, Christine adds with bitter irony, against chivalry, in his ingratitude toward his hostess. Although Christine borrowed three-quarters of her examples for *La Cité des Dames* from *De Claris Mulieribus* (see Jeanroy), in a French translation of the latter, the *Des cleres femmes*, she is not dependent on Boccaccio's historical version for her treatment in *Cité des Dames* part 2, but rather follows the tradition to be traced to Ovid's *Heroides* through the *Ovide moralisé*.

Medieval literature thus demonstrates a fascinating panorama of opposing possibilities for the depiction of Dido and Aeneas. The Trojan hero could be portrayed as facing a series of obstacles, most notably the love of Dido, which he must overcome to achieve his goal of reaching Italy and attaining the reward of virtue. He could otherwise be seen as the callous traitor who betrayed the love of the Carthaginian queen. Dido, in turn, could be viewed as her historical self, who died a noble death as an example of chaste widowhood. In the Virgilian and the Ovidian models, she was the tragic queen, abandoned by her Trojan guest and suffering a brave but pitiable death. Her story as enacted in the Middle Ages inspired an ever-widening range of moral lessons and profound sentiments, continuing into the Renaissance and modern times.

See also Arthurian Women; *Belle Dame Sans Merci*; Boccaccio, Women in, *De Claris Mulieribus*; Boccaccio, Women in, *Des Cleres et Nobles Femmes*; Boccaccio, Women in, Works Other than *De Claris Mulieribus*; Christine de Pizan; Criseyde; Le Fèvre de Ressons, Jean; Le Franc, Martin; Medea in the Middle Ages

BIBLIOGRAPHY

Primary Sources

Augustine. *Sancti Aureli Augustini Confessionum Libri Tredecim*. Edited by Pius Knöll. Re-edited by Martin Skutella. Bibliotheca scriptorum Graecorum et Romanorum Teubneriana. Leipzig, Germany: Teubner, 1934.

Ausonius, Decimus Magnus. *Epigrammata*. In *Opuscula*, edited by Rudolf Peiper. Bibliotheca scriptorum Graecorum et Romanorum Teubneriana. Leipzig, Germany: Teubner, 1886. Reprinted, Stuttgart, Germany: Teubner, 1976.

Bersuire, Pierre [Petrus Berchorius]. *Reductorium Morale, Liber XV: Ovidius Moralizatus*. Edited by Joseph Engels. Instituut voor Laat Latijn, Werkmateriaal, 3. Utrecht, Netherlands: Rijksuniversiteit, 1966.

Boccaccio, Giovanni. *Amorosa Visione*. Edited by Vittore Branca. Florence, Italy: Leo Olschki, 1944.

———. *De Casibus Virorum Illustrium*. Edited by Pier Giorgio Ricci and Vittorio Zaccaria. In *Tutte le Opere di Giovanni Boccaccio*, 9. Milan, Italy: Arnoldo Mondadori, 1983.

———. [*De claris mulieribus*]. *Famous Women*. Edited and translated by Virginia Brown. I Tatti Renaissance Library, 1. Cambridge, Mass.: Harvard University Press, 2001. [Bilingual Latin-English ed.].

———. *Genealogie Deorum Gentilium Libri*. Edited by Vincenzo Romano. In *Giovanni Boccaccio Opere*, 10–11. *Scrittori d'Italia*, 200, 201. Bari, Italy: G. Laterza, 1951.

———. *L'Elegia di Madonna Fiammetta*. Edited by Vincenzo Pernicone. In *Giovanni Boccaccio Opere*, 4. *Scrittori d'Italia*, 171. Bari, Italy: G. Laterza, 1939.

———. [*Esposizioni sopra il Dante*]. *L'Ultima Opera di Giovanni Boccaccio*. Edited by Giorgio Padoan. Università di Padova, Pubblicazioni della Facoltà di lettere e filosofia, 34. Padua, Italy: Cedam, 1959.

Carmina Burana. Edited by Benedikt K. Vollmann. Bibliothek des Mittelalters, 13. Frankfurt, Germany: Deutscher Klassiker Verlag, 1987. [Bilingual Latin-German ed.].

———. *The Love Songs of the* Carmina Burana. Translated by E. D. Blodgett and Roy A. Swanson. Garland Library of Medieval Literature, 49B. New York and London: Garland, 1987.

Caxton, William. *Eneydos*. Edited by Mathew T. Culley and Frederick J. Furnivall. Early English Text Society, e.s., 57. London: Trubner, 1890. Reprint Oxford: Oxford University Press, 1962.

Chaucer, Geoffrey. *The House of Fame*. Edited by John M. Fyler. In *The Riverside Chaucer*, edited by Larry D. Benson, 347–73. Boston: Houghton Mifflin, 1987.

———. *The Legend of Good Women*. Edited by M. C. E. Shaner. In *The Riverside Chaucer*, 3: 608–13. Boston: Houghton Mifflin, 1987.

Dante Alighieri. *Convivio*. Edited by Ernesto G. Parodi and F. Pellegrini. In *Le Opere di Dante*. Società dantesca italiana. Florence, Italy: Bemporad e Figlio, 1921. Reprint 1960.

———. *La Divina Commedia di Dante Aliahieri*. Edited by C. H. Grandgent. Boston: D. C. Heath, 1933.

———. *De Monarchia*. Edited by Pier Giorgio Ricci. In *Opere di Dante*, 5. Società dantesca italiana. Milan, Italy: Arnoldo Mondadori, 1965. [Bilingual Latin-Italian ed.].

Excidium Troiae. Edited by E. Bagby Atwood and Virgil K. Whitaker. Mediaeval Academy of America, 44. Cambridge, Mass.: Mediaeval Academy of America, 1944.

Fulgentius. *Fabii Planciadis Fulgentii v. c. Opera*. Edited by Rudolf Helm. Addenda by Jean Préaux. Bibliotheca scriptorum Graecorum et Romanorum Teubneriana. Leipzig, Germany: Teubner, 1898. Reprint Stuttgart, Germany: Teubner, 1970.

Gower, John. *Confessio Amantis*. In *The English Works of John Gower*, edited by George C. Macaulay, vol. 1. Early English Text Society, e.s. 81. London: K. Paul, Trench, Trubner, 1900. Reprint Oxford: Clarendon Press, 1970.

Jerome [Eusebius Hieronymus]. *Adversus Iovinianum*. *Patrologia Latina*, 23: 211–338. Paris: J.-P. Migne, 1883.

———. *Epistolae*. Edited by Isidore Hilberg, vol. 3. Corpus Scriptorum Ecclesiasticorum Latinorum, 56. Addenda by Margit Kampter. Enlarged ed. Vienna, Austria: Osterreichischen Akademie der Wissenschaften, 1996.

Justin [Marcus Junian(i)us Justinus]. *Epitoma Historiarum Philippicarum Pompei Trogi*, Edited by Otto Seel. Bibliotheca scriptorum Graecorum et Romanorum Teubneriana. Revised edition. Stuttgart, Germany: Teubner 1972.

Landino, Cristoforo. *Disputationes Camaldulenses*. Edited by Peter Lohe. Studi e testi Istituto nazionale di studi sul Rinascimento, 6. Florence, Italy: Sansoni,1980.

Lydgate, John. *Fall of Princes*. Edited by Henry Bergen. 4 vols. Early English Text Society, e.s. 121–24. London: Humphrey Milford/Oxford University Press, 1924–1927.

Ovid (Publius Ovidius Naso). *Heroides, Amores*. In *Ovid*, 1. Translated by Grant Showerman. Loeb Classical Library. 2nd ed. Cambridge, Mass.: Harvard University Press; London: Heinemann, 1977. [Bilingual Latin-English ed.].

Ovide moralisé: Poème du commencement du quatorzieme siècle. Edited by Cornelis de Boer. 5 vols. Amsterdam, Netherlands: J. Müller, 1915–38.

Petrarca, Francesco. *Africa*. Edited by Nicola Festa. In *Edizione Nazionale delle Opere di Francesco Petrarca*, vol. I. Florence, Italy: G. Sansoni, 1926.

————. *Epistolae de Rebus Senilibus*, in *Opera quae extant omnia*. Basel, Switzerland, 1554.

————. *Rime e Trionfi*. Edited by Ferdinando Neri. 2nd ed. revised by Ettore Bonora. Classici italiani. Turin, Italy: Unione tipografico-editrice Torinese, 1966.

Pizan, Christine de. *Epistre au Dieu d'Amours*. Edited by Thelma S. Fenster. In *Poems of Cupid, God of Love*, edited by Thelma Fenster and Mary C. Erler. Leiden, Netherlands: Brill, 1990.

————. [*Livre de la Cité des Dames*] *Citté delle dame*. Edited by E. J. Richards. Translated (Italian) by Patrizia Caraffi. 2nd revised ed. Milan, Italy: Luni, 1998.

————. *Book of the City of Ladies*. Translated with commentary by E. J. Richards. Foreword by Natalie Zemon Davis. Revised ed. New York: Persea, 1997.

————. *Le Livre de la Mutacion de Fortune*. Critical ed. by Suzanne Solente. 4 vols. Société des Anciens Textes Francais. Paris: Picard, 1959–1966.

Primera Crónica General de España. Edited by Ramón Menéndez Pidal et al., vol. 1. Universidad de Madrid. Facultad de Filosofia y Letras. Madrid, Spain: Editorial Gredos, 1955.

Roman d'Eneas. Edited and translated by Aimé Petit. Lettres Gothiques. Paris: Livre de Poche, 1997. [Bilingual ed. Old French-English ed.].

Servius (Maurus Servius Honoratus). *Servianorum in Vergilii Carmina Commentariorum Editionis Harvardianae, 2* (Aeneid *1–2*). Edited by Edward K. Rand et al. Lancaster, Penn.: American Philological Association, 1946.

————. *Vol. 3* (Aeneid *3–4*). Edited by Arthur F. Stocker and Albert H. Travis. Oxford: Oxford University Press, 1965.

Silvestris, Bernardus. *Commentum quod dicitur Bernardi Silvestris super sex libros Eneidos Virgilii*. Edited by Julian W. Jones and Elizabeth F. Jones. Lincoln and London: University of Nebraska Press, 1977.

Tertullian [Quietus Septimius Florens Tertullianus]. *Le Mariage unique/De Monogamia*. Edited by Paul Mattei. Sources chretiennes, 343. Paris: Éditions du Cerf, 1988. [Bilingual Latin-French ed.].

Timaeus. *Die Fragmente der griechischen Historiker*. Edited by Felix Jacoby, vol. 3B, no. 566, fragment 82. Leiden, Netherlands: Brill, 1950.

Virgil [Publius Vergilius Maro]. *P. Vergili Maronis Opera*. Edited by Roger A. B. Mynors. Oxford Classical Texts. Corrected ed. Oxford: Oxford University Press, 1972.

Secondary Sources

Allen, Don Cameron. *Mysteriously Meant: The Rediscovery of Pagan Symbolism and Allegorical Interpretation in the Renaissance*. Baltimore: Johns Hopkins University Press, 1970.

Austin, Roland G. *P. Vergili Maronis Aeneidos Liber Quartus*. Edited with a commentary. Revised ed. Oxford: Clarendon Press, 1963.

Baswell, Christopher. *Virgil in Medieval England: Figuring the* Aeneid *from the Twelfth Century to Chaucer*. Cambridge: Cambridge University Press, 1995.

Billanovich, Giuseppe. *Restauri Boccacceschi*. Rome: 1945. [esp. 135–43].

————. *Petrarca Letterato, I: Lo scrittoio del Petrarca*. Storia e letteratura, 16. Rome: Edizioni di "Storia e letteratura," 1947. [esp. 144–56].

Blumenfeld-Kosinski, Renate. *Reading Myth: Classical Mythology and Its Interpretations in Medieval French Literature*. Figurae. Stanford, Calif.: Stanford University Press, 1997.

Bono, Barbara J. *Literary Transvaluation: From Vergilian Epic to Shakespearian Tragicomedy*. Berkeley and Los Angeles: University of California Press, 1984.

Cerbo, Anna. "Didone in Boccaccio." *Annali, Istituto Universitario Orientale, Napoli, Sezione Romanza* 21 (1979): 177–219.

Chance, Jane. *The Mythographic Chaucer: The Fabulation of Sexual Politics*. Minneapolis: University of Minnesota Press, 1995. [esp. ch. 2].

Cormier, Raymond. *One Heart, One Mind: The Rebirth of Virgil's Hero in Medieval French Romance*. Romance Monographs, 3. Oxford: University of Mississippi Romance Monographs, Inc., 1973.

Desmond, Marilynn. *Reading Dido: Gender, Textuality, and the Medieval* Aeneid. Medieval Cultures, 8. Minneapolis: University of Minnesota Press, 1994.

Dronke, Peter. "Dido's Lament: From Medieval Latin Lyric to Chaucer." In *Kontinuität und Wandel. Lateinische Poesie von Naevius bis Baudelaire. Franco Munari zum 65. Geburtstag*, edited by Ulrich

J Stache et al., 364–90. Hildesheim, Germany: Weidmann, 1986. Reprinted in Peter Dronke, *Intellectuals and Poets in Medieval Europe*, 431–56. Storia e letteratura, 183. Rome: Edizioni di storia e letteratura, 1992.

Friend, Albert C. "Chaucer's Version of the *Aeneid*." *Speculum* 28 (1953): 317–23.

Fyler, John. *Chaucer and Ovid*. New Haven, Conn.: Yale University Press, 1979.

Hall, Louis Brewer. *The Story of Dido and Aeneas in the Middle Ages*. Diss. Ph.D. University of Oregon, 1958. Ann Arbor, Mich.: UMI, 1978.

Jeanroy, Alfred. "Boccacce et Christine de Pisan: Le *De Claris Mulieribus*, Principale Source du Livre de *La Cité des Dames*." *Romania* 48 (1922): 93–105.

Jones, Julian Ward, Jr. "A Twelfth-Century Interpretation of Vergil." *Vergilius* 28 (1982): 51–57.

Kallendorf, Craig. "Cristoforo Landino's *Aeneid* and the Humanist Critical Tradition." *Renaissance Quarterly* 36 (1983): 519–46.

———. *In Praise of Aeneas: Virgil and Epideictic Rhetoric in the Early Italian Renaissance*. Hanover, N.H.: University Press of New England, 1989.

Lectures médiévales de Virgile. Actes du Colloque (Rome, 25–28 Octobre 1982). Collection de l'École française de Rome, 80. Rome: École française de Rome, 1985.

Leube, Eberhard. *Fortuna in Karthago: Die Aeneas–Dido–Mythe Vergils in den romanischen Literaturen vom 14. bis zum 16. Jahrhundert*. Heidelberg, Germany: Carl Winter, 1969.

Lida de Malkiel, Maria Rosa. *Dido en la literatura española: su retrato y defensa*. Colección Tamesis : Serie A, Monografias, 37. London: Tamesis, 1974.

Lord, Mary Louise. "Dido as an Example of Chastity: The Influence of Example Literature." *Harvard Library Bulletin* 17 (1969): 22–44, 216–32.

Margolis, Nadia. "*Flamma, Furor,* and *Fol'Amors*: Fire and Feminine Madness from the *Aeneid* to the *Roman d'Eneas*." *Romanic Review* 78 (1987): 131–47.

Minnis, Alistair J., and A. B. Scott, with David Wallace, eds. *Medieval Literary Theory and Criticism c.1100–c.1375: The CommentaryTradition*, 317–18, 366–72. Revised ed. Oxford: Oxford University Press, 1991.

Monfrin, Jacques. "Les Translations Vernaculaires de Virgile au Moyen Age." In *Lectures Médiévales de Virgile: Actes du colloque organisé par l'Ecole française de Rome*, 221–41. Rome: Ecole française de Rome, 1985.

Olsen, Birger Munk. "Virgile et la renaissance du XIIe siècle." In *Lectures Médiévales de Virgile (see above)*, 31–48. Rome: Ecole française de Rome, 1985.

Padoan, Giorgio. "Didone (Dido)." In *Enciclopedia Dantesca*. Vol 2: 430–31. Rome: Istituto della Enciclopedia italiana, 1970.

Quilligan, Maureen. *The Allegory of Female Authority: Christine de Pizan's Cité des Dames*. Ithaca, N.Y. and London: Cornell University Press, 1991.

Rudd, Niall. *The Classical Tradition in Operation*. Robson Classical Lectures, 2. Toronto: University of Toronto Press, 1994. [esp. ch. 1].

MARY LOUISE LORD

DOMESTIC PROSELYTIZATION. *See* **Clotilde, St.**

DOMNA H. *See* **H., Domna**

DONNÉS. *See* **Marriage**

DONZELLA, COMPIUTA. *See* **Compiuta Donzella**

DOROTHEA OF MONTAU, ST. (1347–1394). Dorothea was Prussia's first enclosed anchoress (a religious woman living in strict solitude) and, as such, became an object of veneration credited with miracles, even during her lifetime. As is the case with other women visionaries, her mystical raptures were the vehicle by which she transcended the limitations of her gender, education, and social status, and achieved a fair degree of fame. Dorothea dictated her revelations in German to her confessor, John of Marienwerder, who, with a few exceptions, recorded them in Latin, as contained in the *Liber de festis* (*Book of Holy Feasts*), the *Septililium* (*The Seven Graces*), the major biographies of her in Latin (*Vita Prima, Vita Lindana, Vita Latina*), and in German. She also dictated a short treatise on the spiritual life, *Die geistliche Lehre* (*The Spiritual Doctrine*) and probably composed a number of prayers and poems, which are now lost.

Dorothea is a product of the mystical tradition that became an important aspect of female religious expression in the later Middle Ages. Her role as wife and mother and her bourgeois social status also herald a movement away from the formerly narrow notions of female sanctity, whereby in the infrequent instances when women were the centers of cults, they were martyrs or virginal, cloistered, members of the nobility. Like her slightly older contemporary, Bridget, or Birgitta, of Sweden (c.1303–1373), whose career and revelations profoundly inspired her, Dorothea was beholden to her confessor for the recording of her ecstatic insights. Although Dorothea was aware of the many problems of her era and regarded herself as a kind of intermediary between God and the people of Prussia, her visions reflected no particular political orientation, nor did she play an active role in public life, as did other famous female mystics such as Birgitta of Sweden or Catherine of Siena (c.1347–1380).

Dorothea was born in 1347 at Montau, West Prussia (now in Poland, bordering on northern Germany), the seventh of nine children born to William Swartz, a Dutch peasant, and his wife, Agatha. At the early age of six, following a traumatic accident with scalding, Dorothea embraced a vigorous regimen of prayers and asceticism that would characterize her entire life. In 1363, at the age of sixteen, Dorothea was married to Adalbert, a prosperous weaponsmith in Danzig many years her senior. Dorothea's mystical raptures continued into her married life, and her ascetical practices increased in severity. Her husband, although possessing a conventional piety, had little understanding or patience for Dorothea's intense spirituality and periodically abused her both verbally and physically. Their marriage produced nine children, yet only one daughter, Gertrude, survived infancy, eventually becoming a nun at the Benedictine convent at Kulm. In 1380, after seventeen years of marriage, Dorothea convinced Adalbert to release her from the fulfillment of the conjugal debt and to agree to a vow of chastity. Beginning in 1382, Dorothea embarked on a series of pilgrimages accompanied by Adalbert. He did not accompany her to Rome for the Jubilee year of 1390, and during this period he died. Dorothea moved to Marienwerder, an important town in East Prussia, (now Kwidzyn, Poland) in 1391. Here she placed herself under the guidance of her new confessor, John of Marienwerder (1343–1417), a member of the Teutonic Order (a papally approved order of German knights founded 1190, during the Crusades) and an able theologian. He supported her in her wish to become an anchoress, and she was officially enclosed in a cell attached to the cathedral of Marienwerder on May 2, 1393, where she remained until her death on June 25, 1394. In the course of their three-year relationship, John of Marienwerder recorded and described Dorothea's confessions and ecstasies, later organizing the material into the various *vitae* (biographies)—several in Latin, one in German—and other works that he produced after her death, partially as a means of promoting her case for canonization. Despite John's energetic efforts on Dorothea's behalf, however, Dorothea's case failed due to the flagging fortunes of the Teutonic knights and the controversy that had sprung up around her name. Although locally worshipped in Prussia from the fifteenth century, she was only officially canonized January 9, 1976.

Of the various *vitae* produced by John, the German life in particular is thought to bear the imprint of Dorothea's mode of expression. John also assembled her mystical doctrine into two works: the *Liber de festis*, so-called because arranges her visions around the important liturgical feasts, and the *Septililium*, which examines the seven graces that Dorothea received in terms of her revelations. The last twenty-one chapters of the *Septilimum* are direct transmissions of Dorothea's confessions in German. Dorothea can also be directly credited with a small treatise on the spiritual life, which she dictated for her daughter in German (*Die geistliche Lehre*). Apart from the exceptions mentioned above, the bulk of Dorothea's thought survives in Latin.

Because Dorothea had no formal education and may have been completely illiterate, we can only speak of her doctrine in the form in which it was presented by her confessor. Yet Dorothea did retain a limited degree of authorial control in that John would read her what he had written, to which she often made changes. Moreover, in his various *vitae*, John seems at pains to maintain Dorothea's point of view. Dorothea's doctrine bears the general imprint of the teaching of the Dominicans and the Teutonic Knights as well as the influence of mystical authors like the Scottish-born Parisian Richard of St. Victor (d. 1173), the German Dominican Johannes Tauler (d. 1361), and especially Birgitta of Sweden. Dorothea's revelations are characterized by an intense Eucharistic devotion (focusing on the Blood and Body of Christ) and an exacting *imitatio Christi* (imitation of Christ) with a particular emphasis on His passion—themes that are generally representative of late medieval devotional trends. Dorothea also developed wounds similar to stigmata (Christ's wounds on the Cross) and experienced a divine renewal of the heart, the latter phenomenon coinciding with the awakening of her inner senses and marking the beginning of her mystical union with God. John of Marienwerder places particular emphasis on the many different kinds of love that Dorothea experienced in the course of her mystical raptures. Her feast day is June 25 (also October 30).

See also *Ancrene Riwle*; Birgitta of Sweden, St.; Catherine of Siena, St.; Hagiography (Female Saints); Kempe, Margery

BIBLIOGRAPHY

Primary Sources
Dorothea of Montau. [*Die geistliche Lehre*]. "Die Geistliche Lehre der Frau Dorothea von Montau an ihre Tochter im Frauenkloster zu Kulm." Edited by Richard Stachnik. *Zeitschrift für Ostforschung* 3 (1954): 589–96.
Marienwerder, Johannes. *Liber de Festis Magistri Johannis Marienwerder: Offenbarungen der Dorothea von Montau*. Edited by Anneliese Triller, Ernst Borchert and Hans Westphal. Forschungen und Quellen zur Kirchen- und Kulturgeschichte Ostdeutschlands, 25. Cologne, Germany: Böhlau, 1992. [Latin text, German commentary].
———. *Septililium*. Edited by Franz Hipler. Pt. 1 in *Analecta Bollandiana* 2–4 (1883–1885): 207–51; pt. 2 in *Christliche Lehre und Erziehung in Ermland*, 68–103. Braunsberg, Germany: E. Peter, 1877.
———. *Vita Prima* and *Vita Lindana*. In *Acta Sanctorum*, 30 Oct., 13: 493–560.
———. *Vita Dorotheae Montoviensis magistri Johannis Marienwerder*. Edited by Hans Westphal. Forschungen und Quellen zur Kirchen- und Kulturgeschichte Ostdeutschlands, 1. Graz, Austria: Böhlau, 1964.

————. *The Life of Dorothea von Montau: A Fourteenth-Century Recluse.* Translated by Ute Stargardt. Studies in Women and Religion, 39. Lewiston N.Y.: Edwin Mellen Press, 1997.

Die Akten des Kanonisationsprozesses Dorotheas von Montau von 1394 bis 1521. Edited by Richard Stachnik and Anneliese Triller. Forschungen und Quellen zur Kirchen- und Kulturgeschichte Ostdeutschlands, 15. Cologne: Böhlau, 1978.

Secondary Sources

Elliott, Dyan. "Authorizing a Life: The Collaboration of Dorothea of Montau and John Marienwerder." In *Gendered Voices: Medieval Saints and Their Interpreters*, edited by Catherine M. Mooney, 168–91. Foreword by Caroline W. Bynum. Middle Ages. Philadelphia: University of Pennsylvania Press, 1999.

————. *Spiritual Marriage: Sexual Abstinence in Medieval Wedlock.* Princeton, N.J.: Princeton University Press, 1993.

Hörner, Petra. *Dorothea von Montau: Überlieferung, Interpretation: Dorothea und die osteuropäische Mystik.* Information and Interpretation, 7. Frankfurt and New York: Peter Lang, 1993.

Kieckhefer, Richard. *Unquiet Souls. Fourteenth-Century Saints and Their Religious Milieu.* Chicago and London: University of Chicago Press, 1984.

Stargardt, Ute. "The Political and Social Background of the Canonization of Dorothea von Montau," *Mystics Quarterly* 11 (1985): 107–22.

DYAN ELLIOTT

DOUBLE MONASTERIES (7th–12th centuries). Double monasteries constituted an important development in seventh-century monasticism: associated monastic houses of monks and nuns forming a single physical and juridical unit. This movement placed women in partnership with men in the work of the Church. The first such houses were built in central and northern Gaul under the influence of Irish missionaries. The first double monastery may have been Faremoutiers-en-Brie, in northern France, founded around 617 by Burgundofara with the help of the monks Chagnoald and Waldabert. Earlier nunneries had been in the cities, and when nuns wished to live in isolated areas, the presence of the monks provided protection and the opportunity to receive the sacraments. Some of the monasteries permitted substantial contact between monks and nuns, sharing a common church and singing antiphonally (in a pattern of responses within a liturgical text). Other monasteries imposed greater segregation of the sexes, with monks and nuns occupying separate churches; the abbess would speak to the monks under her rule only through a window. The favorable reputation of the houses indicates the care with which the relations between monks and nuns were governed: only Coldingham in England suffered association with any scandal. Discipline in the early monasteries was strict; for example, the Rule of Waldebert of Luxeuil (629–670) decrees that nuns as well as monks were to perform manual labor.

The double monasteries were famous for their learning and devotion, providing schools for both boys and girls. The English nobility sent their daughters to Gaul either to become nuns at the double monasteries or to be educated. A related feature of double monasteries is that women were not subordinate to men but functioned as their collaborators and often their spiritual leaders. In fact, male leadership was the exception everywhere but in Spain, where double monasteries were under the rule of an abbot. Otherwise the houses were usually governed by an abbess, or occasionally were under the joint administration of an abbess and an abbot. As an example, the German monastery of Heidenheim, founded by St. Willibald, was originally under the rule of his brother Wynnebald, who was succeeded by their sister Waldburg. The abbess had both sacerdotal and administrative powers; she heard confession and administered benediction. Nuns held administrative offices such as librarian and positions of authority such as that of portress—a doorkeeper.

After the double monasteries had succeeded in attracting postulants from various parts of Europe, they were introduced into other countries including Spain, although Isidore of Seville and his brother Leander urged the complete separation of men and women. When the double monastery was introduced into England, it combined the continental form with aspects of monasticism borrowed from the Irish. Peter Hunter Blair traces a specific link between the continental and English monasteries. The abbess of Chelles, Bertilla, sent men, women, and books to England to help in the foundation of double monasteries, and there is a link between Chelles and Whitby through the abbess Hild and her sister Hereswith. Many of the most important Anglo-Saxon monasteries were double houses, and the abbesses were women of noble or royal rank. Like Abbess Bertilla of Chelles, Hild of Whitby and Athelthryth of Ely exerted unparalleled influence over this movement. The double monastery became so important a part of the English monastic system that Frank M. Stenton doubts the existence of any houses founded only for nuns.

St. Boniface took the English form of the double monastery to Germany, where he encouraged their foundation under the Benedictine Rule. The result of bringing the double monasteries under this rule during the late eighth and the ninth centuries was that greater segregation of the sexes came to be mandated with the nuns more strictly cloistered. The effort to protect the chastity of the nuns led to the curtailment of their way of life and freedom of movement and, eventually, the end of the system of the double monastery. In Carolingian France, the abbesses were no longer permitted to exercise sacerdotal functions like hearing confession, and the nuns were no longer permitted to educate boys. The abbesses consequently ceased to play a role in public life. In England, the Danish invasions of the ninth century destroyed most of the double monasteries, which were not restored during the tenth-century Benedictine Reform. In France, the double monasteries were replaced by separate houses of canons and canonesses, and the restructuring meant the end of the period in which male and female monasteries were equal in status and influence, and nuns habitually played a major role both in the Church and in secular affairs.

See also Æthelthryth, St.; Berthgyth; Boniface, St., Mission and Circle of; Convents; Hild (Hilda), St.; Leoba; Petronilla of Chemillé; Rules for Canonesses, Nuns, and Recluses

BIBLIOGRAPHY
Bateson, Mary. *Origin and Early History of Double Monasteries.* Transactions of the Royal Historical Society, n.s., 13. London, 1899.
Eckenstein, Lina. *Woman under Monasticism: Chapters on Saint-Lore and Convent Life Between* A.D. *500 and* A.D. *1500.* Cambridge: Cambridge University Press, 1896. Reprint, New York: Russell & Russell, 1963.
Godfrey, John. "The Double Monastery in Early English History." *Ampleforth Journal* 79 (1974): 19–32.
Heinrich, Mary Pia. "The Canonesses and Education in the Early Middle Ages." Ph.D. diss., Catholic University of America, 1924.
Hilpisch, Stephanus. *Die Doppelkloster. Entstehung und Organisation.* Beiträge zur Geschichte des alten Monchtums und des Benediktinerordens, 15. Münster: Aschendorff, 1928.

Hollis, Stephanie. *Anglo-Saxon Women and the Church: Sharing a Common Fate.* Woodbridge, Sussex, U.K.: Boydell Press, 1992.

Johnson, Penelope D. *Equal in Monastic Profession: Religious Women in Medieval France.* Chicago: University of Chicago Press, 1991.

Levison, Wilhelm. *England and the Continent in the Eighth Century.* Oxford: Clarendon Press, 1946. Reprint 1966.

Mitchell, Barbara. "Anglo-Saxon Double Monasteries." *History Today* (Oct. 1995): 33–39.

Nicolson, John. "*Feminae gloriosae*: Women in the Age of Bede," in *Medieval Women*, edited by Derek Baker, 15–30. Oxford: Basil Blackwell, 1978.

Stenton, Frank M. *Anglo-Saxon England.* 3rd. ed. Oxford: Clarendon Press, 1971.

Wemple, Suzanne Fonay. *Women in Frankish Society; Marriage and the Cloister.* Philadelphia: University of Pennsylvania Press, 1981.

ALEXANDRA HENNESSEY OLSEN

DOWER. From the Latin *dotare* (to endow), the dower is the portion of a deceased husband's estate allowed by law to the widow for her life. Although the dower was originally allotted to the wife at the time of the husband's death, over time it came to be assigned at the time of marriage. Throughout the Middle Ages, the dower was a widespread custom as a primary means of providing support for a widow. Significantly, particularly in northern France, the dower was assigned on the husband's own properties at the time of the marriage; it was not based on the couple's joint holdings or on the bride's (future widow's) own dowry and/or inheritance. The widow enjoyed only usufruct (the right to usage of and profits from the land) privileges of dower lands, these ultimately passing on to the husband's heirs (Evergates), but adept noblewomen nevertheless could exercise considerable power over their fiefs and also serve as guardians of their sons (Reyerson and Kuehn). The dower also remained a distinct entity from the dowry—property brought by the woman into her marriage. Both entities—dower and dowry—were considered inviolable in most countries although there are a number of cases in which a woman was denied her rightful dower or dowry. However, in some specific cases in which a husband owed a substantial amount to creditors prior to his death, the wife's claim to her dower or dowry was protected by law. In these cases, the dower or dowry were considered debts against the husband's estate and were awarded to the wife prior to the liquidation of the husband's assets to creditors. Furthermore, women who received no inheritance were often allowed to withdraw the dower or dowry from the husband's estate before other heirs or creditors were paid.

The typical percentage of the estate conveyed to the dowager (the recipient of the dower) was rated at one-third of the real estate owned by the husband at any time during a marriage. In both rural and urban situations, the husband was obligated by law to assign one-third of his goods and or land to his wife at the time of their betrothal. A widow had a life interest in her dower, but it reverted to her late husband's heirs at the time of her death (*Coutumiers*, trans Amt). Early thirteenth-century Norman law, in specifying that "a widow shall have as her dower up to one-third of the inheritance of the donor, except the chief dwelling, which remains to the heir," also affirmed that, in the event a dwelling was given to the woman in her dower, she could keep this with the exception of the "tower or castle." In the face of this general principle, certain differences in redistribution prevailed in various cities. In Florence, the widow either stayed with her husband's family or returned to her natal home, to preserve her dower's capital; for the same reason she did not usually remarry. Dowered widows in Ghent (now in Belgium) had benefits more like their counterparts in London, except for being denied custody of their children, who were brought up instead by the husband's family (Hanawalt and Dronzek). German laws, especially by the fifteenth century, allowed the wife and widow considerable independence in disposing of her assets, with the same provision for one-third inheritance as in England and France (Uitz). In medieval Wales, by contrast, women could not inherit land nor could title to land be inherited through the female line, according to native Welsh law, until the late thirteenth century, when English influence spread to some parts and certain Welsh princes did dower their wives. The disparity of customs in late-medieval Wales created problems for widows seeking to collect (Richards). Even in England and France, as late-medieval legal systems became increasingly dominated by lawyers (one thinks of the laments of Christine de Pizan in works like the *Mutacion de Fortune* [*Mutations of Fortune*, 1403]), dowered widows confronted new obstacles, thus requiring their own attorneys (Walker), although such had always been the case, unless the woman plaintiff had suffered physical abuse, since women had always been denied legal training (Reyerson and Kuehn).

See also Chaucer, Alice; China, Women in; Christine de Pizan; Dowry; Fatimid Egypt, Women in; Jewish Women in the Middle Ages; Marriage; Norse Women; *Sachsenspiegel* and *Schwabenspiegel*; Salic Law; Widows

BIBLIOGRAPHY

Primary Sources

Christine de Pizan. [*Mutacion de Fortune*, trans. extract]. "Here is Told how She Collected Only the Shards of Her Father's Treasure." Translated by Nadia Margolis. In *The Writings of Christine de Pizan*, edited by Charity Cannon Willard, 116–17. New York: Persea, 1994.

Les Coutumiers de Normandie, I: Le Très Ancien Coutumier de Normandie, edited by Ernest-Joseph Tardif, chs. 4–5, 79. Rouen: E. Cagniard, 1881. Reprint Geneva: Slatkine, 1977. [Latin, Anglo-Norman and French texts].

———. Translated extracts in Emilie Amt. *Women's Lives in Medieval Europe: A Sourcebook*, 53–54, 57–59. New York and London: Routledge, 1993. [Also contains pertinent extracts, with useful commentary, translated from other historical sources: Sicilian law 64–65; 13C Magdeburg 71–72; 12C England 156; 14C England 185].

Feudal Society in Medieval France: Documents from the County of Champagne. Translated and edited by Theodore Evergates, esp. no. 43. Middle Ages Series. Philadelphia: University of Pennsylvania Press, 1993.

Liber Augustalis, or Constitutions of Melfi, Promulgated by the Emperor Frederick II for the Kingdom of Sicily in 1231. Edited and translated by James M. Powell, Book 3: Titles 13, 15. Syracuse, N.Y.: Syracuse University Press, 1971. These extracts reprinted in Amt, 64–65. *See above under* Coutumiers.

Secondary Sources

Evergates, Theodore. "Aristocratic Women in the County of Champagne." In *Aristocratic Women in Medieval France*, edited by T. Evergates, 74–110. The Middle Ages. Philadelphia: University of Pennsylvania Press, 1999.

Hanawalt, Barbara A., and Anna Dronzek, "Women in Medieval Urban Society." In *Women in Medieval Western European Civilization*, edited by Linda E. Mitchell, 31–45. Garland Reference Library of the Humanities, 2007. New York and London: Garland, 1999.

———. "The Widow's Mite: Provisions for Medieval London Widows." In *Upon My Husband's Death: Widows in the Literature and Histories of Medieval Europe*, edited by Louise Mirrer, 21–45. Studies in Medieval and Early Modern Civilization. Ann Arbor: University of Michigan Press, 1992.

Herlihy, David. *Medieval Households*. Cambridge, Mass.: Harvard University Press, 1985.

Maxeiner, Andrea D. B. "Dower and Jointure: A Legal and Statistical Analysis of the Property Rights of Married Women in Late Medieval England." Ph.D. Diss. Catholic University of America, 1990.

Molho, Anthony. *Marriage Alliance in Late Medieval Florence*. Cambridge, Mass.: Harvard University Press, 1994.

Reyerson, Kathryn, and Thomas Kuehn. "Women and Law in France and Italy." In *Women in Medieval Western European Civilization*, 131–41. *See above under* Hanawalt.

Richards, Gwenyth. "Medieval Welsh Noblewomen: The Case of Margaret Bromfield." *Eras: Monash University School of Historical Studies Online Journal* (2002).

Uitz, Erika. *Women in the Medieval Town*. Translated by Sheila Marnie. London: Barrie & Jenkins, 1990. Original *Die Frau in der mittelalterlichen Stadt*. Leipzig, Germany: Edition Leipzig, 1988.

Walker, Sue Sheridan. "'Litigant Agency' in Dower Pleas in the Common Law Courts in Thirteenth and Early Fourteenth Century England." Online at Web site: www.law.uchicago.edu/legalhistory/ lhp/resources/litigant.pdf.

DAVID K. BELL

DOWRY. Dowry, from the Latin *dos* or gift, refers to the property brought by a woman to her husband at the time of marriage. In twelfth-century Western Europe, it became customary for the bride's family to provide a gift, typically money or some form of real property, as a means of enhancing the bride's desirability. In theory, this desirability became mutually dependent on or conjoined with the potential for profit; within the system of dowry, the bride-to-be was objectified as a specific value commensurate with the property, money, or bonds promised to the groom at the time of betrothal. Some women were prevented from marrying precisely because their families lacked the resources to do so. One's fairness by no means guaranteed marriage; nubile women ultimately were only as attractive as their dowries permitted them to be. In the extreme, some women were forced to "marry" the Church or join beguinages (communities of Beguines: noncloistered but pious women), medieval halfway-houses, or religious courts established in part for women devoid of the resources necessary to marry, although, as shall be discussed later, dowries were often still involved even in these cases. While dowagers (dowered widows) could be significant landholders, a woman's dowry evolved as the main source of female investment capital and a significant economic force concomitant to the growth of urban commerce from the thirteenth century onward (Riemer; Angelos).

Because of the dowry's inherent connection to economics, the theory of supply and demand exerted a particular impact on whether or not the prices of dowries were inflated or deflated. If more women sought husbands than vice-versa, the average dowry would become distended; conversely, the median dowry would be depreciated if more bachelors sought brides than the reverse.

From the standpoint of familial strategy, the dowry was a prominent means of fashioning or perpetuating the fortunes of and authority wielded by great European families. In terms of the simultaneous benefit to both genders, the dowry was of particular service to the husband in that it provided an instant means by which to establish a household. But it also assured the wife of financial security in the event that she suffered adverse treatment at the hands of her husband. If the husband transgressed his marital vows by committing adultery or by engaging in abusive behavior that might have resulted in divorce, the marriage gift was to be returned directly to the woman or to her family. The dowry therefore assumed the dual character of being a financially pragmatic incentive to the husband prior to marriage and as a mechanism for deterring treacherous behavior during marriage. The dowry's rescindability was analogous to a type of prenuptial agreement or a kind of marital insurance of particular benefit to the wife.

Historically, the custom of presenting the dowry at the time of marriage can be traced to the marriage law of the Romans, in which it was recognized that the "burdens of matrimony" were such that youthful couples would be at a severe financial disadvantage on entering society. The transfer of property from the families of the bride and groom was "a principle conduit by which the old generation transferred wealth to support the enterprise (and encourage the fertility) of the young." Roman social convention originally dictated that the bride's family would provide the gift or donation to the husband and specified "that it remain forever with him" due to the presumed excessive responsibility placed on him in providing for his wife. However, around the third century, a curious pattern developed in which it also became the responsibility of the husband's family to provide a form of the true dowry, the *donatio* or *dos ex maritos*. The gifts given to Dido by Aeneas in Virgil's *Aeneid* (19 B.C.E.) have been recognized by scholars as an excellent literary-historical manifestation of the *dos ex maritos* or husband's donation. In a sense, this "reverse dowry"—also practiced in Islam as dictated by the *Quran* (*Koran*, seventh century)—equalized the terms within which the marriage transaction transpired and temporarily provided brides with more bargaining power than grooms. The dowry promised by the bride's family was often derived from the *dos ex maritos* and in turn given back to the husband. Until legislation was passed by the Emperor Justinian (r. 527–565) requiring that prenuptial gifts from both parties be equal, the family of the bride often was able to escape the original intent of having to make provision for the "burdens of matrimony" by deducting the true dowry out of the groom's *donatio*.

In the Middle Ages, the system of dowry was introduced into southern Europe around 1140 with very little deviation from the Roman model. The impact of the reverse dowry is notable in that it was expected of the groom to provide a gift of commensurate value to that of the bride. The uniform terms of the reverse dowry and true dowry inherited from the Romans were not maintained for long, however, as the percentage of the groom's gift declined to only one-fourth of the bride's true dowry in the middle part of the twelfth century.

Similarly, medieval Scandinavian custom involved the prospective groom's payment of a *mundr* (bride price)—as did Mediterranean and German customs—to obtain the woman. In exchange for the bride price, the bride's father would provide the dowry, equaling the sum of the woman's inheritance. The monetary component of the arrangement also fixed its legality (Jochens).

The European tendency gradually became the norm as the true dowry began to increase in proportion to the decline of the average reverse dowry, and the dowry's role shifted from that of wedding gift to the woman's full share in her patrimony. As the rights of medieval women to own property were being restricted, marriage laws paralleled this trend by becoming increasingly favorable to men. The system of dowry ultimately became an extension of the bias against women and returned almost uniformly to the initial model advocated by Roman law. In general, northern urban women experienced fewer restrictions in inheritance rights than those in southern Europe. Cash dowries were more prevalent in urban Italy and Flanders by the mid-fourteenth century, which both provided the woman with financial independence from her husband and a kind of severance from her own family; she could make no further claims on her father's property and other assets, yet could inherit from their mothers and other relatives, at least in northern Italy, as "nondotal" assets (Hughes; Angelos). A woman's dotal (dowry-related) and nondotal assets were protected by the state.

In the thirteenth century, dowries were often provided for out of Christian charity to young women lacking the resources to marry. Furthermore, dowries also applied to spiritual marriages, that is, to the Church, in the form of "monastic dowries." Families of means with disfigured daughters, or ones feared otherwise too unattractive to find husbands, or simply those wishing to become nuns, would donate their daughters' dowries—in some cases, only money, not property, to avoid complications—to the monastery. But by the early to mid-twelfth century, this practice would be condemned as a form of simony (the buying and selling of Church offices) and thus outlawed by the Fourth Lateran Council (1215; Johnson).

See also Beguines; China, Women in; Dower; Fatimid Egypt, Women in; *Frauenfrage*; Jewish Women in the Middle Ages; Law, Canon, Women in; Leonor López de Córdoba; Marriage; Norse Women; *Sachsenspiegel* and *Schwabenspiegel*

BIBLIOGRAPHY

Primary Sources

Les Coutumiers de Normandie, I: Le Très Ancien Coutumier de Normandie, edited by Ernest-Joseph Tardif, ch. 80. Rouen: E. Cagniard, 1881. Reprint Geneva: Slatkine, 1977. [Latin, Anglo-Norman, and French texts].

———. Translated extract in Emilie Amt. *Women's Lives in Medieval Europe: A Sourcebook*, 54–55, 59–60. New York and London: Routledge, 1993. [Also contains pertinent extracts translated from other European historical sources: Sicilian law 63, 65–66; 12C England 156; 14C Spain, 159; 13C French nunneries 250–51; 14C Flemish Beguines 264; 13C Jewish 288; 7C Muslim 299].

Feudal Society in Medieval France: Documents from the County of Champagne. Translated and edited by Theodore Evergates, esp. nos. 27–28, 31. Middle Ages Series. Philadelphia: University of Pennsylvania Press, 1993.

Liber Augustalis, or Constitutions of Melfi, Promulgated by the Emperor Frederick II for the Kingdom of Sicily in 1231. Edited and translated by James M. Powell, Book 2: Title 8; 3: 17. Syracuse, N.Y.: Syracuse University Press, 1971. [These extracts reprinted in Amt, 63, 65–66. *See above under* Coutumiers].

Secondary Sources

Amt, Emilie. *Women's Lives in Medieval Europe. See above under* Coutumiers. [Excellent selection and commentary].

Angelos, Mark. "Urban Women, Investment, and the Commercial Revolution of the Middle Ages." In *Women in Medieval Western European Civilization*, edited by Linda E. Mitchell, 257–72. Garland Reference Library of the Humanities, 2007. New York and London: Garland, 1999.

Bynum, Caroline W. "The 'Cruel Mother': Maternity, Widowhood, and Dowry in Florence in the Fourteenth and Fifteenth Centuries." In *Debating the Middle Ages: Issues and Readings*, edited and introduced by Lester K. Little and Barbara H. Rosenwein, ch. 13. Malden, Mass.: Blackwell, 1998.

Chojnacki, Stanley. "The Power of Love: Wives and Husbands in Late Medieval Venice." In *Women and Power in the Middle Ages*, edited by Mary Erler and Maryanne Kowaleski, 126–48. Athens and London: University of Georgia Press, 1988.

Evergates, Theodore. "Aristocratic Women in the County of Champagne." In *Aristocratic Women in Medieval France*, edited by T. Evergates, 74–110. The Middle Ages. Philadelphia: University of Pennsylvania Press, 1999.

Hanawalt, Barbara A., and Anna Dronzek, "Women in Medieval Urban Society." In *Women in Medieval Western European Civilization*, 31–45. *See above under* Angelos.

Herlihy, David. *Medieval Households*. Cambridge, Mass.: Harvard University Press, 1985.

Hughes, Diane Owen. "From Brideprice to Dowry in Mediterranean Europe." *Journal of Family History* 3 (1978): 262–96. Reprint in Kaplan, 25–58. *See below*.

Jochens, Jenny. "Marriage and Divorce." In *Medieval Scandinavia: An Encyclopedia*, edited by Phillip Pulsiano and Kirsten Wolf et al., 408–10. Garland Reference Library of the Humanities, 934. New York and London: Garland, 1993.

Johnson, Penelope D. *Equal in Monastic Profession: Religious Women in Medieval France*. Women in Culture and Society. Chicago and London: University of Chicago Press, 1991.

Kaplan, Marion A., ed. *The Marriage Bargain: Women and Dowries in European History*. New York: Harrington Park Press, 1985. [Important essays by various authors].

Klapisch-Zuber, Christiane. "The 'Cruel Mother': Maternity, Widowhood, and Dowry in Florence in the Fourteenth and Fifteenth Centuries." In C. Klapisch-Zuber, *Women, Family and Ritual in Renaissance Italy*, translated by Lydia G. Cochrane, 117–31. Chicago: University of Chicago Press, 1985. Original "Maternité, veuvage et dot à Florence." *Annales, E. S. C.* 38.5 (1983): 1097–1109.

Molho, Anthony. *Marriage Alliance in Late Medieval Florence*. Cambridge, Mass.: Harvard University Press, 1994.

Reyerson, Kathryn, and Thomas Kuehn. "Women and Law in France and Italy." In *Women in Medieval Western European Civilization*, 131–41. *See above under* Angelos.

Riemer, Eleanor S. "Women, Dowries, and Capital Investment in Thirteenth-Century Siena." In Kaplan, 59–80. *See above*.

Uitz, Erika. *Women in the Medieval Town*. Translated by Sheila Marnie. London: Barrie & Jenkins, 1990. Original *Die Frau in der mittelalterlichen Stadt*. Leipzig, Germany: Edition Leipzig, 1988.

DAVID K. BELL

DRESS, COURTLY WOMEN'S (12th century). Throughout the twelfth century, the vocabulary of dress was a simple one, but in the mid-1100s—a sort of "renaissance" for so many aspects of medieval European culture—a distinct sense of fashion, with all its sociopolitical and economic significance, emerged within the courts of northern Europe. Parallels occur in Scandinavian women's dress and in Middle Eastern textiles at that time, thereby revealing an interrelation of medieval Christian, Jewish, and Muslim societies through courtly women's dress. Chief among the sources of evidence used are the sculptures of women in church portals, those on wax seals affixed to legal documents, and in courtly literary descriptions of the women protagonists' clothing. Other clues come from stained glass images, pottery painting, manuscript illuminations, and, in another dimension, from remnants of more durable fabrics.

In the early 1100s, the costume worn by both men and women of the upper echelons of northern-French society comprised a *chemise* (shirt), a *bliaut* (blouse-like tunic), and a *manteau* (overcoat). Two significant shifts in clothing silhouette and materials divide the century into thirds: the first shift occurred in the 1130s and the second took place in the 1160s. Much about fashionable dress can be learned from the extremely detailed attire of the larger-than-life-size statues installed between the 1130s and the 1160s in the jambs of church portals. While many mid-twelfth-century column-figures have been damaged or lost, visual evidence exists for a group of column-figures from programs of sculpture at twenty great churches in France and one in England. Seventeen of these programs feature women, as found in churches or cathedrals (named in parentheses) in the following cities: Angers (St.-Maurice), Bourges (St.-Étienne), Chartres (Notre-Dame), Corbeil (Notre-Dame),

Dijon (St. Bénigne), Étampes (Notre-Dame-du-Fort), Ivry-la-Bataille (Notre-Dame), Le Mans (Saint-Julien), Nesle-la-Reposte (abbey of Notre-Dame), Paris (Notre-Dame; St. Germain-des-Prés), Provins (St.-Aioul; St.-Thibault), Rochester (Rochester Cathedral), Saint-Denis (Basilica), Saint-Loup-de-Naud (priory church), and Vermenton (Notre-Dame). From these we have accounted for twenty-nine women column-figures, carved with such precision that the garment construction can be discerned and the textiles identified. Each of the "hands" of various artist-masons, or *ymagiers*—literally, "image-makers"—bears its individual traits, yet all the *ymagiers* portray contemporary clothing with a clarity and meticulousness normally confined to small-scale sculpture. Significantly, even though the characters themselves are often fictive or legendary (from biblical or historical lore), their dress is realistically drawn from the sculptors' own time, the twelfth century, in a manner often identifying the sculptor's particular patron and his or her beliefs. When such personages appear at the doors of great churches dressed in the clothing of the contemporary elite, the viewer connects the hierarchy among the column-figures with established hierarchies of real life. The Church, patron of monumental sculpture, employed sculpture programs to shape reality, condoning some behaviors and discouraging others, always with the salvation of the faithful as its ultimate goal. The elevated figures in the sacred precinct within the portal jambs express the patrons' affirmation and participation in the divine plan for the world. Likewise, extended secular power is affirmed by column-figures wearing costumes recognizable both as the fashion of the court and as Eastern in origin, the prestige associated with biblical personages may be transferred to the contemporary authority, the Capetian king of France, for example, Philip Augustus (1165–1223). Philip would double the size of his kingdom, go on Crusade to the Holy Land, implement sweeping judicial and social reform, and stimulate commerce, as exemplified in the great Fairs of Champagne, in which textiles featured prominently.

In Normandy, domain of the Plantagenet royal family (beginning in 1154 with King Henry II of England), among the sculpted figures in the jamb of the main doorway of the cathedral of Saint-Julien in Angers are two women depicted wearing clothing in the style of the earlier part of the century. The costume of the woman in the right side of the jamb is particularly clearly represented, complete with fastening pins and laces. Her chemise, a floor-length undergarment with long, narrow, rucked sleeves, is visible at her neckline and where she has lifted her dress at the hem. The ankle-length tunic she wears over the chemise is the *bliaut*, with its close-fitting bodice, a flaring skirt, and long, hanging sleeve cuffs. It is laced up the side and cinched with a belt at the natural waistline. Cords fastened her *manteau*, a long cloak cut as a half-circle, around both shoulders.

Twenty-two of the women column-figures installed at mid-century were depicted wearing the version of the *bliaut*, fashionable in northern-French court dress in the 1130s, called the *bliaut gironé* (skirted tunic). This is an elaborate dress of costly materials, described frequently in twelfth-century literature (Goddard). In the county of Blois, a territory aligned with the French king Louis VII, on the left jamb of the left portal of the west façade of Chartres Cathedral, the woman column-figure is dressed in a *bliaut gironé* (Fig. 1). This *bliaut* was made in two pieces, with a snug bodice (*cors*) and a skirt (*gironée*) that was finely pleated into a fitted, low waistband. The "warp" threads of the *gironée* fabric ran horizontally; that is, the finished sides of the piece of fabric, the selvages, were used at the waist and as the *gironée* hem, so the pleats of the "weft" threads hung nearly vertically. In some examples, the lower edge appears to have been edged with a decorative strip, embroidery or tablet-woven band. Most women also wore a doubly wrapped belt, a *ceinture*, with long pendant ends, usually ornamented. The center of this *ceinture* was placed over the woman's diaphragm in front. It crossed around her back and returned to be knotted over her pelvic bone, emphasizing her womb (Fig. 4). This long *ceinture* is similar to the belts represented on figures along the Silk Road and trade routes to the East, and its emphasis on the fecund womb is connected to the twelfth-century interest in Mary's womb as a vessel for the Incarnation of Christ.

A distinguishing characteristic of the mid-century fashionable *bliaut* is the overlong hanging sleeve cuff. This cuff may taper to a long point and be so long that it must be knotted to avoid dragging on the floor (Fig. 1), or it may take the form of a broad trumpet turned back upon itself. The sleeve and hanging cuff construction is especially clear in a woman column-figure second from left on the center portal of Chartres Cathedral (Fig. 2). The broad panel of the hanging cuff was turned from the wrist back over the forearm, and the band of understitching securing it can be seen at the turnback along the wrist fold. The extended sleeve points of the eleventh-century women of the Bayeux Tapestry were formally extended to very long hanging sleeve cuffs signaling a twelfth-century lady's status at court as in the Chartres sculptures (Fig. 3).

Additional sculpted evidence comes from sigillography, the study of figured wax seals, just coming into use during the mid-twelfth century to authenticate legal documents, rather than signatures, through the fourteenth century. As Theodore Evergates explains, legal transactions were arranged orally before witnesses and relatives, and their act of consent (*laudatio*) was later commemorated in a document validated by a seal. Seals may identify the sigillant (the seal's bearer) by name and social rank, specify the relationships of the persons involved, and give exact locations of the action validated by the seal. These seals display motifs and designs expressing their owners' self-perceptions (Bedos-Rezak). Though these elements may be stylized and standardized among sigillographic images, the costumes depicted in these proto-portraits of men and women strongly resemble those of the column-figures.

Until nearly 1200, many of the sigillographic proto-portraits of close relatives of Louis VII continued to feature the conservative, formal fashion of the court: the *manteau* and the *bliaut gironé*, recognizable because of its lowered waist and the closely set, vertical pleats of the gironée, with hanging sleeve cuffs and narrow undersleeves to the wrist. The *bliaut gironé* appears on the seals of Eleanor of Aquitaine and two of the three seals of Agnès de Champagne, the sister-in-law of Eleanor's daughter Marie. Long cuffs dominate women's seals even after the *bliaut gironé* was replaced by the *cote*, as seen in the proto-portrait of Marie, daughter of Eleanor and Louis VII of France (see illustration in Marie de Champagne entry, p. 000). The fashionable silhouette of the last third of the century is represented on the north lateral portal at Saint-Étienne, cathedral of Bourges, in the duchy of Burgundy. A shift of the fashion center from Paris southward to the courts of Champagne and Blois occurred in the mid-1160s, following the marriages of Marie and her sister Alix and the birth of Louis VII's heir, the future Philip Augustus. The seal provided tangible, material proof of the sigillant's assent to a document. Similar assent to a policy or allegiance to a lord might be asserted by having the stone column-figures dressed in fashions associated with that lord's court, a maneuver discernible in the Bourges sculptures, since Louis VII was liege lord of the duke of Burgundy and the counts of Champagne and Blois—that is, these lords were among Louis's vassals and thus swore loyalty to him.

Fig. 1

Fig. 2

Fig. 4

Fig. 3

Chartres Cathedral portals showing examples of medieval courtly dress.

Thanks to the sculptors' careful handiwork, scholars have determined that courtly clothing was constructed of silk, very fine linen, and woolen cloth. Each fabric is recognizable from the characteristic drapery folds sculpted by artists working in relatively naturalistic mode. The thickness and weight of these textiles derive both from their original material and the techniques used in preparing, spinning, weaving, and finishing the cloth. Silk is composed of extremely thin and long filaments, which can be woven into substantial or featherweight textiles. Finely woven silks lend themselves to minuscule pleating, and silk cloth retains an airy volume disproportionate to its weight. Linen rumples into creases with crisp corners, made as it is from long cellulose flax fibers, and the surface of linen can be polished or pressed in wrinkles and pleats. Woolen stuffs may be woven with gossamer thinness, and the yarn preserves the springiness of the sheep's fleece, giving the cloth a three-dimensionality even when lightweight. When woolen cloth has been fulled (bulked up) and sheared after weaving, the relatively thick finished fabric will drape in broad, heavy folds.

However, the artists intended their precise representation of clothing not for us modern scholars but for their discriminating twelfth-century audience. Then, as now, dress reflected contemporary values—in commercial, political, spiritual, or social spheres—hence communicating the wearer's status and role within these domains. The envisioned audience would have recognized the fabrics and dress of the column-figures, especially since the sculpture was originally brilliantly painted. In literature and commercial documents, these luxury materials were also identified according to their places of origin, further details appealing to readers prone to fascination with "elsewhere": the prestige of coming from a beautiful, mysterious place beyond one's usual environs, such as the Orient.

Elite women of northern Europe acquired exotic textiles through returning ambassadors, pilgrims, and crusaders, and also through commercial trade. The softer silhouette made possible by fine northern goods appeared during the 1160s in artwork and at the courts of northern France, just as the Fairs of Champagne established themselves as major commercial centers in northern Europe. European trade with the East had continued despite the Muslim invasions in the ninth and tenth centuries. Analysis of the precious, highly diverse trove of Jewish written materials (religious, secular, personal, financial) preserved in the late ninth-century Geniza (Hebrew = "hiding place"; a chamber next to the synagogue housing documents unfit for use in worship) discovered at Cairo, Egypt (in the nineteenth century, now mostly at Cambridge University), reveals some of the French courts' sources for fine stuffs. Certain of these documents show, for instance, that Egyptian Jewish merchants had been trading with northern Europe since at least the ninth century, and that textiles and spices were prime commodities in the eleventh and twelfth centuries. Dyestuffs and mordants (chemicals for fixing coloring in fabric) were included in the "spice" category while silk and flax were by far the most commonly shipped fibers (see Goitein).

Fine textiles tell the economic history of their origins: Egypt, particularly around the Nile delta, produced so much flax that in the Middle Ages it was known as the land of fine linen, and a fabulously fine white linen was produced only in Iran at the Rahban canal as a result of the canal's water chemical content. Since silkworm cultivation had not yet been developed in France by twelfth century, any silk used in France must have been imported from workshops in Spain, Sicily, the Levant, or the Far East. Constantinople, capital of Byzantium and last vestige of the Roman Empire, also produced suitably imperial silks often inaccessible to westerners. Marie de France, author of the popular *Lais* (short romances, usually in verse, c.1170), in a sense "weaves" the Oriental mystique of silk into the plot of one of her lais, *Le Fresne* ("Ash Tree"; also the heroine's name). Marie's courtly readers would have appreciated the inestimable value of the rosette-decorated silk obtained by Fresne's lordly father "from Constantinople" (vv. 121–25) in which the mother wraps the infant heroine (with an inscribed ring tied to her), specifically to denote her noble birth (vv. 132–34), before abandoning her at a convent to avoid unfairly wrought scandal. At the end of the story, the long-lost Fresne, now an adult, is recognized by her mother because of this silk and the ring to end the tale happily (vv. 423–60). The Grecian cities of Thebes and Andros, along with Sicily, produced the specific types of silks mentioned in twelfth-century literature, while Syria, Gaza and lands farther east were sources of lower-priced silks and compound cloths.

Returning to our church-portal column-figure sculpture as testimony to the European taste for acquired styles, we may observe arguably Eastern touches in such details as the understitching of sleeve cuffs, stitches supporting bejeweled borders, tablet-woven bands bordering panels, the shaping of hanging sleeve cuffs, and crisply stitched knife-pleats set into shaped waistbands. Elements adapted from Islamic dress may include the shaped upper shoulder documented in Egyptian garments by Granger-Taylor, the lowered waistband evident in women's costumes painted on Islamic lusterware (glazed pottery covered with a metallic overglaze to produce an iridescent sheen, by Egyptian and Persian artisans), and the upper armband and knotted cummerbund of the terra-cotta Persian Islamic princely figures seen, for example, at the Metropolitan Museum in New York. The border bands recall the Arabic term *tiraz*, which can refer either to the tapestry-woven or embroidered inscription band worked as part of a textile, or to the garment bearing the band, or to the workshop where the cloth was woven or ornamented. The distinctive strips of tapestry applied to or inserted into *tiraz* fabrics were also reproduced in the layering of an individual costume, as on women at Chartres (Figs. 1 and 4) and at Saint-Loup-de-Naud in the county of Champagne (Golombek and Gervers). Such striped arrangements disappeared in sculpture installed after the mid-1160s, when the fashion shifted to the more substantial northern linens and woolens. The finely woven and fulled woolen cloth represented in sculpture at the northern-French towns of Senlis and Mantes, and the transept portals at Chartres, can be none other than Flemish *scarlet*, a very fine, expensive woolen cloth produced in various colors, the staple of the Champenois and Flemish textile trade.

Fragments of costumes and extant textiles can sometimes serve to refute misconceptions concerning the reliability of medieval costume representation in sculpture. For example, art historians have considered the fine pleating of skirts and aprons (*gironées*) as mere conventions imposed by the columnar, architectonic confines of mid-twelfth-century portal sculpture. But examination of extant pieces of finely pleated *gironées* demonstrate that the ymagiers had in fact faithfully reproduced the lines of the actual fabric and clothing item style. Most *court bliauts gironés* illustrated in French portal sculpture are represented as if they had been made of linen or silk. Margarita Nockert has identified the finely pleated woolen fabrics found at Gamla Lödöse and other West Scandinavian sites as the northern equivalent of the *gironées* worn by the Chartres west portal women. These fabrics were finely pleated in the warp direction, and the width of each piece was increased with gores. The largest fragments are eighty-nine centimeters long, and the hems are partly quilted (note the patterned hems of Figs. 3 and 4). Finely pleated linen undergarments like the column-figures' chemises have been found at the great burial site excavated in 1871–1895 at Birka, near Stockholm, Sweden. Apparently the filling-out effect of pleating and rucking or goffering (other types of pleating) was made permanent by binding and boiling the bound fabrics, though in some cases, the crisp ridges of the pleats are fixed by stitches along the peak of the folds. These archaeological textiles represent provincial substitutes for the soft, billowing effect of silk or linen of northern French courtly dress.

Returning to literary evidence for more on the sociopolitical language of courtly women's dress, we note female characters clothed much like the women column-figures to convey similar interrelationships of gender, social status, and power. For example, along with clothing's social-rank definition discussed above in *Fresne*, in another lai, entitled *Lanval*, Marie de France evokes the erotic allure of a *bliaut's* lacings such as those seen at Angers. Lanval, who has spurned the vengeful queen's advances in favor of his secret lady, faces severe punishment. When describing the lady's enchanting arrival to rescue him at Arthur's court, Marie depicts her sumptuous attire, then focuses on this lacing (vv. 565–68): "Ele ert vestue en itel guise/ de chainse blanc e de chemise,/qui tuit li costé li pareient,/ ki de dous parz lacié esteient"("She was dressed in this fashion: in a *chemise* and a *tunique* that revealed both her sides, since the lacing was on each side")—revealing her incomparably white, soft skin along her torso. Jane Burns has recently noted how women's dress in *Lanval* underscores not only their social status but also their individual gender and personal values. In particular, Lanval's beautiful lady's priceless, deep-purple and white silks not only link her with the mythical beauties of old (Dido, Lavinia, even Venus), but also confer on her the status of feudal lord, worthy of King Arthur (never mind the queen), while Lanval is merely her passive lover. Other works of vernacular literature mention the *bliaut gironé*. By contrast, in the thirteenth century, a more "unisex" approach to dress arises in both literature and the visual arts, even in the Muslim world (see Heller), which perplexes some modern historians: is this trend a mark of dowdiness or elegant simplicity?

Much can be discerned, therefore, in the transformation of the women of the courts' simple chemise, *bliaut*, and *manteau* costume of the beginning of the twelfth century into the more elaborate *bliaut gironé*, *ceinture*, and *manteau* for the second third of the century. The fashionable courtly attire of statues in the liminal zone of church portals suggests divine sanction (analogous to the wax seals for mortals), if not for individuals, then for temporal power, social rank and behavior, for military, political and economic dominance both at home and abroad. Such are the implications of clothing's multileveled language.

See also Courtesy Books; Dress, Religious Women's (Western, Christian); Eleanor of Aquitaine; Embroidery; Guilds, Women in; Marie de France; Spinners and Drapers

BIBLIOGRAPHY

Primary Sources
Evergates, Theodore. *Feudal Society in Medieval France. Documents from the County of Champagne.* Philadelphia: University of Pennsylvania Press, 1993.
Marie de France. *Lais.* Edited by Karl Warnke. Translation (Modern French), introduction, and notes by Laurence Harf-Lancner. Lettres gothiques. Paris: Livre de Poche, 1990.
———. *The Lais of Marie de France.* Translated with introduction and notes by Robert Hanning and Joan Ferrante. Durham, N.C.: Labyrinth Press, 1978. Reprint 1982.

Secondary Sources

Bedos-Rezak, Brigitte. *Form and Order in Medieval France, Studies in Social and Quantitative Sigillography.* Aldershot, U.K.: Variorum, 1993.

Burns, E. Jane. *Courtly Love Undressed: Reading Trough Clothes in Medieval French Culture.* Middle Ages. Philadelphia: University of Pennsylvania Press, 2002.

Goddard, Eunice R. *Women's Costume in French Texts of the Eleventh and Twelfth Centuries.* Baltimore: Johns Hopkins University Press; Paris: Presses Universitaires de France, 1927.

Goitein, Shelomo D. *A Mediterranean Society, the Jewish Communities of the Arab world as portrayed in the documents of the Cairo Geniza.* 6 vols. Berkeley and Los Angeles: University of California Press, 1967–1993.

Golombek, Lisa, and Veronika Gervers. "Tiraz Fabrics in the Royal Ontario Museum." In *Studies in Textile History,* edited by Veronika Gervers, 82–93. Toronto: Royal Ontario Museum, 1977.

Gordon, Stuart, ed. *Robes and Honor: The Medieval World of Investiture.* New York: Palgrave/St. Martin's, 2001.

Granger-Taylor, Hero. "The Construction of Tunics." In *Early Islamic Textiles,* edited by Clive Rogers, 10–12. Brighton, U.K.: Rogers & Podmore, 1983.

Heller, Sarah-Grace. Review of Burns (*see above*). BMR online. 19 Feb. 2003.

Jacoby, David. "Silk in Western Byzantium before the Fourth Crusade. Jerusalem." *Byzantinische Zeitschrift* 84–85.2 (1991–1992): 452–500.

Katzenellenbogen, Adolf. *The Sculptural Programs of Chartres Cathedral: Christ, Mary, Ecclesia.* Baltimore: Johns Hopkins University Press, 1959.

Lombard, Maurice. *Études d'économie médiévale, 3: Les Textiles dans le monde musulman du VIIe au XIIe siécles.* Civilisations et Sociétés, 61. Paris and New York: Mouton, 1978.

Lopez, Robert S. "Silk Industry in the Byzantine Empire." In *Speculum* 20 (1945): 1–42.

Luchaire, Achille. *Études sur les Actes de Louis VII: Histoire des institutions monarchiques de la France sous les premiers Capétiens.* Paris: Archives nationales/École des Chartes, 1885.

Muthesius, Anna. "The Byzantine Silk Industry: Lopez and Beyond." *Journal of Medieval History,* 19.1–2 (March–June, 1993): 1–33.

———. "From Seed to Samite: Aspects of Byzantine Silk Production." *Textile History* 20.2 (autumn 1989): 135–49.

Nockert, Margarita. "Medeltida dräkt i bild och verklighet." In *Den Ljusa Medeltiden* [Festschrift Aron Andersson], edited by Lennart Karlsson et al., 191–96. Stockholm Museum of National Antiquities, 4. Stockholm: Statens Historiska Museum, 1984.

Quicherat, Jules. *Histoire du Costume en France depuis les temps les plus reculés jusqu'à la fin du XVIIIe siècle.* 2nd ed. Paris: Hachette, 1877.

Stauffer, Annemarie, with A. Schmidt-Colinet. *Textiles d'Egypte de la collection Bouvier, Antiquité tardive, période copte, premiers temps de l'Islam.* Fribourg, Switzerland: Musée d'art et d'histoire; Bern: Benteli Verlag, 1991.

Viollet-le-Duc, Eugène-Emmanuel. *Dictionnaire raisonné du mobilier français de l'époque carlovingienne à la Renaissance.* 6 vols. Paris: A. Morel, 1872–1875. [vols. 3–4].

JANET E. SNYDER

DRESS, RELIGIOUS WOMEN'S (WESTERN, CHRISTIAN). Religious women's dress in medieval Western society served important cultural, visual, and symbolic purposes. Perceptions about the clothing of the religious changed considerably over time and space, as did the status and position of the female clergy. For the earlier period, the primary sources are textual—written descriptions—whereas from the thirteenth century onward there are also numerous visual representations, particularly in manuscript illuminations. Since both types of sources often idealize or polemicize religious women, each rhetorical presentation requires consideration of its specific cultural context. Throughout the Middle Ages, there arose movements to reform, streamline, and standardize practices within each of the various religious groups, and such tendencies significantly reflected themselves in each group's dress.

In the early medieval written sources, the change into distinctive clothing (*mutatio vestium*) established the virtuous social status of religious women. Patristic writers (early Church authors) such as St. Jerome (c.345–420) would invariably contrast the vain and provocative dress customs of worldly women with the humble self-denial implicit in the holy virgins' "vile," crude garments (Jerome, Epistle 128). Another example is St. Augustine's praise of holy women's neglect of personal physical cleanliness as a path toward spiritual purity (Augustine, Epistle 211). The Church Fathers did not specify the proper color and cut of religious dress; instead these men dwelled only on the forbidden extravagances and vanities—costly dyes, fine cloth finishes, precious decoration, and overall seductive intent.

In the later Middle Ages, by contrast, aspects of clothing prescribed in the rules for nuns and other, noncloistered religious women's commu-

The Augustinian Hermit nuns receiving their rule from a bishop. Attired in dark grey, each wears a large, loose scapular clearly seen over the simple tunic. Ms Typ 156H, f 1v, from a Rulebook for Santa Giustina, Venice, 1550. © Houghton Library, Cambridge, Mass.

nities became increasingly explicit, detailing garment dimensions, color, and textile quality. During this entire phase, dress codes dictated to women generally sought to diminish women's social significance and sexuality, yet the concept of a uniform, expressing a collective, corporate identity through clothing's shape and color, emerged relatively late and in response to the proliferation of new religious orders and their requirements for distinctive identities in medieval society. By this time (thirteenth century), religious orders were ranked: the First Order being comprised of monks, the Second Order referred to nuns, and the Third Order, also called Tertiaries, included medicant orders ("begging," nonproperty owning, bound by vows of poverty and penance, like the Franciscans and Dominicans), and noncloistered religious communities of both genders. All of these orders lived by regulations based on one of the three rules approved by the Church: (1) that devised by St. Benedict of Nursia for his monks (c.540), (2) that attributed to St. Augustine of Hippo (who lived in North Africa 354–430, but whose texts were not really codified as his rule until the late eleventh century in Western Europe), or (3) the *Regula*

primitiva of St. Francis (1209, 1223). Since these rules governed all aspects of life within or outside the cloister, they inevitably affected styles of religious dress.

Whether professed as nuns or affiliated as Tertiaries, religious women shared with their male counterparts a historicizing (as in the familiar modern term, "retro"), ungendered form of dress. Thus, well after European secular society had abandoned classical garment types and introduced distinctions between male and female dress components, the religious continued to dress as people did in the Late Antique period (fourth to sixth centuries), wearing the simple, long-sleeved, ankle-length woolen *tunica* (tunics), always with a cloth, leather, or cord girdle. The girdle functioned both as a dress component and means of penance, since it divided the body into the significant upper and lower zones while chafing uncomfortably as an ever-present reminder of vigilance along the wearer's pious path of self-mortification. Similarly, many orders allowed undergarments in the form of full-length linen or wool shifts; other orders prohibited them or allowed only coarse, hempen *camisiae* (shirts).

Northern Italian nuns' dress as reflected in this representation of the Council of Pisa, 1409. © Houghton Library, Cambridge, Mass.

Although the early rules decreed that cloth should be produced in-house for the community's needs, surviving accounts show market purchases in bulk of the woolen fabrics. Abbesses and nuns who did spin and weave were commended for this extra virtue.

Those participating in the liturgy within the church choir wore wide-sleeved, loose woolen *cucullae* (hoods, cowls) or choir robes over the girdled tunic. The apron-like *scapular* (from Latin *scapulae* = "shoulder blades"), originally worn over the tunic as shoulder protection during manual work, was prescribed for many orders; in depictions it often hides the girdle. The scapular took many shapes, from oversized to abbreviated and vestigial. During the service, it was removed, or covered by the choir robe. Mantles were donned when leaving the religious house and in cold weather.

Leather shoes were standard among most orders (described as "calced," from Latin *calceatus* = "shod"), though some discalced orders distinguished their individual asceticism by insisting on mere sandals or bare feet in imitation of Christ, as emulated by Eastern Church monks since Matthew 10:10 and later introduced in the West by St. Francis (early

1200s). The rules also spell out the number of tunics and mantles permitted in changes of clothing for laundering and for sleeping as opposed to daytime wear. No matter how worn out, these garments were always eventually donated to the abject poor.

Female and male religious did differ in their headdress: men wore a hooded cowl to cover their tonsured heads; women had veils to cover theirs. Women's tonsure consisted in cutting the hair back to the ears four to six times annually. Novices (entry-level nuns), Tertiaries, and lay sisters wore white linen veils; the black veil, worn over a white linen under-veil, was reserved for the professed nun having served a probationary period as a novice and spoken her vows before the bishop. These ceremonies consecrating the black veil were held during certain feast days of the liturgical (Church services-oriented) year, such as the Ascension of Christ. Noncontemplative members of the monastic community, such as the lay sisters, took simple or no vows; they generally wore a modified version of the dress prescribed for the cloistered nuns; for example, minus the hoods (cucullae).

Benedictine nuns, fully cloistered and contemplative, were known as the Black Ladies or Black Nuns, and on the average accounted for almost half of all the women's religious houses in the European Middle Ages. This early order's clothing underscored Benedictine frugality, as reflected in their use of the cheapest local cloth, but this practice was later gradually abandoned. Although St. Benedict's Rule does not specify what color the dress should be, by the early twelfth century, female and male Benedictines alike wore black, ample robes of fine dyed wool; hence the men were called "Black Monks" in England (not to be confused with the term "Blackfriars," denoting the Dominicans). Most Benedictine houses were richly endowed, and their usually royal or aristocratic inhabitants were portrayed in their two-part robes, consisting of a wide-sleeved cuculla, like the choir robes of other orders, and a tunic revealing only the narrow sleeves and lower hems.

The new, reformed orders adopted rules in strict compliance with the Rule of St. Benedict; among these were the communities of Fontevrault (founded c.1115; reformed fourteenth to fifteenth centuries) and Cîteaux (the Cistercians, 1098; peaked twelfth century)—both in France—as well as the Camaldolese (1012–1023), Vallombrosan (1036—at Vallombrosa, near Florence; reformed fifteenth century), Olivetan (1319; named after Monte Olivete in Siena), and Humiliate (feminine of Humiliati = "the Humble Ones"; mid-twelfth century; reorganized for papal approval 1201) orders, in what is now Italy. As signs of their rehabilitation within the Church, all at first attired themselves in undyed, unprocessed woolens (see Hélyot, vol. 4), in off-white to dark-neutral tones. Later, most of these orders, outlasting their original reformist fervor and yielding to an urge for refinement, wore fine, whitened woolens for their tunics, with variations between large and small scapulars, with mantles often in black. The Carthusians (founded 1084 at the Grande Chartreuse in the French Alps), who also followed a form of the Benedictine Rule, likewise began with undyed, then progressed to white, clothing. The Sempringham Order of Gilbertine nuns (founded there by St. Gilbert, early twelfth century) in Lincolnshire, England, aspired to Cistercian ideals—a stricter interpretation of the Benedictine Rule—even though the community was guided by canons following the Augustinian Rule. The nuns of this unique purely English order were prescribed undyed wool and sheepskin garments.

Orders whose rules derived from St. Augustine's Rule rarely displayed the linear growth of the Benedictine-based branches and showed greater diversity in dress color. The order of canonesses, whether "canonesses secular" (who lived as community but without renouncing individual property) under a bishop, or "canonesses regular" (who lived under semi-monastic rule) under an abbot, offered the only alternative to the closed, contemplative life of the Benedictines after the ninth-century determinations of the Councils at Châlons and Aix (McNamara). Augustinian canonesses wore either solid black or combinations of black and white, but not all white. In wills left by secular canonesses, one finds mention of blue, purple, and red apparel as well. The Augustinian Rule, reformulated in the late eleventh century, also came to be widely used for women's communities unwilling or unable to adopt the Benedictine Rule, as in the case of the above-cited Gilbertines. These groups were joined by various Italian eremitical (hermit-like) sects, consolidated as Augustinian Hermits, one of the mendicant orders. Nuns of this order, known in England as "Austin," dress in all black, with visible black leather belts.

The numerous members of the Hospitaller orders, originating after the successful Crusade reconquest of Jerusalem (1099), and remaining linked to later Crusades, began by nursing with extraordinary care the sick impoverished in hospitals, from whence their name. Just as the males became known as Knights Hospitaller or Knights of St. John of Jerusalem, the women could become Sisters of St. John. They functioned as canonesses regular and thus lived in more closed communities than did most of the men (Cross et al.). The Sisters' mantles bore distinguishing marks: usually large crosses applied at the chest or shoulders as signs of their special profession and corporate identity, much like the heraldry used by the male Hospitallers. Close to these sisters were the Trinitarian (Order of the Holy Trinity, founded at Meaux, northern France, 1198) nuns, who strictly adhered to the Augustinian Rule while caring for the unfortunate and helping to ransom captives. Also cloistered, they wore white garments with scapulars and cloaks marked with blue-and-red crosses.

The Premonstratensians (because of their origins in Prémontré, northern France), were also called the Norbertines (after St. Norbert, their founder, in 1120). Their more austere version of the Augustinian Rule prohibited them from eating meat, among other restrictions. While the men were known as the "White Canons" in England, the nuns wore undyed, coarse woolens with very small, black head cloths. Depictions of German Premonstratensian nuns show them dressed in white with cloth-band "crowns" on their heads, over their black veils. Many of the Italian orders of penance adopted the Augustinian Rule when requested by Church officials to conform, thus their appellation of *Mantellate* ("Mantled Women"), indicating their utter simplicity of life and dress practice (Esposito). The Carmelites (founded late twelfth century), another Augustinian-Ruled mendicant order, wore brown tunics, white mantles, and black scapulars. The Dominican nuns—the Second Order—had black veils with white tunics and black mantles, shoes and stockings, while their Tertiary sisters wore white veils (Fontette). The Bridgettines or Birgittines (originally founded by St. Birgitta [English = Bridget] of Sweden 1370) of the Order of St. Savior, relegated to adopting the Augustinian Rule (instead of the controversial Bridgettine Rule), observed very specific dress customs, including the wearing of ash-grey, heavy woolen tunics and mantles, and the black veil crowned with the white linen band dotted with red, inherited from the German Cistercian and Premonstratensian nuns (Kroos).

Other important religious communities such as the beguines, the Sisters of Common Life, and the many penitent movements, often chose the Augustinian Rule when forced to conform to the Church's doctrines. Surviving rules from particular convents contain more prescriptive than descriptive details, offering scant evidence of prolonged, standardized dress codes (Rehm). These religious often participated actively in textile manufacture and charitable works. Accordingly, the shapeless grey mantle of the beguines and the short, ragged ones of the penitents were easily recognizable along the medieval landscape.

The brief and simple Rule of St. Francis (*Regula Primitiva*), though the last of the three major rules to be formulated, was the first to be sanctioned by Rome (orally by Innocent III in 1209; officially, as a *Regula bullata*, by Honorius III in 1223). This rule governed the Franciscan mendicant congregations. The first version of his rule for nuns inspired St. Clare in establishing her order, which she cofounded with Francis in 1212–1214 as the Poor Clares (in French: *Clarisses*), so-named for their lives of complete poverty, a papal privilege, at San Damiano, near Assisi, Italy. However, the Franciscan Rule was not adopted by Clare's order as a whole until 1253, superseding two earlier, lesser rules (Cross et al.). Their garments, rope-girdled tunics of undyed, poor-quality wool, earned them the name "Grey Sisters," just as their brothers were called Grey Friars, and even though their habits are now more generally brown. The Poor Clares' attire was depicted either with or without a scapular (Hélyot, vol. 7); the latter case heeding more closely their very austere Franciscan rule—the harshest yet adopted for women, which was consequently modified for some of their convents.

Problems encountered when attempting to interpret and identify religious women's dress are inherent in both textual and visual representations. Practices of the First (professed male) Orders tend to be the ones most recorded in the Rules. It has generally been assumed that the Second Order (professed women) followed the clothing regulations of their male counterparts. But the sources suggest that considerable fluidity, nonconformity, and borrowing occurred within and among the orders of nuns, sometimes within a short interval of time. Thus, in England, the term White Nuns or White Ladies could denote Cistercians, some reformed Benedictines, and some Augustinian orders (Thompson). This has been attributed to the difficulties encountered by the various orders when seeking to establish themselves by attracting and selecting members, and by each order evolving, then maintaining, distinctive identities. Such collective goals were impeded by the narrower range of privileges allowed nuns, compared to monks within the same order—for example, the Premonstratensian and Cistercian nuns were far more restricted than their male counterparts— by the General Chapters (governing bodies) of each order and also by the papacy. In view of this inequality, the lack of uniformity in images of Cistercians is particularly revealing, even when we factor in artistic license. They are clad in a range of light to dark neutrals, even black and blue, with veils and under-veils marked differently, sometimes with a type of cross.

Excessively lavish attire among religious women was a frequent target of their contemporary critics looking for signs of moral weakness within certain orders. Such sinful *luxuria* also finds visual representation as artistic tropes, in which nuns adorn themselves in ample, sumptuous gowns rivaling those of fashionable laywomen. This may well indicate that female members of well-endowed monasteries were allowed to dress in accordance with their families' social status, in sharp contrast to orders such as the Poor Clares, whose often aristocratic adherents truly renounced all wealth and comfort. Their privilege was granted officially by Pope Gregory IX, who also gave them their first rule. However, it is essential to recognize that the dire straits of many small, underfunded houses of the later Middle Ages were suffered neither by choice nor privilege, and that their members' lack of serviceable clothing was condemned by visiting bishops (Johnson).

Inevitably, both texts and images afford limited information into actual dress standards and practices among medieval religious women, whether cloistered—and therefore "invisible"—or not. Attesting the presence of a double standard for religious dress early on, the Rule of St. Benedict urges men needing to leave the monastery on errands out in public to put on their best clothes. By contrast, the few surviving clothing objects of famous medieval women religious, such as the mantle of St. Clare and St. Birgitta's hairshirt, are humble and "vile," yet today venerated as relics.

See also Ancrene Riwle; Beguines; Birgitta of Sweden, St.; Clare of Assisi, St.; Convents; Double Monasteries; Nunneries, Merovingian; Music in Medieval Nunneries; Nunneries, Merovingian; Relics and Medieval Women; Rules for Canonesses, Nuns, and Recluses; Spinners and Drapers; Virginity

BIBLIOGRAPHY

Primary Sources
Anon. *Liber de diversis ordinibus et professionibus qui sunt in Ecclesia.* Edited by Giles Constable and B. Smith. Oxford Medieval Texts. Oxford: Clarendon Press, 1972.
Augustine, St. [Letters, orig. Latin]. *Epistulae.* Edited by Alois Goldhaber, vol. 57. 5 vols. Corpus Scriptorum Ecclesiasticorum Latinorum, 34:1, 34:2, 44, 57, 58. Vienna: Tempsky, 1895–1923.
———. [Rule] *Augustine of Hippo and His Monastic Rule.* Edited by George Lawless. Oxford: Clarendon Press; New York: Oxford University Press, 1987.
Benedict, St. [Rule]. *Three Middle-English Versions of the Rule of St. Benedict and Two Contemporary Rituals for the Ordination of Nuns.* Edited by Ernst A. Kock. Early English Text Society, o.s. 120. London: Kegan, Paul et al., 1902. Reprint New York: Kraus, 1973.
Caesarius, St. [*Regula sanctorum virginum*] *The Rule of the Nuns of St. Caesarius of Arles.* Translated by M. C. McCarthy. Catholic University of America Studies in Medieval History, n.s. 16. Washington, D.C.: CUA Press, 1960.
Clare, St. *Clare of Assisi: Early Documents.* Edited and translated by Regis J. Armstrong. Mahwah, N.J.: Paulist Press, 1988.
Jerome [Hieronymus], St. *The Letters of Saint Jerome.* Translated by Charles C. Mierow. Introduction and notes by Thomas C. Lawlor. Ancient Christian Writers, 33. London, U.K., and Westminster, Md.: Newman Press, 1963.

Secondary Sources
Braun, Joseph. *Tracht und Attribute der Heilige in der deutschen Kunst.* Stuttgart, Germany: J. B. Metzler, 1943. 3rd ed. Berlin: Mann, 1973. Reprint 1988.
Cardon, Dominique. *La Draperie au Moyen Âge: Essor d'une grande industrie européenne.* Paris: CNRS, 1999.
Cross, F. L., ed. *The Oxford Dictionary of the Christian Church.* 3rd ed. by E. A. Livingstone. Oxford and New York: Oxford University Press, 1997.
Esposito, Anna. "St. Francesca and the Female Religious Communities of Fifteenth-Century Rome." In *Women and Religion in Medieval and Renaissance Italy,* edited by Daniel Bornstein and Roberto Rusconi. Translated by Margery J. Schneider, 197–218. Chicago: University of Chicago Press, 1996.
Fontette, Micheline de. *Les Religieuses à l'âge classique du droit canon: Recherches sur les structures juridiques des branches féminines des ordres.* Paris: J. Vrin, 1967.
Harvey, Barbara. *Monastic Dress in the Middle Ages: Precept and Practice.* Canterbury: William Urry Trust, 1988.
Hélyot, Hippolyte. *Histoire des ordres monastiques, religieux et militaires et des congrégations séculières de l'un et l'autre sexe.* 8 vols. Paris: Gosselin, 1714–1719.
Jenkins, David, ed. *The Cambridge History of Western Textiles.* 2 vols. Cambridge: Cambridge University Press, 2003.
Johnson, Penelope. *Equal in the Monastic Profession: Religious Women in the Middle Ages.* Chicago: University of Chicago Press, 1991.

Koslin, Désirée G. *The Dress of Monastic and Religious Women as Seen in Art from the Early Middle Ages to the Reformation*. New York: New York University Press, 1999.

———, and Janet E. Snyder, eds. *Encountering Medieval Textiles and Dress: Objects, Texts, Images*. The New Middle Ages. New York: Palgrave Macmillan, 2002.

———. "The Robe of Simplicity: Initiation, Robing, and Veiling of Nuns in the Middle Ages." In *Robes and Honor: The Medieval World of Investiture*, edited by Stewart Gordon, 255–74. New York: Palgrave Macmillan, 2001.

Kroos, Renate. "Der Codex Gisle." *Niederdeutsche Beiträge zur Kunstwissenschaft* 12 (1973): 117–34.

McNamara, Jo Ann K. *Sisters in Arms: Catholic Nuns through Two Millennia*. Cambridge, Mass.: Harvard University Press, 1996.

Rehm, Gerhard. *Die Schwestern vom Gemeinsamen Leben in nordwestlichen Deutschland*. Berliner Historische Studien, 11. Berlin: Duncker & Humboldt, 1985.

Thompson, Sally. *Women Religious*. Oxford: Clarendon Press; New York: Oxford University Press, 1991.

DÉSIRÉE G. KOSLIN

DROIT DU SEIGNEUR. *See **Jus Primae Noctis***

EADBURGA, ST. *See* **Bugga**

EANGYTH. *See* **Boniface, St., Mission and Circle of**

EBNER, CHRISTINE (1277–1356). A prioress and major author of the Middle-High German convent chronicle known as the *Engeltaler Schwesternbuch* (Engeltal Sister-Book), Christine is known for recording her mystical life and revelations (*Offenbarungen*), an early example of Franconian (from the German province) literature (see Lewis). Christine's family, originally descended from the class of imperial *ministeriales* (lower-ranking aristocrats serving in administrative and similar posts), later rose to join the patrician, upper-class burghers after settling in Nuremberg. Christine was born on Good Friday, the tenth child of Seyfried Ebner and his wife Elisabeth Kuhdorf. At age twelve she entered the Dominican nunnery of Engeltal near Nuremberg. The Dominican Order (Order of Preachers, or Blackfriars, founded by the Spaniard St. Dominic at Bologna in 1215) emphasized an austere daily regimen, and even physical self-abuse, together with the avid study of spiritual texts—even nuns knew how to read Latin—and intense prayer for both monks and nuns. Having supposedly learned to read the Latin Psalter by age ten, Christine qualified as an "educated girl" (*puella litterata*; see Ehrenschwendtner), though Latin and Middle-High German coexisted in the nuns' liturgy by that time (Lewis). After following the harsh routine of convent life, Christine experienced her first vision in 1291. Although she faced much opposition in her efforts to reform the Engeltal convent, she was elected prioress in 1345.

Her renown as a visionary began to grow after 1297, attracting noteworthy groups like the flagellants—bands of men who went about whipping themselves in public penitential parades to atone for the sins of the world—to seek her advice in 1349, and no less than German Emperor Charles IV to request her blessing in 1350, when he visited her with his whole court. The mystic and priest, Heinrich of Nördlingen (d. 1379), advisor and friend to the mystic Margareta Ebner (not related), also began to correspond with Christine in 1338. Heinrich introduced her to the other women mystics, like Mechthild of Magdeburg (c.1207–1282?), author of *Das Fliessendes Licht der Gottheit* (*The Flowing Light of Divinity*)—so influential in Christine's style. Heinrich acquainted Christine with famous male mystics as well: John (Johannes) Tauler (d. 1361) and Henry Suso (Heinrich Seuse) (c.1295–1366). In 1351, Henry arrived in Nuremberg for a three-week visit.

Christine composed the *Büchlein von der Gnaden Überlast* (*Little Book of the Abundance of Grace*), a chronicle of her convent and considered one of the best sources of late-medieval mysticism in the 1340s. Christine probably dictated her works rather than write them herself—a common practice at that time. Imagery of a nuptial union with Christ forms a key enabling aspect in that it provided her with the authority to proclaim to her convent sisters the endless love of God, at whose command she continues to record her visions, like Moses and other prophets.

After her death in 1356, she was soon worshiped as a saint, but the outbreak of the Reformation (as of 1517) prevented this cult from spreading. Her confessor, the Dominican Konrad of Füssen, and her fellow sisters wrote her biography. Konrad had encouraged her to write down her visions, which she continued for forty years until her death, whereupon Konrad copied them. These revelations resemble in many respects the writings of German women mystics like Gertrud the Great (1256–1301/2) and Mechthild of Hackeborn (1241–1299).

See also Anna of Munzingen; Bride of Christ/*Brautmystik*; Elsbeth von Oye; Gertrude the Great, of Helfta, St.; Langmann, Adelhaid; Mechthild of Hackeborn; Mechthild of Magdeburg; Sister-Books (*Schwesternbücher*); Stagel, Elsbeth

BIBLIOGRAPHY

Primary Sources
Ebner, Christine. *Offenbarungen*. Württemburgische Landesbibliothek MS Cod. Theol. 2° 282. [Since no complete reliable edition exists, this manuscript must be consulted].

———. *Das Büchlein von der Gnaden Uberlast von Christine Ebner*. Edited by Wilhelm Oehl. Paderborn, Germany: Schöningh, 1924. [Useful introduction].

———. *Der Nonne von Engelthal Buchlein von der Gnaden Uberlast*. Litterarischer Verein in Stuttgart. Edited by Karl Schröder. Stuttgart and Tübingen, Germany: Bibliothek des literarischen Vereins, 1871.

———. *Deutsches Nonnenleben: Das Leben der Schwestern zu Töss und Der Nonne von Engeltal Büchlein von der Gnaden Überlast*. Translated (Modern German) and annotated by Margarete Weinhandl. Katholikon, 2. Munich, Germany: Recht, 1921.

Secondary Sources
Bürkle, Susanne. "Die 'Gnadenvita' Christine Ebners: Episodenstruktur-Text-Ich und Autorenschaft." In *Deutsche Mystik im abendländischen Zusammenhang: Neu erschlossene Texte, neue methodische Ansätze, neue theoretische Konzepte*, edited by Walter Haug and Wolfram Schneider-Lastin, 453–513. Tübingen: Niemeyer, 2000.

Ehrenschwendtner, Marie-Luise. "*Puellae litteratae*: The Vernacular in the Dominican Convents." In *Medieval Women in their Communities*, edited by Diane Watt, 49–71. Cardiff: University of Wales Press, 1997.

Garber, Rebecca. *Feminine Figurae: Representations of Gender in Religious Texts by Medieval German Women Writers, 1100–1375*. Studies in Medieval History and Culture, 10. New York and London: Routledge, 2003.

Gehring, H. "The Language of Mysticism in South German Dominican Convent Chronicles of the XIVth Century." Ph.D. diss. University of Michigan 1957.

Kramer, Dewey Weiss. "'Arise and Give the Convent Bread': Christine Ebner, The Convent Chronicle of Engelthal, and the Call to Ministry among Fourteenth Century Religious Women." In *Women as Protagonists and Poets in the German Middle Ages: An Anthology of Approaches to Middle High German Literature*, edited by Albrecht Classen, 187–207. Göppinger Arbeiten zur Germanistik, 528. Göppingen, Germany: Kümmerle, 1991.

Lewis, Gertrud Jaron. *By Women, for Women, about Women: The Sister-Books of Fourteenth-Century Germany.* Studies and Texts, 125. Toronto: Pontifical Institute of Mediaeval Studies, 1996.

Ringler, Siegfried. "Die Rezeption mittelalterlicher Frauenmystik als wissenschaftliches Problem, dargestellt am Werk der Christine Ebner." In *Frauenmystik im Mittelalter*, edited by Peter Dinzelbacher and Dieter K. Bauer, 178–200. Ostfildern (Stuttgart), Germany: Schwabenverlag, 1985.

———. "Christine Ebner." In *Mein Herz schmilzt wie Eis am Feuer. Die religiöse Frauenbewegung des Mittelalters in Porträts*, edited by Johannes Thiele, 146–59. Stuttgart, Germany: Kreuz Verlag, 1988.

Volpert, Anneliese. "Christine Ebner." In: *Fränkische Klassiker: Eine Literaturgeschichte in Einzeldarstellungen*, edited by Wolfgang Buhl, 149–59. Nuremberg, Germany: Nürnberger Presse, 1971.

ALBRECHT CLASSEN

EBNER, MARGARETA (c.1291–1351). A German mystic who composed letters, Margareta was born to upper-middle-class parents in Donauwörth, who sent her to the Dominican convent Maria Medingen, near Dillingen, when she was only a child. She was not related to Christine Ebner, whose family came from Nuremberg. Her life as a mystic began when she became bedridden from a long and difficult illness commencing February 6, 1312, probably caused by a psychological breakdown. Totally isolated for most of the time in the convent, she dedicated herself entirely to prayer and meditation and soon experienced a vision of a lost soul in Purgatory, who told her of her blessedness in God. When the priest Heinrich of Nördlingen visited her on October 29, 1332, he was immediately struck by her personality and persuaded her to interpret her visions as mystical experiences. He saw in them the realization of his own ideals of a personal union with God. She made it possible for him to share her mystic revelations, whereas he induced her to write them down beginning in 1344. Heinrich spread the word of her experiences in Swabia, Alsace, and Basel, and even introduced her to the famous mystic Johannes Tauler (d. 1361).

It was particularly the *Gottesfreunde* (Friends of God) who took pains to make her acquaintance, whereby she soon formed the center of a very active circle of friends who corresponded with each other. This group included the abbot Ulrich III Nibling of Kaisheim, but most significant for Margareta was Heinrich of Nördlingen. Because Heinrich supported—in contrast to Margareta and her convent—the Avignonese pope during the Papal Schism between Avignon and Rome, he had to remove himself from the court of Emperor Ludwig IV of Bavaria (1287?–1347), the pope's personal enemy. Consequently, both Heinrich and Margareta remained in touch through numerous letters of which, however, only one by her to him and fifty-six by him to her have come down to us, apart from a few other letters by her to other people. In contrast to letters by earlier mystics, this correspondence was very private in tone and written in German, not Latin. They reveal more about their emotions for each other than about spiritual matters. Margareta's revelations were composed in the Swabian dialect of her time and addressed to Heinrich in the form of an autobiography. She emphasizes her experiences of Christ's Passion and her encounter with the Christ child. Sometimes she would try to force these visions to recur, or induce stigmatization—a phenomenon attempted by many mystics in which, on her own body, she would reproduce Christ's wounds and actually bleed—but without success. She occasionally inserted some verses in her work, influenced by Mechthild of Magdeburg's *Fliessendes Licht der Gottheit* (*Flowing Light of Divinity*), which Heinrich had strongly recommended she read. She wrote her revelations in her own hand, only once in a while helped by another sister, Elsbeth Schepach. Her writings survive as remarkable historical and literary documents of her time and of the life of a woman mystic. The original manuscripts were meticulously copied and thus preserved the original style and the author's personal directness. She also composed *Der Ebnerin Paternoster* (*The Ebnerin's Prayer to Our Father*), a paraphrase of the Lord's Prayer. All of her works reveal her intensely individual insights on political and historical events and personages surrounding her, such as the plague and pogroms, Holy Roman Emperor Charles IV (1316–1378) and local politics in Nuremberg. Her writings have also been interpreted as clear reflections of her inner physical and psychological agony during her disease, in other words, as psychosomatic phenomena. After her death on June 20, 1351, she was buried in the convent's chapter house, which was soon transformed into a separate chapel.

See also Mechthild of Magdeburg

BIBLIOGRAPHY

Primary Sources
Ebner, Margareta. *Offenbarungen* (*Revelations*). Württemburgische Landesbibliothek MS Cod. Theol. 2° 282. [Since no complete reliable edition exists, this manuscript must be consulted].
———. *Der Ebnerin Paternoster* (*The Ebnerin's Prayer*). Edited by Philip Strauch. In *Margaretha Ebner und Heinrich von Nördlingen. Ein Beitrag zur Geschichte der deutschen Mystik*. Freiburg-im-Breisgau and Tübingen, Germany: Mohr, 1882. Reprint Amsterdam: P. Schippers, 1966.
———. *Major works/Margaret Ebner*. Translated and edited by Leonard P. Hindsley. Introduced by Margot Schmidt and Leonard P. Hindsley. Preface by Richard Woods. Classics of Western Spirituality. New York: Paulist Press, 1993.

Secondary Sources
Ehrenschwendtner, Marie-Luise. "*Puellae litteratae*: The Vernacular in the Dominican Convents." In *Medieval Women in their Communities*, edited by Diane Watt, 49–71. Cardiff: University of Wales Press, 1997.
Garber, Rebecca. *Feminine Figurae: Representations of Gender in Religious Texts by Medieval German Women Writers, 1100–1375*. Studies in Medieval History and Culture, 10. New York and London: Routledge, 2003.
Haas, Alois M. "Traum und Traumvision in der deutschen Mystik." In *Spätmittelalterliche geistliche Literatur in der Nationalsprachen*, edited by James Hogg, 122–55. Salzburg: Institute für Anglistik und Amerikanistik,Universität Salzburg, 1983.
Hindsley, Leonard P. "Monastic Conversion: The Case of Margaret Ebner." In *Varieties of Religious Conversion in the Middle Ages*, edited by James Muldoon, 31–46. Gainesville: University Press of Florida, 1997.
Pfister, Oskar. "Hysterie und Mystik bei Margaretha Ebner." In *Zentralbibliothek für Psychoanalyse. Medizinische Monatsschrift und Seelenkunde* 1 (1910–1911): 468–85.
Preger, Wilhelm. *Geschichte der deutschen Mystik im Mittelalter*, vol. 2, 277–306. Leipzig: Dörffling Franke, 1881. Reprint Aachen: Zeller, 1962.
Muschg, Walter. *Die Mystik in der Schweiz, 1200–1500*. Frauenfeld and Leipzig: Huber, 1935. 290–304.
Ringler, Siegfried. "Marguerite Ebner." In *Dictionnaire de Spiritualité*, vol. 10, cols. 338–40. Paris: Beauchesne, 1980.
Schneider, R. *Die selige Margareta Ebner: Dominikanerin des Klosters Maria Meding*. St. Ottilien, Germany: EOS, 1985.
Walz, Angelus. "Gottesfreunde um Margarete Ebner." *Historisches Jahrbuch* 72 (1953): 253–65.
Weitlauff, Manfred. "Ebner, Margareta." In *Die deutsche Literatur des Mittelalters, Verfasserlexikon*, 2nd ed. by Kurt Ruh et al., 2: 303–6. Berlin and New York: de Gruyter, 1982.

———. "'dein got redender munt ...'." In *Religiöse Frauenbewegung und mystische Frömmigkeit im Mittelalter*, edited by Peter Dinzelbacher, 303–52. Cologne, Germany and Vienna: Böhlau, 1988.

Zoepf, Ludwig. *Die Mystikerin Margereta Ebner (ca. 1291–1351)*. Leipzig and Berlin: Teubner, 1914.

ALBRECHT CLASSEN

EGBURG (early 8th century). Egburg was an English abbess (possibly of Repton or Hackness), one of the missionary Boniface's correspondents writing to him from England. Little else is known about Egburg (Old English = Ecgburga). Theorizing on the meaning of her name (*ec-burg* = outside town, ergo a remote place), which characterizes Repton (in Derbyshire, England), Lina Eckenstein identifies her with the daughter of King Ealdwulf, the abbess of Repton, who sent a coffin and a winding sheet to St. Guthlac of Croyland. George F. Browne, in contrast, surmises that she was a Northumbrian of royal family, naming her brother Oshere as the Consul of the Northumbrians who defeated the Picts in 710, and her sister Wethburga as the abbess mentioned on a monument at Hackness. Browne also hypothesizes that Egburg succeeded her sister as abbess there.

Like Berthgyth, Egburg is known from her correspondence with St. Boniface (c.675–754)—a single letter—in the Boniface Collection. She addresses him by his Anglo-Saxon name, "Wynfrith," and calls him *abbas* (abbot). These facts indicate that the letter was written before 719, when Boniface received a letter from Pope Gregory II addressing him as Boniface, the name by which he was thereafter known. Michael Tangl dates the letter between 716 and 718, considering it one of the earliest of the collection.

In the letter, Egburg speaks of the affection between herself and Boniface and its importance given the death of Oshere and the departure of Wethburga for Rome. She expresses her confidence in God and asks for the prayers of Boniface, in a tone revealing mutual affection between master and assistant. Stylistically, her letter shows the influence of Aldhelm (c.640–c.709)—"the first English man of letters" and author of various complex Latin poetic and prose works—especially in her use of phrases like "*ille superi rector Olimpi*" ["the Lord of high Olympus"]. As with other Anglo-Saxon learned missionaries under Boniface, her style and themes recall the tradition deriving from the sixth-century Christian Latin poet Arator—composer of a hexametric version of the Book of Acts elaborating on biblical symbolism—and Prudentius—the influential fourth-century Latin didactic Christian poet. Such authors sought to merge Christian tradition with that of classical, and thus pagan, Latin heroic verse. This Christian-Latin poetic presence in Egburg's letter attests this tradition's availability to women as well as men in her milieu, and its practice in even personalized forms of writing.

See also Berthgyth; Boniface, St., Mission and Circle of; Epistolary Authors, Women as

BIBLIOGRAPHY

Primary Sources

Egburg. *Die Briefe des heilgen Bonifatius und Lullus*. Edited by Michael Tangl. Monumenta Germaniae Historica: Epistolae Selectae, vol. 1. 2nd ed. Berlin: Weidmann, 1955.

———. *Epistolae merovingici et karolini aevi*. Edited by Ernst Ludwig Dümmler, vol. 1, 428–30. Berlin: Weidmann, 1891. Reprint 1957.

———. *Sancti Bonifacii Epistolae. Codex Vindobonensis 751 des osterreichischen Nationalbibliothek*. Edited by Franz Unterkircher. Graz, Austria: Akademische Druck und Verlagsanstalt, 1971. [Facsimile ed. of Vienna ms.].

———. *The Letters of St. Boniface.* Translated by Ephraim Emerton. Records of Civilization, 31. New York: Columbia University Press, 1940. Reprint New York: Octagon, 1973.

———. *The English Correspondence of Saint Boniface.* Translated by Edward Kylie. New York: Cooper Square, 1966.

Secondary Sources

Browne, George F. *Boniface of Crediton and His Companions.* London: Society for Promoting Christian Knowledge, 1910.

Eckenstein, Lina. *Woman under Monasticism: Chapters on Saint Lore and Convent Life Between* A.D. *500 and* A.D. *1500.* Cambridge: The University Press, 1896. Reprint New York: Russell & Russell, 1963.

ALEXANDRA HENNESSEY OLSEN

EGERIA (fl. 381–385). A Galician nun named variously Egeria, Echeria, Etheria, and Aetheria, she authored a pilgrimage treatise, the *Peregrinatio ad loca sancta* (*Pilgrimage to the Holy Land*)—one of the most ancient works describing the rituals of the early Christian Church. It is also the only authentic substantial document of fourth-century Latin written by a woman.

All that we know of Egeria as a person is that she came from Galicia, northwestern Spain, and that she was extremely pious, despite being part of "feeble womanhood," according to the Spanish hermit, Valerius of El Bierzo, in his letter praising Egeria from c.650. She may well have belonged, as Marcelle Thiébaux surmises, to a consecrated community of women in Galicia, or, as others suggest, in Gaul (mostly, ancient France): one not necessarily enclosed, thus allowing her to move about.

Her itinerary's narrative style, despite its manuscript's mutilated form at the beginning and end of the text, is characterized by the "hieratic grandeur" of her Church Latin (though in an unusual Latin dialect), by the richness of her liturgical (pertaining to Church services) vocabulary, by her incisive knowledge of the Old and New Testaments, and by her reliance on the Greek *Onomasticon* of the renowned Church historian, Eusebius of Caesarea (c.260–c.340)—an important work on biblical topography—which she consulted in its Latin version by St. Jerome (390).

Her pilgrimage takes place during a decisive phase in the formation of Christianity. Topographically, Egeria's three-year itinerary as laid out in the *Peregrinatio*, can be divided into ten separate sections: (1) her departure from Constantinople and her arrival at Jerusalem in time for Easter and a visit to the Holy Places (381); (2) visit to Egypt, in particular to Alexandria and the monastic houses of the Thebaid (centered at Thebes, capital of the Upper Nile, and cradle of Christian monasticism) (381–383); (3) visit to the land of Galilee and return to Jerusalem (383); (4) pilgrimage to Mount Sinai (383–January 384); (5) excursion from Jerusalem to Mount Nebo to observe the splendid panorama of the Promised Land (January or February 384); (6) journey to Carneas, Job's city (February or March 384); (7) departure from Jerusalem for Antioch (March 384); (8) return journey from Antioch to Edessa, especially to pray at the tomb of St. Thomas, *ad ecclesiam et ad martyrium sancti Thomae* (April 384); (9) journey, through Tarsus, to the city of Seleucia of Isauria to visit St. Thecla's martyrium (shrine) and to meet with one of her dear friends, the deaconess Marthana (May 384); (10) return to Constantinople after traversing the regions of Cappadocia, Galatia, and Bythinia, with Egeria announcing her intent to visit St. John's martyrium at Ephesus in the future (June or July 384).

Somewhat oddly, Egeria does not mention many contemporary living personages (not even Emperor Theodosius I, r. 378–395), but she does relish identifying and contemplating sites and persons named in the Bible (for people like Egeria, equivalent to real history). Especially in the first part of her account, she notes, for example, the site on which Lot's wife was turned to salt, Moses's footsteps, the site of the Golden Calf's construction. In part 2, she describes the liturgy and Church offices, primarily in the Church of Jerusalem, thereby providing valuable documentation as to how and when now-traditional, fixed holy days and daily rituals (including the disposition of the canonical hours, which regulated each day's prayers) were actually celebrated back then: along with Easter, Holy Week (including a most vivid description of the processions to the holy places associated with Christ's Passion: the Mount of Olives and Veneration of the Cross) and Whitsuntide (eve of the feast of the Holy Spirit's descent among the Apostles fifty days after Easter); from her we learn that the Feast of the Nativity was held on January 6; Egeria's is the first known mention of the Feast of the Purification (of the Virgin Mary, also later called Candlemas), then held February 14, now February 2. There were other famous early pilgrimages to the Holy Land, such as the *Itinerarium* of the so-called Pilgrim of Bordeaux (333), the *Peregrinatio S. Paula* (*Pilgrimage of St. Paula*, 383), the *De locis sanctis* of Eucherius (*On Holy Places*, 440), the *De situ Terrae Sanctae* of Theodosius (*Description of the Holy Land*, 530) and the *Perambulatio locorum sanctorum* (*Travels through Holy Places*, 530), but these tell mainly of buildings and places, whereas Egeria's *Peregrinatio* is quite unique in its focus on the above-listed details, all presented with keen intelligence and a talent for observation.

Her treatise was first discovered in 1884 by Gian Francesco Gamurrini (1835–1923) in the Library of the Brotherhood of St. Mary in Arezzo, Italy. When Gamurrini published it in 1887, he attributed it to St. Sylvia of Aquitaine, sister of the Roman prefect Rufinus—figures from Palladius's *Lausiac History* (c.419), a popular source—and thus titled it *Peregrinatio Silviae*. It was the Visigoth-Mozarabic specialist Dom Marius Férotin who, in 1903, linked the work with the Egeria (whom he called "Etheria") extolled in Valerius's epistle. Until this rediscovery, Egeria's work had been lost for seven hundred years, though transcribed at the famous scriptorium at Montecassino by Petrus Diaconus (Peter the Deacon) at the order of the abbot Desiderius, the future pope Victor III (1057–1086).

The importance of Egeria's *Peregrinatio* in the history of Christianity derives not only from its contribution to the topography of Palestine and its documentation of the liturgical rites of the Church of Jerusalem but also from its considerable value as a milestone in women's religious writing. Her travelogue has been translated several times into English, also French and, most recently, Portuguese.

See also Macrina the Younger, St.; Melania the Elder, St.; Scribes and Scriptoria; Thecla, St.

BIBLIOGRAPHY

Primary Sources
Egeria [*Peregrinatio* and Valerius's letter on her]. *Journal de voyage: itinéraire*. Critical edition, introduction and translation (French) by Pierre Maraval. *Lettre sur la Bse. Égérie de Valerius du Bierzo*. Edited and translated (French) by Manuel C. Díaz y Díaz. Sources chrétiennes, 296. Revised ed. Paris: Éditions du Cerf, 1997. [Authoritative texts: Latin originals with French translations, maps and commentary; replaces the old 1948 Sources chrétiennes ed. by Hélène Petre].
———. *Egeria's Travels to the Holy Land*. Translated with documents and notes by John Wilkinson. 3rd ed., revised Warminster, U.K.: Aris & Phillips, 1999. Original London: SPCK, 1971.

―――. *S. Silvae Aquitanae Peregrinatio ad loca sancta*. Edited by Gian Francesco [here, Latinized to Johannes Franciscus] Gamurrini. Revised ed. Rome: Vatican, 1888. Original Rome: F. Cuggiani, 1887. [Latin text, now for historical interest only].

―――. [Annotated extracts, English]. "A Pilgrim to the Holy Land." In *The Writings of Medieval Women: An Anthology*, edited and translated by Marcelle Thiébaux, 23–48. Garland Library of Medieval Literature, 100B. 2nd ed. New York and London: Garland, 1994. [Useful introduction].

―――. "The Pilgrimage of Egeria." Introduced and translated by Patricia Wilson-Kastner. In *A Lost Tradition*, edited and translated by P. Wilson-Kastner et al. Washington, D.C.: University Press of America, 1981. [Excellent notes, freer trans. than Gingras's; but more exacting than Wilkinson's].

―――. *Diary of a Pilgrimage*. Edited and translated by George Gingras. Ancient Christian Writers. New York: Newman Press, 1970. [Heavily annotated; most scholarly trans.].

Secondary Sources

[See notes to above editions].

Férotin, Dom Marius. "Le Véritable Auteur de la *Peregrinatio Silviae*." *Revue des Questions Historiques* 74. 2 (1903): 363–97.

Holloway, Julia B. Web site (2004): http://www.umilta.net/egeria.html

SANDRO STICCA

ELAINE. Elaine is a name borne by at least three different Arthurian characters: Elaine of Astolat (demoiselle d'Ascolat, Fair Maid of Astolat), Elaine of Corbenic, and the Elaine who is sometimes Lancelot's mother.

Elaine of Astolat dies of her unrequited love for Lancelot. A barge bearing her dead body arrives at Camelot; in it is a letter explaining that she died because Lancelot rejected her. In Malory's retelling (c.1469), where Elaine is first named (Elaine le Blank, Fair Maid of Astolat), her story is simply and eloquently told, and in a long deathbed speech she declares that she loved Lancelot "oute of mesure."

Elaine of Corbenic, mother of Galahad, goes unnamed in French texts but is named by Malory. Descended from Joseph of Arimathea, to whom legend attributes the bringing of the Grail to Britain, and daughter of King Pelles (in some texts, one of the Fisher Kings), she comes of a holy line. She seduces Lancelot through the use of an enchantment, persuading him that she is Guinevere and thus conceiving a child with him.

Sometimes Lancelot's mother bears the name Elaine. In the Prose *Lancelot*, Elaine of Benoic, wife of King Ban, suffers a double blow when her husband's death is followed immediately by the loss of her son, whom she sees carried down into the water by the Lady of the Lake.

See also Arthurian Women; Enchantresses, Fays (*Fées*), and Fairies; Guinevere; Lady of the Lake

BIBLIOGRAPHY

Primary Sources

Malory, Sir Thomas. *Morte Darthur*. Edited by John Matthews. London: Cassell, 2000.

[Prose *Lancelot*]. *Lancelot: roman en prose du XIIIe siècle*. Edited by Alexandre Micha. 9 vols. Textes Littéraires Français 247, 249, 262, 278, 283, 286, 288, 307, 315. Geneva: Droz, 1978–1983. [Old French texts only].

Lancelot-Grail: The Old French Arthurian Vulgate and Post-Vulgate in Translation. General editor Norris J. Lacy. Translated by N. Lacy et al. Garland Reference Library of the Humanities, 941, 1826, 1878, 1896, 1964. 5 vols. New York: Garland, 1993–1996.

Secondary Source

Fenster, Thelma S., ed. *Arthurian Women: A Casebook*. Arthurian Characters and Themes, 3. New York: Garland, 1996. [Collection of critical essays on wide-ranging aspects, with introduction].

THELMA S. FENSTER

ELEANOR OF AQUITAINE (1122/24–1204). Eleanor (or in French, Aliénor) of Aquitaine, one of the most remarkable women of the Middle Ages, was the wife of two kings and the mother of two more, as well as an influential patron of arts and letters. Although she never ruled a kingdom in her own right, she wielded more influence than many monarchs, demonstrating what a courageous and determined woman could achieve despite the misogynistic forces within the Church and society. The granddaughter of the earliest known troubadour, Duke William (Guilhem) IX of Aquitaine (r. 1127–1137), she was not a writer herself, but scholars credit her patronage, largely through her daughters, with much of the dissemination of the hallmark concept of *fin'amors* (courtly love) and the Arthurian legends throughout France and England. In addition, while queen of France she subsidized the rebuilding of Saint-Denis near Paris, often considered the first Gothic church; while queen of England, she introduced southern-French artistic influence into English manuscript illuminations.

Born around 1122/24, Eleanor was raised in Aquitaine at the brilliant court of her father, William X, from whom she doubtless acquired her penchant for artistic patronage, since, like his father before him, William welcomed troubadour poets and artists into his retinue. When her father died during a pilgrimage to Santiago de Compostela in 1137, his will placed the fifteen-year-old Eleanor, heiress to the prosperous duchy of Aquitaine in southwestern France, under the protection of King Louis VI (The Fat) of France (1081–1137), who quickly whisked her away from her home to marry his younger son, the monkish crown prince Louis Capet (c.1120–1180). Originally destined for an ecclesiastical career, this son had become heir to the throne of France when his elder brother, Philippe, died in a fall from his horse in 1131. Shortly after his marriage to Eleanor in 1137, his father died, forcing the ill-prepared boy of sixteen to take up the scepter and assume the royal title of Louis VII with Eleanor as his equally youthful queen.

However, Eleanor's failure to produce a child after seven years of marriage provoked speculation that the couple's overly close consanguinity had left her barren; both were descended from King Robert II the Pious (972–1031), a fact muted by the link on Eleanor's side consisting of an illegitimate birth as well as by Louis VI's eagerness to annex Aquitaine. When no less than Abbot Bernard of Clairvaux signaled to them that their union transgressed within the "forbidden degrees" of lineage, Eleanor struck a bargain with him during Abbot Suger's dedication celebration for the church of Saint-Denis (1144): she would urge her husband to seek peace with longstanding foe Thibaut of Champagne in exchange for Bernard's prayers that she give birth. Eleanor's first diplomatic effort did indeed soon yield both peace—if an uneasy one—between king and count, and a child (1145)—though a daughter, Marie—instead of the long-awaited male heir.

Having endured the dreary northern-French Capetian palace and its king with a certain impatience, the vivacious Eleanor jumped at the opportunity to accompany her husband on the Second Crusade, actually joining him in taking the cross at Vézelay, farther south, in Burgundy, from the hands of Abbot Bernard himself in 1146. The journey to Constantinople and then Antioch, in what is now modern Turkey, was a grand adventure that also returned her to her southern roots, since her uncle, Raymond de Toulouse, ruled the latter. Unfortunately, this visit elicited unsavory rumors about her relationship with her uncle and a hasty departure of the French crusaders with a reluctant Eleanor in virtual captivity. The failed crusade and Louis's doubts about the legitimacy of their marriage caused the couple to return home via Rome, where Pope Eugene made every effort to help them save their troubled marriage by attempting to dispel their anxieties and promising them a son. Eleanor's ensuing pregnancy renewed their hopes, but at the same time, Abbot Suger of Saint-Denis died (1151), leaving the king under the primary influence of the uncompromising Bernard of Clairvaux, who had never particularly cared for Eleanor and who blamed her, in part, for the failure of the crusade. After

Effigies of Eleanor of Aquitaine at Fontevraud and two Kings. Courtesy of North Wind Picture Archives.

Eleanor gave birth to another daughter, Alix, the king, at Bernard's advice, divorced his wife on grounds of consanguinity in 1152 and married Constance of Castile (c.1140s–1160).

Seizing on this legal opportunity to escape a miserable situation, Eleanor not only offered no resistance but also soon contracted a second marriage, much to Louis VII's surprise and political malaise, with Young Henry Plantagenet (1133–1189)—duke of Normandy, count of Anjou, and claimant to the throne of England—eleven years her junior. As if further to vindicate her worth, within fourteen years, less time than the duration of her entire first marriage, Eleanor bore Henry five sons and three daughters.

Most scholars believe that it was during her marriage to Henry that Eleanor made her greatest contribution as a patron of medieval literature. Just as her father had fostered the first important troubadours Cercamon and Marcabru, she is thought to have invited, among others, renowned troubadour Bernart de Ventadorn, who composed "A la reïna dels Normans" ("To the Queen of the Normans") in her honor, to join her court in Normandy. Another protégé, the Anglo-Norman poet Wace, recast Geoffrey of Monmouth's Latin chronicle, the *Historia regum Britanniae* (*History of the Kings of Britain*) into a vernacular novelistic version called *Le Roman de Brut* (*Romance of Brute/Brutus*, in which Brute is a descendant of Aeneas, Rome's founder, and mythical ancestor of the English), which, according to Layamon's later Middle-English adaptation, he dedicated to Eleanor (c.1155). The *Brut* would serve as a milestone in spreading and cultivating Arthurian literature throughout western Europe, just as another work possibly inspired or commissioned by her—Benoît de Sainte-Maure's *Roman de Troie* (*Romance of Troy*, c.1165)—would do for ancient classical Greek and Roman epic themes, not only for their literary beauty but also as key political myths for reconstructing the kingdom's noble heritage. Moreover, Eleanor's husband Henry replaced old Wace with the more stylish Benoît as his official chronicler, to compose a history of the dukes of Normandy c.1170, left unfinished. Despite all this, Karen Broadhurst has recently argued for a considerably more limited version of Eleanor and Henry's patronage, after reexamining the evidence and concluding that Henry commissioned only two chronicles and that Eleanor commissioned no texts at all.

Such cultural achievements flourished despite Eleanor's stormy relationship with Henry II, crowned king of England in 1154. His infidelities, particularly his liaison with Rosamond Clifford, and Eleanor's determination to rule her own lands resulted in their setting up separate courts in 1168. His was a peripatetic court moving constantly through his territories in Normandy and England, with Young Henry as heir. Hers settled splendidly in Poitiers, the capital of her own familial lands, to which she continued to attract distinguished poets and noble ladies to recreate the exuberant life of her forefathers in Aquitaine for her favorite son Richard to inherit, but which would remain under English domination until the Hundred Years War (1337–1453).

But her overriding concern politically from this point on lay in the advancement of her seven remaining children (the first, William, died at age three), whenever possible at their father's expense. In January 1169, Eleanor's husband, Henry II, and former husband, Louis VII, met at Montmirail to sign a peace treaty. There King Henry bestowed on his three eldest sons—Henry, Richard, and Geoffrey—the titles of king, duke, and count, respectively, while in reality retaining the actual powers of these titles for the rest of his life. Marriages were also performed or planned between the two kings' offspring. At Montmirail one of Louis's daughters by Constance, Alais (not to be confused with daughter Alix by Eleanor), was betrothed to Eleanor's second son, Duke Richard; earlier (1160), Louis's other daughter by Constance of Castile had, at the age of three, married Henry the Young King, as he would become known, thus providing the groom's father, Henry II, with the Vexin territory, in Normandy, as her dowry. The three young princes, impatient to assume the power their titles implied, with the full support of their mother and military assistance from King Louis VII and his sons-in-law, took up arms against their father in 1173. The uprising failed, but Henry II, deciding to take no more chances, marched into Poitiers with his soldiers and took his errant queen captive.

Eleanor would remain in her husband's custody for the rest of his life, a period of some sixteen years. By the time of Henry II's death in July 1189, Henry the Young King was also dead, and her favorite son and heir to her lands, Richard Coeur-de-Lion (the Lionhearted), as he would come to be called, took the throne, ruled from 1189–1199, and freed his mother from her imprisonment. Her sixty-seven years only strengthened her ability to aid her son as advisor and even his emissary on several occasions. When Richard left the kingdom to lead the Third Crusade in 1191, Eleanor remained behind to watch over his interests, joining him only briefly at Messina, Sicily, to accompany Berengaria of Navarre and oversee his marriage to her. Eleanor had personally selected her as his bride at the court of Sancho of Navarre, in what is now Spain, after Richard set aside his Montmirail betrothal to Alais Capet, by convincing the clergy that she had been his father's mistress. When Richard, returning from the crusade, was captured by the duke of

Austria, Eleanor went to Mainz, Germany, personally to negotiate his release from the emperor on February 4, 1194. That same year she retired from public life to take up residence at the double monastery of Fontevraud (or Fontevrault, northwestern France) one of the few remaining double monasteries (housing both men and women, headed by an abbess). It was there that she had King Henry buried, placing him once and for all under female dominion.

Of her ten children, the "eaglets," from her two marriages—Marie and Alix with Louis VII; William, Henry, Matilda, Richard, Geoffrey, Eleanor, Joanna, and John with Henry II— she would outlive all but two. Her beloved Richard was killed by a stray arrow in 1199 and also buried at Fontevraud, leaving Eleanor's youngest son, the cynical and cunning John Lackland, to ascend the throne of England, where he remained until 1216. Even at age eighty Eleanor was a still valued presence, her last influential act being to leave Fontevraud to accompany from the court of Castile a bride for Prince Louis of France, the son of Philip Augustus, himself the long-awaited son of Louis VII (by his third wife Adèle of Champagne). Never afraid to commingle lineages with her former husband's Capetian family, Eleanor wisely chose her own granddaughter, Blanche of Castile, who would prove to be much like Eleanor herself in terms of her intelligence and force of character. Her eldest, Marie de Champagne, would belie her father's disappointment over her gender and rule her court as a true Capet, while arguably surpassing her mother as artistic patron.

Eleanor died on April 1, 1204, aged eighty-two, and was buried at Fontevraud beside her son Richard and husband Henry. Her influence on twelfth-century history and culture exceeded that of any other woman of her time. Her descendants would rule many territories in England, France, Germany, and Spain for generations to come.

See also Blanche of Castile; Ermengard of Narbonne; Marie de Champagne; Petronilla of Chemillé; Rosamond, Fair

BIBLIOGRAPHY

Primary Sources
Benedict of Peterborough. *Gesta Regis Henrici Secundi* (*Chronicle of the Reigns of Henry II and Richard I, A.D. 1169–1192*). Edited by William Stubbs. 2 vols. Rolls Series, 49. London, 1867.
Suger, Abbot. *Vie de Louis le Gros par Suger suivie de l'Histoire du roi Louis VII*. Edited by Auguste Molinier. Paris: Picard, 1887.

Secondary Sources
Bienvenue, Jean-Marc. "Aliénor d'Aquitaine et Fontevraud." *Cahiers de civilisation médiévale* 29 (1986): 15–27.
Broadhurst, Karen M. "Henry II of England and Eleanor of Aquitaine: Patrons of Literature in French?" *Viator* 27 (1996): 53–84.
Flori, Jean. *Aliénor d'Aquitaine: la reine insoumise*. Biographie Payot. Paris: Payot, 2004.
Hivergneaux, Marie. "Aliénor d'Aquitaine: le pouvoir d'une femme à la lumière de ses chartes, 1152–1204." In *La Cour Plantagenêt, 1154–1204: actes du colloque tenu à Thouars du 30 avril au 2 mai 1999*, edited by Martin Aurell. Civilisation médiévale, 8. Poitiers: Université de Poitiers, Centre national de recherche scientifique, Centre d'études supérieures de civilisation médiévale, 2000.
Kelly, Amy. *Eleanor of Aquitaine and the Four Kings*. Cambridge, Mass.: Harvard University Press, 1950.
Kibler, William W., ed. *Eleanor of Aquitaine: Patron and Politician*. Symposia in the Arts and Humanities, 3. Austin and London: University of Texas Press, 1976.
Labande, Edmond-René. "Pour une image véridique d'Aliénor d'Aquitaine." *Bulletin de la Société des Antiquaires de l'Ouest* (1952): 175–234.

Lejeune, Rita. "Rôle littéraire d'Aliénor d'Aquitaine et de sa famille, I: Aliénor d'Aquitaine." *Cultura neolatina* 14 (1954): 5–57.

Lomenech, Gérard. *Alienor d'Aquitaine et les troubadours*. Luçon, France: Sudouest, 1997.

McCash, June Hall Martin. "Eleanor of Aquitaine and Marie de Champagne: A Relationship Reexamined." *Speculum* 54 (1979): 698–711.

Meade, Marion. *Eleanor of Aquitaine: A Biography*. New York: Hawthorn, 1977.

Owen, D. D. R. *Eleanor of Aquitaine: Queen and Legend*. Oxford, U.K. and Cambridge, Mass.: Blackwell, 1993.

Pernoud, Régine. *Eleanor d'Aquitaine*. New ed. Paris: Librairie Générale Française, 1983. [English trans., *Eleanor of Aquitaine*. New York: Coward-McCann, 1968].

"Re-presenting Eleanor of Aquitaine: Roundtable, Panel Discussion" *Medieval Feminist Forum* 37 (Spring 2004): 9–26.

Richardson, H. G. "Letters and Charters of Eleanor of Aquitaine." *English Historical Review* 74 (1959): 193–213.

Shadis, Miriam. "Piety Politics, and Power: The Patronage of Eleanor of Aquitaine and Her Daughters, Berenguela of Léon and Blanche of Castile." In *The Cultural Patronage of Medieval Women*, edited by J. H. McCash, 202–27. Athens: University of Georgia Press, 1996.

Turner, Ralph V. "Eleanor of Aquitaine and Her Children: An Inquiry into Medieval Family Attachment." *Journal of Medieval History* 14 (1988): 321–35.

Vones-Liebenstein, Ursula. *Eleonore von Aquitanien: Herrscherin zwischen zwei Reichen*. Personlichkeit und Geschichte, 160–61. Göttingen, Germany: Muster-Schmidt, 2000.

Weir, Alison. *Eleanor of Aquitaine: By the Wrath of God, Queen of England*. London: Jonathan Cape, 1999. U.S. ed. *Eleanor of Aquitaine: A Life*. New York: Ballantine, 2000.

Wheeler, Bonnie, and John C. Parsons, eds. *Eleanor of Aquitaine: Lord and Lady*. New York: Palgrave Macmillan, 2003.

JUNE HALL MCCASH

ELEANOR OF BRITTANY (c.1182–1241). Nicknamed "La Brette" in France and "the pearl of Brittany" in England, the fair Eleanor is remembered as a pawn and victim of English royal political intrigue, causing her to be imprisoned for much of her life. She was the only surviving daughter of Geoffrey, duke of Brittany (1158–1186)—son of King Henry II of England (1133–1189) and Eleanor of Aquitaine (1122–1204)—and Constance of Brittany (1161–1201), daughter and heiress of Conan IV of Brittany. Constance and Geoffrey were married in 1181, and Eleanor was born sometime afterward. When Geoffrey was killed at a tournament, the infant Eleanor became the heiress to the duchy of Brittany, and King Philip II Augustus of France (1165–1223) claimed her wardship. But Henry II was able to stave him off until 1187, when the birth of Eleanor's brother, Arthur, Geoffrey's posthumous son and thus future duke of Brittany, nullified her claim.

Henry's son and successor, Richard I (the Lionhearted, 1157–1199), attempted to arrange three marriages for Eleanor during his reign. The first, and most fleeting (c.1192), involved Richard's ambitious diplomacy in the Crusades, as part of which he offered Eleanor's hand to Saphadin, brother of the redoubtable Muslim reconqueror of Jerusalem, Salah al-din Yusuf (Saladin, 1137–1193), but this never materialized. The second plan came about as part of Richard's ransom to release him from prison in Austria: Eleanor was to marry the margrave of Austria's son, Leopold. She was sent to him in 1194 in the charge of Baldwin of Bethune, but they aborted their journey and returned on news of Leopold's death. The third arrangement, made as a peace settlement between Richard and Philip of

France (1195), sought to join Eleanor and Philip's son, Louis. This arrangement also failed. The beautiful Eleanor, so frequently used as a diplomatic enticement, would never marry.

On King Richard's death (1199) and at his request, the teenaged Arthur's claim to the throne was passed over in favor of his uncle John ("Lackland," c.1167–1216). Arthur then shifted alliance to Philip, who gave him all of Richard's considerable French lands and whose lords recognized Arthur as king. In 1202, while attempting to take Poitou (his paternal grandmother, Eleanor of Aquitaine's domain), Arthur—the "hope of Brittany"— was captured in battle at Mirebeau by King John and imprisoned at Falaise castle in Normandy. At the same time, Arthur's sister Eleanor was also captured and imprisoned in England. The contemporary *Chronicle* of Thomas Castleford alleges that Eleanor was ravished with her brother and neither one was ever heard from again; French (*Chroniques de Normandie*) and other chronicles were even more mystified as to her whereabouts. But subsequent documented appearances of Eleanor contradict Castleford's account, at least in her case. Though nothing was ever concretely proven, strong rumors of King John's murder of the young Duke Arthur (c.1203) caused Philip to announce that John would forfeit Arthur's French fiefdoms if he did not return Arthur and Eleanor. Unable to convince Pope Innocent III of the wrongfulness of Arthur's murder, Philip was none-theless able to exploit public chagrin at the disappearance of the two siblings as an excuse to conquer Normandy.

Unlike her brother, Eleanor was not killed by King John. However, to ensure that she could never incite a rebellion nor produce an heir to challenge his right to the throne, John imprisoned her in various parts of his kingdom at different intervals over the ensuing almost four decades: Burgh Castle, Westmorland, then later in Bower Castle, Yorkshire, and finally in Corfe Castle, Dorset. Though accounts vary, Eleanor seems to have been well treated in her captivity. Her allowance from the Exchequer enabled her to have servants and fine furnishings; she was also permitted decent, even elegant, clothing. She passed the time with John's wife, Queen Isabella, and with the daughters of the king of Scotland, who were also hostages. In 1214, John took Eleanor with him to La Rochelle in Brittany where he may have been planning to install her in the palace of Philip's ally Peter of Dreux, count of Brittany, whom John had recently captured. Nothing seems to have come of this scheme. A fanciful story in the *Lanercost Chronicle* mentions that she once tried to stab Henry III when he came to visit her and later, in remorse, Henry surrendered his crown to her. She wore it for three days but returned it on seeing that Henry's son Edward was a strong boy and worthy of the royal inheritance.

Eleanor thus remained imprisoned, either in Corfe or Bristol, until her death on August 10, 1241. Buried in St. James's, Bristol, her remains were later transferred by royal command to the convent of Amesbury in Wiltshire. At her death, the duchy of Brittany and the earldom of Richmond passed to her nephew, John of Brittany, son of her half-sister, Alice of Brittany.

See also Eleanor of Aquitaine

BIBLIOGRAPHY

Primary Sources
Castleford, Thomas. *Castleford's Chronicle, or The Boke of Brut.* Critical ed. by Caroline D. Eckhardt. Early English Text Society, 305–6. Oxford and New York: Oxford University Press, 1996.

Cockayne, George E. *Complete Peerage*. Edited by Geoffrey H. White. 12 vols. London: St. Catherine Press, 1910–1953.

Chronicon de Lanercost (1201–1346). Edited by Joseph Stevenson. Bannatyne Club, 65. Edinburgh, 1839. [Latin text, English notes and appended documents].

Chroniques de Normandie. Edited by Francisque Michel. Rouen: Periaux/Édouard, 1839.

Green, Mary A. E., ed. *Letters of Royal and Illustrious Ladies of Great Britain* . . . , 1: 24–27. 3 vols. London: H. Colburn, 1846.

Rotuli Litterarum Patentium in Turri Londonensi Asservati. Edited by Thomas D. Hardy. London: Public Records Commission/Eyre & Spottiswoode, 1835. [Court of Chancery records].

Secondary Sources

Guilloreau, L. "Aliénor de Bretagne, quelques détails relatifs à sa captivité." *Revue de Bretagne* (1907): 58–65.

Kelly, Amy. *Eleanor of Aquitaine and the Four Kings*. Cambridge, Mass.: Harvard University Press, 1950.

Lloyd, Alan. *The Maligned Monarch: A Life of King John of England*. Garden City, N.Y.: Doubleday, 1972.

Warren, Wilfred L. *King John*. London: Eyre Methuen, 1981. Reprint New Haven: Yale University.

ELIZABETH MCCUTCHEON

ELEANOR OF CASTILE (1241–1290). Eleanor of Castile was the first wife of Edward I of England, and the daughter of Ferdinand III of Castile and his second wife Jeanne de Dammartin, countess of Ponthieu. After their father's death in 1252, Eleanor's half-brother Alphonso X resurrected Castilian claims to the Plantagenet duchy of Gascony in southern Aquitaine, allegedly derived from Alphonso VIII's marriage in 1170 to Eleanor Plantagenet, daughter of Henry II of England and Eleanor of Aquitaine. After lengthy negotiations, Eleanor of Castile married Edward, eldest son of Henry III of England, at the royal convent of Las Huelgas near Burgos on November 1, 1254, when Alphonso X released his Gascon pretensions to Edward. Little is known of Eleanor's life in England before 1258, when she supported Edward's new political alliance with his uncles, Henry III's Lusignan half-brothers. After the Lusignans were expelled from England in 1259, Eleanor shared Edward's 1260–1262 "exile." In the baronial crisis of 1263–1265, she imported mercenaries from Ponthieu to support the royalist cause; after the barons defeated Henry III at Lewes in 1264, Eleanor was rumored to be hiring Castilian troops, but in fact had no funds to do so. After Henry's victory at Evesham in 1265, she thus sought grants of land and money from him, and found new followers among the former rebels she worked to reconcile with him. By 1270, when she accompanied Edward on crusade, she had assembled estates that provided a nucleus for later additions, and had recruited efficient administrators to manage her revenues.

No evidence supports the legend that, at Acre in the Holy Land, Eleanor sucked the poisoned wounds an Arab assassin inflicted on Edward. The story first appears in an Italian chronicle written in the 1320s. Only one contemporary English chronicle mentions the incident, and says merely that Eleanor had to be led weeping from Edward's bedside before an intrepid surgeon saved his life by excising the inflamed flesh. In Sicily early in 1273, the couple heard of Henry III's death in November 1272. After Edward spent several months reforming the administration in Aquitaine and taking the barons' homages there, the couple reached England for their coronation on August 19, 1274.

In 1274–1275, Edward enlarged Eleanor's dower assignment and, to help organize her finances, granted her many Christian debts to Jewish moneylenders. She rounded out her dower assignment by using these debts to acquire the estates pledged to secure the loans. By profiting from these usurious debts she caused scandal across England, incurring Archbishop John Pecham's censure and the popular indignation noted by contemporary chroniclers. After 1281 she exploited such debts less often, but still added to her estates; by 1290, they produced above £2500 yearly. Her officials administered her lands strictly, and rigorously exacted debts owed her; they initiated many conflicts with other landlords, and Pecham criticized their oppression of her tenants. On her deathbed, Eleanor begged Edward to redress any wrongs thus committed in her name, but the damage had been done. The English considered her harsh and greedy and, as Pecham warned her in 1283, many therefore blamed her for the strictness of Edward's rule.

A faithful and respectful husband, Edward in fact limited Eleanor's share in official matters. Only after she inherited the county of Ponthieu at her mother's death in 1279 could she claim a personal role in administrative and diplomatic matters. Previously, her diplomatic activities had rested on her ability to exploit her kinship to other European ruling houses, and the marriages she arranged for her cousins. Though she was always occupied with acquiring and managing her estates, her life was also structured by the rhythms of motherhood; of her sixteen children, six survived her. Though the demands of her rank often kept her apart from them, she was an attentive parent and constantly interacted with the caregivers she carefully chose for her family. A vigorous supporter of the universities, Eleanor maintained a personal scriptorium and was a knowing patron of vernacular letters. Her personal piety appears to have borne a strong Dominican stamp; she was an active monastic founder but because she favored the Dominicans, Benedictine and Augustinian chroniclers ignored these activities. What else is known of her individual preferences, including the many goods she purchased from merchants active in the East, implies a refinement and discretion also evident in her cautious promotion of the many cousins she settled in England. Few of these were men, who would have needed property and income, to the potential resentment of the English who had criticized such largesse to foreigners by Henry III and his wife. Eleanor instead patronized female relatives, for whom she easily found willing English noble husbands.

Eleanor died near Lincoln of a feverish illness on November 28, 1290, aged forty-nine. Her funeral procession's route to Westminster was marked by twelve monumental stone crosses of which three survive, at Geddington, Hardingstone (near Northampton), and Waltham. With her fine tomb in Westminster Abbey, these crosses greatly influenced Eleanor's posthumous reputation. A laudatory eulogy of her was written by a chronicler at St. Albans monastery in 1307–1308 with a likely eye to flattering her son, the newly acceded Edward II. Expanded by a second St Albans writer around the middle of the fourteenth century, and again by Thomas Walsingham in the 1390s, this encomium became a second element in Eleanor's evolving renown. The sixteenth-century antiquary, William Camden, provided a third by popularizing in England the tale of Eleanor's selfless heroism at Acre, and by representing the crosses as Edward's tribute to the wife who risked her life to save his. From Walsingham's elaborated St. Albans eulogy, the Acre legend and the crosses, Camden created a glowing account of Eleanor of Castile's life and character that was further embroidered by the popular nineteenth-century biographer of English queens, Agnes Strickland, and in the twentieth by Thomas Costain. While this highly favorable image has largely persisted to the present day, it differs markedly from the opinions many of Eleanor's contemporaries held of her.

See also Dower; Dowry; Eleanor of Aquitaine; Scribes and Scriptoria

BIBLIOGRAPHY

Primary Sources
The Court and Household of Eleanor of Castile in 1290 [London BL MS Add 35294]. Edited with commentary by John C. Parsons. Toronto: Pontifical Institute, 1977.
Walsingham, Thomas. *The St. Albans Chronicle 1406–1420* [Oxford, Bodley MS 462]. Edited by V. H. Galbraith. Oxford: Clarendon Press, 1937.

Secondary Sources
Parsons, John C. *Eleanor of Castile: Queen and Society in Thirteenth-Century England*. New York: St. Martin's, 1995.
Prestwich, Michael. *Edward I*. Berkeley and Los Angeles: University of California Press, 1988.

JOHN CARMI PARSONS

ELEONORE OF AUSTRIA (1433–1480). Eleonore has been credited with the German translation of a rather popular French prose romance, *Ponthus et Sidoine*, into Middle-High German as *Pontus und Sidonia*. Born in Scotland, she was the daughter of James I of Scotland and Jane, daughter of John Beaufort, Earl of Somerset. As one of six daughter of the art connoisseur James I of the House of Stuart, Eleonore was raised in Scotland and France. After her marriage to Archduke Sigmund of Tyrol and Vorderösterreich (Outer Austria) in 1449, she resided at the court of Innsbruck, Austria, which she helped develop into one of the major cultural centers of the German-speaking world. Her contacts with various humanist writers (writers schooled in Classical Greek, Latin, and sometimes Hebrew, who actively used their learning for the public good) of that period made her famous in literary circles. Thus she is praised by Heinrich Stainhowel in the preface to his German version of the Italian humanist Giovanni Boccaccio's mid-fourteenth-century *De claris mulieribus* (*Famous Women*, 1473) as the brightest shining light of womanhood. However, Stainhowel's encomium mentions no literary activity on her part, nor do we find such allusions in other sources.

Her place in literary history is therefore based entirely on her alleged authorship of *Pontus und Sidonia*, the German version of an anonymous French prose romance *Ponthus et la belle Sidoyne* composed in Brittany (c.1400), itself derived from the twelfth-century *chanson de geste* (heroic-epic poem) *Horn et Rimenhild*. The plot of this work consists in a skillful blend of chivalric adventure and combat in the tradition of the *chansons de geste* (warfare against Muslim invaders, exile, and reconquest of homeland), of courtly romance elements (exemplary courtship in the *fin'amors* tradition between prince and princess, betrayal by others, happy reunion), and also, politically, within the conservative *Miroir du Prince* ("Princely Mirror [of proper conduct]") tradition. *Pontus und Sidonia* was at least as successful as its French precursor and set the tone for numerous similar works in the sixteenth and seventeenth centuries, becoming one of the most popular German chapbooks (the so-called *Volksbücher*), judging by the number of references to it and its many reprintings. While the first printed edition of *Pontus und Sidonia* came out in 1483, three years after Eleonore's death, the work itself must have been written before 1465, the date of its first known manuscript copy.

The opening paragraph of the printed edition declares Eleonore's authorship, yet unfortunately, if one compares the stylistic aplomb of the *Pontus und Sidonia* to the less adequate language of several of her autograph letters, it seems more likely that this translation was done by a cleric at the Innsbruck court, perhaps with Eleonore's help, as Margarete Köfler and Werner Maleczek contend. The later attribution to Eleonore may have been arranged by her husband to gain them both fame, and perhaps also for commercial reasons.

See also Boccaccio, Women in, *De Claris Mulieribus*; Elisabeth of Nassau-Saarbrücken

BIBLIOGRAPHY

Primary Sources
Eleonore von Österreich. Pontus und Sidonia. Edited by Reinhard Hahn. Texte des späten Mittelalters und der frühen Neuzeit, 38. Berlin: Erich Schmidt, 1997. [Middle-High German text, German notes].
———. *Pontus und Sidonia in der Verdeutschung eines Ungennanten aus dem 15. Jahrhundert*. Critical ed. by Karin Schneider. Texte des späten Mittelalters, 15. Berlin: Erich Schmidt, 1961.
———.*Pontus und Sidonia: Augsburg 1485*. Facsimile edition with afterword by Gerhard Diehl and Ruth Finckh. Deutsche Volksbücher in Faksimiledrucken, A: 15. Hildesheim, Germany: Olms, 2002.
Le Roman de Ponthus et Sidoine. Critical ed. by Marie-Claude de Crécy. Textes Littéraires Français, 475. Geneva: Droz, 1997.
King Ponthus and the Fair Sidoine. Translated by Frank Jewitt Mather. *PMLA* 12 (1897): 1–150. [Only known available English translation].

Secondary Sources
Köfler, Margarete, and Silvia Caramelle. *Die beiden Frauen des Erzherzogs Sigmund von Österreich-Tirol*. Schlern-Schriften, 269. Innsbruck: Universitätsverlag Wagner, 1982.
Mackenson, L. "Elisabeth von Österreich." In *Deutsche Literatur des Mittelalters. Verfasserlexikon*, edited by Wolfgang Stammler, vol. 1: 543–47. Berlin: de Gruyter, 1933.
Maleczek, Werner. "Die Sachkultur am Hofe Herzog Sigismunds von Tirol." In *Adelige Sachkultur des Spätmittelalters. Internationaler Kongres, Krems, 22–25. September 1980*, 133–67. Veröffentlichungen des Instituts fur Mittelalterliche Realienkunde Österreichs, 5. Vienna: Österreichischen Akademie der Wissenschaften, 1982.
Steinhoff, Hans Hugo. "Eleonore von Österreich." In *Deutsche Literatur des Mittelalters. Verfasserlexikon*, edited by Kurt Ruh, 2: 470–73. Berlin: de Gruyter, 1980.

KARL A. ZAENKER

ELISABETH OF HUNGARY/THURINGIA, ST. (1207–1231). Not to be confused with the later Dominican nun, Elisabeth of Hungary (1293–1337), St. Elisabeth was born at Pressburg (now Bratislava, Czechoslovakia), the daughter of King Andrew II of Hungary and his consort, Gertrude. At the age of four she was moved to Germany, to the court of the landgrave of Thuringia, to be betrothed to his son, the future Ludwig IV. The future couple was raised together, virtually as sister and brother, at court. She was married to Ludwig in 1221, and, it was said, the two of them deeply loved each other. However, though a landgravine, or landgrave's wife (a sort of countess), she never quite acclimated

Saint Elisabeth of Hungary visiting the hospice she founded. Dated 1853. © The Art Archive/ Musée des Beaux Arts Lyons/Dagli Orti.

herself to the frivolous whirlwind of activities at court; rather, having been predisposed toward the ascetic life since childhood, she stayed aloof from the festivities. Not surprisingly, she became influenced by the Franciscans, newly arrived in Germany, an order whose members took an oath of poverty and devoted themselves to charitable works. Meanwhile, Ludwig went on the Crusade and was killed (1227), leaving Elisabeth a widow vulnerable to persecution by his brother and successor, Heinrich Raspe, who not only cut off her charities (claiming these were depleting his state's finances) but left her almost destitute, whereupon she decided to renounce worldly existence. Given asylum by her uncle and austerely ascetic spiritual guide, Conrad of Marburg (c.1180–1233)—a fiery preacher of the Crusades under Pope Innocent III, then attached to Ludwig's court, and later papal inquisitor—Elisabeth could fulfill her self-mortifying desires beyond her dreams. Conrad subjected her to the harshest treatment; not only did he hold her to a life of privation but he also made her give up her children, beat her, and ordered her to devote herself entirely to caring for the sick and impoverished. Because of her devout spirituality, Elisabeth, despite her delicate nature's abuse under Conrad's stern regimen, managed boundless compassion for the poor, the downtrodden, the homeless, and ailing at Marburg, where she established a hospital for them with Conrad as the lay preacher in the chapel, which was dedicated to St. Francis.

She died in 1231, and, because numerous miracles around her grave were reported, she was canonized four years later by Pope Gregory IX. The Elisabethskirche (Church of St. Elisabeth), an outstanding example of German Gothic architecture, was erected in Marburg to enshrine her relics between 1235 and 1283, but the relics were removed in 1539 by Philip of Hesse, a zealous supporter of the reformer Marburg Luther, to end the pilgrimages to her shrine, which by then rivaled those to Santiago de Campostela. Nevertheless, Elisabeth's cult in Germany and Austria was, and remains, rekindled. In modern times, Richard Wagner would romantically recreate her as his minstrel hero's tragic spiritual redeemer in the opera *Tannhäuser* (1845). Her feast day is November 17.

Conrad recorded her accomplishments in letters to Pope Gregory IX (1232). These, together with the testimony of four women attendants at her death (*Libellus de dictis quatuor ancillarum*), taken by the third papal commission (1235), comprise the contemporary sources for Elisabeth's life and served as the testimony for her canonization, further aided by multileveled support from the order known as the Teutonic Knights, who maintained the momentum of her canonization after Conrad's murder in 1233. Then would come her biography, in 1236, by the noted hagiographer, the Cistercian Caesarius of Heisterbach (c.1180–1240), and later, the *Vita sanctae Elizabethae* (*Life of St. Elisabeth*, 1289–1297), composed in Latin by the Dominican monk Theodoric, or Dietrich, of Apolda (b. 1228) at Thuringia. In these legends, Elisabeth's sufferings, charitable works, and self-denial are interpreted in parallel with the life of Christ.

See also Hagiography (Female Saints); Relics and Medieval Women

BIBLIOGRAPHY

Primary Sources
Caesarius of Heisterbach. [*Vita S. Elisabethae*]. Edited by Albert Huyskens. In *Die Wundergeschichten des Caesarius von Heisterbach*, general editor, Alfons Hilka, 3: 329–90. Publikationen der Gesellschaft für rheinische Geschichtskunde, 43. Bonn, Germany: Hanstein, 1933. [Latin text, German notes].
Conrad of Marburg. [Letters concerning Elisabeth]. In *Quellenstudien zur Geschichte der heil. Elisabeth: Landgräfin von Thüringen*, edited by Albert Huyskens. Marburg, Germany: Elwert, 1908.
Libellus de dictis quatuor ancillarum. In *Quellenstudien*, 110–40. *See above entry.*
Theodoric of Apolda. *Die Vita der heiligen Elisabeth des Dietrich von Apolda*. Edited by Monika Rener. Veröffentlichungen der Historischen Kommission für Hessen, 53. Marburg: Elwert, 1993.

Secondary Sources
Ancelet-Hustache, Jeanne. *L'Or dans al fournaise: vie de Sainte Élisabeth de Hongrie*. Paris: Éditions franciscaines, 1962.
"Elizabeth, St, of Hungary." In *The Oxford Dictionary of the Christian Church*. Edited by F. L. Cross. Revised by E. A. Livingstone, 540. 3rd ed. Oxford and New York: Oxford University Press, 1997.
Petrakopoulos, Anja. "Sanctity and Motherhood: Elizabeth of Thuringia." In *Sanctity and Motherhood: Essays on Holy Mothers in the Middle Ages*, edited by Anneke B. Mulder-Bakker, 259–96. Garland Medieval Casebooks, 14. New York and London: Garland, 1995.

EDITH BRIGITTE ARCHIBALD

ELISABETH OF NASSAU-SAARBRÜCKEN (c.1397–1456).

One of the first writers of prose romances in German, Countess Elisabeth was born to Duke Frederick V of Lorraine, and Margarethe of Vaudemont and Joinville in Vézelise, near Nancy, in northeastern France. Her father ruled over a French-speaking court in Lorraine, and Elisabeth was raised by a literate mother steeped in the tradition of the late-medieval *chansons de geste* (heroic epic poems). She married Philip I, Count of Nassau-Saarbrücken, an important German family, in 1412, at about age fifteen, and soon learned to combine the tasks of raising her sons and, especially after being widowed (1429), administering her dower lands.

Moreover, she set about translating French chivalric literature into German, no doubt encouraged by her family ties with both France—especially its leading cultural centers in Lorraine and Burgundy—and Germany, particularly in Heidelberg—home of the younger Countess Palatine Mechthild (Matilda), the foremost patroness of German literature in southern Germany during the later fifteenth century.

The French sources of the four romances attributed to Elisabeth are rhymed *chansons de geste* connected loosely with the romanticized figure of Charlemagne (c.742–814) and his successors and enemies. In an ambiguous phrase at the end of one of her translations, *Loher und Maller*, Elisabeth's mother, Margarethe of Vaudemont, is credited with having written the French version of this poem. It is more likely, however, that Margarethe had manuscript copies of the anonymous thirteenth- and fourteenth-century French *chansons de geste* (some of which could have been in the form of compiled adaptations, summaries, and extracts) made for herself or her daughter as a basis for the translations. Elisabeth must have completed her translations into German prose by 1437, the date found in the *subscriptio* (signature) of the manuscript of her penultimate work, *Loher und Maller*.

The first of Elisabeth's romances is commonly referred to as *Herpin*. Its lengthier title in Simrock's edition, *Der weibe Ritter oder Geschichte von Herzog Herpin von Bourges und Seinem Sohne Low* (*The Knight-Errant, or Tale of Duke Harpin of Bourges and His Son Leon*), indicates the three major strands of the narrative relating the trials of Charlemagne's maligned and exiled retainer Herpin and of his son Low. Various fairy tale motifs season the plot, for example, young Low (from the late-fourteenth-century French epic, *Lion de Bourges*) is nurtured by a lioness; four fairies cast their spells over the infant; a grateful ghost (= the white knight) comes to Low's aid in his later combat; he obtains a magic horn that can be blown only by him. The work was reprinted several times between 1514 and 1659.

The second romance, *Sibille*, on the other hand, did not achieve this degree of popularity and exists only in the sumptuous set of folio manuscripts of Elisabeth's works produced after her death by her son Johann. It is the story of the unjustly maligned consort of Charlemagne, Sibille, who, while in exile, gives birth to Ludwig and is finally restored to honor and reunited with the emperor.

The third romance, *Loher und Maller*, takes the reader a generation later to the struggle for the imperial title between Ludwig and his brother Loher, a fictional combination of Merovingian Clothar I (sixth century) and of the Carolingian Lothar (ninth century). Loher is banned from the French court and while in exile wins the hand of the Eastern Roman emperor's daughter. With the aid of his devoted friend Maller, Loher fights the heathens, the Greeks, and the Franks, is crowned emperor by the pope, loses his beloved wife in childbirth, accidentally kills Maller, and ends his life in despair as a hermit. This work, existing in various manuscript copies (fifteenth century) and early prints (sixteenth century), was rediscovered and reprinted in an abridged and modernized form by an outstanding woman of letters of the Romantic movement, Dorothea von Schlegel (1763–1839), in 1806, under the name of her beloved husband Friedrich von Schlegel (1772–1829), one of the most prominent Romantic poets and critics.

The last and most interesting of Elisabeth's romances is *Huge Scheppel*, based on the French epic poem *Hugues Capet* (early to mid-fourteenth century), itself based on a mere yarn depicting its historical hero and founder of the royal Capetian dynasty (r. 987–996) as usurper of the throne, perhaps to flatter its readers of the rising bourgeoisie. The countess's translation faithfully preserves the tale of dynastic change from the Carolingians to the Capetians, via the ascent of Hugh, the butcher's grandson, to the French throne by winning the deceased Ludwig's daughter through a series of ruthless feats of arms. "Der schneed Gebuwer" ("the loathsome peasant"), as he is called by his aristocratic enemies, succeeds in erasing the blemish of his lowly birth by beating the nobility at their own game: whether by warfare, dueling, or murdering (the butcher's grandson excels in that, as the author slyly remarks), and by courting and seducing noble ladies. His ten bastard sons, who appear at court at an inopportune moment, increase his fame rather than his disgrace: "ist wol in Buelschaft groß Thorheit; so ist ouch grosse Freud vnnd Wollust darin" ("while there is great folly in the pursuit of love, there is also great joy and pleasure in it").

Modern critics have pointed out that Elisabeth merely produced a close translation of the French originals without adapting them to the new prose medium and without restructuring the contents accordingly. The crudeness of her source texts, both in describing violent combat and the seemingly emotionless erotic encounters, is only slightly mitigated. Indeed, the purpose of Elisabeth's literary activity seems to have been to introduce German courtly audiences to subject matter popular among the contemporary French aristocracy, with the only intervention being her German prose—no glossing or alteration out of political or other concerns. Her use of prose, common in late medieval French fiction but hitherto used only for religious or factual texts in Germany, thus marks a shift toward a trend that would last for over two centuries in German literature, producing numerous offshoots (for example, *Pontus und Sidonia*, attributed to Eleonore of Austria). In their many printed versions, such chapbooks (the so-called *Volksbücher* = literally, common people's books) would eventually reach well-to-do bourgeois readers, well into the eighteenth century, who would marvel at the glorious exploits and tribulations of these romantic heroes and heroines while also being morally reassured that, since all are vulnerable to the caprice of Fortune's Wheel, submission to God's will is essential in everyone's life.

Elisabeth died at Saarbrücken. Her tomb can still be seen in the Collegiate Church of St. Amual in that city, now in Germany, near the French border.

See also Dower; Eleonore of Austria

BIBLIOGRAPHY

Primary Sources

Elisabeth of Nassau-Saarbrücken, trans. *Herpin*. In *Die deutschen Volksbücher*, edited by Karl Joseph Simrock, 11: 213–445. Basel, 1892. Reprint Hildesheim, Germany: Olms, 1974.

———. *Der Roman von der Königin Sibille in drei Prosafassungen d. 14. u. 15. Jahrhunderts*, Critical ed. by Hermann Tiemann, 117–86. Veröffentlichungen aus der Staats- und Universitätsbibliothek Hamburg, 10. Hamburg: Hauswedell, 1977. [Also gives texts of sources in original languages: Old Spanish, Old and Middle French, Early New High German].

———. *Loher und Maller* (abridged) in Friedrich Schlegel, *Sammlung von Memoiren und Romantischen Dichtungen des Mittelalters aus Altfranzosischen und Deutschen Quellen*, ed. Liselotte Dieckmann, 377–456. Kritische Friedrich-Schlegel-Ausgabe, 33. Paderborn, Germany: Schoeningh; Zürich, Switzerland: Thomas, 1980.

———. Huge Scheppel, Königin Sibille, ubertragen aus dem Französischen von Elisabeth von Nassau-Saarbrücken: Hamburg Staats- und Universitätsbibliothek, cod. 12 in scrinio. *Facsimile edition with introduction by Dirk Müller*. Munich: Helga Langenfelder, 1993.

———. *Hug Schapler*, Straßburg 1500. Facsimile edition with afterword by Marie-Luise Linn. Deutsche Volksbücher in Faksimiledrucken, 5. Hildesheim: Olms, 1974.

———. *Hug Schapler*. In *Volksbücher vom sterbenden Rittertum*, edited by Heinz Kindermann, 23–114. Entwicklungsreihen, Reihe: Volks-und Schwankbücher, 1. Weimar and Leipzig, Germany: Böhlau, 1928.

Secondary Sources

Frey, Winfried, Walter Raitz et al. *Einführung in die deutschen Literatur des 12. bis 16. Jahrhunderts*. Vol. 3: *Bürgertum und Fürstenstaat—15/16. Jahrhundert*. 69–91. Opladen, Germany: Westdeutscher Verlag, 1981.

Liepe, Wolfgang. *Elisabeth von Nassau-Saarbrücken. Entstehung und Anfänge des Prosaromans in Deutschland.* Halle, Germany: Niemeyer, 1920.

———. "Die Entstehung des Prosaromans in Deutschland." In W. Liepe, *Beitrage zur Literatur- und Geistesgeschichte*, edited by Eberhard Schultz, 9–28. Neumünster, Germany: Wachholtz, 1963.

KARL A. ZAENKER

ELISABETH OF SCHÖNAU, ST. (1129–1165). Elisabeth of Schönau was a German Benedictine mystic who authored visionary journals and letters and was closely associated with Hildegard of Bingen (1098–1179). Judging by the far larger number of manuscripts (145 known, according to Anne Clark) of Elisabeth's works than those of now better-known women mystics, she enjoyed an exceptionally wide readership in her own time. She strongly criticized not only the Cathars (a powerful heresy reigning throughout southern Europe at that time) but also members of the orthodox clergy, whose neglect of their pastoral duties inadvertently fostered the spread of Catharism and other ills. On the positive side, her visions helped to validate hagiographical (on saints' lives) and Marian (on the Virgin Mary) legends and even doctrines. Elizabeth Petroff, among other scholars, affirms Elisabeth's position as transitional between the older Hildegard and later mystics such as Hadewijch of Brabant (d. 1260), Mechthild of Magdeburg (c.1207–c.1282/94), and Julian of Norwich (1342–1416?).

Most of what we know of her life derives from three main sources: scattered autobiographical references in her own writings, her brother, Ekbert's, introductory comments to her visions and his letters to three relatives describing his sister's final moments. Elisabeth was born in Bonn, in what is now northwestern Germany, on the Rhine, to a family of the lesser nobility with well-established ties to the Church, given several family members serving as bishops and abbots. At age twelve she entered the Benedictine monastery at Schönau (100km southeast of Bonn), which was originally founded for men (1114), but later added a nunnery (c.1126) through the influence of the Hirsau reform movement. While still in her teens, she took her vows at Schönau, where she would spend the rest of her life, save for a visit to see Hildegard at Rupertsberg in 1156.

Elisabeth first began experiencing trance-like visions at age twenty-three, apparently the result of severe depression and/or physical illness pushing her to the brink of suicide in 1152. Her abbot directed her to record them herself or dictate accounts of them to other nuns. Because she believed that part of her God-given mission was to share her visions with the supportive group of women always surrounding her (Petroff), Elisabeth was ready to do so, and her abbot seems to have been equally willing to preach the message of these first visions locally, where they were received with interest. A major factor in the greater promotion of her visions, however, was the arrival of her brother, Ekbert (or Egbert), previously a canon at Bonn, who decided to enter the Benedictine community at Schönau (c.1155) and become his sister's secretary, at the abbot's request.

It was Ekbert who would publish Elisabeth's visions in Latin—not without a certain amount of editing and perhaps more substantial intervention—for the "edification of the faithful." Thanks to him, and to the renown his distribution of her works would generate for his sister, Elisabeth's six-year productive span (1155–1161) would yield three books of visions, three other visionary texts, and twenty-two surviving letters counseling other monastics, including important German bishops, as well as three to Hildegard, discussing the meaning of Elisabeth's visions.

Her works consist in the visionary journals *Libri Visionem primus, secundus, tertius* (*Books of Visions First, Second, Third*), begun during her first illness, from the feast of Pentecost, May 18, 1152, to September 23, 1157. Her visions encompass meetings with saints, the Virgin Mary, and the feminine aspect of Jesus; she also endures taunting by bizarrely diabolical bestial figures and children, sometimes dressed as clerics. Though these three books were never circulated in their entirety, but rather in large parts (referred to as separate titles), these powerfully articulated visionary works exerted great impact in their time.

In the *Liber Viarum Dei* (*Book of the Ways of God*, 1156–1157), she speaks in the first person about a vision "which the angel of God most high announced to Elisabeth, handmaid of Christ" occurring from the Feast of the Pentecost, June 3, 1156 to August 22, 1157. Throughout the work, strongly influenced by Hildegard's magisterial *Scivias* (whose Latin title means "Know [the ways of God]"), if less ambitious, Elisabeth discusses the various paths of God as first symbolized by a mountain with ten paths leading to its summit. But her concept of these ways gains in breadth and variety as her narrative unfolds, embracing men and women, of the clergy and laity, chaste and unchaste, of all ages and professions, asking each to examine his or her particular path and instructing each in how to perfect it. This book would become required reading in numerous men's and women's monasteries over the following century.

At about this time (c.1157) Elisabeth was promoted to *magistra* (mother superior) of her nuns, though still under the abbot's authority. Soon afterward (c.1159), two other books followed: one on Mary's Assumption and the other on saintly relics. *De resurrectione beatae Mariae virginis* (*On the Resurrection of the Blessed Virgin Mary*), broaches the controversy as to whether, after her death, Mary's body accompanied her soul to heaven. Elisabeth, on the basis of her visionary "interview" with the Virgin, confirms the Assumption to have happened forty days after her death, thereby contributing to a doctrine first upheld by St. Augustine (d. 430) and later defended by Thomas Aquinas and Albert the Great (thirteenth century). The *Liber revelationum de sacro exercitu virginum Coloniensum* (*Book of Revelations on the Sacred Band of Virgins of Cologne*) reports Elisabeth's conversation with the English princess Ursula and her 11,000 Virgins, known as the Martyrs of Cologne, a popular saints' legend (c. fourth to fifth centuries). Elisabeth's contemporaries became all the more engrossed in this legend on the discovery in 1106 of what were thought to be these women's actual bones during civil engineering excavations to extend Cologne's walls, and also because, in saintly cults, bones were and are considered sacred relics. Elisabeth's recorded revelations, in which she "interrogates" the spirits of these martyrs, attests to the authenticity of these bones as relics, enriched St. Ursula's hagiographical tradition, and provided a boon to area churches seeking relics, thus making the *Revelatio* her most popular work. Two of Elisabeth's letters identify more relics from Cologne.

Inevitably in visionary works produced by the divinely inspired seer and her supposedly passive, literate "editor," the modern reader wonders whose voice is really speaking; how much filtering has occurred between spiritual vision and real-world text. Ekbert and, to a lesser extent, the abbot of Schönau, had her ask concrete questions of the spirits encountered in her visions, sometimes almost incurring angelic wrath at the outset. By framing the record of her visions in this way, Ekbert certainly controlled much of the direction of his sister's work, even though she did not always pursue his line of questioning very rigorously, as Anne Clark has shown. Ekbert's influence increases noticeably by the third book of visions (Clark 2002). Ekbert injects an additional divine note by reproducing these visions as bilingual (Latin and German), while simultaneously acknowledging his sister's virtual ignorance of Latin (although this is contradicted elsewhere in references to Elisabeth's background); he states that "when the Angel's words were in Latin I left them unchanged, but when they were in German I translated them" (trans. Thiébaux). Nonetheless, Elisabeth's voice is clearly heard, according to comparative studies of her letters, her visionary accounts edited by Ekbert, and Ekbert's own writings. Scholars tend, therefore, to label her books a combined effort, with the common goal of transmitting her very inspiring and useful (for their instructive and validating potential) visions among the Christian faithful.

As Clark and others observe, Elisabeth's persona resembles Hildegard's (especially in the latter's *Scivas*) in representing herself as *ancilla Dei* (handmaiden of God) rather than the Bride of Christ/*Brautmystik* image common to so many female mystics seeking to effect a mystical union with Him. Both women saw themselves as "earthen vessels" of the "Living Light," in Hildegard's words in a letter to Elisabeth (see trans. Thiébaux). However, Elisabeth's visions were less intellectually creative and more pragmatic in their instruction and solutions—and thus more accessible—than Hildegard's. Marcelle Thiébaux remarks on Elisabeth's "saintly intercession in reverse: dead souls in purgatory require earthly penance to free them," which we could add to her propensity for verifying saintly relics, so as to define Elisabeth's theology as one of mortal validation, through both suffering and insight, of the heavenly, as a way of attracting believers. Furthermore, Petroff notes the martyrological aspect of Elisabeth's self-representation in the *Liber Visionem Secundus*: the result of her physical suffering combined with visionary intensity, as underscored by stylistic echoes of St. Perpetua's *Passio* (*Passion*, written in 203). Despite their obvious differences, both the cloistered aristocratic German nun of Schönau and the Roman patrician matron martyred in the amphitheater at Carthage can be said to have composed visionary diaries.

Elisabeth died, deeply mourned, at the Schönau monastery in 1164/5, as reverently recorded by Ekbert in *De Obitu Elisabethae* (*On Elisabeth's Passing*). Her remains were interred there near the altar to Mary, then later (c.1420–1430) moved to a chapel dedicated to her (destroyed by fire in 1723). By the end of the fifteenth century, Elisabeth's visions had been translated in to Provençal, German, and Icelandic (Clark 1992); her vision on the Assumption of Mary was rendered into Anglo-Norman and Old French, naming their author "Ysabeau" (Thiébaux; Strachey). She was canonized in 1584. Her nun's cap today rests on the altar on the right side in the Schönau monastery church.

See also Bride of Christ/*Brautmystik*; Hadewijch; Hildegard of Bingen, St.; Julian of Norwich; Mechthild of Magdeburg; Perpetua, St.; Relics and Medieval Women

BIBLIOGRAPHY

Primary Sources

Ekbert and Elisabeth of Schönau. "Intermiscentur Ekberti abbatis Schongagiensis et Sanctae Elisabeth sororis eius germanae." In *Patrologia Latina*, vol. 195, edited by J.-P. Migne. Paris: Migne, 1855. [Mainly for reception-historical interest; see Roth below].

———. *Die Visionen von der hl. Elisabeth und die Schriften der Aebte Ekbert und Emecho von Schönau.* Edited by F. W. E. Roth. Brünn, Germany: Studien Aus dem Benedictiner- und Cistercienser-Orden, 1884. [Latin texts, German commentary including biographies].

———. [Corrections to Roth's text]. Kurt Köster. In *Archiv für mittelrheinische Kirchengeschichte* 3 (1951): 243–315; 4 (1952): 79–119.

———. *Visionem* [extracts]. In *Ein Zeuge mittelalterlicher Mystik in der Schweiz*, edited by Emil Speiss. Rorschach: C. Weder, 1935. [Based on a sixteenth-century-manuscript discovered in Switzerland. Latin texts, German commentary. Also includes excerpts and analysis of Mechthild's work].

———. *Complete Works*. Translated and introduced by Anne L. Clark. Preface by Barbara Newman. New York: Paulist Press, 2000.

———. [*Revelatio*, Letter 1 to Hildegard]. "Handmaid of God." In *The Writings of Medieval Women: An Anthology*, edited and translated by Marcelle Thiébaux, 349–84. Garland Library of Medieval Literature, 100B. 2nd ed. New York and London: Garland, 1994. [Excellent introduction and notes, including Ursula's legend].

———. [Vision 2 extracts, including *De resurrectione Virginis*]. Translated by Thalia Pandiri. In Petroff, 159–70. *See below under* Secondary Sources.

Secondary Sources

Clark, Anne L. *Elisabeth of Schönau: A Twelfth-Century Visionary*. The Middle Ages. Philadelphia: University of Pennsylvania Press, 1992.

———. "Holy Woman or Unworthy Vessel? The Representations of Elisabeth of Schönau." In *Gendered Voices: Medieval Saints and Their Interpreters*, edited by Catherine M. Mooney. Foreword by Caroline W. Bynum. The Middle Ages. Philadelphia: University of Pennsylvania Press, 1999.

———. "The Priesthood of the Virgin Mary: Gender Trouble in the Twelfth Century." *Journal of Feminist Studies in Religion* 18 (2002): 5–24.

Ferrante, Joan M. *To the Glory of Her Sex: Women's Roles in the Composition of Medieval Texts*. Women of Letters. Bloomington: Indiana University Press, 1997. [See esp. 19–21, 141–52].

Garber, Rebecca. *Feminine Figurae: Representations of Gender in Religious Texts by Medieval German Women Writers, 1100–1375*. Studies in Medieval History and Culture, 10. New York and London: Routledge, 2003.

Other Women's Voices Web site: http://home.infionline.net/~ddisse/schonau.html [Excellent updated resource with useful links to translated texts and criticism].

Petroff, Elizabeth A., ed. *Medieval Women's Visionary Literature*. New York: Oxford University Press, 1986. [See esp. 140–43].

Strachey, J. P. *Poem on the Assumption*. Cambridge: Cambridge University Press, 1924.

NADIA MARGOLIS

ELISABETH VON THÜRINGEN (DIE HEILIGE). *See* **Elisabeth of Hungary/ Thuringia, St.**

ELIZABETH OF YORK (1465–1503). Queen of England whose marriage helped end the Wars of the Roses and mother to Henry VIII, Elizabeth also authored letters and verse in English. Perhaps the most remarkable feature of the life of Elizabeth of York is that, amidst her tumultuous life and times, she acted as calm conciliator and comforter. Although apparently never the prime mover in any one event—some would even consider her a mere pawn—she nonetheless emerges at their real center. Her unswerving faith in her God, her family, her land, and herself made Elizabeth a beloved figure in her own time and thereafter as an epitome bridging medieval and Renaissance ideals of queenship.

Daughter of the strong, passionate King Edward IV (1422–1483) and the beautiful, controversial Elizabeth Woodville (c.1437–1492), she was also niece to Richard III (1452–1485), and to Margaret of York (1446–1503), sister to Edward V (1470–1483),

Coin commemorating marriage of Elizabeth of York to King Henry VII, 1486. © The Art Archive.

wife and queen-consort to Henry VII (1457–1509), mother to Henry VIII (1491–1547), and grandmother to Elizabeth I (1533–1603). Her father loved her, his first-born, despite loud proclamations of unequivocal desire for a son as his first child, and so raised her to be strong and responsible. With her mother, Elizabeth shared whatever extreme vicissitudes historical events bestowed or inflicted on them: from the fullest pageantry and honor attainable in late medieval royal life to years of virtual imprisonment, mortal risk, formal declaration of illegitimacy, then eventual restoration. Many of these misfortunes were dealt them by Elizabeth's paternal uncle, Richard III. On the death of his brother, Edward IV (1483), Richard managed to succeed him (instead of Edward's son and Elizabeth's brother, Edward V) by gaining control of the boy king, nullifying the widowed queen-mother Elizabeth Woodville's influence, having both her sons declared illegitimate, and then having them secretly murdered in the Tower. The ambitious Richard also may have contemplated seeking young Elizabeth of York in marriage, but when this failed to materialize, he later at least acquiesced in plots probably against her life and certainly against her honor as part of his campaign to delegitimize her branch's claim to the throne. According to gossip and fanciful stories of the day, Elizabeth also took an active and dangerous part in the 1483 failed Buckingham's rebellion against Richard, led by supporters of the Earl of Richmond, after her brothers' murders. Conversely, however, other stories speak of her strong interest in and even attraction to this uncle. One is more inclined to envision Elizabeth's patient endurance, supporting her mother and sisters and grieving for her brothers, amidst other tribulations.

From early youth Elizabeth loved to read and did so prodigiously in several languages. Such activities sustained her in periods of confinement, and serve to confirm stories of her reading to her mother and sisters for solace and diversion until Richard met his death in the battle of Bosworth Field in 1485, the last of the Yorkist kings. The victorious Earl of Richmond returned to succeed him as Henry VII, not without Yorkist reprisals over the ensuing years.

This Henry, of the Tudor family and rival house of Lancaster in the Wars of the Roses, had good reason to dread Elizabeth, of the House of York, since her claim to the throne was unquestionably stronger than his. He amortized this threat by marrying her in 1486, a politically fortunate if personally unhappy union. Henry's treatment of Elizabeth during the early years of their marriage betokened his uncertainty. Yet his bride, in never pressing her claim, seemed to have understood Henry's doubts and accommodated them for the sake of her country. She accepted her status as queen-consort rather than queen to Henry VII, thanks to which the Wars of the Roses ended with the death of her uncle Richard, the houses of York and Lancaster allied and the Tudor dynasty was born. In the wake of this newfound peace, a quiet yet firm bond of affection developed between Henry and Elizabeth. She also negotiated marriage contracts among important noble families.

The focus of much writing, from broadside ballads—like the *Most Pleasant Song of Lady Bessy*—to folk legends to Renaissance dramas, and despite her interest in literature, she herself wrote little that has survived save for a few letters and inscriptions in books, at least one doubly inscribed by her and Henry, thus documenting the mutual love characterizing their later years. Her motto was "Humble and Reverent," and she was referred to by her own people's successive generations as Elizabeth the Good. Somewhat unjustly, Henry's poor reputation as king came to be based almost entirely on his actions during the period of his decline occurring after her death. Henry's and Elizabeth's hopes that their first-born, Arthur, would become the monarch to lead England into a glorious new age were dashed after Arthur's death five months after his marriage to Katharine of Aragon in 1501. Elizabeth herself died long before their second son, Henry, born in 1491, would become no less than Henry VIII. It was through her eponymous granddaughter, Elizabeth I, the first reigning queen by this name, that Elizabeth of York's personal example and aspirations were finally realized.

See also Beaufort, Margaret; Margaret of York; Woodville, Elizabeth

BIBLIOGRAPHY

Primary Sources
Commynes, Philippe de. *Mémoires*. Edited by Joseph Calmette and G. Durville. 3 vols. Paris: Honoré Champion, 1924.
———. *The Memoirs of Philippe de Commynes*. Edited by Samuel Kinser and translated by Isabelle Cazeaux. 2 vols. Columbia: University of South Carolina Press, 1969–1973.
Nicolas, Nicholas Harris, Sir, ed. *Privy Purse expenses of Elizabeth of York: Wardrobe Accounts of Edward IV*. London: W. Pickering, 1830. Reprint New York: Barnes & Noble 1972. [Also contains notes and a memoir of Elizabeth by Nicolas].
[See notes to works listed below].

Secondary Sources
Chrimes, S. B. *Henry VII*. New Haven, Conn.: Yale University Press, 1999.
Clive, Nancy. *This Sun of York*. New York: Macmillan, 1973.
Griffiths, Ralph A., and Roger S. Thomas. *The Making of the Tudor Dynasty*. New York: St. Martin's, 1985.
Harvey, Nancy Lenz. *Elizabeth of York, Mother of Henry VIII*. New York: Macmillan, 1973.
Laynesmith, J. L. *The Last Medieval Queen: English Queenship 1445–1503*. Oxford and New York: Oxford University Press, 2004.
Strickland, Agnes. *Memoirs of the Queens of Henry VIII and of His Mother, Elizabeth of York*. Philadelphia: Blanchard and Lee, 1853. [One-volume digest of Strickland's 14-vol. *Lives of the Queens of England*].

WILLIAM PROVOST

ELSBETH VON OYE (c.1290–1340). Born to the Zürich family "von Ouw" or to the "Unter Oyen" clan of Uri, Elsbeth entered the Dominican convent of Oetenbach at the age of six. Her revelations feature horrific descriptions of self-inflicted suffering juxtaposed with *auditiones* (hearings) in which God instructs and exhorts her to suffer further. Her visions attain mystical union through an ethereal exchange of blood and marrow, initiated in response to the actual blood that flows whenever she impales her body on a cross of nails.

Elsbeth's spiritual biography is included in the Oetenbach Sisterbook (henceforth: OSB), one of many collections of exemplary nuns' lives (*vitae*) composed in Dominican convents of south-central Europe. Schneider-Lastin's discovery of the long-lost second volume of the OSB, containing the actual text of Elsbeth's *vita*, has confirmed that the OSB reached its final form after 1449 under the direction of the reformer Johannes Meyer. Almost a century earlier, another friar adapted the Oetenbach account by deleting all personal references and highlighting the didactic dialogue with references to the Divine. This "K" (= Karlsruhe, Germany) version achieved greater popularity than the revelations of celebrated mystics like Mechthild of Magdeburg (c.1207–c.128); anonymous variants are documented in twenty codices of the next three centuries. The K-version was read well into the seventeenth century in the Low Countries, where the Carthusian monk Matthäus Tanner translated it into Latin. Written in Elsbeth's own hand, the Zürich manuscript stands alone among medieval devotional texts as an artifact of mystical composition. The many corrections and erasures bear witness to its status as Elsbeth's "notebook." At least three other hands subsequently contributed revisions, most notably a vehement defense of Elsbeth's spirituality appended to the original text some forty years later. It is a matter of dispute as to whether the erasures constitute evidence of male-centered scribal—now termed "patriarchal"—censorship (Haenel), dissension within the convent itself (Opitz), or Elsbeth's own editorial changes (Schneider-Lastin).

Elsbeth's extreme asceticism has long hindered her acceptance into the canon, or traditional body, of medieval literature. Although many medievalists still dismiss Elsbeth as an hysteric, feminist research into marginalized women writers has prompted the reexamination of her contributions to Dominican convent culture. Fanatical asceticism like Elsbeth's certainly provoked alarm and censure by powerful Dominican confessors like Meister Eckhart (c.1260–c.1328) and Henry Suso (c.1295–1366). Yet Elsbeth is also celebrated in the prologue to her spiritual biography for the "distance that she maintained from all creatures, her devotion to solitude, the inwardness of her spirit, and above all for her burning love and desire to suffer as did our Lord Jesus Christ."

See also Mechthild of Magdeburg; Sister-Books (*Schwesternbücher*); Stagel, Elsbeth

BIBLIOGRAPHY

Primary Sources

[Wolfram Schneider-Lastin is preparing a critical edition of the Zürich manuscript, the "K" version, and the second volume of the Oetenbach Sisterbook. Until this edition appears, the texts are accessible only in manuscript form]:

Elsbeth's revelations: Zürich, Zentralbibliothek. Cod. Rh 159, 1–160.

"K" version: Karlsruhe, Badische Landesbibliothek. Cod. St. Peter, pap. 16, 192r–205r.

The Oetenbach Sisterbook, Vol. II: Breslau, Universitätsbibliothek. Codex IV F 194a. Volume I of the Oetenbach Sisterbook has been edited. See Jakob Baechtold's and H. Zeller-Werdmüller's edition, "Die Stiftung des Klosters Oetenbach und das Leben der seligen Schwestern daselbst," in *Zuercher Taschenbuch auf das Jahr 1889*. NF 12: 213–76.

Secondary Sources

Abegg, Regine. "Das Dominikanerinnenkloster Oetenbach—Bau und Ausstattung." In *Bettelorden, Bruderschaften und Beginen in Zürich Stadtkultur und Seelenheil im Mittelalter*, edited by Barbara Helbling, 167–78. Zürich: Verlag Neue Zürcher Zeitung, 2002. Blank, Walter. "Die Nonnenviten des 14. Jahrhunderts." Diss. Freiburg, 1962.

Dinzelbacher, Peter. *Mittelalterliche Frauenmystik*. Paderborn, Germany: Schöningh, 1993.

Gsell Monika, "Das fleißende Blut der 'Offenbarungen' Elsbeths von Oye." In *Deutsche Mystik im abendländischen Zusammenhang: neu erschlossene Texte, neue methodische Ansätze, neue theoretische Konzepte. Kolloquium Kloster Fischingen 1998*, edited by Walter Haug and Wolfram Schneider-Lastin, 455–82. Tübingen, Germany: Niemeyer, 2000.

Haenel, Klaus. "Textgeschichtliche Untersuchungen zum sogenannten 'Puchlein des lebens und der offenbarung swester Elsbethen von Oye.'" Ph.D. diss., Göttingen, 1958.

Heusinger, Sabine von. "Die Geschichte des Frauenklosters Oetenbach." In *Bettelorden, Bruderschaften und Beginen in Zürich Stadtkultur und Seelenheil im Mittelalter*, edited by Barbara Helbling, 159–65. Zürich: Verlag Neue Zürcher Zeitung, 2002.

Lewis, Gertrud Jaron. *Bibliographie zur deutschen Frauenmystik des Mittelalters*. Bibliographien zur deutschen Literatur des Mittelalters,10. Berlin: Schmidt, 1994.

———. *By Women, for Women, about Women: The Sister-Books of Fourteenth-Century Germany*. Texts & Studies, 125. Toronto, Canada: Pontifical Institute of Mediaeval Studies, 1996.

Muschg, Walter. *Die Mystik in der Schweiz.1200–1500*. Frauenfeld-Leipzig, Germany: Huber, 1935.

Neumann, Hans. "Elsbeth von Oye." In *Verfasserlexikon zur deutschen Literatur des Mittelalters*. Edited by Kurt Ruh et al., 2nd ed., vol. 4: 511–14. Berlin and New York: de Gruyter, 1979.

Ochsenbein, Peter. "Die Offenbarungen Elsbeths von Oye als Dokument leidensfixierter Mystik." In *Abendländische Mystik im Mittelalter. Symposium Kloster Engelberg*, edited by Kurt Ruh, 423–42. Stuttgart, Germany: Metzler, 1986.

———. "Leidensmystik in Dominikanischen Frauenklöstern des 14. Jahrhunderts am Beispiel der Elsbeth von Oye." In *Religiöse Frauenbewegung und mystische Frömmigkeit im Mittelalter*, edited by Peter Dinzelbacher and Dieter Bauer, 353–72. Cologne, Germany: Böhlau, 1988.

Opitz, Claudia. *Evatöchter und Bräute Christi. Weiblicher Lebenszusammenhang und Frauenkultur im Mittelalter*. Weinheim, Germany: Deutsche Studien-Verlag, 1990.

Ringler, Siegfried. *Viten- und Offenbarungsliteratur in Frauenklöstern des Mittelalters: Quellen und Studien*. Münchener Texte und Untersuchungen zur deutschen Literatur des Mittelalters, 72. Munich, Germany: Artemis Verlag, 1980.

Schneider-Lastin, Wolfram. "Die Fortsetzung des Oetenbacher Schwesternbuchs und andere vermisste Texte in Breslau." *Zeitschrift für deutsches Altertum* 124 (1995): 201–10.

———. "Das Handexemplar einer mittelalterlichen Autorin. Zur Edition der Offenbarungen Elsbeths von Oye." *Editio* 8 (1994–1995): 54–70.

Thali, Johanna. "Gehorsam, Armut und Nachfolge im Leiden. Zu den Leitthemen des 'Oetenbacher Schwesternbuchs'." In *Bettelorden, Bruderschaften und Beginen in Zürich Stadtkultur und Seelenheil im Mittelalter*, edited by Barbara Helbling, 199–213. Zürich: Verlag Neue Zürcher Zeitung, 2002.

Tinsley, David F. "The Spirituality of Suffering in the Revelations of Elsbeth von Oye." *Mystics Quarterly* 21 (1995): 121–47.

———. "Gender, Paleography, and the Question of Authorship in Late Medieval Dominican Spirituality." *Medieval Feminist Newsletter* 26 (fall 1998): 23–29.

DAVID F. TINSLEY

EMBROIDERY. By the late Middle Ages, both men and women practiced the craft of embroidery professionally, but female virtue and fine needlework had been equivalents since ancient times. Embroidery was a daily occupation for the medieval matron, her daughters, and the female household members, and it was a prescribed activity for nuns and laysisters in religious houses. It added worth to textiles, which themselves represented great value in material and expended labor. The presence of embroidery on garments and textiles required good needles, costly threads, and training; and it conveyed notions of status, prestige, and religious/symbolic meaning beyond its decorative aspects. Necklines, sleeves, and hems on the clothes of important persons often had embroidered borders, serving as protection, reinforcement, and visual effect. Allover or large motifs were embroidered on royal and

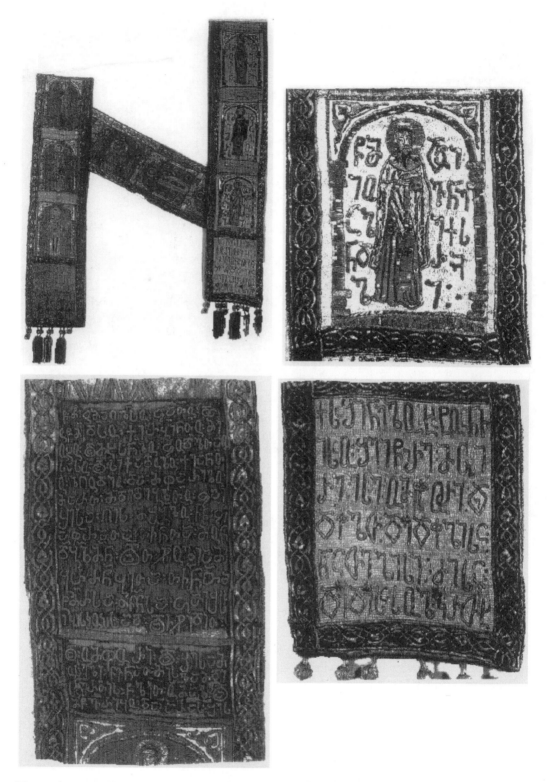

Thirteenth-century Georgian embroidery from the Tsaishi Omophore (a bishop's vestment worn over the shoulders). *Top*: Tsaishi Omophore in entirety (*left*) and details: *right* (and *bottom*, *left* and *right*). Courtesy Irina Nicolaishvili.

aristocratic dress and on the vestments of the upper clergy; in medieval depictions, it is easy to establish ranking systems through the degree of dress elaboration. Curtains, wall hangings, horse trappings, and textile furnishings of the privileged class also featured stitched wealth. The lower classes would not have access to materials or possess skills to deploy embroidery.

The materials needed for embroidery had to be of the highest quality to withstand stress during the process and perform well in subsequent use. Fabric substrates were made of linen, sometimes wool or silk, and threads of the same fibers were used for the stitching. Linen was used in its natural or bleached color, whereas wool and silk could be dyed in a range of brilliant shades. Gold and gilt-silver elements, pearls and colored stones used in the embroidery imparted particular status, especially for sacred and ceremonial purposes. The high regard for embroidered textiles is evident in medieval inventories and in the fact of their preservation; a disproportionate number of the surviving medieval textiles are embroidered. Medieval embroidery practices are frequently depicted in scenes from the Life of the Virgin, especially during her education in the temple. Small and large frames were used to keep the substrate taut, and a variety of devices were at hand for winding and reeling the threads (Wyss). Both St. Clare and St. Birgitta encouraged needle skills in the rules for their respective orders (Poor Clares, Bridgettines/Birgittines), prescribing simple and humble dress and domestic textiles for everyday use, but promoted cloth and vestments adorned with gold and pearls for the liturgy and the glory of God. Birgitta specified that the workshop should be equipped with good chairs, daylight, and a podium from which the abbess would supervise the work.

In terms of technique, embroidery is defined as an "accessory structure to a fabric" (Emery), and may be divided into counted thread work and free embroidery; both types were practiced in the Middle Ages. They share a standard repertory of stitches, which in turn can be subdivided structurally into flat, looped, and knotted, and of which numerous variations and intercombinations exist. In counted thread work, uniform stitches are worked into a woven fabric substrate, conforming in length and number to the weave's interstices and interlacings. It is well suited to small geometric repeating units, deliberately duplicated, and filling larger spaces. The continuity and formulaic aspects of counted work agree well with a life devoted to interiority and meditation, as in the nunnery, and with communal tasks in the women's quarters of a lord's mansion. In free embroidery, stitches form motifs and figures on a substrate regardless of its structure. It is possible to embroider freely without underdrawing, but it is more common to follow an applied outline, transmitted by tracing, pouncing, or freehand copying from a model or pattern. Grandly conceived examples of medieval embroideries of this type, such as the celebrated *Opus Anglicanum* (English Work)—for such was the prestige of English embroidery—vestments of the thirteenth and fourteenth centuries, required a trained artist's conception and a highly developed division of labor for the transmission to fabric and the faithful execution in colored threads. These English embroideries are often characterized by features such as the time-consuming split stitch in silk floss and liberal use of underside couching of the metallic threads. The participation of women in these exemplars may well have been marginal, since their membership in medieval professional guilds was discouraged. Nevertheless, individual English women were named as embroiderers in inventories, and payments to women do appear in the records; a few short-lived needlewomen's guilds were also taken up in the tax rolls of the cities of Rouen, Cologne, and Paris (Dale; Staniland). In embroidery as in all other social and cultural contexts of life in the Middle Ages, we must presume an ongoing and active contribution of women's work, although textual information is lacking.

More securely attributable to the embroidery skills of women are the surviving examples of the so-called *Opus Teutonicum* (German Work) of the thirteenth to fifteenth centuries; this nineteenth-century term denotes the all-white linen-on-linen counted thread work from convents in Westphalia and Lower Saxony. Medieval white work has been described as an economic option to expensive colored silks, but it can also be seen as informed by the fiber's biblical significance of purity and virginity, an appropriate textile expression for the modesty and humility associated especially with Cistercian sensibilities (Kroos). Counted work was also rendered in polychrome wool and silk threads on linen substrates; examples are extant in medieval vestments and liturgical textiles in Austria, Georgia, Germany, and Switzerland. Long-legged cross stitch was a northern medieval specialty, large polychrome altar hangings in this technique have survived in Icelandic and Scandinavian treasuries, with documentation describing them as episcopal commissions made in female religious houses (Gudjónsson; Branting and Lindblom).

Through the teaching, practice, and handed-down traditions of embroidery skills, links may be established between women of privilege in secular domiciles and those in religious settings since they had common social origins. In the nunneries, some arrived as postulants to become professed nuns; others retired there as widows after a full life in the world. Young women received an education there and then brought back embroidery skills and stylistic conventions to their secular lives. In the late medieval period, visitation records rarely fail to criticize the frivolous nature of the embroidery observed by the bishops during their inspections of women's religious houses. A few medieval textiles and vestments of vernacular simplicity have survived in the sacristies of parish churches across Europe; they indicate diversity in embroidered expression removed from urban sophistication at a time when women's engagement in new devotional practices was also at hand.

See also Birgitta of Sweden, St.; Clare of Assisi, St.; Dress, Courtly Women's; Dress, Religious Women's (Western, Christian); Guilds, Women in; Norse Women; Rules for Canonesses, Nuns, and Recluses; Spinners and Drapers

BIBLIOGRAPHY

Abegg, Margaret. *Apropos Pattern for Embroidery, Lace and Woven Textiles*. Bern: Abegg-Stiftung, 1998.

Branting, Agnes, and Anders Lindblom. *Medeltida vävnader och broderier i Sverige*. 1928. Reprint Stockholm and Lund, Sweden: Signum, 1997.

Dale, Marian K. "The London Silkwomen of the Fifteenth Century." *Economic History Review*, 1st Series: 4 (1933). Reprint in *Sisters and Workers in the Middle Ages*, edited by Judith M. Bennett et al., 26–38. Chicago: University of Chicago Press, 1989.

Emery, Irene. *Primary Structures of Fabrics: A Classification*. Washington, D.C.: The Textile Museum, 1964.

Gourlay, Kristina E. "A Positive Representation of the Power of Young Women: The Malterer Embroidery Re-Examined." In *Young Medieval Women*, edited by Katherine J. Lewis, Noel J. Menuge, and Kim M. Phillips, 69–102. New York: St. Martin's, 1999.

Gudjónsson, Elsa E. *Traditional Icelandic Embroidery*. Reykjavik: Icelandic Review, 1982.

Koslin, Désirée. "Turning Time in the Bayeux Embroidery." *Textile and Text* 13 (1990): 28–45.

———, and Janet Snyder, eds. *Encountering Medieval Dress and Textiles: Objects, Texts, Images*. New York: Palgrave, 2003.

Kroos, Renate. *Niedersächsische Bildstickereien des Mittelalters*. Berlin: Deutsche Verlag für Kunstwissenschaft, 1970.

Lowry, Priscilla. "Women in Nunneries: Monasticism and Opus Anglicanum." *Embroidery* 53 (November 2002): 28–29.

Staniland, Kay. *Medieval Craftsmen: Embroiderers*. London: British Museum, 1991.

Warner, Patricia C. "Opus Anglicanum—The Technique." *Bulletin du CIETA* 78 (2001): 41–45.

Wyss, Robert L. "Die Handarbeiten der Maria: Eine ikonographische Studie unter Berücksichtigung der textile Techniken." In *Artes Minores: Dank an Werner Abegg*, edited by Michael Stettler and Mechtild Lemberg, 113–88. Bern: Abegg-Stiftung, 1973.

DÉSIRÉE G. KOSLIN

EMMA (d. 836). Emma, revered wife of the preeminent Carolingian scholar Einhard (c.770–840), exemplifies one of those early medieval women's lives that tantalize by what is only glimpsed in the surviving records, among which are two of her letters in Latin. Her birthdate and most of her life is unknown, but when the distinguished monk and scholar, Servatus Lupus (800–863), who had visited the couple, heard of her death, he sent a letter of consolation to Einhard, then perhaps sixty years of age, sometime in early 836.

The outlines of Einhard and Emma's marriage may be reconstructed from Einhard's grief-stricken letter of reply—all correspondence composed in Latin—and from Lupus's further correspondence, as found in Servatus Lupus, *Epistulae* (*Letters*), 2–4 (see also 1 and 5). Einhard, or Eginhard, the biographer and trusted friend of the Frankish emperor Charlemagne (742–814), had married late, around forty years of age, and Emma lived with him for perhaps a dozen years at the court of Charlemagne's son and successor, Louis the Pious (778–840) at Aachen (Aix-la-Chapelle), in what is now Germany. About twenty years before her death, Einhard had received lands at Michelstadt and Mulinheim, Germany, where he built a church and monastery, renamed Seligenstadt, "the City of the Blessed." The two retired from court in 828, and Seligenstadt was their residence from 830 until Emma's death. Here, according to Einhard, they jointly administered the monastery, presumably as lay abbot and abbess. Einhard seems to suggest that with the retirement to Seligenstadt, Emma, who had formerly been his "most faithful wife," became his "dearest sister and companion." Like many Christian couples before them, they apparently thenceforth practiced celibate marriage, that is, renounced sexual relations. Every indication by Einhard and Lupus—the latter seems to have understood the marriage as the embodiment of Carolingian pastoral ideals—is that the marriage had been "companionate" in both senses of the word. It had been built on companionship on a community of love or affection in that the spouses as companions had shared life's experiences and helped each other attain goals, ultimately heaven, by mutual aid and solicitude; and then, at Seligenstadt, the spouses had become celibate.

Among Einhard's letters there are two that were either written or dictated by Emma. As to the first, a serf had married a free woman and then had fled for sanctuary to Seligenstadt, which because of its possession of relics of Saints Marcellinus and Peter brought from Italy, knew a stream of visitors. The serf asked Emma to intercede with his lord and lady. Emma did so, acting in her own right to save the marriage, which apparently had been entered into without the approval of the lord concerned. In the second letter Emma, this time in a nonmarital matter, again acted in her own person, advising justness and honesty. One can surmise from another of Einhard's letters that Seligenstadt was indeed a place of sanctuary, to which came those who wished to place their cases before God, the saints, and Einhard and Emma.

See also Celibacy; Epistolary Authors, Women as; Marriage; Relics and Medieval Women

BIBLIOGRAPHY

Primary Sources

Einhard. [Letters on Emma]. *See below under* Lupus.

Emma. [2 *Letters*]. In *Epistolae Karolini Aevi*, edited by Karl Hampe, 3: 37–38. *Monumenta Germaniae Historica*. Berlin: Hahn, 1899. [Epistle 3 also mentions Emma].

———. In *Charlemagne's Courtier: The Complete Einhard*, edited and translated by Paul E. Dutton, 137, 158–59, 168–71, 175–84. Peterborough, Ont., Canada and Orchard Park, N.Y.: Broadview Press, 1998.

Lupus of Ferrières [Servatus Lupus]. *Epistulae*. Critical ed. by Peter K. Marshall. Bibliotheca Scriptorum Graecorum et Romanorum Teubneriana. Leipzig, Germany: B. G. Teubner, 1984.

———. In *Charlemagne's Courtier* (see above under Emma). [Letters between Lupus and Einhard on Emma's death].

Secondary Source

Toubert, Pierre. "La théorie du mariage chez les moralistes carolingiens." In *Il matrimonio nella società altomedievale: 22–28 aprile 1976*, 1: 233–82. Settimane di Studio del Centro Italiano di Studi sull'Alto Medioevo, 24. 2 vols. Spoleto: Presso la sede del Centro, 1977.

GLENN W. OLSEN

EMMA/ÆLFGIFU (pre-1018–1052). Ælfgifu, as she was named in Anglo-Saxon, was an ambitious, role-defining queen of England (whose career intertwined with two other women also named Ælfgifu), wife of English kings Æthelred II and Cnut and mother of kings Harthacnut and Edward the Confessor. Emma, as she was originally named, was born in Normandy (now in northern France) to Gunnor of Denmark and Richard I, duke of Normandy, as were her siblings, the future Richard II of Normandy and Robert, future archbishop of Rouen. Perhaps to gain an ally in Richard II as well as profit by Emma's Danish connections, Æthelred II ("the Unready") married Emma in 1002 to help defend his precarious kingdom from the powerful Danes. It was on her marriage that Emma changed her name to Ælfgifu, in honor of her husband's grandmother, St. Ælfgifu (Stafford 1997). Æthelred and Emma/Ælfgifu (for the sake of clarity here, henceforth "Emma") had three children: Edward (the Confessor, 1005–1066), Alfred (b. c.1011/12), and a daughter, Godgifu (b. 1007). At Æthelred's death in 1016, Emma fled to Normandy with her children, while Edmund Ironside succeeded Æthelred briefly as king of England, only to die that same year soon after making peace with Æthelred's victorious nemesis, Cnut of Denmark. Cnut then ascended the throne of England and in 1017 married Emma, who returned from Normandy leaving her children behind. Cnut's concubine or wife prior to his marriage to Emma, yet another Ælfgifu—of Northampton—and her son, the future Harold Harefoot, would later become the target of a defamation campaign by Cnut's new, legal bride, Emma, to protect the rights of Cnut's and Emma's new, legal son, Harthacnut. Apparently Emma's assumption of the name Ælfgifu would thus unify even more currents under her queenly persona than anyone's political designs could have originally foreseen.

As Pauline Stafford demonstrates (1993, 1997), if Emma was a self-effacing queen to Æthelred, she became a forceful ruler alongside Cnut, for whom she acted occasionally as regent during his absences fighting to protect his realm, which by now included Denmark and Norway as well as England. After Cnut's death in 1035, Emma seized control of the treasury along with her husband's mercenaries to ensure her son's succession. But Harthacnut's claim was challenged by Harold Harefoot and his mother Ælfgifu of Northampton. Harold prevailed, despite Emma's maneuvers and attempts to undermine Harold's and his mother's legitimacy, mainly because Emma's one-time ally, Earl Godwine, shifted alliances. Emma consequently retreated to Bruges, in Flanders, until Harold's death in 1040, after which Harthacnut's reign (1040–1042) enabled Emma to regain some control over the kingdom. Meanwhile, Edward, Emma's son by Æthelred, virtually ignored by his mother while he grew up in Normandy, was returned to England as a sort of co-ruler in 1041 by his maternal favored half-brother, King Harthacnut, whom he succeeded when the latter died in 1042. Crowned King Edward (the Confessor) of England (1043), the once-neglected son retaliated against his mother, depriving her of much of her wealth and power. Though Emma's position at court was later partially restored, she lived out the remaining ten years of her life as a dowager at Winchester, whose church she and Cnut had endowed. Edward went on to rule as one of England's most hallowed kings (d. 1066) and to be canonized in the twelfth century.

Emma's notoriety lay not only in her unique interrelation of the roles of wife, mother, queen, and even earthly projection of heavenly queen (Mary) in pursuit of political power, but also in commissioning her chaplain (or some similar anonymous figure) to compose her biography—one of the first significant biographies of a laywoman. Its style reflects advanced literacy in that it contains echoes of the great Classical Roman poet Lucretius (98?–55 B.C.E.) and possibly others. Its tone is very laudatory, as its title (Latin: *encomium* = "praise") implies—the *Encomium Emmae reginae* (*Encomium of Queen Emma*) from c.1037. Likewise, the frontispiece illustration to its manuscript, British Library MS Add. 33241, reflects Emma's awareness, quite unprecedented for a woman of her time, of her own power, superior even to that of her kingly sons (Keynes 1998; Stafford 1997; Neuman de Vegvar).

BIBLIOGRAPHY

Primary Sources

Anglo-Saxon Charters: An Annotated List and Bibliography. Edited by P. H. Sawyer. London: Royal Historical Society, 1968.

Anglo-Saxon Chronicle, MS C (for the year 1051). In *English Historical Documents*, 2, edited by D. C. Douglas and G. Greenaway, 116. 2nd ed. London: Methuen, 1981. Reprint, London and New York: Routledge, 1996.

[Anon.]. *Encomium Emmae Reginae*. Edited by Alistair Campbell. Camden 3rd Series, vol. 72. London: Royal Historical Society, 1949. Reprint, with a supplementary introduction by Simon Keynes. Camden Classic Reprints, 4. Cambridge and New York: Cambridge University Press, 1998.

Keynes, Simon. *The Diplomas of King Æthelred "the Unready": A Study in Their Use as Historical Evidence*, 263. Cambridge: Cambridge University Press, 1980.

Secondary Sources

Neuman de Vegvar, Carol. "A Paean for a Queen: The Frontispiece to the *Encomium Emmae Reginae*." In *Anglo-Saxon History: Basic Readings*, edited by David A. E. Pelteret. New York and London: Garland, 2000.

Stafford, Pauline. *Queen Emma and Queen Edith: Queenship and Women's Power in Eleventh-Century England*. Oxford: Blackwell, 1997.

———. "Emma: The Powers of the Queen in the Eleventh Century." In *Queens and Queenship in Medieval Europe: Proceedings of a Conference Held at King's College London, April 1995*, edited by Anne J. Duggan, 3–38. Woodbridge, Suffolk, U.K.: Boydell Press, 1997.

―――. "The Portrayal of Royal Women in England: Mid-Tenth to Mid-Twelfth Centuries." In *Medieval Queenship*, edited by John C. Parsons, 143–67. New York: St. Martin's, 1993; 1998.

―――. "Powerful Women in the Early Middle Ages: Queens and Abbesses." In *The Medieval World*, edited by Peter Linehan and Janet L. Nelson, 398–415. London and New York: Routledge, 2001.

NADIA MARGOLIS

ENCHANTRESSES, FAYS (*FÉES*), AND FAIRIES. These entities are almost as elusive for us to define as they have been for their pursuers to contain physically through the ages. We first have a linguistic problem: the French *fée* is not really a fairy. Originally, the two are indeed the same and roughly correspond to the Old French *fae*, which means supernatural, without prejudice of gender or even of nature: a tree or an animal can be a "fae" as well as a man or a woman. Later, the English would retain the term "fairy" in relation to the "Little People" and elves, while in France the *fées* specify a quasi-synonym for the English "enchantress," or—unavoidably—"witch." They can also resemble the prophetic, mysterious sibyls. In many ways, the less frequently employed English homonym "fay" is preferable because it retains something of the original French meaning.

The classical image of the Fay is that of a beautiful woman, waiting for a man in pleasant natural settings, near the sea or by a fountain in a garden or forest. She offers the knight-errant her love, which means essentially her body, to be enjoyed immediately without any apparent liability. This embodies the archetypal masculine dream: to be permitted to take a woman without having to play by any rules, free of the strictures of "courtly love." But it also involves an element of menace, since this situation gives the powers of choice and of decision to the woman, and further emphasizes woman's sexual propensities, eliciting the potential male dread of femininity and desire. Fairies/fays also promise to bestow all kinds of earthly prosperity on the lover in exchange for a promise: it may be that the mortal lover must not speak about the fay, or that he must not ask her a particular question, or that he is required to marry her and provide her with the opportunity of becoming a Christian soul. Usually, of course, the man breaks his promise, and the lovers are parted. Sometimes the fay exacts vengeance from the delinquent.

As Laurence Harf-Lancner has demonstrated, there are two types of fays: the first modeled on Morgan (Morgue); the second on Mélusine. More often the first type tends to snatch the young men they desire to their own land, which is part of the Other World, although it may look suspiciously like the normal, human world. This deceptive normality sometimes produces regrettable incidents, such as when a knight becomes homesick and tries to return to his own world, without realizing that a large span of time has elapsed: when he gets off his horse, he usually falls to dust, or, at the least, is very much perturbed by the fact that he does not recognize any of his old friends and relatives. In contrast, the Mélusine type of fay tends to enter the world of her human lover, endowing it with all kind of riches while so doing, and trying very hard to behave like a proper Christian. Initially, there is no moral value implied in the dealings of mortals with fays.

These women of the Other World derive from the Celtic mythology that easily found its way into the Breton romances of the twelfth and especially the thirteenth centuries. When mankind first settled in Great Britain, the previous tenants were expelled and forced to seek refuge underground, in the burial mounds enclosing the noble dead. They came to be known as the "Sidh people," and retained many characteristics of the mythological creatures from which they descended. Among other things, they were deeply interested in the lives and dealings of mortals, and frequently came out to set up mutually beneficial relationships. The Sidh women enlisted men, and knights to help them vanquish their foes, or just went about their own business, which included singing by the sea or near a fountain, bathing naked, or, more generally, displaying a remarkable propensity for seduction and sexual love. Even during the twelfth century, fays hardly ever are the main characters in a novel, with the possible exception of some *Lais féeriques* ("Fairy tales:" this type of *lai* being a short verse-narrative relating a tale of love's trials, death, and

Fairies and elves on their nightly ritual dance. From *Olaus Magnus Historia de Gentibus Septentrionalibus* (*On the History of Scandinavia*). © The Art Archive/Dagli Orti (A).

often supernatural/otherworldly intervention) like *Graelant* and *Guingamor*. Such fays usually appear in the margins of the story, through more or less enigmatic allusions. Morgan is the most often mentioned, in her capacity as an enchantress and physician who has mixed up some remarkable balm to cure madness, or mortal wounds. Conversely, a few feminine figures offer no fay-like qualities, even if they are apparently quite humanized. Indeed, in the thirteenth-century prose novels, the narrative voice goes to great lengths to absolve the suspiciously fay-like characters of any relation to the supernatural or pagan Other World. Many texts explain that all these wise women, the Lady of the Lake as well as Morgan, were commonly called "fairies" but were in fact simply well-educated women who knew the Seven Arts (grammar, logic, rhetoric, arithmetic, geometry, music, astronomy) and also magic, necromancy (Old French: *ingremance*), which was considered to be a science. It seems that being an enchantress is more respectable than being a fay: magic as an acquired art, even a black one, is not as subversive as the very existence of nonhuman, virtually immortal creatures. This tradition continues into the fourteenth century in the anonymous *Roman de Perceforest* (*Romance of Perceforest*), a vast work merging the medieval romance cycle on Alexander the Great (*Roman d'Alexandre*) with those recounting the quest for the Holy Grail (*La Quête du saint Graal*). The *Perceforest*, while introducing "the damsels of the forest" as a generic category (among whom one may notice the direct ancestress of the Lady of the Lake, named, by some strange coincidence, Sibyl [*Sybille*]), emphatically denies their being fairies, and returns to the by then almost banal, scientific explanation of their nature. However, toward the end of the Middle Ages (late fourteenth century), there seems to have occurred a phenomenon one could dub the Return of the Fay: these later versions' emphasis on her clearly supernatural aspects rather than the previous tendency to absorb the fay into her human surroundings, rendering her almost indistinguishable from a "normal" woman. This leads to the figure of Mélusine, who is not only a fairy mistress providing her lover (or here, husband) with abundant sons and lands, but who is also a hybrid creature with the avowed purpose of marrying a good Christian and thereby acquiring an immortal soul so as to enter Paradise after her death. Mélusine embodies ancient elements, existing in more overtly diabolical form in the folk tales contained in such twelfth-century Latin compilations as those by Gautier (Walter) Map or Gervais of Tilbury. She also makes visible the connection between the fay and other supernatural creatures—the mermaid, for instance, whose "second" career is only beginning at the end of the Middle Ages. At about the same time, the connection of the fairies with an underground Other-World appears more clearly than ever, with the many variations on the legend of Tannhaüser, or of the *Paradis de la Reine Sibille* (*Queen Sibyl's Paradise*): another place in which one enjoys all kinds of sinful pleasures, first and foremost the less-than-courtly sensual love of the queen or goddess, Venus or Sibyl. This very un-Christian paradise features images of the Celtic goddesses, later recycled as fairies, but also definitely likens them to demons: the entrance to Queen Sibyl's Paradise, Mongibel in Sicily, is well known as one of the entrances to Hell.

The Lady of the Lake (*La Dame du Lac*), variously named Viviane, Niniane, Niviene, and so forth, is one of the principal fays or fairy characters in Old-French literature—almost as important as Morgan—whom she constantly opposes. Her biography mainly includes the episodes concerning her relationship with Merlin the magician and her role as Lancelot's foster mother (hence "Lancelot of the Lake"). Her character differs widely in the various versions of the Merlin literary tradition (almost as extensive as King Arthur's, and whose origins date back to at least the eighth-century Celtic legends) and its continuations. Portrayals of the Lady of the Lake and Merlin may be said to correlate inversely with each other throughout these different narratives; that is, whenever an author tries to rehabilitate Merlin by excusing his flaws, especially his lechery ("lecherie"), the Lady of the Lake appears as a rather negative character; whereas in texts offering a very positive representation of her, Merlin is darkened as much as possible. In any case, there is a wide range of possibilities as far as her dealings with Merlin are concerned. In the *Post-Vulgate Merlin* (that continuation, previously called the *Merlin-Huth*, following the so-called Prose *Merlin* is itself dated from the mid-thirteenth century), for example, her early avatar as the huntress-maiden ("demoiselle chasseresse") Niviène, a medievalized version of the Classical mythological hunter-goddess Diana (Indeed, Niviène is her goddaughter in the *Merlin*). Niviène truly loathes Merlin, because she knows he wishes only to lie with her and steal her virginity. Because of this fear, she not only steals Merlin's charms and magical formulas, but also convinces him to enter an old grave in which she pretends she wants to rest with him after her death. Once Merlin enters it, she seals the stone coffin with her charms, and Merlin is never heard from again. However, Niviène experiences some remorse for having deprived King Arthur of his best counselor, and so undertakes to act as Merlin's replacement. By contrast, in the "Historical Continuation" of the *Merlin* (*Les Premiers faits du roi Arthur*), as well as in the *Livre d'Artus* (*Book of Arthur*), also post-1235, she first appears as a very young girl, burning with curiosity, who agrees to give her love to Merlin, provided he teach her magic. Though she seems genuinely fond of him, she prevents him from lying with her by magical means, and she eventually imprisons him in the all-too-familiar "prison of air," more out of fear that he will leave her and seduce other women than out of hatred. In the *Merlin Prophesies* (*Prophesies de Merlin*), a late Arthurian compilation, she explicitly regrets having to kill Merlin, but must do so to avoid Morgan's slanders. Besides, in this text, she has a lover (*ami*): Meliadus, Tristan's half-brother, whose jealousy she does not wish to arouse. Appearing in Merlin's prophecies as the "White Serpent," whom Merlin was not able to vanquish, she serves as a target and model for a certain number of misogynist judgments about women. She inhabits the Lake, like a mermaid or water nymph. In Sir Thomas Malory's English (despite its French title) *Morte d'Arthur* (*Death of King Arthur*, c.1469), she presides over the "damsels of the Lake." According to the French *Vulgate Lancelot* (thirteenth century), she pines over her childless state, and therefore seizes the first opportunity to acquire a child, Lancelot, when his mother leaves him alone while attempting to help his grief-stricken father, King Ban de Benoic. Like a number of fays, the Lady of the Lake's persona tends to incur an evolution toward rationalization: the *Lancelot* author explains clearly that she is not a *fee*, but a very wise and well-educated woman, often wrongly call fays. It is also said that her lake is nothing but a mirage, and that behind it she lives in a beautiful but quite natural castle. She performs very little magic in the course of the romance narratives in which she appears, although she reputedly knows everything that befalls her protégé Lancelot, and is always ready to intervene and arrange matters on his behalf. She is often associated, especially via Malory's account, with the enigmatic figure who furnishes Arthur with his sword Excalibur, and whose raised arm takes the sword back into the lake (or the sea) after Arthur is mortally wounded. All in all, she belongs rather to the category of "nurturing" fairies, who give their mortal lovers, or their children, all manner of earthly prosperity.

Mélusine, according to Laurence Harf-Lancner's classification, embodies the second, more positive type of fay; instead of capturing the best and bravest knights for herself, in some outerworldly paradise that turns out to be a prison, she helps her chosen hero (Raimondin) to acquire riches, lands, and political power as befits his worth. The *geis* (promise/taboo) imposed by Mélusine is here introduced as the absolute requirement for the wedding, a sort of taboo-as-prenuptial agreement, as if fays by this time, hardened by tales of damsels in distress, sought to protect themselves from unfaithful knights. Raimondin is henceforth bound by his supernatural wife to a very strong promise: he must not try seeing her on Saturday nights while she sequesters herself, with all the disturbing connotations of infidelity that this taboo may suggest. Mélusine is helpful to him in three areas: (1) she bestows on him boundless wealth, (2) bears his numerous progeny, and (3) helps him to reclaim his rightful lands. Her generosity is typical of that of many fairies.

Significantly, Mélusine's positive influence is not entirely without grave risks, although one is tempted at first to downplay them. Once Raimondin, after jealousy overcomes him and, breaking the taboo, he spies on her while she assumes her true form one Saturday, discovers at last that he has married a "serpent-woman," he loses her and his happiness forever. Even worse, since Mélusine's true nature connects her to the animal world, as well as to the archenemy of humankind (Genesis), the serpent has thus led her husband into the double mortal sin of bestiality and of consorting with the Devil. Furthermore, each of the numerous sons Mélusine bears her husband wears upon his body the mark of his mother's diabolical origin. Mélusine however has but one wish: to relinquish her fairy nature and gifts, to become a good Christian; to die as such and to be allowed to enter Heaven. Unlike other accounts of fays, who tend generally to appear as adults without any reference to their birth or childhood, Mélusine is shown to have descended from a lineage portending (or condemning her to) her destiny. Mélusine's mother was herself a fairy, who married a mortal king to obtain the same reward her daughter would seek for her generation. In contrast to Mélusine's marriage, which produces only sons, her mother's produces three daughters: Palestine, Melior, and Mélusine. Because their father deserted their mother, the daughters take it upon themselves to inflict on him a dire retribution. But their mother takes her husband's side and in her turn condemns them to various lives of penance, of which Mélusine's metamorphosis is one.

Within Mélusine's literary tradition we find in effect three, or even four, novels where we expected but one. First, Mélusine's imposition of a taboo inevitably to be broken by the fay's lover—despite the threat of losing all—is indeed one of the most basic attributes of fairy tales, as we find earlier, in Marie de France's twelfth-century *Lanval* (the hero, Lanval, meets and falls in love with and wins a fairy-princess who forbids him to mention her to anyone). Second, *Mélusine* embodies a dynastic-foundation myth. Mélusine gives Raimondin ten sons, ensuring the prosperity of his lineage and its expansion throughout the Mediterranean Sea and Europe: glorious dreams of the Lusignan house (ruling family of the Poitou region family in France), already somewhat deflated by the time Jehan d'Arras wrote his *Mélusine* (1393). Third, associated with this political myth, Mélusine helps Raimondin, through her good advice, to regain his rightful lands and to become one of the great lords of Poitou. This function of diplomatic advisor is new for a fay: Mélusine's words of advice have nothing to do with magic or any supernatural capacity; they just show good sense and a careful study of the given situation. Fourth, supernatural and eternal elements nevertheless return strongly at the end of the story, when Mélusine is obliged to fly away as a winged serpent-woman, deprived by Raimondin's fault of all she ever wanted to win. She returns, however, not only during his lifetime (to care for her last child), but over the course of subsequent generations, to announce the death of any member of the Lusignan family, whose fortune and fall were both achieved through her. She then becomes an iconographic motif, as depicted, for example, in the *Tres Riches Heures du Duc de Berry* (fourteenth century), the protectress of the city of Lusignan, and joins the figures of protective and, on the whole, beneficent "familiars" or "family demons."

See also Arthurian Women; Lady of the Lake; Marie de France; Medea in the Middle Ages; Melusine; Morgan le Fay; Norse Women; Witches

BIBLIOGRAPHY

Primary Sources
Coudrette. *Mélusine*. Translated (Modern French) with commentary by Laurence Harf-Lancner. Paris: Garnier-Flammarion, 1993.
Graelent, Guingamor. In *Les lais anonymes des XIIᵉ et XIIIᵉ siècles*. Critical ed. by Prudence Mary O'Hara Tobin. publications remanes et française, 143. Geneva: Droz, 1992.
———. *Two Breton Lays*. Edited and Translated by Russell Weingartner. Garland Library of Medieval Literature, 37. New York: Garland, 1985.
[Grail Legends, French]. *Le Livre du Graal*, vol. 1. Critical ed. and translation (Modern French) by Philippe Walter et al. Paris: Éditions de la Pléiade/Gallimard, 2001. [Contains *L'Estoire de Joseph, Merlin, Les Premiers faits du roi Arthur (Suite-Vulgate du Merlin)*].
———. Volume 2. Edited by Philippe Walter et al. Paris: Éditions de la Pléiade/Gallimard, 2003. [Contains *La Marche de Gaule, Galehaut*, and most of the *Lancelot*].
Hutton, Ronald. *Witches, Druids and King Arthur*. London: Hambledon & London, 2003.
Jean d'Arras. *Mélusine: Roman du XVe siècle par Jean d'Arras*. Edited by Louis Stouff. Dijon: Bernigaud & Privat, 1932. Reprint Geneva: Slatkine, 1974.
———. *Le Roman de Mélusine ou l'Histoire des Lusignan*. Modern French translation with introduction and notes by Michèle Perret. Paris: Stock, 1979.

Lancelot: roman en prose du XIIIe siècle. Edited by Alexandre Micha. 9 vols. Textes Littéraires Français, 247, 249, 262, 278, 283, 286, 288, 307, 315. Geneva: Droz, 1978–1983.

Malory, Thomas. *Le Morte d'Arthur.* In *Malory: Complete Works.* Edited by Eugène Vinaver. Originally 1954. 2nd ed. Oxford and New York: Oxford University Press, 1971.

Marie de France. *Lais.* Edited and translated by Philippe Walter. Paris: Folio classique/Gallimard, 2000. [Bilingual Old French-Modern French ed.].

———. *The Lais of Marie de France.* Translated by Glyn S. Burgess and Keith Busby. Original ed. 1986. New Edition. Harmondsworth, Middlesex, U.K. and New York: Penguin, 1999.

[Merlin, Romance of, French]. *La Suite du Roman de Merlin.* Critical ed. by Gilles Roussineau. 2 vols. Geneva: Droz, 1996.

[Various fairy tales]. *Lais féeriques des XIIe et XIIIe siècles.* Edited and translated by Alexandre Micha. Paris: Garnier-Flammarion, 1992. [Bilingual Old French-Modern French ed.].

Secondary Sources

Blank, Walter. "Zur narrativen Bildstruktur im Mittelalter," In *Bildhafte Rede in Mittelalter und früher Neuzeit*, edited by W. Harms and K. Speckenbach with H. Vogel, 8: 25–41. Tübingen, Germany: Max Niemeyer, 1992.

Gallais, Pierre. *La Fée à la fontaine et á l'arbre.* Amsterdam: Rodopi, 1992.

Harf-Lancner, Laurence. *Les Fées au Moyen Âge: Morgane et Mélusine ou la naissance des fées.* Paris: Champion, 1984.

Hutton, Ronald. *Witches, Druids, and King Arthur.* London: Hambledon & London, 20 Melusine.

Lecouteux, Claude. *Fées, sorcières et loups-garous.* Paris: Imago, 1992.

Lundt, Bea. *Mélusine und Merlin im Mittelalter: Entwurfe und Modelle weiblicher Existenz im Beziehungs—Diskurs der Geschlechter. Ein Beitrag zur Historischen Erzählforschung.* Munich: Wilhelm Fink, 1991.

———. "Schwestern der *Mélusine* im 12. Jahrhundert: Aufbruchs-Phantasie und Beziehungs—Vielfalt bei Marie de France, Walter Map und Gervasius von Tilbury." In *Auf der Suche nach der Frau im Mittelalter, Fragen, Quellen, Antworten*, edited by Bea Lundt, 233–53. Munich: Wilhelm Fink, 1991.

Maddox, Donald, and Sara Sturm-Maddox, eds. *Melusine of Lusignan. Founding Fiction in Late Medieval France.* Athens and London: University of Georgia Press, 1996. [Collection of essays by major medievalists in the U. S. and Europe]

Website. http://www.surlalunefairytales.com/boardarchives/2003/nov2003/womentransformation.html

ANNE BERTHELOT

ENGELBINA VON AUGSBURG (13th century). Engelbina was a recluse at St. Ulrich or St. Stephen in Augsburg, Germany. She is mostly noted for her translations of the writings of Saints Gregory the Great (c.540–604), Paul (d. c.65), Augustine (354–430), and Bernard of Clairvaux (1090–1153) into German. The soul is the Bride and Christ is the Bridegroom, a standard theme that finds its way into her mystical prose writings, which ecstatically describe the *unio mystica* (mystical union) of the mortal soul with Christ. All of her works are located at Munich in the Bayerische Staatsbibliothek Manuscript Cgm 94.

See also Bride of Christ/*Brautmystik*

BIBLIOGRAPHY
"Engelbina von Augsburg." In *Deutsches Literatur-Lexikon*, edited by Wilhelm Kosch and Bruno Berger, vol. 4. Bern and Munich: Francke, 1972.

"Engelbina von Augsburg." In *Die Deutsche Literatur des Mittelalters: Verfasserlexikon*, edited by von Wolfgang Stammler, vol. 1. Berlin and Leipzig: de Gruyter, 1933.

EDITH BRIGITTE ARCHIBALD

ENID. Enid appears as Geraint's wife in the Welsh *Geraint* and as Erec's wife in Chrétien de Troyes's Old French *Erec et Enide* (1160–1170), in the Middle-High German *Erec* of Hartmann von Aue, in the Old Icelandic *Erex Saga*, and later in Tennyson's *Idylls of the King*, and elsewhere. In Chrétien's poem, Enid is the beautiful daughter of a poor vavassor whom Erec brings back to Arthur's court and marries. After their marriage, the men of the court whisper that Erec has become too attached to Enid. When, reluctantly, she reports this to Erec, he sets off to seek adventure and commands Enid to accompany him. Unlike many other Arthurian women who show varying degrees of fairy qualities, Enid has no magical endowments to help her in her trial, although the fairy-like woman who keeps a knight in captivity in the Joie de la Cort episode turns out to be her cousin.

In the *Erex Saga*, an Old Norse prose rendering of Chrétien's poem, the story follows the general shape of its model, but in the episode where, in the French version, the Count of Limors forces Enid to marry him (in one of the events that test both her skill and faithfulness), the Scandinavian text makes an important change: Earl Placidus agrees with the court that it is against God's law for anyone to marry Evida (Enid) without her consent.

See also Arthurian Women; Enchantresses, Fays (*Fées*), and Fairies

BIBLIOGRAPHY

Primary Sources
Chrétien de Troyes. *Erec et Enide*. Edited and translated [Modern French] by Jean-Marie Fritz. Lettres gothiques. Paris: Livre de Poche, 1992. [Bilingual, Old French and Modern French ed. with commentary].
———. *Erec and Enide*. Translated by Ruth H. Cline. Athens: University of Georgia Press, 2000.
———. *Erec and Enide*. Translated by Carleton W. Carroll. In *Chrétien de Troyes. Arthurian Romances*, edited by William W. Kibler. Harmondsworth, U.K.: Penguin, 1991.
Erex saga Artuskappa. Edited by Foster W. Blaisdell. Copenhagen: Munksgaard, 1965.
———. Translated by Foster W. Blaisdell and Marianne E. Kalinke. Lincoln: University of Nebraska Press, 1977.
Hartmann von Aue. *Erec*. Critical edition by Albert Leitzmann. 5th ed. by Ludwig Wolff. Tübingen, Germany: Niemeyer, 1972.
———. *Erec*. Translated by J. W. Thomas. Lincoln: University of Nebraska Press, 1982.

Secondary Sources
Fenster, Thelma S., ed. *Arthurian Women: A Casebook*. Arthurian Characters and Themes, 3. New York: Garland, 1996. [Collection of critical essays on wide-ranging aspects, with introduction].
Lacy, Norris, and Geoffrey Ashe et al. *The Arthurian Handbook*. 2nd ed. Garland Reference Library of the Humanities, 1920. New York and London: Garland, 1997.

THELMA S. FENSTER

EPISTOLARY AUTHORS, WOMEN AS. Apart from a few outstanding female poets such as Marie de France (fl. 1167–1190) and Christine de Pizan (c.1365–after 1429), or women mystic writers such as Hildegard of Bingen (1098–1179) and Hrotsvitha of Gandersheim (tenth century), medieval poetry seems to be exclusively dominated by male authors. Even in those poems where a female voice speaks out, as in the works of Reinmar the Elder (late twelfth century) and Walther von der Vogelweide, (d. c.1220), a close analysis reveals them to be a mask for the male singer. These so-called *Frauenstrophen* (women's stanzas) only serve the male poet in setting up a more sophisticated dramatic dialogue in his song.

Nevertheless, for the last thirty years, under the influence of the feminist movement, medieval scholarship has gradually eroded the canonical viewpoint that medieval women did not occupy a significant position in the poetic arts. Likewise, although women are not known as rulers, religious leaders (with some exceptions), or even as knights, there were a considerable number of influential, powerful, and highly learned women in the Middle Ages. Yet strong misogynist attitudes, in part still prevailing in modern times, almost succeeded in preventing medieval women from assuming an active role as poets. In consequence, many literate women were forced to express themselves through the epistle—a formalized letter-writing style with its own prescribed standards since Classical Latin times—instead of the more widespread literary genres reserved for their male counterparts (e.g., epic poem, chronicle, love ballad, learned treatise, and romance), whether in private exchanges or more public philosophical meditations. It was via the epistle, then, that women often formulated and enunciated their ideas, dreams, hopes, and emotions in letters both to female and male correspondents, with the rare exception of those women named previously.

As early as the eighth century, several religious women such as the abbess Eangyth, her daughter Heaburg, and the nun Leoba, addressed interesting and very expressive letters to their spiritual father, the missionary Saint Boniface during his proselytizing efforts in central Germany. These letters attain serious literary status because of their intentional combination of private-emotional matters and public or political issues, all written in a stylized literary form. More complete understanding of this female literacy is still limited because of longstanding scholarly and critical neglect of women's letters as worthwhile literature. However, this lack of primary sources is now being remedied as appreciably more early women's literature is being edited, translated, and studied for classroom use, the general reader, and advanced research. Thanks to such progress, specialists in early women's writing can observe these correspondents' unique rhetorical strategies, powerful emotional language, sophisticated metaphor, and other stylistic features indicating the unexpectedly high level of training and intellectualism manifested in these epistolary masterpieces. Some of these poems literally hide or encase outstanding examples of women's experimentation with some almost-forbidden genres, lyric poetry in particular.

Yet on closer examination, we may discern the origins of the unheralded educational access allowed those fortunate few women intellectuals and poets. From the tenth century onward, certain groups of women in medieval society soon excelled in scholastic learnedness, and a remarkably wider group of women than men were able at least to read and write and thus to control the most basic tools for the composition of letters with their own hands and to read those sent by friends, relatives, or others. Most of them, however, since they belonged to the upper echelons of the aristocratic society, such as the German empresses Gisela of Swabia (d. 1043), Agnes of Poitou (d. 1077), and Judith of Bohemia (d. 1140) resorted, in all likelihood, to their clerics for the composition of letters.

When Heloise (c.1100–c.1164) composed her famous letters in Latin to her teacher, lover, and later, husband, Abelard, she thereby raised her voice as a female author. Under Abelard's tutelage, she soon rivaled Abelard and other contemporaries in Latin eloquence— a feat so astounding that the authenticity of her letters (were they written by her or by Abelard, along with his own signed by him?) has been debated by several scholars. Most recently, Christopher Baswell, while conceding her authorship of the letters signed by her, has nonetheless assessed Heloise's Latinity with greater reserve than her most fervent advocates, such as Constant Mews. In any case, her letters reveal the supreme eloquence that a woman could achieve after years of scholastic training.

In turn, the thirteenth- and fourteenth-century Anglo-French aristocracy produced, among its female members, a sizable and refined body of epistolary literature. For instance, we find Blanche, duchess of Brittany, writing to King Henry III of England (1207–1272) several letters sometime between 1263 and 1270, which are important for their political and personal messages and for their literary quality. Aline la Despensere addressed several letters to Bishop Walter de Merton (d. 1277), founder of Merton College, at Oxford University. Other female authors who appear among the epistolary collections of this time are Henry's wife, Queen Eleanor of Provence (1221–1291) and Alianore de Clare (1290s–1320s), wife of Hugh le Despenser (d. 1326), himself a descendant of the abovementioned Aline and a key figure in the power struggle between the barons and King Edward II of England.

The later Middle Ages, particularly since the middle of the fifteenth century, witnessed a tremendous increase in writing skills among a large group of men and women of all upper social classes. Basic literary knowledge became an integral part of life for a wide range of bourgeois women. The Pastons, the Celys, the Stonors, and the Plumptons, all British families of merchants and royal clerks, have left us a vast body of letters, which were, to a large extent, written by the female family members. Thus even in the world of the urban bourgeoisie, women gained a strong literary profile although still limited to "epistolarity." Traditionally, literary scholars have criticized these letters as formulaic and impersonal, but their real value as products of a female literary culture still awaits final judgment. So far it is certain, however, that letters written by women represent a note-worthy and conspicuous body of literary documents that shed a sharp light on medieval women as authors.

The fourteenth-century saint, Catherine of Siena (1347–1380), and the Swedish mystic St. Birgitta of Sweden (1303–1373) both resorted to the literary genre of letters as a crucial tool for their political endeavors to resolve the Great Schism of the Papacy to convince St. Saint Catherine, above all, carried out a large correspondence with practically all important personalities of her time and thus transformed the letter into an essential source of information both the addressee and the author of each letter. Quite understandably, Saint Catherine's letters are widely praised as early documents of female literacy in the Italian Trecento. Birgitta often voiced strong concerns to political leaders and members of the Church, which could easily be read as threats. Consequently, her mystically inspired letters aroused much criticism and opposition, thus proving that, although limited as to literary genre choices, women could still effectively participate in the religious and political culture of their times via this one mode of epistolarity.

The German women mystics such as Hildegard of Bingen, Mechthild von Magdeburg (c.1210–1282/94), Herrad of Hohenburg (1125/30–1195), and Elsbeth Stagel (c.1300–1360) claim a fundamental share in German female epistolary literature. Similar to the Renaissance letters that contain much of the poets' philosophy and thoughts, their epistolary works often convey the crucial messages of their visions, raptures, and spiritual encounters. Because these mystics often conveyed their extraordinary spiritual experiences through the written word, in letters, and not merely by some type of oral recitation, this greater permanency guaranteed the mystics wider and more lasting influence.

The literary genre of letters was not only cultivated by women mystics, but equally by women of all social classes and intellectual levels, for public and private matters and styles. Georg Steinhausen has provided us with one of the most important epistolary collections of the German Middle Ages, which, above all, includes a noteworthy number of women authors. To some extent they belonged to a religious order or a convent, but the majority of them stemmed from a secular background, either aristocratic or bourgeois. The letters by one epistolary author offers especially interesting insights into the conditions of women in the later Middle Ages and their cultural development. Around 1370, the Countess of Cleve (northwest Germany) created a kind of epistolary circle that, apart from a few male correspondents, mostly included other women. The same phenomenon of a characteristically female cultural center, established through an intense exchange of letters, can be observed in the case of Countess Beatrix of the Palatinate, the duchess Ursula von Münsterberg, or her stepmother Anna von Brandenburg (all late fourteenth century). Likewise, in early fifteenth-century France, Christine de Pizan frequented a circle of Parisian secular intellectuals, often notaries, lawyers and diplomats. Christine, in her *Livre des Trois Vertus* (*Book of the Three Virtues*, 1405–1406) advises women on the art of letter-writing, both in form and content. In her *Livre du duc des vrais amans* (*Book of the Duke of True Lovers*, 1404–1405), we find a harbinger of the epistolary novel in the correspondence between two women, on the dangers and temptations of courtly love, motivating the story.

Margareta von Schwangau (d. c.1459), wife of the famous South-Tyrolean poet Oswald von Wolkenstein (1376/77–1445), occupies a significant role in the history of medieval female epistolarity. While her husband is highly acclaimed for his unique lyric poetry, Margareta's literary achievements lie in her letters addressing her husband and other relatives. Whereas Oswald utilized some of his poems to extoll his love for his wife, her letters document the changing attitude toward love, sex, and marriage in the fifteenth century. Probably under the influence of both parents, their daughter, Maria von Wolkenstein, member of the St. Clare convent in Brixen, South Tyrol, Germany, likewise displayed her literary abilities in the form of letters. An attempt to express herself in more poetic forms probably would have resulted in total rejection by society.

Another outstanding example of feminine literary skills via letters is Margherita di Domenico Bandini, who exchanged an astonishingly large number of letters with her husband, Francesco di Marco Datini, a fourteenth-century merchant of Prato, Italy. Today, husband-and-wife authors have left us a clearly focused mirror of the social and economic life in late-medieval Tuscany, additionally enhanced by female literacy.

Perhaps the most militant women letter-writers surfaced in the early fifteenth century in France. Christine de Pizan, mentioned above in another category of epistolary writing, participated as the only woman in the infamous Debate of the *Roman de la Rose* (*Romance of the Rose*, 1401–1404). She fired lacerating prose epistles at several notable Parisian humanists, taking them to task for their entrenched misogynistic attitudes (by their praise of Jean de Meun's brilliant but irreverent *Roman de la Rose* of c.1275) in France's first *querelle des femmes* (quarrel about women's status and character) and other intellectual-literary debates through the centuries. Christine also composed political and moral-didactic epistles such as her *Epistre Othea* (*Othea's Epistle* [*to the Trojan Prince Hector*])—a compendium or moralized mythological tales for educating princes— and *Epistre a la reine* (1405)—imploring Queen Isabeau of France to intervene for peace in her civil war–torn kingdom. Joan of Arc, a quasi-mythical figure of the Hundred Years War between France and England (1337–1453) and a patron saint of France in modern times, composed forceful letters that played a role almost as great as her sword and banner. Her letters, dictated to her scribes (her literacy being rudimentary at best) and sent to none less than King Henry of England and the English as a whole, plus other high-ranking pro-English dignitaries and towns, urged them to submit to the Dauphin and even provide his armies food and munitions or face divinely ordained destruction. During her campaign therefore, Joan verbally as well as militarily blazed the trail to restore Charles VII to his rightful throne.

Letters have often been interpreted only in terms of what cultural and social information about a certain period they can provide. From a feminist point of view, however, they document the extent to which medieval women were in fact able to reflect on their lives in a sophisticated literary form, to define their existence and their identity as epistolary poets. Considering the large number of letters written by women and taking into account their literary quality, we may conclude that medieval women not only participated in epistolary literature, but in fact widely determined its development and form as an independent literary genre within the general framework of medieval poetry.

Although women were rarely allowed literary publicity or an active role as poetesses, they seem to have conquered their own little but significant niche in literature in the form of epistolarity.

See also Amalasuntha; Beaufort, Margaret; Birgitta of Sweden, St.; Boniface, St., Mission and Circle of; Catherine of Siena, St.; *Chanson de Femme* (Women's Song); Christine de Pizan; Heloise; Herrad of Hohenburg/Landsberg; Hildegard of Bingen, St.; Humanists, Italian Women, Issues and Theory; Joan of Arc, St.; Leoba; Margareta von Schwangau; Marie de France; Murasaki Shikibu; Paston, Margaret; *Roman de la Rose*, Debate of the; Scribes and Scriptoria; Walladah

BIBLIOGRAPHY

Primary Sources

Catherine of Siena. *Letters*. Translated with introduction and notes by Suzanne Noffke, O. P. 2 vols. MRTS, 202–03. Tempe: Arizona Center for Medieval and Renaissance Studies, 2000–2001.

"Christine de Pizan's *Epistre a la reine*." Edited by Angus J. Kennedy. *Revue des langues romanes* [Special issue: Christine de Pizan]. 92: 2 (1988): 253–64.

———. *Epistre Othea*. Critical ed. by Gabriella Parussa. Texts Littéraires Français, 517. Paris: Droz, 1999.

———. *Livre du duc des vrais amans*. Critical ed. by Thelma Fenster. Binghamton, N.Y.: MRTS, 1995.

———. [Same as above, English version] *Book of the Duke of True Lovers*. Translated with an introduction and notes by Thelma Fenster; lyric poetry translated by Nadia Margolis. New York: Persea, 1991.

———. *Livre des Trois Vertus*. Edited by Charity C. Willard and Eric Hicks. Bibliothèque du XVe siècle, 50. Paris: Honoré Champion, 1989.

——— [Selections, English]. *The Writings of Christine de Pizan*. Edited by Charity Willard. New York: Persea, 1994.

——— [Selections, English]. Edited and translated by Renate Blumenfeld-Kosinski. Kevin Brownlee, co-translator. New York: W. W. Norton, 1997.

Despensers. In *Recueil de lettres Anglo-Françaises (1265–1399)*, edited by F. J. Tanquerey. Paris: E. Champion, 1916.

Heloise and Abelard. *Letters*. Translated with introduction and notes by Betty Radice. Harmondsworth, U.K. and New York: Penguin, 1974.

————. *The Lost Love Letters of Heloise and Abelard: Perceptions of Dialogue in Twelfth-Century France.* Edited by Constant J. Mews. Translated by Neville Chiavaroli. New York: St. Martin's, 1999.

Hildegard von Bingen: *Briefwechsel*. Critical ed. and translation [Modern German] by Adelgundis Führkötter. Salzburg: Müller, 1965.

Joan of Arc. *Lettres*. In Régine Pernoud and Marie-V. Clin. *Jeanne d'Arc*. Paris: Fayard, 1986.

————. [English version of above]. *Joan of Arc: Her Story*. Translated and edited by Jeremy DuQuesnay Adams. New York: Saint Martin's Griffin, 1999.

Leoba and Heaburg. In *Die Briefe des Heiligen Bonifatius und Lullus*, edited by Michael Tangl. *Monumenta Germaniae Historica*. Epistolae Selectae I. 2nd ed. Berlin: Weidmann, 1955.

[Various authors], [German]. *Deutsche Mystikerbriefe des Mittelalters 1100–1550*. Edited by Wilhelm Oehl. Munich and Vienna: Langen-Müller, 1931. Reprint Darmstadt: Wissenschaftliche Buchgesellschaft, 1972.

————. [German]. In Georg Steinhausen. *Geschichte des deutschen Briefes, Zur Kulturgeschichte des deutschen Volkes*. 2 vols. Berlin: Gaertner, 1889–1891. Reprint Zurich: Weidemann, 1968.

————. [Selections, Latin]. *Oxford Book of Late Medieval Verse and Prose*. Edited by Douglas Gray. Oxford: Clarendon Press, 1985.

Secondary Sources

Baswell, Christopher. *See below under* Dinshaw.

Camargo, Martin. *The Middle English Verse Love Epistle*. Studien zur englischen Philologie, n.s. 28. Tübingen, Germany: Niemeyer, 1991.

Cherewatuk, Karen, and Wiethaus, Ulrike, eds. *Dear Sister: Medieval Women and the Epistolary Genre*. Middle Ages Series. Philadelphia: University of Pennsylvania Press, 1993.

Classen, Albrecht. "Female Epistolary Literature from Antiquity to the Present: An Introduction." *Studia Neophilologica* 60 (1988): 3–13.

————. "Margareta von Schwangau: Epistolary Literature in the German Late Middle Ages." *Medieval Perspectives* 1 (1986): 41–53.

Cünnen, Janina. *Fiktionale Nonnenwelten. Angelsächsische Frauenbriefe des 8. und 9. Jahrhunderts*. Anglistische Forschungen, 287. Heidelberg: Carl Winter, 2000.

Dinshaw, Carolyn, and David Wallace, eds. *The Cambridge Companion to Medieval Women's Writing*. Cambridge: Cambridge University Press, 2003.

Ferrante, Joan M. *To the Glory of Her Sex: Women's Roles in the Composition of Medieval Texts*. Bloomington: Indiana University Press, 1997.

Grundmann, Herbert. "Die Frauen und die Literatur im Mittelalter. Ein Beitrag zur Frage nach der Entstehung des Schriftums in der Volkssprache." *Archiv für Kulturgeschichte* 26 (1936): 129–61.

Ho, Cynthia. "Words Alone Cannot Express: Epistles in Marie de France and Murasaki Shikibu. In *Crossing the Bridge: Comparative Essays on Medieval European and Heian Japanese Woman Writers*, edited by Barbara Stevenson and Cynthia Ho, 133–52. New York and Houndmills, Basingstoke, U.K.: Palgrave, 2000.

Kohl, Stephan. *Das englische Spätmittelalter. Kulturelle Normen. Lebenspraxis*. Texte, Studien zur englischen Philologie, n.s. 24. Tübingen: Niemeyer, 1986.

The Late Medieval Epistle [Special issue, edited by Carol Poster and Richard Utz]. *Disputatio* 1. Evanston, Ill.: Northwestern University Press, 1996.

Mews, Constant J. *See above*, Primary Sources, *under* Heloise.

Wheeler, Bonnie, ed. *Listening to Heloise: The Voice of a Twelfth-Century Woman*. New York: St. Martin's, 2000.

ALBRECHT CLASSEN

ERMENGARD OF NARBONNE (c.1130–c.1196). Ermengard, viscountess of Narbonne, was a major patron of troubadour poets both male and female. She succeeded her father, Viscount Aymeri II, in 1134 when he was killed before the walls of Fraga, near

Lérida (northeastern Spain). She was only four or five years old at the time. Her two older brothers had died young, and only she and her younger sister Ermessend remained. Sometime around 1139, Alphonse Jordan, count of Toulouse, took over her city of Narbonne, then one of the major Mediterranean ports of Occitania (now southern France) and in 1142 he married her. The marriage provoked a military response from the count's rivals for power in the region—the count of Barcelona, the Trencavel rulers of the neighboring cities of Carcassonne, Béziers, Agde, and Nîmes, and the lord of Montpellier. Defeated, Alphonse was forced to give up both the city and the viscountess. The allies then quickly married her to one of their own allies, Bernard of Anduze. From then on, Ermengard ruled her city by herself. Bernard never again appears with her in any document. Her allies on this occasion, and their successors, remained her allies until the very last years of her life.

In the 1140s, Occitania was inflamed by conflicts over the claims to power of two other women, Stephania of les Baux and Eleanor of Aquitaine. Before she was twenty years old, Ermengard was a full partner in the wars that ensued here as well as in Spain. She was with her army at the siege of Tortosa in 1148 (whose success gave Narbonne trading rights in the newly conquered city), a partner to a major alliance against Alphonse Jordan's son, Count Raymond V of Toulouse in 1157, a partner with the Trencavels and the count of Barcelona in the siege of les Baux in 1162–1163, one of the go-betweens who negotiated peace between Raymond Trencavel and Count Raymond V in 1163; later she helped to negotiate the marriage between Raymond Trencavel's son Roger and Adalais the daughter of Count Raymond V.

In Narbonne, Ermengard's palace stood next to the main market square and the old Roman bridge that crossed the Aude River, which carried goods to and from the port at its mouth downstream. She drew a significant portion of her revenues from tolls and market taxes and so was particularly attentive to promoting commerce. She ordered a new road to be built from Narbonne to Roussillon inland from the old Roman coastal road (which had probably become impassable during the rainy season). She also sent embassies to negotiate commercial and military treaties with Pisa (1164, 1174) and Genoa (1166, 1181)

Ermengard's patronage of several troubadours was one of the most enduring cultural consequences of her diplomatic and financial successes. Scholars commonly assume that she is the one referred to as "ma domna de Narbones" ("my lady of Narbonne") in the lyrics of Bernart de Ventadorn, Peire d'Alvernhe, Giraut de Bornelh, and Azalais de Porcairagues, and as "mon Tort n'avetz" ("my You-are-wrong") in those of Peire Roger. Long after her death, a later troubadour invented a story of a love affair between Ermengard and Peire. Her name even reached a poet far to the north in the Orkney Islands, where a bard recounting the deeds of Earl Rognvaldr turned her into a young blonde queen whose city the Earl visits on his way to the Holy Land. As a result of her connection to the troubadours, another writer turned her into a judge of an imaginary "court of love."

Ermengard had no children. She adopted her sister's younger son Aymeri as her successor, and when he died suddenly, she replaced him with his older brother, Pedro de Lara. In 1194, impatient to succeed his aging aunt, Pedro ousted her from the city. Almost all of Ermengard's allies had died, replaced by their young sons. Though some local lords remained faithful to her, she was unable to regain control of the viscounty. She took refuge in the house of the Templars (a charitable Christian military order) at le Mas Deu in Roussillon, and there on her deathbed, in the company of strangers, she dictated her will on April 30, 1196.

See also Azalais de Porcairagues; Eleanor of Aquitaine

BIBLIOGRAPHY
Cheyette, Fredric L. *Ermengard of Narbonne and the World of the Troubadours.* Ithaca, N.Y. and London: Cornell University Press, 2001.

FREDRIC L. CHEYETTE

EUCHERIA (6th century). Eucheria of Marseilles was a Merovingian poetess, of whom one poem survives, a witty epigram inveighing against a lowborn suitor. She married the Frankish aristocrat Dynamius, who was also a grammarian frequenting a circle of poets and learned men in the Mediterranean seaport of Marseilles, then a great cultural center as well. We know of Eucheria's authorship through her circle's most enduring member, the Italian Latin poet Venantius Fortunatus (d. c.610), also a friend of the illustrious St. Radegund (c.518–587).

Eucheria and her husband's circle had developed their own distinctive Latin literary style—complex and ornate—whose influence is evident in her extant poem, usually known by its opening line, "Aurea concordi quae fulget fila metallo" ("I would entwine together golden threads, glittering like metal"). It consists of sixteen distichs (two-verse units). It is strikingly strange in its content, as twenty-five pairs of completely incompatible items are juxtaposed: golden threads and horsehair, goat skins with bejeweled clothing, a purple rose with a hemlock, a deer with an ass, and owl with a nightingale and others—exemplifying the so-called *impossibilia* motif. Eucheria's entire system of reasoning, as it appears in the poem, is based on a dualist classification of reality, which she arbitrarily proposes with the twenty-eight incongruous pairs (*adynata*) taken from the world of nature, all of which serve her sole purpose of finally rejecting a poor rustic lover. Another *topos* or motif at work here is that of the World Turned Upside Down—frequently used in satire, as Ernst-Robert Curtius has shown: the lowly are on top, slaves lead masters, the coarse is more valued than the refined, and so forth. But the poem reveals itself as more than a clever poetic game: the final two verses reveal the poetess's primary intention of symbolizing certain social distinctions, in which all the sets of *adynata* are literary signs reflecting incompatibilities between social classes. Peter Dronke notes the existence of an extra couplet in another version of the poem occurring, however, in only one of the five manuscripts containing her poem.

Her grandson, also named Dynamius, would carry on the family literary tradition, albeit in a more reverent mode, in his epitaph for his grandparents.

See also Radegund, St.

BIBLIOGRAPHY

Primary Sources
Dynamius (grandson). [Epitaph for Dynamius and Eucheria]. In *Monumenta Germaniae Historica. Auctores Antiquiores* 6: 2. 194.
Eucheria. "Aurea concordi quae fulget fila metallo." In *Dichterinnen des Altertums und des fruhen Mittelalters*, edited and translated (German) by Helene Homeyer, 185–87. Paderborn, Germany: Ferdinand Schoningh, 1979.

―――. "Words Flowing Like Golden Fringes." In *The Writings of Medieval Women: An Anthology*, edited and translated by Marcelle Thiébaux, 125–33. Garland Library of Medieval Literature, 100B. 2nd ed. New York and London: Garland, 1994. [Excellent introduction and notes, plus English translation of poem].

―――. In *Women Writers of Ancient Greece and Rome: An Anthology*. Edited by Ian Plant. Norman: University of Oklahoma Press, 2004.

Secondary Sources

Curtius, Ernst Robert. *European Literature and the Latin Middle Ages*. Bollingen Foundation. N.Y.: Pantheon, 1953. Original *Europäische Literatur und lateinisches Mittelalter*. Bern: Francke, 1948. [See esp. 94–98, on *adynata*, *impossibilia*, and upside-down world (*die verkehrte Welt*); on Venantius Fortunatus, passim].

Dronke, Peter. *Women Writers of the Middle Ages: A Critical Study of Texts from Perpetua (†203) to Marguerite Porete (†1310)*. Cambridge: Cambridge University Press, 1984.

Pauly, August Friedrich. "Eucheria." In *Real Encyclopädie der Altertumswissenschaft*, revised by Hans Gartner and Albert Wunsch, 6: 1. 882. Munich: Druckenmüller, 1980.

Riché, Pierre. *Education and Culture in the Barbarian West, Sixth through Eighth Centuries*. Translated by John J. Contreni. Foreword by Richard Sullivan. Columbia: University of South Carolina Press, 1976. Original *Éducation et culture dans le monde barbare: VIe–VIIIe siècles*. 3rd ed. Paris: Seuil, 1962.

ARISTOULA GEORGIADOU

EUDOCIA (c.400–460). Born in Athens, the Eastern (Byzantine) empress and poet Aelia Eudocia Augusta is remembered for her Christian and Homeric poetry, composed in Greek, and for her controversial political and religious activities.

Eudocia (or Eudokia) was the daughter of the philosopher Leontios, one of the last pagan philosophers teaching in Athens, who named her Athenaïs. After receiving a thorough education in the classics from her father, she traveled to Constantinople where she met the future empress, then saint, Pulcheria (399–453), the pious, domineering elder sister of the weak-willed Emperor Theodosius II (401–450). Athenaïs married Theodosius in 421, after having converted to Christianity, and assumed the name Eudocia. She took the additional name of Augusta (a title given to empresses of the house of Theodosius) in 423. In 438, Eudocia journeyed to Jerusalem on a pilgrimage and returned with St. Stephen's remains, for which she built a small shrine (439).

There seems to have been a power struggle around 440, possibly tinged with sexual scandal, or some sort of upheaval at the imperial court in Constantinople, involving Pulcheria, Theodosius, and Eudocia. One popular account, by the near-contemporary chronicler John Malalas (b. 490), has her committing adultery with Paulinus, a handsome high official, which Emperor Theodosius inadvertently discovered by sending a distinctively huge apple as a gift to his wife, who sent it to Paulinus, who, unaware that it had originated with the emperor, sent it to him as a gift. Theodosius recognized the returning apple, but concealed it to entrap his wife, whom he asked about the apple as his gift to her. Her reply, claiming she had eaten it, infuriated him so that he ordered the execution of Paulinus. Pulcheria also banished Eudocia on this account, or for another reason.

Whatever the truth, Eudocia permanently left the court, returning to Jerusalem, where she built monasteries with the help of funding from Theodosius, and defended the rights of Jews and other non-Christians. Eudocia remained in Jerusalem for the rest of her life, retaining her title as Augusta, in her palace in Bethlehem. She seemed to embody the shifting movements within the early Church and Eastern Empire, through the Monophysite controversy—herself becoming a Monophysite (one believing in Christ incarnate as one nature united out of two, human and divine)—the death of Theodosius (450), and the accession of Pulcheria and Marcian to the throne. Eudocia returned to orthodox Catholicism on conversion by a letter from Pope Leo in 453, but then later, in 457, because of renewed disaffection with Christianity, joined the Eastern Orthodox Church. She died in Jerusalem on October 20, 460, and was buried in the church of St. Stephen, which she had erected.

Eudocia wrote poetic paraphrases of several books of the Bible and an address to the people of Antioch (a line or so from each survives). The Greek Church historian Socrates Scholasticus (d. 450) mentions a poem celebrating Theodosius's victory over the Persians in 422. One of her two major surviving works is the *Homerocentones* (Homeric centos)—long believed the work of others (e.g., a certain Patricius, whom Eudocia credits in her prologue, explaining her near-total reworking of him), with only partial credit to her if at all, until the late 1990s—of which we now have 2,344 verses. The cento, a genre already pioneered for women in the Latin Virgilian mode by Proba (third century), is an ancient one, named for its "patchwork" tendencies. The cento poet begins by taking passages from a famous pagan Classical poet, like Virgil or, in Eudocia's case, Homer, the ancient Greek author of the *Iliad* and *Odyssey*, which she then weaves or "stitches" in her own verses in a new context (see indexes to Homeric lines in Usher ed. 1999), deliberately exploiting the prestigious authorial echoes either for satirical-parodic or serious purposes. Eudocia's purpose is serious: she uses the pagan Classical form to express her Christian beliefs, adapting Greek mythology, as well as meter, to biblical tales from both testaments. Whether Proba's example inspired Eudocia is uncertain, although Theodosius did apparently own a copy of Proba's work (Usher 1998).

Her other principal surviving work, the *Martyrdom of St. Cyprian*, concerns the early fourth-century magician Cyprian of Antioch, whose (probably false) conversion legend has been compared to that of Faust, and who suffered death with his beloved Justina (Eudocia calls her Justa) during Emperor Diocletian's persecutions (303–313); their alleged relics are now at housed at St. John Lateran in Rome. A significant amount (801 vv.) of this verse account survives. Book 1 (from which we have 322 lines) describes how the pure maiden Justa resists, then converts, the evil Cyprian, who ends up as Bishop of Antioch. Book 2 (of which 479 lines survive) has Cyprian tell his life story. From a summary of the *Martyrdom* by the ninth-century scholar and patriarch of Constantinople, Photius (*Bibliotheca*, 184), it is clear that Book 3 described how Justa and Cyprian were almost grilled to death in a giant frying pan and were finally beheaded. The narrative is disrupted by lengthy speeches and descriptions and is rather uneven. Some inconsistencies arise between Books 1 and 2 concerning the time of Justa's temptation and Cyprian's conversion in relation to where these events occurred. On the other hand, Marcelle Thiébaux suggests that the split between the *Martyrdom*'s first two books reveals "a remarkable psychic split, with the author plainly exploring in each one of her two sides" (Thiébaux ed. and trans.). These problems are probably the result of Eudocia's use of different sources for each book. She also displays some clumsiness at the dactylic hexameter, the standard verse form for Greek and Latin heroic-epic poetry. Nevertheless, Eudocia admirably demonstrates a thorough knowledge of Homer and deft use of standard poetic devices.

She also significantly represents the tradition of Christian writers who were not prepared to exclude all pagan elements from their work, an impression greatly confirmed by the discovery of a poem by Eudocia in praise of the baths at Hammat Gader in Israel. In the poem's seventeen surviving lines, Eudocia describes her observations by an attempt at epic style as she lists the various parts of the spa. Here the classicizing trend is dominant and the specifically Christian elements are few.

See also Comnena, Anna; Proba, Faltonia Betitia

BIBLIOGRAPHY

Primary Sources

Aelia Eudocia. *Homerocentones.* Critical ed. by Mark D. Usher. Bibliotheca Scriptorum Graecorum et Romanorum Teubneriana. Stuttgart and Leipzig: B. G. Teubner, 1999. [Greek text, Latin commentary].

———. *De martyrio S. Cypriani.* Edited by Arthur Ludwich. In *Eudociae Augustae Claudiani. Carminum Graecorum reliquiae.* Leipzig: Teubner, 1897.

———. *Martyrdom of St. Cyprian.* Translated and introduced by G. Ronald Kastner. In *A Lost Tradition: Women Writers of the Early Church,* edited by Patricia Wilson-Kastner et al., 149–69. Washington, D.C.: University Press of America, 1981. [English trans. with introduction].

———. [*Martyrdom of St. Cyprian,* extracts]. "Calumniated Empress and Poet." In *The Writings of Medieval Women: An Anthology,* edited and translated by Marcelle Thiébaux, 49–69. Garland Library of Medieval Literature, 100B. 2nd ed. New York and London: Garland, 1994. [Best biographical introduction and notes, English trans.].

———. [Hammat Gader Poem]. Translated in J. Green and Y. Tsafir, "Greek Inscriptions from Hammat Gader." *Israel Exploration Journal* 32 (1982): 77–91.

———. In *Women Writers of Ancient Greece and Rome: An Anthology.* Edited by Ian Plant. Norman: University of Oklahoma Press, 2004.

Malalas, John. *Chronicle of John Malalas.* Translated by Elizabeth Jeffreys et al., 195. Melbourne: Australian Association for Byzantine Studies, 1986.

Photius. *Bibliotheca.* Edited and translated (French) by René Henry. Collection Byzantine. 8 vols. Paris: Société des Belles Lettres, 1959–1977. [Greek text, French translation and commentary].

———. *The Bibliotheca: A Selection.* Translated with notes by N. G. Wilson. London: Duckworth, 1994.

Socrates Scholasticus. [*Ecclesiastical History*]. *Kirchengeschichte.* Critical ed. by Günther C. Hansen. Introductory essay by Manja Sirinjan. Griechischen Schriftsteller der ersten drei Jahrhundert. Neue Folge, 1. Berlin: Akademie Verlag, 1995. [Authoritative Greek text, German essay and commentary].

———. *Ecclesiastical History.* Translated by Andrew C. Zenos. In *Nicene and Post-Nicene Fathers. Second Series,* edited by Philip Schaff and Henry Wace, vol. 2. Peabody, Mass.: Hendrickson, 1994. Original New York: Christian Literature Publishing, 1890.

Secondary Sources

Cameron, Alan. "The Empress and the Poet: Paganism and Politics at the Court of Theodosius II." In *Later Greek Literature,* edited by John J. Winkler and Gordon Williams, 217–91. Yale Classical Studies, 27. Cambridge: Cambridge University Press, 1982.

Holum, Kenneth G. *Theodosian Empresses: Woman and Imperial Dominion in Late Antiquity.* Berkeley: University of California Press, 1982.

Martindale, J. R. *The Prosopography of the Later Roman Empire,* 2: 408–9. Cambridge: Cambridge University Press, 1980.

Other Women's Voices Web site: http://home.infionline.net/~ddisse/eudocia.html [Excellent updated resource with useful links to translated texts and criticism].

Tsatsou, Ioanna. *Empress Athenais-Eudocia, a Fifth-Century Byzantine Humanist: Women of Byzantium.* Translated by Jean Demos. Brookline, Mass.: Holy Cross Orthodox Press, 1977.

Usher, Mark D. *Homeric Stitchings: The Homeric Centos of the Empress Eudocia.* Lanham, Md.: Rowman & Littlefield, 1998.

———. "Prolegomenon to the Homeric Centos." *American Journal of Philology* 118 (1997): 305–21.

Van Duen, Peter. "The Poetical Writings of Empress Eudocia: An Evaluation." In *Early Christian Poetry*, edited by Jan den Boeft and A. Hilhorst. Supplements to Vigiliae Christianae, 22. Leiden, Netherlands and New York: E. J. Brill, 1993.

DAVID LARMOUR

EUSTOCHIUM, ST. (367–419). Julia Eustochium was a favorite member of St. Jerome's esteemed circle of learned Roman matrons choosing, under his guidance, to renounce all wealth and comfort and lead an ascetic Christian life. It was she who inspired Jerome's famous treatise on virginity, in a letter addressed to her (*Epistola* 22).

The third daughter of the Roman senator Toxotius and the noble matron, Paula (347–404), Eustochium was thus descended from the illustrious, aristocratic Gracchis and Scipiones. Paula's other children were Blesilla, the eldest (d. 384) Paulina, and Rufina, who passed away shortly after their marriages, and the youngest, a boy, also named Toxotius. Toxotius's marriage to Laeta, produced Paula, who, like her famous grandmother, would later become a spiritual daughter of St. Jerome.

Jerome (Eusebius Hieronymus, c.345–420), was one of the most learned men of Late Antiquity. *Homo trilinguis* (A man fluent in three languages), as he proudly proclaimed himself, he was versed in Hebrew (while a hermit in the Syrian desert), Greek, and Latin (while a student in Rome). In the wake of dissension within the Eastern Church, Jerome left Constantinople and returned to Rome, at the invitation of Pope Damasus in 382, to serve as the pope's secretary. This Roman phase in Jerome's life, which lasted until 385, was to be a most fruitful one not only because it allowed him, at Damasus's request, to begin a new Latin translation of the Bible—the monumental Vulgate—but also because it provided him with the opportunity to meet a group of noble Christian Roman ladies interested in asceticism: Marcella, Asella, Marcellina, Felicitas, Lea, Furia, Paula, her daughter Eustochium, and others. At Marcella's palace on the Aventine hill, Jerome gave them spiritual guidance and scriptural instruction in the form of conferences. Particularly close to Jerome were Marcella and Paula, both widows, and Eustochium, concerning whom, he states in his *Epistola* (Letter) 127: 5, "It was at Marcella's cell that Eustochium, paragon of virgins, was trained." His use of the word "cell" was not frivolous, for these affluent women now actually emulated desert hermits in the middle of Rome. Eustochium was his exemplary and beloved pupil, to whom he generally refers in his prefaces as "virgo Christi, filia" ("virgin in Christ, daughter"). She remained his faithful companion until her death in 419, a year before his own. Jerome dedicated several works to her, among which, the eighteen prologues to the eighteen books on Isaiah and the fourteen prefaces to the fourteen books on Ezekiel.

In particular, Eustochium's name is tied in a special way to the most celebrated of Jerome's 154 letters, *Epistola* 22, "Ad Eustochium" ("To Eustochium") and which can be considered the most widely known treatise on virginity. Written in the early spring of 384, this letter is an exhortation to the life of virginity by urging Eustochium to shun the society of both married women and women in general. Although primarily concerned with the spiritual education of Eustochium, this letter, which became a classic in the ascetic-monastic tradition, must be seen in the context of Jerome's program of reform of the mores of Roman society undertaken with the approval of Pope Damasus. The basic purpose of the letter "To Eustochium" is simply to expound on and underscore his belief that virginity was the ideal state for Christians and that the best that can be said about marriage is that it should be tolerated, for it engenders virgins. In chapter 20 of the letter, Jerome frames marriage in its proper perspective by comparing its function to others in nature: "I praise weddings, I praise marriage, but because they generate virgins for me: from thorns I gather roses, from the earth gold, from the shell the pearl." He also addressed to her *Epistolae* 31 and 108.

In the wake of Jerome's departure from Rome in August of 384 under open criticism and allegations of misbehavior related to his highly publicized letter on virginity, Eustochium and her mother, Paula, were to follow him several weeks later to Palestine and on to Antioch (now in southern Turkey), where Bishop Paulinus and Jerome awaited them. Soon, under the guidance of their mentor, Eustochium and Paula embarked on a pilgrimage throughout the Holy Land lasting from winter 385 into summer 386, exploring holy cities and places and finally settling in Bethlehem. There, with funds provided by the wealthy Paula, they built a monastery for men and a convent for women. These monasteries were to remain the homes of Paula, Eustochium, and Jerome for the rest of their lives. In this profoundly sacred atmosphere, Eustochium dedicated herself further to the study of the Holy Scriptures under Jerome's tutelage, who considered her his prize pupil, again, mainly because of her virginity (*Epistola* 66: 27). On Paula's death in 404, Eustochium directed the convent founded by her mother, while continuing to stimulate Jerome toward completing several scriptural and exegetical works (commentaries on the meaning of the Scriptures). Eustochium died in early 419, her death deeply felt and lamented by Jerome, as he expressed in his epitaph for her tomb (see McNamara). When he, too, died, Jerome was buried in a grotto facing the tomb of Eustochium and Paula, all of whom became saints. Paula's feast day is January 26; Eustochium's September 28; Jerome's September 30.

See also Desert Mothers; Syrian-Christian Women; Virginity

BIBLIOGRAPHY

Primary Sources

Eustochium and Paula. *De locis sanctis* (386). Edited by Titus Tobler. In *Itinera hierosolymitana et descriptiones Terrae Sanctae bellis sacris interiora*, edited by T. Tobler and Auguste Molinier, 1: 3. 2 vols. Geneva: J.-G. Flick, 1879–1885.

———. *The Letter of Paula and Eustochium to Marcella: About the Holy Places*. Translated by Aubrey Stewart. Notes by C. W. Wilson. New York: AMS Press, 1971. Original, London: Palestine Pilgrims Text Society, 1889.

Jerome. *Lettres*. Critical ed. and trans. (French) by Jérôme Labourt, 1: xv–xxxvii. Paris: Société des Belles Lettres, 1949. [Latin text, French trans. and commentary].

———. *The Letters of St. Jerome*. Translated by Charles C. Mierow, 3–12. Introduction and notes by Thomas Comerford Lawler. New York: Newman Press, 1963. [English only].

Secondary Sources

Antin, Paul. "Eustochium." In *Dictionnaire de spiritualité . . .*, edited by Marcel Viller et al., 4: 1715–18. Paris: Beauchesne, 1961.

Bernet, Anne. *Saint Jérôme*. Étampes, France: Clovis, 2002.

Dumm, D. "St. Jerome and the Theology of Virginity." *Benedictine Review* 9 (1954): 28–35.

Kelly, J. N. D. "Marcella, Paula, Eustochium." In *Jerome: His Life, Writings and Controversies*, 91–103. London: Duckworth, 1975.

McNamara, Jo Ann. "Cornelia's Daughters: Paula and Eustochium." *Women's Studies* 11 (1984): 9–27. Online: http://www.umilta.net/cornelia.html

Miller, Patricia Cox. "'The Blazing Body': Ascetic Desire in Jerome's Letter to Eustochium." In Miller, *The Poetry of Thought in Late Antiquity*, ch. 6. Aldershot, U.K. and Burlington, Vt.: Ashgate, 2001.

Moreschini, Claudio. "Jerome and His Learned Lady Disciples." In *La Città e il libro I/The City and the Book I. International Congresses in Florence's Certosa, 30 May–1 June 2001: Section 2: La Bibbia Christiana/ The Christian Bible*. Online: http://www.florin.ms/aleph2.html

Rebenich, Stefan. *Jerome*. The Early Church Fathers. New York and London: Routledge, 2002.

Serrato Garrido, Mercedes. *Ascetismo femenino en Roma: estudios sobre San Jerónimo y San Agustín*. Cádiz, Spain: Universidad de Cádiz, 1993.

Steininger, Christine. *Die ideale christliche Frau: Virgo-Vidua-Nupta; Eine Studie zum Bild der idealer christlicher Frau bei Hieronymus und Pelagius*. St. Ottilien, Germany: EOS, 1997.

SANDRO STICCA

ÉVANGILE AUX FEMMES ("WOMEN'S GOSPEL"). *See* **Marie de Compiègne**

FAIR HELEN OF CONSTANTINOPLE. *See* Belle Hélène de Constantinople

FAIR MAID OF KENT. *See* **Joan, Fair Maid of Kent**

FAIR ROSAMOND. *See* **Rosamond, Fair**

FAIRIES. *See* **Enchantresses, Fays (Fées), and Fairies**

FALCONIA. *See* **Proba, Faltonia Betitia**

FALTONIA. *See* **Proba, Faltonia Betitia**

FATIMID EGYPT, WOMEN IN (969–1171). Egypt in the Fatimid period was largely a rural society, although it had a number of large and flourishing cities from which come all surviving documentary and literary material. It is not possible, therefore, to write about the lives of the vast majority of the female population living in the medieval Egyptian countryside. From the Arabic literary sources, primarily court histories, we learn nothing of the lives of ordinary women and only little of the lives of women at court. Our most abundant evidence for the period comes from the Judeo-Arabic documents of the Cairo Geniza, emanating from the urban Jewish communities of Egypt from the tenth through the thirteenth centuries.

The primary roles for women in all religious communities were as wives and mothers. Since marriage meant leaving the house of the father, therefore leaving his protection, both economic and social safeguards were needed to protect women. Both Jewish and Islamic law and practice considered the husband's marriage gift to be the property of the wife. This gift was paid in two installments, a smaller immediate installment and a larger deferred installment due if the woman were divorced or widowed. The marriage gift in

Fatimid Egypt was always made in gold, which was the standard material for coins. The most important general social safeguard was marriage within the extended family (often to a cousin). But other, more specific, stipulations appear in marriage contracts, particularly the requirement that the wife remain in the same town as her parents or other close male relatives.

In the urban environment, women constituted a part of local economies as consumers, property owners, and as property. They cannot, however, be considered as part of the mainstream and their economic activities were largely restricted. Although women were able to own property independently, most of their possessions were acquired through gift, dowry, or inheritance, rather than as the result of commercial activities. Married women, especially among the lower classes, usually did some kind of work in addition to household duties. There were a limited number of occupations available to them, most of them related to the lives of women: bride-combers (responsible for the dressing and combing of brides), wet-nurses, midwives, women teachers of needlework and other female crafts, washers of the female dead, doctors. Outside of these occupations, women worked in Egypt's flourishing textile industry unraveling silk or flax filaments, spinning fibers, or weaving. They appear only infrequently as dressmakers, since tailoring was secondary to fiber and color in medieval Egyptian clothing. Female brokers sold the products of female industry largely by going house-to-house, rather than in the marketplace, which was a male domain. Though by no means common, there are also instances of women who achieved a high degree of independence because their husbands were absent much of the time, or they were divorced or widowed and had inherited money from their fathers.

As slaves, women were the property of Christians, Jews, and Muslims in medieval Egypt. Among Christians and Jews, female slaves served primarily as domestic help, personal servants, and nurses of children for the affluent. Among Muslims, female slaves were the sexual property of male masters and thus served the additional function of producing legitimate, free offspring for their masters without the encumbrances of marriage.

Medieval Egypt was a predominantly Islamic society, and the practices of local Muslims had a significant impact on other religious communities. For example, Jewish women sometimes stipulated in their marriage contracts that they would not consent to live in apartments with common courtyards with Muslim women because they wished to avoid being subject to the stricter rules of seclusion prevailing among Muslims. The Jewish jurist Maimonides specified that the wife has the right to leave the house to visit her father's residence, to attend gatherings of mourning, to go to festivities, to visit female friends and relatives, and to receive visits from them; but he also insisted that husbands should not permit this more than once or twice a month. Islamic law and practice permits a man to have up to four wives at one time. And though by no means a common practice among them, there is evidence of polygyny among Jews in Fatimid Egypt.

At the court, women attended sessions for instruction in the Fatimids' Ismaili doctrine, but they appear to have played no significant role in spreading the faith. Women in Fatimid Egypt, as in the rest of the medieval Islamic world, were not entitled to exercise sovereign power. At the Fatimid court, there is insufficient evidence to determine to what extent women were able to wield political influence behind the scenes. In Fatimid times, the harem was not yet the highly developed political institution that it would become in Ottoman times. Though there is evidence that royal women were able to accumulate significant amounts of wealth, the proliferation of monumental building sponsored by elite men and women that is so characteristic of Mamluk Egypt (1250–1517) had not yet begun. There is only one Fatimid woman whose life and political career are known in any detail: Sitt al-Mulk (d. 1025), the sister of the notorious caliph al-Hakim, whose erratic behavior she considered a threat to dynastic stability. She engineered his murder, as well as the death of a cousin who might have succeeded him. She ensured the smooth transition of power to al-Hakim's son al-Zahir, and she instituted a number of social policies that won her the praise of chroniclers.

See also Concubines; Dowry; Marriage; Slaves, Female

BIBLIOGRAPHY

Primary Source
Goitein, Shlomo Dov. *A Mediterranean Society*. 6 vols. Berkeley and Los Angeles: University of California Press, 1967–1988. Abridged ed. one vol., edited by Jacob Lassner. Berkeley: University of California Press, 1999.

Secondary Sources
"Fatimids." In *The Encyclopaedia of Islam*. New ed. Edited by Martijn T. Houtsma et al. 9 vols. Leiden, Netherlands and New York: Brill, 1993.
Gleave, Robert M. "Marrying Fatimid Women: Legal Theory and Substantive Law in Shi'i Jurisprudence." *Islamic Law & Society* 6.1 (February. 1999): 38–68.
Lev, Yaacov. *State and Society in Fatimid Egypt*. Arab History and Civilization, 1. Leiden and New York: Brill, 1991.
———. "The Fatimid Princess Sitt al-Mulk." *Journal of Semitic Studies* 32 (1987): 319–28.
Marmon, Shaun E. "Slavery, Islamic" and "Concubinage, Islamic." In *Dictionary of the Middle Ages*. 13 vols. New York: Scribner, 1982–1989.

PAULA SANDERS

FAYS. *See* **Enchantresses, Fays (Fées), and Fairies**

FEDELE, CASSANDRA (1465/66–1558). This important Italian woman humanist, who authored numerous letters and three orations, seems to have been the daughter of a member of the Venetian citizenry of some literary renown, although her family origins are not clear. Her father, Angelo, "was respected by the members of the Venetian patriciate," suggesting possible patron–client relations between the Venetian nobility and the Fedele family. There appears to have been a family tradition of Classical learning, extending back to Cassandra's great-grandfather, and unusually for a woman, Cassandra continued it into her generation. Her father had her tutored in Latin and Greek by the Servite (an Augustinian-Dominican order founded by Florentine aristocrats c.1233) theologian and humanist Gasparino Borro, possibly in part to bring himself into greater public notice, as the father of the unusual prodigy of an intellectually gifted and trained daughter. By the age of twelve, she was said to have mastered Latin and Greek, rhetoric, history, philosophy, and sacred studies. Not only did she meet and correspond with many notable humanists of her day, receiving high praise in return from some of them, including Angelo Poliziano (Politian, 1454–1494), but she also spoke in public on the value of literary studies, before the University of Padua, the people of Venice, and the Venetian doge.

Fedele's correspondence and involvement with humanist learning continued until her marriage, which did not take place until she was thirty-three or thirty-four, very late in life for a woman of her time and class. She married a physician from Vicenza, Gian-Maria Mapelli, with whom she traveled to and stayed in Crete (1515–1520), and only one letter of hers, on theology, addressed to Girolamo Monopolitano, survives from the period of the marriage. Her husband died after twenty-two years of marriage, at which point she began to write again. This time, however, she wrote to find some kind of financial support, for she appears to have been left impoverished and unable to support herself. In 1547, Pope Paul III and the Venetian senate appointed her lay prioress (at age eighty-two) of the orphanage of San Domenico di Castello, in Venice, where she lived until she died in 1558 and was given a state funeral. She had delivered her last public oration (in honor of the visiting queen of Poland) just two years earlier.

Of all the Italian women humanists of the Renaissance, Fedele and Isotta Nogarola (1418–1466) garnered the most public attention in their own day. Fedele especially, because of her late marriage and long life, achieved both literary and what we might call political reputation, at least according to her own account. She numbered among her correspondents such powerful women as Queen Isabella of Spain (1451–1504, who invited her to her court in 1488), the queen of Hungary, the queen's sister Eleanora, and Eleanor of Aragon, duchess of Ferrara. One of her frequent male correspondents was Ludovico Maria Sforza (1451–1508), who also wrote commending her to the Venetian Senate. She exchanged letters with Alessandra Scala (1475–1506), learned daughter of the chancellor of Florence, as well as with Poliziano and other members of the literary and artistic circle around Lorenzo de' Medici (1449–1492). Isabella and Ferdinand of Spain sought permission for her to visit their court in Castile, but were denied it by the Venetian Senate on the grounds that the city could not spare one of its most illustrious ornaments.

Unlike her contemporary Laura Cereta (1469–1499), Fedele never systematically collected her approximately one hundred known letters, although they were clearly intended for at least quasi-public consumption; the one exception is a group of four letters and an oration, printed together during her lifetime. She wrote to the same kinds of correspondents that humanist men tended also to address, and wrote them the same kinds of letters: letters designed both to praise the learning and accomplishments of the addressee, and to demonstrate her own learning and accomplishments. Her apparent failure to develop either a full-fledged career as a humanist on the male model, or a clear and strong "feminine" voice, has to a certain degree disappointed her modern interpreters, who tend to view her as a conventionally minded product of masculine ambition, or as having overly internalized her culture's evidently ambivalent, belittling, attitudes toward learned women. But Fedele's evident skill in attracting the patronage of the politically and intellectually powerful and her ability to write within the highly structured conventions of humanist letter writing make her an important contributor both to humanist culture and to the intellectual and cultural history of women.

She and her contemporaries' responses to her also offer an excellent opportunity to examine the complex relationship between male humanist constructions of virtue and women's learning and women's responses to those constructions. One of the most famous letters of praise to a humanist woman is Poliziano's to Fedele; we possess in addition the rest of the correspondence between them, a total of four letters. Her letter book also contains a number of other letters of praise, including three lengthy poems reminiscent of

FÉES

the one Antonio Loschi wrote to Maddalena Scrovegni (1356–1429), and an epigram by that Italian philologist and physician living in France, Julius Caesar Scaliger (1484–1558), ringing in changes on the theme of the virility of the learned woman.

See also Cereta, Laura; Humanists, Italian Women, Issues and Theory; Nogarola, Isotta; Scala, Alessandra; Scrovegni, Maddalena

BIBLIOGRAPHY

Primary Sources

Fedele, Cassandra. [Letters]. *Clarissimae feminae Cassandrae Fidelis venetae epistolae et orationes posthumae* [. . .]. Edited by Jacopo Filippo Tomasini. Padua: Franciscus Bolzetta, 1636.

———. *Letters and Orations.* Edited and translated with introduction and notes by Diana Robin. Chicago: University of Chicago Press, 2000. [Contains all but five of her known letters; also has her three orations].

Secondary Sources

Cavazzana, Cesira. "Cassandra Fedele erudita veneziana del rinascimento." *Ateneo Veneto* 29 (1906): 2: 73–91, 249–75, 361–97.

Robin, Diana. "Cassandra Fedele's *Epistolae* (1488–1521): Biography as Ef-facement," in *The Rhetorics of Life-Writing in Early Modern Europe: Forms of Biography from Cassandra Fedele to Louis XIV*, edited by Thomas F. Mayer and D. R. Woolf, 187–203. Ann Arbor: University of Michigan Press, 1995.

———. "Cassandra Fedele." In *Italian Women Writers: A Bio-Bibliographical Sourcebook*, edited by Rinaldina Russell, 119–27. Westport, Conn. and London: Greenwood, 1994.

———. "Woman, Space, and Renaissance Discourse." In *Sex and Gender in Medieval and Renaissance Texts: The Latin Tradition*, edited by Barbara K. Gold, Paul Allen Miller, and Charles Platter, 9–10, 169–71. SUNY Medieval Studies. Albany: State University of New York Press, 1997.

JENNIFER FISK RONDEAU

FÉES. *See* **Enchantresses, Fays (Fées), and Fairies**

FILIPA DE LENCASTRE (1437–1497). Filipa, or, in English, Philippa, of Lancaster, was a Portuguese princess (*infanta*), poet, and translator-adapter of devotional and spiritual works. Filipa benefited both from her family's royal status and cultivated tastes. Her grandfather King João I (Joo or John the Great) of Portugal, negotiated his kingdom's independence from Spain (c.1140) and presided over its first literary and chivalric flowering, later sustained by Portuguese colonial and maritime trade expansion—thanks primarily to one of his sons, and thus Filipa's uncle, Henry the Navigator (1394–1460). Because King João, of the Portuguese Avis dynasty, had married Philippa of Lancaster (Portugese = Filipa de Lencastre) (1360–1415), daughter of John of Gaunt, to secure his treaty with England, his descendants belonged both to the houses of Avis and Lancaster, or "Lencastre" in Portuguese; Filipa probably received her name from her paternal grandmother. Filipa's father, the *infante* (crown prince) Don Pedro, duke of Coimbra, composed learned political and moral treatises before dying tragically in 1449 in battle at Alfarrobeira. Princess Filipa has also been overshadowed by her sister, Queen Isabel of Portugal (d. 1455), and especially by her romantic brother, also named Pedro (1429–1466), who was constable of Portugal, was afterward exiled as king of Aragon, and was an important transition poet who inaugurated the practice of writing in Castilian (a Spanish dialect), a fashion that would last two centuries. Filipa herself spent much of her life in retirement in the convent of Odivellas near Lisbon, quietly cultivating the religious-erudite poetry introduced by her paternal forbears, the princes of Avis, but with greater lasting success than these men (Bell 1925). Her brother, Pedro, though an accomplished man of the world, composed his longest poem, in Castilian, the *Menosprecio del Mundo* (*Contempt for the World*) as an attempt to understand his life's misfortunes and seek solace in philosophy. By contrast, Filipa's extant works are all in Portuguese.

Aside from her family, a major influence on her work was Laurentius Justinianus (Lorenzo Justiniano or Lawrence Justinian, 1381–1456), patriarch of Venice and later canonized, author of several religious works, two of which Filipa translated and adapted. To her Portuguese rendering of his *De Vita Solitaria*, the *Tratado da vida solitaria* (*Treatise on the Solitary Life*), in the widespread medieval-humanistic genre praising the reclusive, contemplative life, she added her own rhymed tract. The second work, *In Disciplinam et perfectionem Monasticæ conversationis*, translated by her as *Regra perfecam da conversaçam dos Monges* (*Rule for the Proper Behavior of Monks*), emphasizes spiritual perfection and disdain for the world. Both of these works by Lorenzo and their reworking by Filipa deserve qualification as "humanistic" because they reflect the distinct character of late-medieval and Renaissance spiritual writing—more individualistic and questioning in their piety, more in tune with readers schooled in the Latin classics yet active in civic affairs—than their medieval predecessors. There is considerable debate as to who translated or adapted this second work. Some scholars, in part influenced by early publishers, credit Infanta Dona Catherina. Adept at combining piety with poetry, Filipa's style of translation is lively; her language vibrant, strong, and beautiful. She also seems to have composed a brief treatise advising on the wars with Castile, the *Conselho* (*Counsel*), as preserved in a seventeenth-century commentary on her by one Francisco Brandão, dedicated to King João IV, thus demonstrating Filipa's posterity to some extent. At least one of her own poems also survives: her twelve-line dedicatory poem to her book of homilies on the Gospels, titled "Ao Bom Jesus" ("To the Good Jesus"), conveying the strong desire for a personal knowledge of God via sacred and profane literary motifs. She bequeathed this homiliary, which she also illustrated, to the convent at Odivellas, having worked for a year on the illuminations (Greer).

See also Artists, Medieval Women; Convents

BIBLIOGRAPHY

Primary Sources

Filipa de Lencastre. "Ao Bom Jesus." In *The Oxford Book of Portuguese Verse*, edited by Aubrey Bell, 79. Oxford: Clarendon Press, 1925. 2nd ed. 1952.

———. *Conselho, e voto da Senhora Dona Felippa filha do Infante Dom Pedro, sobre as tercarias, & guerras de Castella*. Edited with commentary by Francisco Brandão, 9–15. Lisbon: Lourenço de Anveres, 1643.

Lawrence Justinian, St. *In Disciplinam, & perfectionem Monasticæ conversationis, De Vita solitaria*. In *Sancti Laurentii Justiniani Opera omnia*, facsimile reprint of 1751 Venice ed. by J. B. Albritius and J. Rosa, 1: 96–164; 2: 126–60. 2 vols. Introduction by Giorgio Cracco. Florence: L.S. Olschki, 1982.

———. *Livro que seescreve da regra perfecam da conversacam dos monges. Compilado per Lourenço Justiniano. Da perfeição da vida monastica, e da vida solitaria. Traduzidos do latim em portuguez pela*

Serenissima Senhora Infanta D. Catherina. First ed. Coimbra, Portugal: B. Galharde, 1531. 2nd ed. Lisbon: S. T. Ferreira, 1791. [Note translations attributed to Catherina].

Secondary Sources
Bell, Aubrey F. G. *The Oxford Book of Portuguese Verse*. Oxford: Clarendon Press, 1925. 2nd ed. 1952.
————. *Portuguese Literature*. Oxford: Clarendon Press, 1922. Reprint 1970.
Buescu, Maria L. Carvalhão. *Literatura portuguesa medieval*. Lisbon: Universidade Aberta, 1990.
Greer, Germaine. *The Obstacle Race*. New York: Farrar, Strauss & Giroux, 1979.
Martins, Mário. *Estudos de Literatura Medieval*. Braga, Portugal: Livraria Cruz, 1956.

NADIA MARGOLIS

FIRST NIGHT, RIGHT OF. *See* Jus Primae Noctis

FONTEVRAUD. *See* **Petronilla of Chemillé**

FOOTBINDING (late 10th century–early 20th century). Footbinding, the Chinese practice of binding young girls' feet tightly with a long cloth strip to prevent them from growing to normal size, began in the tenth or eleventh centuries and lasted until the early twentieth century. Footbinding spread from the entertainment quarters to the families of the elite, and from there to wider and wider segments of the population. By the eleventh century, women in the entertainment quarters were praised for their small, narrow, arched feet, and by the twelfth century, women outside this circle, including daughters and wives of the educated elite, were binding their feet, though probably not in the numbers they would in later centuries. Although footbinding seems to modern eyes (including modern Chinese eyes) a powerful symbol of the constraints placed on women, to Chinese men and women in the Song period (960–1276) it was looked on as a form of beautification, of a way of making women more feminine and graceful. It is notable that, unlike most other features of Chinese culture in this period, footbinding never spread to China's neighbors, such as Korea, Japan, Tibet, Mongolia, or Vietnam, but rather remained a uniquely Chinese custom.

See also China, Women in

BIBLIOGRAPHY
Blake, Fred. "Foot-binding in Neo-Confucian China and the Appropriation of Female Labor." *Signs* 19.3 (1994): 676–712.
Ebrey, Patricia Buckley. *The Inner Quarters: Marriage and the Lives of Chinese Women in the Sung Period*, 37–43. Berkeley: University of California Press, 1993.
Ko, Dorothy. *Every Step a Lotus: Shoes for Bound Feet*. Berkeley: University of California Press, 2001. [Profusely illustrated].
Levy, Howard S. *Chinese Footbinding: The History of a Curious Erotic Custom*. New York: Bell, 1966.
Wang, Ping. *Aching for Beauty: Footbinding in China*. Minneapolis: University of Minnesota Press, 2000.

PATRICIA BUCKLEY EBREY

FOURNIVAL, RICHARD DE. *See Response du Bestiaire*

FRANCESCA DA RIMINI (d. 1285). Francesca, Dante's legendary adulteress murdered by her husband along with her lover, Paolo Malatesta, was in real life the daughter of Guido da Polenta, who headed one of Ravenna's most powerful families. In 1275, her father arranged her marriage to Giovanni Malatesta, called Giovanni the Lame, from the neighboring city of Rimini, apparently in recompense for political services. After moving to Rimini, Francesca engaged in a love affair with Giovanni's younger brother Paolo for a number of years, until her husband discovered them together and killed both lovers.

The facts surrounding these accusations of adultery and murder were probably embellished by the medieval chroniclers who commented on the scandal. One popular legend attributed to the so-called Anonymous Florentine recounts that because Giovanni was ashamed of his appearance, he sent Paolo in his place to meet Francesca. She believed that the proxy bridegroom was indeed Giovanni, the two fell in love, and then continued the affair until their tragic deaths.

The story of Francesca and Paolo also provided the basis for literary treatments as early as the fourteenth century, when Dante immortalized the couple in Canto V of the *Inferno*, the first part of his *Divina Commedia* (*Divine Comedy*, 1321). While there is no mention of the proxy bridegroom tale in Dante's brief poetic account, he adds a fictional note of his own by inscribing the couple with the tradition of courtly love exemplified in medieval romance. According to the poem, when Dante encounters the sinners in Hell's Circle of the Lustful, Francesca explains to him that their sexual relationship was initiated by reading a description of the first kiss exchanged between Lancelot and Guinevere. Boccaccio, in his unfinished *Commentary on the Divine Comedy* (c.1360–1373), evaluates this detail as an example of artistic license, but appears to accept the veracity of the chronicles concerning Paolo as a stand-in for his brother.

Influenced by Dante, as well as playwrights and novelists, other poets have written works about Francesca da Rimini. Nineteenth-century readers and audiences in particular seem to have been fascinated by her, perhaps due in part to a resurgence in interest about the medieval period in general. Among the best-known staged versions of her story are those by Gabriele D'Annunzio (1902), Stephen Phillips (1900), and George Henry Boker (1853), plus an opera by Sergei Rachmaninoff (c.1920), a symphonic poem by Tchaikovsky (1877), and visual representations by such painters as Ary Scheffer and Ingres.

See also Beatrice; Laura; Rosamond, Fair

BIBLIOGRAPHY

Primary Sources
Annales forolivienses ab origine urbis usque ad annum MCCCCLXXII, in *R.I.S. XXII*, Città de Castello, 1903.
Clementini, C. *Raccolto istorico della fondatione di Rimino, e dell-origine e vite de' Malatesti*. Rimini, Italy, 1617.
Salimbene da Parma. *La Cronaca*. Edited by G. Pochettino. Sancasciano Val di Pesa [no date].

Secondary Sources
Boccaccio, Giovanni. *Comento alla Divina Commedia*. Edited by Domenico Guerri. Bari, Italy: G. Laterza, 1918.

Boker, George Henry. *Francesca da Rimini*. In *Plays and Poems*, vol. 1. 1853. Reprint New York: AMS Press, 1967.

Chubb, Thomas Caldecot. *Dante and His World*. Boston and Toronto: Little, Brown, 1966.

D'Annunzio, Gabriele. *Francesca da Rimini*. Milan: Treves, 1910.

Dante Alighieri. *Inferno*. Translated by John D. Sinclair. New York: Oxford University Press, 1939. Reprint 1961, 1971. [Italian and English ed.].

Evans, Oliver H. *George Henry Boker*. Boston: Twayne, 1984.

Holmes, George. *Florence, Rome, and the Origins of the Renaissance*. Oxford: Oxford University Press, 1986.

Matteini, Nevio. *Francesca da Rimini*. Bologna: Capelli, 1965.

Philipps, Stephen. *Paolo and Francesca: A Tragedy in Four Acts*. New York: Dodd, Mead, 1927.

Prescott, Orville. *Princes of the Renaissance*. New York: Random House, 1969.

DIANA L. MURPHY

FRAU AVA. *See* **Ava, Frau**

FRAUENDIENST. *See* **Minne**

FRAUENFRAGE. *Frauenfrage* is the German term for the "woman question" or "woman problem" identified by historians of later medieval Europe. In the late nineteenth century, the German historian Karl Bücher posited a demographic peculiarity in European cities of the thirteenth and following centuries: a significant majority of the population was female, posing for late medieval society what Bücher called the *Frauenfrage*. This gender imbalance meant many unmarried women had to support themselves through work ranging from begging and prostitution to engagement in lucrative trade and crafts. Ever since its presentation, Bücher's thesis has strongly influenced scholarship on women in the later Middle Ages, especially among those who study the social and economic aspects of women's lives in the heavily urbanized regions of Flanders and the Rhine River basin (encompassing parts of present-day Switzerland, France, Germany, Belgium, Luxembourg, and the Netherlands). The concept has also influenced other research. Religious historians, for example, have linked the *Frauenfrage* to new women's religious institutions including the *beguinages* (groups of pious laywomen known as *beguines*), to distinctive female mystical pursuits and writings of the later Middle Ages, and even to women's participation in heretical movements. Here, too, an "excess" of women is sometimes thought to have been at the root of a great deal of activity and accomplishment outside marriage and child-rearing. Some historians have criticized the whole idea of *Frauenfrage*, suggesting that the gender imbalance of later medieval times has been much exaggerated; others find it an inadequate explanation for the vitality of female religiosity after 1200. Still others, like Ernst Werner, accept the thesis but have extended it backward in time to the eleventh and twelfth centuries and outward in space to rural Europe. Bücher's concept of *Frauenfrage* remains central to scholarly consideration of women's history over a century after its first statement.

See also Beguines; Convents; Petronilla of Chemillé; Widows

BIBLIOGRAPHY

Primary Sources
Bücher, Karl. *Die Frauenfrage im Mittelalter*. Tübingen: H. Laupp, 1882; 2nd ed. 1910.

Secondary Sources
Bolton, Brenda. "Mulieres Sanctae." *Studies in Church History* 10 (1973): 77–97. Reprint in *Women in Medieval History*, edited by Susan Mosher Stuard, 141–58. Philadelphia: University of Pennsylvania Press, 1976.
Herlihy, David. *Opera Muliebria: Women and Work in Medieval Europe*. New York: McGraw-Hill, 1990.
Koch, Gottfried. *Frauenfrage und Ketzertum im Mittelalter*. Berlin: Akademie-Verlag, 1962.
Simons, Walter. *Cities of Ladies: Beguine Communities in the Medieval Low Countries, 1200–1565*. Philadelphia: University of Pennsylvania Press, 2001.
Stuard, Susan Mosher, ed. *Women in Medieval History and Historiography*. Philadelphia: University of Pennsylvania Press, 1987.
Tunc, Suzanne. *Les Femmes au pouvoir: deux abbesses de Fontevraud aux XIIe et XVIIe siècles*. Paris: Cerf, 1993.
Werner, Ernst. "Zur Frauenfrage und zum Frauenkult im Mittelalter: Robert v. Arbrissel und Fontevrault." *Forschungen und Fortschritte* 29 (1955): 269–76.

BRUCE L. VENARDE

FRAUENLIED. The term *Frauenlied* signifies a popular literary genre of musical origin whose name (plural: *Frauenlieder*) comes from the German for "women's song." As with many folk genres, scholars have posited various theories concerning its origins. In a seminal article published in 1949, Theodor Frings showed that the poetry of courtly love composed in French, Provençal, and German during the High Middle Ages derived from an international genre of oral poetry either composed by women or spoken by female protagonists. He thus called the genre *Frauenlieder*. More recently (1990), Ingrid Kasten has taken a broader view, that such songs may be any "whose lyric subject is woman." Frings found parallels to the emotions expressed in Portuguese, Serbian, Russian, and Greek courtly lyrics; in 1952, Leo Spitzer revealed additional similarities in Mozarabic lyrics. In 1962, Kemp Malone added the Old English "Wulf and Eadwacer" and "The Wife's Lament" to the genre, demonstrating that, despite such scant literary remains, a genre of *Frauenlieder* indeed existed during the early Middle Ages. The work of Frings, Spitzer, and Malone establishes conclusively that the genre developed in societies widely separated geographically and culturally and that the songs probably antedate lyrics by men or in the male voice.

Spitzer and Peter Dronke see the source of the *Frauenlieder* in women's dance songs, which in the later Middle Ages evolved into the carol. Thus popular in origin, the *Frauenlieder* flourished alongside the more aristocratic heroic literature. Dronke's assertion that ecclesiastical councils between the sixth and the ninth centuries repeatedly condemned the singing of love songs, specifically those by girls, enables us to consider the extant texts as mere remnants and that these songs were more widespread. Whatever poems have survived are nonnarrative and suggest, rather than actually relate, their story by being highly allusive. They sometimes focus on love from the woman's point of view, for example, telling of a woman frankly inviting a man to share sexual activity and thus assuming the role of active lover rather than the more conventional passive one typified by such male-centered poetic traditions as the Italian *dolce stil nuovo* (sweet new style). In other instances, the woman expresses her loneliness and sorrow for the absence of a loved one, or a young girl grieves over lost love. The *Frauenlieder* often focus on sorrow: the necessity of grief, loss, and pain. In a manner uncommon to medieval poetry, the *Frauenlieder* refer to nature, linking the woman's emotion to some aspect of nature, especially the sea that separates lovers. Only the Mozarabic *muwashshah*, because of its urban setting, omits this self-association of lover-narrator with nature.

Like all vernacular oral poetry, the *Frauenlieder* have become known to us only from their appearance in manuscripts, an oral-to-literate distillation which has inevitably altered their fundamental nature to some extent. Some poems in Latin are extant from the eleventh and twelfth centuries. The written *Frauenlieder* consequently exist in a more learned, and often sacred, context than that fostered by their origins. Their popularity in Europe may be deduced from the fact that there is a Carolingian proclamation from 789 forbidding nuns to compose and send *winileodas* (Germanic=songs for a lover), under penalty of expulsion from the convent, probably because of their sensuous nature. One intriguing but unanswerable question about the *Frauenlieder* concerns their authorship since they are anonymous: does the existence of a female narrator imply a female author, or is a male author assuming a female voice? Fragmentary but substantial evidence suggests that at least some of the *Frauenlieder* were composed by women: for example, the necessity of prohibiting the composition of *winileodas* by nuns. As further documentation, the speaker of "The Wife's Lament" identifies herself as female by her use of feminine inflections, *minre sylfre* (to myself). Because scholars also suspect that Old English poetry may have been composed orally and that the lyrics are records of oral performance, the existence of the feminine inflections raises the intriguing possibility that the author of "The Wife's Lament" was a woman composing before an audience. Applying the literary theories of Julia Kristeva to the two Old English *Frauenlieder*, Patricia Belanoff has argued that the *Frauenlieder* exhibit the semiotic (symbol-oriented), rather than the semantic (tone-oriented), level of language indicative of female lyrics rather than female-voiced projections of a male poet. Granting that at least some *Frauenlieder* were composed by women, we may deem them valid precursors of courtly poetry, particularly that of the *trobairitz*, or women troubadours.

See also *Alba* Lady; *Chanson de Femme*; *Muwashshah*; Rhetoric, Women and; *Trobairitz*; *Trouvères*, Women

BIBLIOGRAPHY

Primary Sources
[Extracts, in English]. Dronke, Peter. "Personal Poetry by Women." In *Women Writers* (*see below*), 84–106.
Kasten, Ingrid, ed. and trans. *Frauenlieder des Mittelalters*. Universal-Bibliothek, 8630. Stuttgart, Germany: Philipp Reclam, 1990.

Secondary Sources
Belanoff, Patricia A. "Women's Song, Women's Language: *Wulf and Eadwacer* and *The Wife's Lament*." In *New Readings on Women in Old English Literature*, edited by Helen Damico and Alexandra Hennessey Olsen, 193–203. Bloomington: Indiana University Press, 1990. Dronke, Peter. *The Medieval Lyric*. New York: Harper & Row, 1969. Revised ed. Cambridge: D. S. Brewer, 1996.
———. *The Medieval Poet and His World*. Rome: Edizioni di Storia e Letteratura, 1984.

————. *Women Writers of the Middle Ages: A Critical Study of Texts from Perpetua (†203) to Marguerite Porete (†1310)*. Cambridge: Cambridge University Press, 1984.

Frings, Theodor. *Minnesinger und Troubadours*. Berlin: Deutsche Akademie der Wissenschaften, 1949.

Klinck, Anne L. "Lyric Voice and the Feminine in Some Ancient and Medieval Frauenlieder." *Florilegium* 13 (1994): 13–36.

————, and Ann Marie Rasmussen, eds. *Medieval Woman's Song: Cross-Cultural Approaches*. Philadelphia: University of Pennsylvania Press, 2002.

Malone, Kemp. "Two English *Frauenlieder*." In *Studies in Old English Literature in Honor of Arthur G. Brodeur*, edited by Stanley B. Greenfield, 106–17. Eugene: University of Oregon, 1963.

Spitzer, Leo. "The Mozarabic Lyric and Theodor Frings' Theories." *Comparative Literature* 4 (1952): 1–22.

ALEXANDRA HENNESSEY OLSEN

FRAUENTURNIER (late 13th century). The story of *Das Frauenturnier (The Ladies' Tournament)* was composed at the end of the thirteenth century, probably in the region of East Franconia, whose major city was Bamberg, in what is now Germany. Though the name of the author is unknown, the title is attested in the medieval manuscripts. As it indicates, *Das Frauenturnier* depicts women engaged in military sport. It opens with a detailed description of how forty knights pool their military resources to deter aggressors and live in peace. One day, when the knights are away on a diplomatic mission, their wives decide to hold a tournament in pursuit of honor. They don their husbands' armor and adopt the names of male kin for the purposes of the game. One maiden, whose kinsmen are too poor to joust, selects the name of a historical personage, Duke Walram of Limbourg. She emerges as the victor in the hard-fought (and richly narrated) tournament. On their return, the knights decide not to punish their wives, but forbid any future jousting. News of the ladies' tournament begins to circulate. When the duke hears of the maiden's deeds, he decides to honor her with a visit. Moved by her poverty, which has prevented her from finding a husband, Walram dowers her and marries her to a rich man.

Das Frauenturnier is a German adaptation of similar stories that had circulated earlier in France, known as the *Tournoiement des dames*. What it shares with the French tales is the idea that women can act "like men" in unusual or emergency circumstances. Bearing arms is shown to be conventionally rather than naturally masculine. The German version, however, is distinctive for its debate on women's honor, conducted by the ladies themselves; for its implicit criticism of the dowry system of marriage; and for its appreciative view of women's community.

Honor is "the public figure one cuts and the respect one elicits." It was fundamental to medieval selfhood in society. For elite women, honor was tied to prescriptive rules of conduct that are reflected in literary texts, and which became codified in conduct books in later medieval centuries. In *Das Frauenturnier*, a woman described only as "bold" asserts that the women should secure honor in the same manner as their men folk—through the pursuit of military glory and sport. She is countered by a "wise" or "experienced" woman, who depicts honor passively as loving ones husband and preserving ones femininity. On the surface, this exchange looks like a conflict between a foolish character and a conventional one. Yet as the plot unfolds, their ideas of honor are shown to be linked. Wifely honor is possible only if the marriage system provides husbands. The bold woman's tournament

349

plan, and the public acclaim it generates for the victorious maiden, secures for her the marriage on which the wise woman's concept of honor depends. The problem at the core of *Das Frauenturnier* is the impoverishment of families of knightly standing, specifically its effects on unmarried women. The narrator pointedly contrasts the impact of poverty on the maiden's father and on herself. The father, the romance type of the poor vavasour, suffers a decline of reputation but remains a member of his knightly peer group. She, however, is "made to pay" in that the size of her dowry determined whom she could marry. A woman with a small dowry could have been compelled to marry below her birth standing and assume her husband's social identity. This outcome of cross-class marriage was codified by the most prominent contemporary custumal, *Der Sachsenspiegel* (*The Saxon Mirror*). *Das Frauenturnier* gives no hint of the social fate of women who did not marry (and did not follow a religious vocation), either through choice or through lack of dowry. Here, as in many contemporary literary and nonliterary sources, marriage is assumed.

Moreover, the maiden in *Das Frauenturnier* has no say in the negotiation between her father and Duke Walram on the size of her dowry. Her father maintains his paternal authority by assuring the duke that his daughter will be content with a small amount of money and a marriage beneath her family status. The narrator thus portrays a marriage system presided over by men who act as guardians, in which a maiden's status is negotiated as a cash equivalent through dowry. In Germany at the time *Das Frauenturnier* was composed, elite marriages involved a web of gift exchanges between the families of both bride and groom, not just dowry. The narrator thus spotlights aspects of a more complex historical reality to make a point, perhaps about worsening local traditions, or to warn about an increasing importance of dowry in marriage formation.

It is also noteworthy that the narrator explores men's and women's communities. Most of the narrator's attention is on the forty knights' way of life in which alliance and negotiation supplant warfare. The men's peaceful outlook is expressed in the scene where they decide to forgive their wives rather than punish them. As one observes, they are already "battered enough" by the tournament and should not receive additional beatings. The men's appreciation of the women's jousting skill suggests a degree of comfort with deviations from gender norms among those members of the knightly strata for whom the story was intended. There is also a passage praising the way the women sustain a mutual bond. We are told that they settle their differences by "talking among themselves." The text emphasizes group process in the resolution of differences. The ladies do not elect a "headman" as the knights do. Rather, leadership is ad hoc and based on one's rhetorical skills, as shown by the woman who prevails in the debate on honor to become mistress of the tournament. The goal of the women's community is pleasure and conviviality, which the text depicts as a worthy and valued goal. Depictions of women's communities are not common in Middle-High German secular literature, or at least not in the most commonly read texts. The most important comparisons are found in the Arthurian romances of early thirteenth-century leading poets such as Hartmann von Aue's *Iwein* (the episode of the enslaved clothmakers) or Wolfram von Eschenbach's *Parzival* (the four hundred ladies and four queens enchanted by an evil magician). These women-only communities are coerced, not voluntary; they are based on shared suffering, not pleasure; and they are dissolved by the heroic chivalry of a single knight, not by the women's own actions.

The unconventional approaches to gender are especially striking in *Das Frauenturnier* since it is a poem in which the threshold between fiction and history is easily crossed.

Although not a tournament poem in a strictly generic sense, it adapts the generic trait of naming an historical personage. The generous duke was almost certainly Walram IV of Limburg who ruled from 1247 to 1279. His second marriage was to the niece of King Otakar II of Bohemia. Walram's connections to the Bohemian crown suggest why *Das Frauenturnier* was preserved in a manuscript from Bohemia, Heidelberg University Library Cpg 341, dated c.1300. The poem's setting "across the Rhine," accords with Walram's Limburg connection. There is no obvious historical reason to explain Walram's image as a benefactor of undowered maidens. Perhaps the fact that his daughter by his first wife, Ermengard, was heir to Limburg, had a bearing on the tale's perception of him as an advocate for women. The story may be found in three other manuscripts as well.

See also Convents; Dowry; *Sachsenspiegel* and *Schwabenspiegel*; *Tournoiement des Dames*

BIBLIOGRAPHY

Primary Source

"Der vrouwen turnei." In *Gesamtabenteuer: Hundert altdeutsche Erzählungen*. Edited by Friedrich Heinrich von der Hagen, vol. 1, 371–82. Stuttgart and Tübingen, Germany, 1850. Reprint Darmstadt: Wissenschaftliche Buchgesellschaft, 1961.

Secondary Sources

Rosenfeld, Hans-Friedrich. "Das Frauenturnier." *Die deutsche Literatur des Mittelalters: Verfasserlexicon*. 2nd ed., vol. 2, cols. 882–83. Berlin and New York: Walter de Gruyter, 1980."Walram IV, duke of Limburg (1247–1279)." In *Allgemeine deutsche Biographie*, 40: 775–76. Reprint Berlin: Duncker & Humblot, 1971. Original 1895.

Westphal-Wihl, Sarah. *"The Ladies' Tournament*: Marriage, Sex and Honor in Thirteenth-Century Germany." *Signs* 14 (1989): 371–98. Reprint in *Sisters and Workers in the Middle Ages*, edited by Judith M. Bennett et al., 162–89. Chicago: University of Chicago Press, 1989.

SARAH WESTPHAL-WIHL

FREDEGUND. *See* **Brunhild**

GALLA PLACIDIA (c.390–450). "Rome's last empress" and an accomplished builder of churches, Galla Placidia was the daughter of Theodosius (d. 395), the last Roman emperor to rule over an undivided empire, and the sister and half-sister of the next two emperors who divided it into two parts. In Rome at the time of its fall (408–410), she was captured by Alaric I, king of the Visigoths (d. 410) and spent some years wandering with his army, although she is said to have always been accorded imperial honors. In 414 she married Alaric's successor, Ataulf, at Narbonne (now in southern France), and reigned with him over the Goths, to the scandal of the Roman world. After Ataulf's death, she was ransomed and returned to her imperial relatives (416). The following year, she was married to the esteemed Roman general, then emperor, Constantius III (d. 421), who co-ruled the West with her half-brother, Honorius (384–423). She bore Constantius a son who, at the age of six, became emperor of the West as Valentinian III (r. 425–455). As regent for this son, she exercised a powerful influence for some twenty years (although after 433, the general Flavius Aetius [d. 454] attained power as leader of the military campaigns), building churches and palaces in Ravenna, which had replaced Rome as capital of the Western Empire. Of these buildings only her mausoleum remains, a building outstanding for its remarkable mosaics. It appears, however, that she was never buried in the tomb prepared for her there.During her regency she also fueled the ambitions of Pope Leo I, helping to increase his political influence as well as his ecclesiastical power during a doctrinally turbulent time for Christianity. Staunchly Catholic, she supported Leo in his repudiation of the heretical monophysitism of Eutyches, abbot of Constantinople (d. 454). Monophysitism holds that the Incarnate Christ consists in one nature, not two—Divine and Human; Eutyches added that this one nature is "not consubstantial with us." Galla Placidia was the first of a series of women who played an important role in the history of the Byzantine era, although it has been suggested that Byzantine historians reflected a certain "feminism" in attributing to women an excessive role in the politics of the period. But the mosaics at Ravenna, in which women figure prominently, raise doubts about the validity of such a theory.

See also Syrian-Christian Women; Theodora

BIBLIOGRAPHY
Herzhaft, Gérard. *Galla Placidia*. Les Romanesques. Paris: Ramsay, 1987.
Ketvel, Urho. *Galla Placidia myöhäisantiikin vaikuttajanainen*. Helsinki: Yliopistopaino, 2000.

Oost, Stewart I. *Galla Placidia Augusta: A Biographical Essay*. Chicago: University of Chicago Press, 1968.

Richlin, Amy. "Julia's Jokes, Galla Placidia, and the Roman Use of Women as Political Icons." In *Stereotypes of Women in Power: Historical Perspectives and Revisionist Views*, edited by Barbara Garlick, Suzanne Dixon, and Pauline Allen, ch. 3. New York: Greenwood Press, 1992.

Rizzardi, Clementina, et al. *Il Mausoleo di Galla Placidia a Ravenna*. Mirabilia Italiae, 4. Modena, Italy: Panini, 1996.

Sirago, Vito Antonio. *Galla Placidia e la trasformazione politica dell'Occidente*. Université de Louvain. Recueil de travaux d'histoire et de philologie, 4: 25. Louvain, Belgium: Bureau de recueil/ Bibliothèque de l'Université, 1961. [Sirago is the leading Galla Placidia scholar].

———. *Galla Placidia: la nobilissima (392–450)*. Donne d'Oriente e d'Occidente, 1. Milan: Jaca, 1996.

CHARITY CANNON WILLARD

GARSENDA OF FORCALQUIER (c.1170–post-1225). "La Comtessa de Proensa" (Countess of Provence), a *trobairitz* (woman troubadour) and also regent of an important political and literary court, has traditionally been identified with Garsenda (or Carsenda) as the coauthor of the exchange of *coblas* (two-stanza dialogue poem) in Occitan, the medieval language of southern France. Their poem is known by its opening line, "Vos que.m semblatz dels corals amadors" ("You who seem to me a true-hearted lover"), which she composed with the troubadour Gui de Cavaillon. She figures as "Garsenda" in two troubadour *vidas* (poetic biographies).

According to trobairitz specialist Stanislaw Stronski, she was born Garsenda de Sabran to Raines de Claustral and Garsenda de Forcalquier; she was also the granddaughter of Guilhem (William) IV, last count of Forcalquier, in the lower Alps part of Provence (extreme southeastern France). In 1193, bringing Forcalquier as her dowry, she married Alphonse II, count of Provence (d. 1209), to whom in 1205 she bore a son who, upon his father's death, would become Count Raimon-Berangar IV of Provence (1209–1245). She ruled effectively as Raimon's regent, but without official title or authority, since those were claimed by Alphonse's brother, King Peire (Pedro/Peter) II of Aragon (d. 1213) from 1209 to 1216, while Raimon lived with his late father's family at Aragon. But by 1216, Pedro had died and Raimon returned to his mother's court, inaugurating the second, officially sanctioned, phase of Garsenda's regency, lasting until 1219 or 1220, when Raimon attained his majority and married Beatrice of Savoy, now the new countess of Provence. Garsenda then withdrew from what had been a formidable reign, amid that region's political power struggles, to enter the convent of La Celle, in Brignolles, Var (southeastern France), taking her vows in 1225, where she is presumed to have spent the remainder of her life.

Her *coblas* exchange with Gui de Cavaillon (fl. 1220–1229) is thought to have been composed between 1200 and 1209, when Gui, a knight of high estate, frequented the court of Provence, a major literary center (Bruckner et al.; Rieger). Gui and Garsenda's exchange imitates the rhyme and meter of the troubadour Gaucelm Faidit's (fl. 1172–1203) "Ja mais nuill temps" (Riquer). It is preserved in only two manuscripts: one called "F" in Rome at the Vatican Library, Chigi L.IV, 106; the other, called "T," in Paris at the Bibliothèque nationale de France, fr. 15211. While in MS *T* the poem is anonymous, in MS *F* it is ascribed by its rubric (heading) to "la contesa de Proensa" and to "Gui de Cavaillo." However, collateral evidence supplied by the vidas of Gui and of Elias de Barjols (fl. 1191–1230) suggests that Garsenda of Provence is the countess referred to in the rubric. Gui's *vida* recounts that he was a baron of Provence, well loved by the ladies, and the author of quality *coblas d'amor* (couplets on love). It says farther on that "it was believed that he was the lover of the Countess Garsenda, wife of the Count of Provence, who was the brother of the King of Aragon" (Boutière and Schutz, 505). As we have noted, Alfonso's brother was indeed Peire II of Aragon. Elias de Barjols' *vida* identifies him as a *joglar* (or minstrel) in the service of Alfonso of Provence who "fell in love with the Countess Carsenda, wife of the Count, following the latter's death in Sicily, and who composed his good and beautiful songs about her for as long as she lived" (Boutière and Schutz, 215). Four of Elias's songs are in fact dedicated to Garsenda. While these details would seem to validate the historicity of the information presented in "Vos que.m semblatz" and its rubric, it might also be that the pertinent passages in Gui's *vida* were composed solely to explain the circumstances of the composition of the *coblas* exchange and to identify the Comtessa de Proensa. Indeed, many of the troubadour vidas were composed for similar reasons, drawing a part of their "factual" content from the lyrics they prefaced rather than from reliable historical sources (Poe).

"Vos que.m semblatz dels corals amadors" is composed of two stanzas, the first of which is spoken by the persona of the countess, the second by the persona of Gui, he who seems to her "a true-hearted lover," though not without some reservation. Saying that because of him she suffers, the feminine poetic voice reproaches her masculine interlocutor for his *vulpillatge* (faint-heartedness) in wooing her. She points out that a lady can hardly reveal her true feelings for fear of rejection and urges Gui to avoid doing ill to both of them. Gui responds that it is her high station alone that makes him hesitant to seek her love. Rather, believing that his desires will be obvious in his deeds, which will be worth more than empty words, he wishes to serve her so nobly that no harm might come of it. While Garsenda's *cobla*, which reveals precisely the desire she claims that ladies must conceal, exhibits wit and a fine sense of irony, Gui's equally subtle reply preserves the status quo that Garsenda would alter.

See also Dowry; *Trobairitz*

BIBLIOGRAPHY

Primary Sources
Elias de Barjol. [Songs to Garsenda] In *Bibliographie des Troubadours*, edited by Alfred Pillet and Henry Carstens. Reprint New York: Burt Franklin, 1968. [See no. 132 (Elias's code) and then his poems numbered 1, 7, 9, 10 for their location].
————. [*Vidas* of Gui by Elias and anon.]. In *Biographies des troubadours. Textes provençaux des XIIIᵉ et XIVᵉ siècles*, edited by Jean Boutière and Alexander H. Schutz, revised with I.-M. Cluzel, 215–16, 505–7. Les Classiques d'Oc, 1. Paris: Nizet, 1964.
Garsenda and Gui. "Vos que.m semblatz dels corals amadors." In *Los Trovadores: Historia literaria y textos*, edited by Martín de Riquer, 3: 1191–92. Barcelona: Planeta, 1975. [Text, Spanish translation, historical commentary].
————. "Vos que.m semblatz dels corals amadors." In *Songs of the Women Troubadours*, edited and translated by Matilda Tomaryn Bruckner, Laurie Shepard and Sarah White, 54–55, 162–63. Garland Library of Medieval Literature, 97A. New York and London: Garland, 1995. New ed. 2000. [Most recent, authoritative: original texts, notes, introduction, and English translation].
————. "Vos que.m semblatz dels corals amadors." In *Trobairitz: Der Beitrag der Frau in der altokzitanischen höfischen Lyrik. Edition des Gesamtkorpus*, edited by Angelica Rieger, 206–13. Beihefte der Zeitschrift für romanische Philologie, 233. Tübingen, Germany: Max Niemeyer Verlag, 1991. [Most authoritative, German trans. and commentary].

Secondary Sources

[See also notes to above editions].

Poe, Elizabeth Wilson. *From Poetry to Prose in Old Provençal. The Emergence of the "Vidas," the "Razos," and the "Razos de trobar."* Birmingham, Ala.: Summa, 1984.

Stronski, Stanislaw. "Notes sur quelques troubadours et protecteurs des troubadours célèbres par Elias de Barjols." *Revue des Langues Romanes* 50 (1907): 5–44.

MERRITT R. BLAKESLEE

GAUDAIRENCA (late 13th century). Guadairenca was the only known *trobairitz* (woman troubadour, writing in the southern-French language labeled Old Provençal or Old Occitan) from the Aude region in southern France (other trobairitz came from other southern-French areas). Gaudairenca was also the estranged wife of the troubadour Raimon de Miraval (fl. 1191–1229), a poor knight but prolific and popular poet from near Carcassonne. Little is known of her life, and no works attributed to her have survived. That she lived and composed at all is confirmed only through the distorting prism of three literary sources: the work of as many male authors, including her husband. Troubadour scholars have been attempting to piece together her puzzle since the late eighteenth century. Gaudairenca's story is thus also a saga of modern scholarly discovery in dissecting the poetic-versus-real-life intricacies of troubadour culture.

Early in the thirteenth century, the Catalan troubadour Uc [= Hugh] de Mataplana (fl. 1185–1213) composed a *sirventes* (lyric poem on nonamorous topics, often politically satirical) directed at Miraval on the subject of his marriage and naming Gaudairenca in the *envoi*, the poem's final dedicatory stanza, as edited by noted scholar Martín de Riquer. Miraval replied with his own *sirventes*, echoing Uc's metrics and rhymes and citing Uc's wife in its envoi in responding to the accusations as made in Uc's song (Topsfield; Riquer). Finally and most elaborately, several fourteenth-century manuscripts include two *razos* (early commentaries to the poems) recounting, and no doubt embellishing, events behind the exchange of sirventes, according to the classic scholarship on troubadour biography by Jean Boutière and Alexander Schutz and, more recently, William Burgwinkle. Ever since its early mention in 1774 by one of the great French Enlightenment medievalists, La Curne de Sainte-Palaye, the story of Gaudairenca and Miraval's relations has wisely been taken with a grain of salt. But even Sainte-Palaye himself, who finds the story "suspect d'infidélité ou d'erreur" ("perhaps unfaithful or erroneous"), concludes that "il y a sans doute un fond de vrai" ("there is doubtless some basis in truth"). No doubt he was accurate in this assessment. But where the historical basis ends and romantic embellishment begins is less clear. According to the story developed in the *razos*, Lord Raimon de Miraval courted a lady named Aimengarda de Castras, nicknamed "la belle Albigeoise" ("the fair Albigensian") from modern-day Castres in the region around Albi, in southern France. Albigensian heretical doctrine authorized a husband to repudiate his wife for another, and to do so was apparently not uncommon (Topsfield). Aimengarda maintained she would surrender to Miraval only if he abandoned his wife to marry her. That was supposedly reason enough for Gaudairenca to be turned out by Miraval, who justified himself with the claim that "he did not want a wife who knew how to compose poetry." When he gaily ("fort alegres") instructed Gaudairenca to return to her parents, she pretended to be quite angry, "feis se fort irada," while wisely summoning instead Lord Guillem Bremon, her own suitor. Rather than go home to her mother, she was given to Bremon in marriage, and with Miraval's blessing. He thus not only abandoned his wife but also married her off. Bremon was delighted with the arrangement, and so was Raimon. The story does not end there. Aimengarda then congratulated Miraval and told him to prepare their marriage celebrations. Meanwhile, she summoned another, successful suitor, Lord Olivier de Saisac, and took him as her husband the very next day, and he was the happiest man in the world (*fo lo plus alegres hom del mon*). Thus the would-be deceiver Miraval was himself deceived, for only he was left alone and miserable (*fort fo dolens et tristz*). He naturally lamented the double cross and with it the double loss of lady and wife, regretted by him in that order. According to one *razo*, he went about like a madman for fully two years thereafter.

Internal evidence from the songs undermines as much as it underscores the historical credibility of these events. Uc's accusation, as echoed in the *razos*, is that Raimon spurned his courtly wife because of her worthy conduct and praiseworthy poetry. While his *sirventes* accuses Raimon of turning out Gaudairenca, he intimates that husband and wife may yet be reconciled. Probably for that reason, troubadour expert René Nelli presumes that Raimon could and would eventually have taken Gaudairenca back. Raimon, in his reply, does not deny that he dismissed Gaudairenca in the first place, but only that he did so on the advice of a servant, which was indeed another criticism leveled at him by Uc in his *sirventes*. Raimon counters Uc's reproaches by justifying marital separation in unspecified cases and by insisting that he has always supported the dual causes of love and poetry. Thus Raimon cautiously separates cause and effect: his professed support for poetry on the one hand, and the acknowledged rejection of Gaudairenca on the other. The marital status of the other participants in this episode has not been confirmed, nor even their identities positively established, despite Nelli's contention. Consequently, as is so often the case with *vidas* (short biographies, often by contemporaries) and *razos*, it remains uncertain how much of the detail to Raimon's marital status lies in the realm of history or legend. In either case, the songs and especially the *razos* take on new meaning as a result of the strong role they award to Gaudairenca, concurrently Raimon's discarded wife and fellow poet. According to several parallel troubadour *vidas*, a pledge of compensation (*esmenda*) from a lady lures a poet like Gaucelm Faidit (fl. c.1170–1205) into renouncing his current love.

In these variations on essentially the same story, the poets and would-be lovers all find themselves jilted and mocked by their first love, who perfidiously does not keep her word. The novel element in the Gaudairenca episode and especially in the courtly career of Raimon, however, is the strength of character shown by his decisive wife. In contradistinction to long-suffering Griselda in the novella popularized by the fourteenth-century Italian author Boccaccio, this proto-feminist version of the jettisoned wife shows that she need not patiently await her husband's beck and recall. Rather, this wife promptly and wisely contracts a new marriage with her longstanding lover, who is more noble, in both senses, and certainly more devoted than her doubly poor husband. As for her now former husband, Raimon's sorry plight may be read as a tongue-in-cheek resolution of the many troubadour *tensos* (debate poems) in which poets debate the relative "virtues" of distant ladies (who give little or nothing) and near-at-hand women (who grant their all). To the more familiar such oppositions of *domna* (lady) versus *femna* (woman) and *domna* (lady) versus *piucella* (maiden) is now added the more obvious one juxtaposing *domna* (lady) versus *moiller* (wife). Unfortunately for Raimon, according to the razos, in renouncing his wife and proposing to his lady, he relinquishes the company of one and fails to win the favors of the other. In sum, he enjoys neither his lady nor his wife. He, too, is tested as a spouse, but unlike Griselda and Gaudairenca, Raimon fails to pass muster. As one *razo* notes, after the ladies made fun of Raimon they mocked "many troubadour knights."

Gaudairenca's case, as the ribald moral tales called *fabliaux* do for northern France, allows us to examine complex troubadour attitudes toward marriage and mistresses. Marriage and especially wives are not usually so flattered by the *vidas*. Gaucelm Faidit's regular lady may have been a reformed bawd. Another, lesser-known, poet, Gausbert de Puycibot, finds his jilted legal other supposedly turned to prostitution. In the 2,700 Old Occitan lyrics preserved, not one seems to sing on a positive note the joys of marriage. When it is at issue at all, which is rarely, some troubadours poke fun at the hypocrisy of marriage; the Gascon satirists bewail the widespread abuse of a sanctified union (Paden). In Old-French lyric, when a single *trouvère* claims to be married, his song is nothing less than a calculated attempt to legitimize the child born out of wedlock to him and his mistress (Rosenberg). In sum, the *maritalis affectio*, or harmonious marital contract, on which the medieval institution of marriage reposes seems entirely lacking here. Still, the example of Gaudairenca as wife triumphant is richer and more complex than her fabliau situation suggests, not simply because she is yet another medieval woman who has the last laugh over her foolhardy, wayward spouse, but principally because she is herself a poet. In this sense, her story is not only a social statement by virtue of the uncommon issues it raises and a literary artifact given its architectonic balance and mirror composition. It is above all a rare document attesting the reception of the trobairitz as serious literary-historical figures.

Gaudairenca's case is also an example of the perils of having two poets in one household. Precisely the very poetic and musical skills that Raimon should have appreciated in his wife served him instead as a pretext for rejecting her. Lady Gaudairenca was likely an "intellectual woman" ("mujer intelectual" as Riquer states) and very clever (a "fine mouche" as Nelli says). As such, she must have been more than a match for her husband. No double standard reigned in this household. The *razo* specifies that Raimon praised his lady in story and song ("en contan et en cantan"), much as Gaudairenca had a talent for *coblas* (couplets, strophes) and particularly *dansas* (dances) about her suitor. A strict parallelism is thus maintained: each sings the charms of her or his lover. Thus far, husband and wife would seem to practice courtly love on an equal footing. We know from his *vida* that Raimon owned a part of a small castle; there Gaudairenca would have held a modest court, as Uc's *sirventes* intimates. However, when the moment of truth and its consequences arrives, the greater wisdom of the wife is made abundantly clear in the *razo*. Raimon is tricked into renouncing his wife in vain hopes of marrying a lady who ultimately will neither satisfy his desires nor make good on her marriage proposal to him. Concurrently but contrastively, Gaudairenca, when renounced by her husband, at once finds fulfillment and marriage in the arms of her lover. That is, she rewrites the end of the famous twelfth-century romance by Chrétien de Troyes, *Cligès*, in which the protagonist makes his lover his wife: "de s'amie a feite sa fame." That would become, in Gaudairenca's case, "she made of her lover her husband." It is perhaps not by chance that the names of Gaudairenca's two husbands in literature (if not in life), Raimon (de Miraval) and (Guillem) Bremon, should overlap formally in the *razos*. Was B-remon a second Raimon—better still—to pun on the French for "second": a *bis*-Raimon? Certainly they show significant differences in their treatment of Gaudairenca the serial monogamist. Gaudairenca remains by far the strongest figure ("feis se fort irada!") at the heart of the triangle tying her to and untying her from the husband and lover who become former husband and new husband. Gascon satirist Marcabru voices a sour intolerance of overlapping when he denounces "celha qui ja ab dos o tres," she who sleeps with two or three. His stance flies in the face of a medieval fascination with just such tales of great women devourers of men found also in real life, such as Eleanor of Aquitaine (one woman with two royal husbands) and Almodis of La Marche (with three successive spouses, the third having kidnapped her) referred to in William of Malmesbury's twelfth-century chronicles.

Gaudairenca's shadowy existence has provoked further linguistic, genealogical, and topographic theories to support the poetic-historical evidence. For example, the *razos* and sirventes name Raimon/Bremon's wife "Caudairenca" or "Caudairenga" and propose an etymology and genealogy based on a paternal Caudeira, whose name also suggests a cauldron or "hot spot" in general. Paul Andraud adds that in Castres—the hometown of her rival Aimengarda—there are the remains of a castle called La Tour Caudière. But the name used most often today is Gaudairenca, which marries the Occitan suffix -*enca* and a reflex of Late Latin *gaudire*, suggesting an undead metaphor for the storytellers who recognize its meaning as "she who enjoys herself," in contrast to the husband who enjoys neither his lady nor his wife. This then is all that we have to attach to Gaudairenca's name and persona. It is precious little, and it is a great deal. As René Nelli concludes facetiously, "Etrange destinée que celle de la gloire de Gaudairenca, la trobairitz, dont la postérité n'a retenu qu'une aventure un peu folle et très gracieuse, qui ne lui est peut-être jamais arrivée!" ("What a strange destiny for the glory of Gaudairenca the woman troubadour, of whom posterity has retained but one slightly foolish, if elegant, episode—if that itself ever happened!").

See also *Alba* Lady; Capellanus, Andreas; Eleanor of Aquitaine; Ermengard of Narbonne; Grazida (Grazida Lizier); Griselda; Isolde; *Miroir de Mariage* (*Mirror of Marriage*); *Trobairitz*

BIBLIOGRAPHY

Primary Sources
Boutière, Jean, and Alexander H. Schutz, eds. *Biographies des troubadours*. Paris: Nizet, 1973.
Burgwinkle, William E., trans. *Razos and Troubadour Songs*. New York: Garland, 1990.
Rieger, Angelica. *Trobairitz: Der Beitrag der Frau in der altokzitanischen höfischen Lyrik, Edition des Gesamtkorpus*, 98–105. Beihefte der Zeitschrift für romanische Philologie, 233. Tübingen: Niemeyer, 1991.
Topsfield, Leslie, ed. *Les Poésies du troubadour Raimon de Miraval*. Paris: Nizet, 1971.

Secondary Sources
Andraud, Paul. *La Vie et l'oeuvre du troubadour Raimon de Miraval*. Paris: Bouillon, 1902.
Gégou, Fabienne. "En lisant les vidas.... Lumière nouvelle sur les trobairitz." *Marche romane* 33 (1983): 101–7.
La Curne de Sainte-Palaye, J.-B. *Histoire littéraire des troubadours* [...]. Edited by Claude-François-Xavier Millot. Paris: Durand, 1774.
Nelli, René. "De quelques 'Poetae minores': Gaudairenca." In *Actualité des Troubadours (Les Troubadours de l'Aude)* [special issue of] *Pyrénées* 1 (1941): 179–81.
Paden, William D., et al. "The Troubadour's Lady: Her Marital Status and Social Rank." *Studies in Philology* 72 (1975): 28–50.
Riquer, Martín de. "El trovador Huguet de Mataplana." In *Studia hispanica in Honorem Rafael Lapesa*, 1: 455–94, esp. 488–92. Madrid: Cátedra-Seminapio Menéndez Pidal, 1972.
Rosenberg, Samuel. "Observations on the *Chanson* of Jacques d'Autun (R. 350/51)." *Romania* 96 (1975): 552–60.

ROY ROSENSTEIN

GEERTRUIDE VAN OOSTEN (c.1300–1358). Geertruide (Gertrude) van Oosten (or van Delft) was a Dutch beguine and mystic. According to her *vitae* (biographies), she was born into a humble peasant family at Voorburg, near The Hague, around the year 1300. Having reached adulthood, she went to Delft, an important town in the Netherlands, where she worked as a maidservant in a number of households. Disappointed in an affair of the heart, she resolved to devote the rest of her life to the service of God and entered the beguinage (community of beguines, a uniquely liberal, independent category of religious, yet lay, women; males = beghards) in Delft. Generally speaking, the first *vitae* are in agreement with one another, and they give insight into beguine life and spiritually in their earliest stages in Holland much like the *Vita Maria d'Oignies* (*Life of Marie d'Oignies*) did rather earlier for the beguines in the diocese of Liège in what is now eastern Belgium, and neighboring principalities.

When she first entered the beguinage, she was compelled to beg to support herself, a practice not normally acceptable among the beguines. Thereafter, she became engaged in caring for the sick and other forms of charitable work commonly pursued by the beguines. In her spiritual life, which was rich and profound, Gertrude concentrated on the infancy and passion of Christ in particular, with the result that in 1340 she received the stigmata (visible or felt wounds like those of Christ on the Cross). However, fearing that the stigmata might be the cause of spiritual pride and vanity, Gertrude prayed for their removal, which duly happened. Not only did her stigmata attract widespread attention, but Gertrude was also widely known for her prophetic statements and revelations. Furthermore, in the company of two other beguines she often sang hymns on the bridges of Delft, or in "other advantageous places," for the edification of the passersby. And in 1351, when the city of Delft was threatened militarily during the domestic wars between the Hoeks and the Kabeljauws, Gertrude led the beguines of Delft in hours-long prayer in the parish church to check the danger and destruction facing the city. She died in 1358 and was buried in the cemetery of the Old Church in Delft, since the beguinage did not yet have its own church and cemetery.

The *vitae* of Gertrude, detailed in the following bibliography, attribute two hymns to her, *Het daghet in den Oosten* (*Ab Oriente dies nascitur* [*It dawns in the East*]) and *Jesus die is ghecomen* (*Jesus who has come*), respectively, as well as spiritual exercises titled *Asceses seu Exercitia quaedam familiaria* (B. Gertrudi van Oosten) (*Some Customs or Private Exercises [of the Blessed Gertrude van Oosten]*). However, two hymns beginning "Het daghet in den Oosten" have come down to us from the late Middle Ages, but both S. Axters and M. Goossens come to the conclusion that only the hymn that continues "Die Maen schijnt overal" ("The Moon Shines Everywhere") could have been written by Gertrude who, according to the *vitae*, owed her nickname, van Oosten, to the fact that she was the author of this hymn. The other hymn beginning "Het daghet in den Oosten" dates from after her death. However, the two hymns are both Christianized versions of older, profane songs. Axters accepts Gertrude's authorship of *Jesus die is ghecomen*, but Goossens doubts her authorship, for various reasons. He suggests that the hymn may have been written c.1500 by the anonymous author of a number of hymns, namely a Franciscan tertiary of the convent Barberadael at Den Dungen near 's Hertogenbosch (= Bois-le-Duc [The Duke's Woods]). Finally, it is only in the *vita* published by J. G. van Ryckel (1631) that the name of Gertrude is mentioned in connection with the *Asceses seu Exercitia*, which follow the *vita* itself. However, Goossens argues that if these *Asceses* were originally the work of

Gertrude herself, then, judging by their contents, van Ryckel must have altered them to the point where they bear but little resemblance to the original. In summary, Goossens doubts whether this supposed record of Gertrude's daily practices has any connection with her whatsoever.

See also Beguines; Hagiography (Female Saints); Music, Women Composers and Musicians

BIBLIOGRAPHY

Primary Sources

"De Venerabili Virgine Gertrude ab Oosten Beghina Delphensi in Belgio." In *Acta Sanctorum*, 1: 348–53. Antwerp, 1643. [Based on an older, undated manuscript from Utrecht, which is no longer extant].

Het Leven van die Heylighe ende waerdighe maecht Geertruyd van Oosten Baghijnken tot Delft. 2nd ed. Louvain, 1589. [Biography drawing on a number of older sources, including the well-known set of chronicles titled *Divisiekroniek* (Leiden, 1517) and, most likely, the lost Utrecht manuscript referred to above].

Vita. In *Generale Legende der Heylighen*, edited by P. de Ribadeneira and H. Rosweyden. Antwerp, 1619.

———. In *Het Leven der H. Maeghden*, edited by H. Rosweyden, 39–47. Antwerp, 1626. [Vita citing *Divisiekroniek* as its source].

———. In Laurentius Surius. *De probatis sanctorum vitis*, 7: 14–18. Cologne, 1581.van Ryckel, J. G. *Vita S. Beggae.* Louvain, 1631. [Gertrude, 357–61].

Secondary Sources

Axters, Stephanus. *Geschiedenis van de Vroomheid in de Nederlanden, Vol. II: De Eeuw van Ruusbroec*, 163–69. Antwerp: De Sikkel, 1953.

Bredero, Adrian Hendrik. "De Delftse begijn Gertruid van Oosten (ca. 1320–1358) en haar niet-erkende heiligheid." In *De Nederlanders in Late Middeleeuwen*, edited by E. H. de Boer and J. W. Marsilje, 83–97. Utrecht: Het Spectrum, 1987.

Carasso-Kok, Marijke. *Repertorium van Verhalende Historische Bronnen uit de Middeleeuwen*, 35–36. The Hague: Martinus Nijhoff, 1981.

de Moor, Geertruida. "Geertruid van Oosten." In *Delftse Vrouwen van Vroeger door Delftse Vrouwen van Nu*, edited by H. M. Bonebakker-Westerman et al., 17–32. Delft: Delftse Vrouwenraad, 1975.Goossens, Mathias. "Enige Bemerkingen Betreffende Geertruid van Oosten." *Studia Catholica*, 29 (1954): 207–16.

Kieckhefer, Richard. *Unquiet Souls: Fourteenth-Century Saints and Their Religious Milieu.* Chicago and London: University of Chicago Press, 1984.

Knuttel, Johannes A. N. *Het Geestelijke Lied in de Nederlanden voor de Kerkhervorming.* Rotterdam: Brusse, 1906. Reprint Groningen: Bouma; Amsterdam: Bert Hagen, 1974.

Renna, Thomas. "Hagiography and Feminine Spirituality in the Low Countries." *Cîteaux. Commentarii Cistercienses* 39 (1988): 285–96.

GERRIT H. GERRITS

GENEVIEVE (GENOVEFVA), ST. *See* **Clotilde, St.**

GERTRUDE THE GREAT, OF HELFTA, ST. (1256–1301/02). Gertrude, or more correctly, Gertrud of Helfta, was a noted German mystic who wrote in Latin and Middle-High German, with only her Latin works surviving. Born to parents now unknown on January 6, 1256, as a child of five she entered the convent of Helfta where she would spend her entire life. Demonstrating strong intellectual propensities from early on, her thorough schooling included the seven *artes liberales* (grammar, logic, rhetoric, arithmetic, geometry, astronomy, and music). Soon thereafter, she dedicated herself to comprehensive studies in theology.

Helfta (Helpede), in the region called Thuringia—in today's Germany, near Eisleben in Sachsen-Anhalt—was a convent founded at Mansfeld in 1229 and moved to Helfta in 1258. The nuns of Helfta were Cistercian-oriented Benedictines, that is, they followed the Benedictine rule more strictly than other Benedictines. Under its second and most famous abbess, Gertrud of Hackeborn (b. 1232; in office: 1251–1292)—with whom Gertrud of Helfta is often confused—and under the spiritual guidance of Dominican monks of nearby Halle, the Helfta convent developed into a renowned center of culture and mysticism. The Helfta community would be dissolved in 1546 after its buildings were destroyed during the Peasants' War in 1525. The convent church was rebuilt and completed in 1999, while reconstruction of the entire convent continues.

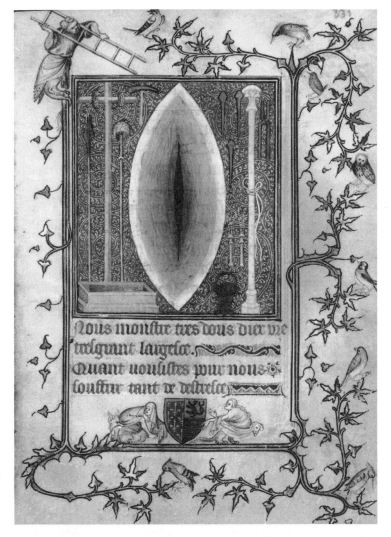

"The Wound of Christ" from the psalter and prayer book of Bonne de Luxembourg (fol. 331r.). © Metropolitan Museum, New York City, Cloisters, 1969 (69.86).

Of Gertrud's lost Middle-High German secular poetry and theological treatises, only an occasional German term or short passage can be found interspersed with her Latin prose. Her Latin work consists of the *Legatus divinae pietatis* (*The Herald of Loving Kindness*), to become a classic of Christian mysticism, and the *Exercitia spiritualia* (*Spiritual Exercises*), a book of meditations and prayers (the title is not Gertrud's) later becoming influential in Catholic devotional practice. She is also one of the writers responsible for disseminating Mechthild of Hackeborn's work, perhaps originally composed in German, but preserved only in its Latin version, *Liber specialis gratiae* (*Book of Special Grace*).

The prime experience inaugurating her writing occurred on January 27, 1281. Yet she did not begin composing her memorial, now Book 2 of the *Legatus*, until 1289, on sensing

361

a divine call to communicate her inner transformation and mystical experiences. It is characteristic of Gertrud that the experience of *unio mystica* (mystical union) liberates her so that she feels unrestrained by petty rules and regulations. Nonconformist in many ways, she often suggests areas in need of reform within the Church. She perceives herself to be divinely authorized to guide her fellow nuns spiritually and advise laypeople. It is perhaps because of these potentially presumptuous passages that her work endured some censorship.

The *Legatus* is comprised of five books, of which only Book 2 was written by Gertrud herself; the other books were finalized by others from her notes. Book 1 represents a *vita* (life) of Gertrud, presumably written by a sister of her convent after Gertrud's death; Books 3 through 5 contain an account of Gertrud's spiritual experiences based on Gertrud's dictation, notes, and conversations. Not surprisingly, these other books (1, 3–5) differ in style, content, and in their more didactic tone from Gertrud's own Book 2. Their moralizing reflects a transition from literature of revelation to the convent chronicles. The *Legatus* is extant in five manuscripts: the best being the 1412 one now at Munich, in the Bayerische Staatsbibliothek, clm. 15332; then one from 1487, at Vienna, Österreichische Nationalbibliothek, cod. 4224, and another (fifteenth century) at Trier, Germany, in the Stadtbibliothek, cod. 77/1061. Two others are partial manuscripts, also from the fifteenth century: one at Mainz, Stadtbibliothek, cod. 13, and the other (dated 1473) at Darmstadt, in the Hessische Landesbibliothek, cod. 84. The first complete edition of her Latin work was produced in 1536, printed by a Carthusian monk at Cologne (Köln), Johann Gerecht of Landsberg (Lanspergius), made Gertrud's work more widely available and even ended up preserving it when earlier sources became lost.

Such is the case with the *Exercitia spiritualia*, of which no known manuscript exists, and thus survives only in Johannes Justus Lanspergius's first edition of 1536. The *Exercitia*'s authenticity was established through a comparison with Book 2 of the *Legatus*. For about two hundred years, beginning in the middle of the seventeenth century, excerpts of prayers from Gertrud's work (by Martin von Cochem in 1666) were widely circulated, translated, and imitated throughout the Western world. Gertrud of Helfta's writing was influenced by the style and diction of the famous French mystic and preacher, Bernard of Clairvaux (1090–1153) and in general by texts of the daily liturgy and Scriptures, especially the Song of Songs and Psalms. A predominant characteristic of Gertrud's work is the intertwining of liturgy with mystical meditations in which Bride-of-Christ imagery (*Brautmystik*) assumes central position. She also reports a vision of the birth and delivery of the Christ child within her own heart—a motif not uncommon among the mystical nuns and beguines. At times Gertrud's effusive sweetness in using terms of endearment may divert today's reader from the fact that her prose is also highly poetic and—like many mystical works—characterized by startling oxymora (rhetorical juxtaposition of opposites) and a wealth of almost brutal imagery.

Within the theological context of the thirteenth century, the themes that capture Gertrud's interest most are the Eucharist and the veneration of the heart of Jesus. The heart as the intellectual, spiritual, and affective center of the human being in medieval thinking becomes the focus of Gertrud's mystical love of Christ. Her interpretation, based on John 7: 37ff. and 13: 23–25, is best symbolized in the famous visual trope of the love between Christ and his disciple John, also evoked by Anna of Munzingen. Her veneration of Jesus's heart, closely intertwined with and inseparable from the theme of God/Jesus as

Mother, is expressed in the remarkable poetic imagery of the *Legatus* and *Exercitia*. Gertrud of Helfta and Mechthild of Hackeborn, together with Luitgard of Aywieres and Beatrijs van Nazareth, are credited in Church history as the first writers to focus on the Sacred Heart of Jesus, laying the basis for a cult that became popular in the Baroque period (seventeenth and eighteenth centuries) and the nineteenth century.

The unique traits of Gertrud of Helfta's writings lie in her emphasis on joy, praise, and thanksgiving. Her "freedom of the heart" (*libertas cordis*), an inner detachment, causes her not to dwell on the human condition as sinful and suffering but rather to burst out at every possible occasion into songs of jubilation—no doubt also as a way of coping with her own lifelong illness. Her mystical *jubilus* (*Exercitia*, 6) is a masterpiece of mystical poetry.

One of three Helfta nuns contributing to the literature of medieval mysticism, Gertrud of Helfta remains less known than her close associates, the abbess Gertrud of Hackeborn's sister, Mechthild of Hackeborn, and the beguine Mechthild of Magdeburg. Contemporary reception of Gertrud's work, judging by the small number of surviving manuscripts, was at best lukewarm. A Middle-High German translation, *Ein botte der götlichen miltekeit* of her now famous *Legatus*, appearing about a hundred years after her death, is a shortened, moralizing version, mainly of Books 3 through 5. The numerous later editions and translations of her writings all relied on Lanspergius's 1536 edition until the first critical edition of Gertrud's work was published by the Benedictines of Solesmes, France, in 1875, now superseded by the Sources Chrétiennes edition (1967–1986). It was the Solesmes edition that first pointed out the error, already to be found in a 1505 printing of *Ein botte* and perpetuated in some instances even until today, that Gertrud of Helfta and the abbess Gertrud of Hackeborn were the same person.

Although Gertrud's writings, together with books by other mystics, were condemned in 1573 by the Jesuit general Mercurian, her fame nevertheless began to spread into Italy, France, Spain, and Central and South America. During the seventeenth century, she became the patroness of the West Indies. Due to the markedly Benedictine spirituality of her writings, Gertrud has been venerated as a saint within the Benedictine order since 1606. Though she was never canonized through the usual bureaucratic process, in 1738, Pope Clement XIII extended her cult to the entire Church. Her feast day is now the same as the day of her death, November 16. Gertrud is the only German woman ever to receive the title "the Great."

See also Anna of Munzingen; Beatrijs van Nazareth/van Tienen; Beguines; Bride of Christ/*Brautmystik*; Mechthild of Hackeborn; Mechthild of Magdeburg; Rules for Canonesses, Nuns, and Recluses

BIBLIOGRAPHY

Primary Sources
Gertrud of Helfta. *Ein botte der götlichen miltekeit*. Translated (Modern German) by Otmar Wieland. Ottobeuren, Germany: Bayerische Benediktineracademie; Augsburg: Winfried-Werk, 1973.
———. *Revelationes Gertrudianae ac Mechtildianae*. Edited by the Benedictine Monks of Solesmes. Poitiers and Paris: Oudin, 1875.
———. *Œuvres spirituelles*. Edited and translated (Modern French) by Jacques Hourlier, Albert Schmitt, et al. Sources chrétiennes, 127, 139, 143, 255, 331. Paris: Éditions du Cerf, 1967–1986. [Bilingual Latin-French ed. with notes].
———. [*Exercitia Spiritualia*]. *Spiritual Exercises*. Translated with notes and introduction by Gertrud Jaron Lewis and Jack Lewis. Cistercian Fathers, 49. Kalamazoo, Mich.: Cistercian Publications, 1989.

———. [*Legatus divinae pietatis*, Book 3]. *The Herald of God's Loving Kindness*. Translated by Alexandra Barratt. Cistercian Fathers, 63. Kalamazoo, Mich.: Cistercian Publications, 1999.

———. [*Legatus divinae pietatis*, Books 1–2]. *The Herald of God's Loving Kindness*. Translated by Alexandra Barratt. Cistercian Fathers, 35. Kalamazoo, Mich.: Cistercian Publications, 1991.

Mechthild of Hackeborn. [*Liber spiritualis gratiae*]. *The Booke of Gostlye Grace*. Edited by Teresa Halligan. Toronto: Pontifical Institute of Medieval Studies, 1979. [Middle English translation with modern notes].

Secondary Sources

Bynum, Carolyn Walker. *Jesus as Mother: Studies in the Spirituality of the High Middle Ages*. Berkeley and Los Angeles: University of California Press, 1982.

Cross, F. T., et al. "Gertrude the Great, St." In *The Oxford Dictionary of the Christian Church*. 3rd ed. Oxford and New York: Oxford University Press, 1997.

Dinzelbacher, Peter. *Vision und Visionsliteratur im Mittelalter*. Stuttgart: Hiersmann, 1981.

Ehrenschwendtner, Marie-Luise. "Puellae litteratae: The Vernacular in the Dominican Convents." In *Medieval Women in their Communities*, edited by Diane Watt, 49–71. Cardiff, Wales: University of Wales Press, 1997.

Holsinger, Bruce W. *Music, Body and Desire in Medieval Culture: Hildegard of Bingen to Chaucer*. Figurae: Reading Medieval Culture. Stanford, Calif.: Stanford University Press, 2001.

Jenkins, Eve B. "St. Gertrude's Synecdoche: The Problem of Writing the Sacred Heart." *Essays in Medieval Studies* 14 (1998): 29–37.

Ruh, Kurt. "Gertrud von Helfta: Ein neues Gertrud-Bild." *Zeitschrift für deutsches Altertum und deutsche Literatur* 121 (1992): 1–20.

———. *Geschichte der abentländischen Mystik. II: Frauenmystik und Franziskanische Mystik der Frühzeit*. Munich: Beck, 1993.

Petroff, Elizabeth Alvida. *Medieval Women's Visionary Literature*. New York and Oxford: Oxford University Press, 1986.

Voaden, Rosalynn. "All Girls Together: Community, Gender and Vision at Helfta." In *Medieval Women in their Communities*, edited by Diane Watt, 72–91. Cardiff: University of Wales Press, 1997.

ALBRECHT CLASSEN

GERTRUDE OF NIVELLES, ST. (626–659). One of the most popular saints of northern Europe, Gertrude was the first abbess of Nivelles, in modern-day Belgium, and an ascetic mystic. She was noted for her hospitality toward pilgrims and for helping Irish monks, among others, and was also revered as the saintly guardian against plagues of vermin. Mice and rats often figure in pictorial representations of her. Gertrude's biography consists of two *vitae* (lives): an anonymous *vita* (c. 670) possibly composed by a priest at Nivelles (Effros; McNamara), and a second life written probably by an Irish monk at Fosse after 693.

Born in Landen, Belgium, she was a daughter of Pippin (Pepin) of Landen (Pippin the Elder), palace mayor to Dagobert, king of Austrasia (comprising what are now eastern France, western Germany and the Netherlands) and founder of the Carolingian dynasty (Charlemagne's family). Her mother, Itta (Ida), was very devout. Gertrude herself had chosen the religious life when young, and thus her *vita* begins with her refusal to follow King Dagobert's plans to marry her off for his political gain, as he schemed to do with other saintly ladies such as Rictrude and Sadalberga. We know her pious mother Ida supported her in this choice. Her father may have too, for political reasons. For Gertrude, becoming a nun provided a safe haven from various pressures in addition to fulfilling her spiritual needs (McNamara et al.). Both mother and daughter took their vows and founded the Nivelles convent after the deaths of Dagobert and Pippin (640). Pippin and Ida had another daughter, Begga, who did marry—the son of Pippin's palace ally, Arnulf, bishop of Metz. Begga (d. 693)—who also took the veil after being widowed, founded an abbey at Andennes, and later became a saint. Precisely what monastic rule governed Nivelles, a double monastery (housing monks and nuns as separate communities under one roof), is not known, perhaps a mix of Columban and Benedictine. An excellent convent administrator, Gertrude also practiced austere self-denial. Her ascetic routine took such a severe toll on her health that she had to resign in 656, whereupon her niece, St. Wilfetrudis, took over the monastery, and Gertrude devoted herself entirely to scriptural study, penance, and prayer until her death three years later at age thirty-three, the same as Christ's at His death, as many have noted.

Gertrude is also known for her unusual request to be buried simply in a hair shirt and old woman pilgrim's veil (like Melania [d. 438/9], "clad only in her virtues"). The significance of her burial garb has been analyzed recently by Bonnie Effros as one intended to convey the virtuous Gertude's "amuletic powers," whose "transmission also authenticated Gertude's status by linking her with authority of cosmological significance which transcended the boundaries of the present context." Thanks to Ida's, Gertrude's, and Begga's renown, and the second *vita* of Gertrude dated after Begga's death in 693, Nivelles became a saintly cult center, replacing an ancient pagan shrine in that same place. This sacred continuity and family connection greatly aided the Pippinids (Pepin's family, ancestors of the Carolingians) in their eventually successful attempt to wrest the throne permanently from the Merovingians a century later (McNamara et al.). Meanwhile, Gertrude's brother Grimoald briefly overthrew the Merovingians and ruled Austrasia after her death, until he himself was killed. The abbey of Nivelles then suffered persecution by the Merovingian royal family. Yet by felicitous backlash, this mistreatment triggered renewed veneration of Gertrude in the heart of the Pippinid power base, and thus achieved the protection Grimoald had hoped to obtain for his sister's abbey as well as sacred validation of their family's (Pippinid-Carolingian) right to the throne. Despite her humble choice of mortuary costume, Gertrude's tomb, moved to the basilica of St. Peter, is of marble, centrally located, and swathed in miracles surrounding her relics. Her feast day is March 17, for which she is also the patron saint of gardeners.

See also Aldegund, St.; Chelles, Nun of; Double Monasteries; Hagiography (Female Saints); Melania the Younger, St.; Nunneries, Merovingian; Radegund, St.; Relics and Medieval Women; Rules for Canonesses, Nuns, and Recluses

BIBLIOGRAPHY

Primary Sources
Anonymous. *Vita sanctæ Gerterudis.* Revised ed. by Bruno Krusch. *Monumenta Germaniae Historica. Scriptores Rerum Merovingicarum,* 2: 447–74. Hannover, Germany: Hahn, 1956. Original 1888. [Latin texts of both lives based on two manuscripts, A and B, mainly B].
———. "Gertrude, Abbess of Nivelles." Translated by John Cox. In *Sainted Women of the Dark Ages.* Edited by Jo Ann McNamara et al., 220–34. Durham, N.C.: Duke University Press, 1992. [Translated from the B *Vita*].

Secondary Sources
Dierkens, Alain. *Abbayes et chapitres entre Sambre et Meuse (VIIᵉ–XIᵉ siècles): contribution à l'histoire religieuse des campagnes du haut moyen âge.* Sigmaringen, Germany: Jan Thorbecke, 1985.

Effros, Bonnie. "Symbolic Expressions of Sanctity: Gertrude of Nivelles in the Context of Merovingian Mortuary Custom." *Viator* 27 (1996): 1–10.

Essen, Léon van der. *Étude critique et littéraire sur les vitæ des saints mérovingiens de l'ancienne Belgique.*
Université de Louvain, 17. Louvain, Belgium: Bureaux de recueil, 1907.

McNamara, Jo Ann, et al. *See above under* Primary Sources

NADIA MARGOLIS

GHERARDESCA OF PISA (c.1200/1207–c.1267). The Blessed Gherardesca of Pisa,
Italian Apocalyptic visionary, was a Tertiary (member of a mendicant, or Third Order who
does not take vows) in the Camaldolensian order (so-named for its founding monastery at
Camaldoli, Italy, c.1020). In the Latin text of the *Acta Sanctorum* (May 29), she is cited as
"Beata Gerardesca Pisana, Tertiary Camaldolensian." The only surviving material on her
is a *vita* (biography) written by her unnamed confessor and friend, a brother in the same
order, to whom she dictated visions, revelations, and sermons. She probably spoke in Italian, since there is no mention of her knowing Latin, but her words are recorded in Latin in
the *vita*, following standard practice. The *vita* as we have it is fragmentary, and the *Acta
Sanctorum* text is based on the fragment of the last *vita*, beginning: "Incipit historia sive
vita Sanctae Gerardeschae, de civitate Pisana, quae apud monasterium S. Savini re-
quiescit" ("Here begins the story or life of Sant Gherardesca, of the city of Pisa, who rests
at the monastery of St. Savino"). It is part of a collection of lives of various saints
belonging to the Monastery of St. Sylvester in Pisa.

Gherardesca of Pisa's biography is composed largely of verbatim accounts of her visionary experiences, often introduced by a simple "and then Gherardesca spoke" or "the
saint opened her mouth and said." Some of the visions are fragmentary due to the poor
condition of the unique Latin manuscript, but others seem to have been edited to conceal
the identity of persons who were still alive. Her biographer sees her as a prophetess and
hints that she met with much hostility from some of the brothers in the Camoldolese
monastery near where she had her hermitage as a tertiary. She often speaks of one monk
in particular, of whom she was very fond and with whom she always wished to share her
spiritual consolations; her confessor/biographer never admits that this "certain monk" is
himself, but in context it is clear that they are the same man.

Nothing is mentioned about her family origins; this is unusual, especially considering
that the *vita* was written by her contemporary in Pisa, and that she was well known both
as a visionary and as a mediator of disputes. She belonged to the noble family of the Della
Gherardesca; monastic recruiting among the aristocracy was common at that time (see
Benvenuti Papi). We are told in passing that a relative of hers was abbot of St. Savino, but
the only immediate family member mentioned, not by name, is her strong-willed mother,
with whom she had a difficult relationship. Gherardesca's vocation was precocious. At
seven she ran away from home to join a convent, which she later left at her mother's
urging, and then even married to please her. Her biography's manner of retelling this
episode probably reflects her own ambivalence: "When she had been there for some time,
and her mother had been grieving sorely over her absence, she was induced by her
mother's pain—or perhaps it was because she had not yet reached the maturity of age—at
any rate, in all simplicity, at the voice of her mother, she left the monastery."

Unhappy in marriage, she tried to compensate for it by imitating as far as possible the austere life she had lived at the convent, by mortifying her flesh with fasting and prayers, and by being a public example of good works. She did not become pregnant, which evidently disturbed her mother more than it did her. A rather odd incident follows, which evidently circulated as evidence of her special status. Her mother "prayed ceaselessly to the Lord that her daughter might be given a son," and finally the Lord settled the issue by appearing to her in a dream saying that her would give Gherardesca St. John the Evangelist as her son. In token of this, he gave her three healing herbs: sage, savin, and rosemary, which she promptly flaunted to her neighbors as a sign of His special affection for her. The mother's joyous and vain response was deemed inappropriate, however, causing ulcerous sores to erupt on her arms from the herbs, which He only deigned to heal in a mood of clemency, after two years.

Gherardesca, believing more and more firmly that she could not "earn eternity in the world," convinced her husband to enter the religious life with her. The very day he consented to this, Gherardesca rushed him to the abbot of St. Savino, a relative of hers, who immediately received both of them into the "sacred assembly of the monks of the monastery." Now Gherardesca was happy; she began to smile again, and radiated her happiness out from the cell to which she was assigned, just outside the male monastery. Her spiritual gifts grew in this environment, and her visions were often announced by the appearance of an eagle, the symbol of John the Evangelist.

Perhaps because of her preoccupation with "earn[ing] eternity," many of Gherardesca's visions concerned the afterlife. The content and style of her visions were influenced by the Apocalypse of St. John (Book of Revelations), her favorite saint. Some of them are remarkably vivid and moving, and suggest Dante in their scope and imagery; for example, she details an allegorical vision of a journey to heaven, hell, and purgatory. (Dante was born in nearby Florence in 1265, about the year Gherardesca died.) Also like Dante, Gherardesca was sensitive to music, and most of her visions of heaven, or of St. John the Evangelist, are filled with auditory as well as visual imagery. She was evidently trained in several types of meditation, for sometimes her visions seemed to derive from meditations on the life of Christ and his mother (the system of meditation taught to most women), while others are more abstract. "[She] was thinking with great circlings of her mind about the enormity and nature of Divine Potency." She sought the divine potency everywhere, in heaven and on earth, even in a piece of straw: "For in that straw there appeared to the saint the whole life eternal with the omnipotence of God."

Her visions, even those that began abstractly, were almost always structured around a symbolic object—a ring, a flowering branch, a crown—or around specific landscapes or cityscapes. Her lengthy vision of the heavenly Jerusalem begins with a mental ascent through the heavens: "In a circle surrounding it [Jerusalem] there were seven citadels [...] rising high up in the mountains and hewn out of costly stone, each with stairs for ascending and descending made of precious jewels." Some of her narratives are quite clearly sermons, utilizing material from her visions interpreted allegorically by the use of scriptural references. For example, in chapter 4, paragraph 40, she tells about the souls freed from the pains of Purgatory who were hastening to the joys of eternal glory, citing the Psalms, Ecclesiastes, and Isaiah as authorities in her three-phased prescription for the soul's cleanliness, anointment with precious unguents and acquisition of virtue. As a visionary, Gherardesca exhibited many of the physical traits associated with mysticism; she was often seen to levitate during prayer, and sometimes her body was so lifeless during and immediately after a vision that she seemed to be dead. Her gift of prophecy (by which medieval authors usually mean mind-reading and predicting the future) involved her in familial and monastic interrelationships requiring great caution and tact, since she knew more than anyone else about sins her colleagues and neighbors were committing.

One reads this *vita*, her one extant text, with pain; Gherardesca was obviously a gifted woman deprived of the opportunity to develop her abilities. Without her "certain monk" of whom she was so fond, we would not even know of her creativity.

Though she was buried in the church of St. Savinus in Pisa, as her *vita*'s opening states, the church suffered such damage in the medieval wars between Pisa and Florence that there is no possibility of determining her grave. The presence of a contemporary cult is also indicated by a portrait of her on a panel painting belonging to the Pisan church of St. Michael in the City; here she is depicted as one among a number of Camaldolensian saints. Neither the day nor the year of her death is known for certain, but her feast is celebrated on May 29.

See also Agnes of Assisi, St.; Angela of Foligno, Blessed; Convents; Umiltà of Faenza, St.

BIBLIOGRAPHY

Primary Sources
Anonymous Camaldolensian Monk. "Vita de B. Gerardesca Pisana, Ordinis Camaldulensis tertiaria." In *Acta Sanctorum May VII. 29 Maii*, 160–75. Antwerp, 1688.
———. Translated with commentary in Elizabeth A. Petroff, *Consolation of the Blessed*, 85–120. New York: Alta Gaia, 1979.
———. "The Life of Blessed Gherardesca of Pisa." Translated with commentary by Elizabeth A. Petroff. *Vox Benedictina* 9.2 (1992): 227–86.

Secondary Sources
[See also commentary to translations listed above].
Benvenuti Papi, Anna. "Mendicant Friars and Female *Pinzochere* in Tuscany: From Social Marginality to Models of Sanctity." In *Women and Religion in Medieval and Renaissance Italy*, edited by Daniel Bornstein and Roberto Rusconi, 84–103. Translated by Margery J. Schneider. Chicago: University of Chicago Press, 1996. Original *Mistiche e devote nell'Italia tardomedievale*. Naples: Liguori, 1992. [See p. 96 n. 8].
Frugoni, Chiara. "Female Mystics, Visions, and Iconography." In *Women and Religion*, 130–64. *See above entry*. [See esp. pp. 131, 134–35].
Weinstein, Donald, and Rudolph M. Bell. *Saints and Society: The Two Worlds of Western Christendom, 1000–1700*. Chicago: University of Chicago Press, 1982.

ELIZABETH A. PETROFF

GILDS, WOMEN IN. *See* **Guilds, Women in**

GODIVA, LADY (11th century). Godiva was an English noble benefactor and the wife of Earl Leofric of Mercia, a major English kingdom. The legend of Lady Godiva tells of how she freed the town of Coventry from high taxes collected by her husband Leofric, an Anglo-Saxon earl. Guided by her love of the Virgin Mary, Godiva could not witness the hardships or endure the complaints of the townspeople and begged Leofric to lift the heavy taxes and tolls he had imposed on them. He initially refused to grant her request, but finally agreed to it on one condition: she had to ride naked on horseback through the town center. Godiva complied, but her long hair hid her nudity. After she accomplished her task, the earl released the town from its financial obligations. Later versions of the legend report that the people were so grateful that they went inside and closed their shutters so as not to see her. Only Tom the town tailor desired to see this beautiful naked woman and tried to look out his window as she rode by. "Peeping Tom" was instantly struck blind.

Historical sources document the existence of Godiva (Godgifu) and Leofric as well-placed members of the Anglo-Saxon nobility. They were the countess and count of Mercia and the parents of Aelfgar, Earl of East Anglia, in England. Leofric died in 1057 and Godiva soon after the Norman Conquest (1066). She is mentioned in the *Domesday Book*—a survey and census of most of England compiled in 1086 at the order of William the Conqueror—simply as a landholder in Staffordshire, England. The *Anglo-Saxon Chronicles* establish them both as respected patrons of the Church, noting especially Godiva's piety and devotion to the Virgin Mary. Together they endowed various English monasteries such as Coventry, Wenloc, Evesham, and Lenton. The story of the ride, however, is clearly apocryphal and does not appear until Roger of Wendover (d. 1236) included it in his thirteenth-century chronicle, the *Flores historiarum* (*Flowers of History*). Matthew Paris (d. 1259) subsequently copied the legend into his *Chronica Maiora* (*Great Chronicle*), and Ranulph Higden (d. 1364) related it in his popular world history, the *Polychronicon* (literally, *Multi-Chronicle*). The widespread use of these three histories, which all treat the story as a historical event, ensured the legend's continued inclusion in other chronicles and histories through the seventeenth century, when the figure of Peeping Tom first appeared.

The legend is easily traced through these monastic chronicles, but assessing the legend's popularity outside monastic circles is more difficult. Higden's *Polychronicon* provides the first evidence of the legend's oral transmission. Ranulph Higden, a monk in the Benedictine Abbey of St. Wereburg in Chester, England, gave an abbreviated account, but he added a minor element to the legend that had not appeared in earlier versions: that despite Godiva's ride, horses were not exempt from tolls. Coventry, as well as the monastery of St. Albans, where Roger of Wendover and Matthew Paris had resided, and Chester, Higden's home, were all located along the old Roman road known as Watling Street. The road was a convenient conduit for stories as people moved along it, and Higden's refashioning and addition suggest that he knew the tale from sources other than monastic chronicles.

Occasional medieval references to the legend can be found within Coventry itself. A stained glass window in the Holy Trinity Church, erected in the fourteenth century in honor of Godiva and Leofric, contained the verse: "I Luriche, for love of thee doe make Coventry tol-fre" ("I, Leofric, for the love of thee, make Coventry toll-free") (Aquilla-Clarke; Warner). In 1495, as part of a revolt against an increase in tolls on wool and cloth, some citizens nailed to the door of St. Michael's Church the following verse: "Be it known and understand this Cite shuld be free and nowe is bonde [bound]. Dame Good Eve made it free; and nowe the custome for wool and the draperie" (Aquilla-Clarke). By the sixteenth and seventeenth centuries, the city and its guilds celebrated Godiva's ride with a

Mass, guild elections, and a fair with a procession. It appears that the story enjoyed an active oral tradition in medieval England.

Most scholarship on the legend has focused on its alleged pagan roots, and, indeed, the need for a sacrifice to maintain land may be of pre-Christian origin. At least four similar legends exist that ostensibly record events from the English Middle Ages. These also tell of wives whose husbands forced them to circumscribe a particular piece of land under difficult and sometimes fatal circumstances to free it from legal or financial obligations. The medieval parochial practice of beating the bounds similarly defined the status of particular parcels of land with respect to a group or individual. Yet the legend of Godiva first appears within the context of growing urban freedoms during the thirteenth and fourteenth centuries. Like other English towns, Coventry sought control of its own economic affairs. Even though its central location made it a lucrative place that its overlords, the Earl of Chester and the Prior of Coventry, were loath to relinquish, Coventry received a charter of incorporation from Edward III in 1345, after years of litigation and violent confrontation. The legend helped to legitimate and to justify this struggle by providing the city with a foundation myth that predated its struggles in the twelfth and thirteenth centuries.

In the Godiva legend, Coventry's concerns over its legal status found expression in women's images and activities. Godiva's role as mediator, her long hair, and her nudity simultaneously invoked the Virgin Mary, Mary Magdalene, and Eve, and the blending of their images and the symbols associated with them made Godiva an ambiguous figure and made the legend a powerful commentary on Coventry's own history and position within medieval society. By both defining and undermining appropriate female behavior, the legend expressed and resolved the tensions emerging from Coventry's changing legal status and evolving community identity. Godiva's ride displayed heightened ambiguities about her status as both a noble servant and pious whore, which gave expression to Coventry's own ambiguous position between subordination and independence. Even before the legend's first appearance, Godiva had been linked to the Virgin Mary through her various acts of piety, and within the legend, Godiva's role as intercessor on behalf of the town strengthened this tie. Her nudity and long hair identified her with Eve and the Magdalene, who both have long hair and are naked in medieval iconography. In both graphic art and literature nudity connoted—ambivalently—the prelapsarian (before the Fall of Man and Expulsion from Eden) state of grace and the abandonment of worldly possessions on the one hand, and lust and sexual dishonor on the other. Eve's naked body symbolized both humanity's innocence and its depravity. Likewise, long hair served to identify not only women's femininity but also their sexuality. Married women bound up their hair and kept it covered, while prostitutes were threatened with having their hair cut off. Yet the Magdalene became a hermit after renouncing her life as a prostitute and paradoxically the only clothing or covering she had was her long hair. Nudity and hair were thus markers of status or position whose presence in the legend conveyed contradictory or ambivalent meanings.

As Godiva moved through the town, the meaning of these markers changed to reflect changes in the town's status. Initially she was the town's mediator and supplicant, willing to sacrifice her own honor for the town. Her husband's demands in exchange for the town's freedom changed her image to one of potential wantonness, since loosening her hair and removing her clothes invited comparisons with Eve as temptress and Magdalene as prostitute. But her success at both freeing Coventry and maintaining her honor restored to her the honor due the penitent and virtuous Magdalene and the prelapsarian Eve. Indeed, her name, Godiva—meaning "gift of God"—was often then pronounced, and spelled, to resemble "Good-Eve," which, as Marina Warner shows, she was. As she gave up her clothes, so Leofric gave up his power over the town. Her nudity was the nudity of innocence and renunciation, her unbound hair, the protection of the selfless servant of God. At all points Godiva behaved as some sort of ideal woman, but she was none of these ideal women. Rather, she operated as a liminal figure who articulated, through the complex imagery of the female body, Coventry's rite of passage from unfree to free city.

The role and position of women was something that a variety of medieval institutions felt obliged to define and to regulate, and this in turn let credibility and authority to those institutions, be it the church or the city. Godiva herself embodies the different female roles regulated by various urban laws—virgin, wife, and prostitute. Her ride, therefore, liberates Coventry through symbolic actions instantly recognizable to the populace as legitimizing the town's own rights. And since the main issue deals with money, the legend represents in particular the struggle for control of Coventry's market, site of Godiva's ride: there where people exchange goods, Godiva changes the city's legal status. In a metaphorical sense then, Godiva's noble, female body may be interpreted as comparable to the currency of exchange, thus equating Coventry's goals of increased economic autonomy with freer notions of female propriety.

Yet it could be argued that our appreciation of Godiva's historical value was made possible by her widespread and enduring literary fascination beyond the chronicles. Modern authors inspired by her legend range from Walter Landor's influential *Imaginary Conversations* and Tennyson's poem in the Victorian spirit of the nineteenth century, to twentieth-century novelists like Austria's religious dramatist Max Mell and Italy's Alberto Moravia. Works in the visual and plastic arts also abound (Hafele; Warner), like the bronze statue of her done in 1949 by Sir William Reid Dick, which stands in Coventry.

See also Guilds, Women in; Mary, Blessed Virgin, in the Middle Ages; Prostitution; Shore, Elizabeth (Jane); Virginity

BIBLIOGRAPHY

Primary Sources

Higden, Ranulph. Polychronicon Ranulphi Higden monachi Cestrensis, *Together with the English Translations of John Trevisa and of an Unknown Writer of the Fifteenth Century.* Edited by Churchill Babington and Rev. Joseph Rawson Lumby. Rolls Series, 41. 9 vols. London: Longman, Green, 1865–1886. Reprint Nendeln, Liechtenstein: Kraus Reprints, 1964.

Paris, Matthew. *Matthaei Parisiensis, monachi Sancti Albani, Chronica majora,* Vol. 1. Edited by Henry Richards Luard. Rolls Series, 57. 7 vols. London, Longman, 1872–1883.

Roger of Wendover. *Rogeri de Wendover Chronica; sive, Flores historiarum, nunc primum.* Edited by Henry O. Coxe. 4 vols. London: English Historical Society, 1841–1842.

Landor, Walter Savage, 1775–1864. *Imaginary Conversations of Literary Men and Statesmen.* 2nd series. 2 vols. London: James Duncan, 1829. [Godiva and Leofric in vol. 2].

Mell, Max. *Die drei Grazien des Traumes: funf Novellen* Leipzig, Germany: Insel-Verlag, 1906.

Moravia, Alberto. [*Un'altra vita*]. *Lady Godiva, and Other Stories.* Translated from the Italian by Angus Davidson. London: Secker & Warburg, 1975.

Tennyson, Alfred. "Godiva, a Tale of Coventry." In *Poems,* 281–84. London: Macmillan, 1893.

Secondary Sources

Aquilla-Clarke, Ronald, and Patrick A. E. Day. *Lady Godiva: Images of a Legend in Art & Society.* Catalog of an exhibition held at the Herbert Art Gallery and Museum. Coventry, U.K.: Leisure Services, Arts and Museums Division, 1982.

Bolton, Diane K. "The Legend of Lady Godiva." In *Victoria County Histories: Warwickshire*, edited by W. B. Stephens, vol. 3. London: Institute for Historical Research, 1969.

Burbidge, F. Bliss. *Old Coventry and Lady Godiva.* Birmingham, U.K.: Cornish Bros., 1952.

Davidson, H. R. Ellis. "The Legend of Lady Godiva." *Folklore* 80 (1969): 107–21.

Donoghue, Daniel. *Lady Godiva: A Literary History of the Legend.* Oxford: Blackwell, 2003.

French, Katherine L. "The Legend of Lady Godiva and the Image of the Female Body." *Journal of Medieval History* 18 (1992): 3–19.

Hafele, Karl. *Die Godivasage und ihre Behandlung in der Literatur: mit einem Überblick über die Darstellungen der Sage in der bildenden Kunst.* Anglistische Forschungen, 66. Heidelberg, Germany: Carl Winter, 1929.

Hartland. E.Sidney. "Peeping Tom and Lady Godiva." *Folklore* 27 (1890): 207–26.

Phythian-Adams, Charles. *Violation of a City: Coventry and the Urban Crisis of the Late Middle Ages.* Cambridge: Cambridge University Press, 1975.

Warner, Marina. *Monuments and Maidens: The Allegory of the Female Form.* New York: Atheneum, 1985.

KATHERINE L. FRENCH

GONZAGA, CECILIA (1425–1451). An Italian humanist and scholar, she was the daughter of Gianfrancesco Gonzaga (1395–1444) and Paola Malatesta da Rimini, and the granddaughter of Battista da Montefeltro Malatesta (1383–1450). Her early education included a mastery of Greek and Latin under the instruction of Vittorino da Feltre (1378–1446), a noted humanist teacher. Pressured by her father to marry the Oddantonio di Montefeltro, duke of Urbino, Cecilia Gonzaga wished to enter a convent instead. A letter written to her by the patrician Venetian humanist and theologian, Gregorio Correr (1409–1464), encouraging her commitment to a religious life supports the hypothesis that she desired also to continue her studies rather than assume a worldly role that would truncate them. Fortunately, Oddantonio proved so hateful to his subjects that her father renounced that arrangement but still disapproved of eighteen-year-old Cecilia's entering a convent, despite her mother's and Vittorino's support. But when Gianfrancesco Gonzaga died in 1444, his daughter was able to take the veil, in the company of her mother.

Gonzaga is perhaps more representative of Italian women humanists than she is unique. According to King, these women were in part tragic figures, forbidden a career in scholarship by rigid and limiting social roles, and unlikely, by virtue of their scholarship, to find satisfaction in those conventional roles. They tended either to enter convents, as Gonzaga did on her father's death, or marry and put scholarship aside, as did Costanza Varano (1428–1447) and Cassandra Fedele (1465/6–1558). In any case, few continued their studies, but those who did included Isotta Nogarola (1418–1466) and Laura Cereta (1469–1499). Gonzaga is also important as a recipient of letters from other humanists, including Costanza Varano and Gregorio Correr. Such correspondence gives us a sample of the qualities sought after and attributed to these learned women: Varano refers to Gonzaga's "noble erudition and unique eloquence," her "great knowledge of rhetoric," her "benevolence, hope and charity." She also refers to the cares and responsibilities that could impede the pursuit of letters for a woman, including self-doubt and the care of a sick mother.

Correr's letter, like Bruni's to Battista Montefeltro Malatesta, gives us an insight into social consensus on the activities and priorities appropriate to women, as well as a view of studies suitable for religious women in particular. Correr praises virginity for Cecilia, but only in the context of the convent: if she remains in the world she must marry or she will fall. As for her studies once she is in the convent, he says, "I forbid utterly the reading of secular literature, particularly the works of the poets." He urges her to read the Psalter instead of Virgil, the Gospel instead of Cicero, the Greek and Latin fathers instead of religious works in the vernacular ("nursery tales and dreamers' fantasies, such as that book by I don't know which silly woman entitled *A Mirror of Simple Souls*" [an anonymous thirteenth-century French dialogue involving allegorical-moral figures translated into Middle English and other fourteenth- and fifteenth-century languages]). Her creative powers she may use in translating spiritual passages into the vernacular "for unlettered virgins," and in writing poetry recounting the stories found in Scripture. This ban on

Medallion commemorating Cecilia Gonzaga, daughter of Gianfranco Gonzaga. © The Art Archive/Galleria Franchetti Venice/Dagli Orti (A).

secular literature is not gender specific, however, but applies to all religious, both men and women.

See also Battista da Montefeltro Malatesta; Cereta, Laura; Fedele, Cassandra; Humanists, Italian Women, Issues and Theory; Nogarola, Isotta; Varano, Costanza

BIBLIOGRAPHY

Primary Sources
Correr, Gregorio. "Letter to the Virgin Cecilia Gonzaga, on Fleeing this Worldly Life." In *Her Immaculate Hand: Selected Works by and about the Women Humanists of Quattrocento Italy*, translated with commentary in Margaret King and Albert Rabil, Jr., 93–105. Medieval & Renaissance Texts & Studies, 20. Binghamton, N.Y.: Center for Medieval & Early Renaissance Studies, 1983. [Excellent introduction and notes].
Varano, Costanza. "Letter to Cecilia Gonzaga." In King and Rabil, 53–55. *See above entry.*

Secondary Source
King, Margaret L. "Book-Lined Cells: Women and Humanism in the Early Italian Renaissance." In *Beyond Their Sex: Learned Women of the European Past*, edited by Patricia H. Labalme, 66–90. New York: New York University Press, 1980.

REGINA PSAKI

GORMONDA OF MONTPELLIER (early 13th century). Gormonda of Montpellier, or de Montpeslier, as she was called in early southern-French language, was a woman troubadour, or *trobairitz*, author of the first-known political poem written in France by a woman. This poem, titled "Greu m'es a durar" ("It's hard to bear it") after its opening verse, consists in a single preserved *sirventes* (sometimes spelled *sirventès*)—a reproachful, song-like poetic genre presumably originating among servants despising their masters, hence its name—written as a parodic rebuttal to Guilhem Figueira's (b. c.1195) popular and lengthy attack on Rome and its papacy. Modern scholar Joseph Salvat characterizes Guilhem's poem, also a *sirventes* as its title-first line suggests—"D'un sirventes far" ("To make a *sirventes*")—as the most brazen anti-papal satire of the Middle Ages. Both poems were evidently composed during the final years of the Albigensian Crusade (1208–1229) waged by the Church and northern-French to rein in the powerful counts of Toulouse and their heretical Cathar sect prior to the Inquisition.

Gormonda de Monpeslier was, as her name implies, a resident of Montpellier, in southern France. She probably completed her 220-line poem—one of the longest works and one of the few *sirventes* ever composed by a *trobairitz*—not long after Guilhem composed his (c.1228), certainly after the death of King Louis (1226) but before the treaty ending the war between Louis IX and Raimon VII of Toulouse, signed in mid-April 1229. Gormonda's poem as we now have it may only be a fragment, lacking three stanzas, as accepted by scholars like Matilda Bruckner. This surmise derives mainly from the fact that Guilhem's poem extends over twenty-three stanzas, while Gormonda's contains only twenty, and that her twenty stanzas closely parallel his first twenty as part of her refutational strategy. However, other critics explain the disparity by asserting that only the first twenty stanzas of Guilhem's poem had become widely circulated. Whatever the case, Gormonda's *sirventes*, as analyzed by Katharina Städtler, stands as the clearest political statement ever conveyed in any *trobairitz* pen, whereby she consistently and vehemently contradicts Guilhem, stanza by stanza, to demolish the falseness of his words. In defending the Church, Gormonda favors King Louis VIII's recent siege of Avignon, and laments his death in Auvergne as he returned to Paris on November 8, 1226. She sees Louis's demise as the inevitable fulfillment of one of Merlin's prophecies, thus denying Guilhem's accusation that the death of "good King Louis" had been the result of the "false preaching" of the Church. She goes on to extol Rome as a symbol of the Christian faith, thus strongly refuting Guilhem's bitter portrayal of the papal city as a "greedy wolf," a "tonsured serpent" fathered by a viper, and an "intimate friend" of the devil. It is, Guilhem concludes, not surprising that the world falls into error, "for you [Rome] have cast the century into torment and war." Gormonda's reply is a call to arms, a war cry supporting the Albigensian Crusade (the Church's longstanding war against the Cathar heretics of southern France): "Qui vol esser sals,/ades deu la crotz penre/per ereties fals/dechazer e mespenre" ("Whoever wishes to be saved must take the cross to destroy and bring ruin to false heretics"]. She left no uncertainty as to whom she referred when she wrote: "Roma, lo reys grans/qu'es senhers de dreytura/als falses Tolzans/don gran malaventura" ("Rome, may the great king/who is lord of justice/Bring grave misfortune to the false people of Toulouse").

Guilhem Figueira, a native of Toulouse, is not only targeted by this general deploration, but also by a malediction aimed at him specifically, when Gormonda implores Rome to execute as a heretic "lo folh rabioz/qui tan dich fals semena" ("the rabid fool who spread such false words"). Gormonda must have taken pleasure in the subsequent capitulation of Count Raimon of Toulouse and the humiliating treaty he was forced to sign. No doubt she agreed with the author of Guilhem's *vida* (biographical sketch), probably a cleric, who contended that Guilhem wrote not for those who conducted themselves among the barons and good people, but was honored rather by "harlots" and "innkeepers."

Virtually nothing is known of Gormonda beyond her loyal, even militant, devotion to the Church, leading Städtler to suggest a Dominican affiliation. Early scholars, disparaging her as merely a "pious" woman, treated her poem more as a curiosity than a work of art. More recent critics like Städtler and Suzanne Thiolier-Méjean have revised this judgment. Without going so far as Joseph Salvat's dismissal of her poem for its lack of "souffle puissant de l'accusateur" ("polemical-accusative fire power"), we concede that while her use of imagery often pales beside Guilhem's, her poem nonetheless possesses an undeniable vitality and conviction of its own. The political-poetic confrontation between Gormonda and Guilhem, remarkably devoid of gender problems, encapsulates the fervent spiritual divisiveness threatening the flourishing, uniquely refined culture of Occitania (Languedoc region, southern France) during the thirteenth century.

See also Gaudairenca; *Trobairitz*

BIBLIOGRAPHY

Primary Sources
Gormonda. In *Songs of the Women Troubadours*, edited and translated by Matilda Tomaryn Bruckner, Laurie Shepard, and Sarah White, 106–19, 182–85. New York and London: Garland, 1995. New ed. 2000. [Most authoritative: original texts, notes, and English translation].
————. In *Les Poétesses provençales du moyen âge et de nos jours*, edited by Jules Véran, 112–14. Paris: A. Quillet, 1946.
———— and Guilhelm. In *Guilhem Figueira: ein provenzalischer Troubadour*, edited by Emil Levy, 8, 74–78. Berlin: Liebrecht, 1880.

Secondary Sources
Anglade, Joseph. *Les Troubadours*, 194–95. Paris: Armand Colin, 1924.
Rieger, Angelica. "Un *sirventès* féminin—la *trobairitz* Gormonda de Montpeslier." In *Actes du premier congrès international de l'Association internationale d'Études occitanes*, edited by Peter T. Ricketts, 423–55. Westfield College, London: AIEO, 1987.
Salvat, Joseph. "Guilhem Figueira." In *Dictionnaire des lettres françaises: Le Moyen âge*, edited by Geneviève Hasenohr and Michel Zink, 599. Paris: Livre de Poche, 1992.
Städtler, Katharina. "The *Sirventès* by Gormonda de Monpeslier." In *The Voice of the Trobairitz: Perspectives on the Women Troubadours*, edited by William Paden, 129–55. Philadelphia: University of Pennsylvania Press, 1989.
Thiolier-Méjean, Suzanne. *Les Poésies satiriques et morales des troubadours du XIIe siècle à la fin du XIIIe siècle*, 359, n. 2. Paris: Nizet, 1978.

JUNE HALL MCCASH

GRAZIDA (Grazida Lizier) (1298–c.1320s). The accused heretic and adulteress Grazida lived in the village of Montaillou in southwestern France. She is known only through a five-page document recorded by the Inquisition under Jacques Fournier, bishop of Pamiers (1318–1325), during his investigation of suspected heretics in the region. Her deposition states that she was the daughter of Fabrisse and Pons Clergue, but that her mother was forced out of the Clergue household because she refused to accept the dualistic religion of Catharism, the faith professed by many of the villagers. Having lost the security of a *domus* (respectable household), Fabrisse became a tavern-keeper and Grazida grew up with the stigma of illegitimacy. At the age of fourteen or fifteen, she was seduced by Pierre Clergue, the parish priest, with her mother's knowledge and consent. Grazida herself describes the relationship as one of mutual love, although she admits to being troubled by the discovery that the priest was her mother's cousin. Not long after their initial encounters, Pierre arranged a marriage between Grazida and Pierre Lizier, but continued to have sexual relations with her as well as with other women in Montaillou. It appears that the Inquisitors' primary intention was to use Grazida's testimony as a means to indict the priest on the grounds of heresy. Grazida was interrogated twice and imprisoned for more than seven weeks between the two sessions. Her deposition offers an intriguing glimpse of heterodox views that express skepticism concerning the doctrines of both Catharism and Catholicism. It also provides insight into Grazida's personal beliefs concerning love, sexuality, and morality.

BIBLIOGRAPHY

Primary Sources
[Grazida's testimony]. *Le Registre d'Inquisition de Jacques Fournier*. Edited by Jean Duvernoy, vol. 1. 3 vols. Toulouse: Privat, 1965. [Latin text based on Vatican MS Vat. reg. lat. 4030].
———. *Le Registre d'Inquisition de Jacques Fournier*. Edited and translated [Modern French] by Jean Duvernoy. Introduction by Emmanuel Le Roy Ladurie, vol. 1. 3 vols. Paris and The Hague: Mouton, 1978.
———. In Dronke, 265–69. *See below.* [Latin text].

Secondary Sources
Biller, Peter. "Cathars and Material Women." In *Medieval Theology and the Natural Body*, edited by Peter Biller and A. J. Minnis, 61–107. York Studies in Medieval Theology, 1. Woodbridge, Suffolk, U.K. and Rochester, N.Y.: Boydell & Brewer/York Medieval Press, 1997.
Decaux, Alain. *Histoire des Françaises I: La Soumission*. Paris: Perrin, 1972.
Dronke, Peter. *Women Writers of the Middle Ages: A Critical Study of Texts from Perpetua (†203) to Marguerite Porete (†1310)*. Cambridge: Cambridge University Press, 1984.
Le Roy Ladurie, Emmanuel. *Montaillou*. Paris: Gallimard, 1975.

DIANA L. MURPHY

GRISELDA (fl. 1350s). Also called Griseldis, Griselidis, Grisildis, Grissell (plus others), Griselda, whose name would become synonymous with unflagging womanly patience and constancy, was, according to the standard plot, a peasant woman who married a marquis after promising absolute obedience to him. To test this promise, the marquis took away her two children under the pretext of killing them, publicly repudiated her, and sent her home wearing only an undergarment; then he recalled her to prepare the castle for his presumed second marriage. After she had endured all the tests willingly and without complaint, he restored the children to her and happily reinstated her as his wife.

This curious story captivated the European imagination from its earliest written versions by fourteenth-century authors including Giovanni Boccaccio (c.1313–1375) and Petrarch (Francesco Petrarca, 1304–1374) in Italy and Geoffrey Chaucer (c.1343–1400) in England. Though the versions by these authors are the most famous, Griselda's story has been rewritten repeatedly in twenty-two European languages (Morabito 1988) over the ensuing six centuries in the dominant literary forms of each epoch: poems, short stories, plays, novellas, novels, opera librettos. As an oral folktale it has been so popular that modern scholars Antti Aarne and Stith Thompson assigned it its own number, 887, in their classic analytical inventory, *The Types of the Folktale*. Although this story may have had an earlier form, its first known appearance occurs as the final tale in Giovanni Boccaccio's *Decameron* (X, 10), dating from 1351–1353, as related by Dioneo, the most ironic and cynical of the *Decameron*'s narrators. Dioneo ascribes no specific meaning to the story, but the marquis himself explains the testing by saying that he did it purposefully "to show you how to be a wife, to teach these people how to choose and keep a wife, and to guarantee my own peace and quiet." Before beginning the story, Dioneo remarks that the tale is marked more by "senseless brutality" than by "munificence," the topic of the day. At the tale's end, he comments that the marquis would have been rightly served had Griselda taken a lover during her period of banishment.

Griselda, 1855. © Corporation of London/Topham-HIP/The Image Works.

The story's controversial nature is hinted at in Boccaccio's endlink when the seven women in the audience begin to discuss it animatedly, some agreeing with it, others disagreeing. Tantalizingly, Boccaccio does not tell us what the women say, and the discussion ends abruptly with the announcement that the young people may safely return to Florence. Ernstpeter Ruhe has observed recently a thematic counterpoint in the *Decameron* between the Griselda story and the so-called Hawk Tale (V, 9) in representing womanly constancy. However one reads Griselda, the controversy, beginning in the 1350s, has yet to end.

Petrarch, in old age, translated Boccaccio's story into Latin in 1373 in a letter to the *Decameron*'s author (Petrarch, *Seniles*, 18.3). After revising the translation in 1374, he published it in the form of a letter to a young man contemplating marriage. Perhaps because of this particular audience, Petrarch specifically cautions that the story should not he applied to contemporary wives, but should be seen as a spiritual model of how human beings should behave towards the adversities sent them by God.

From Petrarch's Latin version, the story became accessible throughout Europe. The French were quick to see that, in spite of Petrarch's caution, it made an ideal model for wives; in the 1380s, it appeared as such in Philippe de Mézières's *Livre de la vertu et du sacrement de mariage et du reconfort des dames mariees* (*Book of the Sacrament of Marriage and Comfort for Married Ladies*). Far outstripping the moral treatise encompassing it, the Griselda tale, once separated, reappeared in various French versions: at the end of a courtesy manual for women by Geoffroi de La Tour Landry known as the *Livre du Chevalier de la Tour Landry* (*Book of the Knight of the Tower*, 1371) or the beginning of Jean Le Fèvre's apology for women, the *Livre de Leesce* (*Book of Joy*, 1380–1387), and the combination courtesy-household-falconry manual called the *Mesnagier de Paris* (*The Goodman of Paris*, 1393). In this last, a book of instructions for his young wife, the Goodman of Paris apologizes to her for having inserted the Griselda story—which he says is not meant to apply to her—but he has put it there, he says, because it is so widely known and discussed. The 1395 theatrical adaptation of Philippe's *Vertu du sacrement*, titled *L'Estoire de Griseldis* (or the *Mystère de Griseldis*)—for a long time erroneously attributed to Philippe himself (disproven by Raynaud de Lage)—became the first serious secular play in French.

Petrarch's Latin version also gained favor through an anonymous French prose translation (now in Paris, Bibliothèque nationale de France MS fr. 12459). Some manuscripts of Laurent de Premierfait's monumental French translation (1414) of Boccaccio's *Decameron* even contain this Petrarchan version in place of Laurent's direct translation from Boccaccio for the Griselda tale. Fortunately, the intertwined destinies of what finally amounts to two prose and two verse texts of the Griselda tale in late-medieval France have been thoroughly and systematically studied by Elie Golenistcheff-Koutouzoff (1933). Printed in 1484, the anonymous French prose version would enter into the French popular literary canon, not only in Charles Perrault's collected fairy tales (1694–1695, to which we English readers owe the Mother Goose stories), but also in the primary source of children's reading before the Revolution of 1789, the *Bibliothèque bleue* (Blue Library: so called because all volumes in the collection were bound in blue; S. Lefèvre).

Most important for the medieval Griselda, however, was that this anonymous French translation also served as one of Chaucer's sources for the *Clerk's Tale* in his *Canterbury Tales* (c.1387–1400), whose literary relationships first received serious scholarly examination by J. B. Severs in 1942. Since Chaucer's other source was Petrarch's revised 1374 translation of Boccaccio, his inspiration derived from two different "layers" of the same author, same tale. Although Chaucer's Clerk cites "Fraunceys Petrack" as his source and restates Petrarch's religious moral at the end of the story, he throws the interpretation of the tale into chaos in his *envoi* (final benediction closing the tale). He says that Griseldas do not exist; Griselda is dead and buried in Italy. He urges wives not to put up with husbands of that sort, jokingly threatening them with Chichevache, the starving cow who eats patient wives. Meanwhile, Harry Bailly, the Host who leads the Canterbury pilgrimage, sighs wistfully that he wishes his wife could hear that story—commentary lightheartedly reflecting the background influence of Philippe de Mézières's counsel of prudence to wives (Collette). While Linda Georgianna perceives a "grammar of assent" in the *Clerk's Tale*, feminist critics like Natalie Grinnell discern a challenge to patriarchal authority.

Despite three brilliant renderings of the story by three of the finest writers of the fourteenth century—Boccaccio, Petrarch, and Chaucer—it nonetheless proved confusing, disagreeable, or somehow otherwise inadequate to many of its readers. And thus were spawned numerous later versions of the story. Although some were simple translations of Petrarch, others strengthened a particular meaning, like the English tracts with titles specifying that Griselda was an example for married women and would-be married women. She has also earned comparisons to Job (Astell), Christ (Cottino-Jones), and the Virgin Mary (Wimsatt). Yet others dealt with troubling aspects of the tale, like the marquis's dubious motivation of a "merveillous desir" to test his wife or Griselda's apparent coldness to the death of her two children. Others saw neglected aspects of the story such as the political implications of a marriage that was so unequal socially or the unhealthy implications of such absolute sovereignty. There are some specific examples of diversely motivated modifications: the celebrated French humanist rhetorician Nicolas de Clamanges (c.1363–1437) tried to usurp and replace the Griselda story with a more quintessentially French tale of conjugal female sacrifice, *Floridan et Elvide* (*Floridan and Elvida*), which failed to catch on. In a more courtly setting, the beleaguered Piedmont marquis, Thomas III of Saluzzo, looked to Griselda, his revered ancestor (for, as Walter's wife, she was marchioness of Saluzzo), as a role model for coping with imprisonment in his 1396 *Livre du Chevalier errant* (*Book of the Wandering Knight*). Christine de Pizan (1364/5–c.1430), the Franco-Italian champion of her gender in her poetry, histories, and political treatises, inserted Griselda's story in her revisionist feminist history, *Le Livre de la Cité des dames* (*The Book of the City of Ladies*, 1404–1405), as an example of a very strong woman. Martin Le Franc would honor not only Christine and other famous women in his *Champion des Dames* (*The Ladies' Champion*) but also Griselda, in 1440–1442. Yet another male-authored homage to female virtue, Olivier de la Marche's verse *Parement et triomphe des dames* (*The Ladies' Apparel and Triumph*), recited her legend in 1493–1494.

Authors from countries outside France also took an interest in her at around this time, such as the German humanist Heinrich Steinhowel (1412–1482), who translated Petrarch's version as the *Historia Griseldis* (see Bertelsmeier-Kierst; Hess). She also found a place in fifteenth-century Italian poetry, in a collection titled *Cantari di Griselda*, preserved in a manuscript at Parma (MS Parmense 2509 in the Biblioteca palatina); and also in Spain, in *Historia de Griseldis*, composed at Seville, c.1544 (Conde and Infantes), and Portugal (see Wannenmacher). Later on, there would emerge Swedish renditions (see Swahn) and an Islandic version by Thorvald Rognvaldsson (1600–1680; see Hermansson). While Griselda's story seems quintessentially medieval, the cultural-political climate following the Protestant Reformation seems to have significantly renewed the tale's appeal, particularly in England, after which it continued to exert its influence throughout modern times (Morabito). Nineteenth-century rewrites include *Belinda*, by British novelist Maria Edgeworth (1820); French playwright Armand Silvestre's *Griselidis, mystère en trois actes* (1891) imitated medieval dramatic forms; by contrast, Gerhart Hauptmann stressed the story's inherent sadomasochism in his 1909 *Griselda*. Interesting among the twentieth-century incarnations are Julian J. Cuningham's 1926 *Griselda, or the Lady's Trial* in rhyme royal, Clara Malraux's 1940s *Portrait de Griseldis*, and Sheila Bishop's 1965 *Impatient Griselda*, along with Jean-Paul Sartre's 1964 memory in *Les Mots* (*The Words*) of admiring, as a child, the "sadism" of Griselda's relentless virtue. More recent examples include playwright Thomas Babe's radical 1963 drama and a piece by Joyce Carol Oates (see Evans). In 1984, Geraldine McCaughrean retold the story for children.

In music, famed Italian Baroque (eighteenth century) composers Alessandro Scarlatti and Antonio Vivaldi, and nineteenth-century French composer Jules Massenet all composed operas based on Griselda's plight and triumph.

Like writers and musicians, visual artists found the story attractive as well. The Griselda tale became the most frequently illustrated one from the one hundred comprising Boccaccio's *Decameron*. These Griselda illustrations were executed in a wide variety of visual media: manuscript illuminations, incunabula (printed editions dated before 1500), woodcuts, *cassoni* (decorated wedding chests especially popular in fifteenth-century Florence), paintings, frescoes, embroidery, engravings for independent sale, book illustrations, watercolors, and drawings. Most of the artists were anonymous, but among the identified cassoni painters in Florence were Apollonio di Giovanni and Francesco Pesellino. In Flanders, Simon Marmion was probably the artist whose beautiful illumination graces the story's text in *La Fleur des histoires* (*The Flower of Histories*) contained in the Brussels (Belgium) Bibliothèque Royale Albert 1er MS 9232. The Master of the Ulm Boccaccio designed a series of original woodcuts for Johann Zainer's 1473 edition of Steinhowel's *Historia Griseldis*; in the eighteenth century, Gravelot (Hubert François Bourguignon) did the designs for an illustrated *Decameron*; in 1896, pre-Raphaelite artist Edward Burne-Jones illustrated the story for William Morris's Kelmscott Press edition of Chaucer's works. Moreover, a German art exhibit touring in the 1970s included three Griselda works: a watercolor and two ink drawings.

Even today, 650 years after Boccaccio first told the Griselda story, its complex psychological, marital, feminist, political, and religious issues retain their power to fascinate and repel readers.

See also Belle Hélène de Constantinople; Boccaccio, Women in, Works other than *De Claris Mulieribus*; Chaucer, Geoffrey, Women in the Work of; Christine de Pizan; Le Fèvre de Ressons, Jean; Le Franc, Martin; *Miroir de Mariage* (*Mirror of Marriage*); Power of Women; *Sachsenspiegel* and *Schwabenspiegel*; *Vertu du sacrement de marriage, Livre de la*

BIBLIOGRAPHY

Primary Sources

Boccaccio, Giovanni. *Griselda* (*Decamerone, X, 10*). Edited by Luca Carlo Rossi. La Memoria, 229. Palermo, Sicily: Sellerio, 1991.

———. *Decameron*. Translated by Guido Waldman. Introduction and notes by Jonathan Usher. World's Classics. Oxford, U.K. and New York: Oxford University Press, 1993, 1998.

Cantari di Griselda. Edited by Raffaele Morabito. Testi di letteratura italiana. L'Aquila, Italy: Japadre, 1988.Chaucer, Geoffrey. *Canterbury Tales*. Edited by F. N. Robinson. In *The Riverside Chaucer*, edited by Larry D. Benson. 3rd ed. Boston: Houghton Mifflin, 1987.

Christine de Pizan. [*Cité des dames*] *Città delle dame*. Edited by Earl J. Richards. Translated (Italian) with introduction by Patrizia Caraffi. Milan: Luni, 1998.

———. Translated with commentary by Rosalind Brown-Grant. Harmondsworth, Middlesex, U.K.: Penguin, 1999.

L'Estoire de Griseldis, en rimes et par personnages (*1395*). Critical ed. by Mario Roques. Textes Littéraires Français, 74. Geneva: Droz, 1957.

L'Estoire de Griseldis. Edited by Barbara M. Craig. Lawrence: University of Kansas Press, 1954.

Historia de Griseldis. Edited by Juan Carlos Conde and Victor Infantes. Viareggio (Lucca), Italy: M. Baroni, 2000. [*see article by same editors below*].

La Tour Landry, Geoffroi de. *Le Livre du Chevalier de la Tour Landry pour l'enseignement de ses filles*. Edited by Anatole de Montaiglon. Paris: P. Jannet, 1854.

———. *Book of the Knight of the Tower*. Translated by William Caxton. Edited by M. Y. Offord. Early English Text Society. Supplementary series, 2. London and New York: Oxford University Press, 1971.

Le Franc, Martin. *Le Champion des dames*. Edited by Robert Deschaux. 5 vols. Classiques Français du Moyen Âge, 127–31. Paris: Honoré Champion, 1999.

Le Mesnagier de Paris. Critical ed. by Georgine Brereton and Janet M. Ferrier. Revised and trans. (Modern French) by Karin Uelstchi. Lettres gothiques. Paris: Livre de Poche, 1994.

Olivier de la Marche. *Le Triomphe des dames*. Critical ed. by Julia Kalbfleisch. Rostock, Germany: Adler/Warkentien, 1901.

Petrarca, Francesco. *Griselda* (*De insigni obedientia et fide uxoria, Seniles xvii, 3*). Edited by Luca Carlo Rossi. La memoria, 229. Palermo: Sellerio. [Bilingual Italian-Latin ed.].

————. In Cazal, *L'Histoire* [Modern French trans.]. *See under* Secondary Sources, *below*.

Philippe de Mézières. *Le Livre de la vertu du sacrement de mariage, edited from Paris*, B. N. MS fr. 1175). Critical ed. by Joan B. Williamson. Washington, D.C.: Catholic University of America Press, 1993.

Thomas III, Marquis of Saluzzo. "An edition of the *Chevalier errant*." Edited by Marvin J. Ward. Ph.D. diss. University of North Carolina, Chapel Hill. 3 vols. Ann Arbor, Mich.: UMI, 1984.

Secondary Sources

Aarne, Antti. *The Types of the Folktale*. Translated and enlarged by Stith Thompson. 2nd rev. ed. Helsinki: Academia Fennica, 1964.

Astell, Ann W. "Translating Job as Female." *Translation: Theory and Practice in the Middle Ages*, edited by Jeanette Beer, 59–69. Kalamazoo: Western Michigan University, 1997.

Berger, Gunter. "*Mouvance, variance* und die Folgen: Griselda und ihre 'nachkommen'." In *Alte und neue Philologie*, edited by Martin-Dietrich Glessgen and Franz Lebsanft, 255–65. Tübingen, Germany: Niemeyer, 1997.

Bertelsmeier-Kierst, Christa. *'Griseldis' in Deutschland : Studien zu Steinhowel und Arigo*. Germanisch-romanische Monatsschrift, 8. Heidelberg, Germany: Carl Winter, 1988.

Branca, Vittore. "Boccaccio Visualizzato III: 1. Nuove segnaliazioni di manoscritte e dipinte." *Studi sul Boccaccio* 17 (1988): 100.

Bronfman, Judith. *Chaucer's Clerk's Tale: The Griselda Story Received, Rewritten, Illustrated*. Garland Studies in Medieval Literature, 11. New York: Garland, 1994.

————. "Griselda, Renaissance Woman." In *The Renaissance Englishwoman in Print: Counterbalancing the Canon*, edited by Anne M. Haselkorn and Betty S. Travitsky, 211–23. Amherst: University of Massachusetts Press, 1990.

Brownlee, Kevin. "Commentary and the Rhetoric of Exemplarity: Griseldis in Petrarch, Phillipe de Mézières, and the *Estoire*." *South Atlantic Quarterly* 91(1992): 865–90.

Cazal, Françoise, et al., eds. *L'Histoire de Griselda: une femme exemplaire dans les littératures européennes*. Toulouse, France: Presses Universitaires du Mirail, 2001. [Commentary and translated selections of Griselda texts from different European countries in Modern French].

Collette, Carolyn P. "Chaucer and the French Tradition Revisited: Philippe de Mézières and the Good Wife." In *Medieval Women: Text and Contexts in Late Medieval Britain: Essays for Felicity Riddy*, edited by Jocelyn Wogan-Browne et al., 151–68. Turnhout, Belgium: Brepols, 2000.

Conde, Juan Carlos, and Victor Infantes. "Noticia de una version castellana de la *Historia de Griseldis*." *Cultura neolatina* 58 (1998): 331–37.

Cottino-Jones, Marga. "Fabula vs. Figura: Another Interpretation of the Griselda Story." *Italica* 50: 38–52.

Evans, Elizabeth. "Joyce Carol Oates' 'Patient Griselda'." *Notes on Contemporary Literature* 6 (1976): 205.

Georgianna, Linda. "The *Clerk's Tale* and the Grammar of Assent." *Speculum* 70 (1995): 793–821.

Golenistcheff-Koutouzoff, Elie. *L'Histoire de Griseldis en France au XIVe et au XVe siècles*. Paris: E. Droz, 1933.

Grinnell, Natalie. "Griselda Speaks: The Scriptural Challenge Patriarchal Authority in 'The Clerk's Tale'." *Critical Matrix: The Princeton Journal of Women, Gender & Culture* 9 (1995): 79–94.

Grossel, Marie-Geneviève. "Sainte paysanne et épouse fidèle: l'image de Griseldis à l'épreuve des Miroirs de mariage." In *Autour d'Eustache Deschamps: Actes du Colloque de l'Université de Picardie, Amiens, 5–8 Novembre 1998*, edited by Danielle Buschinger, 103–26. Amiens, France: Presses du Centre d'Études Médiévales, Université de Picardie, 1999.

Hermannsson, Halldor, ed. *The Story of Griselda in Iceland*. Islandica, 7. Ithaca, N.Y.: Cornell University Library, 1914.

Hess, Ursula. *Heinrich Steinhowels "Griseldis": Studien zur Text- Und Uberlieferungsgeschichte einer fruhhumanistischen Prosanovelle*. Münchener Texte und Untersuchungen zur deutschen Literatur des Mittelalters, Bd. 43. Munich, Germany: C. H. Beck, 1975.

Kirkpatrick, Robin. "The Griselda Story in Boccaccio, Petrarch, and Chaucer." In *Chaucer and the Italian Trecento*, edited by Piero Boitani, 231–48. Cambridge: Cambridge University Press, 1983.

Lefèvre, Sylvie. "Griseldis." In *Dictionnaire des lettres françaises: Le Moyen Âge*, edited by Geneviève Hasenohr and Michel Zink, 581. Paris: Livre de Poche, 1992.

Maddox, Donald. "Early Secular Courtly Drama in France: *L'Estoire de Griseldis*." In *The Expansion and Transformations of Courtly Literature*, edited by Nathaniel B. Smith and Joseph T. Snow, 156–70. Athens: University of Georgia Press, 1980.

———. "The Hunting Scenes in *L'Estoire de Griseldis*." In *Voices of Conscience: Essays on Medieval and Modern French Literature in Memory of James D. Powell and Rosemary Hodgins*, edited by Raymond J. Cormier and Eric Sellin, 78–94. Philadelphia: Temple University Press, 1977.

Morabito, Raffaele. "La Diffusione della Storia di Griselda dal XIV al XX secolo." *Studi sul Boccaccio* 17 (1988): 237–85.

———. *Una sacra rapresentazione profana: fortune di Griselda nel Quattrocentro italiano*. Beihefte zur Zeitschrift fur romanische Philologie, 253. Tübingen, Germany: Max Niemeyer, 1993.

———, ed. *Diffrazioni. Griselda 1. La circolazione dei temi e degli intrecci narrativi: il caso Griselda* (*Atti del convegno di studi, L'Aquila, 3–4 dicembre 1986*). L'Aquila, Italy: Japadre, 1988.

———, ed. *Diffrazioni. Griselda 2. La storia di Griselda in Europa* (*Atti del Convegno: Modi dell'intertestualità: la storia di Griselda in Europa, L'Aquila, 12–14 maggio 1988*). L'Aquila, Italy: Japadre, 1990.

Raynaud de Lage, Guy. "Sur l'attribution de *l'Estoire de Griseldis*." *Romania* 79 (1958): 267–71.

Rossi, Luca Carlo. "In margine alla 'Griselda' latina di Petrarca." *Acme: Annali della Facoltà . . . Milano* 53 (2000): 139–60.

Ruhe, Ernstpeter. "Griselda und der Falke: Intratextueller Dialog im *Decameron*." *Archiv für das Studium der neuern Sprachen und Literaturen* 233 (1996): 59–64.

Severs, J. Burke. *The Literary Relationships of Chaucer's Clerkes Tale*. New Haven, Conn.: Yale University Press, 1942.

Swahn, Sigbrit. "Notes bibliographiques sur 'Griselda' en Suède." *Merveilles & Contes* 1 (1987): 161–70.

Wannenmacher, Franz X. *Die Griseldissage auf der iberischen halbinsel*. Strassburg, Germany (now Strasbourg, France): Universität Strassburg, 1894.

Watson, Paul. "A Preliminary List of Subjects from Boccaccio in Italian Painting, 1400–1550." *Studi sul Boccaccio* 15 (1986): 149–66.

Wimsatt, James I. "The Blessed Virgin and the Two Coronations of Griselda." *Medievalia* 6 (1980): 187–207.

JUDITH BRONFMAN

GUALDRADA DE' RAVIGNANI (c.1165–c.1226). Renowned for her civic and personal virtue, the daughter of a citizen of Florence belonging to the lesser feudal nobility, Gualdrada married Count Guido Guidi in about 1180. Their four sons would mature to play important roles in Florentine military and political affairs. Gualdrada achieved fame in her city because she was reputed to have refused a kiss from the Emperor Otto IV when ordered by her father to accept it. Writing at the turn of the thirteenth century, Dante Alighieri alludes to her as "la bona Gualdrada" ("the good Gualdrada") in *Inferno* 16, while Giovanni Villani recounts this legend in his *Nuova Cronica* (*New Chronicle*); slightly later, Giovanni Boccaccio (c.1313–1375) cites her among the only six contemporary women—most of the 106 female portraits having been drawn from pagan antiquity—discussed in his *De mulieribus claris* (*Famous Women*); while in the mid-sixteenth century, Giorgio Vasari had her likeness painted on a ceiling in one of Duchess Eleanora's rooms in the Palazzo Vecchio.

Although the legend of Gualdrada spurning the emperor's kiss is untrue, legal documents created during her lifetime reveal that she helped significantly toward resolving local territorial disputes between the Guidi and the Florentines. When the latter dispatched armed men to demand tax payments from the monastery of Rosano (whose patrons were the Guidi), Gualdrada persuaded the Florentines to leave without collecting payment. Likewise, after the nuns of this same convent, encouraged by the Florentines, rebelled against Guidi patronage, the family decided to relinquish its patronage rights. Gualdrada had the necessary severance documents drawn up and represented the Guidi family during the ceremony.

See also Boccaccio, Women in, *De Claris Mulieribus*; Boccaccio, Women in, *Des Cleres et Nobles Femmes*; Boccaccio, Women in, Works Other than *De Claris Mulieribus*

BIBLIOGRAPHY

Primary Sources
Davidsohn, Robert. "Una monaca del duodecimo secolo." *Archivio storico italiano*. Series 5, vol. 22 (1898): 225–41.
Passerini, Luigi. "Una monaca del duodecimo secolo." *Archivio storico italiano*. Series 3, vol. 23 (1876): 61–79, 205–17, 385–403.

Secondary Sources
Benson, Pamela. "Eleanora de Toledoamong the Famous Women: Iconographic Innovation after the Conquest of Siena." In *The Cultural World of Eleanora de Toledo, Duchess of Florence and Siena*, edited by Konrad Eisenbichler, ch. 6. Burlington, Vt. and London: Ashgate, 2004.
———. "Gualdrada's Two Bodies: Female and Civic Virtue in Medieval Florence." In *The Body and Soul in Medieval Literature*, edited by Piero Boitani and Anna Torti, 1–15. J. A. W. Bennett Memorial Lectures, 10th series, Perugia, Italy: 1998; Cambridge: D. S. Brewer, 1999.
———. "Transformations of the 'Buona Gualdrada' Legend from Boccaccio to Vasari: A Study in the Politics of Florentine Narrative." In *Women in Italian Renaissance Culture and Society*, edited by Letizia Panizza, 401–20. Oxford: Legenda (European Humanities Research Centre), 2000.

PAMELA BENSON

GUDA. *See* **Scribes and Scriptoria**

GUGLIELMA OF MILAN. *See* **Guglielmites**

GUGLIELMITES (late 13th century). The Guglielmites were feminist religious radicals of Milan, in northern Italy, who were prosecuted for heresy and eradicated by the Inquisition of Lombardy in 1300. The Guglielmites, fewer than fifty enthusiasts, were condemned for their belief that God was about to inaugurate an Age of the Holy Spirit, supplanting the Roman Church of Christ with four new gospels, a college of female cardinals, and a female pope. Their pope was Maifreda da Pirovano, self-elected as the vicar not of Christ but of Guglielma Boema, a local saint whom they considered the Holy Spirit incarnate. Guglielma, rumored to be the legitimate sister of King Wenceslas IV of Bohemia (1361–1419), had been a lay associate of the Humiliati (= "the Humbled Ones," a preaching movement practicing self-mortification and care of the sick and poor as means of doing penance) of Biassono and of the Cistercian monastery of Chiaravalle, both also in Italy. Pious Catholics of Milan, spiritually starved by a Church–state struggle and interdict from 1262 to 1277, when services in the churches, even marriages and Masses, were forbidden, found in Guglielmina (they used the affectionate diminutive) a figure around whom religious hope could rally. Many followers, mostly women, took from the perfectly orthodox preaching of Guglielmina their moral and spiritual guidance. Her personal piety included imitation of the life and sufferings of Jesus; she was rumored to have the stigmata (wounds like Christ's on the Cross) as did St. Francis of Assisi (1181/82–1226). The Cistercian monks bought her a house to live in, and after her death (August 24, 1279), her body was ritually transferred as that of a saint to a chapel in Chiaravalle where the date of her death was celebrated as a saint's feast.

The monks attributed miraculous cures to St. Guglielma and her cult attracted scores of devotees. Some of her spiritual family carried the cult to an extreme, in a way suggested by the prophecies of Joachim da Fiore (d. 1202). Andrea Saramita, a lay brother of Chiaravalle, and Sister Maifreda da Pirovano of the Humiliati of Biassono, became the nucleus of a radical sect, mostly women, to whom Guglielma was God the Holy Spirit incarnate, who would bring the Jews and "pagan Saracens" (Muslims, even though these too were monotheistic) into the Church. Maifreda said Mass on the tomb of St. Guglielma, distributed the bread from that Mass as the Eucharist of the Holy Spirit, and declared that she would be pope when God deposed the pseudo-pope Boniface VIII. In the Inquisition that inevitably followed, the prophetic faith was condemned and some of its adherents died as relapsed heretics. Because the cult of St. Guglielma had become the occasion of such a dangerous heresy, it was also violently suppressed, and her body was exhumed and burned.

See also Clare of Assisi, St.; Joan, Pope; Prous Boneta, Na

BIBLIOGRAPHY

Primary Source
Tocco, Felice, ed. "Il processo dei Guglielmiti," *Rendiconti: Reale Accademia dei Lincei, Classe di scienze morali, storiche e filologiche*, ser. 5, 8 (1899): 309–469.

Secondary Sources
McNamara, JoAnn. "*De quibusdam mulieribus*: Reading Women's History from Hostile Sources." In *Medieval Women and the Sources of Medieval History*, edited by Joel T. Rosenthal, 237–58. Athens: University of Georgia Press, 1990.
Newman, Barbara. *God and the Goddesses: Vision, Poetry, and Belief in the Middle Ages.* The Middle Ages. Philadelphia: University of Pennsylvania Press, 2003.
———. "WomanSpirit, Woman Pope." In *From Virile Woman to WomanChrist: Studies in Medieval Religion and Literature*, edited by B. Newman, 182–223. Philadelphia: University of Pennsylvania Press, 1995.
Wessley, Stephen E. "The Thirteenth-Century Guglielmites: Salvation through Women." In *Medieval Women*, edited by Derek Baker, 289–304. Studies in Church History. Subsidia, 1. Oxford: Basil Blackwell, 1978.

DANIEL WILLIMAN

GUILDS, WOMEN IN. The guild (or gild) in medieval Europe was a major economic and social institution for a great number of wage-earning male and female workers. The primary purpose of these early corporations and monopolies was to sustain and promote skilled trades and selected crafts by establishing ordinances and setting standards regarding membership, apprenticeship, remuneration, and workmanship. The guilds also sought to control competition by regulating sale prices and fees. Most of these early entities also took a protective interest in its membership, in the event of a member's insolvency, disability, or personal crisis. In 1414, for example, the London-based Merchant Taylors Company built almshouses for "their poore brethren and sisters"; and impecunious members of the Carpenters Company received pecuniary benefits and clothing, as well as spiritual counseling.

As scholars have shown, the origin of these early economic cooperatives dates from ancient German tribal and religious "gilds" or brotherhoods, which, by the eleventh century, had developed into fraternities of merchants and craftsmen. The early German guilds were formed to protect commercial enterprise against restrictions imposed by feudal governments. With the rise of towns and cities in the twelfth century, and with the rapid expansion in trade across Europe, guilds rapidly multiplied to include women as well as new groups of professionals. The merchant guilds, for example, distinguished themselves by virtue of their size, prosperity, and power in town polity.

The membership of women in the early guilds offers modern scholars an important

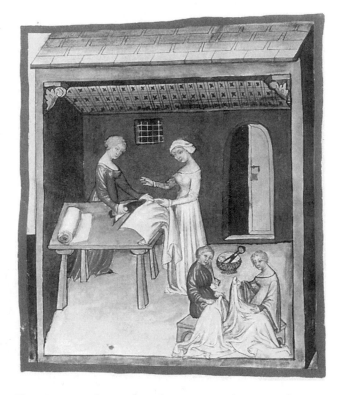

Two women in the textile trades, cutting and preparing linen. From *Tacuinum Sanitatis* MS s.n. 2644, folio 105v, Italian, c.1385. Courtesy of the Dover Pictorial Archive.

historical model of the contribution of women to the rise of urban centers and urban production and, in some cases, their aggressive penetration of the rising market economy. As David F. Crouch has recently shown from surviving archival documents and data, pious women in Yorkshire, England, during period 1389 to 1547, were attracted to religious guilds; such communities served Englishwomen's spiritual needs, just as women on the Continent were nourished spiritually by the beguinages or beguines (nonmonastic communities of pious laywomen). Yet, as David Herlihy notes, secular women in northern Italy, for example, who were eager to embrace active and traditionally male-dominated roles in public affairs, were met with stern resistance: "The guild almost everywhere limited participation of women in the trade it represented; usually, it grudgingly allowed only the widows and daughters of masters to practice the art. And women were altogether excluded from guild offices." But what often appears to be negative evidence of women's presence in the guild economy may be interpreted more neutrally as blank spots (or data gaps) in existing records, as there is adequate evidence, certainly in medieval England, of women's prominent representation in the secular (nonpious) trades, even when married. Such cases went unnoted in contemporary records precisely because they were not unusual, as legal historian Janet S. Loengard points out in response to Marian K. Dale's landmark study of London silkwomen of the fifteenth century. In northern Europe, medieval women evidently enjoyed the same economic positions and prerogatives as men: women could legally inherit property, manage estates, belong to most guilds, and administer the family business

Two midwives, assisting with a birth. From *Tacuinum Sanitatis* MS s.n. 2644, folio 105v Italian, c.1385. Courtesy of the Dover Pictorial Archive.

if widowed or left alone for a period of time by husbands or sons. After specific training in an apprenticeship, unmarried women could trade with relative freedom as independent *femme sole* (single woman) traders, or they could trade as *femmes coverts* (married women). In this latter case, their rights were significantly restricted since married women were regarded legally as theproperty and responsibility of their husbands. Most guildswomen were typically married to guildsmen, and they commonly worked in tandem with husbands, sons, or male kin in strong family partnerships, such as that between male and female brewers, c.1300–1600, as examined by Judith M. Bennett. Guildswomen working outside of a family orbit as *femmes soles* traders tended to concentrate in towns or in the many new urban centers throughout Europe. When the spinning wheel and a more effective type of loom were introduced in the thirteenth century, women distinguished themselves as cloth-workers, spinners (spinsters), weavers, and carders. Sometimes guildswomen held managerial and supervisory positions as guild-mistresses. In such capacity, they directed the daily work and training of employees and apprentices.

Scholars have reached valuable, if differing, conclusions on medieval women in the trade and crafts guilds by culling pertinent data from extant contemporary literature, chronicles, letters, wills, business and legal documents, urban tax rolls, and manor and census records. One important repository of information on the representation of women in medieval guilds is the famous *Livre des métiers de Paris* (*Book of Trades of Paris*), compiled c.1269 by Étienne Boileau (c.1200–1269), Grand Provost of Paris in 1250, at the behest of King Louis IX (Saint Louis) (1214–1270). This book of occupations records the regulation of Paris guilds and it also documents, for example, that five out of some 110 guilds were essentially female monopolies; furthermore, only a very few guilds systematically excluded female membership. Boileau's data, as well as Parisian tax rolls of 1292 and 1300, document that 108 out of 321 professions were open to females. The professions Boileau names include the corporations of surgeons, butchers, glass-blowers, bit-and-bridle makers, and chain-mail forgers. In addition to Boileau's *Livre* and surviving medieval tax rolls, there exists a precedent-setting English statute of 1363, published in the *Liber Albus* (*The White Book*), a compilation of ordinances and regulations on guild membership, apprenticeship, and legal responsibilities of master-traders. This important fourteenth-century English statute restricts men to a single trade, but permits women to work in several: "But the intent of the King and his Council is that women, that is to say Brewers, Bakers, Carders, Spinners, and Workers [in] Linnen and Silk [. . .] and all others that do use and work all handy works, may freely use and work as they have done before this time without [. . .] being retrained by this Ordinance." Other surviving archival records from this period reveal that in 1455, for example, more than one thousand London guildswomen were employed in silkwork, as studied by Dale.

Female entertainers in France offer themselves as an attractive model of the professional incorporation of talented women via the guild system. The Guild of Singers and Players of Paris included many female members, some of whom were attached to the households of Henry III and the Countess of Blois. Furthermore, household account books of Louis IX in 1239 record that 100 sous were paid to a professional female entertainer, one "Melang, cantatrix" ("Melanie, singer"). Scholars also have identified useful data in fourteenth-century Parisian account books, showing that professional female entertainers were often resident in some of France's great royal or aristocratic castles. Available statistics on minstrels in early fourteenth-century Parisian guilds name eight "menestrens et menestrelles" ("minstrels and minstrelesses") among some thirty-seven singers, namely Isabelet la Rousselle, Marie la Chartaine, Liegart wife of Bienviegnant, one Marguerite, Jehane la Ferpiere, Alison wife of Guerin, Adeline wife of G. Langlois, and Isabiau la Lorraine. Extant records of the great cultural patron John, duke of Berry (1340–1416), document payments in 1372 to female musicians from Lyons, Paris, and Le Puy.

While guildswomen enjoyed relative freedom in the practice of their trades or crafts, their status was significantly, indeed systematically, challenged and progressively diminished by the patriarchal establishment in the field of "the healing artes." Such was the perspective of historians of women in medicine prior to Monica Green's extensive reassessment of the relationship between male and female healers' guilds. On the one hand, there is the older, traditional view of medieval medicine and caretaking as essentially a male monopoly, supported (ideologically and legally) by the Church, royalty, and secular authorities. Historians have made much of the prosecution of one Jacqueline de Alemania in 1322 by the University of Paris medical faculty, which charged her with practicing without authorization from the faculty or without a license from the chancellor. The Inquisition and witch hunts contributed to the decline of women in the medical guilds throughout the later Middle Ages (1300s–1500s). And by the eighteenth century, as Barbara Brandon Schnorrenberg has shown, the licensing of women healers and surgeons had become so rigorous and prejudicial that the majority of women were literally run out of the medical profession: women's traditional and natural skills in gynecology and obstetrics were systematically denied them by an oppressive male medical establishment. Yet on the other hand, Green, based on her identification and interpretation of a relatively overlooked body of contrarian evidence, proposes a more nuanced and varied approach to the roles of midwife and female healer. While admitting to increasing male control, especially after the fifteenth century, Green's view seeks to neutralize and rectify, to some extent, the heretofore "victimization school" of medieval women in the medical arts.

Women's so-called oldest profession, prostitution, also has its place in any summary of the early guilds. Prostitutes' guilds were essentially an early form of the brothel, and these mercenary sex communities were regulated in such a way as to afford each brothel owner some sort of autonomy while plying her trade in an orderly fashion; thus, the medieval sex trade was in truth an accepted component of the municipal structure and social organization of early urban centers. Ruth Mazo Karras has valuably examined the regulation and inner workings of the early English brothels, though she declines to give them the status of guilds. By the end of the seventeenth century, with the rise of new trade, sophisticated forms of commercial exchange, and nascent forms of capitalism, most of the guilds began to decline in power. In France, the guilds were abolished during the French Revolution. In Austria, England, Germany, and Italy, they persisted until the late nineteenth century.

Contemporary pictorial sources of guildsworkers, available to us today in the decorative borders or margins of medieval manuscripts, was often the work of trained guildswomen illuminators and manuscript painters. This unit of guildswoman further documents women's representation as professional wage-earning workers. That women merchants are portrayed as *sprechers* (speakers) in religious books, such as the *Hours of the Virgin* (Flemish, c.1525; provenance, Viscount Astor, Oxford), tells us today that their pictorial representation was not limited to secular texts. Also, women weavers are the subject of informing miniatures in certain manuscripts of the *Cité des dames* (*City of Ladies*), the pioneering 1404–1405 feminist text by Christine de Pizan (c.1465–1430?). Furthermore, women apothecaries are figured in the *Tacuinum Sanitatis* (Italian, *Il libro di casa Cerruti*), or, the *Book of Secrets of Health* (c.1385). The manuscript sheets of this Italian-Latin text were richly illustrated, even though, as with several manuals of this sort, the original parent-text (the Arabic *Taqwīm al-sihhah* or *Secrets of Health* by Ibn Bōtlan [d. 1068]) contained few or no illustrations, and certainly not of women in guilds. Pictorial images of women merchants in gold and silver also make a strong showing in such manuscripts as Platearius's *Livre des symples medichines* (Paris, Bibliothèque nationale de France, MS fr. 9136, folio 344). Women are abundantly depicted in a variety of trades—spinners, carders, and weavers; artists and portrait-painters—alongside mythic women warriors, queens, and saints in illuminated manuscripts of French translations, c.1400–1415, of Boccaccio's fourteenth-century Latin catalogues of illustrious women and men—a major source for Christine de Pizan—his *De claris mulieribus* and *De casibus virorum illustrium* (French, *Des cleres et nobles femmes*; *Des cas des nobles hommes et femmes* [*Of Illustrious Women*; *Of the Fates of Noble Men and Women*]). The "signification" of pictorial images of women in medieval translations and renderings of Boccacio's great texts is the subject of a recent edition, with commentary, by Brigitte Buettner. Women musicians and traveling *jougleresses* (singers) and *trobairitz* (female troubadours) may be viewed in a book of hours preserved in the liturgical collection of Oxford University's Bodleian Library (MS Rawlinson E36, f. 90), as well as in the secular manuscripts of these early women composers. Likewise, other contemporary manuscripts, preserved in the great libraries of Austria, Belgium, England, France, and the United States, bear many colorful and corroborating images of professional women bookbinders and book workers, miners, sculptors, writers, copyists and scribes, and surgeons. More accessible formats for viewing such images now exist in the printed and online catalogues of many of the great world libraries, and also in the "Medieval Women" series of calendars, note cards, address books, and the like, researched and edited by Sally Fox, and sold in many museum gift shops. Such commodification of visual images of medieval women at work in their everyday professions reflects a growing interest in this fascinating group of women achievers.

Scholars' recent reassessment of women's representation in the medieval guild system, which rapidly came to dominate the nascent market economies of England and

Continental Europe, valuably shows that the majority of medieval guildswomen worked collaboratively with their male counterparts, but that they also managed to achieve a measure of economic independence, if not (in some cases) notoriety and fame. The prominence of women in the medieval guilds patently confutes the longstanding typologies of medieval women as, for example, white-gloved royals and nobles, as religious ecstatics, and as dubious practitioners of the medical arts.

See also Artists, Medieval Women as; Boccaccio, Women in Works Other than *De Claris Mulieribus*; Embroidery; Law, Canon, Women in; Medicine and Medieval Women; Music, Women Composers and Musicians; Prostitution; Scribes and Scriptoria; Spinners and Drapers; *Trobairitz*

BIBLIOGRAPHY

Primary Sources

Boileau, Étienne. *Le Livre des métiers d'Étienne Boileau*. Edited by René de Lespinasse and François Bonnardot. Histoire générale de Paris. Paris: Imprimerie nationale, 1879. [*Liber albus*]. *Munimenta Gildhallae Londoniensis. Liber albus, Liber custumarum, et Liber Horn*. Edited by Henry Thomas Riley. 3 vols. Rolls Series, 12. London: Longman, Brown, Green, Longmans, and Roberts, 1859–1862.

[*Tacuinum sanitatis*]. *The Medieval Health Handbook*: Tacuinum sanitatis (*by Ibn Botlân*). Edited with commentary by Luisa Cogliati Arano. Translated and adapted by Oscar Ratti and Adele Westbrook from the original Italian ed. New York: George Braziller, 1976. [Reproduces illustrations from five different manuscripts].

———. *The Four Seasons of the House of Cerruti*. Translated by Judith Spencer. New York: Facts on File, 1984. [Reproduces miniatures from the Vienna, Österreichische Nationalbibliothek MS series nova 2644].

Secondary Sources

Adams, Carol J., et al. *From Workshop to Warfare: The Lives of Medieval Women*. Cambridge and New York: Cambridge University Press, 1983.

Bennett, Judith M. *Ale, Beer and Brewsters in England: Women's Work in a Changing World, 1300–1600*. New York and Oxford: Oxford University Press, 1996.

———, and Amy M. Froide, eds. *Singlewomen in the European Past: 1250–1800*. Philadelphia: University of Pennsylvania Press, 1999.

Boissonnade, Prosper. *Life and Work in Medieval Europe: From the Fifth to the Fifteenth Century*. With an introduction by Eileen Power. New York: Dorset Press, 1987. [See "Women" entries in index (11 categories)].

Bowers, Jane, and Judith Tick, eds. *Women Making Music: The Western Art Tradition, 1150–1959*. Urbana: University of Illinois Press, 1986.

Buettner, Brigitte. *Boccaccio's* Des cleres et nobles femmes: *Systems of Signification in an Illuminated Manuscript*. Seattle and London: College Art Association/University of Washington Press, 1996.

Coornaert, Emile. *Les Corporations en France avant 1789*. Paris: Gallimard, 1968.

Crouch, David J. F. *Piety, Fraternity, and Power: Religious Gilds in Late Medieval Yorkshire, 1389–1547*. Woodbridge, Suffolk, U.K. and Rochester, N.Y.: Boydell Press, 2000.

Dale, Marian K. "London Silkwomen of the Fifteenth Century." *Economic History Review*, 1st ser. 4 (1933): 324–35. Reprint in *Sisters and Workers in the Middle Ages*, edited by Judith M. Bennett et al., 26–38. Chicago: University of Chicago Press, 1989.

Davies, Matthew. "Artisans, Guilds and Government in London." In *Daily Life in the Middle Ages*, edited by Richard Britnell, 125–50. Stroud, Gloucestershire, U.K.: Sutton, 1998.

Egbert, Virginia Wylie. *The Medieval Artist at Work*. Princeton, N.J.: Princeton University Press, 1967.

Ferrell, Robert G. *Women in Medieval Guilds*. Six pages, with bibliography. http://66.82.75.68/wimguild2.html.

Fox, Sally, ed. *Medieval Women*. New York Graphic Society. Boston and Toronto: Little, Brown, 1988. [In various formats].

Gross, Charles. *The Gild Merchant: A Contribution to British Municipal History*. 2 vols. Oxford: Clarendon Press, 1890.

Green, Monica. "Women's Medical Practice and Health Care in Medieval Europe." In *Sisters and Workers in the Middle Ages*, 39–78. *See under* Dale, *above*.

"Guilds: London, England, Europe: Exploring the History of Europe's Guilds and Livery Companies from 1000 to 1900." Conference sponsored by the Centre for Metropolitan History, Institute of Historical Research, School of Advanced Study, University of London. 31 October 2003–1 November 2003, Senate House, London. Organizers I. A. Gadd et al. http://www.history.ac.uk/cmh/guilds2.html (illustrated).

Hanawalt, Barbara A. *Women and Work in Preindustrial Europe*. Bloomington: Indiana University Press, 1986.

Herlihy, David. "The Towns of Northern Italy." In *Medieval Women and the Sources of Medieval History*, edited by Joel T. Rosenthal, 133–54. Athens and London: University of Georgia Press, 1990.

Hilton, Rodney H. "Women Traders in Medieval England." *Women's Studies* 6 (1984): 139–55.

Karras, Ruth Mazo. "The Regulation of Brothels in Later Medieval England." In *Sisters and Workers*, 100–134. *See under* Dale, *above*.

Kowaleski, Maryanne, and Judith M. Bennett. "Crafts, Gilds, and Women in the Middle Ages: Fifty Years after Marian K. Dale." In *Sisters and Workers*, 11–25. *See under* Dale, *above*.

Loengard, Janet S. "'Legal History and the Medieval Englishwoman' Revisited: Some New Directions." In *Medieval Women and the Sources*, 210–36. *See under* Herlihy, *above*.

Menuge, Noël James. *Medieval Women and the Law*. Suffolk, U.K., and Rochester, N.Y.: Boydell & Brewer Ltd., 2003.

Mundy, John Hine, and Peter Riesenberg. *The Medieval Town*. Princeton, N.J.: Van Nostrand, 1958. Reprint 1967.

Power, Eileen. *Medieval Women*. Edited by M. M. Postan. Cambridge: Cambridge University Press, 1975.

Schnorrenberg, Barbara Brandon. "Is Childbirth Any Place for a Woman? The Decline of Midwifery in the Eighteenth-Century England." *Studies in Eighteenth-Century Culture* 10 (1981): 393–408. [A classic, early essay on this debate, from a feminist perspective].

Shahar, Shulamith. *The Fourth Estate: A History of Women in the Middle Ages*. London and New York: Methuen, 1983.

Staley, Edgcumbe. *The Guilds of Florence*. London: Methuen, 1906.

Thrupp, Sylvia. "The Gilds." In *The Cambridge Economic History of Europe*, edited by M. M. Postan et al., 3: 230–80. Cambridge: Cambridge University Press, 1963.

———. *The Merchant Class of Medieval London, 1300–1500*. Chicago: University of Chicago Press, 1948.

Uitz, Erika. *Women in the Medieval Town*. Translated by Sheila Marnie. London: Barrie & Jenkins, 1990. Originally *Die Frau in der mittelalterlichen Stadt*. Leipzig, Germany: Edition, 1988.

Unwin, George. *The Gilds and Companies of London*. London: George Allen & Unwin, 1938.

Waller, A. C. "The Guild of Women Binders." In *Guilds of Book Workers Journal* 24 (1986): 25–37.

Young, L. S. "The Guild of Book Workers: A Brief History." In *The Guild of Book Workers*, edited by Susanne Borghese et al., 54–72. New York: Guild of Book Workers, 1981.

MAUREEN E. MULVIHILL

GUILIELMA DES ROSERS (fl. mid-13th century). Guilielma was the coauthor of the *tenso* (or dialogue poem, in Occitan, the medieval language of southern France) with an Italian male troubadour, Lanfranc Cigala. Their poem, known by its opening verse "Na Guillelma, man cavalier arratge" ("Lady Guilielma, several knights voyaging"), exemplifies the finely honed erotic-intellectual tension often typical of medieval love-debate poetry.

Of the six manuscripts that preserve the poem entirely or in part, one (called M, in Paris, Bibliothèque nationale de France, fr. 12474) gives no attribution, while the rest ascribe it jointly to the Italian troubadour Lanfranc Cigala (fl. 1235–1278) and *Na*

Guilhelma de Rosers, or, more simply, to *Na Guilielma*, as in the "a" manuscript (see notes to ed. Rieger). What little can be conjectured about her identity is based on the sparse data provided by her name, by what is known of Lanfranc Cigala, and by an apparent reference to her in the anonymous *canso* (love song) "Quan Proensa ac perduda proeza" ("When Provence has lost its noble prowess"). According to his *vida* (poetic biography), Lanfranc Cigala, a knight and judge from Genoa, the Italian west coast port, was a great lover who delighted in the poetic arts. He visited Provence in 1241 as legate to Raimon-Berangar of Provence and was assassinated near Monaco in 1278 (Boutière and Schutz). The anonymous author of "Quan Proensa ac perduda proeza" laments that a "Na Guilielma," said to be from "Rogier," has left Provence and now embellishes Genoa. While there are several towns in southern France that might be identified with Rosers/Rogier, two seem, because of their proximity to the Italian littoral, to be most likely. Present-day Rosières lies near Largentière in the Ardèche, just beyond the Rhône river that marks the western boundary of Provence proper. Since the troubadours used *Proensa* (Provence) in its larger sense, it is certainly possible that Rosières and Rosers/Rogier are one and the same. Yet the other possibility, Rougiers, lies strictly within the traditional boundaries of Provence and, because of its greater proximity to the Mediterranean coast and Genoa, it is more probably Guilielma's hometown. In any case, scholars surmise that Guilielma, from one of the above towns in Provence, at one point in her life left Provence to take up residence in Genoa, and that she was known to Lanfranc Cigala. It is impossible to determine whether she knew Lanfranc in France or Italy. Nor do we know the homeland of her husband, if she had one (as her title *Na* [Lady] would seem to indicate).

Because it is ostensibly a debate over a theoretical point of love, "Na Guilielma, man cavalier arratge" is a *partimen* (or debate poem), a subgenre of the tenso in which the first speaker propounds a problem and offers the second his or her choice of positions to defend, the first then taking the opposing position. The long *razo* (a prose introduction purporting to explain the circumstances in which the lyric was composed) recounts the story of two knights who, having been summoned by their ladies, set off together on a night of bad weather. En route, they encounter a group of knights lost in the storm. One turns aside to help the travelers, while the other continues toward his lady. Lanfranc's persona, having heard the story, asks Na Guilielma which of the two knights behaved more laudably. Her persona replies that while the first acted well, the second, who kept his word to his lady, acted better. Lanfranc argues that he who saved the travelers from death acted out of love, which is the source of all *cortezia* (courtliness), which, like *proeza* (prowess, nobility), is a key virtue in the troubadour world. He clearly implies that, in acting in a way that enhances his merit, a knight renders himself more worthy of his lady's love and, hence, enhances her status. When Guilielma continues to criticize the first knight, Lanfranc taxes her with egotism. He observes, in a metaphor laden with sarcasm and scarcely concealed sexual innuendo, that a lover, like a tournament horse, must be treated with moderation and wisdom if he is to joust well and not lose his strength. Guilielma retorts that a lady of noble birth and great worth must have a man in her service, even if her knight is not present. She remarks gaily that the lover who does not keep his word is the more likely to lose his strength at the critical moment. In their final exchange in the two *tornadas* (concluding half-stanzas), it becomes clear that, far from being theoretical, the debate is an intensely personal one. Lanfranc declares that he has the necessary ardor and strength to vanquish her by lying down. He professes to regret their acrimonious argument and announces his wish to be vanquished by her, a euphemism for sexual congress. Guilielma replies that she has the necessary ardor to consent to his proposition, declaring that she will defend herself with typically feminine ruses against the hardiest suitor. The work, a witty and suggestive exercise in sexual politics, recounts a skirmish in the war of the sexes in which the initial struggle for dominance is resolved to the mutual satisfaction of the erstwhile antagonists.

See also Trobairitz; Tournoiement des Dames

BIBLIOGRAPHY

Primary Sources

Anon. "Quan Proensa ac perduda proeza." In *Bibliographie des Troubadours*, edited by Alfred Pillet and Henry Carstens. Reprint New York: Burt Franklin, 1968. [See no. 461, poem 204].

Guilielma des Rosers and Lanfranc. "Na Guillelma, man cavalier arratge." In *Songs of the Women Troubadours*, edited and translated by Matilda Tomaryn Bruckner, Laurie Shepard and Sarah White, 74–77, 170–72. New York and London: Garland, 1995. New ed. 2000. [Most recent, authoritative: original texts, notes, introduction and English translation].

———. "Na Guillelma, man cavalier arratge." In *Trobairitz: Der Beitrag der Frau in der altokzitanischen höfischen Lyrik. Edition des Gesamtkorpus*, edited by Angelica Rieger, 230–33. Beihefte der Zeitschrift für romanische Philologie, 233. Tübingen, Germany: Max Niemeyer Verlag, 1991. [Most authoritative, German trans. and commentary].

———. "Na Guillelma, man cavalier arratge." In *I Trovatori d'Italia*, edited by Giulio Bertoni, 99, 377–83, 567–69. Modena, Italy: Umberto Orlandini, 1915. Reprint Geneva: Slatkine, 1974. [Pioneering ed. based on MS "a" (Florence, Biblioteca Riccardiana 2814 and Modena, Bibliotecta Estense, Campori g. N.8. 4, 11, 12, 13); Italian translation, notes, historical commentary].

Lanfranc Cigala. [Works]. *Il Canzoniere di Lanfranco Cigala*, critical ed. and trans. (Italian) by Francisco Branciforti, 172–80. Biblioteca dell'*Archivum Romanicum*, ser. 1, 37. Florence: Olschki, 1954.

[*Vida* of Lanfranc, *razo* of their *tenso*]. In *Biographies des troubadours. Textes provençaux des XIIIe et XIVe siecles*, edited by Jean Boutière and Alexander H. Schutz, revised with I.-M. Cluzel, 569–75. Les Classiques d'Oc, 1. Paris: Nizet, 1964.

Secondary Sources

[See also notes to above editions].

Bruckner, Matilda Tomaryn. "Debatable Fictions: The *Tensos* of the *Trobairitz*." In *Literary Aspects of Courtly Culture: Selected Papers from the Seventh Triennial Congress of the International Courtly Literature Society*, edited by Donald Maddox and Sara Sturm-Maddox, 19–28. Cambridge: D. S. Brewer, 1994.

Eméric-David, Toussaint-Bernard. "Guillelma de' Rosieri, Simon Doria, Jacopo Grillo." In *Histoire Littéraire de la France*, 19: 565–66. Paris: Firmin Didot; Treuttel & Wurtz, 1838.

MERRITT R. BLAKESLEE

GUINEVERE (from the 6th century). The queen of King Arthur's court and often reputed lover of Lancelot, Guinevere is known in French as Guenevere or Guenièvre, and also by other European linguistic variations (including those in medieval German, Italian, and Dutch) deriving from the Welsh Gwenhwyfar (White Phantom). One of the most popular female literary characters ever, Guinevere has been portrayed both positively and negatively, from the early Welsh portrayal of her as seductress to her most complex and compelling characterization in Malory (c. 1469), only to flourish in further reincarnations to this day. As with other major legendary figures, historians have sought real-life equivalents to Guinevere, Arthur, and his principal knights by evaluating and collating the various accounts.

Because medieval historiographers, despite their drier, more solemn tone, were actually no more reliable than the predictably fictitious poets and romanciers, such scientific efforts, though fascinating, have met with uneven certitude (see Ashe; Goodrich). In such cases, the character's "reality"—here, Guinevere's—must combine data on her supposed mortal life with narratives of her literary precedents and especially of her afterlife, respecting all the inevitably accumulated national-cultural layering and degrees of assimilation.

Epic precedents for Guinevere include Dido in Virgil's *Aeneid* (19 B.C.E.), the epic of Rome's founding, a resemblance already spotted and cultivated by certain medieval authors (see Neuendorf), and in the person of Aino of the Finnish national epic *Kalevala* (originally oral; not compiled as a written text until the mid-nineteenth century). These investigations liken all three—Dido, Aino and Guinevere—to each other in their queenly bearing at each legend's beginning, and observe

Imprisoned Queen Guinevere sent into exile by ship. From fifteenth-century French manuscript of *Le roman du roi Arthur et les compagnons de la Table Ronde* (*Book of King Arthur and the Knights of the Round Table*) by Chrétien de Troyes. © The Art Archive/Biblioteca Nazionale Turin/Dagli Orti.

how all three then suffer their downfall due to their "moral misconduct" in the end. In her comparison of Aino to Guinevere, Norma Lorre Goodrich also uncovers fairy tale analogues in the Russian tradition (in the figure of Mistress of the Copper Mountain) as well as an earlier, classical Sleeping Beauty.

Guinevere herself was the daughter King Leodagan of the Scottish eastern Picts, and supposed sister of Bedevere (Welsh = Bedwyr), one of Arthur's closest warrior companions, along with Kay (Cai). A tatoo imprinted on her hip in the form of a crown—a mark of royalty and holiness—later proved to distinguish her from the False Guinevere, her half sister (and evil double), who was conceived when Leodagan raped his seneschal Bertolais's wife. The English monk and historian St. Gildas, author of *De Excidio Britanniae* (*On the Destruction of Britain*, sixth century), whose pertinent sections were repeated by the Anglo-Saxon historian known as the Venerable Bede, in his *Historia Ecclesiastica Gentis Anglorum* (*Ecclesiastical History of the English People*, 731), and modern scholars Heinrich

Zimmer and Goodrich all explain that the Picts were not Celtic, nor even Indo European, but rather that they derived from ancient Finnish-Estonian or Iberian tribes who migrated to the British Isles from Siberia and the Volga River area. Pictish law dictated that daughters alone inherited real estate. It was thus mainly through his marriage to Guinevere and her dowry lands land that Arthur, a Celt, became king. Guinevere was educated at the Grail Castle on the Isle of Man in Gaelic territory. Unlike King Arthur, she was literate, for she had been taught calligraphy and symbology by Lady Niniane (also called Nimue, Viviane, and so on), subordinate to or synonymous with the Lady of the Lake, who had abducted and raised Lancelot.

King Leodagan of Carmelide was under siege by the Saxons. King Urien of Wales took Leodagan prisoner, but Merlin and Arthur freed him and demanded that Guinevere be given in marriage to Arthur in recompense. Her dowry was Carmelide, the eastern fortress, or Camelot, modern Sterlingshire (though other studies equate Camelot with Cadbury Castle in Somerset, or Colchester because of its Latin name, *Camulodunum*); the other, equally momentous part of Guinevere's dowry was the Round Table, a rotunda constructed on a stone foundation. Merlin, the prophet and enchanter (original Celtic name, Myrddin, Latinized to "Merlinus" by Geoffrey), advised Arthur to obtain this territory to help him achieve sovereignty over the rebellious English kings. The Prose *Lancelot* (the first half of the larger prose group—prior romances having been composed in verse—called the Vulgate Cycle, Lancelot-Grail Cycle or Pseudo-Map Cycle, c.1215–1235) relates that Guinevere's first abduction took place on the eve of the wedding. Bertolais, stepfather of the False Guinevere, tries to substitute his "daughter," the product of Leodagan's rape of his wife, at the nuptials, after kidnapping Guinevere, but Bertolais's plan is thwarted by a shrewd Merlin, whose guards intervene just in time to save Arthur's bride. Another abduction episode connected with Gildas—not the above-mentioned historiographer-saint's work but in the biography of him (*Vita Gildae*) by the Breton Caradoc Llancarfan (c.1130)—relates how Melwas, king of Somerset, carried off Guinevere from Arthur's court and held her at Glastonbury Abbey, later returning her after negotiations. Caradoc's Melwas episode would supply material for the jealous and evil Meleagant aggrandized as Lancelot's adversary by Chrétien de Troyes in *Lancelot* or *Le Chevalier de la charrete* (*Lancelot*, or *The Knight of the Cart*, c. 1180), the Vulgate Cycle (thirteenth century), and, with increasing richness of plot and portrayal, Malory's *Morte Darthur* (*Death of King Arthur*, c. 1469).

The historical Guinevere may have been crowned queen around the turn of the sixth century, on the August Feast of the Virgin. The ceremony was a festive pageant officiated by Merlin, in his capacity as archbishop. Wace says that the heiress was crowned during a four-day festival attended by the Gaels from Ireland, the Welsh and, of course, the Picts. Thomas Malory, in his *Morte Darthur* counts one hundred mounted warriors in attendance, while Alfred, Lord Tennyson, in his poem on her as one of his *Idylls of the King* (1859–1885) describes Guinevere clothed in grass-green silk with plumes. Geoffrey of Monmouth, in his *Historia regum Britanniae* (*History of the Kings of Britain*, c.1137) depicts her entrance as preceded by four queens bearing white doves. After Guinevere's beautiful, very long hair is anointed to signify her royal rank, the warriors swear their loyalty to her and Arthur officially names her his treasurer and archivist.

The False Guinevere, loathe to relinquish her claim and aided by Bertolais, tricks Arthur during a hunting trip with his men. When Arthur leaves the group, he is captured and taken to Camelot-Carmelide. It is under False Guinevere's spell that Arthur repudiates Queen Guinevere as the false one, and consents to having his wife stand trial. Guinevere not only has a double, but in early Welsh and Irish lore, there are three Guineveres, listed in the so-called Welsh *Triads* (no. 56). But these three Guineveres are not antagonistic; rather, they underscore her godlike multiple aspects, to be discussed later (Fenster).

Galehaut (not to be confused with Galahad), possibly the real-life Irish-Scottish King Domingart, becomes close friends with Lancelot, the queen's companion and bodyguard sent to her by the Lady of the Lake. Lancelot's loyalty to the queen is fixed from the moment she saves him from drowning, and he changes the Dolorous Castle to the Castle of the Holy Grail, or Joyous Guard, in seeking her. The Prose *Lancelot* relates that Arthur yields to the entreaties of the False Guinevere and seeks the death penalty for the queen's alleged imposture and adultery. But Galehaut, urging caution, requests a delay of forty days to weigh the evidence. Arthur refuses. Galehaut declares that if Queen Guinevere were condemned, he would call a mistrial and fight Arthur personally. Lancelot insists on defending her himself. The seneschal Bertolais proclaims a dire sentence on the queen: mutilation and exile. The nobles and knights unanimously refuse to accept this verdict. Lancelot resigns from the Round Table, labeling the judges liars. He declares his intent to fight for Queen Guinevere's honor in judicial combat, during which Lancelot vanquishes three champions with the sword Excalibur, sparing the life of the third at Guinevere's request. Guinevere herself escapes mutilation and exile, but is not reinstated as Arthur's bride or queen. She is given refuge by Galehaut, who offers her his Sorelois estates to occupy as her own land. The False Guinevere and Bertolais, suffering paralyzing strokes, publicly confess their lies; Queen Guinevere is exonerated of all the original charges and declared King Arthur's lawful spouse.

The historical King Mordred, having been crowned in Pictland after King Loth's death, was joined by King Urien. Together they battled King Arthur's forces at Camian in 627. King Arthur died fighting Mordred, his sister's youngest son by King Loth. Many Scots and Picts also died in the battle. Queen Guinevere of Britain was taken hostage by the victorious Picts, originally her own people, and returned safely to Dunbar Castle. Inspired by the account of Giraldus Cambrensis (Gerald of Wales) in his *De Principis Instructione* (*The Instruction of Princes*, 1193), recording the discovery of Arthur's grave at Glastonbury Abbey, those who believe that Arthur died (a point left in doubt in most accounts) at Avalon (his place of refuge after being fatally wounded by Mordred) also contend that Arthur was then buried at Glastonbury, and that Guinevere joined him there at her death. Since that grave and the famous unearthed inscribed cross attesting Arthur and Guinevere's burial there have disappeared since Giraldus, modern historians have yet to verify this evidence.

As may be discerned even in the above summary, several challenges loom before the Guinevere researcher, particularly those related to sources. The earliest sources, or those closest to Guinevere's lifetime of the late fifth and early sixth centuries, are chronicle histories. Later, with the advent of so-called courtly love and the cultivation of chivalry, the literary sources, with their more esthetic allure, begin to rival and even surpass the chronicles in appeal. Guinevere's image has been affected by each historian's or romancier's artistic talent and appeal to his or her public, as the following survey attempts to outline, however rapidly. Generally speaking, for example, while the Welsh Guinevere tradition speaks of her has having borne Arthur sons, the English chronicles specify that she was unfortunately barren, save for the Alliterative *Morte Arthure* of c.1400, which has her give Mordred two sons (Beverly Kennedy).

Geoffrey of Monmouth's *Historia* is one of the earliest and most enduring sources. A medieval-style Oxford don and therefore familiar with Classical literature, Geoffrey highlights Guinevere's Roman background—modeling her to some extent on Dido—and claims that "Modred," as he calls him (revealing his reliance on Cornish or Breton sources for this detail), is Arthur's nephew who jointly ruled Britain with Guinevere in Arthur's absence, enticed her into an adulterous relationship with him, and made himself king. Arthur must then fight him to regain his crown. It is here that Mordred fatally wounds Arthur. Wace (1155), in his Norman-French version of Geoffrey's *History*, titled the *Roman de Brut* (*Romance of Brut/Brutus*), provides ceremonial details and, together with Layamon's *Brut* (c.1200), emphasizes Guinevere's feelings of guilt and fear. Hardyng's *Chronicle* (c.1457) takes a more pragmatic view by saying she was forced to marry Mordred to protect herself. The Vulgate Cycle, composed c.1215–1235, contains further elaboration but its moral perspective changes over time, from one favoring Guinevere in the earlier Prose *Lancelot* to one condemning her, because of the destructive effect of her liaison with Lancelot, by time of the later *Queste del Saint Graal* (*Quest for the Holy Grail*) and *La Mort le roi Artu* (*The Death of King Arthur*).

In Germany, Heinrich von dem Türlin, who penned the lengthy Middle High German version *Diu Crône* (*The Crown*, thirteenth century), adds to the Meleagant (here, Gasozein) abduction episode (in which she is here saved by Gawain) the figure of Guinevere/Ginover's spurned suitor. This nobleman wanted to identify her by seeing her crown-shaped birthmark or tatoo on her hip. The suitor's battle in the forest glade with her brother ends in a stalemate, whereupon Guinevere leads them back to Carlisle on horseback.

Another viewpoint comes from Paris, in 1527, when Hector Boece, first principal of the University of Aberdeen, Scotland, wrote his widely read Latin chronicle, *Scotorum Historiae* (*History and Chronicles of Scotland*), tells us that Queen Guinevere was taken by the Picts after the battle of Camlan, and moreover that her monument was in Meigle, Scotland. Boece's chronicle repeats the anti-Arthur feelings expressed in his main source, John of Fordun's Latin *Chronica Gentis Scotorum* (*Chronicle of the Scottish People*) or *Scotichronicon* (c.1385).

Not surprisingly, it is especially in the literary sources (that is, romances rather than chronicles and histories) that we encounter another challenge, the vexed question inherent in Guinevere's image: her alleged adultery with Lancelot. This is the Guinevere legend's second love triangle: more glorious than the darkly pragmatic one with Mordred, because this one is based on love. The magnitude of this willful offense derives not only from its legal implications (by law she would have been executed had the charges been proven) but also from its causative role in the downfall of Arthur's court, as narrated at the end of the Vulgate Cycle. The adulterous Guinevere tradition was perhaps initially fueled by ancient Celtic queenship rights, which allowed queens, like their husbands, to take lovers without the kind of censure arising in later Christianized versions, even those in the *fin' amors* (courtly love) tradition (Lacy et al.). The most renowned of all courtly romanciers, Chrétien de Troyes, in his *Lancelot* or *Le Chevalier de la charrete* (c.1178)—so titled because Lancelot's riding in a cart significantly dictates his standing among the other characters—was the first to show Guinevere committing adultery with Lancelot, but without condemning the affair. On the contrary, in the true spirit of courtly romance, he was responding to his sophisticated public's interest in the love triangle and the problematics of female desire, particularly as encouraged by his patron, Marie de Champagne, as mentioned in his prologue, which in turn appears subverted by the epilogue, written by Godefroi de Legni, supposedly at Chrétien's behest (Krueger). Chrétien's contemporary, Marie de France, in *Lanval*, chief among her exquisitely-wrought *Lais* (short romances), casts Guinevere (unnamed) very negatively as a conniving, rank-pulling, would-be adulterer who pursues Lanval unsuccessfully and then, once rebuffed, enacts a Potiphar's-Wife-style countermeasure (Genesis 34) by accusing Lanval of making advances toward her and causing him to stand trial; in a sense doing to him what False Guinevere does to Guinevere in other versions. In a significant departure from the orthodox Lancelot-Guinevere tradition, the hero of Ulrich von Zatzikhoven's *Lanzelet* (1194–1205) loves other women (commenting on the doctrine of *minne*, the German equivalent of fin' amors)—but *not* Ginover—as part of his chivalric apprenticeship in becoming an ideal knight and future king. Lancelot is Ginover's champion (though he does not rescue her from her abductor) and also pledged to Arthur in a keenly political setting (Schultz). This positive image of the queen, which would influence the Prose *Lancelot*, is in keeping with the German Arthurian tradition's overall tendency to portray her as the ideal wife to a deserving, most courtly Arthur (Samples). However, Chrétien's adulterous Guinevere, despite the poet's sympathetic framing, established the basis for a derogatory typology whose moral-psychological depths later authors would artfully attempt to probe. As Denis de Rougemont repeatedly affirms in his classic study on the Tristan and Isolde legends and their enduring appeal, *L'Amour et l'Occident* (*Love in the West*), unhappy, transgressive love stories and their intricate repercussions pique human interest far more than happy, respectable ones.

Goodrich, among certain other twentieth-century scholars, asserts that these authors' charges remain unsupported and urges a cautious approach, citing, for example, that Chrétien in *Lancelot* mistranslates "altar" as being analogous to "bed," thereby presenting Lancelot as the queen's lover whereas Goodrich's translation has him serving as her acolyte. Other evidence contradicting the adultery thesis stems from the unsuitable conditions of sixth-century life: a period of invasion, political instability, and frequent imminent danger to body and dwelling, even amidst the nobility. Such discomfort would have hardly encouraged a long-term liaison. Lancelot would more likely have devoted himself to protecting both her person and her reputation. The modern-day defenders of "Pure Guinevere" also point to prohibitive structural and other details within the prisons and other buildings in which she and Lancelot supposedly trysted, together with the incoherence and fragmentation of the various accounts, as evidence undermining the adultery thesis.

Sir Thomas Malory, author of *Le Morte Darthur* printed by the illustrious William Caxton in 1485, because he envisioned the most complete version ever, also presents the most complete and subtle moral tableau, interweaving strands from previous cultures into his own monumental retelling. To cite Lori Walters's interpretation, for example, Malory deemphasized the sexual side of Guinevere and Lancelot's relationship in attempting to redefine "the place of love in the moral order." Malory transforms their story into "a study of secular chivalry," integrating societal and personal needs in a new light. He drew on the widest array of sources, principally the French Prose *Merlin* and the English Alliterative *Morte Arthure*, the Prose *Lancelot* and *Queste del Saint Graal* of the Vulgate Cycle, and the Prose *Tristan*. By the end of Malory's *Morte Darthur*, character and accident of situation are more central than moral judgments, especially concerning the love affair between Guinevere and Lancelot, who end their lives in repentance. Lancelot retreats to a hermitage, and Guinevere becomes a nun in Amesbury, but not before proclaiming to her ladies that Lancelot, whose honorable love of his king (by chivalric standards) is rivaled only by his equally honorable love of his queen (by courtly love standards), is the noblest of knights. Furthermore, Lancelot takes all the blame for their affair and its consequences upon himself (Brewer).

Leaping into the nineteenth century, we find Tennyson's *Idylls of the King* portraying Guinevere's adultery with Lancelot as a moral contaminant infecting the purity of Camelot with evil. Yet despite his monolithic Victorian-age moralizing, Tennyson is also intrigued by her; his Guinevere emerges as the most original of all his *Idylls*, as David Staines argues: her portrayal defines those of all the other women characters. She surpasses even Arthur in heroic bearing, as she lives by her credo, however tragic: "We needs must love the highest when we see it." Tennyson also mentions her ability to foresee the decline of her reputation. But not all authors of this period deplored her morality. Shortly before Tennyson's work, William Morris, inspired by Malory, published a group of Arthurian poems of which the most famous is "The Defence of Guenevere" (1858). It begins dramatically with Guenevere, about to be burned alive publicly for her adultery, attempting to defend herself by eloquently acknowledging her crime while also emotionally evoking the misery that drove her to commit it. She almost manages to persuade Gawaine, who nonetheless finally turns away to leave her to her fate, from which she is rescued at the last minute by Launcelot. Morris's three other Arthurian poems further explore the psychological and moral paradoxes of the lovers' liaison.

Tennyson, whose *Idylls* tend to lack psychological nuance, nonetheless notes Guinevere's gift of foresight, which hints at another side to her, that of prophetess, especially in her dreams, and also her role as priestess, recalling her tutelage under the enchantress Viviane. Her Pict and Druid origins and frequent allusions to her garment (fabrics and color), jewels and metals in her apparel, and her various insignias—crown, dove, pillars, fountains, and, on another level, blood—also foster her supernatural aspect, along with her Welsh triad mentioned earlier. All of these underscore her role as priestess, warrior, and even embodiment of a goddess. In Sharan Newman's *Guenevere Evermore* (1985), Guinevere recognizes herself as a priestess. Newman emphasizes the spiritually pleasing setting, celebrating nature, tranquilly, femininity. By contrast, R. T. Davis's view of Malory's account highlights Guinevere's experience as a warrior who would prefer to be slain herself by Sir Mellyagaunce rather than see her wounded knights suffer. Of the numerous literary continuations of the Arthurian legends, the acknowledged best for the twentieth century is T. H. White's *The Once and Future King*, a collection of four Arthurian epics composed in 1939–1940, which in turn yielded the highly successful musical *Camelot* (1961), also warmly received as a film (1967). *The Once and Future King* depicts a domesticated passion between Guinevere and Arthur, with the king at first ignoring the liaison; another film version, *First Knight* (1995) ends happily despite the love triangle. Of all the films to have commemorated Guinevere, the most artistically rewarding is arguably that by the highly refined and distinctively French "medievophile," Robert

Bresson (d. 1999), in his controversial *Lancelot du Lac* (1974), although one should peruse Kevin Harty's many studies of Arthurian cinema, and those by other critics, before rushing to judgment.

The above discussion can only afford mere glimpses of Guinevere's multimedia history and afterlife, continuously analyzed in volumes of studies edited by such scholars as Thelma Fenster, Norris Lacy, Lori Walters, and, most recently, Alan Lupack.

See also Arthurian Women; Capellanus, Andreas; Dowry; Embroider, Enchantresses, Fays (*Fées*), and Fairies; Isolde; Marie de Champagne; Marie de France; Morgan le Fay

BIBLIOGRAPHY

Primary Sources
Boece, Hector. *The History and Chronicles of Scotland*. Translated from Latin [into Scots] by John Bellenden (1531). Edited by Walter Seton. Continued by R. W. Chambers and Edith C. Batho. 2 vols. Scottish Text Society, 10, 15. Edinburgh and London: Blackwood, 1938–1941.
Chrétien de Troyes. *Lancelot, ou Le Chevalier de la Charrette*. Edited with commentary by Mireille Demaules. Translated [Modern French] by Daniel Poirion. Folio classique. Paris: Gallimard, 1996.
———. *Lancelot: The Knight of the Cart*. Translated by Burton Raffel. Afterword by Joseph J. Duggan. New Haven, Conn.: Yale University Press, 1997.
Geoffrey of Monmouth. *Historia regum Britannie*. Translated with commentary by Neil Wright and Julia C. Crick. 5 vols. Cambridge and Dover, N.H.: D. S. Brewer, 1984–1991.
Heinrich von dem Türlin. *Diu Crône*. Edited by Gottlob H. F. Scholl. Bibliothek des literarischen Vereins Stuttgart, 27. Stuttgart, Germany: Literarischer Verein, 1852. [Middle-High German text only].
———. *The Crown: A Tale of Sir Gawein and King Arthur's Court*. Translated with introduction by John Wesley Thomas. Lincoln: University of Nebraska Press, 1989.
Lancelot du Lac: Roman français du XIIIᵉ siècle. Edited by Elspeth Kennedy. Translated (Modern French) with commentary by François Mosès. Preface by Michel Zink. Lettres gothiques. 3 vols. Paris: Livre de Poche, 1991–1998. *See also below under* Vulgate Cycle.
Layamon. [*Brut*]. *Layamon's Arthur: The Arthurian Sections of Layamon's Brut*. Edited and translated with introduction and notes by W. R. J. Barron and S. C. Weinberg. Revised ed. Exeter, U.K.: University of Exeter Press, 2001.
Malory, Thomas. *Le Morte d'Arthur*. In *Malory: Complete Works*. Edited by Eugène Vinaver. Originally 1954. 2nd ed. Oxford and New York: Oxford University Press, 1971.
Marie de France. *Lanval*. In *Lais*. Edited by Karl Warnke. Translated [Modern French] with introduction and commentary by Laurence Harf-Lancner. Lettres gothiques. Paris: Livre de Poche, 1990.
———. *Lanval*. In *Lais of Marie de France*. Translated with introduction by Glyn S. Burgess and Keith Busby. 2nd ed. New York and London: Penguin, 1999.
Morris, William. *The Defence of Guenevere and Other Poems*. Edited by Margaret Lourie. Garland English Texts, 2. New York: Garland, 1981.
Newman, Sharan. *Guinevere Evermore*. New York: St. Martin's, 1985.
Tennyson, Alfred. *Idylls of the King*. Edited by J. M. Gray. Revised. New York and London: Penguin, 1996. Ulrich von Zatzikhoven. *Lanzelet*. Edited by K. A. Hahn. Frankfurt: Broenner, 1845. [Medieval German text only].
———. *Lanzelet: A Romance*. Translated by Kenneth Gibson. Introduction and notes by Roger S. Loomis. New York: Columbia University Press, 1951.
[Vulgate Cycle]. *Lancelot roman en prose du XIIIᵉ siècle*. Edited by Alexandre Micha. 9 vols. Textes Littéraires français, 247, 249, 262, 278, 283, 286, 288, 307, 315. Geneva: Droz, 1978–1983.
———. *Lancelot-Grail: The Old French Arthurian Vulgate and Post-Vulgate in Translation*. General editor Norris J. Lacy. Translated by N. Lacy et al. Garland Reference Library of the Humanities, 941, 1826, 1878, 1896, 1964. New York: Garland, 1993–1996.

Wace. *Wace's Roman de Brut: A History of the British*. Edited and translated, with introduction by Judith Weiss. Revised ed. Exeter, U.K.: University of Exeter Press, 2002. [Bilingual (Old-French and English) ed.].

White, T[erence]. H[anbury]. *The Once and Future King*. London: Collins, 1958.

Secondary Sources

Ashe, Geoffrey. *The Discovery of King Arthur*. New York: Henry Holt, 1985.

———. ed. *The Quest for Arthur's Britain*. London: Granada Publishing, 1982.

Brewer, Derek. "Paradoxes of Honour in Malory." In Lupack, 33–47. *See below.*

Davies, Reginald Thorne, ed. *King Arthur and His Knights* [Selections from Malory's *Morte Darthur*]. New York: Barnes & Noble, 1967.

Fenster, Thelma, ed. *Arthurian Women: A Casebook*. Arthurian Characters and Themes, 3. Garland Reference Library of the Humanities, 1499. New York and London: Garland, 1996. [Extensive introduction with several pertinent essays by leading specialists].

Goodrich, Norma Lorre. *Guinevere*. New York: Harper Collins, 1991.

Gordon-Wise, Barbara Ann. *The Reclamation of a Queen: Guinevere in Modern Fantasy*. New York: Greenwood, 1991.

Harty, Kevin J. "Arthur? Arthur? Arthur?—Where Exactly is the Cinematic Arthur to be Found?" In Lupack, 135–48. *See below.*

Kennedy, Beverly. "Guenevere." In Lacy, Norris J., ed. *The New Arthurian Encyclopedia*, 215. *See below.*

Korrel, Peter. *An Arthurian Triangle: A Study of the Origin, Development and Characterization of Arthur, Guinevere and Modred*. Leiden: E. J. Brill, 1984.

Krueger, Roberta L. "Desire, Meaning, and the Female Reader: The Problem in Chrétien's *Charrete*." In Walters, 229–45. *See below.*

Lacy, Norris J., ed. *The New Arthurian Encyclopedia*. New York and London: Garland, 1996.

———, and Geoffrey Ashe, with Deborah N. Mancoff. *The Arthurian Handbook*. Garland Reference Library of the Humanities, 1920. 2nd ed. New York and London: Garland, 1997.

Lupack, Alan, ed. *New Directions in Arthurian Studies*. Arthurian Studies, 51. Cambridge: D. S. Brewer, 2002.

Neuendorf, Fiona. "Feminist and Historical Concerns: Guinevere in Geoffrey of Monmouth's *Historia Regum Brittanniae*." *Quondam et Futurus*. 3. 2 (1991–1993): 26–44.

Rougemont, Denis de. *L'Amour et l'Occident*. Paris: Plon, 1939. [Several reprints and translations].

Samples, Susan. "Guinevere: A Re-Appraisal." *Arthurian Interpretations* 3. 2 (1989): 106–18. Reprint in Walters, 219–28. *See below.*

Schultz, James A. "*Lanzelet*: A Flawless Hero in a Symmetrical World." *Beiträge der deutschen Sprache und Literatur* 102 (1980): 160–88. Reprint in Walters, 29–54. *See below.*

Staines, David. "Tennyson's Guinevere and Her *Idylls of the King*." In Lupack, 83–96. *See above.*

Walters, Lori J., ed. *Lancelot and Guinevere: A Casebook*. Arthurian Characters and Themes, 4. Garland Reference Library of the Humanities, 1513. New York: Garland, 1996. Reprint New York: Routledge, 2002. [Extensive literary-historical introduction by Walters and sixteen essays by leading specialists].

ANNE DAGHISTANY AND KRISTIAN KIMBRO

ħ

H., DOMNA (fl. 1220–c.1240). The mysterious "Lady H." coauthored a *tenso*, or dialogue poem, concerning proper male lover's conduct, with a male troubadour known only as "Rofin," as signaled in the poem's title and opening verse, "Rofin, digatz m'ades de cors" ("Rofin, now tell me from the heart"). Such male- and female-voiced poems offer much insight into concepts of love within the refined milieu of the troubadours and *trobairitz* (women troubadours) and how seriously we are to take them.

Four of the five troubadour *chansonniers* (manuscripts containing collections of lyrics) that contain the *tenso* attribute it jointly to "Domna H." and to an otherwise unknown male poet named "Rofin" (or "Rosin"), while the fifth ascribes it only to "H." The traditional *tenso* is a dialogue poem composed jointly by two real authors, each of whom speaks in his or her own voice and is accorded rigorously equal space in the text. The poem of Domna H. and Rofin is a *partimen* (debate poem), a subgenre of the *tenso* in which the first speaker proposes a theoretical problem and offers the second his choice of positions to defend, then taking the opposing position. Domna H.'s persona, after having asserted that Rofin is knowledgeable in matters of love and courtesy, asks him to give his opinion on a dilemma faced by a lady of her acquaintance who has two suitors. The setting involves a ritual known as the *assag* (test) or *jazer* (lying together) between courtly lovers, if one accepts René Nelli's theory that such tests really existed (Nelli 1974), the lady has invited each lover in turn into her bed, after first obtaining from each his oath (*sagramen*) that he would do no more than hold and kiss her. While the second "no.l ausa far per re" ("dared do no more"), the first, disregarding his oath, possessed the lady.

Rofin's persona deplores the *follors* (folly; unconscionable actions) of the impetuous lover, arguing that he who respected the lady's wishes is alone worthy to receive her love. Domna H. replies sharply that the compelling desire that prevented the impetuous lover from seeing, from hearing, and from distinguishing good from evil is a measure of his love, suggesting by implication that the obedient lover's passion is inferior. Since no agreement seems possible, the speakers propose to consult an arbiter. Domna H. suggests "N'Agnesina" ("Lady Agnesina"), whom she calls *midons* ("my lady"), while Rofin, who has the last word, insists that N'Agnesina submit the question to a still higher authority: "Na Cobeitosa de Tot Be" ("Lady Desirous of All Good").

"Rofin, digatz m'ades de cors" is problematic in two respects: in the historicity of its protagonists and putative authors and in its intentionality and ideology. While it has been suggested that the sexual explicitness of Domna H.'s remarks was required her concealment beneath an incognito (Perkal-Balinsky, 16), early scholars, who assumed the historical accuracy of the information provided by the rubric (manuscript heading for the poem) and the proper names within the text, undertook to discover her identity. In the eighteenth century, Francesco Quadrio proposed to identify her with Huguette de Forcalquier, a figure mentioned by none less than Jehan de Nostredamus in his apocryphal *Vies des plus célèbres et anciens poètes provençaux* (*Lives of the Most Famous and Oldest Provençal Poets*) or with "some Hermissenda or Helen" (Nostredamus, 2: 134). Later, Camille Chabaneau tentatively and tersely suggested the name "Helis"—nothing more, while Oskar Schultz-Gora, who believed "N'Agnesina" to be the daughter of Bonifazio di Saluzzo (d. 1212), from the Piedmont in Italy, and "Na Cobeitosa" to be a real-life Na Cobeitosa d'Este, hypothesized accordingly that Domna H. was the Italian woman troubadour [H]Alais de Videllana (or di Viadana) and dated the work to 1220–1240. Most recently, Angelica Rieger, looking at various intertextual links among the different troubadours of Provence and Northern Italy, favors Hugueta of Baux, praised by the troubadour Blancatz (ed. Rieger, 299–304), seconded by Matilda Bruckner (ed. Bruckner et al., 173). A lesser, but equally intriguing quest has puzzled over Rofin's identity or more precisely, since most researchers accept its role as a *senhal* (code name), the meaning of his name, ranging from Meg Bogin's *Rosin* (nightingale) to Rieger's *Rofin* (ruffian).

However, the second problematic aspect of the text, its intentionality, calls into question the factual accuracy of its historical allusions. Domna H.'s persona, who argues that virtue must yield to lust and who, by her example, testifies to the natural incontinence of the female sex, adopts (and incarnates) a traditionally masculine and misogynistic view of feminine sexuality, as Sarah Kay has also noted, while Rofin's persona, who argues that the lady's person and wishes must be respected and that a lover's self-restraint in the *assag* is proof of durable and sincere love, adopts a point of view that, if not exclusively feminine, would find sympathy with many women. While some critics would explain the work by dismissing Domna H. as "une insatiable" ("a [sexually] insatiable woman"; Nelli 1977, 261), her exaggerated rhetoric and the transposition of gender roles suggest that the work is satirical or playful and thus deliberately subverts the ethic of *fin'amors* (courtly love). In all, even if the characters other than Rofin and Domna H. were real, too many other factors lead us to believe that their *tenso* is an amusing fiction— not an unusual occurrence in these genres—and that Domna H. herself is apocryphal (Torraca, 30–31; Bertoni, 96; Bruckner 1994).

See also Trobairitz

BIBLIOGRAPHY

Primary Sources
Domna H. and Rofin. "Rofin, digatz m'ades de cors." In *Songs of the Women Troubadours*, edited and translated by Matilda Tomaryn Bruckner, Laurie Shepard and Sarah White, 78–83, 172–73. New York and London: Garland, 1995. New ed. 2000. [Most recent, authoritative: original texts, notes, introduction and English trans.].
———. "Rofin, digatz m'ades de cors." In *Trobairitz: Der Beitrag der Frau in der altokzitanischen höfischen Lyrik. Edition des Gesamtkorpus*, edited by Angelica Rieger, 296–99. Beihefte der Zeitschrift für romanische Philologie, 233. Tübingen, Germany: Max Niemeyer Verlag, 1991. [Most authoritative, German trans. and commentary].

Secondary Sources

[See also notes to above editions].

Bertoni, Giulio. *I Trovatori d'Italia. Biografie, testi, traduzioni, note.* Modena: Umberto Orlandini, 1915. Geneva: Slatkine, 1974.

Bogin, Meg. *The Women Troubadours.* New York and London: Paddington Press, 1976.

Bruckner, Matilda Tomaryn. "Debatable Fictions: The *Tensos* of the *Trobairitz.*" In *Literary Aspects of Courtly Culture: Selected Papers from the Seventh Triennial Congress of the International Courtly Literature Society,* edited by Donald Maddox and Sara Sturm-Maddox, 19–28. Cambridge: D. S. Brewer, 1994.

Chabaneau, Camille. *Les Biographies des Troubadours en langue provençale.* Toulouse: E. Privat, 1885. Geneva: Slatkine, 1975.

Kay, Sarah. *Subjectivity in Troubadour Poetry.* Cambridge: Cambridge University Press, 1990.

Nelli, Rene. *L'Érotique des troubadours.* 2: 24–46. 2 vols. New ed. "10/18". Paris: Union Générale d'Éditions, 1974.

———. *Ecrivains anticonformistes du moyen âge occitan. I. La Femme et l'amour.* Paris: Phébus, 1977.

Nostredame, Jean de. *Vies des plus célèbres et anciens poètes provençaux.* Edited by Camille Chabaneau. Paris: Champion, 1913. Reprint Geneva: Slatkine, 1970.

Perkal-Balinsky, Deborah. "The Minor *Trobairitz*: An Edition with Translation and Commentary." Ph.D. diss., Northwestern University, 1986.

Quadrio, Francesco Saverio. *Della storia e della ragione d'ogni poesia.* 5 vols. Bologna-Milan, 1739–1752.

Schultz-Gora, Oskar. *Die provenzalischen Dichterinnen.* Leipzig: Foch, 1888. Reprint Geneva: Slatkine, 1975.

Torraca, Francesco. *Le donne italiane nella poesia provenzale; La "Treva" di G. de la Tor.* Biblioteca Critica della Letteratura Italiana 39. Firenze: G. C. Sansoni, 1901.

MERRITT R. BLAKESLEE

HADEWIJCH (d. 1260). Hadewijch was a Middle-Dutch mystic and beguine (one of a group of pious women leading nonmonastic lives), and an author of letters (*Brieven*; sing. *Brief*), poetry, and visionary prose. Because no historical documents referring to Hadewijch are preserved, for biographical information scholars must resort exclusively to some scarce factual data in her own work, whose interpretation poses difficulty. The most important source in this respect is the *Lijst der Volmaakten* (*List of the Perfect*), an enumeration, from Christ's days to the end of time, of all the perfect lovers of God she had seen in one of her *Visioenen* (*Visions*; sing. *Visioen*). From among her deceased contemporaries, Hadewijch mentions a "Beguine who was killed by Master Robert because of her true love." Specialists concur that she is referring to the inquisitor Robert le Bougre (aptly named: French = "Robert the Bugger"), who operated in the southern Netherlands from 1236 until 1239. Perhaps one might also consider the mention of "seven hermits, who live on the wall of Jerusalem," as a latest possible dating point for this list: Jerusalem having been seized by the Saracens in 1244. Hadewijch must have flourished therefore in the second quarter or about the middle of the thirteenth century.

Her language situates her in the duchy of Brabant, in what are now Belgium and the Netherlands. Some sources claim that she was from Antwerp, but these go back no later than the fifteenth century, thereby leaving this point unresolved. Her perfect command of courtly discourse, her acquaintance with the poetry of the *trouvères* (northern-French versions of the southern-French troubadours: lyric poets) and her ability to read theological writings in Latin—as attested by part of her tenth letter (*Brief 10*) in its adaptation of an extract from (pseudo-?)Richard of Saint Victor's *Explicatio in Cantica Canticorum* (*Exposition on the Song of Songs*, twelfth century) and her eighteenth letter's translation of a passage from chapter 8 of French theologian William of Saint-Thierry's *De natura et dignitate amoris* (*On the Nature and Dignity of Love*, twelfth century)—indicate her privileged origins.

She also was seemingly able to choose freely the people with whom she lived (*Brief 3*, 18–19), since she did not always live in the same place and was even compelled to wander around (*Brieven 26* and *29*, 12; see also what Christ tells her in *Visioen 1*, 291: "you will not know where to lodge for a single night"), from which we can infer that she did not live in a convent. Moreover, among the contemporaries in her *Lijst der Volmaakten*, she shows a marked preference for people either from outside the institutions of the Church, or who only occupied a marginal position within it: female and male hermits, beguines, a castaway priest, or a forgotten master in Paris, lonely in his cell. We may therefore situate her in the early beguine movement, originating in and around her homeland.

Very probably, it is in such a milieu that Hadewijch's work must be placed. All her writings resulted from the necessity to exhort her companions, who just like herself had been touched by God's love, to radical love in return. In her works, she teaches her readers two fundamental and complementary lessons. On the one hand, she shows that fruition—the satiating experience of being one with God—is never exhaustive: God is always greater than what man can possess of Him. God is by definition "over-rich." He is transcendent. In this respect, Hadewijch points out the dangers of purely "affective" mysticism since it conveys the impression of merging completely into God and thus gaining a complete knowledge of the Other in an affective "unknowing." It is beyond doubt that, in the ambience of the religious women's movement of the thirteenth century—one in which mystical *epiphenomena* (Greek = events, like visions and levitations) were much in vogue—Hadewijch's warnings against the blindness of affective mysticism were valid.

But on the other hand, and paradoxically, Hadewijch stresses the point that it is possible to be one with God, already here on earth. God allows himself to be possessed; He is immanent. The high opinion she has of the power of love makes her engage in a polemic with those people, whom in her *Strofische Gedichten* (*Stanzaic Poems*) she calls "the aliens," and behind whom we may suspect philosophically schooled clergymen, who pretend that God is unattainable because of man's lowness (*Visioen 1*, 407). For them God remains out of reach because they do not love. And therefore, in her eighth *Visioen*, a champion, whom we may identify as a theologian, must confess to her: "When I lived as man, I had too little love with affection, and followed the strict counsel of the intellect. For this reason I could not be set on fire with the love that creates such a great oneness, for I did the noble Humanity great wrong in that I withheld from it this affection" (*Visioen 8*, 117–23).

Hadewijch's emphasis on both God's transcendence and His immanence explains why the "two eyes of the soul" (*Brief 18*, 81), reason and love, play such an important part in her spirituality: reason alerts man to God's greatness, but love surmounts over and over again the gap that separates man from God. Accordingly, in the passage she borrowed from French theologian William of Saint-Thierry (1075–1148), she is able to say: "Love and reason are of great mutual help one to the other; for reason instructs love, and love enlightens reason. When reason abandons itself to love's wish, and love consents to be forced and held within the bounds of reason, they can accomplish a very great work" (*Brief 18*, 93–98; see also *Brief 11*, 40–45).

Until now, all theories about the chronological order of Hadewijch's work have turned out to be very questionable. One should thus not draw any conclusions from the order in which Hadewijch's works are discussed here, in moving from her prose to her verse works.

Hadewijch's prose works include her fourteen *Visioenen* and her thirty-one *Brieven* (*Letters*). The collection of *Visioenen* must be considered as a whole and describes Hadewijch's progress towards the perfect oneness with God, or, as she puts it, her development from spiritual "infancy" to "maturity." Time and again, she explains that this oneness here on earth does not only consist in the rewarding experience of God's presence, but that it includes also a second aspect, the experience of God's absence. In this second, painful moment, the mystic learns that she must also become one with Christ in his life and sufferings, and that in this process her will, even in its noblest intentions (charity, friendship, love of the saints), requires conformity with God's will. Only when she has become "full grown" does she receive, directly from God, the explicit order to lead others towards Him: "Lead all the unled according to their worthiness, in which they are loved by me and with which they love and serve me according to my Nature" (*Visioen 8*, 104–7). Moreover, the collection of *Visioenen* itself may be considered as a result of that divine order: by telling of her (visionary) experiences, Hadewijch shows her readers, who are still in their mystical "infancy" (compare to *Visioen 14*, 63) the way they have to follow.

Hadewijch addressed her thirty-one *Brieven* to one or more (unnamed) friends, whom she usually calls "sweet" or "dear child" and from whom presumably she lived separated. The letter, more than the other genres she practiced, offered her space and freedom enough to develop diverse aspects of her love-doctrine so that many *Brieven* can be considered as small treatises, which is a frequent phenomenon in medieval letter collections. But unlike the impersonal treatise, the medieval letter is preeminently the genre of friendship: it requires author and reader to be moved by the same ideal of love. In this way, it enables Hadewijch to bring up her own experience as an example and to exhort the reader directly to put her message into practice. The polished style and the use of verses and of rhyming prose suggest that Hadewijch, like many other medieval epistolary authors, had from the very beginning a larger public of kindred souls in mind than merely the addressee.

Her poetic works include sixteen poems in couplets and forty-five stanzaic poems. The collection of poems in couplets mainly consists in didactic letters in rhymed couplets. In Hadewijch studies, they are mostly called *Mengeldichten* (*Mixed Poems*), but *Rijmbrieven* (*Rhymed Letters*) would no doubt be a better name. The *Mengeldichten 17–29*, that appear, among other places, in two Hadewijch manuscripts are of an entirely different nature and are generally considered as not having been written by her. They seem more closely related to the work of the mystics Eckhart (c.1260–c.1328) and Marguerite Porete (d. 1310) and probably date only from the first half of the fourteenth century. Her religious *Strofische Gedichten* is closely related to the secular *grand chant courtois* (great courtly poetics) of the *trouvères*. The mystical and courtly vocabularies of love are blended to one new poetic language, with which Hadewijch, like the *trouvères*, constantly realizes new variations on the same theme. Like the courtly chansons these poems were meant for an audience, who thought of themselves as an elite, taking part in the supreme adventure of (mystical) love. At the center of this poetry is personified Love, who entraps, shoots, and wounds the lover, who robs him of his mind and heart, who forces him with violence and so forth, but also warns him, cherishes him, grants him full pardon, consoles him, clothes, honors, and nourishes him. Too often, these poems have been read as purely confessional poetry, written by an author who felt desperate, but there can be no doubt that their first function was to teach and to exhort—they are didactic—as is the case with all Hadewijch's works. This spiritual, didactic tendency contrasts distinctly with the earthly, sensuous concerns of courtly love poetry while appropriating courtly-poetic language; the audience is constantly and directly urged to radical love-service. The loving "I" serves as an example: the plaints about the absence of the beloved One must teach the others that they should leave the quiet of deceptive, complacent enjoyment and engage in the adventure of real love.

In the Middle Ages, Hadewijch's work circulated mainly among Carthusians (a strictly contemplative monastic order begun in 1084 in the French Alps), regular canons (clergy living under monastic rule) and in the milieu of then newer *Devotio Moderna*, the Modern Devotion movement that attracted followers intent on deepening their spiritual lives beyond that afforded by the established Church. Three manuscripts (Brussels, Koninklijke Bibliotheek, 2879–80 [ms. A] and 2877–78 [ms. B]; Ghent, Universiteitsbibliotheek 941 [ms. C]) contain the whole of Hadewijch's work, a fourth manuscript (Antwerp, Ruusbroecgenootschap, 385 II [ms. R]) only the *Strofische Gedichten*, the *Rijmbrieven*, and the *Lijst der Volmaakten*. One can also find parts of her work (especially of her *Brieven*) in many other manuscripts, in the form of paraphrases, anthologies, quotations, and the like. In the fourteenth century, excerpts from her *Brieven* were translated into High German under the names of *sante Adelwip* or *sant Adel*. She exerted great influence on the Flemish mystic and Devotio Moderna leader, Jan van Ruusbroec (1293–1381), who quotes her repeatedly, yet without mentioning her name, and on his Flemish pupils John of Louvain and Godfried of Wevel.

From the sixteenth century onward, Hadewijch's work seems to have fallen into almost complete oblivion. It was only in 1838, when two Hadewijch manuscripts were found in the Burgundian (now: Royal) Library in Brussels, that her work began to arouse new interest. Thanks to the abundant scholarship and critical editing by the Jesuit Joseph van Mierlo in the mid-twentieth century, Hadewijch became recognized as one of the great authors in Dutch literature. But it is especially during the last two decades that Hadewijch has become one of the very rare Middle-Dutch authors whose work finds its way to an ever-increasing modern readership in her own country and elsewhere.

See also Beatrijs van Nazareth/van Tienen; Beguines; Capellanus, Andreas; Epistolary Authors, Women as; Mechthild of Magdeburg; *Minne*; Porete, Marguerite; *Trouvères*, Women

BIBLIOGRAPHY

Primary Sources
Hadewijch. *Brieven*. Edited with commentary by Joseph van Mierlo. Leuvense Studiën en Tekstultgaven, 14. Antwerp, Belgium: Standaard-Boekhandel, 1947.
———. *De brieven van Hadewijch*. Edited and translated [Modern Dutch] by Paul Mommaers. Cahiers voor levensverdieping, 55. Averbode, Netherlands: Kok, 1990.
———. *Mengeldichten*. Edited with commentary by Joseph van Mierlo. Leuvense Studiën en Tekstuitgaven, 15. Antwerp: Standaard-Boekhandel, 1952.
———. *Poetry of Hadewijch*. Introductory essay, edition, translation, and notes by Marieke van Baest. Foreword by Edward Schillebeeckx. Studies in Spirituality, supplement 3. Louvain, Belgium: Peeters, 1998.

———. *Strophische Gedichten*. Edited with commentary by J. van Mierlo. Leuvense Studiën en Tekstuitgaven 13. Antwerp: Standaard-Boekhandel, 1942.

———. *Visioenen*. Edited and translated by Frank Willaert. Foreword by Imme Dros. Nederlandse Klassieken 8. Amsterdam: Prometheus/Bert Bakker, 1996.

———. *De Visioenen van Hadewych*. Edited by J. van Mierlo. 2 vols. Leuvense Studiën en Tekstuitgaven, 10, 11. Louvain: De Vlaamsche Boekenhalle, 1924–1925.

———. *Das Buch der Visionen*. [Middle-Dutch with German trans.] Edited and translated, with an introduction by Gerald Hofmann. Mystik in Geschichte und Gegenwart, 1: Christliche Mystik, 12–13. 2 vols. Stuttgart-Bad Cannstatt, Germany: Frommann-Holzboog, 1998.

English Translations Only

———. *Hadewijch. The Complete Works*. Translation and introduction by Mother Columba Hart. Preface by Paul Mommaers. Classics of Western Spirituality. New York: Ramsey; Toronto: Paulist Press, 1980. U.K. ed. London, 1981.

———. *Beguine Sprituality: Mystical Writings of Mechtild of Magdeburg, Beatrice of Nazareth, and Hadewijch of Brabant*. Edited and introduced by Fiona Bowie. Translated by Oliver Davies. New York: Crossroad, 1990.

———. "The Brabant Mystic Hadewijch." Translated by Ria Vanderauwera. In *Medieval Women Writers*, edited by Katharina M. Wilson, 186–203. Athens: University of Georgia Press, 1984. [Some *Brieven* and *Strofische Gedichten*].

———. "Hadewijch of Antwerp. The List of the Perfect." Translated by Helen Rolfson. *Vox Benedictina* 5 (1988): 277–87.

———. "Hadewijch" Translated by Veerle Fraeters. In *Women Writing in Dutch*, edited by Kristiaan Aercke, 61–92. Women Writers of the World. New York: Garland, 1994. [Some *Visioenen*, *Brieven* and *Strofische Gedichten*].

———. [French] *Béguine, écrivain et mystique: portrait et textes de Hadewijch d'Anvers (XIIIe siècle)*. Translation and commentary by André Gozier. Preface by Louis Boyer. Montrouge, France: Nouvelle Cité, 1994.

Secondary Sources

Axters, Stephanus. *Geschiedenis van de vroomheid in de Nederlanden*, vol. 1: *De vroomheid tot rond het jaar 1300*, 335–81. Antwerp: De Sikkel, 1950.

Bynum, Caroline Walker. *Holy Feast and Holy Fast: The Religious Significance of Food to Medieval Women*. Berkeley: University of California Press, 1987.

de Paepe, N. *Hadewijch. Strofische Gedichten. Een studie van de "Minne" in het kader der 12de- en 13de-eeuwse mystiek en profane minnelyriek*. Leonard Willemsfonds, 2. Ghent, Belgium: Secretariaat van de Koninklijke Vlaamse Academie voor Taal-en Letterkunde, 1967.

Faesen, Rob. *Begeerte in het werk van Hadewijch*. Antwerpse Studies over Nederlandse literatuurgeschiedenis, 4. Louvain: Peeters, 2000.

Guest, Tanis M. *Some Aspects of Hadewijch's Poetic Form in the "Strofische Gedichten."* Bibliotheca Neerlandica Extra Muros, 3. The Hague: Martinus Nijhoff, 1975.

Milhaven, John Giles. *Hadewijch and Her Sisters: Other Ways of Loving and Knowing*. Albany: State University of New York Press, 1993.

Mommaers, Paul. *Hadewijch. Schrijfster—Begijn—Mystica*. Cahiers voor Levensverdieping, 3. Averbode: Altiora; Kampen: Kok, 1989.

Newman, Barbara. *From Virile Woman to WomanChrist: Studies in Medieval Religion and Literature*. The Middle Ages. Philadelphia: University of Pennsylvania Press, 1995.

———. *God and the Goddesses: Vision, Poetry and Belief in the Middle Ages*. The Middle Ages. Philadelphia: University of Pennsylvania Press, 2003.

Petroff, Elizabeth Alvilda. "Gender, Knowledge and Power in Hadewijch's *Strofische Gedichten*." In Petroff, *Body and Soul. Essays on Medieval Women and Mysticism*, 182–203. New York: Oxford University Press, 1994.

Reynaert, J. *De beeldspraak van Hadewijch*. Studiën en Tekstuitgaven van Ons Geestelijk Erf, 21. Tielt/Bussum, Belgium: Lannoo, 1981.

———. "Hadewijch: Mystic Poetry and Courtly Love." In *Medieval Dutch Literature in Its European Context*, edited by Erik Kooper, 208–25. Cambridge Studies in Medieval Literature, 21. Cambridge: Cambridge University Press, 1994.

Ruh, Kurt. *Geschichte der abendländischen Mystik . Vol. II: Frauenmystik und Franziskanische Mystik der Frühzeit*. Munich: Beck, 1993. 158–232.

Willaert, Frank. *De Poëtica van Hadewijch in de Strofische Gedichten*. Utrecht, Netherlands: HES Publishers, 1984.

———, and Marie-José Govers. "D. Anhang. 2. Hadewijch." In *Bibliographie zur deutschen Frauenmystik des Mittelalters*. Mit einem Anhang zu Beatrijs van Nazareth und Hadewijch, edited by Gertrud Jaron Lewis, 10, 351–410. Bibliographien zur deutschen Literatur des Mittelalters. Berlin: Erich Schmidt, 1987.

FRANK WILLAERT

HAGIOGRAPHY (FEMALE SAINTS). The term *hagiography* is derived from Greek roots (*hagios* = holy; *graph* = writing) and has come to refer to the full range of medieval literature concerning the saints. The scope of that literature was breathtakingly wide, including such genres as lives of the saints, collections of miracle stories, accounts of the discovery or movement of relics, bulls of canonization, inquests held into the life of a candidate for canonization, liturgical books, sermons, visions, and the like. These works were composed not only in Latin and Greek, but in the full range of vernacular languages as well. The term "hagiography" can also be used to refer to the modern discipline of studying such writings. These two usages were largely developed by modern scholars such as the Bollandists. Medieval writers usually used cognate terms to refer instead to the "holy writings" of the Bible. This entry focuses on works written about the lives of saints and, in particular, of women.

The authors of hagiography did not intend their works to be biography or history in the modern sense. To be sure, many works of hagiography—such as Baudonivia's *Life of St. Radegund* (sixth century) or Raymond of Capua's *Life of St. Catherine of Siena* (fourteenth century)—were written by authors who had firsthand knowledge of their subjects. But even these authors modeled their portraits on existing ideals of sanctity and drew from a large body of traditional and somewhat standardized stories about the saints, known to modern scholars as *topoi* or types, clusters of motifs. Such stories were borrowed, sometimes with little change, from earlier saints' lives and were intended to convey a moral message rather than historically accurate information. Works written centuries after the fact were often little more than bundles of such topoi. Some—such as the anonymous *Life of St. Montana*—were composed by authors who knew nothing about their subject's life or identity. These consisted virtually entirely of stories borrowed from the lives of other saints in which the names and other details have simply been changed. This traditional or typical character is one of the most striking aspects of hagiography. Hagiographic works must sometimes be used with extreme caution, recognizing that they reveal more about the religious and cultural world of their authors than about the lived lives of their subjects.

Hagiography must be understood in reference to the concept of sanctity and as part of the practice of the cult of saints. Christian saints were quite simply and literally "holy people" (in Latin *sancti* [men] or *sanctae* [women]; in Greek *hagios* or *hagia*). According to certain theological definitions of sanctity, anyone who entered heaven was a saint. In practice, however, Christian communities honored only a limited number of people with the title of saint. Crucial to such official recognition of sainthood was the celebration of a feast that marked the day of the saint's death, that is, the day considered to be that person's birth into the kingdom of heaven. Thus, in practice a person becomes a saint only when he or she is accepted as such by an audience and is provided the blessing of an institutional authority. In late Antiquity and the early Middle Ages, bishops controlled the celebration of such feasts. By the thirteenth century, the papacy came to assert its authority over this process (or canonization as it came to be known) for the Western (or Roman Cath-

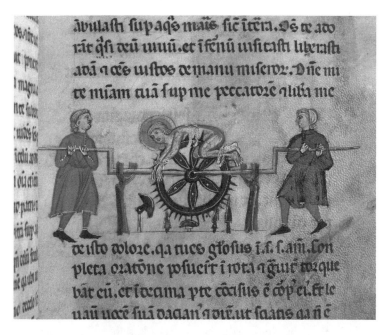

Martyrdom of Saint Margaret of Antioch, third-century virgin and martyr. From late-thirteenth-century manuscript *Scenes from the Life of Saint Margaret*. © The Art Archive/Biblioteca Capitolare Verona/Dagli Orti.

olic) Church as a whole. More limited cults, however, continued to be fostered at the local level, while varied forms of episcopal and imperial authority continued to be decisive in Eastern (or Orthodox) churches. Because of the varied ways through which the veneration of saints could be authorized, there was and is no single universally authoritative list of Christian saints. Rather there are many lists, litanies, and calendars of the holy people given public honor by Christian institutions and communities in varied times and places. The composition of a hagiographic text does serve as evidence, however, that its subject once received some form of such public honor. Celebrations of a feast or of the existence of a relic shrine are other indications of officially sanctioned status as a saint.

Sanctity is thus, in at least one important sense, a social or institutional construct, a fact that is important to a consideration of the related subjects of female sanctity and hagiography concerning female saints. Sanctity is an ideal that developed historically: different sorts of people were recognized as saints by Christian communities during different periods. One of the most important factors in the changing character of sanctity over the course of the Middle Ages was gender. The recognition of, or more importantly the failure to recognize, women as saints betrays many of the misogynist traits typical of medieval society and culture. While most medieval theologians conceded a theoretical equality between men and women in their ability to be saved, they almost uniformly saw men as more likely to practice the virtues necessary for salvation. Thus Athanasius (d. 373) claimed that female martyrs demonstrated how something "against nature" (female bravery) could give proof of something "higher than nature" (the truth of Christianity). Moreover, women were excluded from the Christian clergy and thus from the callings that produced the majority of saints recognized during certain periods. Throughout the Middle

Ages women were a distinct minority among those Christians whose reputation for holiness received public celebration and thus earned for them the title of saint.

The first Christians to be recognized as saints were martyrs, those who had died for their "witness" (the meaning of the Greek term *martus*) to the name of Christ and who had thus earned immediate entrance into heaven. A number of contemporary descriptions survive of the deaths of various martyrs. These passions, as they are often called, constitute the earliest known pieces of hagiography; the very earliest is the *Martyrdom of Polycarp* composed around 167. Many passions were, however, written at a much later date and even concerned martyrs whose very existence is apocryphal. Christian women shared the sufferings of martyrdom in significant numbers, and many women figure in the earliest passions. The oldest surviving hagiographic account of a woman, the *Passion of Perpetua and Felicity* (203), preserves Perpetua's remarkable first-person account of the visions that she experienced during the time spent in prison awaiting execution.

Female martyrs were not, however, memorialized to the same degree as their male counterparts. From an early date Christian communities favored prominent clerics and thus, by definition, men, in their recognition of communal heroes. It is therefore not surprising that among some 120 martyrs listed by name in Eusebius's *Ecclesiastical History* (c.313) only fifteen were women. Some women did have their feasts celebrated and their relics venerated by the fourth century: in addition to Perpetua, we know of Agnes of Rome, Eulalia of Merida, Euphemia of Chalcedon, and a handful of others. With the exception of Perpetua, few of the authentically early passions focus on women. It was only in the later fourth century, long after their martyrdoms, that accounts of the lives and deaths of most of the authentic female martyrs on the calendar of saints began to be written. And many of the most familiar female martyrs—including Cecilia of Rome, Margaret of Antioch, and Catherine of Alexandria—were the inventions of hagiographers writing in the seventh century or later. Even in the fourth century, the most influential account of a female martyr was of a fictive saint, that of Thecla included in the apocryphal *Acts* of Paul. The story inspired sharply differing reactions: the holy woman Macrina (d. 379/80) read it and considered Thecla to be her patron, while the controversialist Jerome (d. 419/20) denounced it.

The end of the persecution of Christians marked by the Edict of Milan in 313 did not only allow the growth of the public recognition of the martyrs, but led to the recognition of new types of saints. The first important category was that of bishops, such as Martin of Tours (d. 397), Augustine of Hippo (d. 430), Cyril of Alexandria (d. 444), or the shadowy fourth-century Nicholas of Myra whose cult survives today under the guise of Santa Claus. Women were as fully excluded from this form of sanctity as they were from membership in the clerical hierarchy.

The second important new path to sainthood was asceticism, the rigorous practice of self-denial and even mortification of the body—through disciplines such chastity and fasting—which led to a kind of symbolic martyrdom. Many of the saints of the fourth and early fifth centuries were drawn from the so-called "athletes of Christ" who lived singly or communally in the deserted wastelands of the Roman Empire. For Christian women the ascetic life, in a way similar to martyrdom, promised a means of subverting misogynist ideals. According to contemporary theologians such as Athanasius and Jerome, women could make up for their natural inferiority to men through leading a life vowed to virginity as an ascetic bride of Christ. But the promise was largely illusory. The homeland of the monastic movement was the Egyptian desert. When Palladius (d. 425) wrote his influential record of saintly Egyptian monks, he commented, "I must also commemorate in this book the virile women to whom God granted struggles equal to those of men, so that no one could plead as an excuse that women are too weak to practice virtue successfully." Yet only eleven of his seventy-one chapters concerned nuns.

Women were, on the other hand, preeminent in the smaller ascetic movement centered in the cities of the Roman Empire. A number of women who chose to pursue a life dedicated to chastity and charity within an urban landscape gained a great deal of fame. Records of their lives were composed by male clerics who were friends and relatives to serve as ascetic guidebooks for other women: Gregory of Nyssa (d. c.395) wrote the life of his sister Macrina (d. 379/80), Jerome an epitaph for Paula (d. 404), John Chrysostom (d. 407) letters memorializing Olympias (d. 410), Gerontius a life of Melania (d. 439). While all these men considered their subjects "holy," the only one who was unequivocally regarded a "saint" was Melania.

The circulation of and audience for the lives of these women, however, paled in comparison to that for the stories of Thecla and the other apocryphal female martyrs mentioned above (some of whom were described as having been inspired to their martyrdoms by having heard or read the story of Thecla). A new type of apocryphal female saint—and with it a new genre of hagiography—began to develop in the fifth century, that of the lascivious woman, usually a prostitute or actress, who converted to Christianity and repented her former life through dramatic asceticism. These legends, concerning characters such as Pelagia of Antioch and Mary the Egyptian, bore strong literary ties to classical Greek romances. It is ironic that these fictive female ascetics should have attained a much greater importance in medieval Christianity than their real-life counterparts. These stories of apocryphal female martyrs and penitents had their roots in the Christian east, but became very popular in the Latin West at a later date.

Over the course of the fifth century, imperial authority and many of the institutions of Roman government crumbled in the Latin West, but just as the Roman Empire survived in the Greek East, transforming itself into the empire usually called Byzantium, so too did the late antique traditions of hagiography and sanctity. Through the seventh century it was the monastic life of the desert that produced most Byzantine saints, and the cities and monasteries of Egypt, Syria, and Palestine that produced most hagiography. Alongside the stories of male stylites (as one distinctive type of desert ascetic who lived on pillars were known), the stories of Mary the Egyptian and other penitent women flourished not only in Greek, but in Syriac, Armenian, and other eastern languages. Literary production, including hagiography, declined in the latter seventh and eighth centuries, partially as a result of the twin blows of the Islamic conquests and the battles of iconoclasm. In the renewal of hagiography during the later ninth and tenth centuries, generally considered the golden age of Byzantine hagiography, the old themes were repeated, but in a slightly different key. Wise abbots who guided their communities, such as Athanasius the Athonite (d. 1003), replaced the extravagant ascetics of the Palestine desert, while chaste matrons of the upper classes, such as Mary the Younger (d. 902/3), stood in for repentant prostitutes. The ninth and tenth centuries, however, also witnessed the development of menologia: standardized collections of brief saints' lives organized by the liturgical calendar and intended to provide readings for monastic communities and other spiritually minded people. These collections included few women. Still, the old Roman models of female sanctity endured in Byzantine Christianity through the eleventh century. Asceticism itself came under attack from some intellectuals, and hagiographic composition declined through the twelfth and early thirteenth centuries. It revived under the Palailogan dynasty of the late Middle Ages, but largely as a form of polemic in the varied controversies of the period. Concerned almost exclusively with males of the military and monastic elites, there was no room for saintly women, except in rewriting of stories of earlier saints. Among the hagiographers there was one woman, Theodora Raoulaina (d. 1300), herself a member of the Palaiologan family.

Far to the west, in Ireland, a Christian tradition developed during the early Middle Ages that had little to do with the traditions of the Roman world. Through the efforts of missionaries from Britain and Gaul, the myriad Celtic kingdoms of the island were converted to Christianity in the first half of the fifth century. The Irish quickly adopted and adapted monasticism. The severely ascetic ideals of the Egyptian desert mingled with native concepts of holiness producing a unique form of monasticism, especially severe in its ascetic rigor, but tempered by a boundless enthusiasm for the wonders of the natural world. The early Irish monastic movement produced a large number of men and women of saintly reputation, so much so that by the eleventh century Ireland had become known as "the isle of saints." A handful of Latin works that can be securely dated to the seventh century celebrated the lives of the greatest Irish saints: the chief missionary bishop, Patrick (d. c.461); the wandering abbot, Columba (d. 597); and the extraordinary abbess of Cell Dara, Brigit (d. c.523). Later hagiographic works in both Latin and Irish, however, are notoriously difficult to date with any accuracy, and virtually all were written at a great remove from the lives of their subjects. While some 119 Irish female saints were recorded in the Martyrology of Tallaght, lives have survived for only four (Brigit, Monenna [d. c.518], Ite [d. c.570], and Samthann [d. 739]).

Between these geographical and cultural extremes, the early Middle Ages witnessed the development of barbarian kingdoms as successors to the Roman Empire in the Latin West. For over a century after the fall of the city of Rome to the Goths, sanctity in these regions was a domain almost exclusively inhabited by male clerics, and those mostly from the ever-diminishing ranks of the old Roman elite. The cults and legends of the old martyrs endured, but new saints were bishops such as Caesarius of Arles (d. 542) and Germanus of Paris (d. 576) or abbots such as Severinus of Noricum (d. 482) and Benedict of Nursia (d. c.540). Their hagiographers were men of similar background: Gregory of Tours (d. 593/94) and Venantius Fortunatus (d. 610) in Gaul, Ennodius of Pavia (d. 521), and Gregory the Great (d. 604) in Italy. There was little room for female leaders in the world of this elite struggling for its survival, but the virgin ascetic Geneviève (d. c.500) became one of the patrons of Paris by helping to organize the defense of the city against Hunnish and Frankish attacks. By the late sixth century, however, members of the converted Germanic peoples were entering the clergy and the monasteries. Among the nobleman who became bishops and abbots were some, particularly among the Franks, who adopted a fiercely ascetic lifestyle, borrowed in part not from continental monastic traditions, but from the influence of Columbanus (d. 615) and other missionary Irish monks. They represented a new type of sanctity, mixing noble blood and asceticism, which was peculiar to the new ruling elites of the barbarian kingdoms.

Women played a distinctive role in these developments, in the persons of new saints who came almost exclusively from royal families or from the ranks of the abbesses of important convents. Sanctity was particularly associated with queens of Merovingian

Frankland (for example, Radegund [d. 587] and Balthild [d. 680]), Anglo-Saxon East Anglia (Aethelthryth [d. 679] and Sexburga [d. c.700]), and Ottonian Saxony (Mathilda [d. 968] and Adelheid [d. 999]). Female saints also included daughters of these and other clans of the high nobility who served as abbesses of important convents such as Nivelles (Gertrude d. 659), Gandersheim (Hathumoda d. 874), Wilton (Edith d. 984), and Villich or Willich (Adelaide d. 1015). As with their male contemporaries, some combination of noble blood and exceptional asceticism marked these women as holy. This was the dominant model of female sanctity in the west from the sixth century to the year 1100. The lives written about these women served as a kind of "mirror for princes" addressed to the female elite of the emerging European kingdoms. Although most were written by male clerics, the Frankish nun Baudonivia wrote the second part of the *Life of Radegund*, becoming the earliest hagiographer to identify herself as a woman. Other female authors from this period include the eighth-century Hugeberc of Heidenheim, the tenth-century Hrotsvit of Gandersheim, and the eleventh-century Bertha of Vilich (or Willich). Their subjects included male as well as female saints. Female sanctity seems to have been regarded as potentially dangerous by much of the episcopal hierarchy. Throughout these centuries, fewer and fewer people became celebrated as saints after their deaths. Increasingly, the cult of saints focused on cherished patrons from the distant past, such as martyred bishops or founding abbots. The bulk of hagiography written from the eighth to the eleventh centuries concerned such figures, and few of those were female. The major exception was the development in the Latin West of the traditions of virgin martyrs. Even the lives of those contemporary female saints considered previously tended to have a restricted circulation. Few survive in more than a handful of manuscripts, and few of these women were included in liturgical calendars outside the regions in which they had lives. Female sanctity was a strictly controlled form of charisma in the earlier Middle Ages.

In the later eleventh and twelfth centuries, the revival of eremitic monasticism, the growth of the *vita apostolica*, and the wider reform of ecclesiastical institutions all made the western church more open to seeing contemporary figures as saints. Cults honoring people as different as Thomas Becket (d. 1170) and Francis of Assisi (d. 1226) covered Western Europe within a few years of their deaths. The period witnessed the composition of many lives of contemporary holy men, but only a few of holy women. According to one calculation, only eighteen of the 153 people recognized as saints during the twelfth century were women. Several male founders of new monastic orders for women, such as Robert of Arbrissel (d. 1116) and Gilbert of Sempringham (d. 1189), became saints, but none of their female disciples attained similar status. Although convents flourished in England, a life was composed for only one English holy woman of the twelfth century, Christina of Markyate (d. c.1155). The attempt to win a papal bull of canonization for Hildegard of Bingen (d. 1179), who had been recognized as a holy woman and visionary by contemporaries including Bernard of Clairvaux and Pope Eugenius, failed in 1233.

The foundations had been laid, however, for a remarkable flowering of female piety, and with it female sanctity, in the thirteenth century. The variety of options open to women interested in practicing the religious life had increased dramatically. Beguinages (groups of lay nuns called beguines) and other informal urban communities, and later groups affiliated with the mendicant orders, offered women lives of ascetic spirituality outside the boundaries of the traditional rural cloister. These new movements were particularly vibrant in the cities of the Low Countries and northern Italy. By the 1230s, Jacques de Vitry and Thomas of Cantimpré had begun to write an influential series of lives concerning beguines and nuns in the region of Liège. Their many subjects included Mary of Oignies (d. 1213), Christina Mirabilis of St. Trond (d. c.1224), and Juliana of Mont Cornillon (d. 1258). A similar trend can be found in Italy celebrating women associated with new, particularly mendicant, orders, including Bona of Pisa (d. 1207), Clare of Assisi (d. 1253), and Margaret of Cortona (d. 1297). Nor was the older tradition of royal sanctity dead, rather it had been translated to the recently Christianized realms of central Europe, whose ruling clans produced such holy women as Elisabeth of Hungary/Thuringia (d. 1231), Margaret of Hungary (d. 1270), and Agnes of Bohemia (d. 1282). Yet this tradition had also been transformed, for these women expressed their asceticism in association with the mendicant orders. According to one calculation, more than one quarter of the thirteenth-century Christians accorded posthumous veneration (themselves in excess of five hundred) were women, probably the highest percentage of any period of the Middle Ages. It was also during this century that the papacy fully asserted control over the official recognition of sanctity, or canonization. Still the vast majority of late medieval holy people did not receive a papal bull of canonization, but rather a more local cult or form of authorization. Of the seventy-two processes of canonization undertaken by the papacy between 1198 and 1418, thirteen concerned women, while there were but seven women among the thirty-five successes.

The lives of thirteenth-century holy women championed their generally novel approach to the religious life. They exhibited the concerns with voluntary poverty, urban charity, and public teaching so prominent in the mendicant movements. Yet there were aspects that were distinctively female. In addition to the visions that had long been characteristic of female sanctity, these women focused their devotions on the reception of the Eucharist, often rejecting all other forms of food in fasts of heroic—even mortal—length. They thus developed a form of piety that centered on food, whose preparation had always been the work of women in medieval society, and which was replicated in the practices of few male saints. At the same time, this piety illuminates the dependency of religious women on male clerics, for only a priest could consecrate the Eucharist or provide the sacrament of confession. The lived lives of these women created a new model of female holiness, which the works recording those lives transmitted to new audiences and new generations. Most of those works were written by male confessors who held a position of authority over the women. At the same time, many autobiographical writings, particularly those detailing visions, survive from these holy women. Taken together, these writings allow historians to chart the dialectical processes by which a reputation for sanctity was negotiated and developed.

A different tradition of female sanctity was also developing in western Christendom over the course of the central and high Middle Ages, that is the traditions of the ancient female martyrs and saintly penitents. Largely traveling from the Christian East, these began to mature in Latin hagiography in the ninth century, beginning a process of development that would continue for the rest of the Middle Ages. Simultaneously, cults focused on the relics of such women as Mary Magdalene and Catherine of Alexandria (some also imported from the East) grew. By the thirteenth century, the legends of these early Christian women were widely disseminated and incorporated into hagiographic collections intended for preachers. The most important of these was the *Legenda Aurea* (*Golden Legend*), completed by the Dominican James of Voragine in 1258. Thirty-one of the 182 legends included in this collection concerned female saints, all of them figures from the New Testament or the early Church.

The legends of martyrs and penitents also served as the primary inspiration for the development of hagiography about women in the vernacular languages, traditions that began as early as the ninth century. In Anglo-Saxon, the enigmatic poet Cynewulf composed accounts of the discovery of the True Cross by Helena and a passion of Juliana, probably toward the beginning of the century. The earliest surviving literary work in any Romance language is the Old French *séquence* or *Cantilène de Sainte Eulalie* (*Song of St. Eulalia*), a brief liturgical piece from the late ninth century celebrating the martyr of Merida. It was in these languages—and in their relatives, Anglo-Norman and Middle English—that hagiography about female saints flourished in the years before 1300. By the late tenth century, for example, the Anglo-Saxon monk Aelfric (d. c.1010) had included a number of female martyrs such as Cecilia and Agnes, but only one native female saint (Æthelthryth or Audrey), in his large prose hagiographic corpus. Over the course of the twelfth century, verse lives were composed about women in Old French (Catherine of Alexandria, Geneviève of Paris, Margaret of Antioch, and Mary of Egypt) and Anglo-Norman (Catherine of Alexandria and Faith). Many of these works, notably the so-called "Katherine Group," which is one of the masterpieces of Middle English, were composed specifically for audiences of religious women. Far to the north, a group of sagas was composed about a similar group of ancient female saints, but these do not seem to have come into vogue until the late thirteenth century. Other vernacular traditions do not offer the same richness before 1300. Early works are known from Middle Irish (into which the life of Brigit was translated, possibly as early as the ninth century), Old Church Slavonic (a now lost, and probably contemporary, life of the martyred princess Ludmilla [d. 921]), and Old Provençal (the earliest surviving example of which is the *Chanson de Sainte Foi*, 1030/70), but female saints never became a staple of these flourishing literary traditions. Lives of female saints are not found until later in Middle-High German (*Legenden von der heiligen Juliana* of the Priester Arnold, post-1150), Castilian (*Estoria de Santa Maria Egipçiaca* [*Story of St. Mary of Egypt*], c.1235), and Catalan (*Cançó de Santa Fe* [*Song of the Holy Ghost*], post-1250). Until 1300 it was the virginal martyr and the penitent prostitute of antiquity who served as the dominant models of female sanctity in vernacular works and the sermon literature, that is in works intended for a broad audience. In contrast, contemporary males such as Thomas Becket, Francis, and Dominic were relatively common in those literatures. Some exceptions, however, did exist, notably Rutebeuf's poem on the recently deceased princess Elizabeth of Thuringia, dedicated (post-1258) to Queen Isabelle of Navarre, and Ebernand of Erfurt's Heinrich und Kunigunde, written in support of the canonization of the German royal couple around 1200. It should also be noted that collections of miracles associated with that very special female saint, the Virgin Mary, became a staple of both Latin and vernacular literatures over the course of the twelfth and thirteenth centuries.

These two traditions that had developed over the course of the high Middle Ages—contemporary women associated with mendicant and other urban religious groups as well as the martyrs and penitents of antiquity—continued to set the pattern for female piety and sanctity in the fourteenth and fifteenth centuries. Yet these traditions were slowly, as it were, transcribed into new keys. Many contemporary holy women continued to be associated with the mendicants, most particularly in Italy: Agnes of Montepulciano (d. 1417), Catherine of Siena (d. 1380), Colette of Corbie (d. 1447), and Catherine of Genoa (d. 1510). The development of a new lay ideal of sanctity within the married state also began to include women. Yet this still involved chastity, for saintly wives such

Delphina of Puimichel (d. 1361) and Dorothea of Montau (d. 1394) either kept their unions strictly chaste or took a vow of chastity after years of childbearing. Other women who lived much of their lives as laywomen, such as Birgitta (Bridget) of Sweden (d. 1373) and Francesca Romana (d. 1440), founded new religious orders for women as alternatives to the mendicants. Devotion to the Passion of Christ and bodily mortification began to take a central place in their spiritual and penitential practices, accompanied by a heightened emotionalism often expressed in the so-called "gift of tears." While poverty and fasting remained important, a new stress was placed on visionary powers in the lives of most late medieval holy women. Their own accounts of ecstatic experiences were written, by themselves or by scribes, in works that remain highpoints of the vernacular literatures: Mechthild of Magdeburg's *Flowing Light of the Godhead* (original written Low German before 1268, translated into Middle-High German c.1344), Julian of Norwich's *Showings* (Middle English after 1373), Catherine of Bologna's *Seven Spiritual Weapons* (Italian, published after her death in 1463). The lives of these women also came to be far more available in the vernacular, some of them even written by female friends and disciples.

The traditions of the female martyrs and penitents became much more widely available to and known by the pious laity in the later Middle Ages. The *Golden Legend* and other important hagiographic collections were translated into virtually every vernacular language. Such collections—which occasionally, as in like Osbern Bokenham's *Legends of Holy Women* (c.1443), contained only female saints—were common in manuscripts and early printed books. Even the widespread *Lives of the Fathers* contained models of female sanctity, as penitents such as Mary the Egyptian entered the translated versions. These stories still served the purposes of preachers, but were also read by an ever-growing literate lay audience. Paintings, statues, woodcuts, and other art objects (some virtually mass produced) also commonly incorporated the traditions of early Christian women. Stories and images together became part of a fervent culture of devotion. Those practices of devotion, and indeed the entire panoply of the cult of saints, were vigorously attacked by the Protestant reformers of the sixteenth century. Yet both traditions of female sanctity—that of contemporary visionary women and that of the ancient martyrs—remained central to the religious culture of Catholic regions in the early modern period.

See also Æthelthryth, St.; Agnes of Bohemia, Blessed; Aldegund, St.; Baudonivia; Beguines; Bertha of Vilich; Birgitta of Sweden, St.; Bokenham, Osbern; Catherine of Bologna, St.; Catherine of Siena, St.; Christina of Markyate; Christina Mirabilis; Clare of Assisi, St.; Colette of Corbie, St.; Desert Mothers; Dorothea of Montau, St.; Elisabeth of Hungary/Thuringia, St.; Hildegard of Bingen, St.; Hrotsvitha of Gandersheim; Joan of Arc, St.; Julian of Norwich; Juliana of Mont-Cornillon; Macrina the Elder, St.; Macrina the Younger, St.; Mary, Blessed Virgin, in the Middle Ages; Mechthild of Magdeburg; Melania the Elder, St.; Melania the Younger, St.; *Mulieres Sanctae*; Perpetua, St.; Relics and Medieval Women; Syrian-Christian Women; Thecla, St.; Virginity

BIBLIOGRAPHY

Primary Sources and Guides
Bibliotheca hagiographica graeca. Edited by François Halkin, 3d ed., 3 vols. Subsidia hagiographica, 47. Brussels: Société des Bollandistes, 1969.
Bibliotheca hagiographica latina antiquae et mediae aetatis. 3 vols. Subsidia hagiographica, 6, 70. Brussels: Société des Bollandistes, 1898, 1986.

Bibliotheca Sanctorum. 13 vols. Rome: Istituto Giovanni XXIII, 1961–1970.

Cazelles, Brigitte, ed. and trans. *The Lady as Saint: A Collection of French Hagiographic Romances of the Thirteenth Century*. Philadelphia: University of Pennsylvania Press, 1993.

Farmer, David, ed. *The Oxford Dictionary of Saints*. Revised ed. Oxford: Oxford University Press, 1992.

McNamara, Jo Ann, et al., eds. and transs. *Sainted Women of the Dark Ages*. Durham, N.C.: Duke University Press, 1992.

Petersen, Joan, ed. and trans. *Handmaids of the Lord: Contemporary Descriptions of Feminine Asceticism in the First Six Christian Centuries*. Cistercian Studies Series, 143. Kalamazoo, Mich.: Cistercian Publications, 1996.

Petroff, Elizabeth, ed. and trans. *Consolation of the Blessed*. New York: Alta Gaia Society, 1979.

———, ed. *Medieval Women's Visionary Literature*. Oxford: Oxford University Press, 1986.

Medieval Hagiography: An Anthology. Edited by Thomas Head. Translations by various authors. Garland Reference Library of the Humanities, 1942. New York and London: Garland, 2000. Paperback ed. New York and London: Routledge, 2001.

Talbot, Alice-Mary. *Holy Women of Byzantium: Ten Saints' Lives in English Translation*. Washington, D.C.: Dumbarton Oaks, 1996.

Vies des saints et des bienheureux. Edited by Jules Baudot, Paul Antin, and Jacques Dubois. 13 vols. Paris: Letouzey et Ane, 1935–1959.

Secondary Sources

Benvenuti Papi, Anna. *"In castro poenitentiae": santità e societa femminile nell'Italia medievale*. Rome: Herder, 1990.

Bitel, Lisa. *Land of Women: Tales of Sex and Gender from Early Ireland*. Ithaca, N.Y.: Cornell University Press, 1996.

Bynum, Caroline Walker. *Holy Feast and Holy Fast: The Religious Significance of Food to Medieval Women*. Berkeley: University of California Press, 1987.

Coakley, John. "Gender and the Authority of Friars: the Significance of Holy Women for Thirteenth-Century Franciscans and Dominicans." *Church History* 60 (1991): 445–60.

Dinzelbacher, Peter. *Heilige oder Hexen? Schicksale auffälliger Frauen in Mittelalter und Frühneuzeit*. Zurich: Artemis and Winkler, 1995.

Dubois, Jacques, and Jean-Loup Lemaître. *Sources et méthodes de l'hagiographie médiévale*. Paris: Éditions du Cerf, 1993.

Elliott, Dyan. *Spiritual Marriage: Sexual Abstinence in Medieval Wedlock*. Princeton, N.J.: Princeton University Press, 1993.

Elm, Susanna. *"Virgins of God": The Making of Asceticism in Late Antiquity*. Oxford: Oxford University Press, 1994.

Giannarelli, Elena. *La tipologia femminile nella biografia e nell'autobiografia cristiana del IV° secolo*. Studi storici, 127. Rome, 1980.

Grundmann, Herbert. *Religious Movements in the Middle Ages*. Translated by Steven Rowan. Notre Dame, Ind.: Notre Dame University Press, 1995. German original 1935.

Jenkins, Jacqueline, and Katherine Lewis, eds. *St. Katherine of Alexandria: Texts and Contexts in Western Medieval Europe*. Turnhout: Brepols, 2003.

Kitchen, John. *Saints Lives and the Rhetoric of Gender: Male and Female in Merovingian Hagiography*. Oxford: Oxford University Press, 1998.

Klaniczay, Gábor. *Holy Rulers and Blessed Princesses: Dynastic Cults in Medieval Central Europe*. Translated by Éva Pálmai. Cambridge: Cambridge University Press, 2002.

Matter, E. Ann, and John Coakley, eds. *Creative Women in Medieval and Early Modern Italy: A Religious and Artistic Renaissance*. Philadelphia: University of Pennsylvania Press, 1994.

Newman, Barbara. *From Virile Woman to WomanChrist: Studies in Medieval Religion and Literature*. The Middle Ages. Philadelphia: University of Pennsylvania Press, 1995.

Mooney, Catherine. *Gendered Voices: Medieval Saints and their Interpreters*. The Middle Ages. Philadelphia: University of Pennsylvania Press, 1999.

Philippart, Guy. "Hagiographes et hagiographie, hagiologes et hagiologie; des mots et des concepts." *Hagiographica* 1 (1994): 1–16.

————, ed. *Histoire internationale de la littérature hagiographique, latine et vernaculaire, en Occident, des origines à 1550.* 4 vols. Turnhout, Belgium: Brepols, 1994–.

Sheingorn, Pamela, and Kathleen Ashley, eds. *Interpreting Cultural Symbols: Saint Anne in Late Medieval Society.* Athens: University of Georgia Press, 1990.

Schulenburg, Jane Tibbets. *"Forgetful of Their Sex": Female Sanctity and Society, ca. 500–1100.* Chicago: University of Chicago Press, 1996.

Sheingorn, Pamela. *Writing Faith: Text, Sign and History in the Miracles of Sainte Foy.* Chicago: University of Chicago Press, 1999.

Smith, Julia. "The Problem of Female Sanctity in Carolingian Europe c.780–920." *Past and Present* 146 (1995): 3–37.

Thacker, Alan, and Richard Sharpe, eds. *Local Saints and Local Churches in the Early Medieval West.* Oxford and New York: Oxford University Press, 2002.

Vauchez, André. *Sainthood in the Later Middle Ages.* Translated by Jean Birrell. Cambridge: Cambridge University Press, 1997. French original, 2nd ed., 1988.

Wogan-Browne, Jocelyn. *Saints Lives and Women's Literary Culture: Viginity and its Authorizations.* Oxford: Oxford University Press, 2001.

Zarra, Gabriella, and Lucetta Scaraffia, eds. *Donne e fede. Storia delle donne in Italia. Santità e vita religiosa.* Rome: Laterza, 1994.

THOMAS HEAD

HAIDER, URSULA (1413–1498). Ursula Haider, a German Poor Clare abbess and mystic, established and reformed the *Klarissenkloster* (Convent of St. Clare) in Villingen, southern Germany. She also authored some mystical writings.

Born in Leutkirch (Allgäu, southern Germany), she was orphaned as an infant and raised by her grandmother and an uncle who was a priest. At the age of eight she prepared to receive the sacrament to enter a hermitage. Ten years later, at the age of eighteen, she entered the Klarissenkloster at Valdunen, in Vorarlberg (now in western Austria), which, since the Klarissen (Poor Clares) were an order originally founded by St. Clare and St. Francis (1212–1214). This entailed a vow of strict poverty and commitment to a life of prayer, contemplation and manual labor. At age thirty-six, Haider was chosen to be the mother superior at Valdunen. One day, while attending an ordinary funeral at a cemetery with several of her nuns, she heard a voice from out of a rosebush telling her that her grave would not be in that monastery's cemetery, but in Villingen, in the Schwarzwald (Blackforest, southern Germany). After she had served another thirteen years as mother superior at Valdunen, the Franciscan provincial head, Heinrich Karrer, called Ursula along with seven other nuns to go to Villingen (1480). It seems the temporal powers of the city wanted the St. Clare monastery to be an open convent; but the Church wanted to reform it and have the nuns live there and administer it as an enclosed community. Ursula devoted all of her energies to fulfilling this mission, driving all worldliness out of St. Clare's, guiding it wisely and thereby making it a model convent.

Haider's mysticism was strongly influenced by the writings of the important, but controversial, German writer Heinrich von Seuse (Henry Suso, c.1295–1366). She made notes about her visions, speeches, mystical perceptions, and poetry with almost pathological zeal. Her writings were introduced to the laity in 1637 by Juliana Ernstin, who incorporated them into the *Chronik der Bickenklosters zu Villingen* (*Chronicles of the Bickenkloster at Villingen*), now the St. Ursula Women's Convent.

Haider was concerned to impress on her nuns the importance of developing an inner spiritual life, of honoring the heart of Jesus and necessity of a life of quiet contemplation and meditation. As a monastic administrator, she was strong in the face of danger or distress, practical and resourceful. She also dedicated herself to the care of the sick. Ursula died at age eighty-five on January 20, 1498, at Villingen, just as foretold by the voice in the rosebush.

See also Clare of Assisi, St.; Sister-Books (*Schwesternbücher*)

BIBLIOGRAPHY

Primary Sources
Ernstin, Juliana. *Chronik der Bickenklosters zu Villingen 1238 bis 1614*, edited by Karl J. Glatz. Bibliothek des Literarischen Vereins, 151. Tübingen, Germany: Literarischer Verein Stuttgart, 1881.
Haider, Ursula. [Writings]. In *Deutscher Mystikerbriefe des Mittelalters, 1100–1550*, edited by Wilhelm Oehl. Munich: Georg Müller, 1931.

Secondary Sources
Bautz, Friedrich W. "Ursula Haider." In *Biographisch-Bibliograpisches Kirchenlexicon*, 2: 478–79. Online http://www.bautz.de/bbkl/h/haider_u.shtml
"Ursula Haider," etc. In *Deutsches Literatur-Lexikon*, edited by Heinz Rupp and Carl-Ludwig Lang. Berne and Munich: Francke, 1979.

EDITH BRIGITTE ARCHIBALD

HALI MEIDHAD. *See* **Virginity**

HANDLESS MAIDEN. *See* **Belle Hélène de Constantinople**

HAZZECHA OF KRAUFTAL (late 12th century). Born in or near Krauftal in the diocese of Strasbourg (Alsace, France), Hazzecha was abbess of the Benedictine convent at Krauftal, near Zabern in the diocese of Strasbourg, Germany, in the middle of the twelfth century. She wrote several letters to Hildegard of Bingen (1098–1179) describing Hazzecha's difficulties in coping with her unruly convent at Krauftal and indicating her strong dependence on Hildegard for advice. These letters are contained in the so-called Berlin Collection, housed in the Berlin Library, Manuscript Berlin Lat. Qu. 674. In one of the letters, Hazzecha is eager to escape her responsibility as abbess and wants to turn to the life of a hermit (*solitaria vita*). Hildegard advises against this, telling Hazzecha that she is too unsteady for this type of life and that if she failed to persevere, she would be worse off. She reminds Hazzecha of the passage in the Gospel of Matthew 12:45: "Off it goes again to bring back with it this time seven spirits more evil than itself. They move in and settle there. Thus the last state of that man becomes worse that the first. And that is how it will be with the evil generation." Hildegard also warns Hazzecha not to avoid other sinners like herself and not to reject reasonable human solutions to her problems.

In another letter requesting Hildegard's counsel, Hazzecha is considering taking two of her faithful followers either to set up a hermitage or to go on a pilgrimage. Hildegard replies to Hazzecha, in one of the longest letters in the Berlin collection, admonishing her to resist the urge to flee her burdens by flying to spiritual goals that are beyond her. Hildegard tells her to remedy the problems at her convent instead. In particular, she advises Hazzecha to use discretion, which will teach her in true humility and obedience how to correct her own sins and to avoid willfulness and excessive pride. Hildegard maintains that the person who despises her own will out of fear and love of God will listen to the advice of her teachers and thereby become a dwelling place of the Holy Spirit. Regarding Hazzecha's possible pilgrimage to Rome with her two companions, Hildegard reminds her that she is already on a pilgrimage to the heavenly Jerusalem. Hildegard closes with the usual mention that she will pray for her so that through further performance of good works, she will be strengthened in pure holiness and will attain supreme bliss. In general, Hildegard warns her sister-abbess to resist the temptation to rise higher than one's capacities as a solution to present problems.

The nuns of Hazzecha's convent at Krauftal also received a letter from Hildegard, reprimanding them through a story about a fig tree planted in a garden. She says that the tree flourished at first—like the convent at Krauftal—because it was well cared for and because it was watered by a spring. But then evil beasts wanted to hinder the flow of the stream watering the fig tree by filling the stream with stems, reeds, and bellows. Hildegard interprets this allegory by affirming that the beast with the stems signifies bad habits at the convent, the one with the reeds signifies the hollowness and distaste of good works, and the one with the bellows signifies the inflation of presumption. The three beasts are trying to dry up the fig tree, that is, to cause the convent's devotional life to be dry, full of despair, and painful. For three years the man who had planted the tree came and found no fruit, but then, instead of cutting down the tree, he cleared the way blocking the flow of water. And so it is with God: He would not eradicate the convent at Krauftal, but would educate the sisters through discipline, bitterness, and poverty, just as before. It is now time for them to reestablish obedience, good habits, and discipline.

Little else is known about Hazzecha.

See also Hildegard of Bingen, St.

BIBLIOGRAPHY

Primary Sources
Hildegard of Bingen. *Opera omnia.* Edited by J.-P. Migne, 338–41. *Patrologia latina,* 197. Paris: Migne, 1855.
———. *Epistolarium.* Edited by Lieven Van Acker. *Corpus Christianorum. Continuatio Medievalis,* 91–91a. Turnhout, Belgium: Brepols, 1991, 1993.
———. [Works: Selections, English]. *Hildegard of Bingen. Selected Writings.* Translated with an introduction and notes by Mark Atherton. London: Penguin, 2001.
———. *The Letters of Hildegard of Bingen.* Translated by Joseph L. Baird and Radd K. Ehrman. New York: Oxford University Press, 1998. [English translations taken from this work].

Secondary Sources
Dronke, Peter. *Women Writers of the Middle Ages: A Critical Study of Texts from Perpetua* († 203) *to Marguerite Porete* (†1310). Cambridge: Cambridge University Press, 1984.
Newman, Barbara, ed. *Voice of the Living Light: Hildegard of Bingen and Her World.* Berkeley: University of California Press, 1998.

BRUCE HOZESKI

HEABURG. *See* **Bugga**

HELOISE (c.1101–1164). Best remembered for her tumultuous love affair and Latin correspondence with Peter Abelard (1079–1142), one of the foremost intellectual figures of the day, Heloise also became a highly competent abbess and thinker in her own right. There is no reliable information concerning her parentage. She was raised as a child at a house for religious women at Argenteuil, northern France, and confined to the care of her uncle, Fulbert, a canon in the Church of Notre Dame. She seems to have been given an exceptional education in the liberal arts, and at the age of seventeen was considered something of a prodigy. Abelard tells us, too, that she was no mean beauty, when, "puffed up by pride" and at the pinnacle of success at the age of thirty-seven, he began looking around Paris for someone worthy of his lustful intentions. Under the pretext of its favorable location, he succeeded in gaining access as a boarder to Fulbert's home, proposing to give lessons to Heloise in return for his keep (c.1116–1117). That Fulbert should have consented to such an arrangement was still a source of some amusement to Abelard, as he related the events some eighteen years later in his autobiography. For misfortunes there were. Abelard seduced Heloise in good order, but the two fell passionately in love. It was not a cautious relationship. Like Mars and Venus before them, as Abelard has it, they were finally caught in the act. Amidst considerable scandal, the philosopher was evicted from the house. The lovers were able to communicate, however, by way of letters, and it was thus that Heloise soon announced to her lover, "with the utmost joy," that she was with child. Fearing for her safety, Abelard abducted Heloise and carried her off to his native Brittany, where she gave birth to a son, whom she named Astralabius, in c.1118.

Yet their situation proved to be difficult if not untenable, and Abelard approached Fulbert to seek reconciliation. He proposed to marry Heloise, though secretly, to protect the philosopher's reputation among his traditionally Church-affiliated, and thus celibate, colleagues. But such secrecy would have the effect of nullifying any element of reparation to which Fulbert might have thought himself entitled. For her part, Heloise violently disapproved of the plan. In the first place, she argued, her uncle Fulbert would never forgive. But more importantly for Heloise—and her place in literature—she condemned the marriage, and indeed the institution of marriage itself, for contaminating the purity of their love, as she would enunciate in her first letter to Abelard (ed. Radice; 2, ed. Monfrin). Blind to her reasons, Abelard persisted in what proved to be a grievous error: the marriage was celebrated at night in Paris, before Fulbert and witnesses c.1118, with all due regard for secrecy, according to plan. Thus Abelard resumed his teaching, and Heloise returned to Fulbert's home in the cloister of Notre Dame. The situation deteriorated rapidly when Fulbert began to "spread rumors" about the marriage, rumors that Heloise roundly denied. Fulbert then became quarrelsome, and took to inflicting harsh treatments on his niece. For the second time, Abelard abducted Heloise, placing her securely behind the walls of the nunnery at Argenteuil. Thinking that the new husband intended to rid himself permanently of his bride, Fulbert and the men of his family broke into Abelard's lodgings by night and took vengeance "by cutting off those parts with which the offenses against them had been made." Humiliated and mutilated, the philosopher took refuge at the monastery of Saint Denis, just north of Paris. Shortly thereafter, he "obliged a willing Heloise" to take the veil at Argenteuil, while he himself took orders at Saint Denis—all

Abelard visits the cloistered Heloise. From a c.1500 manuscript.
© The British Library/Topham-HIP/The Image Works.

at about the year 1118: it was this, more than his castration by Fulbert's men, that "killed Heloise" by making her thus sacrifice her life for his sake (Southern; Clanchy).

They lived their separate lives until Abelard, hoping to return to Paris and resume his teaching career, wrote a sort of autobiography, the apology for his own life, titled *Historia calamitatum* (*History of My Misfortunes*). This work purports to be addressed to a friend as a letter of consolation (Letter 1, ed. Muckle 1950; text 1, ed. Radice). Although by no means intended for Heloise, her reply to certain passages concerning her directly would make the *Historia* the inaugural letter in the correspondence that was to follow. Heloise reproaches this Abelard for writing a lengthy epistle to a friend, while remaining oblivious to a woman who had meant so much to him and who loved and revered him (Letter 2). The underlying theme of the collection is the subject of writing itself. Heloise was now in a position of spiritual authority at the monastery of the Paraclete ("consoler") near Troyes, in central France, founded by Abelard for her and her sisters following the confiscation of Argenteuil by the powerful Abbot Suger (1089–1151), Abelard's successor at Saint Denis. In her letters she requests, after giving ample proof of her own enduring passion, that her former lover first show some proof of the sincerity of his love. Throughout their correspondence, as recent scholar Michael Clanchy recounts it, Heloise is more openly—indeed, unrepentantly—sensual and passionate in recalling their affair, while Abelard seems more concerned to portray himself as deliberate and calculating in both his career and in love, even when such feigned coldness could not have been the case, while also emphasizing his deeper piety. Eager to reverse the roles of "bad monk" and "good nun," Abelard urges her to renounce their love so that they might both focus their love on God. Heloise then asks him to instruct her, following the manner of the Church Fathers, in the ways of the religious life in her third letter (Letter 6). "Abelard's Rule for Religious Women" (Letters 7, 8; see ed. Muckle 1955) can thus be considered as the logical end of the exchange in the collection appended to the *Historia calamitatum*. When one includes the *Love Letters* (*Epistolae duorum amantium*; ed. Mews 1999), a putative total of 121 letters and poems survives from their relationship. Abelard also composed some thirty-six sermons for the sisters and friars of the Paraclete that reveal much about that community's spiritual life (ed. de Santis).

Because of all the attention lavished on their love affair, it is too often ignored that Heloise lived the major part of her life far from Abelard, as the abbess of the Paraclete, which thanks to her became an important institution for religious women, although Abelard's Rule never really supplanted the Benedictine Rule at the convent (Mews 1995). She authored various texts of an epistolary character, consistent with the course of her duties, and engaged in further correspondence with Abelard, touching on questions of Church dogma and spiritual matters.

Their son, Astralabius, was raised meanwhile by Abelard's sister in the paternal birthplace of Le Pallet, in Brittany, France. Abelard appears to have written a Latin poem of advice to his son. Beyond documentation of Heloise's asking Abbot Peter the Venerable, Abelard's protector at Cluny, to help her son find a prebend (paid ecclesiastical post) in c.1144, not much certitude about Astralabius's later life remains, though references to various clerics bearing his name exist from that time (Clanchy).

Heloise outlived Abelard. It was Peter the Venerable (c.1094–1156)—himself an admirer of young Heloise in his youth, later comparing her to the Amazon Penthesilea and the Old Testament heroine Deborah—who informed her of Abelard's death in 1042 and who dutifully brought his remains to her two years later at the Paraclete, their spiritual home. A legend worthy of courtly romance arose about the tomb Abelard was to share with the one "once dear to [him] in the world, now dearest in Christ" (Luscombe, no. 106). According to accounts from as early as 1207, as Heloise's body was lowered into the crypt, the corpse of Abelard is said to have opened its arms to welcome her. The lovers were, at any rate, interred in a common grave. During the French Revolutionary period (1790s), the bodies were exhumed and examined by noted medical figures before being laid to rest in what is now the famous Père Lachaise cemetery in Paris. The Neogothic monument marking the site is regularly strewn with flowers.

History might well have perpetuated this image, that of the wise and prudent abbess, rather than that of a woman driven by love's passions. Helen Laurie argues that the great twelfth-century courtly *romancier* (novelist) Chrétien de Troyes had access to a copy of their letters. In any case they were legendary well before Jean de Meun first made their letters available in his French translation in the 1270s (Hicks). This romantic image has been attacked as a blatant anachronism from several points of view. The famous, long-standing authenticity debate concerning Heloise's letters to Abelard—ranging from first doubting either lover's authorship of the dossier, including the *Historia*, in favor of an unknown third party—to disputing Heloise's authorship of the letters signed by her, and instead crediting Abelard with all their letters) continues to attract new interest (ed. Mews 1999; Mews 1995; Marenbon; Newman et al.), with the most recent, Christopher Baswell, confirming her authorship. The documents, however, are not really historical by intent, if history is understood as the search for objective, verifiable information about the past. All the letters at issue are written from a rhetorical perspective and show less concern for fact than for values (Moos). Did Abelard really enter Fulbert's household with the intent of seducing Heloise? The question is worth raising, given Abelard's propensity for counterproductive self-portrayal and posterity's sympathy for Heloise. Yet the tenor of Heloise's attack on marriage was traditional, with her major points of argument deriving from the standard male epistolary models, the Roman author Cicero (106–43 B.C.E.) and St. Jerome (340–420). This letter is therefore inauthentic, as is the entire correspondence, from the standpoint of spontaneity and sincerity. Still, do people not live the books they read? Many have found Heloise's evocation of her continuing passion for Abelard unworthy of a woman's pen and far more consistent with the viewpoint of a fatuous and falsifying Abelard, imbued with his own personality and full of self-love. But again, people do not always act according to reason on important matters, and history is full of examples of alienation, not only as concerns the female sex, but whole peoples. The skeptics may never concede, and it is fascinating to follow the debate on fraud, fiction, and borrowing in the writings of "Heloise" and "Abelard." But for reasons inherent to the process of historical criticism, it is doubtful that any definitive argument will ever be pronounced on the matter of passion as historical myth, though Peter von Moos (2003), in refuting Constant Mews's ideas on Heloise and Abelard, has eloquently and incisively discussed the "secular religion of love." If the flowers still fall on the tomb of Heloise and Abelard, it is because the values of the protagonists belong to an order of truth more persuasive than the factual, and that can only be termed historical in the sense that literature belongs to history.

See also Celibacy; Convents; Epistolary Authors, Women as; Humility Topos; Marriage; Rhetoric, Women and; Rules for Canonesses, Nuns, and Recluses

BIBLIOGRAPHY

Primary Sources

Abelard. *Historia calamitatum* [and *Epistolae* (*Letters*) 1–8, or some of these]:

———. *The Letters of Heloise and Abelard*. Translated, with notes and Introduction by Mary Martin McLaughlin. The New Middle Ages. New York: Palgrave Macmillan, forthcoming.

———. *Lettres et vies: Héloïse et Abélard*. Edited and translated by Yves Ferroul. Garnier-Flammarion, 827. Paris: Flammarion, 1996. [Modern French trans. with notes].

———. *Abélard. Historia Calamitatum*. Critical edition by Jacques Monfrin. Bibliothèque des textes philosophiques. Paris: Vrin, 1959. Revised ed. 1978. [Critical ed. of original Latin text of *Historia* plus Letters 2, 4, 5].

———. "Abelard's Letter of Consolation to A Friend." Edited by J. T. Muckle. *Mediaeval Studies* 12 (1950): 163–213. [Only critical ed. of Letter 1].

———. "The Letter of Héloïse on the Religious Life and Abelard's First reply." Edited by J. T. Muckle. *Mediaeval Studies* 17 (1955): 240–81. [Letters 6 and 7].

———."The Personal Letters between Abelard and Héloise,: Edited by J. T. Muckle. *Mediæval Studies* 15 (1953): 47–94. [Latin text of 1–4].

———. *Letters of Abelard and Heloise*. Translated and annotated by Betty Radice. Harmondsworth, U.K.: Penguin, 1974. [English only. Includes *Historia* and monastic regulation letters].

———. *Abélard. Lamentations, Histoire de mes malheurs, Correspondance avec Héloïse*. Edited and translated [Modern French] by Paul Zumthor. Musicology notes by Gérard Le Vot. Babel, 52. Arles, France: Actes Sud, 1992. [Modern French annotated edition, reprints Zumthor's Paris: UGE/ "10/18," 1979 translation of the Correspondence and *Historia* with additional musicological *Planctus* texts].

———. [Sermons]. *I sermoni de Abelardo per le monache del Paracleto*. Edited by Paola di Santis. Medievalia Lovanensia, 1: 31. Louvain: Leuven University Press, 2001.

———. [trans. Jean de Meun]. *La vie et les epistres Pierres Abaelart et Heloys sa fame*. Critical ed. by Eric Hicks. Vol. 1. Paris: Honoré Champion, 1991. [Bilingual Latin-Old-French text: Monfrin's ed. of Abelard's original Latin text with facing Jean de Meun's thirteenth century French translation].

Abelard and Heloise. Lyric Poems, Love Letters, and Treatises (see also eds. by Muckle [1953] and Radice, etc. above):

————. [Love Poems] In Peter Dronke, *Medieval Latin and the Rise of the European Love Lyric.* 2 vols. 2nd ed. Oxford: Oxford University Press, 1968. [Latin texts of poems and letters with commentary, passim].

————. *Epistolae duorum amantium: briefe Abaelards und Heloises?* Edited by E. Könsgen. Leiden: Brill, 1974. [Critical ed. of original Latin with authenticity discussion].

————. *The Lost Love Letters of Heloise and Abelard: Perceptions of Dialogue in Twelfth-century France.* Edited by Constant J. Mews. Translated by Neville Chiavaroli. New York: St. Martin's, 1999.

————. *Two Late Medieval Love Treatises: Heloise's "Art d'Amour" and a Collection of "Demandes d'Amour" from British Library Royal MS 16 F.* Edited by Leslie C. Brooke. Medium Aevum Monographs, n.s. 16. Oxford: Society for the Study of Mediaeval Languages and Literature, 1993.

Other Sources

[Carmina Burana]. *Love Lyrics from the Carmina Burana.* Edited and translated by P. G. Walsh. Chapel Hill and London: University of North Carolina Press, 1993.

Peter the Venerable. *The Letters of Peter the Venerable.* Edited by Giles Constable. Cambridge, Mass.: Harvard University Press, 1967.

Secondary Sources

Baswell, Christopher. "Heloise." In *The Cambridge Companion to Medieval Women's Writing,* edited by Carolyn Dinshaw and David Wallace, 161–71. Cambridge: Cambridge University Press, 2003.

Brown, Catherine. "*Muliebriter*: Doing Gender in the Letters of Heloise." In *Gender and Text in the Later Middle Ages,* edited by Jane Chance, 25–51. Gainesville: University Press of Florida, 1996.

Calabrese, Michael. "Ovid and the Female Voice in the *De Amore* and the Letters of Abelard and Heloise." *Modern Philology* 95 (1997): 1–26.

Clanchy M[ichael]. T. *Abelard: A Medieval Life.* Oxford, U.K. and Cambridge, Mass..: Blackwell, 1997.

Dronke, Peter. *Abelard and Heloise in Medieval Testimonies.* W. P. Ker Lecture no. 26. Glasgow: University of Glasgow Press, 1976.

————. "Francesca and Heloise." *Comparative Literature* 26 (1975): 113–35.

————. "Heloise." In Dronke, *Medieval Women Writers of the Middle Ages: From Perpetua (†203) to Marguerite Porete (†1310),* 107–43. Cambridge: Cambridge University Press, 1984.

Georgianna, Linda. "Any Corner of Heaven: Heloise's Critique of Monasticism." *Mediaeval Studies* 49 (1987): 221–53.

Gilson, Etienne. *Héloïse et Abélard.* Paris: Vrin, 1937. Reprint 1978.

————. *Heloise and Abelard.* Translated by Lawrence K. Shook. Chicago: University of Chicago Press, 1953.

Huchet, Jean-Charles. "La Voix d'Héloïse." *Romance Notes* 25 (1985): 271–87.

Jolivet, Jean, and René Louis. *Pierre Abélard —Pierre le Vénérable. Les Courants philosophiques, littéraires et artistiques en occident au milieu du XIIe siècle; Abbaye de Cluny 2 au 9 juillet 1972.* Paris: CNRS, 1975. [Important collection of essays, some of which are noted separately in this bibliography].

Jones, Nancy A. "By Woman's Tears Redeemed: Female Lament in St. Augustine's Confessions and the Correspondence of Abelard and Heloise." In *Sex and Gender in Medieval and Renaissance Texts: The Latin Tradition,* edited by Barbara K. Gold et al., 15–39. Albany: State University of New York Press, 1997.

Kamuf, Peggy. *Fictions of Feminine Desire: Disclosures of Heloise.* Lincoln: University of Nebraska Press, 1982.

Kauffman, Linda S. *Discourses of Desire: Gender, Genre, and Epistolary Fictions.* Ithaca, N.Y.: Cornell University Press, 1986.

Keller, Jane Eblen. "An Unholy Trinity: Heloise, Eleanor of Aquitaine, Joan of Arc, and the Three Orders." *The Image of Class in Literature, Media, and Society,* edited by Will Wright and Steven Kaplan, 238–44. Pueblo: University of Southern Colorado, 1998.

Laurie, Helen. "The 'Letters' of Abelard and Heloise: A Source for Chrétien de Troyes?" *Studi Medievali* 27 (1986): 123–46.

Luscombe, D. E. "From Paris to the Paraclete: The Correspondence of Abelard and Heloise." *Procedings of the British Academy* 74 (1988): 247–83.

Marenbon, John. "Authenticity Revisited." In Wheeler (*see below*), 19–33.

McLaughlin, Mary Martin. *Heloise and the Paraclete: "Ductrix et Magistra."* The New Middle Ages. New York: Palgrave Macmillan, forthcoming.

———. "Peter Abelard and the Dignity of Women: Twelfth-Century 'Feminism' in Theory and Practice." In Jolivet (*see above*), 287–335.

McLeod, Glenda. "'Wholly Guilty, Wholly Innocent': Self-definition in Heloise's Letters to Abelard." In *Dear Sister: Medieval Women and the Epistolary Genre*, edited by Karen Cherewatuk and Ulrike Wiethaus, 64–86. Philadelphia: University of Pennsylvania Press, 1993.

Mews, Constant J. *Peter Abelard*. Authors of the Middle Ages, 2.5. Aldershot, U.K. and Brookfield, Vt.: Variorum/Ashgate, 1995.

———. "Philosophical Themes in the *Epistolae Duorum Amantium*: The First Letters of Heloise and Abelard." In Wheeler (*see below*), 35–52.

Moos, Peter von. "Die *Epistulae duorum amantium* und die säkulare Religion der Liebe." *Studi medievali*. Ser. 3. 44 (2003): 1–115.

———. "Le Silence d'Héloïse et les idéologies modernes." In Jolivet (*see above*), 425–69.

Newman, Barbara. "Authority, Authenticity, and the Repression of Heloise." *Journal of Medieval and Renaissance Studies* 22 (1992): 121–58.

Silvestre, H. "Héloïse et le témoignage du 'Carmen ad Astralabium'." *Revue d'Histoire Ecclésiastique* 83 (1988): 635–60.

Southern, Richard. "The Letters of Abelard and Heloise." In Southern, *Medieval Humanism and Other Studies*, 86–104. Oxford: Basil Blackwell, 1970.

Vitz, Evelyn B. "Type et individu dans l'autobiographie médiévale: étude de l'*Historia calamitatum*." *Poétique* 6 (1975): 426–45.

Wheeler, Bonnie, ed. *Listening to Heloise: The Voice of a Twelfth-Century Woman*. The New Middle Ages. New York: St. Martin's, 2000. [Important collection of essays, some of which are noted separately above].

ERIC HICKS

HERRAD OF HOHENBURG/LANDSBERG (c.1130–1195/96).

Also often called Herrad of Landsberg, this abbess of Hohenburg is chiefly remembered for her *Hortus deliciarum* (*Garden of Delights*), one of the great florilegia, or encyclopedic collections, to survive from the Middle Ages. Sometime before 1178 she became abbess of a community of Augustinian canonesses located in Alsace (now in northeastern France) at Hohenburg (or Hohenbourg in French, also known as Odilienburg or Mount-Sainte-Odile after its eighth-century founder). She continued the reforms of Abbess Relindis, her predecessor and teacher, who had made Hohenburg a center of learning. The *Hortus*, on which Herrad worked from 1159 and 1175, was a massive undertaking in all senses: the unique codex measured fifty-three by thirty-seven centimeters. The claim that Herrad belonged to the noble family of Landsberg is probably incorrect, but this has not prevented her being referred to as Herrad of Landsberg in scholarly, particularly Anglophone, literature.

While Herrad evidently served as the primary compiler of the florilegium, her own compositions were restricted to a prose preface, a few verses (including an extensive introductory poem), and some glosses. She remarked, "Like a bee inspired by God, I have gathered together this book, *Hortus deliciarum*, in praise and honor of Christ and the Church from varied flowers of sacred and philosophical writings and I have joined them together as if in one mellifluous honeycomb." The title, gleaned from Isidore of Seville's highly influential *Etymologiae* (*Etymologies*, sixth century) heralds texts covering a wide range of theological, spiritual, and historical topics arranged roughly according to the chronology of salvation history. Among the most important nonscriptural sources were the *Ecclesiastica historia* (*Ecclesiastical History*) of Eusebius of Caesarea (d. c.340), the *Elucidarium* (*Book of Elucidation*) and *Speculum Ecclesiae* (*Mirror for the Church*) of Honorius Augustodunensis (d. c.1140), the *Sententiae* (*Sentences*) of Peter Lombard (c.1100–c.1164), and the anonymous early rhetorical source, simply called *Aurea Gemma* (*Golden Gem*). Herrad's learning surpassed the scope of earlier encyclopedias to include some of newly assimilated Arabic learning. Roughly sixty poetic works, some accompanied by musical notation, are interspersed throughout the collection. The ensemble was accompanied by a variety of marginalia (both marginal notes and decorative illuminations) and over 1,200 glosses that explained the intricacies of the texts, including notes that specify the Old High German meaning of Latin terms. This interpretive apparatus was strongly influenced by an earlier encyclopedia known as the *Summarium Heinrici* (*Heinrich's Summary*). Perhaps most significantly, the *Hortus deliciarum* was illustrated with some 336 miniatures of high artistic quality.

The variety of sources indicates the breadth of Herrad's own learning and the strength of her convent's library. The currency of her reading is indicated by her inclusion of passages from the *Scholastica Historica* of Peter Comestor, a work finished only in the early 1170s. The illuminations attest to the wealth of the artistic talent available around Hohenburg: the scribes and artists may well have come from the convent community. Throughout the work, the interplay of word and image is striking. One miniature depicts a "ladder of virtue," which shows a panoply (shining array) of Christians—female and male, religious and lay— struggling toward perfection. Accompanying texts discuss the symbolism. At the foot of the ladder a dragon breathes fire, while at the top the right hand of God offers a crown of virtue. Toward the lower end, the first Christians to fall from the ladder are a married couple. The caption reads, "this knight and his wife represent all faithless lay people who, greedy, proud, and devoted to fornication, love the various delights of this world." At the upper end, it is a virginal woman who grasps the crown of salvation. The message for the canonesses of Hohenburg, many of whom came from knightly families, is clear.

The unique copy of the codex was destroyed by the fire that consumed the municipal library of Strasbourg during the Franco-Prussian War in 1870. The *Hortus deliciarum* is now known only through notes and tracings made by nineteenth-century scholars, especially the first reconstruction by Alexandre Straub and Gustave Keller (1879–1899), which preserve some 240 of the original miniatures, as well as many of the texts. Much of the original, however, has been irretrievably lost.

See also Artists, Medieval Women; Hildegard of Bingen, St.; Scribes and Scriptoria

BIBLIOGRAPHY

Primary Sources
Griffiths, Fiona. "Herrad of Hohenbourg and the Poetry of the *Hortus deliciarum: Cantat tibi cantica.*" In *Women Writing Latin*, edited by Laurie J. Churchill, 2: 231–63. New York: Routledge, 2002.
Herrad of Landsberg. *Hortus Deliciarum*. Critical ed. by Rosalie Green, Michael Evans et al. Studies of the Warburg Institute, 36. 2 vols. London: Warburg Institute, 1979.
———. *Garden of Delights*. Translated by Aristide Caratzas. New Rochelle, N.Y.: Caratzas, 1977. [Revision and English trans. of the Straub and Keller ed. (Strasbourg: Imprimerie Strasbourgeoise, 1879–1899)].

Secondary Sources

Autenrieth, Johanne. "Einige Bemerkungen zu den Gedichten im *Hortus deliciarum* Herrads von Landsberg." In *Festschrift Bernhard Bischoff zu seinem 65. Geburtstag*, edited by Johanne Autenrieth and Franz Brunhölzl, 307–21. Stuttgart, Germany: A. Hiersemann, 1971.

Cames, Gérard. *Allégories et symboles dans l'Hortus deliciarum*. Leiden, Netherlands: E. J. Brill, 1971.

Collard, Judith. "Herrad of Hohenbourg's *Hortus Deliciarum* and the Creation of Images for Medieval Nuns." In *Communities of Women: Historical Perspectives*, edited by Barbara Brookes and Dorothy Page, 39–57. Dunedin, N.Z.: University of Otago Press, 2002.

Curschmann, Michael. "Text-Bilder-Strukturen: Der *Hortus Deliciarum* und die frühmittelhochdeutsche Geistlichendichtung." *Deutsche Vierteljahrsschrift für Literaturwissenschaft und Geistesgeschichte* 55 (1981): 378–418.

Ettlinger, L. D. "Muses and Liberal Arts. Two Miniatures from Herrad of Landsberg's *Hortus Deliciarum*." In *Essays in the History of Art Presented to Rudolf Wittkower*, edited by Douglas Fraser, Howard Hibbard, and Milton J. Lewine, 29–35. London: Phaidon, 1967.

Gillen, Otto. *Ikonographische Studien zum Hortus deliciarum der Herrad von Landsberg*. Kunstwissenschaftliche Studien, 9. Berlin: Deutscher Kunstverlag, 1931.

Griffiths, Fiona. "Herrad of Hohenbourg: A Synthesis of Learning in the *Garden of Delights*." In *Listen, Daughter: The* Speculum Virginum *and the Formation of Religious Women in the Middle Ages*, edited by Constant Mews, 221–43. The New Middle Ages. Basingstoke: Palgrave, 2001.

———. "Nuns' Memories, or, 'Missing' History in Alsace (c.1200): Herrad of Hohenbourg's *Garden of Delights*." In *Medieval Memories: Men, Women and the Past, 700–1300*, edited by Elisabeth van Houts, 132–49. Women and Men in History. New York: Longman, 2001.

Krüger, Annette, and Gabriele Runge. "Lifting the Veil: Two Typological Diagrams in the *Hortus Deliciarum*." *Journal of the Warburg and Courtauld Institutes* 60 (1998): 1–22.

McGuire, Thérèse. "Two Twelfth-Century Women and Their Books." In *Women and the Book: Assessing the Visual Evidence*, edited by Jane Taylor and Lesley Smith, 96–105. London: British Library; Toronto: University of Toronto Press, 1996. [Reproduces and analyzes illuminations from the works of Herrad and of Hildegard of Bingen].

THOMAS HEAD

HILD (HILDA), ST. (614–680). Abbess of Streoneshealh, later, Whitby, in Yorkshire, England, Hild was one of the most important figures in early Anglo-Saxon Christianity. Her life is documented in some detail by the English historian (the Venerable) Bede (early eighth century) in *Historia Ecclesiastica* (*Ecclesiastical History*, iv, 23); other early sources in which she is mentioned are Eddius's *Vita* (*Life of Bishop Wilfrid*) and the eighth-century *Calendar of St. Willibrord*. James Cross argues, on the basis of variations between Bede's account and a vernacular version in the anonymous *Old English Martyrology*, that the latter also draws on an early *Vita* (*Life*) of Hild, now no longer extant. The surprising omission of Hild from the ninth-century Lindisfarne *Liber Vitae Ecclesiae Dunelmensis* (*Book of the Life of Durham Cathedral*) raises the possibility that her name may represent a shortened form of Hildigyth, Hildithryth, or Hildeburh, all of which are represented there.

Like many Anglo-Saxon abbesses, Hild was of royal descent. Her father, Hereric, was the nephew of King Edwin of Northumbria, a major northern English kingdom, in exile with Edwin around the time of Hild's birth in 614. Hereric was killed by poison either before she was born (according to the *Old English Martyrology*) or during her infancy (according to Bede). Nothing is known of the ancestry of her mother, Breguswith, who, in conventional hagiographic fashion, dreamed that, while searching for her exiled husband, she found under her clothes a precious necklace that shone so brightly that it filled all Britain with its light. This dream was, of course, to be fulfilled in her daughter, Hild.

Hild herself was pagan until the age of thirteen, then converted along with Edwin by Paulinus, first bishop of the Northumbrians, in 627. Bede says little of the next twenty years of her life, but it is possible, as Christine Fell suggests, that she may have been married—perhaps to a pagan—and widowed by the time she decided to take religious vows at the age of thirty-three. At first she went to East Anglia, intending to go from there to Gaul to join her sister Hereswith, mother of King Ealdwulf of East Anglia, as a nun at Chelles. After a year, however, Bishop Aidan persuaded her to return to Northumbria, where she founded a religious community on a small estate north of the River Wear. The precise location of the site is now uncertain. A year later, Hild was made abbess of a monastery at Hartlepool, a northern English seaport, founded shortly before by Heiu, the first Northumbrian woman to become a nun. Here Hild established a life according to the monastic rule, and in 655 King Osuiu (Oswy) of Northumbria sent her his infant daughter Ælfflæd, whom he dedicated to God in thanksgiving for his victory over King Penda of Mercia (a realm including most of the English Midlands) at the battle of the river Winwaed. On the basis of strong circumstantial evidence, historians believe that in 657 Hild either founded or refounded the double monastery of Streoneshealh, traditionally identified with Whitby, now a seaport in Yorkshire, northern England, and established the same rule there. She was eventually to be succeeded as abbess by Ælfflæd.

St. Hilda. Detail of stained glass in Kirkby Malham Church, Yorkshire. © Charles Walker/Topfoto/The Image Works.

Under Hild Streoneshealh became a major center of intellectual activity. She placed a strong emphasis on education, so that many of her monks were fitted to enter the priesthood and at least five—Bosa, Ætla, Oftfor, John, and Wilfrid II—became bishops. Her reputation grew to such an extent that her advice was sought by kings and princes, and Bede claims that all who knew her called her mother. Under her rule, Streoneshealh's prestige caused it to be chosen as the venue for the great ecclesiastical synod of 664, known as the Synod of Whitby, to resolve the dispute concerning the dating of Easter. This significant conflict in the Church calendar had arisen between Christians preserving the old Celtic lunar-calendar cycle of eighty-four years, as in Ireland, and the 532-year cycle recently adopted by those once converted by St. Augustine's mission, advocated at

Rome. Hild herself supported the Irish tradition of dating, while others including Bishop Wilfrid spoke in favor of the Roman tradition. The matter was decided in favor of Rome by King Oswy. Wilfrid and Hild clashed again in 679 when he appealed to Rome against his dismissal from his bishopric and was opposed both by her and by the Archbishop of Canterbury.

It was at Streoneshealh during the time of Hild that Caedmon, an illiterate herdsman attached to the monastery, was miraculously inspired to compose the first Christian poetry in English. The way in which the abbess subsequently received him into the religious community and arranged for his instruction in the Scriptures, thus enabling him to continue composing verse on biblical themes, illustrates both her receptiveness to new ideas and her educational zeal. However, Caedmon himself apparently never learned to write, and as Fell points out, the extent of Hild's own literacy is uncertain. No letters from her survive; indeed the only extant texts from Streoneshealh comprise a single letter by her successor Ælfflæd addressed to Abbess Adola of Pfalzel, and an anonymous *Life of St. Gregory* dating from the early eighth century. Both postdate the time of Hild, and the contents and extent of the library at Streoneshealh during her rule are now unknown.

Hild suffered from a chronic illness during the last six years of her life, and died at the age of sixty-six on November 17, 680. According to Bede's account, she had lived thirty-three years in the secular life followed by thirty-three years in the religious life. It is possible, however, that pertinent dates have been manipulated, since thirty-three is a common hagiographical motif based on the age of Christ at his death. Visions of Hild's soul ascending to Heaven in the company of angels were seen at the time of her death by a nun called Begu at the daughter cell of Hackness thirteen miles away, and by an unnamed nun in a remote part of Streoneshealh itself. Hild's burial place is unknown, as is the date of her canonization. Sources written after the Norman Conquest (1066) suggest that her bones were transported to Glastonbury, in southwestern England, during either the eighth or the tenth century following the devastation of Streoneshealh by the Danes, but they have also been claimed by Gloucester, also in the southwest. Her cult appears to have been very localized: of fifteen ancient churches dedicated to Hild, nine are in Yorkshire, two in Durham, and one each in Cumberland and Northumberland—all in northern England. Her feast day is November 17 or 18.

See also Chelles, Nun of; Double Monasteries; Hagiography (Female Saints)

BIBLIOGRAPHY

Primary Sources
[Anon.]. *An Old English Martyrology*. Edited by George Herzfeld, 206–9. Early English Text Society, o.s. 116. London: Kegan Paul, Trench, Trubner, 1900. Reprint New York: Kraus, 1973.
[Bede]. *Bede's Ecclesiastical History of the English People*. Edited and translated by Bertram Colgrave and R. A. B. Mynors, 296–309, 404–21. Oxford: Clarendon Press, 1969.
[Eddius Stephanus]. *The Life of Bishop Wilfrid by Eddius Stephanus*. Edited and translated by Bertram Colgrave. Cambridge: Cambridge University Press, 1927.
[Willibrord] *The Calendar of St. Willibrord from ms. Paris Lat 10837*. Edited by Henry Austin Wilson, 13. Henry Bradshaw Society, 55. London: Harrison, 1918.

Secondary Sources
Cross, James E. "A Lost Life of Hilda of Whitby: The Evidence of the *Old English Martyrology*." In *The Early Middle Ages*, edited by William H. Snyder, 21–43. Acta, 6 (for 1979). Binghamton: State University of New York Press, 1982.

Fell, Christine E. "Hild, Abbess of Streonæshalch." In *Hagiography and Medieval Literature: A Symposium*, edited by Hans Bekker-Nielsen, 76–99. Odense, Denmark: Odense University Press, 1981.

Higham, N. J. *The Kingdom of Northumbria* AD *350–1100*. Stroud, U.K. and Dover, N.H.: Alan Sutton, 1993.

Hunter Blair, Peter. *Northumbria in the Days of Bede*. London: Gollancz, 1976.

———. "Whitby as a Centre of Learning in the Seventh Century." In *Learning and Literature in Anglo-Saxon England: Studies Presented to Peter Clemoes on the Occasion of His Sixty-Fifth Birthday*, edited by Michael Lapidge and Helmut Gneuss, 3–32. Cambridge: Cambridge University Press, 1985.

Nicholson, Joan. "*Feminae Gloriosae*: Women in the Age of Bede." In *Medieval Women*, edited by Derek Baker, 15–29. Studies in Church History: Subsidia, 1. Oxford: Basil Blackwell, 1978.

Wormald, C. P[atrick]. "St. Hilda, Saint and Scholar (614–80)." In *The St Hilda's College Centenary Symposium*, edited by Jane Mellanby, 93–103. Oxford: [n.p.], 1993.

CAROLE HOUGH

HILDEGARD OF BINGEN, ST. (1098–1179). A German Benedictine abbess and founder of two monasteries for women, Hildegard was a renowned visionary and prophet and the first great female theologian of the Catholic Church. A prolific Latin author, she composed three massive tomes of symbolic theology organized around her visions, as well as a liturgical song cycle, an extensive pastoral correspondence, an encyclopedia of natural science and medicine, two saints' lives, and several minor works. Famous in her lifetime as a monastic reformer and audacious preacher, Hildegard was long remembered for her apocalyptic prophecies and locally revered as a miracle-working saint. Though never canonized, she is honored with an officially recognized cult, and one of the monasteries she founded, the Abtei St. Hildegard at Eibingen, Germany, continues to flourish.

Born in the Rhineland village of Bermersheim (diocese of Mainz), Hildegard was the tenth and last child of aristocratic parents, Hildebert and Mechthild. Throughout her eighty-one years she suffered from delicate health, and her physical peculiarities made themselves known from early childhood. At the age of three, according to the memoirs incorporated in her biography, she shuddered at the appearance of a dazzling light that filled her whole field of vision. As she matured, this experience developed into a unique and characteristic form of visual perception. In "the shadow of the living Light," as she called it, Hildegard discerned geometric forms, human figures, buildings, and eventually whole kinetic scenarios that she came to understand as divine revelations. With the aid of dictation from a "heavenly voice," she structured her writings around these visions, explaining that she received them in a state of normal waking consciousness and not in ecstasy or dreams. But she found the experience physically exhausting and suffered from recurrent bouts of debilitating, sometimes paralyzing illness, in spite of which she pursued an extraordinarily vigorous career. Historians of medicine have interpreted her condition as a form of migraine, a diagnosis that seems plausible if it is not construed reductively to "explain" her religious experience.

It may have been her poor health, her precocious intellectual gifts, or simple piety that prompted Hildegard's parents to offer her as a monastic oblate in her childhood. She was given initially as companion to a noblewoman, Jutta of Sponheim, who had established a hermitage near the male monastery of St. Disibod (Disibodenberg). Other women soon joined Jutta and Hildegard, and their community was incorporated as a nunnery under

St. Hildegard of Bingen's vision of God creating an angel to overcome the devil. From 12th-century manuscript at Lucca, Bib. Statale, Cod. Lat. 1942, *De operatione Dei*, I,1. © The Art Archive/Biblioteca Civica Lucca/Dagli Orti.

the Benedictine Rule, the administrative and spiritual code of conduct established by St. Benedict of Nursia (c.540) to foster a perfect following of Christ. Little more is known of Hildegard's life until 1136, when Jutta died and the now middle-aged Hildegard was elected mistress in her stead. Five years after taking up this authoritative post, she received a prophetic call and began, hesitantly at first, to publicize her visions in speech and writing. With the help of two friends, her fellow nun Richardis and the monk Volmar, she took ten years to complete her first and most famous work of visionary theology, the *Scivias* (short for *Scito vias Domini*, or *Know the Ways of the Lord*). In the course of this daunting project, which she believed unprecedented for a woman, Hildegard bolstered her self-confidence as a seer by soliciting the approval of Cistercian abbot Bernard of Clairvaux (1090–1153), a powerful presence in Church affairs and the most celebrated saint of the age. In 1147/1148, her work-in-progress came to the attention of Bernard's protégé, Pope Eugene III, during his sojourn in nearby Trier, in the Rhineland. After assuring himself of Hildegard's orthodoxy, the pope allegedly sent her a letter of "apostolic blessing" that, in effect, gave her the status of a licensed prophet and enabled her to accomplish feats that would otherwise have been unthinkable. Unfortunately, this letter does not survive.

Between 1148 and 1152, Hildegard determined to move her nuns from St. Disibod to a new and independent foundation, the Rupertsberg, near the town of Bingen, on the Rhine. Overcoming initial resistance from her abbot and some of the local nobility, she secured the site of an abandoned Carolingian (eighth century) monastery founded by St. Rupert, to whom she dedicated her new community. The material and spiritual needs of the Rupertsberg— construction, fund-raising, canonical separation from the monks, liturgical music, and pastoral care of the growing sisterhood—dominated Hildegard's life during the next decade. Her pastoral style emphasized moderation and scrupulous moral vigilance, but her love of splendid symbolic gestures distinguished her from the Cistercians and other reform-minded ascetic orders. She scandalized at least one contemporary abbess, for example, by allowing her aristocratic virgins to wear silk veils and golden jewelry when they received communion. It was for her daughters' use that Hildegard wrote her *Liber vitae meritorum* (*Book of Life's Merits*), a lengthy dialogue on virtues and vices cast in the form of an otherworld vision, as well as the rich corpus of liturgical chant collected in her *Symphonia*. The Rupertsberg's unique liturgical style is also attested by the *Ordo virtutum* (*Play of Virtues*), a music-drama Hildegard wrote for her nuns, perhaps to solemnize the profession of novices or the dedication of their new chapel. The *Ordo* has been called the first morality play—despite its distance from the much later vernacular plays—because it dramatizes a headstrong soul's temptations and final victory over Satan. Except for the devil's speaking part, all the roles are scored for female voices. Hildegard further heightened the aura of her nuns' elite and privileged enclave by devising a secret language (*Lingua ignota*) for their private communications.

The growing fame and prosperity of the Rupertsberg mirrored Hildegard's increasing celebrity. Revered as an oracle and spiritual guide, she was sought by pilgrims and correspondents for advice on a wide variety of questions, ranging from problems of monastic discipline to infertility and marital woes. Much of this pastoral activity is reflected in her correspondence, which ranks with the epistles of St. Bernard among the great twelfth-century letter collections. Monastic superiors and clergy constitute the great bulk of Hildegard's correspondents, but several popes and lay rulers, including Emperor Frederick I Barbarossa (c.1122–1190), are represented among them. Letters ostensibly addressed to the abbess must be read with caution, however, for her secretaries were not above introducing pious falsifications to magnify her prestige. The collection also includes occasional writings and even sermons. During the late 1150s and 1160s, Hildegard undertook several preaching tours to advance the cause of monastic and clerical reform, mingling her moral exhortations with fiery apocalyptic warnings and denunciations of the Cathars, the powerful dualistic heretics who had won numerous converts in the Rhineland. Most of her sermons were delivered in religious houses, but more remarkably, Hildegard preached to clergy and laity together in the cathedral towns of Mainz, Trier, and Cologne. In the lengthy papal schism (1159–1176) fomented by Barbarossa, she sided with the "legitimate" pope (supported by the majority of cardinals), Alexander III, against the emperor's successive candidates.

Yet another side of Hildegard's activity is represented by her scientific and medical writings. Her comprehensive encyclopedia of natural history goes by various names: *Physica, Book of Simple Medicine*, and most accurately, *Nine Books on the Subtleties of Different Kinds of Creatures*. This compilation includes a bestiary, a lapidary (on the properties of gems and minerals), and one of the fullest surviving twelfth-century herbals. Its companion volume, *Causae et curae* (*Causes and Cures* or *Book of Compound Medicine*), is a fascinating if rather jumbled manual on diseases and their remedies, notable also for its candid representation of male and female sexuality and character types. These two works contain empirical observation and practical remedies mingled with folklore, charms and incantations, and theological speculation on such topics as the creation of Adam and Eve and the nature of evil. They were long considered to be of doubtful authenticity because they are the only writings for which Hildegard did not claim visionary inspiration, nor were they included in the hefty volume of her "collected works" assembled in an apparent canonization bid. But their genuineness is now accepted by most scholars.

Hildegard's wide-ranging interests—cosmology, ethics, human physiology, salvation history, church reform, and apocalyptic—all come together in the magisterial work of her old age, the *Liber divinorum operum* (*Book of Divine Works*). Like the *Scivias* and *Liber vitae meritorum*, however, the final volume of her trilogy proved too long and unwieldy to be much read in its entirety. Moreover, theological tastes were changing. Hildegard represents not so much the vanguard of a new movement as the consummation of twelfth-century symbolics. Her diffuse and difficult style, as well as her passion to synthesize diverse realms of knowledge in an overarching whole, did not appeal to thirteenth-century readers, who tended to prefer the drier, more analytic genres of systematic theology or the more intimate, confessional style of mystics like Bernard and his imitators. Despite her far-reaching contemporary fame, therefore, Hildegard's reputation soon waned. In later centuries she was remembered chiefly through a compilation of her prophecies produced by the monk Gebeno of Eberbach around 1220. This epitome circulated far more widely than her complete books, and because of it, Hildegard won such posthumous fame in apocalyptic circles that many spurious prophecies came to be ascribed to her.

Locally, however, the abbess was not forgotten. By the time of her death in 1179, her secretary, Guibert of Gembloux, had already begun collecting materials for her *vita*, or sacred biography. The vita was eventually written by two monks, Gottfried of St. Disibod and Theoderich of Echternach, but its most remarkable feature is the inclusion of striking autobiographical fragments. In these passages, Hildegard's first-person voice establishes a new type of female sanctity, soon to be imitated by celebrated hagiographers including Jacques de (or James of) Vitry (c.1165–1240) and Thomas of Cantimpré (c.1201–c.1270). Visually and verbally inspired, chronically ill yet morally indomitable, waging ceaseless war against demons, the seer and prophet triumphs over all adversities through the very depth of her suffering. This memorable self-portrait, along with the image of the thundering doomsday preacher, represents Hildegard's legacy to the later Middle Ages. The astonishing figure she cut in her own era has been rediscovered only in ours.

See also Epistolary Authors, Women as; Hagiography (Female Saints); Jutta of Disibodenberg, Blessed; Medicine and Medieval Women; Music in Medieval Nunneries; Music, Women Composers and Musicians; Rules for Canonesses, Nuns, and Recluses

BIBLIOGRAPHY

Primary Sources

Gottfried of Disibodenberg and Theodoric of Echternach. *Vita Sanctae Hildegardis.* Edited by Monica Klaes. *Corpus Christianorum: Continuatio Mediaevalis.* (=CCCM), 126. Turnhout, Belgium: Brepols, 1993.

————. [Latin and Modern German]. *Vita Sanctae Hildegardis/Leben der heiligen Hildegard von Bingen. Canonizatio Sanctae Hildegardis/Kanonisation der heiligen Hildegard.* Edited, translated, and introduced by Monika Klaes. Fontes Christiani, 29. Freiburg, Germany and New York: Herder, 1998.

Hildegard of Bingen. *Opera omnia.* Edited by J.-P. Migne. *Patrologia latina*, 197. Paris: Migne, 1855. [Complete works, but unreliably edited; see better separate-work editions below].

————. [Works: Selections, English]. *Hildegard of Bingen. Selected writings.* Translated with an introduction and notes by Mark Atherton. London: Penguin, 2001.

————. *Causae et curae.* Edited by Paul Kaiser. Leipzig, Germany: Teubner, 1903.

————. *Hildegard of Bingen: On Natural Philosophy and Medicine. Selections from* Causae et curae. Translated from Latin with introduction, notes and interpretive essay by Margret Berger. Library of Medieval Women. Cambridge and Rochester, N.Y.: D. S. Brewer, 1999.

————. *Epistolarium.* Edited by Lieven Van Acker and Monika Klaes-Hachmöller. CCCM, 91, 91a, 91b. Turnhout: Brepols, 1991, 1993, 2001.

————. *The Letters of Hildegard of Bingen*. Translated by Joseph L. Baird and Radd K. Ehrman. New York and Oxford: Oxford University Press, 1994, 1998.

————. *Liber divinorum operum*. Edited by Albert Derolez and Peter Dronke. CCCM, 92. Turnhout: Brepols, 1996.

————. *Liber vitae meritorum*. Edited by Angela Carlevaris. CCCM, 90. Turnhout: Brepols, 1995.

————. *Book of the Rewards of Life*. Translated by Bruce Hozeski. New York: Garland, 1993.

————. *Ordo virtutum*. In *Nine Medieval Latin Plays*, edited and translated by Peter Dronke, 147–84. Cambridge: Cambridge University Press, 1994.

————. *Ordo virtutum*. Etcetera 101. Amsterdam, Netherlands: Etcetera Records, 1998. Video-cassette.

————. *Physica*. Translated by Priscilla Throop. Rochester, Vt.: Healing Arts Press, 1998.

————. *Scivias*. Edited by Adelgundis Führkötter and Angela Carlevaris. CCCM, 43–43a. Turnhout: Brepols, 1978.

————. *Scivias*. Translated by Mother Columba Hart and Jane Bishop. Classics of Western Spirituality. New York: Paulist Press, 1990.

————. *Symphonia armonie celestium revelationum*. Edited and translated with critical commentary by Barbara Newman. 2nd revised ed. Ithaca, N.Y.: Cornell University Press, 1998.

Jutta and Hildegard: The Biographical Sources. Edited and translated by Anna Silvas. Medieval Women: Texts and Contexts. Turnhout: Brepols, 1998; Brepols Medieval Women Series. University Park: Pennsylvania Stae University Press, 1999.

Thesaurus Hildegardis Bingensis. Series Corpus Christianorum. Thesaurus patrum Latinorum. CETEDOC (Catholic University of Louvain, Louvain-la-neuve). Turnhout: Brepols, 1998. Text-fiche. [Concordance to her works].

Secondary Sources

Burnett, Charles, and Peter Dronke, eds. *Hildegard of Bingen: The Context of her Thought and Art*. London: Warburg Institute, 1998.

Craine, Renate. *Hildegard: Prophet of the Cosmic Christ*. New York: Crossroad, 1997.

Dronke, Peter. *Women Writers of the Middle Ages: A Critical Study of Texts from Perpetua (†203) to Marguerite Porete (†1310)*. Cambridge: Cambridge University Press, 1984.

Flanagan, Sabina. *Hildegard of Bingen, 1098–1179. A Visionary Life*. London: Routledge, 2nd ed., 1998.

Gouguenheim, Sylvain. *La Sibylle du Rhin: Hildegarde de Bingen, abbesse et prophétesse rhénane*. Paris: Presses de al Sorbonne, 1996.

Haverkamp, Alfred, ed. *Hildegard von Bingen in ihrem historischen Umfeld*. Mainz, Germany: P. von Zabern, 2000.

King-Lenzmeier, Anne. *Hildegard of Bingen: An Integrated Vision*. Collegeville, Minn.: Liturgical Press, 2001.

McInerney, Maud Burnett, ed. *Hildegard of Bingen: A Book of Essays*. Garland Medieval Casebooks. New York and London: Garland, 1998.

Newman, Barbara. *Sister of Wisdom: St. Hildegard's Theology of the Feminine*. 2nd ed. Berkeley: University of California Press, 1997.

————, ed. *Voice of the Living Light: Hildegard of Bingen and Her World*. Berkeley: University of California Press, 1998.

Schipperges, Heinrich. *Hildegard of Bingen: Healing and the Nature of the Cosmos*. Translated from the German by John Broadwin. Princeton, N.J.: Markus Wiener, 1997.

Schrader, Marianna, and Adelgundis Führkötter. *Die Echtheit des Schrifttums der heiligen Hildegard von Bingen*. Cologne, Germany and Graz, Austria: Böhlau, 1956.

BARBARA NEWMAN

HOCKTIDE. A gender-specific festival in England, Hocktide falls on the second Monday and Tuesday after Easter. Celebrations involved the married women working together to capture the married men, who gained their freedom by paying a forfeit. On Tuesday, the men captured the women. Its origins are obscure. The chronicler John Roussius claimed that the holiday commemorated the death of King Harthacanute (d. 1042). Elizabethans in the sixteenth century believed that it marked a ninth- or tenth-century Anglo-Saxon victory over the Vikings and that the holiday reenacts the Anglo-Saxon women's decisive role in the triumph. In truth, English towns did not begin to celebrate it until the fifteenth century.

By the mid-fifteenth century, despite the bishop of Worcester's denunciation of it in 1450, parishes had incorporated Hocktide as a women's holiday into their parish fundraising activities. Perhaps the most accessible records of this festival are churchwarden's accounts of St. Mary at Hill in London. Typically, women earned more money at this holiday because their quarries were men, who had more money. This should not distract us, however, from recognizing the amount of organization and leadership women exercised in conducting a successful celebration. The money that they earned went to the parish coffers. In many parishes, the women themselves decided how the parish was to spend this money, thus affording us a glimpse of some of the religious and liturgical priorities of women in the pre-Reformation parish. This holiday, along with other communal activities, ended during the Reformation. Although Coventry revived it with a Hocktide play during the reign of Elizabeth I (1558–1603), the holiday never regained its pre-Reformation popularity.

See also Godiva, Lady; Power of Women

BIBLIOGRAPHY

Primary Sources
Carpenter, John, bishop of Worcester. [1450 Denunciation of Hocktide]. In *Record of Early English Drama: Herefordshire and Worcestershire*, edited by David N. Klausner, 349–50, 553–54. Toronto, Ont.: University of Toronto Press, 1990.
The Medieval Records of a London City Church (St. Mary at Hill): A.D. 1420–1559. Edited by Henry Littlehales. 2 vols. Early English Text Society, o.s. 125, 128. London: Kegan, Paul, Trench, Trübner, 1904–1905. Reprint New York: Kraus, 1975 (2 vols. in one).

Secondary Sources
French, Katherine L. "To Free Them from Binding: Women in the Late Medieval English Parish." *Journal of Interdisciplinary History* 27 (1997): 387–412.
Humphrey, Chris. *The Politics of Carnival: Festive Misrule in Medieval England.* Manchester: Manchester University Press, 2001.
Hutton, Ronald. *The Rise and Fall of Merry England: The Ritual Year, 1400–1700.* Oxford: Oxford University Press, 1994.
MacLean, Sally-Beth. "Hocktide: A Reassessment of a Popular Pre-Reformation Festival." In *Festive Drama*, edited by Meg Twycross, 233–41. Woodbridge, Suffolk, U.K.: Boydell and Brewer, 1996.

KATHERINE L. FRENCH

HOMOSEXUALITY. *See* **Lesbians in the Middle Ages; Transvestism**

HROTSVITHA OF GANDERSHEIM (c.935–c.975). Also known as Hrotswitha, Hrosvitha, Hrotsvit, or Roswitha, she was a German canoness writing in Latin, considered the first dramatist (male or female) of the Middle Ages, that is, after the fall of the ancient

Classical theater. She was likewise one of the first love poets of the Latin Middle Ages, who also composed hagiographic verses (saints' lives in verse) and historical poems in epic style and letters.

Hrotsvitha's artistic activity developed in the cultural and intellectual milieu associated with the rather unique Benedictine abbey of Gandersheim, in Saxony, northwestern Germany, the cloister at which Hrotsvitha received her early religious and cultural education. The monastery was founded in 852 by Duke Liudolf of Saxony and his wife, Oda, and consecrated on All Saints' Day 881. This small abbey was aristocratic, proudly independent, and ruled by women. As Dronke, Gold, and other recent scholars have shown, Gandersheim provided an ideal atmosphere for a literary woman. Although it did not attain the renown of its masculine-ruled counterparts in Germany, its women religious enjoyed more freedom—intellectually and personally—than nuns in other abbeys. In the preface to her plays, Hrotsvitha would refer to herself as "clamor validus Gandeshemensis" ("the strong voice of Gandersheim"). She later celebrated its history her last extant poem, *Primordia Coenobii Gandeshemensis* (*On the Foundation and Early History of Gandersheim Abbey*, c.973).

Born of a noble German family, like the other abbesses of Gandersheim, Hrotsvitha was probably related to Hrotsvitha I, the fourth abbess (919–926). How old she was on entering the abbey is not precisely known—probably c.955, under the rule of abbess Wendelgard, and about the same time that Hrotsvitha's good friend Gerberga II (b. 940), whom she describes as younger (in the preface to her *Legends*), arrived there. Hrotsvitha received a sound education, first under the scholarly direction of the nun Rikkardis, and later under the tutelage of Gerberga, niece of Emperor Otto I and herself a product of the prestigious monastery of St. Emmeram in Regensburg. Hrotsvitha's knowledge of classical and religious literature was the result not only of good teaching but also of the cultural opportunities provided by Gandersheim's intellectual activity, fostered to a significant extent by Emperor Otto's younger brother (and Gerberga's uncle), Bruno, Archbishop of Cologne (925–965). The many learned men whom Bruno brought to Gandersheim contributed the intellectual and literary activity forming the major component of what is often called the "Ottonian Renaissance." The learning that Hrotsvitha acquired at Gandersheim was thus both wide and diversified. She appears to have been familiar with Virgil's epic poem on the founding of Rome, the *Aeneid* (19 B.C.E.), and his shorter, pastoral *Eclogues* (37 B.C.E.); Ovid's wry mytho-historical *Metamorphoses* (first century, C.E.), and Terence's refined comedies (second century B.C.E.). Of the Christian writers she appears to have read the poet Prudentius (fourth century), her most important model, especially his *Peristephanon* (*Concerning the Crowns of the Martyrs*), *Psychomachia* (*Conflict for the Soul*) and *Apotheosis* (on the human and divine natures of Christ). Other influences were Sedulius (fifth century), a poet of the life of Christ; religious poet Venantius Fortunatus (sixth century); and the great philosopher and statesman, Boethius (sixth century), famous for his *De consolatione Philosophiae* (*Consolation of Philosophy*). She credits to laborious and disciplined study her thorough training in the two main pillars of medieval education: the trivium (grammar, rhetoric, dialectic), quadrivium (arithmetic, geometry, astronomy, music); and also the dictaminal arts (formal writing, especially epistles). Above all she was steeped in the large body of hagiographic accounts, especially those categorized as *passiones* (heroic deaths of martyrs) and the *vitae patrum* (lives of the Fathers).

All the extant works of Hrotsvitha, except for the *Primordia*, are contained in the manuscript known as the Emmeran-Munich Codex. This large manuscript was discovered at the monastery of St. Emmeran at Regensburg in 1493 by the humanist Conrad Celtis or Celtes, poet laureate of Germany, who published it at Nuremberg in 1501. Composed entirely in Latin, Hrotsvitha's literary works are grouped into three books. Book 1 consists of eight sacred legends in leonine hexameter verse, the first five of which are preceded by a prose preface and verse dedication to Gerberga II, and the last three by an additional dedication to her. A prose epilogue follows the eight poems. Book 2 contains six dramas followed by a poem of thirty-five lines on a "Vision of St. John." The dramas are preceded by a preface and a prose introduction addressed to her readers. Book 3 is comprised of two historical poems in heroic verse arranged within a complex whole that includes a prefatory dedication to Gerberga II, verse dedication to Otto I and Otto II, the *Gesta Ottonis* (*Deeds of Emperor Otto*), a verse introduction, and the *Primordia*, on the history of Gandersheim abbey.

The eight poems (Celtis's Book 1) are composed in leonine hexameters, that is, in the manner of an otherwise obscure poet named Leo or Leonius, who coined this type of popular Medieval-Latin hexameter, in which the final word of each verse rhymed with the word ending the midway pause (caesura) in the verse immediately preceding it. These poems constitute, chronologically, Hrotsvitha's first literary effort. Composed early in her literary career, some of the poems may have been presented and submitted by Hrotsvitha, the zealous pupil, to the scrutiny of her teacher, Gerberga II, as early as 957. However, it appears that the first five were dedicated to Gerberga in 959, when she was consecrated abbess, and the remaining three composed between 960 and 962. Hrotsvitha found the thematic substance of the eight poems in that inexhaustible collection of hagiographic *exempla*, the *Vitae patrum* (lives of the Holy Fathers). Together with the *Passiones*, describing the heroic death of martyrs, the *Translationes*, concerned with the translating of relics, and the *Miracula*, compilations of miracles performed by saints, the *vitae* are constituent elements of that hagiographic genre so prominent in the early Middle Ages.

The first of Hrotsvitha's eight poems, "Maria," recalls the events leading to the Virgin's miraculous birth, her marriage to Joseph, the birth of the child Jesus, and the flight into Egypt, The second poem, "The Ascension of the Lord," is distinguished by Christ's filial parting words to his mother, whom he recommends to John's care. The third poem, "Gangolfus," narrates the story of Gangolfus, a young Frankish prince, renowned for his beauty and sound mores. It recounts the liaison of his unfaithful wife with a lowborn lover, who murdered Gangolfus. Divine providence intervenes, causing the lover to pour forth his bowels and heart, and condemning the wicked wife to produce detestable intestinal sounds whenever she utters a word, thus marking her as a perennial source of laughter. The fourth poem tells of the martyrdom of Pelagius, a Spanish youth from Córdoba, who is beheaded for refusing the lustful advances of a Moorish ruler. The last of this group of poems narrates the popular story of Theophilus, his bond with the devil in return for worldly pleasures, and his repentance and salvation through the intercession of the Holy Virgin.

The last three of the eight poems are dedicated to Gerberga II. The first of this group deals with Basil of Caesarea, who, concerned for his daughter's salvation, has her associated with consecrated virgins in a monastery. Her manservant develops a passion for her and engages the aid of a magician who promises the devil's help if he agrees never to venerate Christ's name. The agreement is formalized in a written document. Christ, however, intervenes, and the story comes to a solemn climax in a church as the infernal document falls from the heavens to the feet of the praying Basilius. The second poem in this group is concerned with Dionysius of Athens, his conversion to Christianity, his voyage to Paris to convert the Gauls, his martyrdom by beheading, and his own miraculous selection of a final resting place. The last poem focuses on the martyrdom of the virgin Agnes, who, having refused to marry a pagan youth, is condemned by the prefect Simphronius to be stripped of her garments and confined to a brothel. Christ, her divine spouse, intervenes, and Agnes' body is completely covered with her thick, fast-growing tresses. She is finally slain with a sword by the judge Aspatius, and her soul ascends into heaven in resplendent glory.

Hrotsvitha's six dramas—*Gallicanus, Dulcitius, Calimachus, Abraham, Paphnutius/Pafnutius, and Sapientia*—constitute her most important and original literary production. The initial impetus toward the dramatization of the very same hagiographic material that had offered her subject matter for the poems was provided by the comedies of Terence. But although Hrotsvitha affirms that she is trying to imitate Terence, it is obvious that what attracts her is his *dulcedo sermonis* (grace of idiom) and *elegantia* (refinement); thus, her imitation, limited to form and style, is used in quite a different fashion. The preface to her plays reveals that she wished to provide an edifying version of Terence's "immoral"—in this context, pagan secular—comedies. Of her six plays, two, *Dulcitius* and *Sapientia*, are passiones; the other four, *Gallicanus, Calimachus, Abraham*, and *Paphnutius*, are *conversiones*, conversions brought about by the personal perfection and sanctity of holy men. Indeed, in the building of the spiritual edifice, the *aedificium spirituale*, through hagiographic exempla, the concept of edification (*aedificatio*) constitutes the fundamental aim and motivation.

The drama *Gallicanus* deals with Gallicanus' love for Constance, the fourth-century Roman Emperor Constantine's daughter, who has taken a virginal vow. Sent by the emperor to fight in Scitia, Gallicanus is converted by John and Paul, almoners to Constance. The story later relates the martyrdom of John, Paul, and Gallicanus under Julian the Apostate; the curing, through the martyrs' intercession, of their executioner's young son; and the latter's conversion to Christianity. *Dulcitius* recounts the martyrdom of the holy virgins Agape, Chionia, and Irene, whom the Roman governor Dulcitius seeks to violate in their prison cell during the night. Later, the three virgins are ordered by Diocletian to be delivered into the hands of Count Sisinnius, who has Agape and Chionia burned and Irene condemned to enter a brothel and then killed with arrows. In *Calimachus*, young Calimachus conceives a passion for the married Drusiana, who implores God for death so as not to succumb. Calimachus visits her tomb intent on violating her body, is bitten by a serpent, and dies. Through the intercession of John the Apostle they are both restored to life, and Calimachus becomes a Christian.

Abraham is concerned with the fall and repentance of Maria, Abraham's niece, who, seduced by the devil in a monk's habit, abandons the solitary cell in which she has spent twenty years in God's service. Abraham, dressed as a lover, seeks her out in a brothel and, after reclaiming her to Christ, takes her back to the desert, where she does penance for the next twenty years and then dies. In *Paphnutius*, the harlot Thais is converted by the hermit Paphnutius, who, disguised as a lover, seeks her out in a brothel in Alexandria. After sacrificing her riches and renouncing her life, Thais is shut up in a narrow cell to do penance. After three years, through a vision granted to Anthony's disciple Paul, Paphnutius realizes that Thais is saved and stays by her in prayerful vigil until her soul soars into heaven. *Sapientia* (*Wisdom*) relates the martyrdom of the holy virgins Faith, Hope, and Charity. They are put to death by the emperor Hadrian in the presence of their mother, who, after having exhorted them to persevere in their faith during their terrible ordeal, gives them a proper burial and then expires upon their tomb.

Hrotsvitha's third and last group of writings includes the two historical poems in heroic verse, the *Gesta Ottonis* and the *Primordia*. The *Gesta Ottonis* was composed by Hrotsvitha around 968 at the request of Gerberga II and William, archbishop of Mainz. Although Hrotsvitha, after the year 973, added to the poem a verse dedication to Otto II, the *Gesta Ottonis* is primarily a history of the reign of Otto I. Hrotsvitha found composition of this foundation epic difficult because of the historical doubtfulness enveloping the various events. The poem, composed of 1,517 verses, begins with the reign of Henry I (the Fowler) and ends in 948 with the marriage of his descendant, Liudolf, duke of Swabia. The work is marred by omissions and unevenness: the events covering the years 953 to 962 are lost, and the period from 962 to 966 only cursorily presented. Hrotsvitha took greater pleasure in writing the *Primordia*, which narrates the history of the monastery from its founding 852 to 919, the date of the death of Christine, sister of Emperor Otto and third abbess of Gandersheim.

An evaluation of her intellectual production clearly indicates that the six dramas constitute Hrotsvitha's most original artistic contribution. From a historical viewpoint, her imitation of Terence and the insertion of comic scenes in some of her plays amply demonstrate that Hrotsvitha and her later contemporaries were capable not only of correctly classifying Terence's dramas but, moreover, possessed the requisite sophistication to engage herself in a literary genre that would find its greatest illustration in the twelfth century, by means of the *comoedia elegiaca* (elegiac comedy) and in the mimetic tradition. As such, this uncloistered nun of Gandersheim remains the first Christian dramatic writer to have rediscovered classical dramaturgy and created in the process a new literary form: drama in rhymed prose.

Although the year of Hrotsvitha's death is not documented—there is no tomb marking the event—the evidence provided by the Hildesheim Chronicles, and in her own allusions in her works to people and events, had led scholars to believe she died in 1001 and 1003. However, more recent estimates place it circa 975.

See also Hagiography (Female Saints); Humanists, Italian Women, Issues and Theory; Rhetoric, Women and

BIBLIOGRAPHY

Primary Sources

Hrotsvitha. *Opera*. Edited by Conrad Celtis. Hildesheim and N.Y.: Olms, 2000. [Facsimile Reprint of Celtis's 1501 Nuremburg edition with German commentary].

———. *Hrosvit: Opera Omnia*. Edited by Walter Berschin. Bibliotheca Scriptorum Graecorum et Romanorum Teubneriana. Munich and Leipzig, Germany: W. G. Saur Verlag, 2001.

———. *Hrotsvit of Gandersheim: A Florilegium of Her Works*. Translated with an Introduction by Katharina M. Wilson. Woodbridge, Suffolk and Rochester, N.Y.: D. S. Brewer, 1998. [Selections in English].

———. *Hrotsvita, Dramata: Texte et Traduction*. Edited with commentary by Monique Goullet. Paris: Les Belles Lettres, 1999. [Excellent critical ed. in French].

———. *Hrotsvithae Opera*. Edited with commentary by Helene Homeyer. Munich: Schöningh, 1970. [Oft-cited German ed., includes the *Primordia*].

————. *The Non-Dramatic Works of Hrotsvitha*. Translated by Sr. Mary Gonsalva Wiegand. St. Louis: St. Louis University, 1936.

————. *The Plays of Hrotsvit of Gandersheim*. Translated by Katharina Wilson. Garland Library of Medieval Literature, 62. New York: Garland, 1989.

Secondary Sources

Berschin, Walter. "Passion un Theater, Zur dramatischen Struktur einiger Vorlagen Hrotsvits von Gandersheim." In *The Theatre in the Middle Ages*, edited by Herman Braet, Johan Nowé, and Gilbert Tournoy, 1–11. Mediaevalia Lovaniensia, 1: studia 13. Louvain, Belgium: Leuven University Press, 1985.

Bertini, Ferruccio. "Rosvita la poetessa." In *Medioevo al femminile*, edited by F. Bertini, F. Cardini et al., 63–95. Storia e società. Bari: Laterza, 1989.

————. "Simbologia e struttura drammatica nel 'Gallicanus' e nel 'Pafnutius' di Rosvita." In *The Theatre in the Middle Ages*, 45–59. *See under* Berschin *above*.

Chamberlain, David. "Musical Learning and Dramatic Action in Hrotsvit's *Pafnutius*." *Studies in Philology* 77 (1980): 319–43.

D'Angelo, Eugenia. "L'ultima Hrotsvitha: I 'Primordia coenobii Gandeshemensis.'" *Studi Medievali* 27 (1986): 575–608.

Dronke, Peter. "Hrotsvitha." In *Women Writers of the Middle Ages: A Critical Study of Texts from Perpetua (†203) to Marguerite Porete (†1310)*, 55–83. Cambridge: Cambridge University Press, 1984.

Giovini, Marco. *Indagini sui poemetti agiografici di Rosvita di Gandersheim*. Genoa: Università di Genova, 2001.

————. *Rosvita e l'imitari dictando terenziano*. Pubblicazioni del D.AR.FI.CL.ET, n.s., 210. Genoa: D.AR.FI.CL.ET., 2003

Gold, Barbara K. "Hrotswitha Writes Herself: 'Clamor Validus Gandeshemensis.'" In *Sex and Gender in Medieval and Renaissance Texts: The Latin Tradition*, edited by Barbara Gold, Paul A. Miller, and Charles Platter, 41–70. Albany: State University of New York Press, 1997.

Homeyer, Helene. "*Imitatio* und *aemulatio* im Werk der Hrotsvitha von Gandersheim," *Studi Medievali* 9 (1968): 966–79.

McInerney, Maud B. *Eloquent Virgins from Thecla to Joan of Arc*. The New Middle Ages. New York: Palgrave Macmillan, 2003.

Newlands, Carol E. "Hrotsvitha's Debt to Terence." *Transactions of the American Philological Association* 116 (1986): 369–91.

Sticca, Sandro. "Hrotsvitha's *Dulcitius* and Christian Symbolism," *Mediaeval Studies* 32 (1970): 108–27.

————. "Hrotsvitha's *Abraham* and Exegetical Tradition." In *Saggi in Onore di Vittorio D'Agostino*, 359–85. Torino: Giappichelli, 1971.

————. "Sacred Drama and Tragic Realism in Hrotsvitha's *Paphnutius*." In *The Theatre in the Middle Ages*, 12–44. *See above under* Berschin.

Wilson, Katharina M., ed. *Hrotsvit of Gandersheim: Rara Avis in Saxonia?* Medieval & Renaissance Monographs, 7. Ann Arbor, Mich.: MARC, 1987.

————. *Hrotsvit of Gandersheim. The Ethics of Authorial Stance*. Leiden: Brill, 1988.

Zeydel, Edwin H. The Authenticity of Hrotsvitha's Works." *Modern Language Notes* 61 (1946): 50–55.

————. "'Ego Clamor Validus'—Hrotsvitha." *Modern Language Notes* 61 (1946): 281–83.

————. "Were Hrotsvitha's Dramas Performed During Her Lifetime?" *Speculum* 20 (1945): 443–56. [Contains a detailed bibliography].

Sandro Sticca

HUGEBURC OF HEIDENHEIM (d. post-786). Also known as Huneberc, Hugeburc left her native England sometime in the middle decades of the eighth century to join relatives in the monastic community of Heidenheim, north of the Danube in Alamannia (now located in the German state of Baden-Württemberg). She thus became part of a remarkable group of Anglo-Saxon monks and nuns who, under the patronage of Frankish kings in the early eighth century, converted pagan Germanic peoples to Christianity. She died in Alemannia and is remembered only through a single composition, *Vita Willibaldi episcopi Eichstetensis et vita Wynnebaldi abbatis Heidenheimensis* (*The Life of Saints Willibald and Wynnebald*), which records the travels and missionary exploits of two saintly Anglo-Saxon brothers. The known details of her life are only those that can be teased from that text. Indeed, her name was only revealed to modern scholarship in 1931, when Bernhard Bischoff, a noted paleographer, deciphered an ingenious cryptogram in which Hugeburc had concealed her identity.

Heidenheim was founded in 752 by Wynnebald with the help of Willibald, then bishop of nearby Eichstätt. It was a double monastery, that is, it included both male and female communities, a common arrangement in Anglo-Saxon monasticism. When Wynnebald died in 761, he was succeeded not by an abbot, but by his sister Walburga, who governed the whole monastery as abbess. Hugeburc, who arrived after Wynnebald's death, was a kinswoman of Heidenheim's founders and thus likely of some stature in the community.

Hugeburc's composition is in many respects remarkable. She remains the only identified female author of a work of hagiography from the Carolingian period, although it is possible that some anonymous works were composed by women. She was related to the brothers of whom she wrote: "I have flowered from the same genealogical root." Acquainted with Willibald, she based her work on her conversations with him. Thus her narrative has an immediacy and color not often found in hagiography of the Carolingian period. Its centerpiece, an extensive description of Willibald's voyage to the Holy Land, is a crucial source of information on pilgrimage and travel in the early Middle Ages.

In her preface Hugeburc excused at great length the literary shortcomings of her work. Such statements of authorial humility formed a standard *topos* (commonplace) derived from classical rhetoric and common in medieval hagiography. Hugeburc, however, was also concerned to allay misogynist accusations that, as a woman, she was presumptuous in assuming an authorial role. The preface is laced with statements such as, "I am but womanly, stained by the frailty and weakness of my sex, and supported neither by pretense to wisdom nor by exalted aspiration to great power." Hugeburc stressed that her narrative was based not "on the meandering turnings of apocryphal stories, but on dictation from Willibald's own mouth." Such statements led earlier scholars to dismiss her as little more than a scribe who recorded the words of the bishop. Recent analysts, however, have more fully appreciated her literary art and accomplishment. Hugeburc shaped her narrative with vigor and imagination, employing a complex Latin style. She had a gift for imagery, as when she likened her writing to "black tracks ploughed by a pen in a furrowed path on these white plains of parchment." While her prose may include the occasional infelicitous or even ungrammatical phrase, it represents an ambitious attempt to imitate the intricate prose of the great Anglo-Saxon scholar Aldhelm (d. 709/710).

See also Boniface, St., Mission and Circle of; Double Monasteries; Hagiography (Female Saints); Humility Topos

BIBLIOGRAPHY

Primary Sources

Hugeburc of Heidenheim. *Vita Willibaldi episcopi Eichstetensis et vita Wynnebaldi abbatis Heidenheimensis auctore sanctimoniale Heidenheimensis.* Edited by Oswald Holder-Egger, 80–117. *Monumenta Germaniae Historica.* Scriptores in folio, 15: 1. Hannover: Hahn, 1887.

———. In *Soldiers of Christ: Saints' Lives from Late Antiquity and the Early Middle Ages*, edited by Thomas Noble and Thomas Head, 141–64. University Park: Pennsylvania State University Press, 1994. [English translation of the *Life of Willibald or Hodoeporicon* only].

Secondary Works

Berschin, Walter. "Hugeburcs Vita Willibaldi in der biographischen Tradition." *Studien und Mitteilungen zur Geschichte des Benediktinerordens und seiner Zweige* 98 (1987): 31–37.

Bischoff, Bernhard. "Wer ist die Nonne von Heidenheim?" *Studien und Mitteilungen zur Geschichte des Benediktinerordens und seiner Zweige* 49 (1931): 387–88.

Dronke, Peter, *Women Writers of the Middle Ages: A Critical Study of Texts from Perpetua (†203) to Marguerite Porete (†1310)*, 33–34. Cambridge: Cambridge University Press, 1984.

Gottschaller, Eva. *Hugeburc von Heidenheim: Philologische Untersuchungen zu den Heiligenbiographen einer Nonne des achten Jahrhunderts*. Münchener Beiträge zur Mediävistik und Renaissance-Forschung, 12. Munich: Arbeo-Gesellschaft, 1973.

Leonardi, Claudio. "Modelli agiografici nel secolo VIII: da Beda a Ugeburga." In *Les Fonctions des saints dans le monde occidental (IIIe–XIIIe siècle)*, 506–16. Collection de l'École française de Rome, 149. Rome: École française, 1991.

Vitrone, Francesca. "Hugeburc di Heidenheim e le *Vitae Willibaldi et Wynnebaldi*," *Hagiographica* 1 (1994): 43–79.

THOMAS HEAD

HUMANISTS, ITALIAN WOMEN, ISSUES AND THEORY (15th and 16th centuries). The period often labeled as the *Rinascimento* (Renaissance) in Italy actually comprises what was still "medieval" in France and other Western cultures, while India, China, and Japan had already experienced more than one "renaissance" or pioneering movements in which women authors participated. Even within Europe, certain periods within what are commonly known as the "Middle Ages" also find themselves identified as renaissances or pre-renaissances, especially in those of the ninth century under Charlemagne (the Carolingian Renaissance) in which one finds women like Dhuoda and Emma; the twelfth century, yielding Marie de France, and the fourteenth and early fifteenth centuries, of Novella d'Andrea and Christine de Pizan. Yet despite such perplexities of periodization, such terms as "renaissance" (rebirth) and "humanism" (the study of classical Greek and Latin language literature to improve contemporary culture, characterizing all European renaissances) are nonetheless useful in marking significant cultural zeniths. It also provokes the question of whether, in a given culture, a renaissance proves embraces worthy women as much as men, as examined in now-classic essays by Joan Kelly and David Herlihy, and in more recent, contrastingly optimistic analyses by Prudence Allen. Because it was the most evolved in all its manifestations (art, literature and rhetoric, science, philosophy, travel) and the most self-conscious of any Renaissance, the Italian Quattrocento (fifteenth century) and Cinquecento (sixteenth century) has also received the most scholarly attention. These findings can often reward application to earlier golden ages as well, including the position of women.

In the history of modern scholarship on the Italian Renaissance, women who wrote the language (the more sophisticated Classical Latin of Virgil and Cicero, rather than twelfth century medieval scholastic Latin of plodding schoolmasters) and the genres (orations, letters, histories, invectives, satires—in the manner of Classical Greek and Latin authors) of Italian humanism have only recently begun to receive critical attention from historians and literary scholars. It was not always the case. As the traditions of fifteenth-century manuscript compilations and early printed books reveal, the command of Classical Latin demonstrated by some Italian Renaissance women was widely admired and disseminated in its own day. Indeed, in the sixteenth century the fashion for admiring works by and about (especially in praise of) women was so widespread that male writers and editors, among them Baldassare Castiglione (1478–1529), forged poems and letter collections by women to reach what we would call an important target market. Although today we possess significant letter collections of only three humanist women from the fifteenth and early sixteenth centuries (two of them published posthumously), many other women wrote letters that circulated publicly and were collected in manuscripts of model letters to be admired and copied. Only in the modern period, and especially, in the Anglophone tradition at any rate, toward the end of the nineteenth century, were women neglected in the construction of the canon of Italian Renaissance writers, and indeed in the construction of modern myths about the Italian Renaissance generally. In part as a result of this relatively recent "excision from the canon," as one scholar has termed it, more recent efforts to bring Italian women humanists to the attention of contemporary scholars have been dominated by the sense that these women were the victims of a pervasive misogynist patriarchy in their own day, and that their reputations have continued to suffer the same ill-deserved fate ever since.

It is certainly true that the society and intellectual culture of late fourteenth and fifteenth century urban Italy, where these women lived and wrote, provided only the most circumscribed of opportunities within which a woman might pursue interests not obviously related to marriage and family. Virtue (*virtus* in Latin = manhood) was defined distinctly differently for men and for women: for men, it consisted in public deeds and public words, forcefully and eloquently presented, while for women it involved, quite simply, chastity, marked by silence. The expression of elegant classicizing Latin, then, was integral to definitions of a man's virtue; for a woman such expression could only threaten her virtue. The notion that speech, that any capacity for language, represented the antithesis of a woman's virtue found explicit expression in the writings of such male humanists as Leonardo Bruni (1369–1444), Leonbattista Alberti (1404–1472), and Francesco Barbaro (1398–1454), and the assumption that a good woman should be silent pervades such male-authored works as Giovanni Boccaccio's *De mulieribus claris* (*Famous Women*, 1362–1375) and Baldassare Castiglione's *Il Cortegiano* (*The Courtier*, 1518). Even when male humanists write in praise of women's classical learning, they feel obliged to call insistent attention to their chastity, sometimes to the point of erasing eloquence and learning altogether, as in Antonio Loschi's (d. 1441) letters to Maddalena Scrovegni (1356–1429).

The gendering of definitions of virtue in Renaissance humanism—manly speech and action for men, silence and chastity for women—meant that on a certain level men's praise of humanist women could only operate in terms of paradox. Learned women were often praised both for their chastity and for their "manly spirit," which was held to account for their eloquence. They were praised, in other words, for being both woman and man. Women could use this language, too, as Cassandra Fedele (1465–1558) did in describing herself as having abandoned "womanly" knitting needles and taken up the "manly" pen. A learned woman was often described as a virago, a man-woman—in other words, a strange hybrid, a hermaphrodite of sorts, who represented the near-impossible wedding of womanly virtue and speech. Even when she was not somehow masculinized in this fashion, she was seen as extraordinary, nearly impossible because marvelously learned, yet wholly woman or girl, "virgin even," as that most brilliant of all Italian humanists, Poliziano (Politian, 1454–1494), puts it to Cassandra Fedele.

In spite of these ideological and social pressures, some women did manage to write, to speak publicly (albeit rarely), and to pursue classical learning. Almost all of them were members of a few aristocratic families in northern Italy, and only a very few took up pen or voice later in life; the rest were typically young prodigies whose youth seemed in part to guarantee the virginity with which their admirers were so preoccupied. Once married or cloistered, depending in part on their own choice and to a large degree on the plans and ambitions of their families, they tended to fall silent. How, then, are we to assess their achievements? Did they represent the tentative beginnings of what some have chosen to call a kind of feminism, or proto-feminism? Were they extraordinary, exceptional women whose accomplishments under the most difficult and oppressive of circumstances nevertheless paved the way for the achievements of future generations of women? Were they the victims of an overwhelmingly misogynistic patriarchy concerned at all costs with preserving the purity of the patrilineage as a social and intellectual construction? How are we to understand the profoundly ambivalent responses they generated in their male admirers? And what of their writing itself, in those cases, few but telling, where we have a sufficient body of work to comment on its overall character? These are only some of the questions that the lives and writings of such women as Maddalena Scrovegni, Battista Malatesta, the Nogarolas (Angela, Isotta, and Ginevra), Laura Cereta, and Cassandra Fedele invite us to consider.

One central theoretical issue, or perhaps set of issues, that lies behind many of these questions, and behind the work of scholars who have written recently on Italian humanist women, has to do with the assessment of agency and subjectivity in these women's lives and scholarship. In part because we possess such a striking body of specific responses by humanist men to humanist women, the women are invariably read in terms of what men had to say about them. Such readings are necessary—the trope of virtue, to take only the most notable example, is a highly gendered one in humanist discourses, and was bound to figure centrally in men's and women's writing alike. They carry multiple charges, however. If men wrote that women must be chaste, and to be chaste must be silent, yet women acknowledged as virtuous spoke and wrote in public forums, then clearly some ideological slippage is at work. In what particular ways might we detect reflections in humanist women's writing of their responses to the constraints placed on their speech? What indications might we trace traces in humanist men's writings, particularly those not addressed to women, of gendered language that might provide a larger context within which to locate the trope of women's chastity? What larger social and intellectual issues might help to explain both men's efforts to silence women and women's ability to imagine, and sometimes to perform, learned speech? And what of the role of religion in many humanist women's lives, a role that has tended to be viewed as repressive, but that may in fact have offered them a significant degree of agency and specifically the possibility of continuing their learned studies, whether their writings have survived to the present day or not?

Some of these questions and issues have been taken up by recent scholars, but their treatments have tended to foreground the few by now classic male humanist statements on women's virtue—those by Bruni, Barbaro, and Alberti, on what we might call the sociointellectual front, and those by Boccaccio (1313?–1375) and Castiglione, on what we might call the literary front. Thus we tend to find readings of women's writings that emphasize their extraordinary achievement (following a tradition begun by their contemporaries), or that lament the unfulfilled promise of what might have been a groundswell of feminist thought and action (by women or by men). Or, in a perhaps more theoretically sophisticated mode, we find readings that present a particularly feminine voice in, say, Laura Cereta (1469–1499), or that trace "ef-facement" (Diana Robin's term) and self-belittling in Cassandra Fedele. There is little sense in most of these accounts of the problematics of gender, sexuality, and agency so insistently raised, not only by the work of humanist women themselves, but also by men's responses to them and by the gender-saturated social and political discourses shaping the larger culture. Within this larger culture, humanist women critiqued and appropriated the language of eloquent political virtue, gender roles, and the ideology and institution of the family as often as they "fell victim" to their culture's representations of them as inferior or exceptional. Indeed, it is possible to see in the invectives of a Laura Cereta or the political letters of an Isotta Nogarola (1420?–1466) "alternative" voices and strategies to those conventionally recommended by (masculine) humanist culture, alternatives to which men, especially by the end of the fifteenth century, did not have access.

Greater attention to these sorts of gender issues in the study of Italian humanist culture might also permit us to turn a somewhat different gaze on classic texts in humanist political thought that have yet to receive much, if any, examination under the lens of a focus on gender. Leonbattista Alberti's *Della Famiglia* (*On the Family*), for example, is known mainly for the infamous statements about the need for men to control their wives uttered by Giannozzo in Book 3. However, the cumulative gendered and sexual language in the entire work acquires a more balanced, even positive meaning if we look also at what women as well as other men were writing on related subjects: friendship, family, education, civic politics. The male-humanist preoccupation with women's chastity assumes a more overtly political significance if we recall fifteenth-century Italy's obsession with the story of the rape of the Roman matron Lucretia, conventionally held to have been the catalyst for the overthrow of the kings and the establishment of the Roman Republic. Matteo Palmieri's (1406–1475) seemingly sexless body politic turns out to be gendered after all, given his concern with body parts never mentioned in Cicero. The study of humanist culture generally, as produced and developed by men and (a few) women in fifteenth-century Italy, can only be enriched by further attention to these sorts of gender questions raised by the presence of women in that culture, and by their interactions with the men who dominated it.

See also Battista da Montefeltro Malatesta; Boccaccio, Women in, *De Claris Mulieribus*; Boccacio, Women in, *Des Cleres et Nobles Femmes*; Boccaccio, Women in, Works Other than *De Claris Mulieribus*; Cereta, Laura; Christine de Pizan; Dhuoda; Emma; Fedele, Cassandra; Gonzaga, Cecilia; Gualdrada de' Ravignani; Hrotsvitha of Gandersheim; Marie de France; Nogarola, Isotta; Novella d'Andrea; Rhetoric, Women and; Scala, Alessandra; Scrovegni, Maddalena; Sforza, Ippolita; Varano, Costanza; Virginity

BIBLIOGRAPHY

Primary Sources
Alberti, Leonbattista. *Della Famiglia*. In *Opere volgari*, edited by Cecil Grayson, vol. 1. Scrittori d'Italia 235. Bari, 1960. Translated by Renee N. Watkins as *The Family in Renaissance Florence* Columbia: University of South Carolina Press, 1969.

Barbaro, Francesco. *De re uxoria*. Edited by Attilio Gensotto. *Atti e memoria della regia accademia di scienze, lettere ed arti in Padova* n.s. 32 (1916): 6–105.

Bruni, Leonardo. *De studiis et litteris*. In *Leonardo Bruni Aretino. Humanistische-philosophische Schriften mit einer Chronologie seiner Werke und Briefe. Quellen zur Geistesgeschichte des Mittelalters und der Renaissance*, edited by Hans Baron, 1: 5–19. Leipzig, Germany: Teubner, 1928. Reprint Wiesbaden, 1969.

———. In *The Humanism of Leonardo Bruni: Selected Texts*, edited and translated by Gordon Griffiths, James Hankins, and David Thompson, 240–51. Medieval and Renaissance Texts and Studies/ Renaissance Society of America. Binghamton, N.Y.: MRTS, 1987.

Castiglione, Baldessare. *Il Libro del Cortegiano, con una scelta delle opere minori*. Edited by Bruno Maier. Torino: UTET, 1964.

———. *The Book of the Courtier*. Translated with commentary by Charles Singleton. New York: Anchor Doubleday, 1959.

Secondary Sources

Allen, Prudence. *The Concept of Woman. II: The Early Humanist Reformation 1250–1500*. Grand Rapids, Mich.: William Eerdmans, 2002.

Benson, Pamela Joseph. *The Invention of the Renaissance Woman: The Challenge of Female Independence in the Literature and Thought of Italy and England*. University Park: Pennsylvania State University Press, 1992.

Butler, Judith. *Gender Trouble: Feminism and the Subversion of Identity*. London and New York: Routledge, 1990.

Clough, Cecil H. "Daughters and Wives of the Montefeltro: Outstanding Bluestockings of the Quattrocento." *Renaissance Studies* 10:1 (1996): 31–55.

Fahy, Conor. "Three Early Renaissance Treatises on Women" *Italian Studies* 11 (1956): 30–55.

Les Femmes écrivains en Italie au Moyen Âge et à la Renaissance. Actes du colloque international, Aix-en-Provence, 12–14 novembre 1992. Centre Aixois de Recherches Italiennes: Publications de l'Université de Provence, 1994.

Ferguson, Margaret W., Maureen Quilligan, and Nancy J. Vickers. *Rewriting the Renaissance : The Discourses of Sexual Difference in Early Modern Europe*. Women in Culture and Society. Chicago: University of Chicago Press, 1986.

Fiore, Silvia R. "The Silent Scholars of Italian Humanism: Feminism in the Renaissance." In *Interpreting the Italian Renaissance: Literary Perspectives*, ed. Antonio Toscano. Filibrary, 1. Stony Brook, N.Y.: Forum Italicum, 1991.

Freccero, Carla. "Economy, Woman, and Renaissance Discourse." *In Refiguring Woman: Perspectives on Gender and the Italian Renaissance*, edited by Marilyn Migiel and Juliana Schiesari, 192–208. Ithaca, N.Y.: Cornell University Press, 1991.

Herlihy, David. "Did Women Have a Renaissance? A Reconsideration." *Medievalia et Humanistica* n.s. 13 (1985): 1–22.

Hughes, Diane Owen. "Invisible Madonnas? The Italian Historiographical Tradition and the Women of Medieval Italy." In *Women in Medieval History and Historiography*, edited by Susan Mosher Stuard, 23–57. Philadelphia: University of Pennsylvania Press, 1987.

Hutson, Lorna. "The Housewife and the Humanist." In Hutson, *see next entry*.

———, ed. *Feminism and Renaissance Studies*. Oxford Readings in Feminism. Oxford and New York: Oxford University Press, 1999. [Reprints classic essays and new ones].

Jardine, Lisa. "Isotta Nogarola: Women Humanists—Education for What?" *History of Education* 12 (1983), 231–44. Revised in *From Humanism to the Humanities: Education and the Liberal Arts in Fifteenth- and Sixteenth-Century Europe*, edited by Anthony Grafton and Lisa Jardine, 29–57. Cambridge, Mass.: Harvard University Press, 1986. Reprint in Hutson, *see above*.

Jed, Stephanie H. *Chaste Thinking: The Rape of Lucretia and the Birth of Humanism*. Bloomington: Indiana University Press, 1989.

———. "The Tenth Muse: Gender, Rationality and the Marketing of Knowledge." In Hutson, *see above*.

Jones, Ann Rosalind. "Surprising Fame: Renaissance Gender Ideologies and Women's Lyric." In Hutson, *see above*.

Jordan, Constance. *Renaissance Feminism: Literary Texts and Political Models.* Ithaca, N.Y.: Cornell University Press, 1990.

———. "Boccaccio's In-Famous Women: Gender and Civic Virtue in the *De mulieribus claris*," in *Ambiguous Realities: Women in the Middle Ages and Renaissance*, edited by Carole Levin and Jeanie Watson, 25–47. Detroit: Wayne State University Press, 1987.

Kelly, Joan. "Did Women Have a Renaissance?" In Kelly, *Women, History, and Theory*, 19–20. Chicago: University of Chicago Press, 1984. Reprint in Hutson, *see above.*

King, Margaret L. "Book-Lined Cells: Women and Humanism in the Early Italian Renaissance." In *Beyond Their Sex: Learned Women of the European Past*, edited by Patricia H. Labalme, 66–90. New York: New York University Press, 1980. Reprint in *Renaissance Humanism: Foundations, Forms, and Legacy*, 1. Edited by Albert Rabil, Jr. 3 vols. Philadelphia: University of Pennsylvania Press, 1988.

———. "Caldiera and the Barbaros on Marriage and the Family: Humanist Reflections of Venetian Realities." *Journal of Medieval and Renaissance Studies* 6 (1976): 19–50.

———. "Personal, Domestic, and Republican Virtues in the Moral Philosophy of Giovanni Caldiera." *Renaissance Quarterly* 28 (1975): 535–54.

———. "Thwarted Ambitions: Six Learned Women of the Renaissance." *Soundings* 59 (1976): 280–304.

———. *Women of the Renaissance.* Chicago: University of Chicago Press, 1991.

———, and Albert Rabil, Jr., eds. *Her Immaculate Hand: Selected Works by and about the Women Humanists of Quattrocento Italy.* MRTS, 20. Binghamton, N.Y.: MRTS, 1983; 1992.

Klapisch-Zuber, Christiane. *Women, Family, and Ritual in Renaissance Italy.* Translated by Lydia G. Cochrane. Foreword by David Herlihy. Chicago: University of Chicago Press, 1985.

Kuehn, Thomas N. *Law, Family, and Women: Toward a Legal Anthropology of Renaissance Italy.* Chicago: University of Chicago Press, 1991.

LaBalme, Patricia H. "Venetian Women on Women: Three Early Modern Feminists." *Archivio veneto* 197 (1981): 81–109.

Martines, Lauro. "A Way of Looking at Women in Renaissance Florence." *Journal of Medieval and Renaissance Studies* 4 (1974): 15–28.

Migiel, Marilyn. "Gender Studies and the Italian Renaissance." In *Interpreting the Italian Renaissance, See above under* Fiore.

Pitkin, Hanna Fenichel. *Fortune is a Woman: Gender and Politics in the Thought of Niccolò Machiavelli.* Berkeley: University of California Press, 1984.

Robin, Diana. "Cassandra Fedele's *Epistolae* (1488–1521): Biography as Ef-facement." In *The Rhetorics of Life-Writing in Early Modern Europe: Forms of Biography from Cassandra Fedele to Louis XIV*, edited by Thomas F. Mayer and D. R. Woolf, 187–203. Ann Arbor: University of Michigan Press, 1995.

Schibanoff, Susan. "Botticelli's Madonna del Magnificat: Constructing the Women Writer in Early Humanist Italy." *PMLA* 109 (1994): 190–206.

Schiesari, Juliana. "In Praise of Virtuous Women? For a Genealogy of Gender Morals in Renaissance Italy." *Annali d'Italianistica* 7 (1989): 66–87.

Scott, Joan Wallach. "Gender: A Useful Category of Historical Analysis." *American Historical Review* 91 (1986). Reprint in *Gender and the Politics of History*, edited by Scott, 29–50. New York: Columbia University Press, 1988.

Jennifer Fisk Rondeau

HUMILITY TOPOS. The prefatory rhetorical posture of submissiveness and humility as a way of engaging the reader was common in both male and female medieval authors, yet women authors needed to use it by means of a more complex strategy than did male authors. Because this invocation of the author's inadequacy and smallness compared to the reader and topic was so formulaic, it is thus categorized as a *topos*, or commonplace, in medieval writing, as defined within Ernst Robert Curtius's literary typologies for Late Antique and medieval literature. Although the humility topos outwardly resembles a variety of early Christian devotional formula as exemplified in St. Paul's Epistles (as when he refers to himself as "the slave/servant of Jesus Christ"), through deeper analysis the true humility topos relates more closely to conventions of submission used by Roman courtiers and Christians when addressing the elite, as Curtius demonstrates. This humility formula would find its way into love poetry and also political and morally edifying works.

The topos therefore entered Western tradition principally through Classical Latin and Greek pagan rather than Judeo-Christian sources. Both Cicero (106–43 B.C.E.), in his youthful *De Inventione* (*On Rhetorical Invention*, 1: 16. 22) and Quintilian (35–c.95 C.E.), in his *Institutio Oratoria* (*Training of Orators*, 4: 1. 8) recommend such formulas for the *exordium* (beginning of a work), which also reflects the topos's roots in judicial oratory. Such formulas were later associated with epideictic ("show-off") rhetoric as well since the increasing glorification of the Roman emperor demanded a more decidedly obsequious pose on the part of his courtiers and writers. Following the reign of the Emperor Diocletian (r. 284–305), the use of humility formulas significantly increased and gradually spread to late Christian authors eager to appropriate the prestige (while discarding the polytheism) of pagan rhetorical style. References to the first-person author's *mediocritas* thus appear in works by such Late-Antique Christian authors as Lactantius (c.240–320), St. Jerome (c.347–420), and Venantius Fortunatus (c.540–c.600).

In medieval and Classical texts, formulas of submission or inadequacy aim at different aspects, derived from the now dual meaning of the Latin *humilitas*: the original, derogatory "lowliness, meanness" and the Christian virtue of "humility." An author may protest his or her general inadequacy, lack of education, rough and unschooled speech, and/or paltry wisdom and insight. Expressions of authorial fear and agitation, as we find for example in Jerome's *Epistulae* (*Letters*), the claim that one is writing only at the command of a patron, as in Sidonius Apollinaris's *Epistula* 1 (fifth century), or the desire to spare the reader boredom or satiety, as in Dante's *De Monarchia* (*On Monarchy*, c.1313) are also permutations of the humility topos.

Medieval women authors, like their male counterparts, often used such disclaimers in their texts. But this practice inevitably bore consequences beyond women authors' mere self-modeling on male masters, since male, and even female, readers were all too ready to interpret a woman's feigned avowal of inadequacy as truth rather than rhetorical pose. Her self-denigration, so standard for male authors, seemed to affirm misogynistic stereotypes, despite her writing's refutation by its evident high quality. As a countermeasure, more resourceful women writers learned to exploit this double standard in their prefaces. Thus we find Hrotsvitha of Gandersheim (tenth century) in her preface to the *Gesta Ottonis* (*Great Deeds of the Ottonians*), and Christine de Pizan (1365–1430?), in her opening remarks to so many of her moral and political works (often on "manly" topics such as history and warfare), proclaiming straightaway their unfitness, only to continue with the rest of their work as confidently and knowledgeably as any male author. In her *Livre de la Cité des dames* (*Book of the City of Ladies*, 1404–1405), Christine de Pizan as narrator professes humility to establish her probity, not presumptuousness, in attacking the omnipresence of traditional misogyny. Although Christine has a "foible scens" ("feeble sense") and a "foible corps femenin" ("weak feminine body"), she nevertheless is ready to execute the task of building nothing less than a city—a formidable task even in figurative terms,

449

since her "City of Ladies" intends to refute the misogyny of such otherwise great men as St. Augustine by parodying the title of his sacrosanct *De Civitate Dei* (*City of God*) (413–426). There is nothing humble, therefore, in this book dedicated to celebrating women's virtue and accomplishment, despite its prologue. As she tells her heavenly interlocutors, "Et voicy vostre chamberiere preste d'obeir" ("Behold your handmaiden, ready to serve"), Christine's merging of piety with humility, echoing Mary's words at the Annunciation, validates her as author and encourages support for her general revision of women's history.

The persona of humility in women's works also functions as a self-defense mechanism—a rhetorical shield—when pronouncing themselves on controversial topics. In exhibiting this technique, Hildegard of Bingen, the famous twelfth-century mystic of noble birth, refers to herself as a "paupercula et fictile vas" ("poor little earthen vessel," *Epistolarium*, 127) imbued with God's inspiration. Claiming to speak not from herself but from God and protected by the papal authentication of her visions, she castigates emperors and popes from a position whose impregnability springs partly from her self-abasement. Her medical, mystical, and scientific texts, on the other hand, amply demonstrate the learning she claims not to have. Some 250 years later, the more militant and direct Joan of Arc (d. 1431) would also eloquently lash out against lofty officials, claiming that God spoke through her, and suffer martyrdom. But it would be too simplistic to ascribe Joan's fate, far less happy than Hildegard's, to blunt speech and refusal to submit to the Anglo-Burgundian theologians. Despite her youth and gender, Joan was a more direct military, political, and theological threat to her foes than Hildegard the abbess was to hers; each lived in different times. But it is worthwhile to observe how humility played a role in Joan's image as well, since her plain speech and unmitigated piety derived from her truly humble origins—no pose here. Minimally educated but hardly a bumpkin, Joan managed to test her Sorbonne-trained Anglo-Burgundian interrogators just as she had their soldiers, while emulating her militarily and intellectually adroit saints: Michael and Catherine, respectively—in her mission to redeem the "grant pitié du royaume." ("piteous state of the kingdom [France]").

Devising another tactic, other women writers incorporate humility ironically to emphasize self-assurance and accomplishment. Women are fond of using diminutives, not only in the predictable genres of love lyric but also, unlike men, in moral and political works to impart an ironic, pathetic, or pejorative connotation. A striking example, first elucidated by Peter Dronke, shows Hrotsvitha, self-described as armed with only her "ingeniolum" ("little wit"), identifying herself and her authorial program with her heroines' deeds. In her drama *Dulcitius*, for example, modeled on those by the Roman comedian Terence (160s B.C.E.), both Hrotsvitha and her heroines are described as "mulierculi" ("weak little women") and "puellulae" ("little girlies") so as to mimic condescending male diminutives for women. Yet both heroines and author triumph over more privileged, physically stronger but wrong-headed male opponents: the heroines hold steadfastly to the Christian ideal and Hrotsvitha provides more appropriate reading material than Terence. Thus, "cum feminea fragilitas vinceret et virilis robor confusioni subiaceret" ("feminine fragility conquers while virile strength is subjected to confusion"), a victory rendered all the more impressive by the victor's "weaknesses." Centuries later, Christine de Pizan, whose predilection for such diminutives was doubtless further enhanced by her Italianate origins, aided by her "petit engin" ("meager wits"), used them frequently in polemical works ranging from her epistles in the Debate of the *Roman de la Rose* (1401–1402) to the *Ditié de Jehanne d'Arc* (*Tale of*

Joan of Arc, 1429), as well as in her best-known lyric widow's lament, "Seulete suy" ("Alone am I, little me," *Cent Balades*, 11). Writing "seulette a part" ("A lonely little woman apart [from the world]") Christine learned to impart potent new meanings to initially innocuous terms like *femmelette* ("little woman") in shifting from love-lyric to political-philosophical contexts. As Hrotsvitha attempted to outdo her model, Terence, so did Christine with Jean de Meun, author of the more provocative continuation of Guillaume de Lorris's *Roman de la Rose*: both authors trying to retain their masters' virtues while providing more suitable texts for and about women.

Strategic self-diminution can also occur without actual linguistic diminutives. In her correspondence with Abelard, Heloise often juxtaposes her feminine inferiority with Abelard's superiority as a means of persuading him to fulfill her requests (whether emotional, as when reproaching him as neglectful of her, or practical, as when she asks him for a new rule for her monastery, the Paraclete). She bestows on him such epithets as "unicus" ("one and only") and "dominus" ("lord"), in contrast to hers as "ancilla" ("handmaiden") to provoke Abelard's reexamination of their personal history. She often asks him via the humble verb *obsecro* ("I beseech"). In this rhetorical maneuver, along with her rhymes and rhythmic symmetries, Heloise's model is not so much her teacher, lover, and husband Abelard— superb Latinist that he was—as the influential Latin poet Ovid (43 B.C.E.–17 C.E.), in his *Heroides* (*Heroines*; fictive love letters from great women of the past), as Dronke reveals. Heloise also deploys such carefully crafted phrases as "tua melius excellentia quam nostra parvitas novit" ("Your excellence knows this better than my littleness").

In general, although medieval men and women authors were equally prone to using modesty topoi, such formulas should be read with an eye toward rhetorical tradition versus the author's individual adaptation of that tradition, particularly in women's texts. Almost never do they simply reflect a woman's acceptance of her gender's mediocrity. More frequently, they offer reassurance to male readers and a safe place from which female writers may accentuate their own accomplishments or voice criticisms of male authority and its institutions.

See also Christine de Pizan; Epistolary Authors, Women as; Heloise; Hildegard of Bingen, St.; Hrotsvitha of Gandersheim; Hugeburc of Heidenheim; Joan of Arc, St.; Rhetoric, Women and; *Roman de la Rose*, Debate of the

BIBLIOGRAPHY

Primary Sources
[See also extracts cited and translated in Curtius and in Dronke, under Secondary Sources].
Christine de Pizan et al. *Le Débat sur le* Roman de la Rose. Edited by Eric Hicks. Bibliothèque du XVᵉ siècle, 43. Paris: Honoré Champion, 1977. Reprint 1997.
———. *La Querelle de la Rose: Letters and Documents*. Edited and translated by Joseph L. Baird and John R. Kane. Chapel Hill: University of North Carolina Press, 1978. [English trans. only].
———. [*Le Livre de la Cité des dames*]. *Città delle dame*. Edited by E. J. Richards. Introduction and translation by Patrizia Caraffi. Revised ed. Milan: Luni, 1998. [Bilingual Middle-French-Italian ed. with notes].
———. *The Book of the City of Ladies*. Translation with commentary by E. J. Richards. Foreword by Natalie Zemon Davis. New ed. New York: Persea, 1998.
———. *Ditié de Jehanne d'Arc*. Edited and translated by Angus J. Kennedy and Kenneth Varty. Medium Ævum Monographs, n.s. 9. Oxford: Society for the Study of Mediæval Languages and Literature, 1977. [Bilingual Middle-French- English ed. with commentary].

Cicero. *De Inventione*. Critical ed. with Italian translation by Maria Greco. Le Galatina, Italy: M. Congedo, 1998. [Bilingual Latin-Italian ed.].

Heloise. *Abélard. Historia Calamitatum* [and other letters]. Critical ed. by Jacques Monfrin. Bibliothèque des textes philosophiques. Paris: J. Vrin, 1959. Revised ed. 1978. [Latin text].

———. *Letters of Abelard and Heloise*. Translated with introduction by Betty Radice. New York: Penguin, 1974.

Hildegard of Bingen. *Opera omnia*. Edited by J.-P. Migne. *Patrologia latina*, 197. Paris: Migne, 1855. [Complete works, but unreliably edited; Latin text only].

———. [Works: Selections, English]. *Hildegard of Bingen. Selected Writings*. Translated with an introduction and notes by Mark Atherton. London: Penguin, 2001.

Hrotsvitha. *Hrosvit: Opera Omnia*. Edited by Walter Berschin. Bibliotheca Scriptorum Graecorum et Romanorum Teubneriana. Munich and Leipzig, Germany: W. G. Saur Verlag, 2001.

———. *The Plays of Hrotsvit of Gandersheim* Translated by Katharina Wilson. Garland Library of Medieval Literature, 62. New York: Garland, 1989.

Jerome. [Letters]. *Sancti Eusebii Hieronymi Epistulae*. Edited by Isidorus Hilberg. 2nd ed. 3 vols. in 4. Vienna: Österreichischen Akademie der Wissenschaften, 1996. [Latin text only].

Ovid. [*Heroides*]. *Epistulae Heroidum*. Edited by Heinrich Dörrie. Texte und Kommentare, 6. Berlin and New York: Walter de Gruyter, 1971. [Authoritative Latin text].

Quintilian. *Institutio oratoria*. Edited and translated by H. E. Butler. 4 vols. Loeb Classical Library. 1920. Reprint Cambridge, Mass.: Harvard University Press, 1980.

Secondary Sources

Curtius, Ernst Robert. *European Literature and the Latin Middle Ages*. Translated by Willard R. Trask. Princeton, N.J.: Bollingen Foundation, 36. New York: Pantheon, 1953. Reprints, Harper & Row, 1963; Princeton University Press, 1973. Original *Europäische Literatur und lateinisches Mittelalter*. Berlin: A. Francke, 1948.

Dronke, Peter. *Women Writers of the Middle Ages: A Critical Study of Texts from Perpetua (†203) to Marguerite Porete (†1310)*. Cambridge: Cambridge University Press, 1984.

Ferrante, Joan. "Public Postures, Private Maneuvers." In *Women and Power in the Middle Ages*, edited by Mary Erler and Maryanne Kowaleski, 83–102. Athens: University of Georgia Press, 1988.

Margolis, Nadia. "Elegant Closures: The Use of the Diminutive in Christine de Pizan and Jean de Meun." In *Reinterpreting Christine de Pizan*, edited by Earl Jeffrey Richards et al., 111–23. Athensand London: University of Georgia Pres, 1992.

McKinley, Mary. "The Subversive 'Seulette'." In *Politics, Gender, & Genre: The Political thought of Christine de Pizan*, edited by Margaret Brabant, 157–70. Boulder, Colo.: Westview, 1992.

Newman, Barbara. *Sister of Wisdom: St. Hildegard's Theology of the Feminine*. Berkeley and Los Angeles: University of California Press, 1987.

Solterer, Helen. *The Master and Minerva: Disputing Women in French Medieval Culture*. Berkeley and Los Angeles: University of California Press, 1995.

Sullivan, Karen. *The Interrogation of Joan of Arc*. Medieval Cultures, 20. Minneapolis and London: University of Minnesota Press, 1999.

Wilson, Katharina. *Hrotsvit of Gandersheim: The Ethics of Authorial Stance*. Leiden, Netherlands and New York: E. J. Brill, 1988.

GLENDA K. MCLEOD

HUNEBERC. *See* **Hugeburc of Heidenheim**

I

IDA OF NIVELLES. *See* **Beatrijs van Nazareth/van Tienen**

IGERNE. Igerne (Ygerne, Yguerne, Igraine) is King Arthur's mother in numerous medieval Arthurian works. In the twelfth century, in Geoffrey of Monmouth's *Historia Regum Britanniae*, in Wace's *Brut*, in the thirteenth-century *Estoire de Merlin* and the *Suite du Merlin*, Igerne is at first married to Gorlois, Duke of Tintagel. Through Merlin's magic arts, however, she is tricked into believing that Uther Pendragon is Gorlois and sleeps with him, conceiving Arthur. That same night Gorlois is killed in battle and Uther soon marries Igerne. Her "adultery" is handled in notably different ways as the story passes from text to text.

See also Arthurian Women; Morgan le Fay

BIBLIOGRAPHY

Primary Sources

Geoffrey of Monmouth. *Historia regum Britannie.* Edited by Neil Wright and Julia C. Crick. 5 vols. Cambridge and Dover, N.H.: D. S. Brewer, 1984–1991. [Latin texts, English notes].

———. *History of the Kings of Britain.* Translated with introduction by Lewis Thorpe. Revised ed. Harmondsworth, U.K.: Penguin, 1976.

[Grail Legends, French]. *Le Livre du Graal,* vol. 1. Critical ed. and trans. (Modern French) by Philippe Walter et al. Paris: Éditions de la Pléiade/Gallimard, 2001. [Contains *L'Estoire de Joseph, Merlin, Les Premiers faits du roi Arthur (Suite-Vulgate du Merlin)*].

The Romance of Merlin: An Anthology. Edited with an introduction by Peter Goodrich. Arthurian Studies. Garland Reference Library in the Humanities, 867. New York and London: Garland, 1990. [English translations of excerpts from Merlin stories through the ages].

Wace. *Wace's Roman de Brut: A History of the British.* Presented, translated, and introduced by Judith Weiss. Exeter Medieval English Texts and Studies. Revised ed. Exeter, U.K.: University of Exeter Press, 2002. [Bilingual Old-French-English ed.].

Secondary Sources

Fenster, Thelma S., ed. *Arthurian Women: A Casebook.* Arthurian Characters and Themes, 3. New York: Garland, 1996. [Collection of critical essays on wide-ranging aspects, with introduction].

THELMA S. FENSTER

ILLUMINATA. *See* **Bembo, Illuminata**

INGEBORG OF DENMARK/ISAMBOUR OF FRANCE (1176–1237/8). The Danish-born queen-consort to Philip II Augustus (1165–1223), king of France, where she was called "Isambour," represents an outstanding case of a queen successfully fighting for her rights despite marital annulment and spousal abuse. Ingeborg was also a literate woman who authored letters to two popes to plead her cause.

Ingeborg's father was King Waldemar I (the Great) of Denmark (1131–1182); her mother, Sophia of Dacia (now northern Rumania). In retrospect, Ingeborg appears to have been predisposed genetically to marital repudiation: her elder sister, Christine, was also rejected by the German king and emperor Frederic I Barbarossa (d. 1190); her mother, Sophia, widowed at Waldemar's death, became remarried to the Landgrave of Thuringia (now in Germany), who soon sent her back to Denmark.

Ingeborg's elder brother became King Waldemar II of Denmark, with whom Philip Augustus sought to neutralize ancient Danish claims to England. A marriage was thus arranged between Philip and Ingeborg. Because "Ingeborg" proved too harsh to French ears, her name was changed to more fluid "Isambour," also reminiscent of Philip's first wife, Isabelle, who had been much loved by people before her death in 1190. Within days after their wedding on August 14, 1193, Philip manifested an inexplicable sexual aversion to her, after which he repudiated, imprisoned, and generally mistreated her for twenty years. The chronicler Rigord attributes Philip's malaise to the devil or sorcery; William of Newburgh ascribes the problem to Ingeborg's bad breath, hidden deformity, or doubts concerning her virginity. Philip initiated divorce proceedings the following November at Compiègne, on tenuous grounds of consanguinity (via their mutual kinship with Isabelle of Hainault). This left Philip free to remarry (1196) Agnes of Meran, daughter of Berthold IV, duke of Dalmatia, Croatia, and Meran.

On hearing the news, Isambour reputedly uttered "Mala Francia, mala Francia; Roma, Roma!" ("Evil France, evil France; Rome, Rome!"), and thus called on Pope Celestin III (r. 1191–1198) for support beginning that same year (1196). Ingeborg, in her letter to the pope, now preserved with Celestin's other correspondence, cites the devil as cause and also attacks certain evil princes for having "seduced" Philip into taking Agnes as wife. She also inveighs against Philip's marriage to Agnes as bigamy. Furthermore, she claims that if Celestin condones this, he, too, is guilty. Meanwhile, Philip Augustus had children with Agnes. Hoping for better treatment under the new pope, Innocent III (r. 1198–1216), Ingeborg wrote to him in 1198, provoking Innocent to urge Philip to "restore Ingeborg to his marital affection." On Philip's refusal to take Ingeborg back, Innocent interdicts the kingdom of France in 1200 but does not excommunicate Philip and Agnes. Along with the pontifical legate, another of Ingeborg's supporters was Stephen Langton (d. 1228), archbishop of Canterbury and future co-redactor of the Magna Carta. Ingeborg waged her campaign amid the misery of imprisonment, during which she was denied the right to hear Mass, another of Philip's ways of taunting the papacy for meddling in his affairs. Innocent continues the epistolary war of attrition against Philip, whose next defense is denying he and Ingeborg ever had sexual intercourse. In 1205, the French king also faced a new trial for affinity and sorcery. Philip finally admits to intercourse with Ingeborg but denies insemination. In his final letter to Ingeborg (1210), Innocent gives up on restoring Philip to her, and advises her to accept this and console herself by piety, since the "Holy Spirit is the true husband of her and all the faithful." Pope Honorius III (r. 1216–1227) placed her under papal protection.

She commissioned the so-called Ingeborg Psalter (now at Chantilly, Musée de Condé MS 9) at around this time. Beautifully illustrated, it contains all 150 psalms, followed by litanies and canticles of liturgical office. Her favorite psalm was 141, *Voce mea*, and her preferred stories of Théophile and of David. The psalter also contains notations documenting events of her life.

Finally, in 1213, Philip ceased resisting and took Ingeborg back as his queen, if only superficially, probably for political motives, after which they reigned for ten years. Ingeborg's queenship, after his death in 1223, is also an interesting example. She was now independent to act, but she had no children, and thus less influence. Despite their past struggles, she remained true to King Philip's memory—he mentioned her affectionately in his will—so that her stepson Louis VIII (r. 1223–1226) and step-grandson Louis IX (St. Louis, r. 1226–1270) treated her well. Ingeborg, now known as "Queen of Orléans," devoted herself to pious deeds as a benefactor of churches and hospitals, especially the Cistercian hospital church at Corbeil, where she spent her last days.

Although scholars have attempted to prove her letters to Innocent to be the work of her inner circle of notaries, the case remains strong for her authorship, as George Conklin affirms. Stephen, bishop of Tournai praised her literacy and piety—a rare example of documented female literacy at this time and in this milieu. It was also Bishop Stephen who, when Ingeborg was confined in the monastery at Cysoing in Tournai (now in Belgium) defended her in a letter (no. 213) to his friend, the archbishop of Reims, as a "precious pearl," whose beauty reminded one of Helen of Troy; a noble woman to whom queenship brought only imprisonment, poverty, and exile; Stephen even compares Ingeborg to Job.

See also Epistolary Authors, Women as

BIBLIOGRAPHY

Primary Sources
Celestine III. [Letters]. In *Patrologia Latina*, edited by J.-P. Migne, 206: 1277–1278.
Gesta Innocenti III. In *Patrologia Latina*, edited by J.-P. Migne, 214: 4 [Letter to Philip], 95 [Ingeborg's divorce], passim.
Ingeborg Psalter (Chantilly). *Der Ingeborg Psalter/ Le Psautier d'Ingeburge....* Edited by Florens Deuchler. Codices selecti phototypice impressi, 80. Graz, Austria: Akademische Druck, 1985. Original Berlin: de Gruyter, 1967. [Facsimile ed.].
Rigord. *Œuvres de Rigord et de Guillaume le Breton: Historiens de Philippe-Auguste*. Edited by H.-F. Delaborde, 1: 124–25. Société de l'Histoire de France, 210, 224. 2 vols. Paris: Renouard & Loones, 1882–1885.
Stephen of Tournai. [Letter 213]. In *Lettres d'Étienne de Tournai*. Edited by Jules Desilve, 263–65. New ed. Valenciennes, France: Lemaître, 1893.
William of Newburgh. *Chronicles of the Reigns of Stephen, Henry II, and Richard I*. Edited by Richard Howlett, 1: 369. 4 vols. Rolls Series 82. London: Public Record Office, 1884–1889. Reprint Wiesbaden, Germany: Kraus, 1964.

Secondary Sources
Baldwin, John. *The Government of Philip Augustus: Foundations of French Royal Power in the Middle Ages*. Berkeley: University of California Press, 1986.
Conklin, George. "Ingeborg of Denmark, Queen of France, 1193–1223." In *Queens and Queenship in Medieval Europe, Proceedings of a Conference Held at King's College, London, April 1995*, edited by Anne J. Duggan, 39–52. Woodbridge, U.K.: Boydell Press, 1997.
Pernoud, Régine, and Geneviève de Cant. *Isambour, la reine captive*. Paris: Stock, 1987.

NADIA MARGOLIS

Isabeau of Bavaria, followed by two maids of honor, at her wedding to Charles VI, king of France, July 17, 1385. Early nineteenth-century watercolor by La Mesangere after early manuscripts. © The Art Archive/Bibliothèque Municipale Rouen/Dagli Orti.

INGIBIORG (11th century). The first recorded Scandinavian queen of the Scots, Ingibiorg was either the daughter, concubine, or repudiated wife of Thorfinn Sigurdsson of Orkney, a second-generation Christian who had traveled to Rome in 1050 and built the first cathedral at Birsay on his return. She was married to Malcolm III (Canmore) of Scotland, who repudiated her by 1070, prior to his marrying Margaret (c.1047–1093). Ingibiorg bore Malcom a son named Duncan, the future Duncan II, whose inheritance suffered by his mother's repudiation and relegation to concubine status.

See also Concubines; Margaret of Scotland, St.

BIBLIOGRAPHY

Primary Source
[Scottish Regnal Lists F, K, N] In Marjorie O. Anderson, *Kings and Kingship in Early Scotland.* Totowa, N.J.: Rowman & Littlefield, 1973.

Secondary Sources
Sellar, W. H. D. "Marriage, Divorce and Concubinage in Gaelic Scotland." *Transactions of the Gaelic Society of Inverness* 51 (1981): 463–78.
Wall, Valerie. "Queen Margaret of Scotland (1070–93): Burying the Past, Enshrining the Future." In *Queens and Queenship in Medieval Europe. Proceedings of a Conference Held at King's College London, April 1995,* edited by Anne J. Duggan, 27–28. Woodbridge, U.K.: Boydell Press, 1997.

NADIA MARGOLIS

ISABEAU OF BAVARIA (c.1370–1435). Queen of France in notoriously troubled circumstances, the daughter of Stephen, duke of Bavaria, and of Taddea Visconti, Isabeau had been brought from Bavaria to meet Charles VI of France in Amiens in 1385. For him, it was love at first sight, and he married her without a marriage contract or dowry, which was unheard of in medieval France. The marriage proved difficult for Isabeau because from 1392 until his death in 1422, Charles suffered from schizophrenia, and sometimes he treated her with hostility or was unable to recognize her. She continued to bear him children, but was obliged to condone the selection of a mistress (Odette de Champdivers) for his pleasure during those times when it was deemed unwise for her to be with him. The doctors prescribed a program of light-hearted amusement for the king, and this involved Isabeau in a court that became prey to unscrupulous persons. Her invention of new fashions was censured by the Augustinian friar Jacques Legrand, who preached before her in 1405 and attacked the morals of her courtiers.

Personally she seems to have preferred the company of such ladies as Jeanne of Luxembourg, who strove for a saintly life and ultimately refused all offers of marriage. Isabeau was evidently of a sensitive nature. At a wedding ball in 1393, when fire threatened the lives of the king and others who were dancing chained together in disguise, she fainted—in contrast to the more hardy duchess of Berry, who saved the king's life by throwing the train of her gown over him. Isabeau often resided away from Paris and from the pressures of the king's court. She did not deal easily with the Parisians, but members of the royal family considered her a good mediator and used her to help resolve their intermittent quarrels. In 1402 she was given considerable political power, but it is not clear that she enjoyed politics.

In the years of strife following the murder of the king's brother (1407), she sought to set up her eldest son, instead of herself, as a replacement for King Charles during his psychotic episodes, and she relied on her brother (who was not popular with the French) to help groom the young prince, Louis, duke of Guyenne. The result would have been successful but for the prince's untimely death in 1415. Her last son (Charles VII), by his stubborn absence and criminal and treasonous acts, pushed the government to negotiate with Henry V of England. For her role in the subsequent Treaty of Troyes (1420), Isabeau has been accused by historians of having "betrayed" France. The treaty arranged for Henry to marry Isabeau's daughter Catherine and succeed Charles VI. How anti-French the treaty was is debatable, for it safeguarded French customs, laws, and institutions and stipulated that England and France would always be separate.

See also Christine de Pizán; Joan of Arc, St.

BIBLIOGRAPHY

Primary Sources
Chronique du religieux de Saint-Denis. Edited by Louis Bellaguet. 6 vols. Paris: Crapelet, 1839–1852. Reprint in 3 vols. Paris: CTHS, 1994.
Froissart, Jean. *Œuvres.* Edited by Joseph M. B. C. Kervyn de Lettenhove. 26 vols. Brussels: Devaux, 1866–1877.
La chronique d'Enguerran de Monstrelet. Edited by L. Douët-d'Arcq. 6 vols. Paris: Renouard, 1857–1862.

Secondary Sources
Famiglietti, R. C. *Royal Intrigue. Crisis at the Court of Charles VI, 1392–1420.* New York: AMS, 1986.
———. *Tales of the Marriage Bed from Medieval France (1300–1500).* Providence, R.I.: Picardy, 1992.
Grandeau, Yann. "De quelques dames qui ont servi la reine Isabeau de Bavière." *Bulletin philologique et historique du Comité des travaux historiques et scientifiques* (1975): 129–238.
———. "Isabeau de Bavière, ou l'amour conjugal." *Actes du 102ᵉ Congrès national des Sociétés savantes, Limoges, 1977, Section de philologie et d'histoire jusqu'à 1610* (1979): 117–48.
———. "Itinéraire d'Isabeau de Bavière." *Bulletin philologique et historique du Comité des travaux historiques et scientifiques* (1964): 569–670.
Straub, Theodor. *Isabeau de Bavière, Königin von Frankreich. Ausstellung im Herzogskasten, 4. November bis 1. Dezember 1985.* Ingolstadt, Germany: Stadt Ingolstadt, 1985.
———. "Isabeau de Bavière, Legende und Wirklichkeit." *Zeitschrift für bayerische Landesgeschichte* 44 (1981): 131–55.
Thibault, Marcel. *Isabeau de Bavière, reine de France: la jeunesse (1370–1405).* Paris: Perrin, 1903.

RICHARD C. FAMIGLIETTI

ISABEL DE VILLENA (1430–1490). The future religious poet and first female prose writer in Catalan was originally named Elionor Manuel, illegitimate daughter of Enric de Villena (1384–1434). She changed her name to Isabel when she entered the convent of the Holy Trinity in Valencia, eastern Spain, at the age of fifteen. Having been educated at the court of Queen Mary of Castile in Valencia, she became abbess of her convent during a prosperous time for her city. Her only known work, the *Vita Christi* (*Life of Christ*), was composed for her nuns and printed at the request of Queen Isabel of Castile (1451–1504). While she follows in outline the tradition of other religious writers, her *Vita* foregrounds women: the Virgin Mary, Mary Magdalene, Saint Anne, and other women appearing in the Gospels. Villena emphasizes such tasks as washing, sewing, child care, and such courtly activities as dancing, music, and fashion. She also takes part in the endless medieval debate on the good or evil nature of women, challenging misogynistic arguments and holding up Mary as the symbol of female virtue. She was widely known in her time; her intellectual background was dominated by her extensive knowledge of theology and the Scriptures. The *Vita* is didactic (morally pedagogical), biographical, and contemplative; the narration is a series of theological and ascetic reflections on biblical sentences or incidents on an allegorical level. The episodes that narrate daily life are full of color and realism. The most important thematic feature of the work is perhaps that Villena shows a woman in direct spiritual communication with Jesus and the Virgin Mary. The book shows the influence of theologians Ramon Llull (Raymond Lull, c.1232–c.1315) and Francesc Eiximenis (c.1340–c.1409)—the latter also wrote about women in religious life—and has been regarded as a reply to the misogynistic *Espill* (*Mirror*), a long narrative poem by Jaume Roig (d. 1478), who also lived in Valencia and knew the abbess personally.

See also Ava, Frau; Borja, Tecla; Catalan Woman Poets, Anonymous; Christine de Pizan; Courtesy Books; Hagiography (Female Saints); Malmojades, Les; Mary, Blessed Virgin, in the Middle Ages

BIBLIOGRAPHY

Primary Sources
Isabel de Villena. *Llibre anomenat Vita Christi, compost per Sor Isabel de Villena.* Edited by Ramon Miquel i Planas. 3 vols. Barcelona: Biblioteca Catalana, 1916.
———. *Vita Christi.* Edited by Lluïsa Parra. Introduction by Rosanna Cantavella. Barcelona: LaSal, 1987.
Roig, Jaume. *Espill.* Edition and prologue by Vincent Escrivà. Biblioteca d'autors valencians, 1. Valencia: Institució Alfons el Magnànim, 1981. [Catalan text and commentary only].

Secondary Sources
Cantavella, Rosanna. "Isabel de Villena, la nostra Christine de Pisan." *Encontre d'escriptors del Mediterrani. Valencia* 2 (winter–spring 1986): 79–86.
Colón, Germà. *Literatura valenciana del segle XV: Joanot Martorell i Sor Isabel de Villena.* Valencia: Consell Valencià de cultura, 1991.
Fuster, Joan. "Jaume Roig i sor Isabel de Villena" and "El món literari de sor Isabel de Villena." In *Joan Fuster. Obres completes,* 1: 153–210. Barcelona: Ediciones 62, 1968.
Hauf, Albert. *D'Eiximenis a sor Isabel de Villena: Aportació a l'estudi de la nostra cultura medieval.* Montserrat: L'Abadia, 1990.

KATHLEEN MCNERNEY

ISAMBOUR. *See* **Ingeborg of Denmark/Isambour of France**

ISELDA, NA. *See* **Alaisina Yselda**

ISEUT DE CAPIO (b. c.1140). Iseut de Capio (or Capion) was a southern-French female troubadour, or *trobairitz*, who wrote in Occitan (Old Provençal), leaving a single *cobla* (stanza) to her credit, composed as part of a *tenso* (debate poem) with Almuc de Castlenou. In these verses she acts as intermediary in a lovers' quarrel, making a poetic plea to Almuc for mercy (*merce*) on behalf of the latter's lover, named in the related *razo* (commentary) as Gigo de Tornon (Gui de Tournon). Because Almuc is angry and unforgiving over an unspecified deceit Gigo has committed, Iseut assures her that he "sospir'e plaing/e muor languen e.s complaing/e qier perdon humilimen" ("sighs and laments/And dies languishing and complains/And humbly seeks forgiveness"). Despite Iseut's eloquent plea and vow that he will "si tot li voletz fenir/q'el si gart meils de faillir" ("refrain from wrongdoing/If you will end all strife with him"), Almuc is unrelenting since she does not believe in his sincere repentance. However, she holds out a ray of hope to Iseut the mediator, avowing that "si vos faitz lui pentir/leu podes mi convertir" ("if you make him repent,/you can easily change my mind").

Iseut, who bears the name popularized by the legend of Tristan and Iseut (Isolde), may be from Chapieu (Castrum de Capione), located in the commune of Lanuéjouls in the arrondissement of Mende (Lozère, in south-central France), located not far from Chateauneuf-de-Randon, which corresponds to the Provençal word "Castelnou." Other scholars have identified her home as Les Chapelins, similarly located near the commune of Caseneuve, also a linguistic parallel to Castelnou.

See also Almuc de Castelnou; Isolde; *Trobairitz*

BIBLIOGRAPHY

Primary Sources
Boutière, Jean, and Alexander H. Schutz. *Biographies des troubadours: textes provençaux des XIIIᵉ et XIVᵉ siècles.* Paris: Nizet, 1964. [Texts of Provençal vidas. For English trans., *see under* Egan, *below*].
Egan, Margarita, trans. *The Vidas of the Troubadours.* Garland Library of Medieval Literature, 6B. New York: Garland Publishing, 1984.
Iseut de Capio. In *The Women Troubadours*, edited with commentary by Meg Bogin, 92–93, 165–66. New York and London: W. W. Norton, 1980. Original ed. Paddington Press, 1976.
———. In *Songs of the Women Troubadours*, edited and translated by Matilda Tomaryn Bruckner, Laurie Shepard, and Sarah White, 48–50, 160–61. New York: Garland, 1995. Revised ed. 2000. [Most authoritative ed.: original text, English translation, and notes].
Schultz-Gora, Oskar. *Die provenzalischen Dichterinnen: Biographieen und Texte.* Leipzig, Germany: Gustav Foch, 1888. [*See* Egan *above for English trans.*].

Secondary Sources
Brunel, Clovis. "Almois de Châteauneuf et Iseut de Chapieu." *Annales du Midi* 28 (1915–1916): 262–68.
Jeanroy, Alfred. *La Poésie lyrique des troubadours*, 1: 313, n. 2. Toulouse and Paris: Privat, 1934. Reprint Geneva: Slatkine, 1973.

Tristan and Isolde drinking a love potion. © Bibliotheque Nationale de France, Paris.

Nelli, René, ed. *Ecrivains anti-conformistes du moyen-âge occitan: I. La Femme et l'amour*, 247–49. Paris: Phébus, 1977.

Rieger, Angelica. "*En conselh no deu hom voler femna*: les dialogues mixtes dans la lyrique troubadouresque." *Perspectives médiévales* 16 (1990): 47–57.

JUNE HALL MCCASH

ISLAM, WOMEN IN. *See* Fatimid Egypt, Women in; Rābi'a al-'Adawiyya; Wallādah

ISOLDE (early 12th century onward). Isolde is the legendary Irish princess who, while betrothed to King Mark of Cornwall, became bound to his nephew by an overpowering mutual passion when she and Tristan mistakenly consumed a love potion intended for her and Mark. Isolde is also known as Isolt, Ysot, Yseut, Iseut, Iseult, or Isotta, depending on the linguistic and cultural context.

The legend, considered one of the founding myths of Western culture, was extremely popular throughout the Middle Ages in both literature and art. It experienced an important revival in the modern period, owing largely to the success of Wagner's "music-drama," *Tristan und Isolde* (1865). This romantic reinterpretation, which decisively influenced that of Denis de Rougemont in his own monumental *L'Amour et l'Occident* (*Love in the West*) in 1939, depicts the lovers as imbued with a death wish, clearly seeking the realm of Night and Death as a refuge from an oppressive society.

However, quite a different picture of the legend emerges from the medieval versions. In these the lovers are constrained by the power of the potion to violate the most sacred social and religious taboos: Isolde deceives her husband, while Tristan betrays the man who is both his uncle and his lord; considering the importance of the maternal uncle, the lovers' relationship is even tinged with incest. Although the presence of the potion serves to mitigate their culpability, the lovers feel acutely the weight of the sanctions resulting from their liaison and make every effort both to escape death and to achieve social integration.

In the extant fragments of the two earliest verse romances in Old French, those of Béroul and Thomas of Britain (end of twelfth century), the love idyll is so central that it is difficult to speak of Isolde without evoking her lover. Both are celebrated (as they were in lyric poetry from about 1130 on) for their beauty, ardor, and ingenuity. Béroul's long fragment concentrates on the ruses that the lovers deploy to evade the plots hatched by Mark and his evil barons to catch them *in flagrante delecto*. In perpetrating these ruses the lovers act in tandem (and experience considerable delight in the success of their combined ingenuity, a brief yet memorable episode of which is contributed by the later twelfth-century poet, Marie de France, in her "Lai du Chievrefoil" ["Tale of the Goatleaf"]). Thomas's poem, on the other hand, is preserved in several fragments: the recently discovered one relating the drinking of the potion on board ship (see Baumgartner and Short, notes to their edition of Thomas), while the others focus primarily on the end of the story (Tristan's Breton exile, his unconsummated marriage to Isolde of the White Hands, and the lovers' death). Thomas describes the lovers' respective reactions to the anguish of separation and the acute social alienation they experience. While the self-deluded hero contemplates the marriage he will immediately regret, an anxious Isolde remains true to her love and rebuffs a suitor even as he reports that Tristan has wed. But the violent quarrel that erupts between Isolde and her confidante Brangane shortly thereafter reveals that Thomas is intent on portraying the disastrous effects of the lovers' predicament.

A more extensive account of the legend can be found in three long verse redactions dating from the end of the twelfth and beginning of the thirteenth centuries: two in Middle-High German, by Eilhart von Oberge (c.1190) and Gottfried von Strassburg (c.1210), respectively, and one in Old Norse, by Friar Robert (1226). These versions allow us to see how the protagonists were before the potion reordered their priorities. Like her mother, Isolde has learned to exploit the magical properties of herbs, which the women apply as balms to Tristan's wounds on two separate occasions. It is her mother who brews the potion originally intended to infuse love into the marriage that Tristan arranges between Isolde and his uncle. Isolde is depicted as a strong-willed woman whose fury is ignited when she learns that the ailing harpist "Tantris" (note the anagram ruse) is none other than the knight who killed her maternal uncle in combat. Her hatred of Tristan will be transformed into love when they drink the potion. It is significant that in one of the Celtic analogues of the legend, the Irish tale of the elopement of Diarmaid and Gráinne (ninth century), Gráinne falls in love with the nephew of her husband, the Irish chieftain Fionn, and casts a spell (*geis*) on him that obliges him to flee with her. Indeed, in Celtic society women wielded considerable power and independence. By contrast, the potion that appears in the Old-French versions of the legend, both as the drink was conceived by Isolde's mother and as it was actually used, reflects an abrogation, in a patriarchal culture, of the heroine's right to choose her mate freely. In these redactions, Tristan's "separate" life receives more attention than Isolde's. His idyll with Isolde is preceded by his parents' tragic love story (which anticipates his own), his birth, adolescence, and early exploits; his eventual banishment from Cornwall is the occasion to chronicle his adventures in foreign lands and in Eilhart his nascent association with Arthur's knights, an innovation that anticipates the legend's future development in the great prose romances of the later Middle Ages.

Despite the space accorded to Tristan's biography in the verse redactions, the love intrigue remains central. Gottfried in particular, who addresses his poem to "noble hearts," celebrates this refined passion and the great joy that is the lot of those few willing to suffer great sorrow. The lovers' exalted passion contrasts with the shabby values of

461

Mark's courtiers, and it is not difficult to see what specific elements of Gottfried's version Wagner chose to elaborate for his own idiosyncratic interpretation. A premature death prevented Gottfried from completing his masterpiece, and his poem breaks off, coincidentally, at about the point that the extant fragments of Thomas's poem take up the story. Although Gottfried claimed to be following Thomas, the Anglo-Norman poet gives a much bleaker picture of the destructive effects on both Tristan and Isolde (and their spouses and confidants) of this alienating passion. If Thomas is too much a poet to be overtly moralistic, the two poets who attempt to complete Gottfried's poem, Ulrich von Türheim (1235) and Heinrich von Freiburg (1285–1290), present the legend unabashedly as a negative exemplum. While Isolde of the White Hands arouses little sympathy in the earlier versions, in which the death of her ailing husband is precipitated by her false report that his beloved has not responded to his summons, she becomes in the versions of all of Gottfried's German successors the very model of the patient, loving, and virtuous wife. By contrast, Irish Isolde is seen primarily as a faithless woman responsible for the destruction of two marriages, her own and her lover's.

Outside of Germany and Scandinavia, the legend underwent a very different kind of transformation. Starting with the French Prose *Tristan* (written after the Vulgate Cycle, c.1230), more and more attention was accorded Tristan's adventures as a knight errant. The extraordinarily popular Prose *Tristan* influenced all the prose romances of France, Italy, Spain, and England, notably Malory's *Morte Darthur* (1469–1470), which includes *The Book of Sir Tristram de Lyones*. In these works Isolde becomes a more generalized love object: her great beauty sparks the undying love of many other knights (most notably the Saracen Palamedes and Tristan's brother-in-law Kaherdin, both of whom die of unrequited love). As Tristan is drawn into the Arthurian orbit, eventually joining the Round Table, his prowess is seen to rival Lancelot's, just as Isolde's beauty rivals Guinevere's. Since in these romances Mark's character is further blackened, the Cornish lovers appear more justified in their deception than do Lancelot and Guinevere, but the close link established between love and prowess makes it virtually inevitable that the two most valiant knights will win the love of the two most beautiful ladies. Another important innovation in the Prose *Tristan* is the diminished importance accorded the potion: the mutual attraction that Tristan and Isolde feel for each other is established even before they consume the potion. However, in the *Tavola Ritonda* (Italian, second quarter of the fourteenth century), which attempts to restore to the love intrigue a preeminent role, the philter is seen as an extremely potent force that transforms the chaste friendship shared by the virtuous protagonists into an unbridled desire that simultaneously elevates them to the status of secular martyrs and deprives the world of its brightest stars.

The legend had great appeal for medieval artists, who represented the couple not only in the numerous illustrated manuscripts of the romances but also on embroideries, tapestries, ivory and wood boxes, and even misericords (part of the seat, often decorated, in a church stall) and the paving tiles of one abbey. A favorite scene shows the couple consuming the potion on board ship. But the most frequently depicted scene by far was the orchard rendezvous, where Tristan and Isolde stand on either side of a tree while King Mark spies on them from the upper branches. The popularity of this scene can be explained in part by its replication of the iconography of the Fall; the scene can thus be interpreted negatively (the "disobedient" lovers' sinful failure to respect marital, feudal, and familial ties) as well as positively (the ardent lovers' successful duping of the ridiculous cuckold).

In literature, too, the legend was often encapsulated in a few emblematic images, some negative, as in the mind of Fénice, the heroine of Chrétien de Troyes' *Cligés* (c. 1176), who denounces Isolde's willingness to surrender her body to her husband when her heart was committed to her lover. But generally the lovers were viewed with sympathy, since they were victims of fate. Celebrated for their surpassing beauty, boundless ingenuity, and consummate fidelity (including a capacity for great suffering), Tristan and Isolde early joined the pantheon of classical and medieval star-crossed lovers. Dante, in his *Divina Commedia* (*Divine Comedy*, 1321) placed Tristan among the lustful in his Second Circle of Hell, and Isolde is surely one of the unnamed "more than a thousand/shades . . ./whom love parted from our life" (*Inferno*, 5: 67–69).

See also Arthurian Women; Beatrice; Brangain; Guinevere; Marie de France; *Minne*

BIBLIOGRAPHY

Primary Sources
Béroul. *Le Roman de Tristan*. Edited and translated by Stewart Gregory. Faux titre, 57. Amsterdam, Netherlands and Atlanta, Ga.: Rodopi, 1992. [Bilingual Old French-English ed.].
———. In *Tristan et Iseut: les poèmes français, la saga norroise*. Edited by Daniel Lacroix and Philippe Walter. Lettres gothiques. Paris: Livre de Poche, 1989.
Byelorussian Tristan (*Apovests' pro Tryshchana*). Translated by Zora Kipel. Garland Library of Medieval Literature B, 59. New York: Garland, 1988.
Early French Tristan poems. Edited by Norris J. Lacy. Arthurian archives, 1–2. Woodbridge, Suffolk, U.K. and Rochester, N.Y.: D. S. Brewer, 1998. [Bilingual Old French-English critical ed.].
Chrétien de Troyes. *Cligés*. Edited and translated by Charles Méla and Olivier Collet. Lettres gothiques. Paris: Livre de Poche, 1994. [Bilingual Old French-Modern French critical ed.].
———. *Cligés*. Edited by Claude Luttrell and Stewart Gregory. Arthurian Studies. Woodbridge, Suffolk, U.K. and Rochester, N.Y.: D. S. Brewer, 1993.
———. Translated by Ruth Harwood Cline. Athens: University of Georgia Press, 2000.
Eilhart von Oberge. *Tristrant*. Edited by Kurt Wagner. Bonn, Germany: K. Schroeder, 1924.
Gottfried von Strassburg. *Tristan*. Critical ed. by Reinhold Bechstein and Peter Ganz. 2 vols. Deutscher Klassiker des Mittelalters, 4. Wiesbaden, Germany: Brockhaus, 1978.
———. *Tristan, with Surviving Fragments of the* Tristran *of Thomas*. Translated with introduction by Arthur Thomas Hatto. Baltimore: Penguin, 1960. Reprint 1972.
Heinrich von Freiburg. *Tristan und Isolde: Fortsetzung des Tristan-Romans Gottfried von Strassburg*. Edited by Danielle Buschinger. Translated by Wolfgang Spiewok. Greifswalder Beitrage zum Mittelalter, 1. Wodan, 16. Greifswald, Germany: Reineke-Verlag, 1993. [Bilingual Middle-High and Modern German ed.].
Malory, Sir Thomas. *Morte Darthur*. Edited by John Matthews. London: Cassell, 2000.
Marie de France. "Le Lai du Chievrefoil." In *Tristan et Iseut: les poèmes français, la saga norroise. See under Béroul, above*.
[Norse and Middle English versions]. *Die nordische Version der Tristan Sage: Tristrams Saga ok Isondar; Sir Tristrem*. Edited by Eugen Kölbing. 2 vols. Hildesheim, Germany and New York: G. Olms, 1978–1985. Originally published Heilbronn, Germany: Henninger, 1878–1882.
———. [Norse Version] In *Tristan et Iseut: les poèmes français, la saga norroise. See under Béroul, above*.
[Prose *Tristan*]. *Le Roman de Tristan en prose*. Edited by Joël Blanchard, et al. 3 vols. Classiques Français du Moyen Âge, 123, 133, 135. Paris: Honoré Champion, 1997.
Roman de Tristan en prose. Edited by Renée L. Curtis. Arthurian Studies 12–14. Woodbridge, Suffolk: D. S. Brewer, 1985. [The first two volumes are reprints: v. 1, originally Munich: M. Hueber, 1963; v. 2, orig. pub. Leiden: E. J. Brill, 1976].

Roman de Tristan en prose. Edited by Philippe Ménard et al. 9 vols. Textes Littéraires Français, 353, 387, 398, 408, 416, 437, 462, 474. Geneva: Droz, 1987–.

Tavola Ritonda, o l'istoria di tristano. Critical edition by Filippo-Luigi Polidori and Luciano Banchi. 2 vols. Bologna, Italy: G. Romagnoli, 1864–1866.

———. *Tristan and the Round Table. A Translation of* La Tavola Ritonda. Translated and annotated by Anne Shaver. Medieval & Renaissance Texts & Studies, 28. Binghamton: State University of New York Press, 1983.

Thomas of Britain. *Le Roman de Tristan suivi de La Folie Tristan de Berne et La Folie d'Oxford.* Edited by Félix Lecoy. Translation, presentation and notes by Emmanuèle Baumgartner and Ian Short. Champion classiques. Paris: Honoré Champion, 2003. *See also under* Béroul, Gottfried *and* Norse *above.*

Ulrich von Türheim. *Tristan und Isolde des Gottfried von Strassburg. Tristan: eine Fortsetzung.* Edited by Dieter Kuhn with Lambertus Okken. Frankfurt, Germany: Insel Verlag, 1991.

Modern Reconstructions and Renditions (select list)

Bédier, Joseph. *Le Roman de Tristan et Iseut traduit et restauré.* Preface by Gaston Paris. Paris: H. Piazza, 1900.

———. *The Romance of Tristan and Iseult.* Translated by Hilaire Belloc. Vintage Classics. New York: Vintage Books, 1994. First published London: George Allen & Unwin, 1903.

Davidson, Audrey Ekdahl. *Olivier Messiaen and the Tristan Myth.* Westport, Conn.: Praeger, 2001.

Reichenbacher, Helmut. "Richard Wagner's Adaptation of Gottfried von Strassburg's Tristan." *University of Toronto Quarterly* 67 (1998): 762–67.

Suassuna, Ariano. *Fernando e Isaura.* Recife, Brazil: Ediçoes Bagaço, 1994.

Updike, John. *Brazil.* New York: Knopf/ Random House, 1994.

Secondary Sources

Barteau, Françoise. *Les Romans de Tristan et Iseut: Introduction à une lecture plurielle.* Paris: Larousse, 1972.

Baumgartner, Emmanuèle. *Tristan et Iseut. De la légende aux récits en vers.* Paris: Presses Universitaires de France, 1987.

———. *Le "Tristan" en prose: Essai d'interprétation d'un roman médiéval.* Geneva, Switzerland: Droz, 1975.

Blakeslee, Merritt R. *Love's Masks: Identity, Intertextuality, and Meaning in the Old French Tristan Poems.* Cambridge: Brewer, 1989.

Burns, E. Jane. "Why Beauty Laughs: Iseut's Enormous Thighs." In Burns, *Bodytalk: When Women Speak in Old French Romance*, 203–40. Philadelphia: University of Pennsylvania Press, 1993.

Buschinger, Danielle, ed. *La Légende de Tristan au moyen âge.* Göppingen, Germany: Kümmerle, 1982.

———. *Tristan et Iseut, mythe européen et mondial.* Göppingen, Germany: Kümmerle, 1987.

Chocheyras, Jacques. Tristan et Iseut: genèse d'un mythe littéraire. Nouvelle bibliothèque du moyen âge; 36. Paris: H. Champion; Geneva: Slatkine, 1996.

Curtis, Renée L. "The Character of Iseut in the Prose Tristan (Parts I and II)." In *Mélanges de Littérature du moyen âge au XXᵉ siècle offerts à Jeanne Lods*, 173–82. Paris: École Normale Supérieure des Jeunes Filles, 1978.

Dayan, Joan C. "The Figure of Isolde in Gottfried's *Tristan*: Toward a Paradigm of *Minne*." *Tristania* 6 (1981): 23–36.

Deist, Rosemarie. "The Description of Isolde and Iseut and Their Confidantes in Gottfried von Strassburg and Thomas de Bretagne." *Bulletin Bibliographique de la Société Internationale Arthurienne* 48 (1996): 271–82.

Dick, Ernst S. "Gottfried's Isolde: *Coincidentia Oppositorum?*" *Tristania* 12 (autumn 1986–spring, 1987): 15–24.

Félix, Bernard. *Iseult et ses soeurs celtiques: essai sur la liberté du choix amoureux.* Spezet, France: Coop Breizh, 1995.

Frappier, Jean. "La Reine Iseut dans le *Tristan* de Béroul." *Romance Philology* 26 (1972–1973): 215–28.

Grimbert, Joan Tasker, ed. *Tristan and Isolde: A Casebook*. Arthurian Characters and Themes, 2. New York and London: Garland, 1995. Reprint New York and London: Routledge, 2002. [Important collection of essays by major scholars in the field].

Jonin, Pierre. *Les Personnages féminins dans les romans français de Tristan au XIIe siècle*. Aix-en-Provence, France: Ophrys, 1958.

Kilbourn, R. J. A. "Redemption Revalued in *Tristan und Isolde*: Schopenhauer, Wagner, Nietzsche." *University of Toronto Quarterly* 67 (1998): 781–88.

Malzer, Marion. *Die Isolde-Gestalten in den mittelalterlichen deutschen Tristan-Dichtungen: Ein Beitrag zum diachronischen Wandel*. Beiträge zur alteren Literaturgeschichte. Heidelberg, Germany: Carl Winter, 1991.

Rabine, Leslie W. "Love and the New Patriarchy: *Tristan and Isolde*." In Rabine, *Reading the Romantic Heroine: Text, History, Ideology*, 20–49. Ann Arbor: University of Michigan Press, 1985.

Rasmussen, Ann Marie. "'Ez ist ir G'Artet von mir': Queen Isolde and Princess Isolde in Gottfried von Strassburg's *Tristan und Isolde*." In *Arthurian Women: A Casebook*, edited by Thelma S. Fenster, 41–57. New York: Garland, 1996.

Rougemont, Denis de. *L'Amour et l'Occident*. Paris: Plon, 1939.

———. *Love in the Western World*. Translated by Montgomery Belgion. Revised ed. Princeton, N.J.: Princeton University Press, 1983.

Sahel, Claude. *Esthétique de l'amour: Tristan et Iseut*. L'Ouverture philosophique. Paris: L'Harmattan, 1999.

JOAN TASKER GRIMBERT

IVETTA OF HUY (1158–1228). Also called Yvette of Huy, she was an influential beguine leader of the Low Countries. Aside from the Latin/French form Ivetta or Yvette, she was also known as Jutta or Juetta in Dutch and German. The main biographical source for Ivetta was the *vita* (life) written shortly after her death by Hugh of Floreffe. Born into a wealthy patrician family—her father was the bishop of Liège's administrator in Huy, on the river Meuse, in modern-day Belgium and at the time an important commercial center—Ivetta was married against her will at age thirteen and widowed with three children only five years later. She then steadfastly refused to remarry and remained chaste despite various relatives' attempts to intimidate her. Seizing control of the family fortune, she assumed complete responsibility for her sons' education, while also caring for the sick and needy in her own home. Since nowhere is virginity discussed in her *vita*, her refusal to remarry probably derives less from the usual need to preserve her virginity found in never-married celibates than from her strong will to govern her own life and body.

After five more years at home, her two sons now old enough to fend for themselves (the third had died young), and possibly at the urging of relatives and clergy reproaching her way of life, she left her family behind and moved in with the lepers, living in a crude shelter on the outskirts of town. Soon gaining the admiration and financial support of her fellow townsmen, she expanded the *leprosarium* into a flourishing hospital with a fine church and a convent, in which she and a group of followers founded a religious community. This community is thought to have been one of the first (informal) beguine communities in northern Europe, as part of the growing movement by pious laywomen, called beguines (from the French: *Béguines*) to pursue a holy life though outside ecclesiastical orders as in monasteries.

At the age of thirty-three, she had herself enclosed as a recluse in a cell built onto the new chapel by her father. She was ritually immured by the abbot of Orval, the Cistercian abbey of which her eldest son, Henry de Stenay, would soon become abbot himself. Her father and younger son Eustache would also enter Cistercian abbeys. Ivetta now devoted herself to prayer, meditation, and asceticism. She experienced numerous raptures and intimate mystical conversations with Mary and Jesus, which fueled, just as they were fueled by, her gift of prophecy and clairvoyance. Thus, from the confines of her cell, she led the religious community, as *mater et magistra* (mother and teacher), guided the faithful town-dwellers and remained close to her family and friends while keeping an alert eye on the local clergy.

The Cistercian abbot of Floreffe, John of Huy, in whom she confided more than in the local priesthood, took her general confession before she died in 1228. John had his pupil, Hugh of Floreffe, record her life. Writing within a decade of Ivetta's death and receiving his information from both the abbot John and Ivetta's intimate handmaiden, Hugh gives us a fine portrait of this highly original woman. Not being a church official who might have attempted to transform her into a model saint for political reasons, Hugh displays an eye for the social and emotional aspects of Ivetta's life without hiding his own authorial struggle to express her uniqueness. Scarcely anything more is known about Hugh that might shed further light on his perspective. Though he was once credited with the *vitae* (biographies) of Ida of Nivelles and Ida of Zoutleeuw, this is no longer the case, as discussed by Simone Roisin.

Ivetta belongs to the oldest generation of *mulieres sanctae* (holy women) in the Low Countries. These women, attracted to a full-time religious way of life yet still in contact with society, were better suited than their strictly monastic counterparts to confront the various social consequences of rapid commercial growth vs. the crumbling old hierarchy of wealth in their region: ministering to the newly wealthy and even more to the newly poor. If on the former she bestowed a pious humility and caution in regard to their newfound material prosperity, to the former she taught spiritual insight, hope, and comfort. As Hugh implies in calling her *mediatrix* (female mediator) to evoke more than her gift of prophecy, although Ivetta could not dispense grace as a true priest, she could nonetheless obtain forgiveness of sins among her believers by talking to and praying for them—which endowed her with at least as much power as conventional priests at the popular level. Women inspired by Ivetta looked after their fellow citizens' spiritual well-being while at the same time struggling with Church and society's confining ideals for them. Such are the concerns informing Ivetta's developing community (beguinage), which would prove to be very productive for future generations. By acquiring spiritual leadership as a wise, nurturing figure, she elevated and universalized her maternal function from the individual household level to the communal one, functioning as *sapientissima materfamilias* (most learned, wisest matriarch). A person whose charisma gained her the moral authority surpassing that of official clerics, Ivetta must have been regarded as a "living saint" by her contemporaries (Hugh sometimes calls her a *sancta*). Yet she never acquired a cult after her death nor were steps taken by the Church to canonize her, since according to Church law she did not fulfill the requisite conditions, such as performing miracles. This is because her sanctity was of another kind: she did not seek veneration as an assemblage of dead relics, but rather, remembrance as a living mouthpiece of God. She thus served her people's spiritual needs in a highly meaningful way while re-inventing herself as a second Mary Magdalene.

See also Beguines; Hagiography (Female Saints); *Mulieres Sanctae*; Relics and Medieval Women; Virginity; Widows

BIBLIOGRAPHY

Primary Sources
For lack of extant medieval manuscripts of Ivetta's Life by Hugh of Floreffe, see the following:
Vita B. Juettae Inclusae auctore Hugone Floreffiensi. In Acta Sanctorum (AASS), 13 Januarii, 2: 145–69. 3rd ed. Brussels, 1863.
Henriquez, P. F. Chr., ed. *Lilia Cistercii sive sacrarum virginum Cisterciensium Origo, Instituta et Res Gestae.* Douai, France, 1633 [Abridged version of the complete text given above].
———. *Vita of Yvette, Recluse of Huy.* Translated by JoAnn MacNamara. Toronto: Peregrina Publishing, 2000.

Secondary Sources
Walter Simons, *Cities of Ladies. Beguine Communities in the Medieval Low Countries, 1200–1565.* Philadelphia: University of Pennsylvania Press, 2001.
Carpenter, Jennifer. "Juette of Huy, Recluse and Mother (1158–1228): Children and Mothering in the Saintly Life." In *Power of the Weak. Studies on Medieval Women,* edited by Jennifer Carpenter and Sally-Beth MacLean, 57–93. Urbana: University of Illinois Press, 1995.
Cochelin, Isabella. "Sainteté laïque: l'exemple de Juette de Huy." *Le Moyen Âge* 95 (1989): 397–417.
D'Haenens, A. "Ivetta." In *Bibliotheca Sanctorum,* 7: 992–93. Rome: Istituto Giovanni XXIII, 1966.
Mulder-Bakker, Anneke B. "Ivetta of Huy. Mater et Magistra." In *Sanctity and Motherhood. Essays on Holy Mothers in the Middle Ages,* edited by A. B. Mulder-Bakker, 225–58. New York and London: Garland, 1995.
———. *Lives of the Anchoresses: The Rise of the Urban Recluse in Medieval Europe.* Philadelphia: University of Pennsylvania Press, 2005.
Roisin, Simone. *L'Hagiographie cistercienne dans le diocèse de Liège au XIIIe siècle, 148. Louvain, Belgium: Université de Louvain, 1947.

ANNEKE B. MULDER-BAKKER

IZUMI SHIKIBU (c.970–c.1033). A Heian-period author best known for her diary and her many *waka* (Japanese courtly style) poems, of which 240 appeared in later imperial collections, Izumi Shikibu (no relation to her contemporary, Murasaki Shikibu, c.973–1015?) probably takes her name from her first husband, the governor of Izumi province, Japan. All that we know of her life is that she married in 995, that she bore a daughter in 997, and that she was already a reputable poet prior to her marriage. After the events of the love affair described in her diary (to be discussed below) she attached herself (1007) to the court of the powerful Michinaga's daughter, Empress Shoshi/Akiko (patron of Murasaki, another eminent diarist) as an attendant. In 1010, Izumi remarried and migrated to the provinces, never to return to the court, yet continuing to compose poetry. The last official record of her existence dates from 1033 (see "Other Women's Voices").

In the later tenth century, female members of the middle-ranking aristocracy, many of whom served as ladies-in-waiting at court, developed the prose vernacular diary. Because women did not write in the more public, official *kanbun* Chinese, the diaries are written in *hiragana*, a phonetic Japanese syllabary, which allowed women more freedom to develop a personal style, in this case, the vernacular, compared to *kanbun*. The most important of the extant diaries written by women in the Heian period (794–1192) are *Makura no soshi* (*The Pillow Book*) of Sei Shonagon, Lady Murasaki's *Murasaki Shikibu nikki* (*Murasaki Shikibu's Diary*) and Izumi Shikibu's *Izumi Shikibu nikki*. While very different from each other, all three of these works experiment with the genre of diary.

Izumi Shikibu's diary concerns events occurring from c.June 1003 through spring 1004: Izumi, for three years the lover of Prince Tametaka (977–1002), one year after his death is wooed by his younger brother, Prince Atsumichi (981–1007), who eventually takes her to live in the house also occupied by his wife. The diary begins with a page bearing a spray of orange blossoms from the twenty-three-year-old Prince Atsumichi, son of the Emperor Reizei by a secondary consort. Izumi and the Prince Atsumichi begin by exchanging notes; he then visits her in disguise to keep his wife ignorant of the love affair. Izumi and Atsumichi fall deeply in love and the story then follows their frustration in attempting various secret rendezvous, with Izumi finally displacing the wife, who leaves to live with her sister. Atsumichi's death three years later brings about Izumi's profound grief, as she records in the 120 poems of *Izumi Shikibu zokushu*, during this, her most mournful, yet artistically productive phase.

Izumi Shikibu nikki can best be considered a romantic novel, narrated in short sections of prose interspersed with over 140 lyric insertions. Although the extended narrative suggests a *monogatari* (vernacular prose fiction), its tone and content link it with the diaries of Heian court ladies. Unlike conventional diaries, however, Izumi's entries are undated and the omniscient third-person narrator refers to Izumi as merely *onna* ("the Lady"). Although some scholars have suggested other authors because of this quasi-anonymity, most contemporary authorities accept the diary's attribution to Izumi Shikibu.

Izumi Shikibu also mastered the use of *waka* poetry, an integral part of masculine Heian court culture. *Waka* is the term, sometimes interchanged with *tanka* or *uta*, identifying the classical verse form of thirty-one syllables. It is a five-line short poem in the 5-7-5-7-7 syllable pattern, which became the principal Japanese lyric-poetic form. Izumi's most famous *waka* poem, written an early age, adds personal insights to a conventional Buddhist expression of piety: "I go out of the darkness/Onto a road of darkness / Lit only by the far off / Moon on the edge of the mountains" (Trans. Kenneth Rexroth, in "Other Women's Voices").

Izumi Shikibu's prestige as a *waka* poet is evidenced in her poems' inclusion in a series of important poetic collections: first the imperial collection *Goshuishu* (sixty-eight poems), compiled under Emperor Shirakawa (1053–1129), and subsequent collections such as *Hyakunin Isshu*, *Shikashu*, and *Senzaishu*. Her poems and their prefaces demonstrate her individuality, distinctive voice, and forcefulness. Her most characteristic poetry describes the successive stages of her love affairs, generally in terms of enlightened unhappiness or grief. Even after her death, Izumi Shikibu was known (not always favorably) for her many love affairs, leading Murasaki to say of her: "she does have a rather unsavory side to her character but has a genius for tossing off letters with ease and can make the most banal statement sound special"—allowing also that Izumi's "poems are quite delightful" (Murasaki, trans. Bowring, 131).

Although English translations of Izumi's diary were done as early as the 1920s, and by none less than American poet and critic Amy Lowell (d. 1925), more authoritative ones have since been published by Cranston and Miner, both in 1969.

See also Abutsu-ni; China, Women in; Murasaki Shikibu; Sei Shonagon

BIBLIOGRAPHY

Primary Sources
[All are English texts only unless specifically noted otherwise].
Izumi Shikibu. [*Izumi Shikibu nikki*]. "The Diary of Izumi Shikibu." In *Japanese Poetic Diaries*, selected and translated by Earl Roy Miner, 95–153. Center for Japanese and Korean Studies. Berkeley: University of California Press, 1969.

———. *The Izumi Shikibu Diary: A Romance of the Heian Court*. Translated with introduction by Edward Cranston. Harvard-Yenching Institute Monograph series, 19. Cambridge, Mass. Harvard University Press, 1969.

———. [Love poems, select]. *The Ink Dark Moon: Love Poems by Ono no Komachi and Izumi Shikibu*. Translated by Jane Hirshfield with Mariko Aratani. New York: Scribner, 1988. Reprint New York: Vintage, 1990.

Murasaki Shikibu. [*Murasaki Shikibu Nikki; Kashu*]. *Her Diary and Poetic Memoirs: A Translation and Study* by Richard Bowring. Princeton Library of Asian Translations. Princeton, N.J.: Princeton University Press, 1982. Reprint 1985. [English trans. with excellent introduction and notes].

Secondary Sources
Katō, Shuichi. *A History of Japanese Literature*. Translated by David Chibbett. Tokyo: Kodansha International, 1979.

Keene, Donald. *Seeds in the Heart: Japanese Literature from Earliest Times to the Late Sixteenth Century*. New York: Henry Holt, 1993.

———. *Travelers of a Hundred Years. The Japanese as Revealed through 1,000 Years of Diaries*. New York: Henry Holt, 1989.

Mostow, Joshua S. "On Becoming Ukifune: Autobiographical Heroines in Heian and Kamakura Literature." In *Crossing the Bridge: Comparative Essays on Medieval European and Heian Japanese Women Writers*, edited by Barbara Stevenson and Cynthia Ho, 45–60. New York and Houndmills, U.K.: Palgrave/St. Martin's, 2000.

"Other Women's Voices": www.tl.infi.net/~ddisse/izumi.html [one of several excellent, often university-based, Web sites on Izumi, with trans. excerpts, history, etc.].

Walker, Janet. "Poetic Ideal and Fictional Reality in the *Izumi Shikibu nikki*." *Harvard Journal of Asiatic Studies* 37 (1977): 135–82.

CYNTHIA HO

J

JACOBS, BERTA. *See* Bertken, Sister/Berta Jacobs

JACQUES DE VITRY. *See Mulieres Sanctae*

JACQUETTA OF LUXEMBOURG (c.1416–1472). Jacquetta of Luxembourg, duchess of Bedford, was the mother of Queen Elizabeth Woodville (c.1437–1492) and the matriarch of the Woodville family. Her father, Peter (Pierre) of Luxembourg (1390–1433), count of St. Pol, traced his family back to Charlemagne (742–814). Her mother was Marguerite of Baux (Margherita del Balzo of Andria, in southern Italy, 1394–1469). In April 1433, Jacquetta married John of Lancaster, the powerful duke of Bedford (1389–1435), uncle of the young King Henry VI (1421–1471), who was then ruling both England and English-occupied France. They would have no children. After her husband's death in 1435, the duchess shocked her royal nephew by marrying Richard Woodville (Wydeville), a Northamptonshire gentleman who was well beneath her in social class. Although knighted by Henry in 1426, Woodville was only the son of Bedford's chamberlain (chief steward of the duke's household). As far as the English nobility were concerned, Woodville had nothing but looks to recommend him as a husband for the duchess, and the government fined the couple £1,000 for their misalliance. However, marrying Jacquetta brought Woodville into the House of Lancaster and gave him social rank, land, wealth, and at least fourteen children. Woodville served in France during the last phase of the Hundred Years War (1337–1453) in the 1430s and 1440s, helped suppress Jack Cade's populist rebellion in southern England in 1450, and fought for the House of Lancaster during the Wars of the Roses (1455–1485). A series of intermittent civil struggles, the Wars of the Roses involved a succession dispute between two branches of the royal family—the House of Lancaster, led by Henry VI and his wife Margaret of Anjou (1430–1482) and the House of York, led by Richard, duke of York (1411–1460) and his son Edward, earl of March (1442–1483). The war was named for the family emblems employed by the two contending houses—a red rose for Lancaster and a white rose for York.

At the outbreak of civil war, Duchess Jacquetta accompanied her husband to Sandwich on the southeastern coast of England, where Queen Margaret of Anjou had ordered him to assemble a fleet. In January 1460, Jacquetta, Richard Woodville, and their eldest son, Anthony, were captured by Yorkist raiders and carried across the channel to English-held Calais on the northern coast of France. The duchess was released soon thereafter, but her husband and son remained in Yorkist custody. After Queen Margaret defeated the Yorkist leader, Richard Neville, earl of Warwick, at the Second Battle of St. Albans in February 1461, the London authorities sent Jacquetta to the queen as part of a deputation of high-ranking noblewomen charged with gaining Margaret's assurance that her army would not plunder the city.

Meanwhile, demoralized by the Lancastrian defeat at Towton in March 1461, Richard Woodville threw his support to the House of York and its newly recognized king, Edward IV (the former earl of March). In May 1464, Jacquetta witnessed the marriage of her eldest daughter, Elizabeth, to Edward IV, in a secret ceremony held at the Woodvilles' estate. Edward spent the next three days with the Woodvilles, and each night Jacquetta brought her daughter secretly to the king, who made the bride's father Earl Rivers in 1465. The royal favoritism shown the Woodvilles aroused the jealousy of Richard Neville, earl of Warwick, who consequently sought to undermine the family through negative propaganda. Thus, in 1468, Jacquetta and her family were maligned for ruining Sir Thomas Cook, a wealthy London merchant who owned a lavish tapestry supposedly coveted by the duchess. The traditional account holds that when Cook refused Jacquetta's demand that he sell her the tapestry at an unreasonably reduced price, she denounced him as a Lancastrian sympathizer, taking advantage of Cook's former association with the Lancastrian regime. Edward allowed Jacquetta's husband, now constable of England, to prosecute the merchant for misprision of treason (knowing of but failing to report treasonous activity). Cook was fined £8000, and the duchess received her tapestry after her servants ransacked the merchant's house. Modern historians question much of this story and suggest that Jacquetta's and her family's role in the Cook case was greatly exaggerated by Warwick's anticourt propaganda, and that Cook may indeed have been an active Lancastrian.

In August 1469, Warwick rebelled and temporarily captured Edward, while also arresting and executing Rivers. He arrested Jacquetta on vague charges of witchcraft, claiming—according to some sources—that Jacquetta had used black magic to bewitch Edward into marrying her daughter. To defend herself, the duchess wrote to the mayor of London, who intervened on her behalf with the council. When further investigation revealed that the witnesses against her had been bribed, the case collapsed. Jacquetta was released and formally exonerated by Edward in February 1470, although the charge of witchcraft resurfaced in 1483 when Edward's brother, Richard III, exploited it as one of his justifications for taking the throne from Jacquetta's grandson, Edward V.

Jacquetta died in April 1472. Of her many children by Earl Rivers, the most illustrious were her aforementioned daughter Elizabeth Woodville—queen to Edward IV—and Anthony Woodville, who became second earl Rivers (1440–1483) and a noted warrior and scholar; in 1478, he also translated Christine de Pizan's *Proverbes mouraulx* (*Moral Proverbs*), one of the earliest books printed in England by William Caxton.

See also Chaucer, Alice; Christine de Pizan; Margaret of Anjou; Witches; Woodville, Elizabeth

BIBLIOGRAPHY

Primary Sources
[See also bibliographies to secondary sources listed below].
Corporation of London Record Office. Journal VI, folio 10.

Myers, A. R., ed. "The Household of Queen Margaret of Anjou, 1452–3." *Bulletin of the John Rylands Library* 40 (1957–1958): 79–113; 391–431. Reprint in Myers, *Crown, Household and Parliament in Fifteenth-Century England*, edited by Cecil H. Clough, 135–229. London: Hambledon Press, 1985

———. "The Jewels of Queen Margaret of Anjou." *Bulletin of the John Rylands Library* 42 (1959–1960): 113–31. Reprint *see above entry*.

[Parliament Rolls]. [The] *Curious account of the remarkable case of the Duchess of Bedford, in the reign of Edward IV* [...] *charged with having by witchcraft fixed the love of the King on her daughter Queen Elizabeth.* . . . Edited by Thomas Wright. Northampton, U.K.: J. Taylor & Son, 1867.

Secondary Sources

Baldwin, David. *Elizabeth Woodville: Mother of the Princes in the Tower*. Stroud, England: Sutton Publishing, 2002.

Hicks, Michael. "The Changing Role of the Wydevilles in Yorkist Politics to 1483." In *Patronage, Pedigree and Power: In Later Medieval England*, edited by Charles Ross, 60–86. Gloucestershire: Alan Sutton, 1979.

MacGibbon, David. *Elizabeth Woodville: Her Life and Times*. London: A. Barker Ltd., 1938.

Maurer, Helen. *Margaret of Anjou: Queenship and Power in Late Medieval England*. Woodbridge, Suffolk, U.K.: Boydell Press, 2003.

Wagner, John A. *Encyclopedia of the Wars of the Roses*. Santa Barbara, Calif.: ABC-Clio, 2001.

Weir, Alison, *The Wars of the Roses*. New York: Ballantine Books, 1995.

JOHN A. WAGNER

JEANNE D'ÉVREUX (c.1311–1371). Though reigning queen of France for only about four years (1324–1328), Jeanne d'Évreux played a vital role in French political affairs of the fourteenth century, notably in the transition from the Capetian line, of which she was the last queen, to the house of Valois. Celebrated by Christine de Pizan (1365–1430?) as an exemplar of wisdom, fairness, and deep faith, Jeanne was also an important patron and collector. The sources useful in reconstructing her biography include correspondence, journals of the royal treasury, household expenditures and finance records for her properties, records of the religious institutions to which she made donations, her own instructions for her funeral, the inventory of her possessions made after her death, the testimony of the *Grandes Chroniques de France* (*Great Chronicles of France*), and the characterizations by Christine de Pizan in the *Cité des dames* (*City of Ladies*, 1404–1405), the *Livre des Trois Vertus* (*Book of the Three Virtues*, 1405–1406), and the epistles involved in the Debat sus le *Rommant de la rose* (Debate on the *Romance of the Rose*, 1401–1404).

Jeanne d'Évreux was the daughter of Marguerite of Artois (d. 1311) and a brother of the powerful French king, Philip the Fair, named Louis (d. 1319), who became count of Évreux in 1305. Louis and Marguerite married in 1300 and produced five children: Philip (1305–1343), Charles (d. 1336), Marie (d. 1335), Marguerite (d. 1350), and Jeanne. A dispensation granted by Pope John XXII on June 21, 1324, allowed the marriage, on July 5, of Jeanne d'Évreux to her first cousin, Charles IV. The youngest and sole surviving son of Philip the Fair, Charles had assumed the throne in 1322. His first marriage to Blanche of Artois and Burgundy had been annulled in 1322 on grounds of spiritual consanguinity, subsequent to Blanche's imprisonment on charges of adultery. Charles's second marriage to Marie of Luxembourg ended with the death of the queen and their premature infant son in 1324. Though perhaps as young as eleven at the time of her marriage, Jeanne d'Évreux produced her first child, a daughter named Jeanne, before Pentecost in 1325.

The coronation of Jeanne d'Évreux took place at the Sainte-Chapelle in Paris on Pentecost (May 11) 1326. A second daughter, christened Marie, was born at the end of the same year, not long before the death of Princess Jeanne before January 16, 1327. On Christmas Day 1327, around midnight, the king became ill and took to his bed. On the eve of Candlemas (February 1), Charles IV died at Vincennes, leaving the queen expecting a third child. In April 1328, Jeanne d'Évreux gave birth to a third daughter, Blanche. By June, the widowed queen sealed an agreement concerning the succession, which passed to Philip VI, the first Valois king.

In the 1330s, Jeanne d'Évreux concerned herself with maintaining and improving her properties and income retained as her dower (inheritance from her husband), notably at the Hôtel de Navarre in Paris and near Meaux. To fulfill

Jeanne d'Évreux at the Miraculous Tomb of St. Louis. From *The Hours of Jeanne d'Evreux*, c.1324–1328. © The Metropolitan Museum of Art, The Cloisters Collection, 1954.

one of the obligations of her castellany (jurisdiction of her castle) at nearby Brie-Comte-Robert, she insisted on paying homage to the bishop of Paris only by proxy, arguing that it was beneath her royal dignity to kneel before him. In 1341, Jeanne's older daughter, Marie, died. Letters written by the pope to Jeanne d'Évreux in the 1340s indicate the latter's pivotal position as queen for the success of the Valois lineage. One papal letter suggests the son of Edward of England as a possible spouse for Jeanne's youngest daughter, Princess Blanche, a proposal that would have had extraordinary impact on England's claims to the throne of France. Instead, in 1345, Blanche was married to Philip of Orléans, second son of Philip VI and Jeanne of Burgundy. Philip VI took Jeanne's niece, Blanche of Navarre, as his second wife in January 1350, in a private ceremony at Jeanne d'Évreux's residence at Brie-Comte-Robert. Between 1354 and 1358, Jeanne d'Évreux played a key role on behalf of her nephew, Charles the Bad, king of Navarre and count of Évreux, after the death of Jeanne's brother. Despite Charles's treasonous behavior, Jeanne, along with his sister Blanche of Navarre, repeatedly interceded with both Duke John the Good of Burgundy and the Dauphin Charles, once effecting Charles the Bad's pardon for murder, and, on several occasions, preventing his loss of property.

Jeanne's stature with the Valois family is further evidenced by her being chosen to serve as godmother to Charles V's daughter, Jeanne, in 1366 and, two years later, to the future Charles VI. After Jeanne d'Évreux's death in 1371, Charles V ordered a supplementary service in her honor at the royal abbey of Saint-Denis, north of Paris, in which French monarchs were traditionally buried, to compensate for the typically unostentatious funeral that Jeanne herself had prescribed.

Jeanne d'Évreux was a highly important patron, even though only a few works of art created for her survive. Her first known commission dates to 1327: a golden reliquary (a vessel believed to contain a saint's relics, e.g., bones) of St. James that she and Charles IV presented to the Confraternity of Saint-Jacques-aux-Pèlerins (St. James of the Pilgrims), a charitable religious brotherhood, in Paris. Known from inventory descriptions and a seventeenth-century drawing and engraving, the reliquary depicted the royal couple, Jeanne and Charles, kneeling before the saint's image, conforming to types described in the inventory of Jeanne's collection at the time of her death. But Jeanne's patronage began in earnest about a decade after her husband died. In 1340 Jeanne commissioned the sculpture for the high altar of the Cistercian convent of Maubuisson, where her husband's entrails were interred according to his wishes. The sculptural ensemble included images of Charles, herself, and her two daughters, depicted both as relief and free-standing figures. Some of the sculpture from this ensemble is preserved at the Louvre museum in Paris, including the king and queen's funerary effigies, which were commissioned only in 1371, according to the terms of Jeanne's will. In 1340, Jeanne d'Évreux also endowed a chapel at Saint-Denis, the first at the royal necropolis (elaborate cemetery) sponsored by a woman. In addition to a white marble image of the Virgin and Child (from which the chapel came to be known as Notre-Dame-la-Blanche [Our Lady in White]), there were sculpted images of the queen, her deceased husband, and her two daughters. At both Maubuisson and Saint-Denis, and elsewhere, the queen's gifts of monumental sculpture were accompanied by precious works of art. The exquisite silver-gilt reliquary image of the Virgin and Child from the queen's chapel at Saint-Denis preserved at the Louvre is the sole surviving vestige of her generosity, while the original gift included a large silver chasse (case, often for housing relics) and a figure of St. John (Jeanne's patron), which, however, the queen specified would only be bestowed on her death. Another silver image of the Virgin embellished with crystal, like the one at Saint-Denis, and containing relics was presented to the Carmelite church at the place Maubert, Paris, in 1353, after the queen granted funds for the church building. The church's decor included images of Jeanne and Charles set on either side of the Virgin on the sculpted portal. To support this building campaign, Jeanne donated jewels from her coronation and wedding, with instructions that they should be sold as expeditiously as possible. Another of her crowns, chosen by the queen to be used at her funeral, was given to Saint-Denis, where it was preserved until the French Revolution (1789–1799), which deliberately desecrated all royal monuments, including tombs, as part of its antimonarchist political symbolism.

The inventory of Jeanne d'Évreux's possessions at the time of her death includes a number of objects from the collections of her husband, father, brother, nephew and sister-in-law, queens Clemence of Hungary and Marie of Luxembourg, and kings Philip V, and Louis X, as well as gifts from Charles V. Their disparate sources notwithstanding, they display a consistent predilection for goldsmith's work, especially incorporating translucent enamels, a disinterest in ivory, and a taste for the exotic and rare, including Oriental porcelain and cameos.

The Hours of Jeanne d'Évreux, preserved at The Cloisters, New York City, and the Virgin from Saint-Denis at the Louvre are the most celebrated of the few works to survive from the queen's collection. Though the *Hours*, the Cloisters' devotional prayer book, was a gift to her from her husband, it nonetheless represents what we know of the queen's own taste. Its grisaille decoration is also used in the *Breviary of Jeanne d'Évreux*, another type of prayerbook, of which one volume survives in the Musée Condé at Chantilly, near Paris. The playful images appearing in the *Hours*'s margins find their equivalent in objects described in the queen's inventory. Its prayer cycle devoted to St. Louis (Louis IX [1214–1270]), demonstrating the king's lifelong piety, reflects a personal devotion to her great grandfather that is also manifest in the royal tradition of charity toward the poor consistently emulated by Jeanne. At her death, she carefully placed the *Hours* manuscript, along with other objects associated with St. Louis, in the hands of Charles V, a clear indication that she was ever mindful of this Valois king's role as Louis's legitimate successor as patron and divinely anointed monarch of France.

See also Blanche of Castile; Christine de Pizan; Dower; Relics and Medieval Women

BIBLIOGRAPHY

Primary Sources

Anselme de Sainte-Marie. *Histoire généalogique et chronologique de la maison royale de France, des pairs, grand officiers de la couronne et de la maison du roy.* 3rd ed. 9 vols. Paris: Compagnie des Libraires, 1726.

Baron, Françoise. "Le Maitre-Autel de l'abbaye de Maubuisson au XIVe siècle." *Académie des Inscriptions et Belles Lettres. Fondation Eugène Piot, Monuments et Mémoires* 57 [Paris: E. Leroux, 1971]: 130–51.

———. "Les Arts précieux: Paris aux XIVe et XVe siècles d'après les archives de l'hôpital Saint-Jacques-aux-Pèlerins." *Bulletin archéologique du Comité des travaux historiques et scientifiques* n.s. 20–21 (1984–85) [Paris: Bibliothèque nationale, 1988]: 59–141.

Christine de Pizan. *Le Livre de la Cité des Dames.* Paris: Stock, 1986.

———. *Le Livre des Faits et Bonnes Mœurs du roi Charles V le Sage.* Translated by Eric Hicks and Thérèse Moreau. Paris: Stock, 1997.

———. *Le Livre des Trois Vertus.* Edited by Charity C. Willard with Eric Hicks. Bibliothèque du XVe siècle, 50. Paris: Honoré Champion, 1989.

———, Jean Gerson, Jean de Montreuil, Gontier and Pierre Col. *Le Débat sur le Roman de la rose.* Edited by Eric Hicks. Bibliothèque du XVe siècle, 43. Paris: Honoré Champion, 1977. Reprint 1996.

Comptes de la reine Jehanne d'Évreux à Brie-Comte-Robert (texte de référence et commentaires). Brie-Comte-Robert, France: Les Amis du Vieux Château, 1997.

Grandes Chroniques de France. Edited by Jules Viard. Paris: Société de l'Histoire de France, 1920–1953. [vol. 9: Charles IV le Bel, Philippe VI de Valois].

Grandes Chroniques de France: Chronique des règnes de Jean II et de Charles V. Edited by Roland Delachenal. 4 vols. Paris: Renouard; H. Laurens, 1910–1920.

Hours of Jeanne d'Évreux, Queen of France, at the Cloisters. New York: Metropolitan Museum of Art/New York Graphic Society, 1957. [Facsimile of the manuscript with commentary by Harry Bober, *see also* Boehm, Barbara Drake *in* Secondary Sources, *below*].

Leber, Constant. *Collection des meilleurs dissertations, notes et traités particuliers relatifs à l'histoire de France,* vol. 19: 120–69. Paris: G. A. Dentu, 1838.

Longnon, Auguste. *Documents relatifs au comté de Champagne et de Brie, 1172–1361. Vol. 3: Les comptes administratifs.* Paris: Imprimerie nationale, 1914.

Montesquiou-Fezensac, Blaise de, and Danielle Gaborit-Chopin, eds. *Le Trésor de Saint-Denis: Inventaire de 1634.* 3 vols. Paris: A. & J. Picard, 1973.

Secondary Sources

Boehm, Barbara Drake. "Le mécénat de Jeanne d'Évreux." In *1300—l'Art au temps de Philippe le Bel: Actes du colloque international, Galeries nationales du Grand Palais 24 et 25 juin 1998,* edited by

Danielle Gaborit-Chopin and François Avril, 15–31. Paris: École du Louvre/Documentation française, 2001.

———, with Abigail Quandt and William D. Wixom. *The Hours of Jeanne d'Évreux.* Lucerne, Switzerland: Faksimile Verlag. [Commentary for the facsimile].

Holladay, Joan A. "The Education of Jeanne d'Évreux: Personal Piety and Dynastic Salvation in her Book of Hours at the Cloisters." *Art History* 17: 4 (December 1994): 585–611.

Lord, Carla. "Jeanne d"Evreux as a Founder of Chapels: Patronage and Public Piety." In *Women and Art in Early Modern Europe: Patrons, Collectors, and Connoisseurs,* edited by Cynthia Lawrence, 21–36. University Park: Pennsylvania State University Press, 1997.

BARBARA DRAKE BOEHM

JEWISH WOMEN IN THE MIDDLE AGES. In medieval times, most Jews lived outside the land of Israel in the Muslim worlds of Egypt, North Africa, the Middle East, and Spain; far smaller communities lived in Christian Europe. In both milieus, Jews, beyond paying heavy taxes, constituted an autonomous community, governing their own lives and internal affairs according to the Babylonian Talmud, the comprehensive legal and ethical compendium codified in Iraq in the mid-sixth century C.E. While Talmudic legislation recognized women's human rights and physical and emotional needs, rabbinic Judaism generally relegated females to secondary, enabling roles. However, the norms and customs of local environments were also central in defining women's opportunities, since Jews tended to adopt the language, dress, and many of the mores of their gentile neighbors. Women's voices are all but absent from the Jewish Middle Ages; aside from a few letters, the relevant primary sources for this period were written by men. These include *responsa* literature (legal queries and responses) and law codes, marriage and divorce documents, historical chronicles, letters, and ethical wills, and economic, religious, and literary works.

The documents of the Cairo Genizah, an abandoned synagogue and communal archive rediscovered in 1890s, are a major source of information about women in the large and prosperous urban mercantile Jewish communities of the Muslim world, particularly from the ninth to the twelfth century. Polygyny was not uncommon in this environment, and adherence to rabbinic norms and Muslim practice dictated that woman's place was in the home. Nevertheless, Genizah accounts of marital disputes indicate that some wives insisted on freedom of movement. Girls were married at thirteen or fourteen, usually to considerably older husbands chosen by their parents; spouses were often from within the extended family. Marrying daughters outside the family, however, often across considerable distances, was an opportunity for merchant families to form strategic business alliances. The marriage contract (*ketubbah*) detailed each spouse's financial and personal obligations and could record the material objects the bride brought into the marriage and their value. Wealthy parents might insist on special clauses altering Jewish laws and practices unfavorable to women, including guarantees that a husband would leave a divorce document (*get*) with his wife prior to geographic separation; that he would not take another wife, and that he would not be physically abusive. For less fortunate women, Genizah documents reflect problems stemming from polygynous (more than one wife) households and men's sexual relations with female household servants. Agreements grant equal rights to co-wives, the husband generally undertaking to alternate nights with each spouse, while several rabbinic leaders encouraged married men who had affairs with slave girls to emancipate and marry them.

Most women were involved in economic endeavors, mostly through needlework; enterprising brokers collected other women's spun threads, textiles, and embroidery and sold them to merchants. The Genizah also refers to "bride-combers," midwives, female specialists in eye diseases, and "washers," who prepared the dead for burial. Other women taught needle skills, were astrologers, or served as caretakers of synagogues and schools, offices bestowed as communal charity. Wealthy women owned property; a substantial businesswoman of early twelfth-century Cairo was Karima ("The Dear One"), known as al-Wuhsha ("Object of Yearning") the Broker, whose independent life and unconventional activities are documented in Genizah records.

The *responsa* of the Spanish-born sage Moses ben Maimon (Maimonides, 1135–1204), who lived most of his adult life in Cairo, refers to a woman who ran a primary school for boys with her sons, but this evidence of female learning is unusual. Significant religious education or even literacy among Jewish women was rare, although daughters of elite families could be exceptions. A twelfth-century Jewish traveler from France reported the possibly apocryphal story of the daughter of a community leader in Baghdad, an only child, who was so expert in Scriptures and Talmud that she instructed young men through a curtained window. Two poems by Qasmunah survive in an anthology of Arabic poetry. She was probably the daughter of the famous court Jew, Samuel ibn Nagrela haNagid of Granada, Spain (d. 1056), himself an outstanding Hebrew poet. Most frequently, Genizah writers praise women for scrupulously observing home-based laws and for attending synagogue, where they were confined to separate upper galleries. Wealthy women's synagogue donations of Torah scrolls, oil, and books, while piously motivated, may also be read as female strategies for imprinting themselves on a communal and religious realm in which they were otherwise nonentities.

Jewish merchant communities were established in Europe in Roman times. With the advent of Christianity, Jews became subject to increasing legal disabilities and by the thirteenth century were barred from virtually any occupation but money lending and often had to wear distinctive clothing and badges. Toward the end of the Middle Ages, Jews were either expelled altogether (England, 1290; France, 1394; Spain, 1492), or were forced to live in crowded and unpleasant ghettoes (German-speaking Europe and Italy). During these later centuries large numbers of Jews moved east to new opportunities in Poland. Significant Jewish linguistic acculturation to medieval Christian society is evident in women's names; appellations like Alemandina, Blanche, Brunetta, Chera, Columbina, Duzelina, Fleur de Lys, and Glorietta are far more common than Hebrew names. (Jewish women in the Muslim realm also tended to have picturesque names of Arabic derivation.)

Jewish women in Christian Europe, who were active participants in the family economy, had greater mobility and higher status than Jewish women in the Islamic milieu, indicated, in part, by their large dowries, significant portions of their parents' property. Substantial dowries reflected well on a family's social status and assured a wife a prominent financial position in her own household. This social reality and Christian cultural influences explain the *takkanah* (legal alteration) attributed to Rabbi Gershom ben Judah of Mainz (c.960–1028), the first great rabbinic authority of Western European (Ashkenazic) Jewry, forbidding polygyny for Jews in Christian countries. He is also credited with the *takkanah* that no woman could be divorced against her will. Jewish girls were married at eleven or twelve to husbands of almost the same age; motivations for such early unions included the desire to shield offspring from sexual temptations that might lead to sin, as well as the pragmatic economic concern to establish young couples as expeditiously as possible. While settling a young daughter well increased her family's prestige, a broken engagement might harm a family's future marriage possibilities; thus, an eleventh-century *takkanah* imposed a ban of excommunication against those who violated a betrothal agreement; in most cases it was applied to bridegrooms and their families. Another indication of women's prominent social status was the rabbinic prohibition of spousal abuse; wife-beating as grounds for divorce was taken far more seriously in Ashkenaz than in other parts of the Jewish world.

Marital harmony was a central value for medieval Jews; pleasurable sexual activity was seen as an essential component of marriage, and several twelfth- and thirteenth-century rabbinic authorities allowed the use of the *mokh*, a cervical sponge or cap, for marital intercourse without fear of pregnancy. Such positive attitudes about marital sexuality contrasted with Christian religious teachings enjoining celibacy on clerics and restricting sexual activity within marriage to procreation. The Church also forbade divorce, frowned on remarriage after the death of a spouse, and had strict rules on consanguinity that forbade marriages between relatives, including first cousins (a common match in the Jewish community) as incestuous. It is not surprising that Christian writers condemned Jewish sexual behavior, real and imagined, nor that Jews were often perplexed by Christian teachings. Influence from the Christian environment may account for the ambivalence toward sexuality characteristic of the German-Jewish pietists of the twelfth and thirteenth centuries, the *Hasidei Ashkenaz,* whose writings, such as *Sefer Hasidim* (*The Book of the Pious*), express not only an obsessive awareness of the ubiquity of extramarital sexual temptations, but also a profound ambivalence about the joys of licensed sexual activities since they could distract a man from God, who should be the focus of his greatest and most intense devotion.

Women often took the initiative in business matters and were particularly involved in money lending; sometimes they supported their families so their husbands could devote themselves to study. Like the Christian women among whom they lived, Jewish women had significant freedom of movement. An example of a highly successful Jewish businesswoman in thirteenth-century England was Licoricia of Winchester who had direct business dealings with the king. Her five sons, who described themselves as "sons of Licoricia," also became moneylenders, continuing their mother's business after her murder in 1277. Some women were probably artisans who practiced the trades of their fathers or husbands; Christian sources refer to independent Jewish women who practiced medicine. Midwives and wet nurses are well documented in Spain, and the existence of obstetrical treatises in Hebrew, apparently intended for female midwives, indicate that some women were literate in that language.

For most women, education meant literacy in the vernacular (always written in Hebrew characters), mastery of the mathematics essential for complex business transactions, and the acquisition of housekeeping skills that included knowledge of religious regulations required for Jewish domestic observance and marriage. Some women from learned families may have had some knowledge of Hebrew and religious texts. Elite women taught other women and led worship; among those described as women's prayer leaders are Dulce of Worms (d. 1196), wife of Rabbi Eleazar of Worms, and Urania of Worms (thirteenth century), whose headstone epitaph commemorates her as a cantor's daughter who "with sweet tunefulness" led the women's singing. A Latin letter in the Archive of the Crown of

Aragon, dating from 1325, refers to Çeti of Zaragoza as a *"rabissa,"* who served as a salaried synagogue leader of Jewish women for twenty years.

Since most ordinary Jewish women were ignorant of Hebrew and could not read the traditional liturgy and holy books, and since women were not obligated to participate in communal synagogue services, many women recited prayers in the vernacular, a practice sanctioned by the rabbinic leadership. While many of these prayers, some of which were written by women, closely followed the synagogue liturgy, others were intended for events particular to women's lives such as baking Sabbath loaves, or immersion in the ritual bath. With the invention of printing, this women's vernacular literature of supplicatory prayers (*tkhines*), together with simplified "women's Bibles" and ethical writings, began to be available widely.

Many Jewish women, although unconcerned with enlarging their religious knowledge or obligations beyond the household sphere, were genuinely pious. The thirteenth century *Sefer Hasidim* preserves several passages praising women's piety and their philanthropy. Similarly, women appear to have been less likely than men to choose the available option of conversion to Christianity. Chronicles of the First Crusade document the courage of Jewish women who preferred death for themselves and their children to apostasy. Another example of such loyalty is Pulcellina, a moneylender who had extensive dealings with Count Theobald of Blois; she perished together with thirty other Jews as the result of a ritual murder accusation in 1171, apparently fueled by jealousy and intrigue in Theobald's court.

Romantic liaisons between Jews and Christians were not uncommon; an eleventh-century letter found in the Cairo genizah, probably from Monieux, France, sought economic support for a female convert who had left a noble Christian family to become a Jew. Her Jewish husband was killed in an attack on their community, two older children were taken captive, and she was left bereft with an infant. Sexual relationships that crossed religious boundaries were particularly common in areas where contacts between Jews and gentiles were friendly such as Spain, Provence, and Italy; in all locations they were denounced by both Jewish and Christian leaders, and efforts to prevent sexual contacts probably underlie Church decrees that Jewish women wear a badge or humiliating attire at younger ages than Jewish men and attempts to prevent Jews from hiring Christian maidservants.

Serious study of medieval Jewish women is in its infancy. Future research will delineate the varying impact of Jewish law and local custom and culture on the conduct of everyday life, as well as advance more detailed understandings of the involvement of women in business activities and Jewish communal, intellectual, and religious life in the Muslim and Christian worlds.

See also Celibacy; Guilds, Women in; Kharja; Law, Canon, Women in; Law, Women in, Anglo-Saxon England; Marriage; Medicine and Medieval Women; Slaves

BIBLIOGRAPHY

Primary Sources
[Cairo Genizah Archive] Goitein, Shlomo Dov. *A Mediterranean Society*, vol. 3: *The Family*. Berkeley: University of California Press, 1978. All vols. abridged into one, edited by Jacob Lassner (Berkeley: University of California Press, 1999).
[Translations from Various Primary Documents]. Fine, Lawrence, ed. *Judaism in Practice: From the Middle Ages through the Early Modern Period*. Princeton, N.J.: Princeton University Press, 1999.

Secondary Sources

Abramson, Henry. "A Ready Hatred: Depictions of the Jewish Woman in Medieval Antisemitic Art and Caricature." *Proceedings of the American Academy for Jewish Research* 62 (1996): 1–18.

Baskin, Judith R. "Jewish Women in the Middle Ages." In *Jewish Women in Historical Perspective*, edited by Judith R. Baskin, 101–27. 2nd ed. Detroit: Wayne State University Press, 1998.

Einbender, Susan. "Jewish Women Martyrs: Changing Representations." *Exemplaria* 12 (2000): 105–28.

———. "Pucellina of Blois: Romantic Myths and Narrative Conventions." *Jewish History* 12 (1998): 29–46.

Friedman, Mordechai A. "Marriage as an Institution: Jewry under Islam." In *The Jewish Family: Metaphor and Memory*, edited by David Kraemer, 31–45. New York: Oxford University Press, 1989.

Grossman, Avraham. *Pious and Rebellious: Jewish Women in Europe in the Middle Ages.* Jerusalem: Zalman Shazar Center for Jewish History, 2001. [In Hebrew].

Jordan, William C. "Jews on Top: Women and the Availability of Consumption Loans in Northern France in the Mid-Thirteenth Century." *Journal of Jewish Studies* 29 (1978): 39–56.

Melammed, Renée Levine. "Sephardic Women in the Medieval and Early Modern Period." In *Jewish Women in Historical Perspective*, edited by Judith R. Baskin, 128–49. 2nd ed. Detroit: Wayne State University Press, 1998.

Stow, Kenneth R. *Alienated Minority: The Jews of Medieval Latin Europe.* Cambridge, Mass.: Harvard University Press, 1992.

Taitz, Emily. "Women's Voices, Women's Prayers: Women in the European Synagogue of the Middle Ages." In *Daughters of the King: Women and the Synagogue*, edited by Susan Grossman and Rivka Haut, 59–71. Philadelphia: Jewish Publication Society, 1992.

Weissler, Chava. *Voices of the Matriarchs: Listening to the Prayers of Early Modern Jewish Women.* Boston: Beacon Press, 1998.

JUDITH R. BASKIN

JOAN, FAIR MAID OF KENT (1328–1385). The life of Joan, princess of Wales, as recorded in chronicles, historical documents, and story, illustrates how medieval women were both independent agents capable of exercising power, and at the same time constrained by custom and powerful institutions. She was born in 1328, the third child and only daughter of Edmund of Woodstock, earl of Kent and youngest son of Edward I. She became his heir on the death of her brothers and was invested with the livery of her title in 1353. While in her adolescence she contracted marriage with two men. In 1339 she entered into a marriage with Sir Thomas de Holland, and in 1340, during Holland's absence abroad, she married William Montague (Montacute), earl of Salisbury. In 1349 a papal court annulled the second marriage and confirmed the validity of the first marriage. She had one child with Thomas de Holland, a son, Thomas, born in 1350. Widowed in 1360, she married Edward, prince of Wales, known as the Black Prince, on October 10, 1361, reputedly in a clandestine marriage that was later publicly celebrated at the court of Edward III. Chroniclers (Froissart; Chandos Herald) record that she was an extraordinarily beautiful woman; the Chandos Herald describes her as "une dame de grant pris . . . Qe bele fuist|plesante et sage" ("a lady of great worth . . . who was beautiful, pleasful, pleasing and wise"). Modern historians have dubbed her "The Fair Maid of Kent" (*DNB*). Legend has it that she is the countess of Salisbury whose ribbon garter originated the Order of the Garter (Galway; McKisack).

On her marriage to Edward, the Black Prince, Edward III invested the prince of Wales with the title of prince of Aquitaine and Joan and the Black Prince took up residence in Aquitaine in 1362, where they established a luxurious court, in large part supported by her wealth. T. F. Tout notes that her income greatly exceeded her husband's during this period. While she was in France she gave birth to two sons. In 1365, on the birth of the elder, Edward, the Black Prince kept "a great feast, justis, and tournay, of xl [40] knightes and as many squiers, for the love of the princesse, who was brought to bedde of a faire sonne called Edwarde" (Froissart/Berners). A second son, Richard, who would become Richard II, was born in 1367 at Bordeaux.

As was typical of medieval noblewomen, Joan was a partner to the prince of Wales in maintaining the honor, the security, and the stability of their lands. Historians infer from the record of her activities that as princess of Wales she was an active mediator in the complex world she lived in and helped to shape. Froissart recounts several instances of Joan's intervention in political events. One episode tells how, in dealing with various noblemen in southwestern France, she persuaded the count of Foix, to forgive the count of Armagnac a debt of "threscore thousande frankes [60,000 francs]" (Froissart/Berners), and of how she protected the prince's lands when King Henry, "the bastarde of Spayne," threatened "to make warr to the principalyte and to the duchy of Guyen [Guienne], wherwith she was greatly abasshed"; she wrote to the King of France, enlisting his help (Froissart/Berners). In 1370 her elder son, Edward (1365–1370), died and the household returned to England. Over the course of the 1370s, the Black Prince's health worsened, until he died in 1376. His father, Edward III, died shortly thereafter, in 1377, leaving the crown to Richard.

As mother of the king, Joan's household was of paramount importance. The Black Prince's will had designated a group of his retainers as members of a council of *magistri* (master teachers) to raise Richard of Bordeaux. Joan was an important member of this group (McKisack). She also aligned herself with John of Gaunt during this period of Richard's minority (*Chronicon Angliae*; Walsingham). During the years from 1377 to her death in 1385, the historical record shows her interceding in a number of important political disputes, directing the protection of her lands, and moving to consolidate her power and holdings (McKisack; *Close Rolls*, I and II). McKisack notes that while she was an active figure, she was "in no sense a political intriguer." As a widow and as mother of the king, just as she had been as wife in Aquitaine, Joan was uniquely placed to exercise the kind of power another illustrious widow, the French poet and moralizer, Christine de Pizan, would later ascribe to Queen Isabeau of France, also mother of a future king, in her *Epistre a la reine* (*Epistle to the Queen*, 1405): the role of *moyennerresse* ("mediator-ess"), an independent mediator and broker of peace.

The historical record shows that her alignment with John of Gaunt also brought her into contact with the rebellious theologian John Wyclif (1328–c.1384) and with his followers, the group of men loosely described as Lollard knights—priests who, disillusioned with the corrupt Church in England, went about preaching the virtue of poverty. A papal bull of 1377 seems to single her out as an agent in the dangerous game of religion and politics (*Chronicon Angliae*, 1). Her household sounds like a roster of Chaucer's companions; her will mentions Lewis Clifford, William Neville, Simon Burley, John Clanvowe, and Richard Stury (Nicholls). When Richard II marched north to Scotland in 1385, he ordered Sir Lewis

Clifford, Sir Richard Stury, and Sir Philip le Vache, among others, to "assist continually about the person of the King's mother for her comfort and security" (*Close Rolls*, 1381–1385). Margaret Galway has argued that Joan of Kent was Chaucer's patron and a model for the figure of Alceste. While much of the argument has been discredited, it is also true that Joan of Kent's household included the men the *Chaucer Life Records* link closely to him. Her relationship to the art and learning is not clear; McKisack notes that the Franciscan John Somer wrote an astronomical calendar for her.

In the years between 1377, when Richard ascended to the throne, and 1385, when Joan died, her name appears regularly in chronicles, mediating John of Gaunt's difficulties with the city of London (*Chronicon Angliae*, 1, 1377), interrupting a trial of John Wyclif in 1378 (*Historia Anglicana*, 1), present with Richard in the Tower of London during the most chaotic hours of the Peasants' Revolt of 1381 (*Anonimalle Chronicle*), and reconciling Richard and his uncle, John of Gaunt, after a 1385 plot on the duke's life (*Westminster Chronicle*). Joan's last recorded attempt at mediation, in which she appealed for leniency from Richard toward his half-brother, Thomas Holland, who slew the earl of Stafford. On this occasion, saddened because she was unable to bring about peace, as the *Chronicon Angliae* puts it, she lay down and after four or five days made her farewell to the world in early August, 1385.

See also Anne of Bohemia; Chaucer, Geoffrey, Women in the Work of; Christine de Pizan; Isabeau of Bavaria

BIBLIOGRAPHY

Primary Sources
The Anonimalle Chronicle 1333 to 1381. Edited by V. H. Galbraith. Manchester, U.K.: Manchester University Press, 1927.
Berners, Lord. See under Froissart, Jean *below.*
Chandos Herald. *Life of the Black Prince by the Herald of Sir John Chandos*. Edited by Mildred K. Pope and Eleanor C. Lodge. Oxford: Clarendon Press, 1910.
Chaucer Life Records. Edited by Martin M. Crow and Clair C. Olson. Oxford: Oxford University Press, 1966.
Christine de Pizan. In "Christine de Pizan's *Epistre a la reine* (1405)." Edited by Angus J. Kennedy. *Revue des langues romanes* 92 (1988): 253–64. [Authoritative ed. but original Middle-French text only].
———. In *Christine de Pizan:* The Epistle of the Prison of Human Life, *with* An Epistle to the Queen of France *and* Lament on the Evils of Civil War, edited and translated by Josette A. Wisman, 70–83. Library of Medieval Literature: A, 21. New York and London: Garland Publishing, 1984. [Bilingual ed.]
Chronicon Angliae. Edited by Edward Maunde Thompson. 2 vols. London: Longmans, 1874.
Close Rolls. Supplementary Close Roll No. 14 in *Calendar of the Close Rolls: Richard II, vol. 1: 1377–81*. London: Public Record Office, 1914.
DNB = *Dictionary of National Biography from the Earliest Times to 1900*. Edited by Sir Leslie Stephen and Sir Sidney Lee. 22 vols. Oxford: Oxford University Press, 1973.
Froissart, Jean. *Chroniques de J. Froissart*. Edited by Siméon Luce, Gaston Raynaud and Léon Mirot et al. 15 vols. Société de l'Histoire de France. Paris: Jules Renouard, 1869–1975.
———. *The Chronicles of Froissart. Translated out of the French by John Bourchier, Lord Berners annis 1523–25*. 6 vols. The Tudor Translations, 1st Series, 27–32. London: D. Nutt, 1901–1903.
John of Gaunt's Register, 1372–1376. Edited by Sidney Armitage-Smith. 2 vols. Camden 3rd Series, 21. London: Camden Society, 1911.
John of Gaunt's Register, 1379–1383. Edited by Eleanor Lodge and Robert Somerville. 2 vols. Camden 3rd Series, 57. London: Camden Society, 1937.

Knighton's Chronicle 1337–1396. Edited by G. H. Martin. Oxford: Oxford University Press, 1995.

Nicholls, John, ed. *A Collection of All the Wills Now Known to be Extant, of the Kings and Queens of England....* London, 1780.

Walsingham, Thomas. *Historia Anglicana.* 2 vols. Edited by Henry Thomas Riley. London: Longmans, 1863–1864.

The Westminster Chronicle 1381–1394. Edited by L. C. Hector and Barbara F. Harvey, Oxford: Oxford University Press, 1982.

Secondary Sources

Collette, Carolyn P. "Joan of Kent and Noble Women's Roles in Chaucer's World." *Chaucer Review* 33 (1999): 350–62.

Galway, Margaret. "Chaucer's Sovereign Lady: A Study of the Prologue to the *Legend* and Related Poems," *Modern Language Review* 33 (1938): 145–99.

Given-Wilson, Chris. *The Royal Household and the King's Affinity: Service, Politics and Finance in England 1360–1413.* New Haven, Conn.: Yale University Press, 1986.

McKisack, May. *The Fourteenth Century, 1307–1399.* Oxford: Clarendon Press, 1959.

Ormrod, W. M. "In Bed with Joan of Kent: The King's Mother and the Peasant's Revolt." In *Medieval Women: Texts and Contexts in Late Medieval Britain,* edited by Jocelyn Wogan-Browne et al., 277–92. Turnhout, Belgium: Brepols, 2000.

Tout, T. F. *Chapters in the Administrative History of Medieval England,* vol. 5. Manchester: Manchester University Press, 1928.

CAROLYN P. COLLETTE

JOAN, POPE (c.1255). Pope Joan refers to a story that a woman disguised as a man may have occupied the papacy during the ninth century. This fiction, traceable to c.1255 in the chronicle by the Dominican Jean de Mailly, was held to be true throughout the rest of the Middle Ages until steps were taken to refute it during the sixteenth century.

The episode of Pope Joan, whose veracity continues to be fervently debated up through the present day (see Bibliography), enjoyed immense popularity, not only for its novelistic allure but also because it put into play a prohibition fundamental to the Catholic Church: the exclusion of women from the priesthood, let alone the papacy. It also posed the disturbing question: What happens when a supreme, divinely sanctioned power is usurped? The legend thus played a powerful role in the complex controversies surrounding the Church and its leadership from the thirteenth century onward. At the time of the Great Schism (1378–1417), during which at least two popes (one at Avignon, one at Rome) each claimed to be the rightful one, the tale of Pope Joan was cited in legal trials to justify the nullification of a papal election. The Hussites (an early reform movement founded by Jan Hus [John Huss], who was burned for heresy 1415) in the fifteenth century and then the Protestant reform movements in the sixteenth century found in Pope Joan a strikingly useful symbol of Catholic corruption.

Pope Joan's history stabilized rapidly in the following version: in about 850, a woman born in Mainz, Germany, but of English extraction, disguised herself as a man to follow her studious lover into the university, which excluded women. For her part, she distinguished herself so well at her studies that, after a scholarly sojourn at Athens, she was warmly and admiringly received at Rome, where she entered the Church hierarchy, rising to the papal curia (court) and soon was elected pope, succeeding, according to later versions, Leo IV in 855. Her pontificate lasted two years, then was interrupted by scandal.

Pope Joan, hanging in Rome with her child in her arms. © Charles Walker/Topfoto/The Image Works.

Joan, who had not renounced the pleasures of the flesh, found herself pregnant and died during a procession from St. Peter's (the Vatican) to St. John Lateran after giving birth in public. Various versions of the account produced clues, proof, and a recollection of the "popess." Thereafter, the gender of all popes about to be crowned would be verified manually. Furthermore, pontifical processions would take a detour (by the Church of San Clemente) from the direct route between St. Peter's and St. John Lateran to avoid the site where Pope Joan allegedly gave birth. A statue or an inscription would have eternalized the memory of this deplorable incident.

It is difficult to establish the origins of this story, which appeared for the first time in a convent chronicle compiled in c.1255 by the Dominican Jean de Mailly at Metz in Lorraine in northeastern France. The rapidity and geographic breadth of the legend's dissemination led one to suspect a rumor concerning a woman pope had already been circulating for some time, especially around Rome, before being fixed on paper. Whatever its precise roots, the legend spread among primarily Dominican centers via versions by authors Étienne de Bourbon (1261), Arnoldus of Liège (1307), and, especially, Martinus Polonus (Martin the Pole, Martin of Opava/Troppau, author of a widely read universal chronicle, 1280–1285, variant in 1300), and also among the Franciscans. She also figures in male-authored catalogues of women like Boccaccio's *De mulieribus claris* (*Famous Women*, 1362–1375, ch. 101) and Heinrich Agrippa von Nettesheim's *De nobilitate et praecellentia foeminei sexus* (*The Nobility and Excellence of the Feminine Sex*, c.1530, ch. 32)—with the former retaining Joan's scandalous finale and the latter reverently omitting it. Christine de Pizan excludes her from her *Cité des Dames* (*City of Ladies*, 1404–1405), doubtless for feminist reasons. Many authors would allude to her story (see Boureau for a complete list of references to Joan through the centuries). The papacy itself facilitated the legend's enduring credibility by preserving the famous San Clemente detour during the coronation parade, and, in 1474,

Pope Joan's story was entered into the humanist Bartolomeo Platina's *Liber de vita Christi ac de vitis summorum pontificum omnium* (*Lives of the Popes*), published in Venice in 1479.

See also Boccaccio, Women in, *De Claris Mulieribus*; Christine de Pizan; Guglielmites; Law, Canon, Women in; Transvestism

BIBLIOGRAPHY

Primary Sources
[See also notes in Boureau, Secondary Sources, below].
Arnoldus of Liège. [*Alphabetum narrationum*]. *An Alphabet of Tales.* Edited by Mary M. Banks. Early English Text Society, 126–27. London: Kegan Paul, 1904–1905. Reprint Millwood, N.Y.: Kraus, 1972. [Fifteenth century Middle-English ed. from 1307 Latin original, not yet in printed ed.].
Étienne de Bourbon. *Stephani de Borbone Tractatus de diversis materiis praedicabilibus.* Edited by Jacques Berlioz and Jean-Luc Eichenlaub, [fol. 574ra]. Turnhout, Belgium: Brepols, 2002. [Latin text, French intro].
Jean de Mailly. *Chronica Universalis Mettensis. Monumenta Germaniae Historica.* [= MGH], 24: 514.
Martin the Pole. *Chronicon pontificum et imperatorum.* In MGH *Scriptores rerum germanicarum in usum scholarum,* 22: 428.
———. *The Chronicles of Rome. . . .* Edited by Dan Embree. Medieval Chronicles, 1. Woodbridge, U.K. and Rochester, N.Y.: Boydell Press, 1999. [Bilingual Middle English-English ed.].
———. [Continuation of Martin's *Chronicle*]. *Fortsetzungen zur Papst- und Kaiserchronik Martins von Troppau aus England.* Edited Wolfgang-G. Ikas. MGH. *Scriptores rerum Germanicarum,* n.s., 19. Hannover, Germany: Hahn, 2003.

Secondary Sources
Boureau, Alain. *La Papesse Jeanne.* Paris: Aubier, 1988. Reprint Flammarion, 1993.
———. *The Myth of Pope Joan.* Translated by Lydia G. Cochrane. Chicago: University of Chicago Press, 2001.
Helder, Ebba M. van der. *Pope Joan in Legend and Drama: A Case Study in German Medieval Drama.* Gordon Anderson Memorial Lecture, 5. Armidale, New South Wales: University of New England, 1987.
Pardoe, Rosemary A., and Darroll Pardoe. *The Female Pope: The Mystery of Pope Joan.* Wellingborough, U.K.: Crucible; New York: Sterling, 1988.
Stanford, Peter. *The Legend of Pope Joan: In Search of the Truth.* New York: Henry Holt, 1999. Original *The She-Pope.* London: W. Heinemann, 1998.

ALAIN BOUREAU

JOAN OF ARC, ST. (c.1412–1431). Although heroine of France, Joan of Arc remains one of the most disputed figures in history, and the person about whom more has been written, painted, sculpted, and filmed than any other figure save perhaps for Jesus Christ. Infinite controversies surrounded her both during her lifetime and ever thereafter, whether as historical personage or mythical persona. Every detail of her brief life, whether fanciful or true, has been recorded as part of a saintly progress and martyr's passion.

Born in Domremy, in Lorraine, near what is now the border between France and Germany, during the Hundred Years War, Joan had three brothers and one sister. Her parents, Jacques d'Arc (or, depending on dialect, d'Ay, Day, Tart) and Isabelle Romée (so named supposedly for her or an ancestor's pilgrimage to Rome), were relatively well-off country folk. Joan was educated in the manner of most young girls of her milieu, with an emphasis on sewing, cooking, homemaking, and assisting with farm work. Religion also

Sur la Route de la Victoire.

Joan of Arc on the road to victory. Patriotic image from 1916. Courtesy of the Centre Jeanne d'Arc, Orleans.

playing an important part in a young girl's upbringing, Joan's basic beliefs and prayers came mainly from her mother, plus the village priest's sermons and some preaching from local Mendicant friars (Dominicans, Franciscans, and similar nonconvent-bound orders). The neighboring Bois Chenu (Oak Forest) also provided a folkloric venue for local seasonal celebrations as well as a favorite imaginative play area for children. On the less idyllic side, Joan grew up during the latter part of the Hundred Years War (1337–1453), in which France, repeatedly beaten by the English—most resoundingly at Agincourt (1415)—became divided into two major warring factions: the *Bourguignons* (Anglo-Burgundians: loyal to England's claim over France) and the *Armagnacs* (loyal to Charles the dauphin as legitimate king). In 1420, by signing the Treaty of Troyes yielding to the victorious Henry V, the dauphin's mentally unstable father, Charles VI, gave away his son's succession rights to Henry VI of England. Both Henry V and Charles VI died in 1422. Because Joan's village belonged to one of the last pockets of Armagnac resistance to English domination, Domremy and its environs were subjected to brutal raids by the Anglo-Burgundians from 1425 to 1428. Amid all of these events and influences, Joan began to experience mystical visions at age twelve or thirteen: initially frightening, then engaging, confrontations, visually and aurally of light and voices—these later identified as saints Michael, Katherine and Margaret—who would convince her that she was destined to have the Charles the dauphin crowned and liberate France from the English. This latter, postcoronation phase, a bit hazily defined, would later prove crucial to Joan's fate.

Convincing those in power of her mission, even the first phase enabling Charles to have a proper coronation at Reims, would be her first exploit. In May 1428, she tried to persuade her local leader at the "county seat" of Vaucouleurs, Captain Baudricourt, but was rebuffed. After the announcement of the siege of Orléans (1429), a major city on the western side of France held captive by the English, Joan tried twice again with Baudricourt, who sent her to the duke of Lorraine and his son-in-law, René of Anjou, who granted her safe conduct. Baudricourt, impressed by Joan's persistence and zeal (and a mysteriously accurate announcement of the outcome of the Battle of the Herrings), finally agreed to give her an escort to traverse France westward to Chinon, the dauphin's headquarters (since the English held Paris, like much else) in February 1429.

Thus accompanied, she managed to pass through Anglo-Burgundian territory to arrive at Chinon probably in early March 1429; her arrival was preceded by lively rumors about her. Hundreds of pages can be read on her interview with the dauphin. The most salient aspect, the "secret"—whatever she revealed to Charles privately that convinced him of her credibility—has been theorized variously as a prayer, proclamation, or birthmark. Whatever form it took, Joan's secret communication to Charles reassured him that God had forgiven his part in the murder of Duke John of Burgundy (1419, which had moved his son and successor, Philip of Burgundy, to shift his allegiance from the dauphin to England), and also that he, Charles, was the legitimate king of France in God's eyes, despite Anglo-Burgundian propaganda. Charles—after receiving some letters from Jacques Gelu, archbishop of Embrun, and the treatise *De quadam puella* (*On a Certain Girl*), often ascribed to France's most distinguished Churchman, Jean Gerson (1363–1429)—had Joan interrogated at what would be Joan's first trial, before noted theologians at Poitiers (March 11, 1429) (see Fraioli). This and an examination by select noblewomen certified her virginity and the orthodoxy of her religious beliefs, despite Joan's masculine clothing and extraordinary self-pronouncements. Charles therefore gave her some servants and allowed her to ride with a convoy carrying reinforcements to Orléans. She was also given armor and a standard, while she herself obtained her sword at Sainte-Catherine-de-Fierbois (another mystery: how did she know of it?).

At first the battle-hardened French professional soldiers disdained her as a companion-in-arms, and even more so as *chef de guerre* (military leader). The English replied equally rudely to the ultimatum-bearing letter she wrote them (March 22, 1429), imploring them to surrender to Charles. Furthermore, her first contact with John, Bastard of Orléans (1402–1468; so-called because he was the natural son of Louis, duke of Orléans), before his besieged city, on April 29, 1429, was less than blissful.

But after May 4, when the French regained the small fortress of Saint-Loup (about two miles east of Orléans) and cost the English many men, things changed. Joan "the Maid" (*Jeanne la Pucelle*)—she never called herself Joan of Arc (*Jeanne d'Arc*), preferring to capitalize on the mystique of her youth and virginity—showed herself to be not only a sort of good-luck charm, but also managed, by her active presence on the battlefield, to turn the tide of victory. Because she never left them during those months, she managed to win over her royal captains: Xaintrailles, La Hire, Boussac, Gilles de Laval (de Rais, the future Bluebeard), and the bastard of Orléans, count of Dunois, later joined by John, duke of Alençon. On May 6, Joan was present when the French took back the *bastille* (walled, fortified station) of the Augustinians just across the river Loire from Orléans, and then, despite taking an arrow above her breast (as she had predicted), she led the French through the ferocious combat needed to take the bridge to Orléans called Les Tourelles on May 7 and thus end the seven-month siege, with the English leaving without further combat, on May 8, 1429. The procession of Thanksgiving, begun with a mass at the cathedral, held by the grateful Orléanais inaugurated the annual celebration—the oldest French civic holiday—which continues to this day.

Joan had thus accomplished part of her announced mission, but there remained the recapture of Meung, Beaugency, and Patay (this last battle in particular, on June 18, considered by historians to be mirror-opposite revenge for Agincourt) to secure the route to Reims for Charles's coronation. This phase of her campaign was also facilitated by jubilant but forceful letters Joan dictated and sent in advance to certain other towns

(Tournai, Troyes) imploring their support along the coronation route. As a result, Charles was crowned at Reims, anointed with the Holy Chrism that made him the true king of France. Equally commanding at the ceremony, if not more so, was the figure of Joan standing with her banner: an enduring image in royalist iconography.

It was after the coronation that her troubles began, since this next phase was less well defined by her voices. Historians continue to debate its implications. Should she have considered her mission complete at that point? Did she become so imbued with self-importance that she misinterpreted and overstepped the bounds of her voices' orders? Did the new king become jealous of her, or was he simply ill advised? How did Charles the king and Philip, duke of Burgundy, seek to exploit her situation to make a truce? It is difficult to decide who betrayed whom for certain. But the incontrovertible fact is there: Joan's military momentum suffered a major blow in the Île-de-France (region including Paris and environs) as she, with Alençon, attempted unsuccessfully to take Paris by attacking the Saint-Honoré Gate on September 8, 1429, after which the king ordered the Paris campaign abandoned and the royal army dissolved at Gien (September 21). However, to keep Joan occupied without further threatening Charles's political agenda (which had by now excluded her), she was given some men-at-arms and dispatched to deal with a rogue bandit chieftain troublesome to both sides, Perrinet Gressart. After wresting Saint-Pierre-le-Moûtier from him (November 4), Joan then lay siege to Gressart's capital, La Charité-sur-Loire, at which she failed, due to lack of expected reinforcements from neighboring towns, in mid-November.

To placate her without actually helping her that winter, Charles issued letters patent to ennoble her family, through both male and female lines. More hollow gestures of gratitude by La Trémouïlle, Joan's wiliest enemy at the royal court, ushered in the year 1430. Unswerving in her sense of mission, however, Joan nurtured new plans for war and wrote more letters to reassure her supporters during March. Her concerns were justified, for Philip of Burgundy kept delaying the actual promised truce with Charles, and then even planned an offensive in the Île-de-France, aided by the duke of Luxembourg, for April. Even after officially realizing that Philip's truce was but a ruse in early May, Charles by then could do nothing to fortify Joan's army, by now a mix of mostly Franco-Italian (Piemontese) volunteers and mercenaries that had set out in late April to campaign around the Île-de-France: Lagny, Soissons, and Compiègne, north of Paris. At Compiègne, a town supposedly favorable to Joan, she was caught by the enemy outside the city's gates on May 23, 1430—some say the mayor, Flavy, had been bribed by the Anglo-Burgundians to lock her out.

Seized by John of Luxembourg, Burgundy's man, Joan was then ransomed to the English for 10,000 crowns—again little or no apparent attempt by Charles to rescue her—whereupon would begin her arduous prison itinerary, despite the normally short distance between Compiègne (where she was captured) and Rouen (where she would stand trial). She attempted to escape from Beaulieu tower, then from Beaurevoir, after which she ceased to enjoy the privileges accorded a noblewoman prisoner (supervised by other women) and was thereafter guarded by men only. Once at Rouen (December 23, 1430), she was guarded by the soldiers under the earl of Warwick, Richard Beauchamp (1382–1439), the gray eminence behind her trial proceedings. The University of Paris, France's theological and legal bastion, now unfortunately under English control, would conduct and staff Joan's trial. John, duke of Bedford and regent of France (the newly crowned King Charles still carefully lying low) subjected her to an inquisitorial process to discredit her claims of divine inspiration that so demoralized the English, thereby discrediting Charles's legitimacy in the bargain. A French jurist loyal to the English, Pierre Cauchon, bishop of Beauvais, would preside.

The *beau procès* (beautiful trial), as Cauchon called it, was conducted with the utmost procedural rigor, for its promoters desired only one verdict for Joan: guilty. Lasting from January 9 until May 29, 1431, it was both a political trial (against Charles) and a theological one (against Charles's legitimacy and Joan's claims to divine inspiration), to preserve the prestige of the University of Paris and enforce overall discipline against those refusing to submit to the Church Militant (the Church on earth) by presuming direct contact with the Church Triumphant (Church in Heaven), as Joan did. We know from the available trial records, despite some anti-Joan tinkering during their translation from 2French into the official Latin a few years after the trial, that Joan's deportment was admirable throughout. Deprived of any legal council, she replied to her interrogators with conviction, intelligence, and forthrightness. Her interrogators, seasoned men of law and Church officialdom, used their best ingenuity to trick her into portraying herself as a heretic, yet, for example, when they pushed her to describe precisely her "voices" (Saints Michael, Margaret, and Catherine), she showed herself more adept than these men at interpreting popular religious practices. When they asked her about the "secret" or "sign" given to Charles, she replied via an allegory incomprehensible to her judges. They asked her to submit to the Church Militant, but she first declared she did not know what this meant and then, after explanation, refused. Equally vexing for her judges was the question of her insistence on wearing masculine clothing, which she defended on grounds of practicality in battle—and in prison—in the constant company of men throughout her mission, and also because such attire signified her obedience to her voices. In the end, her judges drew up a list of twelve articles of condemnation against her if she did not repent.

The University of Paris thus found her guilty of being a schismatic, a heretic, liar, and diviner—although they failed to convict her of witchcraft. She also suffered food poisoning, many believe from a rotten fish sent her by Cauchon. In session after session, they alternatingly admonished, berated, and threatened her with torture. Exhausted and weak, on May 24, 1431, Joan signed a recantation—the famous Abjuration—of her voices and her male clothing, at the cemetery of Saint-Ouen, and was led back to prison, there donning women's clothes. Her signing the *cedula*, or abjuration form, whose real length was far shorter than the text later preserved in the trial records, infuriated the English against Cauchon and the other judges because in so doing, Joan was escaping condemnation, since she was now a reformed heretic, which carried a far lighter sentence. Joan, however, was dismayed at having been returned to the English prison of men, despite her new status entitling her, she was promised surveillance by women. For this and other still-debated reasons, Cauchon found her (May 28) again dressed in men's clothing. She was also again citing her voices, specifically Saints Margaret and Catherine, as her guides and denied her intent to renounce them at Saint-Ouen. Joan then declared to Cauchon, the vice-inquisitor and several assessors that her voices made her see that she was "damning myself to save my life." Having thus sealed her fate as a relapsed heretic by, as one notary inscribed his manuscript's margin, this "*Responsio mortifera*" ("a fatal response"), Joan was surrendered to secular authorities to await sentencing. This conformed to proper procedure; however, Cauchon's delivering her to the stake without awaiting a separate secular verdict was highly irregular. Nevertheless, Joan was burned alive at the Rouen marketplace on May 30, 1431, in a spectacle that would forever haunt historical consciousness. This despite Warwick's order, after inspecting her corpse to verify her true gender, that all of her ashes and other remains be thrown into the Seine, to avoid having any of her remains later worshiped as saintly relics.

Little was written in her favor right after this event, save for Martin Le Franc (c.1442), yet dissatisfaction over her fate gradually surfaced. Her rehabilitation came about through a combination of circumstances: Charles, at last joined by Philip of Burgundy and sensing his victory over the English, answered Joan's mother's repeated pleading visits to reopen her daughter's case. In 1449, Charles began reviewing the trial and also requested a new trial from Pope Nicholas V, with his counselor Guillaume Bouillé: this "royal investigation" would last until 1452. The "canonical investigation" by the popes then began, with Calixtus III ordering a new trial in 1455. Charles, having finally managed to expel the English from France at this time, was thus able to have his jurists and inquisitors safely complete their inquiry at Paris, Rouen, Domremy, then Orléans, leading to the nullification of Joan's verdict on July 7, 1456. However, most historians agree that it was really Charles who benefited most from these proceedings in the short term.

Yet in the long term, moving testimony given during her nullification trial, together with such early admirers of Joan during her lifetime as Jean Gerson and Christine de Pizan, would furnish material for countless books, works of visual art and music through the centuries. Probably the most potent, whether true or false, according to one witness, Jean Massieu, was the executioner's affirmation that he found her heart intact and full of blood among her ashes, and Ysambart de la Pierre's recollection of a normally rude English soldier heard lamenting, "We have burned a woman saint." These and other details would inspire either praise or derision from many authors, ranging from Villon (1461), Shakespeare (1592), then Chapelain (1656) and Voltaire (1755). But it was the German Schiller's "romantic tragedy," *Die Jungfrau von Orleans* (*The Maid of Orléans*, 1802) that launched an enormous rebirth of scientific as well as literary interest in her throughout Europe. Historians like Jules Michelet came to her rescue, effectively dubbing her the "soul of France." In the ensuing cultural rivalry between France and Germany, Jules Quicherat published his five-volume critical edition of the trials and related documents—the first, most complete printed record—plus chronicle and literary excerpts (1841–1849), a milestone in Joan of Arc studies. Readers of Quicherat's monument went on to compose their own portraits of the heroine from perspectives as international as those of Americans Mark Twain (*Personal Recollections of Joan of Arc*, 1896) and Maxwell Anderson (*Joan of Lorraine*, 1945), British skeptical playwright George Bernard Shaw (*Saint Joan*, 1924), Scots essayist Andrew Lang (1908), German Marxist playwright Bertolt Brecht (*Die heilige Johanna der Schlachthöfe* [*Saint Joan of the Stockyards*], 1929–1930), Japanese antiwar novelist Ishikawa Jun (*Fugen* [*The Bodhisattva*], 1936), and future Venezuelan president Rómulo Gallegos's screenplay (*La Doncella* [*The Maid*], 1945), often in response to the more predictably numerous French versions, of which those by Charles Péguy (*Le Mystère de la charité de Jeanne d'Arc*, plus others, 1897–1913), Anatole France (1908), Joseph

Delteil (1925), Georges Bernanos (*Jeanne, relapse et sainte* [*Joan, Heretic and Saint*], 1929), Paul Claudel (*Jeanne au bûcher* [*Joan of Arc at the Stake*], 1939) and Jean Anouilh (*L'Alouette* [*The Lark*], 1953) remain the most memorable, if highly diverse. However, the prolific appropriation by right-wing French authors and politicians during the twentieth century and nowadays, from the Action Française group (early 1900s) to Jean-Marie Le Pen's Front National Party official adoption of her (1992–), appears to dominate the French scene, for better or worse (Winock). Although (or because) no reliable portrait of Joan survives, an equally varied array of children's book illustrators, academic and avant-garde painters and sculptors have risen to the challenge (see images in Pernoud; Pernoud and Clin; Warner; Rouen Museum catalogue) across the centuries, ever since the notary Clément de Fauquembergue sketched his image of her in the margins of his manuscript (1429) of the Paris Parlement register: the most striking are by Paul Delaroche (1824), J. L. D. Ingres (1854), Louis Boutet de Monvel (1896), Octave Guillonnet (1912), Georges Rouault (1948), and Marc Chagall (early twentieth century); sculptures by the Princess Marie (1840) (see Heimann in Astell and Wheeler), François Rude (1852), Denis Foyatier (1855), Emmanuel Frémiet (1880), Jules-Pierre Roulleau (1892), and the American Anna Hyatt Huntingdon (1915; see Warner 1981, 1989). Filmmakers too tried to retell her story from the earliest days of cinema (Hatot/Lumière in 1898), producing some forty films in all so far, with more promised. Though each one has its virtues, the most artistically important and successful remains that by Danish Protestant Carl-Theodor Dreyer (1927), rivaled only perhaps by Robert Bresson's much rarer, equally ascetic production of 1962 (see Blaetz in Goy-Blanquet; Harty in Wheeler and Wood). To a lesser, but appreciable extent, the world of music has also contributed to her celebrity, for example, in nineteenth-century operas by Tchaikovsky and Verdi, then in Arthur Honneger's oratorio, *Jeanne au bûcher*, with Paul Claudel (1939), Leonard Bernstein for Lillian Hellman's adaptation of Anouilh's *L'Alouette* (*The Lark*, 1955) and Richard Einhorn's *Voices of Light* (1994) inspired by Dreyer's film (the latter now accompanies the video/DVD version of the newly restored Dreyer).

Because Joan's persona galvanized so many different factions, as attested in the above works, plus the Church's own quandary of sanctifying one whom it had condemned, her canonization required a complex process over much time, beginning with Cardinal Dupanloup's (former bishop of Orléans) panegyrics of the 1860s. Pope Leo XIII declared her Venerable in 1894; she was beatified in 1909, and, particularly after World War I soldiers' accounts of visions of the heroine sustaining them through the horrors of the trenches, in addition to Vatican hagiographical politics, Joan was canonized in 1920 by Benedict XV (Kelly in Wheeler and Wood). Her feast day, another topic of recurrent political manipulation, has shifted in France from among three options—May 30 (her martyrdom), May 8 (her Orléans victory), and most recently, May 1 (Workers' Holiday)—depending upon the party in power.

Quicherat's edition of the trials has taken much time to update completely, with Pierre Champion's influential partial text (Condemnation Trial only) of 1920–1921, enriched by the editions of Paul Doncœur, Yvonne Lanhers, Pierre Tisset, and Pierre Duparc (1950s–1980s), with more documentation still being completed at the Centre Jeanne d'Arc at Orléans, which also publishes a bulletin devoted to Joan of Arc studies—such is the vibrantly variegated abundance of her afterlife.

See also Christine de Pizan; Hagiography (Female Saints); Le Franc, Martin; Relics and Medieval Women

BIBLIOGRAPHY
[See also bibliographies to the works listed below].

Primary Sources

Joan's Trial
Champion, Pierre. *Procès de Condamnation de Jeanne d'Arc.* 2 vols. Bibliothèque du XVe siècle, 22–23. Paris: Édouard Champion, 1920–1921. [Notes still useful].
————. *The Trial of Joan of Arc.* Translated and edited by W. P. Barrett. Notes translated by Coley Taylor and Ruth Kerr. New York: Gotham House, 1932. Reprint, Birmingham, Ala.: Notable Trials Library, 1991. Introduction by Alan Dershowitz.
Duparc, Pierre. *Procès en nullité de la condamnation de Jeanne d'Arc.* 5 vols. Société de l'Histoire de France. Paris: Klincksieck, 1977–1989. [Follows Tisset and Lanhers' ed. of Condemnation Trial, below].
Quicherat, Jules, ed., *Procès de Condamnation et de Réhabilitation de Jeanne d'Arc* Société de l'Histoire de France. 5 vols. Paris: Jules Renouard, 1841–1849. Reprint New York: Johnson, 1965.
Tisset, Pierre, and Yvonne Lanhers *Procès de Jeanne d'Arc.* Société de l'Histoire de France, 3 vols. Paris: Klincksieck, 1960–1971.
Scott, Walter Sydney, trans. *The Trial of Joan of Arc.* London: Folio Society, 1956. [Important annotated translation based on Doncœur's findings on the d'Urfé fragment containing original French testimony].

Other Documentation
Journal du Siège d'Orléans (1428–1429); augmenté de Plusieurs documents. . . . Edited by Paul Charpentier and Charles Cuissard. Orléans: H. Herluison, 1896.
[Chronicle and literary excerpts]. *See under* Quicherat, *above,* vols. 4–5.
[Joan's Letters]. *See under* Pernoud and Clin, *below.*

Visual portraits
American Numismatic Society/Joan of Arc Statue Committee. *Joan of Arc Loan Exhibition Catalogue: Paintings, Pictures, Medals, [. . .] etc. American Numismatic Society Building, New York, January 6th to February 8th, 1913.* New York: Wynkoop & Hallenbeck, 1913.
Rouen, Musée des Beaux Arts. *Jeanne d'Arc, les tableaux de l'histoire (30 mai–1er septembre 2003).* Paris: Réunion des Musées nationaux, 2003.

Secondary Sources
Astell, Ann W. *Joan of Arc and Sacrificial Authorship.* Notre Dame, Ind.: University of Notre Dame Press, 2003.
————, and Bonnie Wheeler, eds. *Joan of Arc and Spirituality.* The New Middle Ages. New York: Palgrave/Macmillan, 2003.
Beaune, Colette. *Jeanne d'Arc.* Paris: Perrin, 2004.
Bouzy, Olivier. *Jeanne d'Arc: mythes & réalités.* Orléans: L'Atelier de l'archer, 1999.
Contamine, Philippe. *De Jeanne d'Arc aux guerres d'Italie.* Orléans: Paradigme, 1994.
De Vries, Kelly. *Joan of Arc: A Military Leader.* Phoenix Mill: Sutton, U.K., 1999.
Fraioli, Deborah A. *Joan of Arc: The Early Debate.* Woodbridge, U.K.: Boydell Press, 2000.
Goy-Blanquet, Dominique, ed. *Jeanne d'Arc en garde à vue.* Brussels: Le Cri, 1999.
———— *Joan of Arc, A Saint for All Reasons: Studies in Myth and Politics.* London and Burlington, Vt.: Ashgate, 2003.
Krumeich, Gerd. *Jeanne d'Arc in der Geschichte.* Sigmaringen, Germany: Jan Thorbecke, 1989.
————. *Jeanne d'Arc à travers l'histoire.* Trans. Josie Mély et al. Introduction by Régine Pernoud. Paris: Albin Michel, 1993. [With updated bibliography].

Margolis, Nadia. "Joan of Arc." In *The Cambridge Companion to Medieval Women's Writing*, edited by Carolyn Dinshaw and David Wallace, 256–66. Cambridge: Cambridge University Press, 2003.

———. *Joan of Arc in History, Literature and Film: A Select, Annotated Bibliography*. Garland Reference Library of the Humanities, 1224. New York: Garland, 1990.

Pernoud, Régine. *J'ai nom Jeanne la Pucelle*. Histoire/Découvertes. Paris: Gallimard, 1994. [Excellent collection of images, carefully labelled, of Joan and her contemporaries through the ages].

———, and Marie-Véronique Clin. *Jeanne d'Arc*. Paris: Fayard, 1986.

———. *Joan of Arc: Her Story*. Revised and translated by Jeremy DuQ. Adams. New York: St. Martin's Griffin, 1998. [Perhaps the most comprehensive single-volume work on Joan in her time and thereafter].

Richey, Stephen W. *Joan of Arc: The Warrior Saint*. Westport, Conn.: Praeger, 2003.

Sullivan, Karen. *The Interrogation of Joan of Arc*. Medieval Cultures, 20. Minneapolis: University of Minnesota Press, 1999.

Warner, Marina. *Joan of Arc: The Image of Female Heroism*. New York: Knopf, 1981. [Though not without errors, a pioneering study of Joan's diachronic, international presence in word and image].

———. "Personification and Idealization of the Feminine." In *Medievalism in American Culture*, edited by Bernard Rosenthal and Paul E. Szarmach, 85–111. Medieval & Renaissance Texts & Studies, 55. Binghamton, N.Y.: CMERS, 1989.

Wheeler, Bonnie, and Charles T. Wood, eds. *Fresh Verdicts on Joan of Arc*. New York and London: Garland, 1996.

Winock, Michel. "Jeanne d'Arc." In *Les Lieux de Mémoire. III: Les France. 3: De l'Archive à l'emblème*, edited by Pierre Nora, 675–733. Paris: Gallimard, 1992. [The most complete study of her political afterlife].

FRANÇOISE MICHAUD-FRÉJAVILLE

JÓREIÐR HERMUNDARDÓTTIR Í MIDJUMDAL (c.1239–?).

Jóreiðr í Miðjumdal, a *skáldkona* (woman poet) writing in Old Norse, is credited with eight stanzas of dream-verse in *Íslendinga saga*, part of *Sturlunga saga*, an account of current events written by Jóreiðr's contemporary Sturla Þórðarson (1214–1284). In the sort of Icelandic visionary verse of which Jóreiðr's poetry is typical, the poet attributes the origin of the poetry to a figure seen and heard in a dream or vision. These muse-figures can be male or female, anonymous or named, supernatural or human, contemporary or long dead. In Jóreiðr's case, the dream-figure is one of the grand heroines of pagan legend, Guðrún Gjúkadóttir, from the *Volsunga saga*, the story of Sigurðr, or Sigurd the Volsung.

The account in *Sturlunga saga* tells us that at the time of the verses Jóreiðr was sixteen years old and living in the household of a priest and farmer named Páll in Midjumdal, in southwestern Iceland. The verses, and the frame-story that goes with them, involve Jóreiðr's visions on a number of summer nights in 1255 in which she sees Guðrún Gjúkadóttir dressed in dark clothing (which is often symbolic of violent death in Icelandic tradition) and mounted on a large grey horse. Jóreiðr is concerned about various of her friends and kinsmen who are tangled up in political feuds elsewhere in Iceland, and she asks the dream-woman about their welfare; the dream-woman provides her with answers, sometimes in prose, but mostly in verse, in archaic Eddic style, often with a doubled refrain. (The term for the rather uncommon meter used is *galdralag*—"spell-singing.") Jóreiðr also expresses concern that she, a Christian woman, has been singled out for visits by a heathen ghost; the apparition replies that whether she is Christian or heathen is of no import, but that "I am a friend to my friends."

Jóreiðr's poetry and the frame-story surrounding it are an evocative and faithful mirror of the apprehension and political tension characteristic of her time, the decline of the Icelandic republic. They are also noteworthy for two other reasons, namely: (1) they represent the largest corpus attributed to any single woman skald in the Old Norse period, and (2) they comprise the largest body of counterevidence to the prevailing modern belief that women composed but little poetry after Iceland's conversion to Christianity.

See also Jórunn skáldmær; *Laxdœla Saga*; Norse Women; *Skáldkonur* (Old Norse-Icelandic Women Poets); Steinunn Refsdóttir

BIBLIOGRAPHY

Primary Sources
Den norsk-islandske skaldedigtning. Edited by Finnur Jónsson, 2B: 158. Copenhagen: Gyldendal/ Nordisk Vorlag, 1915.
Den norsk-isländska skaldediktningen. Edited by Ernst Albin Kock, 2: 84–85. 2 vols. Lund, Sweden: C. W. K. Gleerup, 1946–1949.
Sturlunga saga. Translated by Julia McGrew, 1: 431–34. New York: Twayne Publishers, 1971.

Secondary Source
Helgadóttir, GuÐrún. *Skáldkonur fyrri alda,* 1: 131–36. 2 vols. Akureyri, Iceland: Kvöldvökuútgáfan, 1961.

SANDRA BALLIF STRAUBHAAR

JÓRUNN SKÁLDMÆR (fl. c.910). One of the earliest Old Norse women poets (*skáldkonur*) whose work has been preserved, and one of the few enjoying professional status as a *skáld* (skald/scald; poet) at the courts of the early Norwegian kings, Jórunn, whose epithet *skáldmær* means "poet-maiden," composed oral poetry in the then-fashionable *dróttkvætt* style: formal and elegant, on subjects of courtly interest. Her patron was most probably Harald Fairhair, or his son Hálfdan the Black. Unfortunately, all that remains of Jórunn's life's work are several scattered and offhand citations by the great Icelandic skald, Snorri Sturluson (1178–1241), of various stanzas traditionally attributed to her. In addition, although the biographies of many court skalds were recorded in later Icelandic prose sagas, no concrete information has been preserved concerning Jórunn's life and career. Jórunn was certainly Norwegian by birth, while later virtually all the skalds at the Norwegian courts would come from Iceland. It can be presumed, however, that she was a contemporary of kings Harald and Hálfdan, as well as of the court skald Gutthormr Sindri, as internal evidence from her poetry indicates. She is also likely to have been a close colleague of Harald's skald, Thorbjorn Hornklofi, since her poetry exhibits some similarity of diction to his, for example, similar usage of *heiti* (epithets) and, more specifically, *kenningar* (epithets based on wordplay and riddles), and even one entire verse in common.

There are five remaining stanzas and half-stanzas attributed to Jórunn. One half-stanza is used as a model of poetic style by Snorri in *Skáldskaparmál;* the other four are cited by him in his historical sagas—in *Haralds saga hárfagra* and in an introductory section to *Óláfs saga helga*—as part of a poem called *Sendibit* ("biting message"), praising the role of Gutthormr Sindri in reconciling Hálfdan the Black with his father. Modern editors have assumed universally that the *Skáldskaparmál* stanza belongs in *Sendibit* as well; it is equally likely that the original poem contained a number of additional stanzas that are now lost.

The poem is in near-perfect *dróttkvætt* style, using relatively simple diction for the most part, with the exception of the rather baroque stanza printed by most editors as the penultimate one. There were two other women credited with composing verse in the context of the early Norwegian courts: Hildr Hrólfsdóttir and Gunnhildr konungamódir. But unlike Jórunn, who was bound by loyalty, Hildr and Gunnhildr had kinship ties at court and produced only poetry referring to those kinship ties; they are therefore less likely candidates for professional court skalds than Jórunn. Court skalds were often involved in many other aspects of court life, up to and including the defense of their patron kings in battle. It should perhaps be noted here that Jórunn is called "*skjaldmær*" ("shield-maiden"), instead of *skáldmær* ("poet-maiden"), in a variant reading in one manuscript of Snorri's *Óláfs saga helga* (Flateyjarbók MS., currently in the possession of the Arnamagnean Institute, Reykjavík, Iceland). It is an intriguing, but unlikely, speculation that perhaps, in addition to the service of skaldship, she rendered to her king a swordswoman's service as well.

See also Jóreiðr Hermundardóttir í Midjumdal; *Laxdœla Saga*; Norse Women; *Skáldkonur* (Old Norse-Icelandic Women Poets); Steinunn Refsdóttir

BIBLIOGRAPHY

Primary Sources
Corpus poeticum boreale. Edited and translated by Gudbrandur Vígfússon and F. York Powell, 2: 321–322. Oxford: Clarendon Press, 1883.
Den norsk-islandske skjaldedigtning. Edited by Finnur Jónsson, 2B: 53–54. Copenhagen: Gyldendal/ Nordisk Vorlag, 1915.
Den norsk-isländska skaldediktningen. Edited by Ernst Albin Kock, 1: 33–34. 2 vols. Lund, Sweden: C. W. K. Gleerup, 1946–1949.
Snorri Sturluson. *Heimskringla*. Edited by Bjarni Adalbjarnarson, 2: 426–27. Íslenzk fornrit, 27. Reykjavík: Hid íslenzka fornritafélag, 1941.
———. *Heimskringla*. Translated by Lee M. Hollander, 91. Austin: University of Texas Press, 1964.

Secondary Source
Kreutzer, Gert. "Jórunn skáldmær." *Skandinavistik* 2 (1971): 89–98.

SANDRA BALLIF STRAUBHAAR

JUDGMENT OF PARIS. An important story since ancient times to explain the causes of the Trojan War, the Judgment of Paris theme evolved into a fable, all too often to illustrate how "Woman is man's ruin" (see Geoffrey Chaucer, *Nun's Priest's Tale*, v. 3164), a medieval antifeminist credo.

The story of the Judgment stems from ancient Greece, where it formed part of the background to explain the causes of the Trojan War, believed to have occurred in the twelfth century B.C.E. Paris, son of the Trojan king Priam, was asked to judge the beauty of Aphrodite, Hera, and Athena. Swayed by her bribe of the beautiful Greek queen Helen for himself, Paris judged in Aphrodite's favor. When he claimed his prize, she who became popularly known as "Helen of Troy," the Greeks destroyed Troy. Paris and his country were thus undone by the seductive beauty of a woman.

Homer alluded to the story in his epic poem of the Trojan War, the *Iliad* 24.28–30; the now-lost, anonymous Homeric sequel *Kypria* (*Poem of Cyprus*) recounted the Judgment in

parla a son pere omne toue ceulx
qui en presence estoient.

The Judgment of Paris. From *Histoire de la destruction de Troie la grand.* c. 1500. Illustrated by Jean Colombe. © Bibliothèque Nationale de France, Paris.

detail, from what fragmentary evidence tells us. This "classical version" reached the Middle Ages through Ovid and various handbooks. During the Alexandrian period (fourth century, B.C.E.), the plot details included a golden apple, or Apple of Discord, as the prize for the winning goddess: a sort of "prequel" in which Eris, goddess of discord, irked at not being invited to the wedding of two other divinities, Thetis and Peleus, attended nevertheless and tossed out an apple labeled "For the Fairest" to wreak mayhem among the guests, among whom Hera, Athena, and Aphrodite; whereupon begins our story—all to explain the origins of Troy's downfall. In Sophocles's play, *Krisis* (*The Judgment*) (fifth century, B.C.E.), surviving only in fragments, the story had already assumed a moral dimension: Aphrodite as goddess of pleasure opposed Athena, who represented wisdom, reason, and virtue. By the late fourth century B.C.E., a Stoic-philosophical approach to the Judgment saw Paris's choice among the goddesses as an allegory for a young man's choice among lives, in which Aphrodite signified love, Athena war, and Hera royal power. In late-antique Latin literature, the *Mythologiae* (*Mythologies*) of Fulgentius (late fifth century) passed this choice-of-lives scheme on to the Middle Ages. For Fulgentius, Venus (Aphrodite)

represented the life of pleasure, Minerva (Athena) represented the contemplative life because of Athena's old link with wisdom, and Juno (Hera) represented the active life. But only the life represented by Minerva was good; even the active life was condemned. A third approach to the story also dates from ancient Greece. The rationalizing tradition removed the Judgment's supernatural dimension by claiming Paris only dreamed his encounter with the goddesses. The most important exemplar of this version was the *De Excidio Troiae Historia* (*History of the Fall of Troy*) of "Dares the Phrygian" (fifth or sixth century, C.E.).

The Judgment became enormously popular in the Middle Ages. In twelfth-century romances whose titles bear the names of their lover-protagonists, like *Floire et Blancheflor* and *Athis et Prophilias*, for example, the Judgment's inclusion reflects the medieval taste for classical themes as decorative motifs. In *Floire et Blancheflor*, the Judgment's story and characters decorate a cup; in *Athis et Prophilias*, they adorn a tent in a medievalized Athenian setting. In each case, the romance's plot subtly echoes Paris's love adventure. Such incidental uses of the story are found throughout medieval literature.

More significant, however, are the rationalizing and allegorical traditions. The Trojan War centuries later came to be considered a prologue to European history. Emulating Virgil's national epic of Rome, the *Aeneid* (19 B.C.E.), medieval European nations traced their founding heroes to fleeing Trojans. Thus the story of Troy was important in its own right, and histories of the world or individual nations often included a Trojan segment. Most frequently, the version of the Judgment featured in histories was the dream version, because it did not require of medieval Christians a belief in the pagan supernatural.

Paradoxically, the treatment of the war that the Middle Ages regarded as most authoritative derived from a medieval romance: the *Roman de Troie* (*Romance of Troy*) of Benoît de Sainte-Maure (1155–1160). The Italian Guido delle Colonne reworked it as the *Historia Destructionis Troiae* (*History of the Destruction of Troy*, 1270–1287), and his version influenced most subsequent treatments of the Trojan saga, including four English versions, John Lydgate's *Troy Book* (1412–1420) among them. Following Benoît, who followed Dares, Guido made Paris dream his encounter with the goddesses. But in keeping with the episode's dire results for Troy, he implied that demonic influences inspired the dream, and he emphasized the goddesses' link with the pagan supernatural by having Paris request to judge them nude. Robert Mannyng's *Story of England* (c.1338) went further by making the goddesses witches.

Besides its important place in what was considered history, the Judgment was popular as a classical fable ripe for allegorical interpretation. The Fulgentian choice-of-lives scheme informed most medieval allegorizations of the Judgment, from the Platonizing approach of twelfth-century French commentators like William of Conches and Bernard Silvestris to the preachers' manuals of the fourteenth century. Yet these manuals went beyond Fulgentius in that they offered explicitly Christian interpretations of the story. In the *Ovide moralisé* (*Moralized Ovid*, fourteenth century), for example, Paris's choice of Venus was seen as a reenactment of Adam and Eve's original sin. In a version of the Latin *Ovidius Moralizatus* revised under the influence of the *Ovide moralisé*, Venus was *voluptas*—mistress of delights. Paris chose her because the fallen human will tends to follow its own inclinations.

Some Fulgentian interpretations were influenced by a revival of interest in Aristotle that made the active life, represented by Juno, positive rather than negative. But Venus was always condemned, and Paris's choice of her and her gift was always seen as negative.

This longstanding allegorical tradition paved the way for distinctive literary uses of the Judgment. The fourteenth-century dream-vision, deriving from the thirteenth-century *Roman de la Rose* (*Romance of the Rose*), exploited the allegorical significance of figures drawn from classical myth. Guillaume de Machaut's *Dit de la fonteinne amoureuse* (*Tale of the Fountain of Love*, 1360–1361), Jean Froissart's *Espinette amoureuse* (*Hawthorn Bush of Love*, c.1370), and the anonymous *Echecs amoureux* (*Chess Game of Love*, 1370–1380), translated by John Lydgate as *Reson and Sensuallyte* (*Reason and Sensuality*, c.1412), all present young men who reenact Paris's choice. Each inevitably chooses the life of love, and each work uses the Judgment to point a moral. Also, in the mid-fourteenth century, Italian humanist Convenevole da Prato, in his *Panegyricus* for King Robert of Naples, presents Venus as a Medea—witch or sorceress figure—though Aristotelian influence makes his Juno positive.

Only one woman writer treated the Judgment during the Middle Ages: Christine de Pizan (1365–1430?). She downplayed the condemnation of Paris's choice—but not out of loyalty to her sex so much as deference to her courtly audience. Christine used the story in eight works: in her lyric poetry (1399–1402), we find evocations in *Cent Balades* (*One Hundred Ballads*) 87, *Lays* 2, and *Autres Balades* (*Other Ballads*) 7; among her longer works, in the *Epistre Othea* (*Epistle of Othea to Hector*) of 1400–1401, the *Mutacion de Fortune* (*Mutation of Fortune*, 1403, vv. 14908–17600, and prose section 5), and the final section of the *Chemin de long estude* (*Path of Long Study*, 1402–1403). It figures most significantly in the *Othea* and *Chemin*.

The *Othea* (Episodes 60, 68, and 73) exploits the choice-of-lives interpretation. In fact, Christine's aim in the work as a whole is to urge her princely audience to make the right choice—wisdom and chivalry—so the fables devoted to the Judgment echo in miniature her overall theme. The work is dedicated to Louis, duke of Orléans, whom Christine salutes as coming of Trojan stock (while also appealing to the reckless duke's sense of prudence); since history records that his taste in women was highly developed, the Trojan prince Paris would have been a likely literary parallel. But as a court poet Christine knew the value of discretion. She observes blandly, in the *glose* to Fable 73, that though Paris gave the golden apple to Venus, "the good knight [...] ought not to do likewise."

In the *Chemin* (esp. vv. 6154–6299), Paris's love-centered choice and its goddess have completely dropped out of the story, modified even more than in Christine's probable model, Machaut's *Fonteinne amoureuse*. Christine, responding to the civil unrest of her time and France's desperate need for leadership, cites the original story and characters, then recasts the Judgment as a political debate among four queens (instead of three goddesses) who rule the world: Wisdom, Nobility, Chivalry, and Riches—qualities associated with Pallas and Juno (Ehrhart 1990). The queens argue which quality is most important in a ruler, and the poem concludes when Christine, the narrator-stenographer, is sent to find an arbiter; the debate remaining unresolved as she wakens from her dream. Yet Christine has not only modified myth but actually, with daring more characteristic of male authors, "corrected" it to improve her world and to show that women can contribute to this progress rather than to man's downfall (Blumenfeld-Kosinski).

Though the Judgment of Paris was cited in a variety of contexts in the Christian Middle Ages, overall it offered a useful classical parallel for the Judeo-Christian view of woman as temptress.

See also Christine de Pizan; Criseyde; Dido in the Middle Ages; Enchantresses, Fays (*Fées*), and Fairies; Medea in the Middle Ages; Mélusine

BIBLIOGRAPHY

Primary Sources
Athis et Prophilias, Li Romanz de. Edited by Alfons Hilka. 2 vols. Gesellschaft für romanische Literatur, 29, 40. Dresden: Gesellschaft für romanische literatur, 1912–1916.
Benoît de Sainte-Maure. *Le Roman de Troie.* Edited by Leopold Constans. 6 vols. Société des Anciens Textes Français [=SATF]. Paris: Firmin Didot, 1904–1912. Reprint New York: Johnson, 1968.
Christine de Pizan. *Epistre Othea.* Edited by Gabriella Parussa. Textes Littéraires Français, 517. Geneva: Droz, 1999.
———. *Le Livre du chemin de longue estude.* Critical ed. and translation (Modern French) by Andrea Tarnowski. Lettres gothiques. Paris: Livre de Poche, 2000.
———. *Livre de la Mutacion de Fortune.* Critical ed. by Suzanne Solente. 4 vols. SATF. Paris: Picard, 1959–1966.
———. *Œuvres poétiques de Christine de Pisan.* Edited by Maurice Roy. 3 vols. SATF 24. Paris: Firmin Didot, 1886–1896. Reprint New York: Kraus, 1965.
Convenevole da Prato. *Panegyricus.* In *Regia carmina*, critical edition (Latin) and translation (Italian) by Cesare Grassi. Essays by Marco Ciatti and Aldo Petri. 2 vols. Cinisello Balsamo, Italy: Silvana, 1982. [Also reproduces London British Library MS 6.E.IX].

Dares Phrygius and Dictys Cretensis. *Daretis Phrygii de excidio Troiae Historia.* Critical ed. by Ferdinand Meister. Leipzig, Germany: Teubner, 1873.

————. *The Trojan War: The Chronicles of Dictys of Crete and Dares the Phrygian.* Translated by R. M. Frazer Jr. Bloomington: Indiana University Press, 1966.

Floire et Blancheflor. Critical ed. by Margaret M. Pelan. Publications de la Faculté des Lettres, Université de Strasbourg. Textes d'étude,7. Paris: Les Belles Lettres, 1936. Second version Paris: Ophrys, 1975.

Froissart, Jean. *L'Espinette amoureuse.* Critical ed. by Anthime Fourrier. Bibliothèque française et romane. Textes et Documents, 2. Paris: Klincksieck, 1963.

Fulgentius, Fabius Planciades. *Opera.* Edited by Rudolf Helm. Revised by Jean Préaux. Biblioteca scriptorum graecorum et romanorum Teubneriana. Stuttgart, Germany: Teubner, 1970.

————. *Fulgentius the Mythographer.* Translated by Leslie G. Whitbread. Columbus: Ohio State University Press, 1971.

[Guido delle Collonne] Guido de Columnis. *Historia Destructionis Troiae.* Edited by Nathaniel E. Griffin. Cambridge, Mass.: Mediaeval Academy of America, 1936.

[*Kypria*]. *Hesiod, the Homeric Hymns, and Homerica.* Translated by Hugh G. Evelyn-White, 489–91. Loeb Classical Library. Cambridge, Mass.: Harvard University Press, 1936. [Bilingual Greek-English ed.].

Lydgate, John. *Reson and Sensuallyte.* Edited by Ernst Sieper. Notes by F. J. Furnivall. 2 vols. Early English Text Society [=EETS], e.s. 84, 89. London: Oxford University Press, 1901–1903. Reprint 1965.

————. *The Troy Book.* Critical ed. by Henry Bergen. 4 vols. EETS, e.s. 97, 103, 106, 126. London: Kegan Paul et al. and (vol. 4) Humphrey Milford, 1906–1935. Reprint Millwood, N.Y.: Kraus, 1975.

Machaut, Guillaume de. *La Fontaine amoureuse.* Edited and translated (Modern French) with notes by Jacqueline Cerquiglini-Toulet. Paris: Stock, 1993.

Mannyng, Robert. *The Story of England.* Edited by Frederick J. Furnivall. 2 vols. Rolls Series, 87. London: H. M. S. O., 1887. Reprint New York: Kraus, 1965.

Ovide moralisé. Edited by Cornelis de Boer et al. 5 vols. Koninklijke Akademie van Wetenschappen te Amsterdam, Afdeeling Letterkunde, n.s. 15, 21, 30, 37, 43. Amsterdam: J. Müller, 1915–1938. Reprint Wiesbaden, Germany: Martin Sandig, 1966–1968.

Sophocles. [*Krisis*] In *The Fragments of Sophocles,* edited by A. C. Pearson, 29–31. Cambridge: Cambridge University Press, 1917.

Secondary Sources

Blumenfeld-Kosinski, Renate. *Reading Myth: Classical Mythology and its Interpretations in Medieval French Literature.* Figurae. Stanford, Calif.: Stanford University Press, 1997.

Ehrhart, Margaret J. "Christine de Pizan and the Judgment of Paris: A Court Poet's Use of Mythographic Tradition." In *The Mythographic Art: Classical Fable and the Rise of the Vernacular in Early France and England,* edited by Jane Chance, 125–56. Gainesville: University Press of Florida, 1990.

————. *The Judgment of the Trojan Prince Paris in Medieval Literature.* Philadelphia: University of Pennsylvania Press, 1987.

MARGARET J. EHRHART

JUETTE.   *See* **Ivetta of Huy**

JULIAN OF NORWICH (1342–c.1416). The first known woman to author a book in English, Julian of Norwich received, in May 1373, a vision of the crucified Jesus accompanied by sixteen revelations about God's love for humanity, which form the basis of her book, its title now modernized as *A Revelation of Love.* Since their translation into modern English in 1901, these "Showings" (Middle English: "Shewings") have drawn much attention from scholars who value Julian as a pioneering English woman mystical writer who revealed her gifts as a woman theologian—more intellectual than a mere visionary—who contemplated the nature of sin and salvation: mysteries of Christian doctrine that were central to medieval religious life.

Born at the end of 1342, Julian almost certainly lived until after 1416, although there is no evidence to determine the exact year of her death. She lived during a period of social upheaval brought on by the Hundred Years War, the Black Death, and the persecution of heresy throughout Europe. Little is known of Julian's life, however, except for the scant details offered in her book and two other written sources: contemporary wills and the *Book of Margery Kempe*. A number of fourteenth- and fifteenth-century wills mention her as a recluse as of 1393 at the Church of St. Julian in Norwich, an important ecclesiastical city at that time, in the eastern English county of Norfolk. The *Book* by Margery Kempe (c.1373–c.1440), a religious woman from nearby King's Lynn, records visiting and receiving spiritual counsel from Julian at her cell in Norwich in 1413. Even Julian's real name is uncertain (some have called her Juliana), since Julian likely would have been the name she assumed on entering the anchorhold, a place of refuge for female hermits known as anchoresses, adjoining the Church of St. Julian. It is possible that she was associated with the Benedictine community of nuns nearby at Carrow Abbey, but her early life and the extent of her education are unknown. Scholars agree, however, that Julian was a woman of substantial, if not formal, learning at a time when educational opportunities for women were declining. Although she modestly claims to be "a simple, unlettered creature," her writings indicate that she possessed a thorough knowledge of Scripture and the theology of St. Augustine (354–430) and was widely read in Latin and the spiritual classics.

We know from her book that Julian nurtured a lifelong desire to become more intimate with God and with the suffering of Christ. In her youth she prayed for three graces from God: an understanding of Christ's Passion, a bodily sickness, and wounds of compassion, contrition, and affective longing for God. She received these gifts on May 13, 1373, when she was thirty-and-a-half years old. With her mother, a curate, and others by her side, Julian lay near death with a terrible illness when she received a startling vision of Christ on the cross, the starting point from which fifteen subsequent revelations unfolded. Her visions came to her in three forms: as bodily sights, as spiritual or ghostly visions, and as words formed in her understanding.

The spiritual truths contained in these showings were recorded by Julian as *A Vision schewed* [...] *to a devoute woman*, sometime after her visionary experience, in what has become known as the Short Text. It took twenty years of contemplation and theological maturation, however, before Julian understood the meaning of her visions well enough to set them down as *A Revelacion of Love* (original spelling) in what is generally called the Long Text, completed sometime after 1393. Held together by a message of God's all-encompassing love for humanity despite sinful transgressions, this *Book of Showings* (also known as *Revelations of Divine Love* [as in trans. Warrack] and *A Revelation of Love* [trans. Watson]) was meant to comfort her fellow Christians with the understanding that "all shall be well." In masterful but simple Middle English prose, Julian demonstrates a sophisticated understanding of the chief doctrines of the Christian faith and a strong devotion to the affective piety of the late Middle Ages.

At the center of the first thirteen chapters of the Short Text lies a vivid image or "bodily sight" of the Passion of Christ. Julian describes in careful detail the crown of thorns upon Christ's head, the pouring of His blood, and the discoloring and drying of His skin. This image operates throughout her visionary experience as a means of passing from discursive consciousness to an unmediated knowing or "beholding" of God. Through it, Julian comes to understand the Trinity, the Incarnation, and God's union with the human soul. She is assured that the earthly suffering of Christ was an expression of God's "homely" and sustaining love for humanity and a sacrifice Jesus blissfully made to secure our salvation (Coiner).

Chapters 14 through 18 are dominated by what Julian sees as a troubling contradiction between God's omnipotent goodness and the existence of evil (sin) in the world. She is assured, through her revelations, that evil has no essence of being because it works toward the ultimate good. As a necessary part of God's beneficent plan, sin reveals to us our weaknesses and brings us closer to God as we repent and seek forgiveness.

This closer union with God through repentance and prayer constitutes the focus of the remaining six chapters of the Short Text. Julian learns that, despite sin, human creation is united to God through the divine substance of the soul. The perfection of this intimacy is achieved through contemplative prayer, which fills the soul with peace, joy, and love as we come to know and trust in God's merciful acts of salvation through Christ.

Most of the spiritual messages that appear in the Short Text are developed more fully in the Long Text. The most substantial addition, which constitutes one-third of the Long Text, appears in the account of revelation fourteen and contains some of Julian's most controversial insights. It describes the parable of the lord and servant and the motherhood of God, points of Julian's theology that contradict the Church's insistence on the eternal damnation of sinners and the masculinity of the deity. Through her vision of the parable, Julian learns that God harbors no wrath against sinners. Although the fallen servant is unable to do the lord's will, the lord looks on the servant with deep love and compassion. This vision serves as an allegorical narrative of the original sin in which the lord represents God and the servant represents Adam, Jesus, and, by extension, humanity. It demonstrates, tropologically (in morally symbolic terms), the dwelling of God in the human soul, the redemptive power at work through the Incarnation, and the possibility of universal salvation.

Feminist historians have been particularly interested in Julian's theology of the motherhood of God, a motif that, for Julian, best symbolizes these redemptive acts of Christ. Although many medieval devotional writings, like their early Christian precursors, employed the image of mother as a casual metaphor for Christ's acts of grace, Julian is unique in seeing motherhood as the very essence of Christ's love for humanity (Bynum; Bradley). Through His suffering, Julian reasons, Jesus bore us eternal life, and, through the sacraments of the Church, Christ our mother, the second person of the Trinity, nourishes us so that we may grow closer to God in love. Throughout the *Book of Showings*, Julian expresses a strong commitment to Christian orthodoxy. It is very unlikely, therefore, that her emphasis on Jesus as mother was intended as an overt challenge to the medieval Church's devaluing of the feminine in the order of creation. Nonetheless, feminist scholars acknowledge Julian's reconception of the deity as a radical response to the traditional valorization of soul over body and to the characterization of the universal self as male. Her identification of the Trinity as Father, Mother, and Son calls attention to the full participation of all human beings, both male and female, in the divine nature.

During her lifetime, Julian gained a regional reputation as a spiritual advisor, but her work was not read widely until long after her death. Only four extant manuscripts of her book, ranging from the mid-fifteenth to the mid-eighteenth centuries, have survived (see notes to *Book of Showings*, ed. Colledge and Walsh 1978; Glasscoe). Two of the earliest are in the British Library in London: a fifteenth-century manuscript (Additional 37790) of the Short Text and the early seventeenth-century version (Sloane 2499) of the Long Text. Another early seventeenth-century manuscript of the Long Text is at the Bibliothèque nationale de France in Paris (Fonds anglais 41). The first printed text was published in 1670 by the Benedictine Serenus de Cressy. Since Grace Warrack's translation of the *Showings* in 1901 (so successful it underwent its fourteenth printing in 1952), Julian has been received with admiration by Christian theologians and academic scholars who appreciate her revelations for their spiritual, literary, and historical worth. Her cell in Norwich, which was destroyed during the Protestant Reformation (sixteenth century), was rebuilt on its original site in 1952 as a shrine to Julian and to her comforting message of divine love. Since then dozens of "Julian groups" have sprung up throughout Britain, and Julian has become a popular attraction at scholarly conferences on women mystics. Recent work has emphasized Julian's conceptualization of the self as split between the human and the divine, her apophatic (negative-theological, denying human ability to understand him through human reason) escape from discursive consciousness, the originality of her writings on the nature of evil, and her transformation from visionary to theologian.

See also *Ancrene Riwle*; Kempe, Margery; Mechthild of Magdeburg

BIBLIOGRAPHY

Primary Sources
Julian of Norwich. *Revelations of Divine Love*. Edited by Grace Warrack. London: Methuen, 1901.
———. *A Book of Showings to the Anchoress Julian of Norwich*. 2 vols. Edited by Edmund Colledge and James Walsh. Toronto: Pontifical Institute of Mediaeval Studies, 1978.
———. *Showings*. Edited and translated into Modern English from the Critical Text by Edmund Colledge and James Walsh. New York: Paulist Press, 1978.
———. [*Revelations of Divine Love*]. *The Shewings of Julian of Norwich*. Edited by Georgia Ronan Crampton. Kalamazoo, Mich.: University of Rochester/TEAMS, 1994. [Modernized Middle English version].
———. *Revelations of Divine Love (Short Text and Long Text)*. Translated by Elizabeth Spearing. Introduction and notes by A. C. Spearing. London and New York: Penguin Books, 1998.
———. *The Writings of Julian of Norwich: A Vision to a Devout Woman and A Revelation of Love*. Edited by Nicholas Watson and Jacqueline Jenkins. University Park: Pennsylvania State University Press, 2004.
Kempe, Margery. *The Book of Margery Kempe*. Edited by Sanford Brown Meech and Hope Emily Allen, ch. 18. Early English Text Society, o.s. 212. Oxford: Humphrey Milford, 1940.

Secondary Sources
Abbott, Christopher. *Julian of Norwich: Autobiography and Theology*. Studies in Medieval Mysticism, 2. Woodbridge, Suffolk, U.K. and Rochester, N.Y.: D. S. Brewer, 1999.
Baker, Denise N. *Julian of Norwich's "Showings": From Vision to Book*. Princeton, N.J.: Princeton University Press, 1994.
Bradley, Ritamary. "Mysticism in the Motherhood Similitude of Julian of Norwich." *Studia Mystica* 8 (1985): 4–14.
Bynum, Caroline W. *Jesus as Mother: Studies in the Spirituality of the High Middle Ages*. Berkeley and Los Angeles: University of California Press, 1982.

Coiner, Nancy. "The 'Homely' and the *Heimliche*: The Hidden, Doubled Self in Julian of Norwich's Showings." *Exemplaria* 5 (1993): 305–23.

Gillespie, Vincent, and Maggie Ross. "The Apophatic Image: The Poetics of Effacement in Julian of Norwich." In *The Medieval Mystical Tradition in England: Exeter Symposium V. Papers read at the Devon Centre, Dartington Hall, July 1992*, edited by Marion Glasscoe, 53–77. Cambridge, U.K.: D. S. Brewer, 1992.

Glasscoe, Marion. "Visions and Revisions: A Further Look at the Manuscripts of Julian of Norwich." *Studies in Bibliography* 42 (1989): 103–20.

Jantzen, Grace. *Julian of Norwich: Mystic and Theologian*. New York: Paulist Press, 1988.

Lichtmann, Maria R. "I desyrede a bodylye syght: Julian of Norwich and the Body." *Mystics Quarterly* 17 (1991): 12–19.

Neuberger, Verena A. *Margery Kempe: A Study in Early English Feminism*. European University Studies, 14. Anglo-Saxon Language and Literature, 278. Bern, Switzerland and New York: Peter Lang, 1994.

Nolan, Edward Peter. *Cry Out and Write: A Feminine Poetics of Revelation*. New York: Continuum, 1994.

Nuth, Joan. *Wisdom's Daughter: The Theology of Julian of Norwich*. New York: Crossroad, 1991.

Peters, Brad. "The Reality of Evil within the Mystic Vision of Julian of Norwich." *Mystics Quarterly* 13 (1987): 195–202.

Riddy, Felicity. "Julian of Norwich and Self-Textualization." In *Editing Women*, edited by Ann M. Hutchison, 101–24. Toronto: University of Toronto Press, 1998.

Ruud, Jay. "Images of the Self and Self Image in Julian of Norwich." *Studia Mystica* 16 (1995): 82–105.

Voaden, Rosalynn. *God's Words, Women's Voices: The Discernment of Spirits in the Writing of Late-Medieval Women Visionaries*. Woodbridge, Suffolk, U.K. and Rochester, N.Y.: University of York Medieval Press/Boydell Press, 1999.

Watson, Nicholas. "The Composition of Julian of Norwich's *Revelation of Love*." *Speculum* 68 (1993): 637–83.

———. "Julian of Norwich." In *The Cambridge Companion to Medieval Women's Writing*, edited by Carolyn Dinshaw and David Wallace, 210–21. Cambridge: Cambridge University Press, 2003.

Windeatt, Barry. "Julian of Norwich and Her Audience." *Review of English Studies* 28 (1977): 1–17.

LISA GAUDET

JULIANA OF MONT-CORNILLON (1193–1258). Also called Juliana of Liège, Juliana was a religious of the diocese of Liège in Belgium, and is best known for a single vision and its momentous consequences. "From her youth" she was visited by a "great and marvelous sign" that distracted her at prayer: a vision of "the full moon in its splendor, yet with a little breach in its spherical body." After much anguish, Juliana learned from Christ that the moon represented the Church, and its missing chink, a new solemnity that he now wished Christians to observe. This was to be a feast in honor of the Blessed Sacrament, later given the name of Corpus Christi—one of the most significant festivals in late medieval religion. Juliana devoted much of her life to promoting it, although her efforts were crowned with only posthumous success. Pope Urban IV declared Corpus Christi a feast of the universal Church in his bull *Transiturus* (1264), and it was confirmed and effectively promulgated by the Council of Vienne under Clement V (1311–1312). Among the many devout women memorialized in the thirteenth century, the Blessed Juliana is unusual in that her *vita* (life) was composed less to promote her cult than to serve an explicit institutional goal. In the anonymous life, written by a canon of Liège c.1261–1264, Juliana's religious career is inextricably entwined with the vicissitudes of Corpus Christi.

Like the early history of that feast, her checkered life was filled with conflicts and reversals.

Born at Retinne, a town near Liège, in 1193, Juliana came of wealthy but not aristocratic stock. Orphaned at the age of five, she and her sister Agnes were raised by a lay sister of Mont-Cornillon on a farm belonging to that house. Mont-Cornillon, where Juliana made her profession in 1207, was in fact a leper hospital founded by the burghers of Liège, who maintained control over its property and temporal affairs. But the ecclesiastical authorities contested this right, and the personnel—men and women, healthy and sick—were ostensibly bound by obedience to a prior, although many resisted religious observance. Under the prior's authority was a prioress who governed the sisters alone. Juliana succeeded to this office in 1222 and for some years worked with the prior, Godfrey, in a difficult attempt to impose monastic discipline on the house. After Godfrey's death in 1237, a power struggle broke out: the new prior, Roger, collaborated with the lay magistrates against the regimen introduced by Juliana, who retaliated by hiding Mont-Cornillon's original charters from a crowd of rioting citizens. In 1242 she was compelled to flee, taking refuge for several months in the cell of a close friend, the recluse Eve of St.-Martin.

Later that year the bishop of Liège, Robert of Langres, intervened on Juliana's behalf: he deposed Roger for simony, restored Juliana to office, rebuilt her oratory (which had been destroyed in the riot), and imposed the Augustinian Rule (a code of monastic behavior based on the teachings of St. Augustine of Hippo, fourth century) at Mont-Cornillon. Robert was also won over to the cause of Corpus Christi and intended to have the new feast solemnly proclaimed. A liturgical office had already been commissioned by Juliana from her new prior, John. But Robert's plans were forestalled by his death in 1246. The new prince-bishop of Liège—a layman, the notorious Henry of Guelders—lost no time in restoring the civil magistrates' control of Mont-Cornillon and recalling the deposed prior Roger. This time there was no reprieve for Juliana: she fled the house once again, for life, in 1247. With three companions, she searched in vain for a haven at several Cistercian nunneries before finding refuge at the abbey of Salzinnes in Namur, Belgium. But this home, too, proved short-lived. Civil war broke out in 1256 between Henry II of Luxembourg and Marie of Brienne, styled "empress of Namur" because of her marriage to Baldwin of Courtenay, the Latin emperor of Constantinople. The abbess of Salzinnes, a relative of Baldwin, took the empress's part. When the unpopular Marie was routed, the house of Salzinnes was threatened with imminent destruction and the nuns forced to disperse. This trauma proved too much for Juliana's fragile health. She suffered a heart attack but lingered for two more years, dying on April 5, 1258, in a recluse's cell at Fosses.

Through all the vicissitudes of her turbulent life, Juliana maintained a fervent ascetic piety with a penchant for savage fasting. Like many female saints, she is said to have eaten little or nothing "for thirty years and more before her death," and when she did eat, it was not out of desire or need but only "to display a kind of solidarity with human nature." This revulsion from mortal food was the converse of her intense longing for the Eucharist: the holy communion with Christ as symbolized by each worshiper's taking of bread and wine as the body and blood of Christ. Juliana's other devotions were typical of women's piety in her day: she was deeply attached to the Virgin and to Christ's nativity and passion. In her private meditations she internalized the events of the liturgical year. Miracles of telepathy and clairvoyance were ascribed to her, along with gifts of physical and spiritual healing. Ardent bridal spirituality, illness, and battle with demons complete the picture.

Juliana's biographer did not know her personally, but relied on a vernacular life by Eve of St.-Martin and on the information of her confessor, John of Lausanne. Despite these direct sources, however, his *vita* (life of Juliana) leans heavily on hagiographic conventions, making it hard to discern any unique traits of Juliana's spirituality apart from her passionate devotion to the cause of Corpus Christi. Even here Juliana, whose humility extended to the point of painful shyness, "keenly desired that someone else should be regarded as the founder of the new feast." When her own liturgical office was superseded in 1264 by the superb Corpus Christi hymns of Thomas Aquinas, she evidently got her wish. Never canonized, Juliana has remained little known, although the Vatican authorized local celebration of her feast day (April 5) in 1869.

See also Bride of Christ/*Brautmystik* Convents; Hagiography (Female Saints); Rules for Canonesses, Nuns, and Recluses

BIBLIOGRAPHY

Primary Sources
Vita sanctae Julianae virginis. In *Acta Sanctorum*, April tom. 1: 435–75. Paris, 1866.
Vita sanctae Julianae virginis/ Vie de Sainte Julienne de Cornillon. Critical ed. and translation [French] by Jean-Pierre Delville. In *Fête-Dieu* (1246–1996), vol. 2. Institut d'études médiévales de l'Université Catholique de Louvain: Textes, Etudes, Actes, 19. Louvain, Belgium: Louvain-la-Neuve, 1999.
The Life of Juliana of Mont-Cornillon. Translated, with introduction and notes by Barbara Newman. Peregrina translations series, 13. 3rd printing. Toronto: Peregrina Publishing, 1999. Original ed. 1988.

Secondary Sources
Bynum, Caroline Walker. *Holy Feast and Holy Fast: The Religious Significance of Food to Medieval Women.* Berkeley: University of California Press, 1987.
Denis, Émile. *La vraie histoire de Sainte Julienne de Liège et de l'Institution de la Fête Dieu.* Tournai: Casterman, 1935.
Dumoutet, Édouard. *Corpus Domini: aux sources de la piété eucharistique médiévale.* Paris: Beauchesne, 1942.
Fête-Dieu (1246–1996). Institut d'études médiévales de l'Université Catholique de Louvain: Textes, Études, Actes, 19. 2 vols. Louvain, Belgium: Louvain-la-Neuve, 1999.
Goodich, Michael. *Vita Perfecta: The Ideal of Sainthood in the Thirteenth Century.* Stuttgart: Hiersemann, 1982.
Mulder-Bakker, Anneke. *Lives of the Anchoresses.* Philadelphia: University of Pennsylvania Press, 2004.
Roisin, Simone. "L'Efflorescence cistercienne et le courant féminin de piété au XIIIᵉ siècle." *Revue d'histoire ecclésiastique* 39 (1943): 342–78.
Rubin, Miri. *Corpus Christi: The Eucharist in Late Medieval Culture.* Cambridge: Cambridge University Press, 1991.
Vowles, W. "Eva, Recluse, and the Feast of Corpus Christi." *Downside Review* 58 (1940): 420–37.

BARBARA NEWMAN

JUS PRIMAE NOCTIS (13th–18th centuries). The Latin term meaning "the right of the first night," or its more graphic French equivalent, *le droit de cuissage* (literally: "the right to touch thighs [with someone]") gave the Norman lord of old the right to sleep with the daughter of any of his subjects on the first night of her marriage; hence the usage *jus primae noctis*, and another French equivalent, *le droit du seigneur* ("the lord's right").

The privilege was first mentioned in writing at the beginning of the thirteenth century in Normandy. This first allusion to the custom—by the French term *culage* (from *cul* = "bottom," here, vulgarly)—is found in a satirical French *chanson* (song or poem) that evokes the sorry condition of the *vilain*, or lowly peasant dependent upon his lord (Old French spelling modernized):

Roger Adé m'a bien raconté	Roger Adé recounted to me
Que le vilain a échappé à la honte:	How the peasant avoided shame:
Si le vilain marie sa fille	If he marries off his daughter
En dehors de la seigneurie,	Outside the lord's domain,
Le seigneur en a le culage;	The lord has his rights in this;
Il reçoit quatre sous pour le mariage	He receives four shillings for the wedding
La raison de ces quatre sous,	The reason for these four shillings is—
Sire, je vous la dis sur ma foi:	Sire, this I swear to you in good faith—
Il se passait cel jadis que le vilain	It happened in olden times that the peasant
Prenait sa fille par la main	Would take his daughter by the hand
Et la livrait à son seigneur	And deliver her to his lord
Pour qu'il en fasse à sa guise	To do with her as he pleased
A moins qu'il ne lui eut donné	Unless [the peasant] had given him
Une rente, un bien ou une terre	Money, goods or lands
Afin qu'il consente au mariage.	So that he'd consent to the marriage.

This privilege, which would have belonged to the complex set of multiple seigniorial (lordly) laws during the feudal period, would have been maintained throughout the entire Old Régime, right up to the night of August 4, 1789, during the French Revolution, which saw the total abolition of lordly privileges. One of the last traces of the term *jus primae noctis* is its role as threat to the happiness of two servants, Figaro and his prospective bride Suzanne, menaced by the Count Almaviva, in the famous comedy by Beaumarchais, *Le Mariage de Figaro* (*Marriage of Figaro*, 1784), whose incendiary role in the pre-Revolutionary period is well known. Nineteenth-century literary scholars have uncovered some fifty references to this privilege in texts published between the old Norman *chanson* and Beaumarchais's comedy.

This chronology of a custom accentuating the barbarism of feudal lordship and its era has only one problem: it is entirely false. One cannot emphasize this forcefully enough, given the plenitude of received opinions continuing to prevail (witness the presence of *jus primae noctis* in the successful, supposedly historical film *Braveheart*, of 1995): the custom known as the *jus primae noctis/droit de cuissage*) never existed in the medieval West. To be sure, it would be absurd to absolve the Middle Ages of all brutality committed against women, as it would be to assert that lords never imposed their will upon their subjects, notably in sexual matters. But in no case did a recognized law ever sanction this. When the recent French feminist movement protested against sexual harassment in the workplace, calling it *droit de cuissage*, it is not incorrect. For in the Middle Ages as in the twenty-first century, and in all cultures, one finds sexual abuse founded on the culmination of two forces: social power (exercised by the lord or the employer over the vassal or employee) and sexual power (masculine dominance). This type of abuse might be implicitly tolerated or repressed but it was no more guaranteed by law in the Middle Ages than it is in our time.

How then, does one explain the existence of medieval testimony, notably our Norman text, on the *jus primae noctis*? Let us note first off that the *chanson* presents the law (the *culage*, v. 5) as an ancient custom, transformed into a simple fee or tax (four shillings) by the lord's magnanimity. In fact, the great majority of authentic texts evoking this supposed law ascribe it to the past and present it as the origin of the current tax. A number of seigniorial deductions were similarly justified by old-fashioned reasons. The *jus primae noctis* thereby constitutes a foundation myth for seigniorial financial institutions.

Another aspect of the Norman text should command our attention: the *chanson*, signed by a certain "Estout de Goz," otherwise unknown, is found in a cartulary (a set of documents and charters establishing seigniorial rights, property titles or usage privileges for a domain) prepared by the monks of the abbey of Mont-Saint-Michel (on the coast of Normandy) concerning the circumstances of peasants in Verson (now the *département* of Eure, also in Normandy). It lists all the expenses and deductions the peasants would incur if they were under a secular lord; the document immediately preceding this list in the cartulary gives the series of (lighter) taxes and fees payable to the monks by these same peasants. The monks, worried by the maneuvers of a local lord attempting to take over the domain of Verson, therefore had a list of expenses drawn up against seigniorial domination.

This polemical aspect appears essential to the myth's construction. One finds, in documents dating from the fifteenth century onward, that those from the ranks of magistrates and royal officers, hostile to the power of the nobles, contain most frequent mention of the *jus primae noctis/droit de cuissage* as emblematic of the nobility's ruthless arrogance. The Age of Enlightenment repeated this accusation, this time against the Old Régime as a whole: in around 1755, Voltaire invented the actual term *droit de cuissage*; Beaumarchais's *Mariage de Figaro* takes its place within an entire literary tradition, begun at the start of the century, foreshadowing the French Revolution. Then, at the beginning of the Second Empire (1852–1870), affirmation of the existence of the *droit de cuissage* is reinforced by a rising anticlerical republican trend that, during the authoritarian Empire, intended to pit the new world of the Enlightenment and the Revolution against the outdated one of the nobility, the monarchy and the clergy, whose retrograde collusion was configured within a barbaric image of the Middle Ages.

It is from this era that we find testimonies of which a good number are either false or concern only the innocuous tax on marriages contracted outside a seigniorial domain (*formariages*; *fors* = "outside"). Indeed, a marriage occurring outside a domain (see *chanson* above, v. 4) entails a loss for the lord, since the couple's children could, according to customs governing transmission of dependency, come under the domain of another lord. The tax imposed on outside marriages was therefore not a consequence of *jus primae noctis/droit de cuissage*.

There remains a small group of texts that mention an ancient *jus primae noctis* and, in one or two cases, a current law, compensable by a small sum or by a symbolic gift (a portion of a course served at a wedding banquet, for example). These all concerned very minor lords at the end of the Middle Ages, having become almost as poor as their dependents, who invoked the custom as a nostalgic show of force to recall their bygone barbaric power. Such demands were very rare, and surface in *aveux* ("confessions"): private documents, often devoid of all official form, which detail vexing or folkloric customs, and which recall the demands made by communities of young bachelors in regard to a newly married man from outside (the farcical fees the communities charged were, it so happens, called *culages*, as in our Norman *chanson*). Of course, this folklorization of social relationships did not exclude the crudeness of domination, but probably nor did it entail any serious belief. The *jus primae noctis/droit du seigneur*—this masculine myth covering up the reality of sexual abuse—must not be allowed the benefit of a medieval alibi.

See also Concubines; Law, Women in, Anglo-Saxon England; Marriage; *Sachsenspiegel* and *Schwabenspiegel*; Salic Law; Slaves, Female

BIBLIOGRAPHY

Boureau, Alain. *Le Droit de cuissage. La Fabrication d'un mythe*. L'Évolution de l'humanité. Paris: Albin Michel, 1995.

———. *The Lord's First Night: The Myth of the* Droit de cuissage. Translated by Lydia G. Cochrane. Chicago: University of Chicago Press, 1998.

Louis, Marie Victoire. *Le Droit de cuissage: France, 1860–1930*. Patrimoine. Paris: Éditions de l'Atelier/Éditions ouvrières, 1994. [Modern, leftist-feminist context].

Wettlaufer, Jörg. "The *Jus primae noctis* as a Male Power Display: A Review of Historic Sources with Evolutionary Interpretation." *Evolution and Human Behavior* 21 (2000): 111–23.

ALAIN BOUREAU

JUTTA OF DISIBODENBERG, BLESSED

JUTTA OF DISIBODENBERG, BLESSED (1092–1136). Also called Jutta of Sponheim, Jutta is best known as the *magistra* (teacher) and friend of the young Hildegard of Bingen (1098–1179). She was also a German Benedictine nun of the Hirsau reform movement and founder of the women's anchorhold attached to the men's monastery at Disibodenberg (St. Disibod).

The two chief sources for Jutta's life are the *Vita domnae Juttae* (*Life of Jutta*), and the *Epistola* (*Letter*) no. 38 by Guibert of Gembloux, a French-speaking monk who corresponded with Hildegard and others. These and supplementary documents have been collected and translated by Silvas (1998). They depict Jutta overall as a woman of considerable force of character, vigorously sublimated and directed toward God. Her family was of the upper nobility: her father was Count Stephan II of Sponheim (mid-Rhineland); her mother, Sophia of Formbach (Bavaria), was a cousin of the duke of Saxony, later Emperor Lothar III (r. 1125–1138). Their social milieu's spiritual and political affiliation was pro-papal, pro-monastic, and anti-Salian (they shunned the Salian Franks, an old and powerful imperial dynasty, for seeking to regain control over the papacy and territorial German princes). Jutta's "capacious intelligence" became apparent during her early education, including lessons in Latin, which took place at home under her widowed mother's guidance. Falling gravely ill at age twelve, she promised herself to God in celibacy if she recovered. Recover she did, only to find herself considered a highly desirable marriage prospect. As we find in the lives of other holy women pledged to celibacy despite social pressure to marry (Barbara Newman compares Jutta's celibacy defense to that of her English contemporary, Christina of Markyate), she struggled hard to keep her commitment to celibacy, eventually "seeking out" Archbishop Ruthard of Mainz (1089–1109) to have her resolve confirmed. Ruthard would later continue to influence her career, at least indirectly.

On returning home (1105/1106) she submitted herself to a devout widow of Göllheim, Lady Uda, as her *magistra* for three years. Meanwhile, Jutta "burned" to go on pilgrimage. After her mother's death (1109/1110) she was planning to implement this desire when her brother, the future Count Meinhard, to dissuade her, appealed to Bishop (and future saint) Otto of Bamberg (1062/3–1139), at whose counsel she finally decided on becoming an anchoress (a female religious ascetic hermit).

Consequently, on All Saints' Day (November 1) 1112, she took her monastic vows and was solemnly enclosed, at age twenty, within the Benedictine monastery of Disibodenberg, together with Hildegard, aged fourteen, and their servant, also named Jutta. The site, on a hill by the Nahe and Glan rivers and originally an outpost of the diocese of Mainz (western Germany), had recently been restored—and actually was still under construction—thanks to Archbishop Ruthard, who staffed it with Benedictine monks from Mainz and Hirsau, as part of his role in preserving and reforming his domain amid the effects of the investiture controversy (the struggle between pope and emperor for supreme political power; Ruthard's monks were under his own control). At Disibodenberg, Jutta founded the women's anchorhold (cells enclosing the anchoresses) attached to the men's monastery—an arrangement not unusual among Benedictines of the Hirsau reform. As Hildegard's *magistra*, she was also her friend and foster mother, and most likely taught her enough Latin to enable her to chant the Psalter (Book of Psalms) but according to the sources, not much else in terms of literature, the arts or science—all areas in which Hildegard would later leave her mark. Despite her frail health, Jutta prayed fervently and practiced rigorous asceticism: she fasted, held vigils, and mortified her body by wearing an iron chain (which cut grooves into her flesh) and the hairshirt (an abrasive garment woven from coarse hair worn by ascetics and penitents), or by exposing her naked body to the cold or going barefoot in winter. She experienced visions (*Vita*, 8), and was reputed as a wonderworker. Jutta had a particular gift of insight into people's character, becoming spiritual mother to the monks and counselor to the many faithful who came seeking her help. She "fired up" so many young women "toward the love and awe of God," that the abbot gave permission for the expansion of the anchorhold into a school of female disciples. The *Vita* contains a moving eyewitness account of her final hours; she died at Disibodenberg on December 22, 1136. The monks, holding her in high regard, soon began to revere her as a saint.

The author of the *Vita* was Volmar (d. 1173), the monk who would become Hildegard's lifelong secretary and "only beloved son," and that it was written in the early 1140s (see Silvas, notes to trans.). Hildegard herself persuaded Abbot Kuno of Disibodenberg to commission it as Jutta's memorial (*Vita*, 1). The form of piety manifest in this work reflects the influence of the prevailing Benedictine reform movements: the abovementioned localized Hirsau reform and the far more extensive Cluniac revival, originating with the Cluny monastery in Burgundy (founded early tenth century). The model of holiness presented by the *Vita* recalls women saints of the Patristic Age (second to eighth centuries), for example, St. Radegund (c.525–587) (Hotchin; Newman). Constant Mews notes "a strong focus on the anticipation of death" throughout the *Vita* (Mews 1998). Yet there are also seeds of future developments: the earliest testimony to the visionary acumen of Hildegard, who sees in the *Vita* (9) a progress of Jutta's soul after death—much as what Dante would develop more fully in his *Divina Commedia* (*Divine Comedy*, 1321)— through the final assaults of Satan to her rescue by the saints, who lead her in a "majestic dance" into the community of Heaven.

In showing us a Jutta so enmeshed in the spiritual, social and economic fabric of Disibodenberg, the *Vita* casts into relief the enormous uprooting involved in Hildegard's drive to establish a separate community for the nuns at Rupertsberg.

See also *Ancrene Riwle*; Celibacy; Christina of Markyate; Hildegard of Bingen, St.; Radegund, St.; Rules for Canonesses, Nuns, and Recluses

BIBLIOGRAPHY

Primary Sources

Guibert of Gembloux. ["Letter 38: to Bovo."] In *Guiberti Gemblacensis Epistolae*, edited by Albert Derolez, 366–79. *Corpus Christianorum Continuatio Mediaevalis*, 66A. Turnhout, Belgium: Brepols, 1989. [Latin text only].

———. In *Jutta and Hildegard: the Biographical Sources*. Edited and translated by Anna Silvas. Medieval Women: Texts and Contexts, 1. Turnhout: Brepols, 1998; Brepols Medieval Women Series. University Park: Pennsylvania State University Press, 1999. [English translation with commentary].

Volmar. [*Life of Jutta*]. In *Reform and Reformgruppen im Erzbistum Mainz. Vom "Libellus de Willigisi consuetudinibus" zur "Vita domnae Juttae inclusae."* Edited by Franz Staab. In *Reformidee und Reformpolitik im Spätsalisch-Frühstaufischen Reich. Vorträge der Tagung der Gesellschaft für Mittelrheinische Kirchengeschichte vom 11. bis 13. September 1991 in Trier*, edited by Stefan Weinfurter, 119–87 [Anhang II: *Vita domnae Juttae inclusae*, 172–87]. Quellen und Abhandlungen zur Mittelrheinische Geschichte, 68. Mainz: Gesellschaft für Mittelrheinische Kirchengeschichte, 1992. [Latin text only].

———. [*Life of Jutta*]. "Aus Kindheit und Lehrzeit Hildegards Mit einer Übersetzung der Vita iherer Leherin Jutta von Sponheim." Translated by Franz Staab. In *Hildegard von Bingen: Prophetin durch die Zeiten, zum 900 Geburtstag*, edited by Abbess Edeltraud Forster and the Convent of the Benedictine Abbey of St. Hildegard, Eibingen. Freiburg, Germany: Herder, 1997. [German translation and commentary with material on Hildegard's early years by the original editor of Volmar's Latin *Vita*].

———. In *Jutta and Hildegard: the Biographical Sources*. Edited and translated by Anna Silvas. *See above under* Guibert.

Secondary Sources

Flanagan, Sabina, *Hildegard of Bingen, 1098–1179: A Visionary Life*. Revised ed. London: Routledge, 1998.

———. "Oblation or Enclosure: Reflections on Hildegard of Bingen's Entry into Religion." In *Wisdom which Encircles Circles*, edited by Audrey E. Davidson, 1–14. Kalamazoo, Mich.: Medieval Institute Publications, 1996.

Hotchin, Julie. "Enclosure and Containment: Jutta and Hildegard at the Abbey of Disibodenberg." *Magistra* 2. 2 (1996): 103–23.

Mews, Constant J. "Religious Thinker: 'A Frail Human Being' on Fiery Life." In *Voice of the Living Light: Hildegard of Bingen and Her World*, edited by Barbara Newman, 52–69. Berkeley and Los Angeles: University of California Press, 1998.

———. "Seeing is Believing: Hildegard of Bingen and the *Life of Jutta, Scivias,* and the *Commentary on the Rule of Benedict*." *Tjurunga* 51 (1996): 9–40.

Mötsch, Johannes. "Genealogie der Grafen von Sponheim." *Jahrbuch für westdeutsche Landesgeschichte* 13 (1987): 63–179.

Newman, Barbara. " 'Sibyl of the Rhine': Hildegard's Life and Times." In *Voice of the Living Light*, 1–29, *see above under* Mews.

Van Engen, John. "Abbess: 'Mother and Teacher'." In *Voice of the Living Light*, 30–51, *see above under* Mews.

ANNA SILVAS

[Hildegard]. *Scivias. See under* Führkötter *below.*

Lowe, E[lias] A[very], ed. *Codices Latini Antiquiores.* 11 vols. and suppl. Oxford: Clarendon Press, 1934–1971.

Monasticon Italiae, 3: Puglia e Basilicata. Edited by Giovanni Lunardi et al. Cesena, Italy: Badia di S. Maria del Monte, 1986.

Secondary Sources

Avril, François, and Patricia Danz Stirnemann. *Manuscrits enluminés d'origine insulaire, VIIe–XXe siècle.* Paris: Bibliothèque Nationale, 1987.

Beach, Alison I. "Voices from a Distant Land: Fragments from a Twelfth-Century Nuns' Letter Collection." *Speculum* 77 (2002): 34–54.

Bell, David. *What Nuns Read: Books and Libraries in Medieval English Nunneries.* Kalamazoo, Mich.: Cistercian Publications, 1995.

Bischoff, Bernhard. "Die Kölner Nonnenhandschriften und das Skriptorium von Chelles." In *Mittelalterliche Studien,* 1: 16–38. Stuttgart, Germany: Hiersemann, 1966.

———. *Kalligraphie in Bayern, Achtes bis zwölftes Jahrhundert.* Wiesbaden, Germany: L. Reichert, 1981.

———. *Paléographie de l'antiquité romaine et du Moyen Âge occidental.* Translated by Hartmut Atsma and Jean Vezin. Paris: Picard, 1985.

———, and Josef Hofmann. *Libri Sancti Kyliani: Die Würzberger Schreibschule une die Dombibliothek im VIII und IX Jahrhundert.* Quellen und Forschungen zur Geschichte des Bistums und Hochstifts Würzburg, 6. Würzburg, Germany: F. Schoningh, 1952.

Bishop, T[erence]. A. M. "The Prototype of *Liber glossarum.*" In *Medieval Scribes, Manuscripts and Libraries: Essays presented to N. R. Ker,* edited by M[alcolm] B. Parkes and Andrew G. Watson, 69–86. London: Scolar Press, 1978.

Boffey, Julia. "Women Authors and Women's Literacy in Fourteenth- and Fifteenth-Century England." In *Women and Literature in Britain 1150–1500,* edited by Carol M. Meale, 159–82. Cambridge: Cambridge University Press, 1993.

Bondeele-Souchier, Anne. *Bibliothèques cisterciennes dans la France médiévale: répertoire des abbayes d'hommes.* Paris: CNRS, 1991.

Bozzolo, Carla. "La Production manuscrite dans les pays rhénans au XVe siècle (à partir des manuscrits datés)." *Civiltà* 18 (1994): 183–242.

Brownrigg, Linda L., ed. *Medieval Book Production: Assessing the Evidence.* Los Altos, Calif.: Anderson-Lovelace, 1990.

Bruckner, Albert. "Zum Problem der Frauenhandschriften im Mittelalter." In *Aus Mittelalter und Neuzeit, Festschrift zum 70 Geburtstag von Gerhard Kallen [...],* edited by Josef Engel and Hans M. Klinkenberg, 171–83. Berlin: P. Hanstein, 1957.

——— "Weibliche Schreibtätigkeit im schweizerischen Spätmittelalter." In *Festschrift Bernhard Bischoff,* edited by Johanne Autenrieth and Franz Brunhölzl, 441–48. Stuttgart, Germany: Hiersemann, 1979.

Christianson, C. Paul. "A Century of the Manuscript-book Trade in Medieval London." *Medievalia et Humanistica* n.s. 12 (1984): 143–65.

Doyle, A[nthony]. I. "Book Production by the Monastic Orders in England (c.1375–1530): Assessing the Evidence." In Brownrigg, see above, 1–19.

Dronke, Peter. *Women Writers of the Middle Ages: A Critical Study of Texts from Perpetua (†203) to Marguerite Porete (†1310).* Cambridge: Cambridge University Press, 1984.

Ehrenschwendtner, Marie-Luise. "A Library Collected by and for the Use of Nuns: St. Catherine's Convent, Nuremberg." In Smith and Taylor, see below, 123–32.

Ferrante, Joan. *To the Glory of Her Sex: Women's Roles in the Composition of Medieval Texts.* Bloomington and Indianapolis: Indiana University Press, 1997.

Fianu, Kouky. "Familles et solidarités dans les métiers du livre parisien au XIVe siècle. *Médiévales* 19 (1990): 83–90.

———. *Histoire juridique et sociale des métiers du livre à Paris (1275–1521).* Ph.D. diss., Université de Montréal, 1991.

Finnegan, Sr. Mary Jeremy, O.P. *The Women of Helfta: Scholars and Mystics*. Athens and London: University of Georgia Press, 1991.

Frugoni, Chiara. "La Femme imaginée." In *Histoire des femmes en Occident*, edited by Georges Duby and Michelle Perrot. Vol. 2: *Le Moyen Âge*, edited by Christiane Klapisch-Zuber, 357–437. Paris: Plon, 1991.

Führkötter, Adelgundis. *Les miniatures du Scivias: la connaissance des voies de Sainte Hildegarde de Bingen, tirées du codex de Rupertsberg*. Armaria patristica et mediaevalia, 1. Turnhout, Belgium: Brepols, 1977. [miniatures from the facsim. made at Maria-Laach in 1927 of the original text (Hessische Landesbibliothek MS I), which was lost in 1945].

———. *The Miniatures from the Book Scivias—Know the Ways—of St. Hildegard of Bingen from the Illuminated Rupertsberg Codex*. Translated by F. Hockey. Turnhout: Brepols, 1977. [Provides facsimile of the lost Rupertsberg Codex].

Gasse-Grandjean, Marie-José. *Les Livres dans les abbayes vosgiennes du Moyen Âge*. Nancy, France: Presses Universitaires de Nancy, 1992.

Gebele, Eduard. "Hätzlerin, Clara." *Neue Deutsche Biographie* 7: 455–56. Berlin: Duncker & Humbolt, 1966.

Gies, Frances, and Joseph Gies. *Women in the Middle Ages*. New York: Crowell, 1978.

Gousset, Marie-Thérèse. "Parcheminiers et libraires rouennais à la fin du quatorzième siècle d'après un document judiciaire." *Viator* 24 (1993): 233–47.

Greer, Germaine. *The Obstacle Race: The Fortunes of Women Painters and Their Work*. London: Secker & Warburg; New York: Farrar, Straus & Giroux, 1979.

Hamburger, Jeffrey F. "Art, Enclosure and the *Cura Monialium*: Prolegomena in the Guise of a Postscript." *Gesta* 31 (1992): 108–34.

———. *Nuns as Artists: The Visual Culture of a Medieval Convent*. Berkeley: University of California Press, 1997.

———. *The Visual and the Visionary: Art and Female Spirituality in Late Medieval Germany*. New York: Zone Books, 1998.

Hasenohr, Geneviève. "Les Monastères de femmes." In *Histoire des bibliothèques françaises*, t. I: *Les Bibliothèques médiévales du VIe siècle à 1530*, edited by André Vernet, 250–51. Paris: Promodis, 1989.

Hindman, Sandra. *Christine de Pizan's "Epistre Othéa": Painting and Politics at the Court of Charles VI*. Toronto: Pontifical Institute of Mediæval Studies, 1986.

Lauwers, Michel, and Walter Simons. *Béguins et Béguines à Tournai au bas Moyen Âge*. Tournai, Belgium: Archives du chapitre cathedral; Louvain, Belgium: Université catholique de Louvain-la-neuve, 1988.

Lewis, Gertrud Jaron. *By Women, for Women, about Women: The Sister-Books of Fourteenth-Century Germany*. Toronto: Pontifical Institute of Mediaeval Studies, 1996.

Lowe, Kate. "Women's Work at the Benedictine Convent of Le Murate in Florence: Suora Battista Carducci's Roman Missal of 1509." In Smith and Taylor, see below, 133–46.

Mate, Mavis E. *Women in Medieval English Society*. Cambridge: Cambridge University Press, 1999.

Meiss, Millard. *French Painting in the Time of Jean de Berry: The Late Fourteenth Century and the Patronage of the Duke*. 2 vols. New York and London: Phaidon, 1967.

———. *French Painting in the Time of Jean de Berry: The Limbourgs and Their Contemporaries*. 2 vols. New York: Pierpont Morgan/Braziller, 1974.

Oliver, Judith. *Gothic Manuscript Illumination in the Diocese of Liège (c.1250 –c.1330)*. 2 vols. Louvain: Uitgeverij, 1988.

———. "Gothic Women and Merovingian Desert Mothers." *Gesta* 32 (1993): 124–34.

———. "Worship of the Word: Some Gothic *Nonnenbücher* in their Devotional Context." In Smith and Taylor, *see below*, 106–22.

Ouy, Gilbert, and Christine Reno. "Identification des autographes de Christine de Pizan," *Scriptorium* 34 (1980): 221–38.

Pernoud, Régine. *La Femme au temps des cathédrales*. Paris: Stock, 1980.

Pryce, Huw, ed. *Literacy in Medieval Celtic*. Cambridge Studies in Medieval Literature, 33. Cambridge and New York: Cambridge University Press, 1998.

Riché, Pierre. *Éducation et culture dans l'occident barbare, VIe–VIIIe siècles.* Paris: Seuil, 1962. 4th ed., 1995.

———. *Education and Culture in the Barbarian West.* Translated by John Contreni. Columbia: University of South Carolina Press, 1979.

Rouse, Richard H., and Mary A. Rouse. "The Commercial Production of Manuscript Books in Late-Thirteenth-Century and Early-Fourteenth-Century Paris." In Brownrigg, see above, 103–15.

———. *Manuscripts and their Makers: Commercial Book Production in Medieval Paris 1200–1500.* 2 vols. Turnhout: Harvey Miller, 2000.

Smith, Lesley. "Scriba, Femina: Medieval Depictions of Women Writing." In Smith and Taylor, *see below,* 21–44.

———, and Jane H. M. Taylor, eds. *Women and the Book. Assessing the Visual Evidence.* London and Toronto: British Library/University of Toronto, 1996.

Stiennon, Jacques. *Paléographie du Moyen Âge.* 2nd ed. Paris: Armand Colin, 1991.

Stirnemann, Patricia, and Marie-Thérèse Gousset. "Marques, mots, pratiques: leur signification et leurs liens dans le travail des enlumineurs." In *Vocabulaire du livre et de l'écriture au Moyen Âge,* edited by Olga Weijers, 34–55. Turnhout: Brepols, 1989.

Taylor, Andrew. "Authors, Scribes, Patrons and Books." In *The Idea of the Vernacular: An Anthology of Middle English Literary Theory, 1280–1520,* edited by Jocelyn Wogan-Browne et al. University Park: Pennsylvania State University Press, 1999: 353–65.

Wemple, Suzanne Fonay. "S. Salvatore/ S. Giulia: A Case Study in the Endowment and Patronage of a Major Female Monastery in Northern Italy." In *Women of the Medieval World: Essays in Honor of John H. Mundy,* edited by Julius Kirshner and Suzanne F. Wemple, 85–102. London, Oxford, and New York: Blackwell, 1985.

———. "Les Traditions romaine, germanique et chrétienne." In *Histoire des femmes en Occident,* vol. 2: *Le Moyen Âge,* edited by Christine Klapisch-Zuber, 185–216. Paris: Plon, 1991.

———. *Women in Frankish Society, Marriage and the Cloister, 500–900.* Philadelphia: University of Pennsylvania Press, 1981.

Willard, Charity Cannon. "An Autograph Manuscript of Christine de Pizan?" *Studi francesi* 27 (1965): 452–57.

SUZANNE FONAY WEMPLE AND CHRISTINE M. RENO

SCROVEGNI, MADDALENA (1356–1429). The first of the Quattrocento women humanists, Maddalena Scrovegni was born to a Paduan noble family. We know less about her early life and education than we do about most other women humanists, and of her literary production we possess only handful of letters. She is of considerable interest, however, because she is the earliest woman whose humanist career (i.e., the study and emulation of Classical Greek and Latin literature) is attested, thanks to her correspondents. Furthermore, her life and writing demonstrate a relationship between humanist culture and politics that is relatively atypical for a woman humanist. In 1376, she was married to a nobleman from Reggio, who died after only a few years of marriage; by 1381 she had returned to Padua to live with her natal family. There, she became involved with the rest of her family in one of the factional disputes that plagued late medieval Italian civic life. The Scrovegni were leaders of one faction, the Carrara family leaders of the other. In their search for power, the Scrovegni allied themselves with Giangaleazzo Visconti of Milan (d. 1402), but when his forces were defeated by the Carrara, they, including Maddalena, were forced to flee the city in 1390. Maddalena settled, together with some of her family, in Venice, where she lived until her death in 1429.

Scrovegni's extant letters, like some of those of her contemporary and correspondent Angela Nogarola, aunt of Isotta Nogarola (1418–1466), were written in support of the

Visconti cause. One letter, to Giangaleazzo Visconti, produced first an official response from Visconti's secretary, Antonio Loschi (1365–1441), and then, as he tells the story, a second, more "personal" response generated by Loschi's admiration for Scrovegni's learning. Loschi and Scrovegni had more than literary connections, however. Not only were they both supporters of Visconti expansion in the 1380s and 1390s, but Scrovegni's cousin Ugulotto Biancardo was a Visconti captain and a friend of Loschi's.

The political connections are missing altogether from Loschi's separate letters—he wrote a lengthy poem and an accompanying prose commentary—to Scrovegni. Indeed, the occasion he tells us inspired him to write—his admiration for her learning—is also strikingly missing. Although he begins by praising her "virile spirit" (as so many later men would praise the virility of the learned women to whom they wrote), he goes on to write 162 lines in praise of her chastity, which he imagines as a temple located far away on the Scythian plain, where the Amazons rule. In it, Scrovegni sits on a glass throne, surrounded by marble images of chaste figures from Classical Antiquity and by personifications of virtues associated with chastity: purity, modesty, continence, penitence, virginity, and frugality. Chastity is assaulted by the forces of Cupid and Venus, but in the battle that ensues she emerges triumphant. One of the most striking things about the images that Loschi uses, which are common but rarely used in such detail in men's responses to women's learning, is the contrast between the simultaneous power and fragility of chastity. Chastity is here, as almost always in humanist writing, absolutely central to definitions of women's virtue, but it is also always under siege; Loschi tells us that the throne on which Scrovegni/Chastity sits in his imaginary temple is made of glass because nothing else is so clear or beautiful, nor so violable and weak—and, of course, the ensuing attack by Cupid and his lustful throng demonstrates the aptness of the image.

Scrovegni herself, unsurprisingly, seems to have been neither so weak nor so powerful as Loschi imagined her in his poem. She wrote other letters—four in all are extant—in support of the Visconti cause; she was also well-enough known in her own day to have been included in a catalogue of famous women by Petrarch's colleague Lombardo della Seta (now lost), and her story and her letters were collected in manuscripts and early printed books down through the early sixteenth century as models for others (men and women alike) to imitate. She also corresponded with Angela Nogarola, another Visconti partisan, about matters both political and personal; there is a letter from Nogarola to Scrovegni on the death of her brother, written very much in the mode of the classical letter of consolation, but whose sharply drawn contrasts between masculine fortitude in the face of desperate grief and the tears of silly foolish weak little women sound an odd note in a correspondence between women.

Not only do Scrovegni's life, letters, and reputation deserve greater attention than they have received, but Loschi's response to her also offers an unparalleled opportunity to read gender relations in Italian humanism on a larger scale. Loschi's greatest claim to fame in modern historiography is probably as the opponent of the influential humanistic scholar Coluccio Salutati (1331–1406), who was also chancellor of Florence during Florence's wars against the Visconti and a leading proponent of the republican ideology that has come to be called civic humanism (applying one's Classical learning to civic affairs). In their literary debates over the relative merits of republican versus monarchical regimes, and specifically in their uses of gendered tropes (figures of speech) and tropes of rape to talk about political relations, Loschi and Salutati both use and help to create a common literary and political vocabulary that figured prominently, as Loschi's letters to Scrovegni reveal, in humanist responses to women, especially learned women, as well. Reading the Loschi–Scrovegni exchange in the epistolary contexts of their respective correspondents broadens both our understanding of their personal concerns, and our awareness of the political and social vocabularies they deployed in their writing.

See also Humanists, Italian Women, Issues and Theory; Nogarola, Angela; Nogarola, Isotta

BIBLIOGRAPHY

Primary Sources
Delle inscrizioni veneziane. Edited by Emmanuele Antonio Cigogna, 1: 289; 2: 453–55. 2 vols. Venice: Giuseppe Orlandelli, 1824.
Loschi, Antonio, and Coluccio Salutati. [Letters]. In "Antonio Loschi e Coluccio Salutati (con quattro epistole inedite del Loschi)," edited by Vittorio Zaccaria. *Atti dell'Istituto veneto di scienze, lettere, ed arti* 129 (1970–1971): 345–87.
———. "Una epistola metrica inedita di Antonio Loschi a Maddalena Scrovegni." Edited by Vittorio Zaccaria. *Bollettino del Museo Civico di Padova* 46 (1957–8): 153–68.
Nogarola, Angela. [Letters and Poems]. In *Isotae Nogarolae Veronensis Opera quae supersunt omnia*, edited by Eugen Abel, vol. 2. Budapest: F. Kilian, 1886. [Latin only].
Scrovegni, Maddalena. [Letters]. In "Maddalena degli Scrovegni e le discordie tra i Carraresi e gli Scrovegni," edited by Antonio Medin, 260–62. *Atti e memorie dell'Accademia patavina di scienze lettere ed arti* 12 (1896): 243–72. [Latin only].
———. "Letter of the Lady Maddalena [...] to Jacopo delle Verme rejoicing in the conquest of Padua [...]." In *Her Immaculate Hand: Selected Works by and about the Women Humanists of Quattrocento Italy*, translated with commentary by Margaret King and Albert Rabil Jr., 33–35. Medieval & Renaissance Texts & Studies, 20. Binghamton, N.Y.: Center for Medieval & Early Renaissance Studies, 1983. [Excellent introduction and notes].
Salutati, Coluccio. *Epistolario di Coluccio Salutati*. Edited by Francesco Novati. 4 vols. Rome: Istituto Storico Italiano, 1891–1911.
———. *Invectiva Lini Colucii Salutati [...] in Antonium Luschum Vicentinum*. Florence, Italy: Typis Magherianis, 1826.

Secondary Sources
King, Margaret L. "Goddess and Captive: Antonio Loschi's Poetic Tribute to Maddalena Scrovegni (1389), Study and Text." *Medievalia et Humanistica* n.s. 10 (1981): 103–27.
Kohl, Benjamin G. "The Scrovegni in Carrara Padua." *Apollo* 142. 406 (December 1995): 43–47.
Schio, Giovanni da. *Sulla vita e sugli scritti di Antonio Loschi vicentino, uomo di lettere e di stato*. Padua: Tipi del Seminario, 1858.
Witt, Ronald G. *Hercules at the Crossroads: The Life, Works, and Thought of Coluccio Salutati*. Duke Monographs in Medieval and Renaissance Studies, 6. Durham, N.C.: Duke University Press, 1983.

JENNIFER FISK RONDEAU

SEDAZZARI, BERNARDINA. *See* **Catherine of Bologna, St.**

SEI SHONAGON (966–c.1017). Sei Shonagon, the author of *Makura no soshi* (*The Pillow Book*), was rivaled in fame only by Murasaki Shikibu (c.973–c.1015) among Japanese women writers, yet we know little about her life. Like other women of her time, even her name is something of a mystery: *Sei* is the Sino-Japanese pronunciation of the first character in Kiyohara, her father's name; *Shonagon* means "lesser counselor"—her position at court. Neither her father nor husband held that title.

Sei was the daughter of Kiyohara no Motosuke (908–990), a distinguished poet in the preeminent Japanese court poetry tradition of the Heian period known as *waka*. From 993 until 1001 she was in the court service of Empress Sadako/Teishi, the first consort of Emperor Ichijo and thus the center of the court's cultural life. Moreover, Empress Sadako's father, Fujiwara Michitaka, controlled matters as a sort of grey eminence until his death in 995, whereupon his brother, Michinaga, took over, thereby advancing his own daughter, Shoshi/Akiko, as the Emperor Ichijo's potential new favorite. Sadako's standing became precarious for the ensuing five years, during which time Sei remained in her service until Sadako died in childbirth (1000). Empress Shoshi was served by Murasaki Shikibu, which made Sei and Murasaki members of rival literary "salons." Thereafter, the only recorded events of Sei's life were her visits to various temples and shrines. However, the final section of *Makura no soshi* offers information on the circumstances under which she began writing the book, how it first came into circulation, and its reception at court.

Sei Shonagon wrote during the great mid-Heian period of feminine vernacular literature that produced not only the world's first novel, Murasaki Shikibu's *Genji Monogatari* (*Tale of Genji*), but also abundant poetry and a series of diaries mostly by court ladies. These illustrate what life was like for upper-class Japanese women a thousand years ago. In the Heian Period, when the educated male was expected to write both public documents and private memoirs in *kanbun* (Chinese as used in China, plus Japanese forms of Chinese), women took the lead in developing prose writing in a distinctly Japanese style called *hiragana*.

Makura no soshi (*Notes of the Pillow* or *Pillow Book*) is probably a generic name referring to a miscellany, a group of literary jottings, or an informal book of notes that both men and women composed when retiring to their rooms for the evening. The actual term *Pillow Book* may refer to books kept in the drawers in wooden pillows used by ladies of the court who had elaborate hairdos, or perhaps it alludes to a writer's sketchbook of topics for poetry and prose composition, as a kind of thesaurus to be consulted when composing poetry. Though this one by Sei, comprising some 320 sections, is the only collection of its type to have survived, many others may have been written. It is the precursor of the typically Japanese genre *zuihitsu* (literally, following the brush), which is still popular today. Sei Shonagon herself probably did not give the work its name, but rather a later scribe took it from a reference in the epilogue. Since even the earliest surviving manuscript dates from the sixteenth century, it is difficult to determine how faithful this manuscript is to Sei's original plan for her work, which some believe she had intended as a gift for Sadako's daughter (see "Other Women's Voices").

Two elements distinguish *Makura no soshi*: the obvious wit and learning of the author and its stylistic beauty as an example of Japanese writing. Within its sections are 164 catalogues of places, plants, and objects. Some of the best-known sections concern items on which Sei expresses a personal opinion or notes a paradox, such as "Things that Look Pretty but Are Bad Inside," "Things Which Cannot Be Compared," and "Things That Have Lost Their Power." Examples of "Things that Are Near though Distant" include "Paradise" and "Relations between Man and Woman." A wry intercultural note injects itself in such items as

"Words that Look Commonplace but that become Impressive When Written in Chinese Characters." In addition to her lists, Sei provides numerous descriptions of nature, diary entries, character sketches, and court anecdotes. Pioneering translator Arthur Waley deems the *Makura no soshi* "the most important document of the period that we possess." Entries range in length from a line or two to several pages, with no obvious attempt to unify or arrange the various components. The work's celebrated opening, which lists the best times of day for admiring the four seasons, established a tradition eliciting responses from a number of poets. Her epithets, like "dawn of spring" and "evening of autumn" became standard clichés in later waka and *monogatari*—the latter meaning literally, gibberish, idle talk, then came to signify a work of prose fiction in the vernacular.

Murasaki Shikibu refers to Sei in her own diary (*Nikki*) and appears to have read *Makura no soshi*, yet we do not know if the two women ever actually met. Given certain snide remarks by Murasaki about Sei—portraying the latter as "dreadfully conceited"; one who "thought herself so clever, and littered her writings with Chinese characters [which] left a great deal to be desired" (Murasaki, trans. Bowring, 131–32)—we doubt it could have been a pleasant encounter had it occurred. Critics rank Sei's work as second only to Murasaki's *Genji Monogatari* (*Tale of Genji*), whose popularity did indeed outshine that of *Makura no soshi*. However, Sei's book was frequently imitated, particularly in the zuihitsu work, *Tsurezuregusa* (*Essays in Idleness*) by Yoshida Kenko (1282?–1350). Because of her acclaimed intelligence, Sei became the subject of several posthumous legends. In the visual arts as well, Sei Shonagon reappears in the fourteenth-century *Pillow-Book Scroll*, perhaps painted by a female artist (Weidner); a scene from her *Makura no soshi*, also illustrated by a known woman artist in the sixteenth century—Kyohara Yukinobu—exists as well ("Other Women's Voices").

See also Abutsu-ni; China, Women in; Izumi Shikibu; Murasaki Shikibu

BIBLIOGRAPHY

Primary Sources
[All are English texts only unless specifically noted otherwise].
Murasaki Shikibu. [*Murasaki Shikibu Nikki*; *Kashu*]. *Her Diary and Poetic Memoirs: A Translation and Study* by Richard Bowring. Princeton Library of Asian Translations. Princeton, N.J.: Princeton University Press, 1982. Reprint 1985. [English trans. with excellent introduction and notes].
Sei Shonagon. [*Makura no soshi*]. *The Book of Sei Shonogan*. Translated and edited by Ivan Morris. Records of Civilization. Translations from the Asian Classics. 2 vols. New York: Columbia University Press, 1967. [The definitive trans. with extensive notes, tables, etc.].
———. [*Makura no soshi*]. *The Book of Sei Shonogan*. Translated and edited by Ivan Morris. Translations from the Asian Classics. New York: Columbia University Press, 1991. [Abridged, 1-vol. ed.].
———. [*Makura no soshi*]. *The Book of Sei Shonogan*. Translated by Arthur Waley. Boston: Houghton-Mifflin, 1929. [Highly abridged but historically important].
Yoshida Kenko. *Essays in Idleness: The Tsurezuregusa of Kenko*. Translated by Donald Keene. Records of Civilization. Translations from the Asian Classics. 2nd ed. New York: Columbia University Press, 1998.
[Various]. *Classical Japanese Prose. An Anthology*. Edited by Helen Craig McCullough. Stanford, Calif.: Stanford University Press, 1990.

Secondary Sources
Kato, Shuichi. *A History of Japanese Literature*. Translated by David Chibbett. Tokyo: Kodansha International, 1979.

Keene, Donald. *Seeds in the Heart: Japanese Literature from Earliest Times to the Late Sixteenth Century.* New York: Henry Holt, 1993.

Konishi, Jinichi. *A History of Japanese Literature.* Translated by Aileen Gatten. Princeton, N.J.: Princeton University Press, 1984.

Miner, Earl. ed. *Principles of Classical Japanese Literature.* Princeton, N.J.: Princeton University Press, 1985.

"Other Women's Voices" Web site: http://www.tl.infi.net/~ddisse/shonagon.html [Very useful updated resource, with historical information, translated excerpts, and bibliography, plus images].

Morris, Mark. "Sei Shonagon's Poetic Catalogues." *Harvard Journal of Asiatic Studies* 40. 1 (1980): 5–54.

Rimer, J. Thomas. *A Reader's Guide to Japanese Literature.* Tokyo: Kodansha International, 1988.

Weidner, Marsha, ed. *Flowering in the Shadows. Women in the History of Chinese and Japanese Painting.* Honolulu: University of Hawai'i Press, 1990.

CYNTHIA HO

SENTIMENTAL ROMANCE. *See Novela Sentimental/Sentimental Romance*

SFORZA, IPPOLITA (1445–1488). A humanist scholar and patron of letters—the only important woman humanist of her generation—Ippolita was the daughter of Francesco Sforza I, duke of Milan (1401–1466), and Bianca Visconti Sforza and thus from two illustrious noble families. She and her numerous siblings studied Latin with Guiniforte Barzizza, founder of a leading school of humanist studies in Milan, and with Baldo Martorello, himself a student of Vittorino da Feltre (1378–1446). The Sforza children learned Greek from Constantine Lascaris, tutor to other Italian humanists. In 1459, Ippolita gave a striking Latin oration in Mantua commending her family to Pope Pius II (Enea Silvio Piccolomini, 1405–1464), himself a noted humanist scholar. In florid terms she expounds on her own "shyness and timidity because of [her] age, sex, and frailty of mind," at addressing the pontiff, and her unworthiness to do so, but trusts in his forbearance. The hyperbole of self-abnegation and praise is typical of exalted humanist discourse: "But to what end do I dare to praise you? Is it in order to use my crude and childish words to make filthy your golden and nearly divine virtues?" The address solicits the pope's favor for her family on the basis of their conviction that his papacy would fulfill their hopes for Christendom's restoration and for their own family fortunes: "For, indeed, we believe you are a star sent down from heaven to govern the bark of St. Peter [which is today] imperiled and nearly submerged."

Prior to marrying to Alfonso, duke of Calabria (later King Alfonso II) in 1465, Ippolita Sforza gave her only other surviving address: a similarly hyperbolic praise of her mother, a woman noted for her charitable works, generous patronage of humanists, and loyalty to her husband even against her own, powerful family, the Visconti. In her oration, after a lengthy *occupatio* (rhetorical strategy anticipating possible criticism) disclaiming the need for any *captatio benevolentiae* (means of charming her listeners)—but which effectively serves as one—Ippolita professes to "speak plainly . . . and confess what I feel." The address is of course not at all plain, but ornate and convoluted. She praises her mother's virtues both "religious" (piety, charity) and "human" (liberality, character):

For your intelligence shines resplendent with faith in the divine, your memory flowers with hopes of heaven, your will is inflamed and aglow with charity and the zeal of doing good for all humankind; for all these reasons your beautiful soul, created in the likeness of her creator, will attain eternal praise and glory. [. . .] You enrich neighbors and relatives, you favor friends and well-wishers, you mercifully assist the poor with your wealth, so that you seem to have been born not for yourself alone but for the whole world.

After her marriage, Ippolita ceased being a scholar and author and rather, perhaps in emulation of her mother the duchess of Milan, who died three years later, Ippolita, duchess of Calabria, became more of a patroness, political promoter, and dedicatee of letters, gradually acquiring a valuable library at her residence at Castel Capuano in Naples. Fittingly enough, at her death, one Aulo Giano Parrasio (1470–1534) would deliver an oration honoring her memory, in the style of the *Silvae* by the innovative first-century Roman poet Statius (Klein).

See also Humanists, Italian Women, Issues and Theory; Rhetoric, Women and

BIBLIOGRAPHY

Primary Sources
Sforza, Ippolita. [Oration honoring her Mother]. Edited by G. G. Meersseman. "La Raccolta dell'umanista fiammingo Giovanni de Veris 'De arte epistolandi'." *Italia medioevale e umanistica* 15 (1972): 250–51. [Latin text only].
———. [Oration to Pope Pius II]. Edited by C. Corvisieri. In *Notabilia temporum di Angelo de Tummulillis da Sant'Elia*, 231–33. Fonti per la storia d'Italia, 7. Livorno, Italy, 1890. [Latin text only].
———. [Both Orations]. In *Her Immaculate Hand: Selected Works by and about the Women Humanists of Quattrocento Italy*, translated with commentary by Margaret King and Albert Rabil Jr., 45–48. Medieval & Renaissance Texts & Studies, 20. Binghamton, N.Y.: Center for Medieval & Early Renaissance Studies, 1983. [Excellent introduction and notes].

Secondary Source
Klein, Thomas. *Parrasios Epikedion auf Ippolita Sforza: ein Beispiel schöpferischer Aneignung inbesondere der Silven des Statius*. Studien zur Geschichte und Kultur des Altertums, 1: 3. Paderborn, Germany: F. Schöningh, 1987. [Analysis and critical ed. of *Epicedion* (Funeral oration) to Sforza].

REGINA PSAKI

SHORE, ELIZABETH (JANE) (c.1450–1527). Better known as Jane Shore, Elizabeth Shore enmeshed herself in the political intrigues of her time by engaging in sexual liaisons with King Edward IV of England (1442–1483) and with several prominent English courtiers. Shore's connections involved her in the latter part of the Wars of the Roses (1455–1485), in which the House of Lancaster (whose badge was the red rose) and the House of York (symbolized by the white rose) fought over succession to the English throne.

Shore is said to have derived her seductive powers less from her beauty than from her bright personality. In his *History of King Richard III*, Sir Thomas More (1478–1535) described Shore as follows: "Proper she was and fair [. . .] Yet delighted not men so much in her beauty, as in her pleasant behaviour. For a proper wit had she, and could both read well and write, merry of company, ready and quick of answer, neither mute nor full of babble, sometimes taunting without displeasure and not without disport" (cited in Ross 1976, 137).

What little is known of her early life is largely in dispute. Her father was John Lambert, a respected London mercer (merchant of fine textiles) and her mother was Amy Marshall, a grocer's daughter. She was christened Elizabeth in about 1450 and was married, very young, to William Shore, a London goldsmith. Some accounts assert that William Shore was attractive but impotent (Hammond et al.). The origin of the name "Jane" is uncertain; in the historical record, Shore's first name is often left out altogether. Shore probably became the king's mistress around 1470; in 1476, she petitioned the pope for an annulment of her marriage, citing William Shore's impotence. Although King Edward never permitted his lovers any political role, Shore acquired some influence at court, for she was the favorite among Edward's numerous mistresses, and her soothing attentions were said to have calmed the king in moments of anger or displeasure.

After Edward died in April 1483, Shore is thought to have become the mistress of Thomas Grey, marquis of Dorset (1451–1501), the eldest son (by a previous marriage) of Queen Elizabeth Woodville, and also of Dorset's rival, William, Lord Hastings (1430–1483). If this second relationship did indeed occur, it may explain why, at a council meeting in the Tower of London on June 13, 1483, Richard, duke of Gloucester (1452–1485), the brother of Edward IV, accused Shore and Queen Elizabeth of attempting, in collusion with Hastings, to destroy him through sorcery. Gloucester's charges led to Hastings's summary execution and to Shore's arrest. Using Shore as a symbol of the previous regime's debauchery and thereby as a means to advance himself, Richard made her do public penance as a harlot by forcing her to walk through London dressed only in her kirtle (a sort of gown) carrying a lighted taper. She was then imprisoned at Ludgate. Although she may have participated, perhaps as a go-between, in plots against Gloucester involving either Hastings or Dorset, the likelihood of her conspiring with her late lover's widow in sorcery is very remote. Most modern historians agree with contemporary commentators, such as More and the Italian-born humanist historian Polydore Vergil (1470–1555), author of the *Anglica Historia* (*English History*), that Gloucester largely invented these charges to eliminate Hastings, who was loyal to twelve-year-old Edward V and thus a serious obstacle to Gloucester's plans to usurp his nephew's throne. On July 6, 1483, only weeks after Hasting's execution and Shore's arrest, the duke was crowned as King Richard III.

While in prison, Shore managed to charm the king's solicitor, Thomas Lynom, who sought permission to marry her. In a letter to his chancellor, John Russell, bishop of Lincoln, Richard III urged the bishop to dissuade Lynom—apparently for the latter's benefit—from the marriage. The king lamented that Lynom was "marvelous blinded and abused with that late wife of William Shore" (London, British Library ms. Harley 433, fol. 259, cited in Hammond et al.). However, Richard reluctantly instructed Russell to allow the match if Lynom persisted. Some historians believe the marriage never happened because Shore was still living in poverty in London when Henry VIII came to the throne in 1509, although virtually nothing else is known for certain of Shore's life after 1484. Others hold that she and Lynom wed, had a daughter, and that Shore's dire final circumstances, alluded to in her extant will and by More, may have been partially due to Lynom losing his job when Henry VII (1457–1509) overthrew Richard III in 1485.

Jane Shore's place in history has probably been preserved precisely because of this lack of reliable information—we have, for instance, little clue as to her physical appearance beyond More and a likeness crudely etched into her parents' brass memorial at Hinxworth,

Hertfordshire (Hammond et al.). This uncertainty together with the "unfortunate concubine's" "female perversity" as contrasted with the "male entitlement" of the famous men with whom she had affairs (see Shepard) form the legend, drama, and romance that today surround Shore's name. Aside from the mentions in More and Vergil and a dozen plays and poems by sixteenth- through nineteenth-century English and French authors—including Thomas Churchyard's *Tragedy of Shore's Wife* (sixteenth century), Nicholas Rowe's oft-reprinted *Tragedy of Jane Shore* (1714), and an "Epilogue" by Alexander Pope (1740)—little has been written about Shore. Today, with the resurgent interest in women in literature, "the goldsmith's wife," by whatever name, continues to elicit critical discussion.

See also Godiva, Lady; Rosamond, Fair; Woodville, Elizabeth

BIBLIOGRAPHY

Primary Sources

More, Thomas. *History of King Richard III and Selections from the English and Latin Poems.* Edited by Richard S. Sylvester. New Haven, Conn.: Yale University Press, 1976.

Polydore Vergil. *Anglica Historia.* Menston, U.K.: Scolar Press, 1972. [Facsimile of the 1555 York Minster ed.].

———. Edited and translated by Denys Hay. Camden Third Series, 74. London: Royal Historical Society, 1950.

Secondary Sources

Hammond, Peter, et al., eds. *To Prove a Villain: The Real Richard III. Exhibition at London, Royal National Theatre, March 27–April 27, 1991.* Special online ed.: www.r3.org/rnt1991. [Richest trove of information on Shore and her time, including artifacts and documents].

Helgerson, Richard. "Weeping for Jane Shore." *South Atlantic Quarterly* 98 (1999): 451–76.

Ross, Charles. *Edward IV.* New ed. New Haven, Conn.: Yale University Press, 1997.

———. *Richard III.* Berkeley: University of California Press, 1981.

Seward, Desmond. *The Wars of the Roses through the Lives of Five Men and Women in the Fifteenth Century.* London: Constable; New York, Viking, 1995.

Shepard, Alan C. "'Female Perversity,' Male Entitlement: The Agency of Gender in More's *The History of Richard III.*" *The Sixteenth Century Journal* 26 (1995): 311–28.

Steible, Mary. "Jane Shore and the Politics of Cursing." *Studies in English Literature, 1500–1900* 43 (2003): 1–17. [On Churchyard's tragedy].

Wagner, John A. *Encyclopedia of the Wars of the Roses.* Santa Barbara, Calif.: ABC-Clio, 2001.

JOHN A. WAGNER

SISTER-BOOKS (*SCHWESTERNBÜCHER*) (1300–1350). Also called *Nonnenbücher* (nuns' books) or "convent chronicles" in German literary history, the Sister-Books constitute a unique body of women's writing and, more specifically, women's chronicles. Each book records the history and way of life in one particular community, housed within a monastery, whose place-name informs the book's title, for example, the Adelhausen Sister-Book, from the convent in Adelhausen, Germany. Each community belonged to the so-called Second Order within the Order of Preachers (*Ordo praedicatorum*, hence, "O.P.," also called Blackfriars)—the cloistered women of the Dominican Order, founded by St. Dominic in Bologna, Italy, c.1220. Actually, the term "Dominicans" ("hounds of the Lord"), used as an expedient here, did not come into use until the fifteenth century. From its inception, this order held learning and manuscript production in especially high esteem, a trait enhanced during its late-medieval reform phase and yielding, among other texts, the Sister-Books.

SISTER-BOOKS (*SCHWESTERNBÜCHER*)

Nine of these books are extant. Though two of them (those from Adelhausen and Unterlinden) were originally composed in Latin, all of them were transmitted in Middle-High German, since they were produced in the Dominican province of Teutonia, encompassing virtually all Christianized German-speaking areas during the thirteenth century: Alsace, Switzerland, Swabia, and Bavaria. In 1303, this province was then divided into provinces called Teutonia and Saxony. Written "by women, for women, and about women," these works deal retrospectively with the monasteries' beginnings during the first half of the thirteenth century and, in a series of *vitae*, or "lives," relate the lives of various sisters of the monastery to the community's spiritual growth. Unfortunately, the same reform impulse that gave birth to them would also at times alter and shorten their texts, particularly under the well-intentioned editing of confessor and self-styled historian Johannes Meyer (1422–1485), in his efforts to publicize them as part of his reformist program of spiritual renewal within the Order of Preachers. Yet overall, this order deserves credit for preserving these unique milestones in religious women's historiography.

Nineteenth-century scholars, because they were rediscovering the Sister-Books at the same time as they did many of the great mystical writers, mistakenly tended to judge them as works of mysticism, and thus often dismissed the former as weak imitations of the great mystics. Later critical evaluations since the 1950s placed these chronicles more correctly into the highly formulaic tradition of the medieval vitae and legendary works, such as the widely read collection of saints' lives called the *Legenda aurea* (*Golden Legend*). In 1980, Siegfried Ringler's medieval-rhetorical approach further rehabilitated appreciation of the Sister-Books by demonstrating that the many paranormal occurrences or extreme ascetic achievements described should not be taken literally, but rather read as *topoi* (literary commonplaces) or formulas for conveying the heightened spirituality of the sisters in their aspiration toward their own brand of saintliness.

With the exception of Ruth Meyer's 1995 text of the Katharinentaler Sister-Book, text editions of the nine Sister-Books, were done in the nineteenth century and are generally unreliable because many of them were published as diplomatic editions (literally faithful to only one manuscript of a given text, with little or no philological treatment, such as capitalization of proper nouns, standardized spelling, etc.). What few critical editions were done are now outdated. Since almost no extant original Sister-Book manuscripts have been recovered, editors have had to rely on later manuscripts from the fourteenth, and primarily the fifteenth, centuries, with some even later. Structurally speaking, the Sister-Books typically begin with a chronicle, an aspect often ignored in the reception history because of critical preoccupation with the following section, the sisters' vitae.

As early examples of women's historiography, the Sister-Books were based on sources of uneven reliability, ranging from papal bulls of the community's incorporation and chronological lists of prioresses to lengthy obituaries, in documenting what the sister-historians considered their monasteries' essential history. They describe the beginnings of their cloistered community, which usually originated as a *béguinage* (communities of women, called *beguines*, leading pious yet nonmonastic lives), and how, despite initial hardships including extreme poverty, they attracted a great following of young women to their way of life, and gradual acknowledgement by the Church. The chroniclers then concentrate on the sisters' communal spiritual development and fervent dedication to their only goal in life, to become "saintly." Unlike traditional history, and despite a clear awareness of great suffering both within the cloister walls and in the world outside, an underlying theme of

848

joy and celebration of divine graces permeates each Sister-Book. This is most noticeable in the epilogue, a closing hymn of spiritual jubilation called a *jubilus*. Though penned by women in closed communities, the Sister-Books were also intended for sisters in like-minded neighboring monasteries as well. During the great flourishing of Dominican monasteries, it may be assumed that they interacted via close networks united by similar ideals.

The following survey of the nine Sister-Books, listed in the chronological order of their date of composition insofar as it can best be determined, concentrates on the more salient, distinguishing features of each chronicle.

1. The *Adelhausen Sister-Book* was the work of Anna von Munzingen (1318). Though its Latin original has been lost, Middle-High-German and High-German translations of the original are extant. The Adelhausen monastery, founded in 1234 (O.P.—incorporated into the Order of Preachers—in 1245), was located near Freiburg (in the Black Forest, Germany) and followed the more liberal Rule of St. Augustine. It also became known for its artistic achievements, such as manuscript illumination, as in a famous Gradual (liturgical chants, often based on the psalms, answering the scriptural lesson during a service) produced here, needlework, and sculpture, the latter epitomized in one of the many Christ-John statues. After the customary initial historical section, the Adelhausen chronicle portrays the lives of thirty-four nuns, including that of the illustrious Else von der Nuwenstatt, an earlier lengthy piece adapted by Anna von Munzingen.

2. The *Unterlinden Sister-Book* was composed in Latin by Katharina von Gebweiler (Guebweiler, Geverschwihr, etc.) in the monastery of Unterlinden (founded 1232, O.P. 1245) in Colmar (Alsace, now in France) c.1320, this voluminous chronicle was translated into German by Elisabeth Kempf(in) of Unterlinden in 1485. Both a Latin manuscript and Elisabeth Kempf (or Kempfin)'s version are extant. The chronicle starts with a history chapter, then recounts the lives of sisters in thirty-nine chapters. The Unterlinden chronicle contains two traditional *Klosternovellen* (accounts of miracles) and a novella about a betrothal, important for its cultural insights.

3. The *Gotteszell Sister-Book*, for a long time mistaken for part of the Kirchberg Sister-Book (see below) until the late1970s–early 1980s, came from a monastery founded possibly as early as 1227, just outside of Schwäbisch-Gemünd, Württemberg, Germany, then O.P.1246. This Sister-Book's eventual identification as a separate work by modern scholars Klaus Graf and others (see Ringler) derives from its peculiarities: a sparse manuscript tradition, the substance and style of the lives (about 300–400 words per entry, preceded by a much longer, previously composed life of Adelheit von Hiltegarthausen), and geographical-historical details within the text, as well a distinct notice in a 1447 inventory at Engeltal (see below). Graf estimates its date of composition to be c.1320–1330. (Previously the Gotteszell Sister-Book had been given the title of "Ulm Sister-Book"—*Ulmer Schwesternbuch*—because the text contains a reference to the city of Ulm.) The author, an anonymous sister, is a self-confident, skillful writer. She is explicit in her intention to document her community's asceticism and spirituality. The outstanding feature of this convent chronicle is its extended jubilus, in the manner of the great mystics.

4. The *Engeltal Sister-Book* was compiled by accomplished visionary mystical author Christine Ebner von Engelthal (1277–1356) about her own monastery after 1328 and before 1340, in the style and manner typical of the works of this kind (Ringler). Another important member of this community was Adelhaid Langmann (1306–1375). The Engeltal is situated in Franconia, Germany, where it was first built in 1240 (O.P. 1248). Only two manuscripts of it survive. Using a phrase from the text, its first editor titled this Sister-Book *Von der genaden uberlast*, known in English as "The Nun of Engetal's Little Book of the Overwhelming Burden of Graces." The initial chronicle is composed in anecdotal style. There follow some forty-five *vitae* of varied length, in roughly chronological order, so that the last ones deal with sisters whom Christine Ebner claims to have known personally, since she entered this order at age twelve. Phrases such as "[she] was a faithful servant of God [...] and was a real woman," and, concerning another nun, "she was an unconquered human being" ("ein unüberwundener mensch"), stress the community's individualizing self-confidence. Stylistically, too, this convent chronicle differs from the others in its frequent use of direct speech.

5. The *Kirchberg Sister-Book* was presumably written in Middle-High German between 1305 and 1340 in the Kirchberg monastery in Sulz, Württemberg, Germany (founded 1237, O.P. 1245) by Elisabeth von Kirchberg. This author's self-identification as "Elisabeth, whom God took from the Jews," occurs in her life of Sister Irmengard. Beyond the fact that she was indeed of Jewish parentage, entered the monastery at age four, and was a younger friend to Irmengard, we know little about Elisabeth. Her chronicle affords glimpses of Kirchberg community life colored by her personal knowledge of many of the sisters, while inserting previously written information for those nuns preceding her, like Mechthilt von Waldeck (d. 1305).

6. The *Töss Sister-Book* recorded life at Töss Monastery, originally a béguinage situated near Winterthur, northern Switzerland. Founded in 1233 (O.P. 1245), and one of the first Swiss women's monasteries to adopt the Rule of St. Augustine, it became famous for its scriptorium, library, and convent school. Elsbeth Stagel, the main author of this voluminous convent chronicle, is best known for her twenty-five-year spiritual friendship with the Dominican mystic Heinrich Seuse (Suso). Composed during the early 1340s, the Töss Sister-Book begins with the history of the monastery's beginning, and its second part contains a nucleus of two older vitae around which thirty-six biographies are gathered (most notably those of Anna von Klingenow and Jutzi Schulthasin). Benefiting from a relatively well-established manuscript tradition, the Töss Sister-Book has become the best known of all convent chronicles. It was most publicized by the reformer Meyer, who encouraged its distribution among the declining Dominican monasteries in German-speaking areas. It is also the only Sister-Book of which we have an illuminated manuscript (Nuremberg Municipal Library codex Cent. V 10a).

7. The *Oetenbach Sister-Book*, from the Oetenbach monastery (founded 1231, O.P. 1245) near Zürich, Switzerland, was written after 1340 and survives in only one manuscript (mid-fifteenth century). Its unnamed author identifies herself only as one of the Oetenbach sisters. The shortest Sister-Book text known, it is exceptionally well structured. Its remarkably vivid, yet accurate, prefatory chronicle,

proportionately longer than most, draws a parallel between the monastery's simultaneous economic prosperity and the point when "the reputation of their blessed life spread far into the world," attracting daughters of the nobility. The few vitae of this Sister-Book reveal the particular theological interests of the Oetenbach nuns, who lived under the Rule of St. Augustine.

8. The *Diessenhofen Sister-Book*, also referred to as the Katharinental Sister-Book, was written in the early 1340s and survives through a number of manuscripts. Its author has remained unknown (one of the manuscripts, dated 1420, carries the scribe's name, Sister Antonia). The Katharinental monastery was founded by beguines from Winterthur near Diessenhofen (northern Switzerland) in 1242 (O.P. 1245), and during its prime housed a great collection of art. Its approximately sixty rather uneven vitae provide an overall view of a well-organized community, the interrelationships among the sisters, and with the "world outside." The vita of Elsbeth von Stoffeln, presumably pre-authored, is distinctive for its poetic passage on the Holy Spirit. Master Eckhart (c.1260–c.1328), the illustrious mystic, is recorded as having stayed there in 1324.

9. The *Weiler Sister-Book* was composed in 1350 by an author identifying herself only as a sister of the Weiler community. The monastery of Weiler was founded in 1230 near Esslingen, Germany as the first O.P. monastery (1245) in the diocese of Constance. The shift from "I" to "we" after a certain point in the text suggests that several authors were involved in its compilation. Three manuscripts of it are extant. Its convent chronicle mentions some twenty Weiler sisters by name, but the vitae are often very short and rarely display individualizing features, save for a great emphasis on paranormal events. However, as in the other Sister-Books, the reader nevertheless acquires insight into the community's daily functions and intense spirituality.

See also Anna of Munzigen; Beguines; Convents; Ebner, Christine; Elsbeth von Oye; Gertrude the Great, of Helfta, St.; Hagiography (Female Saints); Katharina von Gebweiler/Geberschweier; Langmann, Adelhaid; Stagel, Elsbeth; Unterlinden, Sisters of

BIBLIOGRAPHY

Primary Sources
(Sister-Book texts are listed below alphabetically.)

Adelhausen
"Die Chronik der Anna von Munzingen. Nach der ältesten Abschrift mit Einleitung una funf Beilagen." Edited by Josef König. *Freiburger Diözesanarchiv* 13 (1880): 129–236.

Diessenhofen
Das Katharinentaler Schwesternbuch. Critical ed. by Ruth Meyer. Münchener Texte und Untersuchungen, 104. Tübingen, Germany: Niemeyer, 1995.

Engeltal
Der Nonne von Engelthal Buchlein von der Gnaden Uberlast. Litterarischer Verein in Stuttgart. Edited by Karl Schröder. Tübingen, Germany, 1871.
Deutsches Nonnenleben: Das Leben der Schwestern zu Toss und Der Nonne von Engeltal Buchlein von der Gnaden Uberlast. Translated (Modern German) and annotated by Margarete Weinhandl. Katholikon, 2. Munich: Recht, 1921.

Gotteszell

"Aufzeichnungen über das mystische Leben der Nonnen von Kirchberg bei Sulz Predigerordens während des XIV. und XV. Jahrhunderts." Edited by F. W. E. Roth. *Alemannia* 21 (1893): 123–48

Katharinental
See above, under Diessenhofen.

Kirchberg
See above, under Gotteszell ed., 103–23.

Oetenbach

"Die Stiftung des Klosters Oetenbach und das Leben der seligen Schwestern daselbst, aus der Nürnberger Handschrift." Edited by H. Zeller-Werdmüller and Jakob Bachtold. *Zürcher Taschenbuch*, n.s. 12 (1889): 213–76.

Töss

Das Leben der Schwestern zu Töss, beschrieben von Elsbet Stagel. Deutsche Texte des Mittelalters, 6. Edited by Ferdinand Vetter. Berlin, Germany: Weidmann, 1906.

Deutsches Nonnenleben: Das Leben der Schwestern zu Töss und Der Nonne von Engeltal Buchlein von der Gnaden Uberlast. Translated (Modern German) and annotated by Margarete Weinhandl. Katholikon, 2. Munich: Recht, 1921.

"Ulm"
See above, under Gotteszell.

Unterlinden

"Les *Vitae Sororum* d'Unterlinden (Colmar MS 508)." Critical ed. by Jeanne Ancelet-Hustache. *Archives d'histoire doctrinale et littéraire du Moyen âge* 5(1930): 317–509.

Weiler

"Mystisches Leben in dem Dominikanerinnenkloster Weiler bei Eßlingen im 13. und 14. Jahrhundert." Edited by Karl Bihlmeyer. *Württembergische Vierteljahreshefte für Landesgeschichte*, n.s. 25 (1916): 61–93.

[Selections. English]. "From the German Sister-Books (Thirteenth and Fourteenth Centuries)." In *Ecstatic Confessions*, edited by Martin Buber (German, 1909). Translated by Esther Cameron and edited by Paul Mendes-Flohr, 77–90. San Francisco: Harper & Row, 1985.

Secondary Sources

Lewis, Gertrud Jaron. *By Women, for Women, about Women. Fourteenth Century Dominican Convent Chronicles: The Sister-Books of Fourteenth-Century Germany.* Studies and Texts, 125. Toronto: Pontifical Institute of Mediaeval Studies, 1996.

Ringler, Siegfried. *Viten- und Offenbarungsliteratur in Frauenklostern des Mittelalters. Quellen und Studien.* Münchener Texte und Untersuchungen, 72. Munich and Zürich: Artemis Verlag, 1980. (Old Norse-Icelandic Women Poets)

GERTRUD JARON LEWIS

SKÁLDKONUR (OLD NORSE-ICELANDIC WOMEN POETS). In modern usage, the term *skáld* is usually reserved for named poets whose verse, in principle historical, is included in Finnur Jónsson's authoritative edition (1912–1915). Estimates differ as to the number of skálds whose names are recorded; Hans Kuhn has suggested around three hundred for the period 850–1200.

The dominant skáldic meter is *dróttkvætt*, the meter fit for the *drótt*: the king's retinue. Stanzas in this style are preserved as quotations in vernacular prose works from the twelfth to the fourteenth century. All-male groups like the *drótt* are rarely shy about advertising man's passionate attachment to man and disregard for woman, so it is not surprising that early northern poetry, centered on a prince, should celebrate male bonding, male courage, and male loyalty and be accompanied by a formalized inhospitality toward and silencing of females. Still, the names and, in a few cases, the poems, of a handful of historically situated *skáldkonur* (women poets), have come down to us, a corpus of texts meager in extent, eccentric in distribution, and inevitably suspect in its claims to authenticity.

Eight pre-Christian Norwegian and Icelandic *skáldkonur* are known to compilers of sagas in the thirteenth century. The three earliest are said to have been closely connected to the Norwegian court of Haraldr Finehair. The four-stanza poem attributed to Jórunn Skáldmaer ("skáld-maiden") celebrates the poet Guthormr Sindri, whose verse mollified both Haraldr and his dysfunctional family. Jórunn's stanzas are complex, sophisticated, and probably composed at a later time (Fidjestøl). A quatrain assigned to Gunnhildr, the possibly Danish and certainly malevolent wife of Haraldr's son, Eiríkr Bloodaxe, is almost certainly apocryphal as well (Jesch 1991). The stanza of the third *skáldkona*, Hildr Hrólfsdóttir, warning Haraldr not to mistreat her son Gongu-Hrólfr, ends with a threat and an apparent play on her son's name (Hrólfr = glory-wolf): "It is dangerous to be wolfish to such a wolf (= warrior) of the war-board of Odinn (= shield); he will not be easy on the royal herds if he runs to the woods." Hildr, like women in the sagas more generally, manages her affairs with a kind of aggressive authority unparalleled in any other medieval European literature (Clover 1993).

The Viking-age women poets portrayed by saga authors are as dedicated as their male counterparts to bullying, boasting, satirizing, and other competitive games. At least one such poet pits herself and her god against the new, male Christianity. Two stanzas attributed to Steinunn *skáldkona*, an Icelander also remembered as the mother of the skáld Refr Gestsson, contrast the impotence of a Christ unable to protect his missionary from shipwreck with the power of the god Thor, who destroyed the ship:

> The feller of the giantess's kinsman (= Thor) smashed completely the bison (= ship) of the mew's resting-place (= sea) on the keeper of the bell (= priest, Thangbrandr); the gods pursued the horse of the strand (= ship). Christ did not protect the stepper of the sea's shingle (= ship) when the ship was crushed; I think that God guarded the reindeer of Gylfi (= ship) only a little.
>
> Thor drove off course Thangbrandr's long animal of Thvinnvill (= ship); he shook and bashed the wood of the prow (= ship) and struck it against the land; the plank (= ship) of Atall's land (= sea) is not likely to be seaworthy again, for the fierce storm caused by him (= Thor) smashed it to smithereens.

The two Old English poems entirely in a woman's voice speak only of hopelessness and longing. The Old Norse poetry assigned to Jórunn, Gunnhildr, and Hildr in the kings' sagas, and to Steinunn in various narratives, is public, political, and agonistic. In *dróttkvætt* stanzas composed by *skáldkonur*, there is little of that delight in solitude and meditation; that gentle melancholy and passive acceptance of change, that attachment to transient blossoms and blackbirds so characteristic of women's stanzaic forms from medieval Ireland to Japan.

Typically, female preoccupations and feelings do not seem to go with the job of being an Icelandic woman poet. Thórhildr *skáldkona* in *Njáls saga* is so called because "she was a great word-witch and slanderous." Her single preserved poetic effort—"Ogling is evil, Thráinn,/There is lust in your eyes"—causes her husband to declare himself divorced from her. A couplet in *Laxdœla saga*—"I'm glad I know/I've been abandoned"—is recited by the unloved and unlovely Audr ("neither attractive nor accomplished," reports the narrator). She mutters this shortly after her husband has divorced her and before she goes after him with a sword, exacting the revenge her brothers refused to undertake. Viking-age saga-women, it seems, allow themselves to frame their distress in verse only when vengeance is on their minds. In *Hardar saga ok Hólmverja*, Thorbjǫrg composes and recites a finely wrought stanza on her brother's last stand. This obituary is followed by multiple and far-reaching revenge killings. Thurídr in *Heidarvíga saga*, still raging and frustrated years after her son Hallr's slaying, recites a stanza goading her remaining sons to revenge. No grief with tears that almost run for these *skáldkonur*, and no protestations of undying love for their errant or deceased menfolk. It is in prose that we find the memorable romantic utterances of the medieval North, from Gudrún's "I was worst to the one I loved the most" (*Laxdœla saga*) to Thórdís's joy in *Ljósvetninga saga* at the sight of her approaching lover: "Now there is much to be made of the sunshine and south wind." The only *dróttkvætt* love stanza attributed to a woman, Steingerdr, merely states her sovereign determination to land her man: "I would wed Fródi's brother even if he were blind" (*Kormaks saga*).

The facility with which trollwomen, witches, legendary heroines, shield-maidens, giantesses, queens, dream-women, and Icelandic matrons spout verses in the sagas of time past and time present suggests that literary activity by women was conceivable either at the time the sagas were composed or at the time of the events narrated. It may be significant in this connection that thirteenth-century saga authors were more likely to credit long poems to legendary or supernatural women than to historical Icelandic female ancestors.

Most of the stanzas attributed to women in the sagas of contemporaries and on the sagas of antiquity are in the simple, chant-like meters used in eddic poetry. In Sturla Thórdarson's *Íslendinga saga*, no fewer than seventeen such stanzas are put in the mouths of various dream-women. The fortune-telling witch Heidr in *Örvar-Odds saga* recites a verse to the hero before relating his fate:

> Don't bully me
> Oddr of Jæderen,
> with your kindling sticks
> even though I chatter now and then.
> What the prophetess says
> will turn out to be true,
> for she can foretell
> the fate of each man.

It has been suggested that women were largely responsible for such poetic genres as laments and whettings (*grátljód* and *hvǫt*), visions and prophecies (*spár*), incantations (*seidr*), and healings (*lækningar*). Women are the principal speakers in nine poems included in the standard edition of the *Poetic Edda*, and they are central to the action unfolding in at least twenty-one others. The very title *Edda* (possibly signifying great-grandmother) has seemed to point to the connection between women and an oral poetic tradition. We shall never know who composed these anonymous poems, but we should not for this reason assume that they are all the work of male authors.

Most Old Norse-Icelandic literary references to *skáldkonur* are neutral or unflattering. Saga-writers associate women poets with magic, paganism, death, age, ugliness, and other transgressions. There is, of course, slippage, not only between literature and life, but also between literary types. If we turn to Viking-age runic stones rather than to twelfth- to fourteenth-century manuscripts, we find a medieval Scandinavian woman poet different from the sharp-tongued scolds of the sagas. One of the Bällsta (Sweden) runestones names a certain widow Gyrídr. Her sons, according to the fourteen-line verse inscription, "raised the stones" in memory of their father. She, the poem concludes, "loved her husband and will proclaim this in [her] lament [*grátr*]." The wording is not unambiguous. But if Gýrídr did indeed compose the verse inscription herself, then the first certainly historical poet in early Sweden was a woman (Clover 1986).

See also Chanson de Femme (Women's Song); *Daina*; Enchantresses, Fays (*Fées*), and Fairies; *Frauenlied*; Jóreiðr Hermundardóttir í Midjumdal; Jórunn skáldmær; *Kharja*; *Laxdœla saga*; *Muwashshaḥ*; Norse Women; Steinunn Refsdóttir.

BIBLIOGRAPHY

Primary Source

Jónsson, Finnur, ed. *Den norsk-islandske skjaldedigtning*. Vols. 1A–2A (*Tekst efter håndskrifterne*) and 2B (*Rettet tekst*). Copenhagen: Gyldendal, 1912–1915. Reprint Copenhagen: Gyldendal, 1967 (vol. A) and 1973 (vol. B). [For *skáldkonur*, see in 1B: Hildr 27; Jórunn 53–54; Gunnhildr 54; Steingerdr 85; Thórhildr 95; Steinunn 127–28; Audr 172.4; Thurídr 197. In 2B, Jóreiðr 158–59].

Secondary Sources

Clover, Carol. "Hildigunnr's Lament." In *Structure and Meaning in Old Norse Literature*, edited by John Lindow et al., 141–83. Odense, Denmark: Odense University Press, 1986.

———. "Regardless of Sex: Men, Women, and Power in Early Northern Europe." *Speculum* 68 (1993): 363–88.

Fidjestøl, Bjarne. *Det Norrøne Fyrstediktet*. Universitet i Bergen Nordisk institutts skriftserie, 11. Øvre Ervik, Norway: Alvheim & Eide, 1982.

Gudmundsson, Bardi. *Uppruni Íslendinga*. Reykjavik, Iceland: Bókaútgáfa Menningarsjóds, 1959.

———. *The Origin of the Icelanders*. Translated by Lee M. Hollander. Lincoln: University of Nebraska Press, 1967 [Trans. of eight of the seventeen articles in the original Norse collection].

Helgadóttir, Gudrún P. *Skáldkonur fyrri alda*. 2 vols. Akureyri, Iceland: Kvöldvökuútgáfan, 1961–1963.

Heller, Rolf. *Die literarische Darstellung der Frau in den Isländersagas*. Halle, Germany: Max Niemeyer, 1958.

Jesch, Judith. "Women Poets in the Viking Age: An Exploration." *New Comparison* 4 (1987): 2–15.

———. *Women in the Viking Age*. Woodbridge, Suffolk, U.K. and Rochester, N.Y.: Boydell, 1991.

Jochens, Jenny. "*Vǫluspá*: Matrix of Norse Womanhood." *Journal of English and Germanic Philology* 88 (1989): 344–62.

———. *Women in Old Norse Society*. Ithaca, N.Y.: Cornell University Press, 1995.

Kress, Helga. "The Apocalypse of a Culture: *Völuspá* and the Myth of the Sources/Sorceress in Old Icelandic Literature." In *Poetry in the Scandinavian Middle Ages. Proceedings of the Seventh International Saga Conference* [. . .] *Spoleto, 4–10 September 1988*. Spoleto, Italy: Presso della sede del Centro studi, 1990.

Kreutzer, Gert. "Jórunn skáldmaer." *Skandinavistik* 2 (1972): 89–98.

Kuhn, Hans. *Das Dróttkvætt*. Heidelberg, Germany: Carl Winter, 1983.

Mundal, Else. "Kvinner og dikting: Overgangen frå munnleg til skriftleg kultur—ei ulykke for kvinnene?" In *Förändringar i kvinnors villkor under medeltiden: Uppsatser framlagda vid ett kvinnohistoriskt symposium i Skálholt, Ísland, 22.–25. júní 1981*, edited by Silja Adalsteinsdóttir and Helgi Thorláksson, 11–25. Reykjavik: Háskólútgáfan, 1983.

ROBERTA FRANK

SLAVES, FEMALE. A slave may be defined as a nonfree or "unfree" person; one whose status is devoid of any economic, social (including familial), or legal privilege or rights. He or she is owned and can be compelled by anyone with privilege—a master—to work in some way. A social outsider, an alien, or, as French specialist Pierre Dockès characterizes it, one of the *morts-vivants* (living dead) taken in war but by chance or grace not killed— he or she is exploited within the society in which he or she finds herself. Medieval slavery and the slave trade began as a continuation of the ancient Roman and Greek institutions, while the later Middle Ages marked the end of actual slave societies in Europe, such as they had existed in Ancient Rome and would later exist in the New World in the transatlantic trade, for example, in the American South before the Civil War. Both serfs and slaves belonged to the class of the "unfree," at the lowest rung of the social ladder. Women slaves, because they were both women and slaves, were condemned to two levels of inferiority; their value usually derived, whether directly or indirectly, from their sexual and procreative potential, yet as the following reveals, this sometimes earned them extra protection. They were most frequently employed as concubines, childcare providers, or domestic servants, but also worked in agricultural fields or workshops, tasks more often associated with male slaves.

Medieval slaves were even lower than serfs—since serfs, however miserably, subsisted directly off the land by their own labors as dictated by the feudal-manorial system, benefiting from any surplus. Slaves, no matter how hard they worked, whether on the land or in urban areas, depended on their masters for sustenance, with the master taking all surplus as well. Yet slaves often did receive varying degrees of privilege, albeit minimal, as their masters' "absolute" power was redefined in some societies, again according to local practice (in ninth-century Carolingian Germany for instance, Yoshiko Morimoto finds examples of "servile manses"—alongside free manses, which were parcels of land usually occupied and worked by dues-paying free peasants—inhabited by former slaves or half-free slaves aspiring to become tenant farmers). The resulting wide variety in concepts of a slave's functions, as with a serf's and free peasant's, makes it difficult to define medieval slavery more precisely than the above attempt (see Karras 1988; Bonnassie).

Our word "slave" derives from *sclavus*, signifying either Slav or slave because the early medieval (ninth century) slave trade established itself in the Slavic countries near the Black Sea, then spread to Africa. The use of sclavus to mean "slave" is first attested in German documents and in Arabic as *ṣaqāliba* (tenth to early eleventh centuries) and would spread to every language in similar form to mean "slave," as reflected in such cognates as French *esclave*, Italian *schiavo*, Spanish *esclavo*, and Portuguese *escravo*. But the concept, as well as the additional terminology, of servitude and servants comes from Latin *servus* (pl. *servi*) as used by the Roman historian Tacitus (first century), in his *Germania*, when speaking of slave practices among the German tribes. Interestingly, the female variant of this term was not *serva*, but rather *ancilla*. *Servi* was also the root of the word "serfs," who followed a different course and gradually replaced slaves in agrarian societies for economic reasons and due to problems in enforcement of domination over slaves (see Samson, in Frantzen and Moffat), more than for humane reasons. The Old English general word for slave was *theow* (fem. *theowa*), although the Anglo-Saxons used a variety of terms denoting the different types of slaves of both genders. Elizabeth Girsch has analyzed these terms as evoking, among other things, the "doubly paradoxical nature of metaphorical servitude for women," especially emphasizing their sexual submissiveness, whether these women slaves were purchased as concubines or for nonsexual/procreative duties (Girsch, in Frantzen and Moffatt, 50). The Germans used *Amt*; the Scandinavians *thrall*, whose female equivalents were *ambátt* and an Old Icelandic cognate of the abovementioned Old English, *thý*.

The situation of women slaves is perhaps best understood within the context of the general history of medieval slavery, from the fall of Rome (fifth century) to 1500, even in the following brief outline. Curiously enough, although the Old Testament forbade it among the Jews (they who had themselves been slave to the Egyptians), early Christianity did little to free slaves, even those who had converted. The Church Fathers, such as Augustine (354–430) who, in his *De Civitate Dei* (*City of God*), rationalized the slave–master bond as mirroring a wife's relationship to her husband, and man's relationship to God—all facets of a greater order granting supremacy to the most intellectually powerful (women and slaves being de facto intellectually inferior to free men). Also influential were such basic Christian beliefs as those in a beautiful afterlife as redemptive of any good person's earthly suffering, and that the Church was founded to save men's souls, not their social status or bodies. In practice, too, the clergy did little to free slaves, since they functioned according to a hierarchical order similar to the secular lords', whom they thus assisted in returning fugitive slaves, which, after all were considered property, not real people. These ideas and practices changed in Carolingian times (eighth through ninth centuries), after sufficient numbers of barbarians had been converted to see themselves not only in terms of tribes and kingdoms but as part of a larger Christian society of which no member should be subjected to slavery. The Church still did not preach the abolition of universal slavery, however, since it allowed for the enslavement of non-Christians, including heretics. Yet this measure at least reduced the "enslavable" population in Europe and North Africa and eventually caused its demise in Europe (Bloch, "Ancient Slavery").

During the barbarian invasions (fifth and sixth centuries), the triumphant Visigoths and Ostrogoths enslaved many citizens, mostly in rural Italy and environs, under much harsher conditions than those imposed under the Romans during the Empire. The Germans did not usually enslave their Roman captives, or any other peoples their felt to be of their own class and ethnicity; they therefore looked to outsider populations, like the Slavs, during their incursions. The Anglo-Saxons enslaved the Celts as they overran them. The Anglo-Saxons, Germans, and Spaniards all imposed penal slavery on criminals unable to pay fines or *wergild*. Religion and ethnicity were determining factors in which group enslaved whom during this brutal and chaotic period. Arian Christians enslaved the Catholics (who judged them heretics) in lands the Arians conquered, and the Catholics did likewise wherever they triumphed; Catholic Franks, for example, enslaved many captives in southern Gaul (France) from among the Arian Visigoths. Christians of varying areas and sects enslaved pagans, Muslims, and Jews. Traffic in slaves became both plentiful and far-ranging, scattering once cohesive populations of the vanquished for thousands of miles over land and sea, from the Iberian Peninsula to Scandinavia, Russia, the Near East, and North Africa.

Slaves now had virtually no rights and were subjected to disproportionately cruel punishment for any infraction under the *Edictum Theodorici* (*Edict of Theodoric*), named after the king of the Ostrogoths (d. 526). A marriage between two slaves was not considered legal; the wife was deemed a concubine, and the master could dissolve the marriage or the couple could be separated by each spouse being assigned to work under different, distant masters, such as half-free peasants (*coloni*), by their common master. The Emperor Justinian's reconquest of Italy (c.555) was too brief to improve matters before the Lombards invaded a decade later, replacing the Ostrogoths in northern Italy, driving away, enslaving, or killing even more Romans after appropriating their slaves and lands. Charles Verlinden has determined the slave and other unfree population to have been large and economically necessary, based on the predominant amount of space devoted to their governance in two important documents of the time: the *Leges Rotharis* (*Laws of King Rothar*, 643) and those of King Liutprand (r. 712–744), the latter significantly improving conditions for the unfree. Under the Lombards, slaves either worked in the fields (*rusticani*) or were trained as secretarial and managerial staff employed in their master's house (*servi ministeriales*), with the rural slave valued at half a *servus ministeriale*, or, as the latter were called in Spain, *idonei*. But the rusticani's lot later improved, because they worked at a distance from the master and were tied to the land. Women also worked in the fields as well as in homes, although in agrarian societies male slaves were preferred; the less useful female children may even have been killed (Karras 1994). Domestic female servants often retained the title designating them in Roman times: *ancillae* (sing. *ancilla*).

The principal way for a slave to earn his or her freedom legally (as opposed to fleeing, which frequently happened despite the risk of recapture and punishment) was through manumission, which, under King Liutprand, was often performed in church (*manumissio in ecclesia*) with the slave being granted a charter of emancipation. A slave, if his master agreed, could join the clergy. Slave marriages, with the master's blessing, were now legal. If a slave were murdered, part of his killer's fine would go to the slave's family—thus benefiting his widow and children—instead of completely to the master. This Frankish custom, delayed by Anglo-Saxon law, finally spread to England via Norman Law by the mid-twelfth century under the *Leges Henrici* (*Laws of Henry II*; Bloch, "Personal Liberty"). A slave could marry a free person (the slave was usually the wife), and their children could be freed, especially if they attached themselves to the clergy. Such cases exemplify how different cultures assimilated more egalitarian practices at different rates over time.

After the Carolingians (Charlemagne's family and régime) conquered the Lombards in 774, lordship—both religious and secular—became an increasingly important social institution. Each lord or abbot had dependents, among whom were slaves and serfs. Even though conditions for slaves improved and the number of manumissions rose, fugitive slaves were still common. Scholars of Carolingian-era slavery glean their understanding of these circumstances by examining church records, cartularies (collections of deeds, charters, and titles to estate or monastic property) and polyptychs (inventories of material and human resources compiled for a major landholder), which by this time refer to slaves by a variety of terms depending on their workplace and function. Lombard women slaves, frequently in groups of varying sizes, often formed workshops for weaving cloth and wool. These workshops sometimes traveled to where their product was in demand. Serfs began to outnumber slaves in rural France and Germany, while at the same time the slave trade as a serious commercial entity flourished around the Mediterranean. Southern Italian ports including Amalfi and Venice became prime centers for slave traffic to Muslim countries, with the Venetians pledging not to traffic in Christian slaves with the Muslims. Jewish merchants also played an important role in slave-trading at this time in both the Mediterranean and in the Alps (ninth to tenth centuries; see Verlinden; Phillips). Also to the north, the Danube provided a major conduit for slaves from Russia (e.g., Kiev) and Eastern Europe to and from the Black Sea; women slaves from this Slavic-driven group commanded higher prices than the men (Verlinden).

In Scandinavia, women often served as concubines (thus ambátt came to mean concubine as well as female slave), either for procreation or recreation. As in many societies, a slave woman's children could not inherit. Marriages between slaves were not sanctioned by either civil law or the Church, although slave families were recognized in practice. Investigations of Danish and British Isles burial sites reveal that slaves were important "grave-goods": they were often interred with their masters or mistresses as prized possessions to accompany them in the afterlife, apparently even if the slave was still alive at the master's or mistress's death. Evidence of women slaves buried with their mistresses has been found at these sites (Karras 1988).

Generally speaking, countries that first embraced Roman Christianity appear also as the first to replace slavery with serfdom, while countries remaining pagan the longest were the last to abolish slavery (these also continued to raid Christian countries for slaves and other spoils; Verlinden). Among Christian European countries, France would be the first to have serfdom entirely replace slavery (ninth century), although southern France, because of its proximity to the Mediterranean, retained primarily female slavery in urban areas like Perpignan into the fifteenth century (see Romestan), as did the Italian port of Genoa (see Balard) and other Mediterranean towns because the required type of labor was mainly domestic. The later Byzantine Empire traded in Greek and Mongol slaves as of 1434 (Romestan). In England, slavery declined before the arrival of the Normans and more sharply thereafter (see Pelteret), yet lingered into the twelfth century. Scandinavia's class distinctions, including that between free and unfree, render their slavery's chronological parameters particularly challenging to define, but it seems to have ended in the thirteenth century. In many cases, slavery can be said to have ended not because servitude disappeared but because the differences among slaves, serfs, and lowest-level free persons (e.g., Latin vilani, French villains, English villeins) became indistinguishable (see Karras 1988). The Slavs (including Bulgars and Serbs), even after converting to Christianity (after 988) and thereby ceasing to be a slave source, because they adhered to Byzantine Christianity (the Eastern Church), continued to capture, or traffic in, non-Christian slaves.

Black slaves, distinct from North African white slaves, were traded in Europe as early as the seventh century (Heers 2003) via Muslim caravan traders, as well as Italian, southern-French, and Catalan merchants. These were commonly called "Moors" and were especially numerous in Aragon, Castile, and Portugal, while rarely seen in England before the seventeenth century. White women slaves tended to be more sought after than blacks, although, as William Phillips surmises, the growing number of mulattoes in the Al-Andalus (Islamic Spain) indicates that black women slaves had little difficulty in finding buyers.

Muslim slavery, whether in the Near East or Al-Andalus (conquered in the eighth century) was an entirely different phenomenon from that in Europe, as illustrated by Shaun Marmon and others. Slaves were a much more integral and inevitable part of life in Islamic society. Although the Quran (Koran) and accompanying hadith literature maintained that all humans were free, slave–master was part of God-given inequality, like that of woman to man, and mortals to God. Muslim jurists and theologians saw no need to rationalize the persistence of slavery as did the Christian Church Fathers because to them, slavery was a "primordial fact." Moreover, slaves may have been better off than wives, since the former could be freed by manumission, encouraged by the Quran as an act of charity or atonement on the master's part. Yet perhaps because Muslims were more at ease with the fundamental rightness of slavery than were the Christian Europeans, the Quran also taught that both male and female slaves should be treated kindly and recommended other conditions more favorable than in Europe: a concubine's children by her master were free and legitimate; a slave freed by manumission suffered no social stigma, except that freed women slaves, because they were women, benefited less than freed male slaves; masters were counseled not to force their slaves into prostitution and to foster slave marriages, although sometimes this resulted in a master forcing a marriage between slaves. Slave men were entitled to half the number of wives allowed free men. Inequality functioned both ways, however, as in the question of punishment for adultery: the slave adulterer received half the penalty dealt a free person (Marmon 1988). Female slaves enjoyed better treatment than the males, since slave traders purchased them to be used mainly as either the more select, valuable group of concubines, entertainers, and musicians, or the lesser, "gross" group comprising domestic servants (Verlinden). Most women slaves were used for childbearing—the healthier and more fertile, the higher her price—and household service. Like all slaves in Islam, each type was trained for these tasks as part of a careful initiation process. Such preparation was necessary because, as in the various European cultures obeying the tenet that Christians could not enslave Christians regardless of ethnicity, Muslims could not enslave other Muslims, so that the new slave was always a foreigner, thus requiring socialization. The slaves' free names were discarded in favor of new ones—special slave identities that also made them "kin" to their masters—bestowed on them just prior to their training as slaves. Their new names also bore a sign of their conversion to Islam. This "processing" phase naturally favored slaves acquired when children, although adult women, probably because they were easier to socialize, were less disfavored than adult men, the latter being presumably harder to "tame." Manumission of slaves taken in childhood usually occurred in early adulthood. The nominal kinship with which the slave had been endowed opened the door for "clientage"—an artificial kinship for life, symbolized by the manumitted slave taking part of his former master's name after emancipation. In this way, a master could inherit from his former slave if the slave died without heirs. Some slaves, of both genders, were never freed and remained slaves for life. There was also a very important, highly prized third gender—eunuchs, who were not only entrusted with guarding harems but also with other tasks because they were deemed more apt than intact males (see Marmon 1995; Phillips). All of the above-described traits and combinations varied according to location and time throughout the extensive the medieval Islamic empire, at its zenith during the late eighth and early ninth centuries before breaking up into separate caliphates such as those in Al-Andalus and Egypt, the latter, along with North Africa, Sicily, and Damascus, ruled by the Fatimids (tenth century) and later dynasties into the fifteenth century.

The literature of this culture affords some revealing sidelights. The relationship during this time between the hegemonic, or "master" Arabic culture versus its conquered, "slave" culture (Hispanic, other Romance languages), together with its gendered component (learned language = male; vernacular = female) is even reflected in Mozarabic (here, using both Arabic and Romance languages) literary genres like the *muwashshah*.

In examining the overriding function of medieval female slaves as objects of sexual exploitation, regardless of their original purpose when acquired, Ruth Mazo Karras argues that "dominance, more than desire or descendants, was the most important factor" in this exploitation of women by their masters in many, if not all societies, whether directly or as a means to assert control over slave men and also free men. Men's ability to control sexual access to their women, even using it as a reward to their subordinates, was legal and a mark of prestige. In arriving at these and related conclusions, Karras makes use of another primary source, penitentials (handbooks used by priests as guides to hearing confession and assigning penance), such as the *Poenitentiale Theodorici* (*Penitential of Theodoric*), which document the relatively light penances imposed on masters for sleeping with their slaves in contrast to those meted out for the same act with a virgin or for committing adultery. Karras also highlights the presence of sexually exploitative attitudes in supposedly refined manuals of "fine love" like Andreas Capellanus's *De amore*, when he urges his aristocratic pupil/reader to feel free to take peasant women by force, as though it were a privilege of his class and gender. In addition, Karras notes the unfortunate similarity between the purchase of female slaves for sex and offspring and the custom of bride-price, in which a man literally bought a bride for the same reasons and during the same period as when slavery existed in Europe (Karras 1994).

Finally, with the advent of cities, freedom, and guilds, women could work and trade with dignity and equality on a par with or close to that of men.

See also Capellanus, Andreas; Childhood and Child-Rearing in the Middle Ages; Concubines; Fatimid Egypt, Women in; Guilds, Women in; *Jus Primae Noctis*; Law, Women in, Anglo-Saxon England; Marriage; Music, Women Composers and Musicians; *Muwashshaḥ*; Norse Women; Penitentials, Women in; Prostitution

BIBLIOGRAPHY

Primary Sources
[See bibliographies to Secondary Sources, e.g., Karras 1988, for a more complete list of primary sources].
[Anglo-Saxon Laws: Alfred, Æthelberht, et al.]. *Die Gesetze der Angelsachsen.* Edited by Felix Liebermann, vol. 1. Halle, Germany: Max Niemeyer, 1903.
Capellanus, Andreas. *De amore.* Edited by Emil Trojel, 236. Munich, 1964.
———. Translated by John J. Parry, 150. New York: Columbia University Press, 1990.
Edictum Theodorici. Edited by Giulio Vismara. Ius Romanum Medii Aevi, I, 2 b aa. Milan: Giuffrè, 1967. [Latin text only].
Leges Henrici primi. Edited and translated with commentary by L. J. Downer. Oxford: Clarendon Press, 1972. [Latin and English texts. See C. 70: 2, 4].
Poenitentiale Theodorici, etc. In *Die Bussordnungen der abendländischen Kirche*, edited by F. W. H. Wasserschleben, 1: 14. 12. Graz, Austria: Akademische Druck, 1958. Original Halle: Graeger, 1851. [Latin only].

Secondary Sources
Balard, Michel. "La Femme-esclave à Gênes à la fin du Moyen Âge." In *La Femme au Moyen Âge. Actes du colloque de Maubeuge, 6–octobre 1988*, edited by Michel Rouche and Jean Heuclin, 299–310. Maubeuge: Ville de Maubeuge/Jean Touzot, 1990.
Bloch, Marc. "How and Why Ancient Slavery Came to End. Personal Liberty and Servitude in the Middle Ages, Particularly in France." In *Slavery and Serfdom in the Middle Ages*, trans. by William

R. Beer, 1–32; 33–92. Center for Medieval and Renaissance Studies, U.C.L.A., 8. Berkeley: University of California Press, 1975. [Selected and trans. from Bloch, *Mélanges historiques*, Paris: E. P. H. E., 1963. Reprint Paris: Serge Fleury, 1983].

Bonnassie, Pierre. *From Slavery to Feudalism in Southwestern Europe.* Translated by Jean Birrell. Past and Present. Cambridge and New York: Cambridge University Press; Paris: Maison des Sciences de l'homme, 1991.

Brand, Charles M. "Slave Women in the Legislation of Alexius I." *Byzantinische Forschungen* 23 (1996): 19–24.

Dockès, Pierre. *La Libération médiévale.* Nouvelle Bibliothèque scientifique. Paris: Flammarion, 1979. [A Marxist-revisionist perspective emphasizing pre-medieval slavery].

———. *Medieval Slavery and Liberation.* Translated by Arthur Goldhammer. Chicago: University of Chicago Press, 1982.

Ferrer i Mallol, Maria Teresa, and Josefina Mutgé i Vives, eds. *De l'Esclavitud a la llibertat: esclaus i lliberts a l'edat mitjana.* Actes del Col.loqui Internacional celebrat a Barcelona, 27–29 maig 1999. Anuario de Estudios medievales, 38. Barcelona: Institució Milà i Fontanals, 2000. [Essays on medieval Mediterranean and North African Slavery by Catalan, Spanish or Italian scholars].

Frantzen, Allen J., and Douglas Moffat, eds. *The Work of Work: Servitude, Slavery and Labor in Medieval England.* Glasgow: Cruithne Press, 1994. [Essays by several major scholars].

Hammer, Carl. "A Slave Marriage Ceremony from Early Medieval Germany." *Slavery and Abolition* 16 (1995): 242–49.

Heers, Jacques. *Esclaves et domestiques au Moyen Âge dans le monde méditerranéen.* Paris: Fayard, 1981.

———. *Les Négriers en terres d'Islam: la première traite des noirs, VII\<e\>–XVI\<e\> siècles.* Pour l'histoire. Paris: Perrin, 2003.

Herlihy, David. *Opera muliebra: Women and Work in Medieval Europe.* Philadelphia: Temple University Press, 1990.

Karras, Ruth Mazo. "Concubinage and Slavery in the Viking Age." *Scandinavian Studies* 62 (1990): 141–62.

———. "Desire, Descendants, and Dominance: Slavery, the Exchange of Women, and Masculine Power." In Frantzen and Moffat, 16–29. *See above.*

———. "Servitude and Sexuality in Medieval Iceland." In *From Sagas to Society: Comparative Approaches to Early Iceland,* edited by Gísli Pálsson, 289–304. Enfield Lock, U.K.: Hisarlik Press, 1992.

———. *Slavery and Society in Medieval Scandinavia.* New Haven, Conn.: Yale University Press, 1988.

Lal, Kishori Saran. *Muslim Slave System in Medieval India.* New Delhi, India: Aditya Prakashan, 1994.

Lerner, Gerda. "The Woman Slave." In Lerner, *Women and History, I: The Creation of Patriarchy,* 76–100. New York: Oxford University Press, 1986. [Rather general; highly polemical; emphasizes ancient origins over medieval].

Marmon, Shaun E. *Eunuchs and Sacred Boundaries in Islamic Society.* Studies in Middle Eastern History. New York: Oxford University Press, 1995.

———, ed. *Slavery in the Islamic Middle East.* Princeton, N.J.: Markus Wiener, 1999.

———. "Slavery, Islamic World." In *Dictionary of the Middle Ages,* edited by Joseph R. Strayer, 11: 330–33. New York: Scribner's, 1988.

Morimoto, Yoshiki. "Aspects of the Early Medieval Peasant Economy as Revealed in the Polyptych of Prüm." In *The Medieval World,* edited by Peter Linehan and Janet L. Nelson, 605–20, esp. 612–13. New York and London: Routledge, 2001.

Pelteret, David A. E. *Slavery in Early Mediaeval England: From the Reign of Alfred until the Twelfth Century.* Studies in Anglo-Saxon History. Woodbridge, U.K. and Rochester, N.Y.: Boydell Press, 1995.

Phillips, William D., Jr. *Slavery from Roman Times to the Early Transatlantic Trade.* Minneapolis: University of Minnesota Press, 1985. [Best general synthesis].

Robertson, Claire C., and Martin A. Klein, eds. *Women and Slavery in Africa.* Madison: University of Wisconsin Press, 1983.

Romestan. Guy. "Femmes Esclaves à Perpignan aux XIVe et XVe siècles." In *La Femme dans l'histoire et la société méridionales (IXe–XIXe siècles). Actes du 66e congrès de la Fédération historique du Languedoc-Roussillon (Narbonne, 15 et 16 octobre 1994),* 187–218. Montpellier: Ville de Narbonne/l'Aude, 1995. [Superbly documented with statistical tables, etc.].

Stuard, Susan Mosher. "Urban Domestic Slavery in Medieval Ragusa." *Journal of Medieval History* 9 (1983): 155–71. Reprint in Barbara Hanawalt, ed. *Women and Work in Preindustrial Europe,* 39–55. Bloomington: Indiana University Press, 1986.

Verlinden, Charles. *L'Esclavage dans l'Europe médiévale.* Rijksuniversiteit te Gent. Faculteit van Letteren en Wijsbegeerte, 119, 162. 2 vols. Bruges: De Tempel, 1955. [Vol. 1 on Spain and France; vol. 2 on Italy, the Latin Near East, Byzantium].

NADIA MARGOLIS

SOREL, AGNÈS (d. 1450). Agnès Sorel was the legendary favorite and mistress of Charles VII of France (1403–1461). Born into the lesser nobility, Agnès appeared at the French royal court probably in 1442 as a

Agnès Sorel. © The Art Archive/Château de Loches/Dagli Orti.

member of the household of Isabelle of Lorraine (d. 1453), wife of René, duke of Anjou and "king of Sicily" (1409–1480). Her status changed when she became pregnant by King Charles VII of France. He showered her with money and jewels, and gave her the royal manor of Beauté-sur-Marne and other properties. Agnès wielded great influence at court; she was the first royal mistress of the later Middle Ages to play a political role in France. Her expensive and risqué apparel created a scandal, but she was very beautiful, and the courtiers admired her, which encouraged her to develop grandiose notions.

The bourgeoisie disliked her, and she was poorly received by the Parisians in 1448. In his journal, the anonymous Bourgeois de Paris (Burgess of Paris) wrote that she liked to be called *la belle Agnès* (the beautiful Agnes) and that her presence and behavior caused the queen, Marie of Anjou, much unhappiness. Because of Agnès, he said, the king was setting a poor example for his entourage, and this could unleash great evils on the kingdom. The chronicler Chastellain, who knew Agnès personally, was even more vitriolic in his condemnation of her, but the chronicler Olivier de la Marche declared she did France much good by introducing the king to persons who later served him well. After her untimely death during a trip to Normandy, Agnès's place in the king's affections was eventually taken by her first cousin, the cold and calculating Antoinette de Maignelay. Agnès bore Charles VII probably four children, three of whom survived: Charlotte (wife of Jacques de

Brézé, count of Maulévrier), Marie (wife of Olivier de Coëtivy); and Jeanne (wife of Antoine de Bueil, count of Sancerre).

BIBLIOGRAPHY

Primary Sources
Chastellain, Georges. *Oeuvres*. Ed. Kervyn de Lettenhove. 8 vols. Bruxelles: Heussner, 1863–1866.
Journal d'un bourgeois de Paris, de 1405 à 1449. Edited, with modern French trans. by Colette Beaune. Lettres gothiques. Paris: Livre de Poche, 1990.
————. Edited by Alexandre Tuetey. Paris: Champion, 1881. [For interesting footnotes, the classic scholarly ed.].
Mémoires d'Olivier de La Marche. Edited by Henri Beaune and Jules d'Arbaumont. 4 vols. Paris: Renouard, 1883–1888.

Secondary Sources
Beaucourt, G. du Fresne de. "L'influence politique d'Agnès Sorel." *Revue des questions historiques* 1 (1866): 204–24.
Cavailler, P. "Le compte des executeurs testamentaires d'Agnès Sorel." *Bibliothèque de l'École des Chartes* 114 (1956): 97–114.
Durrieu, Paul. "Les filles d'Agnès Sorel." *Comptes rendus de l'Académie des inscriptions et belles-lettres* (1922): 150–68.
Levêque, Paul-Jacques. *Agnès Sorel et sa légende*. Tours: Imprimerie Nouvelle, 1970.
Peigné-Delacourt, Achille. "Notice sur Agnès Sorel." *Comptes rendus et travaux du Comité archéologique de Noyon* 2 (1867): 2–17.
Philippe, Robert. *Agnès Sorel*. Paris: Hachette, 1983.
Steenackers, François-Frédéric. *Agnès Sorel et Charles VII. Essai sur l'état politique et moral de la France au XVᵉ siècle*. Paris: Didier, 1868.
Vallet de Viriville, Auguste. "Recherches historiques sur Agnès Sorel." *Bibliothèque de l'École des Chartes* 3rd ser. 1 (1849): 297–326, 477–99.

RICHARD C. FAMIGLIETTI

SPINNERS AND DRAPERS. Textile production, especially woolens, employed women more than any other industry during the Middle Ages. In the early centuries, women dominated all of the phases in textile making. Later, with the rise of the cities, women still did the spinning and weaving, whereas at the other end of the continuum, the drapers tended to be men. Spinning in particular evolved as the quintessential (virtuous) women's work both domestically or professionally, in rural and urban settings. The woman at her distaff, wheel or (for weavers), loom thus emerged as the epitome of the properly occupied married or single woman ("spinster") in literature, the visual arts, and even music (in the *chanson de toile*—"song of the cloth" sung by women while spinning, pre-1200).

Pagan heroines, female, saints and the Virgin Mary (redeeming Eve's condemnation after the Fall) were shown placidly spinning before their great moment (Gibson; Raynaud). For other legendary figures, spinning or weaving was their defining moment: Philomela who, according to Ovid's tale, after being raped then deprived of her tongue, embroidered her story onto a tapestry to expose her attacker (*Metamorphoses*, 6: 543–80); Arachne, the gifted spinner and weaver whose vanity caused her to blaspheme the gods and incur the goddess Minerva's wrath and turn the girl into a spider (*Metamorphoses*, 6: 1–140). Atropos, one of the Fates, ended lives with a desultory snip of her thread. As with most gendered stereotypes and hallowed myths, this emblematic association between women and spinning proved both reassuring and confining for working women in real life. For recent scholars including Dominique Cardon and Christiane Raynaud, however, the abundant, reality-based medieval artistic representations of women textile workers, together with archeological discoveries of the remnants of their tools and products, and consultation of municipal legal and merchants' financial documents, provide a clearer picture of how these women lived and worked.

Spinners and drapers constitute two main aspects at virtually either end of the the complex cloth-making process, which also involved cleaning and carding prior to spinning, combing or unwrapping (in the case of silk). The thread was then woven into cloth to be fulled, then dyed, finished, and sheared into bolts of quality *drap* or cloth suitable for cutting and sewing and/or embroidering. Because these crafts, especially spinning, required little brute strength yet appreciable fine muscle control—consistency in the direction and degree of thread torsion was important (Cardon 1999)—and stamina over many hours, they were perfectly suited to women. The various apparent cycles of a surplus of women in urban populations contributed the necessary workforce for this labor-intensive process (Hanawalt and Dronzek).

Women first spun with a distaff, a long staff with its cleft and holes holding the flax or wool. The distaff is usually shown being

Queen Gaia Cecilia with weaving loom and women spinning and carding. From Boccaccio, *Le Livre des Cleres et Nobles Femmes*, French, fifteenth century. © The Art Archive/British Library.

held by the spinner under one arm (usually her left) or propped up or held by someone else on one side of her. She then drew the material from it with her (left) hand, twisting it spirally between the thumb and forefinger of the other (right) hand and wound it around a spindle. Little wonder that this procedure generated so many graceful images in manuscript miniatures—also sexually suggestive ones, in which images the spinner holds the rather phallic-shaped distaff between her legs—though Western European medieval spinners more commonly worked with a freely suspended spindle. It had also produced fine thread since ancient times (see Cardon 1999). The spinning wheel, probably descended from Han Dynasty (second century B.C.E. to 220 C.E.) Chinese silk-winding and spooling wheels, passed through the Middle East where its techniques were further refined for spinning wool and other threads, and entered Europe by the mid-thirteenth century.

Arachne spinning wool on spinning wheel, folio 17r of c.1505 manuscript *La Vie des Femmes Celebres* (*Life of Famous Women*), by Antoine du Four. © The Art Archive / Musée Thomas Dobrée Nantes/Dagli Orti.

Contemporary images depict the spinner either sitting or standing at her wheel: the sitters spun the wheel by turning a handle, while the standing spinner moved the wheel by pushing its spokes with her right hand.

The distaff and spindle combination remained in use for a long time because of its portability—it could be carried along to the fields while the woman tended her flocks, in her home tending her children, or to a city workshop indoors or on a street corner—and for the unsurpassed quality of its thread. Also, because they were women's tools, they were inexpensive, even the decorated ones. The spinning wheel was also relatively portable, though care had to be taken on narrow streets, as mandated by local bylaws such as those in Mallorca (Spain) and Pamiers (France, fourteenth century, to position the spindle away from passing pedestrians (cited in Cardon 1996).

Cardon has studied the felicitous interrelationship between women spinners (*fileuses*) and their distaves and spindles as a rare condition in which a woman could often choose her own hours and place for productively working at her trade and earning her living. As a spinner, her role in cloth-making was as crucial as it was irreversible (one cannot re-spin a poorly spun thread) compared to most of the other stages, and she could thus dictate her own terms and prices.

Unfortunately, as Cardon has also found based on records and other evidence in Aragonese Spain, then England and southern France, the male drapers soon contrived a way to tie these women down—*brider* (bridle) them, as a thirteenth-century narrative puts it. This they accomplished by imposing a new system of *titrage* (measuring weight versus length of the wool thread) that differed from the traditional system, in existence since ancient times, that had profited the spinners because it gave them a certain leeway (i.e., chance to defraud) in the weights of the skeins or hanks of wool. The drapers' new standard of weights severely disadvantaged the spinners by making them wind the hanks so uniformly that the drapers could weigh them more quickly and precisely on delivery, leaving no room for the profitable irregularity from which the spinners had previously benefited. This aroused a certain furor among the now impoverished spinners, who attempted new, fraudulent methods of winding the skeins, but this turned out to be counterproductive as it hurt their reputation for quality and their relations with the draper, on whom they were and always would be dependent. By the mid-fifteenth century, the spinners' and other textile craftspeople's lucrative leeway was further eradicated by strict laws such as one sees in Toulouse (southern France), Florence, and Pisa (Italy).

Women weavers (*tisserandes*), first worked at looms, moving a shuttle by hand, then progressed to larger, more elaborate looms with pedals. The tools of their trade were also very emblematic, as attested in many contemporary illustrations, and the symbolism of "warp and woof (or weft)"—meaning the vertical and horizontal threads on their loom— predates Descartes as a representation of universal order. But the women weavers too suffered by the mid-fifteenth century by being ordered to pay an artisans' tariff to enable them to work. This, along with a general displacement by male weavers (*tisserands*) in guilds, supported by restrictive statutes such as those forbidding unmarried women weavers or those not associated with guilds to run their workshops, caused their numbers to diminish by the fifteenth century. Some women textile workers were able to form guilds, or quasi-guilds called "misteries" (from "mastery"), as was the case with the silkwomen of Paris in the fourteenth century, then London in the fifteenth century (Dale), which regulated their working conditions and protected them as men's guilds did for men.

See also Chanson de Femme (Women's Song); Dress, Courtly Women's; Dress, Religious Women's (Western, Christian); Embroidery; Guilds, Women in; Slaves, Female

BIBLIOGRAPHY

Primary Sources

[See esp. Cardon 1999, in Secondary Sources, for a complete listing of archival manuscript and printed sources and illustrations, also Raynaud for illustrations].

Bofarull y Mascaró, Próspero de, and Francisco de Bofarull y Sans, eds. *Collección de documentos inéditos del Archivo General de la Corona de Aragón*, 40: 296. Barcelona: Monfort, 1876–1910.

Bonaini, Francesco, ed. *Statuti inediti della città di Pisa dal XII al XIV secolo*, 3: 739. Florence: Vieusseux, 1870.

Bridbury, A. R. *Medieval English Clothmaking: An Economic Survey*. London: Heinemann/Pasold Fund, 1982. [Esp. pp. 77, 84].

Doren, Alfred. *Studien aus der Florentiner Wirtschaftgeschichte: 1: Die Florentiner Wollentuchindustrie vom 14. bis zum 16. Jahrhundert*. Stuttgart, Germany: J. G. Cotta, 1901. [See esp. pp. 253–54].

Melis, Federigo, ed. *Aspetti della vita economica medievale*. Siena, Italy: Monte dei Paschi, 1962. [See esp. pp. 465–66].

———. *Documenti per la storia economica dei secoli XIII–XVI*. Istituto F. Datini, 1: 1. Florence: L. Olschki, 1972. [See esp. p. 108].

Mulholland, Mary A., ed. *Early Gild Records of Toulouse*. New York: Columbia University Press, 1941. [See esp. pp. 5, 11].

———. "Statutes on Cloth-Making—Toulouse, 1227." In *Essays in Medieval Life and Thought Presented in Honor of Austin Patterson Evans*, edited by John H. Mundy et al., 167–80. New York: Columbia University Press, 1955.

Pons i Pastor, Antoni, ed. *Libre del mostassaf de Mallorca*. Consejo Superior de Investigaciones Científicas. Escuela de Estudios medievales: textos, 11. Mallorca, 1949. [See esp. p. 56].

Secondary Sources

Cardon, Dominique. "Arachné Ligotée: La Fileuse du Moyen âge face au drapier." *Médiévales* 30 (1996): 13–22.

———. *La Draperie au Moyen Âge: Essor d'une grande industrie européenne*. Paris: CNRS, 1999. [Authoritative, comprehensive, profusely documented and illustrated].

Dale, Marian K. "London Silkwomen of the Fifteenth Century." *Economic History Review* 1st ser. 4 (1933): 324–35. Reprint, with introduction by Maryanne Kowaleski and Judith Bennett, in *Sisters and Workers in the Middle Ages*, edited by Judith M. Bennett et al., 11–38. Chicago: University of Chicago Press, 1989.

Gibson, Gail M. "The Thread of Life in the Hand of the Virgin." In *Equally in God's Image: Women in the Middle Ages*, edited by Julia B. Holloway et al., 46–54. New York: Peter Lang, 1990.

Hanawalt, Barbara A., and Anna Dronzek. "Women in Medieval Urban Society." In *Women in Medieval Western European Culture*, edited by Linda E. Mitchell, 31–46. Garland Reference Library of the Humanities, 2007. New York and London: Garland, 1999.

McRee, Benjamin R., and Trisha K. Dent. "Working Women in the Medieval City." In *Women in Medieval Western European Culture*, 241–56. See above under Hanawalt.

Raynaud, Christiane. "Quand Ève et Sardanapale filaient." *Bulletin du CRISIMA* 1 (2000): 5–80. [Well-documented and illustrated art-historical study of medieval depictions of the various women's textile crafts].

NADIA MARGOLIS

STAGEL, ELSBETH (c.1300–c.1360). Elsbeth Stagel (or Stagelin, Staglin), writer, scribe, and translator, was a nun and later a prioress in the Dominican women's monastery of Töss, close to Winterthur near Zürich, Switzerland. Töss was founded in 1233 and placed under the spiritual direction of the Dominican monks (also known as the Order of Preachers, or Blackfriars, founded by the Spaniard St. Dominic at Bologna in 1220) of Zürich. By 1350 the monastery housed approximately one hundred members. Given the key Dominican preoccupations of preaching and study—for the salvation of souls—the fame of the Töss scriptorium (manuscript workshop), school, and library is not surprising. Because of this, and despite the harsh life of self-imposed poverty and asceticism, the Dominican order by Elsbeth's time had attracted an overwhelming number of women, many of whom came from aristocratic German and Swiss families.

Thus Elsbeth Stagel, probably the daughter of Zürich senator Rudolf Stagel, and who first entered the Töss community at the age of six, received an excellent, if austere, education. She is best known for her association with the Dominican mystic, the Blessed Heinrich Seuse, or Henry Suso (c.1295–1366), a disciple of the highly influential mystic, Master Eckhart (c.1260–c.1328). Elsbeth met Suso c.1336, who visited during his wanderings after his expulsion from Constance, southern Germany (c.1330) by more powerful mystical groups who condemned the teachings of his mentor, Eckhart. Suso's and Elsbeth's ensuing twenty-five-year-long relationship, as documented in their correspondence, is one of the famous spiritual friendships of the Middle Ages. Suso, also known as "Amandus" (Latin = "Loving one") and often characterized in German as the *minnesinger* (courtly love poet) among the mystics, called Elsbeth his *geischliche tohter* (spiritual daughter) and forbade her to continue starving herself and abusing her body as her monastery sisters did. Under his influence, Elsbeth began to study and to copy mystical writings. Eventually she translated a number of Latin works in prose—and even rendered some of Suso's Latin writings—into Middle-High German verse. She may also have been the scribe of the oldest manuscript of Suso's *Büchlein der ewige Weisheit* (*Little Book of Eternal Wisdom*). Their friendship also yielded the basis for Suso's *vita*, or laudatory biography (1365), written for edification and based on material (sermons, letters, conversations) secretly collected by her. The second part of this vita contains an account of Elsbeth's own life, written later by Johannes Meyer (1454). It was Meyer who first attributed the entire *Tösser Schwesternbuch* (Töss Sister-Book), or convent chronicle, to Elsbeth, emphasizing as well her debt to Suso's tutelage, in a manner designed to heighten the book's prestige while subtly undermining Elsbeth's authority, probably out of gender bias.

Although Meyer's assertion has become outdated, scholars still credit Elsbeth with several of the vitae, and possibly the prologue (though this is inconclusive; see Vetter) in the Töss Sister-Book: arguably one of the finest examples of its genre and the first known attempt at biography in German. Prior to Elsbeth's involvement, this chronicle contained a nucleus of two previously written lives, those of Sophia von Klingau and of Mechthilt von Stans, around which the lives of thirty-six other members of the monastery eventually gathered, from the monastery's origins until c.1340, the date of its composition in Middle-High German. Johannes Meyer added another prologue and the vitae of Elsbeth and Suso's mother in 1454. Written for the purpose of spiritually revitalizing monastery life during a period of reform within the Dominican order, the book concentrates on the ascetic "saintly striving" (*hailig ubung*) and the "distinctive signs of grace and wonder" (*die usgenomnen gnaden und wunder*) apparent in the lives of mystically inclined nuns. While still abounding in clichés and repetitions, the work contains some notable passages, and its authors coined a number of powerful new terms, such as the various compounds for love: *minnebewegung* (love-emotion), *minwund* (love-wound), *minzaichen* (love-sign), and so forth. Unfortunately, we cannot determine precisely which ones were devised by Elsbeth.

See also Anna of Munzingen; Ebner, Christine; Elisabeth of Hungary/Thuringia, St.; Elsbeth von Oye; *Frauenfrage*; *Minne*; Sister-Books (*Schwesternbücher*)

BIBLIOGRAPHY

Primary Sources

Stagel, Elsbeth, et al. *Das Leben der Schwestern zu Töss, beschrieben von Elsbeth Stagel, samt der Vorrede von Johannes Meyer*. Critical ed. by Ferdinand Vetter. Deutsche Texte des Mittelalters, 6. Berlin: Weidmann, 1906.

———. *Das Leben des seligen Heinrich Seuse*. Translated (Modern German) by Georg Hofmann and introduced by Walter Nigg. Düsseldorf, Germany: Patmos-Verlag, 1966.

Suso, Henry (Heinrich Seuse). *Buchlein der ewige Weisheit*. Edited by Olga Schneider. 2nd ed. Stein-am-Rhein, Germany: Christiana-Verlag, 1987.

———. *The Exemplar*. Critical ed. by Nicholas Heller. Translated by Ann Edward. 2 vols. Dubuque, Iowa: Priory Press, 1962.

———. *The Letters of Henry Suso to His Spiritual Daughter*. Translated by Kathleen Goldman. London: Blackfriars, 1955. [Translation of twenty-three letters].

[Töss Schwesternbüch, *Vitae*]. *Deutsches Nonnenleben: Das Leben der Schwestern zu Töss*. Edited by Margarete Weinhandl. Katholikon, 2. Munich: Recht, 1921. [Modern German translations].

Secondary Sources

Ancelet-Hustache, Jeanne. *La Vie mystique d'un monastère de Dominicaines au Moyen-Âge d'après la Chronique de Töss*. Paris: Perrin, 1928.

Bynum, Caroline Walker. *Holy Feast and Holy Fast: The Religious Significance of Food to Medieval Women*. Berkeley: University of California Press, 1987.

Ehrenschwendtner, Marie-Luise. "*Puellae litteratae*: The Vernacular in the Dominican Convents." In *Medieval Women in their Communities*, edited by Diane Watt, 49–71. Cardiff: University of Wales Press, 1997.

Grabmann, Martin. *Mittelalterliches Geistesleben. Abhandlungen der Scholastik und Mystik*. Munich: Hueber, 1926.

Krebs, Englebert. "Stagelin, Elsbeth." In *Die deutsche Literatur des Mittelalters – Verfasserlexikon*, edited by Wolfgang Stammler and Karl Langosch, 4: 256–58. Berlin: de Gruyter, 1953.

Lewis, Gertrud Jaron. *By Women, for Women, about Women: The Sister-Books of Fourteenth-Century Germany*. Studies and Texts, 125. Toronto: Pontifical Institute of Mediaeval Studies, 1996.

Tinsley, David F. "Gender, Paleography, and the Question of Authorship in Late Medieval Dominican Spirituality." *Medieval Feminist Newsletter* 26 (fall 1998): 23–29.

Vetter, Ferdinand. See above under Stagel in Primary Sources.

GERTRUD JARON LEWIS

STEINUNN REFSDÓTTIR (fl. c.999). One of the pre-Christian group of Icelandic woman poets, or *skáldkonur*, as they are called in Old Norse, Steinunn Refsdóttir, who lived in Hofgardr, Snaefellsnes, Iceland, is cited in two later prose accounts (*Njáls saga* and *Kristni saga*) as having composed two oral stanzas in the classic skáldic meter *dróttkvætt* (court meter). These were *nídvísur* (lampooning stanzas) in Old Norse addressed by Steinunn, an adherent of the old pagan religion, to an early Christian missionary in Iceland.

It was often the case in the early days of the Icelandic settlement that activity in the poetic tradition, and an accompanying cultural conservatism, ran in families. This was certainly true of Steinunn's family, a prominent western Icelandic family of celebrated skáldic skill. A number of stanzas, for instance, have been preserved attributed to Steinunn's son, Hofgarda-Refr. Beyond kinship ties and the location of the family farm, however, no details are known about Steinunn herself.

The *Njáls saga* account of the poem's delivery places it in the context of a lengthy debate between Thangbrandr the missionary and Steinunn, partisan of the god Thórr. As a conclusion to her argument, Steinunn refers to Thangbrandr's recent shipwreck and recites her two nídvísur, in which she claims that it was Thórr who smashed Thangbrandr's ship while the White Christ stood by, unable to save it. Whether Thangbrandr was impressed with this argument or not is unrecorded, but his mission to Iceland can be counted successful, since the entire country became Christian by an act of parliament the following year (1000 C.E.).

Steinunn's two stanzas are structurally near perfect, according to the rules of dróttkvætt governing alliteration and internal rhyme. In addition, they exhibit a rollicking rhythm appropriate to the sea-going topic; the images are vivid and strong, particularly in the lines describing Thórr's seizing of the ship, shaking it, and dashing it on the sand. Steinunn definitely deserves the place of honor accorded her by modern Icelanders, as one of Iceland's most celebrated early *skáldkonur*.

See also Jóreiðr Hermundardóttir í Midjumdal; Jórunn skáldmær; *Laxdœla saga*; Norse Women; *Skáldkonur* (Old Norse-Icelandic Women Poets)

BIBLIOGRAPHY

Primary Sources

Brennu-Njáls saga. Edited by Einar Ólafur Sveinsson, 265–67. Íslenzk fornrit, 12. Reykjavík, Iceland: Hid íslenzka fornritafélag, 1954.

Den norsk-islandske skjaldedigtning. Edited by Finnur Jónsson, 127–28. Copenhagen: Gyldendal/Nordisk Vorlag, 1915.

Kristni saga. Edited by Bernhard Kahle, 27–28. Altnordische Sagabibliothek, 11. Halle, Germany: Max Niemeyer, 1905.

Njal's Saga. Translated by Magnus Magnusson and Hermann Pálsson, 222. Harmondsworth, Middlesex, U.K.: Penguin, 1960.

Secondary Sources
Guðrún Helgadottir. *Skáldkonur fyrri alda.* Vol. 1. Akureyri, Iceland: Kvöldvökuútgafan, 1961.
Ohlmarks, Åke, *Tors skalder och Vite-Krists: trosskiftetidens isländske furstelovskalder: 980–1013.* Stockholm: Almqvist & Wiksell, 1957.

SANDRA BALLIF STRAUBHAAR

STURION, MARIA. *See* **Maria of Venice (Maria Sturion)**

SYNCLETICA, ST. *See* **Desert Mothers**

SYRIAN-CHRISTIAN WOMEN (1st–12th centuries). Syrian-Christians are Christians for whom the Syriac language has been a primary liturgical, literary, and/or spoken language throughout their history. Syrian-Christianity's distinctive blend of various cultures carried significant implications for its women in most aspects of their spiritual and practical lives.

Introduction. Syrian Christianity encompasses a complex universe. Syriac, a dialect of Aramaic, itself a dialect of Hebrew, developed in the first centuries of the Common Era. It flourished throughout the Middle East, primarily as a language of Christians, in territories that spanned the eastern Roman, early Byzantine Empire (west Syriac) and Persia (east Syriac). Over the course of Late Antiquity, Syriac became established as the *lingua franca* of the vast trade routes that linked the Mediterranean by way of the Silk Road, through India all the way to China. Always a language known in multilingual environments—whether Greco-Roman, Persian, Arab, or others—Syriac developed into a language with a brilliant literary and cultural history of its own, often distinctive in its themes and forms, even while dynamically interacting with other linguistic cultures. For west Syriac writers, this was an exchange in the lively context of the Greco-Roman world; for east Syriac authors, that of Sassanian Persia. By the time of the Arab conquests in the seventh century, however, the terms east or west Syriac had ceased to connote geographical location; instead, they referenced religious identity within a fragmented Christian population.

From the fifth century onward, Syrian Christianity was split into divided churches with competing hierarchies. Differences in customs, traditions, and teachings that had been due largely to geographical diversity increasingly identified themselves with theological positions. The east Syriac writers, based outside Roman territory, reflected a theological conservatism that led to their withdrawal from the Ecumenical councils of the Church within the Roman Empire following the third Ecumenical Council of Ephesus in 431. These developed a *dyophysite* Christological tradition (one stressing the distinction between Christ's two natures, human and divine), often mislabeled as "Nestorianism," and continued to grow as the (Assyrian) Church of the East. The west Syriac writers split into two camps: those who accepted the decisions of the fourth Ecumenical Council of Chalcedon in 451 and remained in communion with the patriarchate of Constantinople, and those who dissented from the Council's Christological decision, preferring a more strongly *miaphysite* Christology (sometimes termed *monophysite*: one that stressed Christ incarnate as one nature united out of two, human and divine). The former would eventually drop Syriac as a language, preferring Greek or Arabic, and would become known as the *Rūm* (= Eastern Roman, or Byzantine, as distinct from Latin *Rome*) Orthodox. The latter, holding fast to their Syriac heritage, would become the Oriental Orthodox church known as the Syrian Orthodox. Somewhat independently, Christians who had settled around the monastery of St. Maron in the mountains of Lebanon took their own path, solidifying ties with Rome during the Crusades. The Maronite Church remains in communion with the Roman Catholics to this day.

The disputes yielding these separate churches were not isolated theological issues. They were controversies bound up with immense social and political upheavals. As such, their circumstances forced crises in which women as well as men took up leadership roles from lay or monastic locations, offering spiritual as well as political authority and guidance. Earlier persecutions of Christians had produced inspiring models of women's capacity for Christian witness in martyrdom (*Martyrdom of Shmona and Guria*, 1: 70; *Persian Martyrs* in Brock and Harvey). Such precedence helped create an ethos in which women's leadership was accepted in times of crisis. The Empress Theodora (d. 548), in contrast to the Chalcedonian policies of her husband Emperor Justinian (r. 527–565), provided protection and patronage for the incipient anti-Chalcedonian hierarchies (Harvey 2001a). John of Ephesus (d. 589), among others, recorded the heroic leadership of Syrian Orthodox nuns and laywomen in the towns and villages of the Eastern Roman Empire, whose pragmatic tactics made it possible for the Syrian Orthodox church to stabilize its separate identity through the worst of the sixth-century persecutions (John of Ephesus; Brock and Harvey).

Lively and brilliant, troubled and divided, Syrian Christianity of the Late Antique and medieval periods provided an array of venues in which women's participation at various levels added distinctive qualities to the history of this tradition.

Religious Symbolism and Gendered Language. Earliest Syrian Christianity is striking for the depth of gendered symbols prevalent in its literature. Most notable is the presentation of the Holy Spirit as a feminine element of the divine Trinity. While the pre-Christian religions of the Syrian regions included powerful goddess figures as well as feminine imagery for the divine, the immediate impetus for a femininely gendered Holy Spirit in Syriac was linguistic. The Syriac word for "spirit," *ruha*, is grammatically a feminine noun. Early Syriac writers showed no hesitation in following the logic of their own language. Prior to the year 400, the Holy Spirit was most often referred to as "She" in Syriac texts, sometimes elaborated with further feminine imagery, often maternal. Yet early Syriac writers showed unusual dexterity in their use of gendered imagery for the divine Trinity of Father, Son, and Holy Spirit. While the Spirit was most often presented as feminine, the usage was not exclusive; sometimes authors would refer to the Spirit with masculine terms. In turn, both the second-century *Odes of Solomon* and the great hymnography of Ephraem Syrus (d. 373) contain arresting images of God as midwife, housekeeper, birth-giver, and of Christ as nursing mother (Brock 1990, 1992; Harvey, 1993a). Apparently such usage startled the ancient ear. By the year 400, perhaps pressured to conform to Greco-Latin conventions, Syriac writers began to change their language, treating ruha as a masculine noun when it referred to the Holy Spirit and showing far more restraint in gendered imagery for the divine. From the late fourth century onward, the Syrian propensity for exploring the feminine dimension of the divine showed itself in a lyrically exalted Mariology—the cultivation and study of the person of the Blessed Virgin (Murray; Brock 1982)—and in the veneration of an impressive host of female martyrs and saints. Some of the great medieval legends of women, known throughout Europe as well as the Middle East, originated in Syriac during this period: Pelagia, the reformed courtesan of Antioch, and Mary, the fallen niece of Abraham of Qidun, are two of the most influential (Brock and Harvey).

The correlation of religious symbols with social reality is a difficult task for the historian, and no less so in the case of Syrian Christianity. On the one hand, there may have been some impact from the early Syriac tradition of the female Holy Spirit on Syrian ecclesiastical organization. In some third- and fourth-century "Church Orders" (documents or collections of documents relating to canon law), a Trinitarian typology is given for understanding Church offices: the bishop stands in the place of God the Father, the—male—deacon as Christ the Son, and the deaconess holds the place of the Holy Spirit (*Didascalia* 9; *Apostolic Constitutions* 2: 26. 6). Yet it would be hard to see any positive influence of this imagery on women's daily lives. In general, Syriac literature shows the familiar ancient Mediterranean pattern of identifying women with the household and domestic sphere, while men dominated public, civic space. Flexibility to this model came from the early Christian emphasis on asceticism, particularly celibacy, as a valued mode of life. For Syrian Christians, it was possible to imagine the female virgin or celibate widow carving out a place of considerable social freedom through a religious lifestyle, even if not attached to a convent (Torjesen; Harvey 1996b, 2001b). Nonetheless, the presentation of women as saints in Syrian tradition most often shows conformity to male ideals (Brock and Harvey; Synek 1993b).

Similarly, under certain circumstances the ecclesiastical offices of widow and deaconess granted women the authority to teach other women—a ministry by women for women. Yet we have evidence that some holy women achieved the stature of spiritual wisdom acknowledged by men as well as women, and by clergy and monastics as well as laypeople. Examples can be found not only in legends such as that of St. Febronia of Nisibis (sixth century), but also in the reminiscences of male authors about holy women influential in their own lives, such as John of Ephesus recalling the ministry of Euphemia of Amida among the city's poor and sick, or the seventh-century Martyrius (also known as Sahdona) remembering the revered village recluse and spiritual mentor Shirin (Brock and Harvey).

Marriage and Family. For Syrian Christians as for others in the ancient Mediterranean world, the ascetic ideals of early Christianity implied a critical attitude toward traditional social patterns. By their very nature, ascetic lifestyles challenged society's unequal distribution of wealth, along with the hierarchical relationship between men and women in marriage and the importance given to procreation. The force of this social critique is widely evident in Syriac literature. Martyr accounts, beginning with the apocryphal *Acts of Thomas* (second century) indicate that non-Christians resented the implications and felt particularly threatened when women chose not to marry (*Persian Martyrs* in Brock and Harvey). In the fifth century, the Persian Church, seeking peace with its non-Christian environment, dissociated its ecclesiastical hierarchy from the ascetic movement. Thus East Syrian canon law from this time permits widowed clerics a second marriage even after receiving higher ordination. The Synod of Akakis (486) further permitted marriage to professed monks (see Chabot, in *Synodicon Orientale*), thus creating rising sympathy for the ascetically oriented miaphysites, or Syrian Orthodox (Selb, vol. 1). In all churches of West Syrian tradition, asceticism was more supported by the ecclesiastical hierarchy, itself largely recruited from monks, than in the Church of the East where the reconciliation of ascetic "charisma" and ecclesiastical "office" took longer.

Despite the early emphasis on ascetic ideals, most Syrian Christians continued to marry and have children. Leading theologians from the fourth century onward confirmed the traditional perspective: children should be considered a blessing (see, for example, Ephrem, *Commentary on Genesis* 2. 30) and marriage a fundamental social institution created by God himself (see, e.g., Aphrahat, *Demonstration* 18. 8), though ascetic life was upheld as a profoundly valued option for Christians.

The traditional institutions of marriage and family, at least in principle, went on to be governed by common usage and inherited legal traditions (Selb, vol. 2). In Semitic cultures it was customary to conclude matrimony in two stages: the families' agreement on the marriage contract (east Syriac: *mkiruta* or *mkurya*, west Syriac: *mekiruta* or *mekura*; literally: purchase) and the leading of the woman to the marital home (the wedding banquet: *mestuta*). Traditionally, an agreement between two families when the bride (and often the bridegroom) was still a child, an initial step sometimes mistakenly termed a "betrothal," established the marriage bond (Selb, vol. 1). The fact that Christianity discouraged divorce led to some adjustments of the traditional practices: medieval synods requested at least a minimum age for a valid marriage contract, as well as the consent of the couple to their families' agreement. But they never questioned the father's traditional right to marry his daughters to husbands of his choice.

The "Christianization" of marriage may be seen through an increasing number of marriage prohibitions imposed by the ecclesiastical authorities. The full establishment of marriage as a sacrament of the Church took about a millennium and was obviously influenced by the Byzantine development. But polygamy and concubinage were disallowed from the very beginning. The marriage of relatives or in-laws became an issue for canonical prohibition at least from the fourth century onward. As in Byzantine and Latin canon law, the respective prohibitions retain a tendency to undermine traditional social structures. Another concern of canonical regulation was mixed marriage. A number of canons prohibit marriage between Christian women and non-Christian men, as well as interconfessional marriage.

Church canons sometimes allow us to glimpse the factual position of married or widowed women. In the east Syrian context, for example, the economic independence of women seems to have been remarkably high. Canon 24 of the Synod of Isoyahb I (585) declares management of the dowry (Syriac: *ferne*) to be the wife's prerogative. According to a synodical letter from the same council, women are sole inheritors if the husband dies without leaving a will, even if there are children; furthermore, a will that would deprive a woman of assets she brought into marriage from her parents' home or that were acquired during marriage should be considered invalid (Chabot, in *Synodicon Orientale*).

The Ascetic Life. There is an obvious tension between the high regard for marriage and family expressed in homiletic (containing homilies: morally edifying sermons) and canonical literature, and the ideal of virginity (Syriac: *btuluta*), which dominates the various genres of spiritual literature in Syriac tradition. Male celibates, who tended to propagate their own choice as the optimal way of life for Christians, as a rule wrote the spiritual literature. Yet hagiography such as the *Life of St. Febronia* may nonetheless give an authentic picture of life in a Syrian convent, where women's friendships and intellectual pursuits were highly valued, and where the surrounding lay community may also have found a "pastoral center" (Synek 1993b).

Entering a convent was but one alternative to "normal" life as a married homemaker and mother. Early Syrian Christianity had developed an impressive variety of ascetic ways of life. As described in the *Life of Febronia*, convents centered on the ideal of segregation of the sexes were a comparatively late development; they also vanished again under Islamic dominion. Syrian women's religious vocations were more often enacted from within households than convents, and often practiced in the public domain (Harvey 1996a). "Spiritual marriage," the way of the *qaddishe* ("holy ones": married couples who practiced abstinence) afforded the possibility of combining the social and economic functions of marriage with an ascetic vocation. Abstinence might be agreed on from the start of a marriage, or taken up after one or two children had been born. Other women were dedicated as virgins (*btulata*) from childhood, or chose an ascetic way of life after being widowed.

Religious grounds were not the only reason for such a choice. Within the given social context, asceticism meant more than renunciation from sexual intercourse and one's own children in favor of a contemplative life. Abstinence from marital relations allowed women to avoid life-threatening pregnancies and the pain of childbirth. Moreover, asceticism offered possibilities of breaking free from restrictive social codes. The choice of an ascetic life allowed avoidance of subjugation to the—male—family head. Freed from their tasks of housekeeping and child-rearing, ascetic women across social and economic borders could devote themselves to new activities. Some undertook extensive social and ecclesiastical ministries; learning, too, became available to women from lower social strata.

Church Offices and Liturgy. Syrian holy women sometimes gained prominent civic roles without the sanction of a designated church office or an "official" monastic identity. One such woman was Euphemia of Amida who, together with her daughter Maria, over time came to run an entire welfare program for the poor and sick in her city (John of Ephesus, 12; Brock and Harvey 1998). Yet the context for such popular recognition of women's spiritual authority surely lay in the visible, public ministries performed by women in ecclesiastical offices, and particularly the Syrian institution of the "Sons and Daughters of the Covenant" (in Syriac: *bnay* and *bnat qyama*), an office developing in the third century. Following vows of chastity and poverty, living in separated households or with their families, the Members of the Covenant devoted themselves to the service of the Christian community through service to the bishop (Harvey 2000). There is rich evidence for bnay and bnat qyama throughout the Syrian Orient until the tenth century. Often they were identified with works of charity: Bishop Rabbula (d. 434) assigned the Daughters of the Covenant to work at the women's hospital in the venerable Syrian-Christian center of Edessa (now Urfa, Turkey). The Members of the Covenant also played an essential part in the liturgical life of Syrian civic communities. Daughters of the Covenant were assigned the task of chanting psalms and *madrashe*, doctrinal hymns, in the morning and evening daily offices, for memorial services, and special feast days. Indeed, these women's choirs were a distinctive feature of late antique, early medieval Syriac churches, appointed specifically to the civic churches of villages, towns, and cities, rather than to convents. Because Syriac Christianity placed particular emphasis on the liturgy as a place of religious instruction, the role of these women's choirs was immensely important (Harvey 2001b). In time the bnay and bnat qyama provided the resources for a well-trained ecclesiastical staff whose members were recruited as children (see Synek 1993a).

Wherever access was difficult or impossible for men due to social protocol, there was a need for female ministries. Early collections of Church canons such as the *Didascalia Apostolorum* (a Church Order from the third century, deriving from a Greek-speaking Syrian milieu, but transmitted in an early Syriac translation) indicate concern about the propriety of such ministries, even while emphasizing their crucial role in the life of the church (see Synek 1993b).

Syrian sources not only know female deacons but also the office of widow (*qashishta*). While the *Didascalia* and, again in the fourth century, the *Apostolic Constitutions*, tried to confine widows' roles within the Christian communities to a devoted life of prayer, another Church Order, the *Testamentum Domini* (fifth century, or, according to recent scholarship, even later) allows them a place among the ordained clergy. Thanks to the reception of the *Testamentum* in later canonical collections such as the *Clementine Octateuch* and the *Synodicon of West Syrian Tradition*, recollections of that particular female ministry will have remained even when the office itself no longer existed in practice.

The competing office of deaconess had a more successful history. While evidence is scarce, it seems to have survived until modern times (Brock 1996), though not everywhere in the Syrian Orient. In the west-Syrian context the deaconesses faded out from the community clergy in the aftermath of the Council of Chalcedon (451). In contrast, convincing east-Syrian evidence for the office of deaconess cannot be found earlier than the late sixth or seventh century, whereupon it designates a community-bound ministry especially for the baptism of women. We might here assume a connection with the fruitful missionary activity of the Church of the East associated with continued adult baptism. In western Syria, deaconesses found a new field of activity in convents, where their ministry was frequently amalgamated with the office of the abbess. Where the monastic ideal sought as complete a separation of the sexes as possible, a man in a convent could create the same problems as a woman in a monastery, or any kind of cohabitation of male and female ascetics. Not surprisingly, women in such convents assumed functions no longer accessible to them in normal parish life (Synek 1993a). The head of a convent was a woman, and a woman acted as overseer of the convents in a given region. Furthermore, there is canonical evidence for female deacons performing a number of liturgical functions during monastic services. Among these were Scripture readings and administering Holy Communion when a male cleric was not at hand.

Despite the greater conservatism of the medieval period in comparison with Late Antique Syrian Christianity, exclusion of women from community service was never definitive. To this day, the custom persists for the priest's wife to step in wherever propriety requires a woman minister, such as in assisting in the baptism of an older girl or an adult woman. From the tenth century onward, the wife of a priest is referred to as a *ba(r)t qyama*—indicating that being a priest's wife was (and is), in a certain sense, regarded as an ecclesiastical office in itself. In one of the latest canons received into the

Western Syrian *Synodicon* (twelfth century), she is even "the spiritual mother to all the believers" (Canon 29 of Johannan of Marde in *Synodicon*, ed. Vööbus).

See also Convents; Desert Mothers; Dower; Dowry; Law, Canon, Women in; Theodora; Virginity

BIBLIOGRAPHY

Primary Sources

"The Acts of Thomas." Critical eds., commentary, and translations by H. J. W. Drijvers. In *New Testament Apocrypha*, revised ed. by Wilhelm Schneemelcher, 2: 322–411. Translated by R. M. Wilson. Louisville, Ky.: Westminster/John Knox Press, 1992. [Greek texts, English trans.].

Aphrahat. [*Demonstrations*]. Edited and translated by D. I. Parisot. In *Aphraatis sapientis persae demonstrations*. Patrologia Syriaca 1, edited by R. Graffin. Paris 1894.

———. *Demonstration* 18. Translated in Jacob Neusner, *Aphrahat and Judaism*. Leiden: E. J. Brill, 1971. [English trans.].

[Apostolic Constitutions]. *Les Constitutions apostoliques*. Edited and translated by Marcel Metzger. Sources Chrétiennes, 320, 329, 336. Paris: Éditions du Cerf, 1985–1987.

Brock, Sebastian P., and Susan Ashbrook Harvey, eds. and transs. *Holy Women of the Syrian Orient*. Revised ed. Berkeley: University of California Press, 1998. [English trans. of Syriac texts about holy women, martyrs, and saints with commentary].

[Clementine Octateuch]. *La Version syriaque de l'octateuque de Clément*. Edited by François Nau. In *Canoniste contemporain* (1907–1913). Reprint Paris: P. Lethielleux, 1913. New ed. by Pio Cipriotti. Paris: P. Lethielleux, 1967.

The Didascalia Apostolorum in Syriac. Edited and translated by Arthur Vööbus. Corpus Scriptorum Christianorum Orientalium [= CSCO] 401–02, 407–08. Scriptores Syri, 175–80. Louvain, Belgium: CSCO, 1979.

Ephraem Syrus, *Commentary on Genesis*. Edited and translated by R. M. Tonneau. In *Sancti Ephraem Syri in Genesim et in Exodum Commentarii*. CSCO, 152–53. Scriptores Syrii 71–72. Louvain: CSCO, 1955.

———. *St. Ephrem the Syrian: Selected Prose Works*. Translated by Edward G. Mathews, Jr. and Joseph P. Amar. Edited by Kathleen McVey, 59–213. Fathers of the Church, 91. Washington, D.C.: Catholic University of America Press, 1994.

John of Ephesus. *Lives of the Eastern Saints*. Edited and translated by E. W. Brooks. Patrologia Orientalis 17–19. Paris: Firmin-Didot, 1923–1925.

"The Martyrdom of Shmona and Guria." In *Euphemia and the Goth with the Acts of Martyrdom of the Confessors of Edessa, Shmona, Guria, and Habib*, edited and translated by F. C. Burkitt. London and Oxford: Text and Translation Society, 1913.

The Odes of Solomon. Edited and translated by James H. Charlesworth, 2nd ed. Missoula, Mont.: Scholars Press, 1977.

The Synodicon in the West Syrian Tradition I–II. Edited and translated by Arthur Vööbus. CSCO, 367–68, 375–76. Scriptores Syri, 161–64. Louvain: CSCO, 1975; 1976.

Synodicon Orientale. Edited and translated by J.-B. Chabot. Paris: Imprimerie nationale, 1902. [Collection of east Syrian councils and canons].

Testamentum Domini Nostri Jesu Christi. Edited and translated by Ignatius E. Rahmani. Mainz, Germany: F. Kirchheim, 1899.

Secondary Sources

Brock, Sebastian P. "Mary in Syriac Tradition." In *Mary's Place in Christian Dialogue*, edited by A. Stacpoole, 182–91. Slough, U.K.: St. Paul Publications, 1982.

———. "The Holy Spirit as Feminine in Early Syriac Literature." In *After Eve: Women, Theology and the Christian Tradition*, edited by J. M. Soskice, 73–88. London: Marshall Pickering, 1990.

———. "Come, Compassionate Mother . . . , come Holy Spirit": A Forgotten Aspect of Early Eastern Christian Imagery." *Aram* 3 (1991): 249–57.

————. "Deaconesses in the Syriac Tradition." In *Woman in Prism and Focus. Her Profile in Major World Religions and Christian Traditions*, edited by Prasanna Vazheeparampil, 205–18. Rome: Mar Thomas Yogam, 1996.

Fiey, Jean M. "Cénobitisme féminin ancien dans les églises Syriennes orientales et occidentales." *L'Orient Syrien* 10 (1965): 281–306.

Harvey, Susan Ashbrook. *Asceticism and Society in Crisis: John of Ephesus and the Lives of the Eastern Saints*. Berkeley: University of California Press, 1990.

————. "Feminine Imagery for the Divine. The Holy Spirit, the Odes of Solomon, and Early Syriac Tradition." *St. Vladimir's Theological Quarterly* 37 (1993a): 111–39.

————. "Women in Early Syrian Christianity." In *Images of Women in Antiquity*, edited by Averil Cameron and Amélie Kuhrt, 288–98, 312. London: Routledge, 1993b.

————. "Sacred Bonding: Mothers and Daughters in Early Syriac Hagiography." *Journal of Early Christian Studies* 4 (1996a) 27–56.

————. "Women in the Syriac Tradition." In *Woman in Prism and Focus. Her Profile in Major World Religions and Christian Traditions*, edited by Prasanna Vazheeparampil, 69–80. Rome: Mar Thomas Yogam, 1996b.

————. "Women's Service in Ancient Syriac Christianity." In *Mother, Nun, Deaconess: Images of Women According to Eastern Canon Law* (= *Kanon* XVI), edited by Carl G. Fürst and Richard Potz, 226–41. Egling, Germany: Kovar, 2000.

————. "Theodora, the 'Believing Queen': A Study in Syriac Historiographical Tradition." *Hugoye* 4. 2 (July 2001a). [Special Issue: *Women in the Syrian Tradition*]. (http://syrcom.cua.edu/Hugoye/Vol4No2/index.html).

————. "Spoken Words, Voiced Silence: Biblical Women in Syriac Tradition." *Journal of Early Christian Studies* 9 (2001b): 105–31.

Hugoye 4. 2 (July 2001). [Special Issue: "Women in the Syrian Tradition"]. (http://syrcom.cua.edu/Hugoye/Vol4No2/index.html).

Murray, Robert. "Mary, the Second Eve in the Early Syriac Fathers." *Eastern Churches Review* 3 (1971): 372–84.

Selb, Walter. *Orientalisches Kirchenrecht*. Vol . 1: *Die Geschichte des Kirchenrechts der Nestorianer*. 2: *Die Geschichte des Kirchenrechts der Westsyrer*. Vienna: Österreichischen Akademie der Wissenschaften, 1981–1989.

Synek, Eva M. "In der Kirche möge sie schweigen." *Oriens Christianus* 77 (1993a): 151–64.

————. "Kultur und Heiligkeit. Ein Beitrag zum spirituellen Erbe des syrischen Mönchtums." *Geist und Leben* 66 (1993b): 359–81.

Torjesen, Karen Jo. "The Role of Women in the Early Greek and Syriac Churches." *The Harp* 4 (1991): 135–44.

EVA MARIA SYNEK AND SUSAN ASHBROOK HARVEY

τ

TEACHERS, WOMEN AS. Women have undergone a long evolution as teachers both secular and religious during the Middle Ages. The following concentrates on women as Christian teachers.

New Testament Definitions of "Teacher" vs. Women. In the Gospels, Jesus himself is called Rabbi, that is, teacher (Greek: *didaskalos*; plural: *didaskaloi*). "As Jesus Christ had delivered Christianity as a teacher, so the early Christians took it upon themselves to teach Christianity" (Neymeyr, 1). In the communities of the New Testament, the office of didaskalos existed as one of those connected with the proclamation of the Word and thus tied to *charismata*, the blessings, usually supernatural, bestowed on all Christians enabling them to fulfill their life's vocation. Whether lists of those didaskaloi included women cannot be clearly deduced because of the New Testament's use of inclusive language. Yet the so-called "teaching prohibitions" (see 1 Cor. 14: 34ff., and esp. 1 Tim. 2: 12ff.) indicate that women must have been teachers to incur prohibition. Prophetic discourse was granted to women as it was to men at least in principle, but already the layers of the New Testament influenced by the Apostle Paul exhibit hostility toward female teaching. These layers were eagerly received in later Church Orders (early c anon law compilations) like the *Didascalia Apostolorum* (third century) and, in their aftermath, the *Apostolic Constitutions* (late fourth century; Synek 1999). In post-biblical times, the distinction between the charismata of prophecy and teaching, among others, helped to reconcile the crucial biblical heritage and the actual participation of women in teaching the Gospel. Thus it is certainly right to stress that in the second century, "the difference between prophetesses and [female] teachers should not be overemphasized" (Jensen 2003, 371).

Contextual analysis of the relevant biblical texts—cited repeatedly against female teachers—and their reception history reveals that only the issue of religious teaching by women was debated, not the conveyance of general facts of life experience and profane knowledge. In the Book of Titus, aged women (Greek: *presbytides*) are even expressly urged to be good teachers for young women (Greek: *kalodidaskalous*). The values to be taught these women speak for themselves: love of man, love of children, discretion, chastity, prudence, and ultimately, subordination to the husband (Titus 2: 13–14). The greatest resistance to the teaching of women is found where the addressees are men. This is explicable by inherited gender ideology: The definition of man as the head of woman was a commonplace to all cultures of Antiquity, pagan as well as Jewish. Accordingly, from the perspective of an average early Christian male, receiving instruction by a woman implied a risk of loosing face. Since religious instruction is linked with authority, allowing women to teach men the Word of God would also mean to grant them authority with respect to men. This idea threatened social order based on hierarchy and fundamental male lordship. As an anonymous fourth-century manuscript shows, out of this construct grew, at least according to the view of some men of the Church, the prohibition for women even to write books "in their own name" (Labriolle, 93–108). The crucial position of teaching women suffered damage as the prevailing gender prejudice combined with a social system dividing the Greek-named spheres of *oikos* (household) and *polis* (city). While the household was seen as the realm of women, the greater public was not.

Nevertheless, female teachers of the Christian doctrine do exist in Church history. Moreover there were women who acted not only de facto as catechists (Christian educators) or theologians, but also women explicitly referred to as "teachers." Hagiographic texts (saints' lives) in particular use the term *didaskalos* as a sort of title for a number of female saints. For all the ambivalence in the assessment of female activities, we note that, in these texts outlining models of ideal Christian behavior, the teaching of women appears quite frequently. The canonical heritage is much more reserved on this point. However, in some contexts, as the instruction of female candidates for baptism in particular, the teaching of some women sorted out by the ecclesiastical authorities was foreseen by Church Orders and canons, which, on the whole, do not encourage female teaching at all. Among those women officially entrusted with ecclesiastical teaching functions at least in some local churches, are deaconesses, widows, and virgins (Synek 1993a). In the medieval Church they were supervised by abbesses. Because such officially approved teaching was generally (though not always) restricted to an all-female audience, it did not overly threaten social order and thus could be more easily accepted than women giving religious instruction in a mixed-gender public context, such as preaching during a regular Sunday service.

The Early Christian Development. When catechesis (religious education) and theology in the larger sense are defined as characteristics of Christian teaching, we must nonetheless take into account that "teaching" can acquire a great variety of meanings under different contexts. Our discussion focuses on the formative period of Christianity, the first millennium.

The early teachers, didaskaloi, of the New Testament were, according to the (debatable) position of Alfred Zimmermann, strongly rooted in the Jewish tradition and "constituted a Jewish-Christian Proto-rabbinate" (Zimmermann, 218). In the Hellenistic Greek context, however, the transmission of knowledge (*gnosis*) came to the fore. If, in the beginning, nonordained and ordained teachers stood side by side, later on a "melting process" occurred. Especially in the East, the baptismal catechesis of women became closely linked to the office of (female) deacon. As deaconesses and, after the consolidation of monasticism, to some extent also as abbesses, women with a particular ecclesiastical mission were teaching in an official way. This does not mean, however, that, with the consolidation of ecclesiastical offices in Late Antiquity, nonordained or consecrated teachers (male and female) disappeared altogether. Ulrich Neymeyr (1989) holds that the melting process was completed by the mid-third century; he concedes that certain characteristics of the older teaching practices survived in monasticism later on (Neymeyr, 238). However, the ruling Church hierarchy, with its tripartite office (bishop–presbyter–deacon) that tended to absorb the teaching of Christian doctrine among other ecclesiastical functions, was not even established fully by the fourth century. Another weakness in Neymeyr's arguments lies in his old-fashioned notion that women teachers were heretics, and thus should be seen as a peculiarity of the Gnostic movement (Neymeyr, 206–14). Gnosticism, a complex movement first prominent in the second century, believed that through *gnosis* (knowledge) was revealed the nature of God, human destiny, and thus redemption; it endured for centuries despite being condemned by the Church. Recent scholarship shows that a clear separation between "heresy" and "orthodoxy" is often no more than a cliché on this point as on others. These theoretical debates will become clearer as we examine actual female teachers who were neither sympathizers with the Gnostic movement nor adherents of the Marcionitic Circle (named for the heretic Marcion [d. c.160] who preached the Christian Gospel as one entirely of love, without laws), nor proponents of the "New Prophecy," an apocalyptic movement that became the Montanist Church (Labriolle; Trevett; Jensen 2003). Instead, we shall show that women teachers participated in the life of the orthodox "Great Church."

Female Teachers Belonging to the "Great Church" (fourth through fifth centuries). The case of the Roman Faltonia Betitia Proba (d. c.370) refutes the theses of Neymeyr in every respect: Proba, a married woman, lived and worked in the fourth century as an unordained theological writer of the mainstream Church (Jensen 1998; Margoni-Kögler). Her work, a Christian epic of Salvation composed in Virgilian verse, was used as a school manual during the Middle Ages and survives to this day. The encyclopedic authority Isidore of Seville (d. 636) listed her in his *Catalogue of Famous Men* as "the only woman among the Men of the Church" (Isidor of Seville, *De viris illustribus* 5; cited in Jensen 2002, 260). In the person of Empress Eudocia (d. 460), Proba found, in the fifth century, a Greek-poetic successor, who wrote, among other things, a cento in Homeric verse (Eudocia, ed. Usher 1999; Usher 1998). Proba and Eudocia prove that, even though male theologians vastly outnumbered women theologians in early Christian times, this does not mean that the latter did not exist at all.

As further examples, we find Jerome (d. 419) and, from his circle of wealthy Roman women smitten with asceticism, Marcella (d. 410), renowned as a brilliant exegete who surpassed many men in her theological knowledge (Krumeich; Petersen-Szemerédy; Feichtinger; Letsch-Brunner). One important feature in Jerome's report appears to be the tension between the high esteem enjoyed by Marcella's teaching and his firm adherence to the aforementioned prohibition of female teaching inspired by Paul: "I do not allow a woman to teach" (1 Tim. 2: 12; quoted in Jerome, *Epistula* 127, *Ad Principiam virginem* 7; see Jensen ed. 2002, 282). A possible compromise is ascribed to Marcella herself: "in what she taught, she admitted to be pupil herself" (Jerome, *Epistula* 127). It is not implausible that Marcella—who, according to Jerome's posthumous narration, the Roman clergy consulted regularly on exegetical questions—occasionally deployed such ruses to soften the threat of her superiority and retain her position as theological authority.

The *Historia Ecclesiastica* (*Church History*) of Theodoret of Cyrrhus (d. c.466) reports on other female teachers (Jensen 2003, 93–103; 148–57). In particular, he memorialized an anonymous deaconess who instructed converts to Christianity in her house. Remarkably, Theodoret's account (*Hist. Eccl.* III, 14; Jensen 2002, 174–76) does not echo any prejudice against the women as teachers, nor does it mention specific restrictions for female teachers as attested in other sources. On the contrary, the episode recreated by Theodoret deals openly with the deaconess's teaching of a young man. The *Historia* also commemorates another woman whom Theodoret explicitly calls a teacher (*Hist. Eccl.* III, 19; Jensen 2002,

184–86). Whether this head of a convent, named Publia, was also a deaconess can no longer be clearly determined; later editors did infer that she was one, but in Theodoret's account there is no reference to a diaconal function.

Aside from the female teachers marginally affiliated with the Catholic Church, there were noteworthy women who were definitely its adherents and engaged in catechetic (Christian-instructional) activities within their own families, even though Neymayr omits this. That women taught their husbands, children, grandchildren, and siblings the fundamental principles of faith, passed on the theological heritage of their time as well as their own theological reasoning is documented by a number of Church Fathers including Gregory of Nazianzus (d. c.390), Gregory of Nyssa (d. c.395) and Basil the Great (of Caesarea, d. c.378). The attempt to reconcile the classical ideal of female submission in marriage with a wife's factual teaching her husband is apparent in the portrait of Nonna by her son, Gregory of Nazianzus: "Although she deemed it best, in accordance with the law of marriage, to be overruled by her husband, in other respects, she was not ashamed to show herself his master in piety" (Gregory of Nazianzus, *Oration* 18. 8). Nonna is portrayed by her son as a leader (Greek: *archegos*) of her husband, "personally guiding him by her deed and word to what was most excellent" (*Oration* 18. 8). At the same time, Gregory pointed out that Nonna's Christian-instructional activities were restricted to her own house; they did not extend to the liturgical sphere in any way.

The abovementioned teachers were based in and around Cappadocia (now Kizil Irmak, east-central Turkey). Another from this region, acting within her family, was Macrina the Elder (d. c.340). As a pupil of Gregory Thaumaturgus (d. c.270), and through whom the highly influential but controversial Origen (d. c.254), Macrina transmitted their teachings to her grandchildren, among whom were Gregory of Nyssa, Basil the Great, and Macrina the Younger (d. 380). Unlike her famous brothers, Macrina the Younger did not engage in personal theological writing, yet she was still explicitly considered a teacher. In his dialogue *De anima et resurrectione* (*On the Soul and the Resurrection*), Gregory of Nyssa eventually credits his theological message to a conversation with his sister. As a woman who transferred her ascetic practice from within her family to the foundation of a monastic community, Macrina the Younger crossed the boundary from the private realm of teaching within the household to the more open realm of monastic teachers, male and female (Albrecht 1986). This made her not merely a teacher to her younger siblings, but of all the "sisters" in her monastic community at Pontus as well.

Deserving of mention along with Macrina the Younger are a number of other contemporary women ascetics of one sort or another, as, for instance, the two Melanias (Melania the Elder, d. c.410, and Melania the Younger, d. 439), and the Desert Mothers Sara, Theodora, and Syncletica, whose sayings were transmitted, along with those of her more numerous male counterparts, in the so-called *Apophthegmata Patrum* (*Sayings of the Fathers*). In their *Vitae* (*Lives*), Syncletica, Macrina, and Melania the Younger are specifically referred to as didaskaloi. To Syncletica and Theodora are also attributed pronouncements on teaching and related topics.

From among the missionaries of post–New Testament period venturing to Georgia, by the western Black Sea, we find the woman apostle-teacher Nino, legendary founder of what became the Georgian Church. Both ancient historians and modern scholarship associate her acts as a Christian prisoner and the conversion of the Georgian royal family (early fourth century). Of course, much of the abundant medieval material on Nino's missionary-catechetic activities, including missionary travels, remains to be verified. But in any case, it certainly adds to the acceptance and prestige of female teaching in medieval Georgia that the historical sources on the conversion of Georgia call Nino "apostle" and "teacher" (Synek 1994, 2000). It also seems significant that consistent parts of the legendary accounts of the conversion of Georgia were attributed to women.

Early Medieval Teachers. Medieval women's monastic communities also yielded some rare examples of women theological writers and hymnodists who, unlike those alleged authors/transmitters of Nino's tradition, can at least be attested as real historical figures. Of twofold interest are two examples of hagiographic literature heralding seventh-century developments; both are attributed to female authors and deal with a teaching woman. Such was Sergia's *Narration on St. Olympias* (d. 408/410; Olympias, "Life," ed. Clark, 145–55). Sergia, the abbess of the St. Olympias monastery in Constantinople, stylizes the founder of her monastery, perhaps best known from the *Epistles* of John Chrysostom (d. 407), as a teacher of the nuns. From the ancient Armenian royal town of Nisibis (now Nisibin, northeastern Syria) comes the *Life of St. Febronia*, written at about the same time as Sergia's narration. This vita portrays a (female) saint, honored as a martyr, in her capacity as nun and teacher (*Febronia*, ed. Harvey and Brock, 150–76). Though this immensely popular biography's author went by the pseudonym of "Abbess Thomais," Febronia was indeed most likely a woman, probably a nun. A woman may also have authored the other, anonymous *Life of St. Olympias* around the fifth century (see notes to "Life of Olympias," ed. Clark, 127–42). However, neither case can yet be determined conclusively.

Unlike the abovementioned hagiographies, cases of theological correspondence between monastic women and male partners reflect all too often that only the male partner's legacy survived. This holds true for such examples as Jerome's brilliant but self-effacing Marcella (fifth century) and for John Chrysostom's female correspondents (fourth century) Olympias and the abbess Euphrosyne, addressed explicitly as didaskale by Theodore of Studios (d. 826; *Epistulae*, 510, pp. 755–56).

The state of source materials on the Byzantine female hymnodists fortunately has fared somewhat better. These women poet-composers, along with male poets such as Romanos (d. after 555) or John of Damascus (d. c.750), rendered theological ideas into verses; they thus taught through music. The musicologist Egon Wellesz lists six names, but later research reduces this number, because Gregoris cannot be ascertained as a historical figure and there is no proof that the historical Martha wrote hymns as did her son Simeon (d. 592; Topping, 83). However, the three remaining nuns (ninth century)—Theodosia, Thekla, and Kassia (or Kassiane), and later, Palaiologina (probably fifteenth century)— reached a wide public because their hymns were incorporated into the liturgy, that is, church services. In a larger sense, we even have sermons by women, though the canons did not allow personal preaching during service. Kassia's troparion (stanza of religious poetry, often sung at Vespers) "About the sinful woman" (Topping, 30–38) has preserved its place in the Byzantine liturgical tradition and is found even in profane Greece in demotic (colloquial Greek) translation with a modern tune.

Finally, scholars have become increasingly aware that the Western Middle Ages also produced female theologians in the aftermath of early Christianity. As examples let us cite two women from the tenth and eleventh centuries who left a rich, complex body of instructive writing: Hrotsvitha of Gandersheim (d. 975; Berschin 2001; Cescutti 1998; Wilson 1988) and the "prophetess of Germany," Hildegard of Bingen (d. 1179; Aris;

Berndt) were both noblewomen raised and educated in convents from infancy. Hildegard would achieve fame not only as multifaceted religious writer but also as a preacher, given her label of prophetess.

Possibilities and Limits for "Matristic" Studies. The rediscovery of the female teachers of Late Antiquity and the Middle Ages has contributed to the discipline of women's studies in general and to the history of women's roles in theology. Significantly, we find them as authors of saints' lives, hymns, personal revelations, and theological treatises. One can say overall that their works contributed very little to speculative school theology, with rare exceptions such as the work of Hildegard. Only by recognizing this variety and intellectual and literary generic scope in women's theological teaching might we develop a true discipline of "Matristic studies" on a par with the venerable patristic studies (devoted to the Church Fathers such as Basil, Augustine, Jerome et al.). Despite the limited sources on such women now available, perhaps more will be uncovered after serious study, though certainly never in the quantity equivalent to patristic sources.

As to the definite contents and specific emphases of female teaching (see Børresen and Vogt 1993; Børresen 2002) we will know comparably little even in the future. Although valid generalizations are impossible to extract from such a limited samples, the quality of what samples we have, as examined previously, shows those women teachers as most deserving and encourages us to probe farther nonetheless. "There is no discipline of Matristics in existence so far and there will never be one inasmuch as matristics is understood only as parallel to Patristics. The discipline of Matristics can come into existence only when scholars open their eyes to women who left their peculiar stamp on the Church, thereby earning the title of Church Mothers" (Albrecht 1988, 326).

See also Desert Mothers; Dhuoda; Eudocia; Eustochium, St.; Hagiography (Female Saints); Hildegard of Bingen, St.; Hrotsvitha of Gandersheim; Law, Canon, Women in; Macrina the Elder, St.; Macrina the Younger, St.; Melania the Elder, St.; Melania the Younger, St.; Music, Women Composers and Musicians; Proba, Faltonia Betitia; Syrian-Christian Women; Thecla, St.; Theodosia

BIBLIOGRAPHY

Primary Sources

Modern Sourcebooks and Anthologies
Jensen, Anne, ed. *Frauen im frühen Christentum.* Traditio Christiana, 11. Bern and New York: Peter Lang, 2002.
Labriolle, Pierre de, ed. and trans. *Les Sources de l'histoire du montanisme.* Collectanea Friburgensia, n.s., 15/24. Fribourg, Switzerland: Librairie de l'Université: Paris: E. Leroux, 1913. [Greek, Latin, and Syriac texts with French trans., introduction, and commentary].
Wellesz, Egon. *A History of Byzantine Music and Hymnography.* 2nd ed. Oxford: Clarendon Press, 1961.
Wilson-Kastner, Patricia, et al., eds. and transs. *A Lost Tradition. Women Writers of the Early Church.* Washington, D.C.: University Press of America, 1981.

Early Collections and Authors
[Apophtegmata Patrum].*The Sayings of the Desert Fathers: The Alphabetical Series.* Translated and introduced by Benedicta Ward. Foreword by M. Anthony. Cistercian Studies, 59. New ed. London: Mowbray. 1981. Original New York and London: Macmillan, 1975, 1980.

[Apostolic Constitutions]. *Les Constitutions apostoliques*. Edited and translated (French) by Marcel Metzger. Sources Chrétiennes, vols. 329, 329, and 336. Paris: Éditions du Cerf, 1985–1987. [Bilingual Greek-French ed.].

Didascalia Apostolorum in Syriac. Edition and translation by Arthur Vööbus. Corpus Scriptorum Christianorum Orientalium, Scriptores Syri, 175, 176, 179, and 180. Louvain: CSCO, 1979.

Eudocia. *Homerocentones Eudociae Augustae*. Edited by Mark D. Usher. Bibliotheca scriptorum Graecorum et Romanorum Teubneriana. Stuttgart: Teubner, 1999.

Gregory of Nazianzus. "Concerning His Own Life." In *Three Poems. Gregory of Nazianzus*, translated by Denis Molaise Meehan, 77–130. The Fathers of the Church, 75. Washington, D.C.: Catholic University of America Press, 1987.

———. *Funeral Orations*. Translated by Leo McCauley, 3–156. Fathers of the Church, 22. Washington, D.C.: Catholic University of America Press, 1987.

Gregory of Nyssa. *De anima et resurrectione*. In *Patrologia Graeca*, edited by J.-P. Migne [= *PG*], 46: 12–160.

———. *On the Soul and the Resurrection*. In *Ascetical Works*, translated by Virginia W. Callahan, ch. 6. Washington, D.C.: Catholic University of America Press, 1967.

Hildegard of Bingen. *Opera omnia S. Hildegardis*. In *Patrologia Latina*, edited by J.-P. Migne, 179.

———. *Novae S. Hildegardis Opera*. Analecta Sacra, vol. 8. Edited by Jean-Baptiste Pitra. Monte Cassino, 1882.

———*The Letters of Hildegard of Bingen*. Translated by Joseph L. Baird and Radd K. Ehrman. New York: Oxford University Press, 1994.

Hrosvit of Gandersheim. *Opera omnia*. Edited by Walter Berschin. Bibliotheca scriptorum Graecorum et Romanorum Teubneriana. Munich and Leipzig: Saur, 2001.

Proba, Faltonia Betitia. *The Golden Bough, the Oaken Cross. The Virgilian Cento of Faltonia Betitia Proba*. Edited by Elizabeth A. Clark and Diane F. Hatch. American Academy of Religion. Texts and Translations, 5. Chico, Calif.: Scholars Press, 1981.

Testamentum Domini Nostri Jesu Christi. Edited and translated (Latin) by Ignatius E. Rahmani. Mainz: F. Kirchheim, 1899. [Bilingual Syriac-Latin ed.; Latin commentary].

Theodore of Studios. *Epistulae*. Edited by Georgios Fatouros. Corpus Fontium Historiae Byzantinae, 31: 1–2. Berlin: de Gruyter 1992.

Theodoret of Cyrrhus, [*Philotheos historia*]. *Histoire des moines de Syrie*. Critical ed. with notes and introduction by Pierre Canivet and Alice Leroy-Molinghen. Sources Chrétiennes, 234, 257. 2 vols. Paris: Éditions du Cerf . 1977–1979. [Bilingual Greek-French ed.].

———. *A History of the Monks of Syria*. Translated with introduction by Richard M. Price. Cistercian Studies, 88. Kalamazoo, Mich.: Cistercian Publications, 1985.

Vitae of Female Teachers

[Febronia]."The Life of St. Febronia." In *Holy Women of the Syrian Orient*, edited by Susan Ashbrook Harvey and Sebastian Brock, 150–76. 2nd ed. Berkeley: University of California Press, 1998.

[Macrinas, both]. *Vie de Sainte Macrine*. Edition and translated (French) by Pierre Maraval. Sources Chrétiennes, 178. Paris: Éditions du Cerf, 1971.

[Melanias, both]. *The Life of Melania the Younger*. Edited by Elizabeth A. Clark. Studies in Women and Religion, 14. New York: Edwin Mellen Press, 1984.

[Nino]. In "Die Bekehrung Georgiens. Mokcevay Kartlisay." German translation by Gertrud Pätsch. *Bedi Karlisa, revue de Kartvelologie* 33 (1975): 288–337.

———. "St. Nino and the Conversion of Georgia." In *Lives and Legends of the Georgian Saints*. English translation by David Marshall Lang, 13–39. London: Allen & Unwin; New York: Macmillan, 1956.

[Olympias]. "The Life of Olympias" and "Sergia's Narration Concerning St. Olympias." In *Jerome, Chrysostom, and Friends. Essays and Translations*, edited by Elizabeth A. Clark, 107–57. New York: Edwin Mellen Press, 1979.

———. *Vie anonyme d'Olympias*. Edited and translated (French) by Anne-Marie Malingrey. Sources Chrétiennes, 13bis. Paris: Éditions du Cerf, 1968.

[Syncletica]. *Vita S. Syncleticae.* [by Pseudo-Athanasius]. In *PG*, 28: 1485–1558.

———. *Vie de Sainte Synclétique.* Translated by Odile B. Bernard. Foreword by Lucien Regnault. Spiritualité Orientale, 9. Bégrolles-en-Mauge, France: Abbaye de Bellefontaine, 1972.

Secondary Sources

Albrecht, Ruth. *Das Leben der heiligen Makrina auf dem Hintergrund der Thekla-Traditionen.* Studien zu den Ursprüngen des weiblichen Mönchtums im 4. Jahrhundert in Kleinasien. Forschungen zur Kirchen- und Dogmengeschichte, 38. Göttingen, Germany: Vandenhoeck & Ruprecht, 1986.

———. "Erinnern, was vergessen ist. Frauen und der Begriff des Weiblichen in der Zeit der Kirchenväte." *Stimmen der Zeit* 206 (1988): 326–33.

Aris, Marc-Aeilko. *Hildegard von Bingen: internationale wissenschaftliche Bibliographie.* Quellen und Abhandlungen zur mittelrheinischen Kirchengeschichte, 84. Mainz, Germany: Gesellschaft für mittelrheinische Kirchengeschichte, 1998.

Berndt, Rainer. *"Im Angesicht Gottes suche der Mensch sich selbst": Hildegard von Bingen (1098–1179).* Erudiri sapientia, 2. Berlin: Akad.-Verlag, 2001.

Børresen, Kari E. "From Patristics to Matristics." In *Selected Articles on Christian Gender Models,* edited by Øyvind Norderval and Katrine Ore. Rome: Herder, 2002.

———, and Kari Vogt, eds. *Women's Studies of the Christian and Islamic Traditions. Ancient, Medieval and Renaissance Foremothers.* Dordrecht, Netherlands: Kluwer, 1993.

Cescutti, Eva. *Hrotsvit und die Männer. Konstruktionen von "Männlichkeit" und "Weiblichkeit" in der lateinischen Literatur im Umfeld der Ottonen. Eine Fallstudie.* Forschungen zur Geschichte der älteren deutschen Literatur, 23. Munich: Fink, 1998.

Clark, Elizabeth A. *Ascetic Piety and Women's Faith. Essays on Late Ancient Christianity.* Studies in Women and Religion, 20. Lewiston, N.Y.: Edwin Mellen Press, 1986.

Dinzelbacher, Peter, ed. *Religiöse Frauenbewegung und mystische Frömmigkeit im Mittelalter.* Cologne: Böhlau: 1988.

Dronke, Peter. *Women Writers of the Middle Ages. A Critical Study of Texts from Perpetua († 203) to Marguerite Porete († 1310).* Cambridge: Cambridge University Press, 1984.

Eisen, Ute E. *Amtsträgerinnen im frühen Christentum. Epigraphische und literarische Studien.* Forschungen zur Kirchen- und Dogmengeschichte, 61. Göttingen: Vandenhoeck & Ruprecht, 1996.

Feichtinger, Barbara. *Apostolae apostolorum. Frauenaskese als Befreiung und Zwang bei Hieronymus.* Studien zur klassischen Philologie, 94. Frankfurt/Main: Peter Lang, 1995.

Frank, Karl Suso. "Asketinnen in den Apophthegmata Patrum." *Erbe und Auftrag* 77 (2001–2003): 211–25.

Gössmann, Elisabeth. *Hildegard von Bingen: Versuche einer Annäherung.* Archiv für philosophie- und theologiegeschichtliche Frauenforschung. Beiheft. Munich: Iudicium, 1995.

Hofmann, Johannes. "Christliche Frauen im Dienst kleinasiatischer Gemeinden des ersten und zweiten Jahrhunderts." In *Vigiliae Christianae* 54 (2000): 283–308.

Jensen, Anne. *Gottes selbstbewußte Töchter. Frauenemanzipation im frühen Christentum?* Theologische Frauenforschung in Europa, vol. 9. 2nd ed. Münster: LIT, 2003.

———. "Prophetin, Poetin und Kirchenmutter. Das theologische Werk Faltonia Betitia Probas (Rom, 4. Jh.)." In *Frauen gestalten Geschichte. Im Spannungsfeld zwischen Religion und Geschlecht,* edited by Barbara Schoppelreich, 33–53. Hannover, Germany: Lutherisches Verlagshaus, 1998.

———. "Women in the Christianization of the West." In *The Origins of Christendom in the West,* edited by Alan Kreider, 205–26. Edinburgh and New York: T. & T. Clark, 2001.

Krumeich, Christa. *Hieronymus und die christlichen feminae clarissimae.* Habelts Dissertationsdrucke: "Alte Geschichte," 36. Bonn: Habelt, 1993.

Letsch-Brunner, Silvia. *Marcella—discipula et magistra. Auf den Spuren einer römischen Christin des 4. Jahrhunderts.* Beihefte zur Zeitschrift für die neutestamentliche Wissenschaft und die Kunde der älteren Kirche, 91. Berlin and New York: de Gruyter, 1998.

Margoni-Kögler, Michael. "Women Promoting Literary Inculturation: A Case Study of the Aristocratic Roman Matron Faltonia Betitia Proba and Her Biblical Epic." In *Gender and Religion—Genre et religion*, edited by Kari E. Børresen, Sara Cabibbo, and Edith Specht Quaderni, 2: 113–41. Rome: Carocci, 2001.

Neymeyr, Ulrich. *Die christlichen Lehrer im zweiten Jahrhundert. Ihre Lehrtätigkeit, ihr Selbstverständnis und ihre Geschichte.* Supplements to *Vigiliae Christianae*, 4. Leiden: Brill, 1989.

Petersen-Szemerédy, Griet. *Zwischen Weltstadt und Wüste: Römische Asketinnen in der Spätantike. Eine Studie zu Motivation und Gestaltung der Askese christlicher Frauen Roms auf dem Hintergrund ihrer Zeit.* Forschungen zur Kirchen- und Dogmengeschichte, 54. Göttingen, Germany: Vandenhoeck & Ruprecht, 1993.

Rebenich, Stefan. *Hieronymus und sein Kreis. Prosopographische und sozialgeschichtliche Untersuchungen.* Historia Einzelschriften, 72. Stuttgart: Steiner, 1992.

Schmidt, Margot, ed. *"Tiefe des Gotteswissens—Schönheit der Sprachgestalt" bei Hildegard von Bingen.* Mystik in Geschichte und Gegenwart, 10. Stuttgart and Bad Cannstatt, Germany: Frommann-Holzboog, 1995.

Synek, Eva M. *Heilige Frauen der frühen Christenheit. Zu den Frauenbildern in hagiographischen Texten des christlichen Ostens.* Das Östliche Christentum, n.s. 43. Würzburg: Augustinus-Verlag, 1994a.

———. "In der Kirche möge sie schweigen." *Oriens Christianus* 77 (1993a): 151–64.

———. "Kultur und Heiligkeit. Zum spirituellen Erbe des syrischen Mönchtums." *Geist und Leben* 66 (1993b): 359–81.

———. *OIKOS. Zum Ehe- und Familienrecht der Apostolischen Konstitutionen.* Kirche und Recht, 22. Vienna: Plöchl, 1999.

———. "Ostkirchenkunde und Frauenforschung: Zu den Müttern unter den Vätern." *Ostkirchliche Studien* 43 (1994b): 170–86.

———. "The Life of St Nino: Georgia's Conversion to its Female Apostle." In *Christianizing Peoples and Converting Individuals.* Edited by Guyda Armstrong and Ian Wood, 3–13. International Medieval Research, 7. Turnhout, Belgium: Brepols, 2000.

Topping, Eva C. *Holy Mothers of Orthodoxy. Women and the Church.* Minneapolis: Light and Life Publishing Company, 1987.

Trevett, Christine. *Montanism: Gender, Authority and the New Prophecy.* Cambridge: Cambridge University Press, 1999.

Usher, Mark D. *Homeric Stitchings: The Homeric Centos of the Empress Eudocia.* Lanham, Md.: Rowman & Littlefield, 1998.

Wilson, Katharina M. *Hrotsvit of Gandersheim. The Ethics of Authorial Stance.* Davis Medieval Texts and Studies, 7. Leiden: Brill, 1988.

Zimmermann, Alfred F. *Die urchristlichen Lehrer.* Wissenschaftliche Untersuchungen zum Neuen Testament. 2nd series, 12. Tübingen: Mohr, 1991.

EVA MARIA SYNEK

TERESA DE CARTAGENA (b. c.1425). An author of spiritual treatises in Spanish, Teresa de Cartagena was born around 1425 into a socially and intellectually distinguished family of converts from Judaism. She entered the Franciscan convent in Burgos, but in April of 1449 she transferred to the Cistercian Order. Afterward, Teresa began to go deaf, and writing became a means of both self-consolation and communication for her. Although Teresa's principal work, the *Arboleda de los enfermos* (*The Grove of the Ailing*) has traditionally been ascribed to the period between 1453 and 1460 (Cantera Burgos, 546), Seidenspinner-Núñez and Kim argue that it was more likely composed in the 1470s. Sometime after the *Arboleda* began to circulate, Teresa was criticized for writing a spiritual treatise, an activity deemed appropriate only for men. In response, she penned a spirited defense of her right to literary expression, the *Admiraçión operum Dey* (*Admiration of the Works of God*).

The *Arboleda de los enfermos* is intended to demonstrate the spiritual benefits of bodily infirmities. The motif of illness, which is used as a metaphor by other writers, is both literal and figurative for Teresa, since she uses her own deafness as an example for her audience. The *Arboleda* thus invokes the authority of both Teresa's own experience and written sources, largely biblical and patristic. At one point, Teresa recalls hearing a sermon in which the preacher invoked the authority of Peter Lombard, the Master of the Sentences. She, however, will invoke Job, whom she dubs the "Master of the Patiences." In so doing, Teresa rejects the standard patriarchal form of authority based on the writings of learned men to invoke the authority of experience, personified in the sufferings of Job.

The main idea of the *Arboleda* is that the suffering borne of sickness is in reality beneficial because, through the cultivation of the virtue of patience, bodily illness can lead to spiritual health and thereby to salvation. Thus, Teresa considers her deafness a blessing, because it has prevented her from hearing worldly noises that were drowning out the healthy doctrines of the Lord. The treatise proper is fundamentally a commentary on Psalm 45: 10 ("Hearken, O daughter, and see, and incline thy ear; and forget thy people and thy father's house") and Psalm 32:9 ("Do not become like the horse and the mule, who have no understanding. With bit and bridle bind fast their jaws, that they may not come near unto thee"). Teresa must listen with the ear of her soul and abandon both her father's house (sinfulness) and her people (earthly desires). Further, the "bit" (reason) and the "bridle" (temperance) must constrain the "jaws" (vain desires). More specifically, it is Teresa's illness that has served as both bit and bridle by preventing her from eating foods harmful to her spiritual health.

Appropriating the biblical parable of the great supper (Luke 14: 16–24), Teresa observes that while God has invited everyone to his heavenly banquet, the sick and suffering are in a sense forcibly dragged to the feast by their afflictions. She personalizes her source, associating her deafness with the crippled, the blind, and the lame mentioned in the Bible. Teresa goes on to compare her affliction to God's cloistering her hearing, for those who are ill can be said to have professed in the convent of the suffering.

The negative reception accorded the *Arboleda* motivated the writing of an apology, the *Admiraçión operum Dey*. Her treatise, Teresa observes, caused great wonderment not because of its contents but because it was written by a woman. She postulates that men were amazed by a woman's writing such a text precisely because men—not women— normally performed such erudite activities. Nonetheless, she argues, God is omnipotent and can just as well grant wisdom to a woman as to a man. Men's intellectual abilities, she reminds her readers, are not inherent in their male status but are, rather, a divine gift.

Teresa then observes that God inspires notable works in both men and women, and his marvelous deeds include inspiring a woman to compose a learned treatise. She admits that such an activity is not normal for women; it is as uncommon as for a woman to take up a sword to defend her country. Nonetheless, the biblical Judith, empowered by divine grace, wielded a sword. If God could inspire Judith to take up the sword, would it not be even easier for him to inspire a woman to take up the pen? Teresa thus defends her act of writing, making explicit the comparison between herself and Judith, for both were divinely empowered to wield typically masculine—dare one say phallic?—instruments.

Although her treatise occasioned astonishment, Teresa cautions that there are two kinds of amazement, one good, the other bad. "Good" amazement is that which is properly directed at the source of all grace, God himself. "Bad" admiration occurs when we express wonderment at the human recipient of divine grace instead of at its source. Teresa thus attempts to control the reception of her defense through a sort of blackmail: readers who do not wish to be guilty of "bad" admiration should not focus on the nun herself (should not criticize her?) and should concentrate instead on God's manifestation through her. Moreover, she feels compelled to respond to one specific criticism that was leveled against her by denying that her treatise was copied from other books. As Deyermond points out, Teresa's detractors were guilty of applying a double standard, for such intertextuality was the rule in medieval literature (25).

Teresa then compares her intellect, which God inspired to write the *Arboleda*, to the blind man whom Christ met on the road to Jericho (Luke 18: 35–43). Suddenly, she injects herself into the biblical narrative, shifting to the first person and imagining herself calling out to Christ from the side of the road. Teresa explains that just as he healed the blind man, Christ, the true physician, cured her and permitted her to see the light. Therefore, let those who doubt that she wrote the *Arboleda* abandon their disbelief and instead marvel at the power of the Lord.

Teresa's feminism is at best reticent, for she is more inclined to emphasize the exceptional nature of her empowerment to carry out a "male" task than to imply that all women should be so empowered. Nonetheless, she must be given due credit for having the courage to defend her right to write in the face of patriarchal hostility to female authorship.

See also Christine de Pizan; Constance of Castile; Jewish Women in the Middle Ages; María de Ajofrín

BIBLIOGRAPHY

Primary Sources

Cartagena, Teresa de. *Arboleda de los enfermos. Admiraçión operum Dey*. Edited by Lewis Joseph Hutton. *Boletín de la Real Academia Española* 16 (1967).

———. *The Writings of Teresa de Cartagena*. Translated by Dayle Seidenspinner-Núñez. Cambridge: D. S. Brewer, 1998.

Secondary Sources

Cantera Burgos, Francisco. *Alvar García de Santa María y su familia de conversos. Historia de la judería de Burgos y de sus conversos más egregios*. Madrid: Instituto Arias Montano, 1952.

Deyermond, Alan. "'El convento de dolençias': The Works of Teresa de Cartagena." *Journal of Hispanic Philology* 1 (1976): 19–29.

Ellis, Deborah S. "Unifying Imagery in the Works of Teresa de Cartagena: Home and the Dispossessed." *Journal of Hispanic Philology* 17 (1992): 43–53.

Rivera Garretas, María-Milagros. "La *Admiración de las obras de Dios* de Teresa de Cartagena y la Querella de las mujeres." In *La voz del silencio, I: Fuentes directas para la historia de las mujeres (siglos VIII–XVIII)*, edited by Cristina Segura Graiño, 277–99. Madrid: Asociación Cultural Al-Mudayna, 1992.

Seidenspinner-Núñez, Dayle. "'El solo me leyó': Gendered Hermeneutics and Subversive Poetics in *Admiración operum Dey* of Teresa de Cartagena." *Medievalia* 15 (December 1993): 14–23.

———, and Yonso Kim. "Historicizing Teresa: Reflections on New Documents Regarding Sor Teresa de Cartagena." *La Corónica* 32:2 (Spring 2004): 121–50.

Surtz, Ronald E. "Image Patterns in Teresa de Cartagena's *Arboleda de los enfermos*." In *La Chispa '87. Selected Proceedings*, edited by Gilbert Paolini, 297–304. New Orleans, La.: Tulane University, 1987.

———. *Writing Women in Late Medieval and Early Modern Spain: The Mothers of Saint Teresa of Avila*. Philadelphia: University of Pennsylvania Press, 1995.

RONALD E. SURTZ

TEXTILES. *See* **Dress, Courtly Women's; Dress, Religious Women's (Western, Christian); Embroidery; Spinners and Drapers**

THECLA, ST. (2nd century). The best known of several early saints named Thecla, this Christian virgin was the reputed pupil of the Apostle Paul, and joins him as protagonists of the *Acta Pauli et Theclae* (*Acts of Sts. Paul and Thecla*), the sole source for her biography. Distinct from the New Testament Book of Acts, of which they were once a part, the *Acta Pauli et Theclae*, composed c.180, belong to what is known as the Apocryphal New Testament—books now excluded from the standard, or canonical, New Testament for doctrinal reasons as determined by the Church.

The *Acta* tell of how Thecla, a virgin of Iconium, an ancient city of Asia Minor (now Konya, Turkey), was converted to Christianity and inspired to dedicate herself to perpetual virginity by the Apostle Paul, who thereby thwarted the marriage plans of her betrothed, Thamyris. Both future saints were condemned for this infraction: Paul was beaten but Thecla, condemned to the stake, was miraculously saved from death. She then followed Paul to Antioch in Pisidia (now southern Turkey), where she was thrown to the wild beasts and again a miracle saved her from death. After this she went to join Paul at that region's seaport city of Myra (Acts 27: 5). He allowed her to serve as a "female Apostle" in proclaiming the Gospel. She eventually went to Seleucia (seaport of Antioch), where she spent the rest of her days, as reported in the *Acta*, and near where she was buried, at Meriamlik. A sizable church was erected over her tomb, which became a major shrine visited by travelers such as Egeria (fl. 381–385), as reported in the latter's *Peregrinatio ad loca sancta* (*Pilgrimage to the Holy Land*, ch. 4). Thecla became revered as the paragon of early Christian womanhood.

Modern scholars including W. M. Ramsay believe that Thecla may have actually existed historically, just as Paul had been a real person, since the details of her story, despite its genre as saint's legend, seem perfectly in keeping with Paul's work of converting virgins in Thecla's homeland. Within Church community, especially the Eastern Church, in cities like Iconium, Seleucia, and Nicomedia, the widely circulated *Acta* led to a great veneration of Thecla, whom the Eastern Church extolled as "Apostle and protomartyr among women." Her cult appeared very early also in Western Europe, particularly in those districts where the Gallican Liturgy prevailed; there is direct proof of this in the fourth century. References to her, which we can assume to be all the same Thecla—pupil of St. Paul—are attached to various locales in the saintly topography of Asia Minor (Ancient Turkey), listed over several days in that famous collection of martyrdom accounts, once (falsely) ascribed to St. Jerome (d. 420), the *Martyrologium Hieronymianum* (*Hieronymian* [*Jerome's*] *Martyrology*). Bede's martyrology (c.730) lists her for September

23, the same day as her feast day, as given in the present Roman Martyrology. The Western Church celebrated her feast day on September 23, until its suppression in 1969. The Greek Church celebrates her feast on September 24.

See also Desert Mothers; Egeria; Hagiography (Female Saints)

BIBLIOGRAPHY

Primary Sources
"Acta Pauli et Theclae." In *Acta apostolorum apocrypha*, edited by Richard A. Lipsius and Maximilian Bonnet, 1: 235–72. Hildesheim, Germany and New York: G. Olms, 1990. Original Leipzig: Mendelsohn, 1891. [Greek and Latin texts only].
"Acts of Paul and Thecla." In *The Apocryphal New Testament*, translated by Montague Rhodes James and revised and edited by James K. Elliott, 364–80. Oxford: Clarendon Press, 1993.
"Acts of Paul and Thecla." In *Anthology of Ancient Greek Popular Literature*, edited by William F. Hansen, ch. 2. Bloomington: Indiana University Press, 1998. [English translations with commentary].
Bede. *See below, next section, under* Quentin.
Martyrologium Hieronymianum. Edited by Giovanni Battista de Rossi and Louis Duchesne, 24, 36, 120, 124, 144. *Acta Sanctorum*, November. Brussels: Polleu & Ceuterick, 1894. [See 22 February, 25 February, 12 September, 23 September, and 17 November].

Secondary Sources
Bremmer, Jan N., ed. *The Apocryphal Acts of Paul and Thecla.* Studies on the Apocryphal Acts of the Apostles, 2. Kampen, Germany: Kok Pharos, 1996. [Important collection of essays].
Davis, Stephen J. *The Cult of St. Thecla: A Tradition of Women's Piety in Late Antiquity.* Oxford Early Christian Studies. Oxford and New York: Oxford University Press, 2001.
McGinn, Sheila. "The Acts of Thecla." In *Searching the Scriptures, 2: A Feminist Commentary*, edited by Elizabeth S. Fiorenza et al., ch. 10. New York: Crossroad, 1994.
McInerney, Maud B. *Eloquent Virgins from Thecla to Joan of Arc.* The New Middle Ages. New York: Palgrave Macmillan, 2003.
Nauerth, Claudia. *Thecla: ihre Bilder in der frühchristlichen Kunst.* Göttinger Orientforschungen, 2: 3. Wiesbaden, Germany: O. Harrassowitz, 1981.
Quentin, Henri. *Les Martyrologes historiques au moyen âge: étude sur la formation du Martyrologe Romain.* Paris: Victor Lecoffre, 1908.
Van den Hoek, Annewiese, and John J. Herrmann Jr. "Thecla the Beast Fighter: A Female Emblem of Deliverance in Early Christian Popular Art." In *In the Spirit of Faith: Studies on Philo and Early Christianity in Honor of David Hay*, edited by David T. Runia and Gregory E. Sterling. Brown Judaic Studies, 332. Providence, R.I.: Brown Judaic Studies, 2001.

DAVID LARMOUR

THEKLA. *See* **Teachers, Women as**

THEODORA (c.500–548). The Byzantine empress Theodora—the first and most illustrious by this name—rose from unlikely origins to marry the emperor Justinian, with whom she co-ruled Byzantium (527–548), the Eastern half of the Roman Empire. Her co-reign markedly influenced Byzantine culture in matters of women's issues in civil law, religion, the prerogatives of imperial power, and the rebuilding of Constantinople as Byzantium's capital.

Because the sources on her life often contradict each other, and because the most substantial and well-known authority—Procopius of Caesarea (c.500–562), in his *Anekdota*

Empress Theodora and her court. Mosaic in Ravenna. Courtesy of North Wind Picture Archives.

or *Historia Arcana* (*Secret History*), a racy counterpart to his more official histories the *History of the Wars* and *De ædificius* (*On Buildings*)—misses no opportunity to depict her unfavorably, modern historians have cautiously reconstructed what was an extraordinary career nonetheless. Theodora was supposedly one of three daughters born to Akakios, a bear-keeper and trainer in Constantinople who belonged to the Green faction (a sports team with political affiliation, since both athletes and politicians displayed themselves in the hippodrome). When Akakios died close to the time of her birth, the family was left impoverished; Theodora's mother remarried in hopes her new husband could obtain her late husband's post, but without success. The daughters thus went to work in the hippodrome to support the family, joining another athletic-political faction, the Blues, to which Theodora would remain a fanatical adherent. Theodora, once of age, followed her elder sister Komito in becoming an actress (a wide-ranging term in those days) and courtesan. Beautiful, intelligent, and resourceful, Theodora became known for her on-stage sexual performances (including one involving geese) as well as those in private, privileged bedrooms, sometimes playing the role of male prostitute as well. For a time she was the concubine of Hekebolos, governor of Libya, only to be sent away on her own, which necessitated her working as a prostitute in Alexandria and other Near-Eastern cities as she made her way back to Constantinople. During this phase she allegedly performed numerous abortions on herself, allowing only one son, John, to survive at the behest of his father, who took him in. It was also during this time that she began a longstanding friendship with a woman in similar circumstances, Antonina, future wife of Belisarius, Justinian's general, whose military exploits would be chronicled by his legal secretary and advisor, Procopius.

She met and captivated the future emperor Justinian (c.482–565) after her return to Constantinople (c.522). They were married most likely in c.523–524 (Garland). They began co-ruling as emperor and empress as of August 527. Theodora was no mere consort to her husband; Justinian definitely listened to her advice. During the crucial early phase of their reign, the couple—thanks to Theodora's courage in confronting the murderously angry rioters—quelled the Nika riots (January 532) that destroyed Constantinople, imperiled their throne, and with it, Byzantine stability. The couple then rebuilt the city as truly splendid capital, whose centerpiece was the magnificently designed, lavishly ornate church of Hagia Sophia (St. Sophia/Holy Wisdom). Justinian also tried to reconstruct the boundaries of the old Roman Empire by (temporarily) recovering the possessions around the Mediterranean, including Rome itself, from the barbarians.

Among their many other accomplishments, they contributed generously to charitable institutions and established a home for reformed prostitutes. Justinian enacted legislation permitting lower-class women such as actresses and tavern-keepers to marry men of senatorial rank: actions some historians ascribe to imperial self-interest more than to modern-style concern for women's rights. Yet for whatever motive, Justinian did promote unprecedented equal rights for women in matters of marriage and divorce. Since Justinian, in his most lasting achievement, formulated the first synthesis of Roman law as the *Corpus Juris civilis* (Body of Civil Law), the basis for modern civil law, such changes were momentous.

The religious tolerance of Justinian and Theodora was also significant in this formative period of Eastern and Western Christianity. While Theodora was a Monophysite (a heretical group emphasizing Jesus's single, divine nature) and protected Monophysite monks and bishops, Justinian espoused orthodox Catholicism (holding that Christ was of two natures: divine and human), but under the influence of John of Ephesus (c.507–586), tolerated Monophytism. Contemporary commentators opined that the couple's dual position in what was then a serious controversy was politically motivated as a type of compromise to extend their influence and keep the peace. However, as Lynda Garland documents, the intelligent Theodora's Monophysite beliefs were rooted in earnest, if sometimes flawed, theological inquiry in consultation with the leading religious figures, hence her faith's enduring effect as the Monophysite church flourished in the East despite her husband's vacillating policies. She also intervened in Western papal politics through her husband.

Procopius has much to say concerning Theodora's ruthlessness and greed for power in exercising her imperial authority, including blaming her and Justinian for successfully plotting the murder of the Ostrogothic Queen Amalasuntha in Italy (535). On this last, recent scholars seem to agree, after examining, in context, the rather covert comments in letters to Theodora from some principal Ostrogoths, as contained in the *Variae* of the Roman senator and monastic founder Cassiodorus (d. c.580; Garland; Evans).

Theodora died, probably of cancer, on June 28, 548, and was buried with full imperial pomp and dignity in the Church of the Holy Apostles, founded by Constantine the Great (d. 337), the original founder of Constantinople. Justinian, though outliving her by many years, never remarried and never recaptured the personal and political vitality he enjoyed with Theodora.

See also Amalasuntha; Eudocia; Syrian-Christian Women; Zoe Karbounopsina

BIBLIOGRAPHY

Primary Sources

Cassiodorus Senator. *Variae*, edited by Theodor Mommsen, 10: 20–21, 10: 23–24. *Monumenta Germaniae Historica. Auctores Antiquissimorum*, 12. Berlin: Weidmann, 1894. [Original Latin text with commentary].

―――. *The Variae of Magnus Aurelius Cassiodorus*. Translated by S. J. B. Barnish, 137–38. Translated Texts for Historians, 12. Liverpool: Liverpool University Press, 1992. [Translated selections with useful commentary].

John of Ephesus. *Lives of the Eastern Saints*. Edited and translated by Ernest W. Brooks. *Patrologia Orientalis*, 17–19. 3 vols. Paris: Firmin Didot, 1923–1925. [Original Syriac with English trans.].

Malalas, John. *Chronographia*. Edited by Johann Thurn. Corpus fontium historiae Byzaninae. Series Berolinensis, 35. Berlin: de Gruyter, 2000. [Original Greek text, preface in German].

―――. *The Chronicle of John Malalas*. Translated by Elizabeth Jeffreys et al. Byzantina Australiensia, 4. Melbourne: Australian Association for Byzantine Studies; Sydney, N.S.W.: Department of Modern Greek, University of Sydney, 1986. [English text only, with notes].

Procopius. *Historia arcana*. In *Opera omnia*, edited by Gerhard Wirth, vol. 3. Bibliotheca scriptorum Graecorum et Romanorum Teubneriana. Munich: Saur, 2001. [Original Greek text, Latin commentary; replaces the 1913 Haury ed. as the authoritative text].

―――. *The Secret History*. Translated by Geoffrey A. Williamson. Introduced by Philip Ziegler. London: Folio Society, 1990. Earlier eds. Harmondsworth, U.K. and Baltimore: Penguin, 1966, 1981.

Secondary Sources

Beck, Hans-Georg. *Kaiserin Theodora und Prokop: der Historiker un sein Opfer*. Munich: Piper, 1986.

Browning, Robert. *Justinian and Theodora*. Revised ed. New York: Thames & Hudson, 1987.

Cameron, Averil. *Procopius and the Sixth Century*. Berkeley: University of California Press, 1985.

Cesaretti, Paolo. *Teodora: ascesa di un'imperatrice*. Le Scie. 2nd ed. Milan: Mondadori, 2002.

Diehl, Charles. *Byzantine Empresses*. Translated by Harold Bell and Theresa de Kerpely. Long Island City, N.Y.: Studion. Original New York: Knopf, 1963. [English ed. combines Diehl's two books on this topic in French].

―――. *Theodora, Empress of Byzantium*. Translated by Samuel R. Rosenbaum. New York: Ungar, 1972. Original *Théodora, impératrice de Byzance*. Paris: Piazza, 1904. [A classic].

Evans, James Allan. *Theodora, Partner of Justinian*. Austin: University of Texas Press, 2002.

Garland, Lynda. *Byzantine Empresses: Women and Power in Byzantium, AD 527–1204*. London and New York: Routledge, 1999.

NADIA MARGOLIS

THEODOSIA (9th century). A poet living in the Byzantine Empire, Theodosia wrote a hymn on St. Ioannikios in Greek. The hymn is about 230 lines in length. In praising Ioannikios, Theodosia employs the commonplaces of Christian hymnography, but her deft use of imagery is a distinguishing feature. Similar images are grouped together, and those drawn from light and athletics are particularly effective.

BIBLIOGRAPHY

Primary Source

Theodosia. [Hymn]. In *Analecta Hymnica Graeca*, edited by Ioseph Schirò et al., 3: 122–33. Rome: Università di Roma, 1972.

Secondary Sources
Emereau, Casimir. "Hymnographie Byzantine." *Échos d'Orient* 25 (1926): 178–79.
Pitra, Jean-Baptiste. *Hymnographie de l'Église grecque*, 55. Rome: Imprimerie de la Civiltà cattolica, 1867.
Szövérffy, Joseph. *A Guide to Byzantine Hymnography*, 2: 48. Brookline, Mass.: Classical Folia, 1979.

DAVID LARMOUR

THEOSEBEIA (5th–6th centuries). Also known as Theosebia Chemica or Theosobia, the Greek poetess Theosebeia wrote a poem in four hexameters lamenting the death of a famous doctor by the name of Ablabius. The poem is a "sepulchral epigram"—a poem, usually in elegiac couplets, recounting the exchange between a tomb and living passer-by—that initially belonged to Agathias's collection of epigrams (sixth century) and later (tenth century), was incorporated into the so-called Palatine or Greek Anthology (as no. 7: 559). Both the illustrious court physician Galen (second century) and Ablabius, are named in the poem, thus indicating that it was composed during the later Greek Empire. Theosebeia may have been the sister of Zosimus, the alchemist from Panoplis, to whom he dedicated his twenty-eight-volume treatise on alchemy.

Theosebeia's poem was strongly influenced by earlier epigrammatists, in particular by Asclepiades (third century B.C.E.) and Antipater of Sidon (fl. c.120 B.C.E.), whose poems are also included in the Greek anthology. The deified Virtue depicted shearing her hair over the tomb of Ajax (*Anthologia Graeca*, 7: 145–46), as she appears in the two earlier epigrammatists, is transformed by Theosebeia into the deified Healing Art shearing her hair on the tomb of Ablabius. On the whole, the poem does not exhibit the typical characteristics seen in the other sepulchral epigrams of the anthology, for example, information about the deceased, his activities, the place of the burial, or some benediction to the passer-by. No words of emotion are seen in these few lines—on the contrary, their dispassionate, austere tone and dry, unadorned style prevail throughout the poem.

BIBLIOGRAPHY

Primary Sources
Theosebeia. [Epigram]. *Epigrammatum Anthologia Palatina*, edited by Friedrich Dübner, 1: 7.559. Paris: Firmin Didot, 1864.
———. [Epigram, Latin trans.]. *Anthologia Graeca Epigrammatum, Palatina cum Planudea*, edited by Hugo Stadtmüller, vol. 2. Bibliotheca scriptorum Graecorum et Romanorum Teubneriana. Leipzig: Teubner, 1894.
———. [Epigram]. *The Greek Anthology*, 2: 301. Edited and translated by W. R. Paton. Loeb Classical Library. 5 vols. London: W. Heinemann; New York: G. W. Putnam, 1925–1927.

Secondary Sources
Jones, A. H. M., J. R. Martindale, and J. Morris. *The Prosopography of the Later Roman Empire*, 1: 908, 994; 2: 1110. Cambridge: Cambridge University Press, 1971.
Paulys Real-Encyclopädie der Klassischen Altertumswissenschaft, 5: 2246. Stuttgart: Metzler, 1934.

ARISTOULA GEORGIADOU

THEUTHILD (d. c.865). Theuthild is not to be confused with Theudechild, abbess of Jouarre (d. c.660). Aside from some Latin epistles to key figures of her time, little is known of this abbess—known alternatively as Teuthildis, Thiathildis, Teathildis—of the royal foundation of Remiremont in the Vosges mountains of what is now eastern France, by the Moselle and Moselotte rivers. Of good birth (related to a seneschal—a royal bailiff—named Adalhard), Theuthild was appointed abbess in or shortly after 820, and the Remiremont *Liber memorialis* (*Book of Memorials*) records her death on October 26, most likely between 862 and 865. Her six brief Latin epistles are contained in a manuscript at Zurich, Staatsarchiv 141. The first two are addressed to Holy Roman Emperor Louis the Pious (r. 814–840), the third to his second wife, Judith of Bavaria (married 819), the fourth to her kinsman Adalhard, the fifth to a nobleman (name illegible), and the final one to an unnamed abbess and her community of sisters. The correspondence shows an active and concerned leader of her convent, whose admirable command of the more ornate Latin of her day earned her writings a place in the formula books used for the instruction of letter writing.

See also Epistolary Authors, Women as; Scribes and Scriptoria

BIBLIOGRAPHY

Primary Source
Parisse, Michel, et al., eds. *La Correspondance d'un évêque carolingien Frothaire de Toul (ca. 813–847) avec les lettres de Theuthilde, abbesse de Remiremont*, 151–63. Paris: Presses de la Sorbonne, 1998.

Secondary Sources
[See notes to above].

PETER K. MARSHALL

TIBORS (c.12th century). Only a fragment of the opening stanza remains from a song composed by this woman troubadour (*trobairitz*), but it may be the oldest extant work in the women troubadours' corpus (body of writing). Historical research suggests that Tibors was the sister of the troubadour Raimbaut d'Aurenga (Raimbaut of Orange [southern France]), which would place her in the second half of the twelfth century. Manuscript H introduces it with a miniature and a *vida* (biography) that identifies Tibors as a lady of Provence, "courteous and well taught, gracious and very learned; and she knew how to compose songs." Her reputation for loving and being loved, honored by all good men and obeyed by all valiant ladies, accords with the fact that she is named as arbiter in a debate poem by Bertran de Saint-Félix and Uc de la Bacalaria and may be the *Na Tibortz de Proensa* (Lady Tibors from Provence) named in a dance poem by Guiraut d'Espanha. The incantatory quality of the extant fragment, which anaphorically (deliberately beginning each verse with the same word or phrase) lines up a series of negations that affirm her desire and love for her beloved *amic*, recalls the persona and tradition of women's songs.

See also Chanson de Femme (Women's Song); *Trobairitz*

BIBLIOGRAPHY

Primary Sources
Boutière, Jean, and Alexander H. Schutz, eds. *Biographies des Troubadours: Textes provençaux des XIIIe et XIVe siècles*. Revised ed. with I. M. Cluzel. Les Classiques d'Oc, 1. Paris: Nizet, 1964.
Tibors. [Fragment]. In *Songs of the Women Troubadours*, edited and translated by Matilda Tomaryn Bruckner, Laurie Shepard, and Sarah White, 138–39, 191–92. New York: Garland, 1995. Revised ed. 2000.

————. In *Trobairitz: Der Beitrag der Frau in der altokzitanischen höfischen Lyrik. Edition des Gesamtkorpus*, edited by Angelica Rieger, 624–44. Beihefte der Zeitschrift für romanische Philologie, 233. Tübingen, Germany: Max Niemeyer, 1991.

Secondary Sources
Pattison, Walter T. *The Life and Works of the Troubadour Raimbaut d'Orange*. Minneapolis: University of Minnesota Press, 1952.
Poe, Elizabeth W. *Compilatio, Lyric Texts and Prose Commentaries in Troubadour Manuscript H (Vat. Lat. 3207)*. The Edward C. Armstrong Monographs on Medieval Literature, 11. Lexington, Ky.: French Forum, 2000.

MATILDA TOMARYN BRUCKNER

TOURNOIEMENT DES DAMES (late 12th–early 14th centuries). The *Tournoiement des Dames* (*Tournament of Ladies*) belongs to a mini-genre depicting female militancy at the zenith of its literal representation in France. Here, the women actually *are* the weapon-wielding, jousting knights, not spectators, as in other genres, equipped only with the power of their erotic gaze and encouraging words to their male lovers prior to and during combat, as in the Arthurian Romances (twelfth to fifteenth centuries). Here, too, a woman does not need a champion such as Martin Le Franc (1440–1442); she is her own champion. Nor is it a chivalric battle between the sexes, but rather a male-style battle among women according to a male narrator assuming the traditionally female role of spectator, and for whom the vision of armor-clad female warriors may be both titillating and disturbing. This work comes more than a century earlier than Christine de Pizan's *Cité des dames* (*City of Ladies*, 1404–1405), in which the women assume the masculine role of builders. While Christine writes in the analogously male genre of historiography in furnishing the women's lives as building material, the feminism exhibited in the *Tournoiement des dames* is thus less deliberate and systematic. Its significance hovers among the spheres of idle male fantasy ("What if?"), social estates satire (the world turned upside down; whereby women, the habitual Fourth Estate, are now on top), and the background of historical controversy (the right of women to join the Crusades), thereby merging the love-as-war thematics of the Roman poet Ovid (first century B.C.E.) with prevailing chivalric concerns. Helen Solterer notes that although women's participation in the Crusades as soldiers had been outlawed by the Church in the eleventh and twelfth centuries, by the reign of Louis IX (r. 1226–1270), French involvement in the Crusades had intensified sufficiently to allow women combatants on both theological and military-logistical grounds, culminating in Pope Innocent III's decrees (1210) allowing women to accompany their husbands and other male relatives to the Middle East. But even before this edict, popular Crusades chroniclers William of Tyre (d. 1186) and Imad al-din described the bravery of these women warriors during the Third Crusade (1189–1193), in Latin and in Arabic, respectively (Solterer).

Four texts constitute the ladies' tournament tradition in France, which would also appear in German as the *Frauenturnier* (thirteenth century). The French texts are, in chronological order: two lyric-verse renditions (late twelfth century) by early *trouvères* Huon d'Oisy (d. 1190) and Richard de Semilly (fl. 1200), and two narrative-verse (octosyllabic couplets) versions, the anonymous *Tournoiement as dames* (*Tournament of Ladies* [*as* is an old-style possessive here = *des*]) from 1265, and one by Pierre Gencien (d. 1298),

Tournoiement des dames de Paris (*Tournament of the Ladies of Paris*), dated 1270–1292. All these claim to take place in the Marne valley, near Paris. Huon's 216-verse poem includes some thirty women-friends and relatives of the poet from his native Picard aristocracy. Richard de Semilly's unfinished poem numbers some thirty alexandrine verses, relating the contest between only two noblewomen, the chatelaine of Montlhéry and Lady Jacqueline of Vitry. Gencien's version differs from its precursors by presenting his ladies' tournament as a dream vision, whereas the others claim to re-create actual jousts (Muraille and Fery-Hue). Gencien's contestants are from the Parisian bourgeoisie, while the earlier poems' women come from the aristocracy. On the other hand, as Guy Muraille contends, Gencien's *Tournoiement*'s literary value pales beside that of his predecessors; its value is purely historical, though Solterer's recent, more theoretical, broadly researched analysis uncovers appreciable richness in Gencien's supposed deficiency.

The troubadour Raimbaut de Vaqueiras contributed a version in Occitan (southern-French language), titled the *Carros*, a lyric-verse allegorical tourney among the ladies of Lombardy (northern Italy), composed in the fall of 1200 at the court of Bonifazio of Monferrato (Piedmont, northwestern Italy), in honor of the latter's daughter, Beatrice. Raimbaut's tone is more negative than his French contemporaries' at the outset, combining not only parody but also biting irony and political commentary. However, its final purpose may be interpreted as more positive, for it seeks to inspire the noble Beatrice to rebuild the decaying fortress of the old, noble ladies of Lombardy (evidently a pre-Christinian city of ladies) by her virtuous example (Muraille and Fery-Hue).

See also Arthurian Women; Boccaccio, Women in, *De Claris Mulieribus*; Christine de Pizan; *Frauenturnier*; Law, Canon, Women in; Le Franc, Martin; Power of Women; Valkyries

BIBLIOGRAPHY

Primary Sources

Anonymous, Huon d'Oisy, Pierre Gencien, Richard de Semilly, and Raimbaut de Vaqueiras. [*Tournoiement des dames* poems]. In *Ludi e spettacoli nel Medioevo. I tornei di dame*. Edited by Andrea Pulega. Cattedra di filologia romanza dell'Università degli studi di Milano. Milan: Istituto editoriale cisalpino-La goliardica, 1970. [French tourneys, 1–63; Raimbaut, 65–80].

Raimbaut de Vaqueiras. *Carros*. In *Poems of the Troubadour Raimbaut de Vaqueiras*, edited and translated by Joseph Linskill. The Hague: Mouton, 1964. [Bilingual Occitan-English ed.].

Secondary Sources

Muraille, Guy, and Françoise Fery-Hue. "Tournoiement des Dames" [and other pertinent articles]. In *Dictionnaire des lettres françaises: Le Moyen Âge*, edited by Geneviève Hasenohr and Michel Zink, 1443–44, etc. Encyclopédies d'aujourd'hui. Paris: Livre de Poche, 1992.

Solterer, Helen. "Figures of Female Militancy in Medieval France." *Signs: Journal of Women in Culture and Society* 16 (1991): 522–49.

NADIA MARGOLIS

TRANSVESTISM. In the Middle Ages transvestism, or cross-dressing, was associated primarily with questions pertaining to gender roles and social status, in contrast to the link between transvestism and sexuality posited in contemporary Western society. Early Christian doctrine adopted the traditional proscriptions of cross-dressing found in Judaic tradition. Deuteronomy 22:5 forbade individuals to wear the clothing appropriate to the opposite sex. As well, both Germanic tradition and Icelandic law prohibited cross-dressing, suggesting that secular prohibitions complemented religious proscriptions.

In the Middle Ages, however, the prohibition against transvestism was interpreted differently for women and men. In general, women who adopted the clothing of men were tolerated, because they were perceived to be attempting to overcome the mental, spiritual, and social limitations inherent in their inferior female sex. It was natural and even praiseworthy for women to try to overcome these limitations and to become more like men. On the other hand, men who dressed as women were censured and suspected either of involvement in witchcraft or attempting, by disguise, to gain access to women for sexual purposes. For example, Gregory of Tours (538/9–594) reports a case in which it was assumed that a man who dressed as a nun did so to gain sexual access to the women in the convent. A fourteenth-century London case of a male transvestite who worked as a prostitute is virtually unique medieval evidence linking male transvestism and sexual activity or sexual identity.

Among the lives of the early saints there are many stories of female transvestite saints: women who, for a variety of reasons, left behind their old lives and entered the service of God, usually in a male monastic community, disguised as men. There are hagiographical accounts of some thirty female transvestites, reputed to have lived between the second and seventh centuries. Most of the lives have numerous variants, although the legends also share some common features. The most well-known story is that of Pelagia, also called Margaritó, who was a prostitute in Antioch. On her conversion to Christianity, she broke with her old life and, with the approval of her patron, Bishop Nonus, adopted male dress and moved to Jerusalem. In Jerusalem she was believed to be a holy man, renowned for asceticism. Her true sex was revealed only at her death.

A similar story is told of another Margarita/Pelagius. This woman so hated the idea of marriage that she fled her nuptial chamber, cutting her hair and dressing as a man. She entered a monastery as a monk named Pelagius, where she was respected for her holiness and ultimately elected prior of the community. Margarita's disguise was so successful that the community's portress (female doorkeeper) accused Pelagius of fathering her child and consequently he was expelled from the community. Margarita/Pelagius then lived as a hermit, and only on her death was her true sex revealed and her innocence proclaimed.

A similar story is told of Marina, who was brought into a monastic community as a child, disguised by her widowed father who feared abandoning his daughter in the world, on his own entry into religious life. Brought up in the community as a boy, Marina worked bringing supplies from the port to the monastery, necessitating overnight stays at an inn. A woman accused Marina of making her pregnant, and she was expelled from the community. Marina, still living as a man, and her infant son begged at the monastery gates until the community finally readmitted them. Shortly afterward, Marina died and the monks discovered her true sex. The woman who had falsely accused Marina became possessed by demons that only left her after she called on the intercession of the holy Marina. Other female saints of the early church who were transvestites include Athanasia/Athanasius, Appollinaris/Dortheus, Eugenia, Euphrosyn, Theodora, and Anastasia Patricia.

These early transvestite saints' lives share a number of characteristics. The women were all successful at disguising their true sex, something they did for religious reasons. They assumed masculine clothing to enter into monastic life and better serve God. A number of them were falsely accused of sexual misconduct, and each chose to accept exile and punishment rather than reveal her sex and her innocence. Only on death was the true sex of the saint revealed and her remarkable piety extolled. Scholars have interpreted this pattern as an indication of social approbation, or at least toleration, of female transvestism. The traditional means for women to grow closer to God was by renunciation of their sexuality and embracing a life of virginity, to become more like men, their intellectual and spiritual superiors. Dressing in male clothing and assuming the life of a man was a logical extension of such a desire. When pursued for spiritual ends, transvestism challenged neither the social order nor the gender hierarchy, and indeed might have been understood to reinforce them.

Alternatively, it has been suggested that the similarity of outline and the obviously legendary characteristics of the lives indicate that the transvestite saints were not historical personages at all. Rather, it is argued that the hagiographical accounts of the early transvestite saints are literary constructions emanating from a male monastic milieu. By developing stories about women hidden within the monastic communities but conforming to monastic ideals of chastity and asceticism, the transvestite saints served to diffuse male sexual anxiety.

Of greater historical veracity is the life of the twelfth-century female transvestite saint, Hildegund. Her *vita* (biography) was written shortly after her death by Engelhard von Langheim and she is mentioned by numerous other witnesses, including the Cistercian author Caesarius of Heisterbach (c.1180–1240). Hildegund was the daughter of a knight from Neuss, in the Rhineland. When her father was widowed she accompanied him on a pilgrimage to Jerusalem. For her own protection her father dressed her as a boy and called her Joseph. Parent and child traveled to the Holy Land, where the father died. After a series of adventures, betrayals, and near escapes, Joseph returned to Germany and entered the service of a cleric. The two traveled to Rome to see the pope, and after another series of misadventures, Hildegund/Joseph returned to Germany and entered the monastery at Schönau. Hildegund's entry into religious life was not as smooth as that of her legendary precursors; she tried to run away but was brought back to the community. Not long afterward, she died of a uterine hemorrhage, in the end not only revealing her true sex but also falling victim to the weakness of her female flesh. Hildegund's story has stronger historical roots and shows something of the conflict and personal tension that could accompany the life of disguise assumed by the female transvestite.

The essential weakness of female nature, even when hidden under male clothing, also underlies the story of the most notorious and reviled of medieval female transvestites, Pope Joan. Joan was reputed to have held the papacy as John VIII, in the ninth century, although most sources for her life date from the thirteenth century. Joan's legend suggests two different understandings of female transvestism. The fact that, disguised as a man, Joan was able to pursue an education and become a great teacher, suggests that perhaps cross-dressing was one way in which women could circumvent the traditional barriers that barred them from education and ecclesiastical preferment. The notion that a female transvestite could successfully ascend to the pinnacle of the ecclesiastical hierarchy also suggests male anxiety at the idea of women and power.

Unlike her predecessors, Joan's assumption of male clothing was not linked exclusively to the pursuit of holiness. She originally adopted male dress to be with the man she loved, the monk Ulfilias, albeit in a chaste relationship. Nevertheless, Joan's female, and hence sexually lascivious, nature was revealed, not on her deathbed but rather during a very public childbirth. The story of Pope Joan would seem to suggest that, unlike the transvestite saints of the early church, women could not suppress their weaker natures and become like men. That weaker nature, although disguised by male clothing, would ultimately reveal itself as unable to resist the temptations of the flesh. Hildegund's female body revealed itself in her mode of death. For Joan, her female nature revealed itself more dramatically, first, in her sexual appetite and, more spectacularly, in her public childbirth.

The idea that a woman's true nature will inevitably show through her male disguise underlies some medieval literary discussions of transvestism. For example, *Le Roman de Silence*, written in the late thirteenth century by Heldris de Cornouailles (Heldris of Cornwall), tells the story of a woman who, for purposes of inheritance, was brought up as a boy. Like the early transvestite saints, she was wrongly accused of sexual improprieties and had a variety of adventures. In the end, however, her true nature asserted itself and the knight, Silence, became the woman, Silentia.

In the high Middle Ages, the evaluation of female transvestism was transformed. Rather than being condoned as a laudable desire to emulate male superiority, female transvestism was perceived as a threat to the established gender hierarchy. Although the Pope Joan legends do not condemn her male dress, by the end of the Middle Ages the suspicion of women in male dress was universal and female cross-dressing strictly prohibited by both ecclesiastical and secular authorities. This change in evaluation is clearly illustrated in the example of Joan of Arc (c.1412–1431). Among the charges originally leveled against Joan was that she wore male clothing and weapons and refused to wear the clothes appropriate to a woman. Joan is reported to have said that it was more proper and convenient for her to dress in male clothing because she lived among men during military campaigns. Although Joan never disguised herself as a man per se nor pretended to be a man, the judges nevertheless forbade her to wear male clothing. Her resumption of male dress, whether from desire, as her enemies alleged, or from necessity, as she maintained, was the convenient catalyst for her execution.

With the execution of Joan of Arc for wearing male clothing, female transvestism was accorded the same harsh treatment before the law that had hitherto been reserved for male transvestism. In the early modern period, regulation of clothing continued to be enforced rigorously and cross-dressing was perceived to be a threat to the established social order and to hierarchical gender relations.

See also Dress, Courtly Women's; Dress, Religious Women's (Western, Christian); Hagiography (Female Saints); Joan, Pope; Joan of Arc, St.; Lesbians in the Middle Ages; Prostitution

BIBLIOGRAPHY

Primary Sources
[Lives of the transvestite saints]. *Acta sanctorum*. [under the appropriate date].
[Lives, English]. *Butler's Lives of the Saints*. Edited and revised by Herbert Thurston and Donald Attwater. 4 vols. London: Burns and Oates, 1956.
[Trial transcript, case of a male transvestite]. In Ruth Mazo Karras and David Lorenzo Boyd, "'Ut cum muliere' A Male Transvestite Prostitute in Fourteenth-Century London." In *Premodern Sexualities*, edited by Louise Fradenburg and Carla Freccero, 99–116. New York: Routledge, 1996.

[*Le Roman de*] *Silence: A Thirteenth-Century French Romance*. Edited (original Old French) and translated by Sarah Roche-Mahdi. East Lansing: Michigan State University Press, 1999. Original ed. Colleagues Press, 1992.

Secondary Sources

Anson, John. "The Female Transvestite in Early Monasticism." *Viator* 5 (1974): 1–32.

Boureau, Alain. *The Myth of Pope Joan*. Translated by Lydia G. Cochrane. Chicago: University of Chicago Press, 2001.

Bullough, Vern L. "Transvestites in the Middle Ages: A Sociological Analysis." *American Journal of Sociology* 79 (1974): 1381–94. Reprint in Bullough, *Sex, Society, and History*. New York: Science History, 1976.

———, and Bonnie Bullough. *Cross-Dressing, Sex, and Gender*. Philadelphia: University of Pennsylvania Press, 1993.

Delcourt, Marie. *Hermaphrodite: Myths and Rites of the Bisexual Figure in Classical Antiquity*. Translated by Jennifer Nicholson. London: Studio, 1956.

Hotchkiss, Valerie R. "Disguise and Despair: The Life of Hildegund von Schönau." In *Women as Protagonists and Poets in the German Middle Ages: An Anthology of Feminist Approaches to Middle High German Literature*, edited by Albrecht Classen, 29–41. Göppingen, Germany: Kümmerle, 1991.

———, ed. *Clothes Make the Man: Female Cross Dressing in Medieval Europe*. New York: Garland, 1996.

Schibanoff, Susan. "True Lies: Transvestism and Idolatry in the Trial of Joan of Arc." In *Fresh Verdicts on Joan of Arc*, edited by Bonnie Wheeler and Charles T. Wood, 31–60. New York: Garland, 1996.

JACQUELINE MURRAY

TROBAIRITZ. *Trobairitz* were the approximately twenty named women troubadours—compared to some four hundred known male troubadours—writing mainly in southern France during the mid-twelfth and into the mid-thirteenth centuries. Their language was Occitan, or *langue d'oc* (so-called for its word for "yes" = *oc*). Their histories, often presented in *vidas* (usually anonymous poetic biographies of the troubadours, composed in the thirteenth century) are often fragmented, elusive, and mixed with romantic fiction, which has stimulated much scholarly investigation with varying degrees of conclusiveness. All were members of the southern-French aristocracy; some wrote poetic dialogues with their male counterparts. Texts of each *trobairitz*'s poem or poems survive except for those by Gaudairenca, wife of a famous troubadour. There were also several anonymous *domnas* (*domna* = lady) whose works survive the names of their creators.

The songs of the *trobairitz* reveal much about the social and artistic autonomy enjoyed by these privileged women, on a level comparable to that of men. The *trobairitz* poems exemplify the high degree of literacy attainable by certain women of this refinedMediterranean society. They composed according to the rules of the inventive (*trobar* = to compose; literally, to find) yet rigorously formalized poetic genres unique to troubadour culture. These include the *tenso* (dialogue, often debate, poem with sub-genres like the *partimen*), the *sirventes* (poem of reproach and blame whether in love or political situations), and the *planh* (lament). The basic poetic unit was the *cobla* (stanza, strophe), itself cultivated in various forms (*coblas unissonans, coblas doblas,* etc.) with the *tornada* containing the poem's final sign-off. The term *canso* was the general name for a love song; these were performed to music—whether composed expressly for the poem or borrowed—although scholars disagree as to how words and melody were actually performed. Poet-lovers, even when using their own names in a poem, speak through a sort of literary mask or persona; others, might use a *senhal* or secret code-name to protect their social reputations—all of which adds to the enduring mystique of the troubadours and *trobairitz*.

Their principal topic was *fin'amor*—so-called fine or courtly love, a transgressive passion because it usually ventured outside the bounds of at least one of the parties' marriages. Yet within this love relationship, undying fidelity was expected between the two lovers, each often imitating the language of feudal law in pledging devotion to his or her beloved. This rarified love was often represented as a puzzle or game, especially in debate poems, at least at the outset, only to erupt into wrenchingly personal revelations on occasion, despite the restrictions of verse and rhyme as well as decorum. Love's suffering is a constant theme—and here, the woman poet's style of suffering can be expressed differently from the man's—but humor is also often present, as are feigned role reversals. In dialogue poems, the lovers take turns protesting (his/her) humility and (the other's) superiority. Many scholars have analyzed the problematics of *fin'amor* within the contexts of the battle of the sexes, sociopolitical power, and troubadour erotic expression, and the degree to which the *trobairitz* contributed a distinctly female viewpoint. Each woman troubadour juggled these themes and stylistic conventions—indeed, the performer of songs was called a *joglar* (a "juggler" of tunes)—in her own way.

As evidenced by the bibliographies to each *trobairitz* entry in this volume, it is thanks to the pioneering work of late-nineteenth-century German scholar Oskar Schultz-Gora, and the non-scholarly but highly influential collection by Meg Bogin, that these once almost forgotten poets have risen from the status of literary curiosities to command much-needed scholarly attention over the past twenty-five years, particularly with the establishment of reliable texts and translations of their complete works, the most authoritative being the extensively annotated critical editions and translations by Angelica Rieger and Matilda Bruckner et al.

For individual trobairitz, see Alaisina Yselda; Alamanda; Almuc de Castelnou; Azalais d'Altier; Azalais de Porcairagues; Bietris de Roman; Carenza, Na; Castelloza, Na; Clara d'Anduza; Comtessa de Dia; Garsenda of Forcalquier; Gaudairenca; Gormonda of Montpellier; Guilielma des Rosers; H., Domna; Iseut de Capio; Lombarda; Maria de Ventadorn; Tibors; Ysabella, Domna.

For patrons of the troubadours, see Eleanor of Aquitaine and Ermengard of Narbonne.

For related topics, see Capellanus, Andreas; *Chanson de Femme* (Women's Song); Isabel de Villena; Marie de France; *Minne*; Music, Women Composers and Musicians; Power of Women; *Trouvères*, Women.

BIBLIOGRAPHY

Bogin, Meg. *The Women Troubadours*. New York and London: Paddington Press, 1976. Reprint New York: W. W. Norton, 1980. [Texts, translations, commentary].

Bruckner, Matilda Tomaryn, Laurie Shepard, and Sarah White, eds. and transs. *Songs of the Women Troubadours*. Garland Library of Medieval Literature, 97A. New York and London: Garland, 1995. New ed. 2000. [Most recent, authoritative: original texts, notes, introduction, and English trans.].

Grimbert, Joan T. "Diminishing the *Trobairitz*, Excluding the Women *Trouvères*." *Tenso* 14(1999): 23–38.

Paden, William D., Jr., ed. *The Voice of the Trobairitz: Perspectives on the Women Troubadours.* Philadelphia: University of Pennsylvania Press, 1989. [Important collection of essays by major scholars].

Rieger, Angelica, ed. and trans. *Trobairitz: Der Beitrag der Frau in der altokzitanischen höfischen Lyrik. Edition des Gesamtkorpus.* Beihefte der Zeitschrift für romanische Philologie, 233. Tübingen, Germany: Max Niemeyer, 1991. [Most authoritative, original texts, German trans., introduction, and commentary].

Schultz-Gora, Oskar. *Die provenzalischen Dichterinnen.* Leipzig, Germany: Gustav Foch, 1888. Geneva: Slatkine, 1975. [Texts in original Occitan, historical commentary in German].

NADIA MARGOLIS

TROTA AND "TROTULA" (12th–16th centuries). Trota was the name of a twelfth-century female healer and medical author from the southern Italian port town of Salerno (just south of Naples), at that time widely reputed as a center of medical learning. *Trotula* (little Trota or perhaps the abbreviated Trota) was the title of a Latin compendium of remedies on women's medicine that circulated widely throughout Europe from the late twelfth century to the end of the Middle Ages. People misconstrued the title as an author's name, hence the genesis of an imagined single author, "Trotula," for the whole compendium. Together the historical woman healer (Trota), her erroneous counterpart (Trotula), and the texts (*Trotula*) have been at the center of a centuries-long debate about women as medical practitioners and medical writers.

Trota (also spelled Trocta or Trotta in medieval documents) was a common name for women in southern Italy from the eleventh through thirteenth centuries. Precise biographical data about the healer Trota are lacking, but several different kinds of evidence give us some indication of the range of her medical skill and confirm her claim to be a medical author.

An anecdote about her, embedded within a medical text called *De curis mulierum* (*On Treatments for Women*), suggests the kind of skill that made Trota famous. A young woman was suffering from intense abdominal pain that other practitioners thought to be an intestinal rupture. The young woman was about to be operated on when Trota was called in "as if she were a master" ("Trota quasi magistra vocata fuit"), a phrase that acknowledges her stature was virtually equivalent to that of a male master (*magister*) of medicine. Trota took the young woman into her home, rediagnosed her condition as flatulence of the uterus, and then proceeded to cure her by means of baths, massages, and external applications. There is no mention here of elaborate medical theory or a rationalized therapeutics (therapy gauged specifically to counteract the hypothesized cause of the disease); both diagnosis and treatment are simple and direct.

The same kind of pragmatic simplicity characterizes the known writings of Trota. Extant are, first, a brief work titled *Practica secundum Trotam* (*Practical Medicine According to Trota*) and, second, excerpts attributed to Trota within a large compendium of medical cures of Salernitan writers. Together, the *Practica* and the Salernitan compendium show that Trota's medical expertise must have been very extensive indeed, covering everything from gastrointestinal disorders to diseases of the ears and eyes. Trota did not confine herself to treating "women's diseases" but was rather a general practitioner.

She did, however, demonstrate a special expertise in women's conditions and it was in this field that she had her greatest historical influence. The text of the *Treatments for Women*, mentioned above as recounting her cure of the young woman with uterine flatulence, is a distillation of Trota's gynecological and cosmetic cures. Even though she did not author the *Treatments* in the form in which it has come down to us, Trota is acknowledged as its principal source—in much the same way that collected students' notes sometimes circulated under a male medical master's name. Sometime near the end of the twelfth century, the *Treatments* was attached to another text on women's medicine, the anonymous *Liber de sinthomatibus mulierum* (*Book on the Conditions of Women*), which was probably the work of a male author, and to a short cosmetic text, also anonymous and in this case of certain male authorship, called simply *De ornatu mulierum* (*On Women's Cosmetics*). On the basis of both style and content, it is obvious that the three works came from different hands. Nevertheless, when combined, the three texts were considered a single ensemble that went by the title *Summa que dicitur Trotula* or *Trotula mulierum* (*The Compendium Called Trotula* or *The Trotula of Women*). The title *Trotula* was thus formed out of the only known author's name associated with any of the three texts. "Trotula," in turn, was itself soon misunderstood as an author's name, and so it was to "Trotula" that these three different texts of obviously different authorship were attributed.

Trota's authentic *Practica* is found today in only

Trotula here holds an orb in her hand, suggesting her status as the leading authority on women's medicine. © London, Wellcome Institute Library, Western MS 544, p. 65 [= f. 33r].

two manuscripts. The *Trotula* ensemble, however, circulated widely throughout medieval Europe: the three independent texts plus the ensemble are now extant in at least 130 copies and rendered into the vernacular numerous times. While the real-life Trota did achieve fame to some degree, even outside of southern Italy and beyond the Alps (as attested by, among others, the satiric account of the thirteenth-century French author Rutebeuf), it was the alleged "Trotula" who was most widely known, both in connection with the gynecological collection circulating under "her" name and as an abstract authority on "women's nature" In this guise she is cited, for example, by Chaucer, in his *Canterbury Tales* (c.1387–1400), when he describes the notorious "book of wikked wyves" in the *Wife of Bath's Prologue*.

The above information on Trota and her work, and its distinction from the more popular *Trotula* ensemble, has emerged only within the past two decades as scholars have returned to the medieval documents themselves. Common knowledge about "Trotula" was hitherto based on the text of *Trotulae curandarum aegritudinum Muliebrium, ante, in et post partum Liber* (*The Unique Book of Trotula on the Treatment of the Diseases of Women Before, During and After Birth*), as edited by Georg Kraut, for a collection of treatises, also containing Hildegard of Bingen's *Physica* (twelfth century), published in Strasbourg by Johannes Schott in 1544. Kraut rearranged the order of the *Trotula* ensemble, obliterating any last traces of separate authorship among the three texts. Then, to compound the confusion, in 1566 another editor introduced the theory that this presumably single text was the work not of a medieval female author but of an ancient male author, a first-century Roman freedman named Eros.

Ever since then, "Trotula" controversy has surrounded the authorship and authenticity, not unlike those haunting Trota's twelfth-century contemporaries Heloise and Hildegard of Bingen. These debates are edifying in themselves for what they show about modern women's history and the powerful effects of gender stereotypes. Yet the real "Trotula Question" is perhaps less about the singular phenomenon of a woman doctor-writer actually existing than about the larger issue: the extent of women's participation in literate culture with respect to male doctor-writers. Trota was clearly just one of many women who practiced medicine in twelfth-century Salerno. Under the generic phrase *mulieres Salernitane* (the Salernitan women), medical writers recounted the healing practices of local women: how they gathered and prepared certain herbs, how they applied them to cure everything from gynecological and pediatric disorders to stomach problems and nervous ailments. Yet none of these women is said to be literate; none of them is credited with being a teacher. Trota stands out because she is apparently the only one who gathered together her cures and committed them to writing. That even she could not participate fully in the new, more formalized scholastic culture developing in Salerno would characterize the way in which female practitioners throughout Europe related to institutional structures of medicine in subsequent centuries.

See also Childhood and Child-Rearing in the Middle Ages; Heloise; Hildegard of Bingen, St.; Medicine and Medieval Women

BIBLIOGRAPHY

Primary Sources
Liber de sinthomatibus mulierum. In *Anglo-Norman Medicine*, 2. Edited by Tony Hunt. Cambridge: Boydell Press, 1996). [Anglo-Norman verse version].
————. In *A History of Jewish Gynaecological Texts in the Middle Ages*, edited and translated by Ron Barkaï. Leiden: Brill, 1998. [Medieval Hebrew version].
The Trotula: A Medieval Compendium of Women's Medicine. Edited and translated by Monica H. Green. Philadelphia: University of Pennsylvania Press, 2001.
———— '*The Knowing of Woman's Kind in Childing*': *A Middle English Version of Material Derived from the 'Trotula' and Other Sources*. Edited by Alexandra Barratt. Medieval Women: Texts and Contexts, 4. Turnhout, Belgium: Brepols, 2001.

Secondary Sources
Green, Monica H. "A Handlist of Latin and Vernacular Manuscripts of the So-Called Trotula Texts, I." *Scriptorium* 50 (1996): 137–75; "Handlist [...], II." *Speculum* 51 (1997): 80–104.
————. "In Search of an 'Authentic' Women's Medicine: The Strange Fates of Trota of Salerno and Hildegard of Bingen." *Dynamis: Acta Hispanica ad Medicinae Scientiarumque Historiam Illustrandam* 19 (1999): 25–54.

———. "The Development of the Trotula." *Revue d'Histoire des Textes* 26 (1996). Reprint as Essay 5 in Green, *Women's Healthcare in the Medieval West: Texts and Contexts*. Variorum Collected Studies, CS680. Aldershot, U.K.: Ashgate, 2000.

———. "'Traittié tout de mençonges': The *Secrés des dames*, 'Trotula,' and Attitudes Towards Women's Medicine in Fourteenth- and Early Fifteenth-Century France." In *Christine de Pizan and the Categories of Difference*, edited by Marilynn Desmond, 146–78. Medieval Cultures. Minneapolis: University of Minnesota Press, 1998. Reprint as Essay 6 in Green, *Women's Healthcare*. See above entry.

MONICA H. GREEN

TROUVÈRES, WOMEN. By the early thirteenth century, the women *trouvères*, writing in *langue d'oïl*, developed as the northern-French counterparts to the southern-French *trobairitz*, whose literary language was medieval Occitan (such terminology is derived from the fact that the northern-French word for yes was *oïl*, while in southern France it was *oc*). Like the *trobairitz*, who were the female analogues to the more numerous troubadours, the women *trouvères*, as their name implies, complemented the better-known male *trouvères* while exhibiting a distinctive voice, especially in certain genres (Doss-Quinby et al., 74). The women *trouvères* also resembled the *trobairitz* in that most of them were noblewomen, and some were among the most influential and powerful people in Western Europe during the twelfth and thirteenth centuries.

Although scholars are not in agreement about the actual number or even existence of historical women *trouvères*, a pioneering volume by Eglal Doss-Quinby et al. makes a strong case for their recognition and identifies eight historical women *trouvères* by name: Blanche of Castile (1188–1252, wife of Louis VIII of France), Duchess of Lorraine (probably Marguerite de Champagne, the daughter—not wife—of Thibaut IV), Dame Margot, Maroie de Dregnau (or Diergnau) of Lille, the Dame de Gosnai, the Dame de la Chaucie, Lorete, and Sainte des Prez, plus others called simply "Dame" (Lady). Among thirteen known debate songs (*jeux-partis* and *tensons*) that appear to have women authors or coauthors, six survive with music, including "Dame, merci, une riens vous demant" ("Lady, I beg you, I ask you one thing") by Blanche of Castile and Thibaut de Champagne; "Amis, ki est li muelz vaillans" ("Friend, who is more worthy"), by an anonymous woman and her male lover, and "Je vous pri dame Maroie" ("I entreat you, Lady Maroie") by Dame Margot and Dame Maroie (*trouvère* title translations from Doss-Quinby et al.). The anonymous *jeu-parti* is set to music of the most widely known troubadour canso: "Can vei la lauzeta mover" ("When I see the lark moving") by Bernart de Ventadorn (fl. c.1147–1170), the most famous of the troubadours. The debate by Dames Margot and Maroie survives in two manuscripts with very different melodies—perhaps by one of these women—and suggesting its admiration. The *Manuscrit du roi* (Paris, Bibliothèque nationale de France, MS fr. 844), called manuscript W by scholarly editors of *trobairitz* poems, preserves several items by women *trouvères* that include music: "Mout m'abelist quant je voi revenir" ("Great is the pleasure I take upon the return"), a *chanson d'amour* (love song) by Maroie de Dregnau, and "Douce dame, ce soit en vos nomer" ("Dear lady, let this one be your call"), a jeu-parti by Perrot de Beaumarchais and an unnamed woman, as well as a Crusade song, "Chanterai por mon corage" ("I will sing for the sake of my heart"), attributed to Dame de Fayel, a fictional heroine in Jakemes's late thirteenth-century *Roman du Chastelain de Coucy* (*Romance of the Lord of Coucy Castle*). Although the text of "Chanterai" is presented from a woman's point of view, men sometimes used this approach, leaving the attribution uncertain. Other monophonic lyrics preserved with music include "Un petit davant lou jor" ("Just before daybreak"), an erotic dawn song (*aube*) by Duchess of Lorraine; "Amours, u trop tart me sui pris" ("Love, to which I have been drawn so late"), a nonliturgical devotional song (*chanson pieuse*) by Blanche of Castile; and some anonymously preserved songs. A lament (*plainte*) also by Duchess of Lorraine is preserved but without music. "Jherusalem, grant damage me fais" ("Jerusalem, you cause me great harm")—without music—is attributed to two different men, but Peter Dronke tentatively ascribes this woman's lament to a woman *trouvère* on the basis of textual and linguistic evidence (Dronke 1996).

Although not a *trouvère* in the proper sense, the northern-French lyric romancier, Marie de France (fl. 1160–1215), renowned for her narratives and who was possibly at the court of Henry II of England, may also be seen as a kind of *trouvère* in that she accompanied herself on the harp in performances of poetry from the *Lais* (*Lays*), one of her most important works, a collection of deftly retold Breton-folklore tales, centered on courtly love affairs, in verse. It appears that written music existed for these narrative lais—poems divided into stanzas of irregular length and with highly variable musical structure, but the manuscript is now lost (Maillard, 66).

See also Alba Lady; Blanche of Castile; *Chanson de Femme* (Women's Song); Marie de France; Music, Women Composers and Musicians; *Trobairitz*

BIBLIOGRAPHY

Primary Source
Doss-Quinby, Eglal, Joan T. Grimbert, Wendy Pfeffer, Elizabeth Aubrey, eds. and transs. *Songs of the Women Trouvères*. New Haven, Conn. and London: Yale University Press, 2001. [Bilingual Old French-English ed. with extensive commentary and music].

Secondary Sources
[See also commentary to ed. cited above].
Dronke, Peter. *The Medieval Lyric*. London: Hutchinson University Library, 1968. 3rd. ed. Cambridge: D. S. Brewer, 1996.
———. *Women Writers of the Middle Ages: A Critical Study of Texts from Perpetua (†203) to Marguerite Porete (†1310)*. Cambridge: Cambridge University Press, 1984.
Maillard, Jean. *Évolution et esthétique du lai lyrique, des origines à la fin du XIVe siècle*. Paris: Centre de Documentation Universitaire, 1963.

J. MICHELE EDWARDS

U

UMILTÀ OF FAENZA, ST. (1226–1310). St. Umiltà was a mystic, a healer, and a teacher—sometimes called in English "St. Humilitas," from the Latin form of her name. The famous abbess of a Vallombrosan (Benedictine) convent in Florence, she wrote and preached a collection of nine powerfully articulated sermons in Latin.

Born Rosanese Negusanti into a wealthy noble family of Faenza, northern Italy, and the only child of Elimonte Negusanti and his wife Richelde, the future Umiltà was precocious in her piety and wished to dedicate herself to a religious life. She resisted the idea of marriage, and refused several high-ranking suitors chosen for her by her family. But when she was about thirteen her father died, and the changed financial circumstances in her family made it necessary for her to marry. She seems to have loved her husband, Ugolotto de'Caccianemici, with whom she had two children. The firstborn, a son, died shortly after he was baptized; a second son, born a few years later, also died in infancy. When her husband fell ill (probably of a venereal disease) and was told to abstain from sex, Rosanese convinced him they should both enter religious orders. As a nun, aged twenty-four, in the double monastery (a monastery enclosing both a nuns' house and a monks' house under one roof) of St. Perpetua in Faenza, she took the name Umiltà, or "Humility." Eagerly pursuing an ascetic life, when she was twenty-eight she left her convent to become a recluse attached to the church of St. Apollinaris in Faenza, where she remained for the next ten or twelve years. A few of her sermons date from this period. At age thirty-eight, she was divinely commanded to leave her enclosure and found a number of new houses, first near Faenza and then in Florence, where she spent twenty-one years, until her death in 1310, at age eighty-four.

Her *vita* (biography) in the standard collection of saints' lives called the *Acta Sanctorum*, was written between 1311 and 1332 by her younger contemporary, Biagio, a priest and monk in the same order. Brother Biagio records that she was miraculously granted literacy in Latin shortly after entering the convent of St. Perpetua. Nine sermons, or meditations in prose, have been preserved; one of them contains a number of Lauds to the Virgin Mary in verse. She composed in Latin, dictating to one of her disciples, Sister Donnina. In her sermons she uses her personal experience as the basis for teaching others, sometimes through a kind of prayer-dialogue and other times through parable. The first three sermons in the collection of her works are primarily doctrinal and were probably written after she had come to Florence, between 1281 and 1310. The remaining six are closer in form to prayer and meditation and convey the sense of an overheard dialogue among Umiltà, God, and various saints. Some of these latter sermons may have been written or delivered during the ten years she was a recluse, as she was beginning to gather a circle of disciples around her, among them St. Margherita of Faenza.

Brother Biagio's *Vita*, based on witnesses' oral accounts and canonization documents gathered in 1332, retells her life as one of unqualified success, for only success could justify her unconventional and independent actions. Her own writings reveal the near despair she often felt at public criticism and at the enormity of the responsibilities she had assumed. She repeatedly ignored the accepted rules for enclosure, escaping from her first convent at night, then leaving her recluse's cell to found new houses; this often required her to live among secular people while building was going on. She must have been very robust physically, as well as strong-willed, for she made a pilgrimage to Rome with St. Margherita for the jubilee of 1300, when she was in her seventies, and around that time she also helped in the building of the convent of St. John the Evangelist in Florence by gathering building stones from the bed of the nearby Mugnone River. She died, from the aftermath of a stroke, on Friday (her chosen death day), May 22, 1310. Various miracles were reported at her tomb soon thereafter. Also during that time, the famed Sienese painter, Pietro Lorenzetti (d. 1348), began his striking polyptych commemorating high points in Umiltà's career (1313–1348); it is now in the Uffizi Gallery, Florence. The renowned painter and sculptor, Arcangelo Orcagna (d. 1368), sculpted her carrying her book and flail; the statue is now in the baptistery of the church of San Michele at San Salvi. Umiltà's body now lies at Bagno a Ripoli, the same place to which her community finally moved in 1972. She was canonized St. Umiltà on March 4, 1948.

St. Umiltà seems to have been guided to an unusual extent by divine figures; she also broke more rules than usual. In her sermons, themselves an unusual activity, even for an abbess, we see a woman who feels herself surrounded at all times by divine beings, angels and saints and invisible forces, protected and advised by them. In the *Vita*, the narrator goes to great lengths to validate the authority by which Umiltà asserts her teaching role, for this was the activity most frowned on by women. She was at a disadvantage on three counts: she learned to read as an adult, and she both wrote and delivered sermons in Latin, a male language, and on doctrine, male territory. Her biographer sees this as evidence of a miracle:

> It was a thing marvelous in all respects, to see the blessed Umiltà, who had never learned letters, not only reading at table [...] but even discoursing and speaking in the Latin language, as if she had studied much in it, dictating sermons and lovely tractates on spiritual things, in which there appeared profound doctrine, very skilled verbal expression, even when speaking of the more sublime mysteries of sacred theology [...]. It is to be considered [...] that her words were not so much accomplished by her, as they were dictated from heaven by the Holy Spirit.

Umiltà, too, sees her sermons as divinely inspired; she is embarrassed at her own audacity, while she is absolutely confident that God's knowledge is speaking through her:

> I am amazed and fearful and I blush concerning these things that I dare to write and dictate, for I have not read them in other books, nor have I applied myself to learning human knowledge; but only the Spirit of God has spoken in me, who fills my mouth with the words that I ought to speak.

This passage, which is quite typical of Umiltà's style, uses seven first-person verbs; the polysyndeton of "miror et timeo atque erubesco" is also an example of the *accumulatio* (the rhetorical effect of accumulation by repeated use of "and" to separate clauses) by that governs the entire paragraph. In effect, the content asserts that she is only a vessel for God's word, but the rhetoric reaffirms a speaking I.

The titles of Umiltà's sermons give some idea of her range and concerns. "On the Birthday of Our Lord" is a meditation on spiritual preparedness for the feast of Christ's nativity; "The Angels, or A Tract on the Court of Paradise" tells of her visionary experiences and reveals the intimate relationship she felt with St. John the Evangelist; "Divine Things" is a meditation on love, divine and human; "Most Devout Lauds in Honor of the Virgin Mary" combines verse and prose in an exposition of the importance for her and her audience of the Virgin Mary. "The Prayer of Weeping and Lamentation," tells of her dark night of the soul, in which she felt the weight of her spiritual responsibility for others. "In Honor of Jesus Christ" is a cry for help in her difficulties, while "Lauds for St. John the Evangelist" and "More Praises for St. John the Evangelist" explore the meaning for her of St. John's role as the beloved of Christ. "In Praise of St. James the Apostle" evokes the welcome in heaven given to the brother of St. John.

The life and writings of St. Umiltà are important for a number of reasons. In the course of her long life she played many roles, in fact, almost all of the roles available to medieval women. In the secular world, she was the pious but indulged daughter of wealthy parents, then a wife and mother; when she joined the monastic world she was first a canoness living in an Augustinian double community, then became a recluse living alone next to a church. A new community of other recluses began to build around her, and when she set off first to the outskirts of Faenza and then to Florence to found new Vallombrosan houses, she was accompanied by a loyal group of disciples who remained close to her for the rest of their lives. Her particularly intimate relationship with St. Margherita of Faenza gives us an unusual glimpse of the kinds of strong friendships medieval women might develop, friendships that undoubtedly helped them to even greater heroism. Her mastery of Latin in the sermons is quite remarkable, and the teachings she provides deserve a full study. Her mysticism develops around two themes: her colloquy with God the Father (a very rare type in Christian mysticism) and her understanding of love. Her love is expressed with an unusual violence and erotic directness resembling that of the Beguines of northern Europe, and is unlike other Italian mystics until the time of Catherine of Siena.

See also Beguines; Catherine of Siena, St.; Convents; Double Monasteries; Hagiography (Female Saints); Rules for Canonesses, Nuns, and Recluses

BIBLIOGRAPHY

Primary Sources
Biagio et al. *Le vite de Umiltà da Faenza: agiografica trecentesca dal latino al volgare*. Edited with introduction by Adele Simonetti. Per verba, 8. Florence: SISMEL/Galluzzo, 1997. [Contains texts of both Latin *Vita S. Humilitatis* and Old Italian *Vita di Umiltà* from MS Riccardiano 1290].

———. "Vita de S. Humilitatis Abbatissa, ordinis Vallumbrosani Florentie." In *Acta Sanctorum May V, 22 Maii*, 203–22. [*Analecta* Supplement contains Latin texts of her sermons].

———. [*Vita*]. Translated with commentary in Elizabeth A. Petroff, *Consolation of the Blessed*, 121–50. New York: Alta Gaia, 1979.

―――. *Santa Umiltà: la vita e i Sermones*. Edited by Piero Zama. Memorie de Romagna. Faenza: Fratelli Lega, 1974. [Contains the Old Italian *Vita* and Italian translations of her *Sermons*].

Umiltà of Faenza. *I sermoni di Umiltà da Faenza: Studio e edizione*. Edited by Adele Simonetti. Biblioteca de "Medioevo latino", 14. Spoleto: Centro italiano di studi sull'alto medioevo, 1995.

―――. [Sermons 2, 5, 6, English] Translated by Richard J. Pioli. In *Medieval Women's Visionary Literature*, edited by Elizabeth A. Petroff, 247–53. New York: Oxford University Press, 1986.

―――. [Sermons 1 and 6, extracts, Latin and Italian]. In *Scrittrici mistiche italiane*, edited by Giovanni Pozzi and Claudio Leonardi, 94–108. Genoa: Marietti, 1988.

Secondary Sources

Holloway, Julia Bolton. *Beata Umiltà: Sguardo sulla Santa Umiltà: Contemplating on Holy Humility*. Facing Italian trans. by Fabrizio Vanni. Florence: Editoriale gli Arcipressi, 2004. [Booklet of color reproductions of Pietro Lorenzetti's paintings with commentary].

―――. http://www.florin.ms/umilta.html [Interesting, reverent Web site providing biography, extracts from her sermons, and color reproductions of Pietro Lorenzetti's paintings].

Marcucci, Luisa. *Santa Umiltà e storie della sua vita*. Milan: Martello, 1962. [An illustrated art-historical study].

Nel settimo centenario della fondazione del monastero di S. Umiltà. Miscellanea storico-religiosa Faenza: Fratelli Lega, 1966. [Vol. of conference papers, several on Umiltà].

Petroff, Elizabeth A. "She Seemed to Have Come from the Desert: Italian Women Saints and the *Vitae Patrum* Cycle" and "The Rhetoric of Transgression in the *Lives* of Italian Women Saints." In Petroff, *Body and Soul: Essays on Medieval Women and Mysticism*, 110–36, 161–81. New York: Oxford University Press, 1994.

ELIZABETH A. PETROFF

UNTERLINDEN, SISTERS OF. The Dominican convent at Unterlinden ("under the linden trees"), in the city of Colmar, in the Alsace, a province now in France, was founded by two pious, aristocratic widows, Agnes of Mittelnheim and Agnes of Herkenheim at the suggestion of a Dominican prior at Strasbourg, capital of Alsace. The widows had come with their children to Unterlinden to live communally. Soon thereafter, in 1232, the convent was moved to Ufmühlen, outside Strasbourg, then back to Unterlinden (1252) for better shelter from the frequent wars in the area. From 1234 until 1268, the spiritual direction of the women's convent was in the hands of the Dominicans of Basel and from 1268 until 1278, of the same order at Fribourg, Switzerland. A papal bull of 1246 canonically incorporated it into the Order of Preachers, thus making the convent officially Dominican. The renowned theologian, philosopher, and scientist Albertus Magnus, or Albert the Great (c.1200–1280) consecrated the convent church in 1269.

From its very beginning, Unterlinden was always a center of mysticism. It maintained close contact with such influential German mystics as Eckhart (c.1260–c.1328)—the famous "Master Eckhart" who stayed there in 1322—Johannes Tauler (d. 1361), and Heinrich Seuse (Henry Suso, c.1295–1366), who were also of the Dominican order. It was especially Heinrich who introduced the nuns to theological speculation and mystical contemplation. Many of the nuns at Unterlinden were from the upper classes or aristocracy, capable of bringing substantial dowries to the convent. A relatively large proportion of these nuns was also sufficiently educated in Latin, philosophy, and theology to comprehend the teachings of the visiting mystics, whether on a truly scholarly level, like Sister Hedwig of Steinbach, or more modestly, like the aged newcomer Tuoda, who often managed to understand the Latin services despite never having learned Latin (Ehrenschwendter).

Other important figures were the prioress Hedwig of Gundelsheim (d. 1281) and Adalhaid of Rheinfelden, prioress (c.1285). These women led mixed lives of intense ascesis (self-denial, including refusal of adequate nourishment), penance, prayer, and contemplation, coupled with participation in convent life, counseling, charitable works, and literary activity, which consisted in recording sermons and extensive letter-writing.

Such personalities were commemorated by Katharina of Unterlinden (von Gueberschwihr or Gebweiler), who, having entered the convent c.1260, recorded the mystical life at the convent through personal reminiscences of deceased nuns and sisters in her *Vitae Sororum* (*Lives of the Sisters*) written in Latin (c.1320) and based on some preexisting written materials. Katharina's *Vitae* remains preserved in a later manuscript, Colmar MS 508 (dated post-1485) and a Parisian fragment. Her descriptive chronicle is the earliest known example of the body of literature known as the Sister-Books (*Schwesternbücher*) and is the only nonvernacular one. Katharina's text was then translated into Middle-High German about 150 years later by Elisabeth Kempf or Kempfin, prioress of Unterlinden (1469–1485), who extended it by incorporating material from another chronicle source at Unterlinden, what is now the Colmar Library Manuscript 576 (Lewis; Geith).

Because of the rigors of their penitential and, in some cases, excessive subjectivity and sentimentality, as well as the physical and psychic tensions generated by the whole community, these women's writings tend to portray them to the modern reader as hysterical, pathological, repressed, totally imitative, or, at best, uninspired. However, these women saw their lives as effective sermons in which their poverty, sufferings, visions, and experiences of oneness with God attempted to counter the shallowness of real-world materialistic society.

The Unterlinden community, obliterated like so many others during the French Revolution, was reestablished at Colmar in 1899, then moved to Orbey-Tannach, France, in 1926. The vestiges of the original Unterlinden buildings—the church, part of its choir, and cloister—now house a municipal museum in which one can still find remnants and art objects from the sisters' daily lives, along with their funerary slabs, among the "newer" fifteenth-century objects (Lewis; Hamburger and Leroy).

See also Katharina von Gebweiler/Geberschweier; Penitentials, Women in; Sister-Books (*Schwesternbücher*)

BIBLIOGRAPHY

Primary Sources
[Colmar MS 576]. *L'Obituaire des Dominicaines d'Unterlinden*. Critical ed. by Charles Wittmer. Strasbourg, France and Zürich, Switzerland: Heitz, 1946.
Katharina von Unterlinden (von Gueberschwihr)."Les *Vitae sororum* d'Unterlinden (Colmar MS 508)." Critical ed. by Jeanne Ancelet-Hustache. *Archives d'histoire doctrinale et littéraire du Moyen âge* 5 (1930): 317–509.

Secondary Sources
Bynum, Carolyn Walker. *Holy Feast and Holy Fast: The Religious Significance of Food to Medieval Women*. Berkeley: University of California Press, 1987.
Ehrenschwendtner, Marie-Luise. "*Puellae litteratae*: The Vernacular in the Dominican Convents." In *Medieval Women in their Communities*, edited by Diane Watt, 49–71. Cardiff: University of Wales Press, 1997.

Geith, Karl-Ernst. "Elisabeth Kempfs Uebersetzung und Fortzetzung der *Vitae sororum* der Katharina von Gueberschwihr." *Annuaire de la Société d'Histoire de Colmar* 32 (1984): 27–42.

———. "Kempf, Elisabeth." *Verflex* 4 (1983): 1115–17.

———. "Zur Textgeschichte der *Vitae sororum* der Katharina von Gueberschwihr." *Mittellateinisches Jahrbuch* 21(1986): 230–38.

Hamburger, Jeffrey, and Catherine Leroy. *Les Dominicaines d'Unterlinden.* Paris: Somogy; Colmar, France: Musée d'Unterlinden, 2000.

Hinnebusch, William A. *The History of the Dominican Order.* 2 vols. New York: Alba House, 1966–1973.

Lewis, Gertrud Jaron. *By Women, for Women, about Women: The Sister-Books of Fourteenth-Century Germany.* Studies and Texts, 125. Toronto: Pontifical Institute of Mediaeval Studies, 1996.

Vox Benedictina: Women and Monastic Spirituality. Edited by Margot H. King. Vol. 5: 4. Toronto: Magistra, 1988.

EDITH BRIGITTE ARCHIBALD

VALKYRIES. A tradition of armed maiden warriors, the Valkyries—from Old Norse *valkyrja* (chooser of the slain)—are the Old Norse manifestation of a figure found under many forms in Indo-European myth; the female versions of Indo-European *dioscuri* (differing from the Classical Greek *dioscuri*; Castor and Pollux) who were male and female "children of the sky." They appear as war goddesses in Irish myth, such as Morrigu (who, in later legend, becomes a witch); and Bodb and Nemaind, both wives of the war god Neir. In Germanic languages other than Old Norse they are called the *ides* (*idis* = semi–divine lady). Maurice Bowra compares them to the female battle-spirits of Yugoslavian legend, the *vile*. They were originally fierce supernatural female attendants of Odin, the Norse war god, who delighted in blood and devoured corpses. Like Odin's ravens and the *einherjar* (dead warriors), the divine warrior women were delegated to choose slain warriors, and they escorted the chosen heroes as they traveled to Valhalla. Because texts from early Indo-European times do not exist, the original religious function of the divine warrior women is obscure, but there is some evidence that the Valkyries were associated with the worship of Freyja, wife of Odin, to whom half of those slain in battle belonged. Some scholars have argued that actual earthly women warriors among the Germanic tribes inspired the depiction of the Valkyries.

The Valkyries have rightly earned attention as a tradition through their recurring, if varied, presence in literature—principally Old Norse but also, as Nora K. Chadwick and Helen Damico have argued, Old English. The Valkyrie plays a significant role in heroic-legendary poems and stories, appearing in two distinct forms: as a malevolent type recalling the original Valkyrie, or as a benevolent guardian spirit. The early thirteenth-century Danish historian Saxo Grammaticus claims that Valkyries can alter their appearance from fearsome to beautiful, while other works depict them as powerful, supernatural giants rescuing heroes from danger.

In the earliest extant Old Norse poetry, the heroic lays, or poems, of the ninth- to twelfth-century mythological collection known as the *Elder* or *Poetic Edda*, the Valkyries are called *skjáldmaer* (shield-maidens) and *hjálmvitr* (helmet-beings), terms emphasizing their warlike nature. The most famous of these legendary beings bear names—such as Brynhild, Sigrun, or Svava—and distinct personalities. They are also capable of experiencing amorous attachments to mortal heroes, yet retain such supernatural characteristics

Representation of the Valkyrie from the *Ring Cycle* by Richard Wagner. © The Art Archive/Richard Wagner Museum Bayreuth/Dagli Orti (A).

as immortality, freedom of movement, and the gift of prophecy. For example, Svava, who protects the hero Helgi, becomes the princess Sigrun, who marries his descendent Helgi and then joins him in his grave. This story suggests that the Valkyries also served as dynastic guardians, not only guarding mortals in both life and death but also ensuring their family's continuity through generations. In the later skáldic poetry, the Valkyries have neither names nor power but are simply messengers of Odin. They are beautiful and wise, but they do not act independently. In both the heroic lays and the skáldic poems, however, the Valkyries play a benevolent role, and they are figures of radiance and wisdom. They appear as dignified royal women riding in armor among a troop of women warriors escorting the slain to Valhalla and welcoming them with mead, the medieval alcoholic beverage made from fermented honey. Carved stones from Gotland and the famous Torslunda dies, sixth-century dies for molding helmet plates, depict a Valkyrie welcoming a hero with a cup or horn; the Valkyrie has her hair in a braid and wears a train, a cloak, and jewelry.

A famous Valkyrie, found in both poetry and prose up through the Middle-High German epic *Nibelungenlied* (c.1203) and later, is Brynhild (Brunhilda). She disobeyed Odin and gave victory to the king not chosen by Odin to be victorious. As a punishment, Odin placed her within a ring of fire in an enchanted sleep, whence she was awakened by the hero Sigurd, thereafter appearing as a human princess and being involved with the events that culminated in Sigurd's death. Brynhild was reborn in Wagner's nineteenth-century operatic national epic, part of which is titled *Die Walküre*. She is still known in popular culture, in her lightest mood, in the American comic strip "Broom Hilda."

The malevolent Valkyries seem to have been influenced by the South Germanic *idis*, a grim war spirit responsible for binding warriors and inflicting paralysis on them according to the Old High German *Die Merseburger Zaubersprüche* (*The First Merseburg Charm*) (ninth/tenth century). This figure appears primarily in the sagas, and she is marked by her ability to bind warriors and inflict paralysis. The names associated with these Valkyries in Old English are the two common nouns for war and battle, *guðr* and *hildr*, and Odin has a

Valkyrie named *Herfjǫturr* ("War fetter"]. The literary reflex of the malevolent Valkyrie is found in the trolls, giantesses, and dream-figures of the sagas who rejoice in human sacrifice and blood. In one saga about Olaf Trygvasson, Thidrandi was wounded by a company of nine warrior women dressed in black, who were opposed by nine dressed in white. The former represented the guardian spirits of the family, angry at their imminent conversion to Christianity, while the latter symbolized their guardians under the new religion.

The Old English cognate of Old Norse *valkyrja*, *wælcyrge*, is consistently pejorative, referring to an evil being associated with slaughter. As manifested in the late Old English period, these female warriors, monstrous in form, hark back to the ancient Greek Eumenides or Erinyes, and Roman *Furiae* or *Dirae* (Furies) and other harmful female beings. Chadwick has argued that such wælcyrge representations influenced the portrayal of Grendel's Mother in *Beowulf* as a *mihtig manscaða* (mighty evil ravager) and a *wælgæst wæfre* (roaming slaughter spirit). Damico has recently reprised Chadwick's argument, pointing out that the malevolent Valkyrie-figure is also found in Modthrytho, who fetters the men who displease her. Damico argues that Old English literature also contains literary versions of the benevolent Valkyrie, even in Modthrytho, who is beautiful and adorned with gold. The benevolent Valkyrie-figure, however, is most prominently found in the figure of Wealhtheow, a human possessing supernatural characteristics similar to the Valkyries of the *Elder Edda*, and in those Christian poems whose heroines—Judith, Juliana, and Elene—are beautiful, adorned with gold, and wise, yet warlike and assertive. The antiquity and frequent presence thereafter of the Valkyrie tradition reflect its continued popularity as a means of commemorating the powerful, autonomous female spirit— whether heroic or destructive—in northern-European national cultures.

See also Enchantresses, Fays (*Fées*), and Fairies; Medea in the Middle Ages; Melusine; Nine Worthy Women; Norse Women; *Skáldkonur* (Old Norse-Icelandic Women Poets)

BIBLIOGRAPHY

Primary Sources
Beowulf. In *Beowulf and the Fight at Finnsburg*, edited by Friedrich Klaeber. 3rd ed. with 1st and 2nd supplements. Lexington, Mass.: D. C. Heath & Co., 1950.
Beowulf. Translated by Burton Raffel. Amherst: University of Massachusetts Press, 1971.
Edda: Die Lieder des Codex Regius nebst verwandten Denkmälern. Edited by Gustav Neckel. 4th ed. Revised by Hans Kuhn. Heidelberg, Germany: Carl Winter, 1962.
Poetic Edda. Translated by Lee M. Hollander. 2nd revised ed. Austin: University of Texas Press, 1977.
Die Merseburger Zaubersprüche. In *Althochdeutsches Lesebuch*, edited by Wilhelm Braune, 89. Tübingen: Max Niemeyer Verlag, 1969.
Nibelungenlied. Edited by Bartsch de Boor. Wiesbaden: F. A. Brockhaus, 1956.
Nibelungenlied. Translated by D. G. Mowatt. Everyman's Library, 312. London and New York: Dent and Dutton, 1965.
Heimskringla: Nóregs Konunga Sögur. Edited by Finnur Jónsson. Copenhagen: G. E. C. Gads, 1911.
Heimskringla: History of the Kings of Norway, by Snorri Sturluson. Translated by Lee M. Hollander. Austin: University of Texas Press, 1964.
Saxo Grammaticus. *Saxonis Gesta Danorum*. Edited by Jorgen Olrik and Hans Raeder. 2 vols. Copenhagen: Levin & Munksgaard, 1931.
———. *The History of the Danes* (Bks. 1–9). Edited by Hilda Roderick Ellis Davidson. Translated by Peter Fisher. 2 vols. Cambridge and Totowa, N.J.: Brewer, Rowman & Littlefield, 1979. Reprint Woodbridge, Suffolk, U.K.: D. S. Brewer, 1980; 1996.

Secondary Sources

Andersson, Theodore M. *Legend of Brynhild*. Islendica, 43. Ithaca, N.Y.: Cornell University Press, 1980.

Bowra, C. M. *Heroic Poetry*. New York: St. Martin's, 1966.

Chadwick, Nora K. "The Monsters and *Beowulf*." In *The Anglo–Saxons: Studies in Some Aspects of their History and Culture Presented to Bruce Dickins*, edited by Peter Clemoes, 171–203. London: Bowes & Bowes, 1959.

Clover, Carol J. "Maiden Warriors and other Sons." In *Matrons and Marginal Women in Medieval Society*, edited by Robert Edwards and Victoria Ziegler, 75–87. Woodbridge, U.K.: Boydell Press, 1995.

Damico, Helen. *Beowulf's Wealhtheow and the Valkyrie Tradition*. Madison: University of Wisconsin Press, 1984.

de Vries, Jan. *Altgermanische Religionsgeschichte*. 3rd ed. 2 vols. Berlin: Walter de Gruyter, 1970.

Davidson, Hilda Roderick Ellis. *The Road to Hel: A Study of the Conception of the Dead in Old Norse Literature*. Cambridge: Cambridge University Press, 1943. Reprint New York: Greenwood Press, 1968, 1977.

Donahue, Charles. "The Valkyries and the Irish War-Goddesses." *PMLA* 56 (1941): 1–12.

Grimm, Jacob. *Teutonic Mythology*. Translated by James Steven Stallybrass. 4 vols. London: George Bell and Sons, 1882–1888.

Grünewald, Maria. *Valkyria und Pallas Athene*. Berlin: Luhr, 1932.

Krappe, Alexander Haggerty. "The Valkyries." *Modern Language Review* 21 (1926): 55–73.

MacCulloch, J[ohn] A[rnott]. *Eddic*. Vol. 2 of *The Mythology of All Races*, edited by Louis H. Gray and George F. Moore. Boston: Archaeological Institute of America/Marshall Jones, 1930. Reprint New York: Cooper Square, 1964.

Saberhagen, Fred. *Gods of Fire and Thunder*. Book of the Gods, 5. New York: Tor, 2002.

Turville–Petre, Gabriel [E. O. G.]. *Myth and Religion of the North: The Religion of Ancient Scandinavia*. New York: Holt, Rinehart, & Winston, 1964. Reprint Westport, Conn.: Greenwood Press, 1977.

Zurmuhl, Sabine. *Leuchtende Liebe, lachender Tod: zum Tochter—Mythos Brunhilde*. Munich: Frauenbuchverlag, 1984.

ALEXANDRA HENNESSEY OLSEN

VARANO, COSTANZA (1428–1447). An Italian humanist and scholar, Costanza was born in Camerino, the granddaughter of the learned Battista da Montefeltro Malatesta (1383–1450). After Battista pleaded unsuccessfully with the Emperor Sigismund (1368–1437) to save the life of Costanza's father, murdered by his brothers in a struggle for control over Camerino, Costanza, her mother, and siblings fled to Pesaro. Costanza's education was partly overseen by her grandmother. In 1444 she married Alessandro Sforza, lord of Pesaro and uncle of another woman humanist, Ippolita Sforza (1445–1488).

At age sixteen, Costanza Varano gave an oration before Bianca Visconti Sforza, duchess of Milan, asking that Camerino be restored to the Varano family. As usual in such petitions, she begins with an elaborate devaluation of her own eloquence and an elevation of her interlocutor's worth and kindness:

> But I must confess my inadequacy and slight skill in speaking; and if your great generosity, clemency and courtesy had not conferred hope and faith on me [isolated here], my soul would draw back, my lips would hesitate, my tongue, limp and stammering, would fall silent.

While she emphasizes Bianca Visconti Sforza's kindness, however, she shrewdly implies that the "favor" she asks is owed her in exchange for services rendered: "For what could be a more excellent kind of piety than to restore to his proper princedom one who, because of his love for that just and glorious prince, your father, lost his ancient and rightful throne?" With equal tact and insistence she continues simultaneously to "plead for [her] clemency" and to reiterate what her own father's loyalty to the Sforza family cost him.

When Costanza married Alessandro Sforza in 1444, Camerino was indeed restored to her family's control, but not perhaps as the result of her oration. In any case, she spoke publicly to the people of Camerino as well, thanking them for giving her family "so clear a title of sovereignty." Her comments on the ideal forms of government are perhaps surprising for twentieth-century readers, but mirror perfectly the political philosophy of her time and caste:

> there are three forms of rule [found] in the world. [Of these] surely the least satisfactory is rule by the people; the second is rule by many citizens outstanding in virtue; the best, however, and far more worthy than all others, as Aristotle justly shows, is rule of kings and princes—that form of rule which, when it had been lost through adverse fortune, you, with one will and heart, by your skill and wisdom, reestablished.

Convinced of her family's right to rule the city, Costanza nevertheless finds it prudent to acknowledge the "so great and unmatched act of faith" of its citizens in restoring them to power, and to "offer eternal and ineffable thanks" for it.

Her letters to Cecilia Gonzaga (1425–1451) and to Isotta Nogarola (1418–1466), both c.1444, present a learned woman's perspective on her own place in intellectual life and in society. She expresses admiration for Nogarola's decision to renounce marriage for scholarship: "For nothing could be more expedient and fruitful for women than to forget the needs of the body and to reach out strenuously for those good which fortune cannot destroy." Costanza herself essentially suspended her studies after her marriage; after bearing her husband two children, she died in 1447.

See also Battista da Montefeltro Malatesta; Gonzaga, Cecilia; Nogarola, Isotta; Sforza, Ippolita

BIBLIOGRAPHY

Primary Sources

Varano, Costanza. [Letter to Isotta Nogarola]. In *Isotae Nogarolae Veronensis Opera quae supersunt omnia*, edited by Eugen Abel, vol. 2: 3–6. Budapest: F. Kilian, 1886. [Latin only].

———. [Orations, Letter to Cecilia Gonzaga]. In *Catalogus codicum manuscriptorum qui in Bibliotheca Riccardiana adservantur*. Edited by J. Lamius, 145–47. Livorno, Italy, 1756.

———. [Oration to Bianca Maria Visconti, Oration to the People of Camerino, Letter to Cecilia Gonzaga, Letter to Isottta Nogarola]. In *Her Immaculate Hand: Selected Works by and about the Women Humanists of Quattrocento Italy*, translated with commentary by Margaret King and Albert Rabil Jr., 39–41, 42–44, 53–54, resp. Medieval & Renaissance Texts & Studies, 20. Binghamton, N.Y.: Center for Medieval & Early Renaissance Studies, 1983. [Excellent introduction and notes].

———. Latin excerpts with English trans. in Parker, below.

Secondary Sources

Feliciangeli, B. "Notizie sulla vita e sugli scritti di Costanza Varano-Sforza." *Giornale Storico della Letteratura Italiana* 23 (1894): 1–75.

King, Margaret L. "Book-Lined Cells: Women and Humanism in the Early Italian Renaissance." In *Beyond Their Sex: Learned Women of the European Past*, edited by Patricia H. Labalme, 66–90. New York: New York University Press, 1980.

Parker, Holt. "Latin and Greek Poetry by Five Renaissance Italian Women Humanists." In *Sex and Gender in Medieval and Renaissance Texts: The Latin Tradition*, edited by Barbara K. Gold, Paul Allen Miller, and Charles Platter, 247–85, esp. 266–67. SUNY Medieval Studies. Albany: State University of New York Press, 1997.

REGINA PSAKI

VEGRI, CATERINA. *See* **Catherine of Bologna, St.**

VERTU DU SACREMENT DE MARIAGE, LIVRE DE LA (1384–1389). Philippe de Mézières (c.1327–1405), a French soldier, diplomat, and moral-political author, wrote, among other works, an important treatise on marriage, the *Livre de la vertu du sacrement de mariage et du réconfort des dames mariées* (*Book of the Virtue of the Sacrament of Marriage and of Solace for Married Ladies*, 1384–1389). The work is dedicated to Jehanne de Châtillon, wife of Philippe's patron, Pierre de Craon, and exists in one surviving copy: Paris, Bibliothèque nationale de France MS. fr. 1175. The *Livre de la vertu* examines and extols marriage as a sacrament and essential social unit. It also includes a French translation of Petrarch's celebrated Latin tale of the patient wife Griselda, thus helping promote a positive image of medieval women some twenty years before the Franco-Italian feminist Christine de Pizan's *Cité des dames* (*City of Ladies*) and *Livre des Trois Vertus* (*Book of the Three Virtues*), both in 1405. Philippe's *Livre de la vertu* reflects the mature wisdom of a multitalented author who offered lessons for peace and harmony in a complex and even dangerous era.

Born to a family of lesser nobles in Mézières, in the northern-French province of Picardy, Philippe began as a mercenary, a soldier of fortune, learning feats of arms in Italy. He soon earned his knighthood and fought in the Near East. During a pilgrimage to the Holy Land (1347) he had a transformative religious vision, in which God spoke to him and exhorted him to found a knightly order based on devotion to Christ (see below). Philippe's cosmopolitan, military, and pious experiences made him an effective agent of reconciliation, both in diplomatic practice between the Western papacy and Eastern Christendom, and within France during the Great Schism's dual papacy (one pope in Rome; one in Avignon, France, from 1378–1417) and the civil upheavals caused by the Anglo-French Hundred Years War (1337–1453). Philippe also involved himself in such eastern Mediterranean causes as that of the King of Armenia's efforts to regain his throne. In all he seems to have served six kings, most notably Charles V (the Wise) of France. He was also the official tutor of Charles's son, the future Charles VI. Philippe founded the chivalric Order of the Passion of Jesus Christ, for which he composed the guidelines in several versions over three decades. This order attempted to reverse a trend toward questioning the old chivalric mores both on the battlefield and at court. In an age of cynical secularization, Philippe hoped to rejuvenate former beliefs and customs by merging them more profoundly with Christian piety. As a man of letters, he recognized the value of his friend, the great Italian poet and moralist Petrarch (1304–1374), as well as that of his predecessor Dante (1265–1321), despite the era's cultural rivalry between France and Italy. All of these authors shared the belief that social good began with the individual; public morality was rooted in the private value system; dutiful, pious, enlightened citizens made for a good, orderly society; and that the morally responsible author could and should contribute to this program of edification. Philippe enunciated his vision allegorically in his major literary work, *Le Songe du vieil pelerin* (*The Old Pilgrim's Vision*, c.1386–1389).

That he penned the *Livre de la vertu* in the same years as the *Songe* indicates his urgent concern to educate women, as well as men, to be responsible members of society. Both sexes would benefit from contemplating the life and Passion of Christ. Thus, Philippe's view of marriage in the *Livre de la vertu* engages, as its foremost scholar Joan Williamson observes, "the mystical union of Christ with the Church and the human soul"; this union will bring both individual human happiness and social harmony through the cultivation of Christ-like selflessness. The theme belongs to a standard Latin genre that Philippe vulgarizes as part of a move toward popular piety (Williamson 1999). Most significantly, as Carolyn Collette remarks, the *Livre de la vertu* incorporates this mystical construct to teach high spiritual ideals for married women, rather than maintaining a traditional focus on virginal single women. Married women can be "spiritual brides of Christ" as well as "physical wives of real men," and a major force for social improvement. Philippe appeals primarily to noblewomen; later, Christine de Pizan would attempt to reach all classes of women in her *Livre des Trois Vertus*.

Throughout the four books comprising his manual, Philippe's voice is highly stylized yet moving, like that of a learned but effective preacher. Heading the hierarchy of virtuous wives and mothers is the Virgin Mary (who is compared to "a fine diamond"). The virtuous husband should embody the qualities of Christ ("a fine ruby"). The allegorical marriage of Christ and Mary therefore symbolizes the ideal union of physical and spiritual. Philippe then moves on to more mortal women, from holy wives to wicked ones such as Rosamund and Joan of Naples. He mixes alchemical, medical, optical, lapidary, and religious-pilgrimage metaphors while citing various historical and legendary women to illustrate the virtues good wives should have. He also recommends remedies for their discontent. He cautions his wifely readers against the dangers of willfulness, yielding to unhappiness, excessive materialism, luxury, pride, and inordinate passion in general. All of these are not only undesirable in a wife personally, but also threatening to social stability. Philippe maintains that the principal virtue for combating such evils is Prudence, an important allegorical figure also found in the work of Philippe's English contemporary, Geoffrey Chaucer (*Canterbury Tales*, c.1387–1400), in the "Tale of Melibee" (see Collette), and in Christine de Pizan's *Livre de Prudence* (*Book of Prudence*, c.1405-1407). Philippe's numerous illustrative examples derive mostly from the Bible, mythology, and history. He includes a paraphrase of Hugh of St. Victor (d. 1141), author of several analyses of the holy sacraments, as to why the human soul should love God.

Philippe saves his most important example of the ideal wife for the end. The immediate source of his story was Petrarch's Latin *Griselda*, itself taken from the Italian version in Boccaccio's *Decameron* of 1351–1353. Philippe translated Petrarch's version into French: the tale describes the unflagging constancy and many sufferings of a wife whose husband tests her mercilessly, before finally rewarding her goodness. Collette compares the role of Griselda to another principal figure in Philippe's work, St. Cecilia. She observes how the then-popular saint's legend exemplified the chaste, spiritually centered marriage, while Griselda represents a saintly figure within a consummated marriage, and thus a real-life model for women. Philippe intends this closing tale of an earthly marriage to mirror the divine union evoked at his book's beginning: a good wife should obey her husband as

Griselda does Walter, and as the soul should obey Christ. Like the more allegorical Prudence, both St. Cecilia and Griselda figure in Chaucer's *Canterbury Tales*, in the "Second Nun's Tale" and "Clerk's Tale," respectively. Philippe emphasized the role of marriage in his diplomatic efforts as well as his writing. His 1395 *Epistre au roi Richart* (*Letter to King Richard II*) urged the widowed English monarch to marry Isabella of France, so as to effect peace between the warring kingdoms and preserve international harmony.

See also Anne of Bohemia; Boccaccio, Women in, *De Claris Mulieribus*; Boccaccio, Women in, *Des Cleres et Nobles Femmes*; Bride of Christ/*Brautmystik*; Chaucer, Geoffrey, Women in the Work of; Christine de Pizan; Griselda; *Miroir de Mariage* (*Mirror of Marriage*); *Sachsenspiegel* and *Schwabenspiegel*; Virginity

BIBLIOGRAPHY

Primary Sources
Philippe de Mézières. *Campaign for the Feast of Mary's Presentation*. Edited by William E. Coleman. Toronto: Pontifical Institute of Mediaeval Studies, 1981.
———. *Letter to King Richard II: A Plea Made in 1395 for Peace between England and France*. Edited, translated, with an introduction by G. W. Coopland. Liverpool, U.K.: Liverpool University Press, 1975. [Bilingual ed.].
———. *Le Livre de la vertu du sacrement de mariage, edited from Paris, B. N. MS fr. 1175)*. Edited with notes and introduction by Joan B. Williamson. Washington, D.C.: Catholic University of America Press, 1993.

Secondary Sources
Brownlee, Kevin. "Commentary and the Rhetoric of Exemplarity: Griseldis in Petrarch, Phillipe de Mézières, and the *Estoire*." *South Atlantic Quarterly* 91(1992): 865–90.
Collette, Carolyn P. "Chaucer and the French Tradition Revisited: Philippe de Mézières and the Good Wife." In *Medieval Women: Text and Contexts in Late Medieval Britain: Essays for Felicity Riddy*, edited by Jocelyn Wogan-Browne et al., 151–68. Turnhout, Belgium: Brepols, 2000.
Esclapez, Raymond. "Philippe de Mézières, *Le Miroir des dames mariées*, vers 1384." In *L'Histoire de Griselda: Une Femme exemplaire dans les littératures européennes*, edited by Jean-Luc Nardone and Henri Lamarque, 141–75. Toulouse, France: Presses Universitaires du Mirail, 2000.
Golenistcheff-Koutouzoff, Elie. *Etude sur "Le livre de la vertu du sacrement de mariage et reconfort des dames mariées" de Philippe de Mézières*. Belgrade, Yugoslavia: Svetlost, 1937.
Grossel, Marie–Geneviève. "Sainte paysanne et épouse fidèle: L'Image de Griseldis à l'épreuve des Miroirs de mariage." In *Autour d'Eustache Deschamps*, edited by Danielle Buschinger, 103–14. Amiens, France: Centre d'Études Médiévales/Université de Picardie-Jules-Verne, 1999.
Iorga, Nicolae. *Philippe de Mézières (1327–1405) et la croisade au XIVe siècle*. Paris: Bouillon, 1896. [still the most complete biographical study].
Maddox, Donald. "Early Secular Courtly Drama in France: *L'Estoire de Griseldis*." In *The Expansion and Transformations of Courtly Literature*, edited by Nathaniel B. Smith and Joseph T. Snow, 156–70. Athens: University of Georgia Press, 1980.
———. "The Hunting Scenes in *L'Estoire de Griseldis*." In *Voices of Conscience: Essays on Medieval and Modern French Literature in Memory of James D. Powell and Rosemary Hodgins*, edited by Raymond J. Cormier and Eric Sellin, 78–94. Philadelphia: Temple University Press, 1977.
Picherit, Jean-Louis G. "De Philippe de Mézières à Christine de Pizan." *Le Moyen Français* 13 (1983): 20–36.
Williamson, Joan B. "Paris B.N. MS fr. 1175: A Collaboration between Author and Artist." In *Text and Image*, edited by David W. Burchmore, 77–92. Binghamton, N.Y.: Center for Medieval & Early Renaissance Studies, 1986.
———. "Philippe de Mézières." In *Dictionary of Literary Biography 208: Literature of the French and Occitan Middle Ages: Eleventh to Fifteenth Centuries*, edited by Deborah Sinnreich-Levi and Ian

S. Laurie, 216–25. Detroit, Washington, D.C. and London: Bruccoli Clark Layman/Gale Group, 1999.

———. "Philippe de Mézières' Book for Married Ladies: A Book from the Entourage of the Court of Charles VI." In *The Spirit of the Court: Selected Proceedings of the Fourth Congress of the International Courtly Literature Society (Toronto 1983)*, edited by Glyn S. Burgess, Robert A. Taylor et al., 393–408. Dover, N.H.: Brewer, 1985.

ANDREA W. TARNOWSKI

VETULA (Old Woman). *See* **Medicine and Medieval Women**

VIBIA PERPETUA. *See* **Perpetua, St.**

VIRGINITY. One of the dominant ideals for medieval women was that of virginity. Virginity, from the Latin *virginitas* (= maidenhood, derived from *virgo* = maiden), refers to the condition of being or remaining permanently in a chaste state; namely, free from the taint of sexual relations, sexually intact (*virgo intacta*). Virginity in its spiritual definition can also refer to one "whose primary relationship is with God." According to the widespread, authoritative *Etymologiae* (*Etymologies*) of Isidore of Seville (d. 636), virgo pertains to the "verdant, young/vigorous period of life, like a slender green branch and a calf"—an etymology taken directly from the influential Virgilian commentator, Servius (early fifth century?). Set apart by her incorruptibility, the virgin was a *quasi virago*, unaware of feminine passion or sensual appetite. In a letter to a congregation of nuns, Hildegard of Bingen describes the virgin as one who "stands in the unsullied purity of paradise, lovely and unwithering, and she always remains in the full vitality of the budding rod." For the Middle Ages, the virginal life was compared to an "angelic" life—the virgin was seen as "sister of the angels," or "dead to earthly desires, breathing only heavenly affections." According to St. Ambrose, "virginity surpasses the condition of human nature, because through it human beings are associated with the angels, yet the virgins' victory is greater than the angels', because angels live without flesh but virgins triumph in the flesh." Virgins were therefore admired for having successfully negated their "unfortunate" biological nature or female sexuality. Acting in a manner "forgetful of their sex," they were able to transcend the "natural weakness" and "limitations" inherent in their gender. They thus attained a higher level that provided them with a spiritual fecundity. In this tradition St. Augustine notes, "it is a noble thing to choose, while still in this life, to imitate the life of the angels rather than to increase in this life the number of mortals. More fruitful and happier is the fecundity that fosters the spirit than that which swells the belly." It was then as sexless, gender-neutral beings, detached from the world and preoccupied with spiritual things, that these women approached a near equality with men. And for their admirable repudiation of their own sexuality, they often won the highest patristic compliment: they were praised for their spiritual virility; for progressing toward perfect manhood.

Although within the medieval Church and particularly within the monastic environment, the rigors of the chaste life were equally upheld for both sexes, there was clearly

Byzantine mosaic of St. Agnes in the Church of San Apollinare Nouvo, sixth century. Courtesy of North Wind Picture Archives.

a disproportionate emphasis on and admiration for female virginity. From the beginning, virginity was not emphasized for men in the same way as it was for women. Virginity never dominated the total mode of perception of the male religious, nor defined the state of masculine perfection as it did for women. Moreover, for women, the condition of being a virgin, virgo intacta, or the loss of one's physical integrity could be tested or verified. Female virginity was also important for medieval economic and social organization, particularly in regard to the determination of kinship and inheritance.

While the virginal life was viewed by the church as the preferred profession for women, on a practical level virginity also provided women with an important choice—namely, an honorable alternative to forced marriage. In addition, the life of the consecrated virgin offered women an effective escape from the very real fears and dangers of childbirth.

Although the ideal of the virginal life was especially prominent in the Middle Ages, it appears to have been rather rare or exceptional in the ancient world. A few precedents can be found in Greco-Roman society with the cults of virgin goddesses (e.g., Athena and Artemis), as well as the Vestal Virgins. It is, however, in the New Testament that the ideal of virginity, as contrasted to marriage, was defined as the *vita perfecta* for the early Christians. In an eschatological context, Christ praised those who became voluntary "eunuchs for the sake of the kingdom of heaven" (Matthew 19: 10–12). In light of the belief in the imminent end of the world, St. Paul also commended virgins and unmarried women who were free to concentrate fully on "the things of the Lord." Paul advocated that although marriage was praiseworthy, it was clearly a compromise; virginity was the preferred choice.

The third and fourth centuries witnessed a growing popularity in the adoption of the virginal life. During this period the profession of virginity came to be recognized by the Church. Despite the perceived weakness of their sex, virgin martyrs became especially prominent in the defense of their new faith and were singled out for their heroics during the persecutions of the early Christians. *The Apostolic Constitutions* of the fourth century assigned virgins (along with widows and deaconesses) a special honored status in the ecclesiastical hierarchy. In the ordering of ecclesiastical space, virgins were to sit by themselves or stand in front of other women. In the liturgical offices, virgins along with widows occupied the first rank after the clergy. Also beginning with the fourth century, a formal liturgical ceremony for the consecration of virgins was established. This ritual, which reflected marriage ceremonies of the period, consisted of the virgin taking the veil and symbolized her mystical marriage with Christ. During the elaborate consecration ceremonies of the Middle Ages, virgins/nuns also received a ring and crown as symbols of "castimony" or their chaste marriage to Christ.

With the third and fourth centuries, treatises on virginity proliferated. In their frequently polemical works, the Church Fathers Tertullian, Cyprian, Ambrose, Jerome, Augustine, and others, exalted the virginal life often at the expense of marriage. According to St. Jerome, "As long as woman is for birth and children, she is different from man as body is from soul. But when she wishes to serve Christ more than the world, then she will cease to be a woman, and will be called a man." Jerome established a clear hierarchy of values within the Christian community based on the degree of a person's renunciation of or withdrawal from sexual activity. He established three separate levels of female chastity with virgin martyrs or virgins accorded the highest value, followed by chaste widows; with married women occupying the third or lowest level. These three states were traditionally compared to the hundredfold, sixtyfold, and thirtyfold fruit found in the biblical parable of the sower (Matt. 13:8). The English abbot and bishop, Aldhelm (d. 709) in his tract, *In Praise of Virginity*, which was dedicated to the abbess and nuns of Barking Abbey, reformulated this classic tripartite division. Although hierarchically ordered, women in each of the categories (as soldiers of Christ) were known to bear arms for one commander in chief. According to Aldhelm, virginity was viewed as the spontaneous desire for celibacy; chastity as continency within marriage (which also included divorced women and widows); and marriage as an association for procreation. In a fascinating series of metaphors he then equated virginity with gold, riches, the sun, a queen, and royal purple; chastity with silver, an average income, a lamp, a lady, re-dyed fabric; and conjugality with bronze, poverty, darkness, a servant, and undyed wool, and so forth.

Many of the patristic tracts of the second to the sixth centuries were concerned with providing guidance for the life of virginity as adopted by individual women who, successfully avoiding the "nuisances of marriage," remained "in the world," that is, living at home or in small informal groups. Their writings furnished detailed ascetic prescriptions for the maintenance of virginity. Fasting, sleep deprivation, mortification of the flesh, and vigils were strongly recommended; a regimen of strict fasting was deemed especially necessary to "control the flesh." St. Augustine's classic description of the virgin notes that she

> fasts, maintains vigils, meditates on the Scripture. Her attire is mean, poverty is the way of her life. She is joyous but has the gift of tears. She is simple but prudent. She is serene and innocent and sweet. From her interior purity, recollection, and devotion emanate the sweet odor of prayer and good works.... Everything about her exterior manner bespeaks her angelic holiness—her dignified bearing, her modest decorum, the comely pallor of her sober countenance, the pure virginal blush of her modesty, the chaste restraint of her downcast eyes, and the silence of her closed lips. When obliged to speak, her voice is gentle, her words prudent. If she must walk among men, she walks as through a desert, oblivious to all about her." (Nugent, p. 107)

The Church Fathers stressed the need for these women to adhere to a life of total virginity, *integritas*, that is, virginity of the body as well as the spirit or will. Virginity thus entailed both physical and spiritual integrity. Although according to Augustine, Aldhelm, Bonaventure, and others, the involuntary loss of physical integrity through rape and other means, left virginity (resting essentially in the will) intact; nevertheless, the onus of proof of integrity of the will (i.e., that no voluntary carnal pleasure was involved) remained the problem of the female victim. One's innocence, no doubt, would have been rather difficult to prove given the contemporary atmosphere of distrust of female sexuality.

Church writers thus underscored the responsibilities and difficulties inherent in this preferred profession as well as its glorious heavenly rewards. They warned those who had adopted the virginal life of the deceptiveness of "false virgins" as well as the stigma surrounding lapsed virgins. They especially instilled within them a profound sense of fear and guilt. To guard their privileged status, St. Jerome noted that brides of Christ must spend their earthly life balanced precariously between a continual fear of defilement and the steadfast hope of eternal life with their bridegroom, Christ. As Brides of Christ, virgins needed to be carefully guarded so as to remain "unwounded" or "untarnished" for their eternal bridegroom. In his celebrated "Letter to Eustochium," Jerome warned Eustochium of the hard road she had chosen: "I do not wish pride to come upon you by reason of your decision [to espouse virginity], but fear. If you walk laden with gold, you must beware of a robber. This mortal life is a race. Here we struggle, that elsewhere we may be crowned." It is then in this context that the Church Fathers emphasized that virgins were prepared to die to preserve their integrity.

One of the areas of special concern for the Church during this early period was the practice of the *virgines subintroductae*, that is, the chaste cohabitation of virgins with unmarried deacons, priests, monks, or bishops. While this practical partnership worked to minimize gender differences and provided women with an element of protection along with necessary sacerdotal assistance, this practice aroused suspicion and was condemned by churchmen.

It was, however, organized or institutionalized virginity, virginity within monasticism, that would be of primary importance in the medieval period. In every aspect of monastic life the virginal ideal, with its concurrent fear of the loss of integritas, was impressed on the brides of Christ. Monastic rules, canons of church councils, saints' lives, sermons, tracts, as well as the art of the period stressed the need for perpetual virginity by the nuns. For example, the iconography of the parable of the Wise and Foolish Virgins, Dinah, the virgin martyrs, the Virgin Mary, as well as Eve, and *luxuria* (or the personification of lust), were especially popular. While encouraging integritas, the various sources of the period also emphasized the "natural weakness" of women and the serious repercussions surrounding the loss of virginity. They described in vivid detail the horrors of childbirth; moreover, they heightened eschatological fears by underscoring the fallen virgin's failure to receive her future privileges and rewards as a bride of Christ. In this tradition are several important and popular works on virginity from the central and late Middle Ages, including the *Speculum Virginum* (Mirror for Virgins, 1140), *Hali Meidhad* (Holy Maidenhood, c.1200), and the *Ancrene Wisse: Guide for Anchoresses* (c.1215–1221).

Female monasteries were then to serve as a type of refuge or haven that would shelter consecrated virgins from the dangers of the world. Many of the convents were therefore located within the walls of the cities and placed under the special protection of a bishop, abbot, or secular ruler. Monasteries were described as virgins' tombs, or "virgin vaults," where the nuns, as *sponsae Christi* or brides of Christ, were to be dead and buried with Christ, only to arise with Him and appear in his glory at the Last Judgment. Special precautions were taken within monasteries to maintain the sexual purity of their inmates. Internal policies stressed the need for a constant vigilance that aimed at minimizing the opportunities for the formation of "particular friendships" or lesbian relations. Detailed regulations were established in regard to proper dormitory behavior. Policies of active and passive enclosure were increasingly established to reduce the various external threats to the female religious. Double or mixed-sex monasteries—those that consisted of monks and nuns—presented special challenges for the maintenance of virginity. They required the strict segregation of the nuns and monks to avoid altogether any suspicions or opportunities for the perilous comingling of the sexes. In this tradition, for example, *The Book of Gilbert of Sempringham* (d. 1189) notes that the nuns of the mixed community of Sempringham were strictly enclosed with provisions for only a single opening or window, which would allow necessaries to be passed in to the inmates, as well as a single locked door for which the male superior kept the key.

Nevertheless, despite the protective ideal established for these female communities, many of the monasteries and their residents became primary targets of violence, rape, and plunder. It is then in these dire situations that the nuns' commitment to the virginal ideal was put into practice. During the period of the Saracen and Viking invasions, for example, sources describe a number of rather shocking instances of the "heroics of virginity." These cases concern the female religious of several monasteries including St. Cyr, Marseilles (738), and Coldingham (c.870). Thus, to avoid being raped by the invaders, and therefore forfeiting their future rewards as brides of Christ as well as the honor of singing in the celestial choir with the 144,000 virgins, these female religious disfigured themselves by cutting off their noses and lips (*virginitas deformitate defensa*). For their heroic defense of their virginity, these nuns won recognition of sanctity as virgin martyrs. The saints' lives of the period also describe other creative strategies adopted by consecrated virgins to avoid sexual assault, including the use of rotten chicken parts placed in their clothing, tonsuring themselves, wearing male dress, taking the veil, and feigning insanity.

Virginity was a means to become a citizen of the heavenly kingdom. As noted by Methodius of Lycia (d. c.311) in his *Banquet*, "Virginity is something supernaturally great, wonderful, and glorious [...] this best and noblest manner of life alone is the root of immortality, and also its flower and first-fruits; and for this reason the Lord promises that those shall enter into the Kingdom of heaven who have made themselves eunuchs." St. Jerome wrote, "nuptials fill the earth; virginity, paradise." Virginity thus became one of the primary prerequisites for female sainthood with a strong percentage of medieval saints recruited from among virginal candidates. One of the popular hagiographic *topoi* depicts virgin saints heroically defying their parents and adopting various strategies to avoid unwanted forced/political marriages. A number of these women were said to have prayed for some kind of illness or physical deformity (such as leprosy, blindness, excessive facial hair, beards, etc.) that would save them from marriage. For example, St. Brigid of Ireland (d. c.525), founder and abbess of Kildare, was able to preserve her virginity by having one of her eyes "burst," thus making her ineligible for marriage. The folkloric figure, St. Wilgefortis (whose name was a corruption of *Virgo Fortis*), was said to have avoided a forced marriage by miraculously growing a beard. In her martyrdom, she then took on the physical appearance of the crucified Christ (*imitatio Christi*). Known by various names such as Liberata, Uncumber, and so forth, she became the patron saint of women who wanted to be liberated from unwanted marriages. Christina of Markyate (d. 1161) was influenced by the virgin models of St. Cecilia, St. Amalburga, St. Æthelthryth, St. Frideswide, and St. Hild, as well as by several virgin martyrs. Having made a private vow of virginity, she was praised for maintaining her virginity despite her parents' wishes for her to marry. After receiving visions from the age of seven, St. Catherine of Siena (d. 1380) took a vow of virginity. At fifteen she adopted the successful strategy of cutting her hair to avoid a forced marriage. The well-known case of Joan of Arc (d. 1431) notes that she had been inspired by the virgin saints Catherine of Alexandria and Margaret of Antioch, who furnished her with role models of virgin martyrs who had refused marriage, as had Joan; their lives also promoted autonomy, defiance of authority, and heroic martyrdom. Joan of Arc maintained that St. Catherine and St. Margaret had promised to lead her to Paradise on the condition that she preserve her virginity. Contemporaries believed that virginity provided the Maid of Orleans with a special virility, power, and strength.

Although the importance of the cult of the Virgin Mary can be noted already in the sources of the early Middle Ages, it is with the twelfth century that the cult became a major force in medieval society and the Church. Following the typological relationship of the Old and New Testament, the Virgin Mary was seen as the new or second Eve. Thus Eve's negative attributes—her personification of woman as body, lust, and reproduction—were translated/inverted with the Virgin Mary into the positive qualities of purity/perpetual virginity. Many of the symbols and attributes used to identify Mary emphasized her unblemished virginity: for example, the lily, enclosed garden, closed gates, and spotless mirror. The Virgin Mary, as both virgin and mother, became the patron of marriage and protector of brides. She was viewed as having a special concern for the health and well-being of members of her own sex. She was especially called on by women to provide assistance during difficult childbirth. Also, as the personification of purity, prototype of the virgin in society (having made a vow to remain a virgin), she became a particularly important role model for consecrated virgins/female religious. In the ceremony of the consecration or veiling of nuns, for example, there are several allusions to the Virgin Mary. Many of their convents were also dedicated to Mary.

While virginity/female bodily intactness remained the preferred status for women in the medieval church, many formerly married women and widows also adopted lives of chastity and entered religious life. Aldhelm, for example, discussed in some detail the relative merits of virgin nuns and formerly married women who had become chaste nuns. He praised those who had adopted a life of chastity, "having been assigned to marital contracts, having scorned the commerce of matrimony for the sake of the heavenly kingdom." Throughout the Middle Ages one can find many examples of these women. A rather well-known case, which underscores the overwhelming importance of the religious ideal of virginity/chastity, can be found in the life of the late medieval English mystic, Margery Kempe (d. c.1440). In her struggle to live a life of chastity, she was reassured that she was a "maiden in [her] soul" and thus believed in her "restored virginity." As bride of Christ, this mother of fourteen therefore adopted the white robes of a virgin.

Other women were praised for entering spiritual marriages that comprised lives of sexual abstinence for reasons of piety. An interesting case can be found in the life of the popular Anglo-Saxon St. Æthelthryth (Audrey; d. 679), queen, founder, and abbess of Ely. Although twice married, she was celebrated for having managed to remain a virgin. However, in a number of these spiritual or unconsummated marriages, these "virginal" wives found themselves to be especially vulnerable and were forced to resort to extra-ordinary/heroic measures to defend their reputations from accusations of adultery. For example, the famous case of the ninth-century empress-saint Richardis (wife of Charles the Fat), notes that the empress offered to prove her innocence, that is, the integrity of her virginity, through an ordeal; similarly, the eleventh-century empress-saint Cunegund underwent an ordeal by fire to prove her virginity.

The ideals of virginity and chastity thus remained of crucial importance for women throughout the medieval period and continue to exercise a major influence up to the modern era. On the one hand, the adoption of the virginal life, with the renunciation of female sexuality, offered medieval women an important and respected alternative— namely, it freed them from forced marriages and the dreaded possibility of dying in childbirth. It allowed them to live together with other likeminded consecrated virgins and follow a religious or monastic life. It also provided them with a type of spiritual parity; that is, opportunities, power, and a certain autonomy within the church and society. For many, the virginal life provided them with a visibility that led to sanctity. It is also interesting to note that in death, as in life, one of the postmortem signs or proofs of virginity/sainthood was that the body of the virgo intacta was said to remain miraculously incorrupt. How-ever, the special gender-based pressures, the frequently unrealistic expectations of virginal or chaste perfection with the underlying burden that this ideal placed on women, required them to protect their reputations and integritas at all costs. This difficult ideal could also be manipulated by the male-dominated Church to reinforce the submission of women to patriarchal authority. For example, during this period the increasingly "protective" measures of gender-based segregation and enclosure, viewed by the Church as necessary for the maintenance of female virginity, unfortunately worked to further circumscribe their lives and activities, and placed a disproportionately heavy burden on women.

See also Æthelthryth, St.; *Ancrene Riwle*; Bride of Christ/*Brautmystik*; Celibacy; Christina of Markyate; Convents; Double Monasteries; Eustochium, St.; *Frauenfrage*; Hagiography (Female Saints); Hild (Hilda), St.; Hildegard of Bingen, St.; Joan of Arc, St.; Kempe, Margery; Marriage; Mary, Blessed Virgin, in the Middle Ages; *Periculoso*; Rules for Canonesses, Nuns, and Recluses

BIBLIOGRAPHY

Primary Sources
Aldhelm. *Aldhelm: The Prose Works*. Edited and translated by Michael Lapidge and Michael Herren. Cambridge and Totowa, N.J.: D. S. Brewer, 1985.
Ambrose. *De virginibus*. Critical ed. by Ignazio Cazzaniga. Corpus scriptorum latinorum Paravianum. Torino, Italy: Paravia, 1948.
———. *De virginitate*. Critical ed. by Ignazio Cazzaniga. Corpus scriptorum latinorum Paravianum. Torino: Paravia, 1954.
———. *On Virginity*. Translated by Daniel Callam. Toronto: Peregrina, 1989.
Ancrene Wisse: Guide for Anchoresses. Translated by Hugh White. London and New York, 1991.
Augustine of Hippo. *De bono coniugali; De sancta uirginitate*. Edited and translated by P. G. Walsh. Oxford Early Christian texts. Oxford: Clarendon Press; New York: Oxford University Press, 2001.
Clemence of Barking. See under Wogan-Browne and Burgess, below.
Gilbert of Sempringham. *The Book of St. Gilbert*. Translated and edited by Raymonde Foreville and Gillian Keir. Oxford and New York: Oxford University Press, 1987.
Hali Meidhad. Edited by Bella Millett. Early English Text Society, 284. Oxford: Oxford University Press, 1982.
Handmaids of the Lord: Contemporary Descriptions of Female Asceticism in the First Six Christian Centuries. Translated and edited by Joan M. Peterson. Cistercian Studies, 143. Kalamazoo, Mich.: Cistercian Publications, 1996. [Selections of writings by various early Christian women].

Hildegard of Bingen. *The Letters of Hildegard of Bingen.* Vol. I. Translated by Joseph L. Baird and Radd K. Ehrman. New York and Oxford: Oxford University Press, 1994.

Isidore of Seville. *Etymologiarum sive originum libri XX.* Edited by Wallace M. Lindsay, Vol. 2: Book 11: 2, 22; Book 12: 1, 32. Oxford: Clarendon Press, 1911.

Jacobus de Voragine. [*Legenda aurea*, English]. *The Golden Legend: Readings on the Saints.* Translated with commentary by William Granger Ryan. 2 vols. Princeton, N.J.: Princeton University Press, 1993.

Jerome. *The Letters of St. Jerome.* Translated by C. Mierow. Introduction and Notes by Thomas C. Lawler. New York: Newman Press, 1963.

Servius. *In Vergilii Bucolica et Georgica Commentarii.* Edited by G. Thilo, 34. Leipzig: Teubner, 1887.

Winstead, Karen A. *Chaste passions: Medieval English Virgin Martyr Legends.* Edited and translated by Karen A. Winstead. Ithaca, N.Y.: Cornell University Press, 2000.

———. *Virgin Martyrs: Legends of Sainthood in Late Medieval England.* Ithaca, N.Y.: Cornell University Press, 1997.

Wogan-Browne, Jocelyn, and Glyn S. Burgess, eds. and transs. *Virgin Lives and Holy Deaths: Two Exemplary Biographies for Anglo-Norman Women.* London: J. M. Dent; Rutland, Vt.: Charles E. Tuttle, 1996. [Clemence of Barking's life of St. Catherine of Alexandria and an anonymous life of Laurence of Rome, trans. from Anglo-Norman, with notes].

Secondary Sources

Allen, Michael R. *The Cult of Kumari: Virgin Worship in Nepal.* 3rd revised and enlarged ed. Kathmandu, Nepal: Mandala Book Point, 1996.

Aspegren, Kerstin. *The Male Woman: A Feminine Ideal in the Early Church.* Uppsala, Sweden and Stockholm: Academia Ubsaliensis/Almquist & Wiksell, 1990.

Atkinson, Clarissa. "'Precious Balsam in a Fragile Glass': The Ideology of Virginity in the Later Middle Ages." *Journal of Family History* 8 (1983): 131–43.

Bernards, Matthäus. *Speculum virginum: Geistigkeit und Seclenleben der Frau im Hochmittelalter.* Beihefte zum Archiv für Kulturgeschichte, 16. Cologne, Germany: Böhlau Verlag, 1955. Reprint 1982.

Bernau, Anke, Sarah Salih, and Ruth Evans, eds. *Medieval Virginities.* Cardiff: University of Wales Press, 2003.

Bitel, Lisa M. *Land of Women: Tales of Sex and Gender from Early Ireland.* Ithaca, N.Y. and London: Cornell University Press, 1996.

Brown, Peter. *The Body and Society: Men, Women, and Sexual Renunciation in Early Christianity.* Lectures on the History of Religions, n.s. 13. New York: Columbia University Press, 1988.

Brundage, James A. *Law, Sex, and Christian Society in Medieval Europe.* Chicago and London: University of Chicago Press, 1987.

Bugge, John. *Virginitas: An Essay in the History of a Medieval Ideal.* The Hague: Martinus Nijhoff, 1975.

Bührer-Thierry, Genevieve, "La reine adultère." *Cahiers de Civilisation Médiévale* 35 (1992): 299–312.

Bullough, Vern, and James A. Brundage, eds. *Sexual Practices and the Medieval Church.* Buffalo: Prometheus Books, 1982.

Bynum, Caroline Walker. *Holy Feast and Holy Fast: The Religious Significance of Food to Medieval Women.* Berkeley: University of California Press, 1987.

Castelli, Elizabeth. "Virginity and Its Meaning for Women's Sexuality in Early Christianity." *Journal of Feminist Studies in Religion* 2 (1986): 61–88.

Chamberlayne, Joanna L. "Crowns and Virgins: Queenmaking during the Wars of the Roses." In *Young Medieval Women,* edited by Katherine J. Lewis, Noel J. Menuge, and Kim M. Phillips, 47–68. New York: St. Martin's, 1999.

"Chasteté." *Dictionnaire de Spiritualité,* 2. 1: 777–810. Paris: Beauchesne, 1937–1967.

"Chasteté." *Dictionnaire de Théologie Catholique* 2.2: 2319–31. Paris: Letouzey, 1908–1950.

Clark, Elizabeth A. *Ascetic Piety and Women's Faith: Essays on Late Ancient Christianity.* Studies in Women and Religion, 20. Lewiston, N.Y.: Edwin Mellen Press, 1986.

Clayton, Mary. *The Cult of the Virgin Mary in Anglo-Saxon England.* Cambridge and New York: Cambridge University Press, 1990.

Coon, Lynda. L. *Sacred Fictions: Holy Women and Hagiography in Late Antiquity.* Philadelphia: University of Pennsylvania Press, 1997.

Cooper, Kate. *The Virgin and the Bride: Idealized Womanhood in Late Antiquity.* Cambridge, Mass.: Harvard University Press, 1996.

Dixon, Laurinda. "The Curse of Chastity: The Marginalization of Women in Medieval Art and Medicine." In *Matrons and Marginal Women in Medieval Society*, edited by Robert R. Edwards and Vickie L. Ziegler, 49–74. Woodbridge, Suffolk, U.K.: Boydell Press, 1995.

Dumm, Demetrius. *The Theological Basis of Virginity According to St. Jerome.* Latrobe, Pa.: St. Vincent Archabbey, 1961.

Elliot, Dyan. *Spiritual Marriage: Sexual Abstinence in Medieval Wedlock.* Princeton, N.J.: Princeton University Press, 1993.

Evans, Ruth. "Virginities." In *The Cambridge Companion to Medieval Women's Writing*, edited by Carolyn Dinshaw and David Wallace, 21–39. Cambridge: Cambridge University Press, 2003.

Gilchrist, Roberta. *Gender and Material Culture: The Archaeology of Religious Women.* London and New York: Routledge, 1994.

Hollis, Stephanie. *Anglo-Saxon Women and the Church: Sharing a Common Fate.* Woodbridge, Suffolk, U.K. and Rochester, N.Y.: Boydell Press, 1992.

Hollywood, Amy. *The Soul as Virgin Wife: Mechthild of Magdeburg, Marguerite Porete and Meister Eckhart.* Notre Dame, Ind. and London: University of Notre Dame Press, 1995.

Kelly, Kathleen Coyne. *Performing Virginity and Testing Chastity in the Middle Ages.* Routledge Research in Medieval Studies, 2. London and New York: Routledge, 2000.

———, and Marina Leslie, eds. *Menacing Virgins; Representing Virginity in the Middle Ages and Renaissance.* Newark: University of Delaware Press; London: Associated University Presses, 1999.

Makowski, Elizabeth M. *Canon Law and Cloistered Women: Periculoso and its Commentators, 1298–1545.* Studies in Medieval and Early Modern Canon Law, 5. Washington, D.C.: Catholic University of America Press, 1997.

McInerney, Maud Burnett. *Eloquent Virgins from Thecla to Joan of Arc.* New York: Palgrave/Macmillan, 2003.

McNamara, Jo Ann. "A New Song: Celibate Women of the First Three Christian Centuries." *Women and History* 6–7 (1983).

———. "Sexual Equality and the Cult of Virginity in Early Christian Thought." *Feminist Studies* 3 (1976): 145–58.

———. *Sisters in Arms: Catholic Nuns through Two Millennia.* Cambridge, Mass. and London: Harvard University Press, 1996.

Metz, René. *La Consécration des vierges dans l'église romaine: étude d'histoire de la liturgie.* Paris: Presses Universitaires de France, 1954.

Mews, Constant J., ed. *Listen, Daughter: The Speculum virginum and the Formation of Medieval Religious Women in the Middle Ages.* Basingstoke, U.K. and New York: Palgrave, 2001.

Miles, Margaret R. *Carnal Knowing: Female Nakedness and Religious Meaning in the Christian West.* Boston: Beacon Press, 1991.

Newman, Barbara. *From Virile Woman to WomanChrist: Studies in Medieval Religion and Literature.* Philadelphia: University of Pennsylvania Press, 1995.

Nightlinger, Elizabeth. "The Female *Imitatio Christi* and Medieval Popular Religion: The Case of St. Wilgefortis." In *Representations of the Feminine in the Middle Ages: Feminea Medievalia*, edited by Bonnie Wheeler, 1: 291–328. Dallas, Texas: Academia, 1993.

Nugent, M. Rosamond. *Portrait of the Consecrated Woman in Greek Christian Literature of the First Four Centuries.* Washington D.C.: Catholic University of America Press, 1941.

Reynolds, Roger E. "*Virgines subintroductae* in Celtic Christianity." *Harvard Theological Review* 61 (1968): 547–66.

Salih, Sarah. *Versions of Virginity in Late Medieval England.* Cambridge: D. S. Brewer, 2001.

Salisbury, Joyce E. *Church Fathers, Independent Virgins.* London and New York: Verso, 1991.

———. "Fruitful in Singleness." *Journal of Medieval History* 8 (1981): 97–106.

Schulenburg, Jane T. *Forgetful of Their Sex: Female Sanctity and Society, ca. 500–1100*. Chicago and London: University of Chicago Press, 1998.

———. "Saints and Sex, ca. 500-1100: Striding Down the Nettled Path of Life." In *Sex in the Middle Ages: A Book of Essays*, edited by Joyce E. Salisbury, 203–31. Garland Medieval Casebooks, vol. 3, New York and London: Garland, 1991.

———. "Strict Active Enclosure and Its Effects on the Female Monastic Experience (ca. 500–1100)." In *Medieval Religious Women, I: Distant Echoes*, edited by John A. Nichols and Lillian Thomas Shank, 51–86. Kalamazoo, Mich.: Cistercian Publications, 1984.

"Virginité chrétienne." *Dictionnaire de Spiritualité*. 16: 924–49. Paris: Beauchesne, 1937–1967.

"Virginity," *New Catholic Encyclopedia*. 14: 701–04. 2nd ed. Detroit: Thomson/Gale; Washington, D.C.: Catholic University of America, 2003.

Warner, Marina. *Alone of All Her Sex: The Myth and Cult of the Virgin Mary*. New York: Knopf, 1976.

Weinstein, Donald, and Rudolf M. Bell. *Saints and Society: The Two Worlds of Western Christendom, 1000–1700*. Chicago and London: University of Chicago Press, 1982.

Wemple, Suzanne F. *Women in Frankish Society: Marriage and the Cloister, 500 to 900*. Philadelphia: University of Pennsylvania Press, 1981.

Wiethaus, Ulrike. "Sexuality, Gender, and the Body in Late Medieval Women's Spirituality." *Journal of Feminist Studies in Religion* 7 (1991): 35–52.

Wogan-Browne, Jocelyn. *Saints' Lives and Women's Literary Culture c. 1150–1300: Virginity and Its Authorizations*. Oxford and New York: Oxford University Press, 2001.

JANE TIBBETTS SCHULENBURG

VISCONTI, VALENTINA (c.1370–1408). Valentina Visconti was the controversial Italian-born wife of Louis, duke of Orléans and younger brother of Charles VI of France. Valentina, the daughter of Gian Galeazzo Visconti, duke of Milan, and of Isabelle of Valois, married Louis, then duke of Touraine, in 1389. In early 1396, pregnant with her fifth child, she left Paris and the royal court due to rumors that she had bewitched the king. Charles VI had become mentally ill in 1392, and during his psychotic episodes he tended to recognize Valentina but oftentimes not his own wife, a circumstance that evidently caused wild speculation as people sought to understand and explain his condition. It seems that Valentina did not return to Paris until her dramatic entry of December 10, 1407, when she begged the king to prosecute the persons who had murdered her husband in November. She then focused on justice and vengeance and on disproving the accusations made by the duke of Burgundy against Louis. Her fixation no doubt significantly influenced her young son, Charles of Orléans, who, after her untimely death, continued her program with a stubbornness that helped push France into a civil war that encouraged eventual English intervention.

Among contemporaries, opinions about Valentina's character varied. The chronicler Froissart (c.1337–post-1404) despised her, and prolific poet and public figure Eustache Deschamps (c.1346–c.1406) and moralist Honorat Bovet (c.1345–c.1410), whom historians used to call Honoré Bouvet or Bonet, championed her. Valentina's reaction to her husband's infidelity is not known, but she was used to the amorous habits of the Visconti men, who produced a significant number of bastards, and she prized her husband's illegitimate son Jean (the famous "Dunois" or "Bastard of Orléans"), who was associated with Joan of Arc and who praised Joan at her nullification trial.

See also Christine de Pizan; Joan of Arc, St.; *Miroir de Mariage* (*Mirror of Marriage*)

BIBLIOGRAPHY

Primary Sources

Camus, J. "La venue en France de Valentine Visconti, duchesse d'Orléans, et l'inventaire de ses joyaux apportés de Lombardie." *Miscellanea di storia italiana* 3rd ser. 5 (1900): 1–64.

Graves, Frances M. *Quelques pièces relatives à la vie de Louis I, duc d'Orléans et de Valentine Visconti, sa femme.* Paris: Honoré Champion, 1913.

Secondary Sources

Collas, Emile. *Valentine de Milan, duchesse d'Orléans.* Paris: Plon-Nourrit, 1911.

Comani, Francesco E. "I denari per la dote di Valentina Visconti." *Archivio storico lombardo* (1901): 37–82.

Coville, Alfred. "Les derniers jours de Valentine Visconti, duchesse d'Orléans (23 novembre 1407–4 décembre 1408)." *Institut de France. Séance publique annuelle des cinq Académies* (*25 octobre 1929*): 35–50.

Famiglietti, R. C. *Royal Intrigue. Crisis at the Court of Charles VI (1392–1420).* New York: AMS, 1986.

Faucon, Maurice. "Le mariage de Louis d'Orléans et de Valentine Visconti." *Archives des missions scientifiques et littéraires* 3rd ser. 8 (1882): 39–99.

Guenée, Bernard. *Un meurtre, une société. L'assassinat du duc d'Orléans, 23 novembre 1407.* Paris: NRF/Gallimard, 1992.

Romano, G. "Valentina Visconti e il suo matrimonio con Luigi di Turaine." *Archivio storico lombardo* (1898): 5–27.

Shultz, C. R. "The Artistic and Literary Patronage of Louis of Orléans and his wife, Valentine Visconti, 1389–1408." Ph.D. diss., Emory University, 1977.

RICHARD C. FAMIGLIETTI

WALBURGE. *See* **Leoba**

WALDETRUDE. *See* **Aldegund, St.**

WALLĀDAH (994–1077/1091). The renowned princess and poetess of al-Andalus, or Muslim Spain, Wallādah was the beautiful, headstrong daughter of the Umayyad caliph, Muhammad III al-Mustakfī, who ruled al-Andalus from 1023 to 1025. For centuries her fame was preserved almost exclusively through the poetry of her lover, Ibn Zaydūn (1003–1071), the most illustrious Hispano-Arabic love poet of his time. His verses documenting their amorous relationship are quoted anonymously in the *Thousand and One Nights* and are considered perhaps the most accomplished of all Hispano-Arabic (or Arab-Andalusian) poetry.

During the century of Wallādah's birth, al-Andalus encompassed all but the north-western portion of Spain. Her birthplace, Córdoba, was not only the caliphate's capital (pop. 100,000), but also a preeminent cultural nexus of East and West, rivaled only by Cairo or Constantinople, and far outstripping northern capitals such as Paris and London in the quality of life, literacy, and artistic accomplishment enjoyed by its citizens. By Wallādah's time, Spanish and Arabic cultures had so thoroughly intermingled that approximately eighty percent of the native Spaniards had converted to Islam; even among those who remained Christian, the majority communicated in Arabic (Marín-Guzmán). In contrast to this pervasive prosperity and enlightenment, political chaos characterized the period in which Wallādah lived. In 1009–1010, warring factions of Arabs and Berbers razed the magnificent palace of al-Zahrā near the center of Córdoba. The ruins of al-Zahrā later became the uniquely lovely meeting place described in Ibn Zaydūn's poetry to Wallādah. In 1023, her father's predecessor as caliph of Córdoba was dragged from hiding and butchered in al-Mustakfī's presence. Despite his reputation as a detestable character interested only in the pleasures of sex and eating, her father succeeded al-Raḥmān as caliph, becoming Muḥammad III. But after only seventeen months, while fleeing his enemies in the disguise of a singing girl, he was poisoned by one of his own officers. By 1031, as Wallādah became a mature woman, the Umayyad Caliphate failed, and Córdoba's dominance was diffused among nearby city-states. Despite such reigning chaos, artistic life continued to flourish, with poetry emerging as the preferred literary form, practiced among all classes ranging from caliphs and statesmen to washerwomen and slave girls. Verses not only communicated invitations, excuses, and insults, they also decorated the walls and fountains of the finest palaces.

The career of Wallādah's lover, Ibn Zaydūn, epitomizes the ideal, if embattled, life of a privileged citizen of this realm. Immediately following the fall of Córdoba's caliphate, the chief magistrate in the new city administration, Ibn Jahwar, named Ibn Zaydūn as his confidential minister for Jewish-Christian affairs. Soon, however, the poet's love for Wallādah provoked intrigue at court and the jealousy of a fellow minister, Ibn Abdūs, who accused Ibn Zaydūn of plotting to return power to the Umayyads, thus causing the poet to be imprisoned. But Ibn Zaydūn escaped, and became an ambassador to other states under the next regime. He went on to serve the courts of two rulers of Seville. Despite his political expertise, Ibn Zaydūn's fame rests primarily on his poetry, particularly his poems to Wallādah, considered to be among his best (see Jayyusi). Poets such as Ibn Zaydūn breathed new life into the principal poetic genre at that time, the *qaṣīda*, a sort of ode without stanzas allowing for no less than full-syllable rhyming. Most notable is his famous "*Qaṣīda* in Nūn," or "Nūniyya" ("Ode in 'Nun'"), fragments of which made their way, albeit anony-

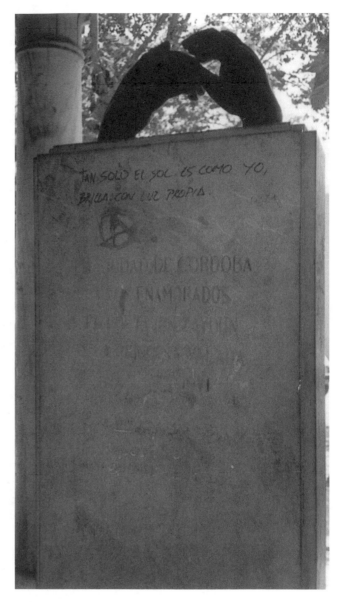

Two clasped hands adorn the monument to lovers Wallādah and Ibn Zaydūn, in Córdoba. Photograph courtesy of Lee Gallo.

mously, into the fifteenth-century collection that became known as the *Thousand and One Nights* (*Arabian Nights* = *Alf laylah wa-laylah*). The "Nūniyya" has also found a place in recent collections of Hispano-Arabic poetry (Monroe). In fact, a major modern scholar, Emilio García Gómez, has published and praised Ibn Zaydūn's "Nūniyya," inspired by Wallādah, with its clever repetition of the rhymed word "nā" (= "our"), as the most beautiful in all Hispano-Arabic love poetry.

Wallādah was also a literary personality in her own right. The seventeenth-century historian and biographer, al-Maqqarī, considers her the worthiest of the poetesses of Muslim Spain, a group whose works and lives were anthologized in the 1980s (Garulo;

Rubiera Mata). Less enthusiastic critics have categorized Wallādah as one of the women poets who survived because of their affiliation with some prominent male figure. The works of the Hispano-Arabic poetesses Ḥafṣah and Nazhūn were preserved for the obscene nature of their verses, a trait generally attributed to Eastern influences (Hoenerbach). But in many cases, the literary posterity of the group endures as the result of pure chance and even then in only fragmentary fashion. Wallādah secured her fame through a mixture of chance and self-determinism. After her father's murder, she opened her home as a literary salon, whereby she gained wide repute for her contests with fellow poets.

Her reported physical beauty further enhanced her mystique: her light skin, blue eyes, and reddish-blond hair may be traced to her Christian-slave mother. Inevitably, descriptions of her morality are less uniformly favorable, with some contemporary biographers including unsubstantiated suggestions of a lesbian relationship with the young poetess, Muhya, whom Wallādah had taken under her wing (Hoenerbach). In any case, the apt pupil would later use her education to satirize her mentor (Garulo). Wallādah defied the *Quran* (*Koran*), the sacred book of Islam, by leaving the harem, refusing to wear a veil, and communicating openly with males outside her family. Such behavior fostered perceptions of her as an unfit princess. Following the tradition of Baghdad, she had two verses embroidered on her robe: "God has destined me for glory," and "I let my lover touch my cheek, and offer my kiss to whoever wishes it." Such unseemly, immodest advertisements could not have helped her moral reputation, nor could her fondness for citing from the infamous poet Abū Nuwās, either revered or reviled among Córdobans for his obscenity and frivolity. Biographers have thus referred to her both as the Sappho and the George Sand of her time. Explanations for her remarkable independence include her status as a wealthy noble growing up in an urban Western environment and the fact that she had no real tribe—no father, brother, or husband—to suffer any resultant shame. Although Wallādah never married (ironically her name means fecund), she maintained a lasting friendship with Ibn Abdūs, whom some say she did marry, and who apparently supported her into her eighties, despite his modest means. The date of her death according to such chroniclers as Ibn Bassan was 1077, whereas Ibn Bâskuwāl calculates it as 1091 (Garulo).

Her extant work includes no *kharja* or *muwashshah*—Hispano-Arabic poetic forms often featuring women's voices—but rather nine short poems (a possible tenth, in a man's voice, is usually attributed to Ibn Zaydūn). These display remarkable eloquence, ingenuity, wit, and learning. Although the extant poetry amounts to fewer than fifty lines, it demonstrates a wide emotional range—tenderness, yearning, vulnerability, despair, disillusionment, haughtiness, volatility, vindictiveness, and vulgarity—as her affair with Ibn Zaydūn evolves. Among her works is an early poem in which she cautions him to arrive on time for a rendezvous scheduled after dark to avoid scandal. Here she confesses a passion more powerful than the forces of nature: one that could "impede the sun's brilliance, cause the moon to flee, and the stars to run away." Later in their affair she wrote him a sincere and vulnerable love lyric or *ghazal*. In this, her longest extant work, she complains of frustrations common to all lovers: separation and incompleteness. She finds herself powerless to escape passion's "embers" and laments: "Time passes, yet I see no end to your long absence,/Nor does patience free me from the bondage of yearning." She then closes the poem with the verse, "May God cause abundant rains in the land where you dwell." For some critics, this poem may imply a death wish. In any case, Ibn Zaydūn responded with a poem assuring her of his affection, accompanied by a subtle critique of her previously mentioned verse beginning "Time passes." It may have been this criticism that prompted a sudden change in her feelings, or it may have been her suspicion of his having an affair with her black slave. That suspicion inspired a fourth poem to him, reprimanding him for choosing "Jupiter" (the dark planet) when already he possessed the "full moon." His own poetry suggests guilt when he refers to the possibility of having committed an error, as he fervently pleads with her to take him back.

Whether she had become depressed over their long periods of separation, outraged by Ibn Zaydūn's criticism of her verses, incensed over his possible infidelity or simply tired of him, it was at this point that Wallādah broke off their romance for good and took Ibn Abdūs as her new suitor with whom she remained through old age. Although historians describe Ibn Abdūs as vain, boring, and intellectually inferior to her, such faults did not deter her from dedicating to him a poem—of only two lines—comparing him to Egypt and praising his generosity. Meanwhile, as a last ploy to win back his beloved, Ibn Zaydūn composed a biting satirical letter against Ibn Abdūs and sent it to Wallādah, requesting that she use it to reject her new lover. Although the letter would win praise for its literary qualities, its author's scheme backfired. Perhaps with Wallādah's complicity, as some historians speculate, Ibn Abdūs avenged himself by having Ibn Zaydūn arrested on trumped-up charges. Wallādah's poetic revenge was the satirical "Hexagon," so titled because it deploys six epithets against Ibn Zaydūn: "thief" (referring to Ibn Abdūs's charge against him) and—with the accusation of sexual deviance typical of many female lovers' invectives, regardless of nationality—"pederast, catamite, fornicator, wittol, and cuckold" (Nichols's translation). In another satire she irreverently mixes allusions to sodomy with references to religious miracles. This poem, like the previous one, paradoxically begins by lauding Ibn Zaydūn's virtues and merits only to turn bitterly sarcastic soon thereafter. By some interpretations, he is metaphorically reduced to his anus which, on spying a desirable male organ perched in a palm tree, transforms itself into a bird. As for the two other extant poems, also satirical, one depicts Wallādah lamenting that the virtuous Ibn Zaydūn curses her unjustly and looks at her as if she were going to castrate his dear servant, Ali; while in the other, she accuses one al-Asbah of selling his son's sexual favors for his own gain.

Wallādah lived among a generation of poets often identified as influential in the development of courtly love ideals among the troubadours and their female counterparts, the *trobairitz*. Her contemporaries contributed the infusion of Neoplatonic elements—such as spiritual and divine language to elevate human love—into secular poetics; for example, precepts from the *Dove's Neck Ring* (*Risála*) of Ibn Hazm are highly evident in Ibn Zaydūn's "Nūniyya" (Monroe). In fact, Henri Pérès has interpreted the relationship between Wallādah and Ibn Zaydūn as particularly exemplary of the courtly love tradition. Today, as if her many years with Ibn Abdūs had never been, a simple monument of two clasped hands stands in the center of Córdoba, commemorating the poets Wallādah and Ibn Zaydūn. Nearby, the most important ongoing Spanish-Islamic archaeological excavation of the last century continues at the site of the lovers' meeting place, the remains of the al-Zahrā palace.

See also *Chanson de Femme* (Women's Song); *Kharja*; Music, Women Composers and Musicians; *Muwashshaḥ*; *Trobairitz*

BIBLIOGRAPHY

Primary Sources
The Arabian Nights = *Alf laylah wa-laylah*. Edited by Muhsin Mahdi. Translated by Husain Haddawy. New York: Norton, 1990.

García Gómez, Emilio, ed. *Qasídas de Andalucía, puestas en verso castellano*. Madrid: Plutarco, 1940.

Garulo, Teresa, ed. *Díwán de las poetisas de al-Andalus*. Madrid: Hiperión, 1985, esp. 141–46. [Spanish trans. with biographies].

Ibn Hazm. *A Book Containing the* Risála *Known as the Dove's Neck Ring, About Love and Lovers*. Edited and translated by A. R. Nykl. Paris: Paul Guenther, 1931.

Ibn Zaydūn al Makhzūmi. *Dīwān*. Edited by Y. Farhāt. Beirut, 1991. [Arabic text only].

———. *The Dīwān of Ibn Zaidun al Makhzumi*. Translated by Arthur Wormhoudt. Oskaloosa, Iowa: William Penn College, 1973. [Arabic and English texts].

———. "Nūniyya." In Monroe (*see below*), 178–87. [Arabic text with English trans.].

Rubiera Mata, María Jesus, ed. *Poesía femenina hispano-árabe*. Madrid: Castalia/Instituto de la Mujer, 1989.

Sobh, Mahmud [Mohammed Subh], ed. *Poetisas arábigo-andaluzas/Shawain al-Andalusiyat*. Granada: Diputaciòn provincial, 1986. [Arabic texts, Spanish trans.].

Secondary Sources
Abu-Haider, J. A. *Hispano-Arabic Poetry and the Early Provençal Lyrics*. Richmond, Surrey, U.K.: Curzon, 2001.

Asfaruddin, Asma. "Poetry and Love: The Feminine Contribution in Muslim Spain." *Islamic Studies* 30 (1991): 157–69.

Cour, Auguste. *Un poète arabe d'Andalousie: Ibn Zaidoun; étude d'après le Díwán de ce poète et les principales sources arabes*. Constantine, Algeria: M. Boet, 1920.

Hoenerbach, Wilhelm. "Notas para una caracterización de Wallādah." *Al-Andalus* 36 (1971): 467–73. Original in German in *Die Welt des Islams* 13 (1971): 20–25.

Jayyusi, Salma Khadra, ed. *The Legacy of Muslim Spain*. Handbuch der Orientalistik, 1: Der Nahe und Mittlere Osten, 12. Leiden: E. J. Brill, 1992.

Lug, Sieglinde. *Poetic Techniques and Conceptual Elements in Ibn Zaydun's Love Poetry*. Washington, D.C.: Catholic University Press of America, 1982.

Marín-Guzmán, Roberto. "Ethnic Groups and Social Classes in Muslim Spain." *Islamic Studies* 30 (1991): 47–49.

Monroe, James T. *Hispano-Arabic Poetry: A Student Anthology*. Berkeley: University of California Press, 1974. [Excellent introduction and bilingual texts].

Nichols, James M. "Wallada, the Andalusian Lyric, and the Question of Influence." *Literature East and West* 21 (1977): 286–91.

Nykl, A[lois]. R[ichard]. "L'Influence arabe-andalouse sur les troubadours." *Bulletin Hispanique* 41 (1939): 305–15. Trans. in Nykl, *Hispano-Arabic Poetry and Its Relations with the Old Provençal Troubadours*. Baltimore: J. H. Furst, 1946.

Pérès, Henri. *La poésie Andalouse en Arabe classique au XIᵉ siècle*. Institut d'Études orientales, Faculté de Lettres d'Alger. Paris: Adrien-Maisonneuve, 1953.

LEE GALLO

WEAVERS. *See* **Spinners and Drapers**

WIDOWS. Widows of all ages were numerous throughout medieval times. They were perhaps the most visible group of single women, unlike the never-married "singlewomen," especially the poor, whose existences have gone virtually unrecorded in local archives

(Bennett and Froide; Farmer). Widows also could have more advantages than other categories of women, in the right combination of circumstances, particularly if they took care to conduct themselves respectably and prudently. Despite the dangers of childbirth, women's life spans tended to outlast men's, thanks to biology, social-military roles, and the practice of pairing younger brides with older grooms, though this was not always true. Widows' rights were protected, at least theoretically, by various secular codes and courts and also by canon law (laws governing the Church and clergy) for all classes. Laws governing widows focused on her recovery of her "mite," consisting mainly in her dower rights (her inheritance from her husband, established during the marriage arrangements) and guardianship of children.

Clerics viewed widows as the third of three main sexually based orders used to classify women, after virgins and wives. Hampered neither by virginity and parents nor by husbands, widows as sexual free agents were thus potentially suspect

A German widow, Witwentracht, in her mourning weeds, sixteenth century. Weigel's *Trachtenbuch*, reproduced in *Fuchs, Illustrierte Sittengeschichte Renaissance*, Erste Band. © Bridgeman Picture Library.

until remarriage or if they vowed themselves to chastity in some way. The fourth- and fifth-century Church Fathers (Ambrose, Jerome, Augustine) considered widowhood a "second virginity," and therefore judged these women's past sins more forgivable if they lived their widowhood virtuously. As such, they were highly valued members of congregations. To hagiographers (authors of saints' lives), it could be a gateway to sainthood, as in Florentine representations of holy women "liberated" from worldly, including carnal, bonds by their husbands' deaths. The moment of a woman's "greatest perfection" (Lawless, in Levy). Gratian's *Decretum*, the unified body of canon law (c.1142), like Roman law (sixth century), categorized the widow above and separately from "ejected" (repudiated) wives and the sinful *meretrix* (who had multiple sexual partners; *Corpus iuris canonici*, D.34 c.16). Moralists also treated secular widows as a potentially admirable category of womanhood and composed advice manuals or courtesy books for them, as in the religious zealot Girolamo Savonarola's *Libro della vita viduale* (*Book on the Widow's Life*, 1491), which counseled widows to lead lives of near-ascetic solitude and sobriety—like nuns—right down to their choice of attire. Joyce de Vries, in reading such advice as typical of male efforts to control what was perceived to be a younger widow's insatiable sexuality (an especially prevalent stereotype in Italy) and newfound freedom, adds that the *Libro* also reflects male society's need to control her financial freedom, since wealthy widows like Caterina Sforza (1463–1509), whose advisor was Savonarola, wielded exceptional power as regents, artistic patrons, and/or intellectual figures, without remarrying and without relying on their husbands' family. To a certain degree, such women were socially masculine and thus threatening—for which they were called "viragos" (see Mitchell)—an aspect they knew to counter by careful public relations, as in the type of portraits they commissioned of themselves, which deliberately downplayed their wealth and power and emphasized their ascetic, pious virtues, per society's wishes. Christine de Pizan (1364/5–1430?), in her "survival manual" for all classes of women, the *Livre des Trois Vertus* (*Book of the Three Virtues*, 1405–1406), urged widows both royal and common, young and old, to learn about and stand up for their legal rights. She also recommends conservative dress and gentle manners to maintain a good reputation, because, as always, she believes that women must learn to excel without arousing evil gossip and disrupting social order, and by working "within the system" to effect positive change. Many financially independent women did, however, retreat from worldly life into the quiet, contemplative life afforded by religious orders or at least affiliate themselves with religious houses as benefactors during the fifteenth century and later (de Vries).

Beyond moral advice and other theological "widow theory" lie questions of medieval canon law in actual practice. As James Brundage has analyzed, canon law recognized widows as disadvantaged persons and provided for them accordingly to offset inadequacies in common or civil law. Canon law policies seem even to have been implemented in practice: for example, canonical court lawyers appear to have acted, even conscientiously, on behalf of poor widows without fee.

Information on how widows dealt with their condition appears to be most plentiful among noblewomen. Linda Mitchell affirms that English and Welsh noble widows could exercise almost as much power as their late husbands—they could draw up their own wills and those for others (see also Lewis in Menuge), hire and fire attorneys and estate managers, recruit their own militias (from which they could supply the king's armies), litigate in the courts, buy and sell property, function as guardians for their children and arrange their marriages, become patrons for religious houses—but could not hold political or religious office. For London, much data can be gleaned from the records of the Husting Court of Deeds and Wills and the Husting Court of Common Pleas. These were common courts, as opposed to royal courts, and thus produce a broader sampling (see Hanawalt 1992; Hawkes, in Menuge). These sources indicate that London widows were well provided for by the city's law, even if no written proof of the dower arrangement existed. If a widow had produced children, she was entitled to one-third of the husband's estate for life; another third went to the children and the final third to the church, for the good of the husband's soul, as was then believed. A London widow with no children received half the estate. The widow also was awarded the principal connubial dwelling (tenement), in dire cases at least the living space of the tenement (Hanawalt 1992). Similar records in Florence and other Tuscan cities have also been studied. Widows there—even the aristocrats—had to contend with a more adversely patriarchal system (Crabb, in Mirrer; Herlihy and Klapisch-Zuber). Florentine widows (fourteenth and fifteenth centuries) whose husband's heirs had deprived her of her dower and/or her home, could resort to a right of refuge in her family since birth called the *tornata* (Klapisch-Zuber). Urban widows dealt with different problems from those of rural populations, although basic legal principles remained the same: a widow had to know how to fend for herself in real life regardless of whatever rights existed for her on paper. Along with the stereotypical beleaguered widow also emerged the derisive one of the scheming, avaricious widow, doubtless first sketched by harried law clerks.

Royal and noble widows, whether in Spain (see Estow, in Mirrer), England (see Mitchell, in Mirrer), France (see Christine de Pizan, *Trois Vertus*; Miskimin, in Mirrer), or elsewhere in Europe, although they usually inherited their husband's power at least temporarily, often suffered from public prejudice against women in power unless they were extremely adept at domestic diplomacy. These difficulties were in addition to the challenges they faced in ruling their husband's realm, especially during wartime (see Rosenthal, in Mirrer). Some once-powerful Carolingian and Anglo-Saxon royal widows (ninth to eleventh centuries), including Emma, her mother Adelaide of Burgundy and grandmother Bertha of Arles, Richildis, and Sexberga, returned to the protection of home near or with family after their downfall or repudiation in remarriage, either to retire in nunneries or to live with their ruling sons or by themselves on dower lands from a previous marriage (Stafford). In Occitania (southern France) a widow head of household retained her status as *domna* (lady), and could act as a free agent in land transactions (see Smith in Menuge).

In urban societies, Barbara Hanawalt and Anna Dronzek have determined marked differences among the cities of London, Florence, and Ghent in the fates of widows' dowry and dower. Florentine society was so patrilineal that the husband's family tended to try to keep the widow's dowry (the goods she had brought to the marriage as a bride), while she either resided with them or returned to her kin. In London and Ghent, widows controlled their dower for life.

A townswoman whose husband's apprentices had not completed their training before he died was allowed by certain guilds to complete his training, but not to take on new apprentices. These guilds might also allow her to continue her husband's trade or craft if she proved competent enough, particularly if demand for the product were high and the workforce low. However, these women usually toiled for lower wages (Shahar). In England, France, Austria, and Germany, some Jewish widows earned a living, sometimes quite successfully, through moneylending, either alone or through family networks (Tallan).

Among the less fortunate, Parisian and English city records counted many single women heads of household among their fiscally poor. These women possessed insufficient dower and could not earn enough on their own (textile work, ale brewing, inn-keeping and similar posts were the most common trades) without resorting to prostitution. Charitable institutions, hospices for women, were endowed by wealthy patrons to shelter widows and reform prostitutes in and around Paris (ten within the city by 1342). But on entering them, the widow probably relinquished much of her independence (Farmer, in Bennett and Froide). Others became domestic servants, as recorded in northern European rolls of the thirteenth to fifteenth centuries. In the early Middle Ages, many joined religious communities. As urban areas developed during what historians interpret as an explosion in lay piety, devout widows, particularly those willing to do penitential manual labor or who were wealthy enough to pay their way, joined lay religious communities such as the Beguines, or gave over their dower to a Second Order (e.g., Poor Clares, Benedictines) to become fully professed nuns. Fortunately, if they had no dependents living with them, these widows were mobile and often used this freedom to leave their conjugal home after their husbands died and seek better wages. Recent demographic historians now count medieval widow migrations as an important statistic, pointing to the fact that, while young men moved about in search of livelihoods much more than did young women, large numbers of older women—usually widows—were forced into nomadism for the same reasons (Farmer 2002). Poor Jewish women in Europe or Egypt, without children or whose children could not or would not help them, could evidently collect some support from charity funds (Tallan; Goitein).

However, Jewish widows in northern Europe enjoyed reasonable benefits by Jewish law. They could not inherit from their husbands beyond what was set down in their *ketubbah* (marriage document), but this wedding-day provision in itself comprised a *nedunya'* (dowry) plus a set sum as prescribed by the Babylonian Talmud (late fifth-century compilation of Jewish law). The widow had absolute control over these assets once she received them and could manage them however she wished (Tallan). In disputes arising from other relatives' attempts to deprive of her rights, she would go before the local rabbi for a judgment. The rabbi, following Jewish law, functioned analogously to the civil courts in gentile societies.

Peasant widows, even those of serfs, had some rights, although dower regulations were observed in varying ways in different locales even within the same country. In general, these widows too received one-third to one-half of her deceased husband's landed property for the duration of her lifetime. If she remarried, a widow risked losing her dower in some areas, but more often was permitted to retain it, which occasioned tensions between her and her offspring and/or her husband's family—to be resolved, sometimes after protracted bitter legal battles, in the courts. The peasant widow was usually also entitled to one-third of the household goods, with another third divided among the offspring and the final third either given to a specific heir designated by the deceased husband or, more commonly, donated to a local church (Shahar). Landholding peasant widows living by themselves were probably among the most fortunate class, since they owned valuable property and yet enjoyed more freedom than their upper-class counterparts (Shahar; Rosenthal in Mirrer), although, as Judith Bennett admonishes after meticulously examining the English community of Brigstock, more nuanced appraisals are required of what rural women really did with their freedom, if and when it really existed (Bennett 1992).

Remarriage patterns varied throughout Europe, across both social ranks and geographic regions. Males—widowers—at least according to English records, remarried far more easily and frequently than women, so much so that records of widowers are scarcer than those for widows (Bennett, in Mirrer). Northwestern European widows frequently remarried, whereas in Italy and much of southern Europe, they rarely remarried (Farmer 2002). In late Barbarian Germany, a man wishing to marry a widow paid a sum called a *reipus* to her family. Frankish German law also influenced canon law in prohibiting a man from marrying his brother's widow (Herlihy 1985). In Florence (northern Italy), two-thirds of women widowed before age twenty remarried, but a sharp decrease in remarriage percentages occurs for women after the age of forty (Klapisch-Zuber). Florentine widows who did not remarry after forty underwent significant social slippage as they became increasingly impoverished with age. As David Herlihy assesses it, though women depended on marriage to define their status, Florentine marriage patterns treated them cruelly (Herlihy 1985). The in-laws of the Florentine widow often barred remarriage to enable them to keep her dowry. One might expect, in precious testimony from a female perspective offered by Christine de Pizan, a young widow of urban middle-class Italian birth but of French citizenry and with English connections, to embody a revealing fifteenth-century convergence of custom. But it is her woman's side that speaks to this aspect, with no mention of dower and family (which she covers earlier); she advises with the widow's personal well-being in mind. She cautions against remarriage for older, wealthy widows, since they have no need of it and risk unhappiness if they make the wrong choice in their new mate; younger widows may stand a better chance of a happy remarriage. She emphasizes the need for widows to develop and trust their own judgment (*Trois Vertus*, 193; *Treasure*, 159–60). Peasant widows choosing not to remarry cultivated their land holdings alone or with hired laborers, or gave their properties to their sons with some sort of agreement providing for her maintenance and protection during the remainder of her life. In other situations, a lord of the manor pressed a peasant widow to remarry (another peasant) to guarantee the supply of crops, labor, or other services due the lord—or, if she did not wish to remarry right then or to that prospective groom chosen by the lord, the widow could pay a sum to the lord. Other widows, such as those in Montaillou, chose to live as a communal household (Shahar). Jewish widows could remarry with rabbinical approval. In cases of "levirate widows" (whose husbands had died without fathering children), these women either had to marry the late husband's brother or be released from this obligation by the brother (Tallan).

Guardianship of children by the mother after the father's death was not automatic, especially among the nobility and if a large inheritance were at stake, in which case the mother/widow often had to contend with several lords, or overlords, even the king. Feudal law awarded guardianship of minor children and possession of their inherited lands to the most closely related lord until the offspring came of age. While joint wardship of either lands or children was not permitted, the children's guardian could be a different person from the one holding the land, but even this did not necessarily mean that the mother would have guardianship of her children if not the land. Undeterred, mothers sought, and sometimes won custody of children or lands or both, as evidenced in the English records known as the various Rolls (Pipe Rolls, Fine Rolls, Patent Rolls; see Walker; Menuge). However, in cities such as London, widows were the preferred guardians of their children (Hanawalt 1993), whereas in Ghent, the children were raised by the deceased husband's family (Hanawalt and Dronzek). By contrast, according to Christiane Klapisch-Zuber, late-medieval Florentine society, in its very complex, male-dominant manipulation of widows, their wealth, and children, fostered the stereotype of the widow as a heartless mother who would abandon her children as well as her husband's by any previous marriage, on his death. This image justified Florentine patriarchal society's controlling treatment of the widow. Sometimes, in order to keep her dower, she left the children with her husband's family. Medieval Jewish widows were not automatically assumed guardians of their minor children either. Once again, the husband's relatives often won this right. However, those widows who were awarded custody used their assets to govern their children's lives, for example, by paying for a son's education or for contracting marriages for a daughter (Tallan).

Whether fighting for her dower or for her children, if she must go to court as a *demanderesse* (woman plaintiff), according to Christine de Pizan, a widow must be mindful of three necessities still valid today: (1) work with and seek advice from wise, knowledgeable attorneys; (2) pursue her case with care and diligence; (3) money for legal fees (*Trois Vertus*, 191; *Treasure*, 158). In northern England, widows addressed their claims to the common law courts (see Hawkes in Menuge). By the early modern period (sixteenth century), European and English widows enjoyed the most extensive economic rights and privileges of any working women (Froide, in Bennett and Froide).

In India, for purposes of comparison, the ancient Hindu custom of *sati* (suttee), in which the widow cremates herself with the body of her dead husband, provided a dramatic way of eliminating disputes between the widow and her husband's heirs (Herlihy 1985). "Becoming sati" meant to become a good woman. Although in Hindu law a woman could choose not to perform this rite, widows' lives in premodern India were so wretched on both social and economic levels that many opted for it, knowing it would bring them eternal veneration for their courage, purity, and devotion. First noted by Greek historians in the fourth century B.C.E., scenes of widows performing sati horrified and fascinated European visitors and colonists in the early modern era, and, in a case occurring as recently as 1987, it created quite a stir worldwide. Yet protests against this custom arose even in ancient and medieval times (Sharma; Hawley).

Throughout Europe, female bereavement was a popular literary theme, especially as evidenced in Spanish and French literature (see Mirrer, pt. 4). It is perhaps most keenly and fully articulated in the lyric poetry of Christine de Pizan, writing from firsthand experience to console herself and others feeling "seulete" ("like a lonely little woman," e.g., *Cent Balades*, 11), before embarking on the more practical mode of the *Trois Vertus*. She returned to this more emotional, consolatory tone now in more public and political prose genres after the English defeated the French at Agincourt (1415), which generated tragic numbers of widows from all classes, even the most noble. Public mourning by a widow was considered appropriate both poetically and socially, though the Italian poet Petrarch (1373) wrote against excessive displays, strongly deriding public female grief at funerals. Metaphorically, in political polemics, as when the city of Rome, "bereaved" either by her fall to the Barbarians or during the Great (papal) Schism, is compared to a supplicant weeping widow by *trecento* (fourteenth-century) Italian poets (Baskins in Levy). Medieval widowhood was therefore a decisive moment overall, with personal and public, legal and financial consequences.

See also Chaucer, Alice; Chaucer, Geoffrey, Women in the Work of; Childhood and Child-Rearing in the Middle Ages; China, Women in; Christine de Pizan; Convents; Courtesy Books; Dower; Dowry; Fatimid Egypt, Women in; *Frauenfrage*; Guilds, Women in; Jewish Women in the Middle Ages; Law, Canon, Women in; Law, Women in, Anglo-Saxon England; Marriage; Matilda of Tuscany/Canossa; Norse Women; *Sachsenspiegel* and *Schwabenspiegel*; Virginity; Witches

BIBLIOGRAPHY

Primary Sources
[A mere sampling. See also notes to works listed in Secondary Sources].

Calendar of Plea and Memoranda Rolls Preserved among the Archives of the Corporation of the City of London at Guildhall. Edited by Arthur H. Thomas. 6 vols. Cambridge: Cambridge University Press, 1929. [These 6 vols. cover 1323–1482].

Calendar of Wills Proved and Enrolled in the Court of Husting, London A.D. *1258–*A.D. *1688. pt. 1 (*A.D. *1258–*A.D. *1348).* Edited, with introduction, by Reginald R. Sharp. London: J. C. Francis, 1889.

Christine de Pizan. *Cent Balades.* In *Œuvres poétiques,* edited by Maurice Roy, 1: 1–100. Société des Anciens Textes Français, 24. Paris: Firmin Didot, 1886. Reprint New York: Johnson, 1965. [French text only; some other poetry in this volume also concerns widowhood].

—————. *One Hundred Ballads* [Selections]. In *The Writings of Christine de Pizan,* [various translators] edited by Charity C. Willard, 41–48. New York: Persea, 1994.

—————. *One Hundred Ballads* [Selections]. In *The Selected Writings of Christine de Pizan,* translated by Renate Blumenfeld-Kosinski and Kevin Brownlee. Edited by R. Blumenfeld-Kosinski. Norton Critical Editions. New York: Norton, 1997.

—————. *Le Livre des Trois Vertus.* Critical ed. by Eric Hicks, 82–90, 188–93. Introduction and notes by Charity C. Willard. Bibliothèque du XVe siècle, 50. Paris: Honoré Champion, 1989.

—————. *The Treasure of the City of Ladies, or Book of the Three Virtues.* Translated and introduced by Sarah Lawson, 81–85, 156–57. Harmondsworth, U.K. and New York: Penguin, 1985.

France. Paris. Archives Nationales. Series X^{1a}, vols. 4, 48, 80.

Gratian. *Corpus iuris canonici.* Edited Emil Richter. Revised by Emil Friedberg, 1: 129. Leipzig: Tauchnitz, 1879. Reprint Graz, Austria: Akademische Druck, 1955. [*See also references in* Brundage].

London. Public Record Office: Early Chancery Proceedings. C1/108/113.

Savonarola, Girolamo. *Libro della vita viduale.* In *Operette spirituale,* edited by Mario Ferrara, 1: 9–62. *Opere di Girolamo Savonarola.* Rome: A. Belardetti, 1976.

Secondary Sources

Barron, Caroline M. "The 'Golden Age' of Women in Medieval London." *Reading Medieval Studies* 15 (1989): 35–59.

—————, and Anne F. Sutton, eds. *Medieval London Widows:1300–1500.* London: Hambledon Press, 1994.

Bennett, Judith M. "Widows in the Medieval English Countryside." In Mirrer, 69–114. *See below.*

—————, and Amy M. Froide, eds. *Singlewomen in the European Past, 1250–1800.* Philadelphia: University of Pennsylvania Press, 1999.

Brundage, James A. "Widows as Disadvantaged Persons in Medieval Canon Law." In Mirrer. 193–206. *See below.*

Carlson, Cindy L., and Angela J. Weisl, eds. *Constructions of Widowhood and Virginity in the Middle Ages.* The New Middle Ages. New York: St. Martin's Press, 1999.

Cavallo, Sandra, and Lyndan Warner, eds. *Widowhood in Medieval and Early Modern Europe.* London: Longman; Harlow, U.K. and New York: Pearson, 1999.

de Vries, Joyce. "Casting Her Widowhood: The Contemporary and Posthumous Portraits of Caterina Sforza." In Levy, 77–92. *See below.*

Farmer, Sharon. *Surviving Poverty in Medieval Paris: Gender, Ideology, and the Daily Lives of the Poor.* Conjunctions of Religion and Power in the Medieval Past. Ithaca, N.Y.: Cornell University Press, 2002.

Foehr-Janssens, Yasmina. *La Veuve en majesté: Deuil et savoir au féminine dans la littérature médiévale.* Publications romanes et françaises, 226. Geneva: Droz, 2000.

Goitein, Solomon D. *A Mediterranean Society: The Jewish Communities of the Arab World as Portrayed in the Documents of the Cairo Geniza.* 6 vols. Berkeley: University of California Press, 1967–93. [See esp. 3: 302–05].

Hanawalt, Barbara. *Growing Up in Medieval London: The Experience of Childhood in History.* New York: Oxford University Press, 1993.

—————. "The Widow's Mite: Provisions for Medieval London Widows." In Mirrer, 21–45. *See below.*

————. *The Ties That Bound: Peasant Families in Medieval England*. New York: Oxford University Press, 1986.

————, and Anna Dronzek. "Women in Medieval Urban Society." In *Women in Medieval Western European Culture*, edited by Linda E. Mitchell, 31–46. Garland Reference Library of the Humanities, 2007. New York and London: Garland, 1999.

Hawley, John S. *Sati, the Blessing and the Curse: The Burning of Wives in India*. New York and Oxford: Oxford University Press, 1994.

Herlihy, David. *Medieval Households*. Cambridge, Mass.: Harvard University Press, 1985.

————, and Christiane Klapisch-Zuber. *Les Toscans et leurs familles: une étude du "catasto" florentin de 1427*. Paris: CNRS/ FNSP/ EHSS, 1978.

————. *Tuscans and Their Families: A Study of the Florentine Catasto of 1427*. Yale Studies in Economic History. New Haven, Conn.: Yale University Press, 1985. [Abridged, rearranged translation of above].

King, Catherine. *Renaissance Women Patrons: Wives and Widows in Italy, c.1300–1550*. Manchester, U.K.: Manchester University Press, 1998.

Klapisch-Zuber, Christiane. "The 'Cruel Mother': Maternity, Widowhood, and Dowry in Florence in the Fourteenth and Fifteenth Centuries." In C. Klapisch-Zuber, *Women, Family and Ritual in Renaissance Italy*, translated by Lydia G. Cochrane, 117–31. Chicago: University of Chicago Press, 1985. Original "Maternité, veuvage et dot à Florence." *Annales, E. S. C.* 38.5 (1983): 1097–1109.

Levy, Allison, ed. *Widowhood and Visual Culture in Early Modern Europe*. Women and Gender in the Early Modern World. Aldershot, U.K. and Burlington, Vt.: Ashgate, 2003.

Loengard, Janet S. "'Of the Gift of her Husband': English Dower and Its Consequences in the Year 1200." In *Women of the Medieval World: Essays in Honor of John Hine Mundy*, edited by Julius Kirshner and Suzanne F. Wemple, 215–255. Oxford and New York: Basil Blackwell, 1985.

Menuge, Noël James. "A Few Home Truths: The Medieval Mother as Guardian in Romance and Law." In Menuge, 77–103. *See entry below*.

————, ed. *Medieval Women and the Law*. Woodbridge, U.K.: Boydell Press, 2000. Reprint 2001, 2003. [Contains several pertinent articles by medieval legal historians].

Mirrer, Louise, ed. *Upon My Husband's Death: Widows in the Literature and Histories of Medieval Europe*. Studies in Medieval and Early Modern Civilization. Ann Arbor: University of Michigan Press, 1992. [An excellent collection of essays on historical and literary aspects].

Mitchell, Linda E. *Portraits of Medieval Women: Family, Marriage, and Politics in England 1225–1350*. The New Middle Ages. New York: Palgrave/Macmillan, 2003.

Nelson, Janet L. "The Wary Widow." In *Property and Power in the Early Middle Ages*, edited by Wendy Davies and Paul Fouracre, 82–113. Cambridge: Cambridge University Press, 1995 [See IX. E. 16].

Parisse, Michel, ed. *Veuves et veuvage dans le Haut Moyen Âge. Table ronde organisée à Göttingen, mars 1991*. Paris: Picard, 1993.

Rivers, Theodore J. "The Legal Status of Widows in Late Anglo-Saxon England." *Medievalia et Humanistica* 24 (1997): 1–16.

Santinelli, Emmanuelle. *Des femmes éplorées? Les Veuves dans la société aristocratique du haut Moyen Âge*. Villeneuve-d'Asq: Presses universitaires du Septentrional, 2003.

Shahar, Shulamith. *The Fourth Estate: A History of Women in the Middle Ages*. Translated by Chaya Galai. Revised ed. London and New York: Routledge, 2003.

Sharma, Arvind, et al. *Sati: Historical and Phenomenological Essays*. Delhi, India: Motilal Banarsidass, 1988.

Smith, Jennifer. "Unfamiliar Territory: Women, Land and Law in Occitania, 1130–1250." In Menuge, 19–40. *See above*.

Stafford, Pauline. *Queens, Concubines and Dowagers: The King's Wife in the Early Middle Ages*. Athens: University of Georgia Press, 1983.

Tallan, Cheryl. "Opportunities for Medieval Northern European Jewish Widows in the Public and Domestic Spheres." In Mirrer, 114–27. *See above*.

Walker, Sue Sheridan. "Widow and Ward: The Feudal Law of Child Custody in Medieval England." In *Women in Medieval Society*, edited and introduced by Susan M. Stuard, 159–72. Philadelphia: University of Pennsylvania Press, 1976.

NADIA MARGOLIS

WITCHES. Witches could be either male or female (the supposed male-centered term "warlock" is now discredited as a modern fiction), but witchcraft became associated much more with women during the Middle Ages, especially with elderly women, for various reasons. Current historians consider European witchcraft a unique phenomenon because it differed both from high magic (astrology and alchemy—in medieval times virtually indistinguishable from true science [see Thorndike]) and low magic (simple sorcery: the weaving and application of magic charms and spells for simple, practical uses without any Satanic component), and it also opposed Christianity by worshiping the Devil, a fact leading to its most ardent persecution. This perception of witches as heinous is not medieval, however, but rather one conceived during the Renaissance. The true "witch craze" occurred from 1450 until 1700, peaking c.1550–1660 (Russell 1989) and thus beyond the scope of the Middle Ages. Contrary to its stereotype as an "irrational" and "dark" era versus the "enlightened" Renaissance and modern times, the Middle Ages served only as a formative period.

In non-European societies, witches never carried the same intensely negative, diabolical stigma, but instead endured both in benign and sinister or mischievous forms (sometimes changing from one to the other) as part of folklore and local myth. In the "transitional"—partly European, partly Asian, partly Christian, partly pagan—culture of Russia, the polymorphous Baba Yaga reigned as the preeminent medieval mythical witch, possibly surviving from an old goddess cult. The Russian Church spoke out against witches, but did not undertake the level of oppression that would occur in Europe (see Hubbs).

European witchcraft did originate in simple sorcery and, to a lesser extent, folklore, from pre-Christian times. This brand of pagan, nature-centered sorcery flourished particularly among Teutonic (early Germanic) and Celtic (Ireland, Brittany, Wales, etc.) peoples. It combined what might now be called natural healing elements from plants and animals with the beliefs and incantations one encounters in folktales and legends to cure illness, invoke an end to drought and other afflictions among loved ones, or to curse and scourge one's enemies, such as one reads in fairy tales and legends. For example, the Valkyries (warrior-maidens in Germanic folklore) possessed both exceptional physical strength and knowledge of sorcery.

Early Christian penitentials (manuals for hearing confession and assigning penance) were already severely penalizing women especially for committing any unusual act that might be deemed sorcery. In 875, the Frankish King Lothar encouraged the denunciation of women who caused divorces by their *malefice* (evil sorcery), as part of a general Carolingian program aimed at establishing proper lay and Church ritual while isolating and condemning sorcery (see Schmitt). The earliest European legal document against witches, the canon *Episcopi*, first appearing in Germany (c.906, later, in c.1142, incorporated into the corpus of canon law by Gratian as part of his *Decretum*, 2 Can. 26.12), invoked belief in a troop of women on horseback led by Berta or Hilda (in German) or

The devil making love to a witch. From Ulrich Molitor's *Von den Unholden und Hexen.* Constance, 1489. Courtesy of the Dover Pictorial Archive.

Diana (the athletic Roman goddess), whom a later version of the canon, by the German Bishop Burchard of Worms (c.1012) in his penitential, characterized as witches and condemned. The canon *Episcopi* offered—then discredited as illusory—the first mention of a nocturnal meeting or Sabbat (Sabbath) involving witches flying, conveyed by demons (a feat called transvection), which would feature strongly in later images of witches.

Meanwhile, pagan festivals of harvest, light, and changing seasons, from which, for example, Halloween and May Day derive, continued alongside Christian religious beliefs into the premodern era peacefully enough unless a defendant's documented observance of such non-Christian rites came in handy for exploitation by a zealous inquisitor. This happened with Joan of Arc, who, however, was finally burned not for witchcraft but for heresy (1431). Indeed, witchcraft was seen as relatively harmless until the final and ultimately crucial formative phase, in which it self-identified with anti-Christian heresies. Only when, as part of heresy, it menaced social and religious order did it become perceived as dangerous.

According to Jeffrey Burton Russell, witchcraft in the eyes of the Church and mainstream society simultaneously separated from simple sorcery/low magic and merged with heresy by the late Middle Ages. To backtrack chronologically for a moment, witchcraft "theory" (beliefs about witches as expressed by theologians and other writers, compiled especially the fifteenth and seventeenth centuries) acquired ideas from several historical events in addition to the above-cited laws and canons. Perhaps the first involved the great waves of heresies (starting in the eleventh century), especially the Cathars (from the Greek *catharos* for pure). This group, probably originating in East, then moving through what is now Bulgaria, flourished in southern France and throughout the Mediterranean countries (see Lansing). An outgrowth of Manicheism and other dualistic faiths (perceiving the world as a continuing battle between good and evil/light and dark/flesh and soul), Catharism taught, among other scandalous ideas, that the Catholic Church was wrong to interpret the biblical allegories literally. Instead, Christ should be understood as an angel whose body was a mere illusion; he thus did not suffer and would not return; his immortality and redemptive powers lay in the Cathar teaching of his doctrine. Cathars also rejected the role of Mary as mother of God; they held instead that she had conceived him literally in one ear and borne him out the other. Significantly, Cathar dogma's image of women was no more favorable than that of the Church Fathers, but they did allow women to become *perfecti*, its elite group of followers, like the men. Other heretical groups that would attract women along with men were the avowedly poor, preaching Waldensians (named after Peter Waldo, late twelfth century), much closer to Catholicism than the Cathars but who again minimized the Virgin Mary's role and were equated with witches by c.1460. The Brethren of the Free Spirit, who believed in humankind's absolute identification with God and thus denied sin, and the Guglielmites (thirteenth century), whose founder, Guglielma of Milan, convinced her followers that she was an incarnation of the Holy Spirit; they also believed in a woman pope (see Shahar). By lessening male-favored gender stereotyping, all of these sects accommodated a certain type of spiritual woman better than did the Church.

Scholasticism (from the twelfth century), based on the teachings of the ancient Greek philosopher Aristotle, was the quintessential medieval philosophical system for rationalizing Christian doctrine as well as science and law (as exemplified in Gratian's *Decretum*). Scholastic thinkers contributed the notion of witches as members of Satan's army who had made a "pact" with the Devil. Although Thomas Aquinas (d. 1274), the Church's "Angelic Doctor," did not advocate persecuting witches, he constructed quasi-scientific explanations of demonic anatomy and physiology that would prove useful to the Inquisitors seeking proof of bodily interaction between witches and devils (Stephens). Established by Pope Gregory IX between 1227 and 1235, the Inquisition against heresy (thirteenth through fifteenth centuries) gave final impetus to the characterization of witchcraft as sinister. Actively applying the scholastic method, with obsessive attention to order, they devised the criminal terminology for the various types of witchcraft and heresy, in addition to the procedures for interrogation, prosecution, and execution. Thus, clearly, the Scholastic intellectuals must share the blame with the later neurotic zealots for the witch craze.

Richard Kieckhefer affirms that, although the greatest number of witches of both genders were persecuted after 1500, during the period between 1300 and 1500, two-thirds of accused witches were women (Kieckhefer 1976). How did witches become women, or vice versa? Common linguistic usage, beliefs, natural circumstances, and theological writings combined to effect this demonization of woman. Some standard words for witches are seen most frequently in their feminine forms: Old English *wicca*, French *sorcière*, Italian *strega*, Latin *strix* (originally screech-owl, then vampire), German *Hexe*, and Russian *ved'ma*. By the later centuries, biology played a part: women tended to resist the famines, plagues, and other privations better than men; they did not usually fight in wars, and thus outlived men, which resulted in a surplus of solitary older women. Even though they no longer possessed the physical beauty capable of enticing men to commit sins of the flesh and related horrors, their survival, haggard looks, and tendency toward eccentric behavior (mainly out of prolonged solitude) elicited contempt and fear, even more than their "female mysteries" had in youth. But during the medieval period (pre-1500), young, mostly married, witches were also numerous. That they often came from the lower classes counted against them, since it showed that the Devil was able to buy them cheaply; were they wealthy, other reasons would be found, as is typical of the plight of persecuted minorities. Women often worked as healers and midwives. Miscarriages were often blamed on witchcraft (Shahar). There also may be a correlation between the increase in women, particularly women preachers (i.e., deeply religious but uninterested in functioning quietly as nuns), joining the more-welcoming heretical sects as they were steadily pushed out of the higher, active roles in the orthodox Church hierarchy that they once held in the early Christian era. Theologically, St. Paul and the Fathers of the Church (early founders of Church doctrine, such as Augustine and Jerome, fifth and sixth centuries) wrote against women as descendants of the deceitful, carnally seductive Eve—the opposite of the Virgin Mary—who must be subjugated and certainly not allowed to teach or preach except in a very limited way. These male theologians also inveighed against paganism, and any reverence toward or incantation honoring demons and the omni-present Devil; their discourse facilitated a connecting women with devilish creatures. Since the Devil, though capable of assuming any shape or gender, traditionally chose to appear as a male, and witches were known to have sexual intercourse with him, another visually and mentally provocative link arose. The medieval visual arts routinely repre-sented the concept of lust as a woman. Shulamith Shahar reminds us of a carved capital in the church at Vézelay, France, depicting Satan playing a woman as though she were a musical instrument, and in the southern-French church of Moissac, a woman is portrayed with serpents hanging from her breasts and a toad upon her genitals, while the Devil looks on.

The earliest contemporary record of a woman gaining occult powers of *maleficium* through sexual congress with the Devil is that of the trial of Alice Kyteler (1324) in Kilkenny, Ireland. Dame Alice, the victim of a typically overzealous bishop and also of greedy children hoping to gain her estate by accusing her of witchcraft and thereby eliminating her, allegedly used dead, unbaptized children's clothes (such children were believed to transmit malefic mania) to prepare magic unguents and potions causing the deaths of her four husbands and bringing harm to other good Christians. Alice's case occasioned the first record of execution for heresy in Ireland. Other women were exe-cuted for heresy, if not exactly *maleficium*: from among the many Cathar martyrs, Gra-zida's testimony survives (early fourteenth century) (Shahar); evidence indicates that Marguerite Porete, belonging to a group akin to the Brethren of the Free Spirit, was martyred in 1310. These events were fueling and being fueled by the early theorists from the start of the Inquisition. In fifteenth-century Germany and France, for instance, var-ious anti-witch, pro-reform treatises appeared: Johann Nider's *Formicarius* (*The Anthill*, c.1436), the anonymous *Errores gazariorum* (*Errors of the Cathars*, c.1450), and the magistrate Claude Tholosan's *Ut magorum et maleficiorum errores* (*Errors of Magicians and Witches*, c.1436; see texts in Ostorero et al.). On the other hand, not all witchcraft theorists were misogynistic, as in the example of Martin Le Franc, provost of Lausanne, Switzerland, author of *Le Champion des dames* (*The Ladies' Champion*, 1442), who praised women, even the recently burned Joan of Arc. He in fact denied that witches actually flew around, carried by demons, at their "synagogues," later called "Sabbat." Le Franc also ridiculed the notion of a pact with the Devil. Nevertheless, despite the production of these tolerant treatises in the French-Swiss border region, witch trials held in this same area resulted in the first mass burning of witches there in 1397. Between 1420 and 1446, eighty-three percent of those found guilty received the death penalty: mostly by burning, some by hanging, and the least number by drowning (Paravy).

The most notorious inquisitor of witches was the Dominican Heinrich Institorus, or Kramer (1430–1505), who, in collaboration with Jacob Sprenger (c.1438–1495)—although Kramer was the principal author—and with papal approval published the *Malleus Maleficarum* (*Hammer against [Female] Witches*) in 1486. Interestingly, at about the same time and later, the term *Malleus Haereticorum* began to be applied to religious leaders who vigorously pursued heretics. Thus the concept of "hammering" came to express a collective ideal in how to treat such offenders. The imprecision of the terms of *malefica/maleficus* (female/male evildoer), compared to more precise terms for witches noted above, is deliberately insidious, since it intends both to widen the Inquisitorial net and connect witches with heretics (anti-Christians) by verbal resonance: *maleficia* (evil deeds) was the complete opposite of the *beneficia* (goodness, good deeds) of the holy sacraments (see Stephens). Prior to publishing this Scholastic manual for recognizing and pursuing witches, the ruthlessly ambitious Heinrich Kramer had gained much influence in Rome, served as inquisitor for southwestern Germany (1474–1490), and convinced Pope Innocent VIII to promote the Inquisition's role in obliterating witchcraft by issuing the bull *Summis desiderantes affectibus* (1484). Kramer's *Malleus*, thanks as much to the advent of printing as to the prevailing mentality among eager readers, attained popularity as one of the most widely read books—not just on witchcraft, but among all early printed books—as attested by the publication of no fewer than fourteen editions of it by 1520. What Justinian (mid-sixth century) and Gratian (mid-twelfth century) did in a positive sense for civil and canon law, respectively, Kramer did for the negative witch-craze phenomenon. The *Malleus* systematically incorporated and clarified the most damning attributes from among accumulated notions of witches as women who had renounced Catholic Christianity, who were completely devoted to the Devil and who sacrificed unbaptized children to him, and—last but not least—who copulated with the Devil. These traits formed the definitive archetype of the witch. Kramer also claimed that women, because of their inferior intelligence, capriciousness, and inability to control their bodily appetites, were more likely to be witches than men. Such misogynous pronouncements appear mostly in part 1, section 6. Because Montague Summers emphasized the text's hostility to women disproportionately in his influential English translation (1928), and because the *Malleus*'s title feminizes witches from the outset (*maleficarum* instead of the masculine or collective *maleficorum*), feminist historians (see Barstow) and those prone to sensationalist scholarship have interpreted the *Malleus* as a primarily misogynistic work, based on less than three percent of the entire text. This misunderstanding, resulting from an excessive reliance on Summers's translation and failure to read the original Latin versions of the *Malleus*, has recently been rectified by Walter Stephens, who, taking his cue from an Italian admirer of Kramer and nephew of the famous humanist of the same family name, Gianfrancesco Pico della Mirandola (1523), reads it as "a hammer for smashing skeptics rather than women" (Stephens, 35; Pico, trans. Alberti, 188). After analyzing the various editions of the *Malleus* and Pope Innocent VIII's bull, Stephens, like Russell, considers these the two most influential works against witchcraft: Innocent's condemnation comes from the highest ecclesiastical source while Kramer, in furnishing the theoretical framework, contributes academic authority. Both texts consider demonic copulation as the origin of witchcraft. Dyan Elliott has also probed at length the carnal lives of demons—their embodiment and disembodiment as demon lovers and demon seeds—and their place in the negative portraiture of women as "polluters" and sexual receptacles for demons, in medieval thought and letters.

Ironically, the savage mass persecution of witches by the Church during the post-medieval centuries coincided precisely with events commonly associated with Western civilization's progress: the Protestant Reformation, Catholic Counter-Reformation, and various manifestations of the Renaissance in science, the arts, printing, and exploration (late fifteenth century through the seventeenth century). Continental Europe equated witches with heretics, and so they were burned at the stake. Russell estimates that during these European witch hunts (not counting the American colonies), at least some 100,000–200,000 people were murdered (Russell 1989). In England, where witches were particularly known to keep "familiars" or "little people," witchcraft was not completely severed from sorcery; convicted witches were hanged, as mandated by English civil law, until James I (r. 1603–1625) introduced the Continental practice of burning (Russell 1989). Some of these victims were completely innocent, yet a substantial proportion resolutely believed themselves to be real witches (Russell 1972). But because actual, effectively diabolical witches of course never existed, the one-sided trials of the hapless defendants, conducted by righteous Christians, must join other murderously pandemic purges caused by *peurs* (great fears, superstitions), such as those of aliens, Roma people, homosexuals, Native Americans, and Jews, in the history of Western culture, as studied by Jean Delumeau, Michael Bailey, and others.

See also Enchantresses, Fays (*Fées*), and Fairies; Grazida (Grazida Lizier); Guglielmites; Joan of Arc, St.; Law, Canon, Women in; Le Franc, Martin; Mary, Blessed Virgin, in the Middle Ages; Medicine and Medieval Women; Melusine; Norse Women; Penitentials, Women in; Porete, Marguerite; Teachers, Women as; Valkyries

BIBLIOGRAPHY

Primary Sources
[See bibliographies to secondary works, esp. Stephens, for a more complete list].
Canon *Episcopi*. In *Corpus iuris canonici*, vol. 1: *Decretum Magistri Gratiani*, edited by Emil L. Richter. Revised by Emil Friedberg, 1030–1031. Leipzig: Tauchnitz, 1879. Reprint Graz, Austria: Akademische Druck, 1959. [Gratian's Latin text; German notes].
———. In Russell 1972, 291–93. [Latin text, English notes; these are the earliest versions, tenth to eleventh centuries].
Hansen, Johannes, ed. *Quellen und Untersuchungen zur Geschichte des Hexenwahns und der Hexenverfolgung im Mittelalter*. Bonn: Georgi, 1901. [Original texts of sources, German notes].
Institorus. *See below under* Kramer.
Kors, Alan C., and Edward Peters, eds. *Witchcraft in Europe 1100–1700: A Documentary History*. Revised ed. by Edward Peters. Middle Ages. Philadelphia: University of Pennsylvania Press, 2001.
Kramer, Heinrich (Institorus). *Malleus Maleficarum 1487*. Facsimile reprint, commentary by Günter Jerouscheck. Hildesheim, Germany: G. Olms, 1992. [Latin text; German notes. Also contains text of papal bull and *approbatio*].
———. *Malleus Maleficarum*. Edited by André Schnyder. Litterae, 113. Göppingen, Germany: Kümmerle, 1991. [Latin text, German notes].
———. *The Malleus Maleficarum of Heinrich Kramer and James Sprenger*. Translated, introduced, and annotated by Montague Summers. London: J. Rodker, 1928. Reprint London: Pushkin Press, 1948; New York: Dover 1971 with bibliographical note from 1948 reprint.
———. *Nürnberger Hexenhammer 1491, Staatsarchiv Nürnberg D 251*. Facsimile reprint. Commentary by Günter Jerouscheck. Hildesheim, Germany: G. Olms, 1992.
[Kyteler, Alice]. *The Sorcery Trial of Alice Kyteler (1324)*. Translated by L. S. Davidson and John O. Ward. Asheville, N.C.: Pegasus, 1993.
Le Franc, Martin. *Le Champion des dames* [excerpt]. In Ostorero et al., 438–508. *See below, next entry*.
Ostorero, Martine, Agostino Paravicini Bagliani, and Kathrin Utz Tremp, eds. *L'Imaginaire du sabbat: Édition critique des textes les plus anciens (1430c.–1440c.)*. Lausanne, Switzerland: Université de Lausanne, 1999. [An important anthology, original languages].
Pico della Mirandola, Gianfrancesco. [*Strix, sive de ludificatione daemonum*]. *Libro detto strega, o delle illusioni del demonio*. Translated by Leandro Alberti (1524). Edited by Albano Biondi. Venice: Marsilio, 1989. [See esp. p. 188].
Weyer, Johann. [*De praestigiis dæmonum, 1563–1583*]. *Witches, Devils and Doctors in the Renaissance*. Translated by Jon Shea. Edited by George Mora et al. Binghamton, N.Y.: Medieval & Renaissance Texts & Studies, 1991.

Secondary Sources

Anglo, Sydney, ed. *The Damned Art: Essays in the Literature of Witchcraft*. London: Routledge & Kegan Paul, 1977.

Ankarloo, Bengt, and Stuart Clark, eds. *The Period of the Witch Trials. Witchcraft and Magic in Europe*. Philadelphia: University of Pennsylvania Press, 2002.

Bailey, Michael. *Battling Demons: Witchcraft, Heresy and Reform in the Late Middle Ages*. Magic in History. University Park: Pennsylvania State University, 2003. [Especially on Nider].

Barstow, Anne Llewellyn. *Witchcraze: A New History of the European Witch Hunts*. San Francisco: Pandora, 1994.

Clark, Stuart. *Thinking with Demons: The Idea of Witchcraft in Early Modern Europe*. Oxford: Clarendon; New York: Oxford University Press, 1997.

Cohn, Norman R. *Europe's Inner Demons: An Enquiry Inspired by the Great Witch Hunt*. New York: New American Library, 1975. Reprint 1977.

———. *The Pursuit of Millennium: Revolutionary Millenarians and Mystical Anarchists of the Middle Ages*. 3rd ed. New York: Oxford University Press, 1970.

Delumeau, Jean. *La Peur en l'Occident*. Paris: Fayard, 1978. Reprint Paris: Hachette, 1999. [See esp. chs.10–Conclusion].

Elliott, Dyan. *Fallen Bodies: Pollution, Sexuality, & Demonology in the Middle Ages*. Middle Ages. Philadelphia: University of Pennsylvania Press, 1999.

Enders, Jody. "Violence, Silence, and the Memory of Witches." In *Violence against Women in Medieval Texts*, edited by Anna Roberts, 210–32. Gainesville: University Press of Florida, 1998.

Ferreiro, Alberto, ed. *The Devil, Heresy and Witchcraft in the Middle Ages: Essays in Honor of Jeffrey B. Russell*. Cultures, Beliefs and Traditions, 6. Leiden and Boston: Brill, 1998.

Hubbs, Joanna. *Mother Russia: The Feminine Myth in Russian Culture*. Bloomington: Indiana University Press, 1988.

Kieckhefer, Richard. *European Witch Trials: Their Foundations in Popular and Learned Culture, 1300–1500*. Berkeley: University of California Press, 1976.

———. *Forbidden Rites: A Necromancer's Manual of the Fifteenth Century*. University Park: Pennsylvania State University Press, 1997.

———. *Magic in the Middle Ages*. Cambridge: Cambridge University Press, 1989. Reprint 2000.

Lansing, Carol. *Power and Purity: Cathar Heresy in Medieval Italy*. New York: Oxford University Press, 1998.

Levack, Brian P., ed. *Articles on Witchcraft, Magic and Demonology*. 12 vols. New York: Garland, 1992. [See esp. vols. 2, 10, 12].

———, ed. *The Witchcraft Sourcebook*. New York and London: Routledge, 2004.

Michelet, Jules. *La Sorcière*. Edited with preface by Paul Viallaneix. Paris: Garnier-Flammarion, 1966.

———. *Satanism and Witchcraft: The Classic Study of Medieval Superstition*. Translated by A. R. Allinson. New York: Citadel, 1992.

Monter, E. William. *Frontiers of Heresy: The Spanish Inquisition from the Basque Lands to Sicily*. Cambridge: Cambridge University Press, 1990.

———, ed. *European Witchcraft*. New York: John Wiley, 1969. [Useful collection of primary texts and essays by major scholars on various key aspects].

Morris, Katherine. *Sorceress or Witch? The Image of Gender in Medieval Iceland*. Lanham, Md.: University Press of America, 1991.

Paravy, Pierrette. "A propos de la genèse médiévale des chasses aux sorcières en Europe dans le traité de Claude Tholosan, juge dauphinois (vers 1436)." *Mélanges de l'École française de Rome* 91 (1979): 333–79.

Peters, Edward. *The Magician, the Witch, and the Law*. Philadelphia: University of Pennsylvania, 1978.

———. *Inquisition*. Berkeley: University of California Press, 1989.

Robbins, Rossell Hope. *The Encyclopedia of Witchcraft and Demonology*. New York: Crown, 1959.

Russell, Jeffrey Burton. *A History of Witchcraft: Sorcerers, Heretics and Pagans*. New York: Thames & Hudson, 1980.

———. "Witchcraft, European." In *Dictionary of the Middle Ages*, edited by Joseph R. Strayer, 12: 658–65. New York: Scribner's, 1989.

———. *Witchcraft in the Middle Ages*. Ithaca, N.Y.: Cornell University Press, 1972.

———, and Mark Wyndham. "Witchcraft and the Demonization of Heresy." *Medievalia* 2 (1976): 1–21.

Schmitt, Jean-Claude. "Sorcellerie." In *Dictionnaire raisonné de l'Occident médiéval*, edited by Jacques Le Goff and Jean-Claude Schmitt, 1084–1096. Paris: Fayard, 1999.

Shahar, Shulamith. *The Fourth Estate: A History of Women in the Middle Ages*. Translated by Chaya Galai. Revised ed. London and New York: Routledge, 2003. [See esp. final chapter].

Stephens, Walter. *Demon Lovers: Witchcraft, Sex, and the Crisis of Belief*. Chicago and London: University of Chicago Press, 2003.

Thorndike, Lynn. *A History of Magic and Experimental Science*, vol. 4. New York: Columbia University Press, 1934.

PETER I. BARTA

WOMEN QUESTION. *See* **Frauenfrage**

WOMEN'S SONGS. *See* **Chanson de Femme** (Women's Song)

WOODVILLE, ELIZABETH (c.1437–1492). Queen-consort to Edward IV of England and influential matriarch of the royal family, Elizabeth Woodville (or Wydeville) was a key figure in the later phases of the Wars of the Roses (1455–1485), the dynastic war of royal succession between the houses of Lancaster (whose symbol was the red rose) and York (symbolized by the white rose).

The daughter of Richard Woodville, a member of the minor gentry, and the more aristocratic Jacquetta of Luxembourg, duchess of Bedford, Elizabeth served as maid of honor in the household of Margaret of Anjou (1430–1482), the French-born wife of the Lancastrian monarch, Henry VI (1421–1471). In about 1450, Elizabeth married John Grey, lord Ferrers of Groby, by whom she had two sons, Thomas and Richard. Thomas Grey, the future marquis of Dorset, was the great-grandfather of the ill-fated "nine days' queen" Lady Jane Grey (1537–1554). When John Grey died fighting for Henry VI at the Second Battle of St. Albans in 1461, his mother denied Elizabeth that portion of the Grey estates to which she was entitled as John's widow. Elizabeth pleaded with Edward IV, the new Yorkist monarch, to intervene on her behalf. The young king was much taken with the attractive widow, but found his amorous advances rebuffed. He could only fulfill his desire by marrying Elizabeth, which he did secretly on May Day 1464. Secrecy was necessary, for the king's marriage was an important diplomatic tool, and union with a subject and a commoner squandered any benefits that might be gained from an advantageous foreign alliance—Edward had already rejected proposals for matches with such royal princesses as Isabella of Castile and Bona of Savoy, sister of the king of France. The disparity in social rank between bride and groom made the marriage an even more scandalous misalliance than was the marriage of Elizabeth's parents in the 1430s.

When revealed later in the year, the marriage—the first royal match with an Englishwoman since the thirteenth century—met with widespread disapproval, especially from

Edward's chief supporter and advisor, Richard Neville, earl of Warwick, who soon found his position at court threatened by Edward's new in-laws. The Woodvilles were a large and ambitious family eager for political influence and financial gain. Edward ennobled Elizabeth's father as Earl Rivers and felt honor bound to find titles, lands, or marriages for his wife's five brothers, seven sisters, and two sons by Grey (Elizabeth eventually bore Edward two sons and eight daughters). Thus, the Woodvilles soon commanded a huge share of the royal patronage, for which they were much maligned then, mainly through Warwick's propaganda, and later by historians. Yet some recent scholars have revised this view, arguing that, save for her father, Earl Rivers (made treasurer in 1466), Elizabeth's family did not receive extravagant rewards and that she herself ran a relatively frugal household (see Pollard; Sutton and Visser-Fuchs).

Elizabeth Woodville. Courtesy of the Perry Casteneda Library.

The Woodvilles' alleged disproportionate claim on the king's bounty, along with their foreign policy favoring the duke of Burgundy (over the king of France), so incensed Warwick and Edward's brother, George Plantagenet, duke of Clarence (1449–1478), that they fomented a rebellion in 1469 and, with French and Lancastrian aid, overthrew Edward in 1470. Because of this perilous situation, Elizabeth gave birth to her first son by the king, the future Edward V, while in sanctuary at Westminster in November 1470. After Edward IV's restoration in April 1471, the Woodville family became the center of an increasingly powerful political faction, led by Elizabeth and her eldest brother, Anthony Woodville, who had become Earl Rivers in 1469 after Warwick executed his father. Probably instrumental in effecting the duke of Clarence's execution in 1478, the Woodvilles, through Rivers's guardianship of the young prince, were well placed to exert control over the future king.

On the death of Edward IV in April 1483, Elizabeth emerged as an important political figure. To ensure Woodville dominance in the new reign, Elizabeth and her eldest son by her first marriage, Thomas Grey, marquis of Dorset, took charge in London while Rivers brought the new king, Edward V, to London. The queen's attempt to have the twelve-year-old king declared of sufficient age to rule aroused strong opposition and created support for Richard, duke of Gloucester (1452–1485), the king's paternal uncle, to

955

establish a protectorate. Driven perhaps by ambition or by fear of a Woodville-dominated crown, Gloucester soon decided to usurp the throne. The duke seized custody of the boy king and executed Elizabeth's brother Rivers and her son, Richard Grey, thereby forcing the queen to again seek sanctuary at Westminster with her remaining children. Meanwhile, Gloucester now ruled as Richard III, basing his claim to the crown, as set out in a document entitled *Titulus Regius* ("The King's Title"), on a canon law technicality that condemned the clandestine marriage of Edward IV and Elizabeth and made their children illegitimate. In June 1483, Richard compelled Elizabeth to surrender her younger son, Richard Plantagenet, duke of York, to him. Lodged in the Tower of London, Elizabeth's two sons disappeared from view in the summer of 1483. Presumed murdered by their uncle, the boys' disappearance provoked outrage against Richard III. Elizabeth's sons have today become the center of the most compelling mystery in English history; their story has been told and their fate debated in various works by various writers and artists since the sixteenth century, including William Shakespeare and Paul Delaroche, who created a moving painting of the princes in 1830. Believing Richard III had murdered her sons, Elizabeth helped foment Buckingham's Rebellion in October 1483. This uprising sought to replace Richard with Henry Tudor, earl of Richmond and son of the Lancastrian heiress Margaret Beaufort (1443–1509). It was agreed by the conspirators (which, besides Elizabeth, included Beaufort and the duke of Buckingham) that Richmond, once he had secured the throne, would marry Elizabeth's eldest daughter, Elizabeth of York. However, the rebellion failed, Buckingham was executed, and Richmond had to abort a planned landing and return to exile in Brittany.

In March 1484, Richard III coaxed Elizabeth out of sanctuary and weaned her from support of Richmond with a promise of good marriages and reception at court for her daughters. However, in August 1485, Richmond defeated and killed Richard III at the Battle of Bosworth Field, thus winning the crown as Henry VII, first king of the house of Tudor. Not wanting to be seen as owing his crown to his wife, Henry delayed his marriage to Elizabeth of York until January 1486. In 1487, suspecting his mother-in-law of supporting a Yorkist plot then forming around one Lambert Simnel—an impostor posing as a claimant to the throne in Ireland—Henry induced Elizabeth to turn her property over to him. The king also imprisoned her eldest son, Thomas Grey, marquis of Dorset. Henry then forced his mother-in-law to enter Bermondsey Abbey, where she died in June 1492.

See also Beaufort, Margaret; Dower; Elizabeth of York; Jacquetta of Luxembourg; Margaret of Anjou

BIBLIOGRAPHY

Primary Source
Myers, A. R., ed. "The Household of Queen Elizabeth Woodville, 1466–67." *Bulletin of the John Rylands Library* 50 (1967–1968): 207–35; 443–81.[See also notes to works listed below].

Secondary Sources
Baldwin, David. *Elizabeth Woodville: Mother of the Princes in the Tower*. Stroud, England: Sutton Publishing, 2002.
Hicks, Michael. "The Changing Role of the Wydevilles in Yorkist Politics to 1483." In *Patronage, Pedigree and Power in Later Medieval England*, edited by Charles Ross, 60–86. Gloucestershire: Alan Sutton, 1979.

———. "Elizabeth Woodville." In *Who's Who in Late Medieval England*, edited by Michael Hicks, 325–27. London: Shepheard-Walwyn, 1991.

MacGibbon, David. *Elizabeth Woodville: Her Life and Times*. London: A. Barker Ltd., 1938.

Pollard, Anthony J. *Late Medieval England, 1399–1509*. Longman History of Medieval England. Essex, U.K.: Longman/Pearson, 2000.

Ross, Charles. *Edward IV*. New Haven, Conn.: Yale University Press, 1998.

Sutton, Anne F., and Livia Visser-Fuchs. "A Most Benevolent Queen." *The Ricardian* 129 (1995): 214–45.

Wagner, John A. *Encyclopedia of the Wars of the Roses*. Santa Barbara, Calif.: ABC-Clio, 2001.

JOHN A. WAGNER

WU, EMPRESS (624/627–705). The flamboyant Wu Zetian or Wu Zhao was China's only female monarch, her promotion to empress having been irregular. The daughter of well-to-do parents—the official Wu Shihuo and Madame Yang (579–670), who was descended from the imperial Sui family—Wu was introduced into Emperor Taizong's palace in her teens to serve as a *cairen* (lady of talents) in 640. But after the emperor died, she was sent to a Buddhist convent, as were the other women at court. A few years later she was brought back, reportedly because the empress of the new emperor, Gaozong (r. 650–683), hoped that Wu's beauty would lure the emperor away from his favorite of the moment. This Wu managed with great success, soon even convincing Gaozong to depose his empress, an action arousing great protest from his ministers. Soon Wu had the former empress brutally killed and achieved total dominance over the emperor, especially during his frequent illnesses, during which she conducted matters at court.

After Emperor Gaozong suffered a stroke in 660, Empress Wu took full charge. At his death in 683, she placed her eldest son, Zhongzong, on the throne, but when he showed signs of independence, she had him deposed in favor of his younger brother, installed as Emperor Ruizong. In 688, Empress Wu's growing ambitions led some princes of the Tang royal family to rebel, but their uprising was quickly suppressed, and Empress Wu took the opportunity to root out opposition, purging many members of the imperial family and officials. In 690, she deposed her second son and proclaimed herself emperor of a new dynasty, the Zhou, making her the only woman to assume the title of emperor in Chinese history.

Empress Wu was undeniably ruthless in eliminating rivals and opponents. At the same time, she deserves credit as an adroit and forceful politician able to enhance the power of both state and throne. Maintaining an aggressive foreign policy, she curbed the power of the aristocratic families from the northwest who had risen to power with the Tang a half century earlier. During her reign, the court frequently moved east to Luoyang, and she recruited many officials from the east through the civil service examination system, leading to a permanent change in the composition of the bureaucracy.

A pious Buddhist, because of her pious mother's influence, Empress Wu was a generous patron of Buddhist and Confucian scholarship and Buddhist establishments, including the great cave temples at Longmen near Luoyang. She drew on Buddhist doctrine to legitimate her ascent to the throne. For instance, she circulated the *Great Cloud Sutra*, a text that predicted the imminent reincarnation of the Buddha Maitreya as a female monarch under whom all the world would be free of illness, worry, and disaster. She also composed poetry in a Buddhist-spiritual vein, even when promoting her political vision, leaving

Wu Tse-Tien, Chinese Empress, shown in her imperial robes. Also pictured is a courtier of a later period, Jo-Fei. © Mary Evans Picture Library.

some forty-six poems (one autobiographical) and numerous essays at least ascribed to her (since detractors claim these poems and essays were mostly ghost-written).

Empress Wu's hold on the government was so strong that she was not deposed until 705, when she was eighty and ailing. And even then, a return to exclusively male domination of the imperial institution was not immediate, for Empress Wu's daughter, the Princess Taiping, and her daughter-in-law, Empress Wei, were major rivals for power for the next several years.

Later historians have viewed Empress Wu not merely as a usurper but as a wanton and evil person, to whom they have attributed stereotypically male and female failings. Like other evil women, she has been depicted, in early life, as vicious in her jealousy of other women in the emperor's harem; for instance, she has been accused of strangling her own infant daughter to accuse the empress of the act and thus have her deposed. But like powerful men, she has been characterized as a profligate who kept numerous male lovers, including a corrupt Buddhist monk.

See also China, Women in; Theodora

BIBLIOGRAPHY

Primary Source
Wu Zetian. [three poems, one literary essay]. In *Women Writers of Traditional China: An Anthology of Poetry and Criticism*, edited with introduction by Kang-i Sun Chang, and Haun Saussy (various translators), esp. 46–51, 669–71. Stanford, Calif.: Stanford University Press, 1999. [English texts only, with useful background commentary, charts, and maps].

Secondary Sources
Fitzgerald, Charles P. *The Empress Wu*. 2nd ed. London: Cresset, 1968.
Guisso, R. W. L. *Wu Tse-t'ien and the Politics of Legitimation in T'ang China*. Bellingham: Western Washington University Program in East Asian Studies Occasional Papers, 1978.
Yen, Chüan-ying. "The Tower of Seven Jewels and Empress Wu." *National Palace Museum* [Taipei] *Bulletin* 22. 1 (March–April 1987): 1–17.

PATRICIA BUCKLEY EBREY

XUE TAO (768–831). Perhaps the most famous courtesan poet of the Tang dynasty, Xue Tao authored over five hundred poems, of which about ninety survive.

Born in Chan'an (now Xi'an, in Shaanxi province, east-central China), Xue Tao was the daughter of a low-ranking official with whom she migrated southward to the state of Shu (now Sichuan province) and began to compose poetry as a child. When she was fourteen or fifteen, her father died, leaving her family stranded in Sichuan province with no means of support. She became registered as a government courtesan (a *geji*), expected to entertain official guests by singing at government functions. She soon acquired a reputation as a witty conversationalist and poet, and met many leading men of letters when they visited Sichuan, including Liu Yuxi, Bo Juyi, and Yuan Zhen. A close relationship with Yuan Zhen developed, and Xue Tao continued to send him her poems after he returned to the capital. However, she never married. In her forties, she was released from her official duties and retired to a house outside the city wall, having apparently saved enough money to live independently at Huanhuaxi. She took on the persona of a Taoist clergywoman but was not cloistered, continuing to receive visitors.

Most of Xue Tao's poems are love poems addressed to her male patrons in their absence. They are noted for the rich sensuous imagery and their musical qualities, as most were intended for singing. The sadness of separation is the main recurrent theme.

See also China, Women in; Li Qingzhao; *Trobairitz*

BIBLIOGRAPHY
Xue Tao. *Brocade River Poems: Selected Works of the Tang Dynasty Courtesan Xue Tao*. Edited and translated by Jeanne Larsen. Princeton, N.J.: Princeton University Press, 1987.
———. [Selections]. In *Autumn Willows: Poetry by Women of China's Golden Age*, translated by Bannie Chow and Thomas Cleary. Ashland, Ore.: Story Line Press, 2003.
———. [10 Selected Poems]. In *Women Writers of Traditional China: An Anthology of Poetry and Criticism*, edited with introduction by Kang-i Sun Chang, and Haun Saussy (various translators), esp. 59–66. Stanford, Calif.: Stanford University Press, 1999. [English texts only, with useful background commentary, charts and maps].

PATRICIA BUCKLEY EBREY

YANG GUIFEI (719–756). China's most celebrated femme fatale and imperial consort of the Tang Emperor Xuanzong (685–762, r. 713–756) was born Yang Yuhuan, the daughter of Yang Xuanyan, an official from a family originating in Shaanxi (central China). Married in 736 to Emperor Xuanzong's eighteenth son, Prince Li Mei, by the early 740s she had attracted the attention of the emperor, who became infatuated with her. She asked to leave the prince and became registered as a Taoist priestess. Then, in 745, Xuanzong had her taken into his own harem, Prince Li Mei was given another wife, and Yang was accorded the title *Guifei* (Precious Consort). Soon several members of her family, including three sisters, were given noble rank and high positions at court and showered with extravagant gifts, such as residences in the capital.

Yang Guifei shared the emperor's passion for music and dance and was a talented performer herself. Together they patronized performers and artists of talent, presiding over what was perhaps China's most brilliant court. This idyllic period lasted less than a decade, however, brought to an end by a civil war that many blamed on the imperial couple's inadequate governance. Two of the key powerholders of the period owed their favor in part to Yang Guifei, and they became rivals. They were Yang Guifei's third cousin, Yang Guozhong, who became chief minister in 752, and the military commander of the northeast, the non-Chinese (he was of Turkic origin) general An Lushan, whom she had found amusing and even "adopted." In 755, An Lushan launched a massive rebellion, quickly attacking and taking both the cities of Luoyang and Chang'an (in modern Henan province, east-central China), and forcing the emperor and his court to flee west toward Sichuan province. While the court was on the road, mutinous troops forced the disconsolate emperor to have his beloved concubine Yang Guifei strangled. He then abdicated. The story of Emperor Xuanzong's intense passion for Yang Guifei and deep sense of loss at her death was immortalized and romanticized by the Buddhist poet Bo (or Bai) Juyi (772–846) in a courtly ballad, "Chang hen ge" ("Song of Everlasting Sorrow"), which found multiple echoes in Chinese women's love poetry into the Ming dynasty (sixteenth century).

In the Chinese historiographical and literary tradition consisting in several novels and dramas, as well as a film by Mizoguchi Kenji, *Princess Yang Kwei Fei* (Yōkihi 1955), Yang Guifei is portrayed not as an evil woman but as an unintentionally dangerous one and

The Chinese beauty Yang Guifei sits on a Chinese-style throne playing the flute. From a hanging scroll painting by the Japanese artist Hosoda Eishi of the Edo period. © The British Museum/Topham-HIP/The Image Works.

sometimes even a political scapegoat. Her exceptional beauty and charm so captivated a ruler than he spent his time trying to please her rather than attending to the business of governing.

See also China, Women in; Concubines; Rosamond, Fair; Shore, Elizabeth (Jane)

BIBLIOGRAPHY

Primary Sources
Bo Juyi. [Poems]. *Bai Juyi, 200 Selected Poems.* Edited and translated by Rewi Alley. Beijing: New World Press, 1983.
———— *Po Chu-I: Selected Poems.* Edited and translated by Burton Watson. New York: Columbia University Press, 2000.
[Various women poets mentioning Yang Guifei]. In *Women Writers of Traditional China: An Anthology of Poetry and Criticism*, edited with introduction by Kang-i Sun Chang, and Haun Saussy (various translators), passim. Stanford, Calif.: Stanford University Press, 1999. [English texts only, with useful background commentary, charts, and maps].

Secondary Sources
Graham, Masako N. *The Yang Kuei-fei Legend in Japanese Literature.* Lewiston, N.Y.: Edwin Mellen Press, 1998.
http://www.amherst.edu/~pwcaddeau/A21/YangGuifei.html [Highly informative Web site with links to related materials on her].
Levy, Howard S. *Harem Favorites of An Illustrious Celestial.* Taichung: Ching-tai, 1958.
Palm, Christoph. *Yang Guifei in der chinesischen Literatur.* Ph.D. diss., Freie Universität, Berlin, 1993.

PATRICIA BUCKLEY EBREY

YOLANDA OF ARAGON (c.1381–1442). Yolanda, or in French, Yolande, a powerful political figure, was duchess of Anjou and "queen of Sicily." The daughter of John I, king of Aragon (now part of Spain), and of Yolande of Bar, Yolanda married, on December 2, 1400, in Arles, Louis II, duke of Anjou and "king of Sicily," to whom she had been contracted to marry in 1390. This union produced five children: Louis III (d. in Italy, November 1434); the illustrious love poet and patron René, duke of Anjou (1409–1480); Charles, count of Maine; Marie, wife of Charles VII of France; and Yolande, wife of Francis I of Brittany. A widow with young children after Louis's death in 1417, Yolanda assumed an important political role—one for which she was well suited. The diversity of her husband's territories made her duties complex. She left in June 1419 for the south and spent four full years governing Provence. In 1423 her son Louis III, then in Italy, where he had been adopted by the queen of Naples, appointed Yolanda administrator of all his lands in France. She exerted considerable influence over Charles VII, who spent several years at her court after his betrothal (December 1413) to her daughter, and he continued to appreciate her counsel.

In 1423, Yolanda hoped to bring about an alliance of Charles with Brittany and his reconciliation with the formidable Duke Philip the Good of Burgundy. She made two trips to Brittany and was ultimately successful there (1424), but her Burgundian efforts were undermined by Charles's favorites. Yolanda managed to have Burgundy's brother-in-law, Arthur of Brittany, "count" of Richemont, appointed constable of France (1425), and with Arthur she worked to purge Charles's court of undesirables. The conflict between Richemont and George of La Trémoille, who became Charles's favorite in 1427, soon led to a civil war that threatened the success of the fight to rid France of the English. After George was ousted in 1433, Yolanda's influence over Charles, which George had sought to extinguish, was strong again, and thereafter she maintained her position through her son Charles, whom she placed at the king's court. Her last known involvement in the king's business dates from 1439, when she attended the meeting of the Estates-General (an assembly convened by royal command during moments of crisis and attended by members of the clergy and the nobility, along with representatives from the towns), in Orléans.

See also Joan of Arc, St.

BIBLIOGRAPHY

Primary Source
Archives nationales, Paris, KK 243 (financial accounts of Yolanda of Aragon, 1409–1427, 1431–1438).

Secondary Sources
Beaucourt, G. du Fresne de. *Histoire de Charles VII.* 6 vols. Paris: Picard, 1881–1891.
Cosneau, Eugène. *Le connétable de Richemont (Arthur de Bretagne, 1393–1458).* Paris: Hachette, 1886.
Orliac, Jehanne d'. *Yolande d'Anjou, la reine aux quatre royaumes.* Paris: Plon, 1933.

RICHARD C. FAMIGLIETTI

YOLANDE OF FLANDERS (1326–1395). A politically influential French countess, Yolande was born on September 15, 1326, the daughter of Robert of Flanders, lord of

Cassel, Gravelines, Dunkerque, Bourbourg, and so forth (d. 1331), and Jeanne of Brittany. Yolande became sole heiress of her father on the death of her brother in about 1332. She was under the guardianship of her mother until Jeanne asked to be discharged in 1337 because of continual problems with the count of Flanders, overlord of Yolande's principal fiefs. Afterward, Yolande was educated at the court of Philip VI of France.

By 1338 she was betrothed to Count Henry of Bar, and they were married c.1340. Henry died on December 24, 1344, and she assumed the guardianship of their two sons, Edward and Robert, but was challenged by their relative Pierre of Bar. Philip VI confirmed her guardianship in 1347 but angered her in 1349 by declaring Edward "of age to govern his estates," for this threatened the longevity of her complete control. Her rash reaction began a long career of intermittent conflict with the crown and the Bar family. In 1352, she agreed to cede the "governorship" of the county of Bar to Jeanne of Bar, daughter of Count Henry III, but within months, after her eldest son's death, she changed her mind and tried unsuccessfully to regain her position by force. Her efforts were supported by her second husband, Philip of Navarre, count of Longueville, whom she married in 1353. Jeanne's power was finally undercut when Yolande prevailed on the (Holy Roman) Emperor Charles IV to declare her son Robert of age in 1354. Yolande's subsequent efforts to control Robert were not always successful. She played a key role in Robert's advancement; he was made a marquis by the emperor (1354) and duke of Bar by the king of France (1355). In 1357 Yolande undertook a war against the bishop of Verdun, during which she counterfeited money, burned a village, and had a priest put to death. Two canons, sent to threaten her with excommunication, disappeared, and she was also accused of their death. She was excommunicated and not absolved for three years.

Yolande was drawn by her husband into supporting his brother Charles the Bad, king of Navarre, in his machinations against France, but Philip died in 1363, and she brought her son to the coronation of Charles V of France in 1364. A marriage was arranged, surely with her help, between Robert and the new king's sister Marie (Robert's father's goddaughter). Later, Yolande turned on Robert when he appointed his relative Henry of Bar his lieutenant. In 1371 she imprisoned Henry, Robert, and others, some of whom were killed. Charles V had her arrested and imprisoned in the Temple in Paris. She escaped in September 1372 but was recaptured and remained in the Temple into October 1373. She governed her lands over the next two decades with concern for her subjects but often with violence when crossed. Accused of ordering another murder, she was again excommunicated (c1377). Her tenacious pursuit of her rights brought her into conflict with Countess Mahaut of Artois and Philip the Bold of Burgundy. During the last year of her life, she was arrested for an unpaid debt. She died on December 12, 1395.

BIBLIOGRAPHY

Primary Source
Delisle, Léopold. *Mandements et actes divers de Charles V (1364–1380)*. Paris: Imprimerie nationale, 1874.

Secondary Sources
Baudot, Jules. *Les Princesses Yolande et les ducs de Bar de la famille de Valois. Première partie: Mélusine.* Paris: Picard, 1900.
Bubenicek, Michelle. *Quand les femmes gouvernent: droit et politique au XIVᵉ siècle: Yolande de Flandre.* Paris: École des Chartes, 2002.

Cockerell, Sydney C. *The book of hours of Yolande of Flanders, a manuscript of the fourteenth century in the library of Henry Yates Thompson.* London: Wittingham/Chiswick, 1905.

Finot, Jules. "Le train de maison d'une grande dame au XIVe siècle. Étude sur les comptes de l'hôtel des sires de Cassel et particulièrement sur ceux d'Yolande de Flandre, comtesse de Bar." *Bulletin historique et philologique du Comité des travaux historiques et scientifiques* (1889): 176–202.

Leuridan, Théodore. "Une dame de Cassel [Yolande de Flandre] faulse monnoyeuse et presbytéricide." *Annales du Comité flamand de France* 20 (1892): 41–62.

Schneider, J. "Yolande de Flandres (1326–1395), comtesse de Bar, dame de Cassel, et les pouvoirs de son temps." In *La femme au Moyen Âge, colloque international. Maubeuge 6–9 octobre 1988.* Maubeuge, France: ville de Maubeuge, 1990, pp. 353–63.

Servais, Victor. *Annales historiques du Barrois de 1352 à 1411.* 2 vols. Bar-le-Duc, France: Contant-Laguerre, 1865–1867.

Smyttère, Philippe-J.-E. de. *Essai historique sur Iolande de Flandre, comtesse de Bar [...]1326–1395.* Lille, France: Lefebvre-Ducrocq, 1877.

RICHARD C. FAMIGLIETTI

YSABELLA, DOMNA (early 13th century). Lady Ysabella, or Isabella, coauthored the *tenso* (dialogue poem) known by its opening verse, "N'Elias Cairel, de l'amor" ("Lord Elias Cairel, about the love"), with the male troubadour Elias Cairel (fl. 1204–1222). Ysabella wrote as a *trobairitz* (woman troubadour) in the southern-French language called Occitan.

In each of the two manuscripts, one called *O* (Rome, Vatican Library, lat. 3208) and the other, *a*¹ (Florence, Biblioteca Riccardiana, 2814), containing it, the poem's rubric (heading) credits the authors as "domna Ysabella" and to "En Elias Cairel" (*en* = lord). While Cairel is a known troubadour, entitling him also to a *vida* (poetic biography), nothing is known of Isabella beyond the scant information contained in the two rubrics. As usual in such cases, literary historians became intrigued by the mystery and advanced various hypotheses about her identity, primarily based on the few known facts about Elias's career. According to his vida, Elias, trained as a goldsmith, traveled extensively as a *jongleur* (minstrel), lived for several years in Italy, then entering the service of Boniface I of Montferrat, a crusading knight, in Greece. There is also the fact that Elias dedicated three poems to a woman named Isabella. The most recent findings identify Ysabella either with Isabella de Montferrat, widow of Boniface's brother, Conrad, or with Isabella Malaspina, Boniface's sister and wife Albert de Malaspina (see ed. Rieger, 282–89). The second possibility is supported by the fact that Elias had dedicated a poem to Guglielmo de Malaspina, coincidentally lamenting a beloved lady's departure for Greece—a connection first suggested by an Ysabella specialist in 1838 (Éméric-David, 496).

"N'Elias Cairel, de l'amor" is an acrimonious exchange, yet not without humor, in which Ysabella's persona berates Elias for having shifted his love (and his song) to another lady. Elias's persona protests that he sang her praises to gain not her love but "per honor e pron" ("for the honor and rewards") that he expected from doing so, as does any *joclar* (minstrel) who celebrates a noble lady. Apparently unfazed by Ysabella's angry outburst, Elias announces that he will betake himself to his beautiful beloved, whose gracious body is matched by her faithful heart. When Ysabella sarcastically suggests that he would do better to return to his monastery—here mentioning a "Patriarch Joannes," another Greek association (ed. Rieger, 280–81; ed. Bruckner et al., 165)—Elias denies that he was ever a monk, saying that she, whose beauty must fade, will soon be fit only to languish in one herself. Then, relenting slightly, he praises Ysabella's beauty and worth, admitting that his change of heart has worked to his detriment. Ysabella seizes on this concession to ask the identity of Elias's new love, but he prudently refuses to reveal the lady's name, citing his fear of slanderers.

Unlike the majority of the Occitan *tensos* between male and female interlocutors, "N'Elias Cairel, de l'amor" is not a theoretical debate on the subject of love but an intensely personal exchange characterized by a high degree of emotional realism. However, this emotional realism guarantees neither Ysabella's historical reality nor that of the situation described in the *tenso*, since the most characteristic feature of the female-voiced Occitan lyric is its emotional authenticity within a narrative fiction of sincerity.

See also Trobairitz

BIBLIOGRAPHY

Primary Sources
Elias Cairel. [three poems to Isabella]. In *Der Trobador Elias Cairel*. Critical ed. by Hilde Jaeschke, 133–44. Romanische Studien, 20. Berlin: Ebering, 1921. Reprint Lübeck: Kraus Reprint 1967. [German translation, notes].

————, and Ysabella. "N'Elias Cairel, de l'amor." In *Songs of the Women Troubadours*, edited and translated by Matilda Tomaryn Bruckner, Laurie Shepard, and Sarah White, 60–63, 164–66. New York and London: Garland, 1995. New ed. 2000. [Most recent, authoritative: original texts, notes, introduction, and English translation].

————. "N'Elias Cairel, de l'amor." In *Trobairitz: Der Beitrag der Frau in der altokzitanischen höfischen Lyrik. Edition des Gesamtkorpus*, edited by Angelica Rieger, 278–82. Beihefte der Zeitschrift für romanische Philologie, 233. Tübingen, Germany: Max Niemeyer, 1991. [Most authoritative, German trans. and commentary].

Secondary Sources
[See also notes to above editions].
Blakeslee, Merritt R. "La Chanson de femme, les *Héroïdes*, et la *canso* occitane à voix de femme: Considérations sur l'originalité des *trobairitz*." In *Hommage à Jean–Charles Payen. "Farai chansoneta novele." Essais sur la liberté créatrice (XIIe–XIIIe s.)*. Edited by Jean-Louis Backus et al., 67–75. Caen, France: Université de Caen, 1989.
Bruckner, Matilda Tomaryn. "Fictions of the Female Voice: The Women Troubadours." *Speculum* 67 (1992): 865–91.
Chambers, Frank. "*Las trobairitz soiseubudas*." In *The Voice of the Trobairitz: Perspectives on the Women Troubadours*, edited by William D. Paden Jr., 45–60. Philadelphia: University of Pennsylvania Press, 1989.
Éméric-David, Toussaint-Bernard. "La Dame Isabelle." In *Histoire Littéraire de la France*, 19: 496–99. Paris: Firmin Didot; Treuttel & Wurtz, 1838.
Shapiro, Marianne. "'Tenson' et 'partimen': La 'tenson' fictive." In *XIV Congresso internazionale di linguistica e filologia romanza: Atti*, edited by Alberto Varvaro, 5: 287–301. Naples: Macchiaroli, 1981.

MERRITT R. BLAKESLEE

Z

ZOE KARBOUNOPSINA (c.885–post-920). The Byzantine Empress and regent Zoe, distinguished from others by the epithet Karbounopsina ("of the coal-black eyes"), in becoming the fourth wife of Emperor Leo VI (866–912), touched off one of the major religious and political issues—the *tetragamia* (fourth marriage), causing a schism within the Eastern Church—in tenth-century Byzantium (Garland; Boojamra) and threatened the legitimacy of Leo's succession.

Leo the Wise, as he was known, needed to marry a fourth time because his previous wives had died without producing an heir. Since his brother Alexander was also childless, and their sisters were all nuns, this problem became all the more crucial to the Macedonian dynasty's continuity. Within two years after the death of his third wife, Eudokia Baiane (901), Leo took Zoe as his mistress. She came of good family, as we are told by chroniclers such as Leo Grammaticus and Theophanes Continuatus: her uncle Himerios was a government archivist, later becoming an admiral, then minister and successful general, as she rose to power. She was also distantly related to the chronicler Theophanes and the general Photeinos (Garland; Jenkins 1966).

The only reason Leo had to marry Zoe, rather than simply keep her as his official mistress, was to legitimize their offspring as heirs; their first-born was a daughter, followed by the long-awaited son, the future Constantine VII (905). Imperial remarriages beyond a second one were severely problematic for the Eastern Church, even in this case, where the patriarch, Nicolas I Mystikos (*mystikos* here meaning he was the imperial private secretary), had just been handpicked by Leo and had blessed Zoe's pregnancy.

As a compromise to appease the extremist Church factions led by other patriarchs, his own ecclesiastical principles, and the emperor's dynastic needs, Nicolas engineered an agreement expelling Zoe from the palace yet allowing Constantine's christening at the Eastern "Vatican," Hagia Sophia, the church of St. Sophia in Constantinople (906). Leo obeyed the pact just long enough to enable his son's baptism before bringing Zoe back for the all-important step, their union's legitimacy, since their son's right to the throne was still contingent on this. Toward this end, Leo had Thomas, a palace priest, preside over their marriage, after which Zoe, now restored to the palace, was proclaimed "Empress of the Romans," according to the chroniclers. These events provoked much contention among various Church figures and the public at large. Leo was banned from all Church services for four years, while Nicolas strove to effect some sort of dispensation for the marriage, begging the imperial couple to separate in the interests of decorum until the Church council could convene, which Leo refused to observe. As far as Leo and his followers were concerned, his marriage was legitimate, Zoe was his empress, and Constantine his heir; to compromise in any way would be to weaken these claims. Leo appealed beyond Patriarch Nicolas to the pope, who ruled in favor of the marriage and sent his legates to have Leo readmitted to St. Sophia. Leo then deposed Nicolas, sent him into exile, and replaced him with Euthymios I, who granted the marriage, though he too opposed third and fourth marriages on principle. The tension Leo's intervention created between Nicolas's loyalists and supporters of Leo and Euthymios resulted in a schism within the Eastern Church.

Euthymios crowned little Constantine co-emperor (908) but deposed and removed Thomas, the priest who had married Leo and Zoe, from the list of serving clergy, and compelled Leo to issue legislation forbidding fourth marriages. The patriarch allowed Leo to take Communion, provided he enter St. Sophia only as a penitent for the remainder of the emperor's life. Finally, Euthymios refused to bestow on Zoe the title of "Augusta" accorded all Byzantine empresses and forbade her name to be recorded in the sacred records, despite her own letters to him in which she pled for her recognition and also for that of the priest Thomas, all in vain (see *Vita Euthymii*, 109, 111). In Euthymios's eyes, Zoe's marriage existed only because of his holy dispensation for the sake of the imperial household; she was entitled to nothing more.

Prior to his death, probably from typhoid fever (912), Leo had named his brother Alexander as his six-year-old son's guardian: somewhat ironic since, at one time, he had suspected Alexander of plotting against him, yet still made him regent over Zoe, who, because of the aforementioned events, lacked adequate standing. Alexander recalled Patriarch Nicolas and expelled Zoe and her attendants (including her favorite eunuch) from the palace, imprisoning her once-favored uncle. Alexander and Nicolas sought retribution up and down the ecclesiastical and political hierarchy in a wave of dismissals, archival deletions, then riots and bloodshed. Zoe feared for her somewhat sickly son's welfare, since Alexander may have been thinking of having him blinded or castrated, prevented from doing so only by Leo's supporters and also by his own death thirteen months after taking power.

This narrowed Zoe's enemies down to one, Nicolas, named head of the council ruling for her son, who banished her to a monastery where she was tonsured as Sister Anna. But Zoe soon staged a coup, taking advantage of a menacing Bulgarian invasion, inner palace supporters, and allies on the ruling council. In the course of a power struggle, Zoe and her eunuch functionaries (a group deriving from her eunuch manservants) gained control of the government, then reached an understanding with Nicolas, whose diplomatic skills she found indispensable. Zoe, now regent (914), had still to deal with the Bulgarians, which entailed a military confrontation. Unfortunately, her generals miscalculated during this confrontation; the Byzantine allies—the Pechenegs—went home, whereupon the fierce Bulgarian leader, Symeon, massacred the entire Roman army, leaving a legendary pile of carnage. Further defeats inflicted by Symeon (917–918) bode poorly for Zoe's government, though she valiantly clung to power for another year. At this point, she was competing with and against Nicolas and also against her incompetent general, Phokas, and admiral, in both of whom she had trusted too much. The admiral, Romanos Lekapenos, who had lost earlier to the Bulgarians, emerged victorious from this rivalry, not

967

only as her son's father-in-law (having married his daughter Helena to the thirteen-year-old Constantine VII in May 919) but also as Caesar (emperor), a few months later.

The unsinkable Nicolas then allied himself with Romanos, and met with a Church patriarchal council at Constantinople (920) to resolve the schism and determine that third marriages were permissible in certain cases, but that fourth marriages were not. Neither Leo VI nor Zoe was mentioned by name in the records. The council's ruling, since it was nonretroactive, did preserve Constantine's legitimacy, despite his father being called a "lecher," his mother a "concubine," and Constantine a "bastard" in a later edict ritually read out to Constantine on Sundays (Garland; Jenkins 1966). Later that same year, Zoe was deposed, sent to the monastery of St. Euphemia in Petrion (in Constantinople), was again tonsured, and reassumed the name Sister Anna.

From this point on, no further mention of her survives. Yet before disappearing, historians remind us, she had surmounted immense obstacles posed by Church and state to fulfill her goal of preserving her husband's continuity by bearing a son and retaining power and prestige until he, Constantine VII, could marry and hope to rule, a position he finally assumed in 945.

See also Concubines; Eudocia; Marriage; Theodora

BIBLIOGRAPHY

Primary Sources
Leo Grammaticus. *Leonis grammatici chronographia. Corpus scriptorum historiae Byzantinae* [=CSHB], 31. Edited by Immanuel Bekker. Bonn: E. Weber, 1842. [Original Greek text, notes in Latin].
Nicolas I (Mystikos), Patriarch. *Letters.* Edited and translated by Romilly Jenkins and L. Westerink. Washington, D.C.: Dumbarton Oaks, 1973. [*See also* Jenkins 1962, ch. 8, *below under* Secondary Sources].
Theophanes, et al. *Theophanes Continuatus* [*Chronographia*]. CSHB, 45. Edited by Immanuel Bekker. Bonn: E. Weber, 1838. [Original Greek text, notes in Latin].
Vita Euthymii patriarchae CP. Edited, translated, and with commentary by Patricia Karlin-Hayter. Bibliothèque de Byzantion, 3. Brussels: Byzantion, 1970. [Original Greek with English trans. and notes].

Secondary Sources
Boojamra, John L. "The Eastern Schism of 907 and the Affair of the Tetragamia." *Journal of Ecclesiastical History* 25(1974): 113–33.
Garland, Lynda. *Byzantine Empresses: Women and Power in Byzantium, AD 527–1204.* London and New York: Routledge, 1999.
Jenkins, Romilly J. H. *Byzantium: The Imperial Centuries, A.D. 610–1071.* London: Weidenfeld & Nicholson, 1966. Reprint Medieval Academy of America Reprints for Teaching, 18. Toronto and Buffalo: University of Toronto Press/Medieval Academy, 1987.
———. "Three Documents Concerning the Tetragamy." *Dumbarton Oaks Papers* 16 (1962): 231–41. Reprint in Jenkins, *Studies on Byzantine History of the Ninth and Tenth Centuries*, ch. 8. London: Variorum, 1970.
Toynbee, Arnold. *A Study of History*, 4:384. Royal Institute for International Affiars. 6 vols. Oxford: Oxford University Press. Original 1939.

NADIA MARGOLIS

Select Bibliography

Bell, Susan Groag, ed. *Women: From the Greeks to the French Revolution.* Stanford, Calif.: Stanford University Press, 1980. Original Wadsworth, 1973.

Bennett, Judith M. *A Medieval Life: Cecilia Penifader of Brigstock, c. 1297–1344.* Boston: McGraw-Hill College, 1998. [Readable, in-depth view of English peasant life through this single case study].

Bitel, Lisa. *Women in Early Medieval Europe, 400–1100.* Cambridge: Cambridge University Press, 2002.

Blamires, Alcuin. *The Case for Women in Medieval Culture.* Oxford: Clarendon Press; New York: Oxford University Press, 1997.

———, ed. *Women Defamed and Woman Defended: An Anthology of Medieval Texts.* Oxford: Clarendon Press, 1992.

Chang, Kang-i Sun, and Haun Saussy, eds. *Women Writers of Traditional China: An Anthology of Poetry and Criticism.* Stanford, Calif.: Stanford University Press, 1999.

Churchill, Laurie, et al., eds. *Women Writing Latin,* vols. 1–2. New York: Routledge, 2002.

Commire, Anne, and Deborah Klezmer, eds. *Women in World History: A Biographical Encyclopedia.* 17 vols. Waterford, Conn.: Yorkin, 1999–2002. [Numerous articles, of varying quality, on a multicultural array of medieval women within the broader spectrum of world history through modern times].

The Defiant Muse. Various editors and translators. 6 vols. New York: Feminist Press, 1986–[1999]. [Ongoing series of bilingual (original language plus English) editions of feminist writing—thus far in the Romance languages, German, Dutch, and Hebrew—from the Middle Ages to the present].

Dinshaw, Carolyn, and David Wallace, eds. *The Cambridge Companion to Medieval Women's Writing.* Cambridge: Cambridge University Press, 2003.

Dronke, Peter. *Women Writers of the Middle Ages: A Critical Study of Texts from Perpetua (†203) to Marguerite Porete (†1310).* Cambridge: Cambridge University Press, 1984. [For the advanced literary student].

Echols, Anne, and Marty Williams. *An Annotated Index of Medieval Women.* New York: Markus Wiener; Oxford: Berg, 1992. [Multi-indexed, brief biographies, and bibliography of a vast range of women].

Farmer, Sharon, and Carol Braun Pasternack, eds. *Gender and Difference in the Middle Ages.* Medieval Cultures, 32. Minneapolis: University of Minnesota Press, 2003. [Stimulating collection of essays on multiculturalism, race, social status and gender (including homosexuality) in word and image].

Holloway, Julia Bolton, et al. [Women Mystics and Pilgrims]. http://www.umilta.net

Labarge, Margaret Wade. *A Medieval Miscellany.* Ottawa, Ont., Canada: Carleton University Press, 1996. [Despite nonspecific title, about half the articles are useful introductions to various aspects of women in medieval society].

Larrington, Carolyne, ed. *Women and Writing in Medieval Europe: A Sourcebook*. London and New York: Routledge, 1995.

Levin, Carole, Debra Barrett-Graves, et al. *Extraordinary Women of the Medieval and Renaissance World*. Westport, Conn. and London: Greenwood Press, 2000.

Linehan, Peter, and Janet L. Nelson, eds. *The Medieval World*. London and New York: Routledge, 2001. Reprint 2003. [Contains several important essays by key specialists on social, legal, and sexual aspects of medieval women's lives, plus film and other topics from innovative perspectives].

McNamara, Jo Ann, et al., eds. and trans. *Sainted Women of the Dark Ages*. Durham, N.C. and London: Duke University Press, 1992.

Mitchell, Linda E., ed. *Women in Medieval Western European Culture*. Garland Reference Library of the Humanities, 2007. New York and London: Garland, 1999. [Despite title, articles also include Byzantine, Jewish, and Islamic women, as well as their place in agriculture, commerce, politics (queeenship), law, literature, and art].

Nicol, Donald M. *The Byzantine Lady: Ten Portraits, 1250–1500*. Canto. Cambridge: Cambridge University Press, 1996. Original 1994.

Other Women's Voices: http://home.infionline.net/~ddisse [Excellent, abundant resource for translations of pre-1700 women's writing around the world].

Pennsylvania, University of. *Celebration of Women Writers (1301–1400)*: http://digital.library.upenn.edu/women/_generate/1301-1400.html

Petroff, Elizabeth A., ed. *Medieval Women's Visionary Literature*. New York: Oxford University Press, 1986.

Power, Eileen. *Medieval Women*. Edited by M. M. Postan. Cambridge: Cambridge University Press, 1975. Reprint 1997. [Good, concise introduction, profusely illustrated].

Rochester, University of. *Women Writers of the Middle Ages*: http://www.library.rochester.edu/index.cfm

Tharu, Susie, and K. Lalita. *Women Writing in India, Volume 1: 600 B.C. to the Early Twentieth Century*. New York: Feminist Press, 1991.

Thiébaux, Marcelle. *The Writings of Medieval Women: An Anthology*. 2nd ed. Garland Reference Library of the Humanities. New York: Garland, 1994.

Trager, James. *The Women's Chronology*. New York: Henry Holt, 1994. [Comparative multicultural chronological table from pre-history to the present].

Wilson-Kastner, Patricia, et al. *A Lost Tradition: Women Writers of the Early Church*. Washington, D.C.: University Press of America, 1981.

Index

[*Note*. Numbers in **boldface** type indicate the location of the primary entry for that topic. Front matter (Roman numeral) page numbers refer to the Introduction in Volume I.]

Contributors

Peter L. Allen
Management Consultant
McKinsey and Company
New York, NY

Edith Brigitte Archibald
Department of Foreign Languages
North Carolina A & T University
Greensboro, NC

Clarissa W. Atkinson
Professor Emerita
Harvard Divinity School
Cambridge, MA

Prateeti Punja Ballal
Department of Comparative Literature
University of Massachusetts
Amherst, MA

Denise-Renée Barberet
Department of Modern Languages and
    Literature
College of the Holy Cross
Worcester, MA

Peter I. Barta
Russian and Cultural Studies
University of Surrey
Surrey, England

Judith R. Baskin
Religious Studies/Schnitzer Foundation for
    Judaic Studies
University of Oregon
Eugene, OR

Jeanette Beer
Department of French
Purdue University
West Lafayette, IN

David K. Bell
Department of History
University of Georgia
Athens, GA

Pamela Benson
Department of English
Rhode Island College
Providence, RI

Anne Berthelot
Department of French
University of Connecticut
Storrs, CT

Merritt R. Blakeslee
Attorney
De Kiefer and Horgan
Washington, DC

Renate Blumenfeld-Kosinski
Department of French
University of Pittsburgh
Pittsburgh, PA

Barbara Drake Boehm
Department of Medieval Art
Metropolitan Museum of Art
New York, NY

Daniel E. Bornstein
Department of History

Texas A & M University
College Station, TX

Alain Boureau
Directeur d'Etudes
L'École des Hautes Études en Sciences
    Sociales
Paris, France

Herman Braet
Faculté des Lettres
University of Antwerp
Antwerp, Belgium

Judith Bronfman
School of Visual Arts
New York, NY

Matilda Tomaryn Bruckner
Department of Romance Languages and
    Literatures
Boston College
Chestnut Hill, MA

Brigitte Buettner
Department of Art
Smith College
Northampton, MA

Glyn S. Burgess
Department of French
The University of Liverpool
Liverpool, England

Michael Calabrese
Department of English
California State University–
    Los Angeles
Los Angeles, CA

Fredric L. Cheyette
Department of History
Amherst College
Amherst, MA

Albrecht Classen
Department of German
University of Arizona
Tucson, AZ

Carolyn P. Collette
Department of English
Mt. Holyoke College
South Hadley, MA

Anne Daghistany
Department of English
Texas Tech University
Lubbock, TX

Craig R. Davis
Department of English
Smith College
Northampton, MA

Sheila Delany
Department of English
Simon Fraser University
Burnaby, British Columbia,
    Canada

Marilynn Desmond
Department of English
Binghamton University–SUNY
Binghamton, NY

Liliane Dulac
Professor Emerita
University of Montpellier
Montpellier, France

Patricia Buckley Ebrey
Department of History
University of Washington
Seattle, WA

George D. Economou
Professor Emeritus
University of Oklahoma
Norman, OK

J. Michele Edwards
Department of Music
Macalester College
St. Paul, MN

Margaret J. Ehrhart
Leonia, NJ

Dyan Elliott
Department of History
Indiana University
Bloomington, IN

Jody Enders
Department of French and Italian
University of California, Santa
    Barbara
Santa Barbara, CA

Richard C. Famiglietti
Picardy Press
Providence, RI

Joel N. Feimer
Department of English Literature
Mercy College
Dobbs Ferry, NY

Thelma S. Fenster
Professor of French and Medieval Studies
Fordham University
New York, NY

Jeanne Fox-Friedman
School of Continuing and Professional Studies
New York University
New York, NY

Deborah A. Fraioli
Department of Modern Languages
Simmons College
Boston, MA

Roberta Frank
Department of English
Yale University
New Haven, CT

Sr. Jane Patricia Freeland (deceased)
Amherst, MA

Katherine L. French
Department of History
SUNY New Paltz
New Paltz, NY

Lee Gallo
Department of Modern Foreign Languages
Morehouse College
Atlanta, GA

Lisa Gaudet
Dauphin, Manitoba, Canada

Aristoula Georgiadou
Department of the Classics and Ancient
   Mediterranean Studies
Pennsylvania State University
State College, PA

Gerrit H. Gerrits
Department of History
Acadia University
Wolfville, Nova Scotia, Canada

Monica H. Green
Department of History
Arizona State University
Tempe, AZ

Joan Tasker Grimbert
Department of French
Catholic University of America
Washington, DC

Sarah Hanley
Departments of History and Law
University of Iowa
Iowa City, IA

Susan Ashbrook Harvey
Department of Religious Studies
Brown University
Providence, RI

Louise M. Haywood
Department of Spanish and Portuguese
Cambridge University
Cambridge, England

Thomas Head
Department of History
Hunter College–CUNY
New York, NY

Eric Hicks (deceased)
Medieval French Literature Section
University of Lausanne
Lausanne, Switzerland

Cynthia Ho
Department of Language and Literature
University of North Carolina–Asheville
Asheville, NC

Carole Hough
Department of English
University of Glasgow
Glasgow, Scotland

Bruce Hozeski
Department of English
Ball State University
Muncie, IN

Karen K. Jambeck
Department of English
Western Connecticut State University
Danbury, CT

Jenny Jochens
Professor Emerita
Towson University
Towson, MD

Catherine M. Jones
Department of French
University of Georgia
Athens, GA

Valentina Jones-Wagner
Comparative Literature Program
Graduate Center–CUNY
New York, NY

Ruth Mazo Karras
Department of History
University of Minnesota, Twin Cities
Minneapolis, MN

Douglas Kelly
Professor Emeritus
University of Wisconsin
Madison, WI

Kristian Kimbro
Department of English
Texas Tech University
Lubbock, TX

Désirée G. Koslin
Fashion Institute of Technology–SUNY
New York, NY

Elizabeth Laidlaw
Edinburgh, Scotland

David Larmour
Department of Classics
Texas Tech University
Lubbock, TX

Gertrud Jaron Lewis
Professor Emerita
Laurentian University
Sudbury, Ontario, Canada

Kimberly A. LoPrete
Department of History
National University of Ireland,
  Galway
Galway, Ireland

Mary Louise Lord
Cambridge, MA

Donald Maddox
Department of French and Italian
University of Massachusetts
Amherst, MA

Nadia Margolis
Leverett, MA

Peter K. Marshall (deceased)
Department of Classics
Amherst College
Amherst, MA

Priscilla Martin
St. Edmund Hall
Oxford University
Oxford, England

June Hall McCash
Department of Foreign Languages and
  Literatures
Middle Tennessee State University
Murfreesboro, TN

Elizabeth McCutcheon
Professor Emerita, History
University of Hawaii at Manoa
Honolulu, HI

Deborah McGrady
Department of French and Italian
Tulane University
New Orleans, LA

Mary Martin McLaughlin
Millbrook, NY

Glenda K. McLeod
Department of English
Gainesville College
Gainesville, GA

Kathleen McNerney
Department of Foreign Languages
West Virginia University
Morgantown, WV

Christine McWebb
Department of French Studies
University of Waterloo
Waterloo, Ontario, Canada

Françoise Michaud-Fréjaville
Faculty of Arts, Languages and
  Humanities

University of Orleans
Orleans, France

Louise Mirrer
Department of Spanish/Vice Chancellor
    for Academic Affairs
CUNY
New York, NY

Anneke B. Mulder-Bakker
Department of History/Medieval
    Studies
Rijksuniversiteit Groningen
Groningen, The Netherlands

Maureen E. Mulvihill
Fellow
Princeton Research Forum
Princeton, NJ

Diana L. Murphy
Unity College
Unity, ME

Jacqueline Murray
Dean of Arts
University of Guelph
Guelph, Ontario, Canada

Barbara Newman
Department of English
Northwestern University
Evanston, IL

Alexandra Hennessey Olsen
Department of English
University of Denver
Denver, CO

Glenn W. Olsen
Department of History
University of Utah
Salt Lake City, UT

John Carmi Parsons
Dallas, TX

Zoja Pavlovskis-Petit
Department of Classics and Comparative
    Literature
Binghamton University–SUNY
Binghamton, NY

Elizabeth A. Petroff
Department of Comparative Literature

University of Massachusetts
Amherst, MA

William Provost
Department of English
University of Georgia
Athens, GA

Regina Psaki
Department of Romance Languages
University of Oregon
Eugene, OR

Christine M. Reno
Department of French
Vassar College
Poughkeepsie, NY

Duncan Robertson
Department of Romance Languages
Augusta State University
Augusta, GA

Jennifer Fisk Rondeau
Department of History
University of Oregon
Eugene, OR

Tova Rosen
Department of Hebrew Literature
Tel Aviv University
Tel Aviv, Israel

Roy Rosenstein
Comparative Literature Program
American University of Paris
Paris, France

Paula Sanders
Department of History
Rice University
Houston, TX

Shigemi Sasaki
University of Tokyo–Meisei
Meisei, Japan

Jane Tibbetts Schulenburg
Department of History and Women's
    Studies
University of Wisconsin
Madison, WI

Gale Sigal
Department of English

Wake Forest University
Winston-Salem, NC

Anna Silvas
School of Classics and History
University of New England
Armidale, New South Wales, Australia

Deborah M. Sinnreich-Levi
English and Comparative Literature
Stevens Institute of Technology
Hoboken, NJ

Janet E. Snyder
Division of Art, College of Creative Arts
West Virginia University
Morgantown, WV

Helen Solterer
Department of Romance Studies
Duke University
Durham, NC

Sandro Sticca
Professor Emeritus
Binghamton University–SUNY
Binghamton, NY

Sandra Ballif Straubhaar
Department of Germanic Studies
University of Texas
Austin, TX

Sara Sturm-Maddox
Department of French and Italian
University of Massachusetts
Amherst, MA

Ronald E. Surtz
Department of Spanish
Princeton University
Princeton, NJ

Eva Maria Synek
Institute for Law and Religion
University of Vienna
Vienna, Austria

Andrea W. Tarnowski
Department of French and Italian
Dartmouth College
Hanover, NH

Steven M. Taylor
Department of French and Medieval Studies

Marquette University
Milwaukee, WI

Marcelle Thiébaux
English Department
St. John's University
New York, NY

Raymond H. Thompson
Arcadia University
Wolfville, Nova Scotia

David F. Tinsley
Department of Foreign Languages
University of Puget Sound
Tacoma, WA

Sylvia Tomasch
Department of English
Hunter College–CUNY
New York, NY

Bruce L. Venarde
Department of History
University of Pittsburgh
Pittsburgh, PA

John A. Wagner
Senior Development Editor
Greenwood Publishing Group
Scottsdale, AZ

Suzanne Fonay Wemple
Professor Emerita
Barnard College
New York, NY

Sarah Westphal-Wihl
German Department
University of South Carolina
Columbia, SC

Duey White
Gretna, LA

Frank Willaert
Universitaire Faculteiten Sint-Ignatius te
  Antwerpen (UFSIA)
University of Antwerp
Antwerp, Belgium

Charity Cannon Willard
Professor Emerita
Romance Languages
Ladycliff College
Cornwall-on-Hudson, NY

Daniel Williman
Department of Classics
Binghamton University–SUNY
Binghamton, NY

Katharina M. Wilson
Department of Comparative
    Literature
University of Georgia
Athens, GA

Anne Bagnall Yardley
Associate Dean Theological School/
    Department of Music

Drew University
Madison, NJ

Karl A. Zaenker
Department of Germanic Studies
University of British Columbia
Vancouver, British Columbia, Canada

Rebecca E. Zorach
Department of Art History
University of Chicago
Chicago, IL

ABOUT THE EDITORS

Katharina M. Wilson is Professor of Comparative Literature at the University of Georgia. She has authored and edited several books on the playwright Hrotsvitha (Hrotsvit), whose plays she has also translated; she coauthored (with Elizabeth Makowski) *Wykked Wyves and the Woes of Marriage: Misogamous Literature from Juvenal to Chaucer* (1990), and has cotranslated (with Christopher Wilson) the works of modern Hungarian author Imre Kertesz. She has also edited and coedited reference works on women writers, both medieval and modern, most pertinently, *Medieval Women Writers* (1984).

Nadia Margolis trained in French and medieval studies primarily at Stanford University and the École des Hautes Études, Paris. She has taught medieval French language and literature at several American institutions, most recently the University of California at Los Angeles. Her books and articles concern various aspects of French medieval literature and culture, particularly on Christine de Pizan, medieval Franco-Italian humanism, and Joan of Arc as medieval and modern cultural icon. Most recently, she coedited (with John Campbell) *Christine de Pizan 2000: Studies in Honour of Angus J. Kennedy* (2000). She has also published translations of Christine's lyric poetry, for example (with Thelma Fenster) in *Christine de Pizan, The Book of the Duke of True Lovers* (1991). She continues to lecture on Christine and on Joan of Arc at universities in the United States, Canada, Europe, and the United Kingdom.